Recommender Systems Handbook

Francesco Ricci • Lior Rokach • Bracha Shapira
Editors

Recommender Systems Handbook

Second Edition

Editors
Francesco Ricci
Faculty of Computer Science
Free University of Bozen-Bolzano
Bolzano, Italy

Lior Rokach
Information Systems Engineering
Ben-Gurion University of the Negev
Beer-Sheva, Israel

Bracha Shapira
Ben-Gurion University of the Negev
Beer-Sheva, Israel

ISBN 978-1-4899-7780-9 ISBN 978-1-4899-7637-6 (eBook)
DOI 10.1007/978-1-4899-7637-6

Springer New York Heidelberg Dordrecht London

Softcover re-print of the Hardcover 2nd edition 2015

Printed on acid-free paper

Springer Science+Business Media LLC New York is part of Springer Science+Business Media (www.springer.com)

Dedicated to

our families in appreciation of their patience and support during the preparation of this handbook

and to

all our students in appreciation of their ideas, patience and stimulus for better understanding the topics covered in this handbook

F.R.
L.R.
B.S.

Preface

Recommender systems are software tools and techniques providing suggestions for items to be of use to a user. The suggestions provided by a recommender system are aimed at supporting their users in various decision-making processes, such as what items to buy, what music to listen, or what news to read. Recommender systems are valuable means for online users to cope with information overload and help them making better choices. They are now one of the most powerful and popular information discovery tools on the web. Several techniques for recommendation generation have been proposed, and during the last decade, many of them have also been successfully deployed in commercial environments.

Development of recommender systems is a multi-disciplinary effort which involves experts from various fields such as artificial intelligence, human computer interaction, data mining, statistics, decision support systems, marketing, and consumer behavior.

The first edition of the handbook, which was published 4 years ago, was extremely well received by the recommender systems community. The positive reception, along with the fast pace of research in recommender systems, motivated us to update the handbook. This second edition aims to refresh the previously presented material and to present new findings in the field. The Recommender Systems Handbook is now offered in a majorly revised edition; about half of the chapters are totally new and the remaining chapters are updated versions of selected chapters already published in the first edition.

Despite these revisions, the goal of this handbook remains unaltered. It still aims to present both fundamental knowledge and more advanced topics by organizing them in a coherent and unified repository of recommender systems' major concepts, theories, methods, trends, challenges, and applications. This is still the unique comprehensive book, which is dedicated entirely to the field of recommender systems. Its informative, factual pages will provide researchers, students, and practitioners in industry with a comprehensive, yet concise and convenient reference source to recommender systems.

This book describes in detail the classical methods, as well as extensions and novel approaches that were more recently introduced. It consists of five parts:

techniques, evaluation of recommender systems, applications, human computer interaction, and advanced topics. The first part presents the most popular and fundamental techniques used nowadays for building recommender systems, such as collaborative filtering, semantic-based methods, data mining, and context-aware methods. The second part focuses on methods and techniques for evaluating the performance and effect of recommender systems by means of both off-line and live user experiments. The third part contains several chapters on diverse applications of recommendation techniques. After a first chapter dedicated to general issues related to the industrial implementation and exploitation of recommender system, the other sections focus on various application domains: music, learning, mobile, social, and reciprocal. The fourth part includes papers addressing the presentation, browsing, explanation, and visualization of the recommendations and important issues related to human decision making and recommender systems. Finally, the last section collects a few papers on some advanced topics such as the exploitation of active learning principles to guide the acquisition of new knowledge, techniques suitable for making a recommender system robust against attacks of malicious users, and recommender systems that aggregate multiple types of user feedbacks and preferences to build more reliable recommendations or recommendations for groups.

We would like to thank all authors for their valuable contributions. We would like to express gratitude for all reviewers who generously gave comments on drafts or counsel otherwise. We would like to express our special thanks to Susan Lagerstrom-Fife and staff members of Springer for their kind cooperation throughout the production of this book. Finally, we wish this handbook will contribute to the growth of this subject, we wish to the novices a fruitful learning path, and to those more experts a compelling application of the ideas discussed in this handbook and a fruitful development of this challenging research area.

Bolzano, Italy
Beer-Sheva, Israel

Francesco Ricci
Lior Rokach
Bracha Shapira

Contents

Part V Advanced Topics

Contributors

Gediminas Adomavicius
Department of Information and Decision Sciences, University of Minnesota, Minneapolis, MN, USA

Xavier Amatriain
Netflix, Los Gatos, CA, USA

Quora, Mountain View, USA

Justin Basilico
Netflix, Los Gatos, CA, USA

Gleb Beliakov
School of Information Technology, Deakin University, Burwood, VIC, Australia

Robert Bell
AT&T Labs – Research, Middletown, NJ, USA

Shlomo Berkovsky
CSIRO, Sydney, NSW, Australia

Dmitry Bogdanov
Music Technology Group, Universitat Pompeu Fabra, Barcelona, Spain

Peter Briggs
HeyStaks Technologies Ltd., NovaUCD, University College Dublin, Dublin, Ireland

Robin Burke
School of Computer Science, Telecommunication and Information Systems, DePaul University, Chicago, IL, USA

Tomasa Calvo
Departamento de Ciencias de la Computación, Universidad de Alcalá, Madrid, Spain

Iván Cantador
Universidad Autónoma de Madrid, Madrid, Spain

Pablo Castells
Universidad Autonoma de Madrid, Madrid, Spain

Li Chen
Hong Kong Baptist University, Hong Kong, China

Maurice Coyle
HeyStaks Technologies Ltd., NovaUCD, University College Dublin, Dublin, Ireland

Paolo Cremonesi
Politecnico di Milano, Milan, Italy

Marco de Gemmis
Department of Computer Science, University of Bari "Aldo Moro", Bari, Italy

Christian Desrosiers
Software Engineering and IT Department, École de Technologie Supérieure, Montreal, QC, Canada

Hendrik Drachsler
Welten Institute Research Centre for Learning, Teaching and Technology, Open University of the Netherlands, Heerlen, The Netherlands

Mehdi Elahi
Free University of Bozen-Bolzano, Bolzano, Italy

Alexander Felfernig
University of Graz, Graz, Austria

Ignacio Fernández-Tobías
Universidad Autónoma de Madrid, Madrid, Spain

Arik Friedman
NICTA, Sydney, NSW, Australia

Gerhard Friedrich
Alpen-Adria-Universitaet Klagenfurt, Klagenfurt, Austria

Ulrike Gretzel
University of Queensland, Brisbane, QLD, Australia

Asela Gunawardana
Microsoft Research, Redmond, WA, USA

Ido Guy
Yahoo Labs, Haifa, Israel

Neil J. Hurley
Insight Centre for Data Analytics, School of Computer Science and Informatics, University College Dublin, Dublin, Ireland

Simon James
School of Information Technology, Deakin University, Burwood, VIC, Australia

Anthony Jameson
DFKI, German Research Center for Artificial Intelligence, Saarbrücken, Germany

Dietmar Jannach
TU Dortmund, Dortmund, Germany

Marius Kaminskas
Insight Centre for Data Analytics, University College Cork, Cork, Ireland

Dain Kaplan
Tokyo Institute of Technology, Tokyo, Japan

George Karypis
Computer Science & Engineering Department, University of Minnesota, Minneapolis, MN, USA

Peter Knees
Department of Computational Perception, Johannes Kepler University Linz, Linz, Austria

Bart P. Knijnenburg
Clemson University, Clemson, SC, USA

Irena Koprinska
School of Information Technologies, University of Sydney, Sydney, NSW, Australia

Yehuda Koren
Google Research, Mountain View, CA, USA

YoungOk Kwon
Sookmyung Women's University, Yongsan-gu, Seoul, Korea

Neal Lathia
Computer Laboratory, University of Cambridge, Cambridge, UK

Pasquale Lops
Department of Computer Science, University of Bari "Aldo Moro", Bari, Italy

Nikos Manouselis
Agro-Know, Vrilissia, Greece

Luc Martens
iMinds - Ghent University, Ghent, Belgium

Judith Masthoff
University of Aberdeen, Aberdeen, UK

Brian McFee
Center for Data Science, New York University, New York, NY, USA

Kevin McNally
Insight Centre for Data Analytics, University College Dublin, Dublin, Ireland

Cataldo Musto
Department of Computer Science, University of Bari "Aldo Moro", Bari, Italy

Fedelucio Narducci
Department of Computer Science, University of Bari "Aldo Moro", Bari, Italy

Xia Ning
Computer Science Department, Purdue University, West Lafayette, IN, USA

Michael P. O'Mahony
Insight Centre for Data Analytics, School of Computer Science and Informatics, University College Dublin, Dublin, Ireland

Josep M. Pujol
Cliqz, Munich, Germany

Francesco Ricci
Faculty of Computer Science, Free University of Bozen-Bolzano, Bolzano, Italy

Lior Rokach
Department of Information Systems Engineering, Ben-Gurion University of the Negev, Beer-Sheva, Israel

Neil Rubens
University of Electro-Communications, Tokyo, Japan

Olga C. Santos
aDeNu Research Group, UNED, Madrid, Spain

Markus Schedl
Department of Computational Perception, Johannes Kepler University Linz, Linz, Austria

Giovanni Semeraro
Department of Computer Science, University of Bari "Aldo Moro", Bari, Italy

Guy Shani
Information Systems Engineering, Ben Gurion University, Beer Sheva, Israel

Bracha Shapira
Department of Information Systems Engineering, Ben-Gurion University of the Negev, Beer-Sheva, Israel

Barry Smyth
Insight Centre for Data Analytics, University College Dublin, Dublin, Ireland

Masashi Sugiyama
Tokyo Institute of Technology, Tokyo, Japan

Nava Tintarev
University of Aberdeen, Aberdeen, UK

Marko Tkalcic
Johannes Kepler University, Linz, Austria

Alexander Tuzhilin
Department of Information, Operations and Management Sciences, Stern School of Business, New York University, New York, NY, USA

Kris Vanhecke
iMinds - Ghent University, Ghent, Belgium

Saúl Vargas
Universidad Autonoma de Madrid, Madrid, Spain

Katrien Verbert
Department of Computer Science, KU Leuven, Leuven, Belgium

Department of Computer Science, Vrije Universiteit Brussel, Brussel, Belgium

Martijn C. Willemsen
Eindhoven University of Technology, Eindhoven, The Netherlands

Kalina Yacef
School of Information Technologies, University of Sydney, Sydney, NSW, Australia

Kyung-Hyan Yoo
William Paterson University, Wayne, NJ, USA

Markus Zanker
Alpen-Adria-Universitaet Klagenfurt, Klagenfurt, Austria

Chapter 1
Recommender Systems: Introduction and Challenges

Francesco Ricci, Lior Rokach, and Bracha Shapira

1.1 Introduction

Recommender Systems (RSs) are software tools and techniques that provide suggestions for items that are most likely of interest to a particular user [17, 41, 42]. The suggestions relate to various decision-making processes, such as what items to buy, what music to listen to, or what online news to read.

"Item" is the general term used to denote what the system recommends to users. An RS normally focuses on a specific type of item (e.g., CDs or news) and, accordingly its design, its graphical user interface, and the core recommendation technique used to generate the recommendations are all customized to provide useful and effective suggestions for that specific type of item.

RSs are primarily directed toward individuals who lack the sufficient personal experience or competence in order to evaluate the potentially overwhelming number of alternative items that a website, for example, may offer [42]. A prime example is a book recommender system that assists users in selecting a book to read. On the popular website, Amazon.com, the site employs an RS to personalize the online store for each customer [32]. Since recommendations are usually personalized, different users or user groups benefit from diverse, tailored suggestions. In addition, there are also non-personalized recommendations. These are much simpler to generate and are normally featured in magazines or newspapers. Typical examples

F. Ricci (✉)
Faculty of Computer Science, Free University of Bozen-Bolzano, Bolzano, Italy
e-mail: fricci@unibz.it

L. Rokach • B. Shapira
Department of Information Systems Engineering,
Ben-Gurion University of the Negev, Beer-Sheva, Israel
e-mail: liorrk@bgu.ac.il; bshapira@bgu.ac.il

F. Ricci et al. (eds.), *Recommender Systems Handbook*,
DOI 10.1007/978-1-4899-7637-6_1

include the top ten selections of books, CDs etc. While they may be useful and effective in certain situations, these types of non-personalized recommendations are not typically addressed by RS research.

In their simplest form, personalized recommendations are offered as ranked lists of items. In performing this ranking, RSs try to predict what the most suitable products or services are, based on the user's preferences and constraints. In order to complete such a computational task, RSs collect information from users regarding their preferences which are either explicitly expressed, e.g., as ratings for products or are inferred by interpreting the actions of the user. For instance, an RS may consider the navigation to a particular product page as an implicit sign of preference for the items shown on that page.

The development of RSs initiated from a rather simple observation: individuals often rely on recommendations provided by others in making routine, daily decisions [41, 51]. For example, it is common to rely on what one's peers recommend when selecting a book to read; employers count on recommendation letters in their recruiting decisions; and when selecting a movie to watch, individuals tend to read and rely on the movie reviews that a film critic has written, which appear in the newspaper they read.

In seeking to mimic this behavior, the first RSs applied algorithms in order to leverage recommendations produced by a community of users and deliver these recommendations to an "active" user, or a user looking for suggestions. The recommendations were for items that similar users, or those with similar tastes, had liked. This approach is termed collaborative-filtering and its rationale follows that if the active user agreed in the past with certain users, then the other recommendations coming from these similar users should be relevant as well as of interest to the active user.

As e-commerce websites began to develop, a pressing need emerged for providing recommendations derived from filtering the whole range of available alternatives. Users found it difficult to arrive at the most appropriate choices from the immense variety of items (products and services) that these websites offered.

The explosive growth and variety of information available on the Web and the rapid introduction of new e-business services (selling products, product comparison, auctions, etc.) frequently overwhelmed users, leading them to make poor decisions. The availability of choices, instead of producing a benefit, started to decrease users' well-being. It was understood that while choice is good, more choice is not always better. Indeed, choice, with its implications of freedom, autonomy, and self-determination can become excessive, and ultimately create a sense that freedom may come to be regarded as a kind of misery-inducing tyranny [49].

In recent years, RSs have proven to be a valuable means of coping with the information overload problem. Ultimately an RS addresses this phenomenon by pointing a user toward new, not-yet-experienced items that may be relevant to the user's current task. Upon a user's request, which can be articulated depending on the recommendation approach by the user's context and need, RSs generate recommendations using various types of knowledge and data about users, the available items, and previous transactions stored in customized databases. The user can then browse the recommendations. One may accept them or not and may provide, immediately or at a later stage, implicit or explicit feedback. This user action and feedback can be stored in the recommender database and may be used for generating new recommendations in the coming user-system interactions.

As previously noted, the study of recommender systems is relatively new compared to research in other classical information system tools and techniques (e.g., databases or search engines). Recommender systems emerged as an independent research area in the mid-1990s [7, 24, 41, 51]. In recent years, the interest in recommender systems has dramatically increased, as the following facts indicate:

1. Recommender systems play an important role in highly-rated Internet sites such as Amazon.com, YouTube, Netflix, Spotify, LinkedIn, Facebook, Tripadvisor, Last.fm, and IMDb. Moreover many media companies are now developing and deploying RSs as part of the services they provide to their subscribers. For example, Netflix, the online provider of on-demand streaming media, awarded a million dollar prize to the team that first succeeded in substantially improving the performance of its recommender system [31].
2. There are conferences and workshops dedicated specifically to the field, namely the Association of Computing Machinery's (ACM) Conference Series on Recommender Systems (RecSys), established in 2007. This conference stands as the premier annual event in recommender technology research and applications. In addition, sessions dedicated to RSs are frequently included in more traditional conferences in the area of databases, information systems and adaptive systems. Additional noteworthy conferences within this scope include: ACM's Special Interest Group on Information Retrieval (SIGIR); User Modeling, Adaptation and Personalization (UMAP); Intelligent User Interfaces (IUI); World Wide Web (WWW); and ACM's Special Interest Group on Management Of Data (SIGMOD).
3. At institutions of higher education around the world, undergraduate and graduate courses are now dedicated entirely to RSs, tutorials on RSs are very popular at computer science conferences, and a book introducing RSs techniques has been published as well [27]. Springer is publishing several books on specific topics in recommender systems in its series: Springer Briefs in Electrical and Computer Engineering. A large, new collection of articles dedicated to recommender systems applications to software engineering has also recently been published [46].
4. There have been several special issues in academic journals which cover research and developments in the RSs field. Among the journals that have dedicated issues to RSs are: AI Communications (2008); IEEE Intelligent Systems (2007); International Journal of Electronic Commerce (2006); International Journal of Computer Science and Applications (2006); ACM Transactions on Computer Human Interaction (2005); ACM Transactions on Information Systems (2004); User Modeling and User-Adapted Interaction (2014, 2012); ACM Transactions on Interactive Intelligent Systems (2013); and ACM Transactions on Intelligent Systems and Technology (2015).

In this introductory chapter, we briefly discuss basic RS ideas and concepts. Our main goal is not to present a self-contained comprehensive survey on RSs but rather to delineate, in a coherent and structured way, the chapters included in this handbook and to help the reader navigate the rich and detailed content that the handbook offers. The reader can also consult these recent introductions or surveys on recommender systems [13, 30, 34, 40, 44]. At the end of this chapter, we have identified some research challenges that we believe are particularly important for the future of the area.

The handbook is divided into five sections: recommendation techniques; recommender systems evaluation; recommender systems applications; recommender systems and human computer interaction; and advanced algorithms.

The first section presents the techniques most popularly used today for building RSs, such as collaborative filtering; content-based, data mining methods; and context-aware methods.

The second section surveys techniques and approaches that have been utilized to evaluate the quality of the recommendations. The section also considers aspects that may affect RS design (domain, device, interfaces, users, etc.). Finally, it discusses methods, challenges and measures to be applied in evaluating the developed systems with user experiments.

The third section includes papers dealing with a number of issues related to how recommendations are presented, browsed, explained and visualized. Among them, this section focuses on user's privacy and the decision making process supported by a recommender system.

The fourth section is fully dedicated to applications of recommender systems. We offer here a broad spectrum of the usage of these techniques in music, mobile computing, dating, social networks, education, and movies.

The last section presents papers on various advanced topics, such as: the exploitation of active learning principles to guide the acquisition of new knowledge; novelty and diversity in the recommendations; suitable techniques for protecting a recommender system against attacks of malicious users; and RSs that aggregate multiple types of user feedback and preferences to build more reliable recommendations.

1.2 Recommender Systems' Function

In the previous section, we defined RSs as software tools and techniques that provide users with suggestions for items that a user may wish to utilize. Now we wish to refine this definition to illustrate a range of possible roles that an RS can play. Firstly, we must distinguish between the role played by the RS on behalf of the service provider, from that of the user of the RS. For instance, a travel recommender system is typically introduced by a travel intermediary such as Expedia.com, or a destination management organization, such as Visitfinland.com, in order to increase its turnover or sell more hotel rooms in the case of Expedia, and increase the number of tourists to the destination in the case of the destination management organization [14, 43]. The user's primary motivations for accessing the two systems would be to find a suitable hotel and interesting events or attractions when visiting a destination.

In fact, there are various reasons as to why service providers may want to exploit this technology:

- *Increase the number of items sold.* This is probably the most important function for a commercial RS, i.e., to be able to sell an additional set of items compared to those usually sold without any kind of recommendation. This goal is achieved because the recommended items are likely to suit the user's needs and wants. Presumably the user will recognize this after having tried several recommendations.[1] Non-commercial applications have similar goals, even if there is no cost for the user that is associated with selecting an item. For instance, a content network aims at increasing the number of news items read on its site. In general, we can say that from the service provider's point of view, the primary goal for introducing an RS is to increase the conversion rate, i.e., the number of users that accept the recommendation and consume an item, compared to the number of simple visitors that just browse through the information.
- *Sell more diverse items.* Another major function of an RS is to enable the user to select items that might be hard to find without a precise recommendation. For instance, in a tourist RS the service provider is interested in promoting all the places of interest in a tourist area, not just the most popular ones. This could be difficult without an RS since the service provider cannot afford the risk of advertising places that are not likely to suit a particular user's taste. Therefore, an RS suggests or advertises unpopular places to the right users.
- *Increase the user satisfaction.* A well designed RS can also improve the experience of the user with the site or the application. The user will find the recommendations interesting, relevant and, with a properly designed human-computer interaction, he or she will also enjoy using the system. The combination of effective, accurate recommendations and a usable interface will increase the user's subjective evaluation of the system. This, in turn, will increase system usage and the likelihood that the recommendations will be accepted.
- *Increase user fidelity.* A user should be loyal to a website which, when visited, recognizes the old customer and treats him as a valued visitor. This is a standard feature of an RS since many RSs compute recommendations, thus leveraging the information acquired from the user during previous interactions such as the user's ratings of items. Consequently, the longer the user interacts with the site, the more refined the user's model becomes: the system's representation of the user's preferences develops and the effectiveness of the recommender output to customize and match to the user's preferences is increased.

[1]This issue, convincing the user to accept a recommendation, is discussed again when we explain the difference between predicting the user interest in an item and the likelihood that the user will select the recommended item.

- *Better understanding of what the user wants.* Another important function of an RS which can be leveraged to many other applications is the description of the user's preferences, which are collected either explicitly or predicted by the system. The service provider may then decide to reuse this knowledge for a number of other goals, such as improving the management of the item's stock or production. For instance, in the travel domain, destination management organizations can decide to advertise a specific region to new customer sectors or advertise a particular type of promotional message derived by analyzing the data collected by the RS (transactions of the users).

We mentioned above some important motivations as to why e-service providers introduce RSs. But users also may want an RS if it will effectively support their tasks or goals. Consequently an RS must balance the needs of these two players and offer a service that is valuable to both.

Herlocker et al. [26], in a paper that has become a classical reference in this field, define eleven popular tasks that an RS can assist in implementing. Some may be considered as the main or core tasks that are normally associated with an RS, such as offering suggestions for items that may be useful to a user. Others might be considered as more "opportunistic" ways to exploit an RS. As a matter of fact, this task differentiation is very similar to what happens with a search engine. Its primary function is to locate documents that are relevant to the user's information need, but it can also be used to check the importance of a webpage (looking at the position of the page in the result list of a query) or to discover the various usages of a word in a collection of documents.

- *Find Some Good Items:* Recommend to a user some items as a ranked list along with predictions of how much the user would like them (e.g., on a scale of one-to-five stars). This is the main recommendation task that many commercial systems address (see, for instance, Chap. 11). Some systems do not show the predicted rating.
- *Find all good items:* Recommend all the items that can satisfy some user needs. In such cases it is insufficient to just find some good items. This is especially true when the number of items is relatively small or when the RS is mission-critical, such as in medical or financial applications. In these situations, in addition to the benefit derived from carefully examining all the possibilities, the user may also benefit from the RS ranking of these items or from additional explanations that the RS generates.
- *Annotation in context:* Given an existing context, e.g., a list of items, emphasize some of them depending on the user's long-term preferences. For example, a TV recommender system might annotate which TV shows displayed in the electronic program guide (EPG) are worth watching (Chap. 15 provides interesting examples of this task).
- *Recommend a sequence:* Instead of focusing on the generation of a single recommendation, the idea is to recommend a sequence of items that is pleasing as a whole. Typical examples include recommending a TV series, a book on RSs after having recommended a book on data mining, or a compilation of musical tracks [28].

- *Recommend a bundle:* Suggest a group of items that fits well together. For instance, a travel plan may be composed of various attractions, destinations, and accommodation services that are located in a delimited area. From the point of view of the user, these various alternatives can be considered and selected as a single travel destination [45].
- *Just browsing:* In this task, the user browses the catalog without any imminent intention of purchasing an item. The task of the recommender is to help the user to browse the items that are more likely to fall within the scope of the user's interests for that specific browsing session. This is a task that has also been supported by adaptive hypermedia techniques [16].
- *Find credible recommender:* Some users do not trust recommender systems, thus they play with them to see how good they are at making recommendations. Hence, a certain system may also offer specific functions to let the users test its behavior in addition to those just required for obtaining recommendations.
- *Improve the profile:* This relates to the capability of the user to provide (input) information to the recommender system about what he or she likes and dislikes. This is a fundamental task that is strictly necessary to provide personalized recommendations. If the system has no specific knowledge about the active user, then it can only provide the same recommendations that would be delivered to an "average" user.
- *Express self:* Some users may not care about the recommendations at all. Rather, what is important to them is that they be allowed to contribute with their ratings and express their opinions and beliefs. The user satisfaction for that activity can still act as leverage, resulting in the user's continued loyalty to the application (as we mentioned prior, in discussing the service provider's motivations).
- *Help others:* Some users are happy to contribute with information, e.g., their evaluation of items (ratings), because they believe that the community benefits from their contribution. This could be a major motivation for entering information into a recommender system that is not used routinely. For instance, with an automobile RS, a user who has already purchased a new car is aware that the rating entered in the system is more likely to be useful to other users rather than to oneself, the next time a new-car-purchase is contemplated.
- *Influence others:* In Web-based RSs, there are users whose main goal is to explicitly influence other users into purchasing particular products. As a matter of fact, there are also malicious users that may use the system simply to promote or penalize certain items (see Chap. 28).

As these various points indicate, the role of an RS within an information system can be quite diverse. This diversity calls for the exploitation of a range of different knowledge sources and techniques. In the next two sections, we discuss the data that an RS manages and the core technique used to identify the right recommendations.

1.3 Data and Knowledge Sources

RSs are information processing systems that actively gather various kinds of data in order to build their recommendations. Data is primarily about the items to suggest and the users who will receive these recommendations. But, since the data and knowledge sources available for recommender systems can be very diverse, ultimately, whether it can be exploited or not depends on the recommendation technique (see also Sect. 1.4). This will become clearer in the various chapters included in this handbook.

In general, there are recommendation techniques that are knowledge-poor, namely, that use very simple and basic data, such as user ratings or evaluations for items (Chaps. 2 and 3). Other techniques are much more knowledge-dependent, in that they use ontological descriptions of the users or the items (Chap. 4), constraints (Chap. 5), or social relations and activities of the users (Chaps. 15 and 17). In any case, as a general classification, data used by RSs refers to three kinds of objects: items, users, and transactions, that is, relations between the users and the items.

Items Items are the objects that are recommended. Items may be characterized by their complexity and their value or utility. The value of an item may be positive if the item is useful to the user, or negative if the item is not appropriate and the user made the wrong decision when selecting it. We note that when a user is acquiring an item, one will always incur in a cost which includes the cognitive cost of searching for the item and the real monetary cost eventually paid for the item.

For instance, the designer of a news RS must take into account the complexity of a news item, i.e., its structure, the textual representation, and the time-dependent importance of any news item. But at the same time, the RS designer must understand that even if the user is not paying for reading news, there is always a cognitive cost associated with searching and reading news items. If a selected item is relevant to the user, this cost is dominated by the benefit of having acquired useful information. Whereas if the item is not relevant, the net value of that item for the user, and its recommendation, is negative. In other domains, e.g., cars, or financial investments, the true monetary cost of the items becomes an important element to consider when selecting the most appropriate recommendation approach.

Items with low complexity and value are: news, webpages, books, CDs, and movies. Items with larger complexity and value are: digital cameras, mobile phones, PCs, etc. The most complex items that have been considered are insurance policies, financial investments, travel, and jobs [39].

RSs, according to their core technology, can use a range of properties and features of the items. For example in a movie recommender system, the genre (comedy, thriller, etc.), as well as the director and actors, can be used to describe a movie and to learn how the utility of an item depends on its features. Items can be represented using various information and representation approaches, e.g., in a minimalist way as a single ID code, or in a richer form, as a set of attributes, and even as a concept in an ontological representation of the domain (Chap. 4).

Users Users of an RS, as mentioned above, may have very diverse goals and characteristics. In order to personalize the recommendations and the human-computer interaction, RSs exploit a range of information about the users. This information can be structured in various ways, and again, the selection of what information to model depends on the recommendation technique.

For instance, in collaborative filtering, users are modeled as a simple list containing the ratings provided by the user for certain items. In a demographic RS, sociodemographic attributes such as age, gender, profession, and education, are used. User data is said to constitute the user model [12, 22]. The user model profiles the user, i.e., encodes her preferences and needs. Various user modeling approaches have been used and, in a certain sense, an RS can be viewed as a tool that generates recommendations by building and exploiting user models [10, 11]. Since no personalization is possible without a convenient user model the user model will always play a central role. For instance, in reconsidering a collaborative filtering approach, the user is either profiled directly by its ratings of items or, using these ratings, the system derives a vector of factor values where users differ in how each factor weights in their model (Chaps. 2 and 3).

Users can also be described by their behavior pattern data, for example, site browsing patterns (in a Web-based recommender system) [54], or travel search patterns (in a travel recommender system) [35]. Moreover, user data may include relations between users such as the trust level of these relations between users (Chap. 16). An RS might utilize this information to recommend items to users that were preferred by similar or trusted users.

Transactions We generically refer to a transaction as a recorded interaction between a user and the RS. Transactions are log-like data that store important information generated during the human-computer interaction and which are useful for the recommendation generation algorithm that the system is using. For instance, a transaction log may contain a reference to the item selected by the user and a description of the context (e.g., the user goal/query) for that particular recommendation. If available, that transaction may also include explicit feedback that the user has provided, such as the rating for the selected item.

In fact, ratings are the most popular form of transaction data that an RS collects. These ratings may be collected explicitly or implicitly. In the explicit collection of ratings, the user is asked to provide an opinion about an item on a rating scale. According to [47], ratings can take on a variety of forms:

- Numerical ratings such as the 1–5 stars provided in the book recommender associated with Amazon.com.
- Ordinal ratings, such as "strongly agree, agree, neutral, disagree, strongly disagree" where the user is asked to select the term that best indicates his or her opinion regarding an item (usually via questionnaire).
- Binary ratings that model choices in which the user is simply asked to decide if a certain item is good or bad.

- Unary ratings can indicate that a user has observed or purchased an item, or otherwise rated the item positively. In such cases, the absence of a rating indicates that we have no information relating the user to the item (perhaps the user purchased the item elsewhere).

Another form of user evaluation consists of tags associated by the user with the items that the system presents. For instance, on Movielens (http://movielens.umn.edu), RS tags represent how MovieLens users feel about a movie, e.g.: "too long," or "acting."

In transactions that collect implicit ratings, the system aims to infer the user's opinion based on the user's actions. For example, if a user enters the keyword "Yoga" at Amazon.com, a long list of books will be provided. In return, the user may click on a certain book on the list in order to receive additional information. At this point, the system may infer that the user is somewhat interested in that book.

In conversational systems, i.e., systems that support an interactive process, the transaction model is more refined. In these systems, user requests alternate with system actions (see Chaps. 10 and 18). That is, the user may request a recommendation and the system may produce a suggestion list. But it can also request additional user preferences to provide the user with better, more refined results. Here, in the transaction model, the system collects the various requests-responses, and may eventually learn to modify its interaction strategy by observing the outcome of the recommendation process [35].

1.4 Recommendation Techniques

In order to implement its core function, identifying useful items for the user, a RS must *predict* that an item is worth recommending. In order to do this, the system must be able to predict the utility of some items, or at least compare the utility of some items, and then decide which items to recommend based on this comparison. The prediction step may not be explicit in the recommendation algorithm but we can still apply this unifying model to describe the general role of an RS. Here, our goal is to provide the reader with a unifying perspective rather than an account of all the different recommendation approaches that will be illustrated in this handbook.

To illustrate the prediction step of an RS, consider for instance, a simple and non-personalized recommendation algorithm that recommends only the most popular songs. The rationale for using this approach is that in the absence of more precise information about the user's preferences, a popular song, i.e., one that is liked (high utility) by many users, will also most-likely appeal to a generic user, or at least with a higher likelihood than another randomly selected song. Hence, the utility of such popular songs is predicted to be reasonably high for this generic user.

This view of the core recommendation computation as the prediction of the utility of an item for a user has been suggested in [2] and recently updated in [44]. Both papers model this degree of utility of the user u for the item i as a (real valued) function $R(u, i)$, as is normally done in collaborative filtering by considering the ratings of users for items. Then, the fundamental task of a collaborative filtering RS is to predict the value of R over pairs of users and items, or in other words, to compute $\hat{R}(u, i)$, where we denote with $\hat{R}$ the estimation, computed by the RS, of the true function R. Consequently, having computed this prediction for the active user u on a set of items, i.e., $\hat{R}(u, i_1), \ldots, \hat{R}(u, i_N)$, the system will recommend the items $i_{j_1}, \ldots, i_{j_K}$ $(K \leq N)$ with the largest predicted utility. K is typically a small number, that is, much smaller than the cardinality of the item data set or the items on which a user utility prediction can be computed, i.e., RSs "filter" the items that are recommended to users.

As mentioned above, some recommender systems do not fully estimate the utility before making a recommendation, but they may apply some heuristics to hypothesize that an item may be of use to a user. This is typical, for instance, in knowledge-based systems. These utility predictions are computed with specific algorithms (see below) and use various kinds of knowledge about users, items, and the utility function itself (see Sect. 1.3) [17]. For instance, the system may assume that the utility function is Boolean and therefore it will just determine whether an item is or is not useful for the user. Consequently, assuming that there is some available knowledge, or possibly none, about the user who is requesting the recommendation, as well as knowledge about items, and other users who received recommendations, the system will leverage this knowledge with an appropriate algorithm to generate various utility predictions and hence recommendations [17].

It is also important to note that sometimes the user utility for an item is observed to depend on other variables, which we generically call "contextual" [44]. For instance, the utility of an item for a user can be influenced by the domain knowledge of the user (e.g., expert versus beginning users of a digital camera), or can depend on the time when the recommendation is requested. Equally, users may be more interested in items (e.g., restaurant) closer to their current location. Consequently, the recommendations must be adapted to these specific additional details and as a result it becomes increasingly more difficult to correctly estimate what the right recommendations are.

This handbook presents several different types of recommender systems that vary in terms of the addressed domain and the knowledge used, but especially with regard to the recommendation algorithm, i.e., how the prediction of the utility of a recommendation is made, as was mentioned at the beginning of this section. Other differences relate to how the recommendations are finally assembled and presented to the user in response to user requests. These aspects are discussed as well, later in this introduction.

To provide an initial overview of the different types of RSs, we want to quote a taxonomy provided by Burke [17] that has become a classical way of distinguishing between recommender systems and referring to them. Burke [17] distinguishes between six different classes of recommendation approaches:

Content-Based The system learns to recommend items that are similar to the ones that the user liked in the past. The similarity of items is calculated based on the features associated with the compared items. For example, if a user has positively rated a movie that belongs to the comedy genre, then the system can learn to recommend other movies from this genre [33].

Classic content-based recommendation techniques aim at matching the attributes of the user profile against the attributes of the items. In most cases, the items' attributes are simply keywords that are extracted from the items' descriptions. Semantic indexing techniques represent the item and user profiles using concepts instead of keywords. Chapter 4 presents a comprehensive survey of semantic indexing techniques to overcome the main problems of classical keyword-based systems. The authors presents two main groups of semantic indexing techniques: top-down and bottom-up. Techniques in the former group rely on the integration of external knowledge sources, such as: ontologies, encyclopedic knowledge (such as Wikipedia) and data from the Linked Data cloud, while techniques in the latter group rely on a lightweight semantic representation based on the hypothesis that the meaning of words depends on their usage in large corpora of textual documents. Chapter 4 demonstrates how to utilize semantic approaches to realize a new generation of semantic content-based recommender systems, by providing a description of their main potentials and limitations.

Collaborative Filtering The original and most simple implementation of this approach [24] makes recommendations to the active user based on items that other users with similar tastes liked in the past. The similarity in taste of two users is calculated based on the similarity in the rating history of the users. This is the reason why [48] refers to collaborative filtering as "people-to-people correlation." Collaborative filtering is considered to be the most popular and widely implemented technique in RS.

Chapter 2 presents a comprehensive survey of neighborhood-based methods for collaborative filtering. Neighborhood-based methods focus on relationships between items or, alternatively, between users. An item-item approach models the preference of a user to an item based on ratings of similar items by the same user. Neighborhood-based methods benefit from considerable popularity due to their simplicity, efficiency, and ability to produce accurate and personalized recommendations. Chapter 2 describes the main benefits of such methods, as well as their principal characteristics.

Moreover, Chap. 2 addresses the essential decisions that are required while implementing a neighborhood-based recommender system, and gives practical information on how to make such decisions. Perhaps the decision that has the greatest impact on the rating prediction and computational performance of the recommender system is the choice between a user-based and an item-based method. In typical commercial recommender systems where the number of users exceeds the number of available items, item-based approaches should be preferred since they provide more accurate recommendations, while being more computationally efficient and requiring less frequent updates. On the other hand, user-based methods usually provide more original recommendations, which may lead users to a more satisfying experience [21].

Finally, the problems of sparsity and limited coverage, often observed in large commercial recommender systems, are discussed by exploring two research directions: dimensionality reduction and graph-based techniques. Dimensionality reduction provides a compact representation of users and items that captures their most significant features. An advantage of such an approach is that it allows for obtaining meaningful relations between pairs of users or items, even though these users have rated different items, or these items were rated by different users. On the other hand, graph-based techniques exploit the transitive relations in the data. These techniques also avoid the problems of sparsity and limited coverage by evaluating the relationship between users or items that are not directly connected. However, unlike dimensionality reduction, graph-based methods also preserve some of the "local" relations in the data.

Chapter 3 presents several recent extensions available for building CF recommenders. Specifically, the authors discuss latent factor models, such as matrix factorization (e.g., Singular Value Decomposition (SVD)). These methods transform both items and users to the same latent factor space. The latent space is then used to explain ratings by characterizing both products and users in term of factors automatically inferred from user feedback. The authors elucidate how SVD can handle additional features of the data, including implicit feedback and temporal information. They also describe techniques to address shortcomings of neighborhood techniques by suggesting more rigorous formulations using global optimization techniques. Utilizing such techniques makes it possible to lift the limit on neighborhood size and to address implicit feedback and temporal dynamics. The resulting accuracy is close to that of matrix factorization models, while offering a number of practical advantages.

Demographic This type of system recommends items based on the demographic profile of the user [13]. The assumption is that different recommendations should be generated for different demographic niches. Many websites adopt simple and effective personalization solutions based on demographics. For example, users are dispatched to particular websites based on their language or country. Or, suggestions may be customized according to the age of the user. While these approaches have been quite popular in the marketing literature, there has been relatively little proper RS research on demographic systems.

Knowledge-Based Knowledge-based systems recommend items based on specific domain knowledge about how certain item features meet users' needs and preferences and, ultimately, how the item is useful for the user. Notable knowledge-based recommender systems are case-based [15, 19, 45]. In these systems, a similarity function estimates how much the user's needs (problem description) match the recommendations (solutions of the problem). Here, the similarity score can be directly interpreted as the utility of the recommendation for the user. Knowledge-based systems tend to work better than others at the beginning of their deployment but if they are not equipped with learning components, they may be surpassed by other shallow methods that can exploit the logs of the human/computer interaction (as in CF).

Constraint-based systems are another type of knowledge-based RS (Chap. 5). In terms of used knowledge, both systems are similar: user requirements are collected, repairs for inconsistent requirements are automatically proposed in situations where no solutions could be found, and recommendation results are explained. The major difference lies in the way solutions are calculated. Case-based recommenders determine recommendations on the basis of similarity metrics whereas constraint-based recommenders predominantly exploit predefined knowledge bases that contain explicit rules about how to relate customer requirements with item features.

Chapter 5 reviews constraint-based recommendation approaches and provide an overview of technologies for the development of knowledge bases for constraint-based recommenders since appropriate tool support can be crucial in practical settings. The authors show that constraint-based methods are particularly well suited for recommending complex products such as financial services or electronic consumer goods.

Moreover, Chap. 5 presents possible forms of user interaction that are supported by constraint-based recommender applications, report scenarios in which constraint-based recommenders have been successfully applied, and review different technical solution approaches.

Community-Based This type of system recommends items based on the preferences of the user's friends. This technique follows the epigram, "Tell me who your friends are, and I will tell you who you are" [4, 9]. Evidence suggests that people tend to rely more on recommendations from their friends than on recommendations from similar but anonymous individuals [52]. This observation, combined with the growing popularity of open social networks, is generating a rising interest in community-based systems or, as they are usually referred, social recommender systems [23]. This type of RS models and acquires information about the social relations of the users and the preferences of the user's friends. The recommendation is based on ratings that were provided by the user's friends. In fact these RSs are following the rise of social-networks and enable a simple and comprehensive acquisition of data related to the social relations of the users.

Hybrid Recommender Systems These RSs are based on the combination of the above mentioned techniques. A hybrid system combining techniques A and B tries to use the advantages of A to fix the disadvantages of B. For instance, CF methods suffer from new-item problems, or, that they cannot recommend items that have no ratings. This does not limit content-based approaches since the prediction for new items is based on their description (features) that are typically easily available. Given two (or more) basic RSs techniques, several ways have been proposed for combining them to create a new hybrid system (see [17] for the precise descriptions).

As we have already mentioned, the context of the user when he or she is seeking a recommendation can be used to better personalize the output of the system. For example, in a temporal context, vacation recommendations in winter should be very different from those provided in summer [8]. Or a restaurant recommendation for a Saturday evening with one's friends should be different from that suggested for a workday lunch with co-workers.

Chapter 6 reviews the topic of context-aware recommender systems (CARS). It presents the general notion of context and how it can be modeled in RSs. As it discusses the possibilities of combining several context-aware recommendation techniques into a single unified approach, the authors also provide a case study of one such combined approach.

Three popular different algorithmic paradigms for incorporating contextual information into the recommendation process are discussed: reduction-based (prefiltering), contextual post filtering, and context modeling. In reduction-based (prefiltering) methods, only the information that matches the current usage context, e.g., the ratings for items evaluated in the same context, are used to compute the recommendations. In contextual post filtering, the recommendation algorithm ignores the context information. The output of the algorithm is filtered/adjusted to include only the recommendations that are relevant in the target context. In the contextual modeling, the more sophisticated of the three approaches, context data is explicitly used in the prediction model.

Recommendation tasks can be solved with the help of techniques that were developed in the field of Data Mining. Chapter 7, presents an overview of the main Data Mining techniques used in the context of Recommender Systems and presents cases where these techniques have been successfully applied. In particular, it discusses the following techniques: preprocessing techniques such as sampling or dimensionality reduction; classification techniques, such as Bayesian Networks, Decision Trees and Support Vector Machines; clustering techniques such as k-means; and finally association rules.

1.5 Recommender Systems Evaluation

Recommender systems research is being conducted with a strong emphasis on practice and commercial applications. One very important issue related to the practical side of RS deployment is the necessity of evaluating the quality and value of the systems. Evaluation is required at different stages of the system's life cycle and for various purposes [1, 26]. At design time, evaluation is required to verify the selection of the appropriate recommender approach. In the design phase, evaluation should be implemented off-line and the recommendation algorithms, i.e., their computed recommendations, are compared with the stored user interactions. An off-line evaluation consists of running several algorithms on the same datasets of user interactions (e.g., ratings) and comparing their performances. This type of evaluation is usually conducted on existing public benchmark data if appropriate data is available, or, otherwise, on collected data. The design of the off-line experiments should follow known experiment design practices [6] in order to ensure reliable results. Off-line experiments can measure the quality of the chosen algorithm in fulfilling its recommendation task. However, such evaluation cannot provide any insight about the user satisfaction, acceptance or experience with the system. The algorithms might be very accurate in solving the core recommendation problem, i.e., predicting user ratings, but for some other reason the system may not be accepted by users, for example, because the performance of the system was not as expected.

Therefore, a user-centric evaluation is also required. It can be performed online after the system has been launched, or as a focused user study. During on-line evaluation, real users interact with the system without being aware of the full nature of the experiment running in the background. It is possible to run various versions of the algorithms on different groups of users for comparison and analysis of the system logs in order to enhance system performance. In addition, most of the algorithms include parameters, such as weight thresholds, the number of neighbors, etc., requiring constant adjustment and calibration.

Focused user studies are conducted when the on-line evaluation is not feasible or too risky. In this type of evaluation, a controlled experiment is planned where a small group of users are asked to perform different tasks with various versions of the system. It is then possible to analyze the user's performance and to distribute questionnaires so that users may report on their experience. In such experiments, it is possible to collect both quantitative and qualitative information about the systems.

In recent years there has been an increased interest in user-centric evaluation procedures and metric for recommender systems. Researchers realized that recommender systems' goals extend beyond the accuracy of the algorithms [30] as tools to provide a helpful and enjoyable, personalized experience that leads to user retention and satisfaction. This approach broadened the range of evaluated aspects of an RS to include aspects such as the form of preference elicitation, the presentation of the recommended results (e.g., one top item, top N items, or predicted ratings), and finally, the evaluation of the explanations provided to the users. Explanations may serve a few goals: the most popular is the justification of results, i.e., explaining to the user why the system decided to recommend a specific item. Other goals may include increasing trust in the system, persuading the user to purchase the recommended item, and helping a user with their decision making. When designing the evaluation of the recommendation explanation, it is important to identify the goal of the explanation and adjust a suitable metric for measuring it.

Chapter 8 details the three previously mentioned types of experiments that can be conducted in order to evaluate recommender systems, namely, off-line, on-line and user studies. It presents their advantages and disadvantages, and defines guidelines for choosing the methods for evaluating them by considering the properties that are to be evaluated. Unlike existing discussions of evaluation in the literature that usually focuses mainly on the accuracy of an algorithm's prediction [26] and related measures, this chapter is unique in its approach to the evaluation discussion since it focuses on property-directed evaluation. It provides a large set of properties (other than accuracy) that are relevant to the system's success. For each of the properties, the appropriate type of experiment and relevant measures are suggested. Among the list of properties are: coverage, cold start, confidence, trust, novelty, risk, and serendipity. The chapter describes the difficulties and pitfalls of each of the properties and guidelines for the selection of the suitable evaluation type and properties for a given recommendation task ad system.

Chapter 9 highlights the importance of user-centric evaluation. It provides detailed and practical guidelines of how to conduct user-centric experiments in order to evaluate the user's experience with the system. The chapter first presents a theoretical user-centric evaluation framework [29] that maps aspects of recommender systems and their interaction with the users that should be evaluated. Then, it provides practical guidelines for students and researchers for conducting user experiments. It presents tips for stating hypotheses, recruiting participants, design of the experiments and statistical analysis of the results. Finally, the chapter provides many examples of actual systems' evaluations from the relevant literature.

Chapter 10 tackles an additional aspect of the user-centric approach to evaluation and highlights an important aspect of RS: explanations of the recommendation results to the users. It examines the reasons that make an evaluation "good" and the effects that explanations might have on RS acceptance. The chapter first explains the interaction between the recommender system and the explanation in terms of preference elicitation methods and the presentation of results, as well as the recommendation algorithm. Then, explanation styles are described, along with examples of explanation in existing systems. The goals of explanations are listed from which metrics that measure the success of explanations in achieving these goals are described. The chapter concludes with challenges related to explanations. This includes the context in which explanations should be shown, and a major challenge in evaluating the interaction between acceptance of recommendation and explanations, as well as how to assure that explanations are indeed helpful and do not lead users to make poor decisions.

1.6 Recommender Systems Applications

Recommender systems research, aside from its theoretical contribution, is generally aimed at practically improving industrial RSs and involves research about various practical aspects that apply to the implementation of the systems. Indeed, an RS is an example of large scale usage of machine learning and data mining algorithms in commercial practice [3]. The common interest in the field, both from the research community and from the industry has leveraged the availability of data for research on one hand, and the evolvement of enhanced algorithms on the other hand. Practical related research in RSs examines aspects that are relevant to different stages in the life cycle of an RS, namely, the design of the system, its implementation, evaluation, maintenance and enhancement during system operation. The Netflix Prize announced in 2006, described in Chap. 11, was an important event for the recommender systems research community and industry, and their mutual interaction. It highlighted the importance of the recommendation of items to users and accelerated the development of many new data mining recommendation techniques. Even though the Netflix Prize initiated a lot of research activities, the prize was a simplification of the full recommendation problem. It consisted of predicting user's ratings while optimizing the Root Mean Square Error (RMSE) between the predicted and actual ratings. Chapter 11 describes lessons learned from the prize awarded in 2009 and provides insights about industrial setting of RSs using the Netflix system as a case study for real-world recommender systems. In addition, the chapter provides the industry perspective about RSs implementation issues that deserve attention while developing a real-world RS. It describes the data centric approach used at Netflix for selecting the best model for a problem in order to provide an optimized personalized experience to the user. In addition, the chapter highlights the need for a suitable scalable system architecture that can support the development and evaluation process of innovative algorithms and deliver recommendations based on large volumes of available data.

The first factor to consider while designing an RS is the application's domain as it has a major effect on the algorithmic approach that should be taken. Montaner et al. [39] provide a taxonomy of RSs and classify existing RS applications to specific application domains. Based on these specific application domains, we define more general classes of domains for the most common recommender systems applications:

- Entertainment—recommendations for movies, music, games, and IPTV.
- Content—personalized newspapers, recommendation for documents, recommendations of webpages, e-learning applications, and e-mail filters.
- E-commerce—recommendations of products to buy such as books, cameras, PCs etc. for consumers.
- Services—recommendations of travel services, recommendation of experts for consultation, recommendation of houses to rent, or matchmaking services.
- Social—recommendation of people in social networks, and recommendations of content social media content such as tweets, Facebook feeds, LinkedIn updates, and others.

As recommender systems become more popular, interest is roused in the potential advantages of new and diverse applications, such as recommending insurance riders, or recommending questions for question-answering systems. As the above list cannot cover all the application domains that are now being addressed by RS techniques: it gives only an initial description of the various types of application domains.

The developer of an RS for a certain application domain should understand the specific facets of the domain, its requirements, application challenges and limitations. Only after analyzing these factors can one be able to select the optimal recommender algorithm and to design an effective human-computer interaction. In the current version of the handbook, some of the chapters in this section describe applications of recommender systems in specific domains. Each of these chapters describes the requirements of an RS for a specific domain, its precise challenges and the suitable technologies and algorithms for addressing them.

One detailed example of an RS designed for a specific domain is described in Chap. 12, which deals with recommender systems for technology-enhanced learning (TEL). TEL, which generally covers technologies that support all forms of teaching and learning activities, aims at designing, developing and testing new methods and technologies to enhance learning practices of both individuals and organizations. As the digital way of education and learning is becoming more popular, the need to integrate the personalization of content into the learning process and the available data for assessing the quality of the algorithms has created opportunities for the rise of the popularity of TEL RSs. Since TEL may benefit greatly from integrating recommender systems technology to personalize the learning process and adjust it to the user's former knowledge, abilities and preferences [55], there is a significant increase in RSs applied to TEL. The chapter presents an extensive survey of RSs for TEL covering 82 systems from 35 countries categorizing them using a classification framework consisting of three main categories, namely: Supported Tasks, Approach, and Operation. An analysis of the 82 systems using the framework resulted in seven clusters of TEL RSs, where each cluster represents a unique form of contribution to the field. The chapter aims at providing an overview about the TEL RS field in order to standardize evaluation settings and measures, as well as providing guidelines for the application of RS technology to TEL.

Yet another popular domain for recommendation is the recommendation of music, presented in Chap. 13. Unique features of music items that pose various challenges for recommendations should be considered when designing and evaluating RSs for music. Such challenges include, for example, the short time that it takes a user to gain an opinion about a recommended item, as compared to a movie or a book, or the fact that the same item can be recommended many times. In addition, music can be recommended as a single item, a playlist, and abstracted by genre, performer, or band. Music RSs, as opposed to many other domains, rely heavily on content-based recommendation which implies specific challenges to the domain [37].

Some new application domains for recommendation evolved with the emergence of new technologies that became very popular. One example, detailed in Chap. 14, is the evolution of mobile technology that accelerated the development of specific RSs for mobile devices utilizing the special capabilities of the devices (e.g., the GPS). Chapter 14 reviews the main components of a location based mobile recommender system. While there are various application domains of mobile context aware RSs (as described in Chap. 6) that may benefit from mobile sensors in order to enrich their users' profiles, Chap. 14 highlights mobile location-based recommendations. Such RS applications recommend places and venues based on the user's location and history of behaviors and preferences. The chapter describes the algorithms that have been applied to recommending venues, and the evaluation procedures for assessing the quality of the recommendations. Looking into the future, the authors suggest additional location based applications such as recommendations for cab drivers on pick-up locations, or recommending where to locate a retail store.

Another example of new RSs that emerged with new technologies are recommender systems related to the social web, and specifically those that target the social media domain. With the rise of social networks (e.g., Facebook, LinkedIn, Tweeter, Flickr, and others), users are overloaded with information, activities and interactions. Social recommender systems are RSs that aim at assisting the user in identifying relevant content (e.g., tweets, feeds or images), and engage only in relevant activities and interactions (e.g., discussions, or comments). Apart from the RSs that have been developed to be dedicated to social media, recommender systems of other domains can benefit from the new types of data that social media introduces about users to enhance the quality of standard RSs [23]. The term Social RS covers many types of RSs that are relevant to the social media platform in which Chap. 15 describes two main types: recommendations of social media content and recommendations of people. For recommendations of social content, the chapter reviews various social content media domains, and provides a detailed case study and insights learned from a recommender system operated in the enterprise which suggests mixed social media items. The chapter lists three different types of people recommendations, namely, the recommendation of familiar people (e.g., classmates, family members) that are not connected in the network; recommendations of interesting people (to connect with, or follow), and recommendations of strangers (to date, to hire, or for various other purposes). It explains the complexity of people-recommendation and lists key topics that should be considered and should be further investigated. The list includes: the need for explanation, privacy concerns, social relationships, trust and reputation, as well as the need to define special evaluation measures.

Chapter 16 highlights a special form of social recommendations, the reciprocal people-to-people recommendations that require the two parties involved in a recommendation to be satisfied. Some examples are: dating recommendations, Human Resource recommendations (recommendations of employees and employers), and recommending groupings of students for learning groups. Besides the unique reciprocal manner of satisfaction that is required from both parties, the chapter highlights other differences between traditional and reciprocal recommendations, including the users' willingness to provide explicit feedback, the fact that users are usually engaged with the system for a long term, and the requirement not to overload users with recommendations.

Within the chapter, the authors provide an overview regarding existing reciprocal recommender systems and demonstrate how the special requirements of reciprocity are considered in system design. A detailed case study, specifically in online dating recommendation, is presented and includes the recommendation hybrid content-collaborative algorithm and its evaluation. One interesting insight shown is that implicit feedback is more effective than explicit for these types of systems.

The social Web is also exploited by modern search engines that rely on recommendation techniques to address Web search challenges and to implement advanced search features. Specifically, various engines attempt to apply some form of personalization and collaboration by generating results to a user query that are not only relevant to the query terms but are also tailored to the user's search history, reputation, and preferences as inferred from the user's own previous activities on the social Web.

Chapter 17 discusses the research goals of Information Retrieval (IR) and personalized Web search from the RS perspective. The authors illustrate how techniques that originated in recent RS research may be applied to address search engine challenges. This chapter focuses on two promising ideas for search engine improvement: personalization and collaboration. It describes a number of different approaches to personalizing Web searches by exploiting user preferences and context information to affect search results. In addition, the chapter discusses recent work in the area of collaborative information retrieval, which attempts to take advantage of the potential for cooperation between friends, colleagues or users with similar needs in implementing a variety of information-seeking tasks. This new line of research, termed social search, benefits from the social medium property of the Web in providing search results that are affected by the experience and preferences of similar users. The authors foresee a convergence of recommender systems and search engines, where a search engine will provide a unique platform for modern recommendation technologies. The authors believe that integrating these sources in search engine algorithms, along with a proactive manner of search experience that strives to understand the users' needs, would result in highly satisfied users that are able to receive the right information at the right time. Another trend that is affecting search engines is the rise of search activities through mobile devices. This introduces new constraints to search and discovery interfaces, but also brings about opportunities for innovations using the mobile sensors that allow enhanced personalization.

1.7 Recommender Systems and Human Computer Interaction

As we have illustrated in the previous sections, researchers have been chiefly concerned with designing a range of technical solutions and leveraging various sources of knowledge to achieve better predictions about what is liked and how much it is liked by the target user. The underlying assumption behind this research activity is that simply presenting these correct recommendations, or the best options, is not sufficient. In other words, the recommendations should speak for themselves, and the user should definitely accept the recommendations if they are correct. This is clearly an overly simplified account of the recommendation problem and the delivery of recommendations is not so straightforward.

In practice, users need recommendations because they do not have enough knowledge to make an autonomous decision. Consequently, it may not be easy for them to evaluate the proposed recommendation. Hence, various researchers have tried to understand the factors that lead to the acceptance of a recommendation by a given user [5, 20, 25, 38, 50, 53].

Swearingen and Sinha [53] were among the first to point out that the effectiveness of an RS is dependent on factors that go beyond the quality of the prediction algorithm. In fact, the recommender must also convince users to try (or read, buy, listen, watch, etc.) the recommended items. This, of course, depends on the individual characteristics of the selected items, and therefore on the recommendation algorithm. The process also depends, however, on the particular human/computer interaction supported by the system when the items are presented, compared, and explained. Swearingen and Sinha [53] found that from a user's perspective, an effective recommender system must inspire trust in the system and it must have a system logic that is at least somewhat transparent. Additionally, the authors note that it should point users towards new, not-yet-experienced items, and should provide details about recommended items, including pictures and community ratings, and finally, it should present ways to refine recommendations.

Swearingen and Sinha [53] and other similarly oriented researchers do not diminish the importance of the recommendation algorithm, but claim that its effectiveness should not be evaluated only in terms of the accuracy of the prediction, i.e., with standard and popular IR metrics, such as Mean Absolute Error (MAE), precision, or Normalized Discounted Cumulative Gain (NDCG) (see Chap. 8). Other dimensions should be measured that relate to the acceptance of the recommender system and its recommendations. These ideas have been remarkably well presented and discussed also by McNee et al. [38]. In that work, the authors propose user-centric directions for evaluating recommender systems, including: the similarity of recommendation lists, recommendation serendipity, and the importance of user needs and expectations in a recommender.

Recommender systems collect tremendous amounts of user data that are necessary for the recommendation purposes. However, the availability of this data may result in this data being used in a way that violates the end-user's expectations of privacy, especially if it is accessed by untrusted parties or misused by malicious agents. Chapter 19 presents the latest in privacy enhanced recommendations. The authors analyze the risks to user privacy imposed by recommender systems, survey the existing solutions, and discuss the privacy implications for the users of the recommenders. In particular, the authors describe several architectures that preserve user privacy by using various decentralized solutions that eliminate a single repository of user modeling data, which would otherwise be the target for malicious attacks on the recommender. In addition, the authors present algorithmic solutions, which either perturb the original user modeling data or apply formal encryption methods. These assure that, even if accessed by an untrusted party, only modified or encrypted user data would be exposed rather than the original data. Lastly, the policy driven solutions are described. These solutions address directives and legislation initiatives that limit the storage, transfer, and exploitation of personal user data.

An essential goal of recommender systems is to help users make better choices [18]. Thus, it is important to understand how people make choices and how the human decision making process can be supported. Chapter 18 begins with a compact overview of the psychology of everyday choice and decision making that is based on a large literature of psychological research and formulated so as to be relevant and accessible to recommender systems research community. The authors explain how recommender systems can be viewed as one of many available tools for facilitating choice. Then, the authors provide a high-level overview of strategies for helping people make better choices, indicating how recommender systems fit into the greater picture of choice. In addition, the main functionalities of RSs are presented: eliciting information to construct preference models, narrowing down a large set of options, helping users choose among a small set of recommended options, and helping users to explore large spaces of options. The authors show how an understanding of human decision making can illuminate research and practice concerning these processes.

As discussed in previous sections, recommender systems often utilize sophisticated algorithms to make recommendations. However, the RS cannot assume the advice provided by a system will always be accepted by its users. Whether a recommendation is seen as credible advice and actually taken into account not only depends on users' perceptions of the recommendation but also of the system as an advice-giver.

In Chap. 20 the authors stress that a recommendation is seen as credible advice and is actually taken into account not only because of the user's perceptions of the recommendation but also due to the fundamental role of the system which is perceived as an advice-giver. Indeed, the literature about persuasion suggests that people are likely to accept recommendations from credible sources and we therefore conclude that the credibility of the RS is vital to increasing the likelihood of recommendation acceptance. Hence, the authors discuss how the credibility of RSs can be enhanced, providing a synopsis of credibility-related research.

Chapter 20 reviews the existing literature on source factors in the context of human-human, human-technology, and human-recommender system interactions. It also discusses system credibility evaluation in light of the increasing popularity of social technology. Source characteristics which have been studied in the context of human and technology interaction, and particularly, in the recommender systems realm are discussed as well. Finally, Chap. 20 concludes that many social cues that have been identified as influential in other contexts have yet to be implemented and tested with respect to recommender systems.

Personality accounts for the most important way in which individuals differ in their enduring emotional, interpersonal, experiential, attitudinal and motivational styles. Studies have shown that personality was especially useful at tackling the issues of the cold start problem and diverse recommendations.

Chapter 21 discusses how personality relates to user preferences and how to use personality in recommender systems. The authors present the Five Factor Model (FFM) of personality. This model appears suitable for usage in recommender systems as it can be easily quantified in terms of features corresponding to the main factors. The acquisition of the personality factors for an observed user can be made explicitly through questionnaires or implicitly using machine learning approaches on modalities like social media streams or mobile phone call logs.

1.8 Advanced Topics

It is clear from the previous pages that RS research is evolving in numerous and diverse directions, and new topics are emerging or becoming more important subjects of investigation. The reader is also encouraged to refer to the proceedings of the last editions of the ACM RecSys conferences and other excellent review papers for additional material [13, 30, 34, 40, 44]. In this handbook, we cover some of these topics. Indeed, some have already been presented, such as: context-aware recommendations (Chap. 6), social-based recommendations (Chap. 15), and reciprocal recommendations (Chap. 16). Other important topics are covered in the last section of this handbook and will now briefly introduce these chapters.

Chapter 22 deals with situations in which the system should recommend information or items that are relevant to a group of users rather than to an individual. For instance, a RS may select television programs for a group to view or a sequence of songs to listen to, based on models of all the group members. Recommending to groups is clearly more complicated than recommending to individuals. Assuming that we know precisely what is good for individual users, the issue is how to combine individual user models. In this chapter, the authors discuss how group recommendation works, what its problems are, and what advances have been made so far.

Chapter 23 discusses the ubiquitous issue of aggregating preferences, criteria or similarities. Normally such aggregation is done by using either the arithmetic mean or maximum/minimum functions. But many other aggregation functions which could deliver flexibility and adaptability, and ultimately more relevant recommendations, are often overlooked. In this chapter the authors review the basics of aggregation functions and their properties and present the most important families, including generalized means, Choquet and Sugeno integrals, ordered weighted averaging, triangular norms and conorms, as well as bipolar aggregation functions. Such functions can model various interactions between the inputs, including conjunctive, disjunctive and mixed behavior.

In Chap. 24, the authors focus on another fundamental problem of RSs: the need to actively look for new data during the operational life of the recommender. This issue is normally neglected on the assumption that there is not much space for controlling the data (e.g., ratings) that the system can collect, since these decisions are taken by the users when visiting the system. Actually, the RS provokes the users with its recommendations and many systems actually explicitly ask for user preferences during the recommendation process. Hence, by tuning the process, users can be pushed to provide a range of different information. Specifically they can be requested to rate particular items since the knowledge of the user's opinions about these items could be estimated as particularly beneficial to the system performance. For instance, the system may be able to provide more diverse recommendations with this additional information, or may improve its prediction accuracy. At this point active learning comes in; it can augment RSs, helping users to become more self-aware of their own likes/dislikes, and lead to more meaningful and useful questions. At the same time, active learning can provide new information to the system that can be analyzed for subsequent recommendations. Hence, applying active learning to RSs enables personalization of the recommending process [36]. This is accomplished by allowing the system to actively influence the items that the user is exposed to (e.g., the items displayed to the user during sign-up or during regular use), as well as by enabling the user to explore his or her interests freely.

Chapter 25 introduces another emerging topic: multi-criteria recommender systems. In the majority of RSs, the utility associated with an item is usually considered a single criterion value, or an overall evaluation or rating of an item by a user. But recently, this assumption has been judged as limited because the suitability of the recommended item for a particular user may depend on several aspects that the user can take into consideration when making his or her choice. The incorporation of multiple criteria that can affect the user's opinions may lead to more effective and accurate recommendations.

Chapter 25 provides an overview of multi-criteria RSs. First, it defines the recommendation problem as a multi-criteria decision-making problem and reviews methods and techniques that can support the implementation of multi-criteria recommenders. Then, it focuses on the category of multi-criteria rating recommender techniques that provide recommendations by modeling the user's utility for an item as a vector of ratings along several criteria. A review of current algorithms that use multi-criteria ratings for calculating the rating prediction and generating recommendations is provided. The chapter concludes with a discussion on open issues and future challenges for these recommenders.

Accurately predicting that the user surely likes a small number of items and suggesting them repeatedly it is not likely to provide a quality service to the user. Likewise, if the suggested items are all quite similar, the system's suggestions will seem repetitive and it may fail to identify peculiar items. Such peculiar items, though they are at the boundary of the user's spectrum of preference, may be unexpected and therefore perceived as more informative or highly desirable to the user.

These topics are discussed in Chap. 26 that is dedicated to novelty and diversity in recommender systems. After having motivated the need for novel and diverse recommendations, the chapter precisely defines these two naturally vague concepts and their relationships. While novelty is a property of the individual recommendations, diversity can only be measured by referring to sets of recommendations, either for a single user or for the full set of users of a recommender system. The quantitative measure of these two properties occupies a substantial amount of the chapter in that this is an important preliminary step prior to focusing on techniques that will improve the system's performance in this respect. This issue is then discussed by presenting a range of techniques aimed at enhancing a recommendation list by editing it with the ultimate goal of increasing the diversification of the recommendations and their novelty. Finally the chapter presents a unifying model that can describe the range of metrics presented thus far. A critical element in this unifying model is that novelty is relative to a context of experience, showing the unexpected relationship between this line of research and that on context-aware recommender systems (see Chap. 6).

As we have referred to already in this introduction, recommender system applications are normally restricted to a particular type of items (movies, CDs, books, etc.). Even though an ecommerce player sells several different types of products (e.g., Amazon), its recommender system treats each product typology independently from the others. This means that if a user has expressed his preferences for a certain category of products (e.g., books), for instance in the form of ratings, this information is ignored when the system computes recommendations for items in another category (e.g., movies). But, it is natural to expect that preferences in a domain are somewhat correlated to preferences in another domain. So, for instance, if two users have bought very similar sets of books, it is likely that some of the movies bought by one of the users may be good recommendations for the other user.

The idea of relating recommendations in different domains by exploiting user data collected in one domain to produce recommendations in another, is at the base of the research on cross-domain recommender systems. These systems and their underlying techniques are illustrated in Chap. 27. It is shown here how leveraging all the user's preferences, collected in several domain specific systems, may be beneficial for generating more comprehensive user models and better recommendations. Cross-domain recommender systems can in fact mitigate the cold-start and sparsity problems in a target domain where not much user data has been collected. Moreover, they can enable cross-selling recommendations, such as building more complex recommendations where items from multiple domains are suggested together (e.g, a movie and a book on a recommended singer). In this chapter, the authors formally define the cross-domain recommendation problem, and try to provide a unifying perspective by merging ideas and approaches which arise in distinct disciplines. The chapter provides an analytical categorization of prior work, and identifies open issues for future research.

The last chapter of this handbook (Chap. 28) surveys articles which deal with security issues. This topic has become a major issue in the past few years. The chapter analyzes algorithms designed to generate more robust recommendations, i.e., recommendations that are harder for malicious users to influence. In fact, collaborative recommender systems are dependent on the goodwill of their users, in that there is an implicit assumption that users will interact with the system with the aim of getting good recommendations for themselves while providing useful data for their neighbors. However, users will have a range of purposes in interacting with RSs and in some cases, these purposes may be counter those of the system owner or those of the majority of the user population. Namely, these users may want to damage the website which hosts the recommender, or to influence the recommendations provided to visitors, e.g., to score some items better or worse rather than to arrive at a fair evaluation.

In this chapter, the authors provide a model of efficient attacks, i.e, attacks that can, at a relatively low cost, produce a large impact on system output. Since these attacks may very well be launched against a site, it makes sense to detect them so that countermeasures can be taken as soon as possible. At the same time, researchers have studied a number of algorithms that are intended to robustly withstand attacks and which have lower impact curves relative to efficient attacks. These approaches are also surveyed in this chapter. With the combination of these techniques, researchers have sought not to eliminate attacks, but rather to control their impact to the point in which they are no longer cost-effective.

1.9 Challenges

The list of newly emerging and challenging RS research topics is not limited to those described in the chapters that we have summarized above. Moreover, covering all of them is not within the scope of this introduction. The reader is referred to the final discussion sections that are included in almost all of the chapters published in this handbook for other crucial problems.

Below, we briefly introduce additional challenging topics that we consider important for the development of the research on RSs.

1.9.1 Preference Acquisition and Profiling

A number of open issues are related to the critical stage of acquiring information about the user preferences and generating usable profiles of the users.

It is clear that in many real-world situations, implicit feedback is much more readily available and requires no extra effort on the user's side. For instance, on a web page it is easy to log the users visiting a URL, or clicking on an ad. The system can treat these actions as a form of positive feedback to the displayed items. It makes sense that information about such previous actions contains highly relevant information for predicting future actions. For that reason many recent approaches focus on the use of the more reliable and readily available implicit feedback (see the final discussion in Chap. 11 that refers to this issue). In cases where we have implicit feedback, the recommendation problem becomes the prediction of the probability that a user will interact with a given item. But, standard recommendation formulation in such a setting is not applicable: there is no negative feedback, all the available data is either positive or missing. The missing data includes both items that the user explicitly chose to ignore because they were not appealing and items that would have been perfect recommendations but were never presented to the user. This issue is discussed in Chap. 11 and effective solutions for tackling it must be still developed further.

Notwithstanding the pros of implicit feedback, this data cannot completely substitute the usage of explicitly user-made evaluations, at last for some of the items. In order to make the acquisition of this information more effective, as is illustrated in Chap. 24, a number of techniques for actively collecting preference data from users, especially in the cold start phase, but also in the full life of a system, have been illustrated. It is however still challenging to select, among the various active learning techniques, the one that is more appropriate to a system when dealing with a particular user in a given stage of the system evolution and for a particular goal (e.g., accuracy vs. coverage). More adaptive solutions which can blend, run-time with several elementary approaches, should be investigated. Moreover, their practical application depends also on their computational cost, which could become prohibitive when multiple strategies must be estimated in real time to find out the best one for that specific scenario.

Hence, in addition to better active learning techniques, simplifying the cognitive cost of preference acquisition is of primary importance. For a recommender system to achieve good recommendation performance, users typically need to provide the system with a certain amount of feedback about their preferences (e.g., in the form of item ratings). This can be an issue in single-rating recommender systems and even more for multi-criteria rating systems that require a more significant level of user involvement, as each user needs to rate an item based on multiple criteria. Therefore, it is important to measure the costs and benefits of adopting alternative rating approaches and scales, and find an optimal solution to meet the needs of both the users and the system designers. For instance, preference disaggregation methods could support the implicit formulation of a preference Multi-Criteria Recommender Systems model (as indicated in Chap. 25).

Another direction of research for easing the preference acquisition process consists of the exploitation of personality, mood and emotions. This is becoming a popular topic, especially because it is clear that more and more techniques will be developed in order to automatically acquire such information. In Chap. 21, the authors stress the challenge of acquiring personality information in a nonintrusive fashion. Nowadays, only the longest questionnaires, which consist of around one hundred questions, can provide an accurate evaluation of the user's personality. Hence, non-intrusive approaches are necessary and the research in this area is just starting. Mining user activity for extracting personality information is an option, but also the fast penetration of portable devices that are life-logging the user's activity can offer a promising platform that is worth exploring.

Another line of research aimed at tackling the cold start problem and reducing the user model elicitation effort is cross-domain recommender systems. These techniques (See Chap. 27) could be used as an alternative path to user preferences' elicitation tools as they are able to build detailed user profiles without the need to collect explicit user assessment of the target domain items. Finally, we want to mention the issue of integrating long-term and short-term user preferences into the process of building a user profile and delivering a recommendation list. Recommender systems may be divided into two classes: those that build a long-term profile, generated by aggregating all the user transaction data collected by the system (e.g., collaborative filtering) and those that are more focused on capturing the ephemeral preferences of the user (e.g., knowledge-based approaches), such as case-based. Obviously both aspects are important and either the precise user task or the availability of items may come into consideration in resolving the preference integration problem. In fact, new research is required to build hybrid models that can correctly decide to what extent to drift toward the contingent user's preferences when there is enough evidence suggesting that the user's short-term preferences are departing from the long-term ones.

1.9.2 Interaction

A major challenge that RS research is now facing is clearly discussed in Chap. 9, in that we still need to broaden the scope of research to the system aspects of a recommender system. This means that aside from the algorithms, which are used to compute the recommendations, the mechanism through which users provide their input and the means by which they receive the systems output, play a significant role and can play an even larger role in determining the success or failure of a recommender system. We still need to better understand the general qualities of alternative solutions to preference elicitation, as we mentioned previously, recommendation presentation and to develop personalized solutions for these phases of the interaction with the system.

It must be observed that while interacting with a recommender system, users make various types of decisions. The most important one is surely selecting an item from the recommendation list. But, before making the final decision, users often have to decide how to explore the information space and what information they must provide to the system. For instance, they could have to select a specific feature (e.g., a camera's size or zoom factor) as search or critiquing criteria, or to select a repair proposal for inconsistent user preferences when interacting with a knowledge-based recommender. Moreover, users often do not know or do not reflect on their preferences beforehand, and the system-supported interaction and visualization contribute to the user construction of their preferences within a specific recommendation scenario. As it has been illustrated in Chap. 18, there are several challenges with the full support of user decision making in a recommender system. Our understanding of the situational context generated by the system and its effect on item selection processes is still incomplete and we need to better connect RS research to psychology and decision making disciplines. While it is clear that RS helps to make decisions, there is still the need for further research that takes theories from decision psychology and cognitive psychology into account when explaining users' preference construction and decision making process in the context of recommender systems.

Considering the user interaction with the recommender system, the topic of explaining the system recommendations still poses a number of interesting and open issues (see Chap. 10). For instance, it is still not completely clear whether explanations bring more overall benefits than risks. In Chap. 10 it is shown that explanations are part of a cyclical process: the explanations affect the acceptance of particular recommendations, the users' mental model of the system, and in turn, this affects the ways users interact with the explanations. But, whether the users are influenced in such a way that their choices are improved is not clear, and explanations may even increase the information overload that the recommendations are supposed to tame. Moreover, while some research has been conducted on explaining recommendations to individual users, explaining recommendations for a group is a much more novel subject. For instance, one might think that accurate predictions of individual satisfaction can also be used to improve the recommender's transparency: showing how satisfied other group members are could improve users' understanding of the recommendation process and perhaps make it easier to accept items they do not like. However, users need for privacy is likely to conflict with their need for transparency and showing the preferences of other users may move the group discussion on the preferences rather than on the recommended items. We definitely need more research on these topics.

In a discussion about the interaction with recommender systems, we cannot forget the issue of the assessment of the value of the recommendations, which is not only related to what extent the recommended items are liked by the user. For instance, the time value of recommendations, which is partially discussed in the chapter on context-aware recommenders (Chap. 6), refers to the fact that a given set of recommendations may not be applicable forever but there could be a time interval when these items can be recommended. This is clear, for instance, when it comes to news items: people want to be informed about the most recent events and news cannot be meaningfully recommended even 1 day after the initial announcement. The time value of a recommendation is clearly dependent on the novelty and diversity of the recommended items. We still need more theoretical, methodological and algorithmic developments around these aspects. For instance, modeling feature-based novelty in probabilistic terms in order to unify discovery and familiarity models would be an interesting line for future work. Aspects such as the time dimension during which items may recover part of their novelty value, or the variability among users regarding their degree of novelty-seeking are examples of issues that require further research and are mentioned in Chap. 26.

Somewhat connected to the novelty and diversity topic is the issue of achieving an effective tradeoff between exploration and exploitation, which is touched upon in the active learning chapter (Chap. 24). This challenge refers to the fundamental dilemma that a designer must properly tackle, or decide whether to keep recommending items that the system can now identify as good recommendations, given the data currently available to the system, or to further explore user preferences (e.g., asking the user to rate additional, particular items) in order to build newer and possibly better recommendations in the future.

1.9.3 New Recommendation Tasks

The application of recommender systems is still dominated by solutions for recommending relatively simple and inexpensive products like movies, music, news and books. While there are systems managing more complex item types, such as financial investments or travel, these item categories are considered as atypical cases. Inevitably, complex domains require more elaborated solutions such as those based on knowledge and largely discussed in Chap. 5. Complex products are typically configurable or offered in several variants. This feature still poses a challenge to recommender systems, which are instead designed to consider different configurations as different items. Identifying the more suitable configuration requires reasoning between the interactions of alternative configurations (classifying and grouping items) and calls for addressing the specificity of the human decision making task generated by the selection of a configuration. In general terms, addressing new types of recommendation domains can call for the introduction of many new and interesting research lines. For instance, Chap. 16 clearly shows how different the recommendation technique must be in domains where reciprocal recommendations are needed, as in dating applications.

As we already indicated in the first edition of this handbook, recommenders that optimize a sequence of recommendations, e.g., a new book every week, are not frequent and we believe that this is still an open issue. It is important to study the sequential dimension of users' decision making both within a recommendation session and between recommendation sessions. Here, we want to further note the importance of such a topic in group recommenders (see Chap. 22). In these systems, sequential recommendations are a natural setting, since stable groups, such as friends or families, repeatedly choose items of the same type, e.g., when deciding where to go for vacation or what to eat at home. A lot more research is needed on algorithms and user interfaces for producing coherent sequences of recommendations. In particular, one should model the effect on users of several contextual conditions such as the manner in which already-shown-items could influence the user evaluation of the next recommendations, or the social role and relationships of the group members.

As it is discussed in Chap. 14 most of the popular recommender systems are now accessed through mobile systems that follow their owners throughout their daily life, and are always within an arm's reach of their owners. In this scenario, as for instance in Google Now, recommender systems can proactively send notifications to their users about items of potential interest that are relevant because of the contextual situation of the user. The challenge is finding true relevant items for the user situation and not overburdening them with a stream of irrelevant interruptions. To address this goal, we must better exploit implicit feedback derived from user usage of the recommendations, but also learn to better identify contextual situations that require push recommendations. We believe that this depends on the detection of contextual changes that are significant to the user and therefore justify a recommendation. For instance, when it is the ideal time for a pause in writing a paper, i.e., the context is changing from work to leisure, a recommendation of a relevant, or personalized, article of sports news can be delivered. Understanding when context changes or could be forced to change and when a user may be receptive to a recommendation push is a challenging issue for further research. As it is also suggested in Chap. 6, in order to develop these new and compelling context aware systems, we need to explore novel engineering solutions to CARS, including: novel data structures, storage systems, user interface components and service oriented architectures.

Another task that we believe should be explored further is guided navigation. This refers to combining classical recommendation lists with tools that let the user navigate more autonomously in the space of possible options. User action interpretation refers to the possibility that in addition to explicit ratings, there could be many more actions performed by the user operating the recommender that can be detected, analyzed and used to build a better prediction model. The idea is that every single user action should be exploited in the recommendation process. But it is challenging to interpret the user's actions, i.e., the intent behind an action, and there are actions that should be discarded because they were not produced by genuine users, such as actions performed by different users on the same browser, or false and malicious registrations or data or log data caused by robots or crawlers.

Finally, we want to note again that in order to deliver a small set of relevant recommendations to the user, correctly predicting the user rating is only one option. An alternative consists of predicting how the user would compare or rank the available options. This is nowadays an important line of research in recommender systems. Chapter 11 discusses this issue in the context of the Netflix recommender.

Finally, we hope that this handbook, as a useful tool for practitioners and researchers, will contribute to further developing knowledge in this exciting and useful research area and provide a baseline for further exploring the above mentioned issues. Currently the research on RSs has greatly benefited from the combined interest and efforts that industry and academia have invested in this field. We therefore wish the best to both groups as they read this handbook and we hope that it will attract even more researchers to work in this highly interesting and challenging field.

References

1. Adomavicius, G., Tuzhilin, A.: Personalization technologies: a process-oriented perspective. Commun. ACM **48**(10), 83–90 (2005)
2. Adomavicius, G., Tuzhilin, A.: Toward the next generation of recommender systems: A survey of the state-of-the-art and possible extensions. IEEE Transactions on Knowledge and Data Engineering **17**(6), 734–749 (2005)
3. Amatriain, X.: Mining large streams of user data for personalized recommendations. SIGKDD Explor. Newsl. **14**(2), 37–48 (2013)
4. Arazy, O., Kumar, N., Shapira, B.: Improving social recommender systems. IT Professional **11**(4), 38–44 (2009)
5. Asoh, H., Ono, C., Habu, Y., Takasaki, H., Takenaka, T., Motomura, Y.: An acceptance model of recommender systems based on a large-scale internet survey. In: Advances in User Modeling - UMAP 2011 Workshops, Girona, Spain, July 11–15, 2011, Revised Selected Papers, pp. 410–414 (2011)
6. Bailey, R.A.: Design of comparative experiments. Cambridge University Press Cambridge (2008)
7. Balabanovic, M., Shoham, Y.: Content-based, collaborative recommendation. Communication of ACM **40**(3), 66–72 (1997)
8. Baltrunas, L., Ricci, F.: Experimental evaluation of context-dependent collaborative filtering using item splitting. User Model. User-Adapt. Interact. **24**(1–2), 7–34 (2014)
9. Ben-Shimon, D., Tsikinovsky, A., Rokach, L., Meisels, A., Shani, G., Naamani, L.: Recommender system from personal social networks. In: K. Wegrzyn-Wolska, P.S. Szczepaniak (eds.) AWIC, *Advances in Soft Computing*, vol. 43, pp. 47–55. Springer (2007)
10. Berkovsky, S., Kuflik, T., Ricci, F.: Mediation of user models for enhanced personalization in recommender systems. User Modeling and User-Adapted Interaction **18**(3), 245–286 (2008)

11. Berkovsky, S., Kuflik, T., Ricci, F.: Cross-representation mediation of user models. User Modeling and User-Adapted Interaction **19**(1–2), 35–63 (2009)
12. Billsus, D., Pazzani, M.: Learning probabilistic user models. In: UM97 Workshop on Machine Learning for User Modeling (1997). URL http://www.dfki.de/~bauer/um-ws/
13. Bobadilla, J., Ortega, F., Hernando, A., Gutierrez, A.: Recommender systems survey. Knowledge-Based Systems **46**(0), 109–132 (2013)
14. Borràs, J., Moreno, A., Valls, A.: Intelligent tourism recommender systems: A survey. Expert Systems with Applications **41**(16), 7370–7389 (2014)
15. Bridge, D., Göker, M., McGinty, L., Smyth, B.: Case-based recommender systems. The Knowledge Engineering review **20**(3), 315–320 (2006)
16. Brusilovsky, P.: Methods and techniques of adaptive hypermedia. User Modeling and User-Adapted Interaction **6**(2–3), 87–129 (1996)
17. Burke, R.: Hybrid web recommender systems. In: The Adaptive Web, pp. 377–408. Springer Berlin / Heidelberg (2007)
18. Chen, L., de Gemmis, M., Felfernig, A., Lops, P., Ricci, F., Semeraro, G.: Human decision making and recommender systems. TiiS **3**(3), 17 (2013)
19. Chen, L., Pu, P.: Critiquing-based recommenders: survey and emerging trends. User Model. User-Adapt. Interact. **22**(1–2), 125–150 (2012)
20. Cosley, D., Lam, S.K., Albert, I., Konstant, J.A., Riedl, J.: Is seeing believing? how recommender system interfaces affect users' opinions. In: In Proceedings of the CHI 2003 Conference on Human factors in Computing Systems, pp. 585–592. Fort Lauderdale, FL (2003)
21. Ekstrand, M.D., Harper, F.M., Willemsen, M.C., Konstan, J.A.: User perception of differences in recommender algorithms. In: Eighth ACM Conference on Recommender Systems, RecSys '14, Foster City, Silicon Valley, CA, USA - October 06 - 10, 2014, pp. 161–168 (2014)
22. Fisher, G.: User modeling in human-computer interaction. User Modeling and User-Adapted Interaction **11**, 65–86 (2001)
23. Golbeck, J.: Generating predictive movie recommendations from trust in social networks. In: Trust Management, 4th International Conference, iTrust 2006, Pisa, Italy, May 16–19, 2006, Proceedings, pp. 93–104 (2006)
24. Goldberg, D., Nichols, D., Oki, B.M., Terry, D.: Using collaborative filtering to weave an information tapestry. Commun. ACM **35**(12), 61–70 (1992)
25. Herlocker, J., Konstan, J., Riedl, J.: Explaining collaborative filtering recommendations. In: In proceedings of ACM 2000 Conference on Computer Supported Cooperative Work, pp. 241–250 (2000)
26. Herlocker, J.L., Konstan, J.A., Terveen, L.G., Riedl, J.T.: Evaluating collaborative filtering recommender systems. ACM Transaction on Information Systems **22**(1), 5–53 (2004)
27. Jannach, D., Zanker, M., Felfernig, A., Friedrich, G.: Recommender Systems: An Introduction. Cambridge University Press (2010)
28. Kaminskas, M., Ricci, F.: Contextual music information retrieval and recommendation: State of the art and challenges. Computer Science Review **6**(2–3), 89–119 (2012)
29. Knijnenburg, B.P., Willemsen, M.C., Gantner, Z., Soncu, H., Newell, C.: Explaining the user experience of recommender systems. User Modeling and User-Adapted Interaction **22**(4–5), 441–504 (2012). DOI 10.1007/s11257-011-9118-4
30. Konstan, J.A., Riedl, J.: Recommender systems: from algorithms to user experience. User Modeling and User-Adapted Interaction **22**(1–2), 101–123 (2012)
31. Koren, Y., Bell, R.M., Volinsky, C.: Matrix factorization techniques for recommender systems. IEEE Computer **42**(8), 30–37 (2009)
32. Linden, G., Smith, B., York, J.: Amazon.com recommendations: Item-to-item collaborative filtering. IEEE Internet Computing **7**(1), 76–80 (2003)
33. Lops, P., de Gemmis, M., Semeraro, G.: Content-based recommender systems: State of the art and trends. In: F. Ricci, L. Rokach, B. Shapira, P.B. Kantor (eds.) Recommender Systems Handbook, pp. 73–105. Springer Verlag (2011)

34. Lu, L., Medo, M., Yeung, C.H., Zhang, Y.C., Zhang, Z.K., Zhou, T.: Recommender systems. Physics Reports **519**(1), 1–49 (2012)
35. Mahmood, T., Ricci, F.: Improving recommender systems with adaptive conversational strategies. In: C. Cattuto, G. Ruffo, F. Menczer (eds.) Hypertext, pp. 73–82. ACM (2009)
36. Mahmood, T., Ricci, F., Venturini, A.: Improving recommendation effectiveness by adapting the dialogue strategy in online travel planning. International Journal of Information Technology and Tourism **11**(4), 285–302 (2009)
37. McFee, B., Bertin-Mahieux, T., Ellis, D.P., Lanckriet, G.R.: The million song dataset challenge. In: Proceedings of the 21st International Conference Companion on World Wide Web, WWW '12 Companion, pp. 909–916. ACM, New York, NY, USA (2012)
38. McNee, S.M., Riedl, J., Konstan, J.A.: Being accurate is not enough: how accuracy metrics have hurt recommender systems. In: CHI '06: CHI '06 extended abstracts on Human factors in computing systems, pp. 1097–1101. ACM Press, New York, NY, USA (2006)
39. Montaner, M., López, B., de la Rosa, J.L.: A taxonomy of recommender agents on the internet. Artificial Intelligence Review **19**(4), 285–330 (2003)
40. Park, D.H., Kim, H.K., Choi, I.Y., Kim, J.K.: A literature review and classification of recommender systems research. Expert Systems with Applications **39**(11), 10,059–10,072 (2012)
41. Resnick, P., Iacovou, N., Suchak, M., Bergstrom, P., Riedl, J.: Grouplens: An open architecture for collaborative filtering of netnews. In: Proceedings ACM Conference on Computer-Supported Cooperative Work, pp. 175–186 (1994)
42. Resnick, P., Varian, H.R.: Recommender systems. Communications of the ACM **40**(3), 56–58 (1997)
43. Ricci, F.: Travel recommender systems. IEEE Intelligent Systems **17**(6), 55–57 (2002)
44. Ricci, F.: Recommender systems: Models and techniques. In: Encyclopedia of Social Network Analysis and Mining, pp. 1511–1522. Springer (2014)
45. Ricci, F., Cavada, D., Mirzadeh, N., Venturini, A.: Case-based travel recommendations. In: D.R. Fesenmaier, K. Woeber, H. Werthner (eds.) Destination Recommendation Systems: Behavioural Foundations and Applications, pp. 67–93. CABI (2006)
46. Robillard, M.P., Maalej, W., Walker, R.J., Zimmermann, T. (eds.): Recommendation Systems in Software Engineering. Springer (2014)
47. Schafer, J.B., Frankowski, D., Herlocker, J., Sen, S.: Collaborative filtering recommender systems. In: The Adaptive Web, pp. 291–324. Springer Berlin / Heidelberg (2007)
48. Schafer, J.B., Konstan, J.A., Riedl, J.: E-commerce recommendation applications. Data Mining and Knowledge Discovery **5**(1/2), 115–153 (2001)
49. Schwartz, B.: The Paradox of Choice. ECCO, New York (2004)
50. van Setten, M., McNee, S.M., Konstan, J.A.: Beyond personalization: the next stage of recommender systems research. In: R.S. Amant, J. Riedl, A. Jameson (eds.) IUI, p. 8. ACM (2005)
51. Shardanand, U., Maes, P.: Social information filtering: algorithms for automating "word of mouth". In: Proceedings of the Conference on Human Factors in Computing Systems (CHI'95), pp. 210–217 (1995)
52. Sinha, R.R., Swearingen, K.: Comparing recommendations made by online systems and friends. In: DELOS Workshop: Personalisation and Recommender Systems in Digital Libraries (2001)
53. Swearingen, K., Sinha, R.: Beyond algorithms: An HCI perspective on recommender systems. In: J.L. Herlocker (ed.) Recommender Systems, papers from the 2001 ACM SIGIR Workshop. New Orleans, LA - USA (2001)
54. Taghipour, N., Kardan, A., Ghidary, S.S.: Usage-based web recommendations: a reinforcement learning approach. In: Proceedings of the 2007 ACM Conference on Recommender Systems, RecSys 2007, Minneapolis, MN, USA, October 19–20, 2007, pp. 113–120 (2007)
55. Verbert, K., Drachsler, H., Manouselis, N., Wolpers, M., Vuorikari, R., Duval, E.: Dataset-driven research for improving recommender systems for learning. In: Proceedings of the 1st International Conference on Learning Analytics and Knowledge, LAK '11, pp. 44–53. ACM, New York, NY, USA (2011)

Part I
Recommendation Techniques

Chapter 2
A Comprehensive Survey of Neighborhood-Based Recommendation Methods

Xia Ning, Christian Desrosiers, and George Karypis

2.1 Introduction

The appearance and growth of online markets has had a considerable impact on the habits of consumers, providing them access to a greater variety of products and information on these goods. While this freedom of purchase has made online commerce into a multi-billion dollar industry, it also made it more difficult for consumers to select the products that best fit their needs. One of the main solutions proposed for this information overload problem are recommender systems, which provide automated and personalized suggestions of products to consumers.

The recommendation problem can be defined as estimating the response of a user for new items, based on historical information stored in the system, and suggesting to this user *novel* and *original* items for which the predicted response is *high*. User-item responses can be numerical values known as ratings (e.g., 1–5 stars), ordinal values (e.g., strongly agree, agree, neutral, disagree, strongly disagree) representing the possible levels of user appreciation, or binary values (e.g., like/dislike or interested/not interested). Moreover, user responses can be obtained explicitly, for

X. Ning
Computer Science Department, Purdue University, West Lafayette, IN, USA
e-mail: xning@iupui.edu

C. Desrosiers (✉)
Software Engineering and IT Department, École de Technologie Supérieure, Montreal, QC, Canada
e-mail: christian.desrosiers@etsmtl.ca

G. Karypis
Computer Science and Engineering Department, University of Minnesota, Minneapolis, MN, USA
e-mail: karypis@cs.umn.edu

F. Ricci et al. (eds.), *Recommender Systems Handbook*,
DOI 10.1007/978-1-4899-7637-6_2

instance, through ratings/reviews entered by users in the system, or implicitly, from purchase history or access patterns [39, 70]. For the purpose of simplicity, from this point on, we will call rating any type of user-item response.

Item recommendation approaches can be divided in two broad categories: personalized and non-personalized. Among the personalized approaches are *content-based* and *collaborative filtering* methods, as well as *hybrid* techniques combining these two types of methods. The general principle of content-based (or cognitive) methods [4, 8, 42, 54] is to identify the common characteristics of items that have received a favorable rating from a user, and then recommend to this user new items that share these characteristics. Recommender systems based purely on content generally suffer from the problems of *limited content analysis* and *over-specialization* [63]. Limited content analysis occurs when the system has a limited amount of information on its users or the content of its items. For instance, privacy issues might refrain a user from providing personal information, or the precise content of items may be difficult or costly to obtain for some types of items, such as music or images. Another problem is that the content of an item is often insufficient to determine its quality. Over-specialization, on the other hand, is a side effect of the way in which content-based systems recommend new items, where the predicted rating of a user for an item is high if this item is similar to the ones liked by this user. For example, in a movie recommendation application, the system may recommend to a user a movie of the same genre or having the same actors as movies already seen by this user. Because of this, the system may fail to recommend items that are different but still interesting to the user.

Instead of depending on content information, collaborative (or social) filtering approaches use the rating information of other users and items in the system. The key idea is that the rating of a target user for a new item is likely to be similar to that of another user, if both users have rated other items in a similar way. Likewise, the target user is likely to rate two items in a similar fashion, if other users have given similar ratings to these two items. Collaborative approaches overcome some of the limitations of content-based ones. For instance, items for which the content is not available or difficult to obtain can still be recommended to users through the feedback of other users. Furthermore, collaborative recommendations are based on the quality of items as evaluated by peers, instead of relying on content that may be a bad indicator of quality. Finally, unlike content-based systems, collaborative filtering ones can recommend items with very different content, as long as other users have already shown interest for these different items.

Collaborative filtering approaches can be grouped in the two general classes of *neighborhood* and *model*-based methods. In neighborhood-based (memory-based [10] or heuristic-based [2]) collaborative filtering [14, 15, 27, 39, 44, 48, 57, 59, 63], the user-item ratings stored in the system are directly used to predict ratings for new items. This can be done in two ways known as *user-based* or *item-based* recommendation. User-based systems, such as GroupLens [39], Bellcore video [27], and Ringo [63], evaluate the interest of a target user for an item using the ratings for this item by other users, called *neighbors*, that have similar rating patterns. The neighbors of the target user are typically the users whose ratings are most correlated to the target user's ratings. Item-based approaches [15, 44, 59], on the other hand, predict the rating of a user for an item based on the ratings of the user for similar items. In such approaches, two items are similar if several users of the system have rated these items in a similar fashion.

In contrast to neighborhood-based systems, which use the stored ratings directly in the prediction, model-based approaches use these ratings to learn a predictive model. Salient characteristics of users and items are captured by a set of model parameters, which are learned from training data and later used to predict new ratings. Model-based approaches for the task of recommending items are numerous and include Bayesian Clustering [10], Latent Semantic Analysis [28], Latent Dirichlet Allocation [9], Maximum Entropy [72], Boltzmann Machines [58], Support Vector Machines [23], and Singular Value Decomposition [6, 40, 53, 68, 69]. A survey of state-of-the-art model-based methods can be found in Chap. 3 of this book.

Finally, to overcome certain limitations of content-based and collaborative filtering methods, hybrid recommendation approaches combine characteristics of both types of methods. Content-based and collaborative filtering methods can be combined in various ways, for instance, by merging their individual predictions into a single, more robust prediction [8, 55], or by adding content information into a collaborative filtering model [1, 3, 51, 65, 71]. Several studies have shown hybrid recommendation approaches to provide more accurate recommendations than pure content-based or collaborative methods, especially when few ratings are available [2].

2.1.1 Advantages of Neighborhood Approaches

While recent investigations show state-of-the-art model-based approaches superior to neighborhood ones in the task of predicting ratings [40, 67], there is also an emerging understanding that good prediction accuracy alone does not guarantee users an effective and satisfying experience [26]. Another factor that has been identified as playing an important role in the appreciation of users for the recommender system is *serendipity* [26, 59]. Serendipity extends the concept of novelty by helping a user find an interesting item he or she might not have otherwise discovered. For example, recommending to a user a movie directed by his favorite director constitutes a novel recommendation if the user was not aware of that movie, but is likely not serendipitous since the user would have discovered that movie on his own.

Model-based approaches excel at characterizing the preferences of a user with latent factors. For example, in a movie recommender system, such methods may determine that a given user is a fan of movies that are both funny and romantic, without having to actually define the notions "funny" and "romantic". This system would be able to recommend to the user a romantic comedy that may not have been known to this user. However, it may be difficult for this system to recommend a movie that does not quite fit this high-level genre, for instance, a funny parody of horror movies. Neighborhood approaches, on the other hand, capture local associations in the data. Consequently, it is possible for a movie recommender system based on this type of approach to recommend the user a movie very different from his usual taste or a movie that is not well known (e.g. repertoire film), if one of his closest neighbors has given it a strong rating. This recommendation may not be a guaranteed success, as would be a romantic comedy, but it may help the user discover a whole new genre or a new favorite actor/director.

The main advantages of neighborhood-based methods are:

- **Simplicity:** Neighborhood-based methods are intuitive and relatively simple to implement. In their simplest form, only one parameter (the number of neighbors used in the prediction) requires tuning.
- **Justifiability:** Such methods also provide a concise and intuitive justification for the computed predictions. For example, in item-based recommendation, the list of neighbor items, as well as the ratings given by the user to these items, can be presented to the user as a justification for the recommendation. This can help the user better understand the recommendation and its relevance, and could serve as basis for an interactive system where users can select the neighbors for which a greater importance should be given in the recommendation [6].
- **Efficiency:** One of the strong points of neighborhood-based systems are their efficiency. Unlike most model-based systems, they require no costly training phases, which need to be carried at frequent intervals in large commercial applications. These systems may require pre-computing nearest neighbors in an offline step, which is typically much cheaper than model training, providing near instantaneous recommendations. Moreover, storing these nearest neighbors requires very little memory, making such approaches scalable to applications having millions of users and items.
- **Stability:** Another useful property of recommender systems based on this approach is that they are little affected by the constant addition of users, items and ratings, which are typically observed in large commercial applications. For instance, once item similarities have been computed, an item-based system can readily make recommendations to new users, without having to re-train the system. Moreover, once a few ratings have been entered for a new item, only the similarities between this item and the ones already in the system need to be computed.

While neighborhood-based methods have gained popularity due to these advantages, they are also known to suffer from the problem of limited coverage, which causes some items to be never recommended. Also, traditional methods of this category are known to be more sensitive to the sparseness of ratings and the cold-start problem, where the system has only a few ratings, or no rating at all, for new users and items. Section 2.5 presents more advanced neighborhood-based techniques that can overcome these problems.

2.1.2 Objectives and Outline

This chapter has two main objectives. It first serves as a general guide on neighborhood-based recommender systems, and presents practical information on how to implement such recommendation approaches. In particular, the main components of neighborhood-based methods will be described, as well as the benefits of the most common choices for each of these components. Secondly, it presents more specialized techniques on the subject that address particular aspects of recommending items, such as data sparsity. Although such techniques are not required to implement a simple neighborhood-based system, having a broader view of the various difficulties and solutions for neighborhood methods may help making appropriate decisions during the implementation process.

The rest of this document is structured as follows. In Sect. 2.2, we first give a formal definition of the item recommendation task and present the notation used throughout the chapter. In Sect. 2.3, the principal neighborhood approaches, predicting user ratings for new items based on regression or classification, are then introduced, and the main advantages and flaws of these approaches are described. This section also presents two complementary ways of implementing such approaches, either based on user or item similarities, and analyzes the impact of these two implementations on the accuracy, efficiency, stability, justifiability and serendipity of the recommender system. Section 2.4, on the other hand, focuses on the three main components of neighborhood-based recommendation methods: rating normalization, similarity weight computation, and neighborhood selection. For each of these components, the most common approaches are described, and their respective benefits compared. In Sect. 2.5, the problems of limited coverage and data sparsity are introduced, and several solutions proposed to overcome these problems are described. In particular, several techniques based on dimensionality reduction and graphs are presented. Finally, the last section of this document summarizes the principal characteristics and methods of neighborhood-based recommendation, and gives a few more pointers on implementing such methods.

2.2 Problem Definition and Notation

In order to give a formal definition of the item recommendation task, we introduce the following notation. The set of users in the recommender system will be denoted by $\mathcal{U}$, and the set of items by $\mathcal{I}$. Moreover, we denote by $\mathcal{R}$ the set of ratings recorded in the system, and write $\mathcal{S}$ the set of possible values for a rating (e.g., $\mathcal{S} = [1, 5]$ or $\mathcal{S} = \{\text{like}, \text{dislike}\}$). Also, we suppose that no more than one rating can be made by any user $u \in \mathcal{U}$ for a particular item $i \in \mathcal{I}$ and write r_{ui} this rating. To identify the subset of users that have rated an item i, we use the notation $\mathcal{U}_i$. Likewise, $\mathcal{I}_u$ represents the subset of items that have been rated by a user u. Finally, the items that have been rated by two users u and v, i.e. $\mathcal{I}_u \cap \mathcal{I}_v$, is an important concept in our presentation, and we use $\mathcal{I}_{uv}$ to denote this concept. In a similar fashion, $\mathcal{U}_{ij}$ is used to denote the set of users that have rated both items i and j.

Two of the most important problems associated with recommender systems are the *rating prediction* and *top-N* recommendation problems. The first problem is to predict the rating that a user u will give his or her unrated item i. When ratings are available, this task is most often defined as a regression or (multi-class) classification problem where the goal is to learn a function $f : \mathcal{U} \times \mathcal{I} \rightarrow \mathcal{S}$ that predicts the rating $f(u, i)$ of a user u for a new item i. Accuracy is commonly used to evaluate the performance of the recommendation method. Typically, the ratings $\mathcal{R}$ are divided into a *training* set $\mathcal{R}_{\text{train}}$ used to learn f, and a *test* set $\mathcal{R}_{\text{test}}$ used to evaluate the prediction accuracy. Two popular measures of accuracy are the *Mean Absolute Error* (MAE):

$$\text{MAE}(f) = \frac{1}{|\mathcal{R}_{\text{test}}|} \sum_{r_{ui} \in \mathcal{R}_{\text{test}}} |f(u, i) - r_{ui}|, \tag{2.1}$$

and the *Root Mean Squared Error* (RMSE):

$$\text{RMSE}(f) = \sqrt{\frac{1}{|\mathcal{R}_{\text{test}}|} \sum_{r_{ui} \in \mathcal{R}_{\text{test}}} (f(u, i) - r_{ui})^2}. \tag{2.2}$$

When ratings are not available, for instance, if only the list of items purchased by each user is known, measuring the rating prediction accuracy is not possible. In such cases, the problem of finding the best item is usually transformed into the task of recommending to an active user u_a a list $L(u_a)$ containing N items likely to interest him or her [15, 59]. The quality of such method can be evaluated by splitting the items of $\mathcal{I}$ into a set $\mathcal{I}_{\text{train}}$, used to learn L, and a test set $\mathcal{I}_{\text{test}}$. Let $T(u) \subset \mathcal{I}_u \cap \mathcal{I}_{\text{test}}$ be the subset of test items that a user u found relevant. If the user responses are binary, these can be the items that u has rated positively. Otherwise, if only a list of purchased or accessed items is given for each user u, then these items can be used as $T(u)$. The performance of the method is then computed using the measures of *precision* and *recall*:

$$\text{Precision}(L) = \frac{1}{|\mathcal{U}|} \sum_{u \in \mathcal{U}} |L(u) \cap T(u)| \, / \, |L(u)| \tag{2.3}$$

$$\text{Recall}(L) = \frac{1}{|\mathcal{U}|} \sum_{u \in \mathcal{U}} |L(u) \cap T(u)| \, / \, |T(u)|. \tag{2.4}$$

A drawback of this task is that all items of a recommendation list $L(u)$ are considered equally interesting to user u. An alternative setting, described in [15], consists in learning a function L that maps each user u to a list $L(u)$ where items are *ordered* by their "interestingness" to u. If the test set is built by randomly selecting, for each user u, a single item i_u of $\mathcal{I}_u$, the performance of L can be evaluated with the *Average Reciprocal Hit-Rank* (ARHR):

$$\mathrm{ARHR}(L) = \frac{1}{|\mathcal{U}|} \sum_{u \in \mathcal{U}} \frac{1}{\mathrm{rank}(i_u, L(u))}, \tag{2.5}$$

where $\mathrm{rank}(i_u, L(u))$ is the rank of item i_u in $L(u)$, equal to ∞ if $i_u \notin L(u)$. A more extensive description of evaluation measures for recommender systems can be found in Chap. 8 of this book.

2.3 Neighborhood-Based Recommendation

Recommender systems based on neighborhood automate the common principle that similar users prefer similar items, and similar items are preferred by similar users. To illustrate this, consider the following example based on the ratings of Fig. 2.1.

Example 2.1. User Eric has to decide whether or not to rent the movie "Titanic" that he has not yet seen. He knows that Lucy has very similar tastes when it comes to movies, as both of them hated "The Matrix" and loved "Forrest Gump", so he asks her opinion on this movie. On the other hand, Eric finds out he and Diane have different tastes, Diane likes action movies while he does not, and he discards her opinion or considers the opposite in his decision.

2.3.1 *User-Based Rating Prediction*

User-based neighborhood recommendation methods predict the rating r_{ui} of a user u for a new item i using the ratings given to i by users most similar to u, called nearest-neighbors. Suppose we have for each user $v \neq u$ a value w_{uv} representing the preference similarity between u and v (how this similarity can be computed will

	The Matrix	Titanic	Die Hard	Forrest Gump	Wall-E
John	5	1		2	2
Lucy	1	5	2	5	5
Eric	2	?	3	5	4
Diane	4	3	5	3	

Fig. 2.1 A "toy example" showing the ratings of four users for five movies

be discussed in Sect. 2.4.2). The k-nearest-neighbors (k-NN) of u, denoted by $\mathcal{N}(u)$, are the k users v with the highest similarity w_{uv} to u. However, only the users who have rated item i can be used in the prediction of r_{ui}, and we instead consider the k users most similar to u that *have rated i*. We write this set of neighbors as $\mathcal{N}_i(u)$. The rating r_{ui} can be estimated as the average rating given to i by these neighbors:

$$\hat{r}_{ui} = \frac{1}{|\mathcal{N}_i(u)|} \sum_{v \in \mathcal{N}_i(u)} r_{vi}. \tag{2.6}$$

A problem with (2.6) is that is does not take into account the fact that the neighbors can have different levels of similarity. Consider once more the example of Fig. 2.1. If the two nearest-neighbors of Eric are Lucy and Diane, it would be foolish to consider equally their ratings of the movie "Titanic", since Lucy's tastes are much closer to Eric's than Diane's. A common solution to this problem is to weigh the contribution of each neighbor by its similarity to u. However, if these weights do not sum to 1, the predicted ratings can be well outside the range of allowed values. Consequently, it is customary to normalize these weights, such that the predicted rating becomes

$$\hat{r}_{ui} = \frac{\sum\limits_{v \in \mathcal{N}_i(u)} w_{uv} \, r_{vi}}{\sum\limits_{v \in \mathcal{N}_i(u)} |w_{uv}|}. \tag{2.7}$$

In the denominator of (2.7), $|w_{uv}|$ is used instead of w_{uv} because negative weights can produce ratings outside the allowed range. Also, w_{uv} can be replaced by w_{uv}^{α}, where $\alpha > 0$ is an amplification factor [10]. When $\alpha > 1$, as is it most often employed, an even greater importance is given to the neighbors that are the closest to u.

Example 2.2. Suppose we want to use (2.7) to predict Eric's rating of the movie "Titanic" using the ratings of Lucy and Diane for this movie. Moreover, suppose the similarity weights between these neighbors and Eric are respectively 0.75 and 0.15. The predicted rating would be

$$\hat{r} = \frac{0.75{\times}5 + 0.15{\times}3}{0.75 + 0.15} \simeq 4.67,$$

which is closer to Lucy's rating than to Diane's.

Equation (2.7) also has an important flaw: it does not consider the fact that users may use different rating values to quantify the same level of appreciation for an item. For example, one user may give the highest rating value to only a few outstanding items, while a less difficult one may give this value to most of the items he likes. This problem is usually addressed by converting the neighbors' ratings r_{vi} to normalized ones $h(r_{vi})$ [10, 57], giving the following prediction:

$$\hat{r}_{ui} = h^{-1}\left(\frac{\sum\limits_{v\in\mathcal{N}_i(u)} w_{uv}\, h(r_{vi})}{\sum\limits_{v\in\mathcal{N}_i(u)} |w_{uv}|}\right). \tag{2.8}$$

Note that the predicted rating must be converted back to the original scale, hence the h^{-1} in the equation. The most common approaches to normalize ratings will be presented in Sect. 2.4.1.

2.3.2 User-Based Classification

The prediction approach just described, where the predicted ratings are computed as a weighted average of the neighbors' ratings, essentially solves a *regression* problem. Neighborhood-based *classification*, on the other hand, finds the most likely rating given by a user u to an item i, by having the nearest-neighbors of u vote on this value. The vote v_{ir} given by the k-NN of u for the rating $r \in \mathcal{S}$ can be obtained as the sum of the similarity weights of neighbors that have given this rating to i:

$$v_{ir} = \sum_{v\in\mathcal{N}_i(u)} \delta(r_{vi} = r)\, w_{uv}, \tag{2.9}$$

where $\delta(r_{vi} = r)$ is 1 if $r_{vi} = r$, and 0 otherwise. Once this has been computed for every possible rating value, the predicted rating is simply the value r for which v_{ir} is the greatest.

Example 2.3. Suppose once again that the two nearest-neighbors of Eric are Lucy and Diane with respective similarity weights 0.75 and 0.15. In this case, ratings 5 and 3 each have one vote. However, since Lucy's vote has a greater weight than Diane's, the predicted rating will be $\hat{r} = 5$.

A classification method that considers normalized ratings can also be defined. Let $\mathcal{S}'$ be the set of possible normalized values (that may require discretization), the predicted rating is obtained as:

$$\hat{r}_{ui} = h^{-1}\left(\underset{r\in\mathcal{S}'}{\arg\max} \sum_{v\in\mathcal{N}_i(u)} \delta(h(r_{vi}) = r)\, w_{uv}\right). \tag{2.10}$$

2.3.3 Regression vs Classification

The choice between implementing a neighborhood-based regression or classification method largely depends on the system's rating scale. Thus, if the rating scale is continuous, e.g. ratings in the *Jester* joke recommender system [20] can take any value between -10 and 10, then a regression method is more appropriate. On the contrary, if the rating scale has only a few discrete values, e.g. "good" or "bad", or if the values cannot be ordered in an obvious fashion, then a classification method might be preferable. Furthermore, since normalization tends to map ratings to a continuous scale, it may be harder to handle in a classification approach.

Another way to compare these two approaches is by considering the situation where all neighbors have the same similarity weight. As the number of neighbors used in the prediction increases, the rating r_{ui} predicted by the regression approach will tend toward the mean rating of item i. Suppose item i has only ratings at either end of the rating range, i.e. it is either loved or hated, then the regression approach will make the safe decision that the item's worth is average. This is also justified from a statistical point of view since the expected rating (estimated in this case) is the one that minimizes the RMSE. On the other hand, the classification approach will predict the rating as the most frequent one given to i. This is more risky as the item will be labeled as either "good" or "bad". However, as mentioned before, taking risks may be desirable if it leads to serendipitous recommendations.

2.3.4 Item-Based Recommendation

While user-based methods rely on the opinion of like-minded users to predict a rating, item-based approaches [15, 44, 59] look at ratings given to similar items. Let us illustrate this approach with our toy example.

Example 2.4. Instead of consulting with his peers, Eric instead determines whether the movie "Titanic" is right for him by considering the movies that he has already seen. He notices that people that have rated this movie have given similar ratings to the movies "Forrest Gump" and "Wall-E". Since Eric liked these two movies he concludes that he will also like the movie "Titanic".

This idea can be formalized as follows. Denote by $\mathcal{N}_u(i)$ the items rated by user u most similar to item i. The predicted rating of u for i is obtained as a weighted average of the ratings given by u to the items of $\mathcal{N}_u(i)$:

$$\hat{r}_{ui} = \frac{\sum\limits_{j \in \mathcal{N}_u(i)} w_{ij}\, r_{uj}}{\sum\limits_{j \in \mathcal{N}_u(i)} |w_{ij}|}. \tag{2.11}$$

Example 2.5. Suppose our prediction is again made using two nearest-neighbors, and that the items most similar to "Titanic" are "Forrest Gump" and "Wall-E", with respective similarity weights 0.85 and 0.75. Since ratings of 5 and 4 were given by Eric to these two movies, the predicted rating is computed as

$$\hat{r} = \frac{0.85 \times 5 + 0.75 \times 4}{0.85 + 0.75} \simeq 4.53.$$

Again, the differences in the users' individual rating scales can be considered by normalizing ratings with a function h:

$$\hat{r}_{ui} = h^{-1}\left(\frac{\sum\limits_{j \in \mathcal{N}_u(i)} w_{ij}\, h(r_{uj})}{\sum\limits_{j \in \mathcal{N}_u(i)} |w_{ij}|} \right). \tag{2.12}$$

Moreover, we can also define an item-based classification approach. In this case, the items j rated by user u vote for the rating to be given to a new item i, and these votes are weighted by the similarity between i and j. The normalized version of this approach can be expressed as follows:

$$\hat{r}_{ui} = h^{-1}\left(\arg\max_{r \in \mathcal{S}'} \sum_{j \in \mathcal{N}_u(i)} \delta(h(r_{uj}) = r)\, w_{ij} \right). \tag{2.13}$$

2.3.5 *User-Based vs Item-Based Recommendation*

When choosing between the implementation of a user-based and an item-based neighborhood recommender system, five criteria should be considered:

- **Accuracy:** The accuracy of neighborhood recommendation methods depends mostly on the ratio between the number of users and items in the system. As will be presented in Sect. 2.4.2, the similarity between two users in user-based methods, which determines the neighbors of a user, is normally obtained by comparing the ratings made by these users on the same items. Consider a system that has 10,000 ratings made by 1000 users on 100 items, and suppose, for the purpose of this analysis, that the ratings are distributed uniformly over the items.[1] Following Table 2.1, the average number of users available as potential neighbors is roughly 650. However, the average number of common ratings used to compute the similarities is only 1. On the other hand, an item-based method usually computes the similarity between two items by comparing ratings made by the same user on these items. Assuming once more a uniform distribution of ratings, we find an average number of potential neighbors of 99 and an average number of ratings used to compute the similarities of 10.

[1]The distribution of ratings in real-life data is normally skewed, i.e. most ratings are given to a small proportion of items.

Table 2.1 The average number of neighbors and average number of ratings used in the computation of similarities for user-based and item-based neighborhood methods

	Average neighbors	Average ratings
User-based	$(\lvert\mathcal{U}\rvert - 1)\left(1 - \left(\frac{\lvert\mathcal{I}\rvert - p}{\lvert\mathcal{I}\rvert}\right)^p\right)$	$\frac{p^2}{\lvert\mathcal{I}\rvert}$
Item-based	$(\lvert\mathcal{I}\rvert - 1)\left(1 - \left(\frac{\lvert\mathcal{U}\rvert - q}{\lvert\mathcal{U}\rvert}\right)^q\right)$	$\frac{q^2}{\lvert\mathcal{U}\rvert}$

A uniform distribution of ratings is assumed with average number of ratings per user $p = \lvert\mathcal{R}\rvert/\lvert\mathcal{U}\rvert$, and average number of ratings per item $q = \lvert\mathcal{R}\rvert/\lvert\mathcal{I}\rvert$

Table 2.2 The space and time complexity of user-based and item-based neighborhood methods, as a function of the maximum number of ratings per user $p = \max_u \lvert\mathcal{I}_u\rvert$, the maximum number of ratings per item $q = \max_i \lvert\mathcal{U}_i\rvert$, and the maximum number of neighbors used in the rating predictions k

	Space	Time	
		Training	Online
User-based	$O(\lvert\mathcal{U}\rvert^2)$	$O(\lvert\mathcal{U}\rvert^2 p)$	$O(\lvert\mathcal{I}\rvert k)$
Item-based	$O(\lvert\mathcal{I}\rvert^2)$	$O(\lvert\mathcal{I}\rvert^2 q)$	$O(\lvert\mathcal{I}\rvert k)$

In general, a small number of high-confidence neighbors is by far preferable to a large number of neighbors for which the similarity weights are not trustable. In cases where the number of users is much greater than the number of items, such as large commercial systems like *Amazon.com*, item-based methods can therefore produce more accurate recommendations [16, 59]. Likewise, systems that have less users than items, e.g., a research paper recommender with thousands of users but hundreds of thousands of articles to recommend, may benefit more from user-based neighborhood methods [26].

- **Efficiency:** As shown in Table 2.2, the memory and computational efficiency of recommender systems also depends on the ratio between the number of users and items. Thus, when the number of users exceeds the number of items, as is it most often the case, item-based recommendation approaches require much less memory and time to compute the similarity weights (training phase) than user-based ones, making them more scalable. However, the time complexity of the online recommendation phase, which depends only on the number of available items and the maximum number of neighbors, is the same for user-based and item-based methods.

  In practice, computing the similarity weights is much less expensive than the worst-case complexity reported in Table 2.2, due to the fact that users rate only a few of the available items. Accordingly, only the non-zero similarity weights need to be stored, which is often much less than the number of user pairs. This number can be further reduced by storing for each user only the top N weights, where N is a parameter [59] that is sufficient for satisfactory coverage on user-item pairs. In the same manner, the non-zero weights can be computed efficiently without having to test each pair of users or items, which makes neighborhood methods scalable to very large systems.

- **Stability:** The choice between a user-based and an item-based approach also depends on the frequency and amount of change in the users and items of the system. If the list of available items is fairly static in comparison to the users of the system, an item-based method may be preferable since the item similarity weights could then be computed at infrequent time intervals while still being able to recommend items to new users. On the contrary, in applications where the list of available items is constantly changing, e.g., an online article recommender, user-based methods could prove to be more stable.
- **Justifiability:** An advantage of item-based methods is that they can easily be used to justify a recommendation. Hence, the list of neighbor items used in the prediction, as well as their similarity weights, can be presented to the user as an explanation of the recommendation. By modifying the list of neighbors and/or their weights, it then becomes possible for the user to participate interactively in the recommendation process. User-based methods, however, are less amenable to this process because the active user does not know the other users serving as neighbors in the recommendation.
- **Serendipity:** In item-based methods, the rating predicted for an item is based on the ratings given to similar items. Consequently, recommender systems using this approach will tend to recommend to a user items that are related to those usually appreciated by this user. For instance, in a movie recommendation application, movies having the same genre, actors or director as those highly rated by the user are likely to be recommended. While this may lead to safe recommendations, it does less to help the user discover different types of items that he might like as much.

  Because they work with user similarity, on the other hand, user-based approaches are more likely to make serendipitous recommendations. This is particularly true if the recommendation is made with a small number of nearest-neighbors. For example, a user *A* that has watched only comedies may be very similar to a user *B* only by the ratings made on such movies. However, if *B* is fond of a movie in a different genre, this movie may be recommended to *A* through his similarity with *B*.

2.4 Components of Neighborhood Methods

In the previous section, we have seen that deciding between a regression and a classification rating prediction method, as well as choosing between a user-based or item-based recommendation approach, can have a significant impact on the accuracy, efficiency and overall quality of the recommender system. In addition to these crucial attributes, three very important considerations in the implementation of a neighborhood-based recommender system are (1) the normalization of ratings, (2) the computation of the similarity weights, and (3) the selection of neighbors. This section reviews some of the most common approaches for these three components, describes the main advantages and disadvantages of using each one of them, and gives indications on how to implement them.

2.4.1 Rating Normalization

When it comes to assigning a rating to an item, each user has its own personal scale. Even if an explicit definition of each of the possible ratings is supplied (e.g., 1="strongly disagree", 2="disagree", 3="neutral", etc.), some users might be reluctant to give high/low scores to items they liked/disliked. Two of the most popular rating normalization schemes that have been proposed to convert individual ratings to a more universal scale are *mean-centering* and *Z-score*.

2.4.1.1 Mean-Centering

The idea of mean-centering [10, 57] is to determine whether a rating is positive or negative by comparing it to the mean rating. In user-based recommendation, a raw rating r_{ui} is transformation to a mean-centered one $h(r_{ui})$ by subtracting to r_{ui} the average $\overline{r}_u$ of the ratings given by user u to the items in $\mathcal{I}_u$:

$$h(r_{ui}) = r_{ui} - \overline{r}_u.$$

Using this approach the user-based prediction of a rating r_{ui} is obtained as

$$\hat{r}_{ui} = \overline{r}_u + \frac{\sum\limits_{v \in \mathcal{N}_i(u)} w_{uv}\, (r_{vi} - \overline{r}_v)}{\sum\limits_{v \in \mathcal{N}_i(u)} |w_{uv}|}. \tag{2.14}$$

In the same way, the *item*-mean-centered normalization of r_{ui} is given by

$$h(r_{ui}) = r_{ui} - \overline{r}_i,$$

where $\overline{r}_i$ corresponds to the mean rating given to item i by user in $\mathcal{U}_i$. This normalization technique is most often used in item-based recommendation, where a rating r_{ui} is predicted as:

$$\hat{r}_{ui} = \overline{r}_i + \frac{\sum\limits_{j \in \mathcal{N}_u(i)} w_{ij}\, (r_{uj} - \overline{r}_j)}{\sum\limits_{j \in \mathcal{N}_u(i)} |w_{ij}|}. \tag{2.15}$$

An interesting property of mean-centering is that one can see right-away if the appreciation of a user for an item is positive or negative by looking at the sign of the normalized rating. Moreover, the module of this rating gives the level at which the user likes or dislikes the item.

Example 2.6. As shown in Fig. 2.2, although Diane gave an average rating of 3 to the movies "Titanic" and "Forrest Gump", the user-mean-centered ratings show that

User mean-centering:

	The Matrix	Titanic	Die Hard	Forrest Gump	Wall-E
John	2.50	-1.50		-0.50	-0.50
Lucy	-2.60	1.40	-1.60	1.40	1.40
Eric	-1.50		-0.50	1.50	0.50
Diane	0.25	-0.75	1.25	-0.75	

Item mean-centering:

	The Matrix	Titanic	Die Hard	Forrest Gump	Wall-E
John	2.00	-2.00		-1.75	-1.67
Lucy	-2.00	2.00	-1.33	1.25	1.33
Eric	-1.00		-0.33	1.25	0.33
Diane	1.00	0.00	1.67	-0.75	

Fig. 2.2 The *user* and *item* mean-centered ratings of Fig. 2.1

her appreciation of these movies is in fact negative. This is because her ratings are high on average, and so, an average rating corresponds to a low degree of appreciation. Differences are also visible while comparing the two types of mean-centering. For instance, the item-mean-centered rating of the movie "Titanic" is neutral, instead of negative, due to the fact that much lower ratings were given to that movie. Likewise, Diane's appreciation for "The Matrix" and John's distaste for "Forrest Gump" are more pronounced in the item-mean-centered ratings.

2.4.1.2 Z-Score Normalization

Consider, two users A and B that both have an average rating of 3. Moreover, suppose that the ratings of A alternate between 1 and 5, while those of B are always 3. A rating of 5 given to an item by B is more exceptional than the same rating given by A, and, thus, reflects a greater appreciation for this item. While mean-centering removes the offsets caused by the different perceptions of an average rating, Z-score normalization [25] also considers the spread in the individual rating scales. Once again, this is usually done differently in user-based than in item-based recommendation. In user-based methods, the normalization of a rating r_{ui} divides the *user*-mean-centered rating by the standard deviation σ_u of the ratings given by user u:

$$h(r_{ui}) = \frac{r_{ui} - \overline{r}_u}{\sigma_u}.$$

A user-based prediction of rating r_{ui} using this normalization approach would therefore be obtained as

$$\hat{r}_{ui} = \overline{r}_u + \sigma_u \frac{\sum\limits_{v \in \mathcal{N}_i(u)} w_{uv}\,(r_{vi} - \overline{r}_v)/\sigma_v}{\sum\limits_{v \in \mathcal{N}_i(u)} |w_{uv}|}. \tag{2.16}$$

Likewise, the z-score normalization of r_{ui} in item-based methods divides the *item-mean-centered* rating by the standard deviation of ratings given to item i:

$$h(r_{ui}) = \frac{r_{ui} - \overline{r}_i}{\sigma_i}.$$

The item-based prediction of rating r_{ui} would then be

$$\hat{r}_{ui} = \overline{r}_i + \sigma_i \frac{\sum\limits_{j \in \mathcal{N}_u(i)} w_{ij}\,(r_{uj} - \overline{r}_j)/\sigma_j}{\sum\limits_{j \in \mathcal{N}_u(i)} |w_{ij}|}. \tag{2.17}$$

2.4.1.3 Choosing a Normalization Scheme

In some cases, rating normalization can have undesirable effects. For instance, imagine the case of a user that gave only the highest ratings to the items he has purchased. Mean-centering would consider this user as "easy to please" and any rating below this highest rating (whether it is a positive or negative rating) would be considered as negative. However, it is possible that this user is in fact "hard to please" and carefully selects only items that he will like for sure. Furthermore, normalizing on a few ratings can produce unexpected results. For example, if a user has entered a single rating or a few identical ratings, his rating standard deviation will be 0, leading to undefined prediction values. Nevertheless, if the rating data is not overly sparse, normalizing ratings has been found to consistently improve the predictions [25, 29].

Comparing mean-centering with Z-score, as mentioned, the second one has the additional benefit of considering the variance in the ratings of individual users or items. This is particularly useful if the rating scale has a wide range of discrete values or if it is continuous. On the other hand, because the ratings are divided and multiplied by possibly very different standard deviation values, Z-score can be more sensitive than mean-centering and, more often, predict ratings that are outside the rating scale. Lastly, while an initial investigation found mean-centering and Z-score to give comparable results [25], a more recent one showed Z-score to have more significant benefits [29].

Finally, if rating normalization is not possible or does not improve the results, another possible approach to remove the problems caused by the rating scale variance is *preference-based filtering*. The particularity of this approach is that it focuses on predicting the relative preferences of users instead of absolute rating values. Since an item preferred to another one remains so regardless of the rating scale, predicting relative preferences removes the need to normalize the ratings. More information on this approach can be found in [12, 18, 32, 33].

2.4.2 Similarity Weight Computation

The similarity weights play a double role in neighborhood-based recommendation methods: (1) they allow to select trusted neighbors whose ratings are used in the prediction, and (2) they provide the means to give more or less importance to these neighbors in the prediction. The computation of the similarity weights is one of the most critical aspects of building a neighborhood-based recommender system, as it can have a significant impact on both its accuracy and its performance.

2.4.2.1 Correlation-Based Similarity

A measure of the similarity between two objects a and b, often used in information retrieval, consists in representing these objects in the form of a vector $\mathbf{x}_a$ and $\mathbf{x}_b$ and computing the *Cosine Vector* (CV) (or *Vector Space*) similarity [4, 8, 42] between these vectors:

$$\cos(\mathbf{x}_a, \mathbf{x}_b) = \frac{\mathbf{x}_a^\top \mathbf{x}_b}{||\mathbf{x}_a|| ||\mathbf{x}_b||}.$$

In the context of item recommendation, this measure can be employed to compute user similarities by considering a user u as a vector $\mathbf{x}_u \in \mathbb{R}^{|I|}$, where $\mathbf{x}_{ui} = r_{ui}$ if user u has rated item i, and 0 otherwise. The similarity between two users u and v would then be computed as

$$CV(u, v) = \cos(\mathbf{x}_u, \mathbf{x}_v) = \frac{\sum\limits_{i \in \mathcal{I}_{uv}} r_{ui}\, r_{vi}}{\sqrt{\sum\limits_{i \in \mathcal{I}_u} r_{ui}^2 \sum\limits_{j \in \mathcal{I}_v} r_{vj}^2}}, \tag{2.18}$$

where I_{uv} once more denotes the items rated by both u and v. A problem with this measure is that is does not consider the differences in the mean and variance of the ratings made by users u and v.

A popular measure that compares ratings where the effects of mean and variance have been removed is the *Pearson Correlation* (PC) similarity:

$$\mathrm{PC}(u,v) = \frac{\sum\limits_{i \in \mathcal{I}_{uv}} (r_{ui} - \overline{r}_u)(r_{vi} - \overline{r}_v)}{\sqrt{\sum\limits_{i \in \mathcal{I}_{uv}} (r_{ui} - \overline{r}_u)^2 \sum\limits_{i \in \mathcal{I}_{uv}} (r_{vi} - \overline{r}_v)^2}}. \tag{2.19}$$

Note that this is different from computing the CV similarity on the *Z*-score normalized ratings, since the standard deviation of the ratings in evaluated only on the common items I_{uv}, not on the entire set of items rated by u and v, i.e. $\mathcal{I}_u$ and $\mathcal{I}_v$. The same idea can be used to obtain similarities between two items i and j [15, 59], this time by comparing the ratings made by users that have rated both these items:

$$\mathrm{PC}(i,j) = \frac{\sum\limits_{u \in \mathcal{U}_{ij}} (r_{ui} - \overline{r}_i)(r_{uj} - \overline{r}_j)}{\sqrt{\sum\limits_{u \in \mathcal{U}_{ij}} (r_{ui} - \overline{r}_i)^2 \sum\limits_{u \in \mathcal{U}_{ij}} (r_{uj} - \overline{r}_j)^2}}. \tag{2.20}$$

While the sign of a similarity weight indicates whether the correlation is direct or inverse, its magnitude (ranging from 0 to 1) represents the strength of the correlation.

Example 2.7. The similarities between the pairs of users and items of our toy example, as computed using PC similarity, are shown in Fig. 2.3. We can see that Lucy's taste in movies is very close to Eric's (similarity of 0.922) but very different from John's (similarity of −0.938). This means that Eric's ratings can be trusted to predict Lucy's, and that Lucy should discard John's opinion on movies or consider the opposite. We also find that the people that like "The Matrix" also like "Die Hard" but hate "Wall-E". Note that these relations were discovered without having any knowledge of the genre, director or actors of these movies.

The differences in the rating scales of individual users are often more pronounced than the differences in ratings given to individual items. Therefore, while computing the item similarities, it may be more appropriate to compare ratings that are centered on their *user* mean, instead of their *item* mean. The *Adjusted Cosine* (AC) similarity [59], is a modification of the PC item similarity which compares user-mean-centered ratings:

$$AC(i,j) = \frac{\sum\limits_{u \in \mathcal{U}_{ij}} (r_{ui} - \overline{r}_u)(r_{uj} - \overline{r}_u)}{\sqrt{\sum\limits_{u \in \mathcal{U}_{ij}} (r_{ui} - \overline{r}_u)^2 \sum\limits_{u \in \mathcal{U}_{ij}} (r_{uj} - \overline{r}_u)^2}}.$$

In some cases, AC similarity has been found to outperform PC similarity on the prediction of ratings using an item-based method [59].

User-based Pearson correlation

	John	Lucy	Eric	Diane
John	1.000	-0.938	-0.839	0.659
Lucy	-0.938	1.000	0.922	-0.787
Eric	-0.839	0.922	1.000	-0.659
Diane	0.659	-0.787	-0.659	1.000

Item-based Pearson correlation

	The Matrix	Titanic	Die Hard	Forrest Gump	Wall-E
Matrix	1.000	-0.943	0.882	-0.974	-0.977
Titanic	-0.943	1.000	-0.625	0.931	0.994
Die Hard	0.882	-0.625	1.000	-0.804	-1.000
ForrestGump	-0.974	0.931	-0.804	1.000	0.930
Wall-E	-0.977	0.994	-1.000	0.930	1.000

Fig. 2.3 The *user* and *item* PC similarity for the ratings of Fig. 2.1

2.4.2.2 Other Similarity Measures

Several other measures have been proposed to compute similarities between users or items. One of them is the *Mean Squared Difference* (MSD) [63], which evaluate the similarity between two users u and v as the inverse of the average squared difference between the ratings given by u and v on the same items:

$$\mathrm{MSD}(u, v) \;=\; \frac{|\mathcal{I}_{uv}|}{\sum\limits_{i \in \mathcal{I}_{uv}} (r_{ui} - r_{vi})^2}. \tag{2.21}$$

While it could be modified to compute the differences on normalized ratings, the MSD similarity is limited compared to PC similarity because it does not allow to capture negative correlations between user preferences or the appreciation of different items. Having such negative correlations may improve the rating prediction accuracy [24].

Another well-known similarity measure is the *Spearman Rank Correlation* (SRC) [36]. While PC uses the rating values directly, SRC instead considers the ranking of these ratings. Denote by k_{ui} the rating rank of item i in user u's list of rated items (tied ratings get the average rank of their spot). The SRC similarity between two users u and v is evaluated as:

Table 2.3 The rating prediction accuracy (MAE) obtained on the *MovieLens* dataset using the mean squared difference (MSD), Spearman rank correlation and Pearson correlation (PC) similarity measures

k	MSD	SRC	PC
5	0.7898	0.7855	0.7829
10	0.7718	0.7636	0.7618
20	0.7634	0.7558	0.7545
60	0.7602	0.7529	0.7518
80	0.7605	0.7531	0.7523
100	0.7610	0.7533	0.7528

Results are shown for predictions using an increasing number of neighbors k

$$\text{SRC}(u, v) = \frac{\sum\limits_{i \in \mathcal{I}_{uv}} (k_{ui} - \overline{k}_u)(k_{vi} - \overline{k}_v)}{\sqrt{\sum\limits_{i \in \mathcal{I}_{uv}} (k_{ui} - \overline{k}_u)^2 \sum\limits_{i \in \mathcal{I}_{uv}} (k_{vi} - \overline{k}_v)^2}}, \tag{2.22}$$

where $\overline{k}_u$ is the average rank of items rated by u.

The principal advantage of SRC is that it avoids the problem of rating normalization, described in the last section, by using rankings. On the other hand, this measure may not be the best one when the rating range has only a few possible values, since that would create a large number of tied ratings. Moreover, this measure is typically more expensive than PC as ratings need to be sorted in order to compute their rank.

Table 2.3 shows the user-based prediction accuracy (MAE) obtained with MSD, SRC and PC similarity measures, on the *MovieLens*[2] dataset [24]. Results are given for different values of k, which represents the maximum number of neighbors used in the predictions. For this data, we notice that MSD leads to the least accurate predictions, possibly due to the fact that it does not take into account negative correlations. Also, these results show PC to be slightly more accurate than SRC. Finally, although PC has been generally recognized as the best similarity measure, see e.g. [24], a more recent investigation has shown that the performance of such measure depended greatly on the data [29].

2.4.2.3 Considering the Significance of Weights

Because the rating data is frequently sparse in comparison to the number of users and items of a system, it is often the case that similarity weights are computed using only a few ratings given to common items or made by the same users. For example, if the system has 10,000 ratings made by 1000 users on 100 items (assuming a uniform distribution of ratings), Table 2.1 shows us that the similarity between two users is computed, on average, by comparing the ratings given by these users to a

---

[2] http://www.grouplens.org/.

single item. If these few ratings are equal, then the users will be considered as "fully similar" and will likely play an important role in each other's recommendations. However, if the users' preferences are in fact different, this may lead to poor recommendations.

Several strategies have been proposed to take into account the *significance* of a similarity weight. The principle of these strategies is essentially the same: reduce the magnitude of a similarity weight when this weight is computed using only a few ratings. For instance, in *Significance Weighting* [25, 46], a user similarity weight w_{uv} is penalized by a factor proportional to the number of commonly rated item, if this number is less than a given parameter $\gamma > 0$:

$$w'_{uv} = \frac{\min\{|\mathcal{I}_{uv}|, \gamma\}}{\gamma} \times w_{uv}. \tag{2.23}$$

Likewise, an item similarity w_{ij}, obtained from a few ratings, can be adjusted as

$$w'_{ij} = \frac{\min\{|\mathcal{U}_{ij}|, \gamma\}}{\gamma} \times w_{ij}. \tag{2.24}$$

In [24, 25], it was found that using $\gamma \geq 25$ could significantly improve the accuracy of the predicted ratings, and that a value of 50 for γ gave the best results. However, the optimal value for this parameter is data dependent and should be determined using a cross-validation approach.

A characteristic of significance weighting is its use of a threshold γ determining when a weight should be adjusted. A more continuous approach, described in [6], is based on the concept of *shrinkage* where a weak or biased estimator can be improved if it is "shrunk" toward a null-value. This approach can be justified using a Bayesian perspective, where the best estimator of a parameter is the posterior mean, corresponding to a linear combination of the prior mean of the parameter (null-value) and an empirical estimator based fully on the data. In this case, the parameters to estimate are the similarity weights and the null value is zero. Thus, a user similarity w_{uv} estimated on a few ratings is shrunk as

$$w'_{uv} = \frac{|\mathcal{I}_{uv}|}{|\mathcal{I}_{uv}| + \beta} \times w_{uv}, \tag{2.25}$$

where $\beta > 0$ is a parameter whose value should also be selected using cross-validation. In this approach, w_{uv} is shrunk proportionally to $\beta/|I_{uv}|$, such that almost no adjustment is made when $|\mathcal{I}_{uv}| \gg \beta$. Item similarities can be shrunk in the same way:

$$w'_{ij} = \frac{|\mathcal{U}_{ij}|}{|\mathcal{U}_{ij}| + \beta} \times w_{ij}, \tag{2.26}$$

As reported in [6], a typical value for β is 100.

2.4.2.4 Considering the Variance of Ratings

Ratings made by two users on universally liked/disliked items may not be as informative as those made for items with a greater rating variance. For instance, most people like classic movies such as "The Godfather" so basing the weight computation on such movies would produce artificially high values. Likewise, a user that always rates items in the same way may provide less predictive information than one whose preferences vary from one item to another.

A recommendation approach that addresses this problem is the *Inverse User Frequency* [10]. Based on the information retrieval notion of *Inverse Document Frequency* (IDF), a weight λ_i is given to each item i, in proportion to the log-ratio of users that have rated i:

$$\lambda_i \;=\; \log \frac{|\mathcal{U}|}{|\mathcal{U}_i|}.$$

In the *Frequency-Weighted Pearson Correlation* (FWPC), the correlation between the ratings given by two users u and v to an item i is weighted by λ_i:

$$\text{FWPC}(u,v) \;=\; \frac{\sum\limits_{i \in \mathcal{I}_{uv}} \lambda_i (r_{ui} - \overline{r}_u)(r_{vi} - \overline{r}_v)}{\sqrt{\sum\limits_{i \in \mathcal{I}_{uv}} \lambda_i (r_{ui} - \overline{r}_u)^2 \sum\limits_{i \in \mathcal{I}_{uv}} \lambda_i (r_{vi} - \overline{r}_v)^2}}. \tag{2.27}$$

This approach, which was found to improve the prediction accuracy of a user-based recommendation method [10], could also be adapted to the computation of item similarities. More advanced strategies have also been proposed to consider rating variance. One of these strategies, described in [31], computes the factors λ_i by maximizing the average similarity between users.

2.4.2.5 Considering the Target Item

If the goal is to predict ratings with a user-based method, more reliable correlation values can be obtained if the target item is considered in their computation. In [5], the user-based PC similarity is extended by weighting the summation terms corresponding to an item i by the similarity between i and the target item j:

$$\text{WPC}_j(u,v) \;=\; \frac{\sum\limits_{i \in \mathcal{I}_{uv}} w_{ij}\, (r_{ui} - \overline{r}_u)(r_{vi} - \overline{r}_v)}{\sqrt{\sum\limits_{i \in \mathcal{I}_{uv}} w_{ij}\, (r_{ui} - \overline{r}_u)^2 \sum\limits_{i \in \mathcal{I}_{uv}} w_{ij}\, (r_{vi} - \overline{r}_v)^2}}. \tag{2.28}$$

The item weights w_{ij} can be computed using PC similarity or obtained by considering the items' content (e.g., the common genres for movies). Other variations of this similarity metric and their impact on the prediction accuracy are described in [5]. Note, however, that this model may require to recompute the similarity weights for each predicted rating, making it less suitable for online recommender systems.

2.4.3 Neighborhood Selection

The number of nearest-neighbors to select and the criteria used for this selection can also have a serious impact on the quality of the recommender system. The selection of the neighbors used in the recommendation of items is normally done in two steps: (1) a global filtering step where only the most likely candidates are kept, and (2) a per prediction step which chooses the best candidates for this prediction.

2.4.3.1 Pre-filtering of Neighbors

In large recommender systems that can have millions of users and items, it is usually not possible to store the (non-zero) similarities between each pair of users or items, due to memory limitations. Moreover, doing so would be extremely wasteful as only the most significant of these values are used in the predictions. The pre-filtering of neighbors is an essential step that makes neighborhood-based approaches practicable by reducing the amount of similarity weights to store, and limiting the number of candidate neighbors to consider in the predictions. There are several ways in which this can be accomplished:

- **Top-*N* filtering:** For each user or item, only a list of the *N* nearest-neighbors and their respective similarity weight is kept. To avoid problems with efficiency or accuracy, *N* should be chosen carefully. Thus, if *N* is too large, an excessive amount of memory will be required to store the neighborhood lists and predicting ratings will be slow. On the other hand, selecting a too small value for *N* may reduce the coverage of the recommendation method, which causes some items to be never recommended.
- **Threshold filtering:** Instead of keeping a fixed number of nearest-neighbors, this approach keeps all the neighbors whose similarity weight's magnitude is greater than a given threshold $w_{\min}$. While this is more flexible than the previous filtering technique, as only the most significant neighbors are kept, the right value of $w_{\min}$ may be difficult to determine.
- **Negative filtering:** In general, negative rating correlations are less reliable than positive ones. Intuitively, this is because strong positive correlation between two users is a good indicator of their belonging to a common group (e.g., teenagers, science-fiction fans, etc.). However, although negative correlation may indicate membership to different groups, it does not tell how different are these groups, or whether these groups are compatible for some other categories of items.

While experimental investigations [25, 26] have found negative correlations to provide no significant improvement in the prediction accuracy, whether such correlations can be discarded depends on the data.

Note that these three filtering approaches are not exclusive and can be combined to fit the needs of the recommender system. For instance, one could discard all negative similarities *as well as* those that are not in the top-N lists.

2.4.3.2 Neighbors in the Predictions

Once a list of candidate neighbors has been computed for each user or item, the prediction of new ratings is normally made with the k-nearest-neighbors, that is, the k neighbors whose similarity weight has the greatest magnitude. The choice of k can also have a significant impact on the accuracy and performance of the system.

As shown in Table 2.3, the prediction accuracy observed for increasing values of k typically follows a *concave* function. Thus, when the number of neighbors is restricted by using a small k (e.g., $k < 20$), the prediction accuracy is normally low. As k increases, more neighbors contribute to the prediction and the variance introduced by individual neighbors is averaged out. As a result, the prediction accuracy improves. Finally, the accuracy usually drops when too many neighbors are used in the prediction (e.g., $k > 50$), due to the fact that the few strong local relations are "diluted" by the many weak ones. Although a number of neighbors between 20 to 50 is most often described in the literature, see e.g. [24, 26], the optimal value of k should be determined by cross-validation.

On a final note, more serendipitous recommendations may be obtained at the cost of a decrease in accuracy, by basing these recommendations on a few very similar users. For example, the system could find the user most similar to the active one and recommend the new item that has received the highest rated from this user.

2.5 Advanced Techniques

The neighborhood approaches based on rating correlation, such as the ones presented in the previous sections, have two important flaws:

- **Limited coverage:** Because rating correlation measures the similarity between two users by comparing their ratings for the same items, users can be neighbors *only if* they have rated common items. This assumption is very limiting, as users having rated a few or no common items may still have similar preferences. Moreover, since only items rated by neighbors can be recommended, the coverage of such methods can also be limited. This limitation also applies to item-based systems, when two items have only a few or no co-ratings.
- **Sensitivity to sparse data:** Another consequence of rating correlation, addressed briefly in Sect. 2.3.5, is the fact that the accuracy of neighborhood-based

recommendation methods suffers from the lack of available ratings. Sparsity is a problem common to most recommender systems due to the fact that users typically rate only a small proportion of the available items [7, 21, 60, 61]. This is aggravated by the fact that users or items newly added to the system may have no ratings at all, a problem known as *cold-start* [62]. When the rating data is sparse, two users or items are unlikely to have common ratings and, consequently, neighborhood-based approaches will predict ratings using a very limited number of neighbors. Moreover, similarity weights may be computed using only a small number of ratings, resulting in biased recommendations (see Sect. 2.4.2.3 for this problem).

A common solution for these problems is to fill the missing ratings with default values [10, 15], such as the middle value of the rating range, or the average user or item rating. A more reliable approach is to use content information to fill out the missing ratings [13, 21, 39, 47]. For instance, the missing ratings can be provided by autonomous agents called *filterbots* [21, 39], that act as ordinary users of the system and rate items based on some specific characteristics of their content. The missing ratings can instead be predicted by a content-based approach [47]. Furthermore, content similarity can also be used "instead of" or "in addition to" rating correlation similarity to find the nearest-neighbors employed in the predictions [4, 43, 55, 66]. Finally, data sparsity can also be tackled by acquiring new ratings with active learning techniques. In such techniques, the system interactively queries the user to gain a better understanding of his or her preferences. A more detailed description of active learning techniques can be found in Chap. 24 of this book.

These solutions, however, also have their own drawbacks. For instance, giving a default value to missing ratings may induce bias in the recommendations. Also, item content may not be available to compute ratings or similarities. This section presents two approaches proposed for the problems of limited coverage and sparsity: *graph-based* and *learning-based* and methods.

2.5.1 Graph-Based Methods

In graph-based approaches, the data is represented in the form of a graph where nodes are users, items or both, and edges encode the interactions or similarities between the users and items. For example, in Fig. 2.4, the data is modeled as a bipartite graph where the two sets of nodes represent users and items, and an edge connects user u to item i if there is a rating given to i by u in the system. A weight can also be given to this edge, such as the value of its corresponding rating. In another model, the nodes can represent either users or items, and an edge connects two nodes if the ratings corresponding two these nodes are sufficiently correlated. The weight of this edge can be the corresponding correlation value.

In these models, standard approaches based on correlation predict the rating of a user u for an item i using only the nodes directly connected to u or i. Graph-based

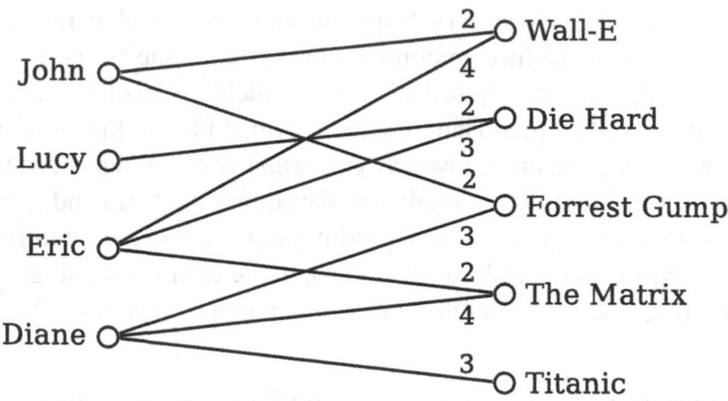

Fig. 2.4 A bipartite graph representation of the ratings of Fig. 2.1 (*only ratings with value in* $\{2, 3, 4\}$ *are shown*)

approaches, on the other hand, allow nodes that are not directly connected to influence each other by propagating information along the edges of the graph. The greater the weight of an edge, the more information is allowed to pass through it. Also, the influence of a node on another should be less if the two nodes are further away in the graph. These two properties, known as *propagation* and *attenuation* [22, 30], are often observed in graph-based similarity measures.

The transitive associations captured by graph-based methods can be used to recommend items in two different ways. In the first approach, the proximity of a user u to an item i in the graph is used directly to evaluate the relevance of i to u [16, 22, 30]. Following this idea, the items recommended to u by the system are those that are the "closest" to u in the graph. On the other hand, the second approach considers the proximity of two users or item nodes in the graph as a measure of similarity, and uses this similarity as the weights w_{uv} or w_{ij} of a neighborhood-based recommendation method [16, 45].

2.5.1.1 Path-Based Similarity

In path-based similarity, the distance between two nodes of the graph is evaluated as a function of the number of paths connecting the two nodes, as well as the length of these paths.

Let R be once again the $|U| \times |I|$ rating matrix, where r_{ui} is the rating given by user u to an item i. The adjacency matrix A of the user-item bipartite graph can be defined from R as

$$A = \begin{pmatrix} 0 & R^{\top} \\ R & 0 \end{pmatrix}.$$

The association between a user u and an item i can be defined as the sum of the weights of all distinctive paths connecting u to i (allowing nodes to appear more than once in the path), whose length is no more than a given maximum length K. Note that, since the graph is bipartite, K should be an odd number. In order to attenuate the contribution of longer paths, the weight given to a path of length k is defined as α^k, where $\alpha \in [0, 1]$. Using the fact that the number of length k paths between pairs of nodes is given by A^k, the user-item association matrix S_K is

$$\begin{aligned} S_K &= \sum_{k=1}^{K} \alpha^k A^k \\ &= (I - \alpha A)^{-1}(\alpha A - \alpha^K A^K). \end{aligned} \tag{2.29}$$

This method of computing distances between nodes in a graph is known as the *Katz* measure [35]. Note that this measure is closely related to the *Von Neumann Diffusion* kernel [17, 38, 41]

$$\begin{aligned} K_{\text{VND}} &= \sum_{k=0}^{\infty} \alpha^k A^k \\ &= (I - \alpha A)^{-1} \end{aligned} \tag{2.30}$$

and the *Exponential Diffusion* kernel

$$\begin{aligned} K_{\text{ED}} &= \sum_{k=0}^{\infty} \frac{1}{k!} \alpha^k A^k \\ &= \exp(\alpha A), \end{aligned} \tag{2.31}$$

where $A^0 = I$.

In recommender systems that have a large number of users and items, computing these association values may require extensive computational resources. In [30], spreading activation techniques are used to overcome these limitations. Essentially, such techniques work by first activating a selected subset of nodes as starting nodes, and then iteratively activating the nodes that can be reached directly from the nodes that are already active, until a convergence criterion is met.

Path-based methods, as well as the other graph-based approaches described in this section, focus on finding relevant associations between users and items, not predicting exact ratings. Therefore, such methods are better suited for item retrieval tasks, where explicit ratings are often unavailable and the goal is to obtain a short list of relevant items (i.e., the top-N recommendation problem).

2.5.1.2 Random Walk Similarity

Transitive associations in graph-based methods can also be defined within a probabilistic framework. In this framework, the similarity or affinity between users or items is evaluated as a probability of reaching these nodes in a random walk. Formally, this can be described with a first-order Markov process defined by a set of n states and a $n \times n$ transition probability matrix P such that the probability of jumping from state i to j at any time-step t is

$$p_{ij} = \Pr\big(s(t+1) = j | s(t) = i\big).$$

Denote $\pi(t)$ the vector containing the state probability distribution of step t, such that $\pi_i(t) = \Pr(s(t) = i)$, the evolution of the Markov chain is characterized by

$$\pi(t+1) = P^{\top}\pi(t).$$

Moreover, under the condition that P is row-stochastic, i.e. $\sum_j p_{ij} = 1$ for all i, the process converges to a stable distribution vector $\pi(\infty)$ corresponding to the positive eigenvector of $P^{\top}$ with an eigenvalue of 1. This process is often described in the form of a weighted graph having a node for each state, and where the probability of jumping from a node to an adjacent node is given by the weight of the edge connecting these nodes.

Itemrank

A recommendation approach, based on the PageRank algorithm for ranking Web pages [11], is ItemRank [22]. This approach ranks the preferences of a user u for new items i as the probability of u to visit i in a random walk of a graph in which nodes correspond to the items of the system, and edges connects items that have been rated by common users. The edge weights are given by the $|\mathcal{I}| \times |\mathcal{I}|$ transition probability matrix P for which $p_{ij} = |\mathcal{U}_{ij}|/|\mathcal{U}_i|$ is the estimated conditional probability of a user to rate and item j if it has rated an item i.

As in PageRank, the random walk can, at any step t, either jump using P to an adjacent node with fixed probability α, or "teleport" to any node with probability $(1-\alpha)$. Let $\mathbf{r}_u$ be the uth row of the rating matrix R, the probability distribution of user u to teleport to other nodes is given by vector $\mathbf{d}_u = \mathbf{r}_u/||\mathbf{r}_u||$. Following these definitions, the state probability distribution vector of user u at step $t+1$ can be expressed recursively as

$$\pi_u(t+1) = \alpha P^{\top}\pi_u(t) + (1-\alpha)\mathbf{d}_u. \tag{2.32}$$

For practical reasons, $\pi_u(\infty)$ is usually obtained with a procedure that first initializes the distribution as uniform, i.e. $\pi_u(0) = \frac{1}{n}\mathbf{1}_n$, and then iteratively updates π_u, using (2.32), until convergence. Once $\pi_u(\infty)$ has been computed, the system recommends to u the item i for which π_{ui} is the highest.

Average First-Passage/Commute Time

Other distance measures based on random walks have been proposed for the recommendation problem. Among these are the *average first-passage time* and the *average commute time* [16, 17]. The average first-passage time $m(j|i)$ [52] is the average number of steps needed by a random walker to reach a node j for the first time, when starting from a node $i \neq j$. Let P be the $n \times n$ transition probability matrix, $m(j|i)$ can be obtained expressed recursively as

$$m(j|i) \;=\; \begin{cases} 0 & , \;\text{if}\; i = j \\ 1 + \sum\limits_{k=1}^{n} p_{ik}\, m(j|k) & , \;\text{otherwise} \end{cases}$$

A problem with the average first-passage time is that it is not symmetric. A related measure that does not have this problem is the average commute time $n(i,j) = m(j|i) + m(i|j)$ [19], corresponding to the average number of steps required by a random walker starting at node $i \neq j$ to reach node j for the first time and go back to i. This measure has several interesting properties. Namely, it is a true distance measure in some Euclidean space [19], and is closely related to the well-known property of resistance in electrical networks and to the pseudo-inverse of the graph Laplacian matrix [16].

In [16], the average commute time is used to compute the distance between the nodes of a bipartite graph representing the interactions of users and items in a recommender system. For each user u there is a directed edge from u to every item $i \in \mathcal{I}_u$, and the weight of this edge is simply $1/|\mathcal{I}_u|$. Likewise, there is a directed edge from each item i to every user $u \in \mathcal{U}_i$, with weight $1/|\mathcal{U}_i|$. Average commute times can be used in two different ways: (1) recommending to u the item i for which $n(u,i)$ is the smallest, or (2) finding the users nearest to u, according to the commute time distance, and then suggest to u the item most liked by these users.

2.5.2 *Learning-Based Methods*

In graph-based methods, the similarity or affinity between users and items in a network is evaluated directly from the network. Learning-based methods, on the other hand, obtain these values by defining a parameteric model that describes the relation between users, items or both, and then computes the model parameters through an optimization process.

Using a learning-based method has significant advantages. First, such methods can capture high-level patterns and trends in the data, are generally more robust to outliers, and are known to generalize better than approaches solely based on local relations. In recommender systems, this translates into greater accuracy and stability in the recommendations [40]. Also, because the relations between users and items are encoded in a limited set of parameters, such methods normally require less memory than other types of approaches. Finally, since the parameters are usually learned offline, the online recommendation process is generally faster.

Learning-based methods that use neighborhood or similarity information can be divided in two categories: factorization methods and adaptive neighborhood learning methods. These categories are presented in the following sections.

2.5.2.1 Factorization Methods

Factorization methods [6, 7, 20, 40, 60, 68, 69] address the problems of limited coverage and sparsity by projecting users and items into a reduced latent space that captures their most salient features. Because users and items are compared in this dense subspace of high-level features, instead of the "rating space", more meaningful relations can be discovered. In particular, a relation between two users can be found, even though these users have rated different items. As a result, such methods are generally less sensitive to sparse data [6, 7, 60].

There are essentially two ways in which factorization can be used to improve recommender systems: (1) factorization of a sparse *similarity* matrix, and (2) factorization of a user-item *rating* matrix.

Factorizing the Similarity Matrix

Neighborhood similarity measures like the correlation similarity are usually very sparse since the average number of ratings per user is much less than the total number of items. A simple solution to densify a sparse similarity matrix is to compute a low-rank approximation of this matrix with a factorization method.

Let W be a symmetric matrix of rank n representing either user or item similarities. To simplify the presentation, we will suppose the latter case. We wish to approximate W with a matrix $\hat{W} = QQ^\top$ of lower rank $k < n$, by minimizing the following objective:

$$\begin{aligned} E(Q) &= ||W - QQ^\top||_F^2 \\ &= \sum_{i,j} \left(w_{ij} - \mathbf{q}_i\mathbf{q}_j^\top\right)^2, \end{aligned} \tag{2.33}$$

where $||M||_F = \sqrt{\sum_{i,j} m_{ij}^2}$ is the matrix Frobenius norm. Matrix $\hat{W}$ can be seen as a "compressed" and less sparse version of W. Finding the factor matrix Q is equivalent to computing the eigenvalue decomposition of W:

$$W = VDV^\top,$$

where D is a diagonal matrix containing the $|\mathcal{I}|$ eigenvalues of W, and V is a $|\mathcal{I}|\times|\mathcal{I}|$ orthogonal matrix containing the corresponding eigenvectors. Let V_k be a matrix formed by the k principal (normalized) eigenvectors of W, which correspond to the axes of the k-dimensional latent subspace. The coordinates $\mathbf{q}_i \in \mathbb{R}^k$ of an item i in this subspace is given by the ith row of matrix $Q = V_k D_k^{1/2}$. Furthermore, the item similarities computed in this latent subspace are given by matrix

$$\begin{aligned}\hat{W} &= QQ^\top \\ &= V_k D_k V_k^\top.\end{aligned} \tag{2.34}$$

This approach was used to recommend jokes in the Eigentaste system [20]. In Eigentaste, a matrix W containing the PC similarities between pairs of items is decomposed to obtain the latent subspace defined by the k principal eigenvectors of W. A user u, represented by the uth row $\mathbf{r}_u$ of the rating matrix R, is projected in the plane defined by V_k:

$$\mathbf{r}'_u = \mathbf{r}_u V_k.$$

In an offline step, the users of the system are clustered in this subspace using a recursive subdivision technique. Then, the rating of user u for an item i is evaluated as the mean rating for i made by users in the same cluster as u. This strategy is related to the well-known spectral clustering method [64].

Factorizing the Rating Matrix

The problems of cold-start and limited coverage can also be alleviated by factorizing the user-item rating matrix. Once more, we want to approximate the $|\mathcal{U}|\times|\mathcal{I}|$ rating matrix R of rank n by a matrix $\hat{R} = PQ^\top$ of rank $k < n$, where P is a $|\mathcal{U}|\times k$ matrix of *users* factors and Q a $|\mathcal{I}|\times k$ matrix of *item* factors. This task can be formulated as finding matrices P and Q which minimize the following function:

$$\begin{aligned}E(P,Q) &= ||R - PQ^\top||_F^2 \\ &= \sum_{u,i} \left(r_{ui} - \mathbf{p}_u \mathbf{q}_i^\top\right)^2.\end{aligned} \tag{2.35}$$

The optimal solution can be obtained by the Singular Value Decomposition (SVD) of R: $P = U_k D_k^{1/2}$ and $Q = V_k D_k^{1/2}$, where D_k is a diagonal matrix containing the k largest singular values of R, and U_k, V_k respectively contain the left and right singular vectors corresponding to these values.

However, there is significant problem with applying SVD directly to the rating matrix R: most values r_{ui} of R are undefined, since there may not be a rating given to i by u. Although it is possible to assign a default value to r_{ui}, as mentioned above, this would introduce a bias in the data. More importantly, this would make the large matrix R dense and, consequently, render impractical the SVD decomposition of R. A common solution to this problem is to learn the model parameters using only the known ratings [6, 40, 67, 69]. For instance, suppose the rating of user u for item i is estimated as

$$\hat{r}_{ui} = b_u + b_i + \mathbf{p}_u \mathbf{q}_i^{\top}, \tag{2.36}$$

where b_u and b_i are parameters representing the user and item rating biases. The model parameters can be learned by minimizing the following objective function:

$$E(P, Q, \mathbf{b}) = \sum_{r_{ui} \in \mathcal{R}} (r_{ui} - \hat{r}_{ui})^2 + \lambda \left(||\mathbf{p}_u||^2 + ||\mathbf{q}_i||^2 + b_u^2 + b_i^2 \right). \tag{2.37}$$

The second term of the function is as a regularization term added to avoid overfitting. Parameter λ controls the level of regularization. A more comprehensive description of this recommendation approach can be found in Chap. 3 of this book.

The SVD model of Eq. (2.36) can be transformed into a similarity-based method by supposing that the profile of a user u is determined implicitly by the items he or she has rated. Thus, the factor vector of u can be defined as a weighted combination of the factor vectors $\mathbf{s}_j$ corresponding to the items j rated by this user:

$$\mathbf{p}_u = |\mathcal{I}_u|^{-\alpha} \sum_{j \in \mathcal{I}_u} c_{uj}\, \mathbf{s}_j. \tag{2.38}$$

In this formulation, α is a normalization constant typically set to $\alpha = 1/2$, and c_{uj} is a weight representing the contribution of item j to the profile of u. For instance, in the SVD++ model [40] this weight is defined as the bias corrected rating of u for item j: $c_{uj} = r_{ui} - b_u - b_j$. Other approaches, such as the FISM [34] and NSVD [53] models, instead use constant weights: $c_{uj} = 1$.

Using the formulation of Eq. (2.38), a rating r_{ui} is predicted as

$$\hat{r}_{ui} = b_u + b_i + |\mathcal{I}_u|^{-\alpha} \sum_{j \in \mathcal{I}_u} c_{uj}\, \mathbf{s}_j \mathbf{q}_i^{\top}. \tag{2.39}$$

Like the standard SVD model, the parameters of this model can be learned by minimizing the objective function of Eq. (2.37), for instance, using gradient descent optimization.

Note that, instead of having both user and item factors, we now have two different sets of item factors, i.e., $\mathbf{q}_i$ and $\mathbf{s}_j$. These vectors can be interpreted as the factors of an asymmetric item-item similarity matrix W, where

$$w_{ij} = \mathbf{s}_i \mathbf{q}_j^{\top}. \tag{2.40}$$

As mentioned in [40], this similarity-based factorization approach has several advantages over the traditional SVD model. First, since there are typically more users than items in a recommender system, replacing the user factors by a combination of item factors reduces the number of parameters in the model, which makes the learning process faster and more robust. Also, by using item similarities instead of user factors, the system can handle new users without having to re-train the model. Finally, as in item-similarity neighborhood methods, this model makes it possible to justify a rating to a user by showing this user the items that were most involved in the prediction.

In FISM [34], the prediction of a rating r_{ui} is made without considering the factors of i:

$$\hat{r}_{ui} = b_u + b_i + \left(|\mathcal{I}_u| - 1\right)^{-\alpha} \sum_{j \in \mathcal{I}_u \setminus \{i\}} \mathbf{s}_j \mathbf{q}_i^\top . \tag{2.41}$$

This modification, which corresponds to ignoring the diagonal entries in the item similarity matrix, avoids the problem of having an item recommending itself and has been shown to give better performance when the number of factors is high.

2.5.2.2 Neighborhood-Learning Methods

Standard neighborhood-based recommendation algorithms determine the neighborhood of users or items directly from the data, using some pre-defined similarity measure like PC. However, recent developments in the field of item recommendation have shown the advantage of learning the neighborhood automatically from the data, instead of using a pre-defined similarity measure [37, 49, 56].

Sparse Linear Neighborhood Model

A representative neighborhood-learning recommendation method is the `SLIM` algorithm, developed by Ning et al. [50]. In `SLIM`, a new rating is predicted as a sparse aggregation of existing ratings in a user's profile,

$$\hat{r}_{ui} = \mathbf{r}_u \mathbf{w}_i^\top , \tag{2.42}$$

where $\mathbf{r}_u$ is the uth row of the rating matrix R and $\mathbf{w}_j$ is a sparse row vector containing $|\mathcal{I}|$ aggregation coefficients. Essentially, the non-zero entries in $\mathbf{w}_i$ correspond to the neighbor items of an item i.

The neighborhood parameters are learned by minimizing the squared prediction error. Standard regularization and sparsity are enforced by penalizing the ℓ_2-norm and ℓ_1-norm of the parameters. The combination of these two types of regularizers in a regression problem is known as elastic net regularization [73]. This learning process can be expressed as the following optimization problem:

$$\begin{aligned} \underset{W}{\text{minimize}} \quad & \frac{1}{2}\|R - RW\|_F^2 + \frac{\beta}{2}\|W\|_F^2 + \lambda\|W\|_1 \\ \text{subject to} \quad & W \geq 0 \\ & \text{diag}(W) = 0. \end{aligned} \tag{2.43}$$

Parameters β and λ control the amount of each type of regularization. Moreover, the non-negativity constraint on W imposes the relations between neighbor items to be positive. The constraint $\text{diag}(W) = 0$ is also added to the model to avoid trivial solutions (e.g., W corresponding to the identity matrix) and ensure that r_{ui} is not used to compute $\hat{r}_{ui}$ during the recommendation process.

Sparse Neighborhood with Side Information

Side information, such as user profile attributes (e.g., age, gender, location) or item descriptions/tags, is becoming increasingly available in e-commerce applications. Properly exploited, this rich source of information can significantly improve the performance of conventional recommender systems [1, 3, 65, 71].

Item side information can be integrated in the SLIM model by supposing that the co-rating profile of two items is correlated to the properties encoded in their side information [51]. To enforce such correlations in the model, an additional requirement is added, where both the user-item rating matrix R and the item side information matrix F should be reproduced by the same sparse linear aggregation. That is, in addition to satisfying $R \sim RW$, the coefficient matrix W should also satisfy $F \sim FW$. This is achieved by solving the following optimization problem:

$$\begin{aligned} \underset{W}{\text{minimize}} \quad & \frac{1}{2}\|R - RW\|_F^2 + \frac{\alpha}{2}\|F - FW\|_F^2 + \frac{\beta}{2}\|W\|_F^2 + \lambda\|W\|_1 \\ \text{subject to} \quad & W \geq 0, \\ & \text{diag}(W) = 0. \end{aligned} \tag{2.44}$$

The parameter α is used to control the relative importance of the user-item rating information R and the item side information F when they are used to learn W.

In some cases, requiring that the aggregation coefficients be the same for both R and F can be too strict. An alternate model relaxes this constraints by imposing these two sets of aggregation coefficients to be similar. Specifically, it uses an aggregation coefficient matrix Q such that $F \sim FQ$ and $W \sim Q$. Matrices W and Q are learned as the minimizers of the following optimization problem:

$$\begin{aligned} \underset{W,Q}{\text{minimize}} \quad & \frac{1}{2}\|R - RW\|_F^2 + \frac{\alpha}{2}\|F - FQ\|_F^2 + \frac{\beta_1}{2}\|W - Q\|_F^2 \\ & + \frac{\beta_2}{2}(\|W\|_F^2 + \|Q\|_F^2) + \lambda(\|W\|_1 + \|Q\|_1) \qquad (2.45) \\ \text{subject to} \quad & W, Q \geq 0, \\ & \text{diag}(W) = 0, \ \text{diag}(Q) = 0. \end{aligned}$$

Parameter β_1 controls how much W and Q are allowed to be different from each other.

In [51], item reviews in the form of short texts were used as side information in the models described above. These models were shown to outperform the SLIM method without side information, as well as other approaches that use side information, in the top-N recommendation task.

2.6 Conclusion

One of the earliest approaches proposed for the task of item recommendation, neighborhood-based recommendation still ranks among the most popular methods for this problem. Although quite simple to describe and implement, this recommendation approach has several important advantages, including its ability to explain a recommendation with the list of the neighbors used, its computational and space efficiency which allows it to scale to large recommender systems, and its marked stability in an online setting where new users and items are constantly added. Another of its strengths is its potential to make serendipitous recommendations that can lead users to the discovery of unexpected, yet very interesting items.

In the implementation of a neighborhood-based approach, one has to make several important decisions. Perhaps the one having the greatest impact on the accuracy and efficiency of the recommender system is choosing between a user-based and an item-based neighborhood method. In typical commercial recommender systems, where the number of users far exceeds the number of available items, item-based approaches are typically preferred since they provide more accurate recommendations, while being more computationally efficient and requiring less frequent updates. On the other hand, user-based methods usually provide more original recommendations, which may lead users to a more satisfying experience. Moreover, the different components of a neighborhood-based method, which include the normalization of ratings, the computation of the similarity weights and the selection of the nearest-neighbors, can also have a significant influence on the quality of the recommender system. For each of these components, several different alternatives are available. Although the merit of each of these has been described in this document and in the literature, it is important to remember that the “best” approach may differ from one recommendation setting to the next. Thus, it is important to evaluate them on data collected from the actual system, and in light of the particular needs of the application.

Finally, when the performance of a neighborhood-based approach suffers from the problems of limited coverage and sparsity, one may explore techniques based on dimensionality reduction or graphs. Dimensionality reduction provides a compact representation of users and items that captures their most significant features. An advantage of such approach is that it allows to obtain meaningful relations between pairs of users or items, even though these users have rated different items, or these items were rated by different users. On the other hand, graph-based techniques exploit the transitive relations in the data. These techniques also avoid the problems of sparsity and limited coverage by evaluating the relationship between users or items that are not "directly connected". However, unlike dimensionality reduction, graph-based methods also preserve some of the "local" relations in the data, which are useful in making serendipitous recommendations.

References

1. Adams, R.P., Dahl, G.E., Murray, I.: Incorporating side information into probabilistic matrix factorization using Gaussian processes. In: P. Grünwald, P. Spirtes (eds.) Proceedings of the 26th Conference on Uncertainty in Artificial Intelligence, pp. 1–9 (2010)
2. Adomavicius, G., Tuzhilin, A.: Toward the next generation of recommender systems: A survey of the state-of-the-art and possible extensions. IEEE Transactions on Knowledge and Data Engineering **17**(6), 734–749 (2005)
3. Agarwal, D., Chen, B.C., Long, B.: Localized factor models for multi-context recommendation. In: Proceedings of the 17th ACM SIGKDD international conference on Knowledge discovery and data mining, KDD '11, pp. 609–617. ACM, New York, NY, USA (2011). DOI http://doi.acm.org/10.1145/2020408.2020504. URL http://doi.acm.org/10.1145/2020408.2020504
4. Balabanović, M., Shoham, Y.: Fab: Content-based, collaborative recommendation. Communications of the ACM **40**(3), 66–72 (1997)
5. Baltrunas, L., Ricci, F.: Item weighting techniques for collaborative filtering. In: Knowledge Discovery Enhanced with Semantic and Social Information, pp. 109–126. Springer (2009)
6. Bell, R., Koren, Y., Volinsky, C.: Modeling relationships at multiple scales to improve accuracy of large recommender systems. In: KDD '07: Proc. of the 13th ACM SIGKDD Int. Conf. on Knowledge Discovery and Data Mining, pp. 95–104. ACM, New York, NY, USA (2007)
7. Billsus, D., Pazzani, M.J.: Learning collaborative information filters. In: ICML '98: Proc. of the 15th Int. Conf. on Machine Learning, pp. 46–54. Morgan Kaufmann Publishers Inc., San Francisco, CA, USA (1998)
8. Billsus, D., Pazzani, M.J.: User modeling for adaptive news access. User Modeling and User-Adapted Interaction **10**(2–3), 147–180 (2000)
9. Blei, D.M., Ng, A.Y., Jordan, M.I.: Latent dirichlet allocation. Journal of Machine Learning Research **3**, 993–1022 (2003)
10. Breese, J.S., Heckerman, D., Kadie, C.: Empirical analysis of predictive algorithms for collaborative filtering. In: Proc. of the 14th Annual Conf. on Uncertainty in Artificial Intelligence, pp. 43–52. Morgan Kaufmann (1998)
11. Brin, S., Page, L.: The anatomy of a large-scale hypertextual Web search engine. Computer Networks and ISDN Systems **30**(1–7), 107–117 (1998)

12. Cohen, W.W., Schapire, R.E., Singer, Y.: Learning to order things. In: NIPS '97: Proc. of the 1997 Conf. on Advances in Neural Information Processing Systems, pp. 451–457. MIT Press, Cambridge, MA, USA (1998)
13. Degemmis, M., Lops, P., Semeraro, G.: A content-collaborative recommender that exploits wordnet-based user profiles for neighborhood formation. User Modeling and User-Adapted Interaction **17**(3), 217–255 (2007)
14. Delgado, J., Ishii, N.: Memory-based weighted majority prediction for recommender systems. In: Proc. of the ACM SIGIR'99 Workshop on Recommender Systems (1999)
15. Deshpande, M., Karypis, G.: Item-based top-N recommendation algorithms. ACM Transaction on Information Systems **22**(1), 143–177 (2004)
16. Fouss, F., Renders, J.M., Pirotte, A., Saerens, M.: Random-walk computation of similarities between nodes of a graph with application to collaborative recommendation. IEEE Transactions on Knowledge and Data Engineering **19**(3), 355–369 (2007)
17. Fouss, F., Yen, L., Pirotte, A., Saerens, M.: An experimental investigation of graph kernels on a collaborative recommendation task. In: ICDM '06: Proc. of the 6th Int. Conf. on Data Mining, pp. 863–868. IEEE Computer Society, Washington, DC, USA (2006)
18. Freund, Y., Iyer, R.D., Schapire, R.E., Singer, Y.: An efficient boosting algorithm for combining preferences. In: ICML '98: Proc. of the 15th Int. Conf. on Machine Learning, pp. 170–178. Morgan Kaufmann Publishers Inc., San Francisco, CA, USA (1998)
19. Gobel, F., Jagers, A.: Random walks on graphs. Stochastic Processes and Their Applications **2**, 311–336 (1974)
20. Goldberg, K., Roeder, T., Gupta, D., Perkins, C.: Eigentaste: A constant time collaborative filtering algorithm. Information Retrieval **4**(2), 133–151 (2001)
21. Good, N., Schafer, J.B., Konstan, J.A., Borchers, A., Sarwar, B., Herlocker, J., Riedl, J.: Combining collaborative filtering with personal agents for better recommendations. In: AAAI '99/IAAI '99: Proc. of the 16th National Conf. on Artificial Intelligence, pp. 439–446. American Association for Artificial Intelligence, Menlo Park, CA, USA (1999)
22. Gori, M., Pucci, A.: Itemrank: a random-walk based scoring algorithm for recommender engines. In: Proc. of the 2007 IJCAI Conf., pp. 2766–2771 (2007)
23. Grcar, M., Fortuna, B., Mladenic, D., Grobelnik, M.: k-NN versus SVM in the collaborative filtering framework. Data Science and Classification pp. 251–260 (2006). URL http://db.cs.ualberta.ca/webkdd05/proc/paper25-mladenic.pdf
24. Herlocker, J., Konstan, J.A., Riedl, J.: An empirical analysis of design choices in neighborhood-based collaborative filtering algorithms. Inf. Retr. **5**(4), 287–310 (2002)
25. Herlocker, J.L., Konstan, J.A., Borchers, A., Riedl, J.: An algorithmic framework for performing collaborative filtering. In: SIGIR '99: Proc. of the 22nd Annual Int. ACM SIGIR Conf. on Research and Development in Information Retrieval, pp. 230–237. ACM, New York, NY, USA (1999)
26. Herlocker, J.L., Konstan, J.A., Terveen, L.G., Riedl, J.T.: Evaluating collaborative filtering recommender systems. ACM Trans. Inf. Syst. **22**(1), 5–53 (2004)
27. Hill, W., Stead, L., Rosenstein, M., Furnas, G.: Recommending and evaluating choices in a virtual community of use. In: CHI '95: Proc. of the SIGCHI Conf. on Human Factors in Computing Systems, pp. 194–201. ACM Press/Addison-Wesley Publishing Co., New York, NY, USA (1995)
28. Hofmann, T.: Collaborative filtering via Gaussian probabilistic latent semantic analysis. In: SIGIR '03: Proc. of the 26th Annual Int. ACM SIGIR Conf. on Research and Development in Information Retrieval, pp. 259–266. ACM, New York, NY, USA (2003)
29. Howe, A.E., Forbes, R.D.: Re-considering neighborhood-based collaborative filtering parameters in the context of new data. In: CIKM '08: Proceeding of the 17th ACM conference on Information and knowledge management, pp. 1481–1482. ACM, New York, NY, USA (2008)
30. Huang, Z., Chen, H., Zeng, D.: Applying associative retrieval techniques to alleviate the sparsity problem in collaborative filtering. ACM Transactions on Information Systems **22**(1), 116–142 (2004)

31. Jin, R., Chai, J.Y., Si, L.: An automatic weighting scheme for collaborative filtering. In: SIGIR '04: Proc. of the 27th Annual Int. ACM SIGIR Conf. on Research and Development in Information Retrieval, pp. 337–344. ACM, New York, NY, USA (2004)
32. Jin, R., Si, L., Zhai, C.: Preference-based graphic models for collaborative filtering. In: Proc. of the 19th Annual Conf. on Uncertainty in Artificial Intelligence (UAI-03), pp. 329–33. Morgan Kaufmann, San Francisco, CA (2003)
33. Jin, R., Si, L., Zhai, C., Callan, J.: Collaborative filtering with decoupled models for preferences and ratings. In: CIKM '03: Proc. of the 12th Int. Conf. on Information and Knowledge Management, pp. 309–316. ACM, New York, NY, USA (2003)
34. Kabbur, S., Ning, X., Karypis, G.: Fism: factored item similarity models for top-n recommender systems. In: Proceedings of the 19th ACM SIGKDD international conference on Knowledge discovery and data mining, KDD '13, pp. 659–667. ACM, New York, NY, USA (2013). DOI 10.1145/2487575.2487589. URL http://doi.acm.org/10.1145/2487575.2487589
35. Katz, L.: A new status index derived from sociometric analysis. Psychometrika **18**(1), 39–43 (1953)
36. Kendall, M., Gibbons, J.D.: Rank Correlation Methods, 5 edn. Charles Griffin (1990)
37. Koenigstein, N., Koren, Y.: Towards scalable and accurate item-oriented recommendations. In: Proceedings of the 7th ACM conference on Recommender systems, RecSys '13, pp. 419–422. ACM, New York, NY, USA (2013). DOI 10.1145/2507157.2507208. URL http://doi.acm.org/10.1145/2507157.2507208
38. Kondor, R.I., Lafferty, J.D.: Diffusion kernels on graphs and other discrete input spaces. In: ICML '02: Proc. of the Nineteenth Int. Conf. on Machine Learning, pp. 315–322. Morgan Kaufmann Publishers Inc., San Francisco, CA, USA (2002)
39. Konstan, J.A., Miller, B.N., Maltz, D., Herlocker, J.L., Gordon, L.R., Riedl, J.: GroupLens: applying collaborative filtering to usenet news. Communications of the ACM **40**(3), 77–87 (1997)
40. Koren, Y.: Factorization meets the neighborhood: a multifaceted collaborative filtering model. In: KDD'08: Proceeding of the 14th ACM SIGKDD Int. Conf. on Knowledge Discovery and Data Mining, pp. 426–434. ACM, New York, NY, USA (2008)
41. Kunegis, J., Lommatzsch, A., Bauckhage, C.: Alternative similarity functions for graph kernels. In: Proc. of the Int. Conf. on Pattern Recognition (2008)
42. Lang, K.: News Weeder: Learning to filter netnews. In: Proc. of the 12th Int. Conf. on Machine Learning, pp. 331–339. Morgan Kaufmann publishers Inc.: San Mateo, CA, USA (1995)
43. Li, J., Zaiane, O.R.: Combining usage, content, and structure data to improve Web site recommendation. In: Proc. of the 5th Int. Conf. on Electronic Commerce and Web Technologies (EC-Web) (2004)
44. Linden, G., Smith, B., York, J.: Amazon.com recommendations: Item-to-item collaborative filtering. IEEE Internet Computing **7**(1), 76–80 (2003)
45. Luo, H., Niu, C., Shen, R., Ullrich, C.: A collaborative filtering framework based on both local user similarity and global user similarity. Machine Learning **72**(3), 231–245 (2008)
46. Ma, H., King, I., Lyu, M.R.: Effective missing data prediction for collaborative filtering. In: SIGIR '07: Proc. of the 30th Annual Int. ACM SIGIR Conf. on Research and Development in Information Retrieval, pp. 39–46. ACM, New York, NY, USA (2007)
47. Melville, P., Mooney, R.J., Nagarajan, R.: Content-boosted collaborative filtering for improved recommendations. In: 18th National Conf. on Artificial intelligence, pp. 187–192. American Association for Artificial Intelligence, Menlo Park, CA, USA (2002)
48. Nakamura, A., Abe, N.: Collaborative filtering using weighted majority prediction algorithms. In: ICML '98: Proc. of the 15th Int. Conf. on Machine Learning, pp. 395–403. Morgan Kaufmann Publishers Inc., San Francisco, CA, USA (1998)
49. Natarajan, N., Shin, D., Dhillon, I.S.: Which app will you use next?: collaborative filtering with interactional context. In: Proceedings of the 7th ACM conference on Recommender systems, RecSys '13, pp. 201–208. ACM, New York, NY, USA (2013). DOI 10.1145/2507157.2507186. URL http://doi.acm.org/10.1145/2507157.2507186

50. Ning, X., Karypis, G.: Slim: Sparse linear methods for top-n recommender systems. In: Proceedings of 11th IEEE International Conference on Data Mining, pp. 497–506 (2011)
51. Ning, X., Karypis, G.: Sparse linear methods with side information for top-n recommendations. In: Proceedings of the sixth ACM conference on Recommender systems, RecSys '12, pp. 155–162. ACM, New York, NY, USA (2012). DOI 10.1145/2365952.2365983. URL http://doi.acm.org/10.1145/2365952.2365983
52. Norris, J.R.: Markov Chains, 1 edn. Cambridge University Press, Cambridge (1999)
53. Paterek, A.: Improving regularized singular value decomposition for collaborative filtering. In: Proceedings of the KDD Cup and Workshop (2007)
54. Pazzani, M., Billsus, D.: Learning and revising user profiles: The identification of interesting Web sites. Machine Learning **27**(3), 313–331 (1997)
55. Pazzani, M.J.: A framework for collaborative, content-based and demographic filtering. Artificial Intelligence Review **13**(5–6), 393–408 (1999)
56. Rendle, S., Freudenthaler, C., Gantner, Z., Lars, S.T.: Bpr: Bayesian personalized ranking from implicit feedback. In: Proceedings of the Twenty-Fifth Conference on Uncertainty in Artificial Intelligence, UAI '09, pp. 452–461. AUAI Press, Arlington, Virginia, United States (2009)
57. Resnick, P., Iacovou, N., Suchak, M., Bergstrom, P., Riedl, J.: GroupLens: An open architecture for collaborative filtering of netnews. In: CSCW '94: Proc. of the 1994 ACM Conf. on Computer Supported Cooperative Work, pp. 175–186. ACM, New York, NY, USA (1994)
58. Salakhutdinov, R., Mnih, A., Hinton, G.: Restricted Boltzmann machines for collaborative filtering. In: ICML '07: Proceedings of the 24th international conference on Machine learning, pp. 791–798. ACM, New York, NY, USA (2007)
59. Sarwar, B., Karypis, G., Konstan, J., Reidl, J.: Item-based collaborative filtering recommendation algorithms. In: WWW '01: Proc. of the 10th Int. Conf. on World Wide Web, pp. 285–295. ACM, New York, NY, USA (2001)
60. Sarwar, B.M., Karypis, G., Konstan, J.A., Riedl, J.T.: Application of dimensionality reduction in recommender systems – A case study. In: ACM WebKDD Workshop (2000)
61. Sarwar, B.M., Konstan, J.A., Borchers, A., Herlocker, J., Miller, B., Riedl, J.: Using filtering agents to improve prediction quality in the grouplens research collaborative filtering system. In: CSCW '98: Proc. of the 1998 ACM Conf. on Computer Supported Cooperative Work, pp. 345–354. ACM, New York, NY, USA (1998)
62. Schein, A.I., Popescul, A., Ungar, L.H., Pennock, D.M.: Methods and metrics for cold-start recommendations. In: SIGIR '02: Proc. of the 25th Annual Int. ACM SIGIR Conf. on Research and Development in Information Retrieval, pp. 253–260. ACM, New York, NY, USA (2002)
63. Shardanand, U., Maes, P.: Social information filtering: Algorithms for automating "word of mouth". In: CHI '95: Proc. of the SIGCHI Conf. on Human factors in Computing Systems, pp. 210–217. ACM Press/Addison-Wesley Publishing Co., New York, NY, USA (1995)
64. Shi, J., Malik, J.: Normalized cuts and image segmentation. Pattern Analysis and Machine Intelligence, IEEE Transactions on **22**(8), 888–905 (2000)
65. Singh, A.P., Gordon, G.J.: Relational learning via collective matrix factorization. In: Proceeding of the 14th ACM International Conference on Knowledge Discovery and Data Mining, pp. 650–658 (2008). DOI http://doi.acm.org/10.1145/1401890.1401969. URL http://doi.acm.org/10.1145/1401890.1401969
66. Soboroff, I.M., Nicholas, C.K.: Combining content and collaboration in text filtering. In: Proc. of the IJCAI'99 Workshop on Machine Learning for Information Filtering, pp. 86–91 (1999)
67. Takács, G., Pilászy, I., Németh, B., Tikk, D.: Major components of the gravity recommendation system. SIGKDD Exploration Newsletter **9**(2), 80–83 (2007)
68. Takács, G., Pilászy, I., Németh, B., Tikk, D.: Investigation of various matrix factorization methods for large recommender systems. In: Proc. of the 2nd KDD Workshop on Large Scale Recommender Systems and the Netflix Prize Competition (2008)
69. Takács, G., Pilászy, I., Németh, B., Tikk, D.: Scalable collaborative filtering approaches for large recommender systems. Journal of Machine Learning Research (Special Topic on Mining and Learning with Graphs and Relations) **10**, 623–656 (2009)

70. Terveen, L., Hill, W., Amento, B., McDonald, D., Creter, J.: PHOAKS: a system for sharing recommendations. Communications of the ACM **40**(3), 59–62 (1997)
71. Yoo, J., Choi, S.: Weighted nonnegative matrix co-tri-factorization for collaborative prediction. In: Z.H. Zhou, T. Washio (eds.) Advances in Machine Learning, *Lecture Notes in Computer Science*, vol. 5828, pp. 396–411. Springer Berlin / Heidelberg (2009)
72. Zitnick, C.L., Kanade, T.: Maximum entropy for collaborative filtering. In: AUAI '04: Proc. of the 20th Conf. on Uncertainty in Artificial Intelligence, pp. 636–643. AUAI Press, Arlington, Virginia, United States (2004)
73. Zou, H., Hastie, T.: Regularization and variable selection via the elastic net. Journal Of The Royal Statistical Society Series B **67**(2), 301–320 (2005)

Chapter 3
Advances in Collaborative Filtering

Yehuda Koren and Robert Bell

3.1 Introduction

Collaborative filtering recommender system (CF) methods produce user specific recommendations of items based on patterns of ratings or usage (e.g., purchases) without need for exogenous information about either items or users. While well established methods work adequately for many purposes, we present several recent extensions available to analysts who are looking for the best possible recommendations.

The Netflix Prize competition that began in October 2006 has fueled much recent progress in the field of collaborative filtering. For the first time, the research

Y. Koren (✉)
Google Research, Mountain View, CA, USA
e-mail: yehudako@gmail.com

R. Bell
AT&T Labs – Research, Middletown, NJ, USA
e-mail: rbell@research.att.com

F. Ricci et al. (eds.), *Recommender Systems Handbook*,
DOI 10.1007/978-1-4899-7637-6_3

community gained access to a large-scale, industrial strength data set of 100 million movie ratings—attracting thousands of scientists, students, engineers and enthusiasts to the field. The nature of the competition has encouraged rapid development, where innovators built on each generation of techniques to improve prediction accuracy. Because all methods are judged by the same rigid yardstick on common data, the evolution of more powerful models has been especially efficient.

Recommender systems rely on various types of input. Most convenient is high quality *explicit feedback*, where users directly report on their interest in products. For example, Netflix collects star ratings for movies and TiVo users indicate their preferences for TV shows by hitting thumbs-up/down buttons.

Because explicit feedback is not always available, some recommenders infer user preferences from the more abundant *implicit feedback*, which indirectly reflects opinion through observing user behavior [20]. Types of implicit feedback include purchase history, browsing history, search patterns, or even mouse movements. For example, a user who purchased many books by the same author probably likes that author. This chapter focuses on models suitable for explicit feedback. Nonetheless, we recognize the importance of implicit feedback, an especially valuable information source for users who do not provide much explicit feedback. Hence, we show how to address implicit feedback within the models as a secondary source of information.

In order to establish recommendations, CF systems need to relate two fundamentally different entities: items and users. There are two primary approaches to facilitate such a comparison, which constitute the two main techniques of CF: *the neighborhood approach* and *latent factor models*. Neighborhood methods focus on relationships between items or, alternatively, between users. An item-item approach models the preference of a user to an item based on ratings of similar items by the same user. Latent factor models, such as matrix factorization (aka, SVD), comprise an alternative approach by transforming both items and users to the same latent factor space. The latent space tries to explain ratings by characterizing both products and users on factors automatically inferred from user feedback.

Producing more accurate prediction methods requires deepening their foundations and reducing reliance on arbitrary decisions. In this chapter, we describe a variety of recent improvements to the primary CF modeling techniques. Yet, the quest for more accurate models goes beyond this. At least as important is the identification of all the signals, or features, available in the data. Conventional techniques address the sparse data of user-item ratings. Accuracy significantly improves by also utilising other sources of information. One prime example includes all kinds of temporal effects reflecting the dynamic, time-drifting nature of user-item interactions. No less important is listening to hidden feedback such as which items users chose to rate (regardless of rating values). Rated items are not selected at random, but rather reveal interesting aspects of user preferences, going beyond the numerical values of the ratings.

Section 3.3 surveys matrix factorization techniques, which combine implementation convenience with a relatively high accuracy. This has made them the preferred technique for addressing the largest publicly available dataset—the Netflix data.

This section describes the theory and practical details behind those techniques. In addition, much of the strength of matrix factorization models stems from their natural ability to handle additional features of the data, including implicit feedback and temporal information. This section describes in detail how to enhance matrix factorization models to address such features.

Section 3.4 turns attention to neighborhood methods. The basic methods in this family are well known, and to a large extent are based on heuristics. Some recently proposed techniques address shortcomings of neighborhood techniques by suggesting more rigorous formulations, thereby improving prediction accuracy. We continue at Sect. 3.5 with a more advanced method, which uses the insights of common neighborhood methods, with global optimization techniques typical of factorization models. This method allows lifting the limit on neighborhood size, and also addressing implicit feedback and temporal dynamics. The resulting accuracy is close to that of matrix factorization models, while offering some practical advantages.

Pushing the foundations of the models to their limits reveals surprising links among seemingly unrelated techniques. We elaborate on this in Sect. 3.6 to show that, at their limits, user-user and item-item neighborhood models may converge to a single model. Furthermore, at that point, both become equivalent to a simple matrix factorization model. The connections reduce the relevance of some previous distinctions such as the traditional broad categorization of matrix factorization as "model based" and neighborhood models as "memory based".

3.2 Preliminaries

We are given ratings for m users (aka customers) and n items (aka products). We reserve special indexing letters to distinguish users from items: for users u, v, and for items i, j, l. A rating r_{ui} indicates the preference by user u of item i, where high values mean stronger preference. For example, values can be integers ranging from 1 (star) indicating no interest to 5 (stars) indicating a strong interest. We distinguish predicted ratings from known ones, by using the notation $\hat{r}_{ui}$ for the predicted value of r_{ui}.

The scalar t_{ui} denotes the time of rating r_{ui}. One can use different time units, based on what is appropriate for the application at hand. For example, when time is measured in days, then t_{ui} counts the number of days elapsed since some early time point. Usually the vast majority of ratings are unknown. For example, in the Netflix data 99 % of the possible ratings are missing because a user typically rates only a small portion of the movies. The (u, i) pairs for which r_{ui} is known are stored in the set $\mathcal{K} = \{(u, i) \mid r_{ui} \text{ is known}\}$. Each user u is associated with a set of items denoted by $\mathrm{R}(u)$, which contains all the items for which ratings by u are available. Likewise, $\mathrm{R}(i)$ denotes the set of users who rated item i. Sometimes, we also use a set denoted by $\mathrm{N}(u)$, which contains all items for which u provided an implicit preference (items that he rented/purchased/watched, etc.).

Models for the rating data are learnt by fitting the previously observed ratings. However, our goal is to generalize those in a way that allows us to predict future, unknown ratings. Thus, caution should be exercised to avoid overfitting the observed data. We achieve this by regularizing the learnt parameters, whose magnitudes are penalized. Regularization is controlled by constants which are denoted as: $\lambda_1, \lambda_2, \ldots$ Exact values of these constants are determined by cross validation. As they grow, regularization becomes heavier.

3.2.1 Baseline Predictors

CF models try to capture the interactions between users and items that produce the different rating values. However, much of the observed rating values are due to effects associated with either users or items, independently of their interaction. A principal example is that typical CF data exhibit large user and item biases—i.e., systematic tendencies for some users to give higher ratings than others, and for some items to receive higher ratings than others.

We will encapsulate those effects, which do not involve user-item interaction, within the *baseline predictors* (also known as *biases*). Because these predictors tend to capture much of the observed signal, it is vital to model them accurately. Such modeling enables isolating the part of the signal that truly represents user-item interaction, and subjecting it to more appropriate user preference models.

Denote by μ the overall average rating. A baseline prediction for an unknown rating r_{ui} is denoted by b_{ui} and accounts for the user and item effects:

$$b_{ui} = \mu + b_u + b_i \tag{3.1}$$

The parameters b_u and b_i indicate the observed deviations of user u and item i, respectively, from the average. For example, suppose that we want a baseline predictor for the rating of the movie Titanic by user Joe. Now, say that the average rating over all movies, μ, is 3.7 stars. Furthermore, Titanic is better than an average movie, so it tends to be rated 0.5 stars above the average. On the other hand, Joe is a critical user, who tends to rate 0.3 stars lower than the average. Thus, the baseline predictor for Titanic's rating by Joe would be 3.9 stars by calculating $3.7-0.3+0.5$. In order to estimate b_u and b_i one can solve the least squares problem

$$\min_{b_*} \sum_{(u,i)\in\mathcal{K}} (r_{ui} - \mu - b_u - b_i)^2 + \lambda_1\Big(\sum_u b_u^2 + \sum_i b_i^2\Big).$$

Here, the first term $\sum_{(u,i)\in\mathcal{K}}(r_{ui} - \mu + b_u + b_i)^2$ strives to find b_u's and b_i's that fit the given ratings. The regularizing term—$\lambda_1(\sum_u b_u^2 + \sum_i b_i^2)$—avoids overfitting by penalizing the magnitudes of the parameters. This least square problem can be solved fairly efficiently by the method of stochastic gradient descent (described in Sect. 3.3.1).

For the Netflix data the mean rating (μ) is 3.6. As for the learned user biases (b_u), their average is 0.044 with standard deviation of 0.41. The average of their absolute values ($|b_u|$) is: 0.32. The learned item biases (b_i) average to -0.26 with a standard deviation of 0.48. The average of their absolute values ($|b_i|$) is 0.43.

An easier, yet somewhat less accurate way to estimate the parameters is by decoupling the calculation of the b_i's from the calculation of the b_u's. First, for each item i we set

$$b_i = \frac{\sum_{u \in \mathrm{R}(i)}(r_{ui} - \mu)}{\lambda_2 + |\mathrm{R}(i)|}.$$

Then, for each user u we set

$$b_u = \frac{\sum_{i \in \mathrm{R}(u)}(r_{ui} - \mu - b_i)}{\lambda_3 + |\mathrm{R}(u)|}.$$

Averages are shrunk towards zero by using the regularization parameters, λ_2, λ_3, which are determined by cross validation. Typical values on the Netflix dataset are: $\lambda_2 = 25, \lambda_3 = 10$.

In Sect. 3.3.3.1, we show how the baseline predictors can be improved by also considering temporal dynamics within the data.

3.2.2 The Netflix Data

In order to compare the relative accuracy of algorithms described in this chapter, we evaluated all of them on the Netflix data of more than 100 million date-stamped movie ratings performed by anonymous Netflix customers between November, 1999 and December 2005 [5]. Ratings are integers ranging between 1 and 5. The data spans 17,770 movies rated by over 480,000 users. Thus, on average, a movie receives 5600 ratings, while a user rates 208 movies, with substantial variation around each of these averages. To maintain compatibility with results published by others, we adopt some standards that were set by Netflix. First, quality of the results is usually measured by the root mean squared error (RMSE):

$$\sqrt{\sum_{(u,i) \in TestSet} (r_{ui} - \hat{r}_{ui})^2 / |TestSet|}$$

a measure that puts more emphasis on large errors compared with the alternative of mean absolute error. (Consider Chap. 8 for a comprehensive survey of alternative evaluation metrics of recommender systems.)

We report results on a test set provided by Netflix (also known as the Quiz set), which contains over 1.4 million recent ratings. Compared with the training data, the test set contains many more ratings by users that do not rate much and are therefore harder to predict. In a way, this represents real requirements for a CF system, which needs to predict new ratings from older ones, and to equally address all users, not just the heavy raters.

The Netflix data is part of the Netflix Prize competition, where the benchmark is Netflix's proprietary system, Cinematch, which achieved a RMSE of 0.9514 on the test set. The grand prize was awarded to a team that managed to drive this RMSE below 0.8563 (10 % improvement) after almost 3 years of extensive efforts. Achievable RMSE values on the test set lie in a quite compressed range, as evident by the difficulty to win the grand prize. Nonetheless, there is evidence that small improvements in RMSE terms can have a significant impact on the quality of the top few presented recommendations [16, 17].

3.2.3 Implicit Feedback

This chapter is centered on explicit user feedback. Nonetheless, when additional sources of implicit feedback are available, they can be exploited for better understanding user behavior. This helps to combat data sparseness and can be particularly helpful for users with few explicit ratings. We describe extensions for some of the models to address implicit feedback.

For a dataset such as the Netflix data, the most natural choice for implicit feedback would probably be movie rental history, which tells us about user preferences without requiring them to explicitly provide their ratings. For other datasets, browsing or purchase history could be used as implicit feedback. However, such data is not available to us for experimentation. Nonetheless, a less obvious kind of implicit data does exist within the Netflix dataset. The dataset does not only tell us the rating values, but also *which* movies users rate, regardless of *how* they rated these movies. In other words, a user implicitly tells us about her preferences by choosing to voice her opinion and vote a (high or low) rating. This creates a binary matrix, where "1" stands for "rated", and "0" for "not rated". While this binary data may not be as informative as other independent sources of implicit feedback, incorporating this kind of implicit data does significantly improves prediction accuracy. The benefit of using the binary data is closely related to the fact that ratings are not missing at random; users deliberately choose which items to rate (see Marlin et al. [19]).

3.3 Matrix Factorization Models

Latent factor models approach collaborative filtering with the holistic goal to uncover latent features that explain observed ratings; examples include pLSA [14], neural networks [22], Latent Dirichlet Allocation [7], and models that are induced by factorization of the user-item ratings matrix (also known as SVD-based models). Recently, matrix factorization models have gained popularity, thanks to their attractive accuracy and scalability.

In information retrieval, SVD is well established for identifying latent semantic factors [9]. However, applying SVD to explicit ratings in the CF domain raises difficulties due to the high portion of missing values. Conventional SVD is undefined when knowledge about the matrix is incomplete. Moreover, carelessly addressing only the relatively few known entries is highly prone to overfitting. Earlier works relied on imputation [15, 24], which fills in missing ratings and makes the rating matrix dense. However, imputation can be very expensive as it significantly increases the amount of data. In addition, the data may be considerably distorted due to inaccurate imputation. Hence, more recent works [4, 6, 10, 16, 21, 22, 26] suggested modeling directly only the observed ratings, while avoiding overfitting through an adequate regularized model.

In this section we describe several matrix factorization techniques, with increasing complexity and accuracy. We start with the basic model—"SVD". Then, we show how to integrate other sources of user feedback in order to increase prediction accuracy, through the "SVD++ model". Finally we deal with the fact that customer preferences for products may drift over time. Product perception and popularity are constantly changing as new selection emerges. Similarly, customer inclinations are evolving, leading them to ever redefine their taste. This leads to a factor model that addresses temporal dynamics for better tracking user behavior.

3.3.1 SVD

Matrix factorization models map both users and items to a joint latent factor space of dimensionality f, such that user-item interactions are modeled as inner products in that space. The latent space tries to explain ratings by characterizing both products and users on factors automatically inferred from user feedback. For example, when the products are movies, factors might measure obvious dimensions such as comedy vs. drama, amount of action, or orientation to children; less well defined dimensions such as depth of character development or "quirkiness"; or completely uninterpretable dimensions.

Accordingly, each item i is associated with a vector $q_i \in \mathbb{R}^f$, and each user u is associated with a vector $p_u \in \mathbb{R}^f$. For a given item i, the elements of q_i measure the extent to which the item possesses those factors, positive or negative. For a given user u, the elements of p_u measure the extent of interest the user has in items that are high on the corresponding factors (again, these may be positive or negative).

The resulting dot product,[1] $q_i^T p_u$, captures the interaction between user u and item i—i.e., the overall interest of the user in characteristics of the item. The final rating is created by also adding in the aforementioned baseline predictors that depend only on the user or item. Thus, a rating is predicted by the rule

$$\hat{r}_{ui} = \mu + b_i + b_u + q_i^T p_u \,. \tag{3.2}$$

In order to learn the model parameters (b_u, b_i, p_u and q_i) we minimize the regularized squared error

$$\min_{b_*, q_*, p_*} \sum_{(u,i) \in \mathcal{K}} (r_{ui} - \mu - b_i - b_u - q_i^T p_u)^2 + \lambda_4 (b_i^2 + b_u^2 + \|q_i\|^2 + \|p_u\|^2) \,.$$

The constant λ_4, which controls the extent of regularization, is usually determined by cross validation. Minimization is typically performed by either stochastic gradient descent or alternating least squares.

Alternating least squares techniques rotate between fixing the p_u's to solve for the q_i's and fixing the q_i's to solve for the p_u's. Notice that when one of these is taken as a constant, the optimization problem is quadratic and can be optimally solved; see [2, 4].

An easy stochastic gradient descent optimization was popularized by Funk [10] and successfully practiced by many others [16, 21, 22, 26]. The algorithm loops through all ratings in the training data. For each given rating r_{ui}, a prediction ($\hat{r}_{ui}$) is made, and the associated prediction error $e_{ui} \stackrel{\text{def}}{=} r_{ui} - \hat{r}_{ui}$ is computed. For a given training case r_{ui}, we modify the parameters by moving in the opposite direction of the gradient, yielding:

- $b_u \leftarrow b_u + \gamma \cdot (e_{ui} - \lambda_4 \cdot b_u)$
- $b_i \leftarrow b_i + \gamma \cdot (e_{ui} - \lambda_4 \cdot b_i)$
- $q_i \leftarrow q_i + \gamma \cdot (e_{ui} \cdot p_u - \lambda_4 \cdot q_i)$
- $p_u \leftarrow p_u + \gamma \cdot (e_{ui} \cdot q_i - \lambda_4 \cdot p_u)$

When evaluating the method on the Netflix data, we used the following values for the meta parameters: $\gamma = 0.005, \lambda_4 = 0.02$. Henceforth, we dub this method "SVD".

A general remark is in place. One can expect better accuracy by dedicating separate learning rates (γ) and regularization (λ) to each type of learned parameter. Thus, for example, it is advised to employ distinct learning rates to user biases, item biases and the factors themselves. A good, intensive use of such a strategy is described in Takács et al. [27]. When producing exemplary results for this chapter, we did not use such a strategy consistently, and in particular many of the given constants are not fully tuned.

[1] Recall that the dot product between two vectors $x, y \in \mathbb{R}^f$ is defined as: $x^T y = \sum_{k=1}^{f} x_k \cdot y_k$.

3.3.2 SVD++

Prediction accuracy is improved by considering also implicit feedback, which provides an additional indication of user preferences. This is especially helpful for those users that provided much more implicit feedback than explicit one. As explained earlier, even in cases where independent implicit feedback is absent, one can capture a significant signal by accounting for which items users rate, regardless of their rating value. This led to several methods [16, 21, 23] that modeled a user factor by the identity of the items he/she has rated. Here we focus on the SVD++ method [16], which was shown to offer accuracy superior to SVD.

To this end, a second set of item factors is added, relating each item i to a factor vector $y_i \in \mathbb{R}^f$. Those new item factors are used to characterize users based on the set of items that they rated. The exact model is as follows:

$$\hat{r}_{ui} = \mu + b_i + b_u + q_i^T \left(p_u + |\mathrm{R}(u)|^{-\frac{1}{2}} \sum_{j \in \mathrm{R}(u)} y_j \right) \tag{3.3}$$

The set $\mathrm{R}(u)$ contains the items rated by user u.

Now, a user u is modeled as $p_u + |\mathrm{R}(u)|^{-\frac{1}{2}} \sum_{j \in \mathrm{R}(u)} y_j$. We use a free user-factors vector, p_u, much like in (3.2), which is learnt from the given explicit ratings. This vector is complemented by the sum $|\mathrm{R}(u)|^{-\frac{1}{2}} \sum_{j \in \mathrm{R}(u)} y_j$, which represents the perspective of implicit feedback. Since the y_j's are centered around zero (by the regularization), the sum is normalized by $|\mathrm{R}(u)|^{-\frac{1}{2}}$, in order to stabilize its variance across the range of observed values of $|\mathrm{R}(u)|$.

Model parameters are determined by minimizing the associated regularized squared error function through stochastic gradient descent. We loop over all known ratings in $\mathcal{K}$, computing:

- $b_u \leftarrow b_u + \gamma \cdot (e_{ui} - \lambda_5 \cdot b_u)$
- $b_i \leftarrow b_i + \gamma \cdot (e_{ui} - \lambda_5 \cdot b_i)$
- $q_i \leftarrow q_i + \gamma \cdot (e_{ui} \cdot (p_u + |\mathrm{R}(u)|^{-\frac{1}{2}} \sum_{j \in \mathrm{R}(u)} y_j) - \lambda_6 \cdot q_i)$
- $p_u \leftarrow p_u + \gamma \cdot (e_{ui} \cdot q_i - \lambda_6 \cdot p_u)$
- $\forall j \in \mathrm{R}(u) : y_j \leftarrow y_j + \gamma \cdot (e_{ui} \cdot |\mathrm{R}(u)|^{-\frac{1}{2}} \cdot q_i - \lambda_6 \cdot y_j)$

When evaluating the method on the Netflix data, we used the following values for the meta parameters: $\gamma = 0.007$, $\lambda_5 = 0.005$, $\lambda_6 = 0.015$. It is beneficial to decrease step sizes (the γ's) by a factor of 0.9 after each iteration. The iterative process runs for around 30 iterations until convergence.

Several types of implicit feedback can be simultaneously introduced into the model by using extra sets of item factors. For example, if a user u has a certain kind of implicit preference to the items in $\mathrm{N}^1(u)$ (e.g., she rented them), and a different type of implicit feedback to the items in $\mathrm{N}^2(u)$ (e.g., she browsed them), we could use the model

$$\hat{r}_{ui} = \mu + b_i + b_u + q_i^T \left(p_u + |\mathrm{N}^1(u)|^{-\frac{1}{2}} \sum_{j \in \mathrm{N}^1(u)} y_j^{(1)} + |\mathrm{N}^2(u)|^{-\frac{1}{2}} \sum_{j \in \mathrm{N}^2(u)} y_j^{(2)} \right). \tag{3.4}$$

The relative importance of each source of implicit feedback will be automatically learned by the algorithm by its setting of the respective values of model parameters.

3.3.3 Time-Aware Factor Model

The matrix-factorization approach lends itself well to modeling temporal effects, which can significantly improve its accuracy. Decomposing ratings into distinct terms allows us to treat different temporal aspects separately. Specifically, we identify the following effects that each vary over time: (1) user biases $b_u(t)$, (2) item biases $b_i(t)$, and (3) user preferences $p_u(t)$. On the other hand, we specify static item characteristics, q_i, because we do not expect significant temporal variation for items, which, unlike humans, are static in nature. We start with a detailed discussion of the temporal effects that are contained within the baseline predictors.

3.3.3.1 Time Changing Baseline Predictors

Much of the temporal variability is included within the baseline predictors, through two major temporal effects. The first addresses the fact that an item's popularity may change over time. For example, movies can go in and out of popularity as triggered by external events such as the appearance of an actor in a new movie. This is manifested in our models by treating the item bias b_i as a function of time. The second major temporal effect allows users to change their baseline ratings over time. For example, a user who tended to rate an average movie "4 stars", may now rate such a movie "3 stars". This may reflect several factors including a natural drift in a user's rating scale, the fact that ratings are given in relationship to other ratings that were given recently and also the fact that the identity of the rater within a household can change over time. Hence, in our models we take the parameter b_u as a function of time. This induces a template for a time sensitive baseline predictor for u's rating of i at day t_{ui}:

$$b_{ui} = \mu + b_u(t_{ui}) + b_i(t_{ui}) \tag{3.5}$$

Here, $b_u(\cdot)$ and $b_i(\cdot)$ are real valued functions that change over time. The exact way to build these functions should reflect a reasonable way to parameterize the involving temporal changes. Our choice in the context of the movie rating dataset demonstrates some typical considerations.

A major distinction is between temporal effects that span extended periods of time and more transient effects. In the movie rating case, we do not expect movie likability to fluctuate on a daily basis, but rather to change over more extended periods. On the other hand, we observe that user effects can change on a daily basis, reflecting inconsistencies natural to customer behavior. This requires finer time resolution when modeling user-biases compared with a lower resolution that suffices for capturing item-related time effects.

We start with our choice of time-changing item biases $b_i(t)$. We found it adequate to split the item biases into time-based bins, using a constant item bias for each time period. The decision of how to split the timeline into bins should balance the desire to achieve finer resolution (hence, smaller bins) with the need for enough ratings per bin (hence, larger bins). For the movie rating data, there is a wide variety of bin sizes that yield about the same accuracy. In our implementation, each bin corresponds to roughly ten consecutive weeks of data, leading to 30 bins spanning all days in the dataset. A day t is associated with an integer $\mathrm{Bin}(t)$ (a number between 1 and 30 in our data), such that the movie bias is split into a stationary part and a time changing part

$$b_i(t) = b_i + b_{i,\mathrm{Bin}(t)}\,. \tag{3.6}$$

While binning the parameters works well on the items, it is more of a challenge on the users side. On the one hand, we would like a finer resolution for users to detect very short lived temporal effects. On the other hand, we do not expect enough ratings per user to produce reliable estimates for isolated bins. Different functional forms can be considered for parameterizing temporal user behavior, with varying complexity and accuracy.

One simple modeling choice uses a linear function to capture a possible gradual drift of user bias. For each user u, we denote the mean date of rating by t_u. Now, if u rated a movie on day t, then the associated time deviation of this rating is defined as

$$\mathrm{dev}_u(t) = \mathrm{sign}(t - t_u) \cdot |t - t_u|^{\beta}\,.$$

Here $|t - t_u|$ measures the number of days between dates t and t_u. We set the value of β by cross validation; in our implementation $\beta = 0.4$. We introduce a single new parameter for each user called α_u so that we get our first definition of a time-dependent user-bias

$$b_u^{(1)}(t) = b_u + \alpha_u \cdot \mathrm{dev}_u(t)\,. \tag{3.7}$$

This simple linear model for approximating a drifting behavior requires learning two parameters per user: b_u and α_u.

A more flexible parameterization is offered by splines. Let u be a user associated with n_u ratings. We designate k_u time points—$\{t_1^u, \ldots, t_{k_u}^u\}$—spaced uniformly across the dates of u's ratings as kernels that control the following function:

$$b_u^{(2)}(t) = b_u + \frac{\sum_{l=1}^{k_u} e^{-\sigma|t-t_l^u|} b_{t_l}^u}{\sum_{l=1}^{k_u} e^{-\sigma|t-t_l^u|}} \tag{3.8}$$

The parameters $b_{t_l}^u$ are associated with the control points (or, kernels), and are automatically learned from the data. This way the user bias is formed as a time-weighted combination of those parameters. The number of control points, k_u, balances flexibility and computational efficiency. In our application we set $k_u = n_u^{0.25}$, letting it grow with the number of available ratings. The constant σ determines the smoothness of the spline; we set $\sigma = 0.3$ by cross validation.

So far we have discussed smooth functions for modeling the user bias, which mesh well with *gradual concept drift*. However, in many applications there are *sudden drifts* emerging as "spikes" associated with a single day or session. For example, in the movie rating dataset we have found that multiple ratings a user gives in a single day, tend to concentrate around a single value. Such an effect need not span more than a single day. The effect may reflect the mood of the user that day, the impact of ratings given in a single day on each other, or changes in the actual rater in multi-person accounts. To address such short lived effects, we assign a single parameter per user and day, absorbing the day-specific variability. This parameter is denoted by $b_{u,t}$. Notice that in some applications the basic primitive time unit to work with can be shorter or longer than a day.

In the Netflix movie rating data, a user rates on 40 different days on average. Thus, working with $b_{u,t}$ requires, on average, 40 parameters to describe each user bias. It is expected that $b_{u,t}$ is inadequate as a standalone for capturing the user bias, since it misses all sorts of signals that span more than a single day. Thus, it serves as an additive component within the previously described schemes. The time-linear model (3.7) becomes

$$b_u^{(3)}(t) = b_u + \alpha_u \cdot \text{dev}_u(t) + b_{u,t} \,. \tag{3.9}$$

Similarly, the spline-based model becomes

$$b_u^{(4)}(t) = b_u + \frac{\sum_{l=1}^{k_u} e^{-\sigma|t-t_l^u|} b_{t_l}^u}{\sum_{l=1}^{k_u} e^{-\sigma|t-t_l^u|}} + b_{u,t} \,. \tag{3.10}$$

A baseline predictor on its own cannot yield personalized recommendations, as it disregards all interactions between users and items. In a sense, it is capturing the portion of the data that is less relevant for establishing recommendations. Nonetheless, to better assess the relative merits of the various choices of time-dependent user-bias, we compare their accuracy as standalone predictors. In order to learn the involved parameters we minimize the associated regularized squared error by using stochastic gradient descent. For example, in our actual implementation we adopt rule (3.9) for modeling the drifting user bias, thus arriving at the baseline predictor

$$b_{ui} = \mu + b_u + \alpha_u \cdot \text{dev}_u(t_{ui}) + b_{u,t_{ui}} + b_i + b_{i,\text{Bin}(t_{ui})} \,. \tag{3.11}$$

Table 3.1 Comparing baseline predictors capturing main movie and user effects

Model	Static	Mov	Linear	Spline	Linear+	Spline+
RMSE	0.9799	0.9771	0.9731	0.9714	0.9605	0.9603

As temporal modeling becomes more accurate, prediction accuracy improves (lowering RMSE)

To learn the involved parameters, $b_u, \alpha_u, b_{u,t}, b_i$ and $b_{i,\text{Bin}(t)}$, one should solve

$$\min \sum_{(u,i)\in\mathcal{K}} (r_{ui} - \mu - b_u - \alpha_u \text{dev}_u(t_{ui}) - b_{u,t_{ui}} - b_i - b_{i,\text{Bin}(t_{ui})})^2$$
$$+ \lambda_7 (b_u^2 + \alpha_u^2 + b_{u,t_{ui}}^2 + b_i^2 + b_{i,\text{Bin}(t_{ui})}^2).$$

Here, the first term strives to construct parameters that fit the given ratings. The regularization term, $\lambda_7(b_u^2 + \ldots)$, avoids overfitting by penalizing the magnitudes of the parameters, assuming a neutral 0 prior. Learning is done by a stochastic gradient descent algorithm running 20–30 iterations, with $\lambda_7 = 0.01$.

Table 3.1 compares the ability of various suggested baseline predictors to explain signal in the data. As usual, the amount of captured signal is measured by the root mean squared error on the test set. As a reminder, test cases come later in time than the training cases for the same user, so predictions often involve extrapolation in terms of time. We code the predictors as follows:

- *Static*, no temporal effects: $b_{ui} = \mu + b_u + b_i$.
- *Mov*, accounting only for movie-related temporal effects: $b_{ui} = \mu + b_u + b_i + b_{i,\text{Bin}(t_{ui})}$.
- *Linear*, linear modeling of user biases: $b_{ui} = \mu + b_u + \alpha_u \cdot \text{dev}_u(t_{ui}) + b_i + b_{i,\text{Bin}(t_{ui})}$.
- *Spline*, spline modeling of user biases: $b_{ui} = \mu + b_u + \frac{\sum_{l=1}^{k_u} e^{-\sigma|t_{ui}-t_l^u|} b_{t_l}^u}{\sum_{l=1}^{k_u} e^{-\sigma|t_{ui}-t_l^u|}} + b_i + b_{i,\text{Bin}(t_{ui})}$.
- *Linear+*, linear modeling of user biases and single day effect: $b_{ui} = \mu + b_u + \alpha_u \cdot \text{dev}_u(t_{ui}) + b_{u,t_{ui}} + b_i + b_{i,\text{Bin}(t_{ui})}$.
- *Spline+*, spline modeling of user biases and single day effect: $b_{ui} = \mu + b_u + \frac{\sum_{l=1}^{k_u} e^{-\sigma|t_{ui}-d_l|} b_{t_l}^u}{\sum_{l=1}^{k_u} e^{-\sigma|t_{ui}-t_l^u|}} + b_{u,t_{ui}} + b_i + b_{i,\text{Bin}(t_{ui})}$.

The table shows that while temporal movie effects reside in the data (lowering RMSE from 0.9799 to 0.9771), the drift in user biases is much more influential. The additional flexibility of splines at modeling user effects leads to better accuracy compared to a linear model. However, sudden changes in user biases, which are captured by the per-day parameters, are most significant. Indeed, when including those changes, the difference between linear modeling ("linear+") and spline modeling ("spline+") virtually vanishes.

Beyond the temporal effects described so far, one can use the same methodology to capture more effects. A primary example is capturing periodic effects. For example, some products may be more popular in specific seasons or near certain holidays. Similarly, different types of television or radio shows are popular throughout different segments of the day (known as “dayparting”). Periodic effects can be found also on the user side. As an example, a user may have different attitudes or buying patterns during the weekend compared to the working week. A way to model such periodic effects is to dedicate a parameter for the combinations of time periods with items or users. This way, the item bias of (3.6), becomes

$$b_i(t) = b_i + b_{i,\text{Bin}(t)} + b_{i,\text{period}(t)} \,.$$

For example, if we try to capture the change of item bias with the season of the year, then $\text{period}(t) \in \{\text{fall, winter, spring, summer}\}$. Similarly, recurring user effects may be modeled by modifying (3.9) to be

$$b_u(t) = b_u + \alpha_u \cdot \text{dev}_u(t) + b_{u,t} + b_{u,\text{period}(t)} \,.$$

However, we have not found periodic effects with a significant predictive power within the movie-rating dataset, thus our reported results do not include those.

Another temporal effect within the scope of basic predictors is related to the changing scale of user ratings. While $b_i(t)$ is a user-independent measure for the merit of item i at time t, users tend to respond to such a measure differently. For example, different users employ different rating scales, and a single user can change his rating scale over time. Accordingly, the raw value of the movie bias is not completely user-independent. To address this, we add a time-dependent scaling feature to the baseline predictors, denoted by $c_u(t)$. Thus, the baseline predictor (3.11) becomes

$$b_{ui} = \mu + b_u + \alpha_u \cdot \text{dev}_u(t_{ui}) + b_{u,t_{ui}} + (b_i + b_{i,\text{Bin}(t_{ui})}) \cdot c_u(t_{ui}) \,. \tag{3.12}$$

All discussed ways to implement $b_u(t)$ would be valid for implementing $c_u(t)$ as well. We chose to dedicate a separate parameter per day, resulting in: $c_u(t) = c_u + c_{u,t}$. As usual, c_u is the stable part of $c_u(t)$, whereas $c_{u,t}$ represents day-specific variability. Adding the multiplicative factor $c_u(t)$ to the baseline predictor lowers RMSE to 0.9555. Interestingly, this basic model, which captures just main effects disregarding user-item interactions, can explain almost as much of the data variability as the commercial Netflix Cinematch recommender system, whose published RMSE on the same test set is 0.9514 [5].

3.3.3.2 Time Changing Factor Model

In the previous section we discussed the way time affects baseline predictors. However, as hinted earlier, temporal dynamics go beyond this, they also affect user preferences and thereby the interaction between users and items. Users change their preferences over time. For example, a fan of the “psychological thrillers” genre may become a fan of “crime dramas” a year later. Similarly, humans change their perception on certain actors and directors. This type of evolution is modeled by taking the user factors (the vector p_u) as a function of time. Once again, we need to model those changes at the very fine level of a daily basis, while facing the built-in scarcity of user ratings. In fact, these temporal effects are the hardest to capture, because preferences are not as pronounced as main effects (user-biases), but are split over many factors.

We modeled each component of the user preferences $p_u(t)^T = (p_{u1}(t), \dots, p_{uf}(t))$ in the same way that we treated user biases. Within the movie-rating dataset, we have found modeling after (3.9) effective, leading to

$$p_{uk}(t) = p_{uk} + \alpha_{uk} \cdot \mathrm{dev}_u(t) + p_{uk,t} \quad k = 1, \dots, f. \tag{3.13}$$

Here p_{uk} captures the stationary portion of the factor, $\alpha_{uk} \cdot \mathrm{dev}_u(t)$ approximates a possible portion that changes linearly over time, and $p_{uk,t}$ absorbs the very local, day-specific variability.

At this point, we can tie all pieces together and extend the SVD++ factor model by incorporating the time changing parameters. The resulting model will be denoted as *timeSVD++*, where the prediction rule is as follows:

$$\hat{r}_{ui} = \mu + b_i(t_{ui}) + b_u(t_{ui}) + q_i^T \left(p_u(t_{ui}) + |\mathrm{R}(u)|^{-\frac{1}{2}} \sum_{j \in \mathrm{R}(u)} y_j \right) \tag{3.14}$$

The exact definitions of the time drifting parameters $b_i(t), b_u(t)$ and $p_u(t)$ were given in (3.6), (3.9) and (3.13). Learning is performed by minimizing the associated squared error function on the training set using a regularized stochastic gradient descent algorithm. The procedure is analogous to the one involving the original SVD++ algorithm. Time complexity per iteration is still linear with the input size, while wall clock running time is approximately doubled compared to SVD++, due to the extra overhead required for updating the temporal parameters. Importantly, convergence rate was not affected by the temporal parameterization, and the process converges in around 30 iterations.

3.3.4 Comparison

In Table 3.2 we compare results of the three algorithms discussed in this section. First is SVD, the plain matrix factorization algorithm. Second, is the SVD++ method, which improves upon SVD by incorporating a kind of implicit feedback. Finally is timeSVD++, which accounts for temporal effects. The three methods are compared over a range of factorization dimensions (f). All benefit from a growing number of factor dimensions that enables them to better express complex movie-user interactions. Note that the number of parameters in SVD++ is comparable to their number in SVD. This is because SVD++ adds only item factors, while

Table 3.2 Comparison of three factor models: prediction accuracy is measured by RMSE (lower is better) for varying factor dimensionality (f)

Model	$f = 10$	$f = 20$	$f = 50$	$f = 100$	$f = 200$
SVD	0.9140	0.9074	0.9046	0.9025	0.9009
SVD++	0.9131	0.9032	0.8952	0.8924	0.8911
Timesvd++	0.8971	0.8891	0.8824	0.8805	0.8799

For all models, accuracy improves with growing number of dimensions. SVD++ improves accuracy by incorporating implicit feedback into the SVD model. Further accuracy gains are achieved by also addressing the temporal dynamics in the data through the timeSVD++ model

complexity of our dataset is dominated by the much larger set of users. On the other hand, timeSVD++ requires a significant increase in the number of parameters, because of its refined representation of each user factor. Addressing implicit feedback by the SVD++ model leads to accuracy gains within the movie rating dataset. Yet, the improvement delivered by timeSVD++ over SVD++ is consistently more significant. We are not aware of any single algorithm in the literature that could deliver such accuracy. Further evidence of the importance of capturing temporal dynamics is the fact that a timeSVD++ model of dimension 10 is already more accurate than an SVD model of dimension 200. Similarly, a timeSVD++ model of dimension 20 is enough to outperform an SVD++ model of dimension 200.

3.3.4.1 Predicting Future Days

Our models include day-specific parameters. An apparent question would be how these models can be used for predicting ratings in the future, on new dates for which we cannot train the day-specific parameters? The simple answer is that for those future (untrained) dates, the day-specific parameters should take their default value. In particular for (3.12), $c_u(t_{ui})$ is set to c_u, and $b_{u,t_{ui}}$ is set to zero. Yet, one wonders, if we cannot use the day-specific parameters for predicting the future, why are they good at all? After all, prediction is interesting only when it is about the future. To further sharpen the question, we should mention the fact that the Netflix test sets include many ratings on dates for which we have no other rating by the same user and hence day-specific parameters cannot be exploited.

To answer this, notice that our temporal modeling makes no attempt to capture future changes. All it is trying to do is to capture transient temporal effects, which had a significant influence on past user feedback. When such effects are identified they must be tuned down, so that we can model the more enduring signal. This allows our model to better capture the long-term characteristics of the data, while letting dedicated parameters absorb short term fluctuations. For example, if a user gave many higher than usual ratings on a particular single day, our models discount those by accounting for a possible day-specific good mood, which does not reflects the longer term behavior of this user. This way, the day-specific parameters accomplish a kind of data cleaning, which improves prediction of future dates.

3.3.5 Summary

In its basic form, matrix factorization characterizes both items and users by vectors of factors inferred from patterns of item ratings. High correspondence between item and user factors leads to recommendation of an item to a user. These methods deliver prediction accuracy superior to other published collaborative filtering techniques. At the same time, they offer a memory efficient compact model, which can be trained relatively easy. Those advantages, together with the implementation ease of gradient based matrix factorization model (SVD), made this the method of choice within the Netflix Prize competition.

What makes these techniques even more convenient is their ability to address several crucial aspects of the data. First, is the ability to integrate multiple forms of user feedback. One can better predict user ratings by also observing other related actions by the same user, such as purchase and browsing history. The proposed SVD++ model leverages multiple sorts of user feedback for improving user profiling.

Another important aspect is the temporal dynamics that make users' tastes evolve over time. Each user and product potentially goes through a distinct series of changes in their characteristics. A mere decay of older instances cannot adequately identify communal patterns of behavior in time changing data. The solution we adopted is to model the temporal dynamics along the whole time period, allowing us to intelligently separate transient factors from lasting ones. The inclusion of temporal dynamics proved very useful in improving quality of predictions, more than various algorithmic enhancements.

3.4 Neighborhood Models

The most common approach to CF is based on neighborhood models. Chapter 2 provides an extensive survey on this approach. Its original form, which was shared by virtually all earlier CF systems, is user-user based; see [13] for a good analysis. User-user methods estimate unknown ratings based on recorded ratings of like-minded users.

Later, an analogous item-item approach [18, 25] became popular. In those methods, a rating is estimated using known ratings made by the same user on similar items. Better scalability and improved accuracy make the item-item approach more favorable in many cases [2, 25, 26]. In addition, item-item methods are more amenable to explaining the reasoning behind predictions. This is because users are familiar with items previously preferred by them, but do not know those allegedly like-minded users. We focus mostly on item-item approaches, but the same techniques can be directly applied within a user-user approach; see also Sect. 3.5.2.2.

In general, latent factor models offer high expressive ability to describe various aspects of the data. Thus, they tend to provide more accurate results than neighborhood models. However, most literature and commercial systems (e.g., those of Amazon [18] and TiVo [1]) are based on the neighborhood models. The prevalence of neighborhood models is partly due to their relative simplicity. However, there are more important reasons for real life systems to stick with those models. First, they naturally provide intuitive explanations of the reasoning behind recommendations, which often enhance user experience beyond what improved accuracy may achieve. Second, they can provide immediate recommendations based on newly entered user feedback.

The structure of this section is as follows. First, we describe how to estimate the similarity between two items, which is a basic building block of most neighborhood techniques. Then, we move on to the widely used similarity-based neighborhood method, which constitutes a straightforward application of the similarity weights. We identify certain limitations of this similarity based approach. As a consequence, in Sect. 3.4.3 we suggest a way to solve these issues, thereby improving prediction accuracy at the cost of a slight increase in computation time.

3.4.1 Similarity Measures

Central to most item-item approaches is a similarity measure between items. Frequently, it is based on the Pearson correlation coefficient, ρ_{ij}, which measures the tendency of users to rate items i and j similarly. Since many ratings are unknown, some items may share only a handful of common observed raters. The empirical correlation coefficient, $\hat{\rho}_{ij}$, is based only on the common user support. It is advised to work with residuals from the baseline predictors (the b_{ui}'s; see Sect. 3.2.1) to compensate for user- and item-specific deviations. Thus the approximated correlation coefficient is given by

$$\hat{\rho}_{ij} = \frac{\sum_{u \in \mathrm{U}(i,j)} (r_{ui} - b_{ui})(r_{uj} - b_{uj})}{\sqrt{\sum_{u \in \mathrm{U}(i,j)} (r_{ui} - b_{ui})^2 \cdot \sum_{u \in \mathrm{U}(i,j)} (r_{uj} - b_{uj})^2}} \,. \tag{3.15}$$

The set $\mathrm{U}(i,j)$ contains the users who rated both items i and j.

Because estimated correlations based on a greater user support are more reliable, an appropriate similarity measure, denoted by s_{ij}, is a shrunk correlation coefficient of the form

$$s_{ij} \stackrel{\text{def}}{=} \frac{n_{ij} - 1}{n_{ij} - 1 + \lambda_8} \rho_{ij} \,. \tag{3.16}$$

The variable $n_{ij} = |\mathrm{U}(i,j)|$ denotes the number of users that rated both i and j. A typical value for λ_8 is 100.

Such shrinkage can be motivated from a Bayesian perspective; see Sect. 2.6 of Gelman et al. [11]. Suppose that the true ρ_{ij} are independent random variables drawn from a normal distribution,

$$\rho_{ij} \sim N(0, \tau^2)$$

for known τ^2. The mean of 0 is justified if the b_{ui} account for both user and item deviations from average. Meanwhile, suppose that

$$\hat{\rho}_{ij}|\rho_{ij} \sim N(\rho_{ij}, \sigma_{ij}^2)$$

for known σ_{ij}^2. We estimate ρ_{ij} by its posterior mean:

$$E(\rho_{ij}|\hat{\rho}_{ij}) = \frac{\tau^2 \hat{\rho}_{ij}}{\tau^2 + \sigma_{ij}^2}$$

the empirical estimator $\hat{\rho}_{ij}$ shrunk a fraction, $\sigma_{ij}^2/(\tau^2 + \sigma_{ij}^2)$, of the way toward zero.

Formula (3.16) follows from approximating the variance of a correlation by $\sigma_{ij}^2 = 1/(n_{ij} - 1)$, the value for ρ_{ij} near 0.

Notice that the literature suggests additional alternatives for a similarity measure [25, 26].

3.4.2 Similarity-Based Interpolation

Here we describe the most popular approach to neighborhood modeling, and apparently also to CF in general. Our goal is to predict r_{ui}—the unobserved rating by user u for item i. Using the similarity measure, we identify the k items rated by u that are most similar to i. This set of k neighbors is denoted by $\mathrm{S}^k(i;u)$. The predicted value of r_{ui} is taken as a weighted average of the ratings of neighboring items, while adjusting for user and item effects through the baseline predictors

$$\hat{r}_{ui} = b_{ui} + \frac{\sum_{j \in \mathrm{S}^k(i;u)} s_{ij}(r_{uj} - b_{uj})}{\sum_{j \in \mathrm{S}^k(i;u)} s_{ij}}. \tag{3.17}$$

Note the dual use of the similarities for both identification of nearest neighbors and as the interpolation weights in Eq. (3.17).

Sometimes, instead of relying directly on the similarity weights as interpolation coefficients, one can achieve better results by transforming these weights. For example, we have found at several datasets that squaring the correlation-based similarities is helpful. This leads to a rule like: $\hat{r}_{ui} = b_{ui} + \frac{\sum_{j \in \mathrm{S}^k(i;u)} s_{ij}^2(r_{uj} - b_{uj})}{\sum_{j \in \mathrm{S}^k(i;u)} s_{ij}^2}$. Toscher et al. [29] discuss more sophisticated transformations of these weights.

Similarity-based methods became very popular because they are intuitive and relatively simple to implement. They also offer the following two useful properties:

1. *Explainability.* The importance of explaining automated recommendations is widely recognized [12, 28]. Users expect a system to give a reason for its predictions, rather than presenting "black box" recommendations. Explanations not only enrich the user experience, but also encourage users to interact with the system, fix wrong impressions and improve long-term accuracy. The neighborhood framework allows identifying which of the past user actions are most influential on the computed prediction.
2. *New ratings.* Item-item neighborhood models can provide updated recommendations immediately after users enter new ratings. This includes handling new users as soon as they provide feedback to the system, without needing to re-train the model and estimate new parameters. This assumes that relationships between items (the s_{ij} values) are stable and barely change on a daily basis. Notice that for items new to the system we do have to learn new parameters. Interestingly, this asymmetry between users and items meshes well with common practices: systems need to provide immediate recommendations to new users (or new ratings by old users) who expect quality service. On the other hand, it is reasonable to require a waiting period before recommending items new to the system.

However, standard neighborhood-based methods raise some concerns:

1. The similarity function (s_{ij}), which directly defines the interpolation weights, is arbitrary. Various CF algorithms use somewhat different similarity measures, trying to quantify the elusive notion of user- or item-similarity. Suppose that a particular item is predicted perfectly by a subset of the neighbors. In that case, we would want the predictive subset to receive all the weight, but that is impossible for bounded similarity scores like the Pearson correlation coefficient.
2. Previous neighborhood-based methods do not account for interactions among neighbors. Each similarity between an item i and a neighbor $j \in \mathrm{S}^k(i;u)$ is computed independently of the content of $\mathrm{S}^k(i;u)$ and the other similarities: s_{il} for $l \in \mathrm{S}^k(i;u) - \{j\}$. For example, suppose that our items are movies, and the neighbors set contains three movies that are highly correlated with each other (e.g., sequels such as "Lord of the Rings 1–3"). An algorithm that ignores the similarity of the three movies when determining their interpolation weights, may end up essentially triple counting the information provided by the group.
3. By definition, the interpolation weights sum to one, which may cause overfitting. Suppose that an item has no useful neighbors rated by a particular user. In that case, it would be best to ignore the neighborhood information, staying with the more robust baseline predictors. Nevertheless, the standard neighborhood formula uses a weighted average of ratings for the uninformative neighbors.
4. Neighborhood methods may not work well if variability of ratings differs substantially among neighbors.

Some of these issues can be fixed to a certain degree, while others are more difficult to solve within the basic framework. For example, the third item, dealing with the sum-to-one constraint, can be alleviated by using the following prediction rule:

$$\hat{r}_{ui} = b_{ui} + \frac{\sum_{j \in S^k(i;u)} s_{ij}(r_{uj} - b_{uj})}{\lambda_9 + \sum_{j \in S^k(i;u)} s_{ij}} \tag{3.18}$$

The constant λ_9 penalizes the neighborhood portion when there is not much neighborhood information, e.g., when $\sum_{j \in S^k(i;u)} s_{ij} \ll \lambda_9$. Indeed, we have found that setting an appropriate value of λ_9 leads to accuracy improvements over (3.17). Nonetheless, the whole framework here is not justified by a formal model. Thus, we strive for better results with a more fundamental approach, as we describe in the following.

3.4.3 *Jointly Derived Interpolation Weights*

In this section we describe a more accurate neighborhood model that overcomes the difficulties discussed above, while retaining known merits of item-item models. As above, we use the similarity measure to define neighbors for each prediction. However, we search for optimum interpolation weights without regard to values of the similarity measure.

Given a set of neighbors $S^k(i;u)$ we need to compute *interpolation weights* $\{\theta_{ij}^u | j \in S^k(i;u)\}$ that enable the best prediction rule of the form

$$\hat{r}_{ui} = b_{ui} + \sum_{j \in S^k(i;u)} \theta_{ij}^u (r_{uj} - b_{uj}) \,. \tag{3.19}$$

Typical values of k (number of neighbors) lie in the range of 20–50; see [2]. During this subsection we assume that baseline predictors have already been removed. Hence, we introduce a notation for the residual ratings: $z_{ui} \stackrel{\text{def}}{=} r_{ui} - b_{ui}$. For notational convenience assume that the items in $S^k(i;u)$ are indexed by $1, \ldots, k$.

We seek a formal computation of the interpolation weights that stems directly from their usage within prediction rule (3.19). As explained earlier, it is important to derive all interpolation weights simultaneously to account for interdependencies among the neighbors. We achieve these goals by defining a suitable optimization problem.

3.4.3.1 Formal Model

To start, we consider a hypothetical dense case, where all users but u rated both i and *all* its neighbors in $\mathrm{S}^k(i;u)$. In that case, we could learn the interpolation weights by modeling the relationships between item i and its neighbors through a least squares problem

$$\min_{\theta^u} \sum_{v \neq u} \left(z_{vi} - \sum_{j \in \mathrm{S}^k(i;u)} \theta_{ij}^u z_{vj} \right)^2 . \tag{3.20}$$

Notice that the only unknowns here are the θ_{ij}^u's. The optimal solution to the least squares problem (3.20) is found by differentiation as a solution of a linear system of equations. From a statistics viewpoint, it is equivalent to the result of a linear regression (without intercept) of z_{vi} on the z_{vj} for $j \in \mathrm{S}^k(i;u)$. Specifically, the optimal weights are given by

$$Aw = b . \tag{3.21}$$

Here, $w \in \mathbb{R}^k$ is an unknown vector such that w_j stands for the sought coefficient θ_{ij}^u. A is a $k \times k$ matrix defined as

$$A_{jl} = \sum_{v \neq u} z_{vj} z_{vl} . \tag{3.22}$$

Similarly the vector $b \in \mathbb{R}^k$ is given by

$$b_j = \sum_{v \neq u} z_{vj} z_{vi} . \tag{3.23}$$

For a sparse ratings matrix there are likely to be very few users who rated i and all its neighbors $\mathrm{S}^k(i;u)$. Accordingly, it would be unwise to base A and b as given in (3.22)–(3.23) only on users with complete data. Even if there are enough users with complete data for A to be nonsingular, that estimate would ignore a large proportion of the information about pairwise relationships among ratings by the same user. However, we can still estimate A and b, up to the same constant, by averaging over the given pairwise support, leading to the following reformulation:

$$\bar{A}_{jl} = \frac{\sum_{v \in \mathrm{U}(j,l)} z_{vj} z_{vl}}{|\mathrm{U}(j,l)|} \tag{3.24}$$

$$\bar{b}_j = \frac{\sum_{v \in \mathrm{U}(i,j)} z_{vj} z_{vi}}{|\mathrm{U}(i,j)|} \tag{3.25}$$

As a reminder, $\mathrm{U}(j,l)$ is the set of users who rated both j and l.

This is still not enough to overcome the sparseness issue. The elements of $\bar{A}_{jl}$ or $\bar{b}_j$ may differ by orders of magnitude in terms of the number of users included in the average. As discussed previously, averages based on relatively low support (small values of $|\mathrm{U}(j,l)|$) can generally be improved by shrinkage towards a common value. Specifically, we compute a baseline value that is defined by taking the average of all possible $\bar{A}_{jl}$ values. Let us denote this baseline value by avg; its precise computation is described in the next section. Accordingly, we define the corresponding $k \times k$ matrix $\hat{A}$ and the vector $\hat{b} \in \mathbb{R}^k$:

$$\hat{A}_{jl} = \frac{|\mathrm{U}(j,l)| \cdot \bar{A}_{jl} + \beta \cdot avg}{|\mathrm{U}(j,l)| + \beta} \tag{3.26}$$

$$\hat{b}_j = \frac{|\mathrm{U}(i,j)| \cdot \bar{b}_j + \beta \cdot avg}{|\mathrm{U}(i,j)| + \beta} \tag{3.27}$$

The parameter β controls the extent of the shrinkage. A typical value would be $\beta = 500$.

Our best estimate for A and b are $\hat{A}$ and $\hat{b}$, respectively. Therefore, we modify (3.21) so that the interpolation weights are defined as the solution of the linear system

$$\hat{A}w = \hat{b}\,. \tag{3.28}$$

The resulting interpolation weights are used within (3.19) in order to predict r_{ui}.

This method addresses all four concerns raised in Sect. 3.4.2. First, interpolation weights are derived directly from the ratings, not based on any similarity measure. Second, the interpolation weights formula explicitly accounts for relationships among the neighbors. Third, the sum of the weights is not constrained to equal one. If an item (or user) has only weak neighbors, the estimated weights may all be very small. Fourth, the method automatically adjusts for variations among items in their means or variances.

3.4.3.2 Computational Issues

Efficient computation of an item-item neighborhood method requires pre-computing certain values associated with each item-item pair for rapid retrieval. First, we need a quick access to all item-item similarities, by pre-computing all s_{ij} values, as explained in Sect. 3.4.1.

Second, we pre-compute all possible entries of $\hat{A}$ and $\hat{b}$. To this end, for each two items i and j, we compute

$$\bar{A}_{ij} = \frac{\sum_{v \in \mathrm{U}(i,j)} z_{vi} z_{vj}}{|\mathrm{U}(i,j)|}\,.$$

Then, the aforementioned baseline value avg, which is used in (3.26)–(3.27), is taken as the average entry of the pre-computed $n \times n$ matrix $\bar{A}$. In fact, we recommend using two different baseline values, one by averaging the non-diagonal entries of $\bar{A}$ and another one by averaging the generally-larger diagonal entries, which have an inherently higher average because they sum only non-negative values. Finally, we derive a full $n \times n$ matrix $\hat{A}$ from $\bar{A}$ by (3.26), using the appropriate value of avg. Here, the non-diagonal average is used when deriving the non-diagonal entries of $\hat{A}$, whereas the diagonal average is used when deriving the diagonal entries of $\hat{A}$.

Because of symmetry, it is sufficient to store the values of s_{ij} and $\hat{A}_{ij}$ only for $i \geqslant j$. Our experience shows that it is enough to allocate one byte for each individual value, so the overall space required for n items is exactly $n(n+1)$ bytes.

Pre-computing all possible entries of matrix $\hat{A}$ saves the otherwise lengthy time needed to construct entries on the fly. After quickly retrieving the relevant entries of $\hat{A}$, we can compute the interpolation weights by solving a $k \times k$ system of Eq. (3.28) using a standard linear solver. However, a modest increase in prediction accuracy was achieved when constraining w to be nonnegative through a quadratic program [2]. Solving the system of equations is an overhead over the basic neighborhood method described in Sect. 3.4.2. For typical values of k (between 20 and 50), the extra time overhead is comparable to the time needed for computing the k nearest neighbors, which is common to neighborhood-based approaches. Hence, while the method relies on a much more detailed computation of the interpolation weights compared to previous methods, it does not significantly increase running time; see [2].

3.4.4 Summary

Collaborative filtering through neighborhood-based interpolation is probably the most popular way to create a recommender system. Three major components characterize the neighborhood approach: (1) data normalization, (2) neighbor selection, and (3) determination of interpolation weights.

Normalization is essential to collaborative filtering in general, and in particular to the more local neighborhood methods. Otherwise, even more sophisticated methods are bound to fail, as they mix incompatible ratings pertaining to different unnormalized users or items. We described a suitable approach to data normalization, based around baseline predictors.

Neighborhood selection is another important component. It is directly related to the employed similarity measure. Here, we emphasized the importance of shrinking unreliable similarities, in order to avoid detection of neighbors with a low rating support.

Finally, the success of neighborhood methods depends on the choice of the interpolation weights, which are used to estimate unknown ratings from neighboring known ones. Nevertheless, most known methods lack a rigorous way to derive these weights. We showed how the interpolation weights can be computed as a global solution to an optimization problem that precisely reflects their role.

3.5 Enriching Neighborhood Models

Most neighborhood methods are local in their nature—concentrating on only a small subset of related ratings. This contrasts with matrix factorization, which casts a very wide net to try to characterize items and users. It appears that accuracy can be improved by employing this global viewpoint, which motivates the methods of this section. We suggest a new neighborhood model drawing on principles of both classical neighborhood methods and matrix factorization models. Like other neighborhood models, the building stones here are item-item relations (or, alternatively, user-user relations), which provide the system some practical advantages discussed earlier. At the same time, much like matrix factorization, the model is centered around a global optimization framework, which improves accuracy by considering the many weak signals existing in the data.

The main method, which is described in Sect. 3.5.1, allows us to enrich the model with implicit feedback data. In addition, it facilitates two new possibilities. First is a factorized neighborhood model, as described in Sect. 3.5.2, bringing great improvements in computational efficiency. Second is a treatment of temporal dynamics, leading to better prediction accuracy, as described in Sect. 3.5.3.

3.5.1 A Global Neighborhood Model

In this subsection, we introduce a neighborhood model based on global optimization. The model offers an improved prediction accuracy, by offering the aforementioned merits of the model described in Sect. 3.4.3, with additional advantages that are summarized as follows:

1. No reliance on arbitrary or heuristic item-item similarities. The new model is cast as the solution to a global optimization problem.
2. Inherent overfitting prevention or "risk control": the model reverts to robust baseline predictors, unless a user entered sufficiently many relevant ratings.
3. The model can capture the totality of weak signals encompassed in all of a user's ratings, not needing to concentrate only on the few ratings for most similar items.
4. The model naturally allows integrating different forms of user input, such as explicit and implicit feedback.
5. A highly scalable implementation (Sect. 3.5.2) allows linear time and space complexity, thus facilitating both item-item and user-user implementations to scale well to very large datasets.
6. Time drifting aspects of the data can be integrated into the model, thereby improving its accuracy; see Sect. 3.5.3.

3.5.1.1 Building the Model

We gradually construct the various components of the model, through an ongoing refinement of our formulations. Previous models were centered around *user-specific* interpolation weights—θ^u_{ij} in (3.19) or $s_{ij}/\sum_{j\in \mathrm{S}^k(i;u)} s_{ij}$ in (3.17)—relating item i to the items in a user-specific neighborhood $\mathrm{S}^k(i;u)$. In order to facilitate global optimization, we would like to abandon such user-specific weights in favor of global item-item weights independent of a specific user. The weight from j to i is denoted by w_{ij} and will be learned from the data through optimization. An initial sketch of the model describes each rating r_{ui} by the equation

$$\hat{r}_{ui} = b_{ui} + \sum_{j\in \mathrm{R}(u)} (r_{uj} - b_{uj})w_{ij}\,. \tag{3.29}$$

This rule starts with the crude, yet robust, baseline predictors (b_{ui}). Then, the estimate is adjusted by summing over *all* ratings by u.

Let us consider the interpretation of the weights. Usually the weights in a neighborhood model represent interpolation coefficients relating unknown ratings to existing ones. Here, we adopt a different viewpoint, that enables a more flexible usage of the weights. We no longer treat weights as interpolation coefficients. Instead, we take weights as part of adjustments, or *offsets*, added to the baseline predictors. This way, the weight w_{ij} is the extent by which we increase our baseline prediction of r_{ui} based on the observed value of r_{uj}. For two related items i and j, we expect w_{ij} to be high. Thus, whenever a user u rated j higher than expected ($r_{uj} - b_{uj}$ is high), we would like to increase our estimate for u's rating of i by adding $(r_{uj} - b_{uj})w_{ij}$ to the baseline prediction. Likewise, our estimate will not deviate much from the baseline by an item j that u rated just as expected ($r_{uj} - b_{uj}$ is around zero), or by an item j that is not known to be predictive on i (w_{ij} is close to zero).

This viewpoint suggests several enhancements to (3.29). First, we can use the form of binary user input, which was found beneficial for factorization models. Namely, analyzing which items were rated regardless of rating value. To this end, we add another set of weights, and rewrite (3.29) as

$$\hat{r}_{ui} = b_{ui} + \sum_{j\in \mathrm{R}(u)} [(r_{uj} - b_{uj})w_{ij} + c_{ij}]\,. \tag{3.30}$$

Similarly, one could employ here another set of implicit feedback, $\mathrm{N}(u)$—e.g., the set of items rented or purchased by the user—leading to the rule

$$\hat{r}_{ui} = b_{ui} + \sum_{j\in \mathrm{R}(u)} (r_{uj} - b_{uj})w_{ij} + \sum_{j\in \mathrm{N}(u)} c_{ij}\,. \tag{3.31}$$

Much like the w_{ij}'s, the c_{ij}'s are offsets added to the baseline predictor. For two items i and j, an implicit preference by u for j leads us to adjust our estimate of r_{ui} by c_{ij}, which is expected to be high if j is predictive on i.

Employing global weights, rather than user-specific interpolation coefficients, emphasizes the influence of missing ratings. In other words, a user's opinion is formed not only by what he rated, but also by what he did not rate. For example, suppose that a movie ratings dataset shows that users that rate "Shrek 3" high also gave high ratings to "Shrek 1–2". This will establish high weights from "Shrek 1–2" to "Shrek 3". Now, if a user did not rate "Shrek 1–2" at all, his predicted rating for "Shrek 3" will be penalized, as some necessary weights cannot be added to the sum.

For prior models (3.17) and (3.19) that interpolated $r_{ui} - b_{ui}$ from $\{r_{uj} - b_{uj} | j \in \mathrm{S}^k(i;u)\}$, it was necessary to maintain compatibility between the b_{ui} values and the b_{uj} values. However, here we do not use interpolation, so we can decouple the definitions of b_{ui} and b_{uj}. Accordingly, a more general prediction rule would be: $\hat{r}_{ui} = \tilde{b}_{ui} + \sum_{j \in \mathrm{R}(u)}(r_{uj} - b_{uj})w_{ij} + c_{ij}$. The constant $\tilde{b}_{ui}$ can represent predictions of r_{ui} by other methods such as a latent factor model. Here, we suggest the following rule that was found to work well:

$$\hat{r}_{ui} = \mu + b_u + b_i + \sum_{j \in \mathrm{R}(u)} [(r_{uj} - b_{uj})w_{ij} + c_{ij}] \tag{3.32}$$

Importantly, the b_{uj}'s remain constants, which are derived as explained in Sect. 3.2.1. However, the b_u's and b_i's become parameters that are optimized much like the w_{ij}'s and c_{ij}'s.

We have found that it is beneficial to normalize sums in the model leading to the form

$$\hat{r}_{ui} = \mu + b_u + b_i + |\mathrm{R}(u)|^{-\alpha} \sum_{j \in \mathrm{R}(u)} [(r_{uj} - b_{uj})w_{ij} + c_{ij}] . \tag{3.33}$$

The constant α controls the extent of normalization. A non-normalized rule ($\alpha = 0$), encourages greater deviations from baseline predictions for users that provided many ratings (high $|\mathrm{R}(u)|$). On the other hand, a fully normalized rule, eliminates the effect of number of ratings on deviations from baseline predictions. In many cases it would be a good practice for recommender systems to have greater deviation from baselines for users that rate a lot. This way, we take more risk with well modeled users that provided much input. For such users we are willing to predict quirkier and less common recommendations. At the same time, we are less certain about the modeling of users that provided only a little input, in which case we would like to stay with safe estimates close to the baseline values. Our experience with the Netflix dataset shows that best results are achieved with $\alpha = 0.5$, as in the prediction rule

$$\hat{r}_{ui} = \mu + b_u + b_i + |\mathrm{R}(u)|^{-\frac{1}{2}} \sum_{j \in \mathrm{R}(u)} [(r_{uj} - b_{uj})w_{ij} + c_{ij}] . \tag{3.34}$$

As an optional refinement, complexity of the model can be reduced by pruning parameters corresponding to unlikely item-item relations. Let us denote by $\mathrm{S}^k(i)$ the set of k items most similar to i, as determined by e.g., a similarity measure s_{ij} or a natural hierarchy associated with the item set. Additionally, we use $\mathrm{R}^k(i;u) \stackrel{\text{def}}{=} \mathrm{R}(u) \cap \mathrm{S}^k(i)$.[2] Now, when predicting r_{ui} according to (3.34), it is expected that the most influential weights will be associated with items similar to i. Hence, we replace (3.34) with

$$\hat{r}_{ui} = \mu + b_u + b_i + |\mathrm{R}^k(i;u)|^{-\frac{1}{2}} \sum_{j \in \mathrm{R}^k(i;u)} [(r_{uj} - b_{uj})w_{ij} + c_{ij}] . \tag{3.35}$$

When $k = \infty$, rule (3.35) coincides with (3.34). However, for other values of k it offers the potential to significantly reduce the number of variables involved.

3.5.1.2 Parameter Estimation

Prediction rule (3.35) allows fast online prediction. More computational work is needed at a pre-processing stage where parameters are estimated. A major design goal of the new neighborhood model was facilitating an efficient global optimization procedure, which prior neighborhood models lacked. Thus, model parameters are learned by solving the regularized least squares problem associated with (3.35):

$$\min_{b_*, w_*, c_*} \sum_{(u,i) \in \mathcal{K}} \left(r_{ui} - \mu - b_u - b_i - |\mathrm{R}^k(i;u)|^{-\frac{1}{2}} \sum_{j \in \mathrm{R}^k(i;u)} \left((r_{uj} - b_{uj})w_{ij} + c_{ij}\right) \right)^2$$
$$+ \lambda_{10} \left(b_u^2 + b_i^2 + \sum_{j \in \mathrm{R}^k(i;u)} w_{ij}^2 + c_{ij}^2 \right) \tag{3.36}$$

An optimal solution of this convex problem can be obtained by least square solvers, which are part of standard linear algebra packages. However, we have found that the following simple stochastic gradient descent solver works much faster. Let us denote the prediction error, $r_{ui} - \hat{r}_{ui}$, by e_{ui}. We loop through all known ratings in $\mathcal{K}$. For a given training case r_{ui}, we modify the parameters by moving in the opposite direction of the gradient, yielding:

- $b_u \leftarrow b_u + \gamma \cdot (e_{ui} - \lambda_{10} \cdot b_u)$
- $b_i \leftarrow b_i + \gamma \cdot (e_{ui} - \lambda_{10} \cdot b_i)$
- $\forall j \in \mathrm{R}^k(i;u)$:

$$w_{ij} \leftarrow w_{ij} + \gamma \cdot \left(|\mathrm{R}^k(i;u)|^{-\frac{1}{2}} \cdot e_{ui} \cdot (r_{uj} - b_{uj}) - \lambda_{10} \cdot w_{ij} \right)$$
$$c_{ij} \leftarrow c_{ij} + \gamma \cdot \left(|\mathrm{R}^k(i;u)|^{-\frac{1}{2}} \cdot e_{ui} - \lambda_{10} \cdot c_{ij} \right)$$

---

[2]Notational clarification: With other neighborhood models it was beneficial to use $\mathrm{S}^k(i;u)$, which denotes the k items most similar to i among those rated by u. Hence, if u rated at least k items, we will always have $|\mathrm{S}^k(i;u)| = k$, regardless of how similar those items are to i. However, $|\mathrm{R}^k(i;u)|$ is typically smaller than k, as some of those items most similar to i were not rated by u.

The meta-parameters γ (step size) and λ_{10} are determined by cross-validation. We used $\gamma = 0.005$ and $\lambda_{10} = 0.002$ for the Netflix data. Another important parameter is k, which controls the neighborhood size. Our experience shows that increasing k always benefits the accuracy of the results on the test set. Hence, the choice of k should reflect a tradeoff between prediction accuracy and computational cost. In Sect. 3.5.2 we will describe a factored version of the model that eliminates this tradeoff by allowing us to work with the most accurate $k = \infty$ while lowering running time.

A typical number of iterations throughout the training data is 15–20. As for time complexity per iteration, let us analyze the most accurate case where $k = \infty$, which is equivalent to using prediction rule (3.34). For each user u and item $i \in \mathrm{R}(u)$ we need to modify $\{w_{ij}, c_{ij} | j \in \mathrm{R}(u)\}$. Thus the overall time complexity of the training phase is $O(\sum_u |\mathrm{R}(u)|^2)$.

3.5.1.3 Comparison of Accuracy

Experimental results on the Netflix data with the globally optimized neighborhood model, henceforth dubbed GlobalNgbr, are presented in Fig. 3.1. We studied the model under different values of parameter k. The solid black curve with square symbols shows that accuracy monotonically improves with rising k values, as root mean squared error (RMSE) falls from 0.9139 for $k = 250$ to 0.9002 for $k = \infty$. (Notice that since the Netflix data contains 17,770 movies, $k = \infty$ is equivalent to $k = 17{,}769$, where all item-item relations are explored.) We repeated the experiments without using the implicit feedback, that is, dropping the c_{ij} parameters from our model. The results depicted by the solid black curve with X's show a significant decline in estimation accuracy, which widens as k grows. This demonstrates the value of incorporating implicit feedback into the model.

For comparison we provide the results of the two previously described neighborhood models. First is a similarity-based neighborhood model (in Sect. 3.4.2), which is the most popular CF method in the literature. We denote this model as CorNgbr. Second is the more accurate model described in Sect. 3.4.3, which will be denoted as JointNgbr. For both these two models, we tried to pick optimal parameters and neighborhood sizes, which were 20 for CorNgbr, and 50 for JointNgbr. The results are depicted by the dotted and dashed lines, respectively. It is clear that the popular CorNgbr method is noticeably less accurate than the other neighborhood models. On the opposite side, GlobalNgbr delivers more accurate results even when compared with JointNgbr, as long as the value of k is at least 500. Notice that the k value (the x-axis) is irrelevant to the previous models, as their different notion of neighborhood makes neighborhood sizes incompatible. Yet, we observed that while the performance of GlobalNgbr keeps improving as more neighbors are added, this was not true with the two other models. For CorNgbr and JointNgbr, performance peaks with a relatively small number of neighbors and declines thereafter. This may

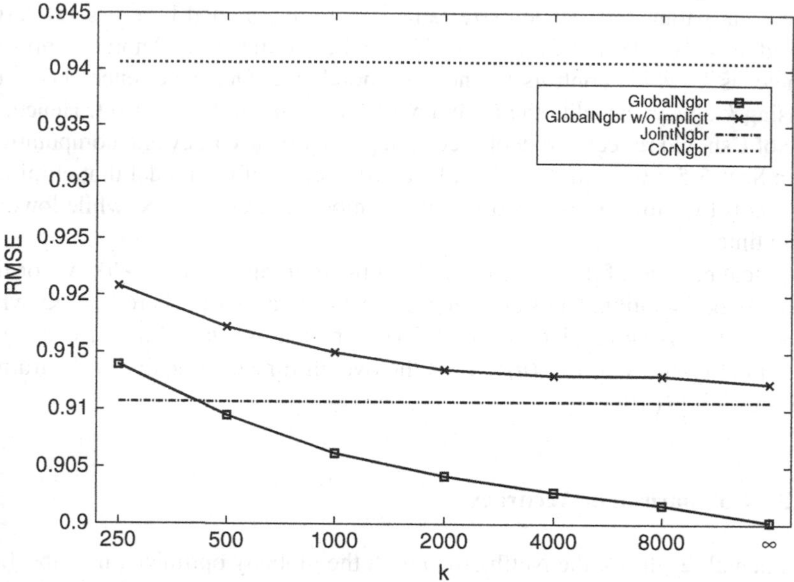

Fig. 3.1 Comparison of neighborhood-based models. Accuracy is measured by RMSE on the Netflix test set, so lower values indicate better performance. We measure the accuracy of the globally optimized model (GlobalNgbr) with and without implicit feedback. RMSE is shown as a function of varying values of k, which dictates the neighborhood size. The accuracy of two other models is shown as *two horizontal lines*; for each we picked an optimal neighborhood size

be explained by the fact that in GlobalNgbr, parameters are directly learned from the data through a formal optimization procedure that facilitates using many more parameters effectively.

Finally, let us consider running time. Previous neighborhood models require very light pre-processing, though, JointNgbr [2] requires solving a small system of equations for each provided prediction. The new model does involve pre-processing where parameters are estimated. However, online prediction is immediate by following rule (3.35). Pre-processing time grows with the value of k. Figure 3.2 shows typical running times per iteration on the Netflix data, as measured on a single processor 3.4 GHz Pentium 4 PC.

3.5.2 A Factorized Neighborhood Model

In the previous section we presented a more accurate neighborhood model, which is based on prediction rule (3.34) with training time complexity $O(\sum_u |\mathrm{R}(u)|^2)$ and space complexity $O(m+n^2)$. (Recall that m is the number of users, and n is the number of items.) We could improve time and space complexity by sparsifying the model through pruning unlikely item-item relations. Sparsification was controlled by the parameter $k \leqslant n$, which reduced running time and allowed space complexity of $O(m+nk)$. However, as k gets lower, the accuracy of the model declines as well.

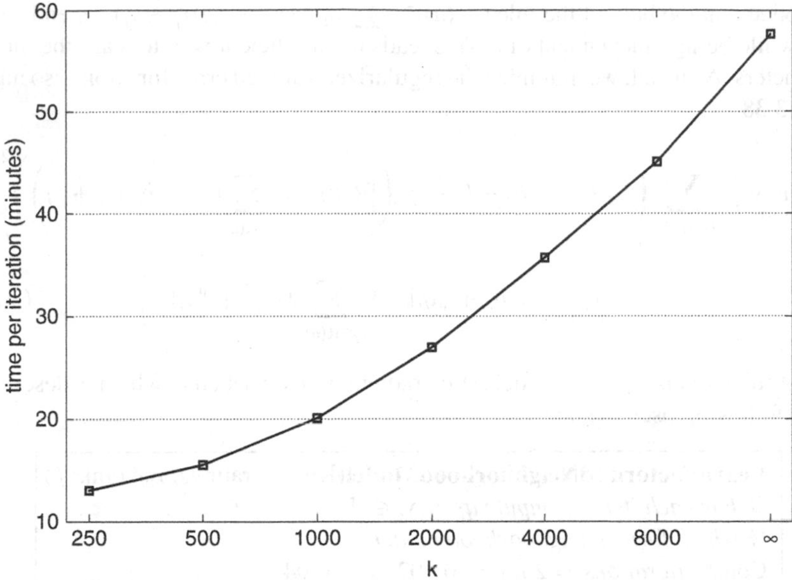

Fig. 3.2 Running time per iteration of the globally optimized neighborhood model, as a function of the parameter k

In addition, sparsification required relying on an external, less natural, similarity measure, which we would have liked to avoid. Thus, we will now show how to retain the accuracy of the full dense prediction rule (3.34), while significantly lowering time and space complexity.

3.5.2.1 Factoring Item-Item Relationships

We factor item-item relationships by associating each item i with three vectors: $q_i, x_i, y_i \in \mathbb{R}^f$. This way, we confine w_{ij} to be $q_i^T x_i$. Similarly, we impose the structure $c_{ij} = q_i^T y_j$. Essentially, these vectors strive to map items into an f-dimensional latent factor space where they are measured against various aspects that are revealed automatically by learning from the data. By substituting this into (3.34) we get the following prediction rule:

$$\hat{r}_{ui} = \mu + b_u + b_i + |\mathrm{R}(u)|^{-\frac{1}{2}} \sum_{j \in \mathrm{R}(u)} [(r_{uj} - b_{uj}) q_i^T x_j + q_i^T y_j] \tag{3.37}$$

Computational gains become more obvious by using the equivalent rule

$$\hat{r}_{ui} = \mu + b_u + b_i + q_i^T \left(|\mathrm{R}(u)|^{-\frac{1}{2}} \sum_{j \in \mathrm{R}(u)} (r_{uj} - b_{uj}) x_j + y_j \right). \tag{3.38}$$

Notice that the bulk of the rule $(|\mathrm{R}(u)|^{-\frac{1}{2}} \sum_{j \in \mathrm{R}(u)} (r_{uj} - b_{uj}) x_j + y_j)$ depends only on u while being independent of i. This leads to an efficient way to learn the model parameters. As usual, we minimize the regularized squared error function associated with (3.38)

$$\min_{q_*, x_*, y_*, b_*} \sum_{(u,i) \in \mathcal{K}} \left(r_{ui} - \mu - b_u - b_i - q_i^T \left(|\mathrm{R}(u)|^{-\frac{1}{2}} \sum_{j \in \mathrm{R}(u)} (r_{uj} - b_{uj}) x_j + y_j \right) \right)^2 + \lambda_{11} \left(b_u^2 + b_i^2 + \|q_i\|^2 + \sum_{j \in \mathrm{R}(u)} \|x_j\|^2 + \|y_j\|^2 \right). \quad (3.39)$$

Optimization is done by a stochastic gradient descent scheme, which is described in the following pseudo code:

```
LearnFactorizedNeighborhoodModel(Known ratings: r_ui, rank: f)
% For each item i compute q_i, x_i, y_i ∈ R^f
% which form a neighborhood model
Const #Iterations = 20, γ = 0.002, λ = 0.04
% Gradient descent sweeps:
for count = 1, ..., #Iterations do
    for u = 1, ..., m do
        % Compute the component independent of i:
        p_u ← |R(u)|^(-1/2) Σ_{j∈R(u)} (r_uj − b_uj) x_j + y_j
        sum ← 0
        for all i ∈ R(u) do
            r̂_ui ← μ + b_u + b_i + q_i^T p_u
            e_ui ← r_ui − r̂_ui
            % Accumulate information for gradient steps on x_i, y_i:
            sum ← sum + e_ui · q_i
            % Perform gradient step on q_i, b_u, b_i:
            q_i ← q_i + γ · (e_ui · p_u − λ · q_i)
            b_u ← b_u + γ · (e_ui − λ · b_u)
            b_i ← b_i + γ · (e_ui − λ · b_i)
        for all i ∈ R(u) do
            % Perform gradient step on x_i:
            x_i ← x_i + γ · (|R(u)|^(-1/2) · (r_ui − b_ui) · sum − λ · x_i)
            % Perform gradient step on y_i:
            y_i ← y_i + γ · (|R(u)|^(-1/2) · sum − λ · y_i)
return {q_i, x_i, y_i | i = 1, ..., n}
```

The time complexity of this model is linear with the input size, $O(f \cdot \sum_u (|\mathrm{R}(u)|))$, which is significantly better than the non-factorized model that required time $O(\sum_u |\mathrm{R}(u)|^2)$. We measured the performance of the model on the Netflix data;

Table 3.3 Performance of the factorized item-item neighborhood model

#Factors	50	100	200	500
RMSE	0.9037	0.9013	0.9000	0.8998
Time/iteration (min)	4.5	8	14	34

The models with $\geqslant 200$ factors slightly outperform the non-factorized model, while providing much shorter running time

see Table 3.3. Accuracy is improved as we use more factors (increasing f). However, going beyond 200 factors could barely improve performance, while slowing running time. Interestingly, we have found that with $f \geqslant 200$ accuracy negligibly exceeds the best non-factorized model (with $k = \infty$). In addition, the improved time complexity translates into a big difference in wall-clock measured running time. For example, the time-per-iteration for the non-factorized model (with $k = \infty$) was close to 58 min. On the other hand, a factorized model with $f = 200$ could complete an iteration in 14 min without degrading accuracy at all.

The most important benefit of the factorized model is the reduced space complexity, which is $O(m + nf)$—linear in the input size. Previous neighborhood models required storing all pairwise relations between items, leading to a quadratic space complexity of $O(m + n^2)$. For the Netflix dataset which contains 17,770 movies, such quadratic space can still fit within core memory. Some commercial recommenders process a much higher number of items. For example, an online movie rental service like Netflix is currently offering over 100,000 titles. Music download shops offer even more titles. Such more comprehensive systems with data on 100,000s items eventually need to resort to external storage in order to fit the entire set of pairwise relations. However, as the number of items is growing towards millions, as in the Amazon item-item recommender system, which accesses stored similarity information for several million catalog items [18], designers must keep a sparse version of the pairwise relations. To this end, only values relating an item to its top-k most similar neighbors are stored thereby reducing space complexity to $O(m + nk)$. However, a sparsification technique will inevitably degrade accuracy by missing important relations, as demonstrated in the previous section. In addition, identification of the top k most similar items in such a high dimensional space is a non-trivial task that can require considerable computational efforts. All these issues do not exist in our factorized neighborhood model, which offers a linear time and space complexity without trading off accuracy.

The factorized neighborhood model resembles some latent factor models. The important distinction is that here we factorize the item-item relationships, rather than the ratings themselves. The results reported in Table 3.3 are comparable to those of the widely used SVD model, but not as good as those of SVD++; see Sect. 3.3. Nonetheless, the factorized neighborhood model retains the practical advantages of traditional neighborhood models discussed earlier—the abilities to explain recommendations and to immediately reflect new ratings.

As a side remark, we would like to mention that the decision to use three separate sets of factors was intended to give us more flexibility. Indeed, on the Netflix data this allowed achieving most accurate results. However, another reasonable choice could be using a smaller set of vectors, e.g., by requiring: $q_i = x_i$ (implying symmetric weights: $w_{ij} = w_{ji}$).

3.5.2.2 A User-User Model

A user-user neighborhood model predicts ratings by considering how like-minded users rated the same items. Such models can be implemented by switching the roles of users and items throughout our derivation of the item-item model. Here, we would like to concentrate on a user-user model, which is dual to the item-item model of (3.34). The major difference is replacing the w_{ij} weights relating item pairs, with weights relating user pairs:

$$\hat{r}_{ui} = \mu + b_u + b_i + |\mathrm{R}(i)|^{-\frac{1}{2}} \sum_{v \in \mathrm{R}(i)} (r_{vi} - b_{vi}) w_{uv} \tag{3.40}$$

The set $\mathrm{R}(i)$ contains all the users who rated item i. Notice that here we decided to not account for implicit feedback. This is because adding such feedback was not very beneficial for the user-user model when working with the Netflix data.

User-user models can become useful in various situations. For example, some recommenders may deal with items that are rapidly replaced, thus making item-item relations very volatile. On the other hand, a stable user base enables establishment of long term relationships between users. An example of such a case is a recommender system for web articles or news items, which are rapidly changing by their nature; see, e.g., [8]. In such cases, systems centered around user-user relations are more appealing.

In addition, user-user approaches identify different kinds of relations that item-item approaches may fail to recognize, and thus can be useful on certain occasions. For example, suppose that we want to predict r_{ui}, but none of the items rated by user u is really relevant to i. In this case, an item-item approach will face obvious difficulties. However, when employing a user-user perspective, we may find a set of users similar to u, who rated i. The ratings of i by these users would allow us to improve prediction of r_{ui}.

The major disadvantage of user-user models is computational. Since typically there are many more users than items, pre-computing and storing all user-user relations, or even a reasonably sparsified version thereof, is overly expensive or completely impractical. In addition to the high $O(m^2)$ space complexity, the time complexity for optimizing model (3.40) is also much higher than its item-item counterpart, being $O(\sum_i |\mathrm{R}(i)|^2)$ (notice that $|\mathrm{R}(i)|$ is expected to be much higher than $|\mathrm{R}(u)|$). These issues have rendered user-user models as a less practical choice.

A Factorized Model All those computational differences disappear by factorizing the user-user model along the same lines as in the item-item model. Now, we associate each user u with two vectors $p_u, z_u \in \mathbb{R}^f$. We assume the user-user relations to be structured as: $w_{uv} = p_u^T z_v$. Let us substitute this into (3.40) to get

Table 3.4 Performance of the factorized user-user neighborhood model

#Factors	50	100	200	500
RMSE	0.9119	0.9110	0.9101	0.9093
Time/iteration (min)	3	5	8.5	18

$$\hat{r}_{ui} = \mu + b_u + b_i + |\mathrm{R}(i)|^{-\frac{1}{2}} \sum_{v \in \mathrm{R}(i)} (r_{vi} - b_{vi}) p_u^T z_v \,. \tag{3.41}$$

Once again, an efficient computation is achieved by including the terms that depends on i but are independent of u in a separate sum, so the prediction rule is presented in the equivalent form

$$\hat{r}_{ui} = \mu + b_u + b_i + p_u^T |\mathrm{R}(i)|^{-\frac{1}{2}} \sum_{v \in \mathrm{R}(i)} (r_{vi} - b_{vi}) z_v \,. \tag{3.42}$$

In a parallel fashion to the item-item model, all parameters are learned in linear time $O(f \cdot \sum_i |\mathrm{R}(i)|)$. The space complexity is also linear with the input size being $O(n + mf)$. This significantly lowers the complexity of the user-user model compared to previously known results. In fact, running time measured on the Netflix data shows that now the user-user model is even faster than the item-item model; see Table 3.4. We should remark that unlike the item-item model, our implementation of the user-user model did not account for implicit feedback, which probably led to its shorter running time. Accuracy of the user-user model is significantly better than that of the widely-used correlation-based item-item model that achieves RMSE = 0.9406 as reported in Fig. 3.1. Furthermore, accuracy is slightly better than the variant of the item-item model, which also did not account for implicit feedback (yellow curve in Fig. 3.1). This is quite surprising given the common wisdom that item-item methods are more accurate than user-user ones. It appears that a well implemented user-user model can match speed and accuracy of an item-item model. However, our item-item model could significantly benefit by accounting for implicit feedback.

Fusing Item-Item and User-User Models Since item-item and user-user models address different aspects of the data, overall accuracy is expected to improve by combining predictions of both models. Such an approach was previously suggested and was shown to improve accuracy; see, e.g. [4, 30]. However, past efforts were based on blending the item-item and user-user predictions during a post-processing stage, after each individual model was trained independently of the other model. A more principled approach optimizes the two models simultaneously, letting them know of each other while parameters are being learned. Thus, throughout the entire training phase each model is aware of the capabilities of the other model and strives to complement it. Our approach, which states the neighborhood models as formal optimization problems, allows doing that naturally. We devise a model that sums the item-item model (3.37) and the user-user model (3.41), leading to

$$\hat{r}_{ui} = \mu + b_u + b_i + |\mathrm{R}(u)|^{-\frac{1}{2}} \sum_{j \in \mathrm{R}(u)} [(r_{uj} - b_{uj})q_i^T x_j + q_i^T y_j]$$
$$+ |\mathrm{R}(i)|^{-\frac{1}{2}} \sum_{v \in \mathrm{R}(i)} (r_{vi} - b_{vi})p_u^T z_v \,. \tag{3.43}$$

Model parameters are learned by stochastic gradient descent optimization of the associated squared error function. Our experiments with the Netflix data show that prediction accuracy is indeed better than that of each individual model. For example, with 100 factors the obtained RMSE is 0.8966, while with 200 factors the obtained RMSE is 0.8953.

Here we would like to comment that our approach allows integrating the neighborhood models also with completely different models in a similar way. For example, in [16] we showed an integrated model that combines the item-item model with a latent factor model (SVD++), thereby achieving improved prediction accuracy with RMSE below 0.887. Therefore, other possibilities with potentially better accuracy should be explored before considering the integration of item-item and user-user models.

3.5.3 Temporal Dynamics at Neighborhood Models

One of the advantages of the item-item model based on global optimization (Sect. 3.5.1), is that it enables us to capture temporal dynamics in a principled manner. As we commented earlier, user preferences are drifting over time, and hence it is important to introduce temporal aspects into CF models.

When adapting rule (3.34) to address temporal dynamics, two components should be considered separately. First component, $\mu + b_i + b_u$, corresponds to the baseline predictor portion. Typically, this component explains most variability in the observed signal. Second component, $|\mathrm{R}(u)|^{-\frac{1}{2}} \sum_{j \in \mathrm{R}(u)} (r_{uj} - b_{uj})w_{ij} + c_{ij}$, captures the more informative signal, which deals with user-item interaction. As for the baseline part, nothing changes from the factor model, and we replace it with $\mu + b_i(t_{ui}) + b_u(t_{ui})$, according to (3.6) and (3.9). However, capturing temporal dynamics within the interaction part requires a different strategy.

Item-item weights (w_{ij} and c_{ij}) reflect inherent item characteristics and are not expected to drift over time. The learning process should capture unbiased long term values, without being too affected from drifting aspects. Indeed, the time changing nature of the data can mask much of the longer term item-item relationships if not treated adequately. For instance, a user rating both items i and j high within a short time period, is a good indicator for relating them, thereby pushing higher the value of w_{ij}. On the other hand, if those two ratings are given 4 years apart, while the user's taste (if not her identity) could considerably change, this provides less evidence of any relation between the items. On top of this, we would argue that those considerations are pretty much user-dependent; some users are more consistent than others and allow relating their longer term actions.

Our goal here is to distill accurate values for the item-item weights, despite the interfering temporal effects. First we need to parameterize the decaying relations between two items rated by user u. We adopt exponential decay formed by the function $e^{-\beta_u \cdot \Delta t}$, where $\beta_u > 0$ controls the user specific decay rate and should be learned from the data. We also experimented with other decay forms, like the more computationally-friendly $(1 + \beta_u \Delta t)^{-1}$, which resulted in about the same accuracy, with an improved running time.

This leads to the prediction rule

$$\hat{r}_{ui} = \mu + b_i(t_{ui}) + b_u(t_{ui}) + |\mathrm{R}(u)|^{-\frac{1}{2}} \sum_{j \in \mathrm{R}(u)} e^{-\beta_u \cdot |t_{ui} - t_{uj}|} ((r_{uj} - b_{uj}) w_{ij} + c_{ij}) . \tag{3.44}$$

The involved parameters, $b_i(t_{ui}) = b_i + b_{i,\mathrm{Bin}(t_{ui})}$, $b_u(t_{ui}) = b_u + \alpha_u \cdot \mathrm{dev}_u(t_{ui}) + b_{u,t_{ui}}$, β_u, w_{ij} and c_{ij}, are learned by minimizing the associated regularized squared error

$$\sum_{(u,i) \in \mathcal{K}} \Bigg(r_{ui} - \mu - b_i - b_{i,\mathrm{Bin}(t_{ui})} - b_u - \alpha_u \mathrm{dev}_u(t_{ui}) - b_{u,t_{ui}} - |\mathrm{R}(u)|^{-\frac{1}{2}} \sum_{j \in \mathrm{R}(u)} e^{-\beta_u \cdot |t_{ui} - t_{uj}|} ((r_{uj} - b_{uj}) w_{ij} + c_{ij}) \Bigg)^2 + \lambda_{12} \left(b_i^2 + b_{i,\mathrm{Bin}(t_{ui})}^2 + b_u^2 + \alpha_u^2 + b_{u,t}^2 + w_{ij}^2 + c_{ij}^2 \right) . \tag{3.45}$$

Minimization is performed by stochastic gradient descent. We run the process for 25 iterations, with $\lambda_{12} = 0.002$, and step size (learning rate) of 0.005. An exception is the update of the exponent β_u, where we are using a much smaller step size of 10^{-7}. Training time complexity is the same as the original algorithm, which is: $O(\sum_u |\mathrm{R}(u)|^2)$. One can tradeoff complexity with accuracy by sparsifying the set of item-item relations as explained in Sect. 3.5.1.

As in the factor case, properly considering temporal dynamics improves the accuracy of the neighborhood model within the movie ratings dataset. The RMSE decreases from 0.9002 [16] to 0.8885. To our best knowledge, this is significantly better than previously known results by neighborhood methods. To put this in some perspective, this result is even better than those reported by using hybrid approaches such as applying a neighborhood approach on residuals of other algorithms [2, 21, 29]. A lesson is that addressing temporal dynamics in the data can have a more significant impact on accuracy than designing more complex learning algorithms.

We would like to highlight an interesting point. Let u be a user whose preferences are quickly drifting (β_u is large). Hence, old ratings by u should not be very influential on his status at the current time t. One could be tempted to decay the weight of u's older ratings, leading to "instance weighting" through a cost function like

$$\sum_{(u,i)\in\mathcal{K}} e^{-\beta_u\cdot|t-t_{ui}|}\Bigg(r_{ui}-\mu-b_i-b_{i,\text{Bin}(t_{ui})}-b_u-\alpha_u\text{dev}_u(t_{ui})$$
$$-b_{u,t_{ui}}-|\text{R}(u)|^{-\frac{1}{2}}\sum_{j\in\text{R}(u)}((r_{uj}-b_{uj})w_{ij}+c_{ij})\Bigg)^2+\lambda_{12}(\cdots)\,.$$

Such a function is focused at the *current* state of the user (at time t), while de-emphasizing past actions. We would argue against this choice, and opt for equally weighting the prediction error at all past ratings as in (3.45), thereby modeling *all* past user behavior. Therefore, equal-weighting allows us to exploit the signal at each of the past ratings, a signal that is extracted as item-item weights. Learning those weights would equally benefit from all ratings by a user. In other words, we can deduce that two items are related if users rated them similarly within a short time frame, even if this happened long ago.

3.5.4 Summary

This section follows a less traditional neighborhood based model, which unlike previous neighborhood methods is based on formally optimizing a global cost function. The resulting model is no longer localized, considering relationships between a small set of strong neighbors, but rather considers all possible pairwise relations. This leads to improved prediction accuracy, while maintaining some merits of the neighborhood approach such as explainability of predictions and ability to handle new ratings (or new users) without re-training the model.

The formal optimization framework offers several new possibilities. First, is a factorized version of the neighborhood model, which improves its computational complexity while retaining prediction accuracy. In particular, it is free from the quadratic storage requirements that limited past neighborhood models.

Second addition is the incorporation of temporal dynamics into the model. In order to reveal accurate relations among items, a proposed model learns how influence between two items rated by a user decays over time. Much like in the matrix factorization case, accounting for temporal effects results in a significant improvement in predictive accuracy.

3.6 Between Neighborhood and Factorization

This chapter was structured around two different approaches to CF: factorization and neighborhood. Each approach evolved from different basic principles, which led to distinct prediction rules. We also argued that factorization can lead to somewhat more accurate results, while neighborhood models may have some practical advantages. In this section we will show that despite those differences, the two approaches share much in common. After all, they are both *linear models*.

Let us consider the SVD model of Sect. 3.3.1, based on

$$\hat{r}_{ui} = q_i^T p_u \,. \tag{3.46}$$

For simplicity, we ignore here the baseline predictors, but one can easily reintroduce them or just assume that they were subtracted from all ratings at an earlier stage.

We arrange all item-factors within the $n \times f$ matrix $Q = [q_1 q_2 \ldots q_n]^T$. Similarly, we arrange all user-factors within the $m \times f$ matrix $P = [p_1 p_2 \ldots p_m]^T$. We use the $n_u \times f$ matrix $Q[u]$ to denote the restriction of Q to the items rated by u, where $n_u = |\mathrm{R}(u)|$. Let the vector $r_u \in \mathbb{R}^{n_u}$ contain the ratings given by u ordered as in $Q[u]$. Now, by activating (3.46) on all ratings given by u, we can reformulate it in a matrix form

$$\hat{r}_u = Q[u]p_u \tag{3.47}$$

For $Q[u]$ fixed, $\|r_u - Q[u]p_u\|_2$ is minimized by

$$p_u = (Q[u]^T Q[u])^{-1} Q[u]^T r_u$$

In practice, we will regularize with $\lambda \geqslant 0$ to get

$$p_u = (Q[u]^T Q[u] + \lambda I)^{-1} Q[u]^T r_u \,.$$

By substituting p_u in (3.47) we get

$$\hat{r}_u = Q[u](Q[u]^T Q[u] + \lambda I)^{-1} Q[u]^T r_u \,. \tag{3.48}$$

This expression can be simplified by introducing some new notation. Let us denote the $f \times f$ matrix $(Q[u]^T Q[u] + \lambda I)^{-1}$ as W^u, which should be considered as a weighting matrix associated with user u. Accordingly, the weighted similarity between items i and j from u's viewpoint is denoted by $s_{ij}^u = q_i^T W^u q_j$. Using this new notation and (3.48) the predicted preference of u for item i by SVD is rewritten as

$$\hat{r}_{ui} = \sum_{j \in \mathrm{R}(u)} s_{ij}^u r_{uj} \,. \tag{3.49}$$

We reduced the SVD model into a linear model that predicts preferences as a linear function of past actions, weighted by item-item similarity. Each past action receives a separate term in forming the prediction $\hat{r}_{ui}$. This is equivalent to an item-item neighborhood model. Quite surprisingly, we transformed the matrix factorization model into an item-item model, which is characterized by:

- Interpolation is made from *all* past user ratings, not only from those associated with items most similar to the current one.
- The weight relating items i and j is factorized as a product of two vectors, one related to i and the other to j.
- Item-item weights are subject to a user-specific normalization, through the matrix W^u.

Those properties support our findings on how to best construct a neighborhood model. First, we showed in Sect. 3.5.1 that best results for neighborhood models are achieved when the neighborhood size (controlled by constant k) is maximal, such that all past user ratings are considered. Second, in Sect. 3.5.2 we touted the practice of factoring item-item weights. As for the user-specific normalization, we used a simpler normalizer: $n_u^{-0.5}$. It is likely that SVD suggests a more fundamental normalization by the matrix W^u, which would work better. However, computing W^u would be expensive in practice. Another difference between our suggested item-item model and the one implied by SVD is that we chose to work with asymmetric weights ($w_{ij} \neq w_{ji}$), whereas in the SVD-induced rule: $s_{ij}^u = s_{ji}^u$.

In the derivation above we showed how SVD induces an equivalent item-item technique. In a fully analogous way, it can induce an equivalent user-user technique, by expressing q_i as a function of the ratings and user factors. This brings us to three equivalent models: SVD, item-item and user-user. Beyond linking SVD with neighborhood models, this also shows that user-user and item-item approaches, once well designed, are equivalent.

This last relation (between user-user and item-item approaches) can also be approached intuitively. Neighborhood models try to relate users to new items by following chains of user-item adjacencies. Such adjacencies represent preference- or rating-relations between the respective users and items. Both user-user and item-item models act by following exactly the same chains. They only differ in which "shortcuts" are exploited to speed up calculations. For example, recommending itemB to user1 would follow the chain user1–itemA–user2–itemB (user1 rated itemA, which was also rated by user2, who rated itemB). A user-user model follows such a chain with pre-computed user-user similarities. This way, it creates a "shortcut" that bypasses the sub-chain user1–itemB–user2, replacing it with a similarity value between user1 and user2. Analogously, an item-item approach follows exactly the same chain, but creates an alternative "shortcut", replacing the sub-chain itemA–user2–itemB with an itemA–itemB similarity value.

Another lesson here is that the distinction that deems neighborhood models as "memory based", while taking matrix factorization and the likes as "model based" is not always appropriate, at least not when using accurate neighborhood models that are model-based as much as SVD. In fact, the other direction is also true. The better matrix factorization models, such as SVD++, are also following memory-based habits, as they sum over all memory stored ratings when doing the online prediction; see rule (3.3). Hence, the traditional separation between "memory based" and "model based" techniques is not appropriate for categorizing the techniques surveyed in this chapter.

So far, we concentrated on relations between neighborhood models and matrix factorization models. However, in practice it may be beneficial to break these relations, and to augment factorization models with sufficiently different neighborhood models that are able to complement them. Such a combination can lead to improved prediction accuracy [3, 16]. A key to achieve this is by using the more localized neighborhood models (those of Sect. 3.4, rather than those of Sect. 3.5), where the number of considered neighbors is limited. The limited number of neighbors might not be the best way to construct a standalone neighborhood model, but it makes the neighborhood model different enough from the factorization model in order to add a local perspective that the rather global factorization model misses.

References

1. Ali, K., and van Stam, W., "TiVo: Making Show Recommendations Using a Distributed Collaborative Filtering Architecture", *Proc. 10th ACM SIGKDD Int. Conference on Knowledge Discovery and Data Mining*, pp. 394–401, 2004.
2. Bell, R., and Koren, Y., "Scalable Collaborative Filtering with Jointly Derived Neighborhood Interpolation Weights", *IEEE International Conference on Data Mining (ICDM'07)*, pp. 43–52, 2007.
3. Bell, R., and Koren, Y., "Lessons from the Netflix Prize Challenge", *SIGKDD Explorations* **9** (2007), 75–79.
4. Bell, R.M., Koren, Y., and Volinsky, C., "Modeling Relationships at Multiple Scales to Improve Accuracy of Large Recommender Systems", *Proc. 13th ACM SIGKDD International Conference on Knowledge Discovery and Data Mining*, 2007.
5. Bennet, J., and Lanning, S., "The Netflix Prize", *KDD Cup and Workshop*, 2007. www.netflixprize.com.
6. Canny, J., "Collaborative Filtering with Privacy via Factor Analysis", *Proc. 25th ACM SIGIR Conf. on Research and Development in Information Retrieval (SIGIR'02)*, pp. 238–245, 2002.
7. Blei, D., Ng, A., and Jordan, M., "Latent Dirichlet Allocation", *Journal of Machine Learning Research* **3** (2003), 993–1022.
8. Das, A., Datar, M., Garg, A., and Rajaram, S., "Google News Personalization: Scalable Online Collaborative Filtering", *WWW'07*, pp. 271–280, 2007.
9. Deerwester, S., Dumais, S., Furnas, G.W., Landauer, T.K. and Harshman, R., "Indexing by Latent Semantic Analysis", *Journal of the Society for Information Science* **41** (1990), 391–407.
10. Funk, S., "Netflix Update: Try This At Home", http://sifter.org/~simon/journal/20061211.html, 2006.
11. Gelman, A., Carlin, J.B., Stern, H.S., and Rubin, D.B., *Bayesian Data Analysis*, Chapman and Hall, 1995.
12. Herlocker, J.L., Konstan, J.A., and Riedl, J., "Explaining Collaborative Filtering Recommendations", *Proc. ACM Conference on Computer Supported Cooperative Work*, pp. 241–250, 2000.
13. Herlocker, J.L., Konstan, J.A., Borchers, A., and Riedl, J., "An Algorithmic Framework for Performing Collaborative Filtering", *Proc. 22nd ACM SIGIR Conference on Information Retrieval*, pp. 230–237, 1999.
14. Hofmann, T., "Latent Semantic Models for Collaborative Filtering", *ACM Transactions on Information Systems* **22** (2004), 89–115.
15. Kim, D., and Yum, B., "Collaborative Filtering Based on Iterative Principal Component Analysis", *Expert Systems with Applications* **28** (2005), 823–830.

16. Koren, Y., "Factorization Meets the Neighborhood: a Multifaceted Collaborative Filtering Model", *Proc. 14th ACM SIGKDD International Conference on Knowledge Discovery and Data Mining*, 2008.
17. Koren, Y., "Factor in the Neighbors: Scalable and Accurate Collaborative Filtering ", *ACM Transactions on Knowledge Discovery from Data (TKDD)*,4(2010):1–24.
18. Linden, G., Smith, B., and York, J., "Amazon.com Recommendations: Item-to-Item Collaborative Filtering", *IEEE Internet Computing* **7** (2003), 76–80.
19. Marlin, B.M., Zemel, R.S., Roweis, S., and Slaney, M., "Collaborative Filtering and the Missing at Random Assumption", *Proc. 23rd Conference on Uncertainty in Artificial Intelligence*, 2007.
20. Oard, D.W.,, and Kim, J., "Implicit Feedback for Recommender Systems", *Proc. 5th DELOS Workshop on Filtering and Collaborative Filtering*, pp. 31–36, 1998.
21. Paterek, A., "Improving Regularized Singular Value Decomposition for Collaborative Filtering", *Proc. KDD Cup and Workshop*, 2007.
22. Salakhutdinov, R., Mnih, A., and Hinton, G., "Restricted Boltzmann Machines for Collaborative Filtering", *Proc. 24th Annual International Conference on Machine Learning*, pp. 791–798, 2007.
23. Salakhutdinov, R., and Mnih, A., "Probabilistic Matrix Factorization", *Advances in Neural Information Processing Systems 20 (NIPS'07)*, pp. 1257–1264, 2008.
24. Sarwar, B.M., Karypis, G., Konstan, J.A., and Riedl, J., "Application of Dimensionality Reduction in Recommender System – A Case Study", *WEBKDD'2000*.
25. Sarwar, B., Karypis, G., Konstan, J., and Riedl, J., "Item-based Collaborative Filtering Recommendation Algorithms", *Proc. 10th International Conference on the World Wide Web*, pp. 285–295, 2001.
26. Takács G., Pilászy I., Németh B. and Tikk, D., "Major Components of the Gravity Recommendation System", *SIGKDD Explorations* **9** (2007), 80–84.
27. Takács G., Pilászy I., Németh B. and Tikk, D., "Matrix Factorization and Neighbor based Algorithms for the Netflix Prize Problem", *Proc. 2nd ACM conference on Recommender Systems (RecSys'08)*, pp. 267–274, 2008.
28. Tintarev, N., and Masthoff, J., "A Survey of Explanations in Recommender Systems", *ICDE'07 Workshop on Recommender Systems and Intelligent User Interfaces*, 2007.
29. Toscher, A., Jahrer, M., and Legenstein, R., "Improved Neighborhood-Based Algorithms for Large-Scale Recommender Systems", *KDD'08 Workshop on Large Scale Recommenders Systems and the Netflix Prize*, 2008.
30. Wang, J., de Vries, A.P., and Reinders, M.J.T, "Unifying User-based and Item-based Collaborative Filtering Approaches by Similarity Fusion", *Proc. 29th ACM SIGIR Conference on Information Retrieval*, pp. 501–508, 2006.

Chapter 4
Semantics-Aware Content-Based Recommender Systems

Marco de Gemmis, Pasquale Lops, Cataldo Musto, Fedelucio Narducci, and Giovanni Semeraro

4.1 Introduction

Content-based recommender systems (CBRSs) rely on item and user descriptions (content) to build item representations and user profiles to suggest items similar to those a target user already liked in the past. The basic process of producing content-based recommendations consists in matching up the attributes of the target user profile, in which preferences and interests are stored, with the attributes of the items. The result is a relevance score that predicts the target user's level of interest in those items. Usually, attributes for describing an item are features extracted from metadata associated to that item, or textual features extracted directly from the item description. The content extracted from metadata is often too short and not sufficient to correctly define the user interests, while the use of textual features involves a number of complications when learning a user profile due to natural language ambiguity. Polysemy, synonymy, multi-word expressions, named entity recognition and disambiguation are inherent problems of traditional keyword-based profiles, which are not able to go beyond the usage of lexical/syntactic structures to infer the user interest in topics.

The ever increasing interest in *semantic technologies* and the availability of several open knowledge sources, such as Wikipedia, DBpedia, Freebase, and BabelNet have fueled recent progress in the field of CBRSs. Novel research works have introduced semantic techniques that shift from a *keyword*-based to a *concept*-based representation of items and user profiles. These observations make very relevant the integration of proper techniques for deep content analytics borrowed

M. de Gemmis • P. Lops (✉) • C. Musto • F. Narducci • G. Semeraro
Department of Computer Science, University of Bari "Aldo Moro", Bari, Italy
e-mail: marco.degemmis@uniba.it; pasquale.lops@uniba.it; cataldo.musto@uniba.it; fedelucio.narducci@uniba.it; giovanni.semeraro@uniba.it

F. Ricci et al. (eds.), *Recommender Systems Handbook*,
DOI 10.1007/978-1-4899-7637-6_4

from Natural Language Processing (NLP) and Semantic Technologies, which is one of the most innovative lines of research in *semantic recommender systems* [61].

We roughly classify semantic techniques into *top-down* and *bottom-up* approaches. Top-down approaches rely on the integration of external knowledge, such as machine readable dictionaries, taxonomies (or IS-A hierarchies), thesauri or ontologies (with or without value restrictions and logical constraints), for annotating items and representing user profiles in order to capture the semantics of the target user information needs. The main motivation behind top-down approaches is the challenge of providing recommender systems with the linguistic knowledge and common sense knowledge, as well as the cultural background which characterize the human ability of interpreting documents expressed in natural language and reasoning on their meaning.

On the other side, bottom-up approaches exploit the so-called geometric metaphor of meaning to represent complex syntagmatic and paradigmatic relations between words in high-dimensional vector spaces. According to this metaphor, each word (and each document as well) can be represented as a point in a vector space. The peculiarity of these models is that the representation is learned by analyzing the context in which the word is used, in a way that terms (or documents) similar to each other are close in the space. For this reason bottom-up approaches are also called distributional models. One of the great virtues of these approaches is that they are able to induce the semantics of terms by analyzing their use in large corpora of textual documents using unsupervised mechanisms, as evidenced by the recent advances of machine translation techniques [52, 83].

This chapter describes a variety of semantic approaches, both top-down and bottom-up, and shows how to leverage them to build a new generation of semantic CBRSs that we call *semantics-aware content-based recommender systems*.

4.2 Overview of Content-Based Recommender Systems

This section reports an overview of the basic principles for building CBRSs, the main techniques for representing items, learning user profiles and providing recommendations. The most important limitations of CBRSs are also discussed, while the semantic techniques useful to tackle those limitations are introduced in the next sections.

The high level architecture of a content-based recommender system is depicted in Fig. 4.1. The recommendation process is performed in three steps, each of which is handled by a separate component:

- CONTENT ANALYZER—When information has no structure (e.g. text), some kind of pre-processing step is needed to extract structured relevant information. The main responsibility of the component is to represent the content of items (e.g. documents, Web pages, news, product descriptions, etc.) coming from information sources in a form suitable for the next processing steps. Data items

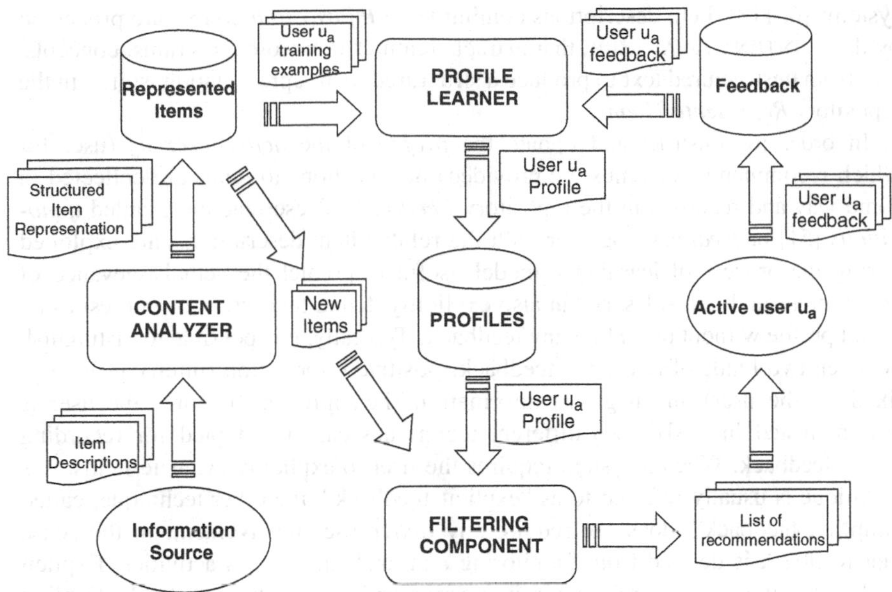

Fig. 4.1 High level architecture of a content-based recommender

are analyzed by feature extraction techniques in order to shift item representation from the original information space to the target one (e.g. Web pages represented as keyword vectors). This representation is the input to the PROFILE LEARNER and FILTERING COMPONENT;

- PROFILE LEARNER—This module collects data representative of the user preferences and tries to generalize this data, in order to construct the user profile. Usually, the generalization strategy is realized through machine learning techniques [86], which are able to infer a model of user interests starting from items liked or disliked in the past. For instance, the PROFILE LEARNER of a Web page recommender can implement a relevance feedback method [113] in which the learning technique combines vectors of positive and negative examples into a prototype vector representing the user profile. Training examples are Web pages on which a positive or negative feedback has been provided by the user;
- FILTERING COMPONENT—This module exploits the user profile to suggest relevant items by matching the profile representation against that of items to be recommended. The result is a binary or continuous relevance judgment (computed using some similarity metrics [57]), the latter case resulting in a ranked list of potentially interesting items. In the above mentioned example, the matching is realized by computing the cosine similarity between the prototype vector and the item vectors.

The first step of the recommendation process is the one performed by the CONTENT ANALYZER, that usually borrows techniques from Information Retrieval systems [6, 118]. Item descriptions coming from *Information Source* are processed by the CONTENT ANALYZER, that extracts features (keywords, n-grams, concepts, ...) from unstructured text to produce a structured item representation, stored in the repository *Represented Items*.

In order to construct and update the *profile* of the *active user* u_a (user for which recommendations must be provided) her reactions to items are collected in some way and recorded in the repository *Feedback*. These reactions, called *annotations* [51] or *feedback*, together with the related item descriptions, are exploited during the process of learning a model useful to predict the actual relevance of newly presented items. Users can also explicitly define their areas of interest as an initial profile without providing any feedback. Typically, it is possible to distinguish between two kinds of relevance feedback: positive information (inferring features liked by the user) and negative information (i.e., inferring features the user is not interested in [58]). Two different techniques can be adopted for recording user's feedback. When a system requires the user to explicitly evaluate items, this technique is usually referred to as "explicit feedback"; the other technique, called "implicit feedback", does not require any *active* user involvement, in the sense that feedback is derived from monitoring and analyzing user's activities. Explicit evaluations indicate how relevant or interesting an item is to the user [111]. Explicit feedback has the advantage of simplicity, albeit the adoption of numeric/symbolic scales increases the cognitive load on the user, and may not be adequate for catching user's feeling about items. Implicit feedback methods are based on assigning a relevance score to specific user actions on an item, such as saving, discarding, printing, bookmarking, etc. The main advantage is that they do not require a direct user involvement, even though biasing is likely to occur, e.g. interruption of phone calls while reading.

In order to build the profile of the active user u_a, the training set TR_a for u_a must be defined. TR_a is a set of pairs $\langle I_k, r_k \rangle$, where r_k is the rating provided by u_a on the item representation I_k. Given a set of item representation labeled with ratings, the PROFILE LEARNER applies supervised learning algorithms to generate a predictive model—the *user profile*—which is usually stored in a *profile repository* for later use by the FILTERING COMPONENT. After the user profile has been learned, the FILTERING COMPONENT predicts whether a new item is likely to be of interest for the active user, by comparing features in the item representation to those in the representation of user preferences (stored in the user profile).

User tastes usually change in time, therefore up-to-date information must be maintained and provided to the PROFILE LEARNER in order to automatically update the user profile. Further feedback is gathered on generated recommendations by letting users state their satisfaction or dissatisfaction with items in L_a. After gathering that feedback, the learning process is performed again on the new training set, and the resulting profile is adapted to the updated user interests. The iteration of the feedback-learning cycle over time enables the system to take into account the dynamic nature of user preferences.

4.2.1 Keyword-Based Vector Space Model

Most content-based recommender systems use relatively simple retrieval models, such as keyword matching or the Vector Space Model (VSM). VSM is a spatial representation of text documents. In that model, each document is represented by a vector in a n-dimensional space, where each dimension corresponds to a term from the overall vocabulary of a given document collection.

Formally, every document is represented as a vector of term weights, where each weight indicates the degree of association between the document and the term. Let $D = \{d_1, d_2, \ldots, d_N\}$ denote a set of documents or corpus, and $T = \{t_1, t_2, \ldots, t_n\}$ be the dictionary, that is to say the set of words in the corpus. T is obtained by applying some standard natural language processing operations, such as tokenization, stopwords removal, and stemming [6]. Each document d_j is represented as a vector in a n-dimensional vector space, so $\overrightarrow{d_j} = \langle w_{1j}, w_{2j}, \ldots, w_{nj} \rangle$, where w_{kj} is the weight for term t_k in document d_j.

Document representation in the VSM raises two issues: weighting the terms and measuring the feature vector similarity. The most commonly used term weighting scheme, TF-IDF (Term Frequency-Inverse Document Frequency) *weighting*, is based on empirical observations regarding text [117]:

- rare terms are not less relevant than frequent terms (IDF assumption);
- multiple occurrences of a term in a document are not less relevant than single occurrences (TF assumption);
- long documents are not preferred to short documents (normalization assumption).

In other words, terms that occur frequently in one document (TF=term-frequency), but rarely in the rest of the corpus (IDF=inverse-document-frequency), are more likely to be relevant to the topic of the document. In addition, normalizing the resulting weight vectors prevent longer documents from having a better chance of retrieval. These assumptions are well exemplified by the TF-IDF function:

$$\text{TF-IDF}(t_k, d_j) = \underbrace{\text{TF}(t_k, d_j)}_{\text{TF}} \cdot \underbrace{log \frac{N}{n_k}}_{\text{IDF}} \tag{4.1}$$

where N denotes the number of documents in the corpus, and n_k denotes the number of documents in the collection in which the term t_k occurs at least once.

$$\text{TF}(t_k, d_j) = \frac{f_{k,j}}{max_z f_{z,j}} \tag{4.2}$$

where the maximum is computed over the frequencies $f_{z,j}$ of all terms t_z that occur in document d_j. In order for the weights to fall in the [0, 1] interval and for the documents to be represented by vectors of equal length, weights obtained by Eq. (4.1) are usually normalized by cosine normalization:

$$w_{k,j} = \frac{\text{TF-IDF}(t_k, d_j)}{\sqrt{\sum_{s=1}^{|T|} \text{TF-IDF}(t_s, d_j)^2}} \tag{4.3}$$

which enforces the normalization assumption.

As stated earlier, a similarity measure is required to determine the closeness between two documents. Many similarity measures have been derived to describe the proximity of two vectors; among those measures, cosine similarity is the most widely used:

$$sim(d_i, d_j) = \frac{\sum_k w_{ki} \cdot w_{kj}}{\sqrt{\sum_k w_{ki}^2} \cdot \sqrt{\sum_k w_{kj}^2}} \tag{4.4}$$

In content-based recommender systems relying on VSM, both user profiles and items are represented as weighted term vectors. Predictions of a user's interest in a particular item can be derived by computing the cosine similarity.

4.2.2 *Methods for Learning User Profiles*

Machine learning techniques generally used in the task of inducing content-based profiles, are well-suited for text categorization [119]. In a machine learning approach to text categorization, an inductive process automatically builds a text classifier from a set of *training documents*, i.e. documents labeled with the categories they belong to.

The problem of learning user profiles can be cast as a binary text categorization task: each document has to be classified as interesting or not with respect to the user preferences. Therefore, the set of categories is $C = \{c_+, c_-\}$, where c_+ is the positive class (user-likes) and c_- the negative one (user-dislikes). Classifiers can be also adopted with a set of categories which is not binary. Besides the use of classifiers, other machine learning algorithms, such as linear regression, can be adopted to predict numerical ratings. The most used learning algorithms in content-based recommender systems are based on probabilistic methods, relevance feedback and k-nearest neighbors [6].

4.2.2.1 Probabilistic Methods

Naïve Bayes is a probabilistic approach to inductive learning, and belongs to the general class of Bayesian classifiers. These approaches generate a probabilistic model based on previously observed data. The model estimates the a posteriori probability, $P(c|d)$, of document d belonging to class c. This estimation is based on the a priori probability, $P(c)$, the probability of observing a document in class c, $P(d|c)$, the probability of observing the document d given c, and $P(d)$, the probability of observing the instance d. Using these probabilities, the Bayes theorem is applied to calculate $P(c|d)$:

$$P(c|d) = \frac{P(c)P(d|c)}{P(d)} \tag{4.5}$$

To classify the document d, the class with the highest probability is chosen:

$$c = argmax_{c_j} \frac{P(c_j)P(d|c_j)}{P(d)}$$

$P(d)$ is generally removed as it is equal for all c_j. As we do not know the value for $P(d|c)$ and $P(c)$, we estimate them by observing the training data. However, estimating $P(d|c)$ in this way is problematic, as it is very unlikely to see the same document more than once: the observed data is generally not enough to be able to generate good probabilities. The naïve Bayes classifier overcomes this problem by simplifying the model through the independence assumption: all the words or tokens in the observed document d are conditionally independent of each other given the class. Individual probabilities for the words in a document are estimated one by one rather than the complete document as a whole. The conditional independence assumption is clearly violated in real-world data, however, despite these violations, empirically the naïve Bayes classifier does a good job in classifying text documents [12, 70].

There are two commonly used working models of the naïve Bayes classifier, the *multivariate Bernoulli* event model and the *multinomial* event model [77]. Both models treat a document as a vector of values over the corpus vocabulary, V, where each entry in the vector represents whether a word occurred in the document, hence both models lose information about word order. The multivariate Bernoulli event model encodes each word as a binary attribute, i.e., whether a word appeared or not, while the multinomial event model counts how many times the word appeared in the document. Empirically, the multinomial naïve Bayes formulation was shown to outperform the multivariate Bernoulli model. This effect is particularly noticeable for large vocabularies [77]. The way the multinomial event model uses its document vector to calculate $P(c_j|d_i)$ is as follows:

$$P(c_j|d_i) = P(c_j) \prod_{t_k \in V_{d_i}} P(t_k|c_j)^{N_{(d_i,t_k)}} \tag{4.6}$$

where $N_{(d_i,t_k)}$ is defined as the number of times word or token t_k appeared in document d_i. Notice that, rather than getting the product of all the words in the corpus vocabulary V, only the subset of the vocabulary, V_{d_i}, containing the words that appear in the document d_i, is used. A key step in implementing naïve Bayes is estimating the word probabilities $P(t_k|c_j)$. To make the probability estimates more robust with respect to infrequently encountered words, a smoothing method is used to modify the probabilities that would have been obtained by simple event counting. One important effect of smoothing is that it avoids assigning probability values equal to zero to words not occurring in the training data for a particular class. A rather simple smoothing method relies on the common Laplace estimates (i.e., adding one to all the word counts for a class). A more interesting method is Witten-Bell [129].

Although naïve Bayes performances are not as good as some other statistical learning methods such as nearest-neighbor classifiers or support vector machines, it has been shown that it can perform surprisingly well in the classification tasks where the computed probability is not important [40]. Another advantage of the naïve Bayes approach is that it is very efficient and easy to implement compared to other learning methods.

4.2.2.2 Relevance Feedback

Relevance feedback is a technique adopted in Information Retrieval that helps users to incrementally refine queries based on previous search results. It consists of the users feeding back into the system decisions on the relevance of retrieved documents with respect to their information needs.

Relevance feedback and its adaptation to text categorization, the well-known Rocchio's formula [113], are commonly adopted by content-based recommender systems. The general principle is to let users to rate documents suggested by the recommender system with respect to their information need. This form of feedback can subsequently be used to incrementally refine the user profile or to train the learning algorithm that infers the user profile as a classifier. Some linear classifiers consist of an explicit profile (or prototypical document) of the category [119]. The Rocchio's method is used for inducing linear, profile-style classifiers. This algorithm represents documents as vectors, so that documents with similar content have similar vectors. Each component of such a vector corresponds to a term in the document, typically a word. The weight of each component is computed using the TF-IDF term weighting scheme. Learning is achieved by combining document vectors (of positive and negative examples) into a prototype vector for each class in the set of classes C. To classify a new document d, the similarity between the prototype vectors and the corresponding document vector representing d are calculated for each class (for example by using the cosine similarity measure), then d is assigned to the class whose document vector has the highest similarity value.

More formally, Rocchio's method computes a classifier $\overrightarrow{c_i} = \langle \omega_{1i}, \ldots, \omega_{|T|i} \rangle$ for the category c_i (T is the *vocabulary*, that is the set of distinct terms in the training set) by means of the formula:

$$\omega_{ki} = \beta \cdot \sum_{\{d_j \in POS_i\}} \frac{w_{kj}}{|POS_i|} - \gamma \cdot \sum_{\{d_j \in NEG_i\}} \frac{w_{kj}}{|NEG_i|} \tag{4.7}$$

where w_{kj} is the TF-IDF weight of the term t_k in document d_j, POS_i and NEG_i are the set of positive and negative examples in the training set for the specific class c_i, β and γ are control parameters that allow to set the relative importance of *all* positive and negative examples. To assign a class $\tilde{c}$ to a document d_j, the similarity between each prototype vector $\overrightarrow{c_i}$ and the document vector $\overrightarrow{d_j}$ is computed and $\tilde{c}$ will be the c_i with the highest value of similarity. The Rocchio-based classification approach does not have any theoretic underpinning and there are guarantees on performance or convergence [108].

4.2.2.3 Nearest Neighbors

Nearest neighbor algorithms, also called lazy learners, simply store training data in memory, and classify a new unseen item by comparing it to all stored items by using a similarity function. The "nearest neighbor" or the "k-nearest neighbors" items are determined, and the class label for the unclassified item is derived from the class labels of the nearest neighbors. A similarity function is needed, for example the cosine similarity measure is adopted when items are represented using the VSM. Nearest neighbor algorithms are quite effective, albeit the most important drawback is their inefficiency at classification time, since they do not have a true training phase and thus defer all the computation to classification time.

4.2.3 Advantages and Drawbacks of Content-Based Filtering

The adoption of the content-based recommendation paradigm has several advantages when compared to the collaborative one:

- USER INDEPENDENCE—Content-based recommenders exploit solely ratings provided by the active user to build her own profile. Instead, collaborative filtering methods need ratings from other users in order to find the "nearest neighbors" of the active user, i.e., users that have similar tastes since they rated the same items similarly. Then, only the items that are most liked by the neighbors of the active user will be recommended;
- TRANSPARENCY—Explanations on how the recommender system works can be provided by explicitly listing content features or descriptions that caused an item to occur in the list of recommendations. Those features are indicators to consult in order to decide whether to trust a recommendation. Conversely, collaborative systems are black boxes since the only explanation for an item recommendation is that unknown users with similar tastes liked that item;
- NEW ITEM—Content-based recommenders are capable of recommending items not yet rated by any user. As a consequence, they do not suffer from the first-rater problem, which affects collaborative recommenders which rely solely on users' preferences to make recommendations. Therefore, until the new item is rated by a substantial number of users, the system would not be able to recommend it.

Nonetheless, content-based systems have several shortcomings:

- LIMITED CONTENT ANALYSIS—Content-based techniques have a natural limit in the number and type of features that are associated, whether automatically or manually, with the objects they recommend. Domain knowledge is often needed, e.g., for movie recommendations the system needs to know the actors and directors, and sometimes, domain ontologies are also needed. No content-based recommendation system can provide suitable suggestions if the analyzed content does not contain enough information to discriminate items the user likes from items the user does not like. Some representations capture only certain aspects of the content, but there are many others that would influence a user's experience. For instance, often there is not enough information in the word frequency to model the user interests in jokes or poems, while techniques for affective computing would be most appropriate. Again, for Web pages, feature extraction techniques from text completely ignore aesthetic qualities and additional multimedia information. Furthermore, CBRSs based on a string matching approach suffer from problems of:
  - POLYSEMY, the presence of multiple meanings for one word;
  - SYNONYMY, multiple words with the same meaning;
  - MULTI-WORD EXPRESSIONS, the difficulty to assign the correct properties to a sequence of two or more words whose properties are not predictable from the properties of the individual words;
  - ENTITY IDENTIFICATION or NAMED ENTITY RECOGNITION, the difficulty to locate and classify elements in text into pre-defined categories such as the names of persons, organizations, locations, expressions of times, quantities, monetary values, etc.
  - ENTITY LINKING or NAMED ENTITY DISAMBIGUATION, the difficulty of determining the identity (often called the reference) of entities mentioned in text.

- OVER-SPECIALIZATION—Content-based recommenders have no inherent method for finding something unexpected. The system suggests items whose scores are high when matched against the user profile, hence the user is going to be recommended items similar to those already rated. This drawback is also called *lack of serendipity* problem to highlight the tendency of the content-based systems to produce recommendations with a limited degree of novelty. To give an example, when a user has only rated movies directed by Stanley Kubrick, she will be recommended just that kind of movies. A "perfect" content-based technique would rarely find anything *novel*, limiting the range of applications for which it would be useful.
- NEW USER—Enough ratings have to be collected before a content-based recommender system can really understand user preferences and provide accurate recommendations. Therefore, when few ratings are available, as for a new user, the system will not be able to provide reliable recommendations.

4.3 Top-Down Semantic Approaches

There is an ever increasing interest in using a deep domain knowledge as part of the recommendation process, in order to deal with the main problems of CBRSs (i.e., limited content analysis, overspecialization) and generate more accurate recommendations. To this purpose, several CBRSs:

- incorporate ontological knowledge, ranging from simple linguistic ontologies, to more complex domain-specific ones [81];
- leverage unstructured or semi-structured encyclopedic knowledge sources, such as Wikipedia [120];
- try to exploit the wealth of the so-called Linked Open Data cloud [39].

The following sections provide an overview of CBRSs, with the aim of imposing a degree of order on the diversity of the knowledge sources and techniques exploited for the representation of items and user profiles. Section 4.3.1 describes the role of ontologies for defining advanced CBRSs, by highlighting the main advantages and drawbacks, while recommendation approaches leveraging encyclopedic knowledge are described in Sect. 4.3.2, with the proposal of new ontological resources which can be effectively used for improving CBRSs. Finally, more recent approaches based on the Linked Open Data cloud are discussed in Sect. 4.3.3.

4.3.1 Approaches Based on Ontological Resources

The leading role of linguistic knowledge is highlighted by the wide use of WordNet [84], which is mostly adopted for the semantic interpretation of content by using Word Sense Disambiguation (WSD) algorithms. In [36, 37], WordNet and WSD algorithms are used to integrate linguistic knowledge in the process of learning user profiles. The basic building block for WordNet is the SYNSET (SYNonym SET), which represents a specific meaning of a word. Hence, items are represented according to a synset-based vector space model, and the user profile includes those synsets that turn out to be most indicative of the user preferences. In addition to the better performance of synset-based profiles, the advantage is that synset-based representations are inherently multilingual. Indeed, concepts (word meanings) remain the same across different languages, while terms used for describing them change in each specific language. Using lexical resources such as MultiWordNet [9], which associates a unique identifier to each possible sense (meaning) of a word, regardless the original language, it is possible to define a bridge between different languages. In [71], a WSD algorithm exploiting MultiWordNet as sense repository is integrated in the design of MARS (MultilAnguage Recommender System), a cross-language recommender system whose effectiveness is comparable to a classical monolingual content-based recommender. Similarly, in [75] the authors present a personal agent for a multilingual news Web site, which adopts a synset-based document representation obtained through a Word Domain Disambiguation algorithm [74] which exploits MultiWordNet.

More recent works still rely on WordNet to define semantic recommender systems. In [25], a semantic approach to news recommendation making use of WordNet is investigated. WordNet synsets are used to compute similarities between unread news articles and articles stored in user profiles by adopting the Wu and Palmer semantic similarity measure [130]. However, in order to cope with the lack of support for named entities, the authors extend the WordNet-based recommendation approach with a similarity based on page counts for named entities stemming from a Web search engine. WordNet and WSD are also adopted in [27] to compute the semantic similarity between short microblog posts in order to recommend tweets related to what a user has issued or trending topics.

In spite of the advantages provided by WordNet, there are several limitations related to its limited coverage for named entities, events, contemporary terms, and in general specific knowledge. With the advent of the Semantic Web [10], ontologies emerged as powerful means for representing domain knowledge in many areas, and for this reason several approaches have been proposed to incorporate ontological knowledge in recommender systems. Ontologies are used to describe domain-specific knowledge and they are commonly handled as hierarchies of concepts with attributes and relations, which establish a terminology to define semantic networks of interrelated concepts and instances. In general, when a domain model is represented as an ontology, items and user models consist of a subset of concepts from the domain ontology, possibly with associated values characterizing their importance. In [82], the recommendation of on-line academic research papers is performed by leveraging a research topic ontology, based on the computer science classifications, for representing both items and user profiles. The match is based on the correlation between the topics in the user profile and those associated to the papers. The same process is adopted in [22, 23] to recommend news. Item descriptions are vectors of TF-IDF scores in the space of ontology concepts, user profiles are represented in the same space, and the item-profile matching is performed as a cosine-based vector similarity, differently from the strategy in [21, 24], in which item and user spaces are clustered in order to build implicit communities of interest which enable recommendation based on the similarities among them. In [121], the similarity between an item and a user profile is based on the existence of the same concepts or related concepts, according to their position in a three-level ontology, while a more advanced recommendation method is described in [16], where a spreading activation algorithm is adopted on ontology-profiles to suggest interesting and novel items to the user. Spreading activation is used in [26] as well, where the propagation from a small number of initial concepts (those which received the user feedback) to other related domain concepts allows to provide finer recommendations and to tackle the cold start problem. The novelty of the approach relies on the definition of a set of contextualized propagation strategies, ranging from the horizontal propagation among siblings, to the anisotropic vertical one among ancestors and descendants, which permits user interests to be propagated differently upward and downward.

The use of ontologies for adding a semantic dimension to items and user profiles may be beneficial for limiting some of the problems of CBRSs and providing better recommendations. Ontology-based user profiles are less ambiguous, and the structure of the ontology may be adopted to define measures able to estimate how semantically related two concepts are. Different types of measures are provided in the literature, ranging from link-based (e.g. Wu and Palmer, Leacock and Chodorow) to node-based ones (e.g. Resnik, Jiang and Conrath, Lin). More details about those measures can be found in [19].

On the other hand, there are difficulties which hinder the use of ontologies in recommender systems. The development of rich and expressive domain-specific ontologies is a time consuming task which has to be performed by human experts, and there are also the onerous tasks of ontology population and maintenance to perform [63]. Hence, there is an increasing attention of many researchers towards the integration of world knowledge which may be extracted from online collaborative resources, in order to exploit the richness of such resources to come up with *semantics-aware recommender systems*.

4.3.2 Approaches Based on Unstructured or Semi-Structured Encyclopedic Knowledge

Studies in Artificial Intelligence (AI) have already recognized the importance of knowledge for problem solving. Back in the early years of AI research, Buchanan and Feigenbaum [18] formulated the knowledge-as-power hypothesis, which postulated that "The power of an intelligent program to perform its task well depends primarily on the quantity and quality of knowledge it has about that task".

Many knowledge sources have become available in the last years, both structured and unstructured [Open Directory Project (ODP), Yahoo!Web Directory, and Wikipedia]. The use of external knowledge sources can be useful to better understand the information items (documents, news, product descriptions) and to extract more meaningful features, in order to design advanced content-based filtering methods able to provide better recommendations. Among unstructured knowledge sources, Wikipedia emerges as the most used source of information for several tasks [8, 42, 59, 96]. The main advantages of using Wikipedia, rather than conventional document archives, as a knowledge source are:

- it is freely available on the Web;
- it is a wide-coverage resource which is under constant development by the community;
- it is available in several languages, hence can be seen as a multilingual corpus;
- it is very accurate [50].

On the other hand, Wikipedia knowledge is available in textual form written by humans for humans, and enough common-sense knowledge is needed to correctly understand the meaning of articles. For this reason, natural language understanding capabilities are required for the interpretation of Wikipedia pages and for making them *machine processable*.

The problem of extracting and using knowledge contained in Wikipedia was studied by several researchers [33, 46, 49]. Different techniques have been defined, which exploit the encyclopedic knowledge contained in Wikipedia for *selecting the most accurate semantic features* to represent the items, or for *generating new semantic features* to enrich the item representation.

The most prominent approaches which perform *feature selection* are Wikify! [33] and Tagme [46]. Wikify! allows to identify important concepts in a text representation by using keyword extraction, and then to link these concepts to the corresponding Wikipedia pages by exploiting WSD techniques. More specifically, Wikify! is a system for automatically cross-referencing documents with Wikipedia [85]. The system is trained on Wikipedia articles, and thus learns to disambiguate and detect links in the same way as Wikipedia editors [45].

Tagme [46] augments a text representation with pertinent hyperlinks to Wikipedia pages, by implementing an anchor disambiguation algorithm which exploits inter-relations between Wikipedia pages, as well as other heuristics. The main advantage of Tagme is its ability to annotate texts which are short and poorly composed, such as snippets coming from search engine result pages, tweets, news, etc.

An approach which leverages Wikipedia knowledge to *generate* new features for enriching items representation is Explicit Semantic Analysis (ESA) [49]. ESA provides a fine-grained semantic representation of text documents as a weighted vector of concepts derived from Wikipedia. Specifically, concepts correspond to Wikipedia articles, e.g. such as WOODY ALLEN, APPLE INC., or MACHINE LEARNING. Explicit Semantic Analysis resembles the well known Latent Semantic Analysis technique [35], whose representation is based on *latent* (and not comprehensible) features, rather than *explicit* (and comprehensible) concepts derived from Wikipedia (concepts explicitly defined and manipulated by humans).

In [48, 49], ESA was adopted for computing semantic relatedness of natural language texts, with better performance with respect to a keyword-based approach. In [43], ESA is adopted to enrich documents and queries to enhance traditional bag-of-words-based retrieval models, while in [8], ESA is used for enriching bag-of-words representing news or blog feeds before their clustering. ESA was also effectively used to augment the bag-of-words representation with Wikipedia-based features in the text categorization task [49].

Finally, the availability of Wikipedia knowledge in several languages and the multilingual alignment of Wikipedia articles allow to have cross-lingual and multilingual services. Potthast et al. [109] proposed a Wikipedia-based multilingual retrieval model for the analysis of cross-language similarity. They demonstrated that, given a query in a specific language, the most similar documents from a corpus in another language were properly ranked. They used Cross-Language Explicit Semantic Analysis (CL-ESA), an extension of ESA for cross-language retrieval. Recently, ESA was also used to develop the Cross-language Service Retriever tool (CroSeR), to support the cross-language linking of e-Government services to the Linked Open Data cloud [98].

4.3.2.1 Explicit Semantic Analysis

The idea behind ESA is to view an encyclopedia as a collection of concepts, each of which accompanied with a large body of text (the article content). The power of ESA is the capability of representing the Wikipedia knowledge base in a way that is directly used by machines, without the need for manually encoded common-sense knowledge. The gist of the technique is to use the high-dimensional space defined by these concepts in order to represent the meaning of natural language texts. ESA allows to leverage Wikipedia knowledge by defining relationships between terms and Wikipedia articles.

More formally, given a set of basic concepts $C = \{c_1, c_2, \ldots, c_n\}$, a term t is represented by a vector of weights $< w_1, w_2, \ldots, w_n >$, where w_i represents the strength of association between t and c_i. The set of concepts C are one to one associated to documents $D = \{d_1, d_2, \ldots, d_n\}$ (the Wikipedia articles). Hence, a sparse matrix T is built, called *ESA-matrix*, where each column corresponds to a concept (title of Wikipedia article), and each row corresponds to a term (word) that occurs in $\bigcup_{i=1\ldots n} d_i$. The entry $T[i,j]$ of the matrix represents the TF-IDF of term t_i in document d_j. Finally, length normalization is applied to each column to disregard differences in document length. This allows to define the semantics of a term t_i as a point in the n-dimensional semantic space of Wikipedia concepts. The weighed vector corresponding to a term t_i is called *semantic interpretation vector*. The semantics of a text fragment $< t_1, t_2, \ldots, t_k >$ (i.e. a sentence, a paragraph, an entire document) is obtained by computing the centroid (average vector) of the semantic interpretation vectors of the individual terms occurring in the fragment. This definition allows to partially perform WSD [49].

As an example consider the text fragment of a news title "Apple patents a Tablet Mac". Without deep knowledge of hi-tech industry and gadgets, one finds it hard to predict the content of the news item. Using Wikipedia it is possible to identify the following related concepts: APPLE COMPUTER (with the correct identification of the concept representing the computer company rather than the fruit), MAC OS, LAPTOP, AQUA (the GUI of Mac OS X), IPOD, and APPLE NEWTON (the name of Apple's early personal digital assistant).

4.3.2.2 CBRSs Leveraging Encyclopedic Knowledge

Even though the above mentioned indexing methods have been adopted for several tasks, they are not yet widely used in the context of learning user profiles and providing recommendations. However, CBRSs may benefit of the Wikipedia-based representation. Indeed, the feature generation process, adopted for example by ESA, can lead to richer item representations, able to improve the overlap between items and profiles. Indeed the new features allow to match items that did not share any keyword with the profile before the feature generation process. ESA is also able to introduce new related concepts for generating less obvious and more serendipitous (unexpected) recommendations.

In [91], an enhanced semantic TV-show representation for Personalized Electronic Program Guides is proposed. ESA is used to enrich the textual descriptions associated to TV shows with additional features extracted from Wikipedia, in order to improve the ranking of the most relevant items for each program genre. ESA is exploited to enrich a classic bag-of-words representation with 20, 40, or 60 new features, and it was adopted to enrich German TV-show descriptions. To this purpose, the German Wikipedia dump (released on October 13th, 2010 with a size of approximately 7.5 GB) was processed in order to obtain the corresponding German ESA-matrix. Results showed that the enhanced bag-of-words representation outperforms the classical bag-of-words one in terms of precision.

Besides the improvement of accuracy, the work carried out in [97] shows that, leveraging encyclopedic knowledge for representing user interests allows to introduce serendipitous topics and to obtain more understandable and transparent user profiles. Transparency is defined as the extent to which keywords in the user profile reflect the actual user interests. In that work user interests have been gathered from Facebook profiles by extracting both interests explicitly declared by users and those implicitly inferred from posts and other published content. The feature generation process implemented by ESA helps to introduce new serendipitous topics of interests, while the feature selection process implemented by Tagme helps to obtain more comprehensible user profiles, more representative of user interests.

These results are confirmed in the user study presented in [96], in which both ESA and Tagme are effectively used to improve the performance of a news recommender. News titles are extracted from a set of RSS feeds, and the profile of interests is built by extracting information from the Facebook and Twitter accounts of the user. The information extracted (news, posts, tweets) are represented using keywords, ESA concepts or Tagme concepts, respectively. The representation obtained by Tagme outperforms the others in terms of transparency and accuracy. This is probably due to the ability of Tagme to effectively annotate very short texts, such as news titles.

The ability of the ESA technique to cope with the cold-start problem is shown in [105], in which a CBRS in the context of non-fiction multimedia recommendation of TED lectures is presented. Using ESA as indexing method for titles and descriptions of talks allows to obtain the best performance with respect to other semantic representations, and this shows that a representation of items based on external knowledge is significantly more useful than the domain knowledge captured intrinsically by the other semantic methods.

4.3.2.3 BabelNet: An Encyclopedic Dictionary

Resources like Wikipedia lack full coverage for the lexicographic senses of lemmas, which is instead provided by a computational lexicon, such as WordNet . In this section we briefly describe a new resource, called BabelNet [100], which integrates the largest multilingual Web encyclopedia, i.e., Wikipedia, and the most popular computational lexicon, i.e., WordNet, to obtain a very large multilingual semantic network. BabelNet integrates the linguistic knowledge contained in WordNet and the encyclopedic knowledge contained in Wikipedia for providing an *encyclopedic dictionary*. It encodes knowledge as a labeled directed graph. *Nodes* are *concepts* extracted from WordNet and Wikipedia, i.e. word senses (synsets) available in WordNet, and encyclopedic entries (Wikipages) extracted from Wikipedia, while *edges* connecting the nodes are labeled with *semantic relations* coming from WordNet, as well as semantically unspecified relations from hyperlinked text coming from Wikipedia. Each node also contains a set of lexicalizations of the concept for different languages, e.g., APPLE for English, MANZANA for Spanish, MELA for Italian, POMME for French, ... These multilingually lexicalized concepts are called *Babel synsets*. The current version (2.0) of BabelNet covers 50 languages, and contains more than nine millions Babel synsets and 262 millions of lexico-semantic relations.

Figure 4.2 presents an excerpt of two results obtained by issuing the query "apple" to BabelNet.[1] The system returns 11 different senses of "apple", such as fruit, the British rock band, the multinational corporation, etc. Clicking on the sense allows to link to the corresponding WordNet synset or Wikipedia page in that specific language. The system also reports the set of glosses extracted from the different resources and the categories extracted from the corresponding Wikipedia pages. For each sense, its semantically related concepts may also be explored. For example, some of the concepts related to apple in the sense of the multinational corporation—*Apple Inc*—are *computer architecture, Power Mac G4, Apple ProDOS, etc.* More information about BabelNet can be found in [100].

BabelNet sense inventory can be effectively used for a variety of tasks, ranging from multilingual semantic relatedness [101], to (multilingual) WSD [99, 102]. The use of BabelNet can also fuel the progress on the research on CBRSs, which could rely on knowledge-richer approaches to represent items and user profiles.

4.3.3 Approaches Based on Linked Open Data

Novel and more accessible forms of information coming from different open knowledge sources represent a new and rapidly growing piece of the big data puzzle. These new sources of open data represent an expanding trove of largely unexploited value, which paves the way to a new generation of recommender systems. Using open or pooled data from many sources, often combined and linked with proprietary big data, can help develop insights difficult to uncover with internal data alone [28]. The Linked Data community has advocated the following set of best principles for collaboratively publishing and interlinking structured data over the Web[2]:

[1]http://babelnet.org/.

[2]http://www.w3.org/DesignIssues/LinkedData.html.

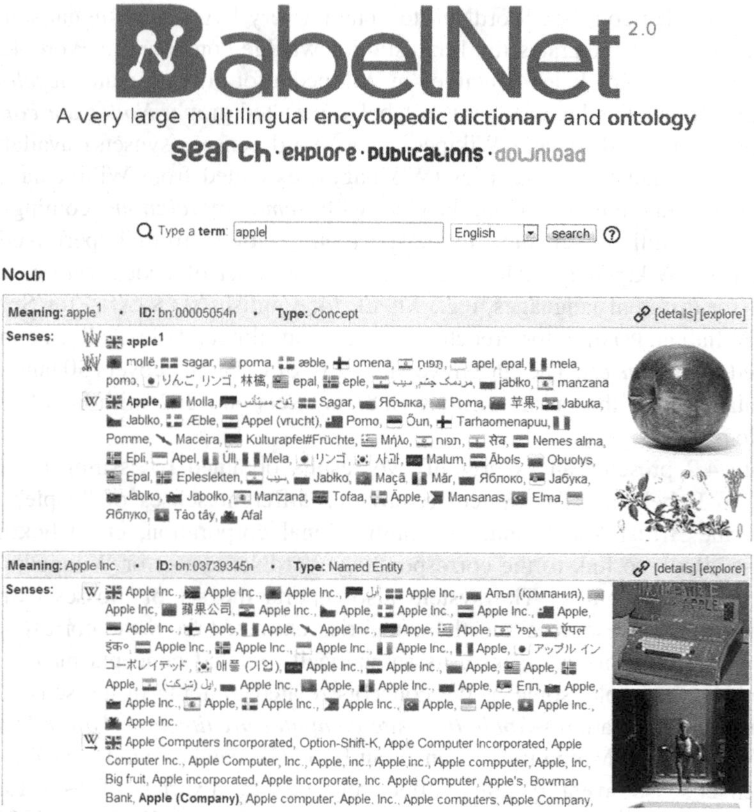

Fig. 4.2 The result obtained by issuing the query "apple" to BabelNet

- the use of URIs (Uniform Resource Identifier) as names for things (arbitrary real-world entities);
- the use of HTTP URIs so those names can be looked up by people (dereferencing);
- the delivery of useful information upon lookup of those URIs using standards such as RDF and SPARQL;
- the inclusion of links to other URIs to discover more things.

This allows the dissemination of structured data on the Web in an interoperable manner using the Semantic Web standards [14].

Over the last years, more and more semantic data are published following the Linked Data principles, by connecting information referring to geographical locations, people, companies, book, scientific publications, films, music, TV and radio programs, genes, proteins, drugs, online communities, statistical data, and reviews in a single global data space, the *Web of Data* [13]. These datasets interlinked with each other form a global graph, called Linked Open Data cloud.

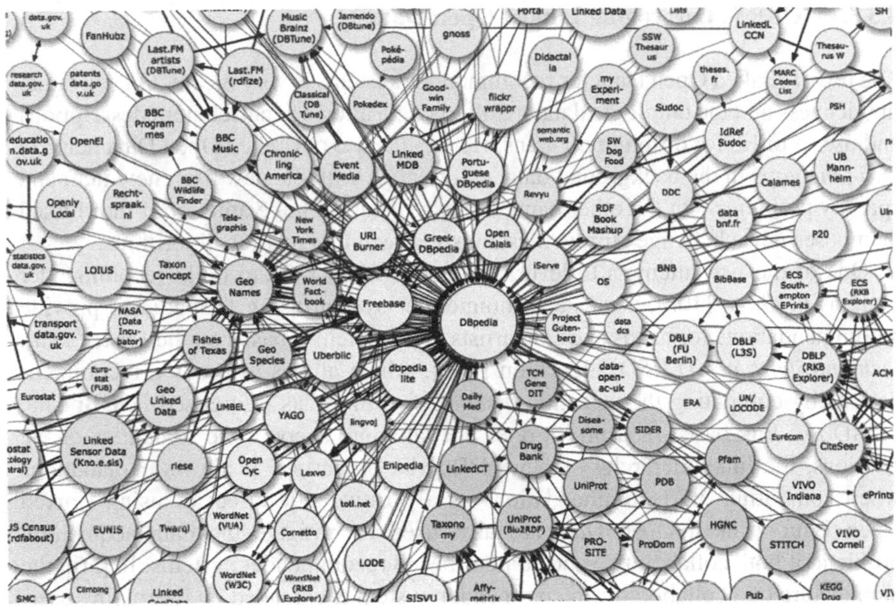

Fig. 4.3 Fragment of the Linked Open Data cloud (as of September 2011)

At the time of writing more than 2100 datasets are available with almost 62 billions of RDF triples.[3] Figure 4.3 shows a fragment of the Linked Open Data cloud, whose nucleus is represented by DBpedia.

The standard mechanism for specifying the existence and meaning of connections between items described in this data is provided by the Resource Description Framework (RDF), which allows to link things by explicitly stating the nature of the connection (typed links). For example, a hyperlink of the type *friend_of* may be set between two people. RDF statements are in the form of *subject-predicate-object* expressions, called *triples*. The *subject* denotes the resource, and the *predicate* denotes an aspect of the resource and expresses a *relationship* between the *subject* and the *object*. Relations are also called *properties*. SPARQL[4] is a SQL-like language for RDF graphs to retrieve and manipulate data stored in RDF format.

In the context of recommender systems, this is useful to interlink diverse information about users, items, and their relations, and to implement reasoning mechanisms that can support and improve the recommendation process [34]. The challenge is to investigate whether and how this large amount of wide-coverage and linked semantic knowledge can significantly improve complex filtering tasks.

[3]http://stats.lod2.eu/.

[4]http://www.w3.org/TR/rdf-sparql-query/ accessed on September 12, 2014.

4.3.3.1 CBRSs Leveraging Linked Open Data

The use of Linked Open Data for recommender systems is very recent. On one hand, the richness and the ontological nature of this data allows to enrich item descriptions and user profiles for different domains. Hence, the use of Linked Open Data helps to *fill in the gaps* in the background data, and to cope with the new user, new item and sparsity problems. On the other hand, the use of such a huge amount of interlinked data poses new challenges for well established recommendation algorithms.

One of the first attempts to leverage Linked Open Data to build recommender systems is *dbrec* [106], a music recommender system using DBpedia to provide recommendations for bands and solo artists. The system is based on the *Linked Data Semantic Distance (LDSD)* algorithm [107], which allows to provide recommendations by computing the semantic distance for all artists referenced in DBpedia. LDSD is a link-based measure; it does not take into account the semantics of the relations, the links hierarchy or other DBpedia properties. It allows explanations when computing the recommendations as a positive side effect of using Linked Open Data. Linked Open Data are also used to mitigate the data acquisition problem of both collaborative and content-based recommender systems. In [56], the architecture of a collaborative recommender system is extended by leveraging user-item connections coming from DBTune [110]; the resulting RDF graph of user-item relations is transformed into a user-item matrix exploited by the recommendation algorithm. In [95], DBpedia is used to enrich the playlists extracted from a Facebook profile with new related artists. Each artist in the original playlist is mapped to a DBpedia node, and other similar artists are selected by taking into account shared properties, such as the genre and the musical category of the artist.

An approach which exploits Linked Open Data for computing cross-domain recommendations is described in [44, 64]. The source and target domains involved in the recommendation scenario are mapped to DBpedia by identifying the classes that belong to the domains of interest, and the relations existing between instances of such classes. Then, a semantic network is defined by querying DBpedia in order to link a specific instance in the source domain with the related instances in the target domain. The recommendation mechanism relies on a graph-based ranking algorithm on the semantic network. The authors focused on a scenario in which recommendations for music artists and tracks are adapted to places of interests, by obtaining very positive results. Similarly to *dbrec*, the approach is able to provide explanations based on the discovered semantic paths between a place of interest and the music artists in the associated semantic network.

A simpler approach to define a CBRS exploiting exclusively Linked Open Data to represent both items and user profiles is proposed in [38]. The ontological information, encoded via specific properties extracted from DBpedia and LinkedMDB [54], is adopted to perform a semantic expansion of the item descriptions, in order to catch implicit relations and hidden information, which are not detectable just looking at the nodes directly linked to the item. The evaluation of different combinations of properties revealed that more properties lead to more accurate recommendations, since this seems to mitigate the limited content analysis issue of CBRSs.

Similarly to the previous work, a CBRS fed exclusively by Linked Open Data is presented in [39]. Data coming from DBpedia [15], LinkedMDB [54] and Freebase [17] are exploited to recommend movies using an adaptation of the Vector Space Model. The RDF graph connecting movies according to some properties is represented as a three-dimensional matrix where each slice refers to an ontology property (e.g. starring, director, genre, ...) and represents its adjacency matrix. A a cell in the matrix is not null if there is a property that relates a subject (on the rows) to an object (on the columns). The weighing scheme is based on TF-IDF and the cosine similarity allows to measure the correlation between two movies. The recommendation step is performed by computing the similarity between the user profile (movies liked and disliked by the user) and movies unknown to the user. The similarity values for each property are combined in a linear fashion, and the best configuration of weights for each property is learned via a genetic algorithm. As in [38], using more ontological information leads to the best performance, and also helps to explain the recommendations by listing, for each property, the values which are common between the movies in the user profile and those suggested.

The same approach devised in [39] is effectively adopted to develop Cinemappy [104] and a recommender system for events [67]. The former is a context-aware CBRS for movies and movie theaters suggestions fed by data coming from localized DBpedia graphs, whose results are enhanced by exploiting contextual information about the user. The latter recommends events, even though some improvements were necessary to deal with the complexity of the domain, such as the social aspect, i.e. the collaborative participation about which friend will attend an event.

All the previous approaches rely on Linked Open Data to catch implicit relations which allow to increase the number of common features between items, or to implement more sophisticated reasoning mechanisms over the graphs. Ultimately, well known reasoning mechanisms for learning content-based user profiles can be adopted on the richer representations provided by leveraging Linked Open Data [89]. An interesting work which goes one step further is presented in [103]; it leverages DBpedia to extract semantic *path-based* features to eventually compute recommendations using a *learning to rank* algorithm. Starting from the common graph-based representation of the content and collaborative data models, all the paths connecting the user to an item are considered in order to have a relevance score for that item. The more paths between a user and an item, the more that item is relevant to that user.

4.3.3.2 (Other) Entity Linking Algorithms

In [1, 2], a semantically-enriched user model based on the analysis of Twitter posts is proposed. Entity linking algorithms are used to enrich and extend user models by identifying the most relevant entities mentioned in the tweets. Similarly, entity linking algorithms are adopted in [94] to enhance item representation in a context-aware content-based recommendation framework. The experimental evaluation showed that entity-based algorithms are able to improve the predictive accuracy of the recommendation framework, in both context-aware and non-contextual recommendation settings.

This section introduces some other known entity linking systems, which can be effectively used to implement semantic CBRSs.

Babelfy[5] [88] is a novel integrated approach to entity linking and word sense disambiguation. Given a lexicalized semantic network, e.g. BabelNet, the approach is based on three steps: (1) the automatic creation of semantic signatures, i.e. related concepts and named entities for each vertex of the semantic network, (2) extraction of all the linkable fragments from a given text, listing all the possible meanings according to the semantic network, and (3) linking based on a high-coherence densest subgraph algorithm.

DBpedia Spotlight [80] has been designed to connect unstructured text to the Linked Open Data cloud by using DBpedia as hub. The output is a set of Wikipedia articles related to a text retrieved by following the URI of the DBpedia instances. The annotation process works in four-stages. First, the text is analyzed in order to select the phrases that may indicate a mention to a DBpedia resource. In this step, spots that are only composed of verbs, adjectives, adverbs and prepositions are disregarded. Subsequently, a set of candidate DBpedia resources is built by mapping the spotted phrase to resources that are candidate disambiguations for that phrase. The disambiguation process uses the context around the spotted phrase to decide for the best choice amongst the candidates.

Other tools allow for the semantic annotation of natural language text, but the techniques used to perform the analysis are not described with sufficient details.

Alchemy[6] offers a NLP processing service able to analyze web pages, documents, and tweets for identifying entities, keywords, concepts, etc. If available, a link to the Linked Open Data cloud is also provided (DBpedia, Yago, Crunchbase, etc.). It also performs sentiment analysis on the input text by assigning a sentiment polarity to the entities identified into the text.

Open Calais[7] exploits NLP and machine learning to find entities within documents. The main difference with respect to other entity recognizers is that Open Calais returns facts and events hidden within the text. Open Calais consists of three main components: (1) a named entity recognizer that identifies people, companies, organizations; (2) a fact recognizer that links the text with position tags, alliance, person-political; (3) an event recognizer whose role is to identify sport, management, change events, labor actions, etc. Open Calais supports English, French and Spanish, and its assets are currently linked to DBpedia, Wikipedia, Freebase, GeoNames.

---

[5]http://babelfy.org.

[6]http://www.alchemyapi.com/.

[7]http://www.opencalais.com/.

NERD (Named Entity Recognition and Disambiguation)[8] [112] is a framework to unify different named entity extractors, such as Alchemy, DBpedia Spotlight, Open Calais, etc., using the NERD ontology, providing a rich set of axioms aligning the taxonomies of those tools. In the NERD ontology a manual mapping between taxonomies coming from different schemas is established, and a concept is included in the NERD ontology as soon as there are at least three extractors that use it.

4.4 Bottom-Up Semantic Approaches

This section focuses on approaches able to produce implicit semantic representation of both items and user profiles that could be defined *lightweight* in contrast to the approaches presented in Sect. 4.3. These techniques are mainly based on the distributional hypothesis, according to which the meaning of words depends on the contexts in which they occur. The most distinguishing aspect of these approaches lies in the fact that the semantic representation is directly learned according to the way terms are used in large corpora of data. Thus, they do not need any *human intervention*, differently from the development of an external resource for semantic content representation or the maintenance of an ontology. Bottom-up semantic approaches just need as much data as possible to learn and represent the meaning of the terms.

The following sections provide the background about Discriminative Models (Sect. 4.4.1), and the basics for the definition of a novel content-based recommendation framework that exploits the strengths of VSM, by tackling its drawbacks at the same time. A novel dimensionality reduction technique, which avoids the need for factorization, is discussed in Sect. 4.4.1.1, and a more sophisticated negation operator to model negative preferences is presented in Sect. 4.4.1.2. A survey of CBRSs built on the ground of the previous methods is finally provided in Sect. 4.4.1.3.

4.4.1 Approaches Based on Discriminative Models

Discriminative Models (DMs) rely on a simple insight: as humans infer the meaning of a word by understanding the contexts in which that word is typically used, discriminative algorithms extract information about the meaning of a word by analyzing its usage in large corpora of textual documents. This means that it is possible to infer the meaning of a term (e.g., *leash*) by analyzing the other terms it co-occurs with (*dog, animal,* etc.) [114]. In the same way, the correlation between different terms (e.g., *leash* and *muzzle*) can be inferred by analyzing the

[8] http://www.wikimeta.com/portfolio_nerd.html.

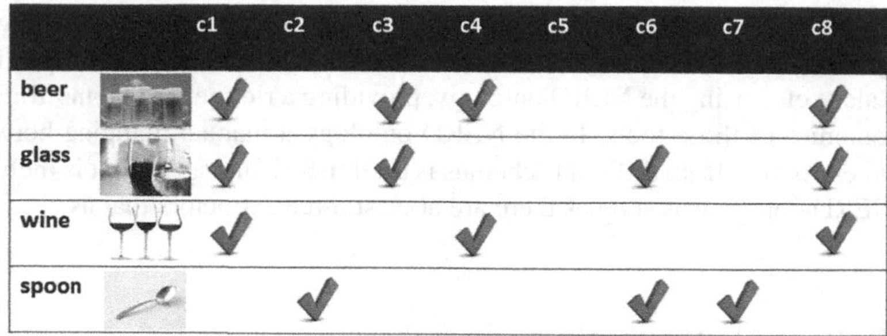

	c1	c2	c3	c4	c5	c6	c7	c8
beer	✓		✓	✓				✓
glass	✓		✓			✓		✓
wine	✓			✓				✓
spoon		✓				✓	✓	

Fig. 4.4 A term-context matrix. The analysis of the usage patterns of the terms allows to state that *beer* and *wine* or *beer* and *glass* are similar, since they are often used together

similarity between the contexts in which they are used. These approaches rely on the *distributional hypothesis* [53], according to which *"Words that occur in the same contexts tend to have similar meanings"*. This means that words are semantically similar to the extent that they share contexts.

DMs represent information about terms usage in a *term-context* matrix (Fig. 4.4), instead of a term-document matrix adopted in the classic VSM. The advantage is that the *context* is a very flexible concept which can be adapted to the specific granularity level of the representation required by the application: for example, given a word, its context could be either a single word it co-occurs with, or a sliding window of terms that surrounds it, or a sentence, or yet the whole document. In [125], it is presented an interesting survey about the three broad classes of VSM to represent semantics, related to the different types of matrix adopted: (1) term-document matrix—usually used to measure similarity of documents, (2) word-context matrix—usually used to measure similarity of terms, and (3) pair-pattern matrix—usually used to measure similarity of relations (the textual patterns in which the pair X,Y co-occurs, e.g. *X cuts Y* or *X works with Y*).

The classical VSM is the simplest DM proposed in literature, in which co-occurrences are computed by considering the whole document as context. This approach uses *syntagmatic* relations between words to assess their semantic similarity. Indeed, words with a similar meaning will tend to occur in the same document, because they are appropriate to define the particular topic of that document. Instead, the approach based on the co-occurrences computed in a context different from the document uses *paradigmatic* relations, because in a small context window we do not expect that similar words (e.g., synonyms) can co-occur, but we could expect that their surrounding words will be more or less the same.

DMs are referred to as *geometrical models* as well, since each term represented by a row of the term-context matrix can be modeled as a vector. In order to compute relatedness between terms, it is possible to exploit distributional measures that rely on the distributional hypothesis, such as spatial measures (e.g., cosine similarity, Manhattan and Euclidean distances), mutual information-based measures (e.g., Lin), or relative entropy-based measures (e.g., Kullback-Leibler divergence) [87].

On one hand, this representation has the advantage of building a language model, typically referred to as `WordSpace` [72], able to learn similarities and connections in a totally unsupervised way, but on the other hand the dimensionality of vectors when adopting finer-grained representations of contexts is a clear issue (*curse of dimensionality*). For example, the adoption of sentences as granularity level for contexts causes an explosion of the number of dimensions of the vector space: by assuming 10–20 sentences per document on average, the dimension of the vector space would be 10–20 times the one using a classical term-document matrix. For this reason, feature selection or *dimensionality reduction* techniques must be adopted.

4.4.1.1 Dimensionality Reduction Techniques

Dimensionality reduction techniques help to transform a high-dimensional space into a lower-dimensionality one.

Latent Semantic Indexing (LSI) [35] is a technique for building a semantic vector space representation based on the application of Singular Value Decomposition (SVD) [68] on the term-document matrix. The approach, largely investigated for representing the meaning of terms through statistical computations applied to a large corpus of text, works in two steps: first, the corpus is represented into a matrix in which each row is a word and each column is a text passage (*document*). Next, SVD is applied in order to decompose the original matrix into two matrices of reduced dimensionality (obtained by selecting the largest eigenvalues) that represent the original rows (*terms*) and the original columns in terms of *latent* orthogonal factors.

As pointed out in [11], the reduced orthogonal dimensions resulting from SVD are less noisy than the original data and capture the latent associations between terms and documents.

The use of LSI in the area of CBRSs has been already investigated in several research work [47, 78], and it has been demonstrated that it is able to outperform other techniques, regardless the application domain. In [122], a feature profile of a user is built using both collaborative and content features, and LSI is exploited to detect the dominant features of a user. Recommendations are provided according to this dimensionally-reduced feature profile, with a better performance with respect to both collaborative and content-based as well as hybrid algorithms. Recently, LSI has been effectively adopted as the content-based component of a hybrid algorithm for recommending TV-shows [7, 32], as well as in the task of recommending source code examples according to user requirements [79]. However, Terzi et al. [124] showed that LSI can underperform compared to other approaches when the set of available data is small and the textual content is too short. This outcome confirms the insight that DMs, regardless the dimensionality technique they adopt, are effective when a lot of data about terms usage is available.

Regardless of its effectiveness, LSI suffers from scalability issues inherited from the use of SVD for dimensionality reduction. Consequently, research has been oriented towards the investigation of more scalable and incremental techniques, such as those based on Random Projections (RP) [126], which has its theoretical basis

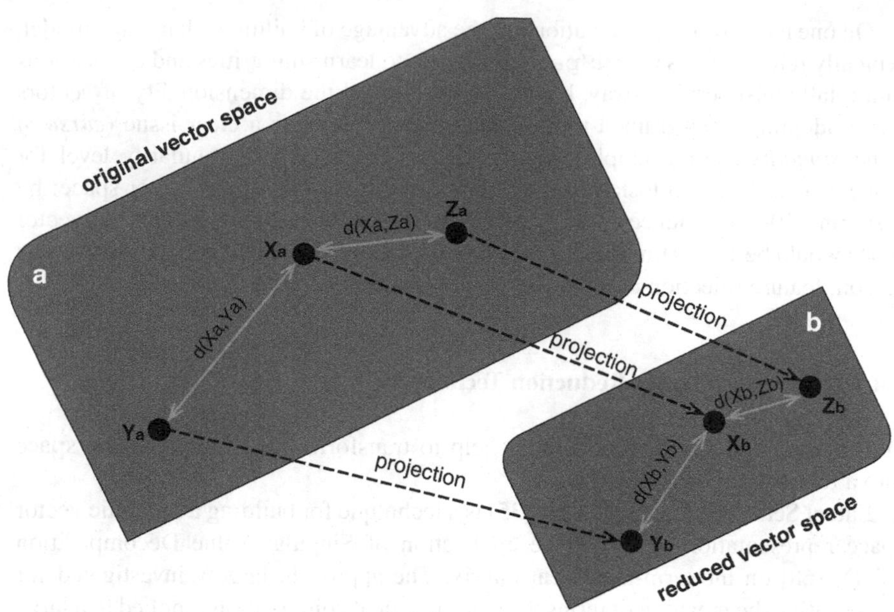

Fig. 4.5 A visual explanation of the Johnson-Lindenstrauss lemma. Z is the nearest point to X in the reduced vector space, as in the original space, even though the *numerical* value of their pairwise similarity is different

in the Hecht-Nielsen's studies about near-orthogonality [55]. These approaches, originally proposed for clustering text documents [69], do not need factorization, and are based on the insight that a high-dimensional vector space can be *randomly* projected into a space of lower dimensionality without compromising distance metrics. By following this approach, a high-dimensional matrix M of size $n \times m$ is transformed into a reduced k-dimensional matrix M^* as follows:

$$M_{n,m} \times R_{m,k} = M^*_{n,k} \tag{4.8}$$

where the row vectors of R are built in a pseudo-random way (more details follow). According to the Johnson and Lindenstrauss' lemma [62], when the random matrix R is built by following specific constraints, distances between points in the reduced vector space are nearly preserved, i.e. remains proportional with respect to those in the original space (see Fig. 4.5), thus it is still possible to perform similarity computations between points in the reduced vector space with a minimum loss of significance, balanced by the gain in efficiency.

This important outcome has been experimentally confirmed in several works [66, 73]. Despite its advantages, the use of RP is still not widespread compared to SVD. In [29, 123], RP is applied to collaborative filtering, while in [105], RP is used to build an item to item similarity matrix leveraging the reduced vector space representation.

RP was used as dimensionality reduction technique for a discriminative model called Random Indexing (RI) [115, 116]. This strategy, based on Kanerva's work on sparse distributed representations [65], is an incremental technique for creating small-scale `WordSpaces` that merges the advantages of discriminative models with the efficiency of dimensionality reduction based on RP. Similarly to LSI, RI represents terms and documents as points in a *semantic* vector space that is built according to the distributional hypothesis. However, differently from it, RI uses RP instead of SVD as technique for dimensionality reduction. Thus, the heavyweight decomposition performed by SVD is here replaced by an incremental (but effective) algorithm as RP, which performs the same process with less computational cost. Thanks to RI it is possible to represent terms (and documents) through a $n \times k$ term-context matrix, which is more compact than the original $n \times m$ term-document matrix, since k is typically set lower than m. One of the strongest points of RI is its flexibility, since the dimension k is a simple parameter thus it can be adapted to the available computational resources, as well as to the requirements of the specific application domain. Basically, the larger the vector space, the higher the precision in representing word similarities, and the higher the computational resources required to represent and update the model.

The k-dimensional representation is obtained by using the following incremental strategy:

1. A k-dimensional randomly generated context vector is assigned to each context. This vector is sparse, high-dimensional and ternary, which means that its elements have values in $\{-1, 0, 1\}$. Values are distributed in a random way, but the number of non-zero elements has to be much smaller. Specifically, a very common choice is to use a Gaussian distribution for the elements of the context vectors. However, much simpler distributions (zero mean distributions with unit variance) can also be used [3];
2. The vector space representation of a *term* is obtained by summing the context vectors of all the contexts which contain the term;
3. The vector space representation of a *document* is obtained by summing the vector space representation of all the terms (created in step 2) which occur in the document.

Step 2 allows to build a `WordSpace`, while step 3 allows to build a `DocSpace`. Both the spaces have the same dimension. In a `WordSpace` it is possible to compute similarities between different terms, while in a `DocSpace` this is possible for documents. The approach is totally incremental: when a new document comes into play, the algorithm randomly generates a new context vector for it (step 1) and updates the `WordSpace`. The technique is scalable because the calculation of the vector space representation of this new document does not need to generate again the whole vector space, but it is simply obtained by summing the context vectors of the terms that occurs in it.

4.4.1.2 Modeling Negation

The above mentioned novel representation inherits a classical issue of VSM, since the information coming from negative evidence (i.e., items user dislikes) is not taken into account. This is an important aspect for recommender systems, since user profiles are built by modeling positive, as well as negative user preferences. Several works rely on an adaptation of the Rocchio algorithm [113] to incrementally refine the user profiles by exploiting positive and negative feedback provided by users. The problems with the Rocchio algorithm is related to the extensive tuning of parameters needed for being effective and to the lack of solid theoretical foundations of the method. Negative relevance feedback is also discussed in [41], in which the idea of representing negation by subtracting an unwanted vector from a query emerged, even if nothing about *how much to subtract* is stated. This is a problem which we try to clarify using the following example, inspired by Widdows [127].

Let us suppose to have a `WordSpace` built on a corpus of documents related to music (in order to leave disambiguation problems out of this discussion). Consider the term vectors of the two words *rock* and *pop*. The query (or profile) (*rock NOT pop*) should allow to represent *rock* only by the aspects of its meaning which are different from, and preferably unrelated to, those of *pop*. If we subtract the whole vector *pop* from *rock*, we might remove features of *rock* which we wanted to keep. Instead, we should subtract exactly the right amount to make the unwanted vector *pop* irrelevant to the desired result. This removal operation is called *vector negation*, which is related to the concept of *orthogonality*, and it is proposed in [127], according to the principles of Quantum Logic. Meanings are unrelated to one another if they have no features in common at all, precisely when their vectors are orthogonal. Hence, we need to make our final query vector (*rock NOT pop*) orthogonal to *pop*. Geometrically, this corresponds to the *orthogonal projection* of the vector *rock* onto the vector *pop*, that is the vector λpop ($\lambda \in \Re$):

$$\lambda = \frac{rock \cdot pop}{pop \cdot pop} \tag{4.9}$$

From this definition, (*rock NOT pop*) is represented as the vector ($rock - \lambda\ pop$), which is orthogonal to the vector *pop*. For simplicity, we do not discuss here about ambiguity problems (e.g. rock could refer also to geology). More details can be found in [127].

4.4.1.3 CBRSs Leveraging Discriminative Models

One of the first attempt to define a CBRS using discriminative models is presented in [120], in which the process of learning user profiles benefits from the infusion of exogenous knowledge coming from Wikipedia. The knowledge contained in Wikipedia is processed using the Semantic Vectors package [128], in order to build a `WordSpace` model in which related words are close to each other in that space.

A more complete approach using discriminative models based on RI and the above mentioned negation operator is described in [92], which presents a novel content-based recommendation framework called enhanced Vector Space Model (eVSM). In eVSM, RI is used to build a user profile in an incremental way, i.e. by summing all the *document vectors* representing documents liked by that user. More complex models were defined by introducing the negation operator to represent in the user profile both positive and negative preferences. To this purpose, instead of a single vector representing a user profile, two vectors were defined, one for positive preferences ($\mathbf{p}_{+u}$) and one for negative ones ($\mathbf{p}_{-u}$).

The same approach was also used to build language-independent user profiles [90], by assuming that in every language each term often co-occurs with the same other terms (expressed in different languages, of course). Hence, representing a content-based user profile in terms of the co-occurrences of its terms, user preferences become inherently independent from the language and this is sufficient to provide the user with cross-language recommendations. Thus, profiles learnt on English movies were used to recommend Italian movies, and vice versa. Results were accurate and comparable to a classical monolingual recommendation setting. This highlights the power of the approach, which is able to tackle a complex multilingual recommendation task without using any complex operations, such as translation or semantic indexing based on WSD [71].

Recently, the eVSM framework has been further evolved to manage contextual information. In [93], contextual eVSM extends eVSM with a context-aware post-filtering algorithm [5]. More specifically, a semantic representation of the context is built and used to influence non-contextual recommendations. The intuition behind the context representation is that there exists a set of terms that are likely more descriptive than others to model items relevant in a certain context. For example, it is likely that restaurant descriptions containing terms such as *candlelight* or *sea view* are more relevant if the user is looking for a restaurant suitable for a romantic dinner. Experiments demonstrated that contextual eVSM is able to outperform non-contextual baselines in most experimental settings, as well as the state of the art algorithm for context-aware collaborative recommendation proposed in [4].

DMs were also adapted to face the sparsity problem of context-aware recommender systems, which need large datasets of contextually tagged ratings, i.e. ratings for items provided in the different contextual situations. In [30], it is described an approach based on the intuition that, when making recommendations in a particular situation, it can be considered as relevant not only the ratings provided by the users in that situation but also to *reuse* ratings provided in similar situations. The similarity among contextual conditions is estimated by identifying the "meaning" of a condition by means of its implicit semantics, that is captured by the usage of the concept. Experiments demonstrated good performance of the proposed approach, which was further improved in [31].

4.5 Summary and Comparison of Approaches

In the previous sections we analyzed top-down and bottom-up semantic approaches for facing well-known problems of CBRSs (i.e., limited content analysis, overspecialization).

In Table 4.1, pros a cons of each approach are summarized with respect to several criteria: transparency of the models, coverage of topics, complexity of NLP techniques required, ease of applying reasoning mechanisms for discovering relationships between items and profiles, support for multilinguality.

In order to capture the semantics of the user information needs, recommender systems based on top-down approaches can exploit different types of exogenous knowledge that allow advanced concept-based content representation: ontological resources, encyclopedic knowledge, and the Linked Open Data cloud. Conversely, recommender systems based on bottom-up semantic approaches rely on methods able to induce the semantics of terms by analyzing their use in large corpora of documents, i.e. they rely on the so-called distributional hypothesis: *words that occur in the same contexts tend to have similar meanings*.

An important difference between the two approaches is related to transparency: the explicit concept-based representation of both items and profiles allows the definition of less ambiguous user profiles and is particularly useful for estimating the semantic similarity between user preferences and item features. Furthermore, the advanced content representation has an impact on the accuracy of recommendations, allows to mitigate the limited content analysis problem, and also helps to provide well-structured explanations of recommendations in terms of matched concepts.

Bottom-up approaches do not allow an explicit representation of concepts, but the meaning of a word is inferred by analyzing its co-occurrence with context features (other words, larger textual units, or documents). Hence, the semantics is implicitly encoded as high-dimensional vectors learned from large corpora of documents. This is the main limitation of these approaches, that do not allow an intelligible explanation of the recommendations.

Another problem is that high-dimensional vectors require novel dimensionality reduction techniques, in order to improve scalability. In [92], we described Random Indexing, a dimensionality reduction technique which avoids the need for factorization, and we showed how effective user profiles can be built in an incremental way by distinguishing between positive and negative user preferences. The novel content-based recommendation framework based on Random Indexing was able to outperform state-of-the-art techniques, and to easily implement language-independent context-aware recommender systems [90]. This is a relevant advantage of bottom-up approaches, which do not require to perform complex NLP tasks such as translation or WSD in order to provide cross-language recommendations.

Furthermore, an important distinction between the two approaches must be considered with respect to the capability of discovering novel relationships among items and profiles, beyond the simple similarity. Indeed, both the approaches give the possibility of inferring new information (e.g. new words or concepts not

Table 4.1 Overview of semantic approaches for CBRSs

Approach	Description	References	Pros	Cons
Top-down	Use of external knowledge to improve the representation of items and user profiles	Ontological resources [16, 21–27, 36, 37, 71, 75, 82, 121]	– High transparency – Standard NLP techniques required, WSD at most – Easily allow reasoning, due to hierarchical organization of concepts	– Limited coverage of named entities, events, etc. – No multilinguality support, unless specific resources are adopted
		Encyclopedic knowledge [91, 96, 97, 105]	– High transparency – Wide coverage of topics – Multilinguality typically supported – Allows reasoning	– More NLP effort needed than using specific ontologies due to unstructured information
		Linked Open Data cloud and entity linking [1, 2, 38, 39, 44, 56, 64, 67, 94, 95, 103, 104, 106]	– Very high transparency – Wide coverage of topics – Allows deeper reasoning especially for cross-domain recommendation	– Strong NLP effort required for linking data to the Linked Open Data cloud
Bottom-up	Use of implicit semantic representation of items and user profiles. The meaning of a term is inferred by analyzing its usage	Latent semantic indexing [7, 32, 47, 78, 79, 122]	– Allows reasoning by capturing latent associations between terms and documents – Multilinguality typically supported	– Low transparency – A lot of data about terms usage required for building a wide language model – Standard NLP effort, but poor scalability due to the need for dimensionality reduction
		Random indexing [29–31, 90, 92, 93, 105, 120, 123]	– Standard NLP effort and good scalability because factorization is notrequired – Allows reasoning – Support for multilinguality based on co-occurrence of terms	– Low transparency – A lot of data about terms usage required for building a wide language model

explicitly included in the item descriptions), which could be exploited to discover those associations, but the reasoning process could be performed in a different way, depending on the type of knowledge it is based on. For example, ontologies represent the domain knowledge in a more formal way, due to their structured representation, and easily allow reasoning, even at an abstract level, by navigating the concept hierarchy. Obviously, reasoning is influenced by the usually limited coverage of topics, because of the cost of the human-based tasks of building, maintaining and populating ontologies. Hence, the research is moving towards the exploitation of freely available knowledge sources, such as Wikipedia. Encyclopedic knowledge covers a wider range of topics compared to ontologies, is generally multilingual, but requires more NLP effort to analyze unstructured information in order to select or even *generate* semantic features to effectively represent items and user profiles. This capability of generating new semantic features, besides those that can be found in item descriptions, can be exploited to discover unexpected and non-trivial relationships between items and between items and user profiles. However, the NLP effort for performing this task is higher compared to using ontologies, due to the absence of an explicit organization of concepts. Similarly, the lack of a structured representation of concepts in bottom-up approaches does not make the implementation of reasoning capabilities as easy as for ontology-based approaches. Anyway, the fact that discriminative models are able to catch *latent* associations between terms can help to find not-trivial correlations among items [120]. On the other side, the graph-based organization of the Linked Open Data cloud facilitates the adoption of even sophisticated reasoning mechanisms, as the one described in [103], that allow deeper reasoning connecting data in different domains and promote cross-domain recommendations. A significant effort here is due to need of linking data to the Linked Open Data cloud.

4.6 Conclusions and Future Challenges

This chapter was structured around two different approaches for introducing semantics in CBRSs: top-down and bottom-up. Both approaches have advantages and drawbacks, and pose new challenges in the development of CBRSs. Many other recommendation scenarios may benefit from semantic-based approaches. In the context of sentiment analysis, concept-based approaches proved to be superior to purely syntactical techniques [20], hence recommender systems which rely on the analysis of opinions written in natural language for extracting user preferences and affective states, might effectively adopt all the techniques presented in this chapter to provide better suggestions.

In conclusion, research on content-based recommender systems produced a variety of solid methods, some of which having their roots in NLP foundations, but still poses some interesting challenges:

- Definition of recommendation methods able to reason on the graph structure of the Linked Open Data cloud to discover latent connections among items and user profiles, as suggested in [39]. Those emerging relations could be exploited for cross-domain recommendations or diversification of suggestions. As an example, the Linked Open Data-enabled Recommender Systems Challenge of the 11th European Semantic Web Conference has shown how Linked Open Data and semantic technologies can boost the creation of a new breed of knowledge-enabled and content-based recommender systems. In particular, one of the tasks of the challenge was devoted to the design of Linked Open Data-enabled recommender systems whose effectiveness was evaluated by considering a combination of both accuracy of the recommendation list and the diversity of items belonging to it. Diversity is a very popular topic in content-based recommender systems, which usually suffer from overspecialization;
- Definition of content-based methods for mining microblogging data and deep analysis of text reviews. In particular, aspect-based opinion mining and sentiment analysis techniques can support the design of recommendation methods that take into account the evaluation of aspects of items expressed in text reviews. As an example, "Aspect Based Sentiment Analysis" was one of the tasks of SemEval 2014, and was devoted to evaluate methods for automated detection of both aspects and the sentiment expressed towards each aspect in text reviews of laptops and restaurants. These methods could be exploited for implicit rating of aspects and can support the development of multi-criteria recommendation techniques;
- Definition of personality-based recommendation methods based on automated recognition of personality. Content-based methods can be exploited to detect personality markers in language through the extraction of linguistic features associated with personality traits [76]. Automated modeling of personality from text can ease the development of systems that incorporate personality aspects into recommendation methods to enhance both recommendation quality and user experience [60]. The design of personality-based and emotion-aware personalized services is an emerging research topic, as shown also by the recent EMPIRE workshops hold in conjunction with the Conference on User Modelling, Adaptation and Personalization.

We hope that this chapter may stimulate the research community to adopt and effectively integrate the discussed techniques in several recommendation scenarios in order to foster future innovations in the area of CBRSs.

Acknowledgements The authors would like to express their deep gratitude to Professor Michael J. Pazzani and Dr. Daniel Billsus for their seminal work on machine learning for user modeling and content-based recommendation systems, which inspired many ideas developed in this chapter.

References

1. Abel, F., Gao, Q., Houben, G.J., Tao, K.: Analyzing User Modeling on Twitter for Personalized News Recommendations. In: J.A. Konstan, R. Conejo, J. Marzo, N. Oliver (eds.) Proc. of the 19th International Conference on User Modeling, Adaption and Personalization, *Lecture Notes in Computer Science*, vol. 6787, pp. 1–12. Springer (2011)
2. Abel, F., Gao, Q., Houben, G.J., Tao, K.: Semantic Enrichment of Twitter Posts for User Profile Construction on the Social Web. In: G. Antoniou, M. Grobelnik, E.P.B. Simperl, B. Parsia, D. Plexousakis, P.D. Leenheer, J.Z. Pan (eds.) Proc. of the 8th Extended Semantic Web Conference, ESWC 2011, Part II, *Lecture Notes in Computer Science*, vol. 6644, pp. 375–389. Springer (2011)
3. Achlioptas, D.: Database-friendly random projections. In: P. Buneman (ed.) PODS. ACM (2001)
4. Adomavicius, G., Sankaranarayanan, R., Sen, S., Tuzhilin, A.: Incorporating contextual information in recommender systems using a multidimensional approach. ACM Trans. Inf. Syst. **23**(1), 103–145 (2005). DOI 10.1145/1055709.1055714. URL http://doi.acm.org/10.1145/1055709.1055714
5. Adomavicius, G., Tuzhilin, A.: Context-Aware Recommender Systems. In: F. Ricci, L. Rokach, B. Shapira, P.B. Kantor (eds.) Recommender Systems Handbook, pp. 217–253. Springer (2011)
6. Baeza-Yates, R., Ribeiro-Neto, B.: Modern Information Retrieval. Addison-Wesley (1999)
7. Bambini, R., Cremonesi, P., Turrin, R.: A Recommender System for an IPTV Service Provider: a Real Large-Scale Production Environment. In: F. Ricci, L. Rokach, B. Shapira, P.B. Kantor (eds.) Recommender Systems Handbook, pp. 299–331. Springer (2011)
8. Banerjee, S., Ramanathan, K., Gupta, A.: Clustering Short Texts Using Wikipedia. In: Proc. of the 30th Annual International ACM SIGIR Conference on Research and Development in Information Retrieval, SIGIR '07, pp. 787–788. ACM, New York, NY, USA (2007). DOI 10.1145/1277741.1277909. URL http://doi.acm.org/10.1145/1277741.1277909
9. Bentivogli, L., Pianta, E., Girardi, C.: MultiWordNet: Developing an Aligned Multilingual Database. In: First International Conference on Global WordNet, Mysore, India (2002)
10. Berners-Lee, T., Hendler, J., Lassila, O.: The Semantic Web. Scientific American **284**(5), 28–37 (2001)
11. Berry, M.W.: Large-scale Sparse Singular Value Computations. International Journal of Supercomputer Applications **6**(1), 13–49 (1992)
12. Billsus, D., Pazzani, M.: Learning Probabilistic User Models. In: Proc. of the Workshop on Machine Learning for User Modeling. Chia Laguna, IT (1997). URL citeseer.nj.nec.com/billsus96learning.html
13. Bizer, C.: The Emerging Web of Linked Data. IEEE Intelligent Systems **24**(5), 87–92 (2009)
14. Bizer, C., Heath, T., Berners-Lee, T.: Linked Data - The Story So Far. Int. J. Semantic Web Inf. Syst. **5**(3), 1–22 (2009)
15. Bizer, C., Lehmann, J., Kobilarov, G., Auer, S., Becker, C., Cyganiak, R., Hellmann, S.: DBpedia - A crystallization point for the Web of Data. Web Semant. **7**(3), 154–165 (2009). DOI 10.1016/j.websem.2009.07.002. URL http://dx.doi.org/10.1016/j.websem.2009.07.002
16. Blanco-Fernandez, Y., Pazos-Arias, J.J., Gil-Solla, A., Ramos-Cabrer, M., Lopez-Nores, M.: Providing Entertainment by Content-based Filtering and Semantic Reasoning in Intelligent Recommender Systems. IEEE Transactions on Consumer Electronics **54**(2), 727–735 (2008)
17. Bollacker, K.D., Evans, C., Paritosh, P., Sturge, T., Taylor, J.: Freebase: a Collaboratively Created Graph Database for Structuring Human Knowledge. In: J.T.L. Wang (ed.) Proc. of the ACM SIGMOD International Conference on Management of Data, SIGMOD 2008, pp. 1247–1250. ACM (2008)
18. Buchanan, B.G., Feigenbaum, E.: Forward. In: R. Davis, D. Lenat (eds.) Knowledge-Based Systems in Artificial Intelligence. McGraw-Hill (1982)

19. Budanitsky, A., Hirst, G.: Evaluating WordNet-based Measures of Lexical Semantic Relatedness. Computational Linguistics **32**(1), 13–47 (2006)
20. Cambria, E., Schuller, B., Liu, B., Wang, H., Havasi, C.: Knowledge-Based Approaches to Concept-Level Sentiment Analysis. IEEE Intelligent Systems **28**(2), 12–14 (2013)
21. Cantador, I., Bellogín, A., Castells, P.: A Multilayer Ontology-based Hybrid Recommendation Model. AI Communications **21**(2), 203–210 (2008)
22. Cantador, I., Bellogín, A., Castells, P.: News@hand: A Semantic Web Approach to Recommending News. In: W. Nejdl, J. Kay, P. Pu, E. Herder (eds.) Adaptive Hypermedia and Adaptive Web-Based Systems, *Lecture Notes in Computer Science*, vol. 5149, pp. 279–283. Springer (2008)
23. Cantador, I., Bellogín, A., Castells, P.: Ontology-based Personalised and Context-aware Recommendations of News Items. In: Proc. of the 2008 IEEE/WIC/ACM International Conference on Web Intelligence and Intelligent Agent Technology-Volume 01, pp. 562–565. IEEE Computer Society (2008)
24. Cantador, I., Szomszor, M., Alani, H., Fernández, M., Castells, P.: Enriching Ontological User Profiles with Tagging History for Multi-domain Recommendations. In: Proc. of the 1st International Workshop on Collective Semantics: Collective Intelligence & the Semantic Web (2008)
25. Capelle, M., Hogenboom, F., Hogenboom, A., Frasincar, F.: Semantic News Recommendation Using Wordnet and Bing Similarities. In: S.Y. Shin, J.C. Maldonado (eds.) Proc. of the 28th Annual ACM Symposium on Applied Computing, SAC '13, pp. 296–302. ACM (2013)
26. Cena, F., Likavec, S., Osborne, F.: Anisotropic Propagation of User Interests in Ontology-based User Models. Inf. Sci. **250**, 40–60 (2013)
27. Chen, X., Li, L., Xu, G., Yang, Z., Kitsuregawa, M.: Recommending Related Microblogs: A Comparison Between Topic and WordNet based Approaches. In: J. Hoffmann, B. Selman (eds.) Proc. of the Twenty-Sixth AAAI Conference on Artificial Intelligence. AAAI Press (2012)
28. Chui, M., Manyika, J., Kuiken, S.V.: What executives should know about open data. McKinsey Quarterly, January 2014 (2014)
29. Ciesielczyk, M., Szwabe, A., Prus-Zajaczkowski, B.: Interactive Collaborative Filtering with RI-based Approximation of SVD. In: Proc. of the 3rd International Conference on Computational Intelligence and Industrial Application (PACIIA), pp. 243–246. IEEE Press (2010)
30. Codina, V., Ricci, F., Ceccaroni, L.: Exploiting the Semantic Similarity of Contextual Situations for Pre-filtering Recommendation. In: S. Carberry, S. Weibelzahl, A. Micarelli, G. Semeraro (eds.) Proc. of the 21st International Conference on User Modeling, Adaptation, and Personalization, UMAP 2013, *Lecture Notes in Computer Science*, vol. 7899, pp. 165–177. Springer (2013)
31. Codina, V., Ricci, F., Ceccaroni, L.: Local Context Modeling with Semantic Pre-filtering. In: Q. Yang, I. King, Q. Li, P. Pu, G. Karypis (eds.) Seventh ACM Conference on Recommender Systems, RecSys '13, pp. 363–366. ACM (2013)
32. Cremonesi, P., Turrin, R., Airoldi, F.: Hybrid Algorithms for Recommending New Items. In: Proc. of the 2nd International Workshop on Information Heterogeneity and Fusion in Recommender Systems, pp. 33–40. ACM (2011)
33. Csomai, A., Mihalcea, R.: Linking Documents to Encyclopedic Knowledge. IEEE Intelligent Systems **23**(5), 34–41 (2008). DOI 10.1109/MIS.2008.86. URL http://dx.doi.org/10.1109/MIS.2008.86
34. de Gemmis, M., Di Noia, T., Lops, P., T.Lukasiewicz, Semeraro, G. (eds.): Proc. of the International Workshop on Semantic Technologies meet Recommender Systems & Big Data, Boston, USA, November 11, 2012, *CEUR Workshop Proceedings*, vol. 919. CEUR-WS.org (2012)
35. Deerwester, S., Dumais, S.T., Furnas, G.W., Landauer, T.K., Harshman, R.: Indexing by Latent Semantic Analysis. Journal of the American Society for Information Science **41**(6), 391–407 (1990)

36. Degemmis, M., Lops, P., Semeraro, G.: A Content-collaborative Recommender that Exploits WordNet-based User Profiles for Neighborhood Formation. User Modeling and User-Adapted Interaction: The Journal of Personalization Research (UMUAI) **17**(3), 217–255 (2007). Springer Science + Business Media B.V.
37. Degemmis, M., Lops, P., Semeraro, G., Basile, P.: Integrating Tags in a Semantic Content-based Recommender. In: P. Pu, D.G. Bridge, B. Mobasher, F. Ricci (eds.) Proc. of the 2008 ACM Conference on Recommender Systems, RecSys 2008, pp. 163–170. ACM (2008)
38. Di Noia, T., Mirizzi, R., Ostuni, V.C., Romito, D.: Exploiting the Web of Data in Model-based Recommender Systems. In: P. Cunningham, N.J. Hurley, I. Guy, S.S. Anand (eds.) Proc. of the Sixth ACM Conference on Recommender Systems, RecSys '12, pp. 253–256. ACM (2012)
39. Di Noia, T., Mirizzi, R., Ostuni, V.C., Romito, D., Zanker, M.: Linked Open Data to Support Content-based Recommender Systems. In: V. Presutti, H.S. Pinto (eds.) I-SEMANTICS 2012 - 8th International Conference on Semantic Systems, pp. 1–8. ACM (2012)
40. Domingos, P., Pazzani, M.J.: On the Optimality of the Simple Bayesian Classifier under Zero-One Loss. Machine Learning **29**(2–3), 103–130 (1997)
41. Dunlop, M.D.: The Effect of Accessing Nonmatching Documents on Relevance Feedback. ACM Trans. Inf. Syst. **15**, 137–153 (1997)
42. Egozi, O., Gabrilovich, E., Markovitch, S.: Concept-based Feature Generation and Selection for Information Retrieval. In: Proc. of the 23rd National Conference on Artificial Intelligence - Volume 2, AAAI'08, pp. 1132–1137. AAAI Press (2008). URL http://dl.acm.org/citation.cfm?id=1620163.1620248
43. Egozi, O., Markovitch, S., Gabrilovich, E.: Concept-Based Information Retrieval using Explicit Semantic Analysis. ACM Transactions on Information Systems **29**(2), 8:1–8:34 (2011).
44. Fernández-Tobías, I., Kaminskas, M., Cantador, I., Ricci, F.: A Generic Semantic-based Framework for Cross-domain Recommendation. In: I. Cantador, P. Brusilovsky, T. Kuflik (eds.) HetRec '11 Proc. of the 2nd International Workshop on Information Heterogeneity and Fusion in Recommender Systems, pp. 25–32. ACM New York (2011)
45. Fernando, S., Hall, M., Agirre, E., Soroa, A., Clough, P., Stevenson, M.: Comparing Taxonomies for Organising Collections of Documents. In: M. Kay, C. Boitet (eds.) Proc. of the 24th International Conference on Computational Linguistics, COLING 2012, pp. 879–894. Indian Institute of Technology Bombay (2012). URL http://www.aclweb.org/anthology/C12-1054
46. Ferragina, P., Scaiella, U.: Fast and Accurate Annotation of Short Texts with Wikipedia Pages. IEEE Software **29**(1), 70–75 (2012)
47. Foltz, P.W., Dumais, S.T.: Personalized Information Delivery: an Analysis of Information Filtering Methods. Communications of the ACM **35**(12), 51–60 (1992)
48. Gabrilovich, E., Markovitch, S.: Computing Semantic Relatedness Using Wikipedia-based Explicit Semantic Analysis. In: M.M. Veloso (ed.) Proc. of the 20th International Joint Conference on Artificial Intelligence, pp. 1606–1611 (2007)
49. Gabrilovich, E., Markovitch, S.: Wikipedia-based Semantic Interpretation for Natural Language Processing. Journal of Artificial Intelligence Research (JAIR) **34**, 443–498 (2009)
50. Giles, J.: Internet Encyclopaedias Go Head to Head. Nature **438**(7070), 900–901 (2005). URL http://dx.doi.org/10.1038/438900a
51. Goldberg, D., Nichols, D., Oki, B., Terry, D.: Using Collaborative Filtering to Weave an Information Tapestry. Communications of the ACM **35**(12), 61–70 (1992). URL http://www.xerox.com/PARC/dlbx/tapestry-papers/TN44.ps. Special Issue on Information Filtering
52. Halevy, A.Y., Norvig, P., Pereira, F.: The Unreasonable Effectiveness of Data. IEEE Intelligent Systems **24**(2), 8–12 (2009)
53. Harris, Z.S.: Mathematical Structures of Language. Interscience, New York, (1968)
54. Hassanzadeh, O., Consens, M.P.: Linked Movie Data Base. In: C.Bizer, T. Heath, T. Berners-Lee, K. Idehen (eds.) Proc. of the WWW2009 Workshop on Linked Data on the Web, LDOW 2009, *CEUR Workshop Proceedings*, vol. 538. CEUR-WS.org (2009)

55. Hecht-Nielsen, R.: Context Vectors: General Purpose Approximate Meaning Representations Self-organized from Raw Data. Computational Intelligence: Imitating Life, IEEE Press pp. 43–56 (1994)
56. Heitmann, B., Hayes, C.: Using Linked Data to Build Open, Collaborative Recommender Systems. In: AAAI Spring Symposium: Linked Data Meets Artificial Intelligence, pp. 76–81. AAAI (2010)
57. Herlocker, L., Konstan, J.A., Terveen, L.G., Riedl, J.T.: Evaluating Collaborative Filtering Recommender Systems. ACM Transactions on Information Systems **22**(1), 5–53 (2004)
58. Holte, R.C., Yan, J.N.Y.: Inferring What a User Is Not Interested in. In: G.I. McCalla (ed.) Advances in Artificial Intelligence, *Lecture Notes in Computer Science*, vol. 1081, pp. 159–171 (1996)
59. Hu, J., Fang, L., Cao, Y., Zeng, H., Li, H., Yang, Q., Chen, Z.: Enhancing Text Clustering by Leveraging Wikipedia Semantics. In: S. Myaeng, D.W. Oard, F. Sebastiani, T. Chua, M. Leong (eds.) Proc. of the 31st Annual International ACM SIGIR Conference on Research and Development in Information Retrieval, SIGIR '08, pp. 179–186. ACM (2008)
60. Hu, R., Pu, P.: A study on user perception of personality-based recommender systems. In: User Modeling, Adaptation, and Personalization, 18th International Conference, UMAP 2010, Big Island, HI, USA, June 20–24, 2010. Proceedings, pp. 291–302 (2010).
61. Jannach, D., Zanker, M., Felfernig, A., Friedrich, G.: Recommender systems: An introduction. Cambridge University Press (2010)
62. Johnson, W., Lindenstrauss, J.: Extensions of Lipschitz Maps into a Hilbert Space. Contemporary Mathematics (1984)
63. Jones, D., Bench-Capon, T., Visser, P.: Methodologies for Ontology Development (1998)
64. Kaminskas, M., Fernández-Tobías, I., Ricci, F., Cantador, I.: Knowledge-based Music Retrieval for Places of Interest. In: C.C.S. Liem, M. Müller, S.K. Tjoa, G. Tzanetakis (eds.) Proc. of the 2nd International ACM workshop on Music information retrieval with user-centered and multimodal strategies, MIRUM '12, pp. 19–24 (2012)
65. Kanerva, P.: Hyperdimensional Computing: An Introduction to Computing in Distributed Representation with High-Dimensional Random Vectors. Cognitive Computation **1**(2), 139–159 (2009)
66. Kaski, S.: Dimensionality Reduction by Random Mapping: Fast Similarity Computation for Clustering. In: Proc. of the International Joint Conference on Neural Networks, vol. 1, pp. 413–418. IEEE (1998)
67. Khrouf, H., Troncy, R.: Hybrid Event Recommendation using Linked Data and User Diversity. In: Q. Yang, I. King, Q. Li, P. Pu, G. Karypis (eds.) Seventh ACM Conference on Recommender Systems, RecSys '13, pp. 185–192. ACM (2013)
68. Klema, V., Laub, A.: The Singular Value Decomposition: its Computation and Some Applications. IEEE Transactions on Automatic Control **25**(2), 164–176 (1980)
69. Kohonen, T., Kaski, S., Lagus, K., Salojarvi, J., Honkela, J., Paatero, V., Saarela, A.: Self Organization of a Massive Document Collection. IEEE Transactions on Neural Networks **11**(3), 574–585 (2000)
70. Lewis, D.D., Ringuette, M.: A Comparison of Two Learning Algorithms for Text Categorization. In: Proc. of the Annual Symposium on Document Analysis and Information Retrieval, pp. 81–93. Las Vegas, US (1994)
71. Lops, P., Musto, C., Narducci, F., de Gemmis, M., Basile, P., Semeraro, G.: MARS: a MultilAnguage Recommender System. In: P. Brusilovsky, I. Cantador, Y. Koren, T. Kuflik, M. Weimer (eds.) HetRec '10 Proc. of the 1st International Workshop on Information Heterogeneity and Fusion in Recommender Systems, pp. 24–31. ACM New York (2010)
72. Lowe, W.: Towards a Theory of Semantic Space. In: Proc. of the Twenty-Third Annual Conference of the Cognitive Science Society, pp. 576–581. Lawrence Erlbaum Associates (2001)
73. Magen, A.: Dimensionality Reductions that Preserve Volumes and Distance to Affine Spaces, and their Algorithmic Applications. In: Randomization and approximation techniques in computer science, pp. 239–253. Springer (2002)

74. Magnini, B., Strapparava, C.: Experiments in Word Domain Disambiguation for Parallel Texts. In: Proc. of SIGLEX Workshop on Word Senses and Multi-linguality, Hong-Kong, October 2000. ACL (2000)
75. Magnini, B., Strapparava, C.: Improving User Modelling with Content-based Techniques. In: M. Bauer, P.J. Gmytrasiewicz, J. Vassileva (eds.) Proc. of the 8th International Conference of User Modeling, *Lecture Notes in Computer Science*, vol. 2109, pp. 74–83. Springer (2001)
76. Mairesse, F., Walker, M.A., Mehl, M.R., Moore, R.K.: Using linguistic cues for the automatic recognition of personality in conversation and text. J. Artif. Intell. Res. (JAIR) **30**, 457–500 (2007). DOI 10.1613/jair.2349. URL http://dx.doi.org/10.1613/jair.2349
77. McCallum, A., Nigam, K.: A Comparison of Event Models for Naïve Bayes Text Classification. In: Proc. of the AAAI/ICML-98 Workshop on Learning for Text Categorization, pp. 41–48. AAAI Press (1998)
78. McCarey, F., Cinnéide, M., Kushmerick, N.: Recommending Library Methods: An Evaluation of the Vector Space Model (VSM) and Latent Semantic Indexing (LSI). In: M. Morisio (ed.) Proc. of the 9th International Conference on Software Reuse, ICSR 2006, *Lecture Notes in Computer Science*, vol. 4039, pp. 217–230. Springer (2006)
79. McMillan, C., Poshyvanyk, D., Grechanik, M.: Recommending Source Code Examples via API Call Usages and Documentation. In: Proc. of the 2nd International Workshop on Recommendation Systems for Software Engineering, pp. 21–25. ACM (2010)
80. Mendes, P.N., Jakob, M., García-Silva, A., Bizer, C.: DBpedia Spotlight: Shedding Light on the Web of Documents. In: C. Ghidini, A.N. Ngomo, S.N. Lindstaedt, T. Pellegrini (eds.) Proceedings the 7th International Conference on Semantic Systems, I-SEMANTICS 2011, pp. 1–8. ACM (2011)
81. Middleton, S.E., De Roure, D., Shadbolt, N.R.: Ontology-based Recommender Systems. In: S. Staab, R. Studer (eds.) Handbook on ontologies, pp. 477–498. Springer (2004)
82. Middleton, S.E., Shadbolt, N.R., De Roure, D.C.: Ontological User Profiling in Recommender Systems. ACM Transactions on Information Systems **22**(1), 54–88 (2004)
83. Mikolov, T., Le, Q.V., Sutskever, I.: Exploiting Similarities among Languages for Machine Translation. CoRR **abs/1309.4168** (2013)
84. Miller, G.: WordNet: An On-Line Lexical Database. International Journal of Lexicography **3**(4) (1990). (Special Issue)
85. Milne, D., Witten, I.H.: Learning to Link with Wikipedia. In: J.G. Shanahan, S. Amer-Yahia, I. Manolescu, Y. Zhang, D.A. Evans, A. Kolcz, K. Choi, A. Chowdhury (eds.) Proc. of the 17th ACM Conference on Information and Knowledge Management, CIKM 2008, pp. 509–518. ACM (2008)
86. Mitchell, T.: Machine Learning. McGraw-Hill, New York (1997)
87. Mohammad, S., Hirst, G.: Distributional Measures of Semantic Distance: A Survey. CoRR **abs/1203.1858** (2012)
88. Moro, A., Raganato, A., Navigli, R.: Entity Linking meets Word Sense Disambiguation: a Unified Approach. Transactions of the Association for Computational Linguistics **2**, 231–244 (2014)
89. Musto, C., Basile, P., Lops, P., de Gemmis, M., Semeraro, G.: Linked Open Data-enabled Strategies for Top-N Recommendations. In: T. Bogers, M. Koolen, I. Cantador (eds.) Proc. of the 1st Workshop on New Trends in Content-based Recommender Systems, ACM RecSys 2014, *CEUR Workshop Proceedings*, vol. 1245, pp. 49–56. CEUR-WS.org (2014)
90. Musto, C., Narducci, F., Basile, P., Lops, P., de Gemmis, M., Semeraro, G.: Cross-Language Information Filtering: Word Sense Disambiguation vs. Distributional Models. In: R. Pirrone, F. Sorbello (eds.) AI*IA, *Lecture Notes in Computer Science*, vol. 6934, pp. 250–261. Springer (2011)
91. Musto, C., Narducci, F., Lops, P., Semeraro, G., de Gemmis, M., Barbieri, M., Korst, J.H.M., Pronk, V., Clout, R.: Enhanced Semantic TV-Show Representation for Personalized Electronic Program Guides. In: Judith.Masthoff, B. Mobasher, M.C. Desmarais, R. Nkambou (eds.) Proc. of the 20th International Conference on User Modeling, Adaptation, and Personalization, UMAP 2012, *Lecture Notes in Computer Science*, vol. 7379, pp. 188–199. Springer (2012)

92. Musto, C., Semeraro, G., Lops, P., de Gemmis, M.: Random Indexing and Negative User Preferences for Enhancing Content-Based Recommender Systems. In: C. Huemer, T. Setzer (eds.) Proc. of the 12th International Conference on Electronic Commerce and Web Technologies, EC-Web 2011, *Lecture Notes in Business Information Processing*, vol. 85, pp. 270–281. Springer (2011)
93. Musto, C., Semeraro, G., Lops, P., de Gemmis, M.: Contextual eVSM: a Content-Based Context-Aware Recommendation Framework Based on Distributional Semantics. In: C. Huemer, P. Lops (eds.) Proc. of the 14th International Conference on E-Commerce and Web Technologies, EC-Web 2013, *Lecture Notes in Business Information Processing*, vol. 152, pp. 125–136. Springer (2013)
94. Musto, C., Semeraro, G., Lops, P., de Gemmis, M.: Combining Distributional Semantics and Entity Linking for Context-Aware Content-Based Recommendation. In: Proc. of the 22nd International Conference on User Modeling, Adaptation, and Personalization, UMAP 2014, *Lecture Notes in Computer Science*, vol. 8538, pp. 381–392. Springer (2014)
95. Musto, C., Semeraro, G., Lops, P., de Gemmis, M., Narducci, F.: Leveraging Social Media Sources to Generate Personalized Music Playlists. In: C. Huemer, P. Lops (eds.) Proc. of the 13th International Conference on E-Commerce and Web Technologies, EC-Web 2012, *Lecture Notes in Business Information Processing*, vol. 123, pp. 112–123. Springer (2012)
96. Narducci, F., Musto, C., Semeraro, G., Lops, P., de Gemmis, M.: Exploiting Big Data for Enhanced Representations in Content-Based Recommender Systems. In: C. Huemer, P. Lops (eds.) Proc. of the 14th International Conference on E-Commerce and Web Technologies, EC-Web 2013, *Lecture Notes in Business Information Processing*, vol. 152, pp. 182–193. Springer (2013)
97. Narducci, F., Musto, C., Semeraro, G., Lops, P., de Gemmis, M.: Leveraging Encyclopedic Knowledge for Transparent and Serendipitous User Profiles. In: S. Carberry, S. Weibelzahl, A. Micarelli, G. Semeraro (eds.) Proc. of the 21st International Conference on User Modeling, Adaptation, and Personalization, UMAP 2013, *Lecture Notes in Computer Science*, vol. 7899, pp. 350–352. Springer (2013)
98. Narducci, F., Palmonari, M., Semeraro, G.: Cross-Language Semantic Retrieval and Linking of e-Gov Services. In: H. Alani, L. Kagal, A. Fokoue, P. Groth, C. Biemann, J. Parreira, L. Aroyo, N. Noy, C. Welty, K. Janowicz (eds.) The Semantic Web - ISWC 2013, *Lecture Notes in Computer Science*, vol. 8219, pp. 130–145. Springer Berlin Heidelberg (2013).
99. Navigli, R., Jurgens, D., Vannella, D.: SemEval-2013 Task 12: Multilingual Word Sense Disambiguation. In: Proc. of the 7th International Workshop on Semantic Evaluation (SemEval 2013), in conjunction with the 2nd Joint Conference on Lexical and Computational Semantics (*SEM 2013), pp. 222–231. Atlanta, USA (2013)
100. Navigli, R., Ponzetto, S.P.: BabelNet: The automatic Construction, Evaluation and Application of a Wide-coverage Multilingual Semantic Network. Artif. Intell. **193**, 217–250 (2012)
101. Navigli, R., Ponzetto, S.P.: BabelRelate! A Joint Multilingual Approach to Computing Semantic Relatedness. In: J. Hoffmann, B. Selman (eds.) Proc. of the Twenty-Sixth AAAI Conference on Artificial Intelligence, AAAI-12. AAAI Press (2012)
102. Navigli, R., Ponzetto, S.P.: Joining Forces Pays Off: Multilingual Joint Word Sense Disambiguation. In: Proc. of the 2012 Joint Conference on Empirical Methods in Natural Language Processing and Computational Natural Language Learning, pp. 1399–1410. Jeju, Korea (2012)
103. Ostuni, V.C., Di, T., Sciascio, E.D., Mirizzi, R.: Top-N Recommendations from Implicit Feedback Leveraging Linked Open Data. In: Q. Yang, I. King, Q. Li, P. Pu, G. Karypis (eds.) Seventh ACM Conference on Recommender Systems, RecSys '13, pp. 85–92. ACM (2013)
104. Ostuni, V.C., Di Noia, T., Mirizzi, R., Romito, D., Sciascio, E.D.: Cinemappy: a Context-aware Mobile App for Movie Recommendations boosted by DBpedia. In: M. de Gemmis, T. Di Noia, P. Lops, T. Lukasiewicz, G. Semeraro (eds.) Proc. of the International Workshop on Semantic Technologies meet Recommender Systems & Big Data, ACM RecSys, *CEUR Workshop Proceedings*, vol. 919, pp. 37–48. CEUR-WS.org (2012)

105. Pappas, N., Popescu-Belis, A.: Combining Content with User Preferences for Non-Fiction Multimedia Recommendation: A Study on TED Lectures. Multimedia Tools and Applications (2014)
106. Passant, A.: dbrec - Music Recommendations Using DBpedia. In: P.F. Patel-Schneider, Y. Pan, P. Hitzler, P. Mika, L. Zhang, J.Z. Pan, I. Horrocks, B. Glimm (eds.) The Semantic Web - ISWC 2010 - 9th International Semantic Web Conference, Revised Selected Papers, Part II, *Lecture Notes in Computer Science*, vol. 6497, pp. 209–224. Springer (2010)
107. Passant, A.: Measuring Semantic Distance on Linking Data and Using it for Resources Recommendations. In: AAAI Spring Symposium: Linked Data Meets Artificial Intelligence, pp. 93–98. AAAI (2010)
108. Pazzani, M.J., Billsus, D.: Content-Based Recommendation Systems. In: P. Brusilovsky, A. Kobsa, W. Nejdl (eds.) The Adaptive Web, *Lecture Notes in Computer Science*, vol. 4321, pp. 325–341 (2007). ISBN 978-3-540-72078-2
109. Potthast, M., Stein, B., Anderka, M.: A Wikipedia-based Multilingual Retrieval Model. In: C. Macdonald, I. Ounis, V. Plachouras, I. Ruthven, R.W. White (eds.) Proc. of the 30th European conference on Advances in information retrieval, ECIR 2008, *Lecture Notes in Computer Science*, vol. 4956, pp. 522–530. Springer (2008)
110. Raimond, Y., Sandler, M.B.: A Web of Musical Information. In: J.P. Bello, E. Chew, D. Turnbull (eds.) International Conference on Music Information Retrieval, pp. 263–268 (2008)
111. Rich, E.: User Modeling via Stereotypes. Cognitive Science **3**, 329–354 (1979)
112. Rizzo, G., Troncy, R.: NERD: a Framework for Unifying Named Entity Recognition and Disambiguation Extraction Tools. In: W. Daelemans, M. Lapata, L. Màrquez (eds.) Proc. of the 13th Conference of the European Chapter of the Association for Computational Linguistics, pp. 73–76. Association for Computational Linguistics (2012)
113. Rocchio, J.: Relevance Feedback Information Retrieval. In: G. Salton (ed.) The SMART retrieval system - experiments in automated document processing, pp. 313–323. Prentice-Hall, Englewood Cliffs, NJ (1971)
114. Rubenstein, H., Goodenough, J.B.: Contextual Correlates of Synonymy. Commun. ACM **8**(10), 627–633 (1965).
115. Sahlgren, M.: An Introduction to Random Indexing. In: Proc. of the Methods and Applications of Semantic Indexing Workshop at the 7th International Conference on Terminology and Knowledge Engineering, TKE (2005)
116. Sahlgren, M.: The Word-Space Model: Using Distributional Analysis to Represent Syntagmatic and Paradigmatic Relations between Words in High-dimensional Vector Spaces. Ph.D. thesis, Stockholm University (2006)
117. Salton, G.: Automatic Text Processing. Addison-Wesley (1989)
118. Salton, G., McGill, M.: Introduction to Modern Information Retrieval. McGraw-Hill, New York (1983)
119. Sebastiani, F.: Machine Learning in Automated Text Categorization. ACM Computing Surveys **34**(1) (2002)
120. Semeraro, G., Lops, P., Basile, P., Gemmis, M.d.: Knowledge Infusion into Content-based Recommender Systems. In: L.D. Bergman, A. Tuzhilin, R.D. Burke, A. Felfernig, L. Schmidt-Thieme (eds.) Proc. of the 2009 ACM Conference on Recommender Systems, RecSys 2009, New York, NY, USA, October 23–25, 2009, pp. 301–304. ACM (2009)
121. Shoval, P., Maidel, V., Shapira, B.: An Ontology-Content-based Filtering Method. International Journal of Information Theories and Applications **15**, 303–314 (2008)
122. Symeonidis, P.: Content-based Dimensionality Reduction for Recommender Systems. In: Data Analysis, Machine Learning and Applications, pp. 619–626. Springer (2008)
123. Szwabe, A., Ciesielczyk, M., Janasiewicz, T.: Semantically Enhanced Collaborative Filtering Based on RSVD. In: P. Jedrzejowicz, N.T. Nguyen, K. Hoang (eds.) Proc. of Computational Collective Intelligence. Technologies and Applications - Third International Conference, ICCCI 2011, Part II, *Lecture Notes in Computer Science*, vol. 6923, pp. 10–19. Springer (2011)

124. Terzi, M., Ferrario, M., Whittle, J.: Free Text In User Reviews: Their Role In Recommender Systems. In: Proc. of the Workshop on Recommender Systems and the Social Web, 3rd ACM Conf. on Recommender Systems, pp. 45–48 (2011)
125. Turney, P.D., Pantel, P.: From Frequency to Meaning: Vector Space Models of Semantics. J. Artif. Intell. Res. (JAIR) **37**, 141–188 (2010)
126. Vempala, S.S.: The Random Projection Method, vol. 65. American Mathematical Society (2004)
127. Widdows, D.: Orthogonal Negation in Vector Spaces for Modelling Word-Meanings and Document Retrieval. In: E.W. Hinrichs, D. Roth (eds.) Proceedings of the 41st Annual Meeting of the Association for Computational Linguistics, pp. 136–143 (2003)
128. Widdows, D., Cohen, T.: The Semantic Vectors Package: New Algorithms and Public Tools for Distributional Semantics. In: Proc. of the 4th IEEE International Conference on Semantic Computing, ICSC 2010, pp. 9–15. IEEE (2010)
129. Witten, I.H., Bell, T.: The Zero-frequency Problem: Estimating the Probabilities of Novel Events in Adaptive Text Compression. IEEE Transactions on Information Theory **37**(4) (1991)
130. Wu, Z., Palmer, M.S.: Verb Semantics and Lexical Selection. In: J. Pustejovsky (ed.) 32nd Annual Meeting of the Association for Computational Linguistics, pp. 133–138. Morgan Kaufmann Publishers / ACL (1994)

Chapter 5
Constraint-Based Recommender Systems

Alexander Felfernig, Gerhard Friedrich, Dietmar Jannach, and Markus Zanker

5.1 Introduction

Traditional recommendation approaches including content-based filtering [59] (see Chap. 4) and collaborative filtering [47] (see Chap. 2) are well-suited for the recommendation of quality and taste products such as books, movies, or news. However, especially in the context of complex products such as cars, computers, real-estate, or financial services those approaches are not the best choice. For example, financial services are typically not contracted very frequently which makes it impossible to collect ratings for one specific item which would be required by collaborative filtering algorithms. Furthermore, users of recommender applications would not be satisfied with recommendations based on years-old item preferences, which would probably be exploited in this context by content-based filtering algorithms.

Knowledge-based recommender technologies help to tackle these challenges by exploiting explicit user requirements and deep knowledge about the underlying product domain [16] for the computation of recommendations. These systems include knowledge sources that are not exploited by collaborative filtering and content-based filtering approaches (e.g., recommendation knowledge in terms of constraints). Compared to collaborative filtering and content-based filtering, knowledge-based recommenders do not face cold-start problems since requirements

A. Felfernig (✉)
Graz University of Technology, Graz, Austria
e-mail: alexander.felfernig@ist.tugraz.at

G. Friedrich • M. Zanker
Alpen-Adria-Universitaet Klagenfurt, Klagenfurt, Austria
e-mail: gerhard.friedrich@aau.at; markus.zanker@aau.at

D. Jannach
TU Dortmund, Dortmund, Germany
e-mail: dietmar.jannach@tu-dortmund.de

F. Ricci et al. (eds.), *Recommender Systems Handbook*,
DOI 10.1007/978-1-4899-7637-6_5

are directly elicited within a recommendation session. However, knowledge-based recommenders suffer from the so-called knowledge acquisition bottleneck meaning that the work of knowledge engineers is required to explicitly encode the knowledge of domain experts into a formal and executable representation.

We can differentiate between two basic types of knowledge-based recommenders: case-based reasoning (CBR) approaches [4, 5, 49] and constraint-based recommenders [16, 81].[1] In terms of the used knowledge and their functionality these systems are often quite similar: user requirements are collected, recommendations are made based on knowledge about the items and how well they match to the requirements, repairs for inconsistent requirements can be proposed in situations where no solutions could be found [18, 19, 55, 81], and explanations for the recommendation results can be provided. The major difference lies in the way solutions are calculated [16]. Case-based recommenders determine recommendations on the basis of similarity metrics [53] whereas constraint-based recommenders predominantly exploit predefined *recommender knowledge bases* that contain explicit rules about how to relate customer requirements with item properties. In this chapter we will focus on constraint-based recommendation technologies. For a detailed review of case-based recommender technologies—see [4, 5, 49].

Technically, a *recommender knowledge base* of a constraint-based recommender system (see [22]) can be defined through two sets of variables (V_C, V_{PROD}) and three different sets of constraints (C_R, C_F, C_{PROD}). These variables and constraints are the major ingredients of a constraint satisfaction problem [72]. A solution for a constraint satisfaction problem consists of concrete instantiations of the variables such that all the specified constraints are fulfilled (see Sect. 5.4).

Customer Properties V_C describe possible requirements of customers, i.e., requirements are instantiations of customer properties. In the domain of financial services *willingness to take risks* is an example of a customer property and *willingness to take risks* = *low* represents a concrete customer requirement.

Product Properties V_{PROD} describe the properties of a given product assortment. Examples of product properties are *recommended investment period, product type, product name,* or *expected return on investment.*

Constraints C_R are systematically restricting the possible instantiations of customer properties, for example, *short investment periods are incompatible with high risk investments.*

Filter Conditions C_F define the relationship between potential customer requirements and the given product assortment. An example of a filter condition is the following: *customers without experiences in the financial services domain should not receive recommendations which include high-risk products.*

---

[1] Utility-based recommenders are often categorized as being knowledge-based, too [5]. For a detailed discussion of utility-based approaches, see [5, 19].

Products Finally, the allowed instantiations of product properties are represented by C_{PROD}. C_{PROD} represents one constraint in disjunctive normal form that defines elementary restrictions on the possible instantiations of variables in V_{PROD}.

A simplified recommender knowledge base for the domain of financial services is the following (see Example 5.1).

Example 5.1. Recommender knowledge base (V_C, V_{PROD}, C_R, C_F, C_{PROD})

V_C = {kl_c: [expert, average, beginner] .... /* level of expertise */
wr_c: [low, medium, high] .... /* willingness to take risks */
id_c: [shortterm, mediumterm, longterm] .... /* duration of investment */
aw_c: [yes, no] .... /* advisory wanted ? */
ds_c: [savings, bonds, stockfunds, singleshares] .. /* direct product search */
sl_c: [savings, bonds] .... /* type of low-risk investment */
av_c: [yes, no] .... /* availability of funds */
sh_c: [stockfunds, singleshares] .... /* type of high-risk investment */ }

V_{PROD} = {$name_p$: [text] .... /* name of the product */
er_p: [1..40] .... /* expected return rate */
ri_p: [low, medium, high] .... /* risk level */
$mniv_p$: [1..14] .... /* minimum investment period of product in years */
$inst_p$: [text] .... /* financial institute */ }

$C_R = \{CR_1: wr_c = high \rightarrow id_c \neq shortterm,$
$CR_2: kl_c = beginner \rightarrow wr_c \neq high\}$

$C_F = \{CF_1: id_c = shortterm \rightarrow mniv_p < 3,$
$CF_2: id_c = mediumterm \rightarrow mniv_p \geq 3 \wedge mniv_p < 6,$
$CF_3: id_c = longterm \rightarrow mniv_p \geq 6,$
$CF_4: wr_c = low \rightarrow ri_p = low,$
$CF_5: wr_c = medium \rightarrow ri_p = low \vee ri_p = medium,$
$CF_6: wr_c = high \rightarrow ri_p = low \vee ri_p = medium \vee ri_p = high,$
$CF_7: kl_c = beginner \rightarrow ri_p \neq high,$
$CF_8: sl_c = savings \rightarrow name_p = savings,$
$CF_9: sl_c = bonds \rightarrow name_p = bonds\}$

$C_{PROD} = \{CPROD_1: name_p = savings \wedge er_p = 3 \wedge ri_p = low \wedge mniv_p = 1 \wedge inst_p = A;$
$CPROD_2: name_p = bonds \wedge er_p = 5 \wedge ri_p = medium \wedge mniv_p = 5 \wedge inst_p = B;$
$CPROD_3: name_p = equity \wedge er_p = 9 \wedge ri_p = high \wedge mniv_p = 10 \wedge inst_p = B\}$

On the basis of such a recommender knowledge base and a given set of customer requirements we are able to calculate recommendations. The task of identifying a set of products fitting a customer's wishes and needs is denoted as *recommendation task* (see Definition 5.1).

Definition 5.1. A *recommendation task* can be defined as a constraint satisfaction problem (V_C, V_{PROD}, $C_C \cup C_F \cup C_R \cup C_{PROD}$) where V_C is a set of variables representing possible customer requirements and V_{PROD} is a set of variables describing product properties. C_{PROD} is a constraint in disjunctive normal form that describes product instances, C_R is a set of constraints describing possible combinations of customer requirements, and C_F (filter conditions) is a set of constraints describing the relationship between customer requirements and product properties. Finally, C_C is a set of unary constraints representing concrete customer requirements.

Example 5.2. Based on the recommender knowledge base of Example 5.1, the definition of a concrete recommendation task can be completed with the following set of requirements C_C=$\{wr_c = low, kl_c = beginner, id_c = shortterm, sl_c = savings\}$.

Based on the definition of a recommendation task, we can introduce the notion of a solution (*consistent recommendation*) for a recommendation task.

Definition 5.2. An assignment of the variables in V_C and V_{PROD} is denoted as *consistent recommendation* for a recommendation task (V_C, V_{PROD}, $C_C \cup C_F \cup C_R \cup C_{PROP}$) iff it does not violate any of the constraints in $C_C \cup C_F \cup C_R \cup C_{PROD}$.

Example 5.3. A consistent recommendation with respect to the recommender knowledge base of Example 5.1 and the customer requirements defined in Example 5.2 is $wr_c = low, kl_c = beginner, id_c = shortterm, sl_c = savings, name_p = savings, er_p = 3, ri_p = low, mniv_p = 1, inst_p = A$.

Once the recommendation rules are defined, the question arises in which form the requirements should be elicited from the user. Simple form-based one-style-fits all approaches can have their limitations for different reasons [42]. Users can have different expertise in the domain and questions about preferences have to be asked in different forms, meaning that the system has to support an adaptive *dialog* (see Sect. 5.3). In addition, in some applications, the specification of some requirements is only required if some other options were chosen. In the literature, different approaches have been made to explicitly *model* how the user interface should behave and react on user actions. The dialog can for example be modeled in the form of finite state models [17] or can be structured even more flexibly in a form where users themselves are enabled to select properties they would like to specify [50].

In this chapter we will discuss the first alternative in more detail where recommendation dialogs are modeled explicitly in the form of finite state models [17]. Transitions between the states are represented as acceptance criteria on the user input. For example, an expert (kl_c = *expert*) who is not interested in a recommendation session regarding financial services (aw_c = *no*) is automatically forwarded to q_4 (search interface that supports the specification of technical product features). Figure 5.1 depicts a finite state model of the intended behavior of a financial services recommender application.

The remainder of this chapter is organized as follows. In Sect. 5.2 we give an overview of knowledge acquisition approaches for the development of recommender knowledge bases and recommender process definitions. In Sect. 5.3 we introduce major techniques for guiding and actively supporting the user in a recommendation dialog. A short overview of approaches to solve recommendation

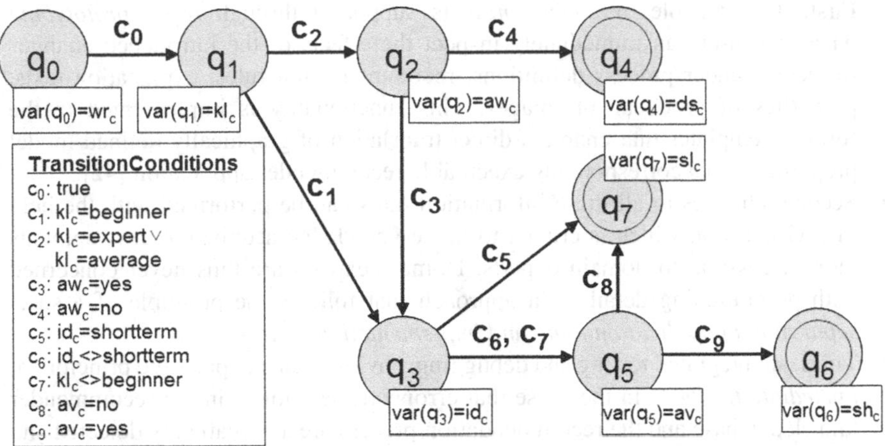

Fig. 5.1 Recommender user interface description: a simple example recommendation process for financial services. The process starts in state q_0, and, depending on the user's knowledge level, is forwarded to either state q_2 or state q_3. In the final state (one of the states q_4, q_6, q_7) the recommended items are presented. Each state q_i has an assigned customer property var (q_i) that represents a question to be asked in this state

tasks is given in Sect. 5.4. In Sect. 5.5 we discuss a number of fielded constraint-based recommender applications. In the final sections, we discuss opportunities for future research in constraint-based recommendation.

5.2 Development of Recommender Knowledge Bases

The major precondition for successfully applying constraint-based technologies in commercial settings are technologies that actively support knowledge engineers and domain experts in the development and maintenance of recommender applications and thus help to limit knowledge acquisition bottlenecks as much as possible. Due to the often very limited programming skills of domain experts, there typically exists a gap between knowledge engineers and domain experts in terms of their know-how regarding knowledge base development [19]. Domain experts are thus in most cases only responsible for knowledge provision but not for the formalization into a machine-interpretable representation (recommender knowledge base).

The following discussions are based on the *CWAdvisor* recommendation environment. A major goal of *CWAdvisor* that was first presented in [36] is to reduce the above mentioned knowledge acquisition bottleneck and its goal is to support the subject matter expert in a way that (s)he can autonomously define and maintain the recommendation logic as far as possible. In the following sections we will review the main functionality and design principles [9] of the *CWAdvisor* environment [19]. For further information on constraint-based recommendation technologies and corresponding environments we refer to [16, 19, 23, 36, 44, 57, 58, 63, 81].

- First, the principle of *concreteness* is supported through *rapid prototyping* where the user can immediately inspect the effects of the introduced changes to recommender process definitions, recommendation rules, explanation texts, properties of products, or images. This functionality is implemented in the form of templates that enable a direct translation of graphically defined model properties into a corresponding executable recommender application [42].
- Second, changes to all these information units can be performed with the help of a visual tool, which is crucial to make knowledge acquisition environments more accessible to domain experts. Domain experts are thus never concerned with programming details—an approach that follows the principle of a strict *separation of application logic and implementation details*.
- Third, an integrated testing and debugging environment supports the principle of *immediate feedback* in the sense that erroneous definitions in the recommender knowledge base and the recommendation process are automatically detected and reported (end-user debugging support). Thus, knowledge bases are maintained in a structured way and not deployed in a productive environment until all test cases specified for the knowledge base are fulfilled. As a direct consequence, domain experts can develop higher levels of trust in the resulting application since erroneous recommendations are avoided.

The Modeling Environment Figure 5.2 shows examples of some of the modeling components in the *CWAdvisor* recommender development environment [19].

This environment can be used for the design of a recommender knowledge base (see Example 5.2), i.e., customer properties (V_C), product properties (V_{PROD}), constraints (C_R), filter conditions (C_F), and the product catalog (C_{Prod}) can be entered with visual tools. The upper part of Fig. 5.2 shows an interface for the design of filter conditions (C_F). In the lower part, an interface for the context-oriented specification of compatibility constraints can be seen. Figure 5.3 shows the *CWAdvisor* Process Designer user interface. This component supports the graphical design of recommendation processes and the interactive dialog. Given such a process definition, the recommender application consisting of a recommendation server and client-side HTML pages is then automatically generated (Fig. 5.4).

Debugging Support In some cases, domain experts make mistakes when defining the recommendation process. For example, the transition conditions between the states could be defined in a wrong way such that not all paths are reachable. Consider again Fig. 5.1. Let us assume that the designer made a mistake and entered the transition condition $c_1' : kl_c = expert$ instead of $c_1 : kl_c = beginner$. In that case, users classified as beginners would get stuck as no related transition is defined. For more complex process definitions, the manual identification and repair of such faults is tedious and error-prone. In [17] an approach is presented which helps to automatically detect and repair such faulty statements. It is based on model-based diagnosis [62] that helps to locate minimal sets of faulty transition conditions.

In addition to a graphical process definition, *CWAdvisor* Designer supports the automated generation of test cases (input sequences including recommended products) [22]. Such test cases can be interpreted as additional constraints that

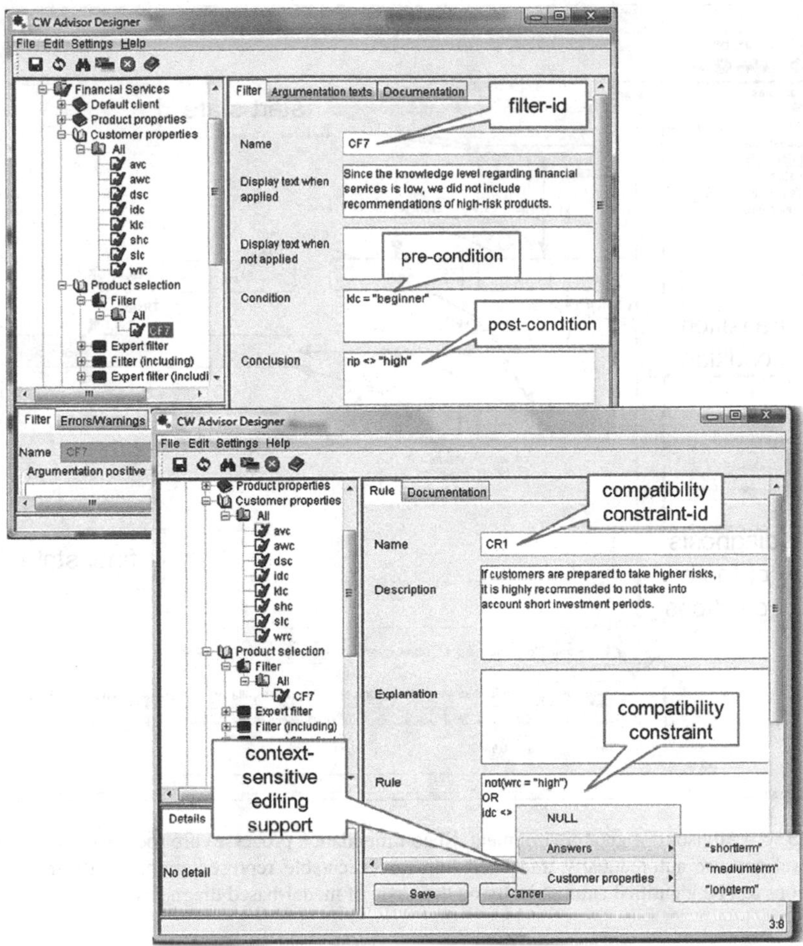

Fig. 5.2 CWAdvisor designer environment. Filter conditions as well as compatibility constraints can be defined in a context-sensitive editing environment

specify combinations of customer properties and product properties to be accepted by the knowledge base. On the one hand, test cases can be exploited for the purpose of regression testing, for example, before the recommender application is deployed in the production environment. On the other hand, test cases can be used to debug faulty recommender knowledge bases and faulty process definitions.

In the following, we will summarize the principles of recommender knowledge base debugging with the help of an example (Example 5.4) [15, 18, 19, 22]. In general, these techniques can be applied to various types of knowledge representations and are not limited to constraint-based techniques that are implemented in *CWAdvisor*.[2]

[2]For simplicity, we omit the specification of V_{PROD}, C_F, and C_{PROD}.

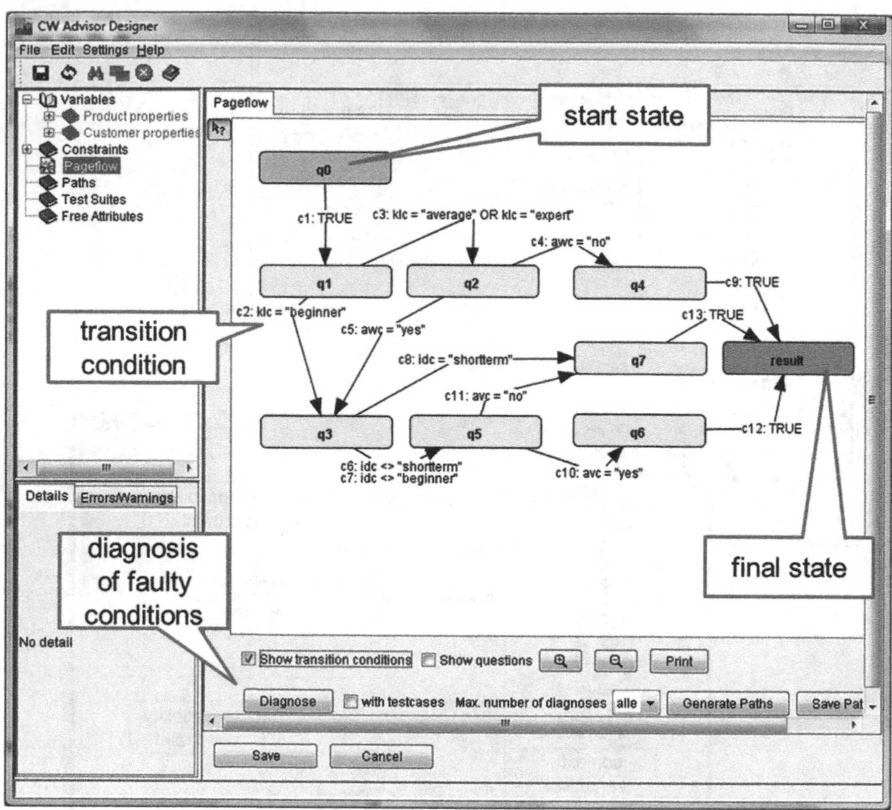

Fig. 5.3 CWAdvisor designer environment. Recommendation processes are specified on a graphical level and are automatically translated into an executable representation. Faulty transition conditions can be identified automatically on the basis of model-based diagnosis

Example 5.4. Faulty recommender knowledge base (V_C, V_{PROD}, C_R, C_F, C_{PROD})

V_C = {rr_c: [1–3%, 4–6%, 7–9%, 9%] .... /* return rate */
wr_c: [low, medium, high] .... /* willingness to take risks */
id_c: [shortterm, mediumterm, longterm] ..... /* duration of investment */ }

$$
\begin{aligned}
C_R = \{ & CR_1: wr_c = medium \rightarrow id_c \neq shortterm \\
& CR_2: wr_c = high \rightarrow id_c = long \\
& CR_3: id_c = long \rightarrow rr_c = 4-6\% \vee rr_c = 7-9\% \\
& CR_4: rr_c \geq 9\% \rightarrow wr_c = high \\
& CR_5: rr_c = 7-9\% \rightarrow wr_c \neq low \}
\end{aligned}
$$

$V_{PROD} = \{\}$ $C_F = \{\}$ $C_{PROD} = \{\}$

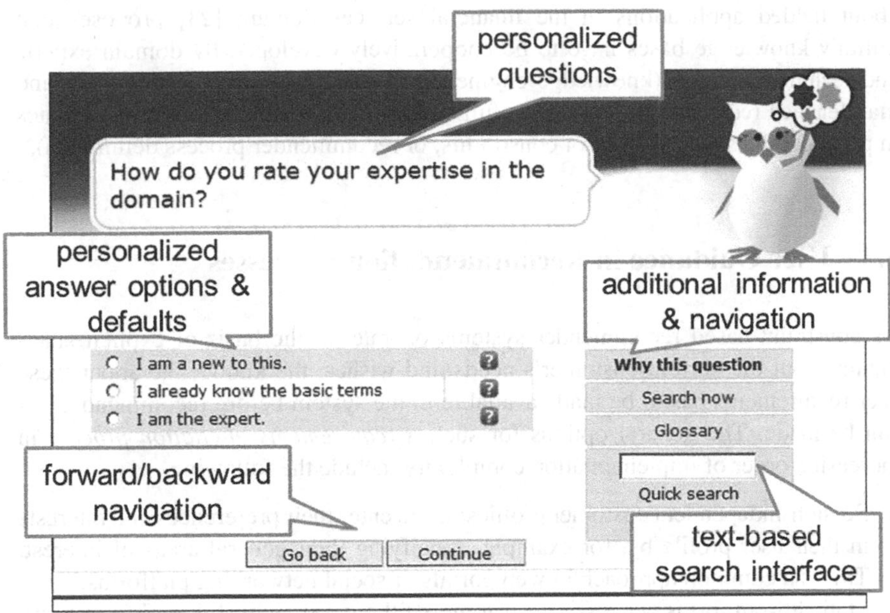

Fig. 5.4 Interactive and personalized preference elicitation example. Customers specify their preferences by answering posed questions

A typical approach to identify faults in a recommender knowledge base is to test the knowledge base with a set of examples (test cases) $e_i \in E$. For simplicity, let us assume that $e_1 : wr_c = high \wedge rr_c \geq 9\%$ is the only example provided by the domain expert. Testing $e_1 \cup C_R$—see the definitions in Example 5.4—results in the empty solution set due to the fact that e_1 is inconsistent with C_R. A more detailed look at the example shows that the constraints CR_2, CR_3 are inconsistent with e_1. CR_2, CR_3 is denoted as *conflict* [45, 62] that can be resolved by simply deleting one of its elements (under the minimality assumption that each individual constraint part of the conflict set also "contributes" to the conflict). For example, if we delete CR_3 from C_R, the consistency of $e_1 \cup C_R$ is restored (the same holds for CR_2).

The calculation of conflict sets can be realized using the conflict detection algorithm proposed by Junker [45]. Based on these conflicts, model-based diagnosis techniques [62] can be applied. The automatically calculated diagnoses then point the domain expert or knowledge engineer to those parts of the knowledge base which, if assumed to be faulty, explain the unexpected inconsistency or failure of the test case.

Experience from commercial projects underline the importance of the above mentioned principles regarding the design of knowledge acquisition and maintenance environments. Within the scope of user studies [15] significant time savings in development and maintenance processes have been detected due to the availability of a graphical development, test, and automated debugging environment. A report about fielded applications in the financial services domain [24] proposes that initially knowledge bases have to be cooperatively developed by domain experts and technical experts (knowledge engineers). Thereafter, many development and maintenance requests can be directly fulfilled by the domain experts (e.g., updates in product tables, adaptations of constraints, or recommender process definitions).

5.3 User Guidance in Recommendation Processes

As constraint-based recommender systems operate on the basis of explicit statements about the current customer's needs and wishes, the knowledge about these user requirements has to be made available to the system before recommendations can be made. The general options for such a *requirements elicitation process* in increasing order of implementation complexity include the following.

1. Session-independent customer profiles: users enter their preferences and interests in their user profile by, for example, specifying their general areas of interest. This is a common approach in web portals or social networking platforms.
2. Static fill-out forms per session: customers fill out a static web-based form every time they use the recommender system. Such interfaces are easy to implement and web users are well-acquainted with such interfaces which are often used on web shops' search for items.
3. Conversational recommendation dialogs: the recommender system incrementally acquires the user's preferences in an interactive dialog, based on, for example, "critiquing" [8], "wizard-like" and form-based preference elicitation dialogs [42], natural-language interaction [34, 71] or a combination of these techniques.

In the context of constraint-based recommendation, in particular the last type of preference elicitation plays an important role. Consider for example the recommendation of complex products such as financial services [24] or electronic consumer goods [36]. Acquiring the preferences in detail can induce a significant cognitive load on the end user interacting with the system. Thus, adequate and adaptive user interfaces are required to make sure that the system is usable for a broad community of online users.

Obviously, the static information available in user-specified customer profiles can also be a valuable input source for a constraint-based recommender. The integration of such general profile information including in particular customer demographics into the recommendation process is straightforward. In many cases, however, this information is comparably unspecific and broad such that the utility of these information pieces can be of limited value in the context of an in-detail knowledge-based recommendation process.

Static fill-out forms for some applications work well for the above-mentioned reasons. However, in knowledge-intensive domains, for which constraint-based recommenders are often built, this approach might be too simplistic, in particular because the online user community can be heterogeneous with respect to their technical background. Thus it appears inappropriate to ask all users the same set of questions or at the same level of technical detail [42].

Finally, we will also not focus on natural language interaction in this chapter as only few examples such as [34, 71] exist, that use a (complementing) natural language recommender system user interface. Despite the advances in the field of Natural-Language-Processing and although human-like virtual advisors can be found as an add-on to different web sites, they are barely used for recommending items to users today, for which there are different reasons. First, such dialogs are often user-driven, i.e., the user is expected to actively ask questions. In complex domains, however, in particular novice users are not capable of formulating such questions about, for example, the right medium-term investment strategy. In addition, the knowledge-acquisition effort for such systems is relatively high, as the system should also be capable of conducting casual conversations. Finally, end users often attribute more intelligence to such human-like avatars than is warranted which carries the risk of leaving them disappointed after interacting with the system [42].

Critiquing Critiquing is an interaction style for knowledge-based recommender systems, which was first proposed in [7] in the context of *Case-Based Reasoning* (CBR) approaches to conversational recommendation. The idea is to present individual items (instances), for example, digital cameras or financial products, to the user who can then interactively give feedback in terms of critiques on individual features. A user might, for instance, ask for a financial product with a "shorter investment period" or a "lower risk". This recommend-review-revise cycle is repeated until the desired item is found. Note that although this method was developed for CBR recommendation approaches,[3] it can also be applied to constraint-based recommendation, as the critiques can be directly translated into additional constraints that reflect the user's directional preferences on some feature.

When compared with detailed search forms that can be found on many online shops, the critiquing interaction style has the advantage that it supports the user in interactively exploring the item space. Moreover, the approach, which is often also called *tweaking*, is relatively easy to understand also for novice users. Developing a critiquing application, however, requires some domain knowledge, for example, about the set of features the user can give feedback on, suitable increment values for number-valued attributes or logical orderings of attributes with enumerated domains. In addition, when mappings from customer needs to product features are required, additional engineering effort is necessary.

The basic critiquing scheme was later on extended to also support *compound critiques* [61, 69], where users can give feedback on several features in a single interaction cycle. In the domain of financial services, a user could therefore ask for a product that has lower risk and a longer investment horizon in one step,

[3]The general idea of exploring a database by criticizing successive examples is in fact much older and was already proposed in the early 1980s in an information-retrieval context [73].

thus decreasing the number of required interaction cycles. While some sort of pre-designed compound critiques were already possible in the initial proposal from [7], it is argued in [61] that the set of possible critiques should be dynamically determined depending on the remaining items in the current user's item space and in particular on the level of diversity among these remaining items. If already selected critiques become inconsistent with new ones, some of the critiques are deleted following criteria such as number of remaining consistent critiques (the more the better). The results of experimental evaluations show that such compound critiques can help to significantly reduce the number of required interaction cycles, thus making the whole interaction process more efficient. In addition, the experiments indicate that compound critiques—if limited to a size that is still understandable to the user—can also help the user understand the logic of generated recommendations.

Additional proposals in the area of critiquing include the use of elaborate visual interfaces [82], the application of the approach in mobile recommender systems [66], the evaluation of critiquing styles regarding decision accuracy and cognitive effort [11], speech recognition based approaches to critiquing [34], and approaches that additionally exploit information in user interaction logs to reduce the number of critiquing cycles [51, 52, 75].

Personalized Preference Elicitation Dialogs Another form of acquiring the user's wishes and needs for a constraint-based recommender system is to rely on explicitly modeled and adaptive preference elicitation dialogs. Such dialog models can for instance be expressed using a *dialog grammar* [3] or by using a finite-state automaton as done in the *CWAdvisor* system [17, 19].

In the *CWAdvisor* system, the end user is guided by a "virtual advisor" through a series of questions about the particular needs and requirements before a recommendation is displayed—see Fig. 5.4 for an example dialog. In contrast to static fill-out forms, the set of questions is personalized, i.e., depending on the current situation and previous user answers, a different set of questions (probably also using a different technical or non-technical language [41]) will be asked by the system.

In the *CWAdvisor* system, the required user interface adaptation is based on manually-engineered personalization rules and on an explicit dialog model in the form of a finite-state automaton as shown in Fig. 5.1. Thus, a method is chosen that represents a compromise between fill-out forms to which web users are well-acquainted and fully free natural language conversations.

Technically, the vertices of the finite-state automaton in Fig. 5.1 are annotated with logical expressions over the constraint variables that are used to capture the user requirements. The process of developing the dialog and personalization model is supported in the *CWAdvisor* system by an end-user oriented graphical process modeling editor (Fig. 5.3). At run time, the interaction-handling component of the framework collects the user inputs and evaluates the transition conditions in order to decide how to continue the dialog—see [19] for more details.

Beside the personalization of the dialog, different other forms of adaptation on the level of content, interaction, and presentation are implemented in the system in order to support the design of preference elicitation and explanation dialogs that help the end user in the best possible way [42].

While highly-dynamic and adaptive web applications can be valuable in terms of ease-of-use and user experience, the technical realization and in particular the maintenance of such flexible user interfaces for a constraint-based recommender can be challenging. The main problem in this context are the strong interrelationships between the "model", the "view" and the control logic of such applications: consider, for instance, the situation, where the dialog model should be extended with a new question (variable), a new answer option (new variable domain), or a complete dialog page (new dialog automaton state). In each case, the web pages that represent the "view" of the recommender application, have to be adapted accordingly. Therefore, toolkits for developing personalized preference elicitation processes, have to provide mechanisms to at least partially automate the process of updating the user interface, see [42] for details of the template-based approach in *CWAdvisor*.

Dealing with Unfulfillable or Too Loose User Requirements The issue of user interface development is not the only challenging problem of personalized preference elicitation in constraint-based recommenders. In the following, we will sketch further aspects that have to be dealt with in practical applications of constraint-based recommendation technologies (see also Chap. 10).

In constraint-based recommenders, the situation can easily arise that no item in the catalog fulfills all the constraints of the user. During an interactive recommendation session, a message such as "no matching product found" is however highly undesirable. The question therefore arises, how to deal with such a situation that can also occur in CBR-based recommenders that in many cases at least initially rely on some query mechanism to retrieve an initial set of cases from the product catalog (case base). One possible approach proposed in the context of CBR-based recommenders is based on *query relaxation* [33, 54, 55, 64]. In the context of CBR recommenders, the set of recommendable items is stored in a database table; the case retrieval process consists of sending a conjunctive query Q (of user requirements) to this case base. Query relaxation then refers to finding a (maximal) subquery Q' of the original query Q that returns at least one item.

The general idea of query relaxation techniques can also be applied to constraint-based recommendation. Consider Example 5.5 (adapted from [39]), where the catalog consisting of four items C_{PROD} is shown in tabular form (Fig. 5.5).

Example 5.5. Query Relaxation

For sake of clarity and simplicity of the example, let us assume that the customer can directly specify the desired properties of the investment product on an "expert screen" of the advisory application. The set of corresponding customer properties V_c thus contains sl_c (investment type), ri_c (risk class), $minimum\_return_c$ (minimum value for expected return) and $investment\_duration_c$ (desired investment duration). The filter constraints (conditions) in this example simply map customer requirements from C_c to item features, i.e., $C_F = \{CF_1 : sl_c = sl_p, CF_2 : ri_c = ri_p, CF_3 : investment\_duration_c >= mniv_p, CF_4 : er_p >= minimum\_return_c\}$.

$name_p$	sl_p (type of low risk inv.)	ri_p (associated risk)	$mniv_p$ (min. investment period)	er_p (expected return)	$inst_p$ (financial institute)
p1	stockfunds	medium	4	5 %	ABank
p2	singleshares	high	3	5 %	ABank
p3	stockfunds	medium	2	4 %	BInvest
p4	singleshares	high	4	5 %	CMutual

Fig. 5.5 Example item catalog (financial services)

Let the concrete customer requirements C_C be the following: $\{sl_c$ = *singleshares*, ri_c = *medium*, *investment_duration*$_c$ = 3, *minimum_return*$_c$ = 5$\}$.

As can be easily seen, no item in the catalog (see Fig. 5.5) fulfills all relevant constraints in the given task, i.e., no consistent recommendation can be found for the recommendation task. When following a "constraint relaxation" approach, the goal is to find a maximal subset of the constraints of C_F, for which a recommendation exists. The maximization criterion is typically selected because the constraints directly relate to customer requirements, i.e., the more constraints can be retained, the better the retrieved items will match these requirements.

While this problem of finding consistency-establishing subsets of C_F does not seem to be too complex at a first glance, in practical settings, computational effectiveness becomes an issue. Given a constraint base consisting of n constraints, the number of possible subsets is 2^n. Since real-world recommender systems have to serve many users in parallel and typically the acceptable response time is about one second, naive subset probing is not appropriate.

Different techniques have therefore been proposed to solve this problem more efficiently. In [54], for instance, an incremental mixed-initiative approach to recover from failing queries in a CBR recommender was suggested. In [64], a relaxation method based on manually-defined feature hierarchies was proposed, which despite its incomplete nature has shown to be an effective help in a travel recommender system. Finally, in [38, 39] a set of complete algorithms for the query relaxation problem in constraint-based recommenders was developed. The algorithms not only support the computation of minimal relaxations in linear time (at the cost of a preprocessing step and slightly increased memory requirements) but also the computation of relaxations that lead to "at least n" remaining items. In addition, also a conflict-directed algorithm for interactive and incremental query relaxation was proposed which makes use of recent conflict-detection technology [45].

The main idea of the linear-time constraint relaxation technique can be sketched as follows. Instead of testing combinations of constraints, the relevant constraints are evaluated individually, resulting in a data structure that assigns to every constraint the list of catalog items that fulfill the constraint—see Fig. 5.6.

The table should be interpreted as follows. Constraint CF_1 on the type of investment (single shares) in line 1 of the table would filter out products $p1$ and $p3$.

ID	Product p1	Product p2	Product p3	Product p4
CF_1	0	1	0	1
CF_2	1	0	1	0
CF_3	0	1	1	0
CF_4	1	1	0	1

Fig. 5.6 Evaluating the subqueries individually. For example, product p1 is filtered out by the filter condition CF_1 under the assumption that $sl_c = singleshares$

Given this table, it can be easily determined which constraints of a given set C_F have to be relaxed in order to have a specific product in the result set, i.e., a product that is consistent with the constraints and the user requirements. For example, in order to have $p1$ in the result set, the constraints CF_1 and CF_3 of C_F have to be relaxed. Let us call this a "product-specific relaxation" for $p1$. The main idea of the method from [39] is that the overall "best" relaxation for given products C_{PROD}, filter conditions C_F and a given set of concrete requirements C_C has to be among the product-specific relaxations. Thus, it is sufficient to scan the set of product-specific relaxations, i.e., no further constraint solving step is required in this phase.

In the example, the relaxation of constraint CF_2 is optimal, when the number of relaxed constraints determines the best choice as only one customer requirement has to be given up. All other relaxations require at least two constraints to be ignored, which can be simply determined by counting the number of zeros in each column. Note that the number of involved constraints is only one possible optimization criterion. Other optimization criteria that take additional "costs of compromise" per constraint into account can also be implemented based on this technique as long as the cost function's value is monotonically increasing with the size of the relaxation.

Technically, the computation of product-specific relaxations can be done very efficiently based on bit-set operations [39]. In addition, the computation can also be precomputed in the initialization phase of the recommender.

Suggesting Alternatives for Unfulfillable Requirements In some application domains, the automated or interactive relaxation of individual constraints alone may not suffice to help the user, whose requirements cannot be fulfilled. Consider, for instance, a situation where the recommender in an interactive relaxation scenario proposes a set of alternatives of constraints to be relaxed. Let us assume that the user accepts one of the proposals, i.e., agrees to relax the constraints related to two variables of V_C, for example, A and B. If, however, the values of A and B are particularly important to him (or mandatory), he will later on put different constraints on these variables. These new values can, however, again cause an inconsistency with the other requirements of the user. This might finally lead to an undesirable situation, in which the user ends up in trying out different values but gets no clear advise, which values to select in order to receive a consistent recommendation.

Overall, it would be thus desirable, if the system could immediately come up with suggestions for new values for *A* and *B*, for which it is guaranteed that some items remain in the result set when user's other requirements are taken into account.

Let us first consider the basic CBR-style case retrieval problem setting as used in [54, 55, 64], in which constraints are directly placed on item features. The constraints in this example shall be $\{sl_p = singleshares,\ ri_p = medium,\ minv_p < 3,$ $er_p >= 5\ \}$. Again, no item fulfills these requirements.

In such a setting, the detailed information about the catalog items can be used to compute a set of suggestions for alternative constraints ("repairs") on individual features. Based on this information, the system could—instead of only proposing the user to relax the constraints on the investment type and on the investment duration—inform the user that "if the single shares requirement is abandoned and the minimum investment duration is set to 4" one or more items will be found. Thus, the user will be prevented from (unsuccessfully) trying a minimum investment duration of 3.

In this example, the calculation of such alternative values can be accomplished by the system by selecting one relaxation alternative (investment duration and investment type) and searching the catalog for items that fulfill the remaining constraints. The values for the investment duration and the investment type (e.g., of product 1 in Fig. 5.5) can be directly taken as suggestions for the end user [20, 25, 28, 37].

While this approach seems intuitive and simple, in practical applications the following problems have to be dealt with.

- The number of possible repairs. In realistic scenarios, the number of possible repair alternatives is typically very large as for every possible relaxation various solutions exist. In practice, however, end users cannot be confronted with more than a few overall alternatives. Thus, the problem is to select and prioritize the repair alternatives.
- The size/length of the repair proposals. Repair suggestions that contain alternative values for more than three features are not easy to understand for end users.
- Computational complexity due to non-trivial constraints. When only simple constraints on product features are allowed, the information from the item catalog can help to determine repairs as described above. In constraint-based systems, however, constraints often relate qualitative user needs to (technical) product features. Consequently, also the repair suggestions must relate to user requirements, which means that the search space of possible repair alternatives is determined by the domains of the user-related variables. In addition, determining whether or not a specific combination of user requirements (i.e., a repair alternative) leads to a non-empty result set, requires a probably costly catalog query.

In order to address these issues at least to some extent, the *CWAdvisor* system uses a combination of query relaxation and different search heuristics and additional domain-specific knowledge for the calculation of repair suggestions in a financial services application [23].

The method implemented in the system was originally proposed in [37] and interleaves the search for relaxations with a bounded search for repair alternatives. The possible relaxations are determined in increasing order of their cardinality. For each relaxation, repair alternatives are determined by varying the values of the variables that are involved in the relaxed constraints. The selection of alternative values can, for instance, be guided by a proximity heuristic that has to be based on an order of domain values. Thus, when varying for instance a user requirement of "at least 5 % expected return rate", the neighboring value of "4 %" is evaluated, assuming that such an alternative will be more acceptable for the end user than an even stronger relaxation. In order to avoid too many similar repair suggestions, the algorithm can be parameterized with several threshold values that, for example, determine the number of repairs for a relaxation, the maximum size of a relaxation and so forth. Overall, anecdotal evidence in the financial service domain indicates that such a repair feature, even if it is based on heuristics, is well-appreciated by end users as a means for shortening the required dialog length. For further discussions on diagnosis and repair approaches in constraint-based recommendation we refer to [20, 29].

Query Tightening Beside having no item in the result set, having *too many* items in the result set is also not desirable in an interactive recommender. In many real-world applications the user is informed that "too many items have been found" and that more precise search constraints have to be specified. Often, only the first few results are displayed (as to, e.g., avoid long page loading times). Such a selection may however not be optimal for the current user, since the selection is often simply based on the alphabetic order of the catalog entries.

In order to better support the user also in this situation, in [65] an *Interactive Query Management* approach for CBR recommenders is proposed, that also includes techniques for "query tightening". The proposed tightening algorithms takes as an input a query Q and its large result set and selects—on the basis of information-theoretic considerations and the entropy measure—three features that are presented to the user as proposals to refine the query.

Overall, an evaluation of *Interactive Query Management* within a travel recommender system that implemented both query relaxation and query tightening [67], revealed that the relaxation feature was well-appreciated by end users. With respect to the tightening functionality, the evaluation indicated that query tightening was not that important to end users who were well capable of refining their queries by themselves. Thus, in [56] a different feature selection method was proposed, that also takes a probabilistic model of feature popularity into account. An evaluation showed that in certain situations the method of [56] is preferable since it is better accepted by end users as a means to further refine their queries.

5.4 Calculating Recommendations

In the introductory section, we have characterized the recommendation task (see Definition 5.1) as a CSP. We will now discuss two problem solving approaches, one based on *constraint satisfaction algorithms* [72] and one based on *conjunctive database queries* [12].

Constraint Satisfaction Solutions for *constraint satisfaction problems* are calculated on the basis of search algorithms that use different combinations of *backtracking* and *constraint propagation*. The basic principle of both concepts will be explained in the following.

Backtracking. In each step, backtracking chooses a variable and assigns all possible values to this variable. It checks the consistency of the assignment with the already existing assignments and the defined set of constraints. If all the possible values of the current variable are inconsistent with the existing assignments and constraints, the constraint solver backtracks which means that the previously instantiated variable is selected again. In the case that a consistent assignment has been identified, a recursive activation of the backtracking algorithm is performed and the next variable is selected [72].

Constraint Propagation. The major disadvantage of pure backtracking-based search is "trashing" where parts of the search space are revisited although the solver has already detected that no solution exists in these parts. In order to make constraint solving more efficient, constraint propagation techniques have been introduced. These techniques try to modify an existing constraint satisfaction problem such that the search space can be significantly reduced. The methods try to create a state of *local consistency* that guarantees consistent instantiations among groups of variables. The mentioned modification steps turn an existing constraint satisfaction problem into an equivalent one. A well known type of local consistency is *arc consistency* [72] which states that for two variables X and Y there must not exist a value in the domain of Y which does not have a corresponding consistent value in X. Thus, arc consistency is a directed concept which means that if X is arc consistent with Y, the reverse must not necessarily be the case.

When using a constraint solver, constraints are typically represented in the form of expressions of the corresponding programming language. Many of the existing constraint solvers are implemented on the basis of Java.

Conjunctive Database Queries Solutions to *conjunctive queries* are calculated on the basis of database queries that try to retrieve items which fulfill all of the defined customer requirements. For details on database technologies and the execution of queries on database tables see, for example, [12].

Ranking Items Given a recommendation task, both constraint solvers and database engines try to identify a set of items that fulfill the given customer requirements. Typically, we have to deal with situations where more than one item is part of a recommendation result. In such situations the items (products) in the result set have to be ranked. In both cases (constraint solvers and database engines), we can apply the concepts of multi-attribute utility theory (MAUT) [74] that helps to determine a ranking for each of the items in the result set. Examples for the application of MAUT can be found in [19, 27].

An alternative to the application of *MAUT in combination with conjunctive queries* are *probabilistic databases* [48] which allow a direct specification of ranking criteria within a query. Example 5.6 shows such a query which selects all products that fulfill the criteria in the WHERE clause and orders the result conform to a built-in similarity metric (defined in the ORDER BY clause).[4] Finally, instead of combining the mentioned *standard constraint solvers with MAUT*, we can represent a recommendation task in the form of soft constraints where the importance (preference) for each combination of variable values is determined on the basis of a corresponding utility operation (for details see, for example, [2]).

Example 5.6. Queries in probabilistic databases

Result = SELECT * /* calculate a solution */
FROM Products /* select items from "Products" */
WHERE x_1=a_1 and x_2=a_2 /* "must" criteria */
ORDER BY score(abs(x_3-a_3), ..., abs(x_m-a_m)) /* similarity-based utility function */
STOP AFTER N; /* at most N items in the solution (result set) */

5.5 Practical Experience from Fielded Applications

The *CWAdvisor* system has been commercialized in 2002 and since then several dozens of different applications have been instantiated and fielded. They have been applied in commercial domains ranging from financial services [23] to electronic consumer goods or tourism applications [44] as well as to application domains that are considered rather untypical for recommender systems such as providing counseling services on business plans [40] or supporting software engineers in selecting appropriate effort estimation methods [60].

Based on this installation base *empirical research* tried to assess the impact and business value of knowledge based recommender systems and identify opportunities for advancing their state-of-the-art. In the following we will differentiate them based on their study design into *user studies*, *evaluations on historical data* and *case studies of fielded applications*.

Experimental User Studies Felfernig and Gula [21] conducted a study to evaluate the impact of specific functionalities of conversational knowledge-based recommenders such as explanations, proposed repair actions or product comparisons. The study assigned users randomly to different versions of the recommender system with varying functionality and applied pre- and post-interaction surveys

[4]For an overview of related similarity metrics we refer to [53].

to identify the users' level of knowledge in the domain, their trust in the system or the perceived competence of the recommender. Quite interestingly, the study showed that the participants appreciated these specific functionalities as they increased their perception of own domain knowledge and their trust in the system's recommendations got strengthened.

The COHAVE project initiated a line of research that investigated how psychological theories might be applied to explain the users' behavior in online choice situations. For instance, asymmetric dominance effects arise if the proposed itemsets contain decoy products that are dominated by other products due to their relative similarity but a lower overall utility [13, 30, 70]. Several user studies in domains such as electronic consumer goods, tourism and financial services showed that knowing about these effects a recommender can increase the conversion rate of some specific items as well as a users' confidence in the buying decision.

Algorithm Evaluations on Historical Datasets are off-line experimentations [35]. A dataset that contains past user transactions is split into a training and a testing set. Consequently, the training set is exploited to learn a model or tune an algorithm's parameters (e.g., importance values for MAUT-based interest dimensions [74]) in order to enable the recommender to predict the historic outcomes of the user sessions contained in the testing set. Such an evaluation scenario enables comparative research on algorithm performance. While the collaborative and the content-based recommendation paradigm have been extensively evaluated in the literature, comparing knowledge-based recommendation algorithms with other recommendation paradigms received only limited attention in the past. One reason is that they are hard to compare, because they require different types of algorithm input: collaborative filtering typically exploits user ratings while constraint-based recommender systems require explicit user requirements, catalog data, and domain knowledge. Consequently, datasets that contain all these types of input data—like the Entree dataset provided by Burke [6]—would allow such comparisons, they are however very rare. One of the few is described in [80]. The dataset stems from a retailer offering premium cigars and it includes implicit ratings that signify the users' purchase actions, the user's requirements input to a conversational recommender and a product catalog with detailed item descriptions. Therefore, offline experiments could be made in which knowledge-based algorithm variants that exploited user requirements were compared with content-based and collaborative algorithms working on ratings. One of the interesting results were that knowledge-based recommenders did not perform worse in terms of serendipity measured by the catalog coverage metric than collaborative filtering. This is especially true if a constraint-based recommender is cascaded with a utility-based item ranking scheme like the *CWAdvisor* system. However, collaborative filtering does better in terms of accuracy, if there are 10 and more ratings known from users. Nevertheless, an evaluation of a knowledge-based recommender always measures the quality of the encoded knowledge base *and* the inferencing mechanism itself.

Another study was instrumented in [79] that focuses on explicit user requirements as the sole input for personalization mechanisms. It compares different hybridization variants of knowledge-based and collaborative algorithms, where collaborative filtering interprets explicit requirements as a form of rating. The retrieval results of knowledge-based recommenders turn out to be very precise, if users formulated some specific requirements. However, when only few constraints apply and the result sets are large, the ranking function is not always able to identify the best matching items. In contrast, collaborative filtering learns the relationships between requirements and actually purchased items. Therefore, the study showed that a cascading strategy in which the knowledge-based recommender removes candidates based on hard criteria and a collaborative algorithm does the ranking works best.

Finally, in [76] a meta-level hybridization approach between knowledge-based and collaborative filtering was proposed and validated. There collaborative filtering learns constraints that map users' requirements onto catalog properties of purchased items and feeds them as input into a knowledge-based recommender that acts as the principal component. Offline experiments on historical data provided initial evidence that such an approach is able to outperform the knowledge base elicited from the domain experts with respect to algorithm's accuracy. Based on these first promising results further research on automatically extracting constraints from historic transaction data will take place.

Case Studies on Productive Systems are the most realistic form of evaluation because users act under real-world conditions and possess an intrinsic motivation to use the system. In [19] experiences from two commercial projects in the domains of financial services and electronic consumer goods are reported. In the latter domain, a conversational recommender for digital cameras has been fielded that was utilized by more than 200,000 online shoppers at a large Austrian price comparison platform. Replies to an online questionnaire supported the hypothesis that advisor applications help users to better orientate themselves when being confronted with large sets of choices. A significantly higher share of users successfully completed their product search when using the conversational recommender compared to those that did not use it. Installations of knowledge-based recommenders in the financial services domain follow a different business model as they support sales agents while interacting with their prospective clients. Empirical surveys among sales representatives showed that the time savings when interacting with clients were considered to be a big advantage which in turn allows sales staff to focus on sales opportunities [19, 23].

In [77] a case study researches how the application of a knowledge-based conversational sales recommender on a Webshop for Cuban cigars affects online shoppers behavior and the sales records in the period before and after introducing the recommender were analyzed. One interesting finding of this study is that the list of top ranked items in the two periods differs considerably. In fact items that were infrequently sold in the period before but very often recommended by the system experienced a very high demand. Thus, the relative sales increase for certain items was positively correlated with how often the recommender proposed these items. The advice given by recommendation applications is thus followed by users and leads to online conversions. Finally, another evaluation of a knowledge-based recommender in the tourism domain was conducted to compare conversion rates, i.e., the share of users that turned into bookers, between users and non-users of the interactive sales guide [78]. This study strongly empirically confirms that the probability of users issuing a booking request is more than twice as high for those having interacted with the interactive travel advisor than for the other non-interacting users.

5.6 Future Research Issues

Constraint-based recommender systems have proven their utility in many fielded applications. Still, we can identify several challenges for improvements. Such improvements will lead to enhancing the *quality* for users, the *broadness* of the application fields, and the *development* of recommender software.

Automated Product Data Extraction A constraint-based recommender is only as good as its knowledge base. Consequently, the knowledge base has to be correct, complete, and up-to-date in order to guarantee high quality recommendations. This implies significant maintenance tasks, especially in those domains where data and recommendation knowledge changes frequently, for example, electronic consumer products. Currently, maintenance is done by human experts who collect product data or update rule-bases. However, in many domains at least the product data is accessible for machines on the web. By exploiting the internet as a resource for data and knowledge almost all necessary pieces for many recommender applications could be collected. The major research focuses in this context are the automated extraction of product data from different information sources and the automated detection and adaptation of outdated product data. This includes the identification of relevant information sources (for instance, Web pages), the extraction of the product data, and the resolution of contradictions in those data. The fundamental problem for machines in that context is the presentation of data in the web. Data in the Web is usually presented with the goal that humans can easily access and comprehend information. Unfortunately, the opposite is true for computers which are currently not particulary capable in interpreting visual information. Therefore, a fundamental research question is how we can enable machines such that they can "read" the web similarly as humans do. In fact, this task goes far beyond recommender systems and is a central endeavor of the Semantic Web and on a more general level of Artificial Intelligence. Although it seems that currently this task is far too ambitious to be solved in the near future, we can exploit the particularities of recommendation domains. For example, when dealing with the extraction of product data from the web, we can search for product descriptions in tabular form, extract the data of these product descriptions, and instantiate a product database [43]. Of course the success of such methods depends on the domain. For example in the domain of electronic consumer products like digital cameras the description of cameras follows a common structure (e.g., data-sheets of different brands are very similar) whereas in other domains like holiday resorts product descriptions are mostly expressed by natural language text. It has to be mentioned that instead of an automated translation of human readable content into machine processable data there is the alternative to provide such machine processable data in addition or instead of human readable content. Indeed, strong market forces like internet search engine vendors might offer improved search services if machine processable information is provided. For example, product vendors supply their data in specific formats and benefit by an improved ranking in search results. However, in this scenario search machine vendors dictate which descriptions of which products are available for recommendation purposes which leads to a strong dependency on single authorities. Therefore, the aim to enable computers to read the web as humans do remain an important point on the research agenda.

Community-Based Knowledge Acquisition The cornerstone of constraint-based recommendation is efficient knowledge acquisition and maintenance [26]. This problem has been addressed in the past in different dimensions, the main focus lying on knowledge representation and conceptualization issues as well as on process models for capturing and formalizing a domain expert's knowledge. Historically, one main assumption of these approaches was that there shall exist one single point of knowledge formalization and in consequence one (user-oriented) conceptualization and a central knowledge acquisition tool. In most cases in real world, however, the domain knowledge is in the heads of different stakeholders, typical examples being cross-department or cross-organization business rules or new types of applications, in which large user communities are sharing knowledge in an open-innovation, web-based environment. Only recently, with the emergence and spread of Web 2.0 and Semantic Web technologies, the opportunities and also the problems of collaborative knowledge acquisition have again become a topic of interest [63]. With regard to the types of knowledge to be acquired, the main focus of these recent developments, however, is on acquiring "structural" knowledge, i.e., on terms, concepts, and relationships among them. New developments aim at going a step further and target at the collaborative acquisition and refinement of domain-constraints and business rules as they represent the most crucial, frequently updated, and thus very costly part in many knowledge-based applications. The main questions to be answered comprise the following: How can we automatically detect and resolve conflicts if knowledge acquisition is distributed between different knowledge contributors? How can we assist the knowledge contributors to acquire knowledge by asking them the "right" questions, i.e., minimizing the interaction needed? How can we generate "good" proposals for changing the knowledge base from different, possibly only partially-defined knowledge chunks, i.e., find plausible (in the eyes of the contributors) changes of the knowledge base? Usually the term *knowledge acquisition* refers to methods supporting the user to formulate rules, constraints, or other logical descriptions depending on the employed language. This task is complicated in recommender systems since in most cases the output includes a preference relation over the recommended items. Consequently, knowledge acquisition has to support also the formulation, debugging, and testing of preference descriptions [31].

A further factor which complicates the search for a satisfying knowledge base is the demand for high quality explanations. Explanations in constraint-based recommender systems are generated by exploiting the content of the knowledge base. In fact, different knowledge bases can provide the equivalent input/output behavior with respect to recommendations but show significant differences in their explanatory quality. Consequently, a further important goal of knowledge acquisition is supporting the formulation of comprehensible knowledge bases which serve the user to gain confidence in the recommendations.

Knowledge bases for recommender systems have to be considered as dynamic. Unfortunately this dynamics are not only caused by changing product catalogs but also by shifts of customer preferences. For example, the pixel resolution of digital photos considered to be sufficient for printing an A4 picture changes over time because of higher quality demands. Consequently, automated detection of such shifts and supporting a subsequent adaptation of the knowledge base are of great interest.

Validation Successfully developing and maintaining recommender knowledge bases requires intelligent testing environments that can guarantee the correctness of the recommendations. In particular in application areas where a certain recommendation quality must be assured (e.g., financial products) a company employing a recommender system has to ensure the quality of the recommendation process and its outcome. Future research should therefore focus on developing mechanisms to automatically configure test suites that both maximize the probability of identifying faulty elements in the recommender knowledge base and minimize the number of test cases needed to achieve this goal. Minimizing the number of test cases is important because domain experts must validate them manually. This validation output fits nicely with supporting knowledge acquisition tasks since any feedback from a knowledge engineer can be exploited for learning recommendation knowledge bases. In particular an interesting research question is to which extend arguments of a user in favor or against a recommendation can be exploited to improve knowledge bases. In [68], for example an algorithm is described which learns constraints based on arguments why an example (e.g., a product) should be recommended or not.

Recommendation of Configurable Products and Services With the production of the Model T, Henry Ford revolutionized manufacturing by employing mass production (the efficient production of many identical products). Nowadays, mass production is in many domains no longer a viable business model, and companies must provide goods and services that fit the customers' individual needs. In this context, mass customization—the production of highly variant products and services under mass production pricing conditions—has become the new paradigm. A phenomenon accompanying mass customization is mass confusion, which occurs when items are too numerous and complex for users to overlook. Developing recommender technologies that apply to configurable products and services can help tackle mass confusion [14]. For example, recommender technology could be adapted to help the uninformed customer to discover her wishes, needs, and product requirements in a domain of almost unlimited product variants. However, recommendation of configurable products pushes the limits of current recommender technologies. Current techniques assume that items to be recommended can be extensionally represented. But configuration domains frequently offer such a high product variance that the set of all possible configurations can only be intensionally characterized by configuration descriptions. Complex configurable systems may comprise thousands of components and connections. In these domains searching for the most preferred configurations satisfying the customer requirements is a challenging task.

Intelligibility and Explanation To be convincing, recommendations must be explained to customers (see also Chap. 10). When they can challenge a recommendation and see why a system recommended a specific product, customers will start to trust that system. In general, explanations are provided for outputs of recommender systems and serve a wide spectrum of tasks, for example, increase transparency and trust, persuade a customer, or improve customer satisfaction just to name some. These explanations depend on the state of the recommendation process and the user profile, for example, the aims, desires, and prior knowledge of the user. The vision of future recommender systems is that information is pro-actively provided to the user such that explanation goals are optimized, i.e., if the recommender recognizes that a customer does not understand the differences between alternative products then explanations of these differences are offered. Conversely, customers with a rich background of a product domain and a clear understanding what they want can be offered a direct link to a recommendation with a detailed technical justification. Consequently, the research challenge is to create an artificial recommender agent that acts flexibly to the needs of customers. Explanations are a cornerstone in such a general endeavor.

Theories of Consumer Buying Behavior A truly intelligent recommender agent adapts to the user. This implies that the recommender has a model of the user which allows predictions about the user's reaction depending on the information provided. In particular, if we have a model about the influencing factors of consumer buying behavior then it is possible to reason about the best next actions a recommender agent can take. Therefore, research in recommender technology can greatly benefit from insights of cognitive and decision psychology [10]. One can argue that such "intelligent" behavior of recommender agents is questionable from an ethical point of view. However, every information provided to a customer influences the user's buying behavior. Therefore, it is important to understand the consequences of communication with the customer thus allowing a more planned recommender design.

Context Awareness and Ambient Intelligence Recommender systems may not only be regarded as simple software tools accessible via a PC or portable device but rather as intelligent agents recommending actions in various situations [1, 46].

For example, in future cars artificial assistants will provide advice for various driving tasks, for example, overtaking, turning, or parking. In order to give recommendations in such environments the recommender has to be aware of the situation and the user's goals. Other typical scenarios are recommendations for tourists during their journeys. In such situations, the recommendations depend not only on customer preferences but also on the context, which can include attributes such as time of the day, season, weather conditions, and ticket availability. Such scenarios are often considered under the term "ambient intelligence", where networked ubiquitous and embedded computer devices can, in addition to traditional input devices, communicate with users based on, for instance, speech and gestures.

Semantic Web The W3C states "The Semantic Web provides a common framework that allows data to be shared and reused across application, enterprise, and community boundaries." In particular Semantic Web technologies offer methods to relate and combine data in the web enabling several improvements to existing techniques. We already mentioned that the extraction of product data and knowledge acquisition can benefit from machine-readable content descriptions. However, we can go a step further and use the information in the Semantic Web to improve the quality of recommendations [32, 83]. In particular, an agent can consider only ratings of trustworthy agents in order to avoid intentional misguidance. Furthermore, the Semantic Web allows us to integrate data of various sources into the reasoning process. On the one hand, this can help to enhance knowledge-based recommendation approaches since knowledge bases can in principle be created and maintained by community effort. However, on the other hand, many research questions for such scenarios arise: How can we assess the quality of these community-engineered knowledge bases? How can we assess the trustworthiness and quality of different knowledge sources? How can we make sure that there is a common agreement on the description of products and services? How can we identify and cope with different semantic interpretations of concepts and values? How can we assess the correctness of recommendations as well as their completeness?

5.7 Summary

In this chapter we have reviewed various aspects of constraint-based recommendation approaches. These technologies are especially applicable when there are large and potentially complex product assortments and/or cold-starting users where collaborative and content-based filtering techniques show serious limitations. The utility of constraint-based recommendation technologies has been demonstrated by several fielded applications that are analyzed in this chapter. Still, a number of perspectives for future research remain including particular aspects of knowledge acquisition and more elaborated forms of user interaction.

References

1. Adomavicius, G., Mobasher, B., Ricci, F., Tuzhilin, A.: Context-aware recommender systems. AI Magazine **32**(3), 67–80 (2011)
2. Bistarelli, S., Montanary, U., Rossi, F.: Semiring-based Constraint Satisfaction and Optimization. Journal of the ACM **44**, 201–236 (1997)
3. Bridge, D.: Towards Conversational Recommender Systems: a Dialogue Grammar Approach. In: D.W. Aha (ed.) EWCBR-02 Workshop on Mixed Initiative CBR, pp. 9–22 (2002)
4. Bridge, D., Goeker, M., McGinty, L., Smyth, B.: Case-based recommender systems. Knowledge Engineering Review **20**(3), 315–320 (2005)
5. Burke, R.: Knowledge-Based Recommender Systems. Encyclopedia of Library and Information Science **69**(32), 180–200 (2000)
6. Burke, R.: Hybrid Recommender Systems: Survey and Experiments. User Modeling and User-Adapted Interaction **12(4)**, 331–370 (2002)
7. Burke, R., Hammond, K., Young, B.: Knowledge-based navigation of complex information spaces. In: 13th National Conference on Artificial Intelligence, AAAI'96, pp. 462–468. AAAI Press (1996)
8. Burke, R., Hammond, K., Young, B.: The FindMe Approach to Assisted Browsing. IEEE Intelligent Systems **12**(4), 32–40 (1997)
9. Burnett, M.: HCI research regarding end-user requirement specification: a tutorial. Knowledge-based Systems **16**, 341–349 (2003)
10. Chen, L., deGemmis, M., Felfernig, A., Lops, P., Ricci, F., Semeraro, G.: Human Decision Making and Recommender Systems. ACM Transactions on Interactive Intelligent Systems **3**(3), article no. 17 (2013)
11. Chen, L., Pu, P.: Evaluating Critiquing-based Recommender Agents. In: 21st National Conference on Artificial Intelligence, AAAI/IAAI'06, pp. 157–162. AAAI Press, Boston, Massachusetts, USA (2006)
12. Elmasri, R., Navathe, S.: Fundamentals of Database Systems. Addison Wesley (2006)
13. Erich C.T., Markus Z.: Decision Biases in Recommender Systems. Journal of Internet Commerce **14**(2), 255–275 (2015). doi:10.1080/15332861.2015.1018703
14. Falkner, A., Felfernig, A., Haag, A.: Recommendation Technologies for Configurable Products. AI Magazine **32**(3), 99–108 (2011)
15. Felfernig, A.: Reducing Development and Maintenance Efforts for Web-based Recommender Applications. Web Engineering and Technology **3**(3), 329–351 (2007)
16. Felfernig, A., Burke, R.: Constraint-based recommender systems: technologies and research issues. In: 10th International Conference on Electronic Commerce, ICEC'08, pp. 1–10. ACM, New York, NY, USA (2008)
17. Felfernig, A., Friedrich, G., Isak, K., Shchekotykhin, K.M., Teppan, E., Jannach, D.: Automated debugging of recommender user interface descriptions. Applied Intelligence **31**(1), 1–14 (2009)
18. Felfernig, A., Friedrich, G., Jannach, D., Stumptner, M.: Consistency-based diagnosis of configuration knowledge bases. AI Journal **152**(2), 213–234 (2004)
19. Felfernig, A., Friedrich, G., Jannach, D., Zanker, M.: An integrated environment for the development of knowledge-based recommender applications. International Journal of Electronic Commerce **11**(2), 11–34 (2007)
20. Felfernig, A., Friedrich, G., Schubert, M., Mandl, M., Mairitsch, M., Teppan, E.: Plausible Repairs for Inconsistent Requirements. In: 21st International Joint Conference on Artificial Intelligence, IJCAI'09, pp. 791–796. Pasadena, CA, USA (2009)
21. Felfernig, A., Gula, B.: An Empirical Study on Consumer Behavior in the Interaction with Knowledge-based Recommender Applications. In: 8th IEEE International Conference on E-Commerce Technology (CEC 2006) / Third IEEE International Conference on Enterprise Computing, E-Commerce and E-Services (EEE 2006), p. 37 (2006)

22. Felfernig, A., Isak, K., Kruggel, T.: Testing Knowledge-based Recommender Systems. OEGAI Journal **4**, 12–18 (2007)
23. Felfernig, A., Isak, K., Szabo, K., Zachar, P.: The VITA Financial Services Sales Support Environment. In: 22nd AAAI Conference on Artificial Intelligence and the 19th Conference on Innovative Applications of Artificial Intelligence, AAAI/IAAI'07, pp. 1692–1699. Vancouver, Canada (2007)
24. Felfernig, A., Kiener, A.: Knowledge-based Interactive Selling of Financial Services using FSAdvisor. In: 20th National Conference on Artificial Intelligence, AAAI/IAAI'05, pp. 1475–1482. AAAI Press, Pittsburgh, PA (2005)
25. Felfernig, A., Mairitsch, M., Mandl, M., Schubert, M., Teppan, E.: Utility-based Repair of Inconsistent Requirements. In: 22nd International Conference on Industrial, Engineering and Other Applications of Applied Intelligence Systems, IEAAIE 2009, Springer Lecture Notes on Artificial Intelligence, pp. 162–171. Springer, Taiwan (2009)
26. Felfernig, A., Reiterer, S., Stettinger, M., Reinfrank, F., Jeran, M., Ninaus, G.: Recommender Systems for Configuration Knowledge Engineering. In: Workshop on Configuration, pp. 51–54 (2013)
27. Felfernig, A., Schippel, S., Leitner, G., Reinfrank, F., Isak, K., Mandl, M., Blazek, P., Ninaus, G.: Automated Repair of Scoring Rules in Constraint-based Recommender Systems. AI Communications **26**(2), 15–27 (2013)
28. Felfernig, A., Schubert, M., Reiterer, S.: Personalized diagnosis for over-constrained problems. In: Proceedings of the 23rd International Joint Conference on Artificial Intelligence. Beijing, China (2013)
29. Felfernig, A., Schubert, M., Zehentner, C.: An efficient diagnosis algorithm for inconsistent constraint sets. Artificial Intelligence for Engineering Design, Analysis, and Manufacturing (AIEDAM) **26**(1), 53–62 (2012)
30. Felfernig, A., Teppan, E.: Decoy Effects in Financial Service E-Sales Systems. In: RecSys11 Workshop on Human Decision Making in Recommender Systems, pp. 1–8 (2011)
31. Felfernig, A., Teppan, E., Friedrich, G., Isak, K.: Intelligent debugging and repair of utility constraint sets in knowledge-based recommender applications. In: ACM International Conference on Intelligent User Interfaces, IUI 2008, pp. 217–226 (2008)
32. Gil, Y., Motta, E., Benjamins, V., Musen, M. (eds.): The Semantic Web - ISWC 2005, 4th International Semantic Web Conference, ISWC 2005, Galway, Ireland, November 6–10, 2005, *Lecture Notes in Computer Science*, vol. 3729. Springer (2005)
33. Godfrey, P.: Minimization in Cooperative Response to Failing Database Queries. International Journal of Cooperative Information Systems **6**(2), 95–149 (1997)
34. Grasch, P., Felfernig, A., Reinfrank, F.: Recomment: towards critiquing-based recommendation with speech interaction. In: Seventh ACM Conference on Recommender Systems, RecSys '13, pp. 157–164. Hong Kong, China (2013)
35. Herlocker, J., Konstan, J., Terveen, L., Riedl, J.: Evaluating Collaborative Filtering Recommender Systems. ACM Transactions on Information Systems **22(1)**, 5–53 (2004)
36. Jannach, D.: Advisor Suite - A knowledge-based sales advisory system. In: R.L. de Mantaras, L. Saitta (eds.) European Conference on Artificial Intelligence, ECAI 2004, pp. 720–724. IOS Press, Valencia, Spain (2004)
37. Jannach, D.: Preference-based treatment of empty result sets in product finders and knowledge-based recommenders. In: 27th Annual Conference on Artificial Intelligence, KI 2004, pp. 145–159. Ulm, Germany (2004)
38. Jannach, D.: Techniques for Fast Query Relaxation in Content-based Recommender Systems. In: C. Freksa, M. Kohlhase, K. Schill (eds.) 29th German Conference on AI, KI 2006, pp. 49–63. Springer LNAI 4314, Bremen, Germany (2006)
39. Jannach, D.: Fast computation of query relaxations for knowledge-based recommenders. AI Communications **22**(4), 235–248 (2009)
40. Jannach, D., Bundgaard-Joergensen, U.: SAT: A Web-Based Interactive Advisor For Investor-Ready Business Plans. In: International Conference on e-Business, pp. 99–106 (2007)

41. Jannach, D., Kreutler, G.: Personalized User Preference Elicitation for e-Services. In: IEEE International Conference on e-Technology, e-Commerce, and e-Services, EEE 2005, pp. 604–611. IEEE Computer Society, Hong Kong (2005)
42. Jannach, D., Kreutler, G.: Rapid Development Of Knowledge-Based Conversational Recommender Applications With Advisor Suite. Journal of Web Engineering **6**, 165–192 (2007)
43. Jannach, D., Shchekotykhin, K.M., Friedrich, G.: Automated ontology instantiation from tabular web sources - the allright system. Journal of Web Semantics **7**(3), 136–153 (2009)
44. Jannach, D., Zanker, M., Fuchs, M.: Constraint-based recommendation in tourism: A multiperspective case study. Journal of Information Technology and Tourism **11**(2), 139–155 (2009)
45. Junker, U.: QUICKXPLAIN: Preferred Explanations and Relaxations for Over-Constrained Problems. In: National Conference on Artificial Intelligence, AAAI'04, pp. 167–172. AAAI Press, San Jose (2004)
46. Kaminskas, M., Ricci, F., Schedl, M.: Location-aware music recommendation using autotagging and hybrid matching. In: 7th ACM Conference on Recommender Systems, RecSys '13, Hong Kong, China, October 12–16, 2013, pp. 17–24 (2013)
47. Konstan, J., Miller, N., Maltz, D., Herlocker, J., Gordon, R., Riedl, J.: GroupLens: applying collaborative filtering to Usenet news. Communications of the ACM **40**(3), 77–87 (1997)
48. Lakshmanan, L., Leone, N., Ross, R., Subrahmanian, V.: ProbView: A Flexible Probabilistic Database System. ACM Transactions on Database Systems **22**(3), 419–469 (1997)
49. Lorenzi, F., Ricci, F., Tostes, R., Brasil, R.: Case-based recommender systems: A unifying view. In: Intelligent Techniques in Web Personalisation, no. 3169 in Lecture Notes in Computer Science, pp. 89–113. Springer (2005)
50. Mahmood, T., Ricci, F.: Learning and adaptivity in interactive recommender systems. In: 9th International Conference on Electronic Commerce, ICEC'07, pp. 75–84. ACM Press, New York, NY, USA (2007)
51. Mandl, M., Felfernig, A.: Improving the performance of unit critiquing. In: 20th International Conference on User Modeling, Adaptation, and Personalization (UMAP 2012), pp. 176–187. Montreal, Canada (2012)
52. McCarthy, K., Y.Salem, Smyth, B.: Experience-based critiquing: Reusing critiquing experiences to improve conversational recommendation. In: ICCBR'10, pp. 480–494 (2010)
53. McSherry., D.: Similarity and compromise. In: ICCBR'03, pp. 291–305. Trondheim, Norway (2003)
54. McSherry, D.: Incremental Relaxation of Unsuccessful Queries. In: P. Funk, P.G. Calero (eds.) European Conference on Case-based Reasoning, ECCBR 2004, no. 3155 in Lecture Notes in Artificial Intelligence, pp. 331–345. Springer (2004)
55. McSherry, D.: Retrieval Failure and Recovery in Recommender Systems. Artificial Intelligence Review **24**(3–4), 319–338 (2005)
56. Mirzadeh, N., Ricci, F., Bansal, M.: Feature Selection Methods for Conversational Recommender Systems. In: IEEE International Conference on e-Technology, e-Commerce and e-Service on e-Technology, e-Commerce and e-Service, EEE 2005, pp. 772–777. IEEE Computer Society, Washington, DC, USA (2005)
57. Paakko, J., Raatikainen, M., Myllarniemi, V., Mannisto, T.: Applying recommendation systems for composing dynamic services for mobile devices. In: 19th Asia-Pacific Software Engineering Conference (APSEC), pp. 40–51 (2012)
58. Parameswaran, A., Venetis, P., Garcia-Molina, H.: Recommendation systems with complex constraints: A course recommendation perspective. ACM Transactions on Information Systems **29**(4), 20:1–20:33 (2011)
59. Pazzani, M.: A Framework for Collaborative, Content-Based and Demographic Filtering. Artificial Intelligence Review **13**(5–6), 393–408 (1999)
60. Peischl, B., Nica, M., Zanker, M., Schmid, W.: Recommending effort estimation methods for software project management. In: International Conference on Web Intelligence and Intelligent Agent Technology - WPRRS Workshop, vol. 3, pp. 77–80. Milano, Italy (2009)
61. Reilly, J., McCarthy, K., McGinty, L., Smyth, B.: Dynamic Critiquing. In: 7th European Conference on Case-based Reasoning, ECCBR 2004, pp. 763–777. Madrid, Spain (2004)

62. Reiter, R.: A theory of diagnosis from first principles. AI Journal **32**(1), 57–95 (1987)
63. Reiterer, S., Felfernig, A., Blazek, P., Leitner, G., Reinfrank, F., Ninaus, G.: WeeVis. In: A. Felfernig, L. Hotz, C. Bagley, J. Tiihonen (eds.) Knowledge-based Configuration – From Research to Business Cases, chap. 25, pp. 365–376. Morgan Kaufmann Publishers (2013)
64. Ricci, F., Mirzadeh, N., Bansal, M.: Supporting User Query Relaxation in a Recommender System. In: 5th International Conference in E-Commerce and Web-Technologies, EC-Web 2004, pp. 31–40. Zaragoza, Spain (2004)
65. Ricci, F., Mirzadeh, N., Venturini, A.: Intelligent query management in a mediator architecture. In: 1st International IEEE Symposium on Intelligent Systems, vol. 1, pp. 221–226. Varna, Bulgaria (2002)
66. Ricci, F., Nguyen, Q.: Acquiring and Revising Preferences in a Critique-Based Mobile Recommender System. IEEE Intelligent Systems **22**(3), 22–29 (2007)
67. Ricci, F., Venturini, A., Cavada, D., Mirzadeh, N., Blaas, D., Nones, M.: Product Recommendation with Interactive Query Management and Twofold Similarity. In: 5th International Conference on Case-Based Reasoning, pp. 479–493. Trondheim, Norway (2003)
68. Shchekotykhin, K., Friedrich, G.: Argumentation based constraint acquisition. In: IEEE International Conference on Data Mining (2009)
69. Smyth, B., McGinty, L., Reilly, J., McCarthy, K.: Compound Critiques for Conversational Recommender Systems. In: IEEE/WIC/ACM International Conference on Web Intelligence, WI'04, pp. 145–151. Maebashi, Japan (2004)
70. Teppan, E., Felfernig, A.: Minimization of Product Utility Estimation Errors in Recommender Result Set Evaluations. Web Intelligence and Agent Systems **10**(4), 385–395 (2012)
71. Thompson, C., Goeker, M., Langley, P.: A Personalized System for Conversational Recommendations. Journal of Artificial Intelligence Research **21**, 393–428 (2004)
72. Tsang, E.: Foundations of Constraint Satisfaction. Academic Press, London (1993)
73. Williams, M., Tou, F.: RABBIT: An interface for database access. In: AAAI'82, pp. 83–87. ACM, New York, NY, USA (1982)
74. Winterfeldt, D., Edwards, W.: Decision Analysis and Behavioral Research. Cambridge University Press (1986)
75. Xie, H., L.Chen, Wang, F.: Collaborative compound critiquing. In: 22nd International Conference on User Modeling, Adaptation, and Personalization (UMAP 2014), pp. 254–265. Aalborg, Denmark (2014)
76. Zanker, M.: A Collaborative Constraint-Based Meta-Level Recommender. In: 2nd ACM International Conference on Recommender Systems, RecSys 2008, pp. 139–146. ACM Press, Lausanne, Switzerland (2008)
77. Zanker, M., Bricman, M., Gordea, S., Jannach, D., Jessenitschnig, M.: Persuasive online-selling in quality & taste domains. In: 7th International Conference on Electronic Commerce and Web Technologies, EC-Web 2006, pp. 51–60. Springer, Krakow, Poland (2006)
78. Zanker, M., Fuchs, M., Höpken, W., Tuta, M., Müller, N.: Evaluating Recommender Systems in Tourism - A Case Study from Austria. In: International Conference on Information and Communication Technologies in Tourism, ENTER 2008, pp. 24–34 (2008)
79. Zanker, M., Jessenitschnig, M.: Case-studies on exploiting explicit customer requirements in recommender systems. User Modeling and User-Adapted Interaction: The Journal of Personalization Research, A. Tuzhilin and B. Mobasher (Eds.): Special issue on Data Mining for Personalization **19**(1–2), 133–166 (2009)
80. Zanker, M., Jessenitschnig, M., Jannach, D., Gordea, S.: Comparing recommendation strategies in a commercial context. IEEE Intelligent Systems **22**(May/Jun), 69–73 (2007)
81. Zanker, M., Jessenitschnig, M., Schmid, W.: Preference reasoning with soft constraints in constraint-based recommender systems. Constraints **15**(4), 574–595 (2010)
82. Zhang, J., Jones, N., Pu, P.: A visual interface for critiquing-based recommender systems. In: ACM EC'08, pp. 230–239. ACM, New York, NY, USA (2008)
83. Ziegler, C.: Semantic Web Recommender Systems. In: EDBT Workshop, EDBT'04, pp. 78–89 (2004)

Chapter 6
Context-Aware Recommender Systems

Gediminas Adomavicius and Alexander Tuzhilin

6.1 Introduction and Motivation

Many existing approaches to recommender systems focus on recommending the most relevant items to individual users and do not take into consideration any contextual information, such as time, place, and the company of other people (e.g., for watching movies or dining out). In other words, traditionally recommender systems deal with applications having only two types of entities, users and items, and do not put them into a context when providing recommendations.

However, in many applications, such as recommending a vacation package, personalized content on a Web site, or a movie, it may not be sufficient to consider only users and items—it is also important to incorporate the *contextual information* into the recommendation process in order to recommend items to users under certain *circumstances*. For example, using the temporal context, a travel recommender system would provide a vacation recommendation in the winter that can be very different from the one in the summer. Similarly, in the case of personalized content delivery on a Web site, it is important to determine what content needs to be delivered (recommended) to a customer and when. More specifically, on weekdays a user might prefer to read world news when she logs on in the morning and the stock market report in the evening, and on weekends to read movie reviews and do shopping.

G. Adomavicius (✉)
Department of Information and Decision Sciences, University of Minnesota,
321 19th Avenue South, Minneapolis, MN 55455, USA
e-mail: gedas@umn.edu

A. Tuzhilin
Department of Information, Operations and Management Sciences, Stern School of Business,
New York University, 44 West 4th Street, Rm 8-85, New York, NY 10012, USA
e-mail: atuzhili@stern.nyu.edu

F. Ricci et al. (eds.), *Recommender Systems Handbook*,
DOI 10.1007/978-1-4899-7637-6_6

These observations are consistent with the findings in behavioral research on consumer decision making in marketing that have established that decision making, rather than being invariant, is contingent on the context of decision making. Therefore, accurate prediction of consumer preferences undoubtedly depends upon the degree to which the recommender system has incorporated the relevant contextual information into a recommendation method.

Over the past 10–15 years, context-aware recommendation capabilities have been developed by academic researchers and applied in a variety of different application settings, including: movie recommenders [6], restaurant recommenders [68], travel recommenders and tourist guides [19, 35, 65, 73, 78, 90], general music recommenders [51, 72, 76], specialized music recommenders (e.g., for places of interest [27], in-car music [18], or music while reading [32]), mobile information search [39], news recommenders [60], shopping assistants [80], mobile advertising [29], mobile portals [85], mobile app recommenders [53], and many others. In particular, *mobile* recommender systems constitute an important special case of context-aware recommenders, where context is often defined by location and time, and there exists a large body of literature dedicated specifically to mobile recommender systems (e.g., see [19, 49, 88] for a few representative examples). In this chapter we focus on the issues related to the general area of context-aware recommender systems and, therefore, we do not provide a separate in-depth review of mobile recommender systems. Readers interested in a systematic coverage of mobile recommender systems are referred to Chap. 14 as well as two recent reviews of the field [54, 77].

Similarly, companies have also started incorporating some contextual information into their recommendation engines for recommending music (e.g., www.last.fm,musicovery.com, and www.sourcetone.com) and movies (e.g., www.moviepilot.de and www.filmtipset.se). For example, when choosing which songs to play for a given user, some interactive radio stations ask the users to specify their current mood by selecting it from a list of well-established types of moods, such as "positive", "energetic", "calm", "dark", etc. The chosen mood is then used by the system as contextual information to recommend only the type of music that best fits the selected mood. As another example, the movie streaming and rental company Netflix knows the location of its customers and uses the locational contextual variables, such as city or zip code as well as time, to provide context-specific recommendations of movies. Similarly, mobile recommender systems (e.g., those deployed on smartphones) provide more relevant recommendations to its customers when they take into account such important contextual information as the GPS-based location and time. As Reed Hastings, the CEO of Netflix, pointed out in the following Youtube video [1] (see the video at 44:40 min), Netflix reportedly can improve the performance of its recommendation algorithms up to 3 % when taking into account such contextual information as the time of the day or user's location. This observation by Hastings was echoed by the participants at the industrial panel held during the CARS workshop at the RecSys'12 conference (http://cars-workshop.org/cars-12/program), where managers from LinkedIn, Netflix,

EchoNest, and Telefonica reiterated the importance of contextual information and described how their recommendation engines utilize contextual information in their businesses.

In this chapter we review the topic of *context-aware recommender systems* (*CARS*). In particular, we discuss the notion of context and how it can be modeled in recommender systems. We also review the major approaches to modeling contextual information in recommender systems and discuss three main algorithmic paradigms for incorporating contextual information into rating-based recommender systems—contextual pre-filtering, post-filtering, and modeling. We also survey recent work on context-aware recommender systems and discuss important and promising directions for future research.

The rest of the chapter is organized as follows. Section 6.2 discusses the general notion of context as well as the general approaches to how it can be modeled in recommender systems. Section 6.3 presents three main algorithmic paradigms for incorporating contextual information into the rating-based recommender systems within the representational framework of modeling contextual information. Finally, some additional discussion and opportunities for future work are presented in Sect. 6.4.

6.2 Context in Recommender Systems

Before discussing the role and opportunities of contextual information in recommender systems, in Sect. 6.2.1 we start by presenting the general notion of context. Then, starting with Sect. 6.2.2, we focus on recommender systems and explain how context is specified and modeled there.

6.2.1 What is Context?

Context is a multifaceted concept that has been studied across different research disciplines, including computer science (primarily in artificial intelligence and ubiquitous computing), cognitive science, linguistics, philosophy, psychology, and organizational sciences. In fact, an entire conference—CONTEXT[1]—is dedicated exclusively to studying this topic and incorporating it into various other branches of science, including medicine, law, and business. Since context is a multidisciplinary concept, each discipline tends to take its own idiosyncratic view that is somewhat different from other disciplines and is more specific than the standard generic dictionary definition of context as "conditions or circumstances

[1]See, for example, http://www.polytech.univ-savoie.fr/index.php?id=context-13-home, http://context-11.teco.edu, or http://context-07.ruc.dk, for recent instances.

which affect some thing" [87]. Therefore, there exist many definitions of context across various disciplines and even within specific subfields of these disciplines. Bazire and Brézillon [25] present and examine 150 different definitions of context from different fields. This is not surprising, given the complexity and the multifaceted nature of the concept. As Bazire and Brézillon [25] observe:

> ... it is difficult to find a relevant definition satisfying in any discipline. Is context a frame for a given object? Is it the set of elements that have any influence on the object? Is it possible to define context a priori or just state the effects a posteriori? Is it something static or dynamic? Some approaches emerge now in Artificial Intelligence [...]. In Psychology, we generally study a person doing a task in a given situation. Which context is relevant for our study? The context of the person? The context of the task? The context of the interaction? The context of the situation? When does a context begin and where does it stop? What are the real relationships between context and cognition?

To bring some "order" to this diversity of views on what context is, Dourish [42] introduces taxonomy of contexts, according to which contexts can be classified into the representational and the interactional views. In the *representational* view, context is defined with a predefined set of observable attributes, the structure (or schema, using database terminology) of which does not change significantly over time. In other words, the representational view assumes that the contextual attributes are identifiable and known a priori and, hence, can be captured and used within the context-aware applications. In contrast, the *interactional* view assumes that the user behavior is induced by an underlying context, but that the context itself is not necessarily observable. Furthermore, Dourish [42] assumes that different types of actions may give rise to and call for different types of relevant contexts, thus assuming a *bidirectional* relationship between activities and underlying contexts: contexts influence activities and also different activities giving rise to different contexts.

In this chapter we focus on what context is *in recommender systems* and try to adapt this multifaceted concept to the specific and idiosyncratic domain of RSes. Furthermore, we will also revisit and enhance the prior definitions of context used in recommender systems, including those provided in [5, 10]. We start with the standard and popular representational approach to modeling contextual information in Sect. 6.2.2, and explore and describe alternative approaches in Sect. 6.2.3.

6.2.2 Representational Approach to Modeling Contextual Information in Recommender Systems

Recommender systems emerged as an independent research area in the mid-1990s, when researchers and practitioners started focusing on recommendation problems that explicitly rely on the notion of ratings as a way to capture user preferences for different items. For example, in case of a movie recommender system, John Doe may assign a rating of 7 (out of 10) for the movie "Gladiator," i.e., set R_{movie}(John_Doe, Gladiator) $= 7$. The rating-based recommender systems typically start with the specification of the initial set of ratings that is either explicitly provided by the users or is implicitly inferred by the system. Once these initial ratings are specified, a recommender system tries to estimate the rating function R

$$R : User \times Item \rightarrow Rating$$

for the (user, item) pairs that have not been rated yet by the users. Here *Rating* is a totally ordered set (e.g., non-negative integers or real numbers within a certain range), and *User* and *Item* are the domains of users and items respectively. Once the function R is estimated for the whole $User \times Item$ space, a recommender system can recommend the highest-rated items for each user, possibly also taking into account item novelty, diversity, or other considerations of recommendation quality [84]. We call such systems *traditional* or *two-dimensional* (2D) since they consider only the *User* and *Item* dimensions in the recommendation process.

In other words, in its most common formulation, the traditional rating-based recommendation problem is reduced to the problem of estimating ratings for the items that have not been seen by a user. This estimation is usually based on the ratings given by the users to other items, and possibly on some other information, such as user demographics and item characteristics. Note that this traditional approach to RSes does not take into the consideration the *contextual information*, such as time, location and the company of other people.

The rating-based *representational approach to context-aware recommender systems* assumes that the contextual information is known and defined by a set of contextual attributes and that these contextual attributes affect ratings. In other words, the ratings are modeled in the rating-based representational approach to CARS as the function of not only items and users, but also of the contextual attributes, i.e., as

$$R : User \times Item \times Context \rightarrow Rating,$$

where *User* and *Item* are the domains of users and items respectively, *Rating* is the domain of ratings, and *Context* specifies the known contextual information associated with the application. To illustrate these concepts, consider the following example.

Example 6.1. Consider the application for recommending movies to users, where users and movies are described as relations having the following attributes:

- Movie: the set of all the movies that can be recommended; it is defined as Movie(MovieID, Title, Length, ReleaseYear, Director, Genre).
- User: the people to whom movies are recommended; it is defined as User(UserID, Name, Address, Age, Gender, Profession).

Further, the contextual information consists of the following three types that are also defined as relations having the following attributes:

- Theater: the movie theaters showing the movies; it is defined as Theater (TheaterID, Name, Address, Capacity, City, State, Country).
- Time: the time when the movie can be or has been seen; it is defined as Time(Date, DayOfWeek, TimeOfWeek, Month, Quarter, Year). Here, attribute DayOfWeek has values Mon, Tue, Wed, Thu, Fri, Sat, Sun, and attribute TimeOfWeek has values "Weekday" and "Weekend".
- Companion: represents a person or a group of persons with whom one can see a movie. It is defined as Companion(companionType), where attribute companionType has values "alone", "friends", "girlfriend/boyfriend", "family", "co-workers", and "others".

Then the rating assigned to a movie by a person also depends on where and how the movie has been seen, with whom, and at what time. For example, the type of movie to recommend to college student Jane Doe can differ significantly depending on whether she is planning to see it on a Saturday night with her boyfriend vs. on a weekday with her parents.

As we can see from this example and other cases, the contextual information Context can be of different *types*, each type defining a certain aspect of context, such as time, location (e.g., Theater), companion (e.g., for seeing a movie), purpose of a purchase, etc. Further, each contextual type can have a complicated structure reflecting complex nature of the contextual information. Although this complexity of contextual information can take many different forms, one popular defining characteristic is the *hierarchical* structure of contextual information that can be represented as trees, as is done in most of the context-aware recommender and profiling systems, including [6, 69]. For instance, the three contexts from Example 6.1 can have the following hierarchies associated with them: *Theater*: TheaterID → City → State → Country; *Time*: Date → DayOfWeek → TimeOfWeek, Date → Month → Quarter → Year.[2]

This *representational* view to CARS assumes that the context is defined with a predefined set of observable attributes, the structure of which does not change significantly over time, and constitutes the most popular approach to incorporating context in RSes. More specifically, many context-aware approaches follow Palmisano et al. [69], and also Adomavicius et al. [6] to some extent, and define the contextual information with a *set* of *contextual dimensions* $\boldsymbol{K}$, each contextual dimension K in $\boldsymbol{K}$ being defined by a set of q attributes $K = (K^1, \ldots, K^q)$ having a hierarchical structure and capturing a particular type of context, such as *Time* or *CommunicatingDevice*. The values taken by attribute K^q define *finer* (more *granular*) levels, while K^1 values define *coarser* (less granular) levels of

[2]For the sake of completeness, we would like to point out that not only the contextual dimensions, but also the traditional User and Item dimensions can have their attributes form hierarchical relationships. For example, the main two dimensions from Example 6.1 can have the following hierarchies associated with them: *Movie*: MovieID → Genre; *User*: UserID → Age, UserID → Gender, UserID → Profession.

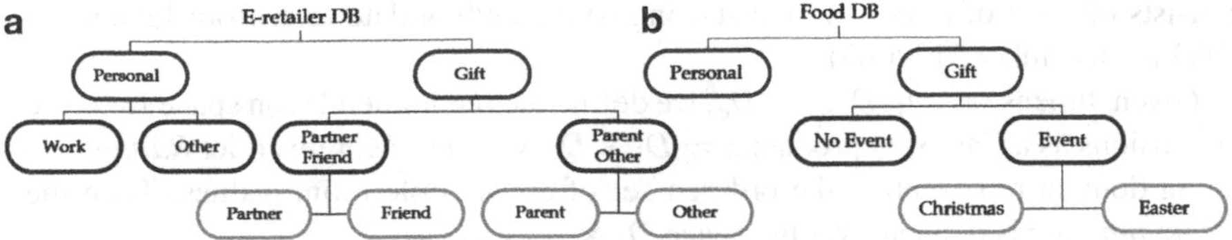

Fig. 6.1 Contextual information hierarchical structure: (**a**) e-retailer dataset, (**b**) food dataset [69]

contextual knowledge. For example, Fig. 6.1a presents a four-level hierarchy for the contextual attribute K specifying the intent of a purchasing transaction in an e-retailer application. While the root (coarsest level) of the hierarchy for K defines purchases in all possible contexts, the next level is defined by attribute $K^1 = \{Personal, Gift\}$, which labels each customer purchase either as a personal purchase or as a gift. At the next, finer level of the hierarchy, "Personal" value of attribute K^1 is further split into a more detailed personal context: personal purchase made for the work-related or other purposes. Similarly, the *Gift* value for K^1 can be split into a gift for a partner or a friend and a gift for parents or others. Thus, the K^2 level is $K^2 = \{PersonalWork, PersonalOther, GiftPartner/Friend, GiftParent/Other\}$. Finally, attribute K^2 can be split into further levels of hierarchy, as shown in Fig. 6.1a.[3]

Contextual information was also defined in [6] as follows. In addition to the classical *User* and *Item* dimensions, additional contextual dimensions, such as *Time*, *Location*, etc., were also introduced using the OLAP-based[4] *multidimensional data (MD) model* widely used in the data warehousing applications in databases [37, 55]. Mathematically, this model can be defined with an n-dimensional *tensor*. Formally, let $D_1, D_2, \ldots, D_n$ be dimensions, two of these dimensions being *User* and *Item*, and the rest being contextual. Each dimension D_i is a subset of a Cartesian product of some attributes (or fields) A_{ij}, $(j = 1, \ldots, k_i)$, i.e., $D_i \subseteq A_{i1} \times A_{i2} \times \ldots \times A_{ik_i}$, where each attribute defines a domain (or a set) of values. Moreover, one or several attributes form a *key*, i.e., they uniquely define the rest of the attributes [75]. In some cases, a dimension can be defined by a single attribute, and $k_i = 1$ in such cases. For example, consider the three-dimensional recommendation space $User \times Item \times Time$, where the *User* dimension is defined as $User \subseteq UName \times Address \times Income \times Age$ and consists of a set of users having certain names, addresses, incomes, and being of a certain age. Similarly, the *Item* dimension is defined as $Item \subseteq IName \times Type \times Price$ and consists of a set of items defined by their names, types and the price. Finally, the *Time* dimension can be defined as $Time \subseteq Year \times Month \times Day$ and

[3]For simplicity and illustration purposes, this figure uses only two-way splits. Obviously, three-way, four-way and, more generally, multi-way splits are also allowed.

[4]OLAP stands for OnLine Analytical Processing, which represents a popular approach to manipulation and analysis of data stored in multi-dimensional cube structures and which is widely used for decision support.

consists of a list of days from the starting to the ending date (e.g. from January 1, 2003 to December 31, 2003).

Given dimensions $D_1, D_2, \ldots, D_n$, we define the recommendation space for these dimensions as a Cartesian product $S = D_1 \times D_2 \times \ldots D_n$. Moreover, let *Rating* be a rating domain representing the ordered set of all possible rating values. Then the *rating function* is defined over the space $D_1 \times \ldots \times D_n$ as

$$R : D_1 \times \ldots \times D_n \rightarrow Rating.$$

For instance, continuing the *User* × *Item* × *Time* example considered above, we can define a rating function R on the recommendation space *User* × *Item* × *Time* specifying how much user $u \in User$ liked item $i \in Item$ at time $t \in Time$, $R(u, i, t)$.

Visually, ratings $R(d_1, \ldots, d_n)$ on the recommendation space $S = D_1 \times D_2 \times \ldots \times D_n$ can be stored in a multidimensional cube, such as the one shown in Fig. 6.2. For example, the cube in Fig. 6.2 stores ratings $R(u, i, t)$ for the recommendation space *User* × *Item* × *Time*, where the three tables define the sets of users, items, and times associated with *User*, *Item*, and *Time* dimensions respectively. For example, rating $R(101, 7, 1) = 6$ in Fig. 6.2 means that for the user with User ID 101 and the item with Item ID 7, rating 6 was specified during the weekday.

The rating function R introduced above is usually defined as a partial function, where the initial set of ratings is known. Then, as usual in the ratings-based

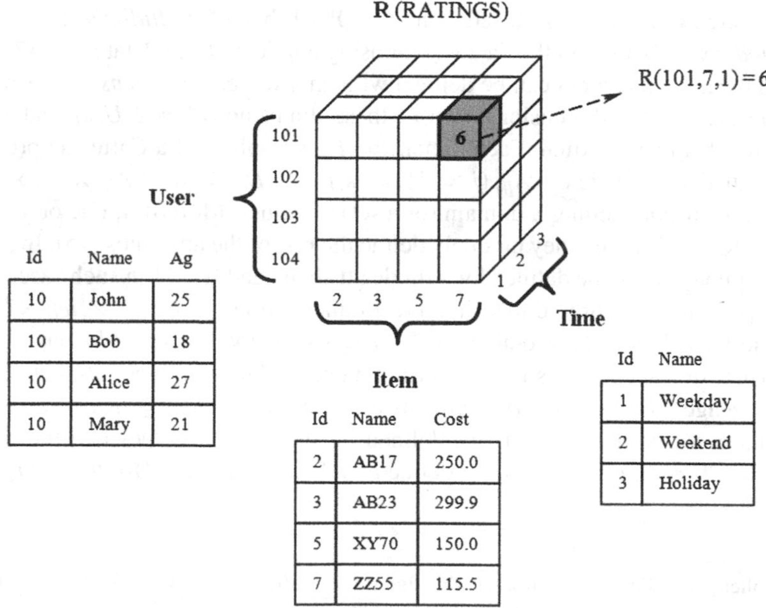

Id	Name	Ag
10	John	25
10	Bob	18
10	Alice	27
10	Mary	21

Id	Name	Cost
2	AB17	250.0
3	AB23	299.9
5	XY70	150.0
7	ZZ55	115.5

Id	Name
1	Weekday
2	Weekend
3	Holiday

Fig. 6.2 Multidimensional model for the *User* × *Item* × *Time* recommendation space

recommender systems, the goal is to estimate the unknown ratings, i.e., make the rating function R total.

The main difference between the multidimensional (MD) contextual model described above and the previously described contextual model lies in that contextual information in the MD model is defined using classical OLAP hierarchies, whereas the contextual information in the previous case is defined with more general hierarchical taxonomies, which can be represented as trees (both balanced and unbalanced), directed acyclic graphs (DAGs), or various other types of taxonomies. Further, the ratings in the MD model are stored in the multidimensional cubes, whereas the ratings in the other contextual model are stored in more general hierarchical structures.

In this section we have provided an overview of the representational approach to modeling contextual information in CARS. The vast majority of CARS research employ this approach, and we will dedicate Sect. 6.3 of this chapter to the discussion of various recommendation techniques that utilize the contextual information using this representational approach in order to provide better recommendations. However, we first discuss several other approaches to modeling contextual information in recommender systems (i.e., besides the representational approach) in Sect. 6.2.3.

6.2.3 Major Approaches to Modeling Contextual Information in Recommender Systems

As mentioned earlier, many existing CARS approaches assume the existence of certain contextual factors (sometimes called contextual dimensions, variables or attributes), such as time, location, and the purchasing purpose, that identify the context in which recommendations are provided. As discussed in Sect. 6.2.2, each contextual factor can be defined by (a) its structure (e.g., defined using trees or OLAP hierarchies) and (b) the values that the contextual variables take. For example, the structure of the Time factor can be defined in terms of Years, Months, Days and Hours. Furthermore, each variable in this structure, Years, Months, Days and Hours, takes the standard set of values, such as the standard 12 months in a year, the standard number of days in a month, hours in a day, etc.

A broader classification of major approaches to modeling contextual information, i.e., classification that goes beyond the standard assumption of the explicit availability of predefined contextual factors with stable (unchanging) structure, is based on the following two aspects of contextual factors [5]: (1) what a recommender system may know about these contextual factors, and (2) how contextual factors change over time.

The first aspect presumes that a recommender system can have different types of knowledge about the contextual factors. This may include knowledge of the list of relevant factors, their structure, and their values. Depending on what is exactly known about the factors (that is, what is observed and what is not), we can classify this knowledge of a recommender system about the contextual factors into the following three categories: fully observable, partially observable, and unobservable [5].

- *Fully observable:* The contextual factors relevant to the application, as well as their structure and their values at the time when recommendations are made, are known *explicitly*. For example, in case of recommending a purchase of a certain product, such as a shirt, the recommender system may know that only the Time, PurchasingPurpose, and ShoppingCompanion factors matter in this application. Further, the recommender system may know the relevant structure of all these three contextual factors, such as having categories of weekday, weekend, and holiday for Time. Further, the recommender system may also know the values of the contextual factors at the recommendation time (for example, when this purchase is made, with whom, and for whom).
- *Partially observable:* Only some of the information about the contextual factors, as described above, is known explicitly. For example, the recommender system may know all the contextual factors, such as Time, PurchasingPurpose, and ShoppingCompanion, but not their structure. Note that there can possibly be different levels of "partial observability." In this chapter, we do not differentiate between them and group various cases of partially observable knowledge into this general category. As another example, mobile recommender systems may know the temporal and geo-spatial contextual factors (e.g., from the system clock and the GPS sensor of the mobile phone), but all other contextual factors may remain unknown.
- *Unobservable:* No information about contextual factors is explicitly available to the recommender system, and it makes recommendations by utilizing only the *latent* knowledge of context in an implicit manner. For example, the recommender system may build a latent predictive model, such as a hierarchical linear or hidden Markov model, to estimate unknown ratings, where unobservable context is modeled using latent variables.

The second aspect of contextual factors is whether and how their structure and their importance changes over time. The settings where the contextual factors are stable over time are classified as static, whereas the factors changing over time are classified as dynamic [5].

- *Static:* The relevant contextual factors and their structure remains the same (stable) over time. For example, in case of recommending a purchase of a certain product, such as a shirt, we can include the contextual factors of Time, PurchasingPurpose, ShoppingCompanion and only these factors during the entire lifespan of the purchasing recommendation application. Furthermore, we assume that the structure of the PurchasingPurpose factor does not change over time: the set of purposes will remain the same throughout the lifespan of the application. The same is applicable to the ShoppingCompanion factor when the same class of shopping companions remains throughout the application.
- *Dynamic:* This is the case when the contextual factors change in some way. For example, the recommender system (or the system designer) may realize over

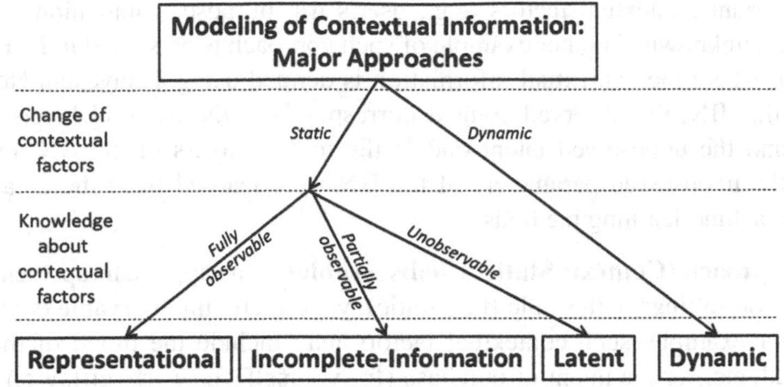

Fig. 6.3 Major approaches to modeling contextual information in recommender systems

time that the ShoppingCompanion factor is no longer relevant for purchasing recommendations and may decide to drop it. Furthermore, the structure of some of the contextual factors can change over time (for example, new categories can be added to the PurchasingPurpose contextual factor over time).

Directly combining the two aspects (i.e., the extent of the recommender system's knowledge about contextual factors and their change over time) could provide 6 (i.e., 3 × 2) possible approaches to modeling contextual information. However, modeling of dynamic contexts represents an already complex task, for which the differentiation between observable and unobservable factors may not be easily formalizable. Therefore, we treat all the approaches to settings with dynamic contextual information as one unified category. In contrast, the modeling approaches for the static context settings are indeed classified further based on the three major cases according to what is known about the contextual factors. This results in four major, distinct approaches to modeling contextual information in recommender systems, as indicated in Fig. 6.3, and we describe them in the remainder of this section.

Representational Approach (Context: Static, Fully Observable) As discussed earlier, this approach corresponds to the *representational* view of context [42], which assumes that all the contextual information in a given application can be modeled with a predefined finite set of observable attributes, where each attribute has a well-defined structure and the structure does not change significantly over time (i.e., is static). The vast majority of the prior work in context-aware recommender systems has focused on this approach and, therefore, we will focus largely on this method in the remainder of this chapter.

Incomplete-Information Approach (Context: Static, Partially Observable) This approach explicitly assumes that only some partial information is known about the contextual factors, which are assumed to have static structure. As mentioned above, an example of the latter case can occur in mobile applications, when the temporal and geo-spatial contextual information is known to the mobile device, but other important contextual factors (e.g., user's trip purpose, companions, mood) may remain unknown. Another example of such approach is presented in Palmisano et al. [69], where the contextual information is defined using a Bayesian Network (BN). In this BN, the observed context corresponds to the external layers of the network and the unobserved latent one to the middle layers of the BN. Further, some of the unobserved parameters of the BN were learned from the data using standard machine-learning methods.

Latent Approach (Context: Static, Unobservable) This approach represents recommendation settings with stable (i.e., static), yet directly unobservable contextual factors. For example, such contextual factors may include the mood of the user (happy, sad, etc.) or the intent of purchase (for yourself, for work, gift, etc.), modeling which could provide recommendation performance improvements. Because the contextual factor structure is stable, it can be modeled with latent variables, and the unobserved contextual information can be learned using machine-learning methods, such as matrix factorization [58], probabilistic latent semantic analysis (PLSA), or hierarchical linear models (HLMs). However, precisely because latent information is not directly observable, it may be difficult to differentiate contextual latent modeling from general-purpose latent modeling approaches in recommender systems (e.g., a variety of general-purpose matrix factorization approaches that are currently popular in recommender systems literature). One possible point of differentiation is that all the latent variables could potentially be associated with the item, user, and/or contextual characteristics. Therefore, the contextual latent variables are those latent characteristics that do not pertain to the user or the item. Although this is an intuitive distinction conceptually, it is hard to operationalize it in practice, and the development of such differentiation methods constitutes an interesting topic of future research and could lead to more nuanced recommendation models and, as a result, potential performance benefits.

Dynamic Approach (Context: Dynamic, Various Observability) This approach represents recommendation settings where the structure (as well as the pertinence) of the contextual information can change over time, e.g., based on passive observations or explicit user feedback. This approach is related to the *interactional* view of context [42], and there are some studies that take the direct interactional approach to modeling contextual recommendations, such as [14] which models context through a short-term memory (STM) interactional approach borrowed from psychology. As another example, Mahmood et al. [65] present a recommender system that adapts the dialogue to the interaction context. This is modeled by a set of dynamic contextual factors representing, for instance, whether the user provided certain information or acted on the recommendations (for example, put an item into the shopping cart). In a dynamic way, step by step, the system adapts the interaction considering a selection of these factors depending on the state of the interaction. In addition, Moling et al. [66] propose a recommendation approach based on a sequential decision making perspective, which allows to blend changing (i.e., less stable) implicit short-term/contextual preferences with more stable long-term user preferences when producing radio channel recommendation. As yet another example, Hariri et al. [45] use a topic-modeling approach to map user's interaction sequence to a sequence of latent topics (representing different contexts) which capture trends in user's current interests. This allows the recommender system to monitor changes in users' interests and dynamically adapt to these changes. As yet another example, consider conversational recommender systems. In standard conversational systems, user feedback is used to iteratively refine the user profile (or the initial user query) resulting in more appropriate recommendations. In a context-aware conversational system, the user feedback may also be used to iteratively modify contextual factors and not just user profiles. For example, in the course of conversation with a user, a restaurant recommender may determine that the user is on a romantic date. This observation, in turn, may result in filtering out restaurants that tend to be noisy or without an adequate wine selection. The iterative refinement of context in conversational recommender systems will introduce a new set of research questions that will require further investigation.

6.2.4 Obtaining Contextual Information

As mentioned earlier, context-aware recommender systems research has been focusing on the representational approach, which assumes that the context is defined with a *predefined* set of contextual attributes, the structure of which does not change over time. The implication of this assumption is that contextual information needs to be identified and acquired before actual recommendations are made. The contextual information can be obtained in a number of ways, including:

- *Explicitly*, i.e., by directly approaching relevant people and other sources of contextual information and explicitly gathering this information either by asking direct questions or eliciting this information through other means. For example, a website may obtain contextual information by asking a person to fill out a web form or to answer some specific questions before providing access to certain web pages. Similarly, a smartphone app may obtain time, location, and motion data from the phone's clock, GPS sensor, and accelerometer, respectively.
- *Implicitly* from the data or the environment, such as a change in location of the user detected by a mobile telephone company. Alternatively, temporal contextual information can be implicitly obtained from the timestamp of a transaction. Nothing needs to be done in these cases in terms of interacting with the user or other sources of contextual information—the source of the implicit contextual information is accessed directly and the data is extracted from it.
- *Inferring* the context using statistical or data mining methods. In other words, contextual information can be "hidden" in the data in some latent form but can still be *implicitly* used to better estimate the unknown ratings. For example, the household identity of a person flipping the TV channels (husband, wife, son, daughter, etc.) may not be explicitly known to a cable TV company; but it can be modeled as a latent variable using various machine learning methods by observing the TV programs watched and the channels visited. This information can then be used to estimate how much this household would like a particular

TV program. It was shown in [69] that this deployment of latent variables, such as intent of purchasing a product (e.g., for yourself vs. as a gift, work-related vs. pleasure, etc.), whose true values were unknown but that were explicitly modeled as a part of a Bayesian Network (BN), indeed improved the predictive performance of the BN classifier. A similar approach of using latent variables is presented in [14]. As another example of inferring contextual information, consider online reviews, such as provided on Yelp, Amazon, and other popular websites. These reviews contain plenty of contextual information describing specific purchasing or consumption experiences, such a restaurant visits. For example, the user may indicate in a review that she went to the restaurant for dinner with her boyfriend to celebrate his birthday. Bauman and Tuzhilin [24] present a method of analyzing such online reviews and extracting contextual information from them. This method is also evaluated on a sample of Yelp reviews, and it is shown that most of the contextual information relevant to that application is extracted using this method. Still another approach toward inferring contextual information, albeit for non-RS related problems, was proposed in [56] where temporal contexts were discovered in web-sessions by decomposing these sessions into non-overlapping segments, each segment relating to one specific context. These contexts were subsequently identified using certain optimization and clustering methods.

It is important to note that, if the acquisition process of the contextual information is done explicitly or even implicitly, it should be conducted as a part of the overall data collection process. This further implies that the decisions of which contextual information should be relevant and collected for an application should be done at the application design stage and well in advance of the time when actual recommendations are provided.

Naturally, not all available contextual factors might be relevant or useful for recommendation purposes. Consider, for example, a book recommender system. Many types of contextual data could potentially be obtained by such a system from book buyers, including: (a) purpose of buying the book (possible options: for work, for leisure, etc.); (b) planned reading time (weekday, weekend, etc.); (c) planned reading place (at home, at school, on a plane, etc.); (d) the value of the stock market index at the time of the purchase. Clearly some types of contextual information can be more relevant in a given application than some other types. For example, in this example, the value of a stock market is likely to be much less relevant as contextual information than the purpose of buying a book.

Because the relevance of contextual factors can vary dramatically from application to application (e.g., location as a recommendation context may matter significantly in one recommendation application, but have absolutely no impact in another), domain expertise typically plays a big role in identifying a candidate set of contextual factors for a given application. For example, for mobile recommendation applications, the following four general types of contextual information are often considered [5, 43]: *physical context* (e.g., time, position, activity of the user, weather, light conditions, temperature), *social context* (e.g., is the user alone or in the group, presence and role of other people around the user), *interaction media context* (e.g., device characteristics—phone/tablet/laptop/etc., media content type—text/audio/video/etc.), *modal context* (e.g., user's state of mind—cognitive capabilities, mood, experience, current goals).

In addition to using the *manual* approach, e.g., leveraging domain knowledge of the recommender system's designer or a market expert in a given application domain, there are also several *computational* approaches to determining the relevance of a given type of contextual information. In particular, numerous existing feature selection procedures from machine learning [57], data mining [63], and statistics [36] can be used during the data preprocessing phase, based on existing ratings data. One methodology of deciding which contextual attributes should be used in a recommendation application (and which should not) is presented in [6]. In particular, Adomavicius et al. [6] propose that a wide range of contextual attributes should be initially selected by the domain experts as possible candidates for the contextual attributes for the application. For example, in a movie recommendation application described in Example 6.1, we can initially consider such contextual attributes as Time, Theater, Companion, Weather, as well as a broad set of other contextual attributes that can possibly affect the movie-watching experiences, as initially identified by the domain experts for the application. Then, after collecting the data, including the rating data and the contextual information, we may apply various types of statistical tests identifying which of the chosen contextual attributes are truly significant in the sense that they indeed affect movie-watching experiences, as manifested by significant deviations in ratings across different values of a contextual attribute. For example, we may apply pairwise t-tests to see if good weather vs. bad weather or seeing a movie alone vs. with a companion significantly affect the movie-watching experiences (as indicated by statistically significant changes in rating distributions). This procedure provides an example of screening all the initially considered contextual attributes and filtering out those that do not matter for a particular recommendation application. For example, we may conclude that the Time, Theater and Companion contexts matter, while the Weather context does not in the considered movie recommendation application. The use of statistical tests for determining the relevance of contextual information has been further explored in subsequent research [67].

Another approach for assessing the relevance of contextual information has been proposed by Baltrunas et al. [20], who developed a survey-based instrument that asks the users to judge what their preferences would be in a wide variety of hypothetical (i.e., imagined) contextual situations. This allows to collect richer contextual preference information in a short timeframe, evaluate the impact of each contextual factor on user preferences based on the collected data, and include into the resulting context-aware system only those factors that were shown to be important. Even though the collected data includes only hypothetical contextual preferences (i.e., preferences for items that users imagined consuming under certain contextual circumstances), the authors demonstrate that the resulting context-aware recommender system was perceived to be more effective by users as compared to the non-context-aware recommender.

The detailed discussion of the specific contextual feature selection procedures is beyond the scope of this chapter; in the remainder of this chapter we will assume that only the relevant contextual information is stored in the data.

In this section we reviewed major approaches to modeling contextual information and also put extra focus on the most popular—representational—approach. Since it has been studied most extensively in the past, we will focus on the major paradigms for incorporating contextual information into the representational approach in the next section.

6.3 Paradigms for Incorporating Representational Context in Recommender Systems

Once the relevant context information has been identified and obtained using the representational approach to CARS, the next step is to use context intelligently in order to produce better recommendations. Different approaches to using contextual information in recommender systems can be broadly categorized into two groups: (1) recommendation via *context-driven querying and search*, and (2) recommendation via *contextual preference elicitation and estimation*. The context-driven querying and search approach has been used by a wide variety of mobile and travel/tourist recommender systems [3, 35, 86]. Systems using this approach typically use contextual information (obtained either directly from the user, e.g., by specifying current mood or interest, or from the environment, e.g., obtaining local time, weather, or current location) to query or search a certain repository of resources (e.g., restaurants) and present the resources that best match a given query (e.g., nearby restaurants that are currently open) to the user. One of the early examples of this approach is the Cyberguide project [3], which developed several *tour guide* prototypes for different hand-held platforms. Abowd et al. [3] discuss different architectures and features necessary to provide realistic tour guide services to mobile users and, more specifically, the role that the contextual knowledge of the user's current and past locations can play in the recommendation and guiding process. Among the many other examples of context-aware tourist guide systems proposed in research literature we can mention GUIDE [38], INTRIGUE [16], COMPASS [86], and MyMap [41] systems.

The other general approach to using contextual information in the recommendation process, i.e., via contextual preference elicitation and estimation, represents a more recent trend in context-aware recommender systems literature [6, 7, 68, 71, 89]. In contrast to the previously discussed context-driven querying and search approach (where the recommender systems typically use the current context information and specified current user's interest as queries to search for the most appropriate content), techniques that follow this second approach attempt to model and learn contextual user preferences, e.g., by observing the interactions of this and other users with the systems or by obtaining preference feedback from the user on various previously recommended items. To model users' context-sensitive preferences and generate recommendations, these techniques typically either adopt existing collaborative filtering, content-based, or hybrid recommendation methods to context-aware recommendation settings or apply various intelligent data analysis techniques from data mining or machine learning (such as Bayesian classifiers or support vector machines).

While both general approaches offer a number of research challenges, in the remainder of this chapter we will focus on the second, more recent trend of the contextual preference elicitation and estimation in recommender systems. We do want to mention that it is possible to design applications that combine the techniques from both general approaches (i.e., both context-driven querying and search as well as contextual preference elicitation and estimation) into a single system. For example, the UbiquiTO system [35], which implements a mobile tourist guide, provides intelligent adaptation not only based on the specific context information, but also uses various rule-based and fuzzy set techniques to adapt the application content based on the user preferences and interests. Similarly, the News@hand system [34] uses semantic technologies to provide personalized news recommendations that are retrieved using user's concept-based queries or calculated according to a specific user's (or a user group's) profile.

To start the discussion of the contextual preference elicitation and estimation techniques for the representational approach to CARS, note that, in its general form, a traditional two-dimensional (2D) (*User* × *Item*) recommender system can be described as a *function*, which takes partial user preference data as its *input* and produces a list of recommendations for each user as an *output*. Accordingly, Fig. 6.4 presents a general overview of the traditional 2D recommendation process, which includes three components: data (input), 2D recommender system (function), and recommendation list (output). Note that, as indicated in Fig. 6.4, after the recommendation function is defined (or constructed) based on the available data, recommendation list for any given user u is typically generated by using the recommendation function on user u and all candidate items to obtain a predicted rating for each of the items and then by ranking all items according to their predicted rating value. Later in this section, we will discuss how the use of contextual information in each of those three components gives rise to three different paradigms for context-aware recommender systems.

As mentioned in Sect. 6.2.2, traditional recommender systems are built based on the knowledge of *partial user preferences*, i.e., user preferences for some (often limited) set of items, and the input data for traditional recommender systems

Fig. 6.4 General components of the traditional recommendation process

is typically based on the records of the form < *user, item, rating* >. In contrast, context-aware recommender systems are built based on the knowledge of *partial contextual user preferences* and typically deal with data records of the form < *user, item, context, rating* >, where each specific record includes not only how much a given user liked a specific item, but also the context in which the item was consumed by this user (e.g., *Context* = Saturday). Also, in addition to the descriptive information about users (e.g., demographics), items (e.g., item features), and ratings (e.g., multi-criteria rating information), context-aware recommender systems may also make use of additional context attributes, such as context hierarchies (e.g., Saturday → Weekend) mentioned in Sect. 6.2.2. Based on the presence of this additional contextual data, several important questions arise: How contextual information should be reflected when modeling user preferences? Can we reuse the wealth of knowledge in traditional (non-contextual) recommender systems to generate context-aware recommendations? We will explore these questions in this chapter in more detail.

In the presence of available contextual information, following the diagrams in Fig. 6.5, we start with the data having the form $U \times I \times C \times R$, where C is additional contextual dimension and end up with a list of contextual recommendations $i_1, i_2, i_3 \ldots$ for each user. However, unlike the process in Fig. 6.4, which does not take into account the contextual information, we can apply the information about the current (or expected) context c at various stages of the recommendation process. More specifically, the context-aware recommendation process that is based

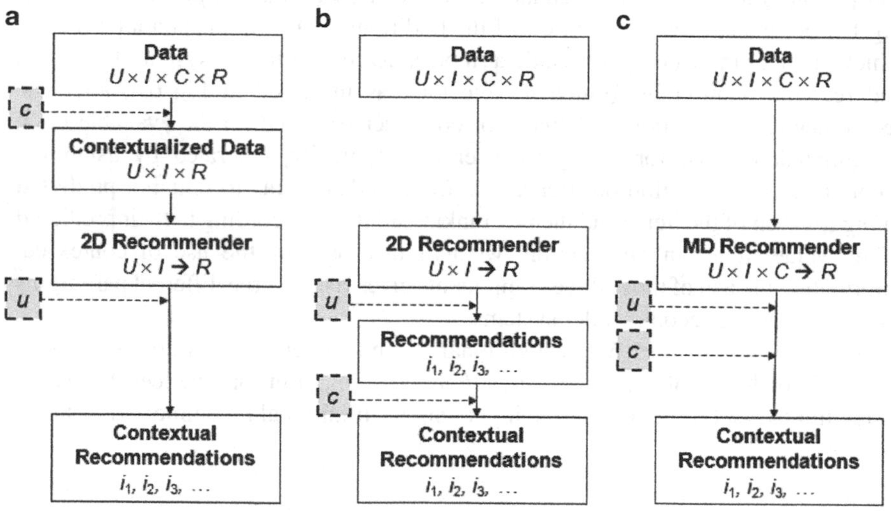

Fig. 6.5 Paradigms for incorporating context in recommender systems. (**a**) Contextual pre-filtering; (**b**) contextual post-filtering; (**c**) contextual modeling

on contextual user preference elicitation and estimation can take one of the three forms, based on which of the three components the context is used in, as shown in Fig. 6.5:

- *Contextual pre-filtering* (or contextualization of recommendation input). In this recommendation paradigm (presented in Fig. 6.5a), contextual information drives data selection or data construction for that specific context. In other words, information about the current context *c* is used for selecting or constructing the relevant set of data records (i.e., ratings). Then, ratings can be predicted using any traditional 2D recommender system on the selected data.
- *Contextual post-filtering* (or contextualization of recommendation output). In this recommendation paradigm (presented in Fig. 6.5b), contextual information is initially ignored, and the ratings are predicted using any traditional 2D recommender system on the *entire* data. Then, the resulting set of recommendations is adjusted (*contextualized*) for each user using the contextual information.
- *Contextual modeling* (or contextualization of recommendation function). In this recommendation paradigm (presented in Fig. 6.5c), contextual information is used directly in the modeling technique as part of rating estimation.

In the remainder of this section we will discuss these three approaches in detail.

6.3.1 Contextual Pre-filtering

As shown in Fig. 6.5a, the contextual pre-filtering approach uses contextual information to select or construct the most relevant 2D (*User* × *Item*) data for generating recommendations. One major advantage of this approach is that it allows deployment of any of the numerous traditional recommendation techniques previously proposed in the literature [9]. In particular, in one possible use of this approach, context *c* essentially serves as a *query* for selecting (filtering) relevant ratings data. An example of a contextual data filter for a movie recommender system would be: if a person wants to see a movie on Saturday, *only* the Saturday rating data is used to recommend movies. Note that this example represents an *exact pre-filter*. In other words, the data filtering query has been constructed using exactly the specified context.

For example, following the contextual pre-filtering paradigm, Adomavicius et al. [6] proposed a *reduction-based approach*, which reduces the problem of multidimensional (MD) contextual recommendations to the standard 2D *User* × *Item* recommendation space. Therefore, as with any contextual pre-filtering approach, one important benefit of the reduction-based approach is that all the previous research on 2D recommender systems is directly applicable in the MD case after the reduction is done. In particular, let $R^D_{User \times Item}$: $U \times I \rightarrow Rating$ be *any* 2D rating estimation function that, given existing ratings D (i.e., D contains records $< user, item, rating >$ for each of the known, user-specified ratings), can calculate a prediction for any rating, e.g., $R^D_{User \times Item}(John, StarWars)$. A three-dimensional rating prediction function supporting the context of time can be defined similarly as $R^D_{User \times Item \times Time}$: $U \times I \times T \rightarrow Rating$, where D contains records $<$

user, *item*, *time*, *rating* > for the user-specified ratings. Then the three-dimensional prediction function can be expressed through a 2D prediction function in several ways, including:

$$\forall (u,i,t) \in U \times I \times T, R^{D}_{User \times Item \times Time}(u,i,t) = R^{D[Time=t](User,Item,Rating)}_{User \times Item}(u,i).$$

Here $[Time = t]$ denotes a simple contextual pre-filter, and $D[Time = t](User, Item, Rating)$ denotes a rating dataset obtained from D by selecting only the records where *Time* dimension has value t and keeping only the values for *User* and *Item* dimensions, as well as the value of the rating itself. That is, if we treat a dataset of three-dimensional ratings D as a relation, then $D[Time = t](User, Item, Rating)$ is simply another relation obtained from D by performing two relational operations: selection and, subsequently, projection.

However, the exact context sometimes can be too narrow. Consider, for example, the context of watching a movie with a girlfriend in a movie theater on Saturday or, i.e., $c =$ (Girlfriend, Theater, Saturday). Using this exact context as a data filtering query may be problematic for several reasons. First, certain aspects of the overly specific context may not be significant. For example, user's movie watching preferences with a girlfriend in a theater on Saturday may be exactly the same as on Sunday, but different from Wednesday's. Therefore, it may be more appropriate to use a more general context specification, i.e., Weekend instead of Saturday. And second, exact context may not have enough data for accurate rating prediction, which is known as the "sparsity" problem in recommender systems literature. In other words, the recommender system may not have enough data points about the past movie watching preferences of a given user with a girlfriend in a theater on Saturday.

Adomavicius et al. [6] introduce the notion of *generalized pre-filtering*, which allows to generalize the data filtering query obtained based on a specified context. More formally, let's define $c' = (c'_1, \ldots, c'_k)$ to be a generalization of context $c = (c_1, \ldots, c_k)$ if and only if $c_i \rightarrow c'_i$ for every $i = 1, \ldots, k$ in the corresponding context hierarchy. Then, c' (instead of c) can be used as a data query to obtain contextualized ratings data.

Following the idea of context generalization, Adomavicius et al. [6] proposed to use not a simple pre-filter $[Time = t]$, which represents the exact context t of the rating (u, i, t), but rather a generalized pre-filter $[Time \in S_t]$, where S_t denotes some superset of context t. Here S_t is called a *contextual segment* [6]. For example, if we would like to predict how much John Doe would like to see the "Gladiator" movie on Monday, i.e., to calculate $R^{D}_{User \times Item \times Time}(JohnDoe, Gladiator, Monday)$, we could use not only other user-specified *Monday* ratings for prediction, but *Weekday* ratings in general. In other words, for every (u, i, t) where $t \in Weekday$, we can predict the rating as $R^{D}_{User \times Item \times Time}(u,i,t) = R^{D[Time \in Weekday](User,Item,AGGR(Rating))}_{User \times Item}(u,i)$. More generally, in order to estimate some rating $R(u, i, t)$, we can use some specific contextual segment S_t as: $R^{D}_{User \times Item \times Time}(u,i,t) = R^{D[Time \in S_t](User,Item,AGGR(Rating))}_{User \times Item}(u,i)$.

Note, that we have used the *AGGR*(*Rating*) notation in the above expressions, since there may be several user-specified ratings with the same *User* and *Item* values for different *Time* instances in dataset D belonging to some contextual segment S_t (e.g., different ratings for *Monday* and *Tuesday*, all belonging to segment *Weekday*). Therefore, we have to aggregate these values using some aggregation function, e.g., averaging, when reducing the dimensionality of the recommendation space. The above three-dimensional reduction-based approach can be extended to a general pre-filtering method reducing an arbitrary n-dimensional recommendation space to an m-dimensional one (where $m < n$). In this chapter we will assume that $m = 2$ because traditional recommendation algorithms are only designed for the two-dimensional *User* × *Item* case. Note that there typically exist multiple different possibilities for context generalization, based on the context taxonomy and the desired context granularity. For example, let's assume that we have the following contextual taxonomies (*is-a* or *belongs-to* relationships) that can be derived from context hierarchies:

- *Company*: Girlfriend → Friends → NotAlone → AnyCompany;
- *Place*: Theater → AnyPlace;
- *Time*: Saturday → Weekend → AnyTime.

Then, the following are just several examples of possible generalizations c' of the above-mentioned context $c =$ (Girlfriend, Theater, Saturday):

- $c' =$ (Girlfriend, AnyPlace, Saturday);
- $c' =$ (Friends, Theater, AnyTime);
- $c' =$ (NotAlone, Theater, Weekend).

Therefore, choosing the "right" generalized pre-filter becomes an important problem. One option is to use a manual, expert-driven approach; e.g., always generalize specific days of week into more general Weekday or Weekend. Another option is to use a more automated approach, which could empirically evaluate the predictive performance of the recommender system on contextualized input datasets obtained from each generalized pre-filter, and then would automatically choose the pre-filter with best performance. An interesting and important research issue is how to deal with potential computational complexity of this approach due to context granularity; in other words, in cases of applications with highly granular contexts, there may exist a very large number of possible context generalizations, for which exhaustive search techniques would not be practical. For such cases, effective greedy approaches would need to be developed. Jiang and Tuzhilin [50] examine optimal levels of granularity of customer segments in order to maximize predictive performance of segmentation methods. Applicability of these techniques in the context-aware recommender systems settings constitutes an interesting problem for future research.

So far, we have discussed applying only one pre-filter at a time. However, as it has been well-documented in recommender systems literature, often a combination (a "blend" or an ensemble) of several solutions provides significant performance improvements over the individual approaches [30, 31, 58, 74]. Therefore, it may also

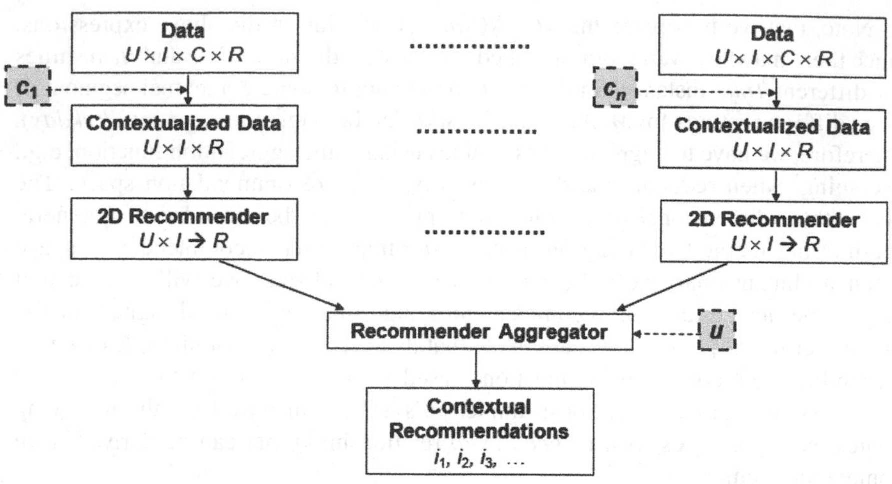

Fig. 6.6 Combining multiple pre-filters

be useful to combine several contextual pre-filters into one model at the same time. The rationale for having a number of different pre-filters is based on the fact that, as mentioned earlier, typically there can be multiple different (and potentially relevant) generalizations of the same specific context. Following this idea, Adomavicius et al. [6] use pre-filters based on the number of possible contexts for each rating, and then combine recommendations resulting from each contextual pre-filter. The general overview of this approach is shown in Fig. 6.6. Note that the combination of several pre-filters can be done in multiple ways. For example, for rating estimation in a specific context, (a) one could choose the best-performing pre-filter, or (b) use an aggregate prediction from the entire "ensemble" of pre-filters.

Also note that the contextual pre-filtering approach is related to the problems of building local models in machine learning and data mining [13]. Rather than building the global rating estimation model utilizing all the available ratings, this approach builds a *local* rating estimation model that uses only the ratings pertaining to the user-specified criteria in which a recommendation is made (e.g., morning). It is important to know if a local model generated by the pre-filtering approach outperforms the global model of the traditional 2D technique, where all the information associated with the contextual dimensions is simply ignored. For example, it is possible that it is better to use the contextual pre-filtering to recommend movies to see in the movie theaters on weekends, but use the traditional 2D technique for movies to see at home. This is the case because pre-filtering, on the one hand, focuses recommendations on a *particular segment* and builds a local prediction model for this segment, but, on the other hand, computes these recommendations based on a *smaller* number of points limited to the considered segment. This tradeoff between having *more relevant* data for calculating an unknown rating based only on the ratings with the same or similar context and having *fewer* data points used in this calculation belonging to a particular segment (i.e., the *sparsity* effect) explains why the pre-filtering recommendation method can outperform traditional 2D recommendation techniques on some segments and underperform on others. Which of these two trends dominates on a particular segment may depend on the application domain and on the specifics of the available data. This observation provides yet another motivation behind the aforementioned ensemble-based approaches [6] that can combine a number of contextual pre-filters along with the traditional 2D technique (i.e., as a default filter, where no filtering is done). This allows to take advantage of more-targeted (local) and well-performing contextual segments were possible, while reverting to the default, traditional 2D technique in other cases.

Among other developments, Ahn et al. [12] use a technique similar to the contextual pre-filtering to recommend advertisements to mobile users by taking into account user location, interest, and time, and Lombardi et al. [64] evaluate the effect of contextual information using a pre-filtering approach on the data obtained from an online retailer. Also, Baltrunas and Ricci [22, 23] take a somewhat different approach to contextual pre-filtering in proposing and evaluating the benefits of the *item splitting* technique, where each item is split into several fictitious items based on the different contexts in which these items can be consumed. Similarly to the item splitting idea, Baltrunas and Amatriain [17] introduce the idea of *micro-profiling* (or user splitting), which splits the user profile into several (possibly overlapping) sub-profiles, each representing the given user in a particular context. The predictions are done using these contextual micro-profiles instead of a single user model. Note that these data construction techniques fit well under the contextual pre-filtering paradigm, because they are following the same basic idea (as the data filtering techniques described earlier)—using contextual information to reduce the problem of multidimensional recommendations to the standard 2D *User* × *Item* space, which then allows to use any traditional recommendation techniques for rating prediction. The idea of generalized contextual pre-filtering has also been adopted in various studies; for example, Zheng et al. [90] use a similar approach (called context "relaxation") for travel recommendations. Furthermore, Codina et al. [40] provide a different approach to generalize the pre-filtering approach; they leverage semantic similarities between different contextual conditions and compute the recommendations based on the ratings taken not just from the single contextual condition, but from the similar contexts as well.

The idea of combining multiple filters is not limited only to pre-filtering and can be extended to post-filtering and contextual modeling approaches (which will be discussed next). In particular, complex contextual information can be split into several components, and the utility of each piece of contextual information may be different depending on whether it is used in the pre-filtering, post-filtering, or modeling stage. For example, time information (weekday vs. weekend) may be most useful to pre-filter relevant data, but weather information (sunny vs. rainy) may be the most appropriate to use as a post-filter. Determining the utility of different contextual information with respect to different paradigms of context-aware recommender systems constitutes an interesting and promising direction for future research.

6.3.2 Contextual Post-filtering

As shown in Fig. 6.5b, the contextual post-filtering approach ignores context information in the input data when generating recommendations, i.e., when generating the ranked list of all candidate items from which any number of top-N recommendations can be made, depending on specific values of N. Then, the contextual post-filtering approach adjusts the obtained recommendation list for each user using context information. The recommendation list adjustments can be made by:

- *Filtering* out recommendations that are irrelevant (in a given context), or
- *Adjusting* the ranking of recommendations on the list (based on a given context).

For example, in a movie recommendation application, if a person wants to see a movie on a weekend, and on weekends she only watches comedies, the system can filter out all non-comedies from the recommended movie list. More generally, the basic idea for contextual post-filtering approaches is to analyze the contextual preference data for a given user in a given context to find specific item usage patterns (e.g., user Jane Doe watches only comedies on weekends) and then use these patterns to adjust the item list, resulting in more "contextual" recommendations, as depicted in Fig. 6.7.

As with many recommendation techniques, the contextual post-filtering approaches can be classified into heuristic and model-based techniques. *Heuristic* post-filtering approaches focus on finding common item characteristics (attributes) for a given user in a given context (e.g., preferred actors to watch in a given context), and then use these attributes to adjust the recommendations, including:

- *Filtering* out recommended items that do not have a significant number of these characteristics (e.g., to be recommended, the movies must have at least two of the preferred actors in a given context), or

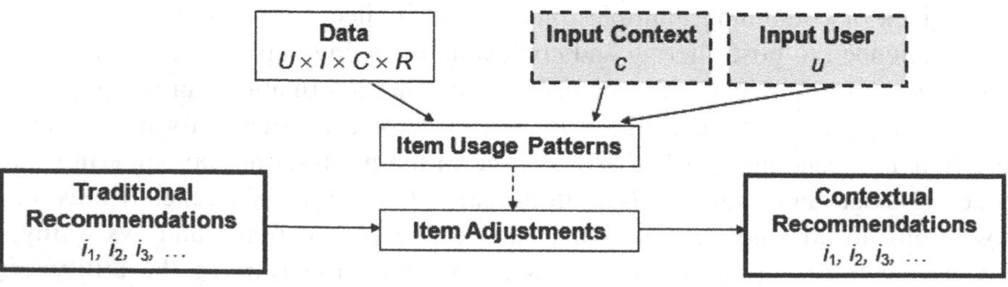

Fig. 6.7 Final phase of the contextual post-filtering approach: recommendation list adjustment

- *Ranking* recommended items based on how many of these relevant characteristics they have (e.g., the movies that star more of the user's preferred actors in a given context will be ranked higher).

In contrast, *model-based* post-filtering approaches can build predictive models that calculate the probability with which the user chooses a certain type of item in a given context, i.e., probability of relevance (e.g., likelihood of choosing movies of a certain genre in a given context), and then use this probability to adjust the recommendations, including:

- *Filtering* out recommended items that have the probability of relevance smaller than a pre-defined minimal threshold (e.g., remove movies of genres that have a low likelihood of being picked), or
- *Ranking* recommended items by weighting the predicted rating with the probability of relevance.

Panniello et al. [71] provide an experimental comparison of the exact pre-filtering method (discussed in Sect. 6.3.1) versus two different post-filtering methods—*Weight* and *Filter*—using several real-world e-commerce datasets. The *Weight* post-filtering method reorders the recommended items by weighting the predicted rating with the probability of relevance in that specific context, and the *Filter* post-filtering method filters out recommended items that have small probability of relevance in the specific context. Interestingly, the empirical results show that the *Weight* post-filtering method dominates the exact pre-filtering, which in turn dominates the *Filter* post-filtering method, thus, indicating that the best approach to use (pre- or post-filtering) really depends on a given application.

As was the case with the contextual pre-filtering approach, a major advantage of the contextual post-filtering approach is that it allows using any of the numerous traditional recommendation techniques previously proposed in the literature [9]. Also, similarly to the contextual pre-filtering approaches, incorporating context generalization techniques into post-filtering techniques constitutes an interesting issue for future research.

6.3.3 Contextual Modeling

As shown in Fig. 6.5c, the contextual modeling approach uses contextual information *directly* in the recommendation function as an explicit predictor of a user's rating for an item. While contextual pre-filtering and post-filtering approaches can use traditional 2D recommendation functions, the contextual modeling approach gives rise to truly multidimensional recommendation functions, which essentially represent predictive models (built using decision trees, regressions, probabilistic models, or other techniques) or heuristic calculations that incorporate contextual information in addition to the user and item data, i.e., $Rating = R(User, Item, Context)$. A significant number of recommendation algorithms—based on a variety of heuristics as well as predictive modeling techniques—have been developed over the last 15 years, and some of these techniques can be extended from the 2D to the multidimensional recommendation settings.

For example, Adomavicius and Tuzhilin [8] proposes to extend the traditional two-dimensional (2D) neighborhood-based approach [28, 81] to the multidimensional case, which includes the contextual information, by using an n-dimensional distance metric instead of the user-user or item-item similarity metrics traditionally used in such techniques. To illustrate how this can be done, consider an example of the three-dimensional *User* × *Item* × *Time* recommendation space. Following the traditional nearest neighbor heuristic that is based on the weighted sum of relevant ratings, the prediction of a specific rating $r_{u,i,t}$ in this example can be expressed as:

$$r_{u,i,t} = k \sum_{(u',i',t') \neq (u,i,t)} W((u,i,t),(u',i',t')) \times r_{u',i',t'},$$

where $W((u,i,t),(u',i',t'))$ describes the "weight" that rating $r_{u',i',t'}$ carries in the prediction of $r_{u,i,t}$, and k is a normalizing factor. Weight $W((u,i,t),(u',i',t'))$ is typically inversely related to the distance between points (u,i,t) and (u',i',t') in multidimensional space, i.e., $dist[(u,i,t),(u',i',t')]$. In other words, the closer the two points are (i.e., the smaller the distance between them), the more weight $r_{u',i',t'}$ carries in the weighted sum. Moreover, Adomavicius and Tuzhilin [8] presents different types of the distance functions used for defining weights $W((u,i,t),(u',i',t'))$; see [8] for additional details.

Another heuristic-based contextual modeling (CM) method is presented in [70], where four variants of the same CM method are considered, i.e., Mdl1, Mdl2, Mdl3, Mdl4. Each of these CM methods requires building a contextual profile $prof(u,c)$ for user u in context c, and then using the contextual profiles of all the users to find the N nearest neighbors of user u in terms of these profiles in context c. The four types of the CM approaches (Mdl1, Mdl2, Mdl3, Mdl4) vary in the constraints by which the neighbors are selected. In Mdl1, there is no constraint in the selection of the N neighbors, i.e., they can be selected based on any context at any level of the hierarchy. In Mdl2, an equal proportion of neighbors is selected from each context c regardless of the context hierarchy. In Mdl3, N neighbors are selected from each context c and each level of the context hierarchy. In Mdl4, an equal proportion of neighbors is selected from each context c at the same level of context hierarchy.

In addition to the heuristic-based contextual modeling techniques, there have been several model-based techniques proposed in the literature. For example, Adomavicius and Tuzhilin [8] present a method of extending a regression-based Hierarchical Bayesian (HB) collaborative filtering model of estimating unknown ratings proposed by Ansari et al. [15] in order to incorporate additional contextual dimensions, such as time and location, into the HB model.

Similarly, Karatzoglou et al. [52] have proposed an extended version of matrix factorization approach based on tensor factorization, which allows to incorporate contextual information into the recommendation process. A alternative matrix-factorization-based approach has been proposed by Baltrunas et al. [21], who extended the traditional matrix factorization technique to context-aware settings by introducing additional model parameters to model the interaction of the contextual factors with ratings.

In addition to extending the traditional *User* × *Item* model-based collaborative filtering techniques to incorporate the contextual dimensions, there have also been some new techniques developed specifically for context-aware recommender systems based on the context modeling paradigm. For example, following the general contextual modeling paradigm, Oku et al. [68] propose to incorporate additional contextual dimensions (such as time, companion, and weather) directly into recommendation space and use machine learning technique to provide recommendations in a restaurant recommender system. In particular, they use support vector machine (SVM) classification method, which views the set of liked items and the set of disliked items of a user in various contexts as two sets of vectors in an n-dimensional space, and constructs a separating hyperplane in this space, which maximizes the separation between the two data sets. The resulting hyperplane represents a classifier for future recommendation decisions (i.e., a given item in a specific context will be recommended if it falls on the "like" side of the hyperplane, and will not be recommended if it falls on the "dislike" side). Furthermore, Oku et al. [68] empirically show that context-aware SVM significantly outperforms non-contextual SVM-based recommendation algorithm in terms of predictive accuracy and user's satisfaction with recommendations. Similarly, Yu et al. [89] use contextual modeling approach to provide content recommendations for smartphone users by introducing context as additional model dimensions and using hybrid recommendation technique (synthesizing content-based, Bayesian-classifier, and rule-based methods) to generate recommendations. Also, Hariri et al. [46] employ the Latent Dirichlet Allocation (LDA) model for use in context-aware recommender systems, which allows to model jointly the users, items, and the meta-data associated with contextual information.

Finally, another model-based approach is presented in [2] where a Personalized Access Model (PAM) is presented that provides a set of personalized context-based services, including context discovery, contextualization, binding and matching services. Then Abbar et al. [2] describe how these services can be combined to form Context-Aware Recommender Systems (CARS) and deployed in order to provide superior context-aware recommendations.

In this section we described various ways to incorporate contextual information into recommendation algorithms within the framework of pre-filtering, post-filtering, and contextual modeling paradigms. Since CARS is still a relatively young sub-area of recommender systems, developing further improvements across all these three paradigms represent a promising research direction.

6.4 Discussion and Conclusions

Context-awareness is being recognized as an important issue in many recommendation applications, which is evidenced by an increasing number of papers on context-aware recommender systems that appear in conferences and journals, as well as by the number and variety of research workshops that have been dedicated specifically to the topics related to context-aware recommender systems. Looking at the current state of the art in context-aware recommender systems, the main research issues, challenges, and directions can be broadly classified into the following four general categories [4]:

- *Fundamentals*, i.e., understanding the notion of context and modeling context in recommender systems.
- *Algorithms*, i.e., developing recommendation algorithms that can incorporate contextual information into recommender systems in advantageous ways.
- *Evaluation*, i.e., in-depth performance evaluation of various context-aware recommendation approaches and techniques, their benefits and limitations.
- *Engineering*, i.e., designing general-purpose architectures, frameworks, and approaches to facilitate the development, implementation, deployment, and use of context-aware recommendation capabilities.

Not surprisingly, the overwhelming majority of existing research on context-aware recommender systems can be classified under the "Algorithms" category [4], i.e., researchers have focused primarily on how to take advantage of contextual information in order to improve the quality of recommendations for different recommendation tasks and applications. Compared to "Algorithms" the other three categories have been relatively under-explored, although there have been more work in the several other areas in recent years.

One recent representative example in the "Evaluation" category is the work by Panniello et al. [70], who performed a comprehensive evaluation and comparison of several contextual pre-filtering, post-filtering, and modeling techniques under variety of conditions, e.g., for different recommendation tasks (find-all vs. top-k), different recommendation utility metrics (accuracy vs. diversity), the granularity of the processed contextual information, as well as other characteristics. Among many findings, the comparison shows that there is no "universally" best technique under all evaluation dimensions. For example, the contextual modeling and post-filtering approaches demonstrate good accuracy performance in many situations, while the exact pre-filtering approach often exhibits better diversity. However, the contextual modeling approaches tend to achieve a comparatively good balance in the accuracy-diversity trade-off. Another example in the "Evaluation" category is the work by Campos et al. [33], who focused on exploring "time" as one of the most valuable and widely used contextual factors in many recommender systems applications. For example, the authors review common evaluation practices and methodological issues related to the comparative evaluation of time-aware recommender systems. They also demonstrate that the choice of the evaluation conditions impacts the performance ranking of different recommendation strategies and propose a methodological framework for a robust and fair evaluation process. These works represent an important step in the direction of improved, standardized and, thus, more reproducible evaluation procedures for context-aware recommender systems.

Developing several large-scale publicly available contextual recommendation datasets for evaluation purposes would provide further stimulus for the CARS research activities and, therefore, this should also be an important priority for the research community.

However, additional research is needed not only in terms of purely algorithmic evaluation, but also in terms of user studies for understanding various behavioral and economic implications of using contextual information in recommender systems (e.g., user acceptance, satisfaction, intrusiveness, privacy, trust, etc.) and preferably not only on the offline data but also in live experiments on real users (i.e., so called A/B testing). One example of such effort is the work by Gorgoglione et al. [44], where the authors study the effects of contextual recommendations on the purchasing behavior of customers and their trust in the provided recommendations, as opposed to the usual predictive accuracy metrics used in most of the other CARS studies. In particular, Gorgoglione et al. [44] describe live controlled experiments performed by the authors with real customers of a major commercial European retailer, in which the authors compare recommendation accuracy, diversity, customers' purchasing behavior and measure customer trust in the provided recommendations across the contextual, content-based, and random recommendations. The authors show that context-aware recommendation techniques outperform traditional (non-contextual) approaches in terms of accuracy, trust, and several economics-based performance metrics across most of their experimental settings. Another interesting example of user studies with context-aware recommender systems is the work by Braunhofer et al. [26]. In this study, the users, after receiving a recommendation from a context-aware system that recommends points-of-interest, were asked to evaluate the system's performance on the following two dimensions: "Does this recommendation fit my preference?" (i.e., "personalization" performance) and "Is this recommendation well-chosen for the situation?" (i.e., "contextualization" performance). In this specific study, the authors show that their proposed technique is able to improve the baseline performance along one of these dimensions—contextualization. Exploring the possible relationships between these two performance dimensions further as well as understanding the performance of other context-aware recommendation techniques with respect to these dimensions represent interesting research directions. In summary, it is important for the CARS community to continue the lines of work described in [26, 44] and to provide strong additional evidence (e.g., via live controlled experiments) of the economic and usability advantages of CARS over the traditional recommendation methods.

Much of the work on context-aware recommender systems has been conceptual, where recommendation techniques are developed, tested on some (often limited) data, and shown to perform well in comparison to certain benchmarks. Historically, there has been little work done on the "Engineering" aspect for CARS, i.e., developing novel data structures, efficient storage methods, and new system architectures. A recent representative example of such system-building work is the study by Hussein et al. [47, 48], where the authors introduce a service-oriented architecture enabling to define and implement a variety of different "building blocks" for context-aware recommender systems, such as recommendation algorithms, context sensors, various filters and converters, in a modular fashion. These building blocks can then be combined and reused in many different ways into systems that can generate contextual recommendations. Another example of such work is Abbar et al. [2], where the authors present a service-oriented approach that implements the Personalized Access Model (PAM) previously proposed by the authors. The implementation is done using global software architecture of CARS developed by the authors and described in [2]. In addition, there has been a number of recent research advances in database community in developing frameworks and techniques for building recommender systems functionality (including some context-aware functionality) directly into relational database engines [61, 62, 82, 83], which provides a number of important benefits in terms of storage, query processing, query optimization, and others.

Another important "Engineering" aspect is to develop richer interaction capabilities with CARS that make recommendations more flexible. As compared to traditional recommender systems, context-aware recommenders have two important differences. The first is *increased complexity*, since CARS involve not only users and items in the recommendation process, but also various types of contextual information. Thus, the types of recommendations can be significantly more complex in comparison to the traditional non-contextual cases. For example, in a movie recommendation application, a certain user (e.g., Tom) may seek recommendations for him and his girlfriend of top 3 movies and the best times to see them over the weekend. The second difference is *increased interactivity*, since more information (i.e., context) usually needs to be elicited from the user in the CARS settings. For example, to utilize the available contextual information, a CARS system may need to elicit from the user (Tom) with whom he wants to see a movie (e.g., girlfriend) and when (e.g., over the weekend) before providing any context-specific recommendations. The combination of these two features calls for the development of more flexible recommendation methods that allow the user to express the types of recommendations that are of interest to them rather than being "hard-wired" into the recommendation engines provided by most of the current vendors that, primarily, focus on recommending top-N items to the user and vice versa. The second requirement of interactivity also calls for the development of tools allowing users to provide inputs into the recommendation process in an interactive and iterative manner, preferably via some well-defined user interface (UI).

Such flexible context-aware recommendations can be supported in several ways. First, Adomavicius et al. [11] developed a *recommendation query language* REQUEST that allows its users to express in a flexible manner a broad range of recommendations that are tailored to their own individual needs and, therefore, more accurately reflect their interests. REQUEST is based on the multidimensional contextual recommendation model described in Sect. 6.2.2 and also in [6]. REQUEST supports a wide variety of features, and the interested reader can find the detailed account of these features as well as the formal syntax and various properties of the language in [11]. In addition, Adomavicius et al. [11] provide a discussion of the expressive power of REQUEST and present a multidimensional recommendation algebra that provides the theoretical basis for this language.

Another proposal to provide flexible recommendations is presented in [59], where the FlexRecs system and framework are described. FlexRecs approach supports flexible recommendations over structured data by decoupling the definition of a recommendation process from its execution. In particular, a recommendation can be expressed declaratively as a high-level parameterized workflow containing traditional relational operators and novel recommendation-specific operators that are combined together into a recommendation workflow.

Furthermore, since a major argument for introducing any recommendation query language is its use by the end-users, it is also very important to develop simple, friendly, interactive, and expressive user interfaces (UIs) for supporting flexible but sometimes complex contextual recommendations. High-quality UIs should reduce the complexity and simplify interactions between the end-users and the recommender system and make them available to wider audiences. For instance, for FlexRecs this may entail building a UI for defining and managing recommendation workflows, while for REQUEST this may involve building front-end UI allowing users to express REQUEST queries using visual and interactive methods. Developing these and other UIs for CARS constitutes a topic of future research.

"Fundamentals" represents arguably the least developed research direction. Context is a complex notion, and there are many diverse approaches of conceptualizing context in recommender systems, some of them still being debated among the researchers. Although the recommender systems community is gradually converging toward the common definition of context, and this chapter represents an attempt to integrate different approaches into one common framework, additional work is still required for the CARS community to arrive at a clear, more formalized definition of context and, therefore, many important questions still remain to be explored in a principled manner. For example, what are underlying theoretical underpinnings for context relevance? Are there systematic approaches for identifying relevant contextual factors (i.e., on which to collect data)? When explicit contextual information is not available, when should we model context as a latent factor vs. ignore modeling the context altogether? What are the tradeoffs of different modeling assumptions (e.g., static vs. dynamic context)? Most of existing research on context-aware recommender systems follows the assumption that contextual dimensions are stable and observable, but implications of other modeling assumptions and approaches should also be explored. These are only some of the examples of various questions that the CARS community can explore further.

In summary, the field of context-aware recommender systems (CARS) is still a relatively new and promising area of research with many interesting and practically important research problems, and much more work is needed to investigate them in a principled and comprehensive manner.

Acknowledgement Research of A. Tuzhilin was supported in part by the National Science Foundation grant IIS-1256036, USA.

References

1. AWS re:Invent 2012, Day 1 Keynote. http://www.youtube.com/watch?v=8FJ5DBLSFe4. YouTube video; Accessed: 2014-06-28
2. Abbar, S., Bouzeghoub, M., Lopez, S.: Context-aware recommender systems: A service-oriented approach. VLDB PersDB Workshop (2009)
3. Abowd, G.D., Atkeson, C.G., Hong, J., Long, S., Kooper, R., Pinkerton, M.: Cyberguide: A mobile context-aware tour guide. Wireless Networks **3**(5), 421–433 (1997)
4. Adomavicius, G., Jannach, D.: Preface to the special issue on context-aware recommender systems. User Model. User-Adapt. Interact. **24**(1–2), 1–5 (2014)
5. Adomavicius, G., Mobasher, B., Ricci, F., Tuzhilin, A.: Context-aware recommender systems. AI Magazine **32**(3), 67–80 (2011)
6. Adomavicius, G., Sankaranarayanan, R., Sen, S., Tuzhilin, A.: Incorporating contextual information in recommender systems using a multidimensional approach. ACM Transactions on Information Systems (TOIS) **23**(1), 103–145 (2005)
7. Adomavicius, G., Tuzhilin, A.: Multidimensional recommender systems: A data warehousing approach. In: L. Fiege, G. Mhl, U. Wilhelm (eds.) Electronic Commerce, *Lecture Notes in Computer Science*, vol. 2232, pp. 180–192. Springer Berlin Heidelberg (2001). DOI 10.1007/3-540-45598-1_17. URL http://dx.doi.org/10.1007/3-540-45598-1_17
8. Adomavicius, G., Tuzhilin, A.: Incorporating context into recommender systems using multidimensional rating estimation methods. In: Proceedings of the 1st International Workshop on Web Personalization, Recommender Systems and Intelligent User Interfaces (WPRSIUI 2005) (2005)
9. Adomavicius, G., Tuzhilin, A.: Toward the next generation of recommender systems: A survey of the state-of-the-art and possible extensions. IEEE Transactions on Knowledge and Data Engineering **17**(6), 734–749 (2005)
10. Adomavicius, G., Tuzhilin, A.: Context-aware recommender systems. In: Ricci et al. [79], pp. 217–253
11. Adomavicius, G., Tuzhilin, A., Zheng, R.: REQUEST: A query language for customizing recommendations. Information System Research **23**(1), 99–117 (2011)
12. Ahn, H., Kim, K., Han, I.: Mobile advertisement recommender system using collaborative filtering: MAR-CF. In: Proceedings of the 2006 Conference of the Korea Society of Management Information Systems,
13. Alpaydin, E.: Introduction to machine learning. The MIT Press (2004)
14. Anand, S.S., Mobasher, B.: Contextual recommendation. WebMine, LNAI **4737**, 142–160 (2007)
15. Ansari, A., Essegaier, S., Kohli, R.: Internet recommendation systems. Journal of Marketing Research **37**(3), 363–375 (2000)
16. Ardissono, L., Goy, A., Petrone, G., Segnan, M., Torasso, P.: Intrigue: personalized recommendation of tourist attractions for desktop and hand held devices. Applied Artificial Intelligence **17**(8), 687–714 (2003)
17. Baltrunas, L., Amatriain, X.: Towards time-dependant recommendation based on implicit feedback. In: Workshop on Context-Aware Recommender Systems (CARS 2009). New York (2009)
18. Baltrunas, L., Kaminskas, M., Ludwig, B., Moling, O., Ricci, F., Aydin, A., Lke, K.H., Schwaiger, R.: Incarmusic: Context-aware music recommendations in a car. In: C. Huemer, T. Setzer (eds.) E-Commerce and Web Technologies, *Lecture Notes in Business Information Processing*, vol. 85, pp. 89–100. Springer Berlin Heidelberg (2011). DOI 10.1007/978-3-642-23014-1_8. URL http://dx.doi.org/10.1007/978-3-642-23014-1_8
19. Baltrunas, L., Ludwig, B., Peer, S., Ricci, F.: Context-aware places of interest recommendations for mobile users. In: A. Marcus (ed.) Design, User Experience, and Usability. Theory, Methods, Tools and Practice, *Lecture Notes in Computer Science*, vol. 6769, pp. 531–540. Springer Berlin Heidelberg (2011). DOI 10.1007/978-3-642-21675-6_61. URL http://dx.doi.org/10.1007/978-3-642-21675-6_61

20. Baltrunas, L., Ludwig, B., Peer, S., Ricci, F.: Context relevance assessment and exploitation in mobile recommender systems. Personal and Ubiquitous Computing **16**(5), 507–526 (2012)
21. Baltrunas, L., Ludwig, B., Ricci, F.: Matrix factorization techniques for context aware recommendation. In: Proceedings of the Fifth ACM Conference on Recommender Systems, RecSys '11, pp. 301–304. ACM, New York, NY, USA (2011). DOI 10.1145/2043932.2043988. URL http://doi.acm.org/10.1145/2043932.2043988
22. Baltrunas, L., Ricci, F.: Context-dependent items generation in collaborative filtering. In: Workshop on Context-Aware Recommender Systems (CARS 2009). New York (2009)
23. Baltrunas, L., Ricci, F.: Experimental evaluation of context-dependent collaborative filtering using item splitting. User Modeling and User-Adapted Interaction **24**(1–2), 7–34 (2014). DOI 10.1007/s11257-012-9137-9. URL http://dx.doi.org/10.1007/s11257-012-9137-9
24. Bauman, K., Tuzhilin, A.: Discovering contextual information from user reviews for recommendation purposes. In: Proceedings of the ACM RecSys Workshop on New Trends in Content Based Recommender Systems (2014)
25. Bazire, M., Brézillon, P.: Understanding context before using it. In: A. Dey, et al. (eds.) Proceedings of the 5th International Conference on Modeling and Using Context. Springer-Verlag (2005)
26. Braunhofer, M., Elahi, M., Ge, M., Ricci, F.: Context dependent preference acquisition with personality-based active learning in mobile recommender systems. In: P. Zaphiris, A. Ioannou (eds.) Learning and Collaboration Technologies. Technology-Rich Environments for Learning and Collaboration - First International Conference, LCT 2014, Held as Part of HCI International 2014, Heraklion, Crete, Greece, June 22–27, 2014, Proceedings, Part II, *Lecture Notes in Computer Science*, vol. 8524, pp. 105–116. Springer (2014). DOI 10.1007/978-3-319-07485-6_11. URL http://dx.doi.org/10.1007/978-3-319-07485-6_11
27. Braunhofer, M., Kaminskas, M., Ricci, F.: Recommending music for places of interest in a mobile travel guide. In: Proceedings of the Fifth ACM Conference on Recommender Systems, RecSys '11, pp. 253–256. ACM, New York, NY, USA (2011). DOI 10.1145/2043932.2043977. URL http://doi.acm.org/10.1145/2043932.2043977
28. Breese, J.S., Heckerman, D., Kadie, C.: Empirical analysis of predictive algorithms for collaborative filtering. In: Proceedings of the Fourteenth Conference on Uncertainty in Artificial Intelligence, vol. 461, pp. 43–52. San Francisco, CA (1998)
29. Bulander, R., Decker, M., Schiefer, G., Kolmel, B.: Comparison of different approaches for mobile advertising. In: Proceedings of the Second IEEE International Workshop on Mobile Commerce and Services, WMCS '05, pp. 174–182. IEEE Computer Society, Washington, DC, USA (2005). DOI 10.1109/WMCS.2005.8. URL http://dx.doi.org/10.1109/WMCS.2005.8
30. Burke, R.: Hybrid recommender systems: Survey and experiments. User Modeling and User-Adapted Interaction **12**(4), 331–370 (2002)
31. Burke, R.: Hybrid web recommender systems. The Adaptive Web pp. 377–408 (2007)
32. Cai, R., Zhang, C., Wang, C., Zhang, L., Ma, W.Y.: Musicsense: Contextual music recommendation using emotional allocation modeling. In: Proceedings of the 15th International Conference on Multimedia, MULTIMEDIA '07, pp. 553–556. ACM, New York, NY, USA (2007). DOI 10.1145/1291233.1291369. URL http://doi.acm.org/10.1145/1291233.1291369
33. Campos, P.G., Díez, F., Cantador, I.: Time-aware recommender systems: a comprehensive survey and analysis of existing evaluation protocols. User Model. User-Adapt. Interact. **24**(1–2), 67–119 (2014)
34. Cantador, I., Castells, P.: Semantic contextualisation in a news recommender system. In: Workshop on Context-Aware Recommender Systems (CARS 2009). New York (2009)
35. Cena, F., Console, L., Gena, C., Goy, A., Levi, G., Modeo, S., Torre, I.: Integrating heterogeneous adaptation techniques to build a flexible and usable mobile tourist guide. AI Communications **19**(4), 369–384 (2006)
36. Chatterjee, S., Hadi, A.S., Price, B.: Regression analysis by example. John Wiley and Sons (2000)
37. Chaudhuri, S., Dayal, U.: An overview of data warehousing and olap technology. ACM Sigmod record **26**(1), 65–74 (1997)

38. Cheverst, K., Davies, N., Mitchell, K., Friday, A., Efstratiou, C.: Developing a context-aware electronic tourist guide: some issues and experiences. In: Proceedings of the SIGCHI conference on Human factors in computing systems, pp. 17–24. ACM (2000)
39. Church, K., Smyth, B., Cotter, P., Bradley, K.: Mobile information access: A study of emerging search behavior on the mobile internet. ACM Trans. Web **1**(1) (2007). DOI 10.1145/1232722.1232726. URL http://doi.acm.org/10.1145/1232722.1232726
40. Codina, V., Ricci, F., Ceccaroni, L.: Exploiting the semantic similarity of contextual situations for pre-filtering recommendation. In: S. Carberry, S. Weibelzahl, A. Micarelli, G. Semeraro (eds.) User Modeling, Adaptation, and Personalization, *Lecture Notes in Computer Science*, vol. 7899, pp. 165–177. Springer Berlin Heidelberg (2013). DOI 10.1007/978-3-642-38844-6_14. URL http://dx.doi.org/10.1007/978-3-642-38844-6_14
41. De Carolis, B., Mazzotta, I., Novielli, N., Silvestri, V.: Using common sense in providing personalized recommendations in the tourism domain. In: Workshop on Context-Aware Recommender Systems (CARS 2009). New York (2009)
42. Dourish, P.: What we talk about when we talk about context. Personal and ubiquitous computing **8**(1), 19–30 (2004)
43. Fling, B.: Mobile Design and Development: Practical Concepts and Techniques for Creating Mobile Sites and Web Apps, 1st edn. O'Reilly Media, Inc. (2009)
44. Gorgoglione, M., Panniello, U., Tuzhilin, A.: The effect of context-aware recommendations on customer purchasing behavior and trust. In: Proceedings of the Fifth ACM Conference on Recommender Systems, RecSys '11, pp. 85–92. ACM, New York, NY, USA (2011). DOI 10.1145/2043932.2043951. URL http://doi.acm.org/10.1145/2043932.2043951
45. Hariri, N., Mobasher, B., Burke, R.: Context-aware music recommendation based on latent topic sequential patterns. In: Proceedings of the Sixth ACM Conference on Recommender Systems, RecSys '12, pp. 131–138. ACM, New York, NY, USA (2012). DOI 10.1145/2365952.2365979. URL http://doi.acm.org/10.1145/2365952.2365979
46. Hariri, N., Mobasher, B., Burke, R.: Query-driven context aware recommendation. In: Proceedings of the 7th ACM Conference on Recommender Systems, RecSys '13, pp. 9–16. ACM, New York, NY, USA (2013). DOI 10.1145/2507157.2507187. URL http://doi.acm.org/10.1145/2507157.2507187
47. Hussein, T., Linder, T., Gaulke, W., Ziegler, J.: Context-aware recommendations on rails. In: Workshop on Context-Aware Recommender Systems (CARS 2009). New York, NY, USA (2009)
48. Hussein, T., Linder, T., Gaulke, W., Ziegler, J.: Hybreed: A software framework for developing context-aware hybrid recommender systems. User Model. User-Adapt. Interact. **24**(1–2), 121–174 (2014)
49. Jannach, D., Hegelich, K.: A case study on the effectiveness of recommendations in the mobile internet. In: Proceedings of the Third ACM Conference on Recommender Systems, RecSys '09, pp. 205–208. ACM, New York, NY, USA (2009). DOI 10.1145/1639714.1639749. URL http://doi.acm.org/10.1145/1639714.1639749
50. Jiang, T., Tuzhilin, A.: Improving personalization solutions through optimal segmentation of customer bases. IEEE Transactions on Knowledge and Data Engineering **21**(3), 305–320 (2009)
51. Kaminskas, M., Ricci, F.: Contextual music information retrieval and recommendation: State of the art and challenges. Computer Science Review **6**(2-3), 89–119 (2012)
52. Karatzoglou, A., Amatriain, X., Baltrunas, L., Oliver, N.: Multiverse recommendation: N-dimensional tensor factorization for context-aware collaborative filtering. In: Proceedings of the Fourth ACM Conference on Recommender Systems, RecSys '10, pp. 79–86. ACM, New York, NY, USA (2010). DOI 10.1145/1864708.1864727. URL http://doi.acm.org/10.1145/1864708.1864727
53. Karatzoglou, A., Baltrunas, L., Church, K., Böhmer, M.: Climbing the app wall: Enabling mobile app discovery through context-aware recommendations. In: Proceedings of the 21st ACM International Conference on Information and Knowledge Management, CIKM '12, pp. 2527–2530. ACM, New York, NY, USA (2012). DOI 10.1145/2396761.2398683. URL http://doi.acm.org/10.1145/2396761.2398683

54. Kenteris, M., Gavalas, D., Economou, D.: Electronic mobile guides: a survey. Personal and Ubiquitous Computing **15**(1), 97–111 (2011)
55. Kimball, R., Ross, M.: The data warehousing toolkit. John Wiley & Sons, New York (1996)
56. Kiseleva, J., Thanh Lam, H., Pechenizkiy, M., Calders, T.: Discovering temporal hidden contexts in web sessions for user trail prediction. In: Proceedings of the 22nd International Conference on World Wide Web Companion, WWW '13 Companion, pp. 1067–1074. International World Wide Web Conferences Steering Committee, Republic and Canton of Geneva, Switzerland (2013). URL http://dl.acm.org/citation.cfm?id=2487788.2488120
57. Koller, D., Sahami, M.: Toward optimal feature selection. In: Proceedings of the 13th International Conference on Machine Learning, pp. 284–292. Morgan Kaufmann (1996)
58. Koren, Y.: Factorization meets the neighborhood: a multifaceted collaborative filtering model. In: Proceedings of the 14th ACM SIGKDD international conference on Knowledge discovery and data mining, pp. 426–434. ACM, New York, NY (2008)
59. Koutrika, G., Bercovitz, B., Garcia-Molina, H.: Flexrecs: expressing and combining flexible recommendations. In: Proceedings of the 35th SIGMOD international conference on Management of data, pp. 745–758. ACM, Providence, RI (2009)
60. Lee, H., Park, S.J.: Moners: A news recommender for the mobile web. Expert Systems with Applications **32**(1), 143–150 (2007). DOI http://dx.doi.org/10.1016/j.eswa.2005.11.010. URL http://www.sciencedirect.com/science/article/pii/S0957417405003167
61. Levandoski, J.J., Ekstrand, M.D., Ludwig, M., Eldawy, A., Mokbel, M.F., Riedl, J.: Recbench: Benchmarks for evaluating performance of recommender system architectures. PVLDB **4**(11), 911–920 (2011)
62. Levandoski, J.J., Eldawy, A., Mokbel, M.F., Khalefa, M.E.: Flexible and extensible preference evaluation in database systems. ACM Trans. Database Syst. **38**(3), 17 (2013)
63. Liu, H., Motoda, H.: Feature selection for knowledge discovery and data mining. Springer (1998)
64. Lombardi, S., Anand, S.S., Gorgoglione, M.: Context and customer behavior in recommendation. In: Workshop on Context-Aware Recommender Systems (CARS 2009). New York
65. Mahmood, T., Ricci, F., Venturini, A.: Improving recommendation effectiveness: Adapting a dialogue strategy in online travel planning. J. of IT & Tourism **11**(4), 285–302 (2009). DOI 10.3727/109830510X12670455864203. URL http://dx.doi.org/10.3727/109830510X12670455864203
66. Moling, O., Baltrunas, L., Ricci, F.: Optimal radio channel recommendations with explicit and implicit feedback. In: P. Cunningham, N.J. Hurley, I. Guy, S.S. Anand (eds.) Sixth ACM Conference on Recommender Systems, RecSys '12, Dublin, Ireland, September 9–13, 2012, pp. 75–82. ACM (2012). DOI 10.1145/2365952.2365971. URL http://doi.acm.org/10.1145/2365952.2365971
67. Odic, A., Tkalcic, M., Tasic, J.F., Kosir, A.: Predicting and detecting the relevant contextual information in a movie-recommender system. Interacting with Computers **25**(1), 74–90 (2013). DOI 10.1093/iwc/iws003. URL http://dx.doi.org/10.1093/iwc/iws003
68. Oku, K., Nakajima, S., Miyazaki, J., Uemura, S.: Context-aware SVM for context-dependent information recommendation. In: Proceedings of the 7th International Conference on Mobile Data Management, p. 109 (2006)
69. Palmisano, C., Tuzhilin, A., Gorgoglione, M.: Using context to improve predictive modeling of customers in personalization applications. IEEE Transactions on Knowledge and Data Engineering **20**(11), 1535–1549 (2008)
70. Panniello, U., Tuzhilin, A., Gorgoglione, M.: Comparing context-aware recommender systems in terms of accuracy and diversity. User Model. User-Adapt. Interact. **24**(1-2), 35–65 (2014)
71. Panniello, U., Tuzhilin, A., Gorgoglione, M., Palmisano, C., Pedone, A.: Experimental comparison of pre-vs. post-filtering approaches in context-aware recommender systems. In: Proceedings of the 3rd ACM conference on Recommender systems, pp. 265–268. ACM (2009)
72. Park, H.S., Yoo, J.O., Cho, S.B.: A context-aware music recommendation system using fuzzy bayesian networks with utility theory. In: Proceedings of the Third International Conference on Fuzzy Systems and Knowledge Discovery, FSKD'06, pp. 970–979. Springer-Verlag, Berlin, Heidelberg (2006). DOI 10.1007/11881599_121. URL http://dx.doi.org/10.1007/11881599_121

73. Park, M.H., Hong, J.H., Cho, S.B.: Location-based recommendation system using bayesian user's preference model in mobile devices. In: Proceedings of the 4th International Conference on Ubiquitous Intelligence and Computing, UIC'07, pp. 1130–1139. Springer-Verlag, Berlin, Heidelberg (2007). URL http://dl.acm.org/citation.cfm?id=2391319.2391438
74. Pennock, D.M., Horvitz, E.: Collaborative filtering by personality diagnosis: A hybrid memory-and model-based approach. In: IJCAI'99 Workshop: Machine Learning for Information Filtering (1999)
75. Ramakrishnan, R., Gehrke, J.: Database Management Systems. USA: McGraw Hill Companies (2000)
76. Reddy, S., Mascia, J.: Lifetrak: Music in tune with your life. In: Proceedings of the 1st ACM International Workshop on Human-centered Multimedia, HCM '06, pp. 25–34. ACM, New York, NY, USA (2006). DOI 10.1145/1178745.1178754. URL http://doi.acm.org/10.1145/1178745.1178754
77. Ricci, F.: Mobile recommender systems. J. of IT & Tourism **12**(3), 205–231 (2010)
78. Ricci, F., Nguyen, Q.N.: Mobyrek: A conversational recommender system for on-the-move travelers. Destination Recommendation Systems: Behavioural Foundations and Applications pp. 281–294 (2006)
79. Ricci, F., Rokach, L., Shapira, B., Kantor, P.B. (eds.): Recommender Systems Handbook. Springer (2011)
80. Sae-Ueng, S., Pinyapong, S., Ogino, A., Kato, T.: Personalized shopping assistance service at ubiquitous shop space. In: Proceedings of the 22nd International Conference on Advanced Information Networking and Applications - Workshops, AINAW '08, pp. 838–843. IEEE Computer Society, Washington, DC, USA (2008). DOI 10.1109/WAINA.2008.287. URL http://dx.doi.org/10.1109/WAINA.2008.287
81. Sarwar, B., Karypis, G., Konstan, J., Reidl, J.: Item-based collaborative filtering recommendation algorithms. In: Proceedings of the 10th international conference on World Wide Web, pp. 285–295. ACM (2001)
82. Sarwat, M., Avery, J., Mokbel, M.F.: A recdb in action: Recommendation made easy in relational databases. PVLDB **6**(12), 1242–1245 (2013)
83. Sarwat, M., Levandoski, J.J., Eldawy, A., Mokbel, M.F.: Lars*: An efficient and scalable location-aware recommender system. IEEE Trans. Knowl. Data Eng. **26**(6), 1384–1399 (2014)
84. Shani, G., Gunawardana, A.: Evaluating recommendation systems. In: Ricci et al. [79], pp. 257–297
85. Smyth, B., Cotter, P.: Mp3 mobile portals, profiles and personalization. In: Web Dynamics, pp. 411–433. Springer Berlin Heidelberg (2004). DOI 10.1007/978-3-662-10874-1_17. URL http://dx.doi.org/10.1007/978-3-662-10874-1_17
86. Van Setten, M., Pokraev, S., Koolwaaij, J.: Context-aware recommendations in the mobile tourist application COMPASS. In: W. Nejdl, P. De Bra (eds.) Adaptive Hypermedia, pp. 235–244. Springer Verlag (2004)
87. Webster, N.: Webster's new twentieth century dictionary of the English language. Springfield, MA: Merriam-Webster, Inc. (1980)
88. Woerndl, W., Huebner, J., Bader, R., Gallego-Vico, D.: A model for proactivity in mobile, context-aware recommender systems. In: Proceedings of the Fifth ACM Conference on Recommender Systems, RecSys '11, pp. 273–276. ACM, New York, NY, USA (2011). DOI 10.1145/2043932.2043981. URL http://doi.acm.org/10.1145/2043932.2043981
89. Yu, Z., Zhou, X., Zhang, D., Chin, C.Y., Wang, X., Men, J.: Supporting context-aware media recommendations for smart phones. IEEE Pervasive Computing **5**(3), 68–75 (2006)
90. Zheng, Y., Burke, R., Mobasher, B.: Differential context relaxation for context-aware travel recommendation. In: C. Huemer, P. Lops (eds.) E-Commerce and Web Technologies, *Lecture Notes in Business Information Processing*, vol. 123, pp. 88–99. Springer Berlin Heidelberg (2012). DOI 10.1007/978-3-642-32273-0_8. URL http://dx.doi.org/10.1007/978-3-642-32273-0_8

Chapter 7
Data Mining Methods for Recommender Systems

Xavier Amatriain and Josep M. Pujol

7.1 Introduction

Recommender Systems (RS) typically apply techniques and methodologies from other neighboring areas such as Human Computer Interaction (HCI) or Information Retrieval (IR). Most of these systems also bear in their core an algorithm that can be understood as a particular instance of a Data Mining (DM) process [5].

The data mining process typically consists of 3 steps, carried out in succession: *Data Preprocessing* [78], *Model Learning*, and *Result Interpretation* (see Fig. 7.1). We will analyze some of the most important methods for data preprocessing in Sect. 7.2. In particular, we will focus on sampling, dimensionality reduction, and the use of distance functions because of their significance and their role in RS. In Sects. 7.3 and 7.4, we provide an overview introduction to the machine learning methods that are most commonly used in RS: classification, clustering and association rule discovery (see Fig. 7.1 for a detailed view of the different topics covered in the chapter).

This chapter does not intend to give a thorough review of Data Mining methods, but rather to highlight the impact that DM algorithms have in the RS field, and to provide an overview of the key DM techniques that have been successfully used. We direct the interested reader to Data Mining and Machine Learning textbooks (see [14, 19, 39, 70, 93], for example) or the more focused references that are provided throughout the chapter.

X. Amatriain (✉)
Netflix, 100 Winchester Cr., Los Gatos, CA 95032, USA

Quora, 150 Castro St., Mountain View, USA
e-mail: xavier@amatriain.net

J.M. Pujol
Cliqz, Rosenkavalierplatz 10, 81925 Munich, Germany
e-mail: josep@cliqz.com

F. Ricci et al. (eds.), *Recommender Systems Handbook*,
DOI 10.1007/978-1-4899-7637-6_7

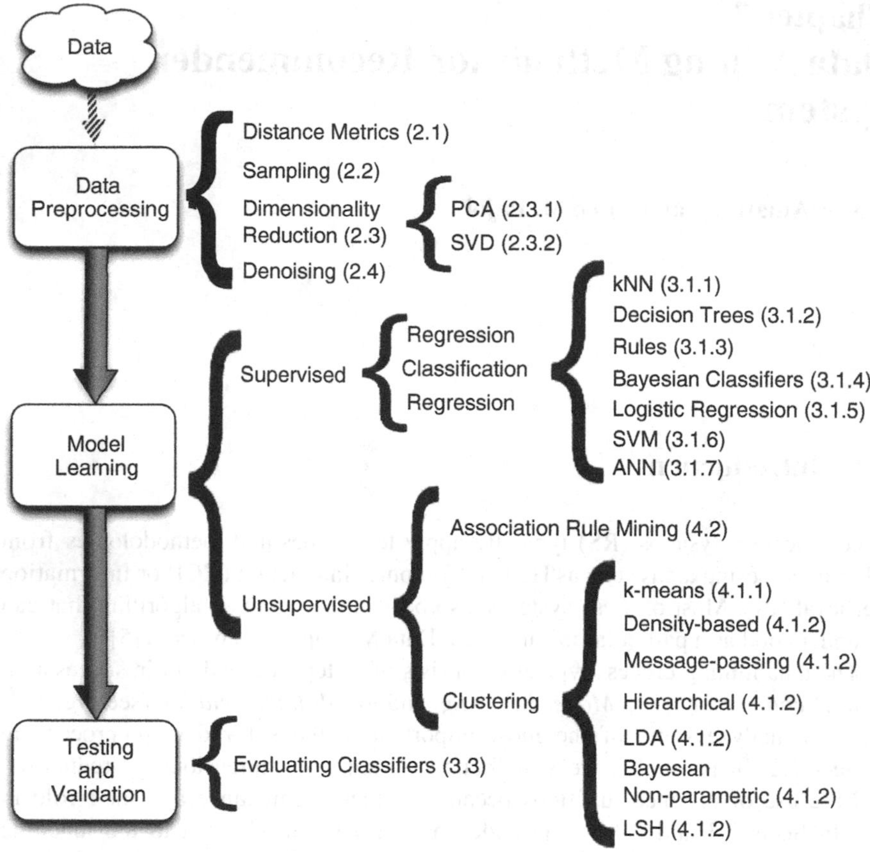

Fig. 7.1 Main steps and methods in a Data Mining process, with their correspondence to chapter sections

7.2 Data Preprocessing

We define *data* as a collection of *objects* and their *attributes*, where an attribute is defined as a property or characteristic of an object. Other names for object include *record*, *item*, *point*, *sample*, *observation*, or *instance*. An attribute might be also be referred to as a *variable*, *field*, *characteristic*, or *feature*. In the context of a typical collaborative filtering setting the objects in our dataset might be each of the ratings we have captured from the users. For each of them we will have typical attributes such as the user and item the rating refers to or the value of the rating itself. We can also add many other features such as the time or the location the rating occurred, or any other characteristic of the item or user such as item popularity, user age, or even the location of the item in the page at the time we received the rating [75].

Real-life data typically needs to be *preprocessed* (e.g. cleansed, filtered, transformed) in order to be used by the machine learning techniques in the model learning step. In this section, we focus on three issues that are of particular importance when designing a RS. First, we review different similarity or distance measures. Next, we discuss the issue of sampling as a way to reduce the number of items in very large collections while preserving its main characteristics. Finally, we describe the most common techniques to reduce dimensionality.

7.2.1 Similarity Measures

One of the preferred approaches to collaborative filtering (CF) recommenders is to use the *k*NN classifier that will be described in Sect. 7.3.1.1. This classification method—as most classifiers and clustering techniques—is highly dependent on defining an appropriate similarity or distance measure.[1]

The simplest and most common example of a distance measure is the Euclidean distance or the *L2 Norm*:

$$d(x,y) = \sqrt{\sum_{k=1}^{n} (x_k - y_k)^2} \tag{7.1}$$

where n is the number of dimensions (attributes) and x_k and y_k are the kth attributes (components) of data objects x and y, respectively.

The Minkowski Distance is a generalization of Euclidean Distance:

$$d(x,y) = \left(\sum_{k=1}^{n} |x_k - y_k|^r \right)^{\frac{1}{r}} \tag{7.2}$$

where r is the degree of the distance. Depending on the value of r, the generic Minkowski distance is known with specific names: For $r = 1$, the *city block*, (*Manhattan*, *taxicab* or *L1 norm*) distance; For $r = 2$, the *Euclidean* distance; For $r \to \infty$, the *supremum* (*L_{max} norm* or *L_∞ norm*) distance, which corresponds to computing the maximum difference between any dimension of the data objects.

The Mahalanobis distance is defined as:

$$d(x,y) = \sqrt{(x-y)\sigma^{-1}(x-y)^T} \tag{7.3}$$

where σ is the covariance matrix of the data.

[1]Note that a similarity measure is not a preprocessing step in itself but rather a prerequisite for being able to execute other data mining processes.

Another very common approach is to consider items as document vectors of an n-dimensional space and compute their similarity as the cosine of the angle that they form:

$$cos(x,y) = \frac{(x \bullet y)}{||x||||y||} \tag{7.4}$$

where $\bullet$ indicates vector dot product and $||x||$ is the norm of vector x. This similarity is known as the *cosine similarity*.

The similarity between items can also be given by their *correlation* which measures the linear relationship between objects. While there are several correlation coefficients that may be applied, the *Pearson correlation* is the most commonly used. Given the covariance of data points x and y Σ, and their standard deviation σ, we compute the Pearson correlation using:

$$Pearson(x,y) = \frac{\Sigma(x,y)}{\sigma_x \times \sigma_y} \tag{7.5}$$

Several similarity measures have been proposed in the case of items that only have binary attributes. First, the *M01*, *M10*, *M11*, and *M00* quantities are computed, where $M01$ = the number of attributes where x was 0 and y was 1, $M10$ = the number of attributes where x was 1 and y was 0, and so on. From those quantities we can compute: The *Simple Matching* coefficient $SMC = \frac{numberofmatches}{numberofattributes}$ $= \frac{M11+M00}{M01+M10+M00+M11}$; the *Jaccard* coefficient $JC = \frac{M11}{M01+M10+M11}$. The *Extended Jaccard* (*Tanimoto*) coefficient is a variation of JC for continuous or count attributes that is computed by $d = \frac{x \bullet y}{\|x\|^2 + \|x\|^2 - x \bullet y}$.

RS have traditionally used either the cosine similarity (Eq. (7.4)) or the Pearson correlation (Eq. (7.5))—or one of their many variations through, for instance, weighting schemes—Chap. 2 details the use of different distance functions for CF. Most of the other distance measures previously reviewed are possible. Spertus et al. [88] did a large-scale study to evaluate six different similarity measures in the context of the Orkut social network. Although their results might be biased by the particular setting of their experiment, it is interesting to note that the best response to recommendations were to those generated using the cosine similarity. Lathia et al. [64] also carried out a study of several similarity measures where they concluded that, in the general case, the prediction accuracy of a RS was *not* affected by the choice of the similarity measure. As a matter of fact and in the context of their work, using a random similarity measure sometimes yielded better results than using any of the well-known approaches.

7.2.2 Sampling

Sampling is the main technique used in DM for selecting a subset of relevant data from a large data set. It is used both in the preprocessing and final data interpretation steps. Sampling may be used because processing the entire data set is computationally too expensive. It can also be used to create *training* and *testing* datasets. In this case, the training dataset is used to learn the parameters or configure the algorithms used in the analysis step, while the testing dataset is used to evaluate the model or configuration obtained in the training phase, making sure that it performs well with previously unseen data. As a matter of fact, in most cases we not only need training and testing, but we also need to think about creating a third validation dataset. The training set is used for model fitting, the validation one for learning hyperparameters, and the testing to see how the model generalizes.

The key issue to sampling is finding a subset of the original data set that is *representative*—i.e. it has approximately the same property of interest—of the entire set. The simplest sampling technique is *random sampling*, where there is an equal probability of selecting any item. However, more sophisticated approaches are possible. For instance, in *stratified sampling* the data is split into several partitions based on a particular feature, followed by random sampling on each partition independently.

The most common approach to sampling consists of using sampling *without replacement*: When an item is selected, it is removed from the population. However, it is also possible to perform sampling *with replacement*, where items are not removed from the population once they have been selected, allowing for the same sample to be selected more than once.

It is common practice to use standard random sampling without replacement with an $80/20$ proportion when separating the training and testing data sets. This means that we use random sampling without replacement to select 20 % of the instances for the testing set and leave the remaining 80 % for training. The $80/20$ proportion should be taken as a rule of thumb as, in general, any value over $2/3$ for the training set is appropriate.

Sampling can lead to an over-specialization to the particular division of the training and testing data sets. For this reason, the training process may be repeated several times. The training and test sets are created from the original data set, the model is trained using the training data and tested with the examples in the test set. Next, different training/test data sets are selected to start the training/testing process again that is repeated K times. Finally, the *average* performance of the K learned models is reported. This process is known as cross-validation. There are several cross-validation techniques. In *repeated random sampling*, a standard random sampling process is carried out K times. In *n-Fold cross validation*, the data set is divided into n folds. One of the folds is used for testing the model and the remaining $n - 1$ folds are used for training. The cross validation process is then repeated n times with each of the n subsamples used exactly once as validation data. Finally, the *leave-one-out (LOO)* approach can be seen as an extreme case of n-Fold cross validation where n is set to the number of items in the data set. Therefore, the algorithms are run as many times as data points using only one of them as a test each time. It should be noted, though, that as Isaksson et al. discuss in [57], cross-validation may be unreliable unless the data set is sufficiently large.

A common approach in RS is to sample the available feedback from the users—e.g. in the form of ratings—to separate it into training and testing. Cross-validation is also common. Although a standard random sampling is acceptable in the general case, in others we might need to bias our sampling for the test set in different ways. We might, for instance, decide to sample only from most recent ratings—since those are the ones we would be predicting in a real-world situation. We might also be interested in ensuring that the proportion of ratings per user is preserved in the test set and therefore impose that the random sampling is done on a per user basis. However, all these issues relate are beyond the scope of this chapter.

7.2.3 Reducing Dimensionality

It is common in RS to have not only a data set with features that define a high-dimensional space, but also very sparse information in that space—i.e. there are values for a limited number of features per object. The notions of density and distance between points, which are critical for clustering and outlier detection, become less meaningful in highly dimensional spaces. This is known as the Curse of Dimensionality. Dimensionality reduction techniques help overcome this problem by transforming the original high-dimensional space into a lower-dimensionality.

Sparsity and the *curse of dimensionality* are recurring problems in RS. Even in the simplest setting, we are likely to have a sparse matrix with thousands of rows and columns (i.e. users and items), most of which are zeros. Therefore, dimensionality reduction comes in naturally. Applying dimensionality reduction makes such a difference and its results are so directly applicable to the computation of the predicted value, that these methods are in fact considered an approach to building a RS, rather than a preprocessing technique. In this case we speak of these techniques as *Matrix Completion Methods*.

In the following paragraphs, we summarize the two most relevant dimensionality reduction algorithms in the context of RS: *Principal Component Analysis (PCA)* and *Singular Value Decomposition (SVD)*.

7.2.3.1 Principal Component Analysis

Principal Component Analysis [59] is a classical statistical method to find patterns in high dimensionality data sets. PCA allows to obtain an ordered list of components that account for the largest amount of the variance from the data in terms of least square errors: The amount of variance captured by the first component is larger

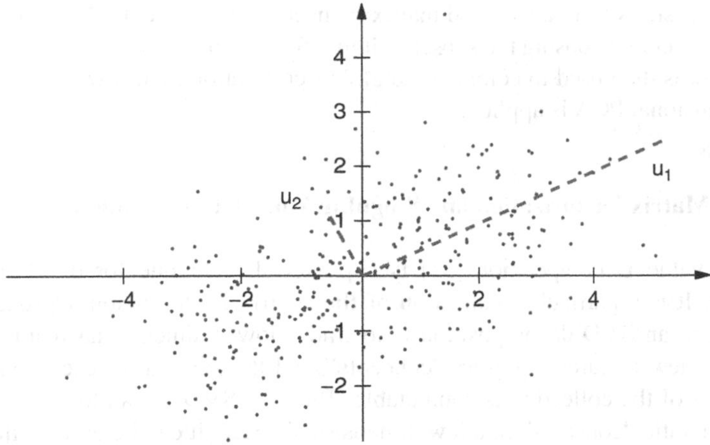

Fig. 7.2 PCA analysis of a two-dimensional point cloud from a combination of Gaussians. The principal components derived using PCS are u_1 and u_2, whose length is relative to the energy contained in the components

than the amount of variance on the second component and so on. We can reduce the dimensionality of the data by neglecting those components with a small contribution to the variance.

Figure 7.2 shows the PCA analysis to a two-dimensional point cloud generated by a combination of Gaussians. After the data is centered, the principal components are obtained and denoted by u_1 and u_2. Note that the length of the new coordinates is relative to the energy contained in their eigenvectors. Therefore, for the particular example depicted in Fig. 7.2, the first component u_1 accounts for 83.5 % of the energy, which means that removing the second component u_2 would imply losing only 16.5 % of the information. The rule of thumb is to choose the target dimensionality m' so that the cumulative energy is above a certain threshold, typically 90 %. PCA allows us to retrieve the original data matrix by projecting the data onto the new coordinate system $X'_{n \times m'} = X_{n \times m} W'_{m \times m'}$. The new data matrix X' contains most of the information of the original X with a dimensionality reduction of $m - m'$.

PCA is a powerful technique, but it does have important limitations. PCA relies on the empirical data set to be a linear combination of a certain basis—although generalizations of PCA for non-linear data have been proposed. Another important assumption of PCA is that the original data set has been drawn from a Gaussian distribution. When this assumption does not hold true, there is no warranty that the principal components are meaningful.

Although current trends seem to indicate that other matrix factorizations techniques such as SVD or Non-Negative Matrix Factorization are preferred for RS, earlier works used PCA. Goldberg et al. proposed an approach to use PCA in the context of an online joke recommendation system [50]. Their system, known as

Eigentaste,[2] starts from a standard matrix of user ratings to items. They then select their *gauge* set by choosing the subset of items for which all users had a rating. This new matrix is then used to compute the global correlation matrix where a standard two-dimensional PCA is applied.

7.2.3.2 Matrix Factorization and Singular Value Decomposition

Singular Value Decomposition [51] is a powerful technique for dimensionality reduction. It is a particular realization of the Matrix Factorization approach. The key issue in an SVD decomposition is to find a lower dimensional feature space where the new features represent "concepts" and the strength of each concept in the context of the collection is computable. Because SVD allows to automatically derive semantic "concepts" in a low dimensional space, it can be used as the basis of *latent-semantic analysis* [34], a very popular technique for text classification in Information Retrieval (IR).

The core of the SVD algorithm lies in the following theorem: It is always possible to decompose a given matrix A into $A = U\lambda V^T$. Given the $n \times m$ matrix data A (n items, m features), we can obtain an $n \times r$ matrix U (n items, r concepts), an $r \times r$ diagonal matrix λ (strength of each concept), and an $m \times r$ matrix V (m features, r concepts). Figure 7.3 illustrates this idea. The λ diagonal matrix contains the *singular values*, which will always be positive and sorted in decreasing order. The U matrix is interpreted as the "item-to-concept" similarity matrix, while the V matrix is the "term-to-concept" similarity matrix.

In order to compute the SVD of a rectangular matrix A, we consider AA^T and A^TA. The columns of U are the eigenvectors of AA^T, and the columns of V are the eigenvectors of A^TA. The singular values on the diagonal of λ are the positive square roots of the nonzero eigenvalues of both AA^T and A^TA. Therefore, in order

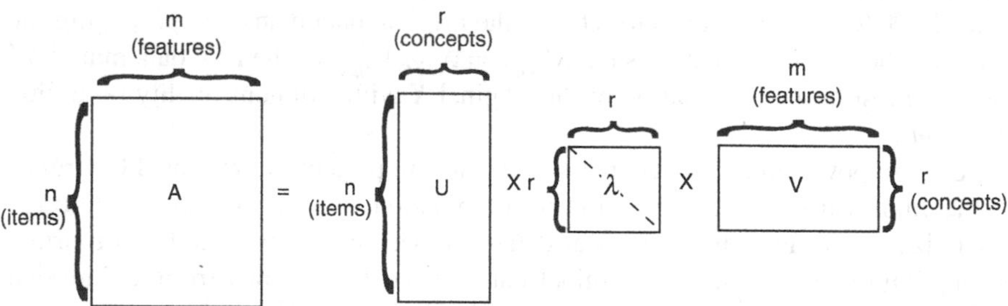

Fig. 7.3 Illustrating the basic Singular Value Decomposition Theorem: an item × features matrix can be decomposed into three different ones: an item × concepts, a concept strength, and a concept × features

[2] http://eigentaste.berkeley.edu.

to compute the SVD of matrix A we first compute T as AA^T and D as A^TA and then compute the eigenvectors and eigenvalues for T and D.

The r eigenvalues in λ are ordered in decreasing magnitude. Therefore, the original matrix A can be approximated by simply truncating the eigenvalues at a given k. The truncated SVD creates a rank-k approximation to A so that $A_k = U_k \lambda_k V_k^T$. A_k is the *closest* rank-k matrix to A. The term "closest" means that A_k minimizes the sum of the squares of the differences of the elements of A and A_k. The truncated SVD is a representation of the underlying latent structure in a reduced k-dimensional space, which generally means that the noise in the features is reduced.

The use of SVD as tool to improve collaborative filtering has been known for some time. Sarwar et al. [85] describe two different ways to use SVD in this context. First, SVD can be used to uncover latent relations between customers and products. In order to accomplish this goal, they first fill the zeros in the user-item matrix with the item average rating and then normalize by subtracting the user average. This matrix is then factored using SVD and the resulting decomposition can be used—after some trivial operations—directly to compute the predictions. The other approach is to use the low-dimensional space resulting from the SVD to improve neighborhood formation for later use in a kNN approach.

As described by Sarwar et al. [84], one of the big advantages of SVD is that there are incremental algorithms to compute an approximated decomposition. This allows to accept new users or ratings without having to recompute the model that had been built from previously existing data. The same idea was later extended and formalized by Brand [23] into an online SVD model. The use of incremental SVD methods has recently become a commonly accepted approach after its success in the Netflix Prize.[3] The publication of Simon Funk's simplified incremental SVD method [47] marked an inflection point in the contest. Since its publication, several improvements to SVD have been proposed in this same context (see Paterek's ensembles of SVD methods [74] or Kurucz et al. evaluation of SVD parameters [63]).

In that sense, Matrix Factorization approaches should be considered as more than a simple preprocessing or dimensionality reduction technique since the whole recommendation problem can be formalized as one of Matrix Completion. We can design a sparse matrix that represents users in rows and items in columns. Each known preference of a user for an item will represent a value in the matrix. All other positions will be unknown. It is in that setting, where coming up with a prediction of how much a user will like an item can be simplified to the task of completing missing values in the matrix (see Chap. 2 for more details on this usage).

It should be noted that different variants of Matrix Factorization (MF) methods such as the Non-negative Matrix Factorization (NNMF) have also been used [94]. These algorithms are, in essence, similar to SVD. The basic idea is to decompose the ratings matrix into two matrices, one of which contains features that describe the users and the other contains features describing the items. Matrix Factorization

---

[3]http://www.netflixprize.com.

methods can handle the missing values by introducing a bias term to the model. This can also be handled in the SVD preprocessing step by replacing zeros with the item average. MF is prone to overfitting. However, there exist MF variants, such as the Regularized Kernel Matrix Factorization, that can avoid the issue efficiently.

7.2.4 Denoising

Data collected for data-mining purposes might be subject to different kinds of noise such as missing values or outliers. Denoising is a very important preprocessing step that aims at removing any unwanted effect in the data while maximizing its information.

In a general sense we define noise as any unwanted artifact introduced in the data collection phase that might affect the result of our data analysis and interpretation. In the context of RS, we distinguish between *natural* and *malicious* noise [72]. The former refers to noise that is involuntarily introduced by users when giving feedback on their preferences. The latter refers to noise that is deliberately introduced in a system in order to bias the results.

It is clear that malicious noise can affect the output of a RS. But, also, we performed a study that concluded that the effects of natural noise on the performance of RS is far from being negligible [7]. In order to address this issue, we designed a denoising approach that is able to improve accuracy by asking some users to re-rate some items [8]. We concluded that accuracy improvements by investing in this pre-processing step could be larger than the ones obtained by complex algorithm optimizations.

7.3 Supervised Learning

7.3.1 Classification

A classifier is a mapping between a feature space and a label space, where the features represent characteristics of the elements to classify and the labels represent the classes. A restaurant RS, for example, can be implemented by a classifier that classifies restaurants into one of two categories (good, bad) based on a number of features that describe it.

There are many types of classifiers, but in general we will talk about either *supervised* or *unsupervised* classification. In supervised classification, a set of labels or categories is known in advance and we have a set of labeled examples which constitute a training set. In unsupervised classification, the labels or categories are unknown in advance and the task is to suitably (according to some criteria) organize the elements at hand. In this section we describe several algorithms to learn supervised classifiers and will be covering unsupervised classification (i.e. clustering) in Sect. 7.4.

7.3.1.1 Nearest Neighbors

Instance-based classifiers work by storing training records and using them to predict the class label of unseen cases. A trivial example is the so-called *rote-learner*. This classifier memorizes the entire training set and classifies only if the attributes of the new record match one of the training examples exactly. A more elaborate, and far more popular, instance-based classifier is the *Nearest neighbor classifier* (kNN) [32]. Given a point to be classified, the kNN classifier finds the k closest points (*nearest neighbors*) from the training records. It then assigns the class label according to the class labels of its *nearest-neighbors*. The underlying idea is that if a record falls in a particular neighborhood where a class label is predominant it is because the record is likely to belong to that very same class.

Given a query point q for which we want to know its class l, and a training set $X = \{\{x_1, l_1\} \ldots \{x_n\}\}$, where x_j is the j-th element and l_j is its class label, the k-nearest neighbors will find a subset $Y = \{\{y_1, l_1\} \ldots \{y_k\}\}$ such that $Y \in X$ and $\sum_1^k d(q, y_k)$ is minimal. Y contains the k points in X which are closest to the query point q. Then, the class label of q is $l = f(\{l_1 \ldots l_k\})$.

Perhaps the most challenging issue in kNN is how to choose the value of k. If k is too small, the classifier will be sensitive to noise points. But if k is too large, the neighborhood might include too many points from other classes. The right plot in Fig. 7.4 shows how different k yields different class label for the query point, if $k = 1$ the class label would be *circle* whereas $k = 7$ classifies it as *square*. Note that the query point from the example is on the boundary of two clusters, and therefore, it is difficult to classify.

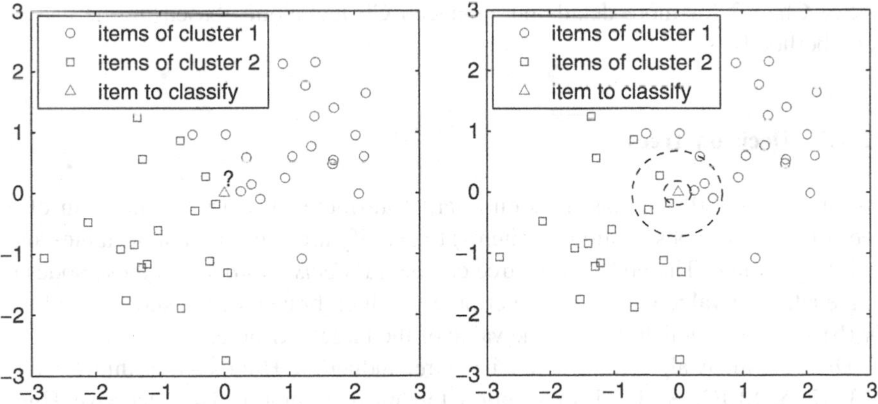

Fig. 7.4 Example of k-nearest neighbors. The *left subfigure* shows the training points with two class labels (*circles and squares*) and the query point (as a *triangle*). The *right sub-figure* illustrates closest neighborhood for $k = 1$ and $k = 7$. The query point would be classified as *square* for $k = 1$, and as a *circle* for $k = 5$ according to the simple majority vote rule. Note that the query points was just on the boundary between the two clusters

kNN classifiers are amongst the simplest of all machine learning algorithms. Since kNN does not build models explicitly it is considered a *lazy learner*. Unlike eager learners such as decision trees or rule-based systems (see Sects. 7.3.1.2 and 7.3.1.3, respectively), kNN classifiers leave many decisions to the classification step. Therefore, classifying unknown records is relatively expensive.

Nearest Neighbor is one of the most common approaches to CF—and therefore to designing a RS. As a matter of fact, any overview on RS—such as the one by Adomavicius and Tuzhilin [1]—will include an introduction to the use of nearest neighbors in this context. One of the advantages of this classifier is that it is conceptually very much related to the idea of CF: Finding like-minded users (or similar items) is essentially equivalent to finding neighbors for a given user or an item. The other advantage is that, being the kNN classifier a lazy learner, it does not require to learn and maintain a given model. Therefore, in principle, the system can adapt to rapid changes in the user ratings matrix. Unfortunately, this comes at the cost of recomputing the neighborhoods and therefore the similarity matrix. This is why we proposed a neighborhood model that uses a reduced set of experts as the source for selecting neighbors [6].

The kNN approach, although simple and intuitive, has shown good accuracy results and is very amenable to improvements. As a matter of fact, its supremacy as the de facto standard for CF recommendation has only been challenged recently by approaches based on Matrix Completion. That said, the traditional kNN approach to CF has experienced improvements in several directions. For instance, in the context of the Netflix Prize, Bell and Koren propose a method to remove *global effects* such as the fact that some items may attract users that consistently rate lower. They also propose an optimization method for computing interpolating weights once the neighborhood is created.

See Chap. 2 for more details on enhanced CF techniques based on the use of neighborhoods.

7.3.1.2 Decision Trees

Decision trees [80] are classifiers on a target attribute (or class) in the form of a tree structure. The observations (or items) to classify are composed of attributes and their target value. The nodes of the tree can be: (a) *decision nodes*, in these nodes a single attribute-value is tested to determine to which branch of the subtree applies. Or (b) *leaf nodes* which indicate the value of the target attribute.

There are many algorithms for decision tree induction: Hunt's Algorithm, CART, ID3, C4.5, SLIQ, SPRINT to mention the most common. The recursive Hunt algorithm, which is one of the earliest and easiest to understand, relies on the *test condition* applied to a given attribute that discriminates the observations by their target values. Once the partition induced by the test condition has been found, the algorithm is recursively repeated until a partition is empty or all the observations have the same target value.

Splits can be decided by maximizing the information gain, defined as follows,

$$\Delta_i = I(parent) - \sum_{j=1}^{k_i} \frac{N(v_j)I(v_j)}{N} \tag{7.6}$$

where k_i are values of the attribute i, N is the number of observations, v_j is the j-th partition of the observations according to the values of attribute i. Finally, I is a function that measures node *impurity*. There are different measures of impurity: Gini Index, Entropy and misclassification error are the most common in the literature.

Decision tree induction stops once all observations belong to the same class (or the same range in the case of continuous attributes). This implies that the impurity of the leaf nodes is zero. For practical reasons, however, most decision trees implementations use pruning by which a node is no further split if its impurity measure or the number of observations in the node are below a certain threshold.

The main advantages of building a classifier using a decision tree is that it is inexpensive to construct and it is extremely fast at classifying unknown instances. Another appreciated aspect of decision tree is that they can be used to produce a set of rules that are easy to interpret (see Sect. 7.3.1.3) while maintaining an accuracy comparable to other basic classification techniques.

Decision trees may be used in a model-based approach for a RS. One possibility is to use content features to build a decision tree that models all the variables involved in the user preferences. Bouza et al. [21] use this idea to construct a Decision Tree using semantic information available for the items. The tree is built after the user has rated only two items. The features for each of the items are used to build a model that explains the user ratings. They use the information gain of every feature as the splitting criteria. It should be noted that although this approach is interesting from a theoretical perspective, the precision they report on their system is worse than that of recommending the average rating.

As it could be expected, it is very difficult and unpractical to build a decision tree that tries to explain all the variables involved in the decision making process. Decision trees, however, may also be used in order to model a particular part of the system. Cho et al. [28], for instance, present a RS for online purchases that combines the use of Association Rules (see Sect. 7.4.2) and Decision Trees. The Decision Tree is used as a filter to select which users should be targeted with recommendations. In order to build the model they create a candidate user set by selecting those users that have chosen products from a given category during a given time frame. In their case, the dependent variable for building the decision tree is chosen as whether the customer is likely to buy new products in that same category. Nikovski and Kulev [71] follow a similar approach combining Decision Trees and Association Rules. In their approach, frequent itemsets are detected in the purchase dataset and then they apply standard tree-learning algorithms for simplifying the recommendations rules.

Another option to use Decision Trees in a RS is to use them as a tool for exploring the space of possible items to present to a user during the coldstarting phase. The basic idea of the approach is to maximize the amount of information obtained with each item presented by considering it a node in a decision tree. Golbandi et al. [49], for instance, detail an efficient tree learning algorithm, specifically tailored to this application.

The use of Decision Trees for ranking has been studied in several settings and their use in a RS for this purpose is fairly straightforward [11, 27]. While it is possible to use individual trees for ranking, it is much more efficient to use ensembles of decision trees for this purpose. The two kinds of tree ensembles that are commonly used both for classification and ranking are Random Forests [25], and Gradient Boosted Decision Trees [45]. Both these techniques are used in collaborative filtering or personalized ranking applications (see [4, 12]).

Finally, trees or trees ensembles can be used as a way to combine different algorithms in an ensemble. The solution to the Netflix Prize, for example, used Gradient Boosted Decision Trees to combine the more than 100 methods that had been trained [61].

7.3.1.3 Ruled-Based Classifiers

Rule-based classifiers classify data by using a collection of "**if** ... **then** ..." rules. The rule *antecedent* or condition is an expression made of attribute conjunctions. The rule *consequent* is a positive or negative classification.

We say that a rule r *covers* a given instance x if the attributes of the instance satisfy the rule condition. We define the *coverage* of a rule as the fraction of records that satisfy its antecedent. On the other hand, we define its *accuracy* as the fraction of records that satisfy both the antecedent and the consequent. We say that a classifier contains *mutually exclusive rules* if the rules are independent of each other—i.e. every record is covered by at most one rule. Finally we say that the classifier has *exhaustive rules* if they account for every possible combination of attribute values—i.e. each record is covered by at least one rule.

In order to build a rule-based classifier we can follow a direct method to extract rules directly from data. Examples of such methods are RIPPER, or CN2. On the other hand, it is common to follow an indirect method and extract rules from other classification models such as decision trees or neural networks.

The advantages of rule-based classifiers are that they are extremely expressive since they are symbolic and operate with the attributes of the data without any transformation. Rule-based classifiers, and by extension decision trees, are easy to interpret, easy to generate and they can classify new instances efficiently.

In a similar way to Decision Tress, however, it is very difficult to build a complete recommender model based on rules. As a matter of fact, this method is not very popular in the context of RS because deriving a rule-based system means that we either have some explicit prior knowledge of the decision making process or that we derive the rules from another model such a decision tree. However a rule-based system can be used to improve the performance of a RS by injecting partial domain knowledge or business rules. Anderson et al. [9], for instance, implemented a CF music RS that improves its performance by applying a rule-based system to the results of the CF process. If a user rates an album by a given artist high, for instance, predicted ratings for all other albums by this artist will be increased.

Gutta et al. [40] implemented a rule-based RS for TV content. In order to do, so they first derived a C4.5 Decision Tree that is then decomposed into rules for classifying the programs. Basu et al. [15] followed an inductive approach using the *Ripper* [30] system to learn rules from data. They report slightly better results when using hybrid content and collaborative data to learn rules than when following a pure CF approach.

7.3.1.4 Bayesian Classifiers

A Bayesian classifier [46] is a probabilistic framework for solving classification problems. It is based on the definition of conditional probability and the Bayes theorem. The Bayesian school of statistics uses probability to represent uncertainty about the relationships learned from the data. In addition, the concept of *priors* is very important as they represent our expectations or prior knowledge about what the true relationship might be. In particular, the probability of a model given the data (*posterior*) is proportional to the product of the *likelihood* times the *prior probability* (or prior). The likelihood component includes the effect of the data while the prior specifies the belief in the model before the data was observed.

Bayesian classifiers consider each attribute and class label as (continuous or discrete) random variables. Given a record with N attributes $(A_1, A_2, \ldots, A_N)$, the goal is to predict class C_k by finding the value of C_k that maximizes the posterior probability of the class given the data $P(C_k|A_1, A_2, \ldots, A_N)$. Applying Bayes' theorem, $P(C_k|A_1, A_2, \ldots, A_N) \propto P(A_1, A_2, \ldots, A_N|C_k)P(C_k)$.

A particular but very common Bayesian classifier is the *Naive Bayes Classifier*. In order to estimate the conditional probability, $P(A_1, A_2, \ldots, A_N|C_k)$, a Naive Bayes Classifier assumes the probabilistic *independence* of the attributes—i.e. the presence or absence of a particular attribute is unrelated to the presence or absence of any other. This assumption leads to $P(A_1, A_2, \ldots, A_N|C_k) = P(A_1|C_k)P(A_2|C_k)\ldots P(A_N|C_k)$.

The main benefits of Naive Bayes classifiers are that they are robust to isolated noise points and irrelevant attributes, and they handle missing values by ignoring the instance during probability estimate calculations. However, the independence assumption may not hold for some attributes as they might be correlated. In this case, the usual approach is to use the so-called *Bayesian Belief Networks (BBN)* (or Bayesian Networks, for short). BBN's use an acyclic graph to encode the dependence between attributes and a probability table that associates each node to its immediate parents. BBN's provide a way to capture prior knowledge in a domain using a graphical model. In a similar way to Naive Bayes classifiers, BBN's handle incomplete data well and they are quite robust to model overfitting.

Bayesian classifiers are particularly popular for model-based RS. They are often used to derive a model for content-based RS. Ghani and Fano [48], for instance, use a Naive Bayes classifier to implement a content-based RS. The use of this model allows for recommending products from unrelated categories in the context of a department store.

Bayesian classifiers can also be used in a CF setting. Miyahara and Pazzani [68], for instance, implement a RS based on a Naive Bayes classifier. In order to do so, they define two classes: *like* and *don't like*. In this context they propose two ways of using the Naive Bayesian Classifier: The *Transformed Data Model* assumes that all features are completely independent, and feature selection is implemented as a preprocessing step. On the other hand, the *Sparse Data Model* assumes that only known features are informative for classification. Furthermore, it only makes use of data which both users rated in common when estimating probabilities. Experiments show both models to perform better than a correlation-based CF.

Pronk et al. [77] use a Bayesian Naive Classifier as the base for incorporating user control and improving performance, especially in cold-start situations. In order to do so they propose to maintain two profiles for each user: one learned from the rating history, and the other explicitly created by the user. The blending of both classifiers can be controlled in such a way that the user-defined profile is favored at early stages, when there is not too much rating history, and the learned classifier takes over at later stages.

In the previous section we mentioned that Gutta et al. [40] implemented a rule-based approach in a TV content RS. Another of the approaches they tested was a Bayesian classifier. They define a two-class classifier, where the classes are *watched/not watched*. The user profile is then a collection of attributes together with the number of times they occur in positive and negative examples. This is used to compute prior probabilities that a show belongs to a particular class and the conditional probability that a given feature will be present if a show is either positive or negative. It must be noted that features are, in this case, related to both content—i.e. genre—and contexts—i.e. time of the day. The posteriori probabilities for a new show are then computed from these.

Breese et al. [24] implement a Bayesian Network where each node corresponds to each item. The states correspond to each possible vote value. In the network, each item will have a set of parent items that are its best predictors. The conditional probability tables are represented by decision trees. The authors report better results for this model than for several nearest-neighbors implementations over several datasets.

Hierarchical Bayesian Networks have also been used in several settings as a way to add domain-knowledge for information filtering [98]. One of the issues with hierarchical Bayesian networks, however, is that it is very expensive to learn and update the model when there are many users in it. Zhang and Koren [99] propose a variation over the standard Expectation-Maximization (EM) model in order to speed up this process in the scenario of a content-based RS.

7.3.1.5 Logistic Regression

Logistic Regression (LR) is perhaps one the most basic probabilistic classification models. Although it is not widely spread in the Recommender Systems literature it is used in the industry, arguably because its simplicity and efficiency.

It is important to note that even though Logistic Regression has the term regression in its name it is not a regression model but a classifier [19]. The term regression is due to legacy since LR is a based on the basic Linear Regression.

In regression models the output is always a continuous value, e.g. the predicted audience of a movie based on a set of features such as production costs, marketing budget, cast, feedback of the preview, etc. On the other hand in a classifier the output is a class label. Following the same example, the output would be whether the movie will be a block-buster or not.

The Linear Regression model is defined by the following linear equation,

$$h_\theta(x) = \theta^\top x \tag{7.7}$$

once we have learned the parameters *theta* using the training set the hypothesis can take any continuous value. The Logistic Regression is similar, but there is an extra function $g(z)$ known as the logistic function,

$$h_\theta(x) = g(\theta^\top x) \tag{7.8}$$

$$g(z) = \frac{1}{1 + e^{-z}} \tag{7.9}$$

The logistic function yields $\frac{1}{2}$ when z is zero. For positive values of z it quickly goes to 1 and symmetrically it goes quickly to zero for negative values of z. Since it guarantees that $0 \leq h_\theta(x) \leq 1$ we can treat the output as a probability of belonging to a particular class. We can predict the class label 1 when $h_\theta(x) \geq \frac{1}{2}$ and class label 0 when $h_\theta(x) < \frac{1}{2}$.

Logistic Regression creates then a decision boundary defined by $\theta^\top x \geq 0$. This hyperplane (a line in the case of a single feature) separates data into two classes.

The concept of decision boundary is also present in other classification methods, notably in Support Vector Machines (see Sect. 7.3.1.6). Unlike in SVM's the decision boundary yield by Logistic Regression is not aware of margins between data, as a consequence, the decision boundary might less resilient to the presence of outliers. On the positive side Logistic Regression is easy to implement, and it is very efficient specially when there is a large number of features.

Zhang et al. [81] evaluated Logistic Regression, together with other probabilistic methodologies, for the case of online reviews with a very small set of users assessing the quality of these reviews. Logistic Regression has also been successfully tested in the context of tag recommendation by Montañés et al. [36]. A final use of both linear and (ordinal) logistic regression can be found in Parra et al.'s work [73]. In this case, regression is used as a way to convert implicit feedback into explicit ratings.

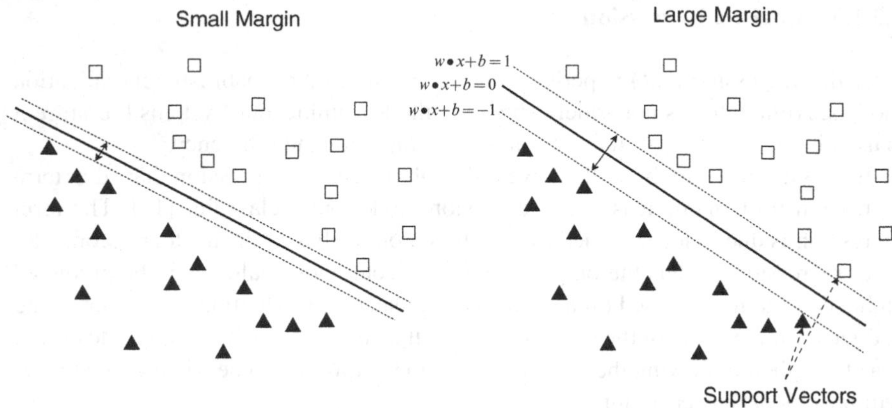

Fig. 7.5 Different boundary decisions are possible to separate two classes in two dimensions. Each boundary has an associated margin

7.3.1.6 Support Vector Machines

The goal of a Support Vector Machine (SVM) classifier [33] is to find a linear hyperplane (decision boundary) that separates the data in such a way that the margin is maximized. For instance, if we look at a two class separation problem in two dimensions like the one illustrated in Fig. 7.5, we can easily observe that there are many possible boundary lines to separate the two classes. Each boundary has an associated margin. The rationale behind SVM's is that if we choose the one that maximizes the margin we are less likely to misclassify unknown items in the future.

A linear separation between two classes is accomplished through the function $w \bullet x + b = 0$. We define a function that can classify items of being of class $+1$ or -1 as long as they are separated by some minimum distance from the class separation function. The function is given by Eq. (7.10)

$$f(x) = \begin{cases} 1, & \text{if } w \bullet x + b \geq 1 \\ -1, & \text{if } w \bullet x + b \leq -1 \end{cases} \tag{7.10}$$

$$Margin = \frac{2}{\|w\|^2} \tag{7.11}$$

Following the main rationale for SVM's, we would like to maximize the margin between the two classes, given by Eq. (7.11). This is in fact equivalent to minimizing the inverse value $L(w) = \frac{\|w\|^2}{2}$ but subjected to the constraints given by $f(x)$. This is a constrained optimization problem and there are numerical approaches to solve it (e.g., quadratic programming).

If the items are not linearly separable we can decide to turn the svm into a *soft margin* classifier by introducing a *slack variable*. In this case the formula to minimize is given by Eq. (7.12) subject to the new definition of $f(x)$ in Eq. (7.13). On the other hand, if the decision boundary is not linear we need to transform data into a higher dimensional space . This is accomplished thanks to a mathematical transformation known as the *kernel trick*. The basic idea is to replace the dot products in Eq. (7.10) by a *kernel* function. There are many different possible choices for the kernel function such as Polynomial or Sigmoid. But the most common kernel functions are the family of Radial Basis Function (RBF).

$$L(w) = \frac{\|w\|^2}{2} + C\sum_{i=1}^{N}\epsilon \tag{7.12}$$

$$f(x) = \begin{cases} 1, & \text{if } w \bullet x + b \geq 1 - \epsilon \\ -1, & \text{if } w \bullet x + b \leq -1 + \epsilon \end{cases} \tag{7.13}$$

Support Vector Machines have recently gained popularity for their performance and efficiency in many settings. SVM's have also shown promising recent results in RS. Kang and Yoo [60], for instance, report on an experimental study that aims at selecting the best preprocessing technique for predicting missing values for an SVM-based RS. In particular, they use SVD and Support Vector Regression. The Support Vector Machine RS is built by first binarizing the 80 levels of available user preference data. They experiment with several settings and report best results for a threshold of 32—i.e. a value of 32 and less is classified as *prefer* and a higher value as *do not prefer*. The user id is used as the class label and the positive and negative values are expressed as preference values 1 and 2.

Xu and Araki [96] used SVM to build a TV program RS. They used information from the Electronic Program Guide (EPG) as features. But in order to reduce features they removed words with lowest frequencies. Furthermore, and in order to evaluate different approaches, they used both the Boolean and the *Term frequency—inverse document frequency* (TFIDF) weighting schemes for features. In the former, 0 and 1 are used to represent absence or presence of a term on the content. In the latter, this is turned into the TFIDF numerical value.

Xia et al. [95] present different approaches to using SVM's for RS in a CF setting. They explore the use of Smoothing Support Vector Machines (SSVM). They also introduce a SSVM-based heuristic (SSVMBH) to iteratively estimate missing elements in the user-item matrix. They compute predictions by creating a classifier for each user. Their experimental results report best results for the SSVMBH as compared to both SSVM's and traditional user-based and item-based CF. Finally, Oku et al. [38] propose the use of Context-Aware Vector Machines (C-SVM) for context-aware RS. They compare the use of standard SVM, C-SVM and an extension that uses CF as well as C-SVM. Their results show the effectiveness of the context-aware methods for restaurant recommendations.

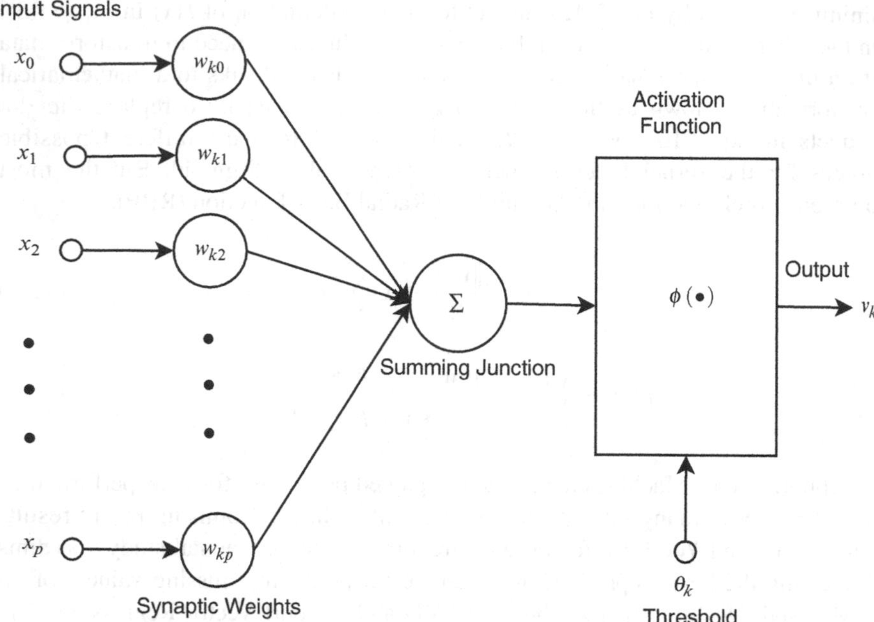

Fig. 7.6 Perceptron model

7.3.1.7 Artificial Neural Networks

An Artificial Neural Network (ANN) [101] is an assembly of inter-connected nodes and weighted links that is inspired in the architecture of the biological brain. Nodes in an ANN are called *neurons* as an analogy with biological neurons. These simple functional units are composed into networks that have the ability to learn a classification problem after they are trained with sufficient data.

The simplest case of an ANN is the *perceptron* model, illustrated in Fig. 7.6. If we particularize the *activation function* ϕ to be the simple Threshold Function, the output is obtained by summing up each of its input value according to the weights of its links and comparing its output against some threshold θ_k. The output function can be expressed using Eq. (7.14). The perceptron model is a linear classifier that has a simple and efficient learning algorithm. But, besides the simple Threshold Function used in the Perceptron model, there are several other common choices for the activation function such as sigmoid, tanh, or step functions.

$$y_k = \begin{cases} 1, & \text{if } \sum x_i w_{ki} \geq \theta_k \\ 0, & \text{if } \sum x_i w_{ki} < \theta_k \end{cases} \tag{7.14}$$

An ANN can have any number of layers. Layers in an ANN are classified into three types: input, hidden, and output. Units in the input layer respond to data that is fed into the network. Hidden units receive the weighted output from the input units. And the output units respond to the weighted output from the hidden units and generate the final output of the network. Using neurons as atomic functional units, there are many possible architectures to put them together in a network. But, the most common approach is to use the *feed-forward ANN*. In this case, signals are strictly propagated in one way: from input to output.

The main advantages of ANN are that—depending on the activation function—they can perform non-linear classification tasks, and that, due to their parallel nature, they can be efficient and even operate if part of the network fails. The main disadvantage is that it is hard to come up with the ideal network topology for a given problem and once the topology is decided this will act as a lower bound for the classification error. ANN's belong to the class of *sub-symbolic* classifiers, which means that they provide no semantics for inferring knowledge—i.e. they promote a kind of *black-box* approach.

ANN's can be used in a similar way as Bayesian Networks to construct model-based RS's. However, there is no conclusive study to whether ANN introduce any performance gain. As a matter of fact, Pazzani and Billsus [76] did a comprehensive experimental study on the use of several machine learning algorithms for web site recommendation. Their main goal was to compare the simple naive Bayesian Classifier with computationally more expensive alternatives such as Decision Trees and Neural Networks. Their experimental results show that Decision Trees perform significantly worse. On the other hand ANN and the Bayesian classifier performed similarly. They conclude that there does not seem to be a need for nonlinear classifiers such as the ANN. Berka et al. [42] used ANN to build an URL RS for web navigation. They implemented a content-independent system based exclusively on *trails*—i.e. associating pairs of domain names with the number of people who traversed them. In order to do so they used feed-forward Multilayer Perceptrons trained with the Backpropagation algorithm.

ANN can be used to combine (or hybridize) the input from several recommendation modules or data sources. Hsu et al. [41], for instance, build a TV recommender by importing data from four different sources: user profiles and stereotypes; viewing communities; program metadata; and viewing context. They use the back-propagation algorithm to train a three-layered neural network. Christakou and Stafylopatis [29] also built a hybrid content-based CF RS. The content-based recommender is implemented using three neural networks per user, each of them corresponding to one of the following features: "kinds", "stars", and "synopsis". They trained the ANN using the Resilient Backpropagation method.

More recently, variations of NN have been used in different collaborative filtering settings. Salakhutdinov et al. used Restricted Boltzmann Machines in the context of the Netflix Prize [83] to predict ratings. This solution is actually part of the current Netflix production system (see Chap. 11).

7.3.2 Ensembles of Classifiers

The basic idea behind the use of *ensembles* of classifiers is to construct a set of classifiers from the training data and predict class labels by aggregating their predictions. Ensembles of classifiers work whenever we can assume that the classifiers are independent. In this case we can ensure that the ensemble will produce results that are in the worst case as bad as the worst classifier in the ensemble. Therefore, combining independent classifiers of a similar classification error will only improve results.

Several approaches are possible to generate ensembles. The two most common techniques are *Bagging* and *Boosting*. In Bagging, we perform sampling with replacement, building the classifier on each bootstrap sample. Each sample has probability $(1-\frac{1}{N})^N$ of being selected—note that if N is large enough, this converges to $1-\frac{1}{e}\approx 0.623$. In Boosting we use an iterative procedure to adaptively change distribution of training data by focusing more on previously misclassified records. Initially, all records are assigned equal weights. But, unlike bagging, weights may change at the end of each boosting round: Records that are wrongly classified will have their weights increased while records that are classified correctly will have their weights decreased. An example of boosting is the AdaBoost algorithm.

The use of ensembles of classifiers is common practice in the RS field. As a matter of fact, any *hybridation* technique [26] can be considered an ensemble as it combines in one way or another several classifiers. An explicit example of this is Tiemann and Pauws' music recommender, in which they use ensemble learning methods to combine a social and a content-base RS [90].

Experimental results show that ensembles can produce better results than any classifier in isolation. Bell et al. [17], for instance, used a combination of 107 different methods in their progress prize winning solution to the Netflix challenge. They state that their findings show that it pays off more to find substantially different approaches rather than focusing on refining a particular technique. In order to blend the results from the ensembles they use a linear regression approach and to derive weights for each classifier, they partition the test dataset into 15 different bins and derive unique coefficients for each of the bins. Different uses of ensembles in the context of the Netflix prize can be tracked in other approaches such as in Schclar et al.'s [86] or Toescher et al.'s [91].

The boosting approach has also been used in RS. Freund et al., for instance, present an algorithm called RankBoost to combine preferences [43]. They apply the algorithm to produce movie recommendations in a CF setting. The winning solution to the Netflix Prize [61] used Gradient Boosted Decision Trees, a tree-based ensemble technique that uses boosting, for the final combination of the individual predictors.

7.3.3 Evaluating Classifiers

The most commonly accepted evaluation measures for RS are the Mean Average Error (MAE) or Root Mean Squared Error (RMSE) between the predicted interest (or rating) and the measured one. These measures compute accuracy without any assumption on the purpose of the RS. However, as McNee et al. point out [67], there is much more than accuracy to deciding whether an item should be recommended. Herlocker et al. [55] provide a comprehensive review of algorithmic evaluation approaches to RS. They suggest that some measures could potentially be more appropriate for some tasks. However, they are not able to validate the measures when evaluating the different approaches empirically on a class of recommendation algorithms and a single set of data.

A step forward is to consider that the purpose of a "real" RS is to produce a top-N list of recommendations and evaluate RS depending on how well they can classify items as being *recommendable*. If we look at our recommendation as a classification problem, we can make use of well-known measures for classifier evaluation such as precision and recall. In the following paragraphs, we will review some of these measures and their application to RS evaluation. Note however that learning algorithms and classifiers can be evaluated by multiple criteria. This includes how accurately they perform the classification, their computational complexity during training , complexity during classification, their sensitivity to noisy data, their scalability, and so on. But in this section we will focus only on classification performance.

In order to evaluate a model we usually take into account the following measures: **True Positives** (*TP*): number of instances classified as belonging to class *A* that truly belong to class *A*; **True Negatives** (*TN*): number of instances classified as not belonging to class *A* and that in fact do not belong to class *A*; **False Positives** (*FP*): number of instances classified as class *A* but that do not belong to class *A*; **False Negatives** (*FN*): instances not classified as belonging to class v but that in fact do belong to class *A*.

The most commonly used measure for model performance is its *Accuracy* defined as the ratio between the instances that have been correctly classified (as belonging or not to the given class) and the total number of instances: $Accuracy = (TP + TN)/(TP + TN + FP + FN)$. However, accuracy might be misleading in many cases. Imagine a 2-class problem in which there are 99,900 samples of class A and 100 of class B. If a classifier simply predicts everything to be of class A, the computed accuracy would be of 99.9 % but the model performance is questionable because it will never detect any class B examples. One way to improve this evaluation is to define the cost matrix where we declare the "cost" of misclassifying class B examples as being of class A. In real world applications different types of errors may indeed have very different costs. For example, if the 100 samples above correspond to defective airplane parts in an assembly line, incorrectly rejecting a non-defective part (one of the 99,900 samples) has a negligible cost compared to the cost of mistakenly classifying a defective part as a good part.

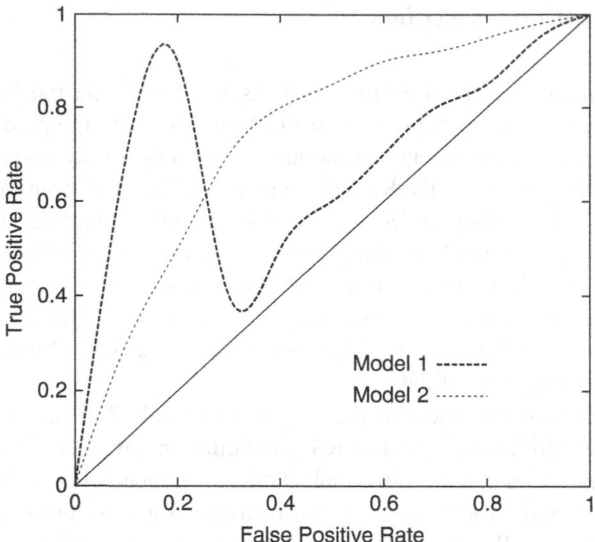

Fig. 7.7 Example of ROC curve. Model 1 performs better for low False Positive Rates while Model 2 is fairly consistent throughout and outperforms Model 1 for False Positive Rates higher than 0.25

Other common measures of model performance, particularly in Information Retrieval, are Precision and Recall. Precision, defined as $P = TP/(TP + FP)$, is a measure of how many errors we make in classifying samples as being of class A. On the other hand, recall, $R = TP/(TP + FN)$, measures how good we are in not leaving out samples that should have been classified as belonging to the class. Note that these two measures are misleading when used in isolation in most cases. We could build a classifier of perfect precision by not classifying any sample as being of class A (therefore obtaining 0 TP but also 0 FP). Conversely, we could build a classifier of perfect recall by classifying all samples as belonging to class A. As a matter of fact, there is a measure, called the F_1-measure that combines both Precision and Recall into a single measure as: $F_1 = \frac{2RP}{R+P} = \frac{2TP}{2TP+FN+FP}$

Sometimes we would like to compare several competing models rather than estimate their performance independently. In order to do so we use a technique developed in the 1950s for analysis of noisy signals: the Receiver Operating Characteristic (ROC) Curve. An ROC curve characterizes the relation between positive hits and false alarms. The performance of each classifier is represented as a point on the curve (see Fig. 7.7).

Ziegler et al. show [100] that evaluating recommender algorithms through top-N lists measures still does not map directly to the user's utility function. However, it does address some of the limitations of the more commonly accepted accuracy measures, such as MAE. Basu et al. [16], for instance, use this approach by analyzing which of the items predicted in the top quartile of the rating scale were actually evaluated in the top quartile by the user. McLaughlin and Herlocker [66] propose a *modified precision* measure in which non-rated items are counted as *not recommendable*. This precision measure in fact represents a lower-bound of the "real" precision. Although the F-measure can be directly derived from the precision-recall values, it is not common to find it in RS evaluations. Huang et al. [56] and Bozzon et al. [22], and Miyahara and Pazzani [68] are some of the few examples of the use of this measure.

ROC curves have also been used in evaluating RS. Zhang et al. [82] use the value of the area under the ROC curve as their evaluation measure when comparing the performance of different algorithms under attack. Banerjee and Ramanathan [13] also use the ROC curves to compare the performance of different models.

It must be noted, though, that the choice of a good evaluation measure, even in the case of a top-N RS, is still a matter of discussion. Many authors have proposed measures that are only indirectly related to these traditional evaluation schemes. Deshpande and Karypis [35], for instance, propose the use of the *hit rate* and the *average reciprocal hit-rank*. On the other hand, Breese et al. [24] define a measure of the utility of the recommendation in a ranked list as a function of the neutral vote. It is also becoming increasingly common to treat a top-N RS as a learning-to-rank problem. In that context, it is common to use ranking metrics such as Mean Average Precision (MAP), Normalized Discounted Cumulative Gain (NDCG), Fraction of Concordant Pairs (FCP), or Mean Reciprocal Rank (MRR).

Chapter 8 focuses on the use of some of these evaluation measures in the context of RS and is therefore a good place to continue if you are interested on this topic.

7.4 Unsupervised Learning

7.4.1 Clustering

The main problem for scaling a CF classifier is the amount of operations involved in computing distances—for finding the best k-nearest neighbors, for instance. A possible solution is, as we saw in Sect. 7.2.3, to reduce dimensionality. But, even if we reduce dimensionality of features, we might still have many objects to compute the distance to. This is where clustering algorithms can come into play. The same is true for content-based RS, where distances among objects are needed to retrieve similar ones. Clustering is sure to improve efficiency because the number of operations is reduced. However, the improve in accuracy is not guaranteed.

Clustering [54] consists of assigning items to groups so that the items in the same groups are more similar than items in different groups: the goal is to discover natural (or meaningful) groups that exist in the data. Similarity is determined using a distance measure, such as the ones reviewed in Sect. 7.2.1. The goal of a clustering algorithm is to minimize intra-cluster distances while maximizing inter-cluster distances.

There are two main categories of clustering algorithms: hierarchical and partitional. Partitional clustering algorithms divide data items into non-overlapping clusters such that each data item is in exactly one cluster. Hierarchical clustering algorithms successively cluster items within found clusters, producing a set of nested cluster organized as a hierarchical tree.

Many clustering algorithms try to minimize a function that measures the quality of the clustering. Such a quality function is often referred to as the objective function, so clustering can be viewed as an optimization problem: the ideal clustering algorithm would consider all possible partitions of the data and output the partitioning that minimizes the quality function. But the corresponding optimization problem is NP hard, so many algorithms resort to heuristics. The main point is that clustering is a difficult problem for which finding optimal solutions is often not possible. For that same reason, selection of the particular clustering algorithm and its parameters (e.g., similarity measure) depend on many factors, including the characteristics of the data. In the following paragraphs we describe the *k*-means clustering algorithm and some of its alternatives.

7.4.1.1 *k*-Means

k-Means clustering is a partitioning method. The function partitions the data set of N items into k disjoint subsets S_j that contain N_j items so that they are as close to each other as possible according a given distance measure. Each cluster in the partition is defined by its N_j members and by its centroid λ_j. The centroid for each cluster is the point to which the sum of distances from all items in that cluster is minimized. Thus, we can define the *k*-means algorithm as an iterative process to minimize $E = \sum_1^k \sum_{n \in S_j} d(x_n, \lambda_j)$, where x_n is a vector representing the n-th item, λ_j is the centroid of the item in S_j and d is the distance measure. The *k*-means algorithm moves items between clusters until E cannot be decreased further.

The algorithm works by randomly selecting k centroids. Then all items are assigned to the cluster whose centroid is the closest to them. The new cluster centroid needs to be updated to account for the items who have been added or removed from the cluster and the membership of the items to the cluster updated. This operation continues until there are no further items that change their cluster membership. Most of the convergence to the final partition takes place during the first iterations of the algorithm, and therefore, the stopping condition is often changed to "until relatively few points change clusters" in order to improve efficiency.

The basic *k*-means is an extremely simple and efficient algorithm. However, it does have several shortcomings: (1) it assumes prior knowledge of the data in order to choose the appropriate k ; (2) the final clusters are very sensitive to the selection of the initial centroids; and (3), it can produce empty cluster. *k*-means also has several limitations with regard to the data: it has problems when clusters are of differing sizes, densities, and non-globular shapes; and it also has problems when the data contains outliers.

Xue et al. [97] present a typical use of clustering in the context of a RS by employing the k-*means* algorithm as a pre-processing step to help in neighborhood formation. They do not restrict the neighborhood to the cluster the user belongs to but rather use the distance from the user to different cluster centroids as a pre-selection step for the neighbors. They also implement a cluster-based smoothing technique in which missing values for users in a cluster are replaced by cluster representatives. Their method is reported to perform slightly better than standard *k*NN-based CF. In a similar way, Sarwar et al. [37] describe an approach to implement a scalable *k*NN classifier. They partition the user space by applying the *bisecting* k-*means* algorithm and then use those clusters as the base for neighborhood formation. They report a decrease in accuracy of around 5 % as compared to standard *k*NN CF. However, their approach allows for a significant improvement in efficiency.

Connor and Herlocker [31] present a different approach in which, instead of users, they cluster items. Using the Pearson Correlation similarity measure they try out four different algorithms: average link hierarchical agglomerative [52], robust clustering algorithm for categorical attributes (ROCK) [53], kMetis, and hMetis.[4] Although clustering did improve efficiency, all of their clustering techniques yielded worse accuracy and coverage than the non-partitioned baseline. Finally, Li et al. [79] and Ungar and Foster [92] present a very similar approach for using k-*means* clustering for solving a probabilistic model interpretation of the recommender problem.

7.4.1.2 Alternatives to *k*-Means

Density-based clustering algorithms such as DBSCAN work by building up on the definition of density as the number of points within a specified radius. DBSCAN, for instance, defines three kinds of points: *core points* are those that have more than a specified number of neighbors within a given distance; *border points* have fewer than the specified number but belong to a *core point* neighborhood; and *noise points* are those that are neither core or border. The algorithm iteratively removes *noise points* and performs clustering on the remaining points.

Message-passing clustering algorithms are a very recent family of graph-based clustering methods. Instead of considering an initial subset of the points as centers and then iteratively adapt those, message-passing algorithms initially consider all points as centers—usually known as *exemplars* in this context. During the algorithm execution points, which are now considered nodes in a network, exchange messages until clusters gradually emerge. *Affinity Propagation* is an important representative of this family of algorithms [44] that works by defining two kinds of messages between nodes: "responsibility", which reflects how well-suited receiving point is to serve as exemplar of the point sending the message, taking into account other

[4]http://www.cs.umn.edu/~karypis/metis.

potential exemplars; and "availability", which is sent from candidate exemplar to the point and reflects how appropriate it would be for the point to choose the candidate as its exemplar, taking into account support from other points that are choosing that same exemplar. Affinity propagation has been applied, with very good results, to problems as different as DNA sequence clustering, face clustering in images, or text summarization.

Hierarchical Clustering, produces a set of nested clusters organized as a hierarchical tree (*dendogram*). Hierarchical Clustering does not have to assume a particular number of clusters in advanced. Also, any desired number of clusters can be obtained by selecting the tree at the proper level. Hierarchical clusters can also sometimes correspond to meaningful taxonomies. Traditional hierarchical algorithms use a similarity or distance matrix and merge or split one cluster at a time. There are two main approaches to hierarchical clustering. In *agglomerative* hierarchical clustering we start with the points as individual clusters and at each step, merge the closest pair of clusters until only one cluster (or k clusters) are left. In *divisive* hierarchical clustering we start with one, all-inclusive cluster, and at each step, split a cluster until each cluster contains a point (or there are k clusters).

To the best of our knowledge, the previous alternatives to k-means have not been applied to RS. On the other hand, other approaches such as Locality-Sensitive Hashing or Bayesian non-parametric models have already proved useful in practical applications.

Locality-sensitive hashing (LSH) [10] is a technique for solving a nearest-neighbor search in high dimensionality spaces. The algorithm relies on the use of hashing functions that preserve "locality" or, in other words, bucket together items that are similar. LSH is an unsupervised method that can be considered as an approach to clustering. However, since it is an approximate solution to the nearest-neighbor problem, it can also be used for supervised classification as explained in Sect. 7.3.1.1. Due to its performance and scalability, LSH is used as a preprocessing step to group similar users in some industrial RS approaches. LinkedIn, for example, has publicly described its application for people recommendation [18].

Latent Dirichlet Allocation (LDA) [20] is a generative unsupervised model that can also be considered a form of clustering. As opposed to the previous methods though, LDA is a mixed membership model in which we consider that each data point may belong to more than a single clusters. A typical application of LDA is to identify topics in collections of documents. In that sense, LDA is also very related to Latent Semantic Analysis, and therefore techniques such as SVD (see Sect. 7.2.3). LDA has been used in different ways for content-based recommendations. For example, Jin et. al use LDA to identify topics in webpages in order to implement a hybrid content/CF recommender system [58]. LDA is also a common approach to tag recommendation (see [62], for example).

Finally, **Bayesian non-parametric models** is a family of methods that combines the power of mixed-membership models such as LDA, and the flexibility of dynamic methods that adapt the number of clusters to the underlying data distribution. **Hierarchical Dirichlet Processes (HDP)** [89] and **Recurrent Chinese Restaurant**

Processes (RCRP) have been used to cluster documents and users to later perform recommendations [3]. These initial results are promising, and highlight the applicability of these flexible approaches for RS.

7.4.2 Association Rule Mining

Association Rule Mining focuses on finding rules that will predict the occurrence of an item based on the occurrences of other items in a transaction. The fact that two items are found to be related means co-occurrence but not causality. Note that this technique should not be confused with rule-based classifiers presented in Sect. 7.3.1.3.

We define an *itemset* as a collection of one or more items (e.g. (Milk, Beer, Diaper)). A *k-itemset* is an itemset that contains k items. The frequency of a given itemset is known as *support count* (e.g. (Milk, Beer, Diaper) = 131). And the *support* of the itemset is the fraction of transactions that contain it (e.g. (Milk, Beer, Diaper) $= 0.12$). A *frequent itemset* is an itemset with a support that is greater or equal to a *minsup* threshold. An association rule is an expression of the form $X \Rightarrow Y$, where X and Y are itemsets. (e.g. $Milk, Diaper \Rightarrow Beer$). In this case the *support* of the association rule is the fraction of transactions that have both X and Y. On the other hand, the *confidence* of the rule is how often items in Y appear in transactions that contain X.

Given a set of transactions T, the goal of association rule mining is to find all rules having $support \geq minsupthreshold$ and $confidence \geq minconfthreshold$. The brute-force approach would be to list all possible association rules, compute the support and confidence for each rule and then prune rules that do not satisfy both conditions. This is, however, computationally very expensive. For this reason, we take a two-step approach: (1) Generate all itemsets whose support $\geq$ minsup (**Frequent Itemset Generation**); (2) Generate high confidence rules from each frequent itemset (**Rule Generation**).

Several techniques exist to optimize the generation of frequent itemsets. On a broad sense they can be classified into those that try to minimize the number of candidates (*M*), those that reduce the number of transactions (*N*), and those that reduce the number of comparisons (*NM*). The most common approach though, is to reduce the number of candidates using the *Apriori principle*. This principle states that if an itemset is frequent, then all of its subsets must also be frequent. This is verified using the support measure because the support of an itemset never exceeds that of its subsets. The Apriori Algorithm is a practical implementation of the principle.

Given a frequent itemset L, the goal when generating rules is to find all non-empty subsets that satisfy the minimum confidence requirement. If $|L| = k$, then there are $2k-2$ candidate association rules. So, as in the frequent itemset generation, we need to find ways to generate rules efficiently. For the Apriori Algorithm we can generate candidate rules by merging two rules that share the same prefix in the rule consequent.

The effectiveness of association rule mining for uncovering patterns and driving personalized marketing decisions has been known for a some time [2]. However, and although there is a clear relation between this method and the goal of a RS, they have not become mainstream. The main reason is that this approach is similar to item-based CF but is less flexible since it requires of an explicit notion of *transaction*—e.g. co-occurrence of events in a given session. In the next paragraphs we present some promising examples, some of which indicate that association rules still have not had their last word.

Mobasher et al. [69] present a system for web personalization based on association rules mining. Their system identifies association rules from pageviews co-occurrences based on users navigational patterns. Their approach outperforms a *k*NN-based recommendation system both in terms of precision and coverage. Smyth et al. [87] present two different case studies of using association rules for RS. In the first case they use the a priori algorithm to extract item association rules from user profiles in order to derive a better item-item similarity measure. In the second case, they apply association rule mining to a *conversational* recommender. The goal here is to find co-occurrent *critiques*—i.e. user indicating a preference over a particular feature of the recommended item. Lin et al. [65] present a new association mining algorithm that adjusts the minimum support of the rules during mining in order to obtain an appropriate number of significant rule therefore addressing some of the shortcomings of previous algorithms such as the a priori. They mine both association rules between users and items. The measured accuracy outperforms previously reported values for correlation-based recommendation and is similar to the more elaborate approaches such as the combination of SVD and ANN.

Finally, as already mentioned in Sect. 7.3.1.2, Cho et al. [28] combine Decision Trees and Association Rule Mining in a web shop RS. In their system, association rules are derived in order to link related items. The recommendation is then computed by intersecting association rules with user preferences. They look for association rules in different transaction sets such as purchases, basket placement, and click-through. They also use a heuristic for weighting rules coming from each of the transaction sets. Purchase association rules, for instance, are weighted higher than click-through association rules.

7.5 Conclusions

This chapter has introduced the main data mining methods and techniques that can be applied in the design of a RS. We have also surveyed their use in the literature and provided some rough guidelines on how and where they can be applied.

We started by reviewing techniques that can be applied in the pre-processing step. First, there is the choice of an appropriate distance measure, which is reviewed in Sect. 7.2.1. This is required by most of the methods in the following steps. The cosine similarity and Pearson correlation are commonly accepted as the best choice. Then, in Sect. 7.2.2, we reviewed the basic sampling techniques that need to be applied in order to select a subset of an originally large data set, or to separating a training and a testing set. Finally, we discussed the use of dimensionality reduction techniques such as Principal Component Analysis and Singular Value Decomposition in Sect. 7.2.3 as a way to address the *curse of dimensionality* problem.

In Sect. 7.3, we reviewed the main classification methods: namely, nearest-neighbors, decision trees, rule-based classifiers, Bayesian networks, logistic regression, support vector machines, and artificial neural networks. We saw that, although *k*NN (see Sect. 7.3.1.1) CF is the preferred approach, all those classifiers can be applied in different settings. Decision trees (see Sect. 7.3.1.2) can be used to derive a model based on the content of the items or to model a particular part of the system. Decision rules (see Sect. 7.3.1.3) can be derived from a pre-existing decision trees, or can also be used to introduce business or domain knowledge. Bayesian networks (see Sect. 7.3.1.4) are a popular approach to content-based recommendation, but can also be used to derive a model-based CF system. In a similar way, Artificial Neural Networks can be used to derive a model-based recommender but also to combine/hybridize several algorithms. Finally, support vector machines (see Sect. 7.3.1.6) are gaining popularity also as a way to infer content-based classifications or derive a CF model.

Choosing the right classifier for a RS is not easy and is in many senses task and data-dependent. In the case of CF, some results seem to indicate that model-based approaches using classifiers such as the SVM or Bayesian Networks can slightly improve performance of the standard *k*NN classifier. However, those results are non-conclusive and hard to generalize. In the case of a content-based RS there is some evidence that in some cases Bayesian Networks will perform better than simpler methods such as decision trees. However, it is not clear that more complex non-linear classifiers such as the ANN or SVMs can perform better.

The choice of the right classifier for a specific recommending task still has nowadays much of exploratory. A practical rule of thumb is to start with the simplest approach and only introduce complexity if the performance gain obtained justifies it. The performance gain should of course balance different dimensions. In Sect. 7.3.3 we reviewed different ways to evaluate the performance of a classifier. Another option is to combine different classifiers in an ensemble. We described different techniques to build ensembles in Sect. 7.3.2.

We reviewed clustering algorithms in Sect. 7.4.1. Clustering is usually used in RS to improve performance. A previous clustering step, either in the user of item space, reduces the number of distance computations we need to perform. The simplicity and relative efficiency of the *k*-means algorithm (see Sect. 7.4.1.1) make it hard to find a practical alternative. We reviewed some of them such as Hierarchical Clustering or Message-passing algorithms in Sect. 7.4.1.2.

Finally, in Sect. 7.4.2, we described association rules and surveyed their use in RS. Association rules offer an intuitive framework for recommending items whenever there is an explicit or implicit notion of *transaction*. Although there exist efficient algorithms for computing association rules, and they have proved more accurate than standard *k*NN CF, they are still not a favored approach.

The choice of the right DM technique in designing a RS is a complex task that is bound by many problem-specific constraints. However, we hope that the short review of techniques and experiences included in this chapter can help the reader make a much more informed decision. Besides, we have also touched upon areas that are open to many further improvements, and where there is still much exciting and relevant research to be done in the coming years.

References

1. G. Adomavicius and A. Tuzhilin. Toward the next generation of recommender systems: A survey of the state-of-the-art and possible extensions. *IEEE Transactions on Knowledge and Data Engineering*, 17(6):734–749, 2005.
2. R. Agrawal and R. Srikant. Fast algorithms for mining association rules in large databases. In *Proceedings of the 20th International Conference on Very Large Data Bases*, 1994.
3. A. Ahmed and E. Xing. Scalable dynamic nonparametric bayesian models of content and users. In *Proceedings of the Twenty-Third International Joint Conference on Artificial Intelligence*, IJCAI'13, pages 3111–3115. AAAI Press, 2013.
4. X. Amatriain. Big & personal: data and models behind netflix recommendations. In *Proceedings of the 2nd International Workshop on Big Data, Streams and Heterogeneous Source Mining: Algorithms, Systems, Programming Models and Applications*, pages 1–6. ACM, 2013.
5. X. Amatriain. Mining large streams of user data for personalized recommendations. *ACM SIGKDD Explorations Newsletter*, 14(2):37–48, 2013.
6. X. Amatriain, N. Lathia, J. M. Pujol, H. Kwak, and N. Oliver. The wisdom of the few: A collaborative filtering approach based on expert opinions from the web. In *Proc. of SIGIR '09*, 2009.
7. X. Amatriain, J. M. Pujol, and N. Oliver. I like it... i like it not: Evaluating user ratings noise in recommender systems. In *UMAP '09*, 2009.
8. X. Amatriain, J. M. Pujol, N. Tintarev, and N. Oliver. Rate it again: Increasing recommendation accuracy by user re-rating. In *Recys '09*, 2009.
9. M. Anderson, M. Ball, H. Boley, S. Greene, N. Howse, D. Lemire, and S. McGrath. Racofi: A rule-applying collaborative filtering system. In *Proc. IEEE/WIC COLA'03*, 2003.
10. A. Andoni and P. Indyk. Near-optimal hashing algorithms for approximate nearest neighbor in high dimensions. *Commun. ACM*, 51(1):117–122, Jan. 2008.
11. B. D. Baets. Growing decision trees in an ordinal setting. *International Journal of Intelligent Systems*, 2003.
12. S. Balakrishnan and S. Chopra. Collaborative ranking. In *Proceedings of the fifth ACM international conference on Web search and data mining*, pages 143–152. ACM, 2012.
13. S. Banerjee and K. Ramanathan. Collaborative filtering on skewed datasets. In *Proc. of WWW '08*, 2008.
14. D. Barber. Bayesian Reasoning and Machine Learning. Cambridge University Press. 2012.
15. C. Basu, H. Hirsh, and W. Cohen. Recommendation as classification: Using social and content-based information in recommendation. In *In Proceedings of the Fifteenth National Conference on Artificial Intelligence*, pages 714–720. AAAI Press, 1998.
16. C. Basu, H. Hirsh, and W. Cohen. Recommendation as classification: Using social and content-based information in recommendation. In *AAAI Workshop on Recommender Systems*, 1998.
17. R. M. Bell, Y. Koren, and C. Volinsky. The bellkor solution to the netflix prize. Technical report, AT&T Labs – Research, 2007.

18. A. Bhasin. Beyond ratings and followers. In *Proceedings of the 6th ACM Conference on Recommender Systems*, RecSys '12, 2012.
19. C. M. Bishop. *Pattern Recognition and Machine Learning (Information Science and Statistics)*. Springer-Verlag New York, Inc., Secaucus, NJ, USA, 2006.
20. D. M. Blei, A. Y. Ng, and M. I. Jordan. Latent dirichlet allocation. *J. Mach. Learn. Res.*, 3:993–1022, Mar. 2003.
21. A. Bouza, G. Reif, A. Bernstein, and H. Gall. Semtree: ontology-based decision tree algorithm for recommender systems. In *International Semantic Web Conference*, 2008.
22. A. Bozzon, G. Prandi, G. Valenzise, and M. Tagliasacchi. A music recommendation system based on semantic audio segments similarity. In *Proceeding of Internet and Multimedia Systems and Applications - 2008*, 2008.
23. M. Brand. Fast online svd revisions for lightweight recommender systems. In *SIAM International Conference on Data Mining (SDM)*, 2003.
24. J. Breese, D. Heckerman, and C. Kadie. Empirical analysis of predictive algorithms for collaborative filtering. In *Proceedings of the Fourteenth Annual Conference on Uncertainty in Artificial Intelligence*, page 43–52, 1998.
25. L. Breiman. Random forests. *Machine learning*, 45(1):5–32, 2001.
26. R. Burke. Hybrid web recommender systems. pages 377–408. 2007.
27. W. Cheng, J. Hühn, and E. Hüllermeier. Decision tree and instance-based learning for label ranking. In *ICML '09: Proceedings of the 26th Annual International Conference on Machine Learning*, pages 161–168, New York, NY, USA, 2009. ACM.
28. Y. Cho, J. Kim, and S. Kim. A personalized recommender system based on web usage mining and decision tree induction. *Expert Systems with Applications*, 2002.
29. C. Christakou and A. Stafylopatis. A hybrid movie recommender system based on neural networks. In *ISDA '05: Proceedings of the 5th International Conference on Intelligent Systems Design and Applications*, pages 500–505, 2005.
30. W. Cohen. Fast effective rule induction. In *Machine Learning: Proceedings of the 12th International Conference*, 1995.
31. M. Connor and J. Herlocker. Clustering items for collaborative filtering. In *SIGIR Workshop on Recommender Systems*, 2001.
32. T. Cover and P. Hart. Nearest neighbor pattern classification. *Information Theory, IEEE Transactions on*, 13(1):21–27, 1967.
33. N. Cristianini and J. Shawe-Taylor. *An Introduction to Support Vector Machines and Other Kernel-based Learning Methods*. Cambridge University Press, March 2000.
34. S. Deerwester, S. T. Dumais, G. W. Furnas, L. T. K., and R. Harshman. Indexing by latent semantic analysis. *Journal of the American Society for Information Science*, 41, 1990.
35. M. Deshpande and G. Karypis. Item-based top-n recommendation algorithms. *ACM Trans. Inf. Syst.*, 22(1):143–177, 2004.
36. I. D. E. Montanés, J.-R. Quevedo and J. Ranilla. Collaborative tag recommendation system based on logistic regression. In *ECML PKDD Discovery Challenge 09*, 2009.
37. B. S. et al. Recommender systems for large-scale e-commerce: Scalable neighborhood formation using clustering. In *Proceedings of the Fifth International Conference on Computer and Information Technology*, 2002.
38. K. O. et al. Context-aware svm for context-dependent information recommendation. In *International Conference On Mobile Data Management*, 2006.
39. P. T. et al. *Introduction to Data Mining*. Addison Wesley, 2005.
40. S. G. et al. Tv content recommender system. In *AAAI/IAAI 2000*, 2000.
41. S. H. et al. Aimed- a personalized tv recommendation system. In *Interactive TV: a Shared Experience*, 2007.
42. T. B. et al. A trail based internet-domain recommender system using artificial neural networks. In *Proceedings of the Int. Conf. on Adaptive Hypermedia and Adaptive Web Based Systems*, 2002.
43. Y. Freund, R. Iyer, R. E. Schapire, and Y. Singer. An efficient boosting algorithm for combining preferences. *J. Mach. Learn. Res.*, 4:933–969, 2003.

44. B. J. Frey and D. Dueck. Clustering by passing messages between data points. *Science*, 307, 2007.
45. J. H. Friedman. Greedy function approximation: a gradient boosting machine. *Annals of Statistics*, pages 1189–1232, 2001.
46. N. Friedman, D. Geiger, and M. Goldszmidt. Bayesian network classifiers. *Mach. Learn.*, 29(2–3):131–163, 1997.
47. S. Funk. Netflix update: Try this at home, 2006.
48. R. Ghani and A. Fano. Building recommender systems using a knowledge base of product semantics. In *In 2nd International Conference on Adaptive Hypermedia and Adaptive Web Based Systems*, 2002.
49. N. Golbandi, Y. Koren, and R. Lempel. Adaptive bootstrapping of recommender systems using decision trees. In *Proceedings of the fourth ACM international conference on Web search and data mining*, pages 595–604. ACM, 2011.
50. K. Goldberg, T. Roeder, D. Gupta, and C. Perkins. Eigentaste: A constant time collaborative filtering algorithm. *Journal Information Retrieval*, 4(2):133–151, July 2001.
51. G. Golub and C. Reinsch. Singular value decomposition and least squares solutions. *Numerische Mathematik*, 14(5):403–420, April 1970.
52. E. Gose, R. Johnsonbaugh, and S. Jost. *Pattern Recognition and Image Analysis*. Prentice Hall, 1996.
53. S. Guha, R. Rastogi, and K. Shim. Rock: a robust clustering algorithm for categorical attributes. In *Proc. of the 15th Int'l Conf. On Data Eng.*, 1999.
54. J. A. Hartigan. *Clustering Algorithms (Probability & Mathematical Statistics)*. John Wiley & Sons Inc, 1975.
55. J. L. Herlocker, J. A. Konstan, L. G. Terveen, and J. T. Riedl. Evaluating collaborative filtering recommender systems. *ACM Trans. Inf. Syst.*, 22(1):5–53, 2004.
56. Z. Huang, D. Zeng, and H. Chen. A link analysis approach to recommendation under sparse data. In *Proceedings of AMCIS 2004*, 2004.
57. A. Isaksson, M. Wallman, H. Göransson, and M. G. Gustafsson. Cross-validation and bootstrapping are unreliable in small sample classification. *Pattern Recognition Letters*, 29:1960–1965, 2008.
58. X. Jin, Y. Zhou, and B. Mobasher. A maximum entropy web recommendation system: Combining collaborative and content features. In *Proceedings of the Eleventh ACM SIGKDD International Conference on Knowledge Discovery in Data Mining*, KDD '05, pages 612–617, New York, NY, USA, 2005. ACM.
59. I. T. Jolliffe. *Principal Component Analysis*. Springer, 2002.
60. H. Kang and S. Yoo. Svm and collaborative filtering-based prediction of user preference for digital fashion recommendation systems. *IEICE Transactions on Inf & Syst*, 2007.
61. Y. Koren. The bellkor solution to the netflix grand prize. *Netflix prize documentation*, 2009.
62. R. Krestel, P. Fankhauser, and W. Nejdl. Latent dirichlet allocation for tag recommendation. In *Proceedings of the third ACM conference on Recommender systems*, pages 61–68. ACM, 2009.
63. M. Kurucz, A. A. Benczur, and K. Csalogany. Methods for large scale svd with missing values. In *Proceedings of KDD Cup and Workshop 2007*, 2007.
64. N. Lathia, S. Hailes, and L. Capra. The effect of correlation coefficients on communities of recommenders. In *SAC '08: Proceedings of the 2008 ACM symposium on Applied computing*, pages 2000–2005, New York, NY, USA, 2008. ACM.
65. W. Lin and S. Alvarez. Efficient adaptive-support association rule mining for recommender systems. *Data Mining and Knowledge Discovery Journal*, 6(1), 2004.
66. M. R. McLaughlin and J. L. Herlocker. A collaborative filtering algorithm and evaluation metric that accurately model the user experience. In *Proc. of SIGIR '04*, 2004.
67. S. M. McNee, J. Riedl, and J. A. Konstan. Being accurate is not enough: how accuracy metrics have hurt recommender systems. In *CHI '06: CHI '06 extended abstracts on Human factors in computing systems*, pages 1097–1101, New York, NY, USA, 2006. ACM Press.

68. K. Miyahara and M. J. Pazzani. Collaborative filtering with the simple bayesian classifier. In *Pacific Rim International Conference on Artificial Intelligence*, 2000.
69. B. Mobasher, H. Dai, T. Luo, and M. Nakagawa. Effective personalization based on association rule discovery from web usage data. In *Workshop On Web Information And Data Management, WIDM '01*, 2001.
70. K. P. Murphy. *Machine Learning: A Probabilistic Perspective*. The MIT Press, 2012.
71. D. Nikovski and V. Kulev. Induction of compact decision trees for personalized recommendation. In *SAC '06: Proceedings of the 2006 ACM symposium on Applied computing*, pages 575–581, New York, NY, USA, 2006. ACM.
72. M. P. O'mahony. Detecting noise in recommender system databases. In *In Proceedings of the International Conference on Intelligent User Interfaces (IUI'06), 29th–1st*, pages 109–115. ACM Press, 2006.
73. D. Parra, A. Karatzoglou, X. Amatriain, and I. Yavuz. Implicit feedback recommendation via implicit-to-explicit ordinal logistic regression mapping. 2011.
74. A. Paterek. Improving regularized singular value decomposition for collaborative filtering. In *Proceedings of KDD Cup and Workshop 2007*, 2007.
75. M. J. Pazzani. A framework for collaborative, content-based and demographic filtering. *Artificial Intelligence Review*, 13:393–408, 1999.
76. M. J. Pazzani and D. Billsus. Learning and revising user profiles: The identification of interesting web sites. *Machine Learning*, 27(3):313–331, 1997.
77. V. Pronk, W. Verhaegh, A. Proidl, and M. Tiemann. Incorporating user control into recommender systems based on naive bayesian classification. In *RecSys '07: Proceedings of the 2007 ACM conference on Recommender systems*, pages 73–80, 2007.
78. D. Pyle. *Data Preparation for Data Mining*. Morgan Kaufmann, second edition, 1999.
79. B. K. Q. Li. Clustering approach for hybrid recommender system. In *Web Intelligence 03*, 2003.
80. J. R. Quinlan. Induction of decision trees. *Machine Learning*, 1(1):81–106, March 1986.
81. T. T. R. Zhang and Y. Mao. Recommender systems from words of few mouths. In *Proceedings of IJCAJ 11*, 2011.
82. J. F. S. Zhang, Y. Ouyang and F. Makedon. Analysis of a low-dimensional linear model under recommendation attacks. In *Proc. of SIGIR '06*, 2006.
83. R. Salakhutdinov, A. Mnih, and G. E. Hinton. Restricted Boltzmann machines for collaborative filtering. In *Proc of ICML '07*, New York, NY, USA, 2007. ACM.
84. B. Sarwar, G. Karypis, J. Konstan, and J. Riedl. Incremental svd-based algorithms for highly scalable recommender systems. In *5th International Conference on Computer and Information Technology (ICCIT)*, 2002.
85. B. M. Sarwar, G. Karypis, J. A. Konstan, and J. T. Riedl. Application of dimensionality reduction in recommender systems—a case study. In *ACM WebKDD Workshop*, 2000.
86. A. Schclar, A. Tsikinovsky, L. Rokach, A. Meisels, and L. Antwarg. Ensemble methods for improving the performance of neighborhood-based collaborative filtering. In *RecSys '09: Proceedings of the third ACM conference on Recommender systems*, pages 261–264, New York, NY, USA, 2009. ACM.
87. B. Smyth, K. McCarthy, J. Reilly, D. O'Sullivan, L. McGinty, and D. Wilson. Case studies in association rule mining for recommender systems. In *Proc. of International Conference on Artificial Intelligence (ICAI '05)*, 2005.
88. E. Spertus, M. Sahami, and O. Buyukkokten. Evaluating similarity measures: A large-scale study in the orkut social network. In *Proceedings of the 2005 International Conference on Knowledge Discovery and Data Mining (KDD-05)*, 2005.
89. Y. W. Teh, M. I. Jordan, M. J. Beal, and D. M. Blei. Hierarchical dirichlet processes. *Journal of the American Statistical Association*, 101, 2004.
90. M. Tiemann and S. Pauws. Towards ensemble learning for hybrid music recommendation. In *RecSys '07: Proceedings of the 2007 ACM conference on Recommender systems*, pages 177–178, New York, NY, USA, 2007. ACM.

91. A. Toescher, M. Jahrer, and R. Legenstein. Improved neighborhood-based algorithms for large-scale recommender systems. In *In KDD-Cup and Workshop 08*, 2008.
92. L. H. Ungar and D. P. Foster. Clustering methods for collaborative filtering. In *Proceedings of the Workshop on Recommendation Systems*, 2000.
93. I. H. Witten and E. Frank. *Data Mining: Practical Machine Learning Tools and Techniques*. Morgan Kaufmann, second edition, 2005.
94. M. Wu. Collaborative filtering via ensembles of matrix factorizations. In *Proceedings of KDD Cup and Workshop 2007*, 2007.
95. Z. Xia, Y. Dong, and G. Xing. Support vector machines for collaborative filtering. In *ACM-SE 44: Proceedings of the 44th annual Southeast regional conference*, pages 169–174, New York, NY, USA, 2006. ACM.
96. J. Xu and K. Araki. A svm-based personal recommendation system for tv programs. In *Multi-Media Modelling Conference Proceedings*, 2006.
97. G.-R. Xue, C. Lin, Q. Yang, W. Xi, H.-J. Zeng, Y. Yu, and Z. Chen. Scalable collaborative filtering using cluster-based smoothing. In *Proceedings of the 2005 SIGIR*, 2005.
98. K. Yu, V. Tresp, and S. Yu. A nonparametric hierarchical bayesian framework for information filtering. In *SIGIR '04*, 2004.
99. Y. Zhang and J. Koren. Efficient bayesian hierarchical user modeling for recommendation system. In *SIGIR 07*, 2007.
100. C.-N. Ziegler, S. M. McNee, J. A. Konstan, and G. Lausen. Improving recommendation lists through topic diversification. In *Proc. of WWW '05*, 2005.
101. J. Zurada. *Introduction to artificial neural systems*. West Publishing Co., St. Paul, MN, USA, 1992.

Part II
Recommender Systems Evaluation

Chapter 8
Evaluating Recommender Systems

Asela Gunawardana and Guy Shani

8.1 Introduction

Recommender systems can now be found in many modern applications that expose the user to a huge collections of items. Such systems typically provide the user with a list of recommended items they might prefer, or predict how much they might prefer each item. These systems help users to decide on appropriate items, and ease the task of finding preferred items in the collection.

For example, the DVD rental provider Netflix[1] displays predicted ratings for every displayed movie in order to help the user decide which movie to rent. The online book retailer Amazon[2] provides average user ratings for displayed books, and a list of other books that are bought by users who buy a specific book. Microsoft provides many free downloads for users, such as bug fixes, products and so forth. When a user downloads some software, the system presents a list of additional items that are downloaded together. All these systems are typically categorized as recommender systems, even though they provide diverse services.

In the past decade, there has been a vast amount of research in the field of recommender systems, mostly focusing on designing new algorithms for recommendations. An application designer who wishes to add a recommender system

[1] www.Netflix.com.

[2] www.amazon.com.

A. Gunawardana
Microsoft Research, One Microsoft Way, Redmond, WA 98052, USA
e-mail: aselag@microsoft.com

G. Shani (✉)
Information Systems Engineering, Ben Gurion University, Beer Sheva, Israel
e-mail: shanigu@bgu.ac.il

F. Ricci et al. (eds.), *Recommender Systems Handbook*,
DOI 10.1007/978-1-4899-7637-6_8

to her application has a large variety of algorithms at her disposal, and must make a decision about the most appropriate algorithm for her goals. Typically, such decisions are based on experiments, comparing the performance of a number of candidate recommenders. The designer can then select the best performing algorithm, given structural constraints such as the type, timeliness and reliability of availability data, allowable memory and CPU footprints. Furthermore, most researchers who suggest new recommendation algorithms also compare the performance of their new algorithm to a set of existing approaches. Such evaluations are typically performed by applying some evaluation metric that provides a ranking of the candidate algorithms (usually using numeric scores).

Initially most recommenders have been evaluated and ranked on their prediction power—their ability to accurately predict the user's choices. However, it is now widely agreed that accurate predictions are crucial but insufficient to deploy a good recommendation engine. In many applications people use a recommender system for more than an exact anticipation of their tastes. Users may also be interested in discovering new items, in rapidly exploring diverse items, in preserving their privacy, in the fast responses of the system, and many more properties of the interaction with the recommendation engine. We must hence identify the set of properties that may influence the success of a recommender system in the context of a specific application. Then, we can evaluate how the system preforms on these relevant properties.

In this chapter we review the process of evaluating a recommendation system. We discuss three different types of experiments; offline, user studies and online experiments.

Often it is easiest to perform offline experiments using existing data sets and a protocol that models user behavior to estimate recommender performance measures such as prediction accuracy. A more expensive option is a user study, where a small set of users is asked to perform a set of tasks using the system, typically answering questions afterwards about their experience. Finally, we can run large scale experiments on a deployed system, which we call online experiments. Such experiments evaluate the performance of the recommenders on real users which are oblivious to the conducted experiment. We discuss what can and cannot be evaluated for each of these types of experiments.

We can sometimes evaluate how well the recommender achieves its overall goals. For example, we can check an e-commerce website revenue with and without the recommender system and make an estimation of the value of the system to the website. In other cases, it can also be useful to evaluate how recommenders perform in terms of some specific properties, allowing us to focus on improving properties where they fall short. First, one must show that a property is indeed relevant to users and affect their experience. Then, we can design algorithms that improve upon these properties. In improving one property we may reduce the quality of another property, creating a trade-off between a set of properties. In many cases it is also difficult to say how these trade-offs affect the overall performance of the system, and we have to either run additional experiments to understand this aspect, or use the opinions of domain experts.

This chapter focuses on property-directed evaluation of recommender algorithms. We provide an overview of a large set of properties that can be relevant for system success, explaining how candidate recommenders can be ranked with respect to these properties. For each property we discuss the relevant experiment types—offline, user study, and online experiments—and explain how an evaluation can be conducted in each case. We explain the difficulties and outline the pitfalls in evaluating each property. For all these properties we focus on ranking recommenders on that property, assuming that better handling the property will improve user experience.

We also review a set of previous suggestions for evaluating recommender systems, describing a large set of popular methods and placing them in the context of the properties that they measure. We especially focus on the widely researched accuracy and ranking measurements, describing a large set of evaluation metrics for these properties. For other, less studied properties, we suggest guidelines from which specific measures can be derived. We provide examples of such specific implementations where appropriate.

The rest of the chapter is structured as follows. In Sect. 8.2 we discuss the different experimental settings in which recommender systems can be evaluated, discussing the appropriate use of offline experiments, user studies, and online trials. We also outline considerations that go into making reliable decisions based on these experiments, including generalization and statistical significance of results. In Sect. 8.3 we describe a large variety of properties of recommender systems that may impact their performance, as well as metrics for measuring these properties. Finally, we conclude in Sect. 8.4.

8.2 Experimental Settings

In this section we describe three levels of experiments that can be used in order to compare several recommenders. The discussion below is motivated by evaluation protocols in related areas such as machine learning and information retrieval, highlighting practices relevant to evaluating recommender systems. The reader is referred to publications in these fields for more detailed discussions [17, 61, 75].

We begin with offline experiments, which are typically the easiest to conduct, as they require no interaction with real users. We then describe user studies, where we ask a small group of subjects to use the system in a controlled environment, and then report on their experience. In such experiments we can collect both quantitative and qualitative information about the systems, but care must be taken to consider various biases in the experimental design. Finally, perhaps the most trustworthy experiment is when the system is used by a pool of real users, typically unaware of the experiment. While in such an experiment we are able to collect only certain types of data, this experimental design is closest to reality.

In all experimental scenarios, it is important to follow a few basic guidelines in general experimental studies:

- **Hypothesis:** before running the experiment we must form an hypothesis. It is important to be concise and restrictive about this hypothesis, and design an experiment that tests the hypothesis. For example, an hypothesis can be that algorithm *A* better predicts user ratings than algorithm *B*. In that case, the experiment should test the prediction accuracy, and not other factors. Other popular hypothesis in recommender system research can be that algorithm *A* scales better to larger datasets than algorithm *B*, that system *A* gains more user trust than system *B*, or that recommendation user interface *A* is preferred by users to interface *B*.
- **Controlling variables:** when comparing a few candidate algorithms on a certain hypothesis, it is important that all variables that are not tested will stay fixed. For example, suppose that in a movie recommendation system, we switch from using algorithm *A* to algorithm *B*, and notice that the number of movies that users watch increases. In this situation, we cannot tell whether the change is due to the change in algorithm, or whether something else changed at about the same time. If instead, we randomly assign users to algorithms *A* and *B*, and notice that users assigned to algorithm *A* watch more movies than those who are assigned to algorithm *B*, we can be confident that this is due to algorithm *A*.
- **Generalization power:** when drawing conclusions from experiments, we may desire that our conclusions generalize beyond the immediate context of the experiments. When choosing an algorithm for a real application, we may want our conclusions to hold on the deployed system, and generalize beyond our experimental data set. Similarly, when developing new algorithms, we want our conclusions to hold beyond the scope of the specific application or data set that we experimented with. To increase the probability of generalization of the results we must typically experiment with several data sets or applications. It is important to understand the properties of the various data sets that are used. Generally speaking, the more diverse the data used, the more we can generalize the results.

8.2.1 Offline Experiments

An offline experiment is performed by using a pre-collected data set of users choosing or rating items. Using this data set we can try to simulate the behavior of users that interact with a recommendation system. In doing so, we assume that the user behavior when the data was collected will be similar enough to the user behavior when the recommender system is deployed, so that we can make reliable decisions based on the simulation. Offline experiments are attractive because they require no interaction with real users, and thus allow us to compare a wide range of candidate algorithms at a low cost. The downside of offline experiments is that they can answer a very narrow set of questions, typically questions about the prediction power of an algorithm. In particular, we must assume that users' behavior when interacting with a system including the recommender system chosen will be modeled well by the users' behavior prior to that system's deployment. Thus we cannot directly measure the recommender's influence on user behavior in this setting.

Therefore, the goal of the offline experiments is to filter out inappropriate approaches, leaving a relatively small set of candidate algorithms to be tested by the more costly user studies or online experiments. A typical example of this process is when the parameters of the algorithms are tuned in an offline experiment, and then the algorithm with the best tuned parameters continues to the next phase.

8.2.1.1 Data Sets for Offline Experiments

As the goal of the offline evaluation is to filter algorithms, the data used for the offline evaluation should match as closely as possible the data the designer expects the recommender system to face when deployed online. Care must be exercised to ensure that there is no bias in the distributions of users, items and ratings selected. For example, in cases where data from an existing system (perhaps a system without a recommender) is available, the experimenter may be tempted to pre-filter the data by excluding items or users with low counts, in order to reduce the costs of experimentation. In doing so, the experimenter should be mindful that this involves a trade-off, since this introduces a systematic bias in the data. If necessary, randomly sampling users and items may be a preferable method for reducing data, although this can also introduce other biases into the experiment (e.g. this could tend to favor algorithms that work better with more sparse data). Sometimes, known biases in the data can be corrected for by techniques such as reweighing data, but correcting biases in the data is often difficult.

Another source of bias may be the data collection itself. For example, users may be more likely to rate items that they have strong opinions on, and some users may provide many more ratings than others. Furthermore, users tend to rate items that they like, and avoid exploring, and hence rating, items that they will not like. For example, a person who doesn't like horror movies will tend not to watch them, would not explore the list of available horror movies for rental, and would not rate them. Thus, the set of items on which explicit ratings are available may be biased by the ratings themselves. This is often known as the *not missing at random* assumption [47]. Once again, techniques such as *resampling* or *reweighting* the test data [70, 71] may be used to attempt to correct such biases.

8.2.1.2 Simulating User Behavior

In order to evaluate algorithms offline, it is necessary to simulate the online process where the system makes predictions or recommendations, and the user corrects the predictions or uses the recommendations. This is usually done by recording historical user data, and then hiding some of these interactions in order to simulate the knowledge of how a user will rate an item, or which recommendations a user will act upon. There are a number of ways to choose the ratings/selected items to be hidden. Once again, it is preferable that this choice be done in a manner that simulates the target application as closely as possible. In many cases, though, we are restricted by the computational cost of an evaluation protocol, and must make compromises in order to execute the experiment over large data sets.

Ideally, if we have access to time-stamps for user selections, we can simulate what the systems predictions would have been, had it been running at the time the data set was collected [11]. We can begin with no available prior data for computing predictions, and step through user selections in temporal order, attempting to predict each selection and then making that selection available for use in future predictions. For large data sets, a simpler approach is to randomly sample test users, randomly sample a time just prior to a user action, hide all selections (of all users) after that instant, and then attempt to recommend items to that user. This protocol requires changing the set of given information prior to each recommendation, which can still be computationally quite expensive.

An even cheaper alternative is to sample a set of test users, then sample a single test time, and hide all items after the sampled test time for each test user. This simulates a situation where the recommender system is built as of the test time, and then makes recommendations without taking into account any new data that arrives after the test time. Another alternative is to sample a test time for each test user, and hide the test user's items after that time, without maintaining time consistency across users. This effectively assumes that the sequence in which items are selected is important, not the absolute times when the selections are made. A final alternative is to ignore time. We would first sample a set of test users, then sample the number n_a of items to hide for each user a, and finally sample n_a items to hide. This assumes that the temporal aspects of user selections are unimportant. We may be forced to make this assumption if the timestamps of user actions are not known. All three of the latter alternatives partition the data into a single training set and single test set. It is important to select an alternative that is most appropriate for the domain and task of interest, given the constraints, rather than the most convenient one.

A common protocol used in many research papers is to use a fixed number of known items or a fixed number of hidden items per test user (so called "given n" or "all but n" protocols). This protocol may be useful for diagnosing algorithms and identifying in which cases they work best. However, when we wish to make decisions on the algorithm that we will use in our application, we must ask ourselves whether we are truly interested in presenting recommendations only for users who have rated exactly n items, or are expected to rate exactly n items more. If that is not the case, then results computed using these protocols have biases that make them unreliable in predicting the performance of the algorithms online, and these protocols should be avoided.

8.2.1.3 More Complex User Modeling

All the protocols that we discuss above make some assumptions concerning the behavior of users, which could be regarded as a user-model for the specific application. While we discuss only very simple user models, it is possible to suggest more complicated models for user behavior [46]. Using advanced user models we can execute simulations of users interactions with the system, thus reducing the need for expensive user studies and online testing. However, care must be made when designing user-models; First, user-modeling is a difficult task, and there is a vast amount of research on the subject (see, e.g. [19]). Second, when the user model is inaccurate, we may optimize a system whose performance in simulation has little correlation with its performance in practice. While it is reasonable to design an algorithm that uses complex user models to provide recommendations, we should be careful in trusting experiments where algorithms are verified using such complex, difficult to verify, user models.

8.2.2 User Studies

Many recommendation approaches rely on the interaction of users with the system (see, e.g., Chaps. 24, 5, 10, and 18). It is very difficult to create a reliable simulation of users interactions with the system, and thus, offline testing are difficult to conduct. In order to properly evaluate such systems, real user interactions with the system must be collected. Even when offline testing is possible, interactions with real users can still provide additional information about the system performance. In these cases we typically conduct user studies.

We provide here a summarized discussion of the principles of user studies for the evaluation of recommender systems. The interested reader can find an in depth discussion in Chap. 9.

A user study is conducted by recruiting a set of test subjects, and asking them to perform several tasks requiring an interaction with the recommender system. While the subjects perform the tasks, we observe and record their behavior, collecting any number of quantitative measurements, such as what portion of the task was completed, the accuracy of the task results, or the time taken to perform the task. In many cases we can ask qualitative questions, before, during, and after the task is completed. Such questions can collect data that is not directly observable, such as whether the subject enjoyed the user interface, or whether the user perceived the task as easy to complete.

A typical example of such an experiment is to test the influence of a recommendation algorithm on the browsing behavior of news stories. In this example, the subjects are asked to read a set of stories that are interesting to them, in some cases including related story recommendations and in some cases without recommendations. We can then check whether the recommendations are used, and whether people read different stories with and without recommendations.

We can collect data such as how many times a recommendation was clicked, and even, in certain cases, track eye movement to see whether a subject looked at a recommendation. Finally, we can ask qualitative questions such as whether the subject thought the recommendations were relevant [30, 32].

Of course, in many other research areas user studies are a central tool, and thus there is much literature on the proper design of user studies. This section only overviews the basic considerations that should be taken when evaluating a recommender system through a user study, and the interested reader can find much deeper discussions elsewhere (see. e.g. [7]).

8.2.2.1 Advantages and Disadvantages

User studies can perhaps answer the widest set of questions of all three experimental settings that we survey here. Unlike offline experiments this setting allows us to test the behavior of users when interacting with the recommender system, and the influence of the recommendations on user behavior. In the offline case we typically make assumptions such as "given a relevant recommendation the user is likely to use it" which are tested in the user study. Second, this is the only setting that allows us to collect qualitative data that is often crucial for interpreting the quantitative results. Also, we can typically collect in this setting a large set of quantitative measurements because the users can be closely monitored while performing the tasks.

User studies however have some disadvantages. Primarily, user studies are very expensive to conduct[39]; collecting a large set of subjects and asking them to perform a large enough set of tasks is costly in terms of either user time, if the subjects are volunteers, or in terms of compensation if paid subjects are employed. Therefore, we must typically restrict ourselves to a small set of subjects and a relatively small set of tasks, and cannot test all possible scenarios. Furthermore, each scenario has to be repeated several times in order to make reliable conclusions, further limiting the range of distinct tasks that can be tested.

As these experiments are expensive to conduct we should collect as much data about the user interactions, in the lowest possible granularity. This will allow us later to study the results of the experiment in detail, analyzing considerations that were not obvious prior to the trial. This guideline can help us to reduce the need for successive trials to collect overlooked measurements.

Furthermore, in order to avoid failed experiments, such as applications that malfunction under certain user actions, researchers often execute pilot user studies. These are small scale experiments, designed not to collect statistical data, but to test the systems for bugs and malfunctions. In some cases, the results of these pilot studies are then used to improve the recommender. If this is the case, then the results of the pilot become "tainted", and should not be used when computing measurements in the final user study.

Another important consideration is that the test subjects must represent as closely as possible the population of users of the real system. For example, if the system is designed to recommend movies, the results of a user study over avid movie fans may not carry to the entire population. This problem is most persistent when the participants of the study are volunteers, as in this case people who are originally more interested in the application may tend to volunteer more readily.

However, even when the subjects represent properly the true population of users, the results can still be biased because they are aware that they are participating in an experiment. For example, it is well known that paid subjects tend to try and satisfy the person or company conducting the experiment [60]. If the subjects are aware of the hypothesis that is tested they may unconsciously provide evidence that supports it. To accommodate that, it is typically better not to disclose the goal of the experiment prior to collecting data. Another, more subtle effect occurs when the payment to subjects takes the form of a complete or partial subsidy of items they select. This may bias the data in cases where final users of the system are not similarly subsidized, as users' choices and preferences may be different when they pay full price. Unfortunately, avoiding this particular bias is difficult.

8.2.2.2 Between vs. Within Subjects

As typically a user study compares a few candidate approaches, each candidate must be tested over the same tasks. To test all candidates we can either compare the candidates *between subjects*, where each subject is assigned to a candidate method and experiments with it, or *within subjects*, where each subject tests a set of candidates on different tasks [24].

Typically, within subjects experiments are more informative, as the superiority of one method cannot be explained by a biased split of users between candidate methods. It is also possible in this setting to ask comparative questions about the different candidates, such as which candidate the subject preferred. However, in these types of tests users are more conscious of the experiment, and hiding the distinctions between candidates is more difficult.

Between subjects experiments, also known as *A-B testing* (All Between), provide a setting that is closer to the real system, as each user experiments with a single treatment. Such experiments can also test long term effects of using the system, because the user is not required to switch systems. Thus we can test how the user becomes accustomed to the system, and estimate a learning curve of expertise. On the downside, when running between subjects experiments, typically more data is needed to achieve significant results. As such, between subjects experiments may require more users, or more interaction time for each user, and are thus more costly then within subjects experiments.

8.2.2.3 Variable Counter Balance

As we have noted above, it is important to control all variables that are not specifically tested. However, when a subject is presented with the output of several candidates, as in within subject experiments, we must counter balance several variables.

When presenting several results to the subject, the results can be displayed either sequentially, or together. In both cases there are certain biases that we need to correct for [1]. When presenting the results sequentially the previously observed results influence the user opinion of the current results. For example, if the results that were displayed first seem inappropriate, the results displayed afterward may seem better than they actually are. When presenting two sets of results, there can be certain biases due to location. For example, users from many cultures tend to observe results left to right and top to bottom. Thus, the user may observe the results displayed on top as superior.

A common approach to correct for such untested variables is by using the *Latin square* [7] procedure. This procedure randomizes the order or location of the various results each time, thus canceling out biases due to these untested variables.

8.2.2.4 Questionnaires

User studies allow us to use the powerful questionnaire tool (e.g. [58]). Before, during, and after subjects perform their tasks we can ask them questions about their experience. These questions can provide information about properties that are difficult to measure, such as the subject's state of mind, or whether the subject enjoyed the system.

While these questions can provide valuable information, they can also provide misleading information. It is important to ask neutral questions, that do not suggest a "correct" answer. People may also answer untruthfully, for example when they perceive the answer as private, or if they think the true answer may put them in an unflattering position.

Indeed, vast amount of research was conducted in other areas about the art of questionnaire writing, and we refer the readers to that literature (e.g. [56]) for more details.

8.2.3 *Online Evaluation*

In many realistic recommendation applications the designer of the system wishes to influence the behavior of users. We are therefore interested in measuring the change in user behavior when interacting with different recommender systems. For example, if users of one system follow the recommendations more often, or if some utility gathered from users of one system exceeds utility gathered from users of the other system, then we can conclude that one system is superior to the other, all else being equal.

The real effect of the recommender system depends on a variety of factors such as the user's intent (e.g. how specific their information needs are), the user's personality (Chap. 21), such as how much novelty vs. how much risk they are seeking, the user's context, e.g., what items they are already familiar with, how much they trust the system (Chap. 6), and the interface through which the recommendations are presented.

Thus, the experiment that provides the strongest evidence as to the true value of the system is an online evaluation, where the system is used by real users that perform real tasks. It is most trustworthy to compare a few systems online, obtaining a ranking of alternatives, rather than absolute numbers that are more difficult to interpret.

For this reason, many real world systems employ an online testing system [40], where multiple algorithms can be compared. Typically, such systems redirect a small percentage of the traffic to different alternative recommendation engine, and record the users interactions with the different systems.

There are a few considerations that must be made when running such tests. For example, it is important to sample (redirect) users randomly, so that the comparisons between alternatives are fair. It is also important to single out the different aspects of the recommenders. For example, if we care about algorithmic accuracy, it is important to keep the user interface fixed. On the other hand, if we wish to focus on a better user interface, it is best to keep the underlying algorithm fixed.

In some cases, such experiments are risky. For example, a test system that provides irrelevant recommendations, may discourage the test users from using the real system ever again. Thus, the experiment can have a negative effect on the system, which may be unacceptable in commercial applications.

For these reasons, it is best to run an online evaluation last, after an extensive offline study provides evidence that the candidate approaches are reasonable, and perhaps after a user study that measures the user's attitude towards the system. This gradual process reduces the risk in causing significant user dissatisfaction.

Online evaluations are unique in that they allow direct measurement of overall system goals, such as long-term profit or user retention. As such, they can be used to understand how these overall goals are affected by system properties such as recommendation accuracy and diversity of recommendations, and to understand the trade-offs between these properties. However, since varying such properties independently is difficult, and comparing many algorithms through online trials is expensive, it can be difficult to gain a complete understanding of these relationships.

8.2.4 Drawing Reliable Conclusions

In any type of experiment it is important that we can be confidant that the candidate recommender that we choose will also be a good choice for the yet unseen data the system will be faced with in the future. As we explain above, we should exercise caution in choosing the data in an offline experiments, and the subjects in a user study, to best resemble the online application. Still, there is a possibility that the algorithm that performed best on this test set did so because the experiment was fortuitously suitable for that algorithm. To reduce the possibility of such statistical mishaps, we must perform significance testing on the results.

8.2.4.1 Confidence and p-Values

The result of a significance test is a significance level or p-value—the probability that the obtained results were due to chance. In practice, we choose a significance test (see below) to match our situation in order to evaluate this probability. Each significance test postulates an underlying random mechanism that may have generated the result. This is termed the null hypothesis. The chosen test then gives us a probability that a result that is at least as good as the one we are testing was produced under the null hypothesis. This probability is the p-value. If the p-value is below a threshold, we are confident that the null hypothesis is not true, and we deem our results significant. Traditionally, people choose $p = 0.05$ as their threshold, which indicates 95 % confidence. More stringent significance levels (e.g. 0.01 or even lower) can be used in cases where the cost of making the wrong choice is higher. Notice, however, that the significance test only tells us that the null hypothesis is unlikely to be true. It does not guarantee that the result was not randomly produced by some other mechanism. Thus, to be confident that we are making meaningful decisions, we need to be careful in choosing a test with a strong null hypothesis that is appropriate for our situation. Below, we discuss how to make this choice. For more details, see, e.g., [4].

8.2.4.2 Paired Results

In order to perform a significance test that algorithm A is indeed better than algorithm B, we often use the results of several independent experiments comparing A and B. Thus, rather than the aggregate results that we typically use to compare systems, confidence testing requires the results of multiple independent sub-experiments. Indeed, the protocol we have suggested for generating our test data (Sect. 8.2.1.2) allows us to obtain such a set of results. Assuming that test users are drawn independently from some population, the performance measures of the algorithms for each test user give us the independent comparisons we need. However, when recommendations or predictions of multiple items are made to the same user, it is unlikely that the resulting per-item performance metrics are independent. Therefore, it is better to compare algorithms on a per-user case.

Given such paired per-user performance measures for algorithms A and B a simple test of significance is the **sign test** [17, 45]. To use the sign test, we compute a score (e.g. RMSE for system accuracy) for each user under algorithms A and B. The sign test makes no assumption on these scores other than that users are independent, and considers the number of times A beats B. The null hypothesis is that whether A beats B or vice-versa is determined by a coin-toss. Thus, it uses the number of times n_A that A beats B (e.g. the number of times that alternative A achieved a lower RMSE than alternative B) If we are interested in a pure winner, i.e., that A would achieve a strictly better RMSE than B, then draws should count against A, that is, they should not be counted in n_A. If we are interested in the case where A should do no worse than B, then draws should be counted in n_A.

Let n be the number of users in J for which the predictions were made. The null hypothesis is that whether A beats B or vice-versa is determined by a coin-toss. We can now compute the probability that we will observe at least n_A times that system A got a better score than system B under the null hypothesis that the two systems are equal using:

$$p = (0.5)^n \sum_{i=n_A}^{n} \frac{n!}{i!(n-i)!} \tag{8.1}$$

when this p-value is below some predefined value (typically, 0.05) we can say that the null hypothesis that the two system have an equal performance is rejected.

The sign test is an attractive choice due to its simplicity, and lack of assumptions over the distribution of cases. When $n_A + n_B$ is large, we can take advantage of large sample theory to approximate Eq. (8.1) by a normal distribution. However, this is usually unnecessary with powerful modern computers. Some authors (e.g. [61]) use the term **McNemar's test** to refer to the use of a χ^2 approximation to the two-sided sign test.

Note that sometimes, the sign test may indicate that system A outperforms system B with high probability, even though the average performance of system B is higher than that of system A. This happens in cases where system B occasionally outperforms system A overwhelmingly. Thus, the reason for this seemingly inconsistent result is that the test only examines the probability of one system outperforming the other, without regard to the magnitude of the difference.

The sign test can be extended to cases where we want to know the probability that one system outperforms the other by some amount. For example, suppose that system A is much more resource intensive than system B, and is only worth deploying if it outperforms system B by some amount. We can define "success" in the sign test as A outperforming B by this amount, and find the probability of A not truly outperforming B by this amount as our p value in Eq. (8.1).

A commonly used test that takes the magnitude of the differences into account is the **paired Student's t-test**, which looks at the average difference between the performance scores of algorithms A and B, normalized by the standard deviation of the score difference. Using this test requires that the differences in scores for different users is comparable, so that averaging these differences is reasonable. For small numbers of users, the validity of the test also depends on the differences being Normally distributed. [17] points out that this assumption is hard to verify when the number of samples is small and that the t-test is susceptible to outliers. He recommends the use of **Wilcoxon signed rank test**, which like the t-test, uses the magnitude of the differences between algorithms A and B, but without making distributional assumptions on the differences. However, using the Wilcoxon signed rank test still requires that differences between the two systems are comparable between users.

Another way to improve the significance of our conclusions is to use a larger test set. In the offline case, this may require using a smaller training set, which may result in an experimental protocol that is not representative of the amount of training data available after deployment. In the case of user studies, this implies an additional expense. In the case of online testing, increasing the amount of data collected for each algorithm requires either the added expense of a longer trial or the comparison of fewer algorithms.

8.2.4.3 Unpaired Results

The tests described above are suitable for cases where observations are paired. That is, each algorithm is run on each test case, as is often done in offline tests. In online tests, however, it is often the case that users are assigned to one algorithm or the other, so that the two algorithms are not evaluated on the same test cases. The **Mann-Whitney test** is an extension of the Wilcoxon test to this scenario. Suppose we have n_A results from algorithm A and n_B results from algorithm B.

The performance measures of the two algorithms are pooled and sorted so that the best result is ranked first and the worst last. The ranks of ties are averaged. For example if the second through fifth place tie, they are all assigned a rank of 3.5. The Mann-Whitney test computes the probability of the null hypothesis that n_A randomly chosen results from the total $n_A + n_B$ have at least as good an average rank as the n_A results that came from algorithm A.

This probability can be computed exactly be enumerating all $\frac{(n_A+n_B)!}{n_A!n_B!}$ choices and counting the choices that have at least the required average rank, or can be approximated by repeatedly resampling n_A of the results. When n_A and n_B are both large enough (typically over 5), the distribution of the average rank of n_A results randomly selected from a pool of $n_A + n_B$ under the null hypothesis is well approximated by a Gaussian with mean $\frac{1}{2}(n_A + n_B + 1)$ and standard deviation $\sqrt{\frac{1}{12}\frac{n_A}{n_B}(n_A + n_B + 1)}$. Thus, in this case we can compute the average rank of the n_A results from system A, subtract $\frac{1}{2}(n_A + n_B + 1)$, divide by $\sqrt{\frac{1}{12}\frac{n_A}{n_B}(n_A + n_B + 1)}$, and evaluate the standard Gaussian CDF at this value to get the p value for the test.

8.2.4.4 Multiple Tests

Another important consideration, mostly in the offline scenario, is the effect of evaluating multiple versions of algorithms. For example, an experimenter might try out several variants of a novel recommender algorithm and compare them to a baseline algorithm until they find one that passes a sign test at the $p = 0.05$ level and therefore infer that their algorithm improves upon the baseline with 95 % confidence. However, this is not a valid inference. Suppose the experimenter evaluated ten different variants all of which are statistically the same as the baseline. If the probability that any one of these trials passes the sign test mistakenly is $p = 0.05$, the probability that at least one of the ten trials passes the sign test mistakenly is $1-(1-0.05)^{10}=0.40$. This risk is colloquially known as "tuning to the test set" and can be avoided by separating the test set users into two groups—a development (or tuning) set, and an evaluation set. The choice of algorithm is done based on the development test, and the validity of the choice is measured by running a significance test on the evaluation set.

A similar concern exists when ranking a number of algorithms, but is more difficult to circumvent. Suppose the best of $N+1$ algorithms is chosen on the development test set. To achieve a confidence $1-p$ that the chosen algorithm is indeed the best, it must outperform the N other algorithms on the evaluation set with significance $1-(1-p)^{1/N}$. This is known as the Bonferroni correction, and should be used when pair-wise significance tests are used multiple times. Alternatively, approaches such as **ANOVA** or the **Friedman test for ranking**, which are generalization of the Student's t-test and Wilcoxon's rank test. ANOVA makes strong assumptions about the Normality of the different algorithms' performance measures, and about the relationships of their variances. We refer the reader to [17] for further discussion of these and other tests for ranking multiple algorithms.

A more subtle version of this concern is when a pair of algorithms are compared in a number of ways. For example, two algorithms may be compared using a number of accuracy measures, a number of coverage measures, etc. Even if the two algorithms are identical in all measures, the probability of finding a measure by which one algorithm seems to outperform the other with some significance level increases with the number of measures examined. If the different measures are independent, the Bonferroni correction mentioned above can be used. However, since the measures are often correlated, the Bonferroni correction may be too stringent, and other approaches such as controlling for false discovery rate [3] may be used.

8.2.4.5 Confidence Intervals

Even though we focus here on comparative studies, where one has to choose the most appropriate algorithm out of a set of candidates, it is sometimes desirable to measure the value of some property. For example, an administrator may want to estimate the error in the system predictions, or the net profit that the system is earning. When measuring such quantities it is important to understand the reliability of your estimates. A popular approach for doing this is to compute **confidence intervals**.

For example, one may estimate that the RMSE of a system is expected to be 1.2, and that it will be between 1.1 and 1.35 with probability 0.95. The simplest method for computing confidence intervals is to assume that the quantity of interest is Gaussian distributed, and then estimate its mean and standard deviations from multiple independent observations. When we have many observations, we can dispense with this assumption by computing the distribution of the quantity of interest with a non-parametric method such as a histogram and finding upper and lower bounds such that include the quantity of interest with the desired probability.

8.3 Recommender System Properties

In this section we survey a range of properties that are commonly considered when deciding which recommendation approach to select. As different applications have different needs, the designer of the system must decide on the important properties to measure for the concrete application at hand. Some of the properties can be traded-off, the most obvious example perhaps is the decline in accuracy when other properties (e.g. diversity) are improved. It is important to understand and evaluate these trade-offs and their effect on the overall performance. However, the proper way of gaining such understanding without intensive online testing or defering to the opinions of domain experts is still an open question.

Furthermore, the effect of many of these properties on the user experience is unclear, and depends on the application. While we can certainly speculate that users would like diverse recommendations or reported confidence bounds, it is essential to show that this is indeed important in practice. Therefore, when suggesting a method that improves one of this properties, one should also evaluate how changes in this property affects the user experience, either through a user study or through online experimentation.

Such an experiment typically uses a single recommendation method with a tunable parameter that affects the property being considered. For example, we can envision a parameter that controls the diversity of the list of recommendations. Then, subjects should be presented with recommendations based on a variety of values for this parameter, and we should measure the effect of the parameter on the user experience. We should measure here not whether the user noticed the change in the property, but whether the change in property has affected their interaction with the system. As is always the case in user studies, it is preferable that the subjects in a user study and users in an online experiment will not know the goal of the experiment. It is difficult to envision how this procedure could be performed in an offline setting because we need to understand the user response to this parameter.

Once the effects of the specific system properties in affecting the user experience of the application at hand is understood, we can use differences in these properties to select a recommender.

8.3.1 User Preference

As in this chapter we are interested in the selection problem, where we need to choose on out of a set of candidate algorithms, an obvious option is to run a user study (within subjects) and ask the participants to choose one of the systems [29]. This evaluation does not restrict the subjects to specific properties, and it is generally easier for humans to make such judgments than to give scores for the experience. Then, we can select the system that had the largest number of votes.

However, aside from the biases in user studies discussed earlier, there are additional concerns that we must be aware of. First, the above scheme assumes that all users are equal, which may not always be true. For example, an e-commerce website may prefer the opinion of users who buy many items to the opinion of users who only buy a single item. We therefore need to further weight the vote by the importance of the user, when applicable. Assigning the right importance weights in a user study may not be easy.

It may also be the case that users who preferred system *A*, only slightly preferred it, while users who preferred *B*, had a very low opinion on *A*. In this case, even if slightly more users preferred *A* we may still wish to choose *B*. To measure this we need non-binary answers for the preference question in the user study. Then, the problem of calibrating scores across users arises.

Finally, when we wish to improve a system, it is important to know why people favor one system over the other. Typically, it is easier to understand that when comparing specific properties. Therefore, while user satisfaction is important to measure, breaking satisfaction into smaller components is helpful to understand the system and improve it.

8.3.2 Prediction Accuracy

Accuracy is by far the most discussed property in the recommendation system literature. At the base of the vast majority of recommender systems lie a prediction engine. This engine may predict user opinions over items (e.g. ratings of movies) or the probability of usage (e.g. purchase).

A basic assumption in a recommender system is that a system that provides more accurate predictions will be preferred by the user. Thus, many researchers set out to find algorithms that provide better predictions.

Assuming accurate and consistent user ratings for items, prediction accuracy is typically independent of the user interface, and can thus be measured in an offline experiment. That being said, the interface used for providing user feedback and preferences over items may influence the gathered ratings [54]. This weakens the generality of the conclusions drawn from such offline experiments. Measuring prediction accuracy in a user study, however, typically measures the accuracy given a set of recommendations or item ratings displayed to the user. This is a different concept from the prediction of user behavior without recommendations, and is closer to the true accuracy in the real system.

We discuss here three broad classes of prediction accuracy measures; measuring the accuracy of ratings predictions, measuring the accuracy of usage predictions, and measuring the accuracy of rankings of items.

8.3.2.1 Measuring Ratings Prediction Accuracy

In some applications, such as in the new releases page of the popular Netflix DVD rental service, we wish to predict the rating a user would give to an item (e.g. 1-star through 5-stars). In such cases, we wish to measure the accuracy of the system's predicted ratings.

Root Mean Squared Error (RMSE) is perhaps the most popular metric used in evaluating accuracy of predicted ratings. The system generates predicted ratings $\hat{r}_{ui}$ for a test set $\mathcal{T}$ of user-item pairs (u, i) for which the true ratings r_{ui} are known. Typically, r_{ui} are known because they are hidden in an offline experiment, or because they were obtained through a user study or online experiment. The RMSE between the predicted and actual ratings is given by:

$$\mathrm{RMSE} = \sqrt{\frac{1}{|\mathcal{T}|} \sum_{(u,i)\in\mathcal{T}} (\hat{r}_{ui} - r_{ui})^2} \tag{8.2}$$

Mean Absolute Error (MAE) is a popular alternative, given by

$$\mathrm{MAE} = \frac{1}{|\mathcal{T}|} \sum_{(u,i)\in\mathcal{T}} |\hat{r}_{ui} - r_{ui}| \tag{8.3}$$

Compared to MAE, RMSE disproportionately penalizes large errors, so that, given a test set with four hidden items RMSE would prefer a system that makes an error of 2 on three ratings and 0 on the fourth to one that makes an error of 3 on one rating and 0 on all three others, while MAE would prefer the second system.

Normalized RMSE (NMRSE) and **Normalized MAE (NMAE)** are versions of RMSE and MAE that have been normalized by the range of the ratings (i.e. $r_{max} - r_{min}$). Since they are simply scaled versions of RMSE and MAE, the resulting ranking of algorithms is the same as the ranking given by the unnormalized measures.

Average RMSE and **Average MAE** adjust for unbalanced test sets. For example, if the test set has an unbalanced distribution of items, the RMSE or MAE obtained from it might be heavily influenced by the error on a few very frequent items. If we need a measure that is representative of the prediction error on any item, it is preferable to compute MAE or RMSE separately for each item and then take the average over all items. Similarly, one can compute a per-user average RMSE or MAE if the test set has an unbalanced user distribution and we wish to understand the prediction error a randomly drawn user might face.

RMSE and MAE depend only on the magnitude of the errors made. In some applications [16, e.g.], the semantics of the ratings may be such that the impact of a prediction error does not depend only on its magnitude. In such domains it may be preferable to use a suitable distortion measure $d(\hat{r}, r)$ than squared difference or absolute difference. For example in an application with a 3-star rating system where 1 means "disliked," 2 means "neutral" and 3 means "liked," and where recommending an item the user dislikes is worse that not recommending an item a user likes, a distortion measure with $d(3,1) = 5$, $d(2,1) = 3$, $d(3,2) = 3$, $d(1,2) = 1$, $d(2,3) = 1$, and $d(1,3) = 2$ may be reasonable.

8.3.2.2 Measuring Usage Prediction

In many applications the recommender system does not predict the user's preferences of items, such as movie ratings, but tries to recommend to users items that they may use. For example, when movies are added to the queue, Netflix suggests a set of movies that may also be interesting, given the added movie. In this case we are interested not in whether the system properly predicts the ratings of these movies but rather whether the system properly predicts that the user will add these movies to the queue (use the items).

In an offline evaluation of usage prediction, we typically have a data set consisting of items each user has used. We then select a test user, hide some of her selections, and ask the recommender to predict a set of items that the user will use. We then have four possible outcomes for the recommended and hidden items, as shown in Table 8.1.

In the offline case, since the data isn't typically collected using the recommender system under evaluation, we are forced to assume that unused items would have not be used even if they had they been recommended—i.e. that they are uninteresting or useless to the user. This assumption may be false, such as when the set of unused items contains some interesting items that the user did not select. For example, a user may not have used an item because she was unaware of its existence, but after the recommendation exposed that item the user can decide to select it. In this case the number of false positives is over estimated.

We can count the number of examples that fall into each cell in the table and compute the following quantities:

$$\textbf{Precision} = \frac{\#\text{tp}}{\#\text{tp} + \#\text{fp}} \tag{8.4}$$

$$\textbf{Recall (True Positive Rate)} = \frac{\#\text{tp}}{\#\text{tp} + \#\text{fn}} \tag{8.5}$$

$$\textbf{False Positive Rate } (1 \text{ - } \textbf{Specificity}) = \frac{\#\text{fp}}{\#\text{fp} + \#\text{tn}} \tag{8.6}$$

Table 8.1 Classification of the possible result of a recommendation of an item to a user

	Recommended	Not recommended
Used	True-positive (tp)	False-negative (fn)
Not used	False-positive (fp)	True-negative (tn)

Typically we can expect a trade off between these quantities—while allowing longer recommendation lists typically improves recall, it is also likely to reduce the precision. In applications where the number of recommendations that can be presented to the user is preordained, the most useful measure of interest is **precision at N** (often written Precision@N).

In other applications where the number of recommendations that are presented to the user is not preordained, it is preferable to evaluate algorithms over a range of recommendation list lengths, rather than using a fixed length. Thus, we can compute curves comparing precision to recall, or true positive rate to false positive rate. Curves of the former type are known simply as precision-recall curves, while those of the latter type are known as a receiver operating characteristic curve[3] or ROC curve. While both curves measure the proportion of preferred items that are actually recommended, precision-recall curves emphasize the proportion of recommended items that are preferred while ROC curves emphasize the proportion of items that are not preferred that end up being recommended.

We should select whether to use precision-recall or ROC based on the properties of the domain and the goal of the application; suppose, for example, that an online video rental service recommends DVDs to users. The precision measure describes the proportion of their recommendations were actually suitable for the user. Whether the unsuitable recommendations represent a small or large fraction of the unsuitable DVDs that could have been recommended (i.e. the false positive rate) may not be as relevant as what proportion of the relevant items the system recommended to the user, so a precision-recall curve would be suitable for this application. On the other hand, consider a recommender system that is used for selecting items to be marketed to users, for example by mailing an item to the user who returns it at no cost to themselves if they do not purchase it. In this case, where we are interested in realizing as many potential sales as possible while minimizing marketing costs, ROC curves would be more relevant than precision-recall curves.

Given two algorithms, we can compute a pair of such curves, one for each algorithm. If one curve completely dominates the other curve, the decision about the superior algorithm is easy. However, when the curves intersect, the decision is less obvious, and will depend on the application in question. Knowledge of the application will dictate which region of the curve the decision will be based on.

Measures that summarize the precision-recall or ROC curve such as **F-measure** [73]—the harmonic mean of the equally weighted precision and recall

$$F = \frac{2 \cdot precision \cdot recall}{precision + recall} \tag{8.7}$$

and the **Area Under the ROC Curve (AUC)** [2] are useful for comparing algorithms independently of application, but when selecting an algorithm for use in a particular task, it is preferable to make the choice based on a measure that reflects the specific needs at hand, such as the actual list length dictated by the application.

[3] A reference to their origins in signal detection theory.

Precision-Recall and ROC for Multiple Users

When evaluating precision-recall or ROC curves for multiple test users, a number of strategies can be employed in aggregating the results, depending on the application at hand.

In applications where a fixed number of recommendations are made to each user (e.g. when a fixed number of headlines are shown to a user visiting a news portal), we can compute the precision and recall (or true positive rate and false positive rate) at each recommendation list length N for each user, and then compute the average precision and recall (or true positive rate and false positive rate) at each N [63]. The resulting curves are particularly valuable because they prescribe a value of N for each achievable precision and recall (or true positive rate and false positive rate), and conversely, can be used to estimate performance at a given N. An ROC curve obtained in this manner is termed a **customer ROC (CROC) curve** [64].

When different numbers of recommendations can be shown to each user (e.g. when presenting the set of all recommended movies to each user), we can compute ROC or precision-recall curves by aggregating the hidden ratings from the test set into a set of reference user-item pairs, using the recommender system to generate a single ranked list of user-item pairs, picking the top recommendations from the list, and scoring them against the reference set. An ROC curve calculated in this way is termed a **Global ROC (GROC) curve** [64]. Picking an operating point on the resulting curve can result in a different number of recommendations being made to each user.

A final class of applications is where the recommendation process is more interactive, and the user is able to obtain more and more recommendations. This is typical of information retrieval tasks, where the user can keep asking the system for more recommended documents. In such applications, we compute a precision-recall curve (or ROC curve) for each user and then average the resulting curves over users. This is the usual manner in which precision-recall curves are computed in the information retrieval community, and in particular in the influential TREC competitions [74]. Such a curve can be used to understand the trade-off between precision and recall (or false positives and false negatives) a typical user would face.

8.3.2.3 Ranking Measures

In many cases the application presents to the user a list of recommendations, typically as vertical or horizontal list, imposing a certain natural browsing order. For example, in Netflix, the "movies you'll love" tab, shows a set of categories, and in each category, a list of movies that the system predicts the user to like. These lists may be long and the user may need to continue to additional "pages" until the entire list is browsed. In these applications, we are not interested in predicting an explicit rating, or selecting a set of recommended items, as in the previous sections, but rather in ordering items according to the user's preferences. This task is typically known as the ranking of items. There are two approaches for measuring the accuracy of such a ranking. We can try to determine the correct order of a set of items for each user and measure how close a system comes to this correct order, or we can attempt to measure the utility of the system's raking to a user. We first describe these approaches for offline tests, and then describe their applicability to user studies and online tests.

Using a Reference Ranking

In order to evaluate a ranking algorithm with respect to a reference ranking (a correct order), it is first necessary to obtain such a reference.

In cases where explicit user ratings of items are available, we can rank the rated items in decreasing order of ratings. However, there are two problems with this approach. First, most users typically have not rated some (usually most) of the items. Second, in many applications, the user ratings are quantized. For example, in the case of Netflix, each user only rates some of the movies, and the ratings are quantized to a 5-star scale. Thus, while we know that a movie rated 4 stars is preferred over a movie rated 3 stars, we do not know which (if either) of two 4-star movies is actually preferred by the user. We also know nothing about the user's preferences over most of the movies, which they have not rated.

Constructing reference rankings from usage data also runs into this problem. We can assume that items that the user actually used are preferred to those that the user was aware of but did not use. However, we do not know how to rank unused items that the user is not known to have been aware of (e.g. items that were never presented to the user, or items that were presented in a manner that the user may have easily missed them). We also do not know how to rank used items against other used items, and unused items the user was aware of against other such items.

Such cases where a ranking over items is incompletely specified is described technically as a *partial order*.

Let $\binom{I}{2}$ denote the set of all unordered pairs of items in I. Let $\succ$ be a partial order over a set of items I. In a partial order, for any two items i_1, i_2, exactly one of the following three conditions holds:

1. One item is a successor of the other, e.g. i_1 is a successor of i_2, denoted $i_1 \succ i_2$, typically meaning that i_1 is preferred to i_2. For example, if the user prefers "Star Wars IV" to "The Matrix", and the list is ranked by preference, then we can write "Star Wars IV" $\succ$ "The Matrix".
2. If the user prefers the items equally, denoted $i_1 = i_2$. For example, a user may be indifferent as to whether he would get a brand A or brand B laptop, as long as they both have the same amount of memory, or may bid the same amount for two items on an auction at eBay.
3. The items may be incomparable. For example, one may not be able to say whether she prefers the latest Coen brothers movie, or the latest U2 disk. Alternatively, as discussed above, we may not have information about the user's preferences on the pair.

A *total order* over a set of items is an order where for each pair of items i_1, i_2, either $i_1 \succ i_2$ or $i_2 \succ i1$. In many cases, the reference ranking is given by a partial order, but the system outputs its recommendations as a total order, although perhaps not on all items. Therefore, we now describe ranking accuracy metrics that allow measurement agreement/disagreement between partial and total orders. To do so, we formally define the concepts of agreement, disagreement, and compatibility.

Let $\succ_1$ and $\succ_2$ be two partial orders over a set of items I, where $\succ_1$ is the reference order and $\succ_2$ is the system proposed order. We define an agreement relation between the orders $\succ_1$ and $\succ_2$ with respect to a pair of items as follows:

- The orders $\succ_1$ and $\succ_2$ *agree* on items i_1 and i_2 if $i_1 \succ_1 i_2$ and $i_1 \succ_2 i_2$.
- The orders $\succ_1$ and $\succ_2$ *disagree* on items i_1 and i_2 if $i_1 \succ_1 i_2$ and $i_2 \succ_2 i_1$.
- The orders $\succ_1$ and $\succ_2$ *are compatible* on items i_1 and i_2 if $i_1 \succ_1 i_2$ and neither $i_1 \succ_2 i_2$ nor $i_2 \succ_2 i_1$. In other words the items are either tied or incomparable under at least one of the orders.

The **Normalized Distance based Performance Measure** (NDPM) [76] is commonly used in information retrieval. It differentiates between correct orders of pairs, incorrect orders and ties. Formally, let $\delta_{\succ_1,\succ_2}(i_1, i_2)$ be a distance function between a reference ranking $\succ_1$ and a proposed ranking $\succ_2$ defined as follows:

$$\delta_{\succ_1,\succ_2}(i_1, i_2) = \begin{cases} 0 & \text{if } \succ_1 \text{ and } \succ_2 \text{ agree on } i_1 \text{ and } i_2, \\ 1 & \text{if } \succ_1 \text{ and } \succ_2 \text{ are compatible on } i_1 \text{ and } i_2, \\ 2 & \text{if } \succ_1 \text{ and } \succ_2 \text{ disagree on } i_1 \text{ and } i_2. \end{cases} \tag{8.8}$$

The total distance over all item pairs in I is:

$$\beta_{\succ_1,\succ_2}(I) = \sum_{(i_1,i_2)\in\binom{I}{2}} \delta_{\succ_1,\succ_2}(i_1, i_2) \tag{8.9}$$

where the summation is over all possible item pairs in I (efficient implementations can sum only over item pairs for which the reference ranking asserts an order).

Let $m(\succ_1) = \text{argmax}_{\succ} \beta_{\succ_1,\succ}(I)$ be a normalization factor which is the maximal distance that any ranking $\succ$ can have from a reference ranking $\succ_1$. In fact, $m(\succ_1)$ is the number of pairs in I for which the reference ranking asserts an ordering, because the worst possible outcome would be to be wrong on all possible pairs. The NDPM score $NDPM(I, \succ_1, \succ_2)$ comparing a proposed ranking of items $\succ_2$ to a reference ranking $\succ_1$ is

$$NDPM(I, \succ_1, \succ_2) = \frac{\beta_{\succ_1,\succ_2}(I)}{m(\succ_1)} \tag{8.10}$$

Intuitively, the NDPM measure will give a perfect score of 0 to rankings over the set I that completely agree with the reference ranking, and the worst score of 1 is assigned to a ranking that completely disagrees with the reference ranking. If the proposed ranking does not contain a preference between a pair of items that are ranked in the reference ranking, it is penalized by half as much as providing a contradicting preference.

The proposed ranking is not penalized for containing preferences that are not ordered in the reference ranking. This means that for any pair of items that was not ordered in the reference ranking any ordering predicted by the ranking algorithm is acceptable. This is because we typically display a list within the application. As such the ranking algorithm is expected to output a total, not a partial order, and should not be penalized for being forced to order all pairs.

A potential downside of NDPM in some applications is that it does not consider the location of disagreements in the reference ranking. In some cases it is more important to appropriately order items that should appear closer to the head of the ranked list, than items that are positioned near the bottom. For example, when ranking movies by decreasing preference, it may be more important to properly order the movies that the user would enjoy, than to properly order the movies that the user would not enjoy. It is sometimes important to give different weights to errors depending on their position in the list.

To this end, we can use the **average precision (AP) correlation** metric [77], which gives more weight to errors over items that appear at earlier positions in the reference ranking. Formally, let $\succ_1$ be the reference ranking and $\succ_2$ be a proposed ranking over a set of items. The AP measure compares the ordering of each item in the proposed ranking $\succ_2$ with respect to its preceding items (successors) in the reference ranking $\succ_1$.

For each $i_1 \in I$, let the set $Z^{i_1}(I, \succ)$ denote all item pairs (i_1, i_2) in I such that $i_2 \succ i_1$. These are all the items that are preferred over i_1 (i.e., preceding tems).

$$Z^i(I, \succ) = \{(i_1, i_2) \mid \forall i_1, i_2 \in I \text{ s.t. } i_2 \succ i_1\} \tag{8.11}$$

We define the indicator function $\delta(i_1, i_2, \succ_1, \succ_2)$ to equal 1 when $\succ_1$ and $\succ_2$ agree on items i_1 and i_2, and zero otherwise.

Let $A^{i_1}(I, \succ_1, \succ_2)$ be the normalized agreement score between $\succ_2$ and the reference ranking $\succ_1$ for all items i_2 such that $i_2 \succ_1 i_1$.

$$A^{i_1}(I, \succ_1, \succ_2) = \frac{1}{|Z^{i_1}(I, \succ_2)| - 1} \sum_{(i_1, i_2) \in Z^{i_1}(I, \succ_2)} \delta(i_1, i_2, \succ_1, \succ_2) \tag{8.12}$$

The AP score of a partial order $\succ_2$ over I given partial order $\succ_1$ is defined as

$$AP(I, \succ_1, \succ_2) = \frac{1}{|I| - 1} \sum_{i \in I} A^i(I, \succ_1, \succ_2) \tag{8.13}$$

The AP score gives a perfect score of 1 where there is total agreement between the system proposed ranking and the reference ranking for every item pair above location i for all $i \in \{1 \ldots |I|\}$. The worst score of 0 is given to systems were there is no agreement between the two ranked lists.

In some cases, we may completely know the user's true preferences for some set of items. For example, we may elicit the user's true ordering by presenting the user with binary choices. In this case, when a pair of items are tied in the reference ranking it means that the user is actually indifferent between the items. Thus, a perfect system should not rank one item higher than the other. In such cases, rank correlation measures such as **Spearman's** ρ or **Kendall's** τ [37, 38] can be used. These measures tend to be highly correlated in practice [22]. Kendall's τ is given by

$$\tau = \frac{C^+ - C^-}{\sqrt{C^u}\sqrt{C^s}} \tag{8.14}$$

where C^+ and C^- are the number of pairs that were correctly, and incorrectly ordered by the system, respectively, C^u is the number of item pairs for which the reference ranking asserts any ordering, and C^s is the number of item pairs for which the evaluated system asserts any ordering.

Utility-Based Ranking

While reference ranking scores a ranking on its correlation with some "true" ranking, there are other criteria for deciding on ordering a list of items. One popular alternative is to order items by decreasing utility. In such cases, we not only care about whether items i_1 and i_2 were ordered incorrectly, but also about the difference in utility between i_1 and i_2. It is not as bad to incorrectly order a pair of items with similar utilities, as to incorrectly order items with very different utilities.

It is also common to assume that the utility of a list of recommendations is additive, given by the sum of the utilities of the individual recommendations. The utility of each recommendation is the utility of the recommended item discounted by a factor that depends on its position in the list of recommendations. One example of such a utility is the likelihood that a user will observe a recommendation at position i in the list. It is usually assumed that users scan recommendation lists from the beginning to the end, with the utility of recommendations being discounted more heavily towards the end of the list. The discount can also be interpreted as the probability that a user would observe a recommendation in a particular position in the list, with the utility of the recommendation given that it was observed depending only on the item recommend. Under this interpretation, the probability that a particular position in the recommendation list is observed is assumed to depend only on the position and not on the items that are recommended.

In many applications, the user can use only a single, or a very small set of items, or the recommendation engine is not used as the main browsing tool. In such cases, we can expect the users to observe only a few items of the top of the recommendations list. We can model such applications using a very rapid decay of the positional discount down the list. The **R-Score** metric [10] assumes that the value of recommendations decline exponentially down the ranked list to yield the following score for each user u:

$$R_u = \sum_j \frac{\max(r_{u,i_j} - d, 0)}{2^{\frac{j-1}{\alpha-1}}} \tag{8.15}$$

where i_j is the item in the jth position, $r_{u,i}$ is user u's rating of item i, d is a task dependent neutral ("don't care") rating, and α is a half-life parameter, which controls the exponential decline of the value of positions in the ranked list. In the case of ratings prediction tasks, r_{ui} is the rating given by the user to each item (e.g. 4 stars), and d is the don't care vote (e.g. 3 stars), and the algorithm only gets credit for ranking items with rating above the "don't care" vote higher than d (e.g. 4 or 5 stars). In usage prediction tasks, $r_{u,i}$ is typically 1 if u selects i and 0 otherwise, while d is 0. Using

$$r_{u,i} = -\log(\text{relative-frequency}(i)) \tag{8.16}$$

if i is used and 0 otherwise can capture the amount of information in the recommendation [66]. The resulting per-user scores are aggregated using:

$$R = 100\frac{\sum_u R_u}{\sum_u R_u^*} \tag{8.17}$$

where R_u^* is the score of the best possible ranking for user u.

In other applications the user is expected to read a relatively large portion of the list. In certain types of search, such as the search for legal documents [28], users may look for all relevant items, and would be willing to read large portions of the recommendations list. In such cases, we need a much slower decay of the positional discount. **Normalized Discounted Cumulative Gain (NDCG)** [33] is a measure from information retrieval, where positions are discounted logarithmically. Assuming each user u has a "gain" $g_{u,i}$ from being recommended item i, the average Discounted Cumulative Gain (DCG) for a list of J items is defined as

$$\text{DCG} = \frac{1}{N}\sum_{u=1}^{N}\sum_{j=1}^{J}\frac{g_{u,i_j}}{\log_b(j+1)} \tag{8.18}$$

where i_j is the item at position j in the list. The logarithm base is a free parameter, typically between 2 and 10. A logarithm with base 2 is commonly used to ensure all positions are discounted. NDCG is the normalized version of DCG given by

$$\text{NDCG} = \frac{\text{DCG}}{\text{DCG}^*} \tag{8.19}$$

where DCG* is the ideal DCG.

We show the two methods here as they were originally presented, but note that the numerator in the two cases contains a utility function that assigns a value for each item. One can replace the original utility functions with a function that is more appropriate to the designed application. A measure closely related to R-score and NDCG is **average reciprocal hit rank (ARHR)** [18] which is an un-normalized measure that assigns a utility $1/k$ to a successful recommendation at position k. Thus, ARHR decays more slowly than R score but faster than NDCG.

Online Evaluation of Ranking

In an online experiment designed to evaluate the ranking of the recommendation list, we can look at the interactions of users with the system. When a recommendation list is presented to a user, the user may select a number of items from the list. We can now assume that the user has scanned the list at least as deep as the last selection. That is, if the user has selected items 1, 3, and 10, we can assume that the user has observed items 1 through 10. We can now make another assumption, that the user has found items 1, 3, and 10 to be interesting, and items 2, 4, 5, 6, 7, 8, and 9 to be uninteresting (see, e.g. [35]). In some cases we can have additional information whether the user has observed more items. For example, if the list is spread across several pages, and only 20 results are presented per page, then, in the example above, if the user moved to the second page we can also assume that she has observed results 11 through 20 and had found them to be irrelevant.

In the scenario above, the results of this interaction is a division of the list into three parts—the interesting items (1, 3, 10 in the example above), the uninteresting items (the rest of the items from 1 through 20), and the unknown items (21 till the end of the list). We can now use an appropriate reference ranking metric to score the original list. This can be done in two different ways. First, the reference list can contain the interesting items at the top, then the unknown items, and the uninteresting items at the bottom. This reference list captures the case where the user may only select a small subset of the interesting items, and therefore the unknown items may contain more interesting items. Second, the reference list can contain the interesting items at the top, followed by the uninteresting items, with the unknown items completely ignored. This is useful when making unreasonable preference assumptions, such as that some unknown items are preferred to the uninteresting items, may have negative consequences. In either case, it should be borne in mind that the semantics of the reference ranking are different from the case of offline evaluations. In offline evaluations, we have a single reference ranking which is assumed to be correct, and we measure how much each recommender deviates from this "correct" ranking. In the online case, the reference ranking is assumed to be the ranking that the user would have preferred given that were presented with the recommender's ranking. In the offline case, we assume that there is one correct ranking, while in the online case we allow for the possibility of multiple correct rankings.

In the case of utility ranking, we can evaluate a list based on the sum of the utilities of the selected items. Lists that place interesting items with high utility close to the beginning of the list, will hence be preferred to lists that place these interesting items down the list, because we expect that in the latter case, the user will often not observe these interesting items at all, generating no utility for the recommender.

8.3.3 Coverage

As the prediction accuracy of a recommender system, especially in collaborative filtering systems, in many cases grows with the amount of data, some algorithms may provide recommendations with high quality, but only for a small portion of the items where they have huge amounts of data. This is often referred to as the *long tail* or *heavy tail* problem, where the vast majority of the items where selected or rated only by a handful of users, yet the total amount of evidence over these unpopular items is much more than the evidence over the few popular items.

The term coverage can refer to several distinct properties of the system that we discuss below.

8.3.3.1 Item Space Coverage

Most commonly, the term coverage refers to the proportion of items that the recommender system can recommend. This is often referred to as **catalog coverage**. The simplest measure of catalog coverage is the percentage of all items that can ever be recommended. This measure can be computed in many cases directly given the algorithm and the input data set.

A more useful measure is the percentage of all items that are recommended to users during an experiment, either offline, online, or a user study. In some cases it may be desirable to weight the items, for example, by their popularity or utility. Then, we may agree not to be able to recommend some items which are very rarely used anyhow, but ignoring high profile items may be less tolerable.

Another measure of catalog coverage is the **sales diversity** [20], which measures how unequally different items are chosen by users when a particular recommender system is used. If each item i accounts for a proportion $p(i)$ of user choices, the **Gini index** is given by:

$$G = \frac{1}{n-1}\sum_{j=1}^{n}(2j-n-1)p(i_j) \tag{8.20}$$

where $i_1, \cdots i_n$ is the list of items ordered according to increasing $p(i)$. The index is 0 when all items are chosen equally often, and 1 when a single item is always chosen.

The Gini index of the number of times each item is recommended could also be used. Another measure of distributional inequality is the **Shannon Entropy**:

$$H = -\sum_{i=1}^{n} p(i) \log p(i) \tag{8.21}$$

The entropy is 0 when a single item is always chosen or recommended, and $\log n$ when n items are chosen or recommended equally often.

Steck [70] further discusses how accuracy methods can be modified to better model the accuracy in the long tail. He suggests a correction for the bias of users towards the more popular items.

8.3.3.2 User Space Coverage

Coverage can also be the proportion of users or user interactions for which the system can recommend items. In many applications the recommender may not provide recommendations for some users due to, e.g. low confidence in the accuracy of predictions for that user. In such cases we may prefer recommenders that can provide recommendations for a wider range of users. Clearly, such recommenders should be evaluated on the trade-off between coverage and accuracy.

Coverage here can be measured by the richness of the user profile required to make a recommendation. For example, in the collaborative filtering case this could be measured as the number of items that a user must rate before receiving recommendations. This measurement can be typically evaluated in offline experiments.

8.3.3.3 Cold-Start Problem

Another related set of issues are the well known cold start problems—the coverage and performance of the system on new items and on new users. Cold start can be considered as a sub problem of coverage because it measures the system coverage over a specific set of items and users. In addition to measuring how large the pool of cold start items or users are, it may also be important to measure system accuracy for these users and items.

Focusing on cold start items, we can use a threshold to decide on the set of cold items. For example, we can decide that cold items are only items with no ratings or usage evidence [64], or items that exist in the system for less than a certain amount of time (e.g., a day), or items that have less than a predefined evidence amount (e.g., less than ten ratings). Perhaps a more generic way is to consider the "coldness" of an item using either the amount of time it exists in the system or the amount of data gathered for it. Then, we can credit the system more for properly predicting colder items, and less for the hot items that are predicted.

It may be possible that a system better recommends cold items at the price of a reduced accuracy for hotter items. This may be desirable due to other considerations such as novelty and serendipity that are discussed later. Still, when computing the system accuracy on cold items it may be wise to evaluate whether there is a trade-off with the entire system accuracy.

8.3.4 Confidence

Confidence in the recommendation can be defined as the system's trust in its recommendations or predictions [26, 72]. As we have noted above, collaborative filtering recommenders tend to improve their accuracy as the amount of data over items grows. Similarly, the confidence in the predicted property typically also grows with the amount of data.

In many cases the user can benefit from observing these confidence scores [26]. When the system reports a low confidence in a recommended item, the user may tend to further research the item before making a decision. For example, if a system recommends a movie with very high confidence, and another movie with the same rating but a lower confidence, the user may add the first movie immediately to the watching queue, but may further read the plot synopsis for the second movie, and perhaps a few movie reviews before deciding to watch it.

Perhaps the most common measurement of confidence is the probability that the predicted value is indeed true, or the interval around the predicted value where a predefined portion, e.g. 95 % of the true values lie. For example, a recommender may accurately rate a movie as a 4 star movie with probability 0.85, or have 95 % of the actual ratings lie within -1 and $+\frac{1}{2}$ of the predicted 4 stars. The most general method of confidence is to provide a complete distribution over possible outcomes [49].

Given two recommenders that perform similarly on other relevant properties, such as prediction accuracy, is can be desirable to choose the one that can provide valid confidence estimates. In this case, given two recommenders with, say, identical accuracy, that report confidence bounds in the same way, we will prefer the recommender that better estimates its confidence bounds.

Standard confidence bounds, such as the ones above, can be directly evaluated in regular offline trials, much the same way as we estimate prediction accuracy. We can design for each specific confidence type a score that measures how close the method confidence estimate is to the true error in prediction. This procedure cannot be applied when the algorithms do not agree on the confidence method, because some confidence methods are weaker and therefore easier to estimate. In such a case a more accurate estimate of a weaker confidence metric does not imply a better recommender.

Example 8.1. Recommenders A and B both report confidence intervals over possible movie ratings. We train A and B over a confidence threshold, ranging of 95 %. For each trained model, we run A and B on offline data, hiding a part of the user ratings and requesting each algorithm to predict the missing ratings. Each algorithm produces, along with the predicted rating, a confidence interval. We compute A_+ and A_-, the number of times that the predicted rating of algorithm A was within and outside the confidence interval (respectively), and do the same for B. Then we compute the true confidence of each algorithm using $\frac{A_+}{A_- + A_+} = 0.97$ and $\frac{B_+}{A_- + A_+} = 0.94$. The result indicates that A is over conservative, and computes intervals that are too large, while B is liberal and computes intervals that are too small. As we do not require the intervals to be conservative, we prefer B because its estimated intervals are closer to the requested 95 % confidence.

Another application of confidence bounds is in filtering recommended items where the confidence in the predicted value is below some threshold. In this scenario we assume that the recommender is allowed not to predict a score for all values. In a top n recommendation scenario, we may allow a system to sometimes suggest less than n items, because it cannot produce a set of n items with sufficient confidence. In this case the precision of the system is not punished when less results are returned, and the shorter list is expected to result only in lower recall. As such, measuring only precision@N in such problems is insufficient, because algorithms have an incentive to provide less recommendations, or even no recommendations, obtaining a meaningless precision of 1.

We can hence design an experiment around this filtering procedure by comparing the accuracy of two recommenders after their results were filtered by removing low confidence items. In such experiments we can compute a curve, estimating the prediction accuracy (typically precision-recall curves) for each portion of filtered items, or for different filtering thresholds. This evaluation procedure does not require both algorithms to agree on the confidence method.

While user studies and online experiments can study the effect of reporting confidence on the user experience [67], it is difficult to see how these types of tests can be used to provide further evidence as to the accuracy of the confidence estimate.

8.3.5 *Trust*

While confidence is the system trust in its ratings (Chap. 20), in trust we refer here to the user's trust in the system recommendation.[4] For example, it may be beneficial for the system to recommend a few items that the user already knows and likes. This way, even though the user gains no value from this recommendation, she observes that the system provides reasonable recommendations, which may increase her trust in the system recommendations for unknown items. Another common way

[4]Not to be confused with trust in the social network research, used to measure how much a user believes another user. Some literature on recommender systems uses such trust measurements to filter similar users [48].

of enhancing trust in the system is to explain the recommendations that the system provides (Chap. 10). Trust in the system is also called the credibility of the system.

If we do not restrict ourselves to a single method of gaining trust, such as the one suggested above, the obvious method for evaluating user trust is by asking users whether the system recommendations are reasonable in a user study [5, 14, 26, 57]. In an online test one could associate the number of recommendations that were followed with the trust in the recommender, assuming that higher trust in the recommender would lead to more recommendations being used. Alternatively, we could also assume that trust in the system is correlated with repeated users, as users who trust the system will return to it when performing future tasks. However, such measurements may not separate well other factors of user satisfaction, and may not be accurate. It is unclear how to measure trust in an offline experiment, because trust is built through an interaction between the system and a user.

8.3.6 Novelty

Novel recommendations (Chap. 26) are recommendations for items that the user did not know about [41]. In applications that require novel recommendation, an obvious and easy to implement approach is to filter out items that the user already rated or used. However, in many cases users will not report all the items they have used in the past. Thus, this simple method is insufficient to filter out all items that the user already knows.

While we can obviously measure novelty in a user study, by asking users whether they were already familiar with a recommended item [12, 34], we can also gain some understanding of a system's novelty through offline experiments. For such an experiment we could split the data set on time, i.e. hide all the user purchases that occurred after a specific point in time. In addition, we can hide some purchases that occurred prior to that time, simulating the items that the user has purchased and is hence familiar with, but did not report their purchase to the system. When recommending, the system is rewarded for each item that was recommended and purchased after the split time, but would be punished for each item that was recommended but purchased prior to the split time.

To implement the above procedure we must carefully model the hiding process such that it would resemble the true preference discovery process that occurs in the real system. In some cases the set of purchased items is not a uniform sample of the set of all items the user is familiar with, and such bias should be acknowledged and handled if possible. For example, if we believe that the user will report more purchases of unique items, and less purchases of popular or common items, then the hiding process should tend to hide more popular items.

In using this measure of novelty, it is important to control for accuracy, as irrelevant recommendations may be new to the user, but still worthless. One approach would be to consider novelty only among the relevant items [79].

Example 8.2. We wish to evaluate the novelty of a set of movie recommenders in an offline test. As we believe that users of our system rate movies after they watch them, we split the user ratings in a sequential manner. For each test user profile we choose a cutoff point randomly along the time-based sequence of movie ratings, hiding all movies after a certain point in the sequence.

Let us assume that user studies on this imaginary system showed that people tend not to report ratings of movies that they did not feel strongly about, but occasionally also do not report a rating of a movie that they liked or disliked strongly. Therefore, we hide a rating of a movie prior to the cutoff point with probability $1 - \frac{|r-3|}{2}$ where $r \in \{1, 2, 3, 4, 5\}$ is the rating of the movie, and 3 is the neutral rating. We would like to avoid predicting these movies with hidden ratings because the user already knows about them.

Then, for each user, each recommender produces a list of 5 recommendations, and we compute precision only over items after the cutoff point. That is, the recommenders get no credit for recommending movies with hidden ratings that occurred prior to the cutoff point. In this experiment the algorithm with the highest precision score is preferred.

Another method for evaluating novel recommendations uses the above assumption that popular items are less likely to be novel. Thus, novelty can be taken into account by using an accuracy metric where the system does not get the same credit for correctly predicting popular items as it does when it correctly predicts non-popular items [65]. Ziegler et al. [80] and Celma and Herrera [12] also give accuracy measures that take popularity into account.

Finally, we can evaluate the amount of new information in a recommendation together with the relevance of the recommended item. For example, when item ratings are available, we can multiply the hidden rating by some information measurement of the recommended item (such as the conditional entropy given the user profile) to produce a novelty score.

8.3.7 Serendipity

Serendipity is a measure of how surprising the successful recommendations are (Chap. 26). For example, if the user has rated positively many movies where a certain star actor appears, recommending the new movie of that actor may be novel, because the user may not know of it, but is hardly surprising. Of course, random recommendations may be very surprising, and we therefore need to balance serendipity with accuracy.

One can think of serendipity as the amount of relevant information that is new to the user in a recommendation. For example, if following a successful movie recommendation the user learns of a new actor that she likes, this can be considered as serendipitous. In information retrieval, where novelty typically refers to the new information contained in the document (and is thus close to our definition of serendipity), [79] suggested to manually label pairs of documents as redundant. Then, they compared algorithms on avoiding recommending redundant documents. Such methods are applicable to recommender systems when some meta-data over items, such as content information, is available (Chap. 4).

To avoid human labeling, we could design a distance measurement between items based on content. Then, we can score a successful recommendation by its distance from a set of previously rated items in a collaborative filtering system, or from the user profile in a content-based recommender [78]. Thus, we are rewarding the system for successful recommendations that are far from the user profile.

Example 8.3. In a book recommendation application, we would like to recommend books from authors that the reader is less familiar with. We therefore design a distance metric between a book b and a set of books B (the books that the user has previously read); Let $c_{B,w}$ be the number of books by writer w in B. Let $c_B = \max_w c_{B,w}$ the maximal number of books from a single writer in B. Let $d(b, B) = \frac{1+c_B-c_{B,w(b)}}{1+c_B}$, where $w(b)$ is the writer of book b.

We now run an offline experiment to evaluate which of the candidate algorithms generates more serendipitous recommendations. We split each test user profile—set of books that the user has read—into sets of observed books B_i^o and hidden books B_i^h. We use B_i^o as the input for each recommender, and request a list of five recommendations. For each hidden book $b \in B_i^h$ that appeared in the recommendation list for user i, the recommender receives a score of $d(b, B_i^o)$. Thus the recommender is getting more credit for recommending books from writers that the reader has read less often. In this experiment the recommender that received a higher score is selected for the application.

One can also think of serendipity as deviation from the "natural" prediction [53]. That is, given a prediction engine that has a high accuracy, the recommendations that it issues are "obvious". Therefore, we will give higher serendipity scores to successful recommendations that the prediction engine would deem unlikely.

We can evaluate the serendipity of a recommender in a user study by asking the users to mark the recommendations that they find unexpected. Then, we can also see whether the user followed these recommendations, which would make them unexpected and successful and therefore serendipitous. In an online study, we can assume that our distance metric is correct and evaluate only how distance from the user profile affected the probability that a user will follow the recommendation. It is important to check the effect of serendipity over time, because users might at first be intrigued by the unexpected recommendations and try them out. If after following the suggestion they discover that the recommendations are inappropriate, they may stop following them in the future, or stop using the recommendation engine at all.

8.3.8 Diversity

Diversity is generally defined as the opposite of similarity (Chap. 26). In some cases suggesting a set of similar items may not be as useful for the user, because it may take longer to explore the range of items. Consider for example a recommendation for a vacation [68], where the system should recommend vacation packages. Presenting a list with five recommendations, all for the same location, varying only on the choice of hotel, or the selection of attraction, may not be as useful as suggesting five different locations. The user can view the various recommended locations and request more details on a subset of the locations that are appropriate to her.

The most explored method for measuring diversity uses item-item similarity, typically based on item content, as in Sect. 8.3.7. Then, we could measure the diversity of a list based on the sum, average, min, or max distance between item pairs, or measure the value of adding each item to the recommendation list as the new item's diversity from the items already in the list [8, 80]. The item-item similarity measurement used in evaluation can be different from the similarity measurement used by the algorithm that computes the recommendation lists. For example, we can use for evaluation a costly metric that produces more accurate results than fast approximate methods that are more suitable for online computations.

As diversity may come at the expanse of other properties, such as accuracy [78], we can compute curves to evaluate the decrease in accuracy vs. the increase in diversity.

Example 8.4. In a book recommendation application, we are interested in presenting the user with a diverse set of recommendations, with minimal impact to accuracy. We use $d(b, B)$ from Example 8.3 as the distance metric. Given candidate recommenders, each with a tunable parameter that controls the diversity of the recommendations, we train each algorithm over a range of values for the diversity parameters. For each trained model, we now compute a precision score, and a diversity score as follows; we take each recommendation list that an algorithm produces, and compute the distance of each item from the rest of the list, averaging the result to obtain a diversity score. We now plot the precision-diversity curves of the recommenders in a graph, and select the algorithm with the dominating curve.

In recommenders that assist in information search, we can assume that more diverse recommendations will result in shorter search interactions [68]. We could use this in an online experiment measuring interaction sequence length as a proxy for diversification. As is always the case in online testing, shorter sessions may be due to other factors of the system, and to validate this claim it is useful to experiment with different diversity thresholds using the same prediction engine before comparing different recommenders.

8.3.9 Utility

Many e-commerce websites employ a recommender system in order to improve their revenue by, e.g., enhancing cross-sell. In such cases the recommendation engine can be judged by the revenue that it generates for the website [66]. In general, we can define various types of utility functions that the recommender tries to optimize. For such recommenders, measuring the utility, or the expected utility of the recommendations may be more significant than measuring the accuracy of recommendations. It is also possible to view many of the other properties, such as diversity or serendipity, as different types of utility functions, over single items or over lists. In this chapter, however, we define utility as the value that either the system or the user gains from a recommendation.

Utility can be measured cleanly from the perspective of the recommendation engine or the recommender system owner. Care must be taken, though, when measuring the utility that the user receives from the recommendations. First, user utilities or preferences are difficult to capture and model, and considerable research has focused on this problem [9, 25, 59]. Second, it is unclear how to aggregate user utilities across users for computing a score for a recommender. For example, it is tempting to use money as a utility thus selecting a recommender that minimizes user cost. However, under the diminishing returns assumption [69], the same amount of money does not have the same utility for people with different income levels. Therefore, the average cost per purchase, for example, is not a reasonable aggregation across users.

In an application where users rate items, it is also possible to use the ratings as a utility measurement [10]. For example, in movie ratings, where a five star movie is considered an excellent movie, we can assume that a recommending a five star movie has a higher utility for the user than recommending a movie that the user will rate with four stars. As users may interpret ratings differently, user ratings should be normalized before aggregating across users.

While we typically only assign positive utilities to successful recommendations, we can also assign negative utilities to unsuccessful recommendations. For example, if some recommended item offends the user, then we should punish the system for recommending it by assigning a negative utility. We can also add a cost to each recommendation, perhaps based on the position of the recommended item in the list, and subtract it from the utility of the item.

For any utility function, the standard evaluation of the recommender is to compute the expected utility of a recommendation. In the case where the recommender is trying to predict only a single item, such as when we evaluate the system on time-based splits and try to predict only the next item in the sequence, the value of a correct recommendation should simply be the utility of the item. In the task where the recommender predicts n items we can use the sum of the utilities of the correct recommendations in the list. When negative utilities for failed recommendations are used, then the sum is over all recommendations, successful or failed. We can also integrate utilities into ranking measurements, as discussed in Sect. 8.3.2.3. Finally, we can normalize the resulting score using the maximal possible utility given the optimal recommendation list.

Evaluating utility in user studies and online is easy in the case of recommender utility. If the utility we optimize for is the revenue of the website, measuring the change in revenue between users of various recommenders is simple. When we try to optimize user utilities the online evaluation becomes harder, because users typically find it challenging to assign utilities to outcomes. In many cases, however, users can say whether they prefer one outcome to another. Therefore, we can try to elicit the user preferences [31] in order to rank the candidate methods.

8.3.10 Risk

In some cases a recommendation may be associated with a potential risk. For example, when recommending stocks for purchase, users may wish to be risk-averse, preferring stocks that have a lower expected growth, but also a lower risk of collapsing. On the other hand, users may be risk-seeking, preferring stocks that have a potentially high, even if less likely, profit. In such cases we may wish to evaluate not only the (expected) value generated from a recommendation, but also to minimize the risk.

The standard way to evaluate risk sensitive systems is by considering not just the expected utility, but also the utility variance. For example, we may use a parameter q and compare two systems on $E[X] + q \cdot Var(X)$. When q is positive, this approach prefers risk-seeking (also called bold [50]) recommenders, and when q is negative, the system prefers risk-averse recommenders.

8.3.11 Robustness

Robustness (Chap. 24) is the stability of the recommendation in the presence of fake information [55], typically inserted on purpose in order to influence the recommendations. As more people rely on recommender systems to guide them through the item space, influencing the system to change the rating of an item may be profitable to an interested party. For example, an owner of an hotel may wish to boost the rating for their hotel. This can be done by injecting fake user profiles that rate the hotel positively, or by injecting fake users that rate the competitors negatively.

Such attempts to influence the recommendation are typically called attacks [43, 52]. Coordinated attacks occur when a malicious user intentionally queries the data set or injects fake information in order to learn some private information of some users. In evaluating such systems, it is important to provide a complete description of the attack protocol, as the sensitivity of the system typically varies from one protocol to another.

In general, creating a system that is immune to any type of attack is unrealistic. An attacker with an ability to inject an infinite amount of information can, in most cases, manipulate a recommendation in an arbitrary way. It is therefore more useful to estimate the cost of influencing a recommendation, which is typically measured by the amount of injected information. While it is desirable to theoretically analyze the cost of modifying a rating, it is not always possible. In these cases, we can simulate a set of attacks by introducing fake information into the system data set, empirically measuring average cost of a successful attack [13, 44].

As opposed to other evaluation criteria discussed here, it is hard to envision executing an attack on a real system as an online experiment. It may be fruitful, however, to analyze the real data collected in the online system to identify actual attacks that are executed against the system.

Another type of robustness is the stability of the system under extreme conditions, such as a large number of requests. While less discussed, such robustness is very important to system administrators, who must avoid system malfunction. In many cases system robustness is related to the infrastructure, such as the database software, or to the hardware specifications, and is related to scalability (Sect. 8.3.14).

8.3.12 Privacy

In a collaborative filtering system, a user willingly discloses his preferences over items to the system in the hope of getting useful recommendations (Chap. 19). However, it is important for most users that their preferences stay private, that is, that no third party can use the recommender system to learn something about the preferences of a specific user.

For example, consider the case where a user who is interested in the wonderful, yet rare art of growing Bahamian orchids has bought a book titled "The Divorce Organizer and Planner". The spouse of that user, looking for a present, upon browsing the book "The Bahamian and Caribbean Species (Cattleyas and Their Relatives)" may get a recommendation of the type "people who bought this book also bought" for the divorce organizer, thus revealing sensitive private information.

It is generally considered inappropriate for a recommender system to disclose private information even for a single user. For this reason analysis of privacy tends to focus on a worst case scenario, illustrating theoretical cases under which users private information may be revealed. Other researchers [21] compare algorithms by evaluating the portion of users whose private information was compromised. The assumption in such studies is that complete privacy is not realistic and that therefore we must compromise on minimizing the privacy breaches.

Another alternative is to define different levels of privacy, such as k-identity [21], and compare algorithms sensitivity to privacy breaches under varying levels of privacy.

Privacy may also come at the expense of the accuracy of the recommendations. Therefore, it is important to analyze this trade-off carefully. Perhaps the most informative experiment is when a privacy modification has been added to an algorithm, and the accuracy (or any other trade-off property) can be evaluated with or without the modification [51].

8.3.13 Adaptivity

Real recommender systems may operate in a setting where the item collection changes rapidly, or where trends in interest over items may shift. Perhaps the most obvious example of such systems is the recommendation of news items or related stories in online newspapers [23]. In this scenario stories may be interesting only over a short period of time, afterwards becoming outdated. When an unexpected news event occurs, such as the tsunami disaster, people become interested in articles that may not have been interesting otherwise, such as a relatively old article explaining the tsunami phenomenon. While this problem is similar to the cold-start problem, it is different because it may be that old items that were not regarded as interesting in the past suddenly become interesting.

This type of adaptation can be evaluated offline by analyzing the amount of information needed before an item is recommended. If we model the recommendation process in a sequential manner, we can record, even in an offline test, the amount of evidence that is needed before the algorithm recommends a story. It is likely that an algorithm can be adjusted to recommend items faster once they become interesting, by sacrificing some prediction accuracy. We can compare two algorithms by evaluating a possible trade-off between accuracy and the speed of the shift in trends.

Another type of adaptivity is the rate by which the system adapts to a user's personal preferences [46], or to changes in user profile [42]. For example, when users rate an item, they expect the set of recommendations to change. If the recommendations stay fixed, users may assume that their rating effort is wasted, and may not agree to provide more ratings. As with the shift in trends evaluation, we can again evaluate in an offline experiment the changes in the recommendation list after adding more information to the user profile such as new ratings. We can evaluate an algorithm by measuring the difference between the recommendation lists before and after the new information was added. The Gini index and Shannon entropy measures discussed in Sect. 8.3.3 can be used to measure the variability of recommendations made to a user as the user profile changes.

8.3.14 Scalability

As recommender systems are designed to help users navigate in large collections of items, one of the goals of the designers of such systems is to scale up to real data sets. As such, it is often the case that algorithms trade other properties, such as accuracy or coverage, for providing rapid results even for huge data sets consisting of millions of items (e.g. [15]).

With the growth of the data set, many algorithms are either slowed down or require additional resources such as computation power or memory. One standard approach in computer science research is to evaluate the computational complexity of an algorithm in terms of time or space requirements (as done, e.g., in [6, 36]). In many cases, however, the complexity of two algorithms is either identical, or could be reduced by changing some parameters, such as the complexity of the model, or the sample size. Therefore, to understand the scalability of the system it is also useful to report the consumption of system resources over large data sets.

Scalability is typically measured by experimenting with growing data sets, showing how the speed and resource consumption behave as the task scales up (see, e.g. [23]). It is important to measure the compromises that scalability dictates. For example, if the accuracy of the algorithm is lower than other candidates that only operate on relatively small data sets, one must show over small data sets the difference in accuracy. Such measurements can provide valuable information both on the potential performance of recommender systems in general for the specific task, and on future directions to explore.

As recommender systems are expected in many cases to provide rapid recommendations online, it is also important to measure how fast does the system provides recommendations [27, 62]. One such measurement is the throughput of the system, i.e., the number of recommendations that the system can provide per second. We could also measure the latency (also called response time)—the required time for making a recommendation online.

8.4 Conclusion

In this chapter we discussed how recommendation algorithms could be evaluated in order to select the best algorithm from a set of candidates. This is an important step in the research attempt to find better algorithms, as well as in application design where a designer chooses an existing algorithm for their application. As such, many evaluation metrics have been used for algorithm selection in the past.

We describe the concerns that need to be addressed when designing offline and online experiments and user studies. We outline a few important measurements that one must take in addition to the score that the metric provides, as well as other considerations that should be taken into account when designing experiments for recommendation algorithms.

We specify a set of properties that are sometimes discussed as important for the recommender system. For each such property we suggest an experiment that can be used to rank recommenders with regards to that property. For less explored properties, we restrict ourselves to generic descriptions that could be applied to various manifestations of that property. Specific procedures that can be practically implemented can then be developed for the specific property manifestation based on our generic guidelines.

References

1. Bailey, R.: Design of comparative experiments, vol. 25. Cambridge University Press Cambridge (2008)
2. Bamber, D.: The area above the ordinal dominance graph and the area below the receiver operating characteristic graph. Journal of Mathematical Psychology **12**, 387–415 (1975)
3. Benjamini, Y., Hochberg, Y.: Controlling the false discovery rate: a practical and powerful approach to multiple testing. Journal of the Royal Statistical Society. Series B (Methodological) pp. 289–300 (1995)
4. Bickel, P.J., Ducksum, K.A.: Mathematical Statistics: Ideas and Concepts. Holden-Day (1977)
5. Bonhard, P., Harries, C., McCarthy, J., Sasse, M.A.: Accounting for taste: using profile similarity to improve recommender systems. In: CHI '06: Proceedings of the SIGCHI conference on Human Factors in computing systems, pp. 1057–1066. ACM, New York, NY, USA (2006)
6. Boutilier, C., Zemel, R.S.: Online queries for collaborative filtering. In: In Proceedings of the Ninth International Workshop on Artificial Intelligence and Statistics (2002)
7. Box, G.E.P., Hunter, W.G., Hunter, J.S.: Statistics for Experimenters. Wiley, New York (1978)
8. Bradley, K., Smyth, B.: Improving recommendation diversity. In: Twelfth Irish Conference on Artificial Intelligence and Cognitive Science, pp. 85–94 (2001)
9. Braziunas, D., Boutilier, C.: Local utility elicitation in GAI models. In: Proceedings of the Twenty-first Conference on Uncertainty in Artificial Intelligence, pp. 42–49. Edinburgh (2005)
10. Breese, J.S., Heckerman, D., Kadie, C.M.: Empirical analysis of predictive algorithms for collaborative filtering. In: UAI, pp. 43–52 (1998)
11. Burke, R.: Evaluating the dynamic properties of recommendation algorithms. In: Proceedings of the Fourth ACM Conference on Recommender Systems, RecSys '10, pp. 225–228. ACM, New York, NY, USA (2010)
12. Celma, O., Herrera, P.: A new approach to evaluating novel recommendations. In: RecSys '08: Proceedings of the 2008 ACM conference on Recommender systems, pp. 179–186. ACM, New York, NY, USA (2008)
13. Chirita, P.A., Nejdl, W., Zamfir, C.: Preventing shilling attacks in online recommender systems. In: WIDM '05: Proceedings of the 7th annual ACM international workshop on Web information and data management, pp. 67–74. ACM, New York, NY, USA (2005)
14. Cramer, H., Evers, V., Ramlal, S., Someren, M., Rutledge, L., Stash, N., Aroyo, L., Wielinga, B.: The effects of transparency on trust in and acceptance of a content-based art recommender. User Modeling and User-Adapted Interaction **18**(5), 455–496 (2008)
15. Das, A.S., Datar, M., Garg, A., Rajaram, S.: Google news personalization: scalable online collaborative filtering. In: WWW '07: Proceedings of the 16th international conference on World Wide Web, pp. 271–280. ACM, New York, NY, USA (2007)
16. Dekel, O., Manning, C.D., Singer, Y.: Log-linear models for label ranking. In: NIPS'03, pp.-1–1 (2003)
17. Demšar, J.: Statistical comparisons of classifiers over multiple data sets. J. Mach. Learn. Res. **7**, 1–30 (2006)
18. Deshpande, M., Karypis, G.: Item-based top-N recommendation algorithms. ACM Transactions on Information Systems **22**(1), 143–177 (2004)
19. Fischer, G.: User modeling in human-computer interaction. User Model. User-Adapt. Interact. **11**(1–2), 65–86 (2001)
20. Fleder, D.M., Hosanagar, K.: Recommender systems and their impact on sales diversity. In: EC '07: Proceedings of the 8th ACM conference on Electronic commerce, pp. 192–199. ACM, New York, NY, USA (2007)
21. Frankowski, D., Cosley, D., Sen, S., Terveen, L., Riedl, J.: You are what you say: privacy risks of public mentions. In: SIGIR '06: Proceedings of the 29th annual international ACM SIGIR conference on Research and development in information retrieval, pp. 565–572. ACM, New York, NY, USA (2006)

22. Fredricks, G.A., Nelsen, R.B.: On the relationship between spearman's rho and kendall's tau for pairs of continuous random variables. Journal of Statistical Planning and Inference **137**(7), 2143–2150 (2007)
23. George, T.: A scalable collaborative filtering framework based on co-clustering. In: Fifth IEEE International Conference on Data Mining, pp. 625–628 (2005)
24. Greenwald, A.G.: Within-subjects designs: To use or not to use? Psychological Bulletin **83**, 216–229 (1976)
25. Haddawy, P., Ha, V., Restificar, A., Geisler, B., Miyamoto, J.: Preference elicitation via theory refinement. Journal of Machine Learning Research **4**, 2003 (2002)
26. Herlocker, J.L., Konstan, J.A., Riedl, J.T.: Explaining collaborative filtering recommendations. In: CSCW '00: Proceedings of the 2000 ACM conference on Computer supported cooperative work, pp. 241–250. ACM, New York, NY, USA (2000)
27. Herlocker, J.L., Konstan, J.A., Riedl, J.T.: An empirical analysis of design choices in neighborhood-based collaborative filtering algorithms. Inf. Retr. **5**(4), 287–310 (2002). DOI http://dx.doi.org/10.1023/A:1020443909834
28. Herlocker, J.L., Konstan, J.A., Terveen, L.G., Riedl, J.T.: Evaluating collaborative filtering recommender systems. ACM Trans. Inf. Syst. **22**(1), 5–53 (2004). DOI http://doi.acm.org/10.1145/963770.963772
29. Hijikata, Y., Shimizu, T., Nishida, S.: Discovery-oriented collaborative filtering for improving user satisfaction. In: IUI '09: Proceedings of the 13th international conference on Intelligent user interfaces, pp. 67–76. ACM, New York, NY, USA (2009)
30. Hu, R., Pu, P.: A comparative user study on rating vs. personality quiz based preference elicitation methods. In: IUI, pp. 367–372 (2009)
31. Hu, R., Pu, P.: A comparative user study on rating vs. personality quiz based preference elicitation methods. In: IUI 0́9: Proceedings of the 13th international conference on Intelligent user interfaces, pp. 367–372. ACM, New York, NY, USA (2009)
32. Hu, R., Pu, P.: A study on user perception of personality-based recommender systems. In: UMAP, pp. 291–302 (2010)
33. Järvelin, K., Kekäläinen, J.: Cumulated gain-based evaluation of ir techniques. ACM Trans. Inf. Syst. **20**(4), 422–446 (2002). DOI http://doi.acm.org/10.1145/582415.582418
34. Jones, N., Pu, P.: User technology adoption issues in recommender systems. In: Networking and Electronic Conference (2007)
35. Jung, S., Herlocker, J.L., Webster, J.: Click data as implicit relevance feedback in web search. Inf. Process. Manage. **43**(3), 791–807 (2007)
36. Karypis, G.: Evaluation of item-based top-n recommendation algorithms. In: CIKM '01: Proceedings of the tenth international conference on Information and knowledge management, pp. 247–254. ACM, New York, NY, USA (2001)
37. Kendall, M.G.: A new measure of rank correlation. Biometrika **30**(1–2), 81–93 (1938)
38. Kendall, M.G.: The treatment of ties in ranking problems. Biometrika **33**(3), 239–251 (1945)
39. Kohavi, R., Deng, A., Frasca, B., Walker, T., Xu, Y., Pohlmann, N.: Online controlled experiments at large scale. In: Proceedings of the 19th ACM SIGKDD International Conference on Knowledge Discovery and Data Mining, KDD '13, pp. 1168–1176. ACM, New York, NY, USA (2013)
40. Kohavi, R., Longbotham, R., Sommerfield, D., Henne, R.M.: Controlled experiments on the web: survey and practical guide. Data Min. Knowl. Discov. **18**(1), 140–181 (2009)
41. Konstan, J.A., McNee, S.M., Ziegler, C.N., Torres, R., Kapoor, N., Riedl, J.: Lessons on applying automated recommender systems to information-seeking tasks. In: AAAI (2006)
42. Koychev, I., Schwab, I.: Adaptation to drifting user's interests. In: In Proceedings of ECML2000 Workshop: Machine Learning in New Information Age, pp. 39–46 (2000)
43. Lam, S.K., Frankowski, D., Riedl, J.: Do you trust your recommendations? an exploration of security and privacy issues in recommender systems. In: In Proceedings of the 2006 International Cónference on Emerging Trends in Information and Communication Security (ETRICS) (2006)

44. Lam, S.K., Riedl, J.: Shilling recommender systems for fun and profit. In: WWW '04: Proceedings of the 13th international conference on World Wide Web, pp. 393–402. ACM, New York, NY, USA (2004)
45. Lehmann, E.L., Romano, J.P.: Testing statistical hypotheses, third edn. Springer Texts in Statistics. Springer, New York (2005)
46. Mahmood, T., Ricci, F.: Learning and adaptivity in interactive recommender systems. In: ICEC '07: Proceedings of the ninth international conference on Electronic commerce, pp. 75–84. ACM, New York, NY, USA (2007)
47. Marlin, B.M., Zemel, R.S.: Collaborative prediction and ranking with non-random missing data. In: Proceedings of the 2009 ACM Conference on Recommender Systems, RecSys 2009, New York, NY, USA, October 23–25, 2009, pp. 5–12 (2009)
48. Massa, P., Bhattacharjee, B.: Using trust in recommender systems: An experimental analysis. In: In Proceedings of iTrust2004 International Conference, pp. 221–235 (2004)
49. McLaughlin, M.R., Herlocker, J.L.: A collaborative filtering algorithm and evaluation metric that accurately model the user experience. In: SIGIR '04: Proceedings of the 27th annual international ACM SIGIR conference on Research and development in information retrieval, pp. 329–336. ACM, New York, NY, USA (2004)
50. McNee, S.M., Riedl, J., Konstan, J.A.: Making recommendations better: an analytic model for human-recommender interaction. In: CHI '06: CHI '06 extended abstracts on Human factors in computing systems, pp. 1103–1108. ACM, New York, NY, USA (2006)
51. McSherry, F., Mironov, I.: Differentially private recommender systems: building privacy into the netflix prize contenders. In: KDD '09: Proceedings of the 15th ACM SIGKDD international conference on Knowledge discovery and data mining, pp. 627–636. ACM, New York, NY, USA (2009)
52. Mobasher, B., Burke, R., Bhaumik, R., Williams, C.: Toward trustworthy recommender systems: An analysis of attack models and algorithm robustness. ACM Trans. Internet Technol. **7**(4), 23 (2007)
53. Murakami, T., Mori, K., Orihara, R.: Metrics for evaluating the serendipity of recommendation lists. New Frontiers in Artificial Intelligence **4914**, 40–46 (2008)
54. Nguyen, T.T., Kluver, D., Wang, T.Y., Hui, P.M., Ekstrand, M.D., Willemsen, M.C., Riedl, J.: Rating support interfaces to improve user experience and recommender accuracy. In: Proceedings of the 7th ACM Conference on Recommender Systems, RecSys '13, pp. 149–156. ACM, New York, NY, USA (2013)
55. O'Mahony, M., Hurley, N., Kushmerick, N., Silvestre, G.: Collaborative recommendation: A robustness analysis. ACM Trans. Internet Technol. **4**(4), 344–377 (2004)
56. Pfleeger, S.L., Kitchenham, B.A.: Principles of survey research. SIGSOFT Softw. Eng. Notes **26**(6), 16–18 (2001)
57. Pu, P., Chen, L.: Trust building with explanation interfaces. In: IUI '06: Proceedings of the 11th international conference on Intelligent user interfaces, pp. 93–100. ACM, New York, NY, USA (2006)
58. Pu, P., Chen, L., Hu, R.: A user-centric evaluation framework for recommender systems. In: Proceedings of the Fifth ACM Conference on Recommender Systems, RecSys '11, pp. 157–164. ACM, New York, NY, USA (2011)
59. Queiroz, S.: Adaptive preference elicitation for top-k recommendation tasks using gai-networks. In: AIAP'07: Proceedings of the 25th conference on Proceedings of the 25th IASTED International Multi-Conference, pp. 579–584. ACTA Press, Anaheim, CA, USA (2007)
60. Russell, M.L., Moralejo, D.G., Burgess, E.D.: Paying research subjects: participants' perspectives. Journal of Medical Ethics **26**(2), 126–130 (2000)
61. Salzberg, S.L.: On comparing classifiers: Pitfalls toavoid and a recommended approach. Data Min. Knowl. Discov. **1**(3), 317–328 (1997)
62. Sarwar, B., Karypis, G., Konstan, J., Reidl, J.: Item-based collaborative filtering recommendation algorithms. In: WWW '01: Proceedings of the 10th international conference on World Wide Web, pp. 285–295. ACM, New York, NY, USA (2001)

63. Sarwar, B., Karypis, G., Konstan, J., Riedl, J.: Analysis of recommendation algorithms for e-commerce. In: EC '00: Proceedings of the 2nd ACM conference on Electronic commerce, pp. 158–167. ACM, New York, NY, USA (2000)
64. Schein, A.I., Popescul, A., Ungar, L.H., Pennock, D.M.: Methods and metrics for cold-start recommendations. In: SIGIR '02: Proceedings of the 25th annual international ACM SIGIR conference on Research and development in information retrieval, pp. 253–260. ACM, New York, NY, USA (2002)
65. Shani, G., Chickering, D.M., Meek, C.: Mining recommendations from the web. In: RecSys '08: Proceedings of the 2008 ACM Conference on Recommender Systems, pp. 35–42 (2008)
66. Shani, G., Heckerman, D., Brafman, R.I.: An mdp-based recommender system. Journal of Machine Learning Research **6**, 1265–1295 (2005)
67. Shani, G., Rokach, L., Shapira, B., Hadash, S., Tangi, M.: Investigating confidence displays for top-*n* recommendations. JASIST **64**(12), 2548–2563 (2013)
68. Smyth, B., McClave, P.: Similarity vs. diversity. In: ICCBR, pp. 347–361 (2001)
69. Spillman, W., Lang, E.: The Law of Diminishing Returns. World Book Company (1924)
70. Steck, H.: Item popularity and recommendation accuracy. In: Proceedings of the Fifth ACM Conference on Recommender Systems, RecSys '11, pp. 125–132. ACM, New York, NY, USA (2011)
71. Steck, H.: Evaluation of recommendations: rating-prediction and ranking. In: Seventh ACM Conference on Recommender Systems, RecSys '13, Hong Kong, China, October 12–16, 2013, pp. 213–220 (2013)
72. Swearingen, K., Sinha, R.: Beyond algorithms: An hci perspective on recommender systems. In: ACM SIGIR 2001 Workshop on Recommender Systems (2001)
73. Van Rijsbergen, C.J.: Information Retrieval. Butterworth-Heinemann, Newton, MA, USA (1979)
74. Voorhees, E.M.: Overview of trec 2002. In: In Proceedings of the 11th Text Retrieval Conference (TREC 2002), NIST Special Publication 500-251, pp. 1–15 (2002)
75. Voorhees, E.M.: The philosophy of information retrieval evaluation. In: CLEF '01: Revised Papers from the Second Workshop of the Cross-Language Evaluation Forum on Evaluation of Cross-Language Information Retrieval Systems, pp. 355–370. Springer-Verlag, London, UK (2002)
76. Yao, Y.Y.: Measuring retrieval effectiveness based on user preference of documents. J. Amer. Soc. Inf. Sys **46**(2), 133–145 (1995)
77. Yilmaz, E., Aslam, J.A., Robertson, S.: A new rank correlation coefficient for information retrieval. In: Proceedings of the 31st Annual International ACM SIGIR Conference on Research and Development in Information Retrieval, SIGIR '08, pp. 587–594. ACM, New York, NY, USA (2008)
78. Zhang, M., Hurley, N.: Avoiding monotony: improving the diversity of recommendation lists. In: RecSys '08: Proceedings of the 2008 ACM conference on Recommender systems, pp. 123–130. ACM, New York, NY, USA (2008)
79. Zhang, Y., Callan, J., Minka, T.: Novelty and redundancy detection in adaptive filtering. In: SIGIR '02: Proceedings of the 25th annual international ACM SIGIR conference on Research and development in information retrieval, pp. 81–88. ACM, New York, NY, USA (2002)
80. Ziegler, C.N., McNee, S.M., Konstan, J.A., Lausen, G.: Improving recommendation lists through topic diversification. In: WWW 0́5: Proceedings of the 14th international conference on World Wide Web, pp. 22–32. ACM, New York, NY, USA (2005)

Chapter 9
Evaluating Recommender Systems with User Experiments

Bart P. Knijnenburg and Martijn C. Willemsen

9.1 Introduction

Traditionally, the field of recommender systems has evaluated the fruits of its labor using metrics of algorithmic accuracy and precision (see Chap. 8 for an overview of recommender systems evaluation practices). Netflix organized a million-dollar contest for just this goal of improving the accuracy of its movie recommendation algorithm [7]. In recent years, however, researchers have come to realize that the goal of a recommender system extends well beyond accurate predictions; its primary real-world purpose is to provide personalized help in discovering relevant content or items [72].

This has caused two important changes in the field. The first change was incited by McNee et al. [83] who argued that "being accurate is not enough" and that one should instead "study recommenders from a user-centric perspective to make them not only accurate and helpful, but also a pleasure to use" (p. 1101). McNee et al. suggest broadening the scope of research regarding the *outcomes* of the evaluation beyond accuracy measures. This suggestion has spawned a research area that evaluates recommender systems in online user experiments with user-centric evaluation metrics that span behaviors (e.g. user retention and consumption) as well as attitudes (e.g. usability, choice satisfaction, and perceived usefulness; cf. [67, 95]).

The author contributed to this chapter while he was at the University of California, Irvine.

B.P. Knijnenburg (✉)
Clemson University, Clemson, SC, USA
e-mail: bartk@clemson.edu

M.C. Willemsen
Eindhoven University of Technology, Eindhoven, The Netherlands
e-mail: m.c.willemsen@tue.nl

F. Ricci et al. (eds.), *Recommender Systems Handbook*,
DOI 10.1007/978-1-4899-7637-6_9

The second change is a broadening of the scope of research regarding the *system aspects* to investigate beyond just the algorithm of the recommender. In essence, recommender systems apply algorithms on user input with the goal of providing some kind of personalized output. This means that aside from the algorithm, there are two important interactive components to any recommender: the mechanism through which users provide their input, and the means by which they receive the system's output. Realizing the importance of these interactive components, McNee et al. [84] suggested that researchers should put more focus on the "Human-Recommender Interaction" and investigate these interactive components. Moreover, in his RecSys 2009 keynote Martin emphasized the importance of this endeavor: he argued that the interactive components of a recommender account for about 50 % of its commercial success, while he provocatively estimated that the algorithm accounts for only 5 % [81]. Indeed, research has shown that the preference elicitation mechanism and the presentation of recommendations have a substantial impact on users' acceptance and evaluation of recommender systems as well as their usage behavior (cf. [19, 67, 96]).

These two changes have gradually evolved the field to take broader perspective on the user experience of recommender systems [72]. However, the majority of current research on recommender systems is still primarily focused on creating better algorithms, and conducts offline machine learning evaluations instead of "live" user experiments. The contribution of that research is thus limited to claims about algorithmic accuracy and precision; without performing any user-centric evaluations it is difficult to extend these claims to the more user-centric objective of recommender systems: giving users a pleasant and useful personalized experience.

Proper evaluation of the user experience of a recommender system requires conducting a *user experiment*,[1] either in the form of a lab experiment or a randomized field trial (which includes—but also extends beyond—conventional A/B tests). This chapter of the Recommender System Handbook is meant as a guideline for students and researchers aspiring to conduct user experiments with their recommender systems, as well as for editors and reviewers of conferences and journals to evaluate manuscripts. To this end, this chapter will provide both theoretical and practical guidelines. The theoretical part starts with the description of the Knijnenburg et al. [67] User-Centric Evaluation Framework for Recommender Systems. We subsequently use this framework to highlight aspects of recommenders and their users that could be the object of study. We outline what has already been tested, and where gaps in the literature exist. In the practical part, we provide guidelines regarding all the steps involved in setting up, conducting and analyzing user experiments. The framework will be used there to motivate and illustrate our practical guidelines.

[1]We use the term "user experiment" to denote the use of experimental conditions and formal measurement as a means of testing theories about users interacting with recommender systems. This as opposed to "user studies", which are typically smaller observational studies used to iteratively improve the usability of a recommender system.

This chapter is meant as a practical primer; a succinct yet comprehensive introduction to user experiments, motivated by numerous examples of published recommender systems studies. The reader who is serious about conducting user experiments is encouraged to continue their learning process beyond this chapter. To this effect we have listed a number of excellent textbooks in the conclusion of this chapter.

9.2 Theoretical Foundation and Existing Work

An essential part of conducting a good experiment is to have a good *research model* (or descriptive theory, cf. [53]) of how the aspects under evaluation interact (see Sect. 9.3.1). Such models are usually based on a synthesis of formal theories and existing research, identifying the unknown parameters, and formulating testable hypotheses regarding these parameters. To add some structure to the process of theory development, it is helpful to conceptualize the interaction between users and recommenders within a theoretical framework. Several of such frameworks exist (cf. [84, 95]), but we choose to structure this chapter around the Knijnenburg et al. [67] User-Centric Evaluation Framework for Recommender Systems.

9.2.1 Theoretical Foundation: The Knijnenburg et al. Evaluation Framework

The Knijnenburg et al. [67] framework consists of two levels (see Fig. 9.1). The top level is a middle range "EP type" theory[2] of how users experience an interactive information system. A middle range theory is a theory about human behavior that is applicable in a specific but reasonably generic situation (in this case: in using an interactive information system). An "EP type" theory is a theory that can be used to explain (E) the described behavior and to predict (P) how users would behave under specific circumstances. The theory that comprises the top level of the Knijnenburg et al. framework combines[3] existing theories of attitudes and behaviors [2–4, 37], technology acceptance [26, 116], and user experience [46, 47]. Specifically, it describes how users' subjective interpretation (Subjective System Aspects, or SSA) of a system's critical features (Objective System Aspects) influences their

[2]See [45] for a taxonomy of different types of theory.

[3]Like Hassenzahl [46, 47], our framework describes the formation of experiences during technology use rather than the longer-term phenomenon of technology acceptance, but it extends this model to behavioral consequences using attitude-behavior theories [2–4, 37] (a theoretical structure that is prominent in technology acceptance models [26, 116]).

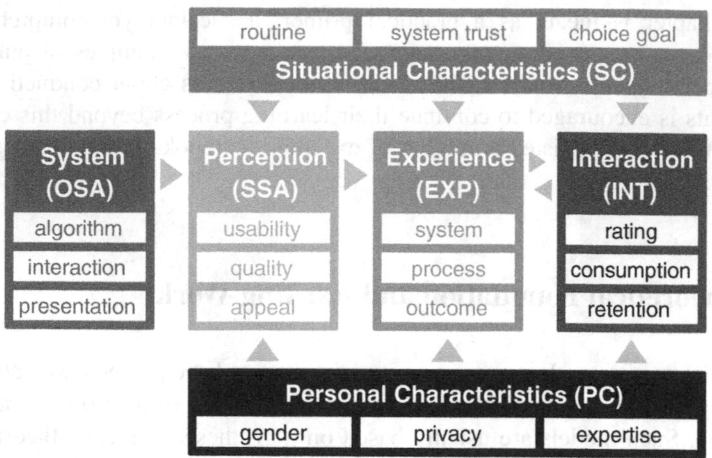

Fig. 9.1 An updated version of the User-Centric Evaluation Framework [67]

experience of (EXP) and interaction with (INT) a system. Note that the top level of the framework can potentially be applied beyond the field of recommender systems.

The lower level of the Knijnenburg et al. framework is a classification of recommender system related constructs under these higher level concepts (inspired by related analysis-type frameworks of recommender system aspects [84, 95, 122]). These constructs can be used to turn the top-level theory into models for specific recommender system evaluation studies. The combination of a top level theory and a lower level taxonomy makes our framework more actionable than [84] (because the EP type theory provides concrete suggestions for specific research hypotheses) and more generic than [95] (because the EP type theory is generative, which makes our framework more easily adaptable to new areas of recommender system research). The Knijnenburg et al. framework has been put to practice in several published and unpublished studies, so we will be able to illustrate many of our practical guidelines with examples from existing applications of this framework.

An updated version[4] of the Knijnenburg et al. [67] evaluation framework is displayed in Fig. 9.1. It represents the user-centric evaluation of recommender systems as six interrelated conceptual components:

Objective System Aspects (OSAs) As recommender systems are typically multi-faceted systems, their evaluation should be simplified by considering only a subset of all system aspects in each experiment. The Objective System Aspects (OSAs) are the aspects of the system that are currently being evaluated. The algorithm can be considered as an OSA, but also the input

[4]The paths from Personal and Situation Characteristics to Subjective System Aspects were added to the original framework (as presented in [67]) based on insights from various experiments with the framework.

(interaction) mechanisms (e.g. the rating scale used to provide feedback on recommendations) or output (presentation) mechanisms (e.g. the number of presented recommendations, or their layout).

Subjective System Aspects (SSAs) Although we are ultimately interested in the effects of OSAs on User Experience (EXP) and Interaction (INT), we need to consider Subjective System Aspects (SSAs) as mediating variables of these effects. SSAs are users' perceptions of the OSAs. SSAs are measured with questionnaires that participants are asked to complete after (or sometimes during) their interaction with the system (see Sect. 9.3.4). The measurement of SSAs is necessary because incremental advances in recommender system aspects (e.g. algorithms) are often small, and may go unnoticed. SSAs help establish whether users *perceive* a certain system aspect, independently of their *evaluation* of the aspect. For example, if an improved system does not lead to the expected increase in user satisfaction, the SSA "perceived recommendation quality" can be used to find out if users simply did not notice the improvement, or if they noticed it but did not really like it. SSAs mediate the effects of OSAs on EXP, thereby explaining how and why OSAs influence EXP, as well as increasing the robustness of this causal link.

User Experience (EXP) The User Experience factors (EXPs) are users' self-relevant evaluations of the qualities of the recommender system. User experience is also measured with questionnaires. Note that experience can relate to different aspects of system usage, namely the evaluation of the recommender system itself (e.g. perceived system effectiveness; system-EXP), the evaluation of the process of using the system (e.g. expressing preferences, and browsing or choosing recommended items; process-EXP), or the evaluation of the chosen items (e.g. choice satisfaction; outcome-EXP). It is important to make these distinctions, because different OSAs may influence different aspects of the experience.

Interaction (INT) The "final step" in the evaluation of a recommender system is the users' interaction with the system (INT). The interaction can be measured objectively by logging the users' clicks. Examples are: the number of recommendations inspected by the user, their rating feedback, and the time they spent using the recommender. Behavior grounds the subjective part of the evaluation in observable behavior. At the same time, the subjective components provide explanations for the (sometimes counterintuitive) observed behaviors.

Personal and Situational Characteristics (PCs and SCs) Although the main objective of most user experiments is to test the effects of OSAs on SSAs, EXPs and INTs, these outcomes can also be influenced by Personal Characteristics (e.g. domain knowledge; PCs) and Situational Characteristics (e.g. choice goals; SCs). PCs and SCs are typically measured by questionnaires,[5] and since they are beyond the influence of the system they can be measured before users interact with the system.

---

[5]In some cases PCs and SCs can be inferred from user behavior, e.g. observing the click-stream can tell us the market segment a user belongs to [44]. SCs can also be manipulated, e.g. by priming users to approach the recommender with either a concrete or abstract mindset [71, 120].

The evaluation framework can be used as a conceptual guideline for developing hypotheses. It can answer questions like:

Which EXP aspects is this OSA likely to influence? For example, an improved algorithm may influence users' evaluation of the recommendations (outcome-EXP), while a new preference elicitation method is likely to influence the perceived effectiveness of the recommendation process (process-EXP). Both may impact users' satisfaction with the system itself (system-EXP).

Which SSAs can be used to explain these effects? For example, certain algorithms may produce more accurate recommendations, while other algorithms may increase the diversity of the recommendations. Both may increase user satisfaction, but for different reasons.

Which PCs and SCs may moderate these effects? For example, users' liking of accurate or diverse recommendations may depend on their choice goals (SC). The most suitable preference elicitation method may depend on users' domain knowledge (PC).

Like most theories [2–4, 26, 37, 116], the theoretical top level of the Knijnenburg et al. [67] evaluation framework is *generative*: experimenters should see the relationships between OSA, SSA, EXP, and INT as a blueprint for their own descriptive models, but define their own set of measurable constructs and manipulations that are tailored to their experiment. This way, the framework can help answer questions that are specifically relevant to the system under evaluation.

9.2.2 Overview of Existing User-Centric Work and Promising Directions

The main contribution of any recommender system user experiment is an empirical evaluation of how selected OSAs influence the user experience, possibly moderated by PCs and SCs. To aid the selection of interesting research topics, we provide a brief overview of OSAs that have been studied in the past, and some promising directions for future work. When writing a related works section for their own papers, researchers are advised to also consult other existing overviews of user-centric research in recommender systems, such as the following:

- Xiao and Benbasat [122] provide a thorough overview and synthesis of 47 empirical user-centric studies on what they call "recommendation agents". Their synthesis consists of a conceptual model that served as inspiration for the Knijnenburg et al. [67] framework. The authors recently updated their overview [123].
- Pu et al. [96] provide an overview of the state-of-the-art of user-centric recommender systems studies. Their synthesis consists of a number of practical design guidelines for recommender systems developers (see also Chap. 10).

- Konstan and Riedl [72] put the rise of user-centric evaluation of recommender systems into a historical context. They focus on user-centric implications of technical aspects of recommender systems.

Here we discuss the most commonly researched OSAs of recommender systems. Envisioning a recommender system as a generic system that processes inputs to produce outputs, the main OSA categories are the input (preference elicitation), processing (algorithm) and output (recommendations and the presentation thereof). Our overview is meant for researchers who wish to evaluate the user experience of recommender systems. Researchers who wish to use recommender systems as a vehicle for researching aspects of human decision making are referred to Chap. 18 for a comprehensive overview.

9.2.2.1 Preference Elicitation Methods

The four most common methods recommender systems use to elicit preferences from users are rating scales, attribute weights, critiques, and implicit behavior. Rating scales are the most commonly employed method. They vary in granularity from binary (thumbs up/down), via the most common star ratings (5 stars or 10 half stars), to sliders (any number of steps). Research has shown that users behave differently depending on the used rating scale [42]. Users seem to prefer the 5-star and 10-half-star scales [15, 23, 28, 42, 106]. The more granular rating methods are more effortful, but also provide more information [60]. Regardless of the rating scale, user-ratings are often inaccurate [5, 100], and helping users with the rating task can increase their accuracy [87].

Preference elicitation via attribute weights originates from the field of decision analysis, where multi-attribute utility theory is used as a standard for rational decision-making [9]. Early work in this area shows that attribute-based recommenders result in better decisions and less effort compared to static browsing tools [48]. This benefit is moderated by domain knowledge: only experts are more satisfied with attribute-based recommenders and their outcomes; for novices, expressing preferences in terms of needs or examples tends to work better [65, 66, 98].

Another method to elicit preferences is example critiquing. In this method, users iteratively provide detailed feedback on example recommendations. Substantial user-centric work in this area (as summarized in [19]) shows that example critiquing systems save cognitive effort and increase decision accuracy. Moreover, aiding users by suggesting critiques seems to improve users' decision confidence [16]. On the other hand, Lee and Benbasat [77] show that a preference elicitation method that highlights trade-offs may increase users' trade-off difficulty.

A recommender system needs a certain number of ratings before it can produce accurate recommendations, but not all users may have rated that many items yet; this is the so-called "cold start problem". Implicit behavioral feedback such as browsing or purchase/consumption actions can be used to compute recommendations in such cases. In [67] we compared the use of explicit and implicit feedback to calculate recommendations. The results of this study showed that an implicit feedback recommender can provide higher-quality recommendations that result in a higher perceived system effectiveness and higher choice satisfaction. The results also showed that users perceived the explicit feedback-based recommendations to be more diverse, though, and diversity is another good quality of recommendation lists (cf. [120, 121, 126], see also Chap. 26). The best solution is thus to create a hybrid system that uses both explicit and implicit feedback. Koren et al. [73] show that such hybrid recommenders are usually more accurate than their implicit and explicit counterparts (see also Chap. 23). In [65] we show that hybrid recommenders are especially satisfying and effective for experts; for novices they seem to be too complex.

Another way to overcome the cold start problem is to encourage users to rate more items. Work on this topic shows that the best way to get users to rate more items is to show them the benefit of rating by presenting good recommendations early on in the interaction [33, 39, 68].

Future work could conduct a more comprehensive evaluation across the listed preference elicitation paradigms, or explore how the most suitable preference elicitation method depends not just on users' personal characteristics [65], but also on situational characteristics such as users' current mindset or choice goal.

9.2.2.2 Algorithms

As mentioned in the introduction, algorithms are often evaluated in an offline setting. More accurate algorithms are often assumed to result in higher quality recommendations and more effective systems, but this is not necessarily always the case. For example, McNee et al. [82] found that users rated their most accurate algorithm as least helpful, and Torres et al. [112] found that users were most satisfied with their least accurate algorithm. Despite the prevalent opinion that recommender systems research should move beyond offline evaluations to user-centric studies [72], surprisingly few research papers about new algorithmic solutions test the effect of the proposed algorithm on users' satisfaction (some exceptions are [25, 29, 31, 99]). Given the results of McNee et al. [82] and Torres et al. [112], we strongly suggest that algorithm developers test whether the accuracy improvements of their algorithms translate to a higher user satisfaction.

9.2.2.3 Recommendations and Their Presentation

The composition and presentation of the list of recommendations has a strong effect on the user experience. Choosing among top recommendations is a difficult task, and may lead to a phenomenon called "choice overload" [12]. Overcoming choice overload is one of the main challenges of research on the presentation of recommendations. Longer lists of recommendations may attract more attention [109], but are generally harder to choose from [6, 12]. Diversifying recommendations seems to be a good antidote against choice overload, because diversified lists are attractive even when short [120, 121, 126]. In fact, non-personalized diversified lists can be as attractive as personalized recommendations [67]. A steady stream of research has considered algorithmic solutions to diversifying recommendations [1, 76, 115, 124, 125]. More research needs to be done on whether these algorithmic solutions indeed result in *perceptibly* more diverse recommendations, and on whether these recommendations reduce choice overload and increase user satisfaction.

The *layout* of the recommendations on the screen determines the amount of attention users pay to each recommendation. In a vertical list, users pay more attention to the first few items than to items lower down the list [12], but this decay is much less when using a grid layout [18]. In a grid layout, items in the top-left of the grid are taken to be the most relevant [57]. Chen and Tsoi [20] show that if recommendations are divided over two pages, the items on the second page get very few clicks. Comparing a list, grid and pie (circular) layout for recommendations, they find a slight user preference for the pie layout. This layout does however take up much more space on the screen.

In many commercial recommender systems the recommendations are organized into distinct *categories*. Chen and Pu [17] have developed a "Preference-Based Organization Interface" that uses categories as a basis for critiquing. In their system, the primary category has the user's top recommendations, and each other category explores a trade-off. Hu and Pu [52] show that this kind of categorization increases the perceived diversity of the recommendations. Beyond this, the categorization of recommendations has not received much attention in academic research but consumer research literature [85, 103] suggests that categorization structures the user's choice task, and helps to overcome choice overload.

Another challenge for recommender systems is to *explain* their recommendations (see [40, 41, 110] for an overview). Explanations can be based on the preferences of similar users (e.g. "this item was rated highly by users similar to you"), similar items (e.g. "this is similar to other items you liked"), or attributes/keywords of interest (e.g. "this has attributes you prefer"). Explanations can be presented textually (e.g. as a number, keyword, text or tag cloud) or visually (e.g. as a histogram or pie chart). Research has found that users like explanations [50], and that they increase users' understanding of the recommendation process [41, 117], their trust in the quality of the recommendations, and the competence and benevolence of the system [24, 36, 119] (more on credibility and trust can be found in Chap. 20). This in turn increases their purchase intentions [118] and their intention to return to the system [94].

Which type of explanation works best? Research comparing different types of explanation strategies has found that explanations based on the preferences of similar users are persuasive: users tend to overestimate the quality of recommendations explained this way [10, 41, 50]. Item- and keyword-based explanations produce more accurate expectations [10, 41] and ultimately lead to more satisfaction [41, 108]. Finally, Pu and Chen demonstrate that carefully organizing the list of recommendations may also be perceived as an implicit explanation [94]. This type of explanation produces little perceived cognitive overhead.

Tintarev and Masthoff [111] explore the idea of personalizing explanations to the user. They show that users tend to like such personalized explanations, but that these may actually be less effective than generic explanations. Social recommenders that use a user's friends instead of anonymous nearest neighbors for recommendation purposes have an additional opportunity for explanation, as they can show how recommendations are linked to the preferences of the user's friends. In [62] we demonstrate that displaying such a "recommendation graph" increases the inspectability of the recommendations, and ultimately users' satisfaction with the system.

There is no doubt that explaining recommendations is beneficial for the user experience, because they help users to increase their understanding of the recommendation process. However, users can also use explanations to justify their choice among the presented recommendations, which could arguably reduce choice overload and increase their decision confidence (see Chap. 18). We reiterate the conclusion by Konstan and Riedl [72] and Tintarev and Masthoff [111] that future work should explore how explanations can help to reduce choice overload and otherwise improve users' decision-making.

Work on the presentation of recommendations generally considers variants of the conventional "Top-N" list of recommendations. Alternative uses of recommendations are becoming more prevalent in practice, though. Examples are "co-recommendations" ("Users who bought this also bought..." [89, 90]) and "smart defaults" (recommendations as default settings for yes/no or multiple-option decisions [61, 105]). The presentation of these types of recommendations has to date not been investigated in much detail.

9.3 Practical Guidelines

We now turn to the practical part of this chapter, where we provide guidelines regarding the different steps involved in recommender system user experiments. Section 9.3.1 (Research Model) deals with developing a research model and hypotheses for the experiment. Section 9.3.2 (Participants) discusses the recruitment of test users. Section 9.3.3 (Manipulations) covers the operationalization of hypotheses into different versions of the system and the process of randomly assigning participants to these versions. Section 9.3.4 (Measurement) explains how to measure and analyze subjective concepts like satisfaction with questionnaires. Section 9.3.5 (Statistical Evaluation), finally, explains how to statistically test the formulated hypotheses. The guidelines are illustrated with existing user-centric work in the recommender systems field where possible.

9.3.1 Research Model

The goal of a user experiment is to test the effect of some Objective System Aspect (OSA) on the user's Experience (EXP) and Interaction (INT). The Knijnenburg et al. [67] framework suggests that such effects are mediated by Subjective System Aspects (SSAs), and possibly moderated by Personal and Situational Characteristics (PCs and SCs). Before conducting the experiment, the specific constructs and their expected interrelations should be presented as a *research model* consisting of a set of testable hypotheses. Each hypothesis consists of an independent variable and a dependent variable. Hypotheses are predictions about how the independent variable influences the dependent variable (and optionally, how a moderating variable qualifies this effect).

9.3.1.1 Determining Which OSAs Will Be Tested

The first step in developing a research model is to determine which OSAs will be tested. In a typical experiment the OSAs are manipulated independent variables (see Sect. 9.3.3): their presence, operation or appearance is altered between different experimental conditions, but these conditions are exactly the same otherwise (similar to A/B testing). This concept of ceteris paribus ("all else remains the same") is important, because it allows the researchers to trace differences in outcomes between conditions back to the manipulated OSA. If aside from the manipulated OSA other aspects differ between conditions as well, then these aspects are said to be *confounded* with the OSA: it is then impossible to determine whether the OSA or any of these other aspects caused the difference in outcomes.

For example, in [68] we manipulated the algorithm by testing a system with an SVD algorithm against the same system that was altered to select random items as recommendations. The items were labeled as "recommendations" in both conditions. If we had given the items different labels in each condition (e.g. "random items" and "recommendations"), then the labeling would have been confounded with the algorithm itself. That is, if users judged the recommendations to have a higher quality, this could be either because they indeed had a higher quality, or because the "recommendations" label simply made users *think* that they had a higher quality. By having the same label for the random items, we ruled out the latter explanation.

9.3.1.2 Selecting Appropriate Outcome Measures (INT and EXP)

The second step in developing a research model is to select appropriate outcome measures (dependent variables). These are typically a combination of observed behaviors (INT) and questionnaire-based feedback (EXP). Although industry executives are typically most interested in objective outcomes that influence conversion rates (i.e. INT), there are reasons why the inclusion of EXP variables is beneficial for industry and academic researchers alike. First of all, users' behavior is often influenced by external factors (e.g. purchases may be gifts rather than a reflection of the user's taste; time on a page may be influenced by their Internet connection speed), so the effects of OSAs on INT are less robust than on EXP. More importantly, studies that test behavioral variables only (i.e. conventional A/B tests) can detect behavioral differences, but they often say very little about *how and why* the behavioral difference occurred. The explanation of behavioral effects is what drives scientific discovery and sound corporate decisions, and a carefully selected combination of EXP and INT variables can provide such explanations.

Knijnenburg et al. [68] provides a good example of the importance of including both EXP and INT variables in an experiment. Looking only at the behavioral outcomes of this study, one would come to the conclusion that the system with the SVD algorithm resulted in a shorter total viewing time and fewer clips clicked than the system with random recommendations. This result may be counterintuitive, until one includes perceived system effectiveness as a mediating EXP variable: The system with the SVD recommender is perceived as more effective, which manifests in less need for browsing, and hence a shorter viewing time and fewer clips clicked. Only after incorporating both EXP and INT variables were we able to explain that the SVD recommender system is indeed effective.

Experiments that measure EXP variables require that the researchers administer questionnaires, which limits the scale of such experiments compared to conventional A/B tests. As such, A/B tests can more effectively test the behavioral effects of a large number of OSAs simultaneously (these tests are more appropriately called "multivariate tests"). The optimal test plan therefore involves both: A/B tests are used to discover interesting effects, while user experiments with questionnaires can follow up these tests to explain how and why these interesting effects come about.

Generally speaking, a well-rounded research effort should use a combination of INT and EXP variables: the EXP variables explain differences in participants' behavior, while the INT variables "ground" the user experience in observable behavior.

9.3.1.3 Explaining the Effects with Theory and Mediating Variables (SSAs)

The inclusion of EXP variables alone is not always sufficient to explain how and why users are more satisfied or behave differently between conditions. Moreover, even if one can demonstrate that a certain OSA makes users more (or less) satisfied, there needs to be a compelling argument about whether this finding is generalizable, or rather just a one-off event. A *theory* that explains the hypothesized effects of a study more thoroughly can provide a sense of its generalizability [45]. In this regard, researchers can consult existing theories of user experience [46, 47], technology acceptance [26, 116], attitudes and behaviors [2–4, 37], or the theory of how users experience technology embedded in the Knijnenburg et al. [67] framework.

Just having a theory for the hypothesized effects is not enough, though; the experiment can (and should) confirm these theories. In the words of Iivari [53], this means translating the conceptual level theories to the descriptive level, which involves not only developing hypotheses regarding expected effects of the OSA on INT and EXP variables, but also hypotheses that explain *how and why* these effects come about.

A theory can also help in fine-tuning experimental conditions to rule out alternative explanations. For example, choice overload theory suggests that choice overload is moderated by the *diversity* of an item set, independent of its *quality* and *size* [34, 103]. In Willemsen et al. [120, 121] we therefore took care to increase the diversity of the recommendations without reducing their quality, and we manipulated the size of the item set independently from the diversity.

Another way to test theoretical explanations is to include mediating SSA variables in the research model. These SSAs serve both as a dependent variable (in the hypothesized effect of OSA → SSA) and an independent variable (in the hypothesized effect of SSA → EXP). For example, experiment FT4 in [67] tested two matrix factorization algorithms, one using explicit feedback (MF-E) and the other using implicit feedback (MF-I), against a system that recommended the (non-personalized) most popular items. The results ([67], Fig. 9) showed that both algorithms (OSAs) result in a more effective system (EXP) than the non-personalized version, but that the reason for this differs per algorithm. Specifically, the MF-I recommendations are perceived to have a higher quality (OSA → SSA), and these higher quality recommendations eventually result in a more effective system (SSA → EXP). On the other hand, the MF-E recommendations are perceived to be more diverse (OSA → SSA), and these diverse recommendations are perceived to have a higher quality (SSA → SSA) and thus result in a more effective system (SSA → EXP). The mediating SSAs explain the different reasons why each algorithm leads to a more effective system.

Finally, it may happen that the outcome variable does not differ between OSA conditions. In some cases, a theoretical examination may point out that different underlying effects could be counteracting each other, effectively cancelling out the total effect of the OSA. One can then demonstrate this theoretical phenomenon by measuring these underlying causes and including them as mediating variables in the research model.

For example, in Bollen et al. [12] we showed that there was no effect of the experimental conditions on overall choice satisfaction, but we were still able to demonstrate the phenomenon of "choice overload" by incorporating the mediating variables item set attractiveness and choice difficulty. Specifically, the results showed that more attractive item sets led to higher choice satisfaction, but that attractive sets were also more difficult to choose from, which in turn reduced choice satisfaction. We thereby demonstrated that good recommendations do not always lead to higher choice satisfaction due to choice overload. Similarly, Nguyen et al. [87] showed that the increased effectiveness of rating support by means of providing exemplars was limited, because it was counteracted by increased difficulty of using this type of support, compared to a baseline rating scale.

9.3.1.4 Include PCs and SCs Where Appropriate

The final step in developing a research model is to determine which PCs and SCs may influence the outcome variable. Incorporating these aspects into the experiment will increase the robustness of the results, so they should be considered even though they are typically beyond the influence of the system.

In some cases, the effect of the OSA on the outcome variable is hypothesized not to hold universally, but only for a specific type of user or in a specific situation. In that case, this PC or SC is said to *moderate* the effect of the OSA on the outcome. Measuring the PC or SC is then crucial to determine the true effect of the OSA.

For example, in [66] we argued that domain novices and experts use different strategies to make decisions, and that their ideal recommender system would therefore require different preference elicitation methods. Our results demonstrated that novices were indeed more satisfied with a case-based preference elicitation method, while experts were more satisfied with an attribute-based preference elicitation method.

9.3.1.5 Practical Tip: Never Formulate a "No Effect" Hypothesis

It is important to note that with every hypothesis comes a *null hypothesis*, which argues the absence of the effect described in the hypothesis. For example:

H_0: There is no difference in perceived recommendation quality between algorithm A and algorithm B.

H_1: Participants perceive the recommendation quality of algorithm A to be higher than algorithm B.

It is common practice in scientific writing to only state H_1 and leave the null hypothesis implicit. Statistical evaluations can never directly "prove" H_1, but they can support it by rejecting H_0 [38]. Importantly though, the absence of support for H_1 does not mean that H_0 is supported instead. In other words, if the aforementioned H_1 is not supported, one cannot claim that there is no difference in perceived recommendation quality between algorithm A and B, only that the current study did not find such an effect. In fact, providing support for the absence of an effect is very difficult to do statistically [11]. Researchers are therefore advised to never formulate a "no effect" hypothesis. Experiments should always be set up in such a way that differences (not equalities) between experimental conditions prove the underlying theory.

9.3.2 Participants

Finding participants to take part in the experiment is arguably the most time-consuming aspect of conducting a user experiment. Participant recruitment involves a tradeoff between gathering a large enough sample for statistical evaluation, and gathering a sample that accurately reflects the characteristics of the target population. Both considerations are discussed below.

9.3.2.1 Sampling Participants

Ideally, the sample of participants in the experiment should be an unbiased (random) sample of the target population. Creating a truly unbiased sample is practically impossible, but if one aspires to extrapolate the study results to real-world situations, then the participants should resemble the users (or potential users) of the tested system as closely as possible.

To avoid "sampling bias", certain practices should be avoided. For example, it is very tempting to ask colleagues, students or friends to participate, but these people will arguably have more knowledge of the field of study than an average user. They may even know what the experiment is about, which may unconsciously cause them to behave more predictably. Your colleagues and friends may also be more excited about the experiment, and they may want to please you, which may lead to socially desirable answers [91, 107]. It is better when participants are "blind", i.e. when they have no "special" connection to the researcher, the system, or the experiment.

Another practice to avoid is to post a link to the study to one's Facebook or Twitter account, and ask for reposts/retweets. Again, the first-degree participants will have a connection with the researcher, and should therefore be discarded. Participants who responded to the reposts/retweets will be more likely to resemble "blind" users, but extra checks should be performed on them since they are recruited via a "snowball sampling method" [32, 49, 78, 101].

Participant recruitment messages should be phrased carefully, because their framing may influence who participates in the study and how participants approach the tested system. It is generally better to give a generic description of the study to avoid bias. Specifically, the description should focus on the task ("Test this music recommender and answer a questionnaire") rather than the purpose of the study ("We are studying users' privacy perceptions of a recommender system"). Avoid technical terms, otherwise non-expert users may feel they are not knowledgeable enough to participate (note that even the term "recommender system" itself may not be common parlance for some potential users). Also make sure that the experiment works in all major browsers (even older versions) and on both laptops and tablets.

In some cases it makes sense to limit participation in the experiment to a specific subset of users, especially when some users cannot be given a meaningful experience. For example, in [62] we tested the inspectability and control of social recommenders using TasteWeights, a music recommender that uses overlap between Facebook users' music likes and their friends' music likes to calculate recommendations. We limited participation in this experiment to Facebook users with sufficient overlap between their own music likes and those of their friends. Users with insufficiently overlapping profiles were asked to either add more music likes or leave the study. We argued that this was admissible because a real system would likely do something similar. At the same time though, this meant that our conclusions would only hold for eligible users, and not for the population at large.

9.3.2.2 Determining the Sample Size

User experiments need a reasonable sample size (often reported as *N*) to allow robust statistical evaluation of the hypotheses. Increasing the number of participants increases the statistical power of the experiment. Statistical power is the likelihood of detecting an effect of certain size in a sample, given that the effect indeed exists in the population. To determine the required sample size, researchers should perform a *power analysis* [22, 35] using an estimate (based on previous work) of the expected effect size of the hypothesized effects and an adequate power level (usually 85 %). In recommender systems research manipulations typically have small effects (causing differences of about 0.2–0.3 standard deviations in the dependent variables) and occasionally medium-sized effects (differences of around 0.5 standard deviations). To detect a small effect (0.3 *SD*) with a power of 85 % in a between-subjects experiment, 201 participants are needed *per experimental condition*. To detect a medium-sized effect (0.5 *SD*), 73 participants are needed per condition. Within-subjects experiments need far fewer participants: 102 to detect small effects, and 38 to test medium-sized effects. Note, though, that there are additional sample size requirements for advanced statistical procedures like Factor Analysis (see Sect. 9.3.4.2) and Structural Equation Modeling (see Sect. 9.3.5.3).

The results of "underpowered" studies should be mistrusted, even if they are statistically significant. Due to low power, it is very likely that the experimenters simply "got lucky" and found a spurious effect [88]. And even if the reported effects are real, the effect sizes are inevitably overstated. Moreover, a low *N* means that the study may not have an inductive base that is wide enough to generalize the findings to the entire population, because small samples are likely to be biased.

For example, one of the first user-centric evaluations of a recommender system, conducted by Sinha and Swearingen [104], employs only 19 participants. Even though the authors find some significant results, the study is severely underpowered so the conclusions cannot be generalized beyond this specific sample: the large effect sizes reported are likely to be much smaller (if not absent) in the population.

9.3.2.3 Practical Tip: Run Your Studies on a Crowd-Sourcing Platform

In the past, participants were often recruited through volunteer panels painstakingly built by universities, or through expensive consumer research panels managed by marketing firms. This has changed with the rise of classified advertisements and crowd-sourcing websites such as Craigslist and Amazon Mechanical Turk. Craigslist allows researchers to post user experiments in various cities under Jobs > Etcetera, and is very convenient for creating a geographically balanced sample. Amazon Mechanical Turk[6] is often used for very small tasks, but Turk workers appreciate more elaborate survey studies. A benefit of Mechanical Turk is that it has anonymous payment facilities. Requesters can set certain criteria for workers that are allowed to participate, and experience has shown that it is good practice to restrict participants to U.S. workers with a high reputation [58, 92].

In our experience, the demographics of Craigslist and Mechanical Turk participants reflect the general Internet population, with Craigslist users being a bit higher educated and more wealthy. Turk workers are less likely to complain about tedious study procedures, but are also more likely to cheat [30]. Ample attention and quality checks can prevent cheaters from affecting the results. It is good practice to include a contact email address as well as an open feedback item in the study to catch unexpected problems with the experiment.

9.3.3 Experimental Manipulations

In a typical user experiment, one or more OSAs are manipulated into two or more experimental conditions following the ceteris paribus principle (see Sect. 9.3.1). OSAs can be manipulated in various ways. One can turn the OSA on or off (e.g. display predicted ratings or not), test different versions of the OSA (e.g. implicit versus explicit preference elicitation), or test several levels of the OSA (e.g. display 5, 10 or 20 recommendations). This section explains how to create meaningful experimental conditions, and how to randomly assign participants to them.

9.3.3.1 Selecting Conditions to Test

The goal of many user experiments is to demonstrate the superiority of some new invention: a new algorithm, preference elicitation method, or recommendation display technique. In such experiments, the condition with the new invention (called the *treatment* condition) should be tested against a reasonable *baseline* condition. A baseline should be included even when several treatment conditions are compared against each other, because the baseline condition links the study conditions to the status quo in recommender systems research.

Selecting a baseline can be difficult. For example, one could compare a recommender system against a non-personalized system, but the results of such an unbalanced comparison are usually unsurprising [114]. On the other hand, recommender systems are definitely not always better than their non-personalized variant, so a comparison with a non-personalized system may very well be justified when

[6]Mechanical Turk is currently only available for researchers in the United States, but various alternatives for non-US researchers exist.

testing a recommender in a new domain [21]. Another option is to test against the state-of-the-art (e.g. what has proven to be the best algorithm, preference elicitation method, or recommendation display technique in previous work).

Not all manipulations consist of a specific baseline and treatment condition. Sometimes (especially when the experiment focuses on the users' interaction with the recommender system rather than some new invention) there is no accepted baseline. A range of plausible conditions should then be considered in a way that maximizes the opportunity for the effect to occur, while staying within the realm of plausibility. For example, testing a recommendation list length of 5 versus 300 recommendations is likely to produce a choice overload effect, but finding choice overload in lists of more plausible lengths (e.g. 20 items) is practically much more useful. Making the manipulation too subtle (e.g. testing lists of 5 versus 6 items) may not produce a choice overload effect, or the effect may be so small that many more participants are needed to detect it.

9.3.3.2 Including Multiple Manipulations

The simplest user experiment includes a single manipulation with two experimental conditions. One can also create multiple experimental conditions per manipulation, e.g. when manipulating recommendation list length one can test lengths of 5, 10 and 20. It is also possible to manipulate multiple OSAs in a single experiment, and this is especially interesting when these OSAs are expected to have an *interaction effect* on the outcome variables. Interaction effects occur when a certain manipulation has an effect in certain condition(s) of the other manipulation, but no effect (or the opposite effect) in the other condition(s) of the other manipulation.

For example, in [120] we showed that high-diversity recommendations were perceived as more attractive, were easier to choose from, and led to higher system satisfaction than low-diversity recommendations, but only for short recommendation lists (5 recommendations). In longer lists, there was no difference between high- and low-diversity recommendations. We concluded that giving users recommendation lists that are both short *and* diverse could reduce choice overload.

When multiple OSAs are considered simultaneously like in the example above, these OSAs should be manipulated independently, or *orthogonally* by creating an instance of the system for each possible combination of conditions. The example above considered a 2-by-3 experiment (2 levels of diversity, 3 list lengths), which resulted in 6 experimental conditions.

9.3.3.3 Setting Up Between-Subjects or Within-Subjects Randomization

There are essentially three ways in which participants can be assigned to experimental conditions. In a *between-subjects* experiment, participants are randomly assigned to one of the experimental conditions. A benefit of between-subjects experiments is that the manipulation remains hidden from the participant, since each participant sees only one condition. This also makes the experiment more realistic, because users of real systems usually also only see a single version of the system. The averages of outcome variables are compared between conditions to see if the OSA had an effect on the outcomes. By assigning participants to conditions randomly, any differences between participants are leveled out. These differences can still cause random fluctuations in the outcomes, though, which is why between-subjects experiments typically need a larger N to attain an adequate level of statistical power.

Our study on different interfaces for an energy-saving recommender [65] is a good example of a between-subjects experiment. In the experiment different preference elicitation methods are tested, and users' satisfaction with the chosen energy-saving measures is an important outcome variable in the experiment. Having participants go through the same process of choosing energy-saving measures several times would have been rather weird, and users would have been able to guess the purpose of the different preference elicitation methods, which could have affected the results. With 5 conditions and a number of moderating PCs, the 147 participants recruited for this study were a bare minimum, though.

In a *sequential within-subjects* experiment, participants interact with both experimental conditions, one at a time. A benefit of within-subjects experiments is that differences in outcomes can be compared for each participant, which effectively eliminates the between-participant variability. As a result, fewer participants are needed to attain an adequate level of statistical power. A downside is that participants may be able to guess the experimental manipulation, and that repeating the same experiment several times may feel unnatural. Moreover, participants may react differently the second time they walk through the experiment. Randomizing the order in which participants see the conditions prevents the order from becoming confounded with the condition in the overall analysis.

In [121] we provide a good example of a within-subjects manipulation. In that study we tested three levels of diversification of the recommendations. The three different recommendation lists were presented in random order. Other than containing different items, the lists showed no apparent differences, so it was not possible for participants to guess the purpose of the study. Moreover, the presented lists were sufficiently different that the task of selecting an item from the list did not feel repetitive. Due to the within-subjects setup, the study was able to detect subtle differences between conditions. The study additionally manipulated the list length between-subjects, but no differences between length conditions (or interactions with diversification) were found.

Pu and Chen [94] also use a within-subjects manipulation, to test two different presentation techniques for recommendations. Each participant completes two tasks, one with each presentation technique. To avoid repetitiveness, the tasks involve different recommendation domains (digital cameras and notebooks). The presentation order of domains and techniques are manipulated between-subjects in a 2-by-2 setup; this cancels out any order- and task-effects. They then compare the presentation techniques using within-subjects tests.

In a *simultaneous within-subjects* experiment, participants experience all conditions at the same time. This allows participants to compare the different conditions and choose which one they like best. This again reduces between-participant variability, and also avoids order effects. Note though that the position of experimental conditions should be randomized, because we do not want to confound condition with position on the screen. The advantage of this method is that it can detect very subtle differences between conditions. The downside is that showing two conditions simultaneously is obviously a far cry from a realistic usage scenario.

As an example of a simultaneous within-subjects experiment, Ghose et al. [43] considered a novel ranking algorithm for a hotel and travel search site based on crowd-sourced content. Their study pairs the proposed algorithm with several different baseline algorithms. Each pair is tested as a simultaneous within-subjects experiment, where the two rankings produced by the proposed algorithm and the baseline algorithm are presented side-by-side, and users choose which ranking they prefer. The results show that their proposed algorithm is significantly preferred over 13 different baselines in six different cities. On average, twice as many participants prefer the recommendations of the proposed algorithm to the baseline.

Ekstrand et al. [31] also conducted a simultaneous within-subject design, and they chose this design because they were interested in detecting subtle differences between two recommendation lists produced by common algorithms (user-user, item-item and SVD). Like Ghose et al. [43] Users were asked which list they preferred, but also to indicate perceived *differences between* the lists in terms of the relative satisfaction, novelty and diversity. Importantly, Ekstrand et al. were able to link these perceived differences to objective measures of recommendation quality (e.g., perceived novelty was predicted by popularity rank). The results show that novelty (which was highest for the user-user algorithm) had a negative effect on satisfaction and preference for a list, whereas diversity showed a positive effect.

Increased realism is the main reason why between-subjects experiments are more appropriate than within-subjects experiments in most recommender system studies. Note, however, that even a between-subjects experiment is not completely natural: participants know that they are part of an experiment, and may therefore behave differently. This is called the *Hawthorne effect* [75]. In experiments that involve real systems, the Hawthorne effect can be detected by comparing the behavior of participants in (the baseline condition of) the experiment with the behavior of participants in the real system (or in an A/B test). If behaviors are substantially different, this is likely due to the Hawthorne effect.

9.3.3.4 Practical Tip: Think Big, Start Small

Designing experimental manipulations often involves difficult trade-offs. With several orthogonal manipulations with multiple variants each, the number of experimental conditions will grow exponentially. Since the number of participants needed to attain a certain level of statistical power grows linearly with the number of conditions, it is advisable to keep the number of conditions low.

The best strategy is therefore to think big, but start small: write down all possible versions of all OSAs that are relevant to the study in an experiment plan, but then start investigating the manipulation that seems most likely to cause an effect. If this experiment indeed detects the effect, subsequent experiments can be conducted to test different levels of the manipulation, or to include additional manipulations that may moderate (i.e. interact with) the existing effect.

In [16], for example, Chen and Pu identified several OSAs that may influence the effectiveness and usability of critiquing-based recommender systems: the number of recommendations presented in the first round of preference elicitation, the number of alternatives presented after each round of critiquing, and whether the user initiates the critiquing or the system suggests critiques (for both unit critiques and compound critiques). They systematically explored these parameters in a series of 2-condition experiments. By keeping the setup of the experiments consistent, they were even able to make comparisons across experiments.

Consistent with the "think big, start small" mantra, it is in some cases perfectly acceptable to simplify a system to increase experimental control. For example, the original TasteWeights system [14] allows you to inspect connections between liked items, friends, and recommendations, and control the weights of both liked items and friends. In our user experiment of this system [62] we wanted to test the influence of these features separately, so we split the interaction into two steps: a control step and an inspection step. This allowed us to manipulate the control and inspection OSAs independently, which resulted in a much "cleaner" experimental design.

9.3.4 Measurement

In this section we present best practices for measuring perceptions (SSAs), experiences (EXPs) and personal and situational characteristics (PCs and SCs) using questionnaires. Most importantly, we give the reader a practical example of performing a Confirmatory Factor Analysis (CFA) using MPlus,[7] a state-of-the-art statistical software package, and Lavaan[8] a package for R that has many of the same features.

9.3.4.1 Creating Measurement Scales

Due to their subjective nature, measuring perceptions, experiences, and personal and situational characteristics is not as easy as it may seem. Whereas objective traits can usually be measured with a single question (e.g. age, income), this is not

[7]http://www.statmodel.com/.

[8]http://lavaan.ugent.be/.

advisable for subjective concepts. Single-item measurements such as "On a scale from 1 to 5, how much did you like this system?" are said to lack *content validity*: each participant may interpret the item differently. For example, some may like the system because of its convenience, others may like it because of its ease of use, and again others may like it because the recommendations are accurate. These different interpretations reduce the precision and conceptual clarity of the measurement.

A better approach is to create measurement scales consisting of multiple items[9]; at least 3 but preferably 5 or more. This is a delicate process that usually involves multiple iterations of testing and revising items. It is advisable to first develop around 10–15 items and then reduce it to 5–7 through discussions with domain experts and comprehension pre-tests with test subjects. One to two additional items may still be discarded during the analysis of the actual study results.

The items in most user experiments are phrased as statements (e.g. "The system was easy to use") to which participants are asked to express their agreement on a 5- or 7-point scale (from "strongly disagree" to "strongly agree"). Studies have shown that participants find such items easy to answer. There are a few additional tips for designing good questionnaire items:

- Invest a lot of time in deciding upon a clear definition of the construct to be measured, and check for each item whether it fits the construct definition.
- Include both positively and negatively phrased items. This will make questionnaires less leading, and allows one to explore the flipside of the construct. It also helps to filter out participants who do not carefully read the items. However, avoid the word "not", because it is too easily overlooked.
- Study participants may not have a college degree, so their reading level may be low. Use simple words and short sentences to aid comprehension. Like with the recruitment message, try to avoid technical terms.
- Avoid double-barreled questions. Each item should measure only one thing at a time. For example, if a participant found the system fun but not very useful, they would find it hard to answer the question "The system was useful and fun."

As mentioned, it is a good idea to pre-test the questionnaire items with experts; they can give advice on how to accurately define the concept to be measured, and on whether the proposed questionnaire items cover all aspects of the concept. Furthermore, comprehension pre-tests can be conducted to test how well participants understand the questionnaire items. A comprehension pre-test invites participants to read the questionnaire items aloud and to explain their reasoning while answering the questions. Their think-aloud answers can highlight questionnaire items that are unclear or interpreted incorrectly.

[9]Or, multiple measurement scales for the different constructs (e.g. system satisfaction, ease of use, and recommendation quality), each measured with multiple items.

9.3.4.2 Establishing Construct Validity

Once a set of items has been developed that accurately reflects the concept to be measured (i.e. content validity is established), the next step is to establish *construct validity*, i.e. to make sure that the items comprise a robust and valid measurement scale. For the purpose of statistical analysis, each multi-item measurement scale has to be turned into single variable. Summing the item scores may seem like the most straightforward way of doing this, but Confirmatory Factor Analysis (CFA) is a more sophisticated solution that not only creates the measurement variable but also tests some of the preconditions for construct validity along the way.

Listings 9.1 and 9.2 show example input of a CFA as ran in MPlus and Lavaan. The output of these tools is very similar, so we present it for MPlus only (Listing 9.3). The example CFA is based on an experiment with a social network based music recommender system [62]. This system employs an innovative graph-based interface that shows how the users' Facebook music "likes" overlap with their friends' music "likes", and how these friends' other music "likes" are in turn used to create a set of recommendations. In the graph, users can trace back each recommendation to the friends that "liked" that item, and to the overlapping "likes" that caused these friends to be part of the user's nearest-neighborhood. We argued that this graph would provide a good justification for the recommendations, thereby increasing the perceived recommendation quality (`quality`) and the understandability of the recommender system (`underst`). Moreover, we allowed users to control either the weights of their "likes" or the weights of their friends, and we argued that this would influence their perceived control (`control`). Finally, we argued that perceived recommendation quality, understandability, and control would ultimately increase users' satisfaction with the system (`satisf`).

The CFA validates the four subjective measurement scales of the experiment. Each scale is represented by a latent factor, with each item loading on its designated scale (MPlus: lines 8–11, Lavaan: lines 2–5). The output shows the loadings of the items on the factors (lines 1–30), which are proportional to the extracted variance (lines 42–67). The factors may be correlated with each other (lines 32–40). The solution has no standard scale, so we include code (MPlus: line 12, Lavaan: lines 6–9) to give the factors a standard deviation of 1 and a mean of 0.[10] We also declare all items as ordered categorical (MPlus: line 6, Lavaan: line 12), because they are measured on a 5-point scale. Otherwise, the items would be treated an interval scale, which would assume that the difference between "completely disagree" (1) and "somewhat disagree" (2) is the same as the difference between "neutral" (3) and "somewhat agree" (4). MPlus and Lavaan model ordered categorical variables in a way that does not make this assumption.

---

[10] MPlus and Lavaan use a different parameterization by default by fixing the loading of the first item to 1. We free up these loadings by including an asterisk after (MPlus) or `NA*` before (Lavaan) the first item of each factor. This alternative solution conveniently standardizes the factor scores.

Listing 9.1 CFA input, MPlus

```
DATA: FILE IS twc.dat;   !specify the data file
VARIABLE:  !list the variable names (columns in the data file)
 names are s1 s2 s3 s4 s5 s6 s7 q1 q2 q3 q4 q5 q6
  c1 c2 c3 c4 c5 u1 u2 u3 u4 u5 cgraph citem cfriend;
 usevariables are  s1-u5;   !specify which vars are used
 categorical are s1-u5;   !specify which vars are categorical
MODEL:  !specify each factor as [factorname] by [vars]
 satisf  by s1* s2-s7;   !satisfaction
 quality by q1* q2-q6;   !perceived recommendation quality
 control by c1* c2-c5;   !perceived control
 underst by u1* u2-u5;   !understandability
 satisf-underst@1;   !set the std. dev. of each factor to 1
```

Listing 9.2 CFA input, Lavaan (R package)

```
model <- '   #specify each factor as [factorname] =~ [vars]
 satisf  =~ NA*s1+s2+s3+s4+s5+s6+s7  #satisfaction
 quality =~ NA*q1+q2+q3+q4+q5+q6   #perceived rec. quality
 control =~ NA*c1+c2+c3+c4+c5   #perceived control
 underst =~ NA*u1+u2+u3+u4+u5   #understandability
 satisf  ~~ 1*satisf   #set the std. dev. of each factor to 1
 quality ~~ 1*quality
 control ~~ 1*control
 underst ~~ 1*underst
';
fit <- sem(model, data=twc,   #specify the dataset
 ordered=names(twc));   #specify which vars are categorical
summary(fit, rsquare=TRUE);   #produce model fit and R^2 values
```

Listing 9.3 CFA output

```
MODEL RESULTS
                                                          Two-Taile
                    Estimate       S.E.  Est./S.E.     P-Value
 SATISF    BY
    S1                 0.887      0.018      49.604      0.000
    S2                -0.885      0.018     -48.935      0.000
    S3                 0.770      0.029      26.982      0.000
    S4                 0.821      0.025      32.450      0.000
    S5                 0.889      0.018      50.685      0.000
    S6                 0.788      0.031      25.496      0.000
    S7                -0.845      0.022     -38.426      0.000
 QUALITY   BY
    Q1                 0.950      0.013      72.837      0.000
    Q2                 0.949      0.013      73.153      0.000
    Q3                 0.942      0.012      77.784      0.000
    Q4                 0.805      0.033      24.332      0.000
    Q5                -0.699      0.042     -16.700      0.000
    Q6                -0.774      0.040     -19.428      0.000
```

```
 CONTROL  BY
    C1                   0.711       0.038      18.653      0.000
    C2                   0.855       0.024      35.667      0.000
    C3                   0.906       0.022      41.704      0.000
    C4                   0.722       0.037      19.276      0.000
    C5                  -0.425       0.056      -7.598      0.000
 UNDERST  BY
    U1                  -0.568       0.048     -11.745      0.000
    U2                   0.879       0.019      46.539      0.000
    U3                   0.748       0.031      24.023      0.000
    U4                  -0.911       0.020     -46.581      0.000
    U5                   0.995       0.014      70.251      0.000
 QUALITY  WITH
    SATISF               0.686       0.033      20.541      0.000
 CONTROL  WITH
    SATISF              -0.760       0.028     -26.962      0.000
    QUALITY             -0.648       0.040     -16.073      0.000
 UNDERST  WITH
    SATISF               0.373       0.049       7.581      0.000
    QUALITY              0.292       0.059       4.932      0.000
    CONTROL             -0.396       0.051      -7.736      0.000

R-SQUARE
    Observed                      Residual
    Variable         Estimate     Variance
    S1                   0.788       0.212
    S2                   0.783       0.217
    S3                   0.593       0.407
    S4                   0.674       0.326
    S5                   0.790       0.210
    S6                   0.622       0.378
    S7                   0.714       0.286
    Q1                   0.903       0.097
    Q2                   0.901       0.099
    Q3                   0.888       0.112
    Q4                   0.648       0.352
    Q5                   0.488       0.512
    Q6                   0.599       0.401
    C1                   0.506       0.494
    C2                   0.731       0.269
    C3                   0.820       0.180
    C4                   0.521       0.479
    C5                   0.180       0.820
    U1                   0.322       0.678
    U2                   0.772       0.228
    U3                   0.560       0.440
    U4                   0.831       0.169
    U5                   0.990       0.010
```

As mentioned earlier, an advantage of using CFA over simply summing the item scores is that it can help establish the construct validity of the measurement scales. Specifically, CFA can be used to establish convergent and discriminant validity. Convergent validity determines whether the items of a scale measure a single construct (i.e. that the scale is not a combination of multiple constructs, or simply a collection of items with no common ground), while discriminant validity determines whether two scales indeed measure two separate constructs (i.e. that two scales are not so similar that they actually measure the same construct).

Convergent validity is said to hold when the average variance extracted (AVE) from the items measuring the factor is larger than 0.50. Beyond that, a higher AVE indicates more precise measurement. The AVE can be calculated by averaging the R^2 values for all items of a factor (e.g., lines 54–60 for `satisf` and lines 61–66 for `quality`). The AVE can be improved by iteratively removing items with low loadings. Doing this for the presented data removes items `C5`, `U1` and `U3` from the model, respectively. Bear in mind that at least three items should remain per factor, because a factor with only two items has no free parameters for estimation. Generally speaking, more items provide a better definition of the construct, and aiming for 4–5 items per construct is good practice.

In some cases convergent validity does not hold because a factor actually measures more than one construct. For example, in [63] we found that information disclosure to an app recommender system actually consisted to two correlated factors: demographics disclosure and context data disclosure. If there exists some uncertainty about the factor structure, an Exploratory Factor Analysis (EFA) can be used to discover the correct factor structure.[11] EFA initially makes no assumptions about which items load on which factors, but tries to find a "clean" factor structure (with each item loading on one of the factors) that best fits the data. In [64] we employ this technique to discover the various dimensions of information disclosure in three different datasets. We first run several EFAs with an increasing number of factors to determine the optimal number of dimensions (looking at fit statistics and the conciseness of the model). Then we inspect the model to determine the optimal factor structure, and conduct a CFA to generate the final measurement model.

Discriminant validity is called into question when two scales are too highly correlated (i.e. when the correlation is higher than the square root of the AVE of either of the two factors). In that case the scales measure essentially the same thing, which means that they can be combined, or that one of the scales can be discarded. For example, in FT2 of [67] we originally tried to measure separate factors for perceived usefulness and fun. These factors were however so highly correlated that we ended up integrating them into a single factor.

There is no consensus on the sample size needed for CFA, but 100 participants seems to be a bare minimum, or 200 when unvalidated factors are tested [79]. Larger CFAs probably require even more participants: a rule of thumb is to have at least five participants per questionnaire item.

---

[11]Moreover, even if you are more or less certain about the factor structure of a CFA model, it pays to consult the *modification indices* of the model. The use of modification indices and CFA goes beyond the current chapter, but is thoroughly explained in Kline's [59] practical primer on Structural Equation Models.

9.3.4.3 Practical Tip: Use Existing Scales

Developing measurement scales from scratch is a time-consuming activity. Researching new phenomena often calls for specialized measurement scales, so this effort is in many cases unavoidable. A good tip is to look for related measurement scales and adapt them to the experiment at hand. For example, in [70] we developed scales for privacy concerns and protection as system- and provider-specific versions of existing scales. Surprisingly little scale development work has been done in the Human-Computer Interaction field; the Management Information Systems field is a much better source for related scales.

Most experiments also include some more general constructs that can be copied verbatim from existing work (this is considered good practice, not plagiarism). Two sources for existing scales related to recommender systems are the Knijnenburg et al. [67] framework paper and the ResQue framework developed by Pu et al. [95]. In Knijnenburg et al. [67] we include scales for the following concepts:

- Perceived recommendation quality (SSA)
- Perceived recommendation accuracy (SSA)
- Perceived recommendation variety (SSA)
- Perceived system effectiveness (and fun) (EXP)
- Choice Difficulty (EXP)
- Choice Satisfaction (EXP)
- Effort to use the system (EXP)
- Intention to provide feedback (INT)
- General trust in technology (PC)
- System-specific privacy concern (SC)

Pu et al. [95] include scales for the following concepts (classification ours, only scales with more than two items are included):

- Interface adequacy (SSA)
- Interaction adequacy (SSA)
- Control (SSA)
- Perceived usefulness (EXP)
- Confidence and trust (EXP)
- Use Intentions (INT)

Despite the fact that the measurement properties of these scales have been tested before, it is still wise to perform factor analysis on new experimental data to make sure that the constructs are robustly measured in the context of the new experiment.

9.3.5 Statistical Evaluation

Once the validity of measurements is established and scales have been constructed, the next step is to statistically test the formulated hypotheses. Note that the practice of statistical evaluation is continuously evolving, developing tests that are ever stronger and more robust. One of the most prominent changes is the transition from piecewise statistical testing to integrative approaches that evaluate entire research models and provide simultaneous tests of all hypothesized effects.

As most scholars have been trained in piecewise statistical testing (primarily t-tests, ANOVAs, and regressions), we will briefly discuss this approach first, but assume that the reader is already familiar with the mechanics of conducting such tests. Instead, we will focus mainly on the assumptions that such tests make about the data, and the consequences when these assumptions are violated. Subsequently we will discuss the integrative approach in more detail by giving the reader a practical example of testing a Structural Equation Model (SEM) in MPlus and Lavaan.

9.3.5.1 Piecewise Statistical Testing: T-tests, ANOVAs, and Regressions

Most researchers perform piecewise tests of their hypotheses, which means that they perform a separate test of each dependent variable. The dependent variable is typically a continuous variable that is either an observed behavior (INT) or a measured construct (SSA or EXP). For measured constructs, individual item scores are transformed into a scale score, either by saving the factor scores from the CFA or by simply summing the item scores (after establishing construct validity with a CFA). The independent variables can either be manipulated OSAs (i.e. the experimental conditions), continuous variables (SSA, EXP or INT), or both.

The difference between two experimental conditions (e.g., the effect of a manipulated OSA on a continuous outcome) can be tested with a t-test. For between-subject manipulations (see Sect. 9.3.3), one uses an independent (2-sample) t-test. For within-subjects manipulations, one should use a paired (1-sample) t-test.

The main outcome of a t-test is the t-statistic and its p-value; a smaller p-value signifies more evidence against the null-hypothesis. We typically reject the null hypothesis at $p < 0.05$. It is important to also look at the actual difference in the dependent variable between the experimental conditions: does this difference signify a substantial effect? For example, the difference between spending \$150 and \$151 in an e-commerce recommender may not be substantial enough to be practically relevant, especially if that difference is caused by a computationally expensive new recommendation algorithm.

The difference between more than two conditions can be tested with an ANOVA (or a repeated measures ANOVA in case of a within-subjects design). The ANOVA test produces an F-statistic; its p-value signifies evidence against the null hypothesis that the dependent variable has the same value in all conditions. When this "omnibus" test is significant, it is usually followed up by testing specific conditions against each other.

Multiple manipulations can be tested simultaneously with a factorial ANOVA. Factorial ANOVA tests exist for between-subjects, within-subjects and mixed (both within- and between-subjects) experiments. The factorial ANOVA will provide test statistics for each manipulation as well as the interaction between the manipulations.

Due to the complexity of such interaction effects, it is often helpful to plot the mean of the dependent variable for each (combination of) experimental condition(s). Visually inspecting this plot will give you a good understanding of the effects; the ANOVA results can then be used to find out whether these effects are likely to be real or due to chance variation.

The effect of one or more continuous independent variables on a continuous dependent variable can be tested with a linear regression (or a multilevel regression in case of a within-subjects design). Each independent variable receives a β-weight, which signifies the effect of a 1-unit difference in the independent variable on the dependent variable. A t-statistic and a p-value signify the evidence against the null hypothesis that this β-weight is zero. The regression also has an R^2-value, which is the percentage of the variance of the dependent variable that is explained by the set of independent variables.

Combinations of continuous independent variables and experimental manipulations can be tested with either a linear regression or an ANCOVA; note that all the mentioned tests are essentially special cases of linear regression, so a linear regression can in principle be used in any of the mentioned situations.

9.3.5.2 Assumptions of Statistical Tests

The real art of statistical evaluation is to know when *not* to apply a certain statistical test. Virtually all statistical tests make certain assumptions about the data, and violating these assumptions may invalidate the results of the test.

A very common violation is that of *multiple comparisons*. The purpose of any statistical test is to decide whether an observed effect is "real" or due to chance variation. Taking $p < 0.05$, we essentially allow an error margin of 5 %: only 1 out of every 20 chance variations is expected to test significantly. However, if we have k conditions and we test for differences between all possible pairs of conditions, the *family-wise error* (i.e. the chance that *at least one* chance variation tests significantly) grows considerably. At $k = 5$ this amounts to 10 tests, and the family-wise error rate is 40 %. To prevent this problem, one should always perform an omnibus test (e.g. the F-test in ANOVA) to first make sure that there *are* differences between conditions. Next, one can pick a baseline condition and compare all conditions against that condition, or one can perform all pairwise tests but calculate a more stringent p-value using post-hoc test methods such as the *Bonferroni correction*.

Another common violation is that of *data type* and *non-normality*. The t-test, ANOVA and regression all assume that the dependent variable is a normally distributed interval[12] variable that is unbounded within its predicted range. This is

[12] An important property of the "interval" data type is that differences between values are comparable. This is for instance not true for a rating score: the difference between 1 and 2 stars is not necessarily the same as the difference between 3 and 4 stars (cf. [74]).

by definition true for factor scores (SSA and EXP), but not for most interaction variables (INT) such as number of clicks, time (bounded by zero), star ratings (bounded and discrete), or purchase decisions (yes/no). Certain non-normality problems can be solved by applying a formulaic transformation to the dependent variable to make its distribution more normal. For example, most zero-bounded variables such as time become more normal by applying a log transformation: $x_t = \ln(x + a)$, where a is a fraction of x, chosen in such a way that x_t has a fairly normal distribution. Data type problems can be accounted for by using generalized linear models (GLMs) or robust regression algorithms. For example, logistic regression can test nominal outcomes, and Poisson or negative binomial regressions can model count data. Many textbooks suggest the use of non-parametric tests, but these are old-fashioned solutions to non-normality problems, and typically do not work for non-continuous data types; GLMs and robust regressions are typically much more powerful ways to deal with non-normal data and alternative data types.

Arguably the most severe violation is that of *correlated errors*. This problem occurs when repeated measurements on the same participant are treated as independent. Repeated measurements do not only occur in within-subjects experiments, but also when a certain variable is measured several times, such as the lengths of several sessions from the same participant, or the ratings of several items per session. One can solve this problem by taking the average of the repeated measurements and do the analysis with those average values, but this reduces the number of observations (and thereby the statistical power), and makes it impossible to make inferences about individual sessions/ratings/etc. An alternative solution is to use an advanced regression method that allows one to estimate the error correlations resulting from repeated measurements (i.e. multilevel regression).

Advanced regression techniques have been developed for data that are both non-normal and repeated, e.g. generalized linear mixed models (GLMM) and generalized estimating equations (GEE). The algorithms implementing these methods are under continuous development. Due to the complexities of such analyses, it is a good advice to consult a statistician if your data happens to have such structure.

9.3.5.3 Integrative Statistical Testing: Structural Equation Models

In this section we present the state-of-the-art of statistical testing: Structural Equation Modeling (SEM). SEM is an integrative statistical procedure, because it tests the measurement model and all hypotheses (known as the structural model, or path model) at the same time. Practically speaking, a SEM is a CFA where the factors are regressed on each other and on the experimental manipulations. Observed behaviors (INT) can also be incorporated in SEM.

Listings 9.4–9.6 present example input and output of a SEM as ran in MPlus and Lavaan, using the same example as the CFA ([62], see Sect. 9.3.4.2), but adding the two experimental manipulations of the experiment. The 'control' manipulation has three conditions: In the 'item control' condition participants can set a weight for each their "likes", which in turn determines the weight for each friend that also likes these items. In the 'friend control' condition participants can set a weight for each of their friends directly. Finally, in the 'no control' condition participants do not set any weights at all (i.e. items are weighted equally, and friend-weights are based on the number of overlapping items). This manipulation is represented by two dummies: `citem` is 1 for participants in the 'item control' condition; `cfriend` is 1 for participants in the 'friend control' condition. Both variables are 0 for participants in the 'no control' condition, making this the baseline condition.

The 'inspectability' manipulation has two conditions: In the 'full graph' condition participants get to see the graph-based interface; in the 'list only' condition they get to see a list of recommendations only. This manipulation is represented by the dummy variable `cgraph`, which is 1 for participants in the 'full graph' condition and 0 for participants in the 'list only' baseline condition.[13]

For the CFA part of the model we specify the optimized CFA with the items `C5`, `U1` and `U3` removed (MPlus: lines 8–12, Lavaan: lines 2–9; the CFA output is excluded for brevity). The input now also includes a structural part that specifies the regressions of each dependent variable on the independent variables (MPlus: lines 13–16, Lavaan: lines 10–13). The output of these regressions (lines 18–46) can be interpreted as traditional regression outcomes with β-weights, standard errors, a test statistic, and a p-value. The β-weight for `cgraph` tests the difference between the 'full graph' and 'list only' condition, while the β-weights for `citem` and `cfriend` compare these conditions with the 'no control' condition. We conduct an omnibus test for the effect of the control manipulation on understandability (MPlus: lines 16–17, Lavaan: lines 13 and 17), and the output shows that the overall effect of this manipulation is significant (lines 6–9).

Listing 9.4 SEM input, MPlus

```
1  DATA: FILE IS twc.dat;
2  VARIABLE:
3   names are s1 s2 s3 s4 s5 s6 s7 q1 q2 q3 q4 q5 q6
4    c1 c2 c3 c4 c5 u1 u2 u3 u4 u5 cgraph citem cfriend;
5   usevariables are  s1-c4 u2 u4 u5 cgraph citem cfriend;
6   categorical are s1-u5;
7  MODEL:    !specify regressions as [factor] on [predictors]
8   satisf  by s1* s2-s7;
9   quality by q1* q2-q6;
10  control by c1* c2-c5;
11  underst by u1* u2-u5;
12  satisf-underst@1;
13  satisf  on  quality control underst cgraph citem cfriend;
14  quality on control underst cgraph citem cfriend;
15  control on underst cgraph citem cfriend;
16  underst on cgraph citem cfriend (p1-p3);
17 MODEL TEST: p2=0; p3=0;    !conduct the omnibus test
```

[13] Here we do not discuss the interaction effect between inspectability and control. This interaction can be tested by multiplying their dummies, creating `cgraphitem` and `cgraphfriend`. These dummies represent the additional effect of item- and friend-control in the graph condition (and likewise, the additional effect of the graph in the item- and friend-control conditions).

Listing 9.5 SEM input, Lavaan (R package)

```
model <- '      #specify regressions as [factor] ~ [predictors]
 satisf  =~ NA*s1+s2+s3+s4+s5+s6+s7
 quality =~ NA*q1+q2+q3+q4+q5+q6
 control =~ NA*c1+c2+c3+c4+c5
 underst =~ NA*u1+u2+u3+u4+u5
 satisf  ~~ 1*satisf
 quality ~~ 1*quality
 control ~~ 1*control
 underst ~~ 1*underst
 satisf  ~ quality+control+underst+cgraph+citem+cfriend
 quality ~ control+underst+cgraph+citem+cfriend
 control ~ underst+cgraph+citem+cfriend
 underst ~ cgraph+p2*citem+p3*cfriend
';
fit <- sem(model, data=twc, ordered=names(twc[1:23]));
summary(fit, fit.measures=TRUE);
wald(fit, "p2;p3");   #conduct the omnibus test
```

Listing 9.6 SEM output

```
MODEL FIT INFORMATION
 Chi-Square Test of Model Fit
         Value                                      341.770*
         Degrees of Freedom                             212
         P-Value                                     0.0000
 Wald Test of Parameter Constraints
         Value                                        9.333
         Degrees of Freedom                               2
         P-Value                                     0.0094
 RMSEA (Root Mean Square Error Of Approximation)
         Estimate                                     0.048
         90 Percent C.I.                              0.038  0.057
         Probability RMSEA <= .05                     0.637
 CFI/TLI
         CFI                                          0.990
         TLI                                          0.988

MODEL RESULTS
                                                            Two-Tailed
                    Estimate       S.E.  Est./S.E.    P-Value
                        <CFA output excluded>
 SATISF   ON
    QUALITY            0.434      0.077      5.600      0.000
    CONTROL           -0.833      0.111     -7.492      0.000
    UNDERST            0.109      0.079      1.374      0.169
 QUALITY  ON
    CONTROL           -0.761      0.086     -8.827      0.000
    UNDERST            0.055      0.077      0.710      0.478
 CONTROL  ON
    UNDERST           -0.320      0.070     -4.579      0.000
 SATISF   ON
    CGRAPH             0.036      0.145      0.249      0.803
```

```
33      CITEM              0.104      0.180      0.577      0.564
34      CFRIEND           -0.205      0.183     -1.122      0.262
35   QUALITY  ON
36      CGRAPH             0.105      0.147      0.716      0.474
37      CITEM              0.093      0.158      0.586      0.558
38      CFRIEND            0.240      0.190      1.262      0.207
39   CONTROL  ON
40      CGRAPH            -0.155      0.141     -1.099      0.272
41      CITEM             -0.010      0.171     -0.058      0.954
42      CFRIEND           -0.116      0.165     -0.701      0.483
43   UNDERST  ON
44      CGRAPH             0.524      0.137      3.834      0.000
45      CITEM              0.342      0.166      2.060      0.039
46      CFRIEND            0.484      0.163      2.977      0.003
```

The structural part of a SEM should be specified in accordance with the study hypotheses. However, if we *only* include the hypothesized effects, one may overlook important additional effects. For example, our hypotheses may suggest that the inspectability and control manipulations increase users' understandability and perceived control, that understandability and perceived control increase the perceived recommendation quality, and that this in turn increases system satisfaction. These hypotheses assert that understandability and control have a mediated (indirect) effect on system satisfaction, but it is perfectly plausible that there also be a *direct* effect. Similarly, the hypotheses assert a direct effect of understandability on perceived recommendation quality, but it is possible that this effect is actually mediated by perceived control. A prudent way to specify the structural part of a SEM is therefore to start with a "saturated" path model of the core variables of the study (i.e. OSA, SSA and EXP), and then prune any non-significant effects from this model.

To build a saturated path model, first line up the core variables in the predicted order of cause and effect. The Knijnenburg et al. [67] framework suggests a general order: OSA → SSA → EXP. If there are multiple SSA or EXP, one should try to find theoretical or empirical arguments for a certain causal direction among them. In the example, we argue `cgraph`, `citem` and `cfriend`[14] → `underst` → `control` → `quality` → `satisf`. Next, set up all possible regressions that adhere to the correct causal direction; this is the model we ran in our example. The output of the example shows that several effects in this saturated model are non-significant. The next step is to iteratively prune the model from non-significant effects until all effects are significant at $p < 0.05$ (or for experiments with a very large sample, $p < 0.01$). In our example, we would iteratively remove non-significant effects on lines 25, 28, and 31–42. This "trimmed" SEM is presented graphically in Fig. 9.2; this is a standardized way to present the outcomes of a SEM analysis. Finally, we add the hypothesized effects of SCs, PCs and INTs to the model. The final SEM of our example is presented graphically in Fig. 3 of [62].

[14]By design, experimental manipulations can only be independent variables (i.e. they never have incoming arrows), so they always start the causal chain.

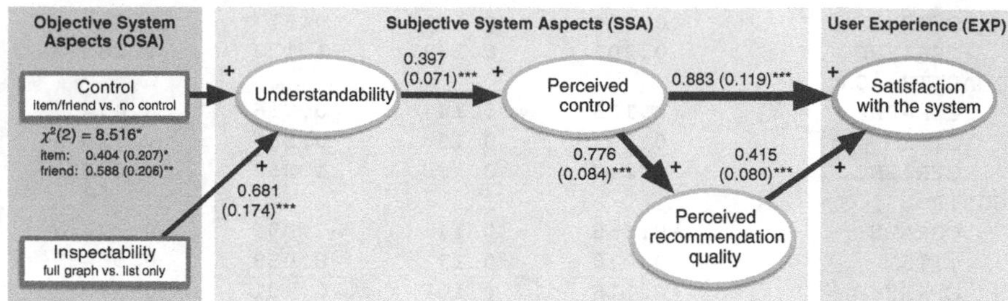

Fig. 9.2 The structural equation model of the trimmed SEM example. Significance levels: $***p < 0.001$, $**p < 0.01$, 'ns' $p > 0.05$. *Numbers on the arrows* (and their *thickness*) represent the β-coefficients (and standard error) of the effect. Factors are scaled to have an SD of 1

The main benefit of SEM over other statistical methods is that it estimates the measured factors and all hypothesized paths in a single model. This has several advantages over a piecewise analysis. First of all, SEM explicitly models the mediated structure of causal effects. For example, Fig. 9.2 shows that the effect of understandability on perceived recommendation quality is *fully mediated* by perceived control. In common terms: understandability leads to better recommendations because (and *only* because) understandability increases users' perceived control over the recommendations. Another example: the effect of perceived control on satisfaction is *partially mediated* by perceived recommendation quality. In common terms: control increases users' satisfaction partially because it leads to better recommendations, and partially because of other, unobserved reasons. These other reasons can be explored in a follow-up study. The ability to argue about the causal structure of a model is the main scientific advantage of SEM over piecewise statistical analyses. Mediated effects can be tested in piecewise models as well, but only in a very cumbersome, post-hoc fashion.

Secondly, in SEM the quality of the entire model itself can be evaluated with a number of fit statistics (lines 1–5 and 10–16). The Chi-square Test of Model Fit tests the difference between the predicted and observed covariance matrix. A significant test means that there is significant misfit between the model and reality. Models are an abstraction of reality, though, so a certain amount of misfit is expected, and this often amounts to significant misfit [8]. The alternative fit indices (*CFI*, *TLI*, and *RMSEA*) give an indication of how much misfit the model contains. Hu and Bentler [51] propose cut-off values for these indices to be: $CFI > 0.96$, $TLI > 0.95$, and $RMSEA < 0.05$ for a good model. The 90 % confidence interval on the *RMSEA* indicates the precision with which the amount of misfit is predicted. This interval will be wider in smaller samples, and should remain below 0.10. The model fit statistics help researchers in their effort to find a well-fitting model.[15]

[15]Like in CFA, more exploratory model efforts can be assisted by the use of modification indices. Please consult [59] for examples.

Finally, there is a technical advantage to fitting the measurement model and the structural model simultaneously. Psychological constructs are never measured with 100 % precision, even when they are measured with multiple items. This lack of precision leads to measurement error, which attenuates the structural effects. In SEM, however, the precision of a factor can be estimated, and the structural effects can be corrected for measurement error, leading to more powerful statistical tests and thus a more robust statistical analysis. Note that despite this additional power, SEM is not a suitable method for analyzing data from small samples; estimating a reasonably complex SEM model requires data from at least 200 participants [55, 59].

9.3.5.4 Practical Tip: Learn More About Structural Equation Modeling

MPlus and the Lavaan R package are but examples of tools to analyze Structural Equation Models. Other tools include AMOS and Lisrel, and several different R packages. We recommend the use of MPlus because it is easy to learn, has a powerful set of advanced modeling features, and it uses non-normality robust estimators by default. It also has good online support and an expansive collection of high quality video lectures covering a wide range of simple and advanced modeling techniques. We advise any reader who is serious about SEM to go to http://www.statmodel.com/ and watch these videos. Beyond these videos, Kline [59] provides a more general introduction to SEM, and Bollen [13] is the most comprehensive technical reference.

9.4 Conclusion

When we first endeavored to explain the process of conducting user experiments in [69], we presented it with the following four steps:

1. Assign participants to conditions
2. Log interaction behavior
3. Measure subjective experience
4. Analyze the collected data

Following an overview of our user-centric evaluation framework and a discussion of interesting recommender system aspects to evaluate, the practical guidelines in this chapter provide a more comprehensive discussion of the steps involved in conducting user experiments. These guidelines first emphasized the formulation of testable hypotheses. They then discussed the importance of collecting an unbiased sample of participants that is large enough to test the hypothesized effects. Next, they covered the development of distinct experimental conditions that manipulate relevant system aspects, as well as different ways of randomly assigning participants to these conditions. The guidelines then covered the practice of measuring subjective constructs that can be used to determine the perceptual and evaluative effects of the experimental manipulations. Finally, they explained in detail how to statistically evaluate the formulated hypotheses with the collected data.

By now it should be clear that learning about user experiments requires working knowledge in several related domains: It involves familiarizing oneself with the basic theory of human-computer interaction and human decision-making, research methods, psychometrics and scale development, and statistics. This chapter has touched upon each of these topics briefly, but we encourage readers to continue their learning process in each of these directions. To this effect, we include a selection of excellent textbooks and other sources below:

On human-computer interaction and human decision-making

- Jacko, "The Human-Computer Interaction Handbook: Fundamentals, Evolving Technologies, and Emerging Applications" [54]: A thorough primer on Human-Computer Interaction. This book covers the principles of human cognition, established interaction paradigms, and HCI design and evaluation practices.
- Kahneman, "Thinking, Fast and Slow" [56]: A very accessible summary of Kahneman's seminal research on human decision-making.
- Smith, Goldstein, and Johnson, "Choice Without Awareness: Ethical and Policy Implications of Defaults" [105]: A recent paper discussing the ethical implications of defaults in decision-making. The paper makes suggestions of how to solve this problem by providing "adaptive defaults" (a type of recommendation).

On research methods

- MacKenzie, "Human-Computer Interaction: An Empirical Research Perspective" [80]: A thorough primer on the design, evaluation and reporting of Human-Computer Interaction experiments.
- Purchase, "Experimental Human-Computer Interaction: A Practical Guide with Visual Examples" [97]: Another primer on experiments; this book contains more details on the evaluation.

On psychometrics and scale development

- DeVellis, "Scale Development, Theory and Applications" [27]: A comprehensive treatment of how to develop measurement scales and assess their quality.
- Schaeffer and Presser, "The Science of Asking Questions" [102]: An in-depth treatment of how to write survey questions.
- Podsakoff, MacKenzie, Lee, and Podsakoff, "Common Method Biases in Behavioral Research" [93]: A paper describing the problem of "Common Method Bias" in survey research, and how to solve or mitigate it.

On statistics

- Utts, "Seeing Through Statistics" [113]: A thorough primer on the statistical evaluation of experimental results.

- Neter, Kutner, Nachtsheim, and Wasserman, "Applied Linear Statistical Models" [86]: A more in-depth treatment of linear statistical methods.
- Kline, "Principles and Practice of Structural Equation Modeling" [59]: An in-depth treatment of structural equation modeling.

We hope that this chapter will spur the adoption of user experiments in the field of recommender systems. We believe that this is an indispensable requirement if the field of recommender systems is indeed to move "from algorithms to user experience" (cf. [72]).

References

1. Adomavicius, G., Kwon, Y.: Improving aggregate recommendation diversity using ranking-based techniques. IEEE Transactions on Knowledge and Data Engineering **24**(5), 896–911 (2012). DOI 10.1109/TKDE.2011.15
2. Ajzen, I.: From intentions to actions: A theory of planned behavior. In: P.D.J. Kuhl, D.J. Beckmann (eds.) Action Control, SSSP Springer Series in Social Psychology, pp. 11–39. Springer Berlin Heidelberg (1985).
3. Ajzen, I.: The theory of planned behavior. Organizational Behavior and Human Decision Processes **50**(2), 179–211 (1991).
4. Ajzen, I., Fishbein, M.: Understanding attitudes and predicting social behaviour. Prentice-Hall, Englewood Cliffs, NJ (1980)
5. Amatriain, X., Pujol, J.M., Tintarev, N., Oliver, N.: Rate it again: Increasing recommendation accuracy by user re-rating. In: Proceedings of the Third ACM Conference on Recommender Systems, RecSys '09, pp. 173–180. ACM, New York, NY, USA (2009). DOI 10.1145/1639714.1639744
6. Basartan, Y.: Amazon versus the shopbot: An experiment about how to improve the shopbots (2001)
7. Bennett, J., Lanning, S.: The netflix prize. In: In KDD Cup and Workshop in conjunction with KDD. San Jose, CA, USA (2007).
URL http://www.cs.uic.edu/~liub/KDD-cup-2007/proceedings/The-Netflix-Prize-Bennett.pdf
8. Bentler, P.M., Bonett, D.G.: Significance tests and goodness of fit in the analysis of covariance structures. Psychological Bulletin **88**(3), 588–606 (1980). DOI 10.1037/0033-2909.88.3.588
9. Bettman, J.R., Luce, M.F., Payne, J.W.: Constructive consumer choice processes. Journal of consumer research **25**(3), 187–217 (1998). DOI 10.1086/209535
10. Bilgic, M., Mooney, R.J.: Explaining recommendations: Satisfaction vs. promotion. In: IUI Workshop: Beyond Personalization. San Diego, CA (2005)
11. Blackwelder, W.C.: "Proving the null hypothesis" in clinical trials. Controlled Clinical Trials **3**(4), 345–353 (1982). DOI 10.1016/0197-2456(82)90024-1
12. Bollen, D., Knijnenburg, B.P., Willemsen, M.C., Graus, M.: Understanding choice overload in recommender systems. In: Proceedings of the fourth ACM conference on Recommender systems, pp. 63–70. Barcelona, Spain (2010). DOI 10.1145/1864708.1864724
13. Bollen, K.A.: Structural equation models. In: Encyclopedia of Biostatistics. John Wiley & Sons, Ltd (2005)
14. Bostandjiev, S., O'Donovan, J., Höllerer, T.: TasteWeights: a visual interactive hybrid recommender system. In: Proceedings of the Sixth ACM Conference on Recommender Systems, RecSys '12, pp. 35–42. ACM, Dublin, Ireland (2012). DOI 10.1145/2365952.2365964

15. Cena, F., Vernero, F., Gena, C.: Towards a customization of rating scales in adaptive systems. In: P.D. Bra, A. Kobsa, D. Chin (eds.) User Modeling, Adaptation, and Personalization, no. 6075 in Lecture Notes in Computer Science, pp. 369–374. Springer Berlin Heidelberg (2010). DOI 10.1007/978-3-642-13470-8_34
16. Chen, L., Pu, P.: Interaction design guidelines on critiquing-based recommender systems. User Modeling and User-Adapted Interaction **19**(3), 167–206 (2009). DOI 10.1007/s11257-008-9057-x
17. Chen, L., Pu, P.: Experiments on the preference-based organization interface in recommender systems. ACM Transactions on Computer-Human Interaction **17**(1), 5:1–5:33 (2010). DOI 10.1145/1721831.1721836
18. Chen, L., Pu, P.: Eye-tracking study of user behavior in recommender interfaces. In: P.D. Bra, A. Kobsa, D. Chin (eds.) User Modeling, Adaptation, and Personalization, no. 6075 in Lecture Notes in Computer Science, pp. 375–380. Springer Berlin Heidelberg (2010). DOI 10.1007/978-3-642-13470-8_35
19. Chen, L., Pu, P.: Critiquing-based recommenders: survey and emerging trends. User Modeling and User-Adapted Interaction **22**(1–2), 125–150 (2012). DOI 10.1007/s11257-011-9108-6
20. Chen, L., Tsoi, H.K.: Users' decision behavior in recommender interfaces: Impact of layout design. In: RecSys' 11 Workshop on Human Decision Making in Recommender Systems, pp. 21–26. Chicago, IL, USA (2011). URL http://ceur-ws.org/Vol-811/paper4.pdf
21. Chin, D.N.: Empirical evaluation of user models and user-adapted systems. User Modeling and User-Adapted Interaction **11**(1–2), 181–194 (2001). DOI 10.1023/A:1011127315884
22. Cohen, J.: Statistical power analysis for the behavioral sciences. Psychology Press (1988)
23. Cosley, D., Lam, S.K., Albert, I., Konstan, J.A., Riedl, J.: Is seeing believing?: How recommender system interfaces affect users' opinions. In: Proceedings of the SIGCHI Conference on Human Factors in Computing Systems, CHI '03, pp. 585–592. ACM, Ft. Lauderdale, Florida, USA (2003). DOI 10.1145/642611.642713
24. Cramer, H., Evers, V., Ramlal, S., Someren, M., Rutledge, L., Stash, N., Aroyo, L., Wielinga, B.: The effects of transparency on trust in and acceptance of a content-based art recommender. User Modeling and User-Adapted Interaction **18**(5), 455–496 (2008). DOI 10.1007/s11257-008-9051-3
25. Cremonesi, P., Garzotto, F., Negro, S., Papadopoulos, A.V., Turrin, R.: Looking for "Good" recommendations: A comparative evaluation of recommender systems. In: P. Campos, N. Graham, J. Jorge, N. Nunes, P. Palanque, M. Winckler (eds.) Human-Computer Interaction – INTERACT 2011, no. 6948 in Lecture Notes in Computer Science, pp. 152–168. Springer Berlin Heidelberg (2011). DOI 10.1007/978-3-642-23765-2_11
26. Davis, F.D.: Perceived usefulness, perceived ease of use, and user acceptance of information technology. MIS Quarterly **13**(3), 319–340 (1989). DOI 10.2307/249008
27. DeVellis, R.F.: Scale development: theory and applications. SAGE, Thousand Oaks, Calif. (2011)
28. Dooms, S., De Pessemier, T., Martens, L.: An online evaluation of explicit feedback mechanisms for recommender systems. In: 7th International Conference on Web Information Systems and Technologies (WEBIST-2011), pp. 391–394. Noordwijkerhout, The Netherlands (2011).
URL https://biblio.ugent.be/publication/2039743/file/2039745.pdf
29. Dooms, S., De Pessemier, T., Martens, L.: A user-centric evaluation of recommender algorithms for an event recommendation system. In: RecSys 2011 Workshop on Human Decision Making in Recommender Systems (Decisions@ RecSys' 11) and User-Centric Evaluation of Recommender Systems and Their Interfaces-2 (UCERSTI 2) affiliated with the 5th ACM Conference on Recommender Systems (RecSys 2011), pp. 67–73. Chicago, IL, USA (2011). URL http://ceur-ws.org/Vol-811/paper10.pdf
30. Downs, J.S., Holbrook, M.B., Sheng, S., Cranor, L.F.: Are your participants gaming the system?: screening mechanical turk workers. In: Proceedings of the 28th SIGCHI conference on Human factors in computing systems, pp. 2399–2402. Atlanta, Georgia, USA (2010). DOI 10.1145/1753326.1753688

31. Ekstrand, M.D., Harper, F.M., Willemsen, M.C., Konstan, J.A.: User perception of differences in recommender algorithms. In: Proceedings of the eighth ACM conference on Recommender systems. Foster City, CA (2014). DOI 10.1145/2645710.2645737
32. Erickson, B.H.: Some problems of inference from chain data. Sociological methodology **10**(1), 276–302 (1979)
33. Farzan, R., Brusilovsky, P.: Encouraging user participation in a course recommender system: An impact on user behavior. Computers in Human Behavior **27**(1), 276–284 (2011). DOI 10.1016/j.chb.2010.08.005
34. Fasolo, B., Hertwig, R., Huber, M., Ludwig, M.: Size, entropy, and density: What is the difference that makes the difference between small and large real-world assortments? Psychology and Marketing **26**(3), 254–279 (2009). DOI 10.1002/mar.20272
35. Faul, F., Erdfelder, E., Lang, A.G., Buchner, A.: G*Power 3: A flexible statistical power analysis program for the social, behavioral, and biomedical sciences. Behavior Research Methods **39**(2), 175–191 (2007). DOI 10.3758/BF03193146
36. Felfernig, A.: Knowledge-based recommender technologies for marketing and sales. Intl. J. of Pattern Recognition and Artificial Intelligence **21**(2), 333–354 (2007). DOI 10.1142/S0218001407005417
37. Fishbein, M., Ajzen, I.: Belief, attitude, intention, and behavior: an introduction to theory and research. Addison-Wesley Pub. Co., Reading, MA (1975)
38. Fisher, R.A.: The design of experiments, vol. xi. Oliver & Boyd, Oxford, England (1935)
39. Freyne, J., Jacovi, M., Guy, I., Geyer, W.: Increasing engagement through early recommender intervention. In: Proceedings of the Third ACM Conference on Recommender Systems, RecSys '09, pp. 85–92. ACM, New York, NY, USA (2009). DOI 10.1145/1639714.1639730
40. Friedrich, G., Zanker, M.: A taxonomy for generating explanations in recommender systems. AI Magazine **32**(3), 90–98 (2011). DOI 10.1609/aimag.v32i3.2365
41. Gedikli, F., Jannach, D., Ge, M.: How should i explain? a comparison of different explanation types for recommender systems. International Journal of Human-Computer Studies **72**(4), 367–382 (2014). DOI 10.1016/j.ijhcs.2013.12.007
42. Gena, C., Brogi, R., Cena, F., Vernero, F.: The impact of rating scales on user's rating behavior. In: D. Hutchison, T. Kanade, J. Kittler, J.M. Kleinberg, F. Mattern, J.C. Mitchell, M. Naor, O. Nierstrasz, C. Pandu Rangan, B. Steffen, M. Sudan, D. Terzopoulos, D. Tygar, M.Y. Vardi, G. Weikum, J.A. Konstan, R. Conejo, J.L. Marzo, N. Oliver (eds.) User Modeling, Adaption and Personalization, vol. 6787, pp. 123–134. Springer, Berlin, Heidelberg (2011). DOI 10.1007/978-3-642-22362-4_11
43. Ghose, A., Ipeirotis, P.G., Li, B.: Designing ranking systems for hotels on travel search engines by mining user-generated and crowdsourced content. Marketing Science **31**(3), 493–520 (2012). DOI 10.1287/mksc.1110.0700
44. Graus, M.P., Willemsen, M.C., Swelsen, K.: Understanding real-life website adaptations by investigating the relations between user behavior and user experience. In: F. Ricci, K. Bontcheva, O. Conlan, S. Lawless (eds.) User Modeling, Adaptation and Personalization, **9146**, 350–356. Springer, Berlin, Heidelberg (2015)
45. Gregor, S.: The nature of theory in information systems. MIS Quarterly **30**(3), 611–642 (2006). URL http://www.jstor.org/stable/25148742
46. Hassenzahl, M.: The thing and i: understanding the relationship between user and product. In: M. Blythe, K. Overbeeke, A. Monk, P. Wright (eds.) Funology, From Usability to Enjoyment, pp. 31–42. Kluwer Academic Publishers, Dordrecht, The Netherlands (2005). DOI 10.1007/1-4020-2967-5_4
47. Hassenzahl, M.: User experience (UX). In: Proceedings of the 20th International Conference of the Association Francophone d'Interaction Homme-Machine on - IHM '08, pp. 11–15. Metz, France (2008). DOI 10.1145/1512714.1512717
48. Häubl, G., Trifts, V.: Consumer decision making in online shopping environments: The effects of interactive decision aids. Marketing Science **19**(1), 4–21 (2000). URL http://www.jstor.org/stable/193256

49. Heckathorn, D.D.: Respondent-driven sampling II: deriving valid population estimates from chain-referral samples of hidden populations. Social problems **49**(1), 11–34 (2002). DOI 10.1525/sp.2002.49.1.11
50. Herlocker, J.L., Konstan, J.A., Riedl, J.: Explaining collaborative filtering recommendations. In: Proc. of the 2000 ACM conference on Computer supported cooperative work, pp. 241–250. ACM Press, Philadelphia, PA (2000). DOI 10.1145/358916.358995
51. Hu, L., Bentler, P.M.: Cutoff criteria for fit indexes in covariance structure analysis: Conventional criteria versus new alternatives. Structural Equation Modeling: A Multidisciplinary Journal **6**(1), 1–55 (1999). DOI 10.1080/10705519909540118
52. Hu, R., Pu, P.: Enhancing recommendation diversity with organization interfaces. In: Proceedings of the 16th International Conference on Intelligent User Interfaces, IUI '11, pp. 347–350. ACM, Palo Alto, CA, USA (2011). DOI 10.1145/1943403.1943462
53. Iivari, J.: Contributions to the theoretical foundations of systemeering research and the PIOCO model. Ph.D. thesis, University of Oulu, Finland (1983)
54. Jacko, J.A.: The human-computer interaction handbook: fundamentals, evolving technologies, and emerging applications. CRC Press, Boca Raton, FL (2012)
55. Jackson, D.L.: Revisiting sample size and number of parameter estimates: Some support for the n:q hypothesis. Structural Equation Modeling: A Multidisciplinary Journal **10**(1), 128–141 (2003). DOI 10.1207/S15328007SEM1001_6
56. Kahneman, D.: Thinking, fast and slow. Macmillan (2011)
57. Kammerer, Y., Gerjets, P.: How the interface design influences users' spontaneous trustworthiness evaluations of web search results: Comparing a list and a grid interface. In: Proceedings of the 2010 Symposium on Eye-Tracking Research & Applications, ETRA '10, pp. 299–306. ACM, Austin, TX, USA (2010). DOI 10.1145/1743666.1743736
58. Kittur, A., Chi, E.H., Suh, B.: Crowdsourcing user studies with mechanical turk. In: Proceedings of the SIGCHI Conference on Human Factors in Computing Systems, pp. 453–456. ACM Press, Florence, Italy (2008). DOI 10.1145/1357054.1357127
59. Kline, R.B.: Principles and practice of structural equation modeling. Guilford Press, New York (2011)
60. Kluver, D., Nguyen, T.T., Ekstrand, M., Sen, S., Riedl, J.: How many bits per rating? In: Proceedings of the Sixth ACM Conference on Recommender Systems, RecSys '12, pp. 99–106. ACM, Dublin, Ireland (2012). DOI 10.1145/2365952.2365974
61. Knijnenburg, B.P.: Simplifying privacy decisions: Towards interactive and adaptive solutions. In: Proceedings of the Recsys 2013 Workshop on Human Decision Making in Recommender Systems (Decisions@ RecSys'13), pp. 40–41. Hong Kong, China (2013). URL http://ceur-ws.org/Vol-1050/paper7.pdf
62. Knijnenburg, B.P., Bostandjiev, S., O'Donovan, J., Kobsa, A.: Inspectability and control in social recommenders. In: Proceedings of the sixth ACM conference on Recommender systems, RecSys '12, pp. 43–50. ACM, Dublin, Ireland (2012). DOI 10.1145/2365952.2365966
63. Knijnenburg, B.P., Kobsa, A.: Making decisions about privacy: Information disclosure in context-aware recommender systems. ACM Transactions on Interactive Intelligent Systems **3**(3), 20:1–20:23 (2013). DOI 10.1145/2499670
64. Knijnenburg, B.P., Kobsa, A., Jin, H.: Dimensionality of information disclosure behavior. International Journal of Human-Computer Studies **71**(12), 1144–1162 (2013). DOI 10.1016/j.ijhcs.2013.06.003
65. Knijnenburg, B.P., Reijmer, N.J., Willemsen, M.C.: Each to his own: how different users call for different interaction methods in recommender systems. In: Proceedings of the fifth ACM conference on Recommender systems, pp. 141–148. ACM Press, Chicago, IL, USA (2011). DOI 10.1145/2043932.2043960
66. Knijnenburg, B.P., Willemsen, M.C.: Understanding the effect of adaptive preference elicitation methods on user satisfaction of a recommender system. In: Proceedings of the third ACM conference on Recommender systems, pp. 381–384. New York, NY (2009). DOI 10.1145/1639714.1639793

67. Knijnenburg, B.P., Willemsen, M.C., Gantner, Z., Soncu, H., Newell, C.: Explaining the user experience of recommender systems. User Modeling and User-Adapted Interaction **22**(4–5), 441–504 (2012). DOI 10.1007/s11257-011-9118-4
68. Knijnenburg, B.P., Willemsen, M.C., Hirtbach, S.: Receiving recommendations and providing feedback: The user-experience of a recommender system. In: F. Buccafurri, G. Semeraro (eds.) E-Commerce and Web Technologies, vol. 61, pp. 207–216. Springer, Berlin, Heidelberg (2010). DOI 10.1007/978-3-642-15208-5_19
69. Knijnenburg, B.P., Willemsen, M.C., Kobsa, A.: A pragmatic procedure to support the user-centric evaluation of recommender systems. In: Proceedings of the fifth ACM conference on Recommender systems, RecSys '11, pp. 321–324. ACM, Chicago, IL, USA (2011). DOI 10.1145/2043932.2043993
70. Kobsa, A., Cho, H., Knijnenburg, B.P.: An attitudinal and behavioral model of personalization at different providers. Journal of the Association for Information Science and Technology. http://onlinelibrary.wiley.com/journal/10.1002/(ISSN)2330-1643/earlyview (In press)
71. Köhler, C.F., Breugelmans, E., Dellaert, B.G.C.: Consumer acceptance of recommendations by interactive decision aids: The joint role of temporal distance and concrete versus abstract communications. Journal of Management Information Systems **27**(4), 231–260 (2011). DOI 10.2753/MIS0742-1222270408
72. Konstan, J., Riedl, J.: Recommender systems: from algorithms to user experience. User Modeling and User-Adapted Interaction **22**(1), 101–123 (2012). DOI 10.1007/s11257-011-9112-x
73. Koren, Y., Bell, R., Volinsky, C.: Matrix factorization techniques for recommender systems. Computer **42**(8), 30–37 (2009). DOI 10.1109/MC.2009.263
74. Koren, Y., Sill, J.: OrdRec: An ordinal model for predicting personalized item rating distributions. In: Proceedings of the Fifth ACM Conference on Recommender Systems, RecSys '11, pp. 117–124. ACM, New York, NY, USA (2011). DOI 10.1145/2043932.2043956
75. Landsberger, H.A.: Hawthorne revisited: Management and the worker: its critics, and developments in human relations in industry. Cornell University (1958)
76. Lathia, N., Hailes, S., Capra, L., Amatriain, X.: Temporal diversity in recommender systems. In: Proceedings of the 33rd International ACM SIGIR Conference on Research and Development in Information Retrieval, SIGIR '10, pp. 210–217. ACM, Geneva, Switzerland (2010). DOI 10.1145/1835449.1835486
77. Lee, Y.E., Benbasat, I.: The influence of trade-off difficulty caused by preference elicitation methods on user acceptance of recommendation agents across loss and gain conditions. Information Systems Research **22**(4), 867–884 (2011). DOI 10.1287/isre.1100.0334
78. Lopes, C.S., Rodrigues, L.C., Sichieri, R.: The lack of selection bias in a snowball sampled case-control study on drug abuse. International journal of epidemiology **25**(6), 1267–1270 (1996). DOI 10.1093/ije/25.6.1267
79. MacCallum, R.C., Widaman, K.F., Zhang, S., Hong, S.: Sample size in factor analysis. Psychological Methods **4**(1), 84–99 (1999). DOI 10.1037/1082-989X.4.1.84
80. MacKenzie, I.S.: Human-Computer Interaction: An Empirical Research Perspective, 1st edn. Morgan Kaufmann Publishers Inc., San Francisco, CA, USA (2013)
81. Martin, F.J.: Recsys'09 industrial keynote: Top 10 lessons learned developing deploying and operating real-world recommender systems. In: Proceedings of the Third ACM Conference on Recommender Systems, RecSys '09, pp. 1–2. ACM, New York, NY, USA (2009). DOI 10.1145/1639714.1639715
82. McNee, S.M., Albert, I., Cosley, D., Gopalkrishnan, P., Lam, S.K., Rashid, A.M., Konstan, J.A., Riedl, J.: On the recommending of citations for research papers. In: Proceedings of the 2002 ACM conference on Computer supported cooperative work, pp. 116–125. New Orleans, LA (2002). DOI 10.1145/587078.587096
83. McNee, S.M., Riedl, J., Konstan, J.A.: Being accurate is not enough: how accuracy metrics have hurt recommender systems. In: Extended abstracts on Human factors in computing systems, pp. 1097–1101. Montréal, Québec, Canada (2006). DOI 10.1145/1125451.1125659
84. McNee, S.M., Riedl, J., Konstan, J.A.: Making recommendations better: An analytic model for human-recommender interaction. In: Extended Abstracts on Human Factors in Computing Systems, CHI EA '06, pp. 1103–1108. ACM, Montréal, Québec, Canada (2006). DOI 10.1145/1125451.1125660

85. Mogilner, C., Rudnick, T., Iyengar, S.S.: The mere categorization effect: How the presence of categories increases choosers' perceptions of assortment variety and outcome satisfaction. Journal of Consumer Research **35**(2), 202–215 (2008). DOI 10.1086/586908
86. Neter, J., Kutner, M.H., Nachtsheim, C.J., Wasserman, W.: Applied linear statistical models, vol. 4. Irwin Chicago (1996)
87. Nguyen, T.T., Kluver, D., Wang, T.Y., Hui, P.M., Ekstrand, M.D., Willemsen, M.C., Riedl, J.: Rating support interfaces to improve user experience and recommender accuracy. In: Proceedings of the 7th ACM Conference on Recommender Systems, RecSys '13, pp. 149–156. ACM, Hong Kong, China (2013). DOI 10.1145/2507157.2507188
88. Nuzzo, R.: Scientific method: Statistical errors. Nature **506**(7487), 150–152 (2014). DOI 10.1038/506150a
89. Oestreicher-Singer, G., Sundararajan, A.: Recommendation networks and the long tail of electronic commerce. Management Information Systems Quarterly **36**(1), 65–83 (2012). URL http://aisel.aisnet.org/misq/vol36/iss1/7
90. Oestreicher-Singer, G., Sundararajan, A.: The visible hand? demand effects of recommendation networks in electronic markets. Management Science **58**(11), 1963–1981 (2012). DOI 10.1287/mnsc.1120.1536
91. Orne, M.T.: On the social psychology of the psychological experiment: With particular reference to demand characteristics and their implications. American Psychologist **17**(11), 776–783 (1962). DOI 10.1037/h0043424
92. Paolacci, G., Chandler, J., Ipeirotis, P.: Running experiments on amazon mechanical turk. Judgment and Decision Making **5**(5), 411–419 (2010). URL http://www.sjdm.org/journal/10/10630a/jdm10630a.pdf
93. Podsakoff, P.M., MacKenzie, S.B., Lee, J.Y., Podsakoff, N.P.: Common method biases in behavioral research: A critical review of the literature and recommended remedies. Journal of Applied Psychology **88**(5), 879–903 (2003). DOI 10.1037/0021-9010.88.5.879
94. Pu, P., Chen, L.: Trust-inspiring explanation interfaces for recommender systems. Knowledge-Based Systems **20**(6), 542–556 (2007). DOI 10.1016/j.knosys.2007.04.004
95. Pu, P., Chen, L., Hu, R.: A user-centric evaluation framework for recommender systems. In: Proceedings of the Fifth ACM Conference on Recommender Systems, RecSys '11, pp. 157–164. ACM, Chicago, IL, USA (2011). DOI 10.1145/2043932.2043962
96. Pu, P., Chen, L., Hu, R.: Evaluating recommender systems from the user's perspective: survey of the state of the art. User Modeling and User-Adapted Interaction **22**(4), 317–355 (2012). DOI 10.1007/s11257-011-9115-7
97. Purchase, H.C.: Experimental Human-Computer Interaction: A Practical Guide with Visual Examples, 1st edn. Cambridge University Press, New York, NY, USA (2012)
98. Randall, T., Terwiesch, C., Ulrich, K.T.: User design of customized products. Marketing Science **26**(2), 268–280 (2007). DOI 10.1287/mksc.1050.0116
99. Said, A., Fields, B., Jain, B.J., Albayrak, S.: User-centric evaluation of a k-furthest neighbor collaborative filtering recommender algorithm. In: Proceedings of the 2013 Conference on Computer Supported Cooperative Work, CSCW '13, pp. 1399–1408. ACM, New York, NY, USA (2013). DOI 10.1145/2441776.2441933
100. Said, A., Jain, B.J., Narr, S., Plumbaum, T., Albayrak, S., Scheel, C.: Estimating the magic barrier of recommender systems: A user study. In: Proceedings of the 35th International ACM SIGIR Conference on Research and Development in Information Retrieval, SIGIR '12, pp. 1061–1062. ACM, Portland, Oregon (2012). DOI 10.1145/2348283.2348469
101. Salganik, M.J., Heckathorn, D.D.: Sampling and estimation in hidden populations using respondent-driven sampling. Sociological Methodology **34**(1), 193–240 (2004). DOI 10.1111/j.0081-1750.2004.00152.x
102. Schaeffer, N.C., Presser, S.: The science of asking questions. Annual Review of Sociology **29**(1), 65–88 (2003). DOI 10.1146/annurev.soc.29.110702.110112
103. Scheibehenne, B., Greifeneder, R., Todd, P.M.: Can there ever be too many options? a Meta-Analytic review of choice overload. Journal of Consumer Research **37**(3), 409–425 (2010). DOI 10.1086/651235

104. Sinha, R., Swearingen, K.: Comparing recommendations made by online systems and friends. In: In Proceedings of the DELOS-NSF Workshop on Personalization and Recommender Systems in Digital Libraries (2001)
105. Smith, N.C., Goldstein, D.G., Johnson, E.J.: Choice without awareness: Ethical and policy implications of defaults. Journal of Public Policy & Marketing **32**(2), 159–172 (2013). DOI 10.1509/jppm.10.114
106. Sparling, E.I., Sen, S.: Rating: How difficult is it? In: Proceedings of the Fifth ACM Conference on Recommender Systems, RecSys '11, pp. 149–156. ACM, Chicago, IL, USA (2011). DOI 10.1145/2043932.2043961
107. Steele-Johnson, D., Beauregard, R.S., Hoover, P.B., Schmidt, A.M.: Goal orientation and task demand effects on motivation, affect, and performance. Journal of Applied Psychology **85**(5), 724–738 (2000). DOI 10.1037/0021-9010.85.5.724
108. Symeonidis, P., Nanopoulos, A., Manolopoulos, Y.: Providing justifications in recommender systems. IEEE Transactions on Systems, Man and Cybernetics, Part A: Systems and Humans **38**(6), 1262–1272 (2008). DOI 10.1109/TSMCA.2008.2003969
109. Tam, K.Y., Ho, S.Y.: Web personalization: is it effective? IT Professional **5**(5), 53–57 (2003). DOI 10.1109/MITP.2003.1235611
110. Tintarev, N., Masthoff, J.: A survey of explanations in recommender systems. In: Data Engineering Workshop, pp. 801–810. IEEE, Istanbul, Turkey (2007). DOI 10.1109/ICDEW.2007.4401070
111. Tintarev, N., Masthoff, J.: Evaluating the effectiveness of explanations for recommender systems. User Modeling and User-Adapted Interaction **22**(4–5), 399–439 (2012). DOI 10.1007/s11257-011-9117-5
112. Torres, R., McNee, S.M., Abel, M., Konstan, J.A., Riedl, J.: Enhancing digital libraries with TechLens+. In: Proceedings of the 2004 joint ACM/IEEE conference on Digital libraries - JCDL '04, pp. 228–236. Tuscon, AZ, USA (2004). DOI 10.1145/996350.996402
113. Utts, J.: Seeing Through Statistics. Cengage Learning (2004)
114. Van Velsen, L., Van Der Geest, T., Klaassen, R., Steehouder, M.: User-centered evaluation of adaptive and adaptable systems: a literature review. The Knowledge Engineering Review **23**(03), 261–281 (2008). DOI 10.1017/S0269888908001379
115. Vargas, S., Castells, P.: Rank and relevance in novelty and diversity metrics for recommender systems. In: Proceedings of the Fifth ACM Conference on Recommender Systems, RecSys '11, pp. 109–116. ACM, Chicago, IL, USA (2011). DOI 10.1145/2043932.2043955
116. Venkatesh, V., Morris, M.G., Davis, G.B., Davis, F.D.: User acceptance of information technology: Toward a unified view. MIS Quarterly **27**(3), 425–478 (2003). URL http://www.jstor.org/stable/30036540
117. Vig, J., Sen, S., Riedl, J.: Tagsplanations: Explaining recommendations using tags. In: Proceedings of the 14th International Conference on Intelligent User Interfaces, IUI '09, pp. 47–56. ACM, Sanibel Island, Florida, USA (2009). DOI 10.1145/1502650.1502661
118. Wang, H.C., Doong, H.S.: Argument form and spokesperson type: The recommendation strategy of virtual salespersons. International Journal of Information Management **30**(6), 493–501 (2010). DOI 10.1016/j.ijinfomgt.2010.03.006
119. Wang, W., Benbasat, I.: Recommendation agents for electronic commerce: Effects of explanation facilities on trusting beliefs. Journal of Management Information Systems **23**(4), 217–246 (2007). DOI 10.2753/MIS0742-1222230410
120. Willemsen, M.C., Graus, M.P., Knijnenburg, B.P.: Understanding the role of latent feature diversification on choice difficulty and satisfaction (manuscript, under review)
121. Willemsen, M.C., Knijnenburg, B.P., Graus, M.P., Velter-Bremmers, L.C., Fu, K.: Using latent features diversification to reduce choice difficulty in recommendation lists. In: RecSys'11 Workshop on Human Decision Making in Recommender Systems, CEUR-WS, vol. 811, pp. 14–20. Chicago, IL (2011). URL http://ceur-ws.org/Vol-811/paper3.pdf
122. Xiao, B., Benbasat, I.: E-commerce product recommendation agents: Use, characteristics, and impact. Mis Quarterly **31**(1), 137–209 (2007). URL http://www.jstor.org/stable/25148784

123. Xiao, B., Benbasat, I.: Research on the use, characteristics, and impact of e-commerce product recommendation agents: A review and update for 2007–2012. In: F.J. Martínez-López (ed.) Handbook of Strategic e-Business Management, Progress in IS, pp. 403–431. Springer Berlin Heidelberg (2014). DOI 10.1007/978-3-642-39747-9_18
124. Zhang, M., Hurley, N.: Avoiding monotony: Improving the diversity of recommendation lists. In: Proceedings of the 2008 ACM Conference on Recommender Systems, RecSys '08, pp. 123–130. ACM, Lausanne, Switzerland (2008). DOI 10.1145/1454008.1454030
125. Zhou, T., Kuscsik, Z., Liu, J.G., Medo, M., Wakeling, J.R., Zhang, Y.C.: Solving the apparent diversity-accuracy dilemma of recommender systems. Proceedings of the National Academy of Sciences **107**(10), 4511–4515 (2010). DOI 10.1073/pnas.1000488107
126. Ziegler, C.N., McNee, S.M., Konstan, J.A., Lausen, G.: Improving recommendation lists through topic diversification. In: Proceedings of the 14th international conference on World Wide Web - WWW '05, pp. 22–32. Chiba, Japan (2005). DOI 10.1145/1060745.1060754

Chapter 10
Explaining Recommendations: Design and Evaluation

Nava Tintarev and Judith Masthoff

10.1 Introduction

In recent years, there has been an increased interest in more user-centered evaluation metrics for recommender systems such as those mentioned in [49]. It has also been recognized that many recommender systems functioned as *black boxes*, providing no transparency into the working of the recommendation process, nor offering any additional information to accompany the recommendations beyond the recommendations themselves [35].

This chapter investigates the role of explanations, such as the one depicted in Fig. 10.1. It is sometimes erroneously assumed that explanations should always justify why items have been recommended. A popular definition of explanation is synonymous with justification. However, to explain also means *"to make clear by giving a detailed description"* [Oxford concise dictionary]. So, an explanation can be an item description that helps the user to understand the qualities of the item well enough to decide whether it is relevant to them or not.

Explanations can serve multiple aims, out which one is transparency: aiming to expose the reasoning and data behind a recommendation. This is the case with some of the explanations hosted on Amazon, such as: *"Customers Who Bought This Item Also Bought*... ". Explanations can also serve other aims such as helping to inspire user trust and loyalty, increase satisfaction, make it quicker and easier for users to find what they want, and persuade them to try or purchase a recommended item. In this way, we distinguish between different explanation such as e.g. explaining the way the recommendation engine works (transparency), and explaining why the user may or may not want to try an item (effectiveness). An effective explanation may be formulated along the lines of *"You might (not) like Item A because*... ". In contrast

N. Tintarev (✉) • J. Masthoff
University of Aberdeen, AB24 3UE Aberdeen, UK
e-mail: n.tintarev@abdn.ac.uk; j.masthoff@abdn.ac.uk

F. Ricci et al. (eds.), *Recommender Systems Handbook*,
DOI 10.1007/978-1-4899-7637-6_10

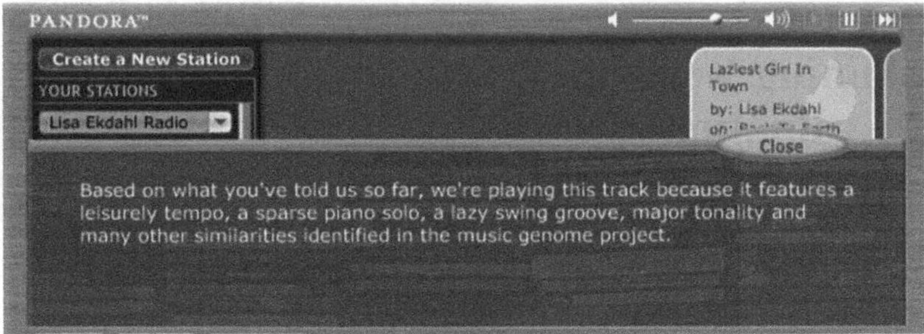

Fig. 10.1 Explanation in the Pandora system, *"Based on what you've told us so far, we're playing this track because it features a leisurely tempo ..."*

to the Amazon example above, this explanation does not *necessarily* describe how the recommendation was selected—in which case it is not transparent.

Explanations in advisory systems are not a new idea: explanations have often been considered as part of the research in the area of advisory expert systems [6, 33, 38, 44, 86]. This research has largely been focused on what kind of explanations can be generated and how these have been implemented in real world systems [6, 38, 44, 86]. The kinds of explanations that could be generated were directly linked to the inference methods, of which the three most common ones were: rule-based methods [42], Bayesian networks [41], and case-based reasoning [23].

Overall, *there are few evaluations of the explanations in these systems*. When they did occur evaluations of explanations have largely focused on *user acceptance* of the system such as [14] or acceptance of the systems' conclusions [87]. An exception is the MYCIN system and its explanation capability which were evaluated in terms of the decision support of the system *as a whole* [33].

New challenges stemming from recommender systems have revived explanation research, after a decline of studies in expert systems in the 90s. One such development is the increase in data: due to the growth of the web, many systems are being used by thousands of users rather than dozens or just a handful of experts. In addition, new algorithms, in particular in the domain of collaborative filtering, have been adapted and developed (see also Chap. 2 on neighborhood based approaches, and Chap. 7 on advances in data mining). These approaches mitigate domain dependence, and allow for greater generalizability, and are more suitable for large and often sparse datasets.

Research on explanations in recommender systems to date has been evaluated much more extensively than in previous advisory systems, and in a much wider range of domains (varying from movies [73] to financial advice [26] to cultural heritage artifacts [20]). We supply an overview of existing systems by studying various properties of the existing explanation facilities.

Explanations are not strictly decoupled from recommendations themselves, the way preferences are elicited, or the way in recommendations are presented: these factors influence each other and the explanations that can be generated. So, in the next section we discuss these types of design choices.

This enables us to discuss how these choices interact with different explanation styles, including a table of explanations in commercial and academic systems (Sect. 10.3). Looking at the different explanation styles we start to sense that the underlying algorithm of a recommender engine may influence the types of explanations that can be generated.

Next, in Sect. 10.4, we discuss what defines a good explanation. We list seven explanatory criteria, and describe how these have been measured in previous systems. These criteria can also be understood as advantages that explanations may offer to recommender systems, answering the question of *why* to explain. Finally, we conclude with future directions in Sect. 10.5.

10.2 Designing the Presentation and Interaction with Recommendations

Every stage of the recommendation process, including both preference elicitation and how recommendations are presented or visualized, requires an interaction model. All of these factors can affect the types of explanations that can be generated. In turn, some of the explanations that can be generated may be more suitable for particular explanatory criteria (which we discuss in Sect. 10.4). Pu et al. [61] also discusses a complementary evaluation framework for preference-based (such as critiquing [46]) recommender systems and focuses on the design of both presentation of recommendations and interaction model. For example one of their guidelines states: *"Showing one search result or recommending one item at a time allows for a simple display strategy which can be easily adapted to small display devices; however, it is likely to engage users in longer interaction sessions or only allow them to achieve relatively low decision accuracy."* (Guideline 9, [61]).

10.2.1 Presenting Recommendations

We summarize the ways of presenting recommendations that we have seen for the systems considered in this paper. While there are a number of possibilities for the *appearance* of the graphical user interface, the actual *structure* of offering recommendations can also vary. We identify the following categories for structuring the presentation of recommendations:

- **Top item.** Perhaps the simplest way to present a recommendation is by offering the user the best item for them. For example *"You have been watching a lot of sports, and football in particular. This is the most popular and recent item from the world cup."*
- **Top N-items.** The system may also present several items at once. *"You have watched a lot of football and technology items. You might like to see the local*

football results and the gadget of the day." Note that while this system could be able to explain the relation between chosen items, it could also explain the rational behind each single item.

- **Similar to top item(s).** Once a user shows a preference for one or more items, the recommender system can offer *similar* items. For example *"You might also like... Oliver Twist by Charles Dickens"*.
- **Predicted ratings for all items.** Rather than forcing selections on the user, a system may allow its users to browse all the available options. Recommendations are then presented as predicted ratings on a scale (say from 0 to 5) for each item. A user might query why a certain item, for example local hockey results, is predicted to have a low rating. The recommender system might then generate an explanation like: *"While this is a sports article, it is about hockey, which you do not seem to like!"*.
- **Structured overview.** The recommender system can give a structure which displays trade-offs between items [59, 88]. The advantage of a structured overview is that the user can see how items compare, and what other items are still available if the current recommendation should not meet their requirements. An example of a structured overview can be seen in Fig. 10.2.

10.2.2 Preference Elicitation

There are different ways in which a user can give input to the recommender system. This interaction is what distinguishes conversational systems from "single-shot" recommendations. They allow users to elaborate their requirements over the course of an extended dialog [62] rather than each user interaction being treated independently of previous history.

The most popular product

	Manufacturer	Price	Processor speed	Battery life	Installed memory	Hard drive capacity	Display size	Weight
⊙	——	$2'095.00	1.67 GHz	4.5 hour(s)	512 MB	80 GB	38.6 cm	2.54 kg

We also recommend the following products because
they are cheaper and lighter, but have lower processor speed

	Manufacturer	Price	Processor speed	Battery life	Installed memory	Hard drive capacity	Display size	Weight
○	——	$1'499.00	1.5 GHz	5 hour(s)	512 MB	80 GB	33.8 cm	1.91 kg
○	——	$1'739.99	1.5 GHz	4.5 hour(s)	512 MB	80 GB	38.6 cm	2.49 kg
○	——	$1'625.99	1.5 GHz	5 hour(s)	512 MB	80 GB	30.7 cm	2.09 kg
○	——	$1'426.99	1.5 GHz	5 hour(s)	512 MB	60 GB	30.7 cm	2.09 kg
○	——	$1'929.00	1.2 GHz	4 hour(s)	512 MB	60 GB	26.9 cm	1.41 kg
○	——	$1'595.00	1 GHz	5.5 hour(s)	512 MB	40 GB	26.9 cm	1.41 kg

Fig. 10.2 Organizational structure, this is a form of structured overview which displays trade-offs between items [59]

We expand on the four ways suggested by McGinty and Smyth [47], supplying examples of current applications.[1] Note that although there are more unobtrusive ways to elicit user preferences, e.g. via usage data [55] or demographics [4], this section focuses on *explicit* feedback from users.

- **The user specifies their requirements.** The user can specify their requirements through a dialog about their preferences in plain English [50, 83]. Such a dialog does not make use of the user's previous interests, nor does it explain *directly*. That is, there is no sentence that claims to be a justification of the recommendation. It does however do so indirectly, by reiterating (and satisfying) the user's *requirements*.
- **The user asks for an alternation.** A more direct approach is to allow users to explicitly critique recommended items [46], for instance using a structured overview (see Sect. 10.2.1). One such system explains the difference between a selected item and remaining items [45].
- **The user rates items.** To change the type of recommendations they receive, the user may want to correct predicted ratings, or modify a rating they made in the past. The *influence based explanation* in Table 10.1 shows which rated titles influenced the recommended book the most [9].
- **The user gives their opinion.** A common usability principle is that it is easier for humans to recognize items, than to draw them from memory. For example, a user could specify whether they think an item is interesting or not, if they would like to see more similar items, or if they have already seen the item previously [10, 69]. Amazon.com has explanations that could support this type of interaction: *"Recommended for you [item] because you purchased [item list]"*. For these types of interactions, the item is part of the explanation. The system can strengthen the recommendation by explaining how or why this item was selected.

Table 10.1 The *influence based explanation* showed which rated titles influenced the recommended book the most. Although this particular system did not allow the user to modify previous ratings, or degree of influence, in the explanation interface, it can be imagined that users could directly change their rating here. Note however, that it would be much harder to modify the degree of influence, as it is computed: any modification is likely to interfere with the regular functioning of the recommendation algorithm [9]

Book	Your rating out of 5	Influence out of 100
Of Mice and Men	4	54
1984	4	50
Till We Have Faces: A Myth Retold	5	50
Crime and Punishment	4	46
The Gambler	5	11

[1] A fifth section on mixed interaction interfaces is appended to the end of this original list.

Figure 10.5 gives another example explanation along these lines, comparing a recommendation with previously rated items.
- **Mixed interaction interfaces.** Recommender systems can also combine different types of interactions [16, 48]. Chen and Pu [16] uses a combination of system generated and user-driven critiques. McNee et al. [48] allowed both user and system to select items to rate, and found that asking users for items to rate increases user loyalty to the system. This tentatively suggests that explanations accompanying these interactions should mention if the critique or item was user or system selected.

10.3 Explanation Styles

By applying a particular algorithm in a recommender systems, certain types of explanations may be easier to generate since the algorithm can produce the type of information that the explanation style uses. In this section we describe explanations that would be supported best by a particular underlying algorithm, or different "explanation styles". We caution that explanations may follow the "style" of a particular algorithm irrespective of whether or not this is how the recommendations have been retrieved or computed. In other words, the explanation style for a given explanation *may, or may not,* reflect the underlying algorithm by which the recommendations are computed. There often is a divergence between how the recommendations are retrieved and the style of the given explanations. Consequently, this type of explanation would not be consistent with the goal of transparency, but may support other explanatory goals.

Transparency is not the only explanatory goal (see Sect. 10.4 on different explanatory aims and ways to measure them) to consider when deciding upon explanation style. For example, for a given system one might find that users are more satisfied with content-based style explanations even though critique-based style explanations are more efficient. The closest tie between explanation styles and explanatory aims inspired by an algorithm can be found in [36], who compared the understandability and scrutability of explanation styles inspired by different algorithms. More generally, there is a small body of studies which have considered the effects of different explanation styles on explanatory goals [20, 35, 56, 77]. This body of work does not tie the explanation style strongly to any specific algorithm. Papadimitriou et al. [56] for example, considers a classification of explanation styles that is independent from algorithms which includes human style explanations, item style explanations and feature style explanations.

Notwithstanding, the underlying algorithm of a recommender engine will to a certain degree influence the types of explanations that can be generated. Table 10.2 summarizes the most commonly used explanation styles (case-based, content-based, collaborative-based, demographic-based, knowledge and utility-based) with examples of each. In this section we describe each style: their *assumed* inputs, processes and generated explanations. For commercial systems where this information is not

Table 10.2 Examples of explanations in commercial and academic systems, ordered by explanation style (case-based, collaborative-based, content-based, conversational, demographic-based and knowledge/utility-based)

System	Example explanation	Explanation style
iSuggest-Usability [36]	See e.g. Fig. 10.5	Case-based
LoveFilm.com	*"Because you have selected or highly rated: Movie A"*	Case-based
LibraryThing.com	"Recommended By User X for Book A"	Case-based
Netflix.com	A list of similar movies the user has rated highly in the past	Case-based
Amazon.com	*"Customers Who Bought This Item Also Bought . . . "*	Collaborative-based
LIBRA [9]	Keyword style (Tables 10.6 and 10.7); neighbor style (Fig. 10.7); influence style (Table 10.1)	Collaborative-based
MovieLens [35]	Histogram of neighbors (Fig. 10.3)	Collaborative-based
Amazon.com	*"Recommended because you said you owned Book A"*	Content-based
CHIP [20]	*"Why is 'The Tailor's Workshop recommended to you'? Because it has the following themes in common with artworks that you like: * Everyday Life * Clothes . . . "*	Content-based
Moviexplain [70]	See Table 10.3	Content-based
MovieLens: *"Tagsplanations"* [81]	Tags ordered by relevance or preference (see Fig. 10.4)	Content-based
News Dude [10]	*"This story received a [high/low] relevance score, because it contains the words f1, f2, and f3."*	Content-based
OkCupid.com	Graphs comparing two users according to dimensions such as "more introverted"; comparison of how users have answered different questions	Content-based
Pandora.com	*"Based on what you've told us so far, we're playing this track because it features a leisurely tempo . . . "*	Content-based
Adaptive place Advisor [72]	Dialog e.g. "Where would you like to eat?" "Oh, maybe a cheap Indian place."	Conversational
ACORN [84]	Dialog e.g. "What kind of movie do you feel like?" "I feel like watching a thriller."	Conversational
INTRIGUE [4]	*"For children it is much eye-catching, it requires low background knowledge, it requires a few seriousness and the visit is quite short. For yourself it is much eye-catching and it has high historical value. For impaired it is much eye-catching and it has high historical value."*	Demographic-based
Qwikshop [45]	*"Less Memory and Lower Resolution and Cheaper"*	Knowledge/utility-based

(continued)

Table 10.2 (continued)

SASY [21]	"*...because your profile has: *You are single; *You have a high budget*" (Fig. 10.6)	Knowledge/utility-based
Top Case [50]	"Case 574 differs from your query only in price and is the best case no matter what transport, duration, or accommodation you prefer"	Knowledge/utility-based
(Internet Provider) [25]	"*This solution has been selected for the following reasons: *Webspace is available for this type of connection ...*" (Fig. 10.8)	Knowledge/utility-based
"Organizational Structure" [59]	Structured overview: "*We also recommend the following products because: *they are cheaper and lighter, but have lower processor speed.*" (Fig. 10.2)	Knowledge/utility-based
myCameraAdvisor [82]	e.g "...cameras capable of taking pictures from very far away will be more expensive ..."	Knowledge/utility-based

public, we offer educated guesses. While conversational systems are included in Table 10.2, we consider conversational systems as more of an interaction style than a specific algorithm.

In the following sections we will give further examples of how explanation styles can be inspired by common algorithms as classified by Burke [12]. For each example we also mention how the recommendations are presented, and the interaction model that was chosen.

For describing the interface between the recommender system and explanation component we use the notation used in [12]: U is the set of users whose preferences are known, and $u \in U$ is the user for whom recommendations need to be generated. I is the set of items that can be recommended, and $i \in I$ is an item for which we would like to predict u's preferences.

10.3.1 Collaborative-Based Style Explanations

For collaborative-based style explanations the assumed input to the recommender engine are user u's ratings of items in I. In user-based collaborative filtering these ratings are used to identify users that are similar in ratings to u. These similar users are often called "neighbors" as nearest-neighbors approaches are commonly used to compute recommendations. A prediction for the recommended item is extrapolated from the neighbors' ratings of i (e.g. using a weighted average over the neighbors predictions).

Commercially, the most well known usage of collaborative-based explanations are the ones used by Amazon.com: *"Customers Who Bought This Item Also Bought ... "*. This explanation assumes that the user is viewing an item which they are already interested in, and the explanation and several recommendations are shown just below it. The approach used on Amazon is a item-based collaborative approach, which recommends items based on item (rating) similarity. This approach is different from the approach described above in that it uses the similarity between items (rather than users) to compute a recommendation. The recommendations are presented in the format of similar to top item. In addition, this explanation suggests a preference elication model whereby ratings are inferred from purchase behavior rather explicitly requested. (Note that Amazon also supplies recommendations in different aspects of the website, some of which use elicit rating elicitation.)

Herlocker et al. suggested 21 explanation interfaces using text as well as graphics [35]. These interfaces varied with regard to content and style, but a number of these explanations directly referred to the concept of neighbors. Figure 10.3 for example, shows how neighbors rated a given (recommended) movie, a bar chart with "good", "ok" and "bad" ratings clustered into distinct columns. Again, we see that this explanation is given for a specific way of recommending items, and a particular interaction model: this is a single recommendation (either top item or one item out of a top-N list), and assumes that the users are supplying rating information for items.

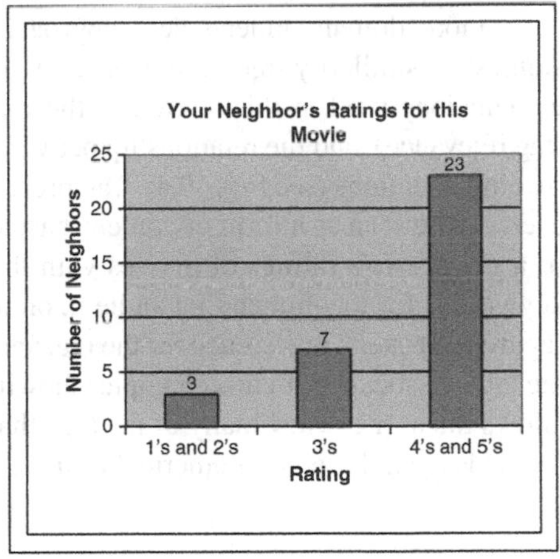

Fig. 10.3 One out of 21 interfaces evaluated for persuasiveness—a histogram summarizing the ratings of similar users (neighbors) for the recommended item grouped by good (5 and 4's), neutral (3s), and bad (2s and 1s), on a scale from 1 to 5 [35]

In the classification of [56], collaborative-based style explanations are a type of human explanation style, since they are based on similar users.

10.3.2 Content-Based Style Explanation

For content-based style explanations the assumed input to the recommender engine are user u's ratings (for a sub-set) of items in I. These ratings are then used to generate a classifier that fits u's rating behavior and use it on i. Recommendations are items that the classifier predicts having the highest ratings.

If we simplify this further, we could say that content-based algorithms consider similarity between items, based on user ratings but considering item properties. In the same spirit, content-based style explanations are based on the items' properties. For example, [70] justifies a movie recommendation according to what they infer is the user's favorite actor (see Table 10.3). While the underlying approach is in fact a hybrid of collaborative- and content-based approaches, the explanation style suggests that they compute the similarity between movies according to the presence of features in highly rated movies. They elected to present users with several recommendations and explanations (top-N) which may be more suitable if the user would like to make a selection between movies depending on the information given in the explanations (e.g. feeling more like watching a movie with Harrison Ford over one starring Bruce Willis). The interaction model is based on ratings of items.

A more domain independent approach is suggested by Vig et al. [81] who suggest a similarity measure based on user specified keywords, or tags. The explanations used in this study use the relationship between keywords and items (tag relevance), and the relationship between tags and users (tag preference) to make recommendations (see Fig. 10.4). Tag preference, or how relevant a tag is for a given user, can be seen as a form of content-based explanation, as it is a weighted average of a given user's ratings of movies with that tag. Tag relevance, or how relevant a keyword is for recommending an item, on the other hand is the correlation between (aggregate) users' preference for the tag, and their preference for a movie with which the tag is associated. In this example, showing recommendations as a single top item allows the user to view many of the tags that are related to the item. The interaction model is again based on numerical ratings.

Table 10.3 Example of an explanation in Moviexplain, using features such as actors, which occur for movies previously rated highly by this user, to justify a recommendation [70]

Recommended movie title	The reason is the participant	Who appears in
Indiana Jones and the Last Crusade (1989)	Ford, Harrison	Five movies you have rated
Die Hard 2 (1990)	Willis, Bruce	Two movies you have rated

Fig. 10.4 Tagsplanation with both tag preference and relevance, but sorted by tag relevance [81]

Your prediction is based on how MovieLens thinks you like these aspects of the film:

Relevance ↓ Your preference

wes anderson

deadpan

quirky

witty

off-beat comedy

notable soundtrack

stylized

The commercial system Pandora explains its recommendations of songs according to musical properties such as tempo and tonality. These features are inferred from users' ratings of songs. Figure 10.1 shows an example of this [1]. Here, the user is offered one song at a time (top item) and gives their opinion as "thumbs-up" or "thumbs-down" which also can be considered as numerical ratings.

In the classification of [56], content-based style explanations are a type of feature based explanation, since they explain the recommendation in terms of similarity of item features to (features of) previously rated items.

10.3.3 Case-Based Reasoning (CBR) Style Explanations

Explanations can also omit mention of detailed item features (e.g. music genre, actor in a movie) and focus primarily on the similar items used to make the recommendation. The items used are thus considered cases for comparison, resulting in case-based style explanations. We note that CBR systems greatly vary with regard to the recommendation algorithm. For example, the FINDME recommender [13] is based on critiquing, and the ranking of items in [2] is based on their presence in travel plans of users who expressed similar interests.

While these CBR systems have also used different methods to present their explanations, we recall that this section, and the sections describing the other explanation styles, are focused on the *style* of the explanation rather than the actual underlying algorithm. As such, each of these systems could in theory have had a case-based style explanation.

The "influence based style explanation" of [9] in Table 10.1 is a type of case-based style explanation. Here, the influence of an item on the recommendation is computed by looking at the difference in the score for the recommended item computed with the influential item, and the score for the recommender item when computed without that influential item. In this case, recommendations were presented as top item, assuming a rating based interaction. Another study computed

Fig. 10.5 Learn by example, or case based reasoning [36]

the similarity between recommended items,[2] and used these similar items as justification for a top item recommendation in the "learn by example" explanations (see Fig. 10.5) [36]. A recent study compared case-based explanations with feature-based explanations. Showing participants previous items (case-based explanations) during the rating process improved accuracy (RMSE) and was considered most useful by participants [52].

In the classification of [56], case-based reasoning style explanations are a type of item style explanations, since they use exemplars of items to justify a recommendation.

10.3.4 Knowledge and Utility-Based Style Explanations

Knowledge-based systems reason over a knowledge-base to solve problems through rules in an inference engine. One common category of knowledge-based system are case-based systems which use examples of previous similar situations or cases to predict an outcome or solution. It is therefore arguable that there is a degree of overlap between knowledge-based, content-based (Sect. 10.3.2) and case-based style explanations (Sect. 10.3.3) which can be derived from either type of algorithm depending on the details of the implementation.

For all knowledge and utility-based style explanations the assumed input to the recommender engine are description of user u's needs or interests. The recommender engine then infers a match between the item i and u's needs. One

[2]The author does not specify which similarity metric was used, though it is likely to be a form of rating based similarity measure such as cosine similarity.

knowledge-based recommender system takes into consideration how camera properties such as memory, resolution and price reflect the available options as well as a user's preferences [45]. Their system may explain a camera recommendation in the following manner: *"Less Memory and Lower Resolution and Cheaper"*. Here, recommendations are presented as a form of structured overview describing the competing options, and the interaction model assumes that users ask for alterations in the recommended items.

Similarly, in the system described in [50] users gradually specify (and modify) their preferences until a top recommendation is reached. This system can generate explanations such as the following for a recommended holiday titled "Case 574": *"Top Case: Case 574 differs from your query only in price and is the best case no matter what transport, duration, or accommodation you prefer"*.

The classification of [56] does not cover this style of explanation.

10.3.5 Demographic-Based Style Explanations

For demographic-based style explanations, the assumed input to the recommender engine is demographic information about user u. From this, the recommendation algorithm identifies users that are demographically similar to u. A prediction for the recommended item i is extrapolated from how the similar users rated this item, and how similar they are to u considering their demographic features.

Surveying a number of systems which use a demographic-based filter e.g. [4, 39, 57], we could only find one which offers an explanation facility: *"For children it is much eye-catching, it requires low background knowledge, it requires a few seriousness and the visit is quite short. For yourself it is much eye-catching and it has high historical value. For impaired it is much eye-catching and it has high historical value."* [4]. In this system recommendations were offered as a structured overview, categorizing places to visit according to their suitability to different types of travelers (e.g. children, impaired). Users can then add these items to their itinerary, but there is no interaction model that modifies subsequent recommendations

To our knowledge, there are no other systems that make use of demographic style explanations. It is possible that this is due to the sensitivity of demographic information; anecdotally we can imagine that many users would not want to be recommended an item based on their gender, age or ethnicity (e.g. *"We recommend you the movie Sex in the City because you are a female aged 20–40."*).

The classification of [56] does not cover this style of explanation.

10.4 Goals and Metrics

Surveying the literature for explanations in recommender systems, we see that recommender systems with explanatory capabilities have been evaluated according to different criteria, and identify seven different goals for explanations of single item recommendations. Here we mention goals that are applicable to single item recommendations, i.e. when a single recommendation is being offered. When recommendations are made for multiple items, such as in a list, additional factors such as diversity (e.g. "this list contains items that are different from each other in order to improve variation") may be relevant.

Table 10.4 states these goals, some of which are similar to those desired (but not evaluated on) in expert systems, cf. MYCIN [8]. In Table 10.5, we summarize previous evaluations of explanations in recommender systems, and the goal by which they have been evaluated. Works that have no clear goal stated, or have not evaluated the system on the explanation goal which they state, are omitted from this table.

In the introduction, we mentioned that expert systems were commonly evaluated in terms of user acceptance and the decision support of the system as a whole. User acceptance can be defined in terms of our goals of satisfaction or persuasion. If the evaluation measures acceptance with the system as whole, such as [14] who asked questions such as *"Did you like the program?"*, this reflects user satisfaction. If rather the evaluation measures user acceptance of advice or explanations, as in [87], the criterion can be said to be persuasion.

It is important to identify these goals as distinct, even if they may interact, or require certain trade-offs. Indeed, it would be hard to generate explanations that do well for all of the goals, in reality it is a trade-off. While personalized explanations may lead to greater user satisfaction, they do not necessarily increase effectiveness [29, 77, 78]. Other times, goals that seem to be inherently related are not necessarily so, for example it has been found that transparency does not necessarily aid trust [20]. For these reasons, while an explanation in Table 10.5 may have been evaluated for several goals, it may not have achieved them all.

The type of explanation that is given to a user is likely to depend on the goals of the designer of a recommender system. For instance, when building a system

Table 10.4 Explanatory goals and their definitions

Aim	Definition
Transparency (Tra.)	Explain how the system works
Scrutability (Scr.)	Allow users to tell the system it is wrong
Trust	Increase users' confidence in the system
Effectiveness (Efk.)	Help users make good decisions
Persuasiveness (Pers.)	Convince users to try or buy
Efficiency (Efc.)	Help users make decisions faster
Satisfaction (Sat.)	Increase the ease of use or enjoyment

Table 10.5 The goals for which explanations in recommender systems have been evaluated. System names are mentioned if given, otherwise we only note the type of recommended items. Works that have no clear goal stated, or have not *evaluated* the system on the explanation goal which they state, are omitted from this table. Note that while a system may have been evaluated for several goals, it may not have achieved all of them. Also, for the sake of completeness we have distinguished between multiple studies using the same system

System (type of items)	Tra.	Scr.	Trust	Efk.	Per.	Efc.	Sat.
(Advice, intrusion detection system) [24]				X			
(Internet providers) [25]			X		X		X
(Financial advice, internet providers) [26]						X	X
(Digital cameras, notebooks computers) [59]			X				
(Digital cameras, notebooks computers) [60]			X	X			
(Image tags and movies) [66]	X			X		X	
(Music) [68]			X				
(Music) [40]	X		X				
(Music) [67]				X	X		
(Movies) [29]	X			X	X	X	X
(Movies) [77, 78]				X	X		X
(Social network news) [51]	X	X	X				
Adaptive place advisor (restaurants) [72]				X		X	
ACORN (movies) [84]							X
CHIP (cultural heritage artifacts) [19]	X		X	X			
CHIP (cultural heritage artifacts) [20]	X		X				X
iSuggest-Usability (music) [36]	X			X			
LIBRA (books) [9]				X			
MovieLens (movies) [35]					X		X
Moviexplain (movies) [70]				X			X
myCameraAdvisor [82]			X				
Qwikshop (digital cameras) [45]				X		X	
SASY (e.g. holidays) [21]	X	X					X
Tagsplanations (movies) [81]	X			X			

that sells books one might decide that user trust is the most important aspect, as it leads to user loyalty and increases sales. For selecting tv-shows, user satisfaction could be more important than effectiveness. That is, in a system focused on pure entertainment it may be more important that a user enjoys using the service, than that they are presented the very best available shows (as long as the shows are "good enough").

In addition, some attributes of explanations may contribute toward achieving multiple goals. For instance, one can measure how *understandable* an explanation is, which can contribute to e.g. user trust, as well as satisfaction.

In this section we describe seven potential aims for explanations (Table 10.4), and suggest evaluation metrics based on previous evaluations of explanation facilities, or offer suggestions of how existing measures could be adapted to evaluate the explanation facility in a recommender system.

10.4.1 Explain How the System Works: Transparency

An anecdotal article in the Wall Street Journal titled "*If TiVo Thinks You Are Gay, Here's How to Set It Straight*" describes users' frustration with irrelevant choices made by a video recorder that records programs it assumes its owner will like, based on shows the viewer has recorded in the past.[3] For example, one user, Mr. Iwanyk, suspected that his TiVo thought he was gay since it inexplicably kept recording programs with gay themes. This user clearly deserved an explanation.

An explanation may clarify *how* a recommendation was chosen. In expert systems, such as in the domain of medical decision making, the importance of transparency has also been recognized [8]. Transparency or the heuristic of "Visibility of System Status" is also an established usability principle [53], and its importance has also been highlighted in user studies of recommender systems [68].

Vig et al. differentiate between transparency and justification [81]. While transparency should give an honest account of how the recommendations are selected and how the system works, justification can be descriptive and decoupled from the recommendation algorithm. The authors cite several reasons for opting for justification rather than genuine transparency. For example some algorithms that are difficult to explain (e.g. latent semantic analysis where the distinguishing factors are latent and may not have a clear interpretation), protection of trade secrets by system designers, and the desire for greater freedom in designing the explanations.

Cramer et al. studied the effect of transparency on other evaluation goals such as trust, persuasion (acceptance of items) and satisfaction (acceptance) in an art recommender [19, 20]. Transparency itself was evaluated in terms of its effect on actual and perceived understanding of how the system works [20]. Actual understanding was based on the correctness of user answers to interview questions such as "Could you please tell me how the system works..." . *Perceived* understanding was extracted from self-reports in questionnaires and interviews, measuring responses to statements such as "I understand what the system bases its recommendations on".

The evaluation of transparency has also been coupled with scrutability (Sect. 10.4.2) and trust (Sect. 10.4.3), but we will see in these sections that these goals can be distinct from each other.

[3]http://online.wsj.com/article_email/SB1038261936872356908.html, retrieved Feb. 12, 2009.

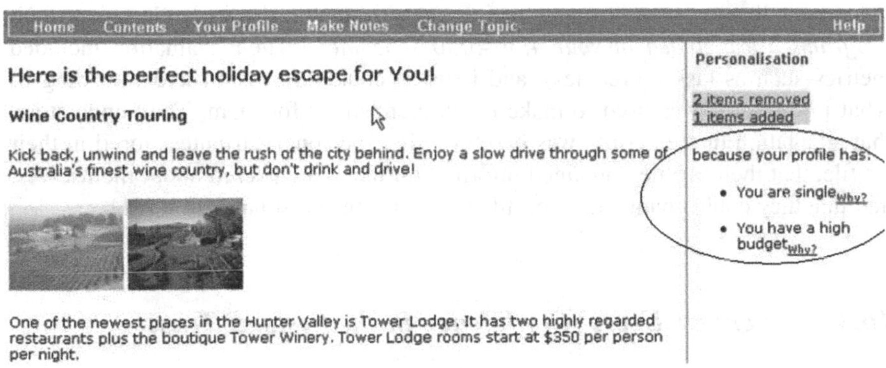

Fig. 10.6 Scrutable holiday recommender [21]. The explanation is in the *circled area*, and the user profile can be accessed via the "why" links

10.4.2 Allow Users to Tell the System It Is Wrong: Scrutability

Explanations may help isolate and correct misguided assumptions or steps. When the system collects and interprets information in the background, as is the case with TiVo, it becomes all the more important to allow the user to modify these assumptions or steps. Explanations can be used in way that helps the users to *correct* reasoning, or make the system *scrutable* [21]. Scrutability is related to the established usability principle of User Control [53]. See Fig. 10.6 for an example of a scrutable holiday recommender. Here the user can ask why certain assumptions (like a low budget) were made. Selecting this option takes them to a page with a further explanation and an option to modify this in their user model.

While scrutability is very closely tied to the goal of transparency, it deserves to be uniquely identified. Transparency in and of itself does not allow users to modify the reasoning in a system, and some systems may only offer partial transparency together with scrutability. The explanation in Fig. 10.1 (*"Based on what you've told us so far, we're playing this track because it features a leisurely tempo* ...") is transparent but not scrutable. Here, the user cannot change the ratings that affected this recommendation. If however, the ratings in Table 10.7 were changeable, we could argue that the explanation was scrutable. However, it is not (fully) transparent even if they offer some form of justification. There is nothing about the explanations in the table that suggests that the underlying recommendations are based on a Bayesian classifier. In such a case, we can imagine that a user attempts to scrutinize a recommender system, and manages to change their recommendations, but still does not understand exactly what happens within the system. In contrast, [30] made a preliminary attempt to make explanations that are both transparent and scrutable.

Czarkowski found that users were not likely to scrutinize on their own, and that extra effort was needed to make the scrutability tool more visible [21]. In addition, it was easier to get users to perform a given scrutinization task such as changing the personalization (e.g. "*Change the personalisation so that only Current Affairs programs are included in your 4:30–5:30 schedule.*") Their evaluation included metrics such as task correctness, and if users could express an understanding of what information was used to make recommendations for them. They understood that adaptation in the system was based on their personal attributes stored in their profile, that their profile contained information they volunteered about themselves, and that they could change their profile to control the personalization [21].

10.4.3 Increase Users' Confidence in the System: Trust

A study of users' trust (defined as perceived confidence in a recommender system's *competence*) suggests that users intend to return to recommender systems which they find trustworthy [15]. Trust in the recommender system could also be dependent on the accuracy of the recommendation algorithm [48]. Trust is also sometimes linked with transparency: previous studies indicate that transparency and the possibility of interaction with recommender systems increases user trust [25, 68].

We note however, that are also cases where transparency and trust were not found to be related [20]. Kulesza et al. [40] also found that poor explanations could decrease how beneficial they were found by users and led to poor mental models.

Consequently, we do not claim that explanations can fully compensate for poor recommendations, but that they can mitigate their effects on user trust. A user may be more forgiving, and more confident in recommendations, if they understand why a bad recommendation (or one based on low confidence) has been made and can prevent it from occurring again. A user may appreciate when a system is 'frank' and admits that it is not confident about a particular recommendation.

In addition, the interface design of a recommender system may affect its trustworthiness. In a study of factors determining web page credibility, the largest proportion of users' comments (46.1 %) referred to the appeal of the overall visual design of a site, including layout, typography, font size and color schemes [28]. Likewise the perceived credibility of a Web article was significantly affected by the presence of a photograph of the author [27]. So, while recommendation accuracy, and the goal of transparency are often linked to the evaluation of trust, design is also a factor that needs to be considered as part of the evaluation.

Questionnaires can be used to determine the degree of trust a user places in a system. An overview of trust questionnaires can be found in [54] which also suggests and validates a five dimensional scale of trust. Note that this validation was done with the aim of using celebrities to endorse products, but was not conducted for a particular domain. Additional validation may be required to adapt this scale to a particular recommendation domain.

A model of trust in recommender systems is proposed in [15, 60], and the questionnaires in these studies consider factors such as intent to return to the system, and intent to save effort. Also [82] query users about trust, but focus on trust related beliefs such as the perceived competence, benevolence and integrity of a virtual adviser. They found that the different trusting beliefs could be improved by explanations with different content. Although questionnaires can be very focused, they suffer from the fact that self-reports may not be consistent with user behavior. In these cases, implicit measures (although less focused) may reveal factors that explicit measures do not.

One such implicit measure could be loyalty, a desirable bi-product of trust. One study compared different interfaces for eliciting user preferences in terms of how they affected factors such as loyalty [48]. Loyalty was measured in terms of the number of logins and interactions with the system. Among other things, the study found that allowing users to independently choose which items to rate affected user loyalty. It has also been thought that Amazon's conservative use of recommendations, mainly recommending familiar items, enhances user trust and has led to increased sales [69]. We encourage readers who would like to learn more about trust in recommender systems to read a previous handbook chapter which is dedicated to this topic [80].

10.4.4 Convince Users to Try or Buy: Persuasiveness

Explanations may increase user acceptance of the system or the given recommendations [35]. Both definitions qualify as persuasion, as they are both attempts to influence the user.

Cramer et al. [20] evaluated the acceptance of recommended items in terms of how many recommended items were present in a final selection of six favorites. In a study of a collaborative filtering- and rating-based recommender system for movies, participants were given different explanation interfaces (e.g. Fig. 10.3) [35]. This study directly inquired how likely users were to see a movie (with identifying features such as title omitted) for 21 different explanation interfaces. Persuasion was thus a numerical rating on a 7-point Likert scale.

In addition, it is possible to measure if the evaluation of an item has changed, i.e. if the user rates an item differently after receiving an explanation. Indeed, it has been shown that users can be manipulated to give a rating closer to the system's prediction [18]. It has also been found that confidence information, or how "sure" a system is about the relevance or non-relevance of a recommendation, can influence user ratings. Shani et al. [66] found that participants were more likely to rate an item that was actually non-relevant as relevant if the system said it was very confident. For (truly) relevant items, the participants were also less likely to remain undecided about the relevance of items (a similar pattern was not found for items that were truly irrelevant).

Both studies were in subjective and low investment domains (movies and images), and it is possible that users may be less influenced by incorrect predictions in high(er) cost domains such as cameras.[4] It has also been found that confidence information can influence user ratings. In addition, too much persuasion may backfire once users realize that they have tried or bought items that they do not really want.

Persuasiveness can be measured in a number of ways, For example, it can be measured as the difference between two ratings: the first being a previous rating, and the second a re-rating for the same item but with an explanation interface [18]. Another possibility would be to measure how much users actually try or buy items compared to users in a system without an explanation facility. These metrics can also be understood in terms of the concept of "conversion rate" commonly used in e-Commerce, operationally defined as the percentage of visitors who take a desired action. For a more in-depth discussion of persuasion in recommender systems the reader may continue in Chap. 20.

10.4.5 Help Users Make Good Decisions: Effectiveness

Rather than simply persuading users to try or buy an item, an explanation may also assist users to make *better* decisions: accepting relevant items and discarding irrelevant ones [66, 77, 78]. Effectiveness is by definition highly dependent on the accuracy of the recommendation algorithm. An effective explanation would help the user evaluate the quality of suggested items according to their own preferences. This would increase the likelihood that the user discards irrelevant options while helping them to recognize useful ones. For example, a book recommender system with effective explanations would help a user to buy books they actually end up liking. Bilgic and Mooney emphasize the importance of measuring the ability of a system to assist the user in making accurate decisions about recommendations based on explanations such as those in Fig. 10.7, and Tables 10.6 and 10.7 [9]. Effective explanations could also serve the purpose of introducing a new domain, or the range of products, to a novice user, thereby helping them to understand the full range of options [25, 59].

Vig et al. measure perceived effectiveness: *"This explanation helps me determine how well I will like this movie."* [81]. Effectiveness of explanations can also be calculated as the *absence of a difference* between the liking of the recommended item prior to, and after, consumption. For example, in a previous study, users rated a book twice, once after receiving an explanation, and a second time after reading the book [9]. If their opinion on the book did not change much, the system was considered effective. This study explored the effect of the whole recommendation process, explanation inclusive, on effectiveness. The same metric was also used to evaluate whether personalization of explanations (in isolation of a recommender

[4]In [76] participants reported that they found incorrect overestimation less useful in high cost domains compared to low cost domains.

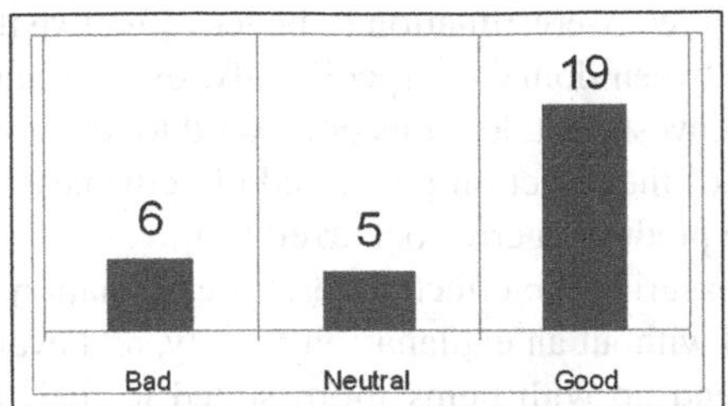

Fig. 10.7 The neighbor style explanation—a histogram summarizing the ratings of similar users (neighbors) for the recommended item grouped by good (5 and 4's), neutral (3s), and bad (2s and 1s), on a scale from 1 to 5. The similarity to Fig. 10.3 in this study was intentional, and was used to highlight the difference between persuasive and effective explanations [9]

Table 10.6 The keyword style explanation by Bilgic and Mooney [9] for an item (a book). The item is being recommended based on a number of keywords such as "HEART" and "MOTHER". The explanation lists keywords that were used in the description of the item, and that have previously been associated with highly rated items

Word	Count	Strength	Explain
HEART	2	96.14	*Explain*
BEAUTIFUL	1	17.07	*Explain*
MOTHER	3	11.55	*Explain*
READ	14	10.63	*Explain*
STORY	16	9.12	*Explain*

Table 10.7 A more detailed explanation for the strength of a keyword (such as "HEART") which shows after clicking on *"Explain"* in Table 10.6. The rows represent all the previous items which influence the strength of the keyword [9]

Title	Author	Rating	Count
Hunchback of Notre Dame	Victor Hugo, Walter J. Cobb	10	11
Till We Have Faces: A Myth Retold	C.S. Lewis, Fritz Eichenberg	10	10
The picture of Dorian Gray	Oscar Wilde, Isobel Murray	8	5

system) increased their effectiveness in the movie domain [76]. In [67] there is a distinction between the likelihood of finding out more about a recommended artist and the actual rating given to the artist after listening to several songs.

While this metric considers the difference between the before and after ratings, it does not discuss the effects of over- contra underestimation.[5] In our work we

[5]By overestimation we mean that the prediction is higher than the final or actual rating, and underestimation when the prediction is lower than it.

found that users considered overestimation to be less effective than underestimation, and that this varied between domains. Specifically, overestimation was considered more severely in high investment domains compared to low investment domains. In addition, the strength of the effect on perceived effectiveness varied depending on where on the scale the prediction error occurred [76].

Another way of measuring the effectiveness of explanations has been to test the same system with and without an explanation facility, and evaluate if subjects who receive explanations end up with items more suited to their personal tastes [19]. This approach has been used in work which measured both perceived effectiveness (helpfulness) and performance accuracy (actual effectiveness) [24].

Other work evaluated explanation effectiveness using a metric from marketing [34], with the aim of finding the single *best* possible item (rather than "good enough items" as above) [16]. Participants interacted with the system until they found the item they would buy. They were then given the opportunity to survey the entire catalog and to change their choice of item. Effectiveness was then measured by the fraction of participants who found a better item when comparing with the complete selection of alternatives in the database. So, using this metric, a low fraction represents high effectiveness.

Effectiveness is the criterion that is most closely related to accuracy measures such as precision and recall [19, 70, 72]. In systems where items are easily consumed, these can be translated into recognizing relevant items and discarding irrelevant options respectively [66]. For example, there have been suggestions for an alternative metric of "precision" based on the number of profile concepts matching with user interests, divided by the number of concepts in their profile [19].

10.4.6 Help Users Make Decisions Faster: Efficiency

Explanations may make it *faster* for users to decide which recommended item is best for them. Efficiency is another established usability principle, i.e. how quickly a task can be performed [53]. This criterion is one of the most commonly addressed in the recommender systems literature (See Table 10.5) given that the task of recommender systems is to find needles in haystacks of information.

Efficiency may be improved by allowing the user to understand the relation between competing options. McCarthy et al. [45], McSherry [50], and Pu and Chen [59] use so called critiquing, a sub-class of knowledge-based algorithms based on trade-offs between item properties, which lends itself well to the generation of explanations. The rules generated by the algorithm can intuitively be translated to rules such as *"Less Memory and Lower Resolution and Cheaper"* [45]. This explanation can help users to find a cheaper camera more quickly if they are willing to settle for less memory and lower resolution. The efficiency of these explanations is closely tied with the efficiency of the query language, but can also be compared from a user-centered perspective in terms of the number of interactions needed by a user to make a choice.

Efficiency is often used in the evaluation of so-called conversational recommender systems, where users continually interact with a recommender system, refining their preferences (see also Sect. 10.2.2). In these systems, the explanations can be seen to be implicit in the dialog. Efficiency in these systems can be measured by the total amount of interaction time, and number of interactions needed to find a satisfactory item [72]. Evaluations of explanations based on improvements in efficiency are not limited to conversational systems however. Pu and Chen for example, compared completion time for two explanatory interfaces, and measured completion time as the amount of time it took a participant to locate a desired product in the interface [59].

Other metrics for efficiency also include the number of inspected explanations, and number of activations of repair actions when no satisfactory items are found [25, 63]. Normally, it is not sensible to expose users to all possible recommendations and their explanations, and so users can choose to inspect (or scrutinize) a given recommendation by asking for an explanation. In a more efficient system, the users would need to inspect *fewer* explanations. Repair actions consist of feedback from the user which changes the type of recommendation they receive, as outlined in the sections on scrutability (Sect. 10.4.2). Examples of user feedback/repair actions can be found in Sect. 10.2.2.

10.4.7 Make the Use of the System Enjoyable: Satisfaction

Explanations have been found to increase user satisfaction with, or acceptance of, the overall recommender system [25, 35, 68]. Gedikli et al. [29] studied the effect of various explanatory aims on satisfaction, and found that user-perceived transparency had a significant positive effect on overall satisfaction with the explanation interfaces (but did not find an effect of efficiency or effectiveness on satisfaction). The presence of longer descriptions of individual items has been found to be positively correlated with both the *perceived* usefulness [75], and ease of use of the recommender system [68]. Also, many commercial recommender systems such as those seen in Table 10.2 are primarily sources of entertainment. In these cases, any extra facility should take notice of the effect on user satisfaction. Figure 10.8 gives an example of an explanation evaluated on the criterion of satisfaction.

When measuring satisfaction, one can directly ask users whether the system is enjoyable to use. Tanaka-Ishii and Frank in their evaluation of a multi-agent system describing a Robocup soccer game ask users whether they prefer the system

This solution has been selected for the following reasons:
• Webspace is available for this type of connection.
• This package is available for you, connections are possible for each location in your state.
• The monthly costs for the internet connection are beyond the limit you defined for the connection.

Fig. 10.8 An explanations for an internet provider, describing the provider in terms of user requirements: "This solution has been selected for the following reasons ...". This explanation has been evaluated on satisfaction, among other aims [25]

with or without explanations [71]. Satisfaction can also be measured indirectly by measuring user loyalty [25, 48] (see also Sect. 10.4.3), and likelihood of using the system for a search task [20].

In measuring explanation satisfaction, it is important to differentiate between satisfaction with the recommendation process,[6] and the recommended products (persuasion) [20, 25]. One (qualitative) way to measure satisfaction with the process would be to conduct usability testing methods such as record a think-aloud protocol for a user conducting a task [43].

In this case, the participants describe their entire experience using the system: what they are looking at, thinking, doing and feeling, as they go about a task such as finding a satisfactory item. Objective notes of everything that users say are taken, without interpretation or influencing the users in any way. Video and voice recordings can also be used to revisit the session and to serve as a memory aid. In such a case, it is possible to identify usability issues and even apply quantitative metrics such as the ratio of positive to negative comments; the number of times the evaluator was frustrated; the number of times the evaluator was delighted; the number of times and where the evaluator worked around a usability problem etc.

It is also arguable that users would be satisfied with a system that offers effective explanations, confounding the two goals. However, a system that aids users in making good decisions, may have other disadvantages that decrease the overall satisfaction (e.g. requiring a large cognitive effort on the part of the user). Fortunately, these two goals can be measured by distinct metrics.

10.5 Future Directions

This section identifies four strands of promising future directions. Firstly, it seems likely that future explanations will reflect the social nature of recommendations. Secondly, explanations may support users in making unexpected discoveries

[6]Here we mean the entire recommendation process, inclusive of the explanations. We note however that the evaluation of explanations in recommender systems are seldom fully independent of the underlying recommendation process.

and understanding which options got filtered out. Thirdly, we discuss whether explanations should always be visible, invoked by the user or by certain contexts. Finally, more research is required to identify when explanations are helpful, and under which circumstances they may be detrimental.

10.5.1 Social Recommendations

Increasingly, recommendations are based not only on similarity between items or rating patterns, but also on information in social networks. While this area of research is still very young, it is likely one that will have a great impact on explanations in the near future. Ongoing research has been studying the impact of recommendations based on people's relationships in online social networks [51, 58, 85], and geographic information [7, 64, 89], in addition to more classical recommendation algorithms. One particular interesting strand regards reciprocal vs. non-reciprocal relationships [32, 58]. Open questions regard how different types of relationships may affect explanation strength, and how this affects the actual (rather than perceived) effectiveness of the explanations. Please refer to Chap. 15 for further reading.

10.5.2 Explanations, Serendipity and the Filter Bubble

Explanations may have a role in helping users accept new and unexpected (serendipitous) items. [51] have looked at visualizing the 'filter bubble', i.e. the limited coverage for an individual user which can result from the filtering inherent to recommendation. In parallel, a growing body of research is studying how to computationally model serendipity for recommender systems [3, 37, 74]. There is also a body of research on visualizations of the recommendation space (see e.g. [31, 79]), and some indication that increasing diversity can help find target items [11]. It remains an open challenge to tie together visual or textual explanations to serendipity. More generally, the link between recommender systems evaluations and explanations evaluation for criteria such as coverage, acceptance and learning rate is still under-developed, although some tentative efforts are being made [65]. Issues relating to diversity and novelty in recommender systems are also discussed in Chap. 26 of this handbook.

10.5.3 When Should Explanations Be Shown?

Another question that remains open is whether the explanation mechanism should be invoked by the user, by a specific context or if they should always be presented to the user.

While explanations in recommender systems may be most beneficial for experienced users [26], explanations research in other types of decision support systems have found that explanations are helpful when something unexpected or undesired happens [22].. There is also some tentative support for the idea that people who actually look at explanations in recommender systems use them more [24].

In general, a proactive approach appears to be the best approach for recommender systems [21, 22]. However, an additional analysis of cognitive load in high cost domains (cf. work in aviation[7]) should be considered, in line with previous research on the trade-off between the cost and benefit of explanations [17, 40].

10.5.4 Explanations: Help or Harm?

Researchers are starting to find that explanations are part of a cyclical process: the explanations affect acceptance of particular recommendations , the user's mental model of the algorithm in the recommender system, and in turn this affects the ways users interact with the explanations. Explanations may affect users' behavior toward the system, and consequently the recommendations that they are given [5, 82]. Overall however, it is still largely unclear how users' mental models are affected by the cyclical and longer-term interaction between explanations and recommendations. Initial work suggests that they can be harmful [5, 20, 24, 66]. For example, [24] found that at least for a small sub-set of users, explanations not only helped accept good decisions but also increased their acceptance of incorrect advice. How to ensure that explanations are helpful (also in the long term) is another promising avenue for future research.

References

1. Pandora (2006). http://www.pandora.com
2. Nutking (2010). http://nutking.ectrldev.com/nutking/jsp/language.do?action=english
3. Adamopoulos, P., Tuzhilin, A.: On unexpectedness in recommender systems: Or how to except the unexpected. In: Workshop on Novelty and Diversity in Recommender Systems in conjuction with Recsys (2011)
4. Adrissono, L., Goy, A., Petrone, G., Segnan, M., Torasso, P.: Intrigue: Personalized recommendation of tourist attractions for desktop and handheld devices. Applied Artificial Intelligence **17**, 687–714 (2003)
5. Ahn, J.W., Brusilovsky, P., Grady, J., He, D., Syn, S.Y.: Open user profiles for adaptive news systems: help or harm? In: World Wide Web (WWW), pp. 11–20. ACM Press, New York, NY, USA (2007)

[7] http://www.aea.net/AvionicsNews/ANArchives/DesignDisplayOct03.pdf, retrieved Nov. 2013.

6. Andersen, S.K., Olesen, K.G., Jensen, F.V.: HUGIN—a shell for building Bayesian belief universes for expert systems. Morgan Kaufmann Publishers Inc., San Francisco, CA, USA (1990)
7. Backstrom, L., Sun, E., Marlow, C.: Find me if you can: Improving geographical prediction with social and spatial proximity. In: World Wide Web (WWW) (2010)
8. Bennett, S.W., Scott., A.C.: The Rule-Based Expert Systems: The MYCIN Experiments of the Stanford Heuristic Programming Project, chap. 19 - Specialized Explanations for Dosage Selection, pp. 363–370. Addison-Wesley Publishing Company (1985)
9. Bilgic, M., Mooney, R.J.: Explaining recommendations: Satisfaction vs. promotion. In: Proceedings of the Wokshop Beyond Personalization, in conjunction with the International Conference on Intelligent User Interfaces, pp. 13–18 (2005)
10. Billsus, D., Pazzani, M.J.: A personal news agent that talks, learns, and explains. In: Proceedings of the Third International Conference on Autonomous Agents, pp. 268–275 (1999)
11. Bridge, D., Kelly, J.P.: Ways of computing diverse collaborative recommendations. In: Adaptive Hypermedia and Adaptive Web-based Systems (2006)
12. Burke, R.: Hybrid recommender systems: Survey and experiments. User Modeling and User-Adapted Interaction **12(4)**, 331–370 (2002)
13. Burke, R.D., Hammond, K.J., Young, B.C.: Knowledge-based navigation of complex information spaces. In: AAAI/IAAI, Vol. 1, pp. 462–468 (1996)
14. Carenini, G., Mittal, V., Moore, J.: Generating patient-specific interactive natural language explanations. Proc Annu Symp Comput Appl Med Care pp. 5–9 (1994)
15. Chen, L., Pu, P.: Trust building in recommender agents. In: WPRSIUI in conjunction with Intelligent User Interfaces, pp. 93–100 (2002)
16. Chen, L., Pu, P.: Hybrid critiquing-based recommender systems. In: Intelligent User Interfaces, pp. 22–31 (2007)
17. Chen, L., Pu, P.: Interaction design guidelines on critiquing-based recommender systems. User Modeling and User-Adapted Interaction **3**, 167–206 (2009)
18. Cosley, D., Lam, S.K., Albert, I., Konstan, J.A., Riedl, J.: Is seeing believing?: how recommender system interfaces affect users' opinions. In: CHI, *Recommender systems and social computing*, vol. 1, pp. 585–592 (2003)
19. Cramer, H., Evers, V., Someren, M.V., Ramlal, S., Rutledge, L., Stash, N., Aroyo, L., Wielinga, B.: The effects of transparency on perceived and actual competence of a content-based recommender. In: Semantic Web User Interaction Workshop, CHI (2008)
20. Cramer, H.S.M., Evers, V., Ramlal, S., van Someren, M., Rutledge, L., Stash, N., Aroyo, L., Wielinga, B.J.: The effects of transparency on trust in and acceptance of a content-based art recommender. User Model. User-Adapt. Interact **18**(5), 455–496 (2008)
21. Czarkowski, M.: A scrutable adaptive hypertext. Ph.D. thesis, University of Sydney (2006)
22. Darlington, K.: Aspects of intelligent systems explanation. Universal Journal of Control and Automation **1**, 40–51 (2013)
23. Doyle, D., Tsymbal, A., Cunningham, P.: A review of explanation and explanation in case-based reasoning. Tech. rep., Department of Computer Science, Trinity College, Dublin (2003)
24. Erlich, K., Kirk, S., Patterson, J., Rasmussen, J., Ross, S., Gruen, D.: Taking advice from intelligent systems: The double-edged sword of explanations. In: Intelligent User Interfaces (2011)
25. Felfernig, A., Gula, B.: Consumer behavior in the interaction with knowledge-based recommender applications. In: ECAI 2006 Workshop on Recommender Systems, pp. 37–41 (2006)
26. Felfernig, A., Teppan, E., Gula, B.: Knowledge-based recommender technologies for marketing and sales. Int. J. Patt. Recogn. Artif. Intell. **21**, 333–355 (2007)
27. Fogg, B., Marshall, J., Kameda, T., Solomon, J., Rangnekar, A., Boyd, J., Brown, B.: Web credibility research: A method for online experiments and early study results. In: CHI 2001, pp. 295–296 (2001)
28. Fogg, B.J., Soohoo, C., Danielson, D.R., Marable, L., Stanford, J., Tauber, E.R.: How do users evaluate the credibility of web sites?: a study with over 2,500 participants. In: Designing for User Experiences (DUX), no. 15 in Focusing on user-to-product relationships, pp. 1–15 (2003)

29. Gedikli, F., Jannach, D., Ge, M.: How should I explain? A comparison of different explanation types of recommender systems. International Journal of Human-Computer Studies **72**(4), 367–382 (2014)
30. Green, S., Lamere, P., Alexander, J., Maillet, F.: Generating transparent, steerable recommendations from textual descriptions of items. In: Recommender Systems Conference (2009)
31. Gretarsson, B., O'Donovan, J., Bostandjiev, S., Hall, C., Höllerer, T.: Smallworlds: Visualizing social recommendations. Computer Graphics Forum **29**(3), 833–842 (2010)
32. Guy, I., Ronen, I., Wilcox, E.: Do you know? recommending people to invite into your social network. In: International Conference on Intelligent User Interfaces, pp. 77–86 (2009)
33. Hance, E., Buchanan, B.: Rule-based expert systems: the MYCIN experiments of the Stanford Heuristic Programming Project. Addison-Wesley (1984)
34. Häubl, G., Trifts, V.: Consumer decision making in online shopping environments: The effects of interactive decision aids. Marketing Science **19**, 4–21 (2000)
35. Herlocker, J.L., Konstan, J.A., Riedl, J.: Explaining collaborative filtering recommendations. In: ACM conference on Computer supported cooperative work, pp. 241–250 (2000)
36. Hingston, M.: User friendly recommender systems. Master's thesis, Sydney University (2006)
37. Hu, R., Pu, P.: Helping users perceive recommendation diversity. In: Workshop on Novelty and Diversity in Recommender Systems in conjunction with Recsys (2011)
38. Hunt, J.E., Price, C.J.: Explaining qualitative diagnosis. Engineering Applications of Artificial Intelligence **1**(3), Pages 161–169 (1988)
39. Krulwich, B.: The infofinder agent: Learning user interests through heuristic phrase extraction. IEEE Intelligent Systems **12**, 22–27 (1997)
40. Kulesza, T., Stumpf, S., Burnett, M., Yang, S., Kwan, I., Wong, W.K.: Conference on visual languages and human-centric computing. In: Too Much, Too Little, or Just Right? Ways Explanations Impact End Users Mental Models (2013)
41. Lacave, C., Diéz, F.J.: A review of explanation methods for bayesian networks. The Knowledge Engineering Review **17:2**, 107–127 (2002)
42. Lacave, C., Diéz, F.J.: A review of explanation methods for heuristic expert systems. The Knowledge Engineering Review **17:2**, 107–127 (2004)
43. Lewis, C., Rieman, J.: Task-centered user interface design: a practical introduction. University of Colorado (1994)
44. Lopez-Suarez, A., Kamel, M.: Dykor: a method for generating the content of explanations in knowledge systems. Knowledge-based Systems **7**(3), 177–188 (1994)
45. McCarthy, K., Reilly, J., McGinty, L., Smyth, B.: Thinking positively - explanatory feedback for conversational recommender systems. In: Proceedings of the European Conference on Case-Based Reasoning (ECCBR-04) Explanation Workshop, pp. 115–124 (2004)
46. McGinty, L., Reilly, J.: On the evolution of critiquing recommenders. In: F. Ricci, L. Rokach, B. Shapira, P.B. Kantor (eds.) Recommender Systems Handbook, pp. 547–576. Springer US (2011)
47. McGinty, L., Smyth, B.: Comparison-based recommendation. Lecture Notes in Computer Science **2416**, 575–589 (2002)
48. McNee, S.M., Lam, S.K., Konstan, J.A., Riedl, J.: Interfaces for eliciting new user preferences in recommender systems. User Modeling pp. pp. 178–187 (2003)
49. McNee, S.M., Riedl, J., Konstan, J.A.: Being accurate is not enough: How accuracy metrics have hurt recommender systems. In: Extended Abstracts of the 2006 ACM Conference on Human Factors in Computing Systems (CHI 2006) (2006)
50. McSherry, D.: Explanation in recommender systems. Artificial Intelligence Review **24(2)**, 179–197 (2005)
51. Nagulendra, S., Vassileva, J.: Providing awareness, understanding and control of personalized stream filtering in a p2p social network. In: Conference on Collaboration and Technology (CRIWG) (2013)
52. Nguyen, T.T., Kluver, D., Wang, T.Y., Hui, P.M., Ekstrand, M.D., Willemsen, M.C., Rield, J.: Rating support interfaces to improve user experience and recommender accuracy. In: Recommender Systems Conference (2013)

53. Nielsen, J., Molich, R.: Heuristic evaluation of user interfaces. In: ACM CHI'90, pp. 249–256 (1990)
54. Ohanian, R.: Construction and validation of a scale to measure celebrity endorsers' perceived expertise, trustworthiness, and attractiveness. Journal of Advertising **19:3**, 39–52 (1990)
55. O'Sullivan, D., Smyth, B., Wilson, D.C., McDonald, K., Smeaton, A.: Improving the quality of the personalized electronic program guide. User Modeling and User-Adapted Interaction **14**, pp. 5–36 (2004)
56. Papadimitriou, A., Symeonidis, P., Manolopoulos, Y.: A generalized taxonomy of explanation styles for traditional and social recommender systems. Data Mining and Knowledge Discovery **24**, 555–583 (2012)
57. Pazzani, M.J.: A framework for collaborative, content-based and demographic filtering. Artificial Intelligence Review **13**, 393–408 (1999)
58. Pizzato, L., Rej, T., Akehurst, J., Koprinska, I., Yacef, K., Kay, J.: Recommending people to people: the nature of reciprocal recommenders with a case study in online dating. User Modeling and User-Adapted Interaction **23**, 447–488 (2013)
59. Pu, P., Chen, L.: Trust building with explanation interfaces. In: IUI'06, Recommendations I, pp. 93–100 (2006)
60. Pu, P., Chen, L.: Trust-inspiring explanation interfaces for recommender systems. Knowledge-based Systems **20**, 542–556 (2007)
61. Pu, P., Faltings, B., Chen, L., Zhang, J., Viappiani, P.: Usability guidelines for product recommenders based on example critiquing research. In: F. Ricci, L. Rokach, B. Shapira, P.B. Kantor (eds.) Recommender Systems Handbook, pp. 547–576. Springer US (2011)
62. Rafter, R., Smyth, B.: Conversational collaborative recommendation - an experimental analysis. Artif. Intell. Rev **24**(3–4), 301–318 (2005)
63. Reilly, J., McCarthy, K., McGinty, L., Smyth, B.: Dynamic critiquing. In: P. Funk, P.A. González-Calero (eds.) ECCBR, *Lecture Notes in Computer Science*, vol. 3155, pp. 763–777. Springer (2004)
64. Ricci, F.: Mobile recommender systems. Information Technology & Tourism **12.3**, 205–231 (2010)
65. Said, A., Bellogin Kouki, A., de Vries, A.P., Kille, B.: Information Retrieval And User-Centric Recommender System Evaluation. In: Extended Proceedings of The 21st Conference on User Modeling, Adaptation and Personalization (UMAP'13), http://ceur-ws.org/Vol-997/umap2013_project_3.pdf CEUR (2013). URL http://oai.cwi.nl/oai/asset/21389/21389B.pdf
66. Shani, G., Rokach, L., Shapira, B., Hadash, S., Tangi, M.: Investigating confidence displays for top-n recommendations. Journal of the American Society for Information Science and Technology **64**, 2548–2563 (2013)
67. Sharma, A., Cosley, D.: Do social explanations work? studying and modeling the effects of social explanations in recommender systems. In: World Wide Web (WWW) (2013)
68. Sinha, R., Swearingen, K.: The role of transparency in recommender systems. In: Conference on Human Factors in Computing Systems, pp. 830–831 (2002)
69. Swearingen, K., Sinha, R.: Interaction design for recommender systems. In: Designing Interactive Systems, pp. 25–28 (2002)
70. Symeonidis, P., Nanopoulos, A., Manolopoulos, Y.: Justified recommendations based on content and rating data. In: WebKDD Workshop on Web Mining and Web Usage Analysis (2008)
71. Tanaka-Ishii, K., Frank, I.: Multi-agent explanation strategies in real-time domains. In: 38th Annual Meeting on Association for Computational Linguistics, pp. 158–165 (2000)
72. Thompson, C.A., Göker, M.H., Langley, P.: A personalized system for conversational recommendations. J. Artif. Intell. Res. (JAIR) **21**, 393–428 (2004)
73. Tintarev, N.: Explaining recommendations. In: User Modeling, pp. 470–474 (2007)
74. Tintarev, N., Dennis, M., Masthoff, J.: Adapting recommendation diversity to openness to experience: A study of human behaviour. In: UMAP (2013)
75. Tintarev, N., Masthoff, J.: Effective explanations of recommendations: User-centered design. In: Recommender Systems, pp. 153–156 (2007)

76. Tintarev, N., Masthoff, J.: Over- and underestimation in different product domains. In: Workshop on Recommender Systems associated with ECAI (2008)
77. Tintarev, N., Masthoff, J.: Personalizing movie explanations using commercial meta-data. In: Adaptive Hypermedia (2008)
78. Tintarev, N., Masthoff, J.: Evaluating the effectiveness of explanations for recommender systems: Methodological issues and empirical studies on the impact of personalization. User Modeling and User-Adapted Interaction **22**, 399–439 (2012)
79. Verbert, K., Parra, D., Brusilovsky, P., Duval, E.: Visualizing recommendations to support exploration, transparency and controllability. In: Proceedings of the 2013 International Conference on Intelligent User Interfaces, IUI '13, pp. 351–362. ACM, New York, NY, USA (2013). DOI 10.1145/2449396.2449442
80. Victor, P., Cock, M.D., Cornelis, C.: Trust and recommendations. In: F. Ricci, L. Rokach, B. Shapira, P.B. Kantor (eds.) Recommender Systems Handbook, pp. 547–576. Springer US (2011)
81. Vig, J., Sen, S., Riedl, J.: Tagsplanations: Explaining recommendations using tags. In: Intelligent User Interfaces (2009)
82. Wang, W., Benbasat, I.: Recommendation agents for electronic commerce: Effects of explanation facilities on trusting beliefs. Journal of Management Information Systems **23**, 217–246 (2007)
83. Wärnestål, P.: Modeling a dialogue strategy for personalized movie recommendations. In: Beyond Personalization Workshop, pp. 77–82 (2005)
84. Wärnestål, P.: User evaluation of a conversational recommender system. In: Proceedings of the 4th Workshop on Knowledge and Reasoning in Practical Dialogue Systems, pp. 32–39 (2005)
85. Webster, A., Vassileva, J.: The keeup recommender system. In: Recsys (2007)
86. Wick, M.R., Thompson, W.B.: Reconstructive expert system explanation. Artif. Intell. **54**(1–2), 33–70 (1992)
87. Ye, L., Johnson, P., Ye, L.R., Johnson, P.E.: The impact of explanation facilities on user acceptance of expert systems advice. MIS Quarterly **19**(2), 157–172 (1995)
88. Yee, K.P., Swearingen, K., Li, K., Hearst, M.: Faceted metadata for image search and browsing. In: ACM Conference on Computer-Human Interaction (2003)
89. Zheng, V.W., Zheng, Y., Xie, X., Yang, Q.: Collaborative location and activity recommendations with GPS history data. In: World Wide Web (WWW) (2010)

Part III
Recommendation Techniques

Chapter 11
Recommender Systems in Industry: A Netflix Case Study

Xavier Amatriain and Justin Basilico

11.1 Introduction

Recommender Systems are a prime example of the mainstream industry use of large-scale machine learning and data mining. Diverse applications in areas such as e-commerce, search, Internet music and video, gaming, and even online dating apply similar techniques that leverage large volumes of data to better fulfill a user's needs in a personalized fashion. These techniques have such wide applicability because they have been demonstrated to be effective in increasing core business metrics such as customer satisfaction and revenue. In this chapter, we will focus on approaches for applying recommendation algorithms with a focus on the problem formulations, algorithms, and metrics. Of course, other aspects such as user interaction design can have a deep impact on the effectiveness of an approach. Those topics are covered in other chapters in the book but are outside the scope of this one.

Given an existing application, an improvement in the recommendation system can have a value of millions of dollars and can be the factor that determines the success or failure of a business. In Sect. 11.2 we will review some of the typical uses of recommendation systems in industry. While a lot of work in recommendation focuses on algorithms, there are other aspects of a recommendation approach that can have a significant impact. For example, adding new data sources or

X. Amatriain (✉)
Netflix, 100 Winchester Cr., Los Gatos, CA 95032, USA

Quora, 150 Castro St., Mountain View, USA
e-mail: xavier@amatriain.net

J. Basilico
Netflix, 100 Winchester Cr., Los Gatos, CA 95032, USA
e-mail: jbasilico@netflix.com

F. Ricci et al. (eds.), *Recommender Systems Handbook*,
DOI 10.1007/978-1-4899-7637-6_11

representations (features) to an existing algorithm. In Sect. 11.4, we will use Netflix as the driving example to describe the use of data, models, and other personalization techniques.

Another important factor we consider is how to measure the success of a given personalization technique. Root mean squared error (RMSE) was the offline evaluation metric chosen for the Netflix Prize (see Sect. 11.3). But there are many other relevant metrics that, if optimized, would lead to different solutions. For example, ranking metrics such as Normalized Discounted Cumulative Gain (NDCG), recall, or area under the ROC curve (AUC), often used in Information Retrieval, can also be used to evaluate recommendations. However, beyond the optimization of a given offline metric, what we are really pursuing is the impact of a technique on the business. To do this, we need to relate the quality of a recommendation to more customer-facing metrics such as click-through rate (CTR) or retention. We will describe an approach of how to make use of offline and online metrics to drive innovation, called "Consumer Data Science," in Sect. 11.6.

A key aspect in building a successful large-scale recommendation system is to choose an appropriate architecture that is capable of running computationally complex algorithms and also produces fresh results with an acceptable latency. In Sect. 11.7, we will describe a three-layer architecture that addresses these concerns. But before we dive into these details, it will be useful to understand the uses of recommender systems across industry. In the next section, we will briefly describe some of the most typical use cases.

11.2 Recommender Systems in Industry

Recommendation systems are used by many Internet-focused companies in a variety of application domains. Each domain has its own unique recommendation challenges. We provide here a short overview of some of the more well-known applications in industry.

Today most e-commerce sites and applications are likely to have some sort of recommendation engine powering their user experience. The first large company to be credited as having included a recommender system at the core of their experience is Amazon. Amazon initially employed a simple item-item collaborative filtering approach [48]. The current Amazon experience includes many different instances of recommendation at different levels: from listings on the homepage to many product pages having lists of other products bought or viewed. Other retail companies such as eBay have followed the lead and incorporated recommendations in their experience, such as post-purchase recommendations [88].

News is also an area that companies have applied recommendation approaches to personalize and focus on the interests of a user. For example, Google News was powered by some kind of recommendations for news articles from the beginning [19, 49]. Yahoo! has also invested in personalizing news and other web content [1, 47]. For news recommendation, some of the key challenges are freshness, where relevant articles may have a very limited time span, and diversity, where there can be a large number of articles about the same topic. However, news has the advantage of textual content, which allows for techniques from natural language processing to be applied to create features that can be used in recommendation, which is especially helpful when user behavioral data is sparse.

Video recommendation has always been an active area of research, so it is not surprising that it is used in industry to recommend a variety of types of video spanning movies, TV shows, and user-generated content. For instance, recommendations have been an important component of the YouTube experience to help navigate the vast amounts of user-generated video [20]. With video, it can be hard to extract good content information without harnessing sophisticated computer vision approaches. While metadata may be available for professionally-created content, harnessing user behavior has been key to building recommendations for videos. In such domains, transitioning from ratings to learning-to-rank has shown to be important. Google, for instance, uses a new family of loss functions and shows its applicability in YouTube and Google Music [90].

Music recommendation is also an active application area where there have been interesting developments in the past years. Pandora, for instance, created a complete business model around the idea of creating personalized music stations. They created an approach that combined traditional collaborative filtering techniques with a curated approach called the Music Genome Project [72]. Similarly, Apple's iTunes application uses information about a user's music library to drive personalized mixes and playlists. More recently, Spotify started getting in the business of providing personalized music recommendations in its service. Their approach to recommendations is currently mostly based on standard matrix factorization techniques [9]. Finally, EchoNest was a well-known startup that provided music recommendation engines powering many different services before being acquired by Spotify. They combined different approaches including collaborative filtering, metadata, and audio signal analysis of the music [46]. Music recommendation has some unique aspects [16], such as the multi-level nature of artists, albums, tracks, and playlists that recommendations can be done across. Music tracks also typically short and often listened to repeatedly, which can lead to interesting approaches for leveraging this data and behavior.

More recently, social network companies have introduced a number of different recommendation avenues. Twitter, for example, introduced their Who to Follow recommendation algorithm to recommend new social connections [29]. LinkedIn used a Survival Analysis approach to understand how likely a user is to change jobs [89]. Google has also published work in recommendation systems for some of their social networks such as Orkut [18]. Yahoo! has also worked on personalizing aspects such as comments on social sites [2] or tags in image collections for Flickr [77]. Recommendation algorithms are also very important in online dating sites. Those recommender systems have some particular requirements. For example, the success of the system is not determined by one user receiving a good recommendation but rather by both parties accepting it [61].

In addition to focusing on a single domain, some companies are applying recommendation approaches across domains and even potentially using data from one domain to recommend in another. Microsoft developed a distributed Bayesian approach to recommendation systems called Matchbox [81]. This solution was deployed in several different contexts. For example, it is the main building block of the content recommendations for the XBox game console [39], including games, apps, video, and music content.

Beyond companies building recommendation systems into their own products, there are also many smaller companies that have focused their activity around developing general recommendation systems or technologies. Commendo [32] and Gravity R&D [82], for example, are recommender system consulting firms that emerged from some of the teams that competed in the Netflix Prize.

While many of the previous examples are interesting from an algorithmic perspective, they also represent the different or complimentary requirements that recommender systems have from an industrial point of view. For example, some important issues that are mentioned in most of these publications, unlike in more academic settings, are scalability, business metrics, and integration of the system in the overall user experience. We will go into these issues in the remainder of this chapter.

11.3 The Netflix Prize

In 2006, Netflix announced the Netflix Prize, a machine learning and data mining competition to predict movie ratings on a 5-star scale. We conducted this competition to find new ways to improve the recommendations we provide to our members, which is a key part of our business. However, we had to come up with a proxy question that was easier to evaluate and quantify: the root mean squared error (RMSE) of the predicted rating. We offered a $1 million prize to whomever came up with a solution that reduced RMSE by 10 % beyond what was obtained by Cinematch, our existing system.

The Netflix Prize put the spotlight on the Recommender Systems area and the value of generating personalized recommendations from user data. It did so by providing a crisp problem definition that enabled thousands of teams to focus on improving a single metric. While this was a simplification of the recommendation problem, many valuable lessons were learned.

11.3.1 Lessons from the Prize

After the first year of competition, the KorBell team won the first Progress Prize with an 8.43 % improvement. They reported more than 2000 h of work in order to come up with the final combination of 107 algorithms that put them at the top of the leaderboard and resulted in this prize. As per the terms of the competition, they shared their resulting solution with the team at Netflix. We looked at the two underlying algorithms with the best performance in the ensemble:

Matrix Factorization (MF) [44][1] (see Sect. 5.3) and Restricted Boltzmann Machines (RBM)[71]. Matrix Factorization by itself provided a 0.8914 RMSE, while RBM alone provided a competitive but slightly worse 0.8990 RMSE. A linear blend of these two reduced the error to 0.88.

Given that a combination of these two algorithms performed well on the competition dataset, we sought to put them to use. To do this, we had to overcome some limitations. For instance, the competition code the authors provided was built to handle 100 million ratings, however we needed to apply it to the more than 5 billion that we have. Also, the code was designed to run on a static dataset and thus not built to adapt as members added more ratings. Once we overcame those challenges, we deployed the two algorithms into production, where they are still used to predict our members ratings for videos.

One of the most interesting findings during the Netflix Prize came out of a blog post. Simon Funk introduced an incremental, iterative, and approximate way to compute a matrix factorization (referred to as SVD) using gradient descent [27]. This provided a practical way to scale matrix factorization methods to large datasets. Another enhancement to matrix factorization methods was Koren et. al's SVD++ [42]. This asymmetric variation enables adding both implicit and explicit feedback, and removes the need for learning user-specific parameters for the implicit part.

The second model that proved successful in the Netflix Prize was the Restricted Boltzmann Machine (RBM). RBMs can be understood as the fourth generation of Artificial Neural Networks: the first being the Perceptron popularized in the 60s; the second being the backpropagation algorithm in the 80s; and the third being Belief Networks (BNs) from the 90s. RBMs are BNs that restrict the connectivity to make learning easier. RBMs can be stacked to form Deep Belief Networks (DBN), which is a form of deep learning. For the Netflix Prize, Salakhutditnov et al. proposed an RBM structure with binary hidden units and softmax visible units with five biases that are initialized with the movies that the user rated [71].

Many other learnings came out of the competition. For example, the matrix factorization methods mentioned above were combined with traditional neighborhood-based approaches [42]. Also, early in the competition, it became clear that it was important to take into account temporal dynamics of user feedback [43]. Another finding of the Netflix Prize was that there is a large amount of noise in the ratings provided by users. This was already known in the literature; Herlocker et al.[30] coined the term "magic barrier" to refer to the limit of accuracy in a recommender system due to the natural variability in ratings. This limit was relatively close to the actual Prize threshold [5], and might be a factor in the substantial effort needed to reduce RMSE by enough to cross the 10 % line.

---

[1]The application of Matrix Factorization to the task of rating prediction closely resembles the technique known as Singular Value Decomposition used, for example, to identify latent factors in Information Retrieval. Therefore, it is common to see people referring to this MF solution as SVD.

After almost 3 years, the final Grand Prize ensemble that won the $1M prize was a truly impressive compilation and culmination of work, blending hundreds of predictive models to finally cross the finish line [8]. The final solution was accomplished by combining many independent models developed by different teams that joined forces. It highlights the power of using ensembles to combine a heterogeneous set of models to achieve maximum accuracy.

At Netflix, we evaluated some of the new methods included in the final solution. The additional accuracy gains that we measured did not seem to justify the engineering effort needed to bring them into a production environment. In addition, our focus on improving Netflix personalization had expanded beyond rating prediction. In the next section, we will explain the different methods and components that produce a complete personalization approach such as the one used by Netflix.

11.4 Recommendation Beyond Rating Prediction

Netflix has discovered through the years that there is significant business value in incorporating recommendations to personalize as much of the user experience as possible. This realization motivated the Netflix Prize described in the previous section and has subsequently driven the effort to personalize the service in many other ways. In Sect. 11.2 we introduced different industrial scenarios for recommender systems. In the following sections we will use Netflix as an example of a fully personalized industrial recommendation system.

Before we go into the details, first let us provide some context about the Netflix service as it relates to personalization. Netflix was originally known as a DVD-by-mail subscription service in the US, which it was at the time the Netflix Prize started. However, it has since grown into an international Internet video streaming subscription service. It allows members to instantly stream movies and TV shows from a catalog to a multitude of devices such as laptops, smart TVs, game consoles, tablets, and mobile phones. One of the key aspects of the Netflix service is that it allows members to watch any video we have available in our catalog at any time on any device. Since we have a large quantity of available videos that a member can watch, a key concern is how to help members find videos in our catalog that they want to watch and will enjoy enough to come back. This is the task where we rely primarily on our recommendation system to help. The videos we have are licensed from content providers or produced ourselves. The cost for serving each video is approximately the same, so we have no incentive for favoring one video over another when doing recommendation. Thus, we take a member-centric approach to recommendation. This is in contrast to other domains such as e-commerce, online advertising, or search where there can be very different amounts of revenue for different items.

11.4.1 Everything Is a Recommendation

Netflix personalization starts on a member's homepage, which the application displays on any device after login. This page consists of groups of videos arranged in horizontal rows that create a two-dimensional grid of videos. Each row has a title that conveys the intended meaningful connection between the group of videos in that row. Most of our personalization is embodied in the way we generate rows, select rows, determine what videos to include in a row, determine the ordering of videos in a row, and determine the ordering rows on a page.

Take as a first example the Top 10 row (see Fig. 11.1). This row is our best guess of the videos a user is most likely to watch and enjoy. Of course, when we say "a user", we really mean everyone in a household using that membership (or profile). It is important to keep in mind that Netflix personalization is intended to handle a household that is likely to have different people with different tastes. That is why with a Top 10 row, someone in a family that watches Netflix is likely to discover items for dad, mom, the children, or the family as a whole. Even for a single person household, we want the recommendations to appeal to a person's range of interests and moods. While there are specific techniques for group recommendations, such as the ones described in Chap. 22, those techniques usually rely on having captured each individual preferences rather than an aggregate. For this and other reasons, in most parts of our system we cater to different people and moods by not only optimizing for *accuracy*, but also for *diversity* [69, 87].

Another important element of Netflix personalization is *awareness*. We want members to be aware of how we are adapting to their tastes. This not only promotes trust in the system, but also encourages members to give feedback, which will result in better recommendations. A way of promoting trust with the personalization is to provide *explanations* for why we decide to recommend a given movie or show (see Fig. 11.2). A video is not recommended because it suits a business needs, but because it matches the information we have from a user: viewing history, explicit feedback of ratings and taste preferences, or even a friends recommendations. See Chap. 10 for more details on how to design good explanations for a recommender system.

On the topic of friends, we have a social feature that allows members to connect through Facebook to find friends who are also Netflix members. Knowing about someone's friends not only gives us another signal to use in our personalization

Fig. 11.1 Example of a Netflix Top 10 row. We promote personalization awareness and reflect on the diversity of a household. Note that the labels are an illustration, since the system does not explicitly know the true household composition

Fig. 11.2 Adding explanation and evidence for recommendations contributes to user satisfaction and requires specific algorithms. Evidence can include your predicted rating, related shows you have watched, or even friends who have interacted with the video

algorithms, but also allows us to create rows based on their social circle to generate recommendations. See Chap. 15 for some examples on how to use social network information to generate recommendations.

Similarity is also an important aspect of personalization. We think of similarity in a very broad sense; it can be between videos or between members, and can be along multiple dimensions such as metadata, ratings, or viewing data. While similarity itself can be used as the basis for a recommendation system, we tend to use various forms of similarity as features in other models or as navigational constructs for the user (see Fig. 11.3). For example, we generate rows of "adhoc genres" based on their similarity to videos that a member has interacted with recently, which we label "Because you watched". Also, we provide a list of similar videos that a user may be interested in on the information page for a video. Of course, there can be many different notions of similarity between two items, each of which can be used for the basis of generating a list of similars. These can be combined by constructing independent similarity models and training an ensemble. Other more sophisticated graphical methods such as SimRank [34] accomplish a similar goal. On the other hand, similarity itself can be personalized using approaches such as Personalized Page Rank [26].

In many services like Netflix, even a situation where a user enters an explicit search query can be turned into a recommendation. An example of this might be the user entering a generic term (e.g. "summer" or "Italian") or the title of an item that is not available in the catalog. In these situations we need to come up with

Fig. 11.3 Similarity can be used to present recommendations in different contexts and in response to certain user actions

good related recommendations. Even the auto-complete suggestions when the user starts typing can be personalized and interpreted recommendation over a constrained set. LinkedIn's Metaphor system is another good example of a complete search recommendation system [64].

In most of the previous contexts, the goal of the recommender system is to present a number of attractive items for a person to choose from. This is usually accomplished by selecting some items and sorting them in the order of expected enjoyment (or *utility*). Since the most common way of presenting recommended items is in some form of list, we need an appropriate *ranking* model that can use a wide variety of information to come up with an optimal ordering of the items. In the next section, we will discuss how to design such a ranking model.

11.4.2 Ranking

The goal of a personalized ranking system is to find the best possible ordering of a set of items for a user within a specific context. At Netflix, we optimize ranking algorithms to put videos that a member is most likely to play and enjoy at the beginning of the list. We do this by learning a scoring function $f_{\mathtt{rank}} : U \times V \rightarrow \mathbb{R}$ that maps from our (user, video) space to a score, which is a real number.

An obvious baseline for a ranking function that optimizes consumption is item popularity. The reason is clear: on average, a member is most likely to watch what most others are watching. However, popularity is the opposite of personalization; it will produce the same ordering of items for every user. Thus, the goal becomes to find a personalized ranking function that is better than item popularity, so we can better satisfy users with varying tastes.

Recall that our goal is to recommend the videos that each member is most likely to play and enjoy. One obvious way to approach this is to use the member's predicted rating of each item as an adjunct to item popularity. Using predicted ratings on their own as a ranking function can lead to items that are too niche or unfamiliar. This is because ratings on their own only indicate what someone who has watched a video will rate it, and ignores that most people would rate lowly most videos if they watched them [80]. It can also exclude items that the member may want to watch even though they may not rate them highly. To compensate for this, rather than using either popularity or predicted rating on their own, we would like to produce rankings that balance both of these aspects. One way to do this is to build a ranking prediction model using these two features.

Let us walk through an example of a very simple scoring approach by choosing our ranking function to be a linear combination of popularity and predicted rating. This gives an equation of the form $f_{\mathtt{rank}}(u, v) = w_1 p(v) + w_2 r(u, v)$, where u represents the user, v is the video (item), $p(v)$ is the popularity of video v, and $r(u, v)$ is the predicted rating for user u of video v. The bias term that is typically

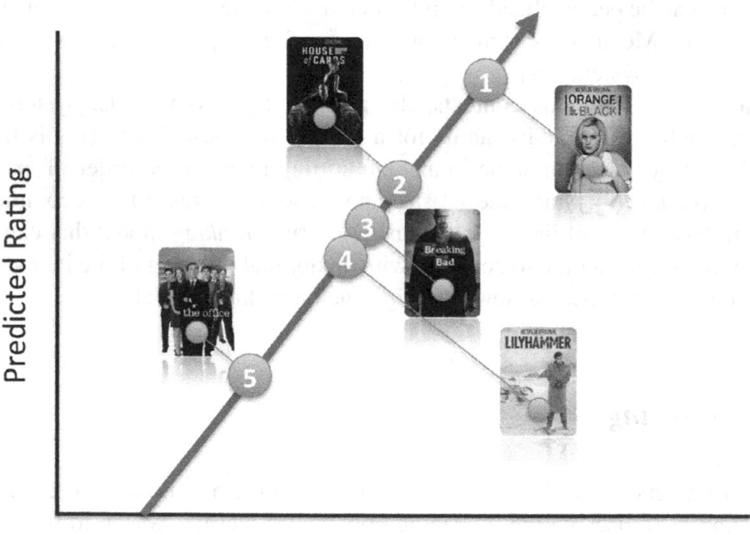

Fig. 11.4 Constructing a basic personalized two-dimensional ranking function based on popularity and predicted rating

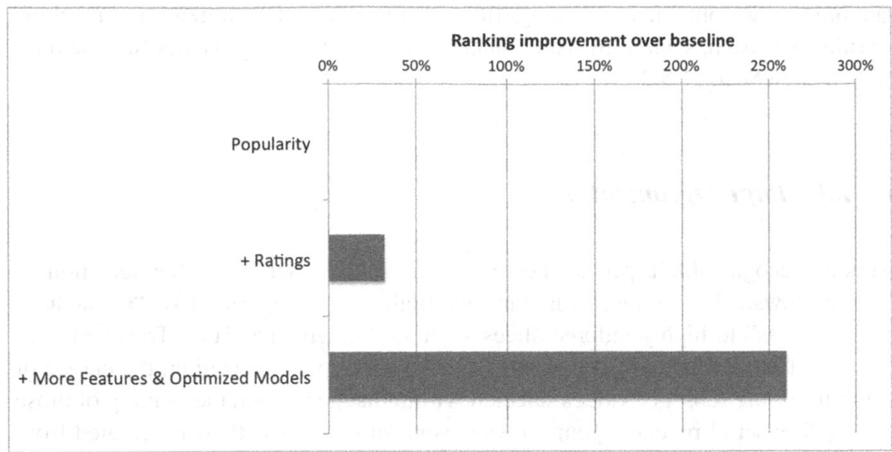

Fig. 11.5 Performance of Netflix ranking system when adding features and optimizing the learning to rank model. An example ranking metric is shown, but the results hold across a range of such metrics

learned as part of a linear model is omitted, since it is a constant and thus does not impact the final ranking. This equation defines a line in a two-dimensional space (see Fig. 11.4).

Once we have such a function, we can pass a set of videos for a given user through it and sort them in descending order according to the score. However, first we need to determine the weights w_1 and w_2 in our model. We can formulate this as a machine learning problem: select positive and negative examples of (user, video) pairs from historical data and let a machine learning algorithm learn the weights that optimize our goal. Treating ranking as a classification or regression problem is known as a pointwise approach in the family of machine learning techniques known as *Learning to Rank*. In addition to recommendations, it is central to application scenarios such as search engines or advertisement targeting. A crucial difference in the case of ranked recommendations is the importance of personalization: we do not expect to optimize a global notion of relevance, but rather a personalized one.

It is interesting to note that in this model, the predicted rating has gone from being the final target variable we are trying to predict to generate a recommendation to being an input to another model that takes into account other features. A model like this that uses outputs of other models as inputs to produce a final prediction are also referred to as *weighted hybrid models* [14].

The previous two-dimensional model is a very basic example of a ranking function. Apart from popularity and predicted rating, we have tried many other features at Netflix related to many aspects of the video, user, and their interaction. Some have shown no positive effect while others have improved our ranking accuracy tremendously. Features can be simple information derived from metadata or be produced by other recommendation algorithms, as with the case of rating prediction. Also, many supervised classification methods beyond simple linear models can be used or adapted for ranking. In addition, algorithms that directly optimize ranking objectives can be used. Figure 11.5 shows an improvement in ranking that we obtained by adding different features and optimizing the machine learning approach, such as by using other learning-to-rank approaches like the ones described in Sect. 11.8.2.

11.4.3 Page Optimization

Another recognizable aspect of personalization in our service is the selection of "genre" rows. These range from familiar high-level categories like "Comedies" and "Dramas" to highly tailored slices such as "Imaginative Time Travel Movies from the 1980s". Each row represents three layers of personalization: the choice of genre itself, the subset of videos selected within that genre, and the ranking of those videos. The set of potential genre rows is very large because they are created from combinations of individual aspects (represented as tags) associated with a video. Thus, the space of genres is much larger than the space of videos, which means selecting them is in itself a recommendation problem. To handle this, row candidates are generated using a member's implicit genre preferences (recent plays, ratings, and other interactions) or explicit feedback provided through our taste preference survey. These elements are used both as input to the selection algorithm as well as evidence to support the recommendations (see Fig. 11.6).

The problem of generating a personalized and optimized page is complex. In the Netflix scenario, there are many thousands of row candidates that can be selected and ranked. As a matter of fact, the catalog of available candidate rows is much larger than the catalog of individual items since the same item can be included in many different rows. On the other hand, when optimizing the page, we are not

Fig. 11.6 Netflix genre rows can be generated from implicit and/or explicit feedback

only optimizing relevance. As with other personalization elements, *freshness* and diversity is taken into account to decide which of the thousands of possible genres to show.

Finally, it is important to note that when optimizing a full page layout, we need to incorporate a model of the user's browsing or attention behavior (see Fig. 11.7) [45, 53]. For example, our model needs to consider whether the probability of the user seeing and clicking the third item in the second row is higher or lower than the probability of seeing and clicking the first item in the fourth row.

To conclude this section, it is worth highlighting how the recommendation approach has evolved at a company like Netflix. Starting from its formulation as a rating prediction problem in the Netflix Prize, it evolved to a one-dimensional ranking, and finally to a full-page personalized optimization problem. This evolution is illustrated in Fig. 11.8.

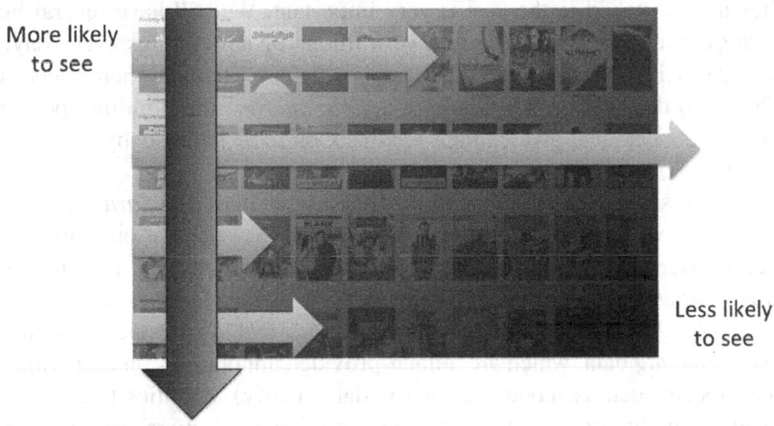

Fig. 11.7 Browsing and attention behavior of users needs to be taken into account when optimizing the whole page experience

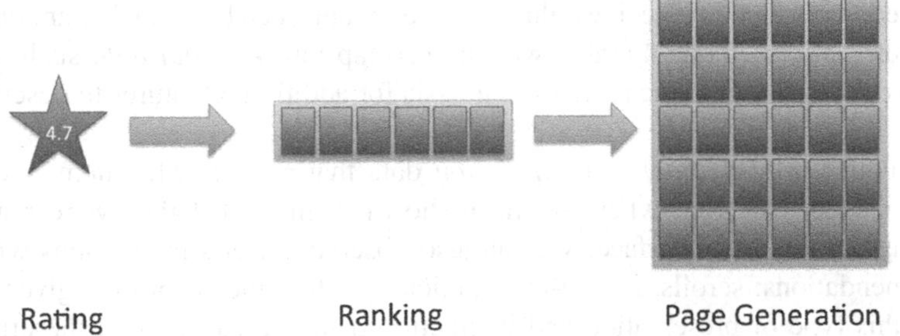

Fig. 11.8 The recommendation approach at Netflix has evolved from focusing on rating prediction to one-dimensional ranking and now to full page optimization

11.5 Data and Models

11.5.1 Data

The discussion of ranking algorithms in the previous section highlights the importance of both data and models in creating an optimal recommendation experience. The availability of high volumes of high-quality user data allows for us to use some approaches that would have been unthinkable in the past. As an example, we will discuss next some of the data sources that we can use at Netflix to inform our recommendations.

We have large amounts of *play* data about what videos users watch, when, for how long, and on what device they watched it; as of 2013 we had around 50 million play events coming into the service every day. Given that helping our users find something to watch is one of our primary goals, this information about what and how they have watched in the past is very important. We still have several billion item *ratings* from users. We also receive millions of new ratings every day; five million per day in 2013. Our users also add millions of items to their *queues* each day. They also directly enter millions of *search queries*; three million per day in 2013. Our users can also give explicit feedback on their interests by completing a signup *onramp* or *taste survey* to express preferences.

On the item side, we already mentioned the use of item *popularity* for ranking. We have many ways of computing popularity such as over various time ranges, aggregating user actions in different ways, or grouping users by region or other similarity metrics. Each item in our catalog also has rich *metadata* such as synopsis, genres, actors, directors, subtitles, parental rating, and user reviews. Items also have associated *tag* data, which are human-provided annotations on each video that describe aspects such as mood (e.g. witty, dark, goofy), qualities (e.g. critically-acclaimed, visually-striking, classic), and storyline (e.g. marriage, time travel, talking animals). Although a manual tagging approach would be unfeasible for other domains with a larger or faster changing catalog, it can be very efficient and practical in a domain like ours where the catalog is in the order of thousands of professionally-produced items. In this case, it would be hard to obtain such high-quality annotations from automatic methods. Finally, we can also tap into *external data* such as box office performance or critic reviews as a basis for additional features to describe an item.

We collect *presentation* and *impression* data that records what items we have recommended to a user, where we have shown them, and if they were rendered on a page in the user interface. We can also observe a user's interactions with the recommendations: scrolls, mouse-overs, clicks, or the time spent on a given page. Using this type of presentation and interaction data, we can look at the effect of showing a recommendation on a user's response. This is important for handling the presentation bias, where a user is more likely to watch a video simply because we put it in a location where they are likely to see it.

Some users choose to provide us with *social* data that we can also use for personalization. Social data may include the social network connections to other users, as well as interactions or activities of those connected users. It can also provide a source of interests (e.g. likes) beyond the scope of items in our catalog or movies and TV shows in general.

There are also many other data sources related to a user or context such as *demographics*, *language preference*, *device*, *location*, or *time* that can be used to derive features for our predictive models.

11.5.2 Models

Many different modeling approaches have been used for building recommendation systems. One thing we have found at Netflix is that with the great availability of data, both in quantity and types, a thoughtful approach is required to model selection, training, and testing. We use all sorts of machine learning approaches: from unsupervised methods such as *clustering* and *dimensionality reduction* algorithms to a number of supervised classifiers that have shown optimal results in various contexts. This is an incomplete list of methods that are useful to know when working in machine learning for personalization: *Linear regression*, *Logistic regression*, *Elastic nets*, *Singular Value Decomposition*, *Matrix Factorization*, *Restricted Boltzmann Machines*, *Markov Chains*, *Latent Dirichlet Allocation* [10], *Association Rules*, *Factorization Machines* [65], *Gradient Boosted Decision Trees* [25], *Random Forests* [12], and clustering techniques from the simple *k-means* to graphical approaches such as *Affinity Propagation* [24] or non-parametric such as *Hierarchical Dirichlet Processes* [85].

There is no easy answer to how to know which model will perform best for a given problem. In general, the simpler a feature space is, the simpler a model can be. But it is easy to get trapped in a situation where a new feature does not show value because the model cannot learn it. Or, the other way around, to conclude that a more powerful model is not useful simply because one does not have the feature space that exploits its benefits. As such, it is important to understand how the problem definition, feature design, and model interact to find an optimal combination of them.

Many other chapters in this book (see Chap. 7 on Data Mining Methods for Recommender Systems for example) focus on describing these and other methods and their applicability to recommender systems.

11.6 Consumer Data Science

An abundance of source data, measurements, and associated experiments allow Netflix to operate as a data-driven organization. We have embedded this approach into our culture from when the company was founded and call it Consumer (Data)

Science. Broadly speaking, the main goal of Consumer Science is to effectively innovate for users by using data to drive product decisions. That is accomplished by evaluating ideas rapidly, inexpensively, and objectively. We do this by running many experiments to test ideas. Once something is tested, we want to know the outcome and also understand why an approach succeeded or failed. This kind of approach guides not only how we improve the personalization algorithms or recommendation systems but also the majority of consumer-facing aspects of a service, from user interface design to streaming technology.

We do this in practice by employing the scientific method and conducting randomized controlled experiments, which are called *AB tests* (or bucket tests) [41]. A standard AB test randomly assigns each user to one of two groups: A and B. Typically group A would be the *control group* that would be given the current default experience. Group B that would have some new variation on that experience that is hypothesized to be better than the current experience. We use the following steps in running such an experiment:

1. **Start with a hypothesis**: Algorithm/feature/design X will increase user engagement with our service and ultimately user retention.
2. **Design a test**: Think about issues such as dependent and independent variables, control, and significance.
3. **Implement the test**: Set up the solution or prototype to run in a production environment where it can serve requests.
4. **Execute the test**: Assign users to the different groups and let them respond to the different experiences.
5. **Analyze the test**: Look for statistically significant changes in business metrics (e.g. retention) and try to explain them through variations in the behavioral metrics (e.g. increased selection of recommendations).

When we execute AB tests at Netflix, we track many different metrics (e.g. viewing hours). However, we ultimately trust user retention as our overall evaluation criteria (OEC) [40] because it is a long-term metric that ties directly to the success of the business as a whole. This is because as a monthly subscription service, the longer that a member stays with us, the more revenue we can collect. Of course, if we want to run tests that measure retention, this means we have to let them run for months to measure the effect. Tests usually have thousands of users and anywhere from 2 to 20 experimental groups exploring variations of a base idea. We typically have many AB tests running in parallel, and can independently run tests on different components as long as there is no conflict between them. AB tests let us try radical ideas or test many approaches at the same time, but their key advantage is that they allow our decisions to be data-driven. It also helps us to only keep changes that objectively demonstrate a significant improvement, at least up to some level of statistical confidence, which helps reduce the complexity of our product, systems, and algorithms.

An interesting follow-up question that we have faced is how to integrate machine learning approaches into this data-driven culture of AB testing at Netflix. We have done this with an *offline-online testing procedure* that tries to combine the best

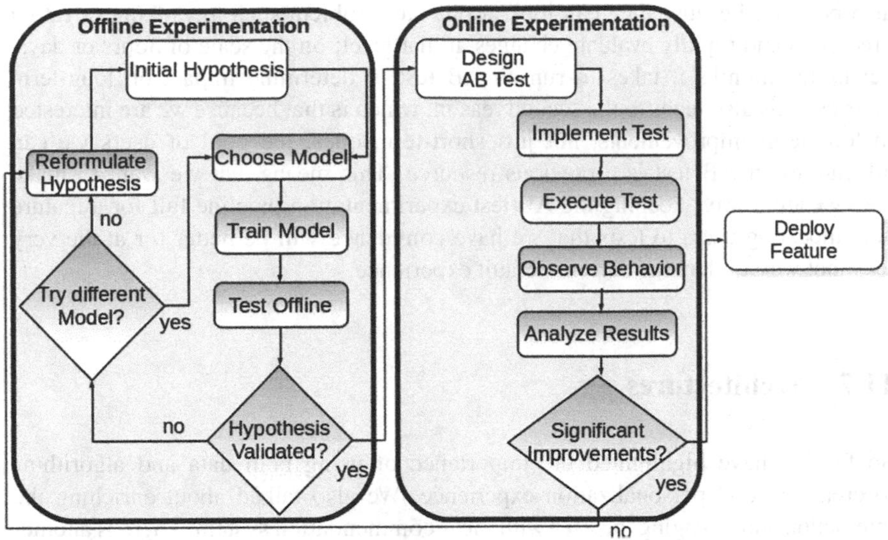

Fig. 11.9 Following an iterative and data-driven offline-online process for innovating in personalization

of both approaches (see Fig. 11.9). The *offline testing* cycle is a process where we test and optimize our algorithms on historical data prior to performing online AB testing. To measure model performance offline we track multiple metrics: from ranking measures such as normalized discounted cumulative gain and their page-level generalizations, to classification metrics such as accuracy, precision, and recall, to regression metrics such as RMSE, and other metrics to track different aspects of recommendation like diversity and coverage (see Chap. 8 for more details on the use of offline metrics for evaluating recommender systems). We also keep track of how well these offline metrics correlate to measurable online metrics in our AB tests. However, since the mapping is not perfect, offline performance is only used as an indication to make informed decisions on follow up steps, not to directly deploy an algorithm without AB testing. Note that this correlation of offline and online metrics is an important practical issue that has just started to get some attention in the academic community [98].

Once offline testing has validated a hypothesis, we are ready to design and launch the online AB test that will demonstrate if an algorithmic change is an improvement from the perspective of user behavior. If it does, we will be ready to deploy the algorithmic improvement to the whole user-base. In fact, this is how we developed the personalization experience described in the previous sections: a sequence of AB tests demonstrating that each successive improvement in personalization was better than an unpersonalized method or the previous personalization approach.

We use this combination of offline and online testing for two primary reasons. The first is that setting up offline tests are typically easier in terms of the engineering involved because they do not need to serve millions of users in real-time. They can also be faster because they can look at one sub-problem such as ranking or rating prediction and rapidly evaluate changes at that level: on the scale of hours or days, versus the months it takes to run an AB test to determine impact on long-term metrics. This also leads to the second reason, which is that because we are interested in long-term improvements, not just short-term ones, the pool of users we can allocate to an AB test is a precious resource. This means that we want to make sure we are always keeping the AB test experimentation pipeline full for a feature and allocating users to tests that we have confidence will be better (or at the very least not worse) than the current default experience.

11.7 Architectures

So far, we have highlighted the importance of using both data and algorithms to create a good personalization experience. We also talked about enriching the interaction and engaging the user with the recommendation system. There is another important piece of the puzzle: how to create a software architecture that can deliver this experience and support rapid innovation. Coming up with a software architecture that handles large volumes of existing data, is responsive to user interactions, and makes it easy to experiment with new recommendation approaches is not a trivial task. In this section we will describe a generic three-layer architecture that addresses these challenges and its particular implementation at Netflix.

We will start by going through the general system architecture in Fig. 11.10. It illustrates a blueprint for multiple personalization algorithm services such as ranking, row selection, and ratings prediction where each provide recommendations involving multi-layered machine learning. To start with, our users generate most of the events and data of interest to the system and at the end our system generates recommendations to show them. The simplest thing we can do with data is to store it for later offline processing, which provides input for *offline jobs*. However, computation can be done offline, nearline, or online. *Online computation* can respond better to recent events and user interaction, but has to respond to requests in real-time.[2] This can limit the computational complexity of algorithms deployed as well as the amount of data that can be processed. *Offline computation* has less limitations on the amount of data and the computational complexity of the algorithms since it runs in a batch manner with relaxed timing requirements. However, it can easily grow stale between updates because the most recent data is not incorporated. One of the key issues in a personalization architecture is how to combine and manage online and offline computation in a seamless manner. *Nearline computation* is an intermediate compromise between these two modes in which we can perform online-like computations, but do not require them to be served

[2]For practical purposes we consider responses below a few hundred milliseconds (e.g. 200) to be real-time.

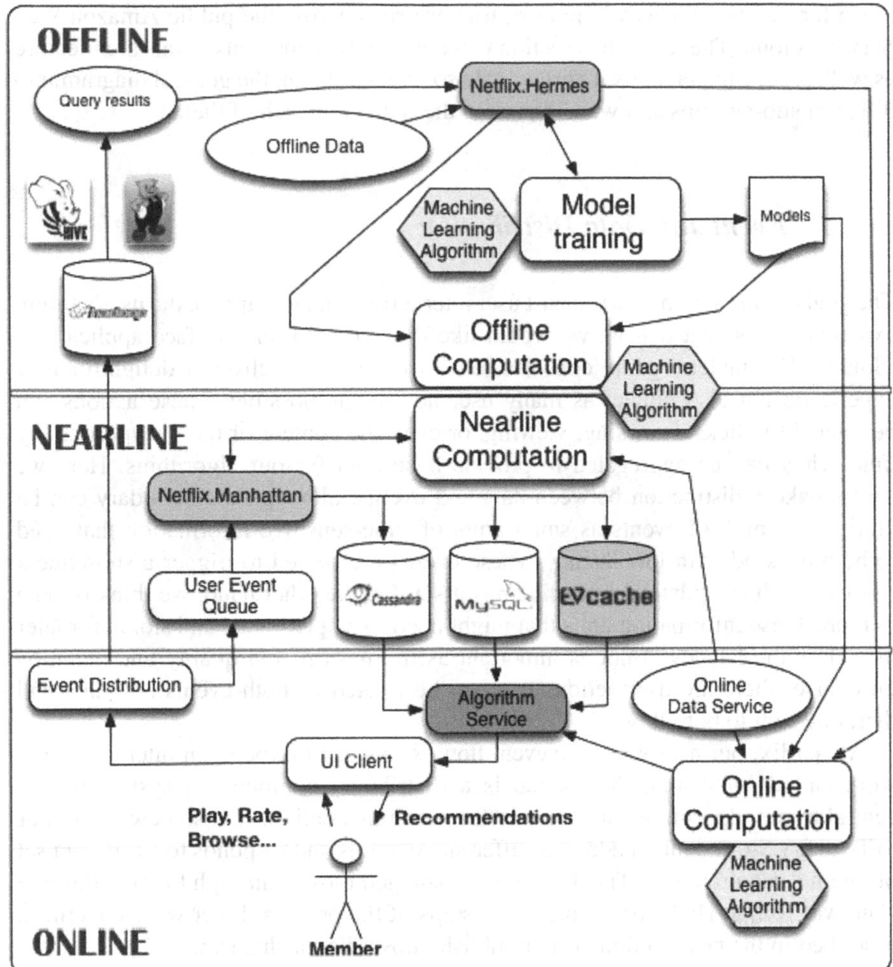

Fig. 11.10 System-level architecture diagram for a recommendation system. The main components of the architecture contains one or more machine learning algorithms

in real-time. *Model training* is another form of computation that uses existing data to generate a model that will later be used during the actual computation of recommendation results. Another part of the architecture describes how the different kinds of events and data need to be handled by the *event and data distribution* system. A related issue is how to combine the different *signals and models* that are needed across the offline, nearline, and online regimes. Finally, we also need to figure out how to combine intermediate *recommendation results* in a way that makes sense for the user.[3] This whole infrastructure runs across the public Amazon Web Services cloud. The rest of this section will detail the components of this architecture as well as their interactions. In order to do so, we will break the general diagram into different sub-systems and we will go into the details of each of them.

11.7.1 Event and Data Distribution

The goal of our system is to use past user interaction data to improve the user's future experience. For that reason, we would like the various user interface applications (Smart TVs, tablets, game consoles, etc.) to not only deliver a delightful user experience but also collect as many user actions as possible. These actions can be related to clicks, browsing, viewing, or even the content of the viewport at any time. They can be aggregated to provide base data for our algorithms. Here we try to make a distinction between data and events, although the boundary can be blurry. We think of events as small units of time-sensitive information that need to be processed with low latency. These events are routed to trigger a subsequent process, such as updating a nearline result set. On the other hand, we think of data as more dense information units that might need to be processed and stored for later use. Here the latency is not as important as the information quality and quantity. Of course, there are user actions that can be treated as both events and data and therefore sent to both flows.

At Netflix, our near-real-time event flow is managed through an internal framework called Manhattan. Manhattan is a distributed computation system that is central to our algorithmic architecture for recommendation. It is somewhat similar to Twitter's Storm, but it addresses different concerns and responds to a different set of internal requirements. The data flow is managed mostly through logging through Chukwa[4] [62] to Hadoop[5] for the initial steps of the process. Later we use Hermes, described in the next section, as our publish-subscribe mechanism.

11.7.2 Offline, Nearline, and Online Computation

As mentioned above, our algorithmic results can be computed either online in real-time, offline in batch, or nearline in between. Each approach has its advantages and disadvantages, which need to be taken into account for each use case.

[3]Intermediate recommendations usually represent lists of items that have been pre-selected and even ranked in advanced but need to undergo further processing such as filtering or re-ranking before being presented to the user.

[4]Chukwa is a Hadoop subproject devoted to large-scale log collection and analysis.

[5]Hadoop is an open-source software framework for storage and large-scale processing of data-sets on clusters of commodity hardware.

Online computation can respond quickly to events and use the most recent data. An example is to assemble a gallery of action movies sorted for a user given the current context. Online components are subject to availability and response time Service Level Agreements (SLA) that specify the maximum latency of the component in responding to requests from client applications while our user is waiting for recommendations to appear. For example, that recommendations need to be returned in at least 250 ms for 99 % of all requests. This can make it harder to fit complex and computationally costly algorithms in this approach. Also, a purely online computation may fail to meet its SLA in some circumstances, so it is always important to have a fast fallback mechanism such as reverting to a precomputed result. Computing online also means that the various data sources involved also need to be available online, which can require additional infrastructure to serve that data.

On the other end of the spectrum, offline computation enables more algorithmic approaches such as complex algorithms and less limitations on the amount of data that is used. A trivial example might be to periodically aggregate statistics from millions of video play events to compile baseline popularity metrics for recommendations. Offline systems also have simpler engineering requirements. For example, relaxed response time SLAs imposed by clients can be easily met. New algorithms can be deployed in production without the need to put too much effort into performance tuning. In the context of Consumer Science we take advantage of this to support rapid experimentation: if a new experimental algorithm is slower to execute, we can choose to simply deploy more cloud compute instances to achieve the throughput required to run an experiment, instead of spending valuable engineering time optimizing performance for an algorithm that may prove to be of little business value. However, because offline processing does not have strong latency requirements, it can not react quickly to changes in context or new data. Ultimately, this can lead to staleness that may degrade the usefulness of recommendations and thus the user experience. Offline computation also requires having infrastructure for storing, computing, and accessing large sets of precomputed results.

Much of the computation we need for personalization involving machine learning algorithms can be done offline. This means that the jobs can be scheduled to be executed periodically and their execution does not need to be synchronous with the request or presentation of the results. There are two main kinds of tasks that fall in this category: model training and batch computation of intermediate or final results. In the model training jobs, we collect relevant existing data and apply a machine learning algorithm to produce a set of model parameters (which we will henceforth refer to as the model). The training process usually involves training several models with different hyper-parameters in order to select the optimal one. This final model will usually be encoded and stored in a file for later consumption. Although most of the models are trained offline in batch mode, we also have some incremental learning techniques where training updates are indeed performed online. Batch computation of results is the offline process defined above in which we use existing models and corresponding input data to compute results that will be used at a later time either for subsequent online processing or direct presentation to the user.

Both of these tasks need refined data to process, which usually is generated by running a database query. Since these queries run over large amounts of data, it can be beneficial to run them in a distributed fashion, which makes them very good candidates for running on Hadoop via either Hive[6] or Pig[7] jobs. Once the queries have completed, we use a mechanism for publishing the resulting data. We have several requirements for that mechanism: First, it should notify subscribers when the result of a query is ready. Second, it should support different repositories (not only HDFS,[8] but also S3[9] or Cassandra, for instance). Finally, it should transparently handle errors, allow for monitoring, and alerting. At Netflix we use an internal tool named Hermes that provides all of these capabilities and integrates them into a coherent publish-subscribe framework. It allows data to be delivered to subscribers in near real-time. In some sense, it covers some of the same use cases as Apache Kafka,[10] but it is not a message/event queue system.

Nearline computation can be seen as a compromise between the two previous modes. In this case, computation is performed exactly like in the online case. However, we remove the requirement to serve results as soon as they are computed and can instead store them, allowing processing to be asynchronous. The nearline computation is done in response to user events so that the system can be more responsive between requests. This opens the door for potentially more complex processing to be done per event. An example is to update recommendations to reflect that a video has been watched immediately after a user begins to watch it. Results can be stored in an intermediate caching or storage backend. Nearline computation is also a natural setting for applying incremental learning algorithms.

In any case, the choice of online/nearline/offline processing is not an either/or question. All approaches can and should be combined. There are many ways to combine them. We already mentioned the idea of using offline computation as a fallback. Another option is to precompute part of a result with an offline process and leave the less costly or more context-sensitive parts of the algorithms for online computation.

Even the modeling part can be done in a hybrid offline/online manner. This is not a natural fit for traditional supervised classification applications where the classifier has to be trained in batch from labeled data and will only be applied online to classify new inputs. However, approaches such as Matrix Factorization are a more natural fit for hybrid online/offline modeling: some factors can be precomputed offline while others can be updated in real-time to create a more fresh result. Other

---

[6]Apache Hive is a data warehouse infrastructure built on top of Hadoop for providing data summarization, query, and analysis.

[7]Pig is a high-level platform for creating MapReduce programs used with Hadoop using a language called Pig Latin.

[8]The Hadoop Distributed File System (HDFS) is a distributed file system designed to run on commodity hardware.

[9]Amazon S3 (Simple Storage Service) is an online file storage web service offered by Amazon Web Services.

[10]Apache Kafka is publish-subscribe messaging rethought as a distributed commit log.

unsupervised approaches such as clustering also allow for offline computation of the cluster centers and online assignment of clusters. These examples point to the possibility of separating our model training into a large-scale and potentially complex global model training and then alighter user-specific model training or updating phase that can be performed online or nearline.

Regardless of whether we are doing an online or offline computation, we need to think about how an algorithm will handle three kinds of inputs: models, data, and signals. Models are usually small files of parameters that have been previously trained offline. Data is previously processed information that has been stored in some sort of database, such as movie metadata or popularity. We use the term *signals* to refer to fresh information we input to algorithms. This data is obtained from live services and can be made of user-related information, such as what the user has watched recently, or context data such as session, device, or time.

11.7.3 Recommendation Results

The goal of our recommendation system is to come up with a personalized set of recommendations. These results can be serviced directly from lists that we have previously computed or they can be generated on the fly by online algorithms. Of course, we can think of using a combination of both where the bulk of the recommendations are computed offline and we add some freshness by post-processing the lists with online algorithms that use real-time signals.

At Netflix, we store offline and intermediate results in various repositories to be later consumed at request time: the primary data stores we use are Cassandra,[11] EVCache,[12] and MySQL.[13] Each solution has advantages and disadvantages over the others. MySQL allows for storage of structured relational data that might be required for some future process through general-purpose querying. However, the generality comes at the cost of scalability issues in distributed environments. Cassandra and EVCache both offer the advantages of key-value stores. Cassandra is a well-known solution for a distributed and scalable NoSQL store. Cassandra works well in some situations, however in cases where we need intensive and constant write operations we find EVCache to be a better fit. The key issue, however, is not so much where to store the results but how to handle the requirements in a way that conflicting goals such as query complexity, read/write latency, and transactional consistency meet at an optimal point for each use case.

---

[11] Apache Cassandra is an open source distributed database management system designed to handle large amounts of data across many commodity servers, providing high availability with no single point of failure.

[12] EVCache is a distributed in-memory data store for the cloud.

[13] MySQL is one of the most popular open source relational databases.

11.8 Research Directions with Industrial Applicability

The Netflix Prize spurred a lot of research advances, but the prize was a simplification of the full recommendation problem. In Sect. 11.4, we illustrated the broader scope of the recommendation problem by presenting Netflix' comprehensive approach. In this section, we will describe some of the latest advances in Recommender Systems by highlighting some of the most promising research directions. Many of these directions are enabled by the availability of larger amounts of different data such as implicit user feedback, contextual information, or social network interaction data.

11.8.1 Beyond Explicit Ratings

Explicit ratings are neither the only feedback we can get from our users nor the best kind of feedback. As already described, explicit feedback is noisy. Another issue is that ratings are provided on an ordinal scale. However, traditional methods wrongly interpret ratings as being linear, for example by computing averages. This issue, however, has been addressed by some recent methods such as OrdRec [95] that treat rating prediction as ordinal regression.

In most real-world situations, implicit feedback is much more readily available than ratings and requires no extra effort on the user side. For instance, with a web page you can have users visiting a URL or clicking on an ad as a positive feedback. In a music service, a user can decide to listen to a song. We already described in Sect. 11.5.1 that Netflix relies on many different kinds of data, the most important of which is user implicit feedback on the service about what a user watched. Also, many of these recommendation applications focus on helping a user choose an action (click, listen, watch), so it makes sense that information about previous such actions contain highly relevant information for predicting future actions. That is why, besides trying to address some of the issues with explicit ratings, there have been many recent approaches that use the more reliable and readily available data from implicit feedback. For example, Bayesian Personalized Ranking (BPR) [66], uses implicit feedback to compute a personalized ranking.

Implicit and explicit feedback can be combined in different ways [59]. Even the SVD++ approach explained in Sect. 11.3.1 can combine explicit and implicit feedback. Another way is to use logistic ordinal regression [60] to provide a mapping. Taking a Bayesian approach like Matchbox [81], also offers a framework to integrate different kinds of feedback such as ordinal ratings or implicit like/don't like preferences.

11.8.2 Personalized Learning to Rank

In Sect. 11.4 we highlighted the importance of ranking in an online recommendation scenario such as Netflix. The traditional pointwise approach to learning to rank described in Sect. 11.4.2 treats ranking as a simple binary classification problem where the only input are positive and negative examples. Typical models used in this context include Logistic Regression, Support Vector Machines, or Gradient Boosted Decision Trees.

There is a growing research effort in finding better approaches to ranking. The pairwise approach to ranking, for instance, optimizes a loss function defined on pairwise preferences from the user. The goal is to minimize the number of preference inversions in the resulting ranking. Once we have reformulated the problem this way, we can transform it back into the previous binary classification problem. Examples of such an approach are RankSVM [17], RankBoost [23], RankNet [13], or BPR.

We can also try to directly optimize the ranking of the whole list by using a listwise approach. RankCosine [91], for example, uses similarity between the ranking list and the ground truth as a loss function. ListNet [15] uses KL-divergence as loss function by defining a probability distribution. RankALS [83] defines an objective function that directly includes the ranking optimization and then uses Alternating Least Squares (ALS) for optimizing.

Across these approaches, we use rank-specific information retrieval metrics to measure the performance of a ranking model. Some of those metrics include Normalized Discounted Cumulative Gain (NDCG), Mean Average Precision (MAP), Mean Reciprocal Rank (MRR), or Fraction of Concordant Pairs (FCP). Ideally, we would like to directly optimize our models those same metrics. However, it is hard to optimize machine-learned models directly on these measures since they are not differentiable and standard methods such as gradient descent or ALS cannot be directly applied.

In order to optimize those metrics, some methods find a smoothed version of the objective function to run gradient descent. CLiMF optimizes MRR [76], and TFMAP [75], optimizes MAP in a similar way. AdaRank [93] uses boosting to optimize NDCG. Another method to optimize NDCG is NDCG-Boost [86], which optimizes the expectation of NDCG over all possible permutations. SVM-MAP [94] relaxes the MAP metric by adding it to the SVM constraints. It is even possible to directly optimize the non-differentiable IR metrics by using techniques such as Coordinate Ascent [84], Genetic Programming, Simulated Annealing [36], or even Particle Swarming [21].

11.8.3 Full Page Optimization

While one-dimensional ranking is already a step beyond rating prediction, we are most interested in optimizing the personalized experience over a complete "page". In order to do that we need to account for several things such as user navigational patterns, attention models and diversity [54]. While this is not a common theme in the literature, there are a few recent papers that are addressing the issue. Amr et. al, for example, present a complete approach to full page optimization in the context of news [3]. Their approach includes a sequential click model for the user and a relevance model that promotes diversity through the use of submodular functions.

11.8.4 Context-Aware Recommendations

Most of the work on recommender systems has traditionally focused on the two-dimensional user/item problem. But we know that in practice many other dimensions might effect a user's preference. In the case of Netflix, for example, the user's preference for shows might depend on variables such as time of the day, day of the week, or viewing device. All of those other dimensions are referred to as context. Using contextual variables represents having to deal with more data and a higher dimensional problem. However, there is the potential for effective improvements in applications that make use of context [28].

Adomavicius and Tuzhilin do a thorough review of approaches to contextual recommendations in Chap. 6 of this book. They categorize context-aware recommender systems (CARS) into three types: contextual pre-filtering, where context drives data selection; contextual post-filtering, where context is used to filter recommendations once they have been computed using a traditional approach; and contextual modeling, where context is integrated directly into the model. Although some standard approaches to recommendation could theoretically accept more dimensions, the only a few models have been adapted in this way. Oku et al.'s Context-aware Support Vector Machines (SVM) [58] extend SVMs with context dimensions to do recommendation. Xiong et al. present a Bayesian Probabilistic Tensor Factorization model to capture the temporal evolution of online shopping preferences [92]. The authors show in their experiments that results using this third dimension in the form of a tensor does improve accuracy when compared to the non-temporal case. Multiverse is another multidimensional tensor factorization approach to contextual recommendations that has proved effective in different situations [35]. Another novel approach to contextual recommendations worth mentioning is the one based on the use of Sparse Linear Method (SLIM) [55].

A Factorization Machine [65] is a novel general-purpose regression model that models interactions between pairs of variables and the target by using factors. Factorization Machines have proved to be useful in different tasks and domains [67]. In particular, they can be efficiently used to model the interaction of contextual variables [68].

11.8.5 Metrics and Evaluation

Another important area of research for recommender systems is the development of metrics that accurately map to user satisfaction with the recommendations. This has been a concern for many years [30, 37, 51, 80], but it is far from being solved. Chapter 8 of this book has a very good survey of the different approaches to evaluating recommender systems.

One of the issues with accuracy metrics is how much they are biased for popularity. Some recent research addresses this by trying to remove this popularity bias [79]. However, accuracy is not the only metric we should look at when evaluating recommendations [52]. Vargas et al., for instance, propose a framework to evaluate also novelty and diversity. In general, we would like to optimize a recommender system to different metrics at the same time. To help with this, there are some recent attempts to introduce a multiple objective optimization function [69, 70]. These approaches deal with how to optimize a recommender system offline by using training data.

However, the ultimate objective should always be to evaluate the system on real users. This is best accomplished through the use of online AB tests. But the use of AB tests can be costly and challenging [40]. Thus, sometimes controlled user experiments might be a tool worth considering [38].

11.8.6 Class Imbalance Problems and Presentation Effects

In the traditional formulation of the recommendation problem, we have pairs of items and users but user feedback values for very few of those dyads. The problem is then formulated as finding a utility function or model to estimate values for missing dyads. However, in cases where we have implicit feedback, the recommendation problem becomes predicting the probability a user will interact with a given item. There is a big shortcoming in using the standard recommendation formulation in such a setting: we do not have negative feedback. All the data we have is either positive or missing. The missing data includes both items that the user explicitly chose to ignore because they were not appealing and items that would have been perfect recommendations but were never presented to the user [78].

One way to address this class imbalance problem is to convert missing examples into both a positive and a negative example, each with a different weight related to the probability that a random exemplar is positive or negative [22]. Another solution is to the implicit feedback values: any feedback value greater than zero means positive preference, while any value equal to zero is converted to no preference [31]. A greater value in the implicit feedback value is used to measure the "confidence" in the fact the user liked the item. For example, in a music listening experience, playing a song would always be considered as positive feedback while the amount of repetitions (or for how long it was listened to) would be interpreted as support.

In many practical situations, we have more information than the simple binary implicit feedback from the user. In particular, we might know whether items not selected by the user were actually displayed to the user. This adds very valuable information, but slightly complicates the formulation of our recommendation problem. We now have three different kinds of values for items: positive, presented but not chosen, and not presented. This issue has been recently addressed by the so-called Collaborative Competitive Filtering (CCF) approach [96]. The goal of CCF is to model not only the collaboration between similar users and items, but also the competition between items for user attention. Another important issue related to how items are presented is the so-called position bias: An item that is presented in the first position of a list is more likely to be seen and chosen than one that is further down [63].

11.8.7 Social Recommendations

Many applications such as Netflix have access to social network data for some users. The use of this new source of data for recommendations is an active area of research, as highlighted in Chap. 15. Most of the initial approaches to social recommendation[14] relied on the so-called *trust-based model* where the trust (or influence) of others is transmitted through the social network connections [6, 57]. However, it is still unclear whether users prefer recommendations from friends to those coming from other users. For instance, in another study [11], the authors found that the selection of users where the recommendation came from did not make much difference, except if the recipients of the recommendation were made aware of it. In any case, it seems clear that social trust can be used in a positive way to generate explanations and support.

There are other uses of social information. For instance, social network data can be an efficient way to deal with user or item cold-start. Social information can, for instance, be used to select the most informative and relevant users or items for modeling [50]. In terms of selecting users, some recent methods propose using social information to select experts [73] in a similar way as collaborative filtering settings [4].

Social-based recommendations can also be combined with the more traditional content-based or collaborative filtering approaches [33]. Social network information can even be efficiently included in a pure collaborative filtering setting, for example by including it in the matrix factorization objective function [56, 97].

[14]It is important to note that the term "social recommendation" was originally used to describe collaborative filtering approaches [7, 74].

11.9 Conclusion

The Netflix Prize abstracted the recommendation problem to a simplified proxy of predicting ratings. It is now clear that this objective, accurate prediction of ratings, is just one of many components in an effective industrial recommendation system. These systems also need to take into account factors such as diversity, context, popularity, interest, evidence, freshness, and novelty. Trying to balance these often competing factors can be a daunting task, but we have found that it is best handled using a range of algorithmic approaches and many types of data.

Recommender systems deployed in the wild, such as those at Netflix, have the difficult goal of optimizing the probability a user chooses something and enjoys it enough to come back to the service. In order to do so, we need to figure out the best way employ all the available data: from user interactions to item metadata. We also need to have optimized approaches, appropriate metrics, rapid experimentation frameworks, solid algorithmic techniques, and scalable architectures embedded within a sound methodology for figuring out what actually improves the user experience. When we put all of this together, we find ourselves continually making progress towards that goal of creating the best possible recommendation experience for our users.

References

1. Agarwal, D., Chen, B.C., Elango, P., Ramakrishnan, R.: Content recommendation on web portals. Commun. ACM **56**(6), 92–101 (2013). DOI 10.1145/2461256.2461277. URL http://doi.acm.org/10.1145/2461256.2461277
2. Agarwal, D., Chen, B.C., Pang, B.: Personalized recommendation of user comments via factor models. In: Proceedings of the Conference on Empirical Methods in Natural Language Processing, EMNLP '11, pp. 571–582. Association for Computational Linguistics, Stroudsburg, PA, USA (2011). URL http://dl.acm.org/citation.cfm?id=2145432.2145499
3. Ahmed, A., Teo, C.H., Vishwanathan, S., Smola, A.: Fair and balanced: Learning to present news stories. In: Proceedings of the Fifth ACM International Conference on Web Search and Data Mining, WSDM '12, pp. 333–342. ACM, New York, NY, USA (2012). DOI 10.1145/2124295.2124337. URL http://doi.acm.org/10.1145/2124295.2124337
4. Amatriain, X., Lathia, N., Pujol, J.M., Kwak, H., Oliver, N.: The wisdom of the few: a collaborative filtering approach based on expert opinions from the web. In: Proc. of 32nd ACM SIGIR, SIGIR '09, pp. 532–539. ACM, New York, NY, USA (2009). DOI 10.1145/1571941.1572033. URL http://dx.doi.org/10.1145/1571941.1572033
5. Amatriain, X., Pujol, J.M., Oliver, N.: I Like It... I Like It Not: Evaluating User Ratings Noise in Recommender Systems. In: G.J. Houben, G. McCalla, F. Pianesi, M. Zancanaro (eds.) User Modeling, Adaptation, and Personalization, vol. 5535, chap. 24, pp. 247–258. Springer Berlin (2009). DOI 10.1007/978-3-642-02247-0_24. URL http://dx.doi.org/10.1007/978-3-642-02247-0_24
6. Andersen, R., Borgs, C., Chayes, J., Feige, U., Flaxman, A., Kalai, A., Mirrokni, V., Tennenholtz, M.: Trust-based recommendation systems: an axiomatic approach. In: Proc. of the 17th WWW, WWW '08, pp. 199–208. ACM, New York, NY, USA (2008). DOI 10.1145/1367497.1367525. URL http://doi.acm.org/10.1145/1367497.1367525

7. Basu, C., Hirsh, H., Cohen, W.: Recommendation as classification: using social and content-based information in recommendation. In: Proc. of AAAI '98, AAAI '98/IAAI '98, pp. 714–720. American Association for Artificial Intelligence, Menlo Park, CA, USA (1998). URL http://dl.acm.org/citation.cfm?id=295240.295795
8. Bell, R.M., Koren, Y.: Lessons from the Netflix Prize Challenge. SIGKDD Explor. Newsl. **9**(2), 75–79 (2007). DOI 10.1145/1345448.1345465. URL http://dx.doi.org/10.1145/1345448.1345465
9. Berndhardsson, E.: Music recommendations at spotify (2013)
10. Blei, D.M., Ng, A.Y., Jordan, M.I.: Latent dirichlet allocation. J. Mach. Learn. Res. **3**, 993–1022 (2003). URL http://dl.acm.org/citation.cfm?id=944919.944937
11. Bourke, S., McCarthy, K., Smyth, B.: Power to the people: exploring neighbourhood formations in social recommender system. In: Proc. of Recsys '11, RecSys '11, pp. 337–340. ACM, New York, NY, USA (2011). DOI 10.1145/2043932.2043997. URL http://doi.acm.org/10.1145/2043932.2043997
12. Breiman, L.: Random forests. Machine learning **45**(1), 5–32 (2001)
13. Burges, C., Shaked, T., Renshaw, E., Lazier, A., Deeds, M., Hamilton, N., Hullender, G.: Learning to rank using gradient descent. In: Proceedings of the 22nd ICML, ICML '05, pp. 89–96. ACM, New York, NY, USA (2005). DOI 10.1145/1102351.1102363. URL http://dx.doi.org/10.1145/1102351.1102363
14. Burke, R.: The adaptive web. chap. Hybrid Web Recommender Systems, pp. 377–408 (2007). DOI 10.1007/978-3-540-72079-9_12. URL http://dx.doi.org/10.1007/978-3-540-72079-9_12
15. Cao, Z., Liu, T.: Learning to rank: From pairwise approach to listwise approach. In: In Proceedings of the 24th ICML, pp. 129–136 (2007). URL http://citeseerx.ist.psu.edu/viewdoc/summary?doi=10.1.1.64.1518
16. Celma, O.: Music Recommendation and Discovery: The Long Tail, Long Fail, and Long Play in the Digital Music Space. Springer (2010)
17. Chapelle, O., Keerthi, S.S.: Efficient algorithms for ranking with SVMs. Information Retrieval **13**, 201–215 (2010). DOI 10.1007/s10791-009-9109-9. URL http://dx.doi.org/10.1007/s10791-009-9109-9
18. Chen, W.Y., Chu, J.C., Luan, J., Bai, H., Wang, Y., Chang, E.Y.: Collaborative filtering for orkut communities: Discovery of user latent behavior. In: Proceedings of the 18th International Conference on World Wide Web, WWW '09, pp. 681–690. ACM, New York, NY, USA (2009). DOI 10.1145/1526709.1526801. URL http://doi.acm.org/10.1145/1526709.1526801
19. Das, A.S., Datar, M., Garg, A., Rajaram, S.: Google news personalization: Scalable online collaborative filtering. In: Proceedings of the 16th International Conference on World Wide Web, WWW '07, pp. 271–280. ACM, New York, NY, USA (2007). DOI 10.1145/1242572.1242610. URL http://doi.acm.org/10.1145/1242572.1242610
20. Davidson, J., Liebald, B., Liu, J., Nandy, P., Van Vleet, T., Gargi, U., Gupta, S., He, Y., Lambert, M., Livingston, B., Sampath, D.: The youtube video recommendation system. In: Proceedings of the Fourth ACM Conference on Recommender Systems, RecSys '10, pp. 293–296. ACM, New York, NY, USA (2010). DOI 10.1145/1864708.1864770. URL http://doi.acm.org/10.1145/1864708.1864770
21. Diaz-Aviles, E., Georgescu, M., Nejdl, W.: Swarming to rank for recommender systems. In: Proc. of Recsys '12, RecSys '12, pp. 229–232. ACM, New York, NY, USA (2012). DOI 10.1145/2365952.2366001. URL http://doi.acm.org/10.1145/2365952.2366001
22. Elkan, C., Noto, K.: Learning classifiers from only positive and unlabeled data. In: Proc. of the 14th ACM SIGKDD, KDD '08, pp. 213–220. ACM, New York, NY, USA (2008). DOI 10.1145/1401890.1401920. URL http://dx.doi.org/10.1145/1401890.1401920
23. Freund, Y., Iyer, R., Schapire, R.E., Singer, Y.: An efficient boosting algorithm for combining preferences. J. Mach. Learn. Res. **4**, 933–969 (2003). URL http://portal.acm.org/citation.cfm?id=964285
24. Frey, B.J., Dueck, D.: Clustering by passing messages between data points. Science **315**, 2007 (2007)

25. Friedman, J.H.: Greedy function approximation: a gradient boosting machine. Annals of Statistics pp. 1189–1232 (2001)
26. Fujiwara, Y., Nakatsuji, M., Yamamuro, T., Shiokawa, H., Onizuka, M.: Efficient personalized pagerank with accuracy assurance. In: Proceedings of the 18th ACM SIGKDD International Conference on Knowledge Discovery and Data Mining, KDD '12, pp. 15–23. ACM, New York, NY, USA (2012). DOI 10.1145/2339530.2339538. URL http://doi.acm.org/10.1145/2339530.2339538
27. Funk, S.: Netflix update: Try this at home. http://sifter.org/ simon/journal/20061211.html (2006). URL http://sifter.org/~simon/journal/20061211.html
28. Gorgoglione, M., Panniello, U., Tuzhilin, A.: The effect of context-aware recommendations on customer purchasing behavior and trust. In: Proc. of Recsys '11, RecSys '11, pp. 85–92. ACM, New York, NY, USA (2011). DOI 10.1145/2043932.2043951. URL http://doi.acm.org/10.1145/2043932.2043951
29. Gupta, P., Goel, A., Lin, J., Sharma, A., Wang, D., Zadeh, R.: Wtf: The who to follow service at twitter. In: Proceedings of the 22Nd International Conference on World Wide Web, WWW '13, pp. 505–514. International World Wide Web Conferences Steering Committee, Republic and Canton of Geneva, Switzerland (2013). URL http://dl.acm.org/citation.cfm?id=2488388.2488433
30. Herlocker, J.L., Konstan, J.A., Terveen, L.G., Riedl, J.T.: Evaluating collaborative filtering recommender systems. ACM Trans. Inf. Syst. **22**(1), 5–53 (2004). DOI http://doi.acm.org/10.1145/963770.963772
31. Hu, Y., Koren, Y., Volinsky, C.: Collaborative Filtering for Implicit Feedback Datasets. In: Proc. of the 2008 Eighth ICDM, *ICDM '08*, vol. 0, pp. 263–272. IEEE Computer Society, Washington, DC, USA (2008). DOI 10.1109/ICDM.2008.22. URL http://dx.doi.org/10.1109/ICDM.2008.22
32. in the Industry, R.S.: Recommendation systems in the industry. Tutorial at Recsys 2009 (2009)
33. Jamali, M., Ester, M.: Trustwalker: a random walk model for combining trust-based and item-based recommendation. In: Proc. of KDD '09, KDD '09, pp. 397–406. ACM, New York, NY, USA (2009). DOI 10.1145/1557019.1557067. URL http://doi.acm.org/10.1145/1557019.1557067
34. Jeh, G., Widom, J.: Simrank: A measure of structural-context similarity. In: Proceedings of the Eighth ACM SIGKDD International Conference on Knowledge Discovery and Data Mining, KDD '02, pp. 538–543. ACM, New York, NY, USA (2002). DOI 10.1145/775047.775126. URL http://doi.acm.org/10.1145/775047.775126
35. Karatzoglou, A., Amatriain, X., Baltrunas, L., Oliver, N.: Multiverse recommendation: n-dimensional tensor factorization for context-aware collaborative filtering. In: Proc. of the fourth ACM Recsys, RecSys '10, pp. 79–86. ACM, New York, NY, USA (2010). DOI 10.1145/1864708.1864727. URL http://dx.doi.org/10.1145/1864708.1864727
36. Karimzadehgan, M., Li, W., Zhang, R., Mao, J.: A stochastic learning-to-rank algorithm and its application to contextual advertising. In: Proceedings of the 20th WWW, WWW '11, pp. 377–386. ACM, New York, NY, USA (2011). DOI 10.1145/1963405.1963460. URL http://doi.acm.org/10.1145/1963405.1963460
37. Karypis, G.: Evaluation of item-based top-n recommendation algorithms. In: CIKM '01: Proceedings of the tenth international conference on Information and knowledge management, pp. 247–254. ACM, New York, NY, USA (2001). DOI http://doi.acm.org/10.1145/502585.502627
38. Knijnenburg, B.P.: Conducting user experiments in recommender systems. In: Proceedings of the sixth ACM conference on Recommender systems, RecSys '12, pp. 3–4. ACM, New York, NY, USA (2012). DOI 10.1145/2365952.2365956. URL http://doi.acm.org/10.1145/2365952.2365956
39. Koenigstein, N., Nice, N., Paquet, U., Schleyen, N.: The xbox recommender system. In: Proceedings of the Sixth ACM Conference on Recommender Systems, RecSys '12, pp. 281–284. ACM, New York, NY, USA (2012). DOI 10.1145/2365952.2366015. URL http://doi.acm.org/10.1145/2365952.2366015

40. Kohavi, R., Deng, A., Frasca, B., Longbotham, R., Walker, T., Xu, Y.: Trustworthy online controlled experiments: five puzzling outcomes explained. In: Proceedings of KDD '12, pp. 786–794. ACM, New York, NY, USA (2012). DOI 10.1145/2339530.2339653. URL http://doi.acm.org/10.1145/2339530.2339653
41. Kohavi, R., Henne, R.M., Sommerfield, D.: Practical guide to controlled experiments on the web: Listen to your customers not to the hippo. In: Proceedings of the 13th ACM SIGKDD International Conference on Knowledge Discovery and Data Mining, KDD '07, pp. 959–967. ACM, New York, NY, USA (2007). DOI 10.1145/1281192.1281295. URL http://doi.acm.org/10.1145/1281192.1281295
42. Koren, Y.: Factorization meets the neighborhood: a multifaceted collaborative filtering model. In: Proceedings of the 14th ACM SIGKDD, KDD '08, pp. 426–434. ACM, New York, NY, USA (2008). DOI 10.1145/1401890.1401944. URL http://dx.doi.org/10.1145/1401890.1401944
43. Koren, Y.: Collaborative filtering with temporal dynamics. In: Proceedings of the 15th ACM SIGKDD, KDD '09, pp. 447–456. ACM, New York, NY, USA (2009). DOI 10.1145/1557019.1557072. URL http://dx.doi.org/10.1145/1557019.1557072
44. Koren, Y., Bell, R., Volinsky, C.: Matrix Factorization Techniques for Recommender Systems. Computer **42**(8), 30–37 (2009). DOI 10.1109/MC.2009.263. URL http://dx.doi.org/10.1109/MC.2009.263
45. Lagun, D., Hsieh, C.H., Webster, D., Navalpakkam, V.: Towards better measurement of attention and satisfaction in mobile search. In: Proceedings of the 37th International ACM SIGIR Conference on Research & Development in Information Retrieval, SIGIR '14, pp. 113–122. ACM, New York, NY, USA (2014). DOI 10.1145/2600428.2609631. URL http://doi.acm.org/10.1145/2600428.2609631
46. Lamere, P.B.: I've got 10 million songs in my pocket: Now what? In: Proceedings of the Sixth ACM Conference on Recommender Systems, RecSys '12, pp. 207–208. ACM, New York, NY, USA (2012). DOI 10.1145/2365952.2365994. URL http://doi.acm.org/10.1145/2365952.2365994
47. Li, L., Chu, W., Langford, J., Schapire, R.E.: A contextual-bandit approach to personalized news article recommendation. In: Proceedings of the 19th International Conference on World Wide Web, WWW '10, pp. 661–670. ACM, New York, NY, USA (2010). DOI 10.1145/1772690.1772758. URL http://doi.acm.org/10.1145/1772690.1772758
48. Linden, G., Smith, B., York, J.: Amazon.com recommendations: Item-to-item collaborative filtering. IEEE Internet Computing **7**(1), 76–80 (2003). DOI 10.1109/MIC.2003.1167344. URL http://dx.doi.org/10.1109/MIC.2003.1167344
49. Liu, J., Pedersen, E., Dolan, P.: Personalized news recommendation based on click behavior. In: 2010 International Conference on Intelligent User Interfaces (2010)
50. Liu, N.N., Meng, X., Liu, C., Yang, Q.: Wisdom of the better few: cold start recommendation via representative based rating elicitation. In: Proc. of RecSys '11, RecSys '11. ACM, New York, NY, USA (2011). DOI 10.1145/2043932.2043943. URL http://doi.acm.org/10.1145/2043932.2043943
51. McLaughlin, M.R., Herlocker, J.L.: A collaborative filtering algorithm and evaluation metric that accurately model the user experience. In: Proc. of SIGIR '04 (2004)
52. Mcnee, S.M., Riedl, J., Konstan, J.A.: Being accurate is not enough: how accuracy metrics have hurt recommender systems. In: CHI '06: CHI '06 extended abstracts on Human factors in computing systems, pp. 1097–1101. ACM Press, New York, NY, USA (2006). DOI 10.1145/1125451.1125659
53. Navalpakkam, V., Jentzsch, L., Sayres, R., Ravi, S., Ahmed, A., Smola, A.: Measurement and modeling of eye-mouse behavior in the presence of nonlinear page layouts. In: Proceedings of the 22Nd International Conference on World Wide Web, WWW '13, pp. 953–964. International World Wide Web Conferences Steering Committee, Republic and Canton of Geneva, Switzerland (2013). URL http://dl.acm.org/citation.cfm?id=2488388.2488471

54. Navalpakkam, V., Jentzsch, L., Sayres, R., Ravi, S., Ahmed, A., Smola, A.: Measurement and modeling of eye-mouse behavior in the presence of nonlinear page layouts. In: Proceedings of the 22Nd International Conference on World Wide Web, WWW '13, pp. 953–964. International World Wide Web Conferences Steering Committee, Republic and Canton of Geneva, Switzerland (2013). URL http://dl.acm.org/citation.cfm?id=2488388.2488471
55. Ning, X., Karypis, G.: Sparse linear methods with side information for top-n recommendations. In: Proc. of the 21st WWW, WWW '12 Companion, pp. 581–582. ACM, New York, NY, USA (2012). DOI 10.1145/2187980.2188137. URL http://doi.acm.org/10.1145/2187980.2188137
56. Noel, J., Sanner, S., Tran, K., Christen, P., Xie, L., Bonilla, E.V., Abbasnejad, E., Della Penna, N.: New objective functions for social collaborative filtering. In: Proc. of WWW '12, WWW '12, pp. 859–868. ACM, New York, NY, USA (2012). DOI 10.1145/2187836.2187952. URL http://doi.acm.org/10.1145/2187836.2187952
57. O'Donovan, J., Smyth, B.: Trust in recommender systems. In: Proc. of IUI '05, IUI '05, pp. 167–174. ACM, New York, NY, USA (2005). DOI 10.1145/1040830.1040870. URL http://doi.acm.org/10.1145/1040830.1040870
58. Oku, K., Nakajima, S., Miyazaki, J., Uemura, S.: Context-aware SVM for context-dependent information recommendation. In: Proc. of the 7th Conference on Mobile Data Management (2006)
59. Parra, D., Amatriain, X.: Walk the Talk: Analyzing the relation between implicit and explicit feedback for preference elicitation. In: J.A. Konstan, R. Conejo, J.L. Marzo, N. Oliver (eds.) User Modeling, Adaption and Personalization, *Lecture Notes in Computer Science*, vol. 6787, chap. 22, pp. 255–268. Springer, Berlin, Heidelberg (2011). DOI 10.1007/978-3-642-22362-4_22. URL http://dx.doi.org/10.1007/978-3-642-22362-4_22
60. Parra, D., Karatzoglou, A., Amatriain, X., Yavuz, I.: Implicit feedback recommendation via implicit-to-explicit ordinal logistic regression mapping. In: Proc. of the 2011 CARS Workshop (2011)
61. Pizzato, L., Rej, T., Chung, T., Koprinska, I., Kay, J.: Recon: A reciprocal recommender for online dating. In: Proceedings of the Fourth ACM Conference on Recommender Systems, RecSys '10, pp. 207–214. ACM, New York, NY, USA (2010). DOI 10.1145/1864708.1864747. URL http://doi.acm.org/10.1145/1864708.1864747
62. Rabkin, A., Katz, R.: Chukwa: A system for reliable large-scale log collection. In: Proceedings of the 24th International Conference on Large Installation System Administration, LISA'10, pp. 1–15. USENIX Association, Berkeley, CA, USA (2010). URL http://dl.acm.org/citation.cfm?id=1924976.1924994
63. Radlinski, F., Kurup, M., Joachims, T.: How does clickthrough data reflect retrieval quality? In: Proc. of the 17th CIKM, CIKM '08, pp. 43–52. ACM, New York, NY, USA (2008). DOI 10.1145/1458082.1458092. URL http://dx.doi.org/10.1145/1458082.1458092
64. Reda, A., Park, Y., Tiwari, M., Posse, C., Shah, S.: Metaphor: A system for related search recommendations. In: Proceedings of the 21st ACM International Conference on Information and Knowledge Management, CIKM '12, pp. 664–673. ACM, New York, NY, USA (2012). DOI 10.1145/2396761.2396847. URL http://doi.acm.org/10.1145/2396761.2396847
65. Rendle, S.: Factorization Machines. In: Proc. of 2010 IEEE ICDM, pp. 995–1000. IEEE (2010). DOI 10.1109/ICDM.2010.127. URL http://dx.doi.org/10.1109/ICDM.2010.127
66. Rendle, S., Freudenthaler, C., Gantner, Z., Thieme, L.S.: BPR: Bayesian personalized ranking from implicit feedback. In: Proceedings of the 25th UAI, UAI '09, pp. 452–461. AUAI Press, Arlington, Virginia, United States (2009). URL http://portal.acm.org/citation.cfm?id=1795167
67. Rendle, S., Freudenthaler, C., Thieme, L.S.: Factorizing personalized Markov chains for next-basket recommendation. In: Proc. of the 19th WWW, WWW '10, pp. 811–820. ACM, New York, NY, USA (2010). DOI 10.1145/1772690.1772773. URL http://dx.doi.org/10.1145/1772690.1772773
68. Rendle, S., Gantner, Z., Freudenthaler, C., Schmidt-Thieme, L.: Fast context-aware recommendations with factorization machines. In: Proc. of the 34th ACM SIGIR, SIGIR '11, pp. 635–644. ACM, New York, NY, USA (2011). DOI 10.1145/2009916.2010002. URL http://doi.acm.org/10.1145/2009916.2010002

69. Ribeiro, M.T., Lacerda, A., Veloso, A., Ziviani, N.: Pareto-efficient hybridization for multi-objective recommender systems. In: Proceedings of the sixth ACM conference on Recommender systems, RecSys '12, pp. 19–26. ACM, New York, NY, USA (2012). DOI 10.1145/2365952.2365962. URL http://doi.acm.org/10.1145/2365952.2365962
70. Rodriguez, M., Posse, C., Zhang, E.: Multiple objective optimization in recommender systems. In: Proceedings of the sixth ACM conference on Recommender systems, RecSys '12, pp. 11–18. ACM, New York, NY, USA (2012). DOI 10.1145/2365952.2365961. URL http://doi.acm.org/10.1145/2365952.2365961
71. Salakhutdinov, R., Mnih, A., Hinton, G.E.: Restricted Boltzmann machines for collaborative filtering. In: Proc of ICML '07. ACM, New York, NY, USA (2007)
72. Science: Rockin' to the Music Genome. Science **311**(5765), 1223d– (2006). DOI 10.1126/science.311.5765.1223d. URL http://www.sciencemag.org
73. Sha, X., Quercia, D., Michiardi, P., Dell'Amico, M.: Spotting trends: the wisdom of the few. In: Proc. of the Recsys '12, RecSys '12, pp. 51–58. ACM, New York, NY, USA (2012). DOI 10.1145/2365952.2365967. URL http://doi.acm.org/10.1145/2365952.2365967
74. Shardanand, U., Maes, P.: Social information filtering: algorithms for automating word of mouth. In: Proc. of SIGCHI '95, CHI '95, pp. 210–217. ACM Press/Addison-Wesley Publishing Co., New York, NY, USA (1995). DOI 10.1145/223904.223931. URL http://dx.doi.org/10.1145/223904.223931
75. Shi, Y., Karatzoglou, A., Baltrunas, L., Larson, M., Hanjalic, A., Oliver, N.: TFMAP: optimizing MAP for top-n context-aware recommendation. In: Proc. of the 35th SIGIR, SIGIR '12, pp. 155–164. ACM, New York, NY, USA (2012). DOI 10.1145/2348283.2348308. URL http://doi.acm.org/10.1145/2348283.2348308
76. Shi, Y., Karatzoglou, A., Baltrunas, L., Larson, M., Oliver, N., Hanjalic, A.: CLiMF: learning to maximize reciprocal rank with collaborative less-is-more filtering. In: Proc. of the sixth Recsys, RecSys '12, pp. 139–146. ACM, New York, NY, USA (2012). DOI 10.1145/2365952.2365981. URL http://dx.doi.org/10.1145/2365952.2365981
77. Sigurbjörnsson, B., van Zwol, R.: Flickr tag recommendation based on collective knowledge. In: Proceedings of the 17th International Conference on World Wide Web, WWW '08, pp. 327–336. ACM, New York, NY, USA (2008). DOI 10.1145/1367497.1367542. URL http://doi.acm.org/10.1145/1367497.1367542
78. Steck, H.: Training and testing of recommender systems on data missing not at random. In: Proc. of the 16th ACM SIGKDD, KDD '10, pp. 713–722. ACM, New York, NY, USA (2010). DOI 10.1145/1835804.1835895. URL http://dx.doi.org/10.1145/1835804.1835895
79. Steck, H.: Item popularity and recommendation accuracy. In: Proceedings of the fifth ACM conference on Recommender systems, RecSys '11, pp. 125–132. ACM, New York, NY, USA (2011). DOI 10.1145/2043932.2043957. URL http://doi.acm.org/10.1145/2043932.2043957
80. Steck, H.: Evaluation of recommendations: Rating-prediction and ranking. In: Proceedings of the 7th ACM Conference on Recommender Systems, RecSys '13, pp. 213–220. ACM, New York, NY, USA (2013). DOI 10.1145/2507157.2507160. URL http://doi.acm.org/10.1145/2507157.2507160
81. Stern, D.H., Herbrich, R., Graepel, T.: Matchbox: large scale online bayesian recommendations. In: Proc. of the 18th WWW, WWW '09, pp. 111–120. ACM, New York, NY, USA (2009). DOI 10.1145/1526709.1526725. URL http://dx.doi.org/10.1145/1526709.1526725
82. Takács, G., Pilászy, I., Németh, B., Tikk, D.: Major components of the gravity recommendation system. SIGKDD Explor. Newsl. **9**(2), 80–83 (2007). DOI 10.1145/1345448.1345466. URL http://doi.acm.org/10.1145/1345448.1345466
83. Takács, G., Tikk, D.: Alternating least squares for personalized ranking. In: Proc. of Recsys '12, RecSys '12, pp. 83–90. ACM, New York, NY, USA (2012). DOI 10.1145/2365952.2365972. URL http://doi.acm.org/10.1145/2365952.2365972
84. Tan, M., Xia, T., Guo, L., Wang, S.: Direct optimization of ranking measures for learning to rank models. In: Proceedings of the 19th ACM SIGKDD International Conference on Knowledge Discovery and Data Mining, KDD '13, pp. 856–864. ACM, New York, NY, USA (2013). DOI 10.1145/2487575.2487630. URL http://doi.acm.org/10.1145/2487575.2487630

85. Teh, Y.W., Jordan, M.I., Beal, M.J., Blei, D.M.: Hierarchical dirichlet processes. Journal of the American Statistical Association **101** (2004)
86. Valizadegan, H., Jin, R., Zhang, R., Mao, J.: Learning to Rank by Optimizing NDCG Measure. In: Proc. of SIGIR '00, pp. 41–48 (2000). URL http://citeseerx.ist.psu.edu/viewdoc/summary?doi=10.1.1.154.8402
87. Vargas, S., Castells, P.: Rank and relevance in novelty and diversity metrics for recommender systems. In: Proceedings of the fifth ACM conference on Recommender systems, RecSys '11, pp. 109–116. ACM, New York, NY, USA (2011). DOI 10.1145/2043932.2043955. URL http://doi.acm.org/10.1145/2043932.2043955
88. Wang, J., Sarwar, B., Sundaresan, N.: Utilizing related products for post-purchase recommendation in e-commerce. In: Proceedings of the Fifth ACM Conference on Recommender Systems, RecSys '11, pp. 329–332. ACM, New York, NY, USA (2011). DOI 10.1145/2043932.2043995. URL http://doi.acm.org/10.1145/2043932.2043995
89. Wang, J., Zhang, Y., Posse, C., Bhasin, A.: Is it time for a career switch? In: Proceedings of the 22Nd International Conference on World Wide Web, WWW '13, pp. 1377–1388. International World Wide Web Conferences Steering Committee, Republic and Canton of Geneva, Switzerland (2013). URL http://dl.acm.org/citation.cfm?id=2488388.2488509
90. Weston, J., Yee, H., Weiss, R.: Learning to rank recommendations with the k-order statistic loss. In: ACM International Conference on Recommender Systems (RecSys) (2013). URL http://dl.acm.org/citation.cfm?id=2507210
91. Xia, F., Liu, T.Y., Wang J.and Zhang, W., Li, H.: Listwise approach to learning to rank: theory and algorithm. In: Proc. of the 25th ICML, ICML '08, pp. 1192–1199. ACM, New York, NY, USA (2008). DOI 10.1145/1390156.1390306. URL http://dx.doi.org/10.1145/1390156.1390306
92. Xiong, L., Chen, X., Huang, T., J. Schneider, J.G.C.: Temporal collaborative filtering with bayesian probabilistic tensor factorization. In: Proceedings of SIAM Data Mining (2010)
93. Xu, J., Li, H.: AdaRank: a boosting algorithm for information retrieval. In: Proc. of SIGIR '07, SIGIR '07, pp. 391–398. ACM, New York, NY, USA (2007). DOI 10.1145/1277741.1277809. URL http://dx.doi.org/10.1145/1277741.1277809
94. Xu, J., Liu, T.Y., Lu, M., Li, H., Ma, W.Y.: Directly optimizing evaluation measures in learning to rank. In: Proc. of SIGIR '08, pp. 107–114. ACM, New York, NY, USA (2008). DOI 10.1145/1390334.1390355. URL http://dx.doi.org/10.1145/1390334.1390355
95. Y, K., Sill, J.: OrdRec: an ordinal model for predicting personalized item rating distributions. In: RecSys '11, pp. 117–124 (2011)
96. Yang, S., Long, B., Smola, A., Zha, H., Zheng, Z.: Collaborative competitive filtering: learning recommender using context of user choice. In: Proc. of the 34th ACM SIGIR, SIGIR '11, pp. 295–304. ACM, New York, NY, USA (2011). DOI 10.1145/2009916.2009959. URL http://dx.doi.org/10.1145/2009916.2009959
97. Yang, X., Steck, H., Guo, Y., Liu, Y.: On top-k recommendation using social networks. In: Proc. of RecSys '12, RecSys '12, pp. 67–74. ACM, New York, NY, USA (2012). DOI 10.1145/2365952.2365969. URL http://doi.acm.org/10.1145/2365952.2365969
98. Yi, J., Chen, Y., Li, J., Sett, S., Yan, T.W.: Predictive model performance: Offline and online evaluations. In: Proceedings of the 19th ACM SIGKDD International Conference on Knowledge Discovery and Data Mining, KDD '13, pp. 1294–1302. ACM, New York, NY, USA (2013). DOI 10.1145/2487575.2488215. URL http://doi.acm.org/10.1145/2487575.2488215

Chapter 12
Panorama of Recommender Systems to Support Learning

Hendrik Drachsler, Katrien Verbert, Olga C. Santos, and Nikos Manouselis

12.1 Introduction

In this chapter we present an extended version of a state-of-the-art review on recommender systems (RS) in the field of education and more specifically of Technology Enhanced Learning (TEL). The chapter is based on a previous study by Manouselis et al. in 2011 [66] in the first Recommender System Handbook, and a Springerbriefs book from 2012 by Manouslis et al. [67].

The initial version from 2011 was limited to 20 recommender systems and got extended by the 2012 publication to 42 systems. The report from 2012 did not only extend the previous review, it also introduced a classification framework that provides a detailed overview over research activities on TEL recommender systems (RecSys). The 2012 publication acts like a map that shows what recommender system approaches have been studied in the TEL field and summarises the main findings. It is also a kind of manual that can inform researchers about most

H. Drachsler (✉)
Welten Institute Research Centre for Learning, Teaching and Technology, Open University of the Netherlands, Heerlen, The Netherlands
e-mail: Hendrik.Drachsler@ou.nl

K. Verbert
Department of Computer Science, KU Leuven, Leuven, Belgium

Department of Computer Science, Vrije Universiteit Brussel, Brussel, Belgium
e-mail: katrien.verbert@cs.kuleuven.be

O.C. Santos
aDeNu Research Group, UNED, Madrid, Spain
e-mail: ocsantos@dia.uned.es

N. Manouselis
Agro-Know, Vrilissia, Greece
e-mail: nikosm@ieee.org

F. Ricci et al. (eds.), *Recommender Systems Handbook*,
DOI 10.1007/978-1-4899-7637-6_12

prominent approaches chosen so far and highlights neglected areas of research that could be taken up by the research community. It tries to standardise the research on TEL RecSys by introducing reference datasets, evaluation methods and procedures, and finally outlines current challenges in the field.

The previous studies are highly cited and had a significant impact on the TEL RecSys field. Since their publication, the community has much more developed into a sustainable and coherent research field. Research results became more transparent and comparable through the use of educational datasets from Educational Resource portals such as *OpenScout* (http://learn.openscout.net/) or *MACE* (http://portal.mace-project.eu) that act as reference datasets like Movielens or Netflix [110]. The research community around TEL RecSys is continuously growing as an increasing amount of research projects, conferences, workshops, special issues in journals and books shows. Examples include the Workshop series of Social Information Retrieval for Technology Enhanced Learning (SIRTEL 2007–2009), the RecSysTEL Workshop series on Recommender Systems for Technology Enhanced Learning [65, 68], the dataTEL workshop series on datasets for Technology Enhanced Learning [25, 26], a specific track on Recommender Systems for Learning (ReSyL) at the 14th IEEE International Conference on Advanced Learning Technologies (ICALT 2014) [27], the data competitions from 2013 until 2014 of the LinkedUp project [19, 21], as well as several special volumes of journals and books [86, 87, 104, 109, 113]. The diversity of the events over the years shows how relevant the research topics and challenges are for the TEL community. Figure 12.1 shows a world map where we indicated the countries that contribute research results to this meta-study. It can be seen that research on TEL RecSys is of global interest.

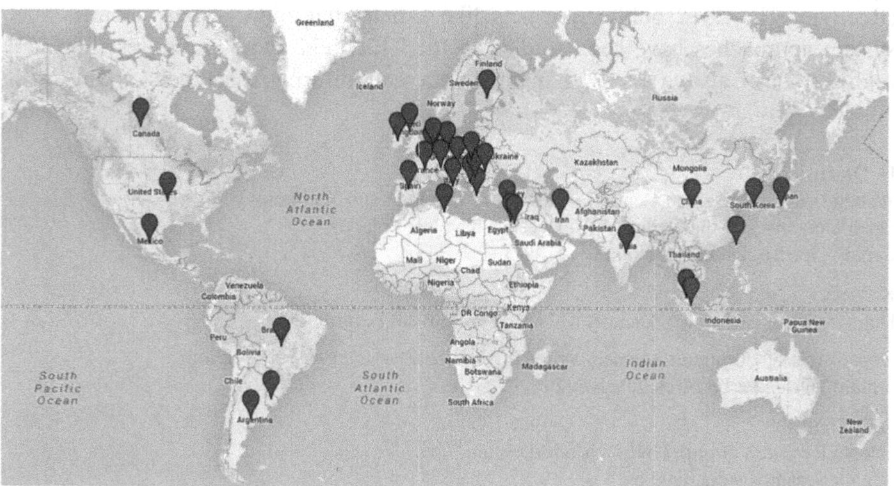

Fig. 12.1 The world map of TEL RecSys research. It highlights countries that contributed research considered for this meta-review study

With the current chapter, we aim to go beyond the previous results by updating the classification framework as well as significantly increasing the amount of recommender systems that have been analysed in the state-of-the-art review. The current review almost doubles the number of systems analysed in the previous study (2012) and includes 82 recommender systems from 35 countries (see Fig. 12.1). Due to the growths of publications in the field, we needed to be more restrictive with the selection of suitable research papers that are added to the review. We therefore mainly considered new publications that are based on empirical data rather than conceptual drafts. We hope to provide a comprehensive overview about the TEL RecSys field, further standardise the research and development, outline new challenges, and increase the common knowledge about the most effective ways to apply recommender system technology in the educational domain.

Finally, we want to emphasis that all the bibliography covered by this chapter is available in an open group created at the Mendeley research platform and will continue to be enriched with additional references (http://bit.ly/recsystel). We would like to invite the reader to sign up for this group and to connect to the community of RecSysTEL researchers. Among gaining access to the collected bibliography, we are looking forward to colleagues that contribute new research articles and findings within this very fast developing research field.

The chapter is structured as follows. First, an overview of the TEL research field is presented. Next, the framework model used to classify the reviewed recommender systems is outlined. After that, the results of the meta review are described, presenting seven clusters in which the TEL RecSys have been grouped. Finally, some conclusions and future challenges are discussed.

12.2 Technology Enhanced Learning (TEL)

Technology Enhanced Learning (TEL) aims to design, develop and evaluate socio-technical innovations for various kinds of learning and education. This involves individual learners but also groups and organisational knowledge management processes. It is therefore an application domain that generally covers technologies that support all forms of teaching and learning activities. The research in this field is very heterogeneous as proven by Kalz and Specht [51] in their study on 3476 research articles collected from the web of science between 2002–2011. TEL research is widespread from web-based information systems over mobile and wearable computing [120] to large scale physical simulators that are used in medicine, military or public transport education [22, 119].

Within this diverse research area, research on personalisation technologies is a strong topic with a large amount of national and international funded research grants. Personalisation of learning gets even more important with the increasing use of digital learning environments like learning object repositories, learning management systems, personal learning environments, and devices for mobile learning scenarios that take into account the learners' needs [8].

The uptake of personalised learning approaches and especially recommender systems nowadays is reasonable due to the high demand on interpreting data that is stored in educational institutions. In fact, we have never been so close to investigate the phenomena of learning as in the days of "big data". Almost all digital behavior of learners is stored and saved on servers of educational institutes. Not so long ago, collecting data was limited in terms of cost, time requirements, scope, and authenticity of the data, as this was typically done using single groups or classes for an experiment. The digital way of learning has made data collection an inherent process of delivering educational content to the students. That means that the analysis of learning behavior is no longer only related to representative pilot studies rather than to the usage of the entire student population. This trend has even become faster with the appearance of Massive Open Online Courses (MOOCs) [72] and the emerging of the Learning Analytics field [41]. MOOCs provide massive amounts of student data and therefore provide new opportunities for recommender systems to offer personalised learning support. Learning Analytics is currently the research field within TEL that focuses on understanding and supporting learners based on their data.

As a consequence, recommender systems have become extremely interesting for TEL research. These efforts resulted in a number of interesting observations as described in [67]: (1) There is a significant increase of recommender systems applied in TEL due to the digitalisation of learning and the growths of educational data; (2) The information retrieval goals that TEL recommenders try to achieve are sometimes different to the ones identified in other systems (e.g. product recommenders). For instance, many TEL RecSys try to suggest most suitable learning activities to learners by taking into account their knowledge level. This level is measured by prior- or self-assessment methods and taken into account to build personalised sequences through the learning content or activities; (3) There is a need to standardise the evaluation of TEL recommenders as the effects of the systems on the learners are in the focus of the research—rather than the most accurate algorithm; and (4) TEL RecSys research tries to evaluate its impact on educational stakeholders ultimately in user studies, rather than in data-driven studies. The evaluation criteria therefore go beyond traditional recommender system criteria such as precision, recall, or F1 measures and include specific learning related evaluation criteria such as effectiveness and efficiency of the learning process.

12.3 Classification Framework for TEL RecSys Review

Several classifications and categories have been used in the past to provide an overview of recommender systems. Hanani et al. [43] provide a general framework for information filtering systems, whereas Schafer et al. [94] and Wei et al. [118] clustered recommender systems in the e-commerce domain by distinguishing information used for recommendations, the types of recommendations, and various techniques. Burke [12] focused especially on the recommendation techniques and listed especially new approaches to the dominating content and collaborative filtering approaches at that time. Adomavicius and Tuzhilin [2] followed up on this technology study and reviewed various systems that they clustered into content-based, collaborative, and hybrid ones. They provided a detailed summary of the different technologies applied by the investigated recommender systems.

There are also publications that provide suitable criteria to categorise and order recommender systems (e.g. [42, 44, 75]). Manouselis and Costopoulou [62] combined all these evaluation criteria in a comprehensive classification framework with three main categories: (1) *Supported Tasks*, (2) *Approach*, and (3) *Operation*. The authors used this framework to analyse and classify 37 multi-criteria recommender systems. This framework was adjusted in 2012 to TEL by adding specific Supported Tasks like *Find peer learners* and *Predict learning performance* [67]. In this chapter, we have used the adjusted version for the following review of the 82 TEL RecSys. A detailed description of the framework and its categories is not available in the chapter due to page limitations. The interested reader can find a summary of the current version of the classification framework under the following URL: https://sites.google.com/site/recsystel/. The additional items (support tasks, methods) that have been added to the original version of the framework [67] have been emphasised in Fig. 12.2.

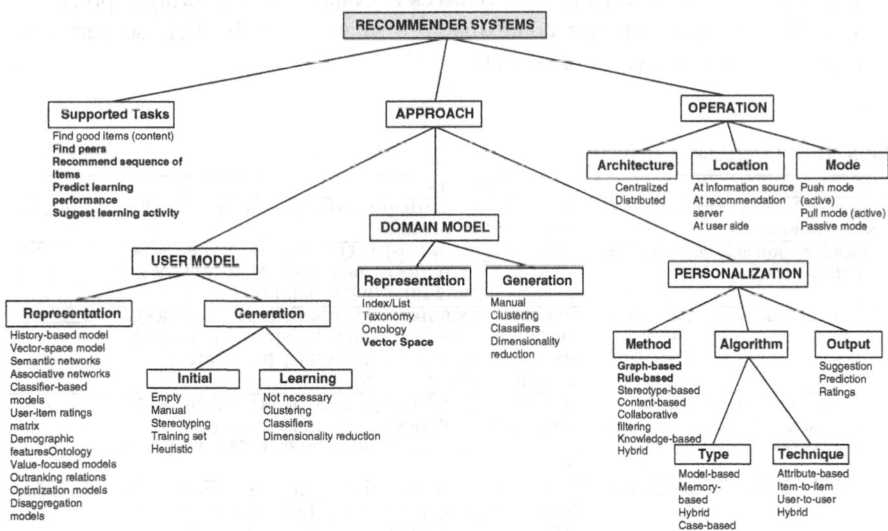

Fig. 12.2 Classification framework for TEL RecSys based on [67]

12.4 Survey Results

12.4.1 Method and Overview of TEL RecSys

The review of recommender systems presented in Table 12.1 compiles a total of 82 systems. These systems have been identified in previous compilations of educational recommender systems [66, 67, 69, 86, 87, 89, 91, 111], and have been extended with works shared in the Mendeley group and complemented with a keyword search in Google Scholar. This review covers 15 years of research on educational recommender systems from 2000 until 2014. The extensive compilation of TEL recommenders offers new insights and trends for the evolution of the research field.

Based on the current state-of-the-art review we have identified seven clusters that group TEL recommenders systems in terms of relevant contributions to the field. Within each cluster, papers are reported in chronological order aimed to represent the research evolution. The clusters identified are the following:

1. TEL RecSys following collaborative filtering approaches as in other domains
2. TEL RecSys that propose improvements to collaborative filtering approaches to take into account the particularities of the TEL domain
3. TEL RecSys that consider explicitly educational constraints as a source of information for the recommendation process
4. TEL RecSys that explore other alternatives to collaborative filtering approaches
5. TEL RecSys that consider contextual information within TEL scenarios to improve the recommendation process

Table 12.1 Overview clusters

	Clusters	
Cluster 1: Recommending resources for learning based on CF (7)	[RS1-2000], [RS3-2003], [RS5-2004], [RS7-2005], [RS8-2005], [RS9-2005], [RS10-2005]	
Cluster 2: Improving CF algorithms with TEL domain particularities (13)	[RS11-2006], [RS14-2008], [RS18-2009], [RS29-2010], [RS30-2010], [RS47-2011], [RS49-2012], [RS63-2013], [RS64-2013], [RS71-2014], [RS72-2014], [RS73-2014], [RS78-2007]	
Cluster 3: Educational contraints as source of information (16)	[RS6-2004], [RS19-2009], [RS31-2010], [RS32-2010], [RS33-2010], [RS50-2012], [RS51-2012], [RS52-2012], [RS53-2012], [RS54-2012], [RS55-2012], [RS56-2012], [RS57-2012], [RS58-2012], [RS74-2014], [RS75-2014]	
Cluster 4: Exploring non-CF techniques to find successful educational recommendations (14)	[RS2-2002], [RS15-2008], [RS20-2009], [RS21-2009], [RS22-2009], [RS34-2010], [RS35-2010], [RS36-2010], [RS59-2012], [RS60-2012], [RS65-2013], [RS66-2013], [RS76-2014], [RS77-2014]	
Cluster 5: Considering contextual information (13)	[RS16-2008], [RS23-2009], [RS37-2010], [RS38-2010], [RS39-2010], [RS40-2010], [RS41-2014], [RS42-2010], [RS43-2010], [RS79-2011], [RS80-2013], [RS81-2013], [RS82-2014]	
Cluster 6: Assessing the educational impact of recommendations (12)	[RS12-2007], [RS24-2009], [RS25-2009], [RS26-2009], [RS44-2010], [RS45-2010], [RS48-2011], [RS61-2012], [RS62-2012], [RS67-2013], [RS68-2013], [RS69-2013]	
Cluster 7: Recommending courses (7)	[RS4-2003], [RS13-2007], [RS17-2008], [RS27-2009], [RS28-2009], [RS46-2010], [RS70-2013]	

6. TEL RecSys that assess the educational impact of the recommendations delivered
7. TEL RecSys that focus on recommending courses (instead of resources within them)

The systems grouped into the mentioned clusters produce recommendations for learners that either contribute additional learning resources, guide their learning process or suggest courses to take. However, recommender systems can also support teachers to improve their courses or monitor their learning resources [9, 32, 37, 38, 59, 96].

Papers included in Table 12.1 have been given an ID in the form of RS+ID+YEAR [RSID-YEAR] to facilitate its follow-up in the remainder of the chapter, since many of the systems analysed have not been named by the authors with a specific acronym.

12.4.1.1 Cluster 1: Recommending Resources for Learning Based on Collaborative Filtering

This first cluster contains seven papers that report the application of collaborative filtering techniques as used in other domains, such as e-commerce, to produce recommendations in TEL scenarios. CoFind [RS1-2000] guides learners to relevant resources that have been previously found as valuable by other learners. The system uses collaborative filtering in combination with folksonomies data [28]. Altered Vista [RS3-2003] considers user evaluations of learning resources and propagates them to users with similar tastes in the form of word-of-mouth recommendations about the qualities of the resources [82]. RecoSearch [RS5-2004] proposes a collaborative filtering infrastructure for authoring, searching, recommending and presenting learning objects to learners [34]. RACOFI [RS7-2005] uses a collaborative filtering engine that works with ratings that users provide for learning resources complemented with an inference rule engine that mines association rules between learning resources [57]. In QSIA [RS8-2005] traditional collaborative filtering is extended with a control mechanism to mark users who should be considered for recommendations [81]. In CYCLADES [RS9-2005] users search, access and rate learning resources available in repositories found through the Open Archives Initiative [4]. The last paper included in this cluster [RS10-2005] proposes a hybrid recommendation service on research papers rated by learners consisting in a clustering module (using data clustering techniques to group learners with similar interests) and a collaborative filtering module (using classic collaborative filtering techniques to identify learners with similar interests in each cluster) [102]. This last work served to span the research to improve collaborative filtering approaches, as compiled in cluster 2.

12.4.1.2 Cluster 2: Improving Collaborative Filtering Algorithms with TEL Domain Particularities

This cluster compiles 13 papers. A considerable amount of researchers have focused on multi-attribute criteria of educational resources in order to cover the complexity of the learning (prior-knowledge, expertise, available study time, etc.) when using collaborative filtering techniques. For instance, in [RS11-2006] resources have been described using SCORM learning resource specification [106]. In [RS78-2007] multi-dimensional ratings provided by the users on learning resources have been considered [63]. [RS29-2010] investigated multi-criteria ratings with data from MERLOT learning object repository [99]. [RS47-2011] considered the relationship (advanced learner, beginner learner) as the third dimension over the typical user x item in collaborative filtering [114]. [RS63-2013] used the learner tree to take into account explicit multi-attribute of resources, time-variant multi-preference of learner and learners' rating matrix for implicit and explicit attribute based collaborative filtering [84]. In [RS71-2014] multi-dimensional ratings on learning objects are considered to correlate one user with another [103].

Other approaches to improve collaborative filtering algorithms have also been proposed. In particular, [RS14-2008] proposes a collaborative recommendation system with query extraction mechanisms [61]. [RS18-2009] stores the ratings made by similar students in the profile together with the learning goal at that time in order to take into account the learner's evolution in time [40]. [RS30-2010] extends a collaborative filtering mechanism with the learners competencies [15]. The RSF system [RS49-2012] presents a collaborative filtering algorithm combined with an embedded web crawler to update learning material [35]. The DELPHOS system [RS64-2013] includes a weighted hybrid recommender (collaborative, content and demographic) that uses different filtering criteria to encode the relative importance of each particular filter. The weights of the filters can be assigned by the user him/herself or automatically calculated by the system [124]. [RS72-2014] shows that a graph-based collaborative filtering algorithm can improve accuracy of generated recommendations even when the user actions data is sparse and provide a balanced distribution of users degree centrality [31]. In [RS73-2014] sentiment analysis techniques on user-generated comments of a repository of educational resources are used to obtain valuable qualitative information for adjusting the perceived rating of a given resource by a specific user [52].

12.4.1.3 Cluster 3: Educational Constraints as Source of Information for the Recommendation Process

The 16 papers in this cluster consider the educational knowledge as information source for the recommendation process in order to produce recommendations that better address the educational goals in TEL scenarios. They require an explicit description of this knowledge in terms of rules, ontologies, concept maps, semantic relations, etc. They can overcome the lack of large datasets needed by collaborative filtering approaches, but in turn may require maintenance efforts to keep the user and domain preferences updated, unless semantic techniques and related approaches are used.

In this line, [RS6-2004] recommends learning objects based on sequencing rules that help users to be guided through the concepts of an ontology of topics [98]. In [RS19-2009] educational standards such as PAPI and IEEE LOM were used within an ontology framework to manage learners properties based on learning styles and reputation metadata [53]. Ontology-based multi-actor learning flows and competence driven user models as described in [RS31-2010] can provide advice on tasks and resources [70]. Ontologies have also been used in [RS55-2012] to recommend resources that match the identified knowledge gaps form the learners [7] and to support creativity such as in [RS54-2012], where a recommender system suggests creativity techniques to the users [100]. Networks of ontologies such as [RS53-2012] that conceptualise different domains and their characteristics to provide semantic recommendations have also been proposed [20].

Another approach to recommend learning resources based on knowledge gaps is CLICK [RS56-2012] that suggests resources to learners by comparing automatically generated domain and learner models from distributed learning repositories [79]. Conceptual relationships have been used in [RS33-2010] to semantically rank lecture slides and the search needs for the users [115]. Conceptual maps have also been built in the METIS system [RS51-2012] to recommend learning activities in the maths domain based on prior knowledge, skills, and abilities of the learners [107]. MetaMender [RS52-2012] supports the description of meta-rules written by domain experts to personalise the information to the learner [123]. In this sense, [RS50-2012] takes the needs and preferences of learners into account to suggest suitable learning resources from distributed learning repositories based on a rule approach [14].

Some issues that deal with the learner situation have also been addressed by several papers. [RS32-2010] considers the limited time available for learning when proposing a utility-based recommender based on concept knowledge modelling [73]. As discussed in [RS57-2012] TEL RecSys can also be used to enhance meta-cognition and make learners aware of the processes of their learning [125]. In this sense, [RS58-2012] recommends widgets for learning activities in the context of personal learning environments for self-regulated learning [78]. In ALEF [RS75-2014] information stored and maintained in the corresponding user and domain models can provide learners recommendations on how to achieve more successful collaboration [6]. Finally, Semantic Affective Educational Recommender Systems (SAERS) [RS74-2014] can provide appropriate emotional support with affective educational-oriented recommendations elicited with TORMES (i.e., Tutor-Oriented Recommendations Modelling for Educational Systems) user centered design methodology in order to recommend the learning activity to carry out [93].

12.4.1.4 Cluster 4: Exploring Non Collaborative Filtering Techniques to Find Successful Educational Recommendations

Specific solutions to produce recommendations for the TEL context have also been explored in the following 14 papers. An initial idea, suggested in [RS2-2002], was to consider data mining techniques (such as association rules mining) in order to build a model that represents learner behaviours, and use this model to suggest activities or shortcuts that can help learners better navigate the digital materials [122]. In this line, in RPL [RS21-2009] web mining techniques were considered together with a scalable search engine to compute recommendations against a repository of educational resources [54]. AHA! adaptive educational system was also extended with recommendations in [RS22-2009] using web usage mining together with hyperlink adaptation to learn learners browsing pathways for personalised link recommendation [83]. Additionally, in [RS66-2013] data mining techniques complemented with user centered design methods were used to identify recommendation opportunities in educational scenarios that promote active participation of learners and strengthen the sharing of learning experiences [88].

Other approaches such as [RS15-2008] have applied fuzzy logic and item response theory to recommending courseware with suitable difficulty levels for learners according to learners' uncertain/fuzzy feedback responses [17]. In [RS60-2012] fuzzy knowledge extraction model is used to extract personalised recommendation knowledge by discovering effective learning paths from past learning experiences through an ant colony optimization model [116]. In [RS65-2013] MPRLS also uses fuzzy logic theory to construct an appropriate learning path based on the learners misconceptions to recommend most suitable materials [46]. Meta-rules derived from a Markov chain model have also been used in [RS20-2009] to calculate transition probabilities of possible learning resources in a sequenced course of study for discovering one or more recommended learning paths [48]. In [RS34-2010] social navigation techniques built upon traces of past user behavior and using the assembled collective wisdom have been used to guide users to the most useful information [11]. Peer-to-peer networks have also been used in [RS36-2010] for searching personalised and useful learning paths suggested by reliable (trusted) peers [13]. Semantic relatedness of open education resources metadata have been considered in [RS35-2010] [97]. [RS59-2012] apply factorisation techniques to generate accurate ratings and perform predictions to recommend most suitable items, as they take temporal effects into account and therefore accurately model and adjust to the increasing knowledge of learners [105]. A graph-based algorithm as defined in [RS76-2014] can be used to create recommendations from cross-platforms in order to make learners aware of relevant activities, resources and peers in self-directed learning scenarios [33]. Finally, geometrical description of the recommender space as in [RS77-2014] can lead to better recommendation and dynamics understanding [77].

12.4.1.5 Cluster 5: Consider Contextual Information in the Recommendation Process

As reported in a recent state-of-the-art review [111] contextual information can be of value to enrich the TEL recommendations process and there are many research opportunities in this direction, as the 13 papers clustered here show.

Some relevant approaches identified in the literature are the following. A2M [RS16-2008] proposed a hybrid approach to select the appropriate recommendation technique depending on the input received from the learning environment and filters the output by the course context and the user features to produce an ordered list of recommendations to be presented to the learner [85]. CoMoLe [RS23-2009] recommends activities (multimedia contents as well as collaborative tools) to learners depending on different criteria (user features, context, etc.), and workspaces through a context-based adaptive mobile educational environment [71]. [RS42-2010] recommends documents to students according to their current activity that is tracked in terms of semantic annotations (with Contextualized Attention Metadata) associated to the accessed resources [10]. [RS38-2010] recommends resources at the workplace using a context driven recommender system to effectively support knowledge workers to meet their individual information needs [95]. In a similar scenario, [RS39-2010] produces contextual recommendations in a knowledge-sharing environment to the employees of large organisations [5]. [RS37-2010] adapts a version of Googles PageRank algorithm to context-aware recommendation in personal learning environments which incorporates different types of relations, including social relations and relations between resources, to standard collaborative filtering techniques [30]. [RS41-2014] considers quality information about learning resources [16].

In some other works, physical sensors are used to collect information from the environment with educational purposes [91]. For instance, [RS43-2010] uses semantic web to adaptively recommend learning content according to various types of context obtained from physical sensors [121]. In the same sense, [RS40-2010] uses a sensor module to collect data from learners and recommends educational resources according to predefined context structure [60]. RFID is used in [RS79-2011] to sense de location of learning resources in the actual environment [117]. SCROLL [RS80-2013] collects context information with the sensors available in smartphones, as well as from the device features and actions done on it [58]. In the BISPA system [RS81-2013], physiological measures aimed to detect learners' affective state are gathered [50]. Finally, AICARP [RS82-2014] proposes an interactive recommendation that is delivered through two complementary sensorial actuators taking as input physiological and environmental information [92].

12.4.1.6 Cluster 6: Assessing the Educational Impact of Recommendations in Educational Scenarios

Throughout more recent development cycles, it has been demanded that TEL recommender systems should be evaluated not only according to technical criteria, but rather by a combination of technical and educational criteria (see a review of 59 papers in [89]). Here, 12 papers compile works in this direction. [RS12-2007] analysed implicit feedback for navigational support in lifelong learning based on self-organisation principles to see the effect on effectiveness (completion rates and amount of progress) and efficiency (time taken to complete) in lifelong learning [49]. [RS68-2013] showed that recommendations can support learners to enhance their effort towards an ascending learning curve and better grades [112]. Additionally, in [RS69-2013] learning effectiveness, learning efficiency, course engagement and knowledge acquisition were measured to evaluate recommendations impact in a MOOC [89]. The study on learners perception as reported in [RS61-2012] suggests that recommenders can significantly enhance virtual learning communities and put the power of determining what constitutes a quality contribution in the hands of the community members [56].

[RS26-2009] evaluated the applicability of recommendations in mash-up environments that combine sources of users from different Web2.0 services [23]. In that context, [RS44-2010] discuss the applicability of recommendations for empowering learners to set up their personal learning environments so that they can connect to networks of learners and collaborate on shared artifacts by using the tools available [74]. Related to this, [RS45-2010] identified the advantages of using a discussion forum within an e-learning system to foster communication between learners [1] and MASSAYO [RS62-2012] suggested that recommendations on blogs contents can support dynamic interactions in the learning environment by improving the discussion as they provide contributions from students with different points of view [45]. In [RS67-2013] students who learned with articles recommended by a mobile learning system based on their preferences and reading proficiency levels achieved significantly better reading comprehension in comparison with the students who read non-adaptive reading materials [47].

Evaluations with users are also useful to compare the best approaches for the recommendations process. [RS24-2009] compared various cost intensive ontology based recommendation strategies with light-weight collaborative filtering strategies regarding their impact on the learning outcomes of the learners in informal learning networks [76]. [RS25-2009] report an experiment with real learners using an hybrid approach for recommending learning resources that combines social-based (using data from other learners) with information-based (using metadata from learner profiles and learning activities) that shows a positive significant effect on efficiency (time taken to complete the learning objects) of the learners after a runtime of 4 months [24]. In LMRF [RS48-2011] learner performance increased when the students use a recommender system based on content-based filtering and good learners ratings, compared to both collaborative and content-based filtering techniques [39].

12.4.1.7 Cluster 7: Recommending Courses

The previous clusters have focused on recommendations that can be provided within a course. However, some research works on TEL recommenders have addressed the problem of recommending appropriate courses to students by taking into account curricula information. The amount of papers that focus on course recommendations is less compared to papers that focus on recommendation tasks within a course or an online environment. Thus, course recommender systems are rather specific and mainly driven by universities that want to support the starting students. Nevertheless, the research on this area has progressed over the years. [RS4-2003] proposed course suggestions for students when they have trouble in choosing courses [18]. A few years later, a course recommender [RS13-2007] was developed for University College Dublin students for their online enrollment application [80]. This was followed up by the famous CourseRank system [RS27-2009] for Stanford University students with more than 70 % of students using the system [55] and another one [RS46-2010] at the University of Pittsburgh, which was evaluated based on a long-term evaluation experiment with students [36]. [RS17-2008] takes into account behavioral patterns to recommends potential courses for learners [101] and [RS28-2009] computes success probabilities of the student if enrolled in a certain course [108]. [RS70-2013] shows the integration of a course recommender in a Moodle instance [3].

12.4.2 Analysis According to the Framework

In the following section we cluster the 82 reviewed TEL RecSys according to the classification framework depicted in Fig. 12.2. We therefore start with the analysis of the *Supported Tasks* illustrated in Table 12.2, afterwards clustered all systems according to their *Approach*, in particular, the *User Model* (Table 12.3), *Domain Model* (Table 12.4), and *Personalisation* characteristics (Table 12.5), and finally *Operation* (Table 12.6). It needs to be mentioned that we could not cluster all systems into all categories exclusively and always end up with a total sum of 82 systems. This has mainly to do with the information that is provided in the papers and is sometimes incomplete. In other cases, the systems fit into several categories (e.g., provide a couple of supported tasks).

From Table 12.2, the following issues can be identified regarding the *Supported Tasks* that TEL RecSys deal with:

- There is a vast majority of TEL RecSys that aim to support the task of *Finding good Items (content)* to support learning activities. In total 61 systems (n=61) aim to support learners by providing new learning content to their current learning process.
- The second most used recommendation tasks is *recommend a sequence of items* to learners (n=13). *Recommend a sequence of items* is a very important task

Table 12.2 Classification of TEL recommenders, according to the Supported Tasks

Supported tasks		
Find good items (61)	[RS1-2000], [RS3-2003], [RS5-2004], [RS7-2005], [RS8-2005], [RS9-2005], [RS11-2006], [RS13-2007], [RS14-2008], [RS17-2008], [RS19-2009], [RS21-2009], [RS22-2009], [RS23-2009], [RS25-2009], [RS26-2009], [RS27-2009], [RS28-2009], [RS29-2010], [RS30-2010], [RS31-2010], [RS32-2010], [RS33-2010], [RS34-2010], [RS35-2010], [RS37-2010], [RS38-2010], [RS39-2010], [RS40-2010], [RS41-2014], [RS42-2010], [RS43-2010], [RS44-2010], [RS45-2010], [RS46-2010], [RS47-2011], [RS48-2011], [RS49-2012], [RS50-2012], [RS52-2012], [RS53-2012], [RS54-2012], [RS55-2012], [RS56-2012], [RS57-2012], [RS58-2012], [RS62-2012], [RS63-2013], [RS64-2013], [RS67-2013], [RS68-2013], [RS70-2013], [RS71-2014], [RS72-2014], [RS73-2014], [RS75-2014], [RS77-2014], [RS78-2010], [RS79-2011], [RS80-2013], [RS81-2013]	
Find peers (9)	[RS3-2003], [RS9-2005], [RS37-2010], [RS38-2010], [RS39-2010], [RS47-2011], [RS54-2012], [RS72-2014], [RS77-2014]	
Recommend sequence of items (13)	[RS6-2004], [RS12-2007], [RS15-2008], [RS20-2009], [RS34-2010], [RS36-2010], [RS51-2012], [RS57-2012], [RS60-2012], [RS65-2013], [RS71-2014], [RS75-2014], [RS77-2014]	
Predict learning performance (1)	[RS59-2012]	
Recommend learning activity (4)	[RS66-2013], [RS69-2013], [RS74-2014], [RS82-2014]	

within TEL RecSys because it is similar to instructional design methods. The aim of an instructional design is to guide a learner through a series of learning activities to achieve a certain competence. This didactical objective can be supported in recommender systems by suggesting the most efficient or effective paths through a plethora of learning resources to achieve a certain competence. Recommender systems with this task often considering the prior knowledge of a learner for their recommendations.

- The *Recommendation of peer learners* is also a very central recommendation task for distance education settings and relatively often applied in TEL RecSys research (n=9). Online learners often feel isolated after a period of time without any physical meeting. Thus, courses with pure online presence tend to have higher dropout rates compared to normal courses or blended learning scenarios. To overcome this situation, recommender systems can be supportive by recommending peer-learners that the target learner can team up within an online course.
- Interesting is that the above mentioned recommendation tasks are applied over all years in research. So there is not one specific recommendations tasks researchers have been focus on in a specific timeframe. In the more recent years some new recommendation tasks have appeared, such as *Predict learning performance* (n=1) and *Suggest a learning activity* (n=4) in contrast to just learning content. These developments show that recommender systems are increasingly applied to filter and personalise information in digital learning environments and are also applied for new educational goals.

Table 12.3 Classification according to the User Model of the Approach category

Approach: User Model		
Representation method	*Vector-space models (29)*	[RS8-2005], [RS9-2005], [RS1-2000], [RS6-2004], [RS11-2006], [RS5-2004], [RS27-2009], [RS56-2012], [RS33-2010], [RS35-2010], [RS59-2012], [RS21-2009], [RS55-2012], [RS46-2010], [RS72-2014], [RS76-2014], [RS73-2014], [RS77-2014], [RS71-2014], [RS67-2013], [RS40-2010], [RS14-2008], [RS23-2009], [RS66-2013], [RS69-2013], [RS60-2012], [RS47-2011], [RS22-2009], [RS74-2014]
	User-item ratings models (13)	[RS3-2003], [RS7-2005], [RS25-2009], [RS78–2010], [RS26-2009], [RS34-2010], [RS46-2010], [RS72-2014], [RS76-2014], [RS13-2007], [RS28-2009], [RS49-2012], [RS63-2013]
	Associative networks (3)	[RS39-2010], [RS40-2010], [RS64-2013]
	History-based (5)	[RS25-2009], [RS20-2009], [RS37-2010], [RS15-2008], [RS65-2013]
	Ontology (18)	[RS25-2009], [RS53-2012], [RS50-2012], [RS52-2012], [RS57-2012], [RS33-2010], [RS32-2010], [RS42-2010], [RS31-2010], [RS54-2012], [RS51-2012], [RS75-2014], [RS58-2012], [RS36-2010], [RS68-2013], [RS62-2012], [RS45-2010], [RS43-2010]
	Demographic features (2)	[RS17-2008], [RS19-2009]
Representation type	*Measurable (17)*	[RS3-2003], [RS8-2005], [RS9-2005], [RS1-2000], [RS6-2004], [RS78–2010], [RS11-2006], [RS5-2004], [RS27-2009], [RS39-2010], [RS21-2009], [RS76-2014], [RS73-2014], [RS71-2014], [RS40-2010], [RS13-2007], [RS63-2013]
	Ordinal / Features (4)	[RS1-2000], [RS77-2014], [RS64-2013], [RS43-2010]
	Probabilistic (3)	[RS9-2005], [RS77-2014], [RS70-2013]
Initial	*Empty (14)*	[RS3-2003], [RS7-2005], [RS9-2005], [RS1-2000], [RS27-2009], [RS16-2008], [RS76-2014], [RS73-2014], [RS71-2014], [RS13-2007], [RS64-2013], [RS49-2012], [RS47-2011], [RS79-2011]
	Manual (24)	[RS78-2010], [RS29-2010], [RS34-2010], [RS46-2010], [RS37-2010], [RS58-2012], [RS67-2013], [RS36-2010], [RS40-2010], [RS70-2013], [RS68-2013], [RS28-2009], [RS62-2012], [RS66-2013], [RS69-2013], [RS15-2008], [RS43-2010], [RS60-2012], [RS65-2013], [RS22-2009], [RS74-2014], [RS17-2008], [RS19-2009], [RS80-2013]
	Stereotype (3)	[RS14-2008], [RS23-2009], [RS45-2010]
Learning	*Clustering (10)*	[RS21-2009], [RS75-2014], [RS40-2010], [RS70-2013], [RS49-2012], [RS66-2013], [RS69-2013], [RS22-2009], [RS74-2014], [RS79-2011]
	Classifiers (15)	[RS9-2005], [RS39-2010], [RS44-2010], [RS38-2010], [RS41–2014], [RS73-2014], [RS77-2014], [RS71-2014], [RS64-2013], [RS49-2012], [RS66-2013], [RS69-2013], [RS15-2008], [RS47-2011], [RS74-2014]

From the analysis of the *User Models* that are illustrated in Table 12.3, the following aspects can be identified:

- Regarding the *Representation method*, most TEL RecSys identified use classic *Vector-space models* with multiple attributes (n=29) to represent the desired features or the user preferences. In addition, many systems rely on *Ontologies* (n=18) that capture various attributes of users and relationships between those attributes. The ontology-based systems are closely followed by *User-item ratings*

Table 12.4 Classification of TEL recommenders, according to the Domain Model

	Approach: Domain Model	
Representation	*Index/List (16)*	[RS3-2003], [RS8-2005], [RS9-2005], [RS5-2004], [RS78–2010], [RS27-2009], [RS20-2009], [RS35-2010], [RS21-2009], [RS46-2010], [RS72-2014], [RS76-2014], [RS13-2007], [RS28-2009], [RS49-2012], [RS65-2013]
	Taxonomy (3)	[RS1-2000], [RS37-2010], [RS70-2013]
	Vector-space model (18)	[RS33-2010], [RS59-2012], [RS72-2014], [RS76-2014], [RS73-2014], [RS77-2014], [RS71-2014], [RS67-2013], [RS48-2011], [RS40-2010], [RS14-2008], [RS23-2009], [RS66-2013], [RS69-2013], [RS15-2008], [RS47-2011], [RS74-2014], [RS17-2008]
	Ontology (23)	[RS6-2004], [RS25-2009], [RS53-2012], [RS50-2012], [RS52-2012], [RS57-2012], [RS33-2010], [RS32-2010], [RS42-2010], [RS31-2010], [RS54-2012], [RS51-2012], [RS55-2012], [RS75-2014], [RS77-2014], [RS36-2010], [RS64-2013], [RS68-2013], [RS62-2012], [RS45-2010], [RS63-2013], [RS43-2010], [RS19-2009]
	Graph (1)	[RS60-2012]
	Rules (1)	[RS22-2009]
Generation	*Manual(26)*	[RS8-2005], [RS9-2005], [RS1-2000], [RS6-2004], [RS78–2010], [RS5-2004], [RS26-2009], [RS27-2009], [RS29-2010], [RS34-2010], [RS67-2013], [RS36-2010], [RS48-2011], [RS13-2007], [RS64-2013], [RS68-2013], [RS23-2009], [RS49-2012], [RS62-2012], [RS45-2010], [RS63-2013], [RS43-2010], [RS47-2011], [RS19-2009], [RS79-2011], [RS81-2013]
	Classifiers (17)	[RS39-2010], [RS56-2012], [RS44-2010], [RS21-2009], [RS75-2014], [RS41–2014], [RS73-2014], [RS71-2014], [RS14-2008], [RS28-2009], [RS66-2013], [RS69-2013], [RS15-2008], [RS60-2012], [RS65-2013], [RS74-2014], [RS19-2009]
	Clustering (8)	[RS39-2010], [RS38-2010], [RS70-2013], [RS66-2013], [RS69-2013], [RS74-2014], [RS17-2008], [RS19-2009]
	Sequential analysis (1)	[RS22-2009]

models (n=13) that capture explicit ratings of users on items. *History-based* and *Demographic features* approaches have been applied less often (n=5 and n=2, respectively). Although there are few *Associative networks* approaches listed in the review (n=3), we believe this approach will become more prominent through the increasing research on the Educational Data Mining field.

- Regarding the *Representation type*, most are based on clear *Measurable* items (n=17). A distinction needs to be made in this category between *implicit* and *explicit* ratings. Some systems apply explicit ratings like star ratings and tags given by the users to the content whereas other systems use implicit ratings extracted from the behaviour of the users such as *user accessed a file, time spend on a resource*, etc. Both types of ratings are together the most common types in TEL RecSys. *Ordinal/Feature* and *Probabilistic* approaches are not applied that often (n=4 and n=3, respectively).
- With regards to the *Generation*, the initial user preferences engaged by the examined systems are usually acquired in a *Manual* way from the users (n=24). In many cases, the user model is initially *Empty* (n=14), and then slowly created throughout the users interactions with the system. *Stereotyping* was also used in some cases (n=3). For learning, there is a trend in the recent years to apply more and more *Clustering* (n=10) or *Classification* (n=15) approaches for learning the initial user model from existing data.

Table 12.5 Classification according to Personalisation characteristics

		Approach: Personalisation
Method	*Collaborative filtering (21)*	[RS3-2003], [RS8-2005], [RS9-2005], [RS1-2000], [RS78–2010], [RS11-2006], [RS5-2004], [RS26-2009], [RS12-2007], [RS44-2010], [RS29-2010], [RS21-2009], [RS37-2010], [RS72-2014], [RS76-2014], [RS73-2014], [RS13-2007], [RS49-2012], [RS63-2013], [RS47-2011], [RS79-2011]
	Content-based (10)	[RS39-2010], [RS38-2010], [RS42-2010], [RS35-2010], [RS21-2009], [RS75-2014], [RS41–2014], [RS70-2013], [RS68-2013], [RS43-2010]
	Hybrid (13)	[RS25-2009], [RS27-2009], [RS56-2012], [RS34-2010], [RS21-2009], [RS46-2010], [RS77-2014], [RS71-2014], [RS48-2011], [RS40-2010], [RS64-2013], [RS14-2008], [RS19-2009]
	Rule-based (22)	[RS6-2004], [RS53-2012], [RS50-2012], [RS52-2012], [RS57-2012], [RS32-2010], [RS31-2010], [RS54-2012], [RS51-2012], [RS55-2012], [RS75-2014], [RS67-2013], [RS70-2013], [RS68-2013], [RS23-2009], [RS28-2009], [RS45-2010], [RS65-2013], [RS22-2009], [RS80-2013], [RS81-2013], [RS82-2014]
	Graph-based (4)	[RS72-2014], [RS76-2014], [RS36-2010], [RS60-2012]
	Knowledge-based (3)	[RS66-2013], [RS69-2013], [RS74-2014]
	Association mining (1)	[RS17-2008]
	Raw retrieval (1)	[RS62-2012]
	Manually selected (1)	[RS52-2012]
Algorithm type	*Model-based (24)*	[RS56-2012], [RS53-2012], [RS50-2012], [RS52-2012], [RS32-2010], [RS38-2010], [RS42-2010], [RS35-2010], [RS59-2012], [RS54-2012], [RS51-2012], [RS55-2012], [RS75-2014], [RS41–2014], [RS67-2013], [RS36-2010], [RS48-2011], [RS70-2013], [RS68-2013], [RS28-2009], [RS15-2008], [RS43-2010], [RS65-2013], [RS22-2009]
	Memory-based (16)	[RS3-2003], [RS8-2005], [RS9-2005], [RS1-2000], [RS78-2010], [RS5-2004], [RS27-2009], [RS12-2007], [RS44-2010], [RS37-2010], [RS13-2007], [RS14-2008], [RS49-2012], [RS47-2011], [RS17-2008], [RS19-2009]
	Hybrid (13)	[RS11-2006], [RS57-2012], [RS34-2010], [RS21-2009], [RS46-2010], [RS76-2014], [RS73-2014], [RS77-2014], [RS71-2014], [RS40-2010], [RS64-2013], [RS23-2009], [RS63-2013],
Algorithm technique	*Attribute-based (17)*	[RS11-2006], [RS39-2010], [RS38-2010], [RS75-2014], [RS41–2014], [RS71-2014], [RS67-2013], [RS36-2010], [RS70-2013], [RS64-2013], [RS68-2013], [RS23-2009], [RS28-2009], [RS43-2010], [RS65-2013], [RS22-2009], [RS17-2008]
	Item-to-item (4)	[RS44-2010], [RS37-2010], [RS48-2011], [RS15-2008]
	User-to-user (10)	[RS3-2003],[RS8-2005], [RS9-2005], [RS78-2010], [RS5-2004], [RS29-2010], [RS36-2010], [RS13-2007], [RS14-2008], [RS49-2012]
	Hybrid (13)	[RS26-2009], [RS27-2009], [RS56-2012], [RS34-2010], [RS51-2012], [RS21-2009], [RS76-2014], [RS73-2014], [RS77-2014], [RS40-2010], [RS63-2013], [RS47-2011], [RS19-2009]
	Vector-space model (2)	[RS42-2010], [RS35-2010]
Output	*Suggestion (54)*	[RS3-2003], [RS9-2005], [RS1-2000], [RS6-2004], [RS25-2009], [RS26-2009], [RS27-2009], [RS39-2010], [RS12-2007], [RS53-2012], [RS50-2012], [RS52-2012], [RS57-2012], [RS44-2010], [RS32-2010], [RS38-2010], [RS42-2010], [RS35-2010], [RS31-2010], [RS34-2010], [RS54-2012], [RS51-2012], [RS21-2009], [RS55-2012], [RS46-2010], [RS75-2014], [RS76-2014], [RS73-2014], [RS77-2014], [RS71-2014], [RS58-2012], [RS67-2013], [RS36-2010], [RS48-2011], [RS40-2010], [RS13-2007], [RS64-2013], [RS68-2013], [RS14-2008], [RS49-2012], [RS45-2010], [RS66-2013], [RS69-2013], [RS15-2008], [RS43-2010], [RS60-2012], [RS65-2013], [RS47-2011], [RS22-2009], [RS17-2008], [RS19-2009], [RS79-2011], [RS80-2012], [RS81-2013]
	Prediction (12)	[RS7-2005], [RS78–2010], [RS29-2010], [RS59-2012], [RS37-2010], [RS41–2014], [RS77-2014], [RS48-2011], [RS70-2013], [RS23-2009], [RS28-2009], [RS63-2013]

Table 12.6 Classification of TEL recommenders, according to the Domain Model of the Approach category

		Operation
Architecture	*Centralised (60)*	[RS3-2003], [RS7-2005], [RS8-2005], [RS1-2000], [RS6-2004], [RS25-2009], [RS78–2010], [RS5-2004], [RS26-2009], [RS27-2009], [RS39-2010], [RS12-2007], [RS20-2009], [RS52-2012], [RS57-2012], [RS44-2010], [RS32-2010], [RS38-2010], [RS29-2010], [RS31-2010], [RS59-2012], [RS54-2012], [RS51-2012], [RS21-2009], [RS55-2012], [RS46-2010], [RS37-2010], [RS72-2014], [RS75-2014], [RS41–2014], [RS76-2014], [RS73-2014], [RS77-2014], [RS71-2014], [RS58-2012], [RS67-2013], [RS36-2010], [RS48-2011], [RS40-2010], [RS13-2007], [RS70-2013],[RS14-2008], [RS23-2009], [RS28-2009], [RS49-2012], [RS62-2012], [RS45-2010], [RS66-2013], [RS69-2013], [RS15-2008], [RS65-2013], [RS47-2011], [RS22-2009], [RS74-2014], [RS17-2008], [RS19-2009], [RS79-2011], [RS80-2013], [RS81-2013], [RS82-2014]
	Distributed (11)	[RS9-2005], [RS56-2012], [RS53-2012], [RS50-2012], [RS42-2010], [RS35-2010], [RS34-2010], [RS64-2013], [RS68-2013], [RS63-2013], [RS43-2010]
Location	*At information source (5)*	[RS7-2005], [RS78–2010], [RS29-2010], [RS59-2012], [RS17-2008]
	At recommendation server (65)	[RS8-2005], [RS9-2005], [RS1-2000], [RS6-2004], [RS25-2009], [RS26-2009], [RS27-2009], [RS39-2010], [RS12-2007], [RS20-2009], [RS56-2012], [RS53-2012], [RS50-2012], [RS52-2012], [RS44-2010], [RS32-2010], [RS38-2010], [RS42-2010], [RS29-2010], [RS35-2010], [RS31-2010], [RS34-2010], [RS59-2012], [RS54-2012], [RS51-2012], [RS21-2009], [RS55-2012], [RS46-2010], [RS37-2010], [RS72-2014], [RS75-2014], [RS41-2014], [RS76-2014], [RS73-2014], [RS77-2014], [RS71-2014], [RS58-2012], [RS67-2013], [RS36-2010], [RS48-2011], [RS40-2010], [RS13-2007], [RS70-2013], [RS64-2013], [RS68-2013], [RS14-2008], [RS23-2009], [RS28-2009], [RS49-2012], [RS62-2012], [RS45-2010], [RS66-2013], [RS69-2013], [RS15-2008], [RS63-2013], [RS43-2010], [RS65-2013], [RS47-2011], [RS22-2009], [RS74-2014], [RS19-2009], [RS79-2011], [RS80-2013], [RS81-2013], [RS82-2014]
Mode	*Pull (active) (20)*	[RS3-2003], [RS8-2005], [RS9-2005], [RS1-2000], [RS78–2010], [RS27-2009], [RS33-2010], [RS38-2010], [RS35-2010], [RS59-2012], [RS46-2010], [RS37-2010], [RS76-2014], [RS71-2014], [RS58-2012], [RS36-2010], [RS64-2013], [RS28-2009], [RS49-2012], [RS45-2010]
	Passive (46)	[RS9-2005], [RS25-2009], [RS26-2009], [RS39-2010], [RS56-2012], [RS50-2012], [RS52-2012], [RS44-2010], [RS32-2010], [RS31-2010], [RS34-2010], [RS54-2012], [RS51-2012], [RS55-2012], [RS72-2014], [RS75-2014], [RS41–2014], [RS76-2014], [RS73-2014], [RS77-2014], [RS71-2014], [RS67-2013], [RS48-2011], [RS57-2012], [RS13-2007], [RS70-2013], [RS68-2013], [RS14-2008], [RS23-2009], [RS49-2012], [RS62-2012], [RS66-2013], [RS69-2013], [RS15-2008], [RS63-2013], [RS43-2010], [RS65-2013], [RS47-2011], [RS22-2009], [RS74-2014], [RS17-2008], [RS19-2009], [RS79-2011], [RS80-2013], [RS81-2013], [RS82-2014]

Analysing the collected systems with respect to the *Domain Model* characteristics (Table 12.4), the following aspects can be identified:

- Regarding *Representation*, there is not one major approach for the domain model for TEL RecSys to recommend items, but three almost equally applied approaches. The most often used approach is: *Ontology* (n=23) followed by *Vector-space* (n=18) approaches and finally *Index/List* (n=16). Only a few systems engage a *Taxonomy* (n=3), *Graph* (n=1) or a *Rule-based* (n=1) approaches. Interestingly, many of the first recommender systems for learning rely on *Index/List* or *Ontologies* representations of domain models and this

approach seem to be kind of stable over all development cycles until today. The *Vector-space* approach is a more recent development starting in 2008.
- Regarding *Generation*, most of the domain models are created in a *manual* way (n=26). However, an increasing amount of systems in the recent years use automated metadata generation with classification (n=17), clustering (n=8) and sequential analysis (n=1) methods.

Table 12.5 presents the analysis of the TEL RecSys based on the *Personalisation* aspect. As the extended review shows a broad variety of Personalisation approaches and different kinds of algorithms have been explored in the 15 years of research in the field.

- In terms of *Methods* used for the personalisation of recommendations, *Rule-based* (n=22) and *Collaborative filtering* (n=21) are the most applied techniques in the TEL field. It is followed by *Hybrid* (n=13), *Content-based techniques* (n=10), *Graph-based* (n=4) and *Knowledge-based* (n=3). Other approaches explored (with n=1) are *Association mining*, *Raw retrieval* and *Manually selected*. Interestingly, some techniques are time independent and are applied over all development cycles in TEL field. Examples for this are Collaborative Filtering (2000–2014), rule-based (2004–2014), whereas other methods are belonging to more recent development cycles such as Hybrid (2009–2014) and Content-based (2008–2014) techniques. There is an increasing interest in Graph-based (2010–2014) and Knowledge-based approaches (2013–2014).
- The *Algorithm type* used in TEL recommenders are as diverse as the personalisation techniques. Although, *Model-based* are dominating (n=24), there have been plenty of research on *Memory-based* systems (n=16), and *Hybrid* (n=13).
- As far as the engaged Algorithm techniques, *Attribute-based* is the most common (n=17), followed by *Hybrid* (n=13), and *User-to-user* (n=10). Few *item-to-item* correlation approaches have been proposed in TEL RecSys (n=4) as well as *Vector space model* (n=2). User-to-user filtering seems the most often techniques over the whole period (2003–2014). Hybrid techniques started to become more relevant from 2009 until theses days, and Attribute-based systems significantly increased in the years 2013 and 2014.
- Regarding the *Output*, a very clear picture is obtained. The produced output is most of the times a *Suggestion* (n=54). However, there are also quite a few systems that predict the evaluation that a user would give to the suggested items in the form of *Prediction* (n=12).

Concerning the *Operation* category of the dimensions, Table 12.6 indicates the following:

- The *Architecture* of the majority of TEL RecSys is *Centralised* (n=60), providing access to a single recommendation repository. Nevertheless, there are a few systems that rely on *distributed architectures* that provide access to a wide range of repositories (n=11).
- Regarding the *Location*, recommendations are usually produced at the recommendation server (n=65). Only a few systems produce them at the information

source (n=5). Recent research on recommender systems is increasingly oriented to produce recommendations on the user side—i.e. for use on mobile devices in situated learning activities. Ongoing work in this area has been described in [111].

- Until now, TEL RecSys *Mode* either provide their recommendations at an active *Pull mode* (n=20) where users request relevant recommendations or in the more often used *Passive mode* where users receive recommendations as part of their natural interaction with the system (n=46).

12.5 Conclusions

This chapter has extended the state-of-the-art reviews of TEL recommenders 2012 by doubling the amount of systems considered. In particular, the current chapter has reviewed 82 TEL RecSys along the 15 years of this specific research field (2000–2014). Research works have come from 35 different countries. The systems compiled and analysed have been classified into 7 exclusive clusters, namely (1) TEL RecSys following collaborative filtering approaches as in other domains; (2) TEL RecSys that propose improvements to collaborative filtering approaches to take into account the particularities of the TEL domain; (3) TEL RecSys that consider explicitly educational constraints as a source of information for the recommendation process; (4) TEL RecSys that explore other alternatives to collaborative filtering approaches; (5) TEL RecSys that consider contextual information within TEL scenarios to improve the recommendation process; (6) TEL RecSys that assess the educational impact of the recommendations delivered; and (7) TEL RecSys that focus on recommending courses (instead of resources within them). The framework proposed in [67] for the analysis of recommender systems has been applied with some extensions. The applied framework has been very valuable to analyse available TEL RecSys from a holistic perspective. However, in some cases it was not easy to extract relevant information from the content reported in the papers and to map those back to the framework categories.

After the state-of-the-art analysis of the field carried out in this chapter, we have perceived that the field is moving and new research approaches are emerging. For instance, initial TEL RecSys used very small and mostly internal datasets, whereas more recent studies apply larger reference datasets before they implement the systems in a real world scenario. Furthermore, the research community tries to make datasets available to other researchers and use additional reference datasets that are publicly available to make the results of their studies more comparable.

In the following sections a trend analysis in TEL RecSys for the last 15 years of research are summarised according to the framework categories.

- **Supported Tasks**. *Finding good Items (content)* is the most applied task for recommender systems in the TEL field. But *Recommendation of sequence of items* that aims to create an effective and efficient learning path through digital contents is also an important task for the TEL community. Along this mainly content driven recommendations, the recommendation of other learners, so-called *peers*, that follow similar learning goals or have the same interest as a target learner are very central tasks. There are some new tasks appearing in the recent years, which go beyond recommending learning content, such as *Predict learning performance* and *Recommend learning activity*.

- **User Model**. There is no clear trend identifiable regarding the user models in TEL RecSys. But there seem to be more research efforts going towards clustering and classification approaches. That is another indicator that the field increasingly adapts ideas and techniques from the educational data mining and learning analytics research communities. In this respect, the interested reader can consult the chapter on Data Mining Methods for Recommender Systems (Chap. 7).
- **Domain Model**. Similar to the user model category, there is not one major approach for modeling the domain within TEL RecSys. The initial systems in the field almost always applied *Index/Lists* and *Ontologies* what is reasonable as TEL RecSys research was mainly driven by two communities: (a) Information Retrieval, and (b) Adaptive Hypermedia. Index/Lists have been used by the information retrieval community within TEL, whereas Ontologies have been extensively used by the Semantic Web and Adaptive Hypermedia community from 1998 until 2010. Both approaches are still used today but we see some converging approaches as described in [21]. In turn, like in the User Model category, more and more classification and clustering approaches are applied for the Domain Model as well. This emphasises once again the growing usage of data mining techniques in the field.
- **Personalisation**. Within the personalisation category we were able to identify some trends over time regarding the used methods. Examples for this are Hybrid and Content-based approaches that started to be reported in 2008 and are increasingly applied in recent years until today. There is an increasing interest in Graph-based (2010–2014) and Knowledge-based approaches (2013–2014). These technologies are mainly applied to address two more common issues within educational datasets: (a) Sparsity, and (b) Unstructured data. When rating data are sparse, users are likely to receive irrelevant recommendations. Therefore, graph-based approaches, which extend the baseline of nearest neighbours in collaborative filtering by invoking graph search algorithms, have been applied successfully in TEL RecSys [31]. Collaborative Filtering and Rule-based approaches are still the most frequently used techniques over all development cycles (2004–2014).
- **Operation**. Regarding the output, most of the TEL RecSys aim to suggest their recommendations directly to the users in a passive mode. The architectures, therefore, are in most of the cases centralised systems and the recommendations are usually created on the side of the recommendation server. There are some federated search approaches mentioned in the recent papers and also recommendations of learning objects from Linked Data sources have become a relevant topic in 2013.

To conclude the chapter, we have reviewed the challenges reported in [67] in the light of the meta-review carried out in this chapter and extended those from the previous publication. These are:

1. **Pedagogical needs and expectations to recommenders**. Recommendation opportunities in educational scenarios that go beyond recommending learning resources need to be further explored. For this, user centered design approaches [88] can be of value, such as to consider recommending learning activities that, for instance, foster communication [1] and metacognition [78, 89, 125]. At the same time, the potential of semantic technologies is being considered to describe the educational domain and therefore enrich the recommendation process [45, 53, 90, 97].
2. **Context-based recommender systems**. As reported in a state-of-the-art review of contextual TEL recommenders [111] contextual information can be of value to enrich the recommendations process and there are many research opportunities in this direction. Context-based recommenders can extend the input and output information to be considered in the recommendations process with the usage of appropriate physical sensors [91], such as reported in [50, 58, 60, 117, 121]. In this sense, the application of affective computing in TEL RecSys can provide added value to the recommendations when emotional and sentiment information is taken into account in the recommendation process [52, 93] and can provide interactive recommendations through sensorial actuators [92]. Details about Context-Aware Recommender Systems can be read in the corresponding Chap. 6.
3. **Visualisation and explanation of recommendations**. An important line of research in this area is the use of visualisation techniques to provide users with insights in the recommendation process. Visualisations can help to explain recommendation results by explicitly exposing relationships among content and people. El-Bishouty et al. [29], for instance, researched the use of visualisation techniques to present the relationship between recommended peer-learners. Visualisation techniques can increase understanding of in- and output for a recommender system. It therefore also contributes to a higher level of trust of the user into the system that mainly acts like a black box to them. In this sense, guidelines for the design of this complex relationships should be taken into account as compiled in the chapter Guidelines for Designing and Evaluating Explanations in Recommender Systems Chap. 10.
4. **Demands for more diverse educational datasets**. In 2011 most TEL recommender studies have still used rather small datasets which were not made public available [64, 65]. Since then, the dataTEL Theme Team of the European network of excellence STELLAR [25] collected an initial set of datasets that can be used by the research community [110]. These days we see many more studies that take advantage of this initial collection of datasets to start their research [31]. But the dataTEL collection can only be a first start to a comprehensive collection of datasets for RecSysTEL research. As TEL is a very diverse research field that starts at school level, over Higher Education until workplace learning and also is differentiated into informal, non-formal and formal learning, a larger collection with more diverse datasets is needed.

5. **Distributed datasets**. Big data architectures (such as Lambda, http://lambda-architecture.net) and technologies (such as Apache Drill, http://incubator.apache.org/drill/) that allow large scale and real time analytics over distributed data, are expected to change the way that research is taking place over federations or aggregations of learning information. Applications developed on top of Linked Open Data such as the ones piloted by the LinkedUp project (http://linkedup-project.eu), are also bringing new requirements to the infrastructures needed to support such research scenarios. We see the need for educational research of e-infrastructure components and services that can host, distribute and virtualise such big data powered recommendation applications for learning also to overcome the sparsity of single data silos.
6. **New evaluation methods that cover technical and educational criteria**. Recommender systems can be analysed to measure the effect on effectiveness (completion rates and amount of progress) and efficiency (time taken to complete) in learning [49, 89], towards an ascending learning curve and better grades [112], including mash-up environments that combine sources of users from different Web2.0 services [23] and mobile learning approaches [47]. For the RecSysTEL field it is important that upcoming developments on TEL RecSys should follow a standardised evaluation method as suggested in [67]. The method consists of four steps:

   a. A selection of datasets that suit the recommendation problem and tasks of the development.
   b. An offline comparison study of different algorithms on the selected datasets including well known datasets (if possible, educational oriented datasets in the same way that Movielens is to movie recommendations) to provide insights into the performance of the recommendation algorithms.
   c. A comprehensive user study in a controlled experimental environment to test psycho-educational effects on the side of the learners as well as on the technical aspects of the designed recommender system.
   d. A deployment of the recommender system in a real life application, where it can be tested under realistic and normal operational conditions with its actual users.

   The above four steps should come along with a complete description of the recommender system according to the classification framework presented in Sect. 12.3. A good example for this research approach is [32]. The used dataset should be reported and made publicly accessible. This would allow other researchers to repeat and adjust any part of the research to gain comparable results and new insights. A detailed description about how to run user studies with recommender systems is also available in Chap. 9.

We hope the panorama of recommender systems to support learning that has been compiled in this chapter helps researchers, developers and users to get a clear view of the field.

Acknowledgements Hendrik Drachsler has been partly supported by the FP7 EU Project LACE (619424). Katrien Verbert is a post-doctoral fellow of the Research Foundation Flanders (FWO). Olga C. Santos would like to acknowledge that her contributions to this work have been carried out within the project Multimodal approaches for Affective Modelling in Inclusive Personalized Educational scenarios in intelligent Contexts (MAMIPEC-TIN2011-29221-C03-01). Nikos Manouselis has been partially supported with funding CIP-PSP Open Discovery Space (297229).

References

1. Abel, F., Bittencourt, I.I., de Barros Costa, E., Henze, N., Krause, D., Vassileva, J.: Recommendations in Online Discussion Forums for E-Learning Systems. TLT 3(2), 165–176 (2010)
2. Adomavicius, G., Tuzhilin, A.: Towards the Next Generation of Recommender Systems: A Survey of the State-of-the-Art and Possible Extensions. IEEE Trans. Knowl. Data Engin., 17(6), 734–749 (2005)
3. Aher, S.B., Lobo, L.: Combination of machine learning algorithms for recommendation of courses in E-Learning System based on historical data. Knowl.-Based Syst. 51: 1–14 (2013)
4. Avancini, H., Straccia, U.: User recommendation for collaborative and personalised digital archives. International Journal of Web Based Communities, 1(2), 163–175 (2005)
5. Beham, G., Kump, B., Ley, T., Lindstaedt, S.: Recommending knowledgeable people in a work-integrated learning system. Procedia Computer Science, 1(2), 2783–2792 (2010)
6. Bielikova, M., Simko, M., Barla, M., Tvarozek, J., Labaj, M., Moro, R., Srba, I., & Sevcech, J.: ALEF: from Application to Platform for Adaptive Collaborative Learning. Special issue on Recommender Systems for Technology Enhanced Learning: Research Trends & Applications, Springer Berlin (2014)
7. Bodea, C., Dascalu, M., Lipai, A.: Clustering of the Web Search Results in Educational Recommender Systems. In: Santos O, Boticario J (eds) Educational Recommender Systems and Technologies: Practices and Challenges, pp. 154–181 (2012)
8. Boticario, J. G., Rodriguez-Ascaso, A., Santos, O. C., Raffenne, E., Montandon, L., Roldon, D., Buendia, F.: Accessible Lifelong Learning at Higher Education: Outcomes and Lessons Learned at two Different Pilot Sites in the EU4ALL Project. In Journal of Universal Computer Science 18 (1), 62–85 (2012).
9. Bozo, J., Alarcon, R., Iribarra, S. (2010) Recommending Learning Objects According to a Teachers Context Model. Sustaining TEL: From Innovation to Learning and Practice. Lecture Notes in Computer Science Volume 6383, 2010, pp 470–475
10. Broisin, J., Brut, M., Butoianu, V., Sedes, F., Vidal, P.: A personalised recommendation framework based on CAM and document annotations. Procedia Computer Science, 1(2), 2839–2848 (2010)
11. Brusilovsky, P., Cassel, L.N., Delcambre, L.M.L., Fox, E.A., Furuta, R., Garcia, D.D., Shipman III, F.M., Yudelson, M.: Social navigation for educational digital libraries, Procedia Computer Science, 1(2), 2889–2897 (2010)
12. Burke, R.: Hybrid Recommender Systems: Survey and Experiments. User Model. User Adapt. Inter., 12, 331–370 (2002)
13. Carchiolo, V., Longheu, A., Malgeri, M.: Reliable peers and useful resources: Searching for the best personalised learning path in a trust- and recommendation-aware environment, Information Sciences, Volume 180, Issue 10, pp. 1893–1907 (2010), ISSN 0020–0255, http://dx.doi.org/10.1016/j.ins.2009.12.023.
14. Casali, A., Gerling, V., Deco, C., Bender, C.: A Recommender System for Learning Objects Personalized Retrieval. In: Santos O, Boticario J (eds) Educational Recommender Systems and Technologies: Practices and Challenges, pp. 182–210. (2012) doi:10.4018/978-1-61350-489-5.ch008

15. Cazella, S.C., Reategui, E.B., Behar, P.A.: Recommendation of Learning Objects Applying Collaborative Filtering and Competencies. Key Competencies in the Knowledge Society pp. 35–43 (2010)
16. Cechinel, C., da Silva Camargo, S., Sánchez-Alonso, S., Sicilia, MA.: Towards automated evaluation of learning resources inside repositories. Special issue on Recommender Systems for Technology Enhanced Learning: Research Trends & Applications, Springer Berlin (2014)
17. Chen, C.M., Duh, L.-J.: Personalized web-based tutoring system based on fuzzy item response theory, Expert Systems with Applications, Volume 34, Issue 4, May 2008, pp. 2298–2315, ISSN 0957-4174, http://dx.doi.org/10.1016/j.eswa.2007.03.010 (2008)
18. Chu, K., Chang, M., & Hsia, Y.: Designing a course recommendation system on web based on the students? course selection records. World conference on educational Educational Multimedia, Hypermedia and Telecommunications, EDMEDIA 2003 (pp. 4–21). Retrieved from http://www.editlib.org/p/18882/ (2003)
19. dAquin, M., Dietze, S., Drachsler, H., Taibi, D.: Using linked data in learning analytics. eLearning Papers, No. 36, ISSN: 1887–1542, www.openeducationeuropa.eu/en/elearning_papers (2014)
20. Diaz, A., Motz, R., Rohrer, E., Tansini, L.: An Ontology Network for Educational Recommender Systems. In: Santos, O., Boticario, J. (eds) Educational Recommender Systems and Technologies: Practices and Challenges, pp. 67–93. doi:10.4018/978-1-61350-489-5.ch004 (2012)
21. Dietze, S., Drachsler, H., Giordano, D.: A Survey on Linked Data and the Social Web as facilitators for TEL RecSys. Recommender Systems for Technology Enhanced Learning: Research Trends & Applications, Eds: Manouselis, N., Verbert, K., Drachsler, H., Santos, O.C., Springer, Berlin (2013)
22. Dourado, A. O., and Martin, C. A.: New concept of dynamic flight simulator, Part I. Aerospace Science and Technology, 30(1), 79–82 (2013)
23. Drachsler, H., Pecceu, D., Arts, T., Hutten, E., Rutledge, L., Van Rosmalen, P., Hummel, H.G.K., Koper, R.: ReMashed-An Usability Study of a Recommender System for Mash-Ups for Learning. In: 1st Workshop on Mashups for Learning at the International Conference on Interactive Computer Aided Learning, Villach, Austria (2009)
24. Drachsler, H., Hummel, H.G.K., Van den Berg, B., Eshuis, J., Berlanga, A., Nadolski, R., Waterink, W., Boers, N., Koper, R.: Effects of the ISIS Recommender System for navigation support in self-organized learning networks. Educational Technology and Society, 12, pp. 122–135 (2009)
25. Drachsler, H., Bogers, T., Vuorikari, R., Verbert, K., Duval, E., Manouselis, N., Beham, G., Lindstaedt, S., Stern, H., Friedrich, M.: Issues and considerations regarding sharable data sets for recommender systems in technology enhanced learning. In: Procedia Computer Science, 1(2), pp. 2849–2858. doi:10.1016/j.procs.2010.08.010 (2010)
26. Drachsler, H., K. Verbert, N. Manouselis, R. Vuorikari, M. Wolpers, S. Lindstaedt. Preface [Special Issue on dataTEL - Data Supported Research in Technology-Enhanced Learning]. In: International Journal Technology Enhanced Learning 4 (1/2) (2012)
27. Drachsler, H., Li, Y., Santos, O.C.: Recommender Systems for Learning. In: Sampson, D. G., Spector, J. M., Chen, N.S., Huang, R., Kinshuk, editor, Proceedings of the IEEE 14th International Conference on Advanced Learning Technologies, pp. 513–538. IEEE (2014).
28. Dron, J., Mitchell, R., Siviter, P., Boyne, C.: CoFIND-an experiment in n-dimensional collaborative filtering. Journal of Network and Computer Applications, 23(2), pp. 131–142 (2000)
29. El-Bishouty MM, Ogata H, Yano Y (2007) Perkam: Personalized knowledge awareness map for computer supported ubiquitous learning. Educational Technology and Society, 10(3):122–134
30. El Helou, S., Salzmann, C., Gillet, D.: The 3A personalised, contextual and relation-based recommender system. Journal of Universal Computer Science, 16(16), 2179–2195 (2010)

31. Fazeli, S., Loni, B., Drachsler, D., & Sloep, P. B. (2014). Which Recommender System Can Best Fit Social Learning Platforms?. In Proceedings of the Ninth European Conference on Technology Enhanced Learning, Open Learning and Teaching in Educational Communities (EC-TEL2014), Graz, Austria.
32. Fazeli, S., Drachsler, H., Brouns, F., Sloep, P. (2014) Towards a Social Trust-Aware Recommender for Teachers. Recommender Systems for Technology Enhanced Learning, Springer, 177–194
33. Fernandez, A., Anjorin, M., Dackiewicz, I., and Rensing, C.: Recommendations from Heterogeneous Sources in a Technology Enhanced Learning Ecosystem. Special issue on Recommender Systems for Technology Enhanced Learning: Research Trends & Applications, Springer Berlin (2014)
34. Fiaidhi, J. RecoSearch: A Model for Collaboratively Filtering Java Learning Objects. International Journal of Instructional Technology and Distance Learning, 1(7), 35–50 (2004)
35. Fraij, F., Al-Dmour, A., Al-Hashemi, R., Musa, A.: An evolving recommender-based framework for virtual learning communities. IJWBC 8(3): 322–332 (2012)
36. Farzan, R., Brusilovsky, P.: Encouraging user participation in a course recommender system: An impact on user behavior. Computers in Human Behavior, 27(1), pp. 276–284 (2011)
37. Gallego, D.; Barra, E.; Gordillo, A; Huecas, G.: Enhanced recommendations for e-Learning authoring tools based on a proactive context-aware recommender. In: IEEE Frontiers in Education Conference, 1393,1395 (2013)
38. Garcia, E., Romero, C., Ventura, S., de Castro, C.: An architecture for making recommendations to courseware authors using association rule mining and collaborative filtering. User Modeling and User-Adapted Interaction, 19(1–2), 99–132 (2009)
39. Ghauth, K. I., & Abdullah, N. A.: The Effect of Incorporating Good Learners' Ratings in e-Learning Content-based Recommender System. Educational Technology & Society, 14 (2), 248–257 (2011)
40. Gomez-Albarran, M., Jimenez-Diaz, G.: Recommendation and Students' Authoring in Repositories of Learning Objects: A Case-Based Reasoning Approach. International Journal of Emerging Technologies in Learning (iJET) 4(1), 35–40 (2009)
41. Greller, W., Drachsler, H.: Translating Learning into Numbers: A Generic Framework for Learning Analytics. In: Educational Technology & Society, 15(3), pp. 42–57 (2012)
42. Han, P., Xie, B., Yang, F., Shen, R.: A scalable P2P recommender system based on distributed collaborative filtering. Expert Systems with Applications, 27, pp. 203–210 (2004)
43. Hanani, U., Shapira, B., Shoval, P.: Information Filtering: Overview of Issues, Research and Systems. User Modeling and User-Adapted Interaction, 11, 203–259 (2001)
44. Herlocker, J.L., Konstan, J.A., Terveen, L.G., Riedl, J.T.: Evaluating Collaborative Filtering Recommender Systems. ACM Transactions on Information Systems, 22, 1, pp. 5–53 (2004)
45. Holanda, O., Ferreira, R., Costa, E., Bittencourt, I.I., Melo, J., Peixoto, M., Tiengo, W.: Educational resources recommendation system based on agents and semantic web for helping students in a virtual learning environment. IJWBC 8(3), pp. 333–353 (2012)
46. Hsieh, T.-C., Lee, M.-C., Su, C.-Y.: Designing and implementing a personalized remedial learning system for enhancing the programming learning. Educational Technology & Society 16(4): 32–46 (2013)
47. Hsu, C.-K., Hwang, G.-J., Chang, C.-K.: A personalized recommendation-based mobile learning approach to improving the reading performance of EFL students, Computers & Education, Volume 63, April 2013, pp. 327–336, ISSN 0360-1315, http://dx.doi.org/10.1016/j.compedu.2012.12.004 (2013)
48. Huang, Y.-M., Huang, T.-C., Wang, K.-T., Hwang, W.-Y.: A Markov-based Recommendation Model for Exploring the Transfer of Learning on the Web. Educational Technology and Society, 12(2),144–162 (2009)
49. Janssen, J., Tattersall, C., Waterink, W., Van den Berg, B., Van Es, R., Bolman, C., et al.: Self-organising navigational support in lifelong learning: how predecessors can lead the way. Computers and Education, 49(3), pp. 781–793 (2007)

50. Kaklauskas, A., Zavadskas, E.K., Seniut, M., Stankevic, V., Raistenskis, J., Simkevioius, C., Stankevic, T., Matuliauskaite, A., Bartkiene, L., Zemeckyte, L., Paliskiene, R., Cerkauskiene, R., Gribniak, V. Recommender System to Analyze Students Academic Performance. Expert Systems with Applications, 40(15), 6150–6165 (2013)
51. Kalz, M., and Specht, M.: Assessing the crossdisciplinarity of technology-enhanced learning with science overlay maps and diversity measures. In: British Journal of Educational Technology, 18 p. (2013)
52. Karampiperis, P., Koukourikos, A., Stoitsis, G.: Collaborative Filtering Recommendation of Educational Content in Social Environments utilizing Sentiment Analysis Techniques. Special issue on Recommender Systems for Technology Enhanced Learning: Research Trends & Applications, Springer Berlin (2014)
53. Kerkiri, T., Manitsaris, A., Mavridis, I.: How e-learning systems may benefit from ontologies and recommendation methods to efficiently personalise resources. IJKL 5(3/4): 347–370 (2009)
54. Khribi, M.K., Jemni, M., Nasraoui, O.: Automatic Recommendations for E-Learning Personalization Based on Web Usage Mining Techniques and Information Retrieval. Educational Technology and Society, 12(4), pp. 30–42 (2009)
55. Koutrika, G., Bercovitz, B., Kaliszan, F., Liou, H., Garcia-Molina, H.: CourseRank: A Closed-Community Social System Through the Magnifying Glass. In: Proc. of the 3rd International AAAI Conference on Weblogs and Social Media (ICWSM'09). San Jose, California (2009)
56. Leino, J.: Case study: recommending course reading materials in a small virtual learning community. IJWBC 8(3): 285–301 (2012)
57. Lemire, D., Boley, H., McGrath, S., Ball, M.: Collaborative Filtering and Inference Rules for Context-Aware Learning Object Recommendation. International Journal of Interactive Technology and Smart Education, 2(3), (2005)
58. Li, M., Ogata, H., Hou, B, Uosaki, N., Mouri, K. Context-aware and Personalization Method in Ubiquitous Learning Log System. Educational Technology & Society, 16 (3), 362–373 (2013)
59. Limongelli, C., Lombardi, M., Marani, A., Sciarrone, F. (2013) A Teaching-Style Based Social Network for Didactic Building and Sharing. AIED 2013, LNAI 7926, pp. 774–777, 2013.
60. Luo, F., Dong, J., Cao, A.: Song. A context-aware personalized resource recommendation for pervasive learning. Cluster Computing, June 2010, Volume 13, Issue 2, pp 213–239 (2010)
61. Mangina, E.E., Kilbride, J.: Evaluation of keyphrase extraction algorithm and tiling process for a document/resource recommender within e-learning environments. Computers & Education, 50(3), pp. 807–820 (2008)
62. Manouselis, N., Costopoulou, C.: Experimental Analysis of Design Choices in Multi-Attribute Utility Collaborative Filtering. International Journal of Pattern Recognition and Artificial Intelligence, Special Issue on Personalization Techniques for Recommender Systems and Intelligent User Interfaces, 21(2), pp. 311–333 (2007)
63. Manouselis, N., Vuorikari, R., Van Assche, F.: Simulated Analysis of MAUT Collaborative Filtering for Learning Object Recommendation. In: Proc. of the Workshop on Social Information Retrieval in Technology Enhanced Learning (SIRTEL 2007). Crete, Greece (2007)
64. Manouselis, N., Vuorikari, R., Van Assche, F.: Collaborative Recommendation of e-Learning Resources: An Experimental Investigation. In: Journal of Computer Assisted Learning, Special Issue on Adaptive technologies and methods in e/m-Learning and Internet-based education, Blackwell Publishing Ltd., 26(4), pp. 227–242, (2010)
65. Manouselis, N., Drachsler, H., Verbert, K., Santos, O.C. (Eds.) Proceedings of the 1st Workshop on Recommender Systems for Technology Enhanced Learning (RecSysTEL 2010). Procedia Computer Science, Volume 1, Issue 2, Pages 2773–2998 (2010)
66. Manouselis, N., Drachsler, H., Vuorikari, R., Hummel, H., and Koper, R.: Recommender systems in technology enhanced learning. In: Rokach, L., Shapira, B., Kantor, P., Ricci, F., editor, Recommender Systems Handbook: A Complete Guide for Research Scientists & Practitioners, pp. 387–409. Springer (2011)

67. Manouselis, N., Drachsler, H., Verbert, K., and Duval, E.: Recommender Systems for Learning. Berlin, Springer, 2012, 90 p.
68. Manouselis, N., Drachsler, H., Verbert, K., and Santos, O.: Proceedings of the 2nd Workshop on Recommender Systems for Technology Enhanced Learning (RecSysTEL 2012). CEUR workshop proceedings, Vol-896, 100 p. (2012)
69. Manouselis, N., Drachsler, H., Verbert, K., Santos, O.C.: Recommender Systems for Technology Enhanced Learning: Research Trends & Applications. Springer (2014)
70. Marino, O., Paquette, G.: A competency-driven advisor system for multi-actor learning environments. Procedia Computer Science, 1(2):2871–2876, doi:10.1016/j.procs.2010.08.013 (2010)
71. Martin, E., Carro, R.M.: Supporting the Development of Mobile Adaptive Learning Environments: A Case Study. TLT 2(1): 23–36 (2009)
72. Masters, K.: A brief guide to understanding MOOCs". The Internet Journal of Medical Education 1 (Num. 2) (2011)
73. Michlik, P., Bielikova, M.: Exercises recommending for limited time learning. Procedia Computer Science, (1)2:2821–2828. doi:10.1016/j.procs.2010.08.007 (2010)
74. Moedritscher, F.: Towards a recommender strategy for personal learning environments. Procedia Computer Science, (1)2:2775–2782. doi:10.1016/j.procs.2010.08.002 (2010)
75. Montaner, M., Lopez, B., de la Rosa, J.L.: A Taxonomy of Recommender Agents on the Internet. Artif. Intell. Rev., 19, pp. 285–330 (2003)
76. Nadolski, R.J., Van den Berg, B., Berlanga, A., Drachsler, H., Hummel, H., Koper, R., Sloep, P.: Simulating Light-Weight Personalised Recommender Systems in Learning Networks: A Case for Pedagogy-Oriented and Rating-Based Hybrid Recommendation Strategies. Journal of Artificial Societies and Social Simulation (JASSS), 12(14) (2009)
77. Nowakowski, S., Ognjanovic, I., Grandbastien, M., Jovanovic, J., Sendelj, R.: Two Recommending Strategies to enhance Online Presence in Personal Learning Environments. Special issue on Recommender Systems for Technology Enhanced Learning: Research Trends & Applications, Springer Berlin (2014)
78. Nussbaumer, A., Berthold, M., Dahrendorf, D., Schmitz, H..C., Kravcik, M., Albert, D.: A Mashup Recommender for Creating Personal Learning Environments. Advances in Web-Based Learning - ICWL 2012. Lecture Notes in Computer Science Volume 7558, pp. 79–88. doi: 10.1007/978-3-642-33642-3_9 (2012)
79. Okoye, I., Maull, K., Foster, J., Sumner, T.: Educational Recommendation in an Informal Intentional Learning System. In: Santos O, Boticario J (eds), Educational Recommender Systems and Technologies: Practices and Challenges, pp. 1–23. doi:10.4018/978-1-61350-489-5.ch001 (2012)
80. O'Mahony, M.P., Smyth, B.: A recommender system for on-line course enrolment: an initial study. RecSys 2007, pp. 133–136 (2007)
81. Rafaeli, S., Dan-Gur, Y., Barak, M.: Social Recommender Systems: Recommendations in Support of E-Learning. International Journal of Distance Education Technologies, 3(2), pp. 29–45 (2005)
82. Recker, M.M., Walker, A.: Supporting "Word-of-Mouth" Social Networks through Collaborative Information Filtering. Journal of Interactive Learning Research, 14(1), pp. 79–99 (2003)
83. Romero, C., Ventura, S., Zafra, A., De Bra, P.: Applying Web usage mining for personalizing hyperlinks in Web-based adaptive educational systems. Computers & Education 53(3), pp. 828–840 (2009)
84. Salehi, M.: Application of implicit and explicit attribute based collaborative filtering and BIDE for learning resource recommendation, Data & Knowledge Engineering, Volume 87, September 2013, pp. 130–145, ISSN 0169-023X, http://dx.doi.org/10.1016/j.datak.2013.07.001 (2013)
85. Santos, O.C.: A recommender system to provide adaptive and inclusive standard-based support along the eLearning life cycle. In: Proceedings of the 2008 ACM conference on Recommender systems, pp. 319–322. ACM (2008)

86. Santos, O. C., & Boticario, J. G.: Educational Recommender Systems and Technologies: Practices and Challenges (pp. 1–362). Hershey, PA: IGI Global. doi:10.4018/978-1-61350-489-5 (2012)
87. Santos, O. C., & Boticario, J. G.: Special Issue on Recommender Systems to Support the Dynamics of Virtual Learning Communities. International Journal of Web Based Communities, Vol. 8 No. 3 (2012)
88. Santos, O.C., Boticario, J.G.: User Centred Design and Educational Data Mining support during the Recommendations Elicitation Process in Social Online Learning Environments. **32**(2), 293–311, (2015). DOI: 10.1111/exsy.12041
89. Santos, O.C., Boticario, J.G., Pérez-Marin, D.: Extending web-based educational systems with personalised support through User Centred Designed recommendations along the e-learning life cycle, Science of Computer Programming, Volume 88, Pages 92–109, ISSN 0167-6423. (2014)
90. Santos, O.C., Boticario, J.G., Manjarrés-Riesco, A.: An Approach for an Affective Educational Recommendation Model. Recommender Systems for Technology Enhanced Learning: Research Trends & Applications, pp 123–143, Springer Berlin (2014)
91. Santos, O. C., Boticario, J.G.: Exploring Arduino for Building Educational Context-Aware Recommender Systems that Deliver Affective Recommendations in Social Ubiquitous Networking Environments. In Proceedings of Web-Age Information Management. Lecture Notes in Computer Science, Volume 8597, 2014, pp 272–286.
92. Santos, O. C., Saneiro, M., Boticario, J., Rodriguez-Sanchez, C. Towards Interactive Context-Aware Affective Educational Recommendations in Computer Assisted Language Learning. New Review of Hypermedia and Multimedia, pp. 1–31. http://dx.doi.org/10.1080/13614568.2015.1058428 (2015)
93. Santos, O.C., Saneiro, M., Salmeron-Majadas, S., Boticario, J.G.: A methodological approach to eliciting affective educational recommendations. In Proceedings of the 14th IEEE International Conference on Advanced Learning Technologies (ICALT14), 529–533 (2014) doi: 10.1109/ICALT.2014.234
94. Schafer, J.B., Konstan, J.A., Riedl, J.: E-Commerce Recommendation Applications. Data Mining and Knowledge Discovery, 5, pp. 115–153 (2001)
95. Schoefegger, K., Seitlinger, P., Ley, T.: Towards a user model for personalised recommendations in work-integrated learning: A report on an experimental study with a collaborative tagging system. Procedia Computer Science, 1(2):2829–2838, doi:10.1016/j.procs.2010.08.008 (2010)
96. Sergis, S., Zervas, P., Sampson, D.G. (2014) Towards Learning Object Recommendations based on Teachers ICT Competence Profiles. 2014 IEEE 14th International Conference on Advanced Learning Technologies, 534–538
97. Shelton, B.E., Duffin, J., Wang, Y., Ball, J.: Linking open course wares and open education resources: creating an effective search and recommendation system. Procedia Computer Science, 1(2), pp. 2865–2870 doi:10.1016/j.procs.2010.08.012 (2010)
98. Shen, L., Shen, R.: Learning content recommendation service based-on simple sequencing specification. In: Liu W et al. (eds) Lecture notes in computer science, pp. 363–370 (2004)
99. Sicilia, M.A., Garcia-Barriocanal, E., Sanchez-Alonso, S., Cechinel, C.: Exploring user-based recommender results in large learning object repositories: the case of MERLOT. Procedia Computer Science, 1(2), pp. 2859–2864. doi:10.1016/j.procs.2010.08.011 (2010)
100. Sielis, G.A., Mettouris, C., Tzanavari, A., Papadopoulos, G.A.: Context-Aware Recommendations using Topic Maps Technology for the Enhancement of the Creativity Process. In: Santos O, Boticario J (eds) Educational Recommender Systems and Technologies: Practices and Challenges, pp. 43–66. doi:10.4018/978-1-61350-489-5.ch003 (2012)
101. Tai, D.W.S., Wu, H.J., Li, P.H.: Effective e-learning recommendation system based on self-organizing maps and association mining. The Electronic Library, 26(3), 329–344 (2008)
102. Tang, T.Y., McCalla, G.: Smart Recommendation for an Evolving E-Learning System: Architecture and Experiment. International Journal on E-Learning, 4(1), pp. 105–129 (2005)

103. Tang, TY., Winoto, P.,ăand McCalla, G.: Further Thoughts on Context-Aware Paper Recommendations for Education. Special issue on Recommender Systems for Technology Enhanced Learning: Research Trends & Applications, Springer Berlin (2014)
104. Tang, T.Y., Daniel, B.K., Romero, C.: Special Issue on Recommender systems for and in social and online learning environments. Expert Systems (2014)
105. Thai-Nghe, N., Drumond, L., Horvith, T., Krohn-Grimberghe, A., Nanopoulos, A., Schmidt-Thieme, L.: Factorization Techniques for Predicting Student Performance. In Santos O, Boticario J (eds) Educational Recommender Systems and Technologies: Practices and Challenges, pp. 129–153. doi:10.4018/978-1-61350-489-5.ch006 (2012)
106. Tsai, K.H., Chiu, T.K., Lee, M.C., Wang, T.I.: A learning objects recommendation model based on the preference and ontological approaches. In: Proc. of 6th International Conference on Advanced Learning Technologies (ICALT'06). IEEE Computer Society Press (2006)
107. Underwood, J.S.: Metis: A Content Map-Based Recommender System for Digital Learning Activities. In: Santos O, Boticario J (eds), Educational Recommender Systems and Technologies: Practices and Challenges, pp. 24–42. doi:10.4018/978-1-61350-489-5.ch002 (2012)
108. Vialardi Sacun, C., Bravo Agapito, J., Shafti, L., Ortigosa, A.: Recommendation in Higher Education Using Data Mining Techniques. EDM 2009: 191–199 (2009)
109. Verbert, K., Duval, E., Lindstaedt, S. and Gillet, D. (eds): Special issue on Context-aware Recommender Systems, Journal of Universal Computer Science, 16(16), pp. 2175–2290 (2010)
110. Verbert, K., Manouselis, N., Drachsler, H., & Duval, E. (2012). Dataset-Driven Research to Support Learning and Knowledge Analytics. Educational Technology & Society, 15 (3), 133–148."
111. Verbert, K., Manouselis, N., Xavier, O., Wolpers, M., Drachsler, H., Bosnic, I., Duval, E.: Context-aware Recommender Systems for Learning: a Survey and Future Challenges. IEEE Transactions on Learning Technologies. 5(4), pp. 318–335 (2012)
112. Vesin, B., Milicevic, A.K., Ivanovic, M., Budimac, Z.: Applying Recommender Systems and Adaptive Hypermedia for e-Learning Personalizatio. Computing and Informatics 32(3), pp. 629–659 (2013)
113. Vuorikari, R., Manouselis, N., and Duval, E. Special issue on social information retrieval for technology enhanced learning. Journal Of Digital Information, 10(2) (2009)
114. Wan, X., Okamoto, T.: Utilizing learning process to improve recommender system for group learning support. Neural Computing and Applications 20(5): 611–621 (2011)
115. Wang, Y., Sumiya, K.: Semantic ranking of lecture slides based on conceptual relationship and presentational structure. Procedia Computer Science, 1(2), pp. 2801–2810. doi:10.1016/j.procs.2010.08.005 (2010)
116. Wang, F.-H.: On extracting recommendation knowledge for personalized web-based learning based on ant colony optimization with segmented-goal and meta-control strategies. Expert Syst. Appl. 39(7), pp. 6446–6453 (2012)
117. Wang, S.L., Wu, C.Y. Application of context-aware and personalized recommendation to implement an adaptive ubiquitous learning system. Expert Systems with Applications, 38(9), 10831–10838 (2011)
118. Wei, C.-P., Shaw, M.J., Easley, R.F.: A Survey of Recommendation Systems in Electronic Commerce. In: Rust RT, Kannan PK (eds) E-Serv.: New Dir. in Theor. and Pract., M. E. Sharpe Publisher (2002)
119. Weidenbach M., Drachsler H., Wild F., Kreutter S., Razek V., Grunst G., Ender J., Berlage T., and Janousek J.: EchoComTEE a simulator for transoesophageal echocardiography. Anaesthesia, 62, 4, pp. 347–353 (2007)
120. Weppner, J., Lukowicz, P., Hirth, M., Kuhn, J. Physics education with Google Glass gPhysics experiment app. In Proceedings of the 2014 ACM International Joint Conference on Pervasive and Ubiquitous Computing: Adjunct Publication (UbiComp '14 Adjunct), 279–282 (2014)
121. Yu, Z., Zhou, X., Shu, L.: Towards a semantic infrastructure for context-aware e-learning. Multimedia Tools Appl. 47(1): 71–86 (2010)

122. Zaiane, O.R.: Building a recommender agent for e-learning systems. Computers in Education, 2002. vol.1, 3–6, doi: 10.1109/CIE.2002.1185862 (2002)
123. Zaldivar, V.A., Burgos, D., Pardo, A.: Meta-Rule Based Recommender Systems for Educational Applications. In: Santos O, Boticario J (eds) Educational Recommender Systems and Technologies: Practices and Challenges, pp. 211–231. doi:10.4018/978-1-61350-489-5.ch009 (2012)
124. Zapata, A., Menendez, V.H., Prieto, M.E., Romero, C.: A framework for recommendation in learning object repositories: An example of application in civil engineering. Advances in Engineering Software 56: 1–14 (2013)
125. Zhou, M., Xu, Y.: Challenges to Use Recommender Systems to Enhance Meta-Cognitive Functioning in Online Learners. In: Santos, O., Boticario, J. (eds) Educational Recommender Systems and Technologies: Practices and Challenges, pp. 282–301. doi:10.4018/978-1-61350-489-5.ch012 (2012)

Chapter 13
Music Recommender Systems

Markus Schedl, Peter Knees, Brian McFee, Dmitry Bogdanov, and Marius Kaminskas

13.1 Introduction

Boosted by the emergence of online music shops and music streaming services, digital music distribution has led to an ubiquitous availability of music. Music listeners, suddenly faced with an unprecedented scale of readily available content, can easily become overwhelmed. Music recommender systems, the topic of this chapter, provide guidance to users navigating large collections. Music items that can be recommended include artists, albums, songs, genres, and radio stations.

In this chapter, we illustrate the unique characteristics of the music recommendation problem, as compared to other content domains, such as books or movies. To understand the differences, let us first consider the amount of time required for a user to consume a single media item. There is obviously a large discrepancy in consumption time between books (days or weeks), movies (one to a few hours), and a song (typically a few minutes). Consequently, the time it takes for a user to form opinions for music can be much shorter than in other domains, which contributes to the ephemeral, even disposable, nature of music. Similarly, in music, a single

M. Schedl (✉) • P. Knees
Department of Computational Perception, Johannes Kepler University Linz, Linz, Austria
e-mail: markus.schedl@jku.at; peter.knees@jku.at

B. McFee
Center for Data Science, New York University, New York, NY, USA
e-mail: brian.mcfee@nyu.edu

D. Bogdanov
Music Technology Group, Universitat Pompeu Fabra, Barcelona, Spain
e-mail: dmitry.bogdanov@upf.edu

M. Kaminskas
Insight Centre for Data Analytics, University College Cork, Cork, Ireland
e-mail: marius.kaminskas@insight-centre.org

F. Ricci et al. (eds.), *Recommender Systems Handbook*,
DOI 10.1007/978-1-4899-7637-6_13

item may be consumed repeatedly (even multiple times in a row), while other media items are typically consumed at most a few times. This implies that a user might not only tolerate, but actually appreciate recommendations of already known items.

On a practical level, another distinguishing property is that music can be directly addressed at different levels of abstraction. For instance, while movie recommenders typically suggest individual items to the user, music recommendation approaches may suggest groupings of items by genre, artist, or albums.

From a practitioner's perspective, we note that collaborative filtering techniques are inherently domain-agnostic, and can be easily applied to music rating data [131, 134].[1] However, in the music domain, explicit rating data is relatively rare, and even when available, tends to be sparser than in other domains [44]. Instead, implicit positive feedback is often drawn from uninterrupted (or unrejected) listening events.

Due to the sparsity of readily available user feedback data, music recommendation techniques tend to rely more upon content descriptions of items than techniques in other domains. Content-based music recommendation techniques are strongly tied to the broader field of music information retrieval (MIR), which aims at extracting semantic information from or about music at different representation levels (e.g., the audio signal, artist or song name, album cover, or score sheet).[2] Many of these approaches apply signal processing and analysis methods directly to music in order to extract musically meaningful features and in turn enable novel search and browsing interfaces. In all these scenarios, as is the case with memory-based collaborative filtering methods (see Chap. 2), the concept of similarity is central. For content-based approaches, item similarity is typically computed between item feature vectors. Section 13.2 provides an overview of content-based music recommendation techniques, including both metadata and signal analysis methods.

From the user's perspective, content can play an important role in influencing preferences for music. Studies in music psychology show that a user's short-term music preferences are influenced by various factors, such as the environment, the emotional state, or the activity of the user [97]. We elaborate on contextual music recommendation approaches in Sect. 13.3. In Sect. 13.4, we present hybrid recommendation approaches which combine collaborative filtering, content-based, and context-based methods.

Because users often listen to several songs in rapid succession—e.g., via streaming radio or a personal music device—some recommender systems have been designed specifically for serial recommendation [59]. Due to the unique

[1]We will not further detail collaborative filtering of music ratings in this chapter. To understand the principles of this technique, we refer the reader to Chap. 2.

[2]To avoid confusion, we note that *content* has different connotations within the MIR and recommender systems communities. MIR makes an explicit distinction between (content-based) approaches that operate directly on audio signals and (metadata) approaches that derive item descriptors from external sources, e.g., web documents [70]. In recommender systems research, as in the remainder of this chapter, both types of approaches are described as "content-based".

constraints and modeling assumptions of serial consumption, the evaluation criteria and algorithmic solutions diverge substantially from the more standard techniques found in the recommender systems literature. Section 13.5 provides an overview of automatic playlist generation, including algorithms and evaluation methodologies.

In Sect. 13.6, we discuss common evaluation strategies, benchmarking campaigns, and data sets used in music recommendation research. Finally, we conclude by highlighting current research challenges in Sect. 13.7.

13.2 Content-Based Music Recommendation

Content information includes any information describing music items that can be extracted from the audio signal, as well as metadata provided by external sources (e.g., web documents, discography data, or tags). In this section, we overview research on content-based approaches to music recommendation, and categorize the existing approaches with respect to the employed information sources.

13.2.1 Metadata Content

Musical metadata comes in several forms, including *manual annotations* provided by experts, *social tags* obtained from collaborative tagging services, and annotations *automatically mined from the web* using text retrieval techniques. Although some studies have demonstrated such metadata may not perform as well as collaborative filtering techniques [54], it can be used to augment or replace collaborative filtering in cold-start scenarios [19, 84].

13.2.1.1 Manual Annotations

Manual annotations include editorial metadata, such as musical genre and subgenre, record label, year and country of release, relations between artists, tracks, and albums, as well as any other associated production information. Additionally, annotations of musical properties such as tempo, mood, and instrumentation can be used to provide detailed summaries of musical content.

There is a number of online databases for editorial metadata, which are built by either music experts or moderated communities of enthusiasts. These databases ensure a certain quality of data, but impose limitations on its structure, e.g., by adhering to genre taxonomies [101]. *MusicBrainz*[3] and *Discogs*[4] provide extensive,

[3]http://www.musicbrainz.org.

[4]http://www.discogs.com.

freely available, community-built information on artists, record labels, and their releases. This information is related to the cultural context of music, but it omits annotations of detailed musical properties beyond genre and musical epoch (e.g., 90s). Although limited, editorial metadata has been used to build simple genre-based recommenders [82], to refine audio content-based methods (e.g., [18]; cf. Sect. 13.2.2), or in hybrid recommenders (e.g., [25]; cf. Sect. 13.4).

Bogdanov et al. [19] build an artist recommender exclusively using metadata from the *Discogs* database. For each artist in the database, a tag weight vector is created by propagating genre, style, record label, country, and year information for each release related to the artist. Relations between artists (aliases, membership in groups) and the role of the artist in each associated release—e.g., main artist, remixing/performing credits on a release, etc.—are taken into account. Artist similarity is measured by comparing sparse tag weight vectors, which are compressed using latent semantic analysis (LSA) [37].

Manual annotations of properties other than genre and epoch are promising, but they are more costly, and difficult to scale to large collections. *Pandora*[5] is an example of a large-scale commercial recommender system using such annotations done by experts [67]. Similarly, *AllMusic*[6] is an example of a commercial database that provides mood annotations in addition to general editorial metadata. However, relatively few academic studies incorporate these manual annotations because they are proprietary, and no public data sets of this kind (and scale) are available for researchers. Existing work therefore resorts to individual, hand-made annotations, for instance of genre, tempo, mood [105, 139], year [139], and emotion [81].

13.2.1.2 Social Tags

In contrast to structured taxonomy-driven expert annotations, information about music items can be collected from social tagging services. Social tagging services allow casual users to provide unstructured text annotations for any item. Social tags, while inherently noisy, can draw from a larger pool of annotators, and noisy annotations can be combined to derive a structured *folksonomy* of tags [135]. The *Last.fm*[7] music tagging service has gained some popularity in academic research by providing open access to an extensive collection of music tags. It includes uncategorized tags describing genres, moods, instrumentation, and locations, as well as personal associations evoked in the users by music (e.g., *favorite* or *seen live*) [58]. The tags can be easily obtained for particular artists or tracks, which can be used to assess similarity between items by comparing respective tag weight vectors [54]. Similarity comparisons can be enhanced by latent semantic analysis techniques to overcome the problem of vector sparsity [74].

---

[5] http://www.pandora.com.

[6] http://www.allmusic.com.

[7] http://www.last.fm.

13.2.1.3 Annotations by Web Content Mining

As an alternative to social tags, keyword annotations can be mined from music-related web pages using text processing techniques. Keywords can be extracted from web pages, blogs and RSS feeds related to music items, as well as lyrics databases. Schedl et al. provide an overview of text mining techniques for measuring artist similarity [123], and create a large-scale music search system which operates on an index of artist term profiles [126]. A similar approach by Barrington et al. [140] limits the keyword mining process to specific web sites with high-quality music information, such as *AllMusic*, *Wikipedia*,[8] *Amazon*,[9] *BBC*,[10] *Billboard*,[11] or *Pitchfork*.[12] An early study by Pazzani and Billsus [108] describes a recommendation approach which used a naïve Bayes classifier to predict user preferences from artist keywords extracted from web pages. Green et al. [54] retrieve keywords from *Wikipedia* artist entries and social tags from *Last.fm*. They propose to generate recommendations based on artist-to-artist similarity, or similarity between artists and a vector of keyword weights summarizing the user's favorite artists. Similarly, McFee and Lanckriet [88] combine social tags and keywords extracted from artist biographies found on *Last.fm* to predict artist similarity ratings. Celma et al. [35] extract keywords from RSS feeds related to music artists, and then generate recommendations by ranking artists by similarity to a set of preferred artists. Finally, Lim et al. [77] learn a song-level similarity function from topic models over bag-of-words representations of lyrics provided by *musiXmatch.com*.

13.2.2 Audio Content

Audio content analysis is advocated by MIR researchers as an alternative or complement to metadata and collaborative filtering methods [12, 29]. Recommender systems based on audio content are not susceptible to popularity bias, and are therefore expected to reveal the "long tail" of music consumption [31]. Music descriptors obtained by audio signal analysis can enhance music search by enabling novel ways for querying and interacting with music collections.

Audio content analysis can provide various types of information which can be incorporated in recommender systems. This information can be broadly divided into two categories: acoustic and musical features computed directly from audio, and semantic annotations inferred or predicted from these acoustic features by machine learning techniques.

---

[8]http://www.wikipedia.org.

[9]http://www.amazon.com.

[10]http://www.bbc.co.uk.

[11]http://www.billboard.com.

[12]http://www.pitchforkmedia.com.

13.2.2.1 Acoustic Features: Timbral, Temporal, and Tonal

Acoustic and musical features used by existing music recommenders include:

- *timbral* features, such as Mel-frequency cepstrum coefficients (MFCCs) [79, 82, 104, 147] and other features related to spectral shape of the signal [17, 32, 76, 92];
- *temporal* and *time-domain* features, characterizing temporal evolution of loudness and timbre [17, 76, 104, 137], rhythmic properties such as beat (tempo) histogram features [17, 55, 76] and onset rate [17, 81], average loudness and dynamics [17, 32];
- *tonal* features, such as harmonic pitch class profiles (chroma) [17, 136, 142] or similar pitch-based features [55, 76, 81], key, scale, chords distribution, and inharmonicity measures [17, 32, 81].

Timbral, temporal, and tonal information address different aspects of music, and can be combined to provide a solid foundation for recommendation algorithms. However, until recently, these different approaches were rarely integrated in academic studies.

Timbral similarity, which compares spectral shapes of the tracks, is probably the most basic and common similarity that can be applied for audio-based music recommendation. Timbre information can be represented as probability distributions of the frame-wise MFCCs, and compared using a number of distance metrics [8, 80, 141]. In particular, Logan [79] considered average, median, and minimum MFCC-based distance from tracks in a target music collection to the preferred tracks and a distance to the summarized MFCC distribution of all preferred tracks. Subjective evaluations of such MFCC-based approaches revealed only average or below-average user satisfaction [17, 82] and suggested their insufficiency compared to approaches with larger feature sets containing a combination of timbral, temporal, and tonal features [17].

Some studies implement wider varieties of acoustic features and include temporal and tonal dimensions of music, which may be complemented with metadata. Pampalk et al. [103, 104] expand timbral similarity based on MFCCs [8] with temporal information that includes fluctuation patterns and derived descriptors of distinctiveness of the fluctuations at specific frequencies and of the overall perceived tempo. Su et al. [137] proposed a music recommender that encodes the temporal evolution of timbral information as time sequences of timbre clusters. The system infers preferred and disliked sequences based on the user's previous track ratings, and matches the feature distribution of recommended tracks to the user's profile.

Celma and Herrera [32] propose an approach based on Euclidean distance, which uses timbre, dynamics, tempo, meter, rhythmic patterns, tonal strength, key, and mode information. This approach is compared to an item-based collaborative filtering distance using listening statistics from *Last.fm*. A large-scale evaluation is conducted, the results of which suggest that the collaborative filtering approach is better able to predict which tracks a user would like, but also produces recommendations which are more familiar to the user. Importantly, this study corroborates that content-based approaches can be effectively incorporated in order to increase novelty of recommendations without a devastating decrease in their quality. Interestingly, average ratings were merely satisfactory: $\approx$3.39 and $\approx$2.87 for collaborative filtering and content-based approaches, respectively, on a 1-to-5 Likert-type liking scale.

Instead of computing similarity between music items and a user profile, some authors propose discriminative models which use audio features to either classify items into *liked* and *disliked* categories or predict user ratings. For example, Grimaldi and Cunningham [55] propose a classification-based approach which uses the tracks rated by a user as *good* and *bad* examples. The authors apply k-nearest neighbors (k-NN) and feature sub-space ensemble classifiers to a set of temporal features derived from beat histograms and tonal features describing harmony. They conclude that the selected audio features are insufficient for the task, except when user preferences are strongly driven by specific genres. Moh et al. [92] propose to classify music into *liked* and *disliked* by using a variety of timbral features, including MFCCs, spectral centroid/rolloff/flux, and zero crossing rate. They evaluate several classification algorithms based on variants of support vector machines (SVMs), as well as a probabilistic Gaussian model to predict user preference.

As an alternative to binary classification, Reed and Lee [116] propose ordinal regression to predict ratings from audio features describing temporal evolution of the MFCCs within each track. Bogdanov [16] investigates the importance of various timbral, temporal, tonal, and semantic features for predicting music preferences. To this end, regression models using these features are built for each particular user in order to predict her ratings.

13.2.2.2 Automatic Semantic Annotation

Currently, collaborative filtering techniques tend to outperform approaches based purely on audio [18, 32, 132]. Audio-based methods are inherently limited in that they cannot (directly) exploit information beyond the pure signal. As a consequence, low-level acoustic descriptors may capture information which has little direct relation to user preference. It is thus desirable to use high-level abstractions or semantic concepts, such as genres, moods, or instrumentation. When these annotations are not provided by human annotators (as described in Sect. 13.2.1), machine learning techniques can be used to predict annotations from audio content.

Bridging the so-called *semantic gap* [6, 33], which arises from the weak linking between human concepts related to musical aspects and the audio-based features, is notoriously difficult. To this end, Barrington et al. [12] propose a semantic music similarity measure which is used for music recommendation. They train Gaussian mixture models (GMMs) of MFCCs for a number of semantic concepts, such as genres, moods, instrumentation, vocals, and rhythm. Thereafter, high-level descriptors are obtained by computing the probabilities of each concept on a frame basis. The resulting semantic annotations of tracks are represented as a distribution over tags, and compared in order to assess similarity. Subsequent work compares this auto-tagging approach to a similarity metric directly derived from

MFCC distributions and finds that the direct MFCC approach is more effective at predicting collaborative filtering similarity between tracks [84]. The authors attribute this finding to the effect of using a fixed set of semantic concepts, which can provide user-interpretable representations, but may prematurely discard useful information for determining similarity. Bogdanov et al. [17] propose a similarity-based recommendation approach grounded on an extensive set of over 60 timbral, temporal, and tonal features together with automatic semantic annotations by genre, mood, instrumentation, and rhythm, created by probabilistic SVMs.

13.3 Contextual Music Recommendation

The topic of context-awareness has gained popularity in recommender systems research in recent years [1] (see Chap. 6 for an extensive review). However, the idea of using context information in computing applications can be traced back to the 1990s. One of the first works in this area defined context as "*information describing where you are, whom you are with, and what resources are nearby*" [127]. In other words, context can be considered as any information that influences the interaction of the user with the system. For instance, in the domain of music recommendation, context can be the situation of the user when listening to recommended tracks (e.g., time, mood, current activity, the presence of other people). Clearly, such information may influence the user's appreciation of music and thus it could be taken into account, in addition to the more conventional knowledge of the user's long-term preferences, when providing recommendations.

Various classifications of contextual information have been proposed in the literature. Adomavicius et al. [1] distinguish between *fully observable*, *partially observable*, and *unobservable* context, where unobservable context may be modeled using latent features that influence the changes in user's short-term preferences [56]. Dey and Abowd [38] suggest distinguishing between the *primary* and *secondary* context. The primary context is defined as the user's location, identity, activity, and time. The authors argue that these four factors are the most important ones when characterizing a user's situation. The secondary context is defined as additional information which can be derived from the primary context factors. For instance, the current weather conditions may be derived from the user's location and time.

In this section, we categorize context information into two general classes—*environment-related* context, which consists of features that can be measured by sensors on the user's mobile device or obtained from external information services e.g., the user's location, current time, weather, temperature, etc., and *user-related* context, which is difficult to measure directly and represents a more high-level information about the user e.g., the user's activity, emotional state, or social environment. Similarly to the relation between primary and secondary context defined by Dey and Abowd [38], environment-related context may be used to derive the user-related context.

13.3.1 Environment-Related Context

A user's environment, such as season, temperature, time of day, noise level, weather conditions, etc., has an influence on the user's state of mind, and therefore indirectly influences her musical preferences. Research has shown that there exists a correlation between characteristics of the listening situation and the preference for music that augments these characteristics [96]. For instance, people tend to prefer different types of music in summer and in winter [109]. Consequently, it may be beneficial to consider environment-related context attributes when recommending music content. Such attributes used in music recommendation research can be classified into the following groups:

- *Location* of the user can be represented by a ZIP code, geographical coordinates, type of landscape (e.g., city, nature), nearby monuments, buildings, landmarks, etc. The surroundings of the user may have a strong impact on her perception and preferences of music. The US music duo Bluebrain is the first band to record a location-aware album.[13] In 2011, the band released two such albums—one dedicated to Washington's park National Mall, and the second dedicated to New York's Central Park. Both albums were released as iPhone apps, with music tracks pre-recorded for specific zones in the parks. As the listener moves through the landscape, the tracks change through smooth transitions, providing a soundtrack to the walk. Despite the large potential of location-aware music services, up to date there has been little research exploring location-related context information in music recommendations.
- *Time* information may refer to the time of day (typically categorized into morning, afternoon, evening, night), or day of week (can be represented by the exact day or can be categorized into working day, weekend). This kind of information is potentially useful since studies have shown that user's music preferences differ depending on the day of the week or moment of the day [60].
- *Weather* information may refer to weather conditions (typically categorized into sunny, overcast, rainy, etc.), to the temperature (e.g., cold, moderate, hot), or to the season. Such information is relevant for music recommendation since the user's music preferences may significantly differ, e.g., in a cold rainy autumn or a hot sunny midsummer [109].
- *Other factors* such as information about the traffic conditions, the noise level, or the amount of ambient light may contribute to the user's state of mind and therefore indirectly influence her music preferences.

One of the first music recommenders to exploit environment-related context was described by Reddy and Mascia [115]. The authors used information about the user's location (represented by a ZIP code), time of day (morning, afternoon, evening, night), day of week, noise level (calm, moderate, chaotic), temperature

[13]http://bluebrainmusic.blogspot.com/.

(frigid, cold, moderate, warm, hot), and weather (rainy, snow, haze, cloudy, sunny, clear). The described system is capable of recommending songs from the user's music library which have to be tagged using a controlled tag vocabulary, where the tags directly represent the values of context attributes. For instance, to recommend a song for a particular location, it has to be tagged with the appropriate ZIP code.

Ankolekar and Sandholm [5] presented a mobile audio application, *Foxtrot*, that allows its users to explicitly assign audio content to a particular location. The authors stressed the importance of the emotional link between music and location. According to the authors, the primary goal of their system is to "*enhance the sense of being in a place*" by creating its emotional atmosphere. *Foxtrot* relies on crowd-sourcing—the users of *Foxtrot* are allowed to assign audio pieces (either a music track or a sound clip) to specific locations (represented by the geographical coordinates of the user's current location), and also specify the visibility range of the audio track—a circular area within which the track is relevant. The system is then able to provide a stream of location-aware audio content to the users.

Braunhofer et al. [24] explored the possibilities to adapt music to the places of interest (POIs) that the user is visiting. This idea is based on the hypothesis that a fitting music track may enhance the sightseeing experience of the user. For instance, during a visit to a Baroque cathedral a user might enjoy hearing a composition by Bach, while the narrow streets in Venice offer a good surrounding to listen to a Vivaldi's concerto. The matching of music and POIs was made by representing both music tracks and POIs with a common set of emotion tags, motivated by music perception research [148]. In a related research, Fernández-Tobías et al. [47] have developed a technique to recommend music content related to POIs using explicit knowledge about musicians and POIs extracted from *DBpedia*[14] [9]. The tag-based [24] and knowledge-based [47] techniques have been combined and evaluated in a web-based user study [68].

Okada et al. [98] describe a mobile music recommender and define context as "*a finite set of sensed conditions collected from a mobile device*", in other words, the authors focus on environment-related context information: ambient noise, location (represented by geographical coordinates), time of day, and day of week. The authors do not provide a detailed technical description of the recommendation algorithm (i.e., how exactly context is used to select music), but rather focus on the architectural design and usability principles of a context-aware mobile music recommender. The authors describe a user study which shows an overall positive evaluation of the system. However, user feedback suggests the need for explanations of the recommendations and more control over the played songs. This leads to an important research question—how to integrate the features of a regular music player and a context-aware recommender.

[14]http://www.dbpedia.org.

13.3.2 User-Related Context

Any contextual information related to the user may be important when recommending music, since music preferences are linked to people's activities, emotions, or social background. Schäfer and Sedlmeier [118] observe different uses of music to serve listeners' needs, such as the ones related to cognitive, emotional, socio-cultural, and physiological functions. The user-related context used in music recommendation research can be classified into the following groups:

- *Activity* information includes an action, typically represented as an element from the set of possible actions (e.g., walking, running, driving), or a numerical attribute defining the user's state (e.g., walking pace or heart rate). This type of context has been shown to have an impact on the user's musical preferences. Foley [52] has shown that people prefer different musical tempo depending on their occupation. North and Hargreaves [97] related personality traits and social lifestyles to music preferences.
- *Emotional state* or mood has a direct influence on the user's music preferences. For example, a user may wish to listen to different types of music when in a sad mood compared to when being happy. Research has shown that music can be used both to moderate the user's emotional condition [72, 118] and to augment the emotions perceived by the listener [96].
- *Social context* information, i.e., the presence of other people, may influence user's music preferences. For instance, people may choose music taking into account the preferences of their companions. Several works have addressed the issue of generating music playlists for groups of users [10, 113]. Mesnage [90] exploited user relations in social networks for music discovery.
- *Cultural context* is closely related to environment-related context (location), however, it defines a more high-level information, e.g., the user's cultural background or belonging to an ethnic group. Koenigstein et al. [71] have exploited the activity of US-based users in peer-to-peer networks to predict the popularity of music tracks in US song charts. Schedl [121] used geo-tagged tweets to extract location-based music listening trends and in turn build a location-aware recommender system.

Compared to the environment-related context, user-related context is difficult to measure directly using mobile sensors or external information services. However, it can be derived to some extent from the environment-related context attributes. For instance, such context attributes as the time of day, ambient noise level, temperature, weather, etc., were used in Bayesian classifiers to predict the user's emotional state [105] or activity [142].

Emotional state of the user is a particularly popular type of context information, which can be exploited to create emotion-based music recommenders, such as *Musicovery*.[15] In addition to adapting music to the user's mood, emotions have been used

[15] http://www.musicovery.com.

to match music with other types of content that can cause an emotional response in users, e.g., text or images [28, 75, 136]. Emotion-based music recommendation is becoming an increasingly popular topic, largely due to advances in automatic music emotion recognition [146].

13.3.3 Incorporating Context Information in Music Recommender Systems

Having described the main types of context information exploited in music recommender systems, we now turn to the major challenge of designing a context-aware recommender—incorporating context information in the recommendation algorithm. Chapter 6 provides a detailed discussion on the paradigms for incorporating context in recommender systems. We therefore refer the reader to the aforementioned chapter for an in-depth discussion on this topic, and here provide only a brief overview of techniques for exploiting context in music recommenders.

Context is known to have an effect on user preferences and information needs [1]. To exploit this information when recommending music, one must establish a degree of relevance between a music track and the contextual information. This information may be obtained on a per user level, e.g., by having users rate music in a particular situation defined by the context attributes, or it can be established globally, by obtaining a relatedness score between a music track and a context attribute. The relevance of particular contextual attributes for music tracks can then be exploited in a recommendation algorithm.

We define four types of approaches to establish a degree of relevance between a music piece and contextual information, as shown in Fig. 13.1:

1. Rating music in context [11, 105] is an extension of the classical collaborative filtering approach. While suffering from the cold-start problem, this is still the state of the art when designing context-aware recommender systems [1].
2. Mapping low-level music features to context attributes [142] is an approach based on machine learning techniques and is closely related to music information retrieval [30] since it involves audio signal analysis. This approach needs training data of music labeled with appropriate context values.
3. Direct labeling of music with context attributes [5, 115] is the most straightforward approach, whose main disadvantage is the high effort required to label music tracks, similarly to rating music in context.
4. Predicting an intermediate context, such as the user's activity [142] or emotional state [24, 105]. This type of approach incorporates the aforementioned techniques—rating in context [105], mapping low-level music features to context [68, 142], or manual labeling of music with context attributes [24].

In summary, context represents an important source of information which can be combined with other sources, such as music content features or user ratings, to provide highly personalized and adaptive music services. Recommender systems

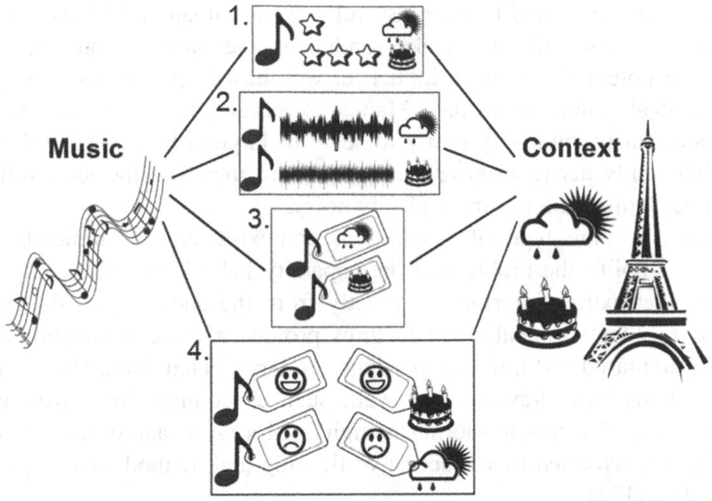

Fig. 13.1 The different types of approaches to establish the relevance of contextual attributes for music

that combine these different sources of information are called hybrid systems. In the next section, we provide a detailed description of hybrid music recommendation and give more details on works that incorporate context information into recommendation algorithms.

13.4 Hybrid Music Recommendation

Since music preference is a complex and multi-faceted concept, it is a logical step to incorporate multiple aspects of musical similarity into recommendation. In the preceding sections, we have discussed different approaches to describe the contents of music and to exploit the context of music consumption. In this section, we discuss hybrid music recommenders, i.e., systems that *"combine two or more recommendation techniques to gain better performance with fewer of the drawbacks of any individual one"* [26]. Before reviewing approaches that integrate different sources, let us briefly reconsider properties of the individual sources used for music recommendation and the entailed advantages and disadvantages.

Like in every other domain, recommendation approaches built upon implicit or explicit user feedback have to deal with the common problems of data sparsity and in particular the cold-start problem. To some extent, this is the same with content-based approaches that rely on external sources for item description. Regardless of whether the content source is editorial metadata, text from the web, or social tags, one or more humans must first create the underlying data. Thus, both of these approaches also exhibit popularity biases in that wider-known items are more likely to have information related to them. By relying on human-crafted data, metadata methods are also susceptible to attacks, vandalism, and manipulation [34, 91]. Even putting aside potential malicious influence, web-based approaches must contend with a great deal of noise in the data. Manual expert annotations, on the other hand, are accurate, but prohibitively costly to scale to large collections [138]. Context features inherently derive from end-users, and are therefore the most difficult to obtain (in academic settings) and typically noisy.

Depending on the type of integration, context-aware recommendation can additionally amplify the problem of data sparsity [1]. Conversely, content-based approaches that extract information directly from the audio signal do not suffer from these problems. Signal-based features provide a static description that can be used for unbiased and time-independent similarity calculation. However, audio content methods have drawbacks as well, such as computational overhead and the requirement of access to the music signal. Moreover, audio content methods are usually outperformed by collaborative filtering and methods that exploit user-generated data [132].

In general, any combination of two or more approaches can be considered a hybrid. For instance, in Sect. 13.2, we described work that combines different types of content-based recommendation. Other approaches combine different aspects of collaborative filtering, such as the *Auralist* framework, which aims at improving user satisfaction by providing diverse and novel recommendations [149]. In the remainder of this section, we focus on work that combines different techniques and information from different sources.

13.4.1 Combining Content with Context Descriptors

To date, there are relatively few methods which combine music content and user context. Schedl [120] presents the *Mobile Music Genius* (MMG) player, which gathers a wide range of user-context attributes during music playback, e.g., time, location, weather, device- and phone-related features (music volume), tasks (running on the device), network, ambient (light, proximity, pressure, noise), motion (accelerometers, orientation), and player-related features (repeat, shuffle, sound effects). MMG then learns relations (using a C4.5 decision tree learner) between these $\sim$100-dimensional feature vectors and metadata (genre, artist, and track are considered), and uses these learned relations to adapt the playlist on the fly when the user's context changes by a certain amount.

Elliott and Tomlinson [45] focus on the particular activities of walking and running. The authors present a system that adapts music to the user's pace by matching the beats per minute of music tracks with the user's steps per minute. Additionally, the system uses implicit feedback by estimating the likelihood of a song being played based on the number of times the user has previously skipped the song. In similar research, de Oliveira and Oliver [99] compare the user's heart rate and steps per minute with music tempo to moderate the intensity of a workout.

Park et al. [105] model a number of context attributes—temperature, humidity, noise, light level, weather, season, and time of day—with Bayesian networks to infer the emotional state of the user: depressing, content, exuberant, or anxious/frantic. The music tracks used in the described system are represented by genre, tempo, and mood attributes. In order to recommend music for the emotional states, users must explicitly express their preferences for each music attribute in every emotional state using a 5-point rating scale. For instance, a user may state that she prefers rock music with a preference rating of 4 in a depressing state, 3 in a content state, and 2 in an exuberant state.

More recently, Wang et al. [142] described a mobile music recommender where the time of day, accelerometer data, and ambient noise are used to predict the user's activity—running, walking, sleeping, working, or shopping. To recommend music for the user's activity context, music tracks had to be labeled with the appropriate activity labels. The authors use a data set of 1200 songs manually labeled with activity values and represented by low-level audio feature vectors for training an auto-tagging algorithm [13].

13.4.2 Combining Collaborative Filtering with Content Descriptors

Collaborative filtering and content descriptors, in particular those extracted from the audio signal, exhibit complementary features. A combination of the two is expected to improve recommendation quality for the following reasons, cf. [26, 27, 31, 41]:

- *Avoiding cold-start problems*: While new items are lacking preference data, audio content analysis and comparison to all existing items can be performed instantly. Thus, when no user feedback is available, a hybrid system could resort to audio similarity for recommendation.
- *Avoiding popularity biases*: Preference data, as well as content metadata, may be focused on popular items only, whereas audio-based information is available uniformly. Including objective content descriptors can remove recommendation biases.
- *Increasing novelty and diversity*: Popularity biases can result in a limited range of recommended items, whereas audio-based approaches are agnostic to whether music is a hit or from the long tail. Therefore, new and lesser known items are more likely to be recommended when both sources are exploited.
- *Combining information on usage with musical knowledge*: Recommendation in the multi-faceted domain of music should benefit from the incorporation of sources reflecting different aspects of music perception.

A straightforward approach to incorporating both preference and content information is to create independent recommenders and combine their outputs using a meta-classifier (*ensemble learning*). Following this direction, Tiemann and Pauws [139] implement an item-based collaborative filtering recommender as well as a content-based recommender that integrates timbre, tempo, genre, mood, and release year features. Both recommenders predict ratings as weighted combinations of the most similar items' ratings. For the final rating prediction, the feature vectors constructed from the individual recommenders' predictions are compared to the output vectors from the learning phase using Euclidean distance and the rating of the most similar vector is predicted. The idea of *fusing outputs* of multiple recommenders is also applied by Lu and Tseng [81], who combine three rankings, namely a ranking according to content similarity based on features extracted from the musical score, a ranking according to user-based collaborative filtering over a data set of user surveys, and an emotion-based ranking in accordance with manual emotion annotations by an expert. In the combination step, a personalization component is introduced. This component reweights the individual rankings according to user feedback gathered in an initial survey in which users specified preference assessments (likes/dislikes) and the underlying reasons (such as preference by tonality, rhythm, etc.) for a sample of tracks.

Instead of fusing multiple outputs in a late stage, preference and content can be *integrated earlier*, for instance to generate a new set of multi-modal features or to adapt similarity measures. The challenge is to combine sources in a manner that avoids the individual drawbacks rather than propagating them. For instance, a simple feature concatenation or unsupervised linear combination can easily preserve the data sparsity problems of preference-based approaches [130].

McFee et al. [84] optimize a content-based similarity metric by learning from a sample of collaborative data. First, a codebook representation of delta-MFCCs is learned to represent songs as a histogram over the derived codewords. Applying metric learning to rank, the resulting feature space is optimized to reflect item similarity according to implicit feedback, i.e., listening histories of users. This allows to find similar items even for novel and unpopular items based on audio content, while maintaining high recommendation accuracy resulting from feedback data.

Van den Oord et al. [100] follow this general direction, but exploit latent space descriptions of both audio features and implicit feedback (song play counts). First, a weighted matrix factorization algorithm [62] is used to learn latent factor representations of users and songs from usage data. Second, log-compressed Mel-spectrograms of randomly sampled 3-second-windows from the songs are presented to a convolutional neural network [61], preserving temporal relations in music to some extent. Here, the latent factor vectors obtained from the weighted matrix factorization step serve as ground truth to train the network. It is shown that this latent factor modeling of audio optimized for latent factor information on usage outperforms traditional MFCC-based vector quantization methods using linear regression or a multi-layer perceptron for latent factor prediction, as well as the metric learning to rank method by McFee et al.

For integrating heterogeneous data into a single, unified, multi-modal similarity space, McFee and Lanckriet [88] propose a multiple kernel learning technique. They demonstrate the applicability of their technique on a music similarity task on the artist level by including five data sources representing different aspects of an artist, namely artist timbre (modeled over all delta-MFCCs extracted from all songs by the artist), auto-tags, social tags, biographical text, and collaborative filtering data. Comparing the unified similarity space with individual similarity spaces (and partial combinations) against a human-annotated ground truth shows that the multiple kernel learning technique outperforms an unweighted combination of individual kernels. It can also be seen that the timbre similarity performs poorly (potentially since it is originally targeting the song level rather that the artist level) and that social tags contribute the most valuable information.

Another group of hybrid music recommenders combines user feedback and content information by means of a *probabilistic framework*. Li et al. [76] propose a probabilistic model in which music tracks are pre-classified into groups by means of both audio content (timbral, temporal, and tonal features) and user ratings. Predictions are made for users considering the Gaussian distribution of user ratings given the probability that a user belongs to a group Yoshii et al. [147] propose a hybrid probabilistic model, in which each music track is represented as a vector of weights of timbres (a "bag-of-timbres"), i.e., as a GMM over MFCCs. Each Gaussian corresponds to a single timbre. The Gaussian components are chosen universally across tracks, being predefined on a certain music collection. Ratings and "bags-of-timbres" are associated with latent variables, conceptually corresponding to genres, and music preferences of a particular listener can be represented in terms of proportions of the genres. A three-way aspect model (a Bayes network) is proposed for this mapping, with the idea that a user stochastically chooses a genre according to her/his preference, and then the genre stochastically "generates" pieces and timbres.

Several approaches follow a *graph-based interpretation* of musical relations to integrate different sources. In the resulting models, the vertices correspond to the songs, and the edge weights correspond to the degree of similarity. Shao et al. [130] build such a model upon a hybrid similarity measure that automatically re-weights a variety of audio descriptors in order to optimally reflect user preference. On the resulting song graph, rating prediction is treated as an iterative propagation of ratings from rated data to unrated data.

Multiple dimensions of similarity can be expressed simultaneously using a *hypergraph*—a generalization in which "hyperedges" can connect arbitrary subsets of vertices. Bu et al. [25] compute a hybrid distance from a hypergraph which contains MFCC-based similarities between tracks, user similarities according to collaborative filtering of listening behavior from *Last.fm*, and similarities on the graph of *Last.fm* users, groups, tags, tracks, albums, and artists, i.e., all possible interactions that can be crawled from *Last.fm*. The proposed approach is compared with user-based collaborative filtering, a content-based timbral approach, and their hybrid combination, on a listening behavior data set. Again, the performance of a timbral approach fell behind the ones working with collaborative filtering, while incorporation of all types of information showed the best results.

McFee and Lanckriet [87] build a hypergraph on a wide range of music descriptors to model and, subsequently, generate playlists by performing random walks on the hypergraph (cf. Sect. 13.5). Hypergraph edges are defined to reflect subsets of songs that are similar in some respect. The different modes of similarity are derived from the *Million Song Dataset* (MSD, cf. Sect. 13.6.3), and include:

- *Collaborative filtering similarity*: connects all songs via an edge that are assigned to the same cluster after k-means clustering for $k = \{16, 64, 256\}$ on a low-rank factorization of the user-song matrix;
- *Low-level acoustic similarity*: connects all songs assigned to the same cluster after k-means clustering for $k = \{16, 64, 256\}$ on audio features;
- *Musical era*: connects songs from the same year or same decade;
- *Familiarity*: connects songs with the same level of popularity (expressed in the categories low, medium, and high);
- *Lyrics*: connects songs assigned to the same topic derived via latent Dirichlet allocation (LDA) [15];
- *Social tags*: connects songs assigned to the same *Last.fm* tag;
- *Pairwise feature conjunctions*: creates a category for any pairwise intersection of the described features and connects songs that match both;
- *Uniform shuffle*: an edge connecting all songs in case no other transition is possible.

The weights of the hypergraph are learned using the *AotM-2011* data set, a collection of over 100,000 unique playlists crawled from *Art of the Mix*[16] (cf. Sect. 13.6.6). In addition to playlist information, this data set also contains a timestamp and a categorical label, such as *romantic* or *reggae*, for each playlist. Experiments on a global hypergraph with weights learned from all playlists and on category-specific hypergraphs trained only on the corresponding subsets of playlists show that performance can be improved when treating specific categories individually ("playlist dialects"). In terms of features, again, social tags have the most significant impact on the overall model, however audio features are more relevant for specific categories such as *hip hop*, *jazz*, and *blues*, whereas lyrics features receive stronger weights for categories like *folk* and *narrative*.

The category labels of the *AotM-2011* data set exhibit further interesting aspects. While most labels refer to genre categories, some refer to a usage scenario or the *user-related context* of a playlist. We discuss these aspects next.

13.4.3 Combining Collaborative Filtering with Context Descriptors

In this section, we review hybrid approaches that incorporate models of user preference and user-related context. As discussed in the previous section, the method proposed by McFee and Lanckriet [87] uses different recommenders for

[16]http://www.artofthemix.org.

different categories, some of which refer to a user's activity (*road trip*, *sleep*), emotional state (*depression*), or social situation (*break up*). The results indicate that the influence of different aspects of musical content can vary dramatically, depending on contextual factors.

The approach by Baltrunas et al. [11] to recommend driving music takes advantage of ratings specifically assigned to each contextual condition (*context-aware collaborative filtering* [1], cf. Sect. 13.3.2). For incorporating environmental (such as *traffic* and *weather*) and user-related factors (such as *mood* and *sleepiness*) into rating prediction, they extend a matrix factorization approach to collaborative filtering by introducing one additional parameter for each pair-wise combination of contextual condition and musical genre to the model. The parameters of the model are then learned using stochastic gradient descent. It is shown that mean absolute error (MAE) decreases when incorporating contextual factors.

Typically, the user-related context is not explicitly available in the observed data. In such cases, hidden context can be modeled by latent factor techniques. Hariri et al. [56] propose a method to apply sequential pattern mining on an LDA model of playlists from *Art of the Mix*, in which songs are represented by social tags from *Last.fm*. While the LDA topics should reflect the contextual factors affecting listening preference—e.g., mood or social setting—sequential pattern mining should capture changes in context over time. Predictions of the listener's current context then provide the additional information to build a context-aware music recommender. Hariri et al. show that the LDA-based context-aware recommender significantly outperforms a simple metadata-based recommendation approach.

Taking a similar approach, Zheleva et al. [150] also apply LDA to a set of listening histories extracted from usage logs of the *Zune Social* platform[17] over a period of 14 weeks. They compare two approaches. The first, called *taste model*, is a direct application of the LDA method developed for text collections and thus refers to overall factors of listening preference. The second, called *session model*, incorporates additional information about listening sessions and aims at capturing latent factors related to mood in a more consistent listening context. Evaluation of the approaches is carried out on the genre level, i.e., instead of predicting individual songs or specific artists, a recommendation consists of a distribution of genres. Furthermore, the discovered taste topics are compared to genres within the two-leveled *Zune Social* genre taxonomy. Evaluation indicates that the context-aware session model is more effective than the time-agnostic taste model. Yang et al. [145] investigate "local preferences," i.e., temporal aspects on a smaller and more consistent time scale. These preferences reflect changes in listening behavior that are strongly influenced by the listening context and occurring events rather than caused by a gradual change in general taste.

The impact of the *temporal context* is not limited to listening sessions. Temporal information is also helpful for modeling long-term patterns in listening behavior

[17]http://zune.net; now *Xbox Music*.

and song life cycles. Dror et al. [43] show that matrix factorization models for music rating prediction can successfully incorporate additional information such as temporal dynamics in listening behavior, temporal dynamics in item histories, and multi-level taxonomy information like genre. Aizenberg et al. [3] apply collaborative filtering methods to the playlists of radio stations associated with the web radio station directory *ShoutCast*.[18] Their goals include prediction of existing radio station programs, as well as predicting the programs of new radio stations. To this end, they model latent factor station affinities as well as temporal effects. We discuss the specifics of sequential recommendation in greater detail in the next section.

13.5 Automatic Playlist Generation

One of the key distinguishing features of music, as compared to other item domains such as books or movies, is that recommendations are often consumed in rapid succession during a listening session. Rather than selecting each song individually, a sequence of songs—a *playlist*—can be automatically generated, and the user would consume the sequence much as if it was a traditional radio broadcast. Automatic playlist generation thus forms a critical component of personalized streaming radio services and portable music devices.

Because the user does not explicitly select or provide feedback for each song in a playlist, the modeling assumptions and evaluation criteria can differ from those of traditional recommender systems (Sect. 8). In this section, we survey evaluation methodologies and algorithmic approaches for automatic playlist generation.

13.5.1 Parallel and Serial Consumption

In most typical recommendation models, the user is first provided with a set of candidate items from which to choose, for example, a page of movie recommendations. The user may then inspect each candidate item before making a selection: in effect, the user can access the candidate recommendations in *parallel*. The selection process may be assisted by presenting the user with a brief summary of each item, such as a star rating, plot synopsis, or capsule review. This approach works well for browsing scenarios in which the user is actively engaged and selecting each item individually.

Unlike browsing a collection, playlist consumption is an inherently *serial* process: only one song is consumed at a time, and the user does not select from a set of alternatives. Typical playlist consumption interfaces mimic conventional

[18]http://www.shoutcast.com.

radio or personal music devices, potentially augmented with a limited set of familiar controls, such as *skip*, *stop*, or *pause*. Because the mode of consumption differs from that of browsing, the semantics and availability of user feedback differ as well. The semantics of explicit per-song feedback are straightforward, but events may be rare due to user disengagement (passive consumption) or fatigue due to consuming a large number of songs in rapid succession.

Implicit feedback can be somewhat more problematic. If a song plays to completion, it may be interpreted as implicit positive feedback, but it is also possible that the user has become disengaged—e.g., by reducing the volume or wandering away—and there is often no way to infer this behavior directly. Negative feedback, on the other hand, must derive from an explicit user action, such as clicking a "stop" or "skip" button [64, 104]. However, as noted by Bosteels et al. [23], great care must be taken when inferring intent from a user's intent action: the user may in fact dislike the recommended song, or she may simply not wish to hear it at that moment due to otherwise obscure contextual factors.

13.5.2 Playlist Evaluation

Sequential playlist consumption differs from traditional recommender system and information retrieval settings, and consequently, several methods have been proposed to evaluate playlist generation algorithms. Because the choice of evaluation criteria influences algorithm design, we first provide a survey of evaluation techniques. At a high level, these techniques fall into four categories which we survey in this section: user studies, semantic cohesion, partial playlist prediction, and generative likelihood.

13.5.2.1 User Studies

Early approaches to evaluating automatic playlist generation systems relied upon user studies. For example, Pauws and Eggen [106] conducted a study in which users were asked to provide a *seed song* in response to a pre-selected contextual query (e.g., *lively music*), which was then used to seed a playlist generation algorithm. Each user then rated the resulting playlist on a scale of 1–10. Later studies followed this general approach by soliciting users for ratings of playlist consistency [111] and similarity to the seed song [20]. Alternatively, Barrington et al. [12] conducted a survey in which users were provided with a seed song and playlists generated by two competing systems, and asked for relative preference of one playlist or the other.

While user studies provide high-quality information, they are notoriously difficult to reproduce, and they do not provide a viable means of automatically evaluating algorithms in a laboratory setting. User evaluation is also difficult to scale to large collections, as the search space of playlists grows exponentially with the number of songs in the collection.

13.5.2.2 Semantic Cohesion

A commonly used alternative to user-centric evaluation is to measure some notion of cohesion over the songs within a playlist. This general strategy is usually applied to song-level metadata, for example, by counting the fraction of songs in the playlist by the same artist [78], or measuring the entropy of the playlist's genre distribution [42, 69, 111]. In cohesion-based playlist evaluation, the metadata in question is obscured from the playlist generation algorithm.

The main drawback of cohesion-based evaluation is that it is essentially user-agnostic, so one cannot directly conclude that an algorithm which produces cohesive playlists will also produce satisfactory recommendations to users. On the contrary, a study conducted by Slaney and White [133] provides evidence that users prefer some degree of diversity in playlists.

13.5.2.3 Partial Playlist Prediction

Rather than evaluate each automatically generated playlist, some authors have evaluated their algorithm's ability to predict the hidden songs in pre-existing playlists from a partial observation. Platt et al. [110] gather a collection of user-generated playlists over a fixed library of songs. For each playlist in the collection, the algorithm is given as input a partial observation of the constituent songs, and as output, produces a ranking over the remaining songs in the library. The algorithm is then evaluated according to the position within the predicted ranking of the remaining songs in the playlist.

Maillet et al. [83] conduct a similar experiment, in which playlists are collected by mining the playback logs of terrestrial broadcast radio stations. Their evaluation methodology is similar to that of Platt et al., except that the partial observations are restricted to immediately preceding song(s), rather than arbitrary partial observations.

Partial prediction evaluation is similar to ranking-based evaluations commonly used in general implicit-feedback collaborative filtering problems [63, 117]. One key distinction, however, is that associations are measured between playlists and songs, not users and songs. Because playlists tend to be much shorter than a user's full listening history, the associations tend to be sparse when compared to a full collaborative filter (see Fig. 13.2). As noted by Platt et al., the sparsity of observations, coupled with the general lack of strong negative feedback, tends to result in an overly pessimistic evaluation [110].

13.5.2.4 Generative Likelihood

The final approach to playlist evaluation is borrowed from the statistical natural language processing community. McFee and Lanckriet [86] argue that because many practical playlist generation algorithms are stochastic, they induce probability

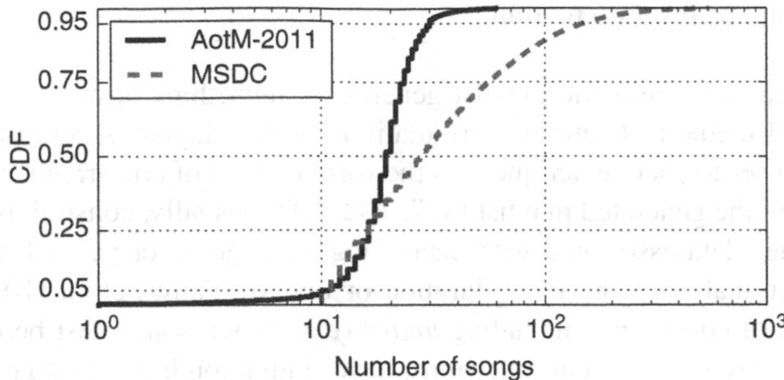

Fig. 13.2 The empirical cumulative distribution function (CDF) of the number of songs in user-generated playlists (*solid line*), and in a user's listening history (*dashed line*). Playlists were gathered from the *Art of the Mix* (AotM-2011) corpus, which includes approximately 10^5 unique playlists [87]. Listening histories were gathered from the *Million Song Dataset Challenge* (MSDC) training set, which contains listening histories for approximately 10^6 users [85]. Ninety-five percent of playlists contain 30 or fewer songs, indicating a high degree of sparsity in the observations. Note that these sets do not span the same user base

distributions over playlists. The induced distribution can thus be interpreted as model of the data (sample playlists), and evaluated in a similar fashion to a natural language model. Concretely, the algorithm is scored according to the likelihood of a test collection of playlists under its corresponding distribution.

In practice, the generative likelihood approach requires a large test corpus of sample playlists. Test corpora can be formed from user-constructed playlists [86, 87], or broadcast or streaming radio logs [93, 94]. However, when evaluating on historical data, rather than intentionally constructed playlists, one must be aware that the data itself may have been generated by an automated process.

The generative likelihood approach only applies to algorithms for which a sample playlist's likelihood can be computed. While this includes broad families of algorithms, such as Markov processes [86], it rules out direct comparisons to deterministic algorithms and black-box methods, e.g., existing streaming radio services. However, the generative likelihood approach does provide a consistent evaluation framework, and a meaningful objective function for designing and optimizing playlist generation algorithms.

13.5.3 Playlist Generation Algorithms

A wide range of algorithmic techniques have been proposed for automatic playlist generation. Most techniques fall into one of three categories, which we survey here. *Constraint satisfaction* methods attempt to construct a playlist which satisfies some user-specified search criteria. *Similarity heuristic* methods build playlists by finding songs which are in some way similar to a query or seed song. Finally, *machine learning* approaches can be used to optimize model parameters over a training set of example playlists.

13.5.3.1 Constraint Satisfaction

Early research into automatic playlist generation algorithms primarily focused on combinatorial methods. Common formulations of the playlist generation problem required the user to encode her query in the form of a set of constraints which must be satisfied by the generated playlist [4, 7, 102, 107]. Usually, constraints would be applied to metadata associated with each song (e.g., genre or year of release), or audio content analysis (e.g., track duration or tempo). Pauws et al. [107] identify several types of constraints, including *unary* (e.g., "each song must be of the *jazz* genre"), *binary* (e.g., "adjacent songs must have similar loudness"), and *global* (e.g., "total duration less than 60 minutes").

Research on constraint-based playlist generation has tailed off in recent years due to several practical limitations. First, constraint satisfaction problems tend to be computationally intractable even for relatively small personal collections, making them unattractive for large-scale applications [7]. Second, because constraint satisfaction is a feasibility problem, and not an optimization problem, there is no explicit notion of *preference* between two satisfactory playlists. Consequently, it may take multiple interactive refinements before the user is satisfied with the recommendations [106]. Finally, constraint generation can be a difficult task for users who may lack the technical sophistication to clearly express their preferences. However, it should be noted that constraint satisfaction forms a necessary component of automatic playlist generators for broadcast radio and streaming services, which may be required by law to conform to certain regulations [48, Sect. 2.7.3].

13.5.3.2 Similarity Heuristics

As an alternative to the query-by-constraint formulations described above, several researchers have proposed methods which allow the user to formulate a query in the form of one or more *seed songs*. Playlists may then be composed by selecting songs which are in some way similar to the seed.

The underlying notion of similarity between songs ultimately determines the song selection, and many different approaches have been proposed in the literature. Most commonly, song similarity is determined by acoustic content features, such as MFCCs, rhythmic descriptors, or automatic semantic annotations [12, 20, 42, 51, 78, 104, 112]. Alternative methods of computing similarity between songs include metadata (e.g., genre or mood) [110], proximity of artists in a social network [49], or textual similarity extracted from web documents [69].

Given one or more seed songs and a song-level similarity function, several methods have been proposed to generate a playlist. In the simplest form, the playlist is constructed by ranking songs by similarity to the seed(s) [12, 78, 110]. More sophisticated approaches construct a graph over songs, and use path-finding algorithms to navigate between seeds, such as shortest path [51], network flow [49], and traveling salesman [69, 112].

13.5.3.3 Machine Learning Approaches

In each of the similarity-based examples above, the notion of similarity between songs is fixed a priori, and is not informed by user activity. However, most recent techniques use some form of machine learning to optimize model parameters from a training set of playlists.

The algorithm proposed by Ragno et al. [114] generates playlists by performing random walks on an undirected graph where edge weights are determined by co-occurrence of songs within training playlists. By relying strictly on playlist co-occurrence, the algorithm is implicitly constrained to only reproduce previously observed sequences. Other authors proposed methods which incorporate tag-based similarity [23], latent topic assignment sequences [56], or combine popularity with artist-level co-occurrence [22] to allow the algorithm to generalize and produce novel sequences.

The above methods use co-occurrence frequency counts to inform song selection, but they are not explicitly optimized for playlist prediction. Maillet et al. [83] propose a method to train a classifier to predict from acoustic features whether an ordered pair of songs form a bigram in observed playlists. By keeping the first song fixed, the classifier's output can be used to induce a ranking over the remaining songs in the library, from which the next song is selected. The proposed method also incorporates direct user feedback by using a weighted tag cloud to reorder the candidate selections. Because the method uses a discriminative classifier, the authors synthesized "negative" training example bigrams by random sampling.

Recently, generative modeling has emerged as a versatile framework for developing playlist generation algorithms. In this view, playlists are generated by sampling sequences from a probability distribution whose parameters are fit to a training sample. This approach lends itself well to generative likelihood evaluation (Sect. 13.5.2.4), as the training and testing criteria match exactly. Existing models in the literature exhibit a range of scale and complexity, including latent topic models [150], low-dimensional song embedding [93], co-embedding of songs and users [94], Markov chain mixtures [86], and cross-modal feature integration [87].

13.6 Data Sets and Evaluation

In this section, we give an overview of frequently used data sets and prominent evaluation campaigns in MIR and music recommendation. In cases where data sets were specifically created for the purpose of running an evaluation campaign we discuss them together.

A comparative overview of data sets is given in Tables 13.1 and 13.2. The former lists statistics of the data sets and the type(s) of editorial metadata included, while the latter details the kind of data that is provided. Note that the statistics in Table 13.1 only indicate figures of the data sets that are publicly available for the individual types of items. The last column "Ratings/Evts." refers to explicit (ratings) or implicit

Table 13.1 Statistics of public data sets for music recommendation research

Data set/items	Songs	Albums	Artists	Users	Ratings/evts.
Yahoo! Music [44]	—— 624,961 in total ——			1,000,990	262,810,175
MSD [14]	1,000,000			1,019,318	48,373,586
Last.fm—360K [31]			186,642	359,347	
Last.fm—1K [31]			107,528	992	19,150,868
MusicMicro [121]	71,410		19,529	136,866	594,306
MMTD [57]	133,968		25,060	215,375	1,086,808
AotM-2011 [87]	98,359		17,332	16,204	859,449

Table 13.2 Features of public data sets for music recommendation research

Data set	Feedback type	Audio files	Item content	User context
Yahoo! Music [44]	Ratings	✗	✗	✗
MSD [14]	Listening events, tags	✗	✓	✗
Last.fm—360K [31]	listening events	✗	✓	✗
Last.fm—1K [31]	Listening events	✗	✓	✓
MusicMicro [121]	Listening events	✗	✓	✓
MMTD [57]	Listening events	✗	✓	✓
AotM-2011 [87]	Playlists	✗	✓	Partial

(listening events) preference indications.[19] In Table 13.2, the column "Feedback type" refers to the kind of user-item-relationship that is addressed (e.g., ratings or listening events), whereas "Item content" indicates the presence or absence of content descriptors (e.g., metadata or audio features). The last column "User context" shows whether contextual data of the user or the listening event is provided (e.g., location or time).[20] Note that the absence of audio files in all data sets (see Table 13.1) would render audio content-based approaches impossible. However, some data sets (e.g., MSD) come with precomputed audio features, such as those provided by *The Echo Nest*.[21] If extracting features directly from the audio file is desired, an alternative solution is to download 30-second-snippets frequently available for preview in major online music stores and compute features on these. Such previews are also offered by *7digital*[22] via their Media Delivery API.[23]

In the following, we give a short introduction to the evaluation of music recommendation techniques in general. Hereafter, we present major evaluation

[19]In AotM-2011, this figure refers to the sum of the length of all playlists, where length is measured as the number of songs.

[20]For AotM-2011 this is partially the case, as not all playlist categories refer to contextual factors.

[21]http://the.echonest.com.

[22]http://www.7digital.com.

[23]http://developer.7digital.com/resources/api-docs.

Table 13.3 Some references to works that make use of the discussed data sets

Data set	References
Yahoo! Music [44]	[53, 73]
MSD [14]	[40, 65, 66, 128]
Last.fm—1K/360K [31]	[39, 144]
MusicMicro [121]	[119, 124]
MMTD [57]	[46, 50, 95, 125]
AotM-2011 [87]	[21, 86]

campaigns and data sets explicitly addressing the task of music recommendation.[24] To give the reader some hints on the usage of each data set, Table 13.3 provides references to corresponding work.

13.6.1 Evaluation Methodologies

In the recommender systems community, evaluation is often conducted by measuring the error of predicted ratings (e.g., root-mean-square error, RMSE). Due to the historical shortage of publicly available rating data for music, evaluation of music recommendation approaches has been carried out for a long time using genre as proxy and modeling a genre prediction task. Given the genre of the seed item(s) and that of the recommended item(s), typical IR performance measures are used (e.g., precision and recall). Using genre as proxy for music preferences, however, can be considered inherently incomplete because listeners might have driving factors for preference other than genres (e.g., happy music with vocals). It further neglects the perceived quality of recommendations, their actual usefulness for the listener [129], and the user's satisfaction [89, 122]—aspects which can only be assessed by asking real users.

Although the number of user studies has increased [143], conducting such studies on real-world commercial music collections remains time-consuming, expensive, and impractical, particularly for academic researchers. Consequently, relatively few studies measuring aspects related to user satisfaction have been published. The study by Celma and Herrera [32] may serve as an example of a proper subjective evaluation experiment, carried out on a larger scale. This study was conducted on 288 participants, each of which provided liking (enjoyment of the recommended music) and familiarity ratings for 19 tracks recommended by three approaches in a blind evaluation. The resulting large total number of evaluated tracks served as a solid basis for statistical testing. Bogdanov [16] proposes to use four subjective measures addressing different aspects of user preference and satisfaction to assess

[24]There exist many more music benchmarking activities which are oriented towards retrieval or annotation, e.g., *MIREX* (http://www.music-ir.org/mirex/wiki) or *MusiClef* (http://www.cp.jku.at/datasets/musiclef).

the quality of recommendations: (1) liking; (2) familiarity with the recommended tracks; (3) listening intention, i.e., readiness to listen to the same track again in the future; and (4) "give-me-more," indicating a request for or rejection of more music that is similar to the recommended track.

13.6.2 Yahoo! Music Dataset and KDD Cup 2011

In 2011, the *KDD Cup*[25] [44] featured a music recommendation task using music ratings data gathered on a large scale and provided by *Yahoo!*.[26] The corresponding data set is simply known as the *Yahoo! Music* data set and currently represents the largest music recommendation data set, including 262,810,175 ratings of 624,961 music items by 1,000,990 users, and spanning the time period from 1999 to 2010. User ratings are given partly on a standard 5-point scale, and partly on a 0–100 scale. Different levels of granularity are covered by the ratings: tracks, albums, artists, and genres. A characteristic of the data set is its high sparsity (99.96 %), even in light of the typically sparse nature of other ratings data sets (for instance, 98.82 % for the *Netflix* set) [44]. This high sparsity renders recommendation tasks particularly challenging.

There were two objectives in *KDD Cup 2011*, which were addressed on separate tracks. The first track was a traditional recommendation task: predict unknown music ratings based on given explicit ratings. The best algorithm achieved an RMSE of 0.84, when assuming a 5-point-scale for rating. It was capable of explaining 59.3 % of the rating variance. The second task aimed at distinguishing *loved* songs from songs never rated. In particular, participants were required to predict three songs for each user in the test set. To this end, the test set contained six songs for each user: three of which the user rated high, three of which the user never rated. As performance measure an error rate was used, corresponding to the fraction of songs wrongly predicted as loved ones. For this second track, a smaller data set was released, roughly 250,000 users, 300,000 items, and 60,000,000 ratings. The best performing algorithm achieved an error rate of 2.47 % [44].

The *KDD Cup 2011* received a lot of attention and had more than 2000 participants. However, it was also the subject of some controversy within the MIR community (see http://musicmachinery.com/2011/02/22/is-the-kdd-cup-really-music-recommendation).

The main criticism stemmed from the total anonymization and absence of any descriptive metadata. Both users and items are represented only by opaque numerical identifiers that do not relate to any semantic entity, such as user name or editorial music metadata. The task was therefore frequently considered as applying collaborative filtering techniques to a huge data set, rather than addressing the

[25] http://www.sigkdd.org/kdd2011/kddcup.shtml.

[26] http://music.yahoo.com.

particularities of music recommendation. The data set and the challenge effectively ignore music domain knowledge, and as a result, prohibit the application of content-based approaches. Nevertheless, the *Yahoo! Music* data set still represents one of the largest collections of user ratings on music items.

13.6.3 Million Song Dataset (MSD) and MSD Challenge 2012

Acknowledging the fact that human music perception is not only influenced by aspects encoded in the audio signal, the proponents of the *Million Song Dataset*[27] (MSD) [14] brought together a wealth of descriptors and information on one million contemporary popular music pieces. As of the time of writing, MSD contains content-based descriptors (e.g., estimates of key, tempo, loudness) and editorial metadata (e.g., artist, title, release year) from *The Echo Nest*, links to *MusicBrainz* and *7digital*, collaborative tags and similarity information from *Last.fm*, term vector representation of song lyrics from *musiXmatch*,[28] user playcount information (called "taste profile") again from *The Echo Nest* (covering almost 50 million `<user, song, playcount>` triples for about one million users), and information about cover songs from *Second Hand Songs*.[29]

Even though it has been criticized by some MIR researchers, foremost for (1) lack of actual audio material and (2) non-transparency of how the content descriptors were obtained, MSD certainly marked a cornerstone of publicly available music-related data sets in terms of size and data variety. In this vein, the proponents encourage MIR research that scales to commercial sizes of music collections. As for criticism (1), although it is true that MSD does not come with the actual digital song files due to copyright reasons, 30-second-snippets can be downloaded easily via links to *7digital*. Criticism (2) originates from the fact that the content descriptors are provided out of the box by *The Echo Nest*, which does not reveal details on how they were computed. Users of MSD however are also free and encouraged to compute their own audio-based features from the *7digital* snippets.

In order to provide an open evaluation contest for music recommendation algorithms that can use a wide variety of data sources, the *MSD Challenge*[30] [85] was organized in 2012. In contrast to *KDD Cup 2011*, which was highly obscured in terms of available data, the MSD Challenge put strong emphasis on allowing for a wide variety of approaches (for instance, including web crawling, audio analysis, collaborative filtering, or use of metadata).

Given full listening histories of one million users and half of the listening histories for another 110,000 test users, the task was to predict the missing hidden

---

[27] http://labrosa.ee.columbia.edu/millionsong.

[28] http://www.musixmatch.com.

[29] http://www.secondhandsongs.com.

[30] http://labrosa.ee.columbia.edu/millionsong/challenge.

listening events for the test users.[31] Mean average precision (MAP) computed on the top 500 recommendations for each listener was used as main performance measure. The winning algorithm achieved a MAP of 17.91 % using a neighborhood method [2]. The proponents of the MSD Challenge further provided some simple reference implementations that recommended songs only based on their popularity, achieving MAP scores between 2.1 % and 2.3 %.

As noted above, several publicly available data sets are strongly tied to their respective evaluation campaigns. This does not mean that they were only used in the corresponding campaigns though; quite the contrary is true. However, there exist a few collections that were proposed independently of benchmarking initiatives. A selection is presented in the following.

13.6.4 Last.fm Dataset: 360K/1K Users

In his book "Music Recommendation and Discovery" [31], Celma proposes the *Last.fm Dataset—360K users* and the *Last.fm Dataset—1K users*.[32] The former contains listening information about almost 360,000 users, but only includes artists they most frequently listened to. The latter provides full listening histories of nearly 1000 users, up to May 2009. While the *360K* set contains `<user, artist, playcount>` triples, the *1K* set further contains information on which songs were played at which time, thus representing the data as `<user, timestamp, artist, song>` quadruples. Both data sets contain user-specific information, including gender, age, country, and date of registering at *Last.fm*. The data has been gathered via the *Last.fm* API.

13.6.5 MusicMicro and Million Musical Tweets Dataset (MMTD)

The importance of temporal and spatial information has been highlighted in context-aware recommender systems in general [1], but also particularly in music recommendation [36, 124]. Until 2013, however, no music-related data set providing both types of information in high granularity was publicly available. Although Celma's data set contains timestamps of listening events, location is only given on the user level. Based on music listening information extracted from microblogs, two data sets were proposed in 2013: *MusicMicro* [121] and the *Million Musical Tweets*

[31] http://www.kaggle.com/c/msdchallenge.

[32] http://ocelma.net/MusicRecommendationDataset.

Dataset (MMTD) [57].[33] The *MusicMicro* set contains about 600,000 listening events by almost 137,000 distinct users and 21,000 artists. MMTD encompasses 1,087,000 listening events by 215,000 *Twitter* users, referring to 25,000 different artists. The latter data set can be regarded as an extension of the former. Temporal information is provided as month and weekday, and spatial information is given as numerical longitude and latitude values, as well as respective countries and cities. In addition, MMTD further includes identifiers linking to *MusicBrainz*, *7digital*, and *Amazon*.

13.6.6 AotM-2011

The *AotM-2011* data set[34] [87] contains playlists crawled from *Art of the Mix*,[35] a portal to share music playlists of any kind. The playlists span the time period from January 1998 to June 2011. The data set contains 101,343 unique playlists, which contain a total of 859,449 events (i.e., song-playlist pairs). Each playlist has had its songs matched to the *Million Song Dataset*, resulting in a total of 98,359 matching tracks. Furthermore, a timestamp of the playlist's upload is provided. Some of the playlists are further annotated with activities. In addition, metadata (name and date of joining the *Art of the Mix* site) is supplied for each user.

13.7 Conclusions and Challenges

In this chapter, we have given a brief overview of the state of the art in music recommender systems. We described the distinguishing characteristics of music recommendation in comparison to other domains, and surveyed content-based, context-aware, hybrid, and serial recommendation methods. We further reviewed common data sets, evaluation strategies and campaigns, and outlined their limitations.

From a practical point of view, there is no single best solution to music recommendation, in terms of features or algorithms. However, a trend towards hybrid approaches, in particular incorporating context-aware aspects is evident.

The overarching challenge for music recommendation research is comprehensive access to large data sets, including not only user ratings, but also contextual information and audio content. From the researcher's perspective, this further motivates the need for efficient and scalable methods which can be applied to large collections. Unfortunately, publicly available data sets with full access to audio are

[33]http://www.cp.jku.at/datasets/musicmicro and http://www.cp.jku.at/datasets/MMTD, resp.

[34]http://bmcfee.github.io/data/aotm2011.html.

[35]http://www.artofthemix.org.

rare and usually small, and therefore not amenable to recommender evaluation. On the other hand, companies that are in possession of large collections are not eager to share their data, be it due to business reasons, user privacy concerns, or legal constraints (i.e., copyright).

Beyond the issues of data access, there is also a need for better understanding how different kinds of data (e.g., semantic descriptions, audio content, or contextual factors) relate to and influence human music perception. Although many of the studies described in this chapter have evaluated some of these effects in isolation or on small data sets, there is still a relative lack of large-scale, comprehensive user studies for music recommendation. Whenever possible, evaluations should be carried out with real users, instead of optimizing for traces of preference that do not reveal any background information or intent [122]. Moreover, even with a better understanding of how individual factors influence music perception, it is still unclear how to best integrate all available sources when developing hybrid recommenders.

Regarding the state of the art in context-aware music recommendation, we note that most systems presented in Sects. 13.3 and 13.4 are research prototypes. While certain music players allow specifying the user's mood or activity as a query, to our knowledge, no fully automated context-aware music recommenders have been released to the public. The research on context-awareness in the music domain is still in its early stages and more work is needed to address such important research topics as understanding the relations between contextual conditions and music [97, 109], explaining context-aware recommendations to users, and determining the right level of user control over the recommendations [98].

If the research community manages to address these challenges and transcend current limitations in music recommendation, many more exciting applications can be expected in the future. These may include music players that "understand" the user's information or entertainment need at any point in time and provide corresponding recommendations, or applications that target specific usage scenarios such as group recommendations.

References

1. Adomavicius, G., Mobasher, B., Ricci, F., Tuzhilin, A.: Context-aware recommender systems. AI Magazine **32**, 67–80 (2011)
2. Aiolli, F.: A preliminary study on a recommender system for the million songs dataset challenge. Preference Learning: Problems and Applications in AI p. 1 (2012)
3. Aizenberg, N., Koren, Y., Somekh, O.: Build your own music recommender by modeling internet radio streams. In: Proceedings of the 21st International Conference on World Wide Web, pp. 1–10. ACM, New York, NY, USA (2012)
4. Alghoniemy, M., Tewfik, A.: Music Playlist Generation Based on Global and Transitional Constraints. In: IEEE Transactions on Multimedia (2003)
5. Ankolekar, A., Sandholm, T.: Foxtrot: a soundtrack for where you are. In: Proceedings of Interacting with Sound Workshop: Exploring Context-Aware, Local and Social Audio Applications, pp. 26–31 (2011)

6. Aucouturier, J.J.: Sounds like teen spirit: Computational insights into the grounding of everyday musical terms. In: J. Minett, W. Wang (eds.) Language, Evolution and the Brain, Frontiers in Linguistics, pp. 35–64. Taipei: Academia Sinica Press (2009)
7. Aucouturier, J.J., Pachet, F.: Scaling Up Music Playlist Generation. In: Proceedings of the IEEE International Conference on Multimedia and Expo (ICME 2002), pp. 105–108. Lausanne, Switzerland (2002)
8. Aucouturier, J.J., Pachet, F., Sandler, M.: "The way it sounds": timbre models for analysis and retrieval of music signals. IEEE Trans. on Multimedia **7**(6), 1028–1035 (2005).
9. Auer, S., Bizer, C., Kobilarov, G., Lehmann, J., Cyganiak, R., Ives, Z.: DBpedia: A nucleus for a web of open data. In: ISWC'08, pp. 722–735 (2008)
10. Baccigalupo, C.G.: Poolcasting: an intelligent technique to customise musical programmes for their audience. Ph.D. thesis, Universitat Autònoma de Barcelona (2009)
11. Baltrunas, L., Kaminskas, M., Ludwig, B., Moling, O., Ricci, F., Lüke, K.H., Schwaiger, R.: InCarMusic: Context-Aware Music Recommendations in a Car. In: International Conference on Electronic Commerce and Web Technologies (EC-Web). Toulouse, France (2011)
12. Barrington, L., Oda, R., Lanckriet, G.: Smarter than genius? Human evaluation of music recommender systems. In: Proceedings of the 10th International Conference on Music Information Retrieval (ISMIR'09), pp. 357–362 (2009)
13. Bertin-Mahieux, T., Eck, D., Maillet, F., Lamere, P.: Autotagger: A model for predicting social tags from acoustic features on large music databases. Journal of New Music Research **37**(2), 115–135 (2008).
14. Bertin-Mahieux, T., Ellis, D.P., Whitman, B., Lamere, P.: The million song dataset. In: Proceedings of the 12th International Society for Music Information Retrieval Conference, pp. 591–596. Miami, USA (2011)
15. Blei, D.M., Ng, A.Y., Jordan, M.I.: Latent Dirichlet Allocation. Machine Learning Research **3**, 993–1022 (2003)
16. Bogdanov, D.: From music similarity to music recommendation: Computational approaches based in audio features and metadata. Ph.D. thesis, Universitat Pompeu Fabra, Barcelona, Spain (2013)
17. Bogdanov, D., Haro, M., Fuhrmann, F., Xambó, A., Gómez, E., Herrera, P.: Semantic audio content-based music recommendation and visualization based on user preference examples. Information Processing & Management **49**(1), 13–33 (2013).
18. Bogdanov, D., Herrera, P.: How much metadata do we need in music recommendation? a subjective evaluation using preference sets. In: Int. Society for Music Information Retrieval Conf. (ISMIR'11), pp. 97–102 (2011)
19. Bogdanov, D., Herrera, P.: Taking advantage of editorial metadata to recommend music. In: Int. Symp. on Computer Music Modeling and Retrieval (CMMR'12) (2012).
20. Bogdanov, D., Serrà, J., Wack, N., Herrera, P., Serra, X.: Unifying Low-Level and High-Level Music Similarity Measures . IEEE Transactions on Multimedia **13**(4), 687–701 (2011)
21. Boland, D., Murray-Smith, R.: Information-theoretic Measures of Music Listening Behaviour. In: Proceedings of the 15th International Society for Music Information Retrieval Conference (ISMIR 2014). Taipei, Taiwan (2014)
22. Bonnin, G., Jannach, D.: Evaluating the quality of playlists based on hand-crafted samples. In: 14th International Society for Music Information Retrieval Conference, ISMIR (2013)
23. Bosteels, K., Pampalk, E., Kerre, E.: Evaluating and analysing dynamic playlist generation heuristics using radio logs and fuzzy set theory. In: Proceedings of the 10th International Society for Music Information Retrieval Conference, ISMIR (2009)
24. Braunhofer, M., Kaminskas, M., Ricci, F.: Location-aware music recommendation. International Journal of Multimedia Information Retrieval **2**(1), 31–44 (2013).
25. Bu, J., Tan, S., Chen, C., Wang, C., Wu, H., Zhang, L., He, X.: Music recommendation by unified hypergraph: combining social media information and music content. In: ACM Int. Conf. on Multimedia (MM'10), pp. 391–400 (2010).
26. Burke, R.: Hybrid recommender systems: Survey and experiments. User Modeling and User-Adapted Interaction **12**(4), 331–370 (2002)

27. Burke, R.: Hybrid web recommender systems. In: The adaptive web, pp. 377–408 (2007)
28. Cai, R., Zhang, C., Wang, C., Zhang, L., Ma, W.Y.: Musicsense: contextual music recommendation using emotional allocation modeling. In: MULTIMEDIA '07: Proceedings of the 15th international conference on Multimedia, pp. 553–556. ACM, New York, NY, USA (2007)
29. Casey, M.A., Veltkamp, R., Goto, M., Leman, M., Rhodes, C., Slaney, M.: Content-based music information retrieval: Current directions and future challenges. Proceedings of the IEEE **96**(4), 668–696 (2008)
30. Casey, M.A., Veltkamp, R., Goto, M., Leman, M., Rhodes, C., Slaney, M.: Content-Based Music Information Retrieval: Current Directions and Future Challenges. Proceedings of the IEEE **96**, 668–696 (2008)
31. Celma, Ò.: Music Recommendation and Discovery – The Long Tail, Long Fail, and Long Play in the Digital Music Space. Springer, Berlin, Germany (2010)
32. Celma, O., Herrera, P.: A new approach to evaluating novel recommendations. In: ACM Conf. on Recommender Systems (RecSys'08), pp. 179–186 (2008)
33. Celma, O., Herrera, P., Serra, X.: Bridging the music semantic gap. In: ESWC 2006 Workshop on Mastering the Gap: From Information Extraction to Semantic Representation (2006). Available online: http://mtg.upf.edu/node/874
34. Celma, O., Lamere, P.: Music recommendation and discovery revisited. In: Proceedings of the 5th ACM Conference on Recommender Systems (RecSys 2011), pp. 7–8. ACM, New York, NY, USA (2011)
35. Celma, O., Ramírez, M., Herrera, P.: FOAFing the music: A music recommendation system based on RSS feeds and user preferences. In: Int. Conf. on Music Information Retrieval (ISMIR'05) (2005)
36. Cunningham, S., Caulder, S., Grout, V.: Saturday Night or Fever? Context-Aware Music Playlists. In: Proceedings of the 3rd International Audio Mostly Conference of Sound in Motion (2008)
37. Deerwester, S., Dumais, S.T., Furnas, G.W., Landauer, T.K., Harshman, R.: Indexing by latent semantic analysis. Journal of the American Society for Information Science **41**, 391–407 (1990)
38. Dey, A., Abowd, G.: Towards a better understanding of context and context-awareness. In: CHI 2000 workshop on the what, who, where, when, and how of context-awareness, vol. 4, pp. 1–6 (2000)
39. Diaz-Aviles, E., Georgescu, M., Nejdl, W.: Swarming to Rank for Recommender Systems. In: Proceedings of the 6th ACM Conference on Recommender Systems. Dublin, Ireland (2012)
40. Dieleman, S., Brakel, P., Schrauwen, B.: Audio-based music classification with a pretrained convolutional network. In: Proceedings of the 12th International Society for Music Information Retrieval Conference (ISMIR 2011). Miami, FL, USA (2011)
41. Donaldson, J.: A Hybrid Social-Acoustic Recommendation System for Popular Music. In: Proceedings of the ACM Recommender Systems (RecSys 2007). Minneapolis, MN, USA (2007)
42. Dopler, M., Schedl, M., Pohle, T., Knees, P.: Accessing Music Collections via Representative Cluster Prototypes in a Hierarchical Organization Scheme. In: Proceedings of the 9th International Conference on Music Information Retrieval (ISMIR'08). Philadelphia, PA, USA (2008)
43. Dror, G., Koenigstein, N., Koren, Y.: Yahoo! Music Recommendations: Modeling Music Ratings with Temporal Dynamics and Item Taxonomy. In: Proceedings of the 5th ACM Conference on Recommender Systems (RecSys 2011). Chicago, USA (2011)
44. Dror, G., Koenigstein, N., Koren, Y., Weimer, M.: The Yahoo! Music Dataset and KDD-Cup'11. Journal of Machine Learning Research: Proceedings of KDD-Cup 2011 competition **18**, 3–18 (2012)
45. Elliott, G.T., Tomlinson, B.: Personalsoundtrack: context-aware playlists that adapt to user pace. In: CHI '06: CHI '06 extended abstracts on Human factors in computing systems, pp. 736–741. ACM, New York, NY, USA (2006)

46. Farrahi, K., Schedl, M., Vall, A., Hauger, D., Tkalčič, M.: Impact of Listening Behavior on Music Recommendation. In: Proceedings of the 15th International Society for Music Information Retrieval Conference (ISMIR 2014). Taipei, Taiwan (2014)
47. Fernández-Tobías, I., Cantador, I., Kaminskas, M., Ricci, F.: Knowledge-based music retrieval for places of interest. In: Proceedings of the 2nd International Workshop on Music Information Retrieval with User-Centered and Multimodal Strategies (MIRUM), pp. 19–24 (2012)
48. Fields, B.: Contextualize your listening: the playlist as recommendation engine. Ph.D. thesis, Department of Computing Goldsmiths, University of London (2011)
49. Fields, B., Rhodes, C., Casey, M., Jacobson, K.: Social playlists and bottleneck measurements: Exploiting musician social graphs using content-based dissimilarity and pairwise maximum flow values. In: ISMIR, pp. 559–564 (2008)
50. Figueiredo, F., Almeida, J.M., Matsubara, Y., Ribeiro, B., Faloutsos, C.: Revisit behavior in social media: The phoenix-r model and discoveries. In: Proceedings of the 7th European Conference on Machine Learning and Principles and Practice of Knowledge Discovery in Databases (ECML PKDD 2014). Nancy, France (2014)
51. Flexer, A., Schnitzer, D., Gasser, M., Widmer, G.: Playlist generation using start and end songs. In: ISMIR, pp. 173–178 (2008)
52. Foley Jr, J.: The occupational conditioning of preferential auditory tempo: a contribution toward an empirical theory of aesthetics. The Journal of Social Psychology **12**(1), 121–129 (1940)
53. Goel, S., Broder, A., Gabrilovich, E., Pang, B.: Anatomy of the Long Tail: Ordinary People with Extraordinary Tastes. In: Proceedings of the 3rd ACM International Conference on Web Search and Data Mining (WSDM 2010). New York, USA (2010)
54. Green, S.J., Lamere, P., Alexander, J., Maillet, F., Kirk, S., Holt, J., Bourque, J., Mak, X.W.: Generating transparent, steerable recommendations from textual descriptions of items. In: ACM Conf. on Recommender Systems (RecSys'09), pp. 281–284 (2009)
55. Grimaldi, M., Cunningham, P.: Experimenting with music taste prediction by user profiling. In: ACM SIGMM Int. Workshop on Multimedia Information Retrieval (MIR'04), pp. 173–180 (2004)
56. Hariri, N., Mobasher, B., Burke, R.: Context-aware music recommendation based on latent-topic sequential patterns. In: Proceedings of the sixth ACM conference on Recommender systems, pp. 131–138. ACM (2012)
57. Hauger, D., Schedl, M., Košir, A., Tkalčič, M.: The Million Musical Tweets Dataset: What Can We Learn From Microblogs. In: Proceedings of the 14th International Society for Music Information Retrieval Conference (ISMIR 2013). Curitiba, Brazil (2013)
58. Haupt, J.: Last.fm: People-powered online radio. Music Reference Services Quarterly **12**(1), 23–24 (2009).
59. Herlocker, J.L., Konstan, J.A., Terveen, L.G., Riedl, J.T.: Evaluating collaborative filtering recommender systems. ACM Trans. on Information Systems **22**(1), 5–53 (2004).
60. Herrera, P., Resa, Z., Sordo, M.: Rocking around the clock eight days a week: an exploration of temporal patterns of music listening. In: ACM Conf. on Recommender Systems. Workshop on Music Recommendation and Discovery (Womrad 2010), pp. 7–10 (2010)
61. Hinton, G., Deng, L., Yu, D., Dahl, G.E., rahman Mohamed, A., Jaitly, N., Senior, A., Vanhoucke, V., Nguyen, P., Sainath, T.N.,, Kingsbury, B.: Deep neural networks for acoustic modeling in speech recognition. IEEE Signal Processing Magazine **29**(6), 82–97 (2012)
62. Hu, Y., Koren, Y., Volinsky, C.: Collaborative filtering for implicit feedback datasets. In: Proceedings of the 2008 Eighth IEEE International Conference on Data Mining, pp. 263–272. IEEE Computer Society, Washington, DC, USA (2008)
63. Hu, Y., Koren, Y., Volinsky, C.: Collaborative filtering for implicit feedback datasets. In: Eighth IEEE International Conference on Data Mining, ICDM, pp. 263–272 (2008)
64. Hu, Y., Ogihara, M.: Nextone player: A music recommendation system based on user behaviour. In: Int. Society for Music Information Retrieval Conf. (ISMIR'11) (2011)

65. Hu, Y., Ogihara, M.: Genre classification for million song dataset using confidence-based classifiers combination. In: Proceedings of the 35th Annual International ACM SIGIR Conference on Research and Development in Information Retrieval (SIGIR) (2012)
66. Humphrey, E.J., Nieto, O., Bello, J.P.: Data driven and discriminative projections for large-scale cover song identification. In: Proceedings of the 14th International Society for Music Information Retrieval Conference (ISMIR 2013). Curitiba, Brazil (2013)
67. Jones, N., Pu, P.: User technology adoption issues in recommender systems. In: Networking and Electronic Commerce Research Conf. (2007)
68. Kaminskas, M., Ricci, F., Schedl, M.: Location-aware Music Recommendation Using Auto-Tagging and Hybrid Matching. In: Proceedings of the 7th ACM Conference on Recommender Systems (RecSys 2013). Hong Kong, China (2013)
69. Knees, P., Pohle, T., Schedl, M., Widmer, G.: Combining Audio-based Similarity with Web-based Data to Accelerate Automatic Music Playlist Generation. In: Proceedings of the 8th ACM SIGMM International Workshop on Multimedia Information Retrieval (MIR'06). Santa Barbara, CA, USA (2006)
70. Knees, P., Schedl, M.: A survey of music similarity and recommendation from music context data. ACM Transactions on Multimedia Computing, Communications and Applications **10**(1), 2:1–2:21 (2013)
71. Koenigstein, N., Shavitt, Y., Zilberman, N.: Predicting billboard success using data-mining in p2p networks. In: Multimedia, 2009. ISM'09. 11th IEEE International Symposium on, pp. 465–470. IEEE (2009)
72. Konecni, V.: Social interaction and musical preference. The psychology of music pp. 497–516 (1982)
73. Koren, Y., Sill, J.: OrdRec: an Ordinal Model for Predicting Personalized Item Rating Distributions. In: Proceedings of the 5th ACM Conference on Recommender Systems (RecSys 2011). Chicago, USA (2011)
74. Levy, M., Sandler, M.: Learning latent semantic models for music from social tags. Journal of New Music Research **37**(2), 137–150 (2008)
75. Li, C.T., Shan, M.K.: Emotion-based impressionism slideshow with automatic music accompaniment. In: MULTIMEDIA '07: Proceedings of the 15th international conference on Multimedia, pp. 839–842. ACM Press, New York, NY, USA (2007)
76. Li, Q., Myaeng, S.H., Kim, B.M.: A probabilistic music recommender considering user opinions and audio features. Information Processing & Management **43**(2), 473–487 (2007)
77. Lim, D., Mcfee, B., Lanckriet, G.R.: Robust structural metric learning. In: S. Dasgupta, D. Mcallester (eds.) Proceedings of the 30th International Conference on Machine Learning (ICML-13), vol. 28, pp. 615–623. JMLR Workshop and Conference Proceedings (2013).
78. Logan, B.: Content-based Playlist Generation: Exploratory Experiments. In: Proceedings of the 3rd International Symposium on Music Information Retrieval (ISMIR 2002), pp. 295–296. Paris, France (2002)
79. Logan, B.: Music recommendation from song sets. In: Int. Conf. on Music Information Retrieval (ISMIR'04), pp. 425–428 (2004)
80. Logan, B., Salomon, A.: A music similarity function based on signal analysis. In: IEEE Int. Conf. on Multimedia and Expo (ICME'01), p. 190 (2001).
81. Lu, C.C., Tseng, V.S.: A novel method for personalized music recommendation. Expert Systems with Applications **36**(6), 10,035–10,044 (2009)
82. Magno, T., Sable, C.: A comparison of signal-based music recommendation to genre labels, collaborative filtering, musicological analysis, human recommendation, and random baseline. In: Int. Conf. on Music Information Retrieval (ISMIR'08), pp. 161–166 (2008)
83. Maillet, F., Eck, D., Desjardins, G., Lamere, P.: Steerable playlist generation by learning song similarity from radio station playlists. In: Proceedings of the 10th International Conference on Music Information Retrieval (2009)
84. McFee, B., Barrington, L., Lanckriet, G.: Learning content similarity for music recommendation. IEEE Trans. on Audio, Speech, and Language Processing **20**(8), 2207–2218 (2012).

85. McFee, B., Bertin-Mahieux, T., Ellis, D., Lanckriet, G.: The million song dataset challenge. In: Proc. of the 4th International Workshop on Advances in Music Information Research (AdMIRe) (2012)
86. McFee, B., Lanckriet, G.: The Natural Language of Playlists. In: Proceedings of the 12th International Society for Music Information Retrieval Conference (ISMIR). Miami, FL, USA (2011)
87. McFee, B., Lanckriet, G.: Hypergraph Models of Playlist Dialects. In: Proceedings of the 13th International Society for Music Information Retrieval Conference (ISMIR 2012). Porto, Portugal (2012)
88. McFee, B., Lanckriet, G.R.: Learning multi-modal similarity. Journal of Machine Learning Research **12**, 491–523 (2011)
89. McNee, S., Riedl, J., Konstan, J.: Being accurate is not enough: how accuracy metrics have hurt recommender systems. In: CHI'06 extended abstracts on Human Factors in Computing Systems, p. 1101 (2006)
90. Mesnage, C.S.: Social shuffle: music discovery with tag navigation and social diffusion. Ph.D. thesis, Università della Svizzera italiana, Lugano, Switzerland (2011)
91. Mobasher, B., Burke, R., Bhaumik, R., Williams, C.: Toward trustworthy recommender systems: An analysis of attack models and algorithm robustness. ACM Transactions on Internet Technology **7**(4) (2007)
92. Moh, Y., Orbanz, P., Buhmann, J.M.: Music preference learning with partial information. In: IEEE Int. Conf. on Acoustics, Speech and Signal Processing (ICASSP'08), pp. 2021–2024 (2008)
93. Moore, J.L., Chen, S., Joachims, T., Turnbull, D.: Learning to embed songs and tags for playlist prediction. In: 13th International Society for Music Information Retrieval Conference, ISMIR, pp. 349–354 (2012)
94. Moore, J.L., Chen, S., Joachims, T., Turnbull, D.: Taste over time: The temporal dynamics of user preferences. In: 14th International Society for Music Information Retrieval Conference, ISMIR (2013)
95. Moore, J.L., Joachims, T., Turnbull, D.: Taste Space Versus the World: An Embedding Analysis of Listening Habits and Geography. In: Proceedings of the 15th International Society for Music Information Retrieval Conference (ISMIR 2014). Taipei, Taiwan (2014)
96. North, A., Hargreaves, D.: Situational influences on reported musical preference. Psychomusicology: Music, Mind and Brain **15**(1–2), 30–45 (1996)
97. North, A., Hargreaves, D.: The social and applied psychology of music. Cambridge Univ Press (2008)
98. Okada, K., Karlsson, B.F., Sardinha, L., Noleto, T.: Contextplayer: Learning contextual music preferences for situational recommendations. In: SIGGRAPH Asia 2013 Symposium on Mobile Graphics and Interactive Applications, p. 6. ACM (2013)
99. de Oliveira, R., Oliver, N.: Triplebeat: enhancing exercise performance with persuasion. In: Proceedings of the 10th international conference on Human computer interaction with mobile devices and services, pp. 255–264. ACM (2008)
100. van den Oord, A., Dieleman, S., Schrauwen, B.: Deep content-based music recommendation. In: C. Burges, L. Bottou, M. Welling, Z. Ghahramani, K. Weinberger (eds.) Advances in Neural Information Processing Systems 26, vol. 26, p. 9. Neural Information Processing Systems Foundation (NIPS), Lake Tahoe, NV, USA (2013)
101. Pachet, F.: Knowledge management and musical metadata. Idea Group (2005)
102. Pachet, F., Roy, P., Cazaly, D.: A combinatorial approach to content-based music selection. Multimedia, IEEE **7**(1), 44–51 (2000)
103. Pampalk, E., Flexer, A., Widmer, G.: Improvements of audio-based music similarity and genre classification. In: Int. Conf. on Music Information Retrieval (ISMIR'05), pp. 628–633 (2005)
104. Pampalk, E., Pohle, T., Widmer, G.: Dynamic playlist generation based on skipping behavior. In: Int. Conf. on Music Information Retrieval (ISMIR'05), pp. 634–637 (2005)
105. Park, H.S., Yoo, J.O., Cho, S.B.: A context-aware music recommendation system using fuzzy bayesian networks with utility theory. In: FSKD 2006. LNCS (LNAI), pp. 970–979. Springer (2006)

106. Pauws, S., Eggen, B.: PATS: Realization and user evaluation of an automatic playlist generator. In: Proceedings of the 2nd International Symposium on Music Information Retrieval, ISMIR (2002)
107. Pauws, S., Verhaegh, W., Vossen, M.: Fast generation of optimal music playlists using local search. In: ISMIR, pp. 138–143. Citeseer (2006)
108. Pazzani, M., Billsus, D.: Learning and revising user profiles: The identification of interesting web sites. Machine Learning **27**(3), 313–331 (1997).
109. Pettijohn, T., Williams, G., Carter, T.: Music for the seasons: Seasonal music preferences in college students. Current Psychology pp. 1–18 (2010)
110. Platt, J.C., Burges, C.J.C., Swenson, S., Weare, C., Zheng, A.: Learning a gaussian process prior for automatically generating music playlists. In: Advances in Neural Information Processing Systems. MIT Press (2002)
111. Pohle, T., Knees, P., Schedl, M., Pampalk, E., Widmer, G.: "Reinventing the Wheel": A Novel Approach to Music Player Interfaces. IEEE Transactions on Multimedia **9**, 567–575 (2007)
112. Pohle, T., Pampalk, E., Widmer, G.: Generating Similarity-based Playlists Using Traveling Salesman Algorithms. In: Proceedings of the 8th International Conference on Digital Audio Effects (DAFx-05), pp. 220–225. Madrid, Spain (2005)
113. Popescu, G., Pu, P.: Probabilistic game theoretic algorithms for group recommender systems. In: Proceedings of the 2nd Workshop on Music Recommendation and Discovery (WOMRAD) (2011)
114. Ragno, R., Burges, C.J., Herley, C.: Inferring similarity between music objects with application to playlist generation. In: Proceedings of the 7th ACM SIGMM international workshop on Multimedia information retrieval, pp. 73–80. ACM (2005)
115. Reddy, S., Mascia, J.: Lifetrak: music in tune with your life. In: Proceedings of the 1st ACM International Workshop on Human-centered Multimedia (HCM), pp. 25–34 (2006)
116. Reed, J., Lee, C.: Preference music ratings prediction using tokenization and minimum classification error training. IEEE Trans. on Audio, Speech, and Language Processing **19**(8), 2294–2303 (2011).
117. Rendle, S., Freudenthaler, C., Gantner, Z., Schmidt-Thieme, L.: Bpr: Bayesian personalized ranking from implicit feedback. In: Proceedings of the Twenty-Fifth Conference on Uncertainty in Artificial Intelligence, pp. 452–461. AUAI Press (2009)
118. Schäfer, T., Sedlmeier, P.: From the functions of music to music preference. Psychology of Music **37**(3), 279–300 (2009)
119. Schedl, M.: #nowplaying Madonna: A Large-Scale Evaluation on Estimating Similarities Between Music Artists and Between Movies from Microblogs . Information Retrieval (2012)
120. Schedl, M.: Ameliorating Music Recommendation: Integrating Music Content, Music Context, and User Context for Improved Music Retrieval and Recommendation. In: Proceedings of the 11th International Conference on Advances in Mobile Computing & Multimedia (MoMM 2013). Vienna, Austria (2013)
121. Schedl, M.: Leveraging Microblogs for Spatiotemporal Music Information Retrieval. In: Proceedings of the 35th European Conference on Information Retrieval (ECIR 2013). Moscow, Russia (2013)
122. Schedl, M., Flexer, A., Urbano, J.: The neglected user in music information retrieval research. Journal of Intelligent Information Systems **41**, 523–539 (2013).
123. Schedl, M., Pohle, T., Knees, P., Widmer, G.: Exploring the Music Similarity Space on the Web. ACM Transactions on Information Systems **29**(3), 1–24 (2011)
124. Schedl, M., Schnitzer, D.: Hybrid Retrieval Approaches to Geospatial Music Recommendation. In: Proceedings of the 36th Annual International ACM SIGIR Conference on Research and Development in Information Retrieval (SIGIR). Dublin, Ireland (2013)
125. Schedl, M., Vall, A., Farrahi, K.: User Geospatial Context for Music Recommendation in Microblogs. In: Proceedings of the 37th Annual International ACM SIGIR Conference on Research and Development in Information Retrieval (SIGIR). Gold Coast, Australia (2014)
126. Schedl, M., Widmer, G., Knees, P., Pohle, T.: A music information system automatically generated via web content mining techniques. Information Processing & Management **47**(3), 426–439 (2011).

127. Schilit, B., Adams, N., Want, R.: Context-aware computing applications. In: Proceedings of the Workshop on Mobile Computing Systems and Applications, pp. 85–90. IEEE Computer Society (1994)
128. Schindler, A., Mayer, R., Rauber, A.: Facilitating comprehensive benchmarking experiments on the million song dataset. In: Proceedings of the 13th International Society for Music Information Retrieval Conference (ISMIR 2012). Porto, Portugal (2012)
129. Shani, G., Gunawardana, A.: Evaluating recommender systems. Recommender Systems Handbook pp. 257–298 (2009).
130. Shao, B., Wang, D., Li, T., Ogihara, M.: Music recommendation based on acoustic features and user access patterns. IEEE Transactions on Audio, Speech, and Language Processing **17**(8), 1602–1611 (2009)
131. Shardanand, U., Maes, P.: Social information filtering: algorithms for automating "word of mouth". In: Proceedings of the SIGCHI conference on Human factors in computing systems, pp. 210–217 (1995)
132. Slaney, M.: Web-scale multimedia analysis: Does content matter? IEEE Multimedia **18**(2), 12–15 (2011)
133. Slaney, M., White, W.: Measuring playlist diversity for recommendation systems. In: 1st ACM workshop on Audio and music computing multimedia, AMCMM '06, pp. 77–82. ACM, New York, NY, USA (2006)
134. Slaney, M., White, W.: Similarity Based on Rating Data. In: Proceedings of the 8th International Conference on Music Information Retrieval (ISMIR 2007). Vienna, Austria (2007)
135. Sordo, M., Celma, O., Blech, M., Guaus, E.: The quest for musical genres: Do the experts and the wisdom of crowds agree? In: Int. Conf. of Music Information Retrieval (ISMIR'08), pp. 255–260 (2008)
136. Stupar, A., Michel, S.: Picasso - to sing, you must close your eyes and draw. In: 34th ACM SIGIR Conf. on Research and development in Information, pp. 715–724 (2011)
137. Su, J.H., Yeh, H.H., Tseng, V.S.: A novel music recommender by discovering preferable perceptual-patterns from music pieces. In: ACM Symp. on Applied Computing (SAC'10), pp. 1924–1928 (2010)
138. Szymanski, G.: Pandora, or, a never-ending box of musical delights. Music Reference Services Quarterly **12**(1), 21–22 (2009).
139. Tiemann, M., Pauws, S.: Towards ensemble learning for hybrid music recommendation. In: ACM Conf. on Recommender Systems (RecSys'07), pp. 177–178 (2007)
140. Turnbull, D.R., Barrington, L., Lanckriet, G., Yazdani, M.: Combining audio content and social context for semantic music discovery. In: Proceedings of the 32nd international ACM SIGIR conference on Research and development in information retrieval, pp. 387–394. ACM (2009)
141. Tzanetakis, G., Cook, P.: Musical genre classification of audio signals. IEEE Trans. on Speech and Audio Processing **10**(5), 293–302 (2002)
142. Wang, X., Rosenblum, D., Wang, Y.: Context-aware mobile music recommendation for daily activities. In: Proceedings of the 20th ACM international conference on Multimedia, pp. 99–108. ACM (2012)
143. Weigl, D., Guastavino, C.: User Studies in the Music Information Retrieval Literature. In: Proceedings of the 12th International Society for Music Information Retrieval Conference (ISMIR 2011). Miami, FL, USA (2011)
144. Weston, J., Wang, C., Weiss, R., Berenzweig, A.: Latent Collaborative Retrieval. In: Proceedings of the 29th International Conference on Machine Learning (ICML). Edinburgh, Scotland (2012)
145. Yang, D., Chen, T., Zhang, W., Lu, Q., Yu, Y.: Local implicit feedback mining for music recommendation. In: Proceedings of the 6th ACM Conference on Recommender Systems, pp. 91–98. ACM (2012)
146. Yang, Y.H., Chen, H.H.: Machine recognition of music emotion: A review. ACM Trans. Intell. Syst. Technol. **3**(3), 40:1–40:30 (2012).

147. Yoshii, K., Goto, M., Komatani, K., Ogata, T., Okuno, H.G.: An efficient hybrid music recommender system using an incrementally trainable probabilistic generative model. IEEE Trans. on Audio, Speech, and Language Processing **16**(2), 435–447 (2008).
148. Zentner, M., Grandjean, D., Scherer, K.R.: Emotions evoked by the sound of music: Characterization, classification, and measurement. Emotion **8**(4), 494–521 (2008)
149. Zhang, Y.C., Séaghdha, D.O., Quercia, D., Jambor, T.: Auralist: Introducing serendipity into music recommendation. In: Proceedings of the Fifth ACM International Conference on Web Search and Data Mining, WSDM '12, pp. 13–22. ACM, New York, NY, USA (2012)
150. Zheleva, E., Guiver, J., Mendes Rodrigues, E., Milić-Frayling, N.: Statistical models of music-listening sessions in social media. In: Proceedings of the 19th international conference on World wide web, WWW '10, pp. 1019–1028. ACM, New York, NY, USA (2010)

Chapter 14
The Anatomy of Mobile Location-Based Recommender Systems

Neal Lathia

14.1 Introduction

The widespread adoption of smartphones—putting both the Internet and sensor-rich hardware into the pockets of millions—is finally bridging the gap between the online and offline worlds. It is now common for mobile phone users to search the web and engage with social media while on the move: the services that were once limited to the desktop computer are now at their fingertips. Furthermore, the vast information repository on the web can now be used to enhance peoples' physical-world experiences. Mobile phones are quickly turning away from being mere portals to the web and towards devices that help users to explore, discover, and interact with their actual surroundings.

One of the key technologies that is enjoying much success in the online world is usage of *recommender systems* to support users' browsing. Online recommender systems take many different shapes: they help users discover movies, music, and e-commerce items of interest, as well as suggesting new friends to connect to in online social networks and providing personalised search results. At the heart of their success is the assumption that a model of users' preferences can be learned by observing their behaviour (expressed as, for example, star-ratings or clicks); huge repositories of data can then be filtered in order to draw out the most interesting results for each person. Mobile phones, instead, have historically been centred on *location*-based services: the underlying paradigm is that the most relevant information for users is about that which is close by. However, the next generation of mobile phones now offer the potential to implement recommender systems to build services that not only leverage users' current location, but also their rich history of preferences and actions. In doing so, a crossroads of multiple lines of research, each

N. Lathia (✉)
Computer Laboratory, University of Cambridge, Cambridge CB3 0FD, UK
e-mail: neal.lathia@cl.cam.ac.uk

F. Ricci et al. (eds.), *Recommender Systems Handbook*,
DOI 10.1007/978-1-4899-7637-6_14

with their own rich literature, is being formed. People's usage of mobile systems is of interest to a wide range of fields within Computer Science, ranging from mobile information retrieval [17], sensor research [22], data mining and knowledge discovery [14], human-computer interaction [49], as well as persuasive [26] and ubiquitous computing [47].

This chapter aims to draw together the various lines of enquiry related to location-based personalisation and mobile recommender systems by presenting a structured survey of the key elements of a mobile location-based recommender system. We do so from the point of view of the recommender system itself, beginning with a broad definition of mobile recommender systems. We then cover three features of mobile recommender systems:

1. **Data.** Recording signals of behaviour that reflect users' preferences is the foundation for any mechanism that aims to recommend new places, activities, or friends. In this regard, a growing body of research has delved into collecting data from users about themselves and their surroundings, via participatory sensing, crowd-sourcing, and game-based incentives. Furthermore, a range of research has investigated how to infer users' activities from such data.
2. **Algorithms.** The principal technique behind recommender systems is *collaborative filtering*. While these are readily applied to mobile systems as well, these algorithms have historically taken a "black-box" approach when computing on user ratings: they do not, for example, need to consider the physical distance between places. We will therefore also discuss supervised learning approaches for mobile recommendations and recent research that augments the efficacy of recommendations by taking into account features relating to space (e.g., where people live) as well as preference.
3. **System Evaluation.** The question of evaluating recommender systems is still actively discussed [35]. We complement this research by surveying how mobile recommender systems have been evaluated to date, and how their evaluation differs from more traditional scenarios.

We conclude our survey by discussing emergent themes and set of directions for future research.

14.1.1 Defining a Mobile Location-Based Recommender System

We begin with a broad definition of the kinds of systems that we describe in this chapter. To date, many *recommender systems* and *location-based systems* have been built and studied as separate entities. Broadly speaking, they can be defined as follows:

- **Recommender Systems** retrieve tailored sets of *items* of interest for each user. A variety of flavours of recommender systems are discussed throughout this

handbook: for example, see the chapter on "Data Mining Methods for Recommender Systems" for approaches that recommend based on users' historical preferences (see Chap. 7), and "Semantics-Aware Content-Based Recommender Systems" for approaches that recommend based on items' features (see Chap. 4).
- **Location-Based Systems** or services retrieve information that is tailored to the user's *current location* [72]. Typical applications here include mapping and route-finding services, applications to find nearby services (e.g., restaurants), location-based social networks where friends share their location with one another, traffic notification services, and advertising. The focus is heavily on location, rather than preference.

Historically, the recommender system literature has been characterised by a focus on recommender systems that users interact with using a personal computer, and recommending items that are potentially not 'consumed' immediately after being recommended, such as movies, music, and the contents of e-commerce catalogues. Although these recommendations may often result in real-world interactions (e.g., a movie being sent to your house), they are nevertheless mostly finding content based on what people like. In other words, any spatial relationships between the items (e.g., where a restaurant is relative to another) are not useful when computing recommendations: the focus is on identifying, via a range of machine learning approaches, implicit relationships between items using the feedback or preferences given by the system's users.

The systems that we focus on here, *mobile location-based recommender systems*, take on characteristics of both of the above: they are accessed via mobile devices, use location data (current or otherwise, e.g. historical), involves and leverages users' movement around a physical space and, most importantly, provide *personalised* recommendations that are tailored to users' preferences. To that end, we exclude systems that do not recommend places (or venues; 'items' that are consumed by visiting a specific geographic location), such as when users access their movie recommender (e.g., Netflix account) via a mobile device [34, 52], or seek personalised app-recommendations with their mobile [39]. In that regard, mobile location-based recommender systems may be viewed as a particular kind of *context-aware* recommender system [2], where spatio-temporal data (about *where* and *when* the system is being used) can be used to further personalise results.

In light of the above, what are the tasks that users of mobile location-based recommender systems are seeking to perform?

1. **Goal-Oriented Search:** Location-based recommender systems often allow users to query for personalised results. Where is the closest restaurants that I would like to have dinner at? Where are nearby shopping areas? These tasks are often associated with a particular intended action (e.g., having dinner, going to a bar), yet with results that can be personalised to each individual.
2. **Location Discovery:** While the above use case captures when users have queries/intents, mobile location-based recommenders can also be used to discover places. What is around me, of interest? What should I see in London? What places are trending nearby, or events happening in my neighbourhood? All these

kinds of questions fuel use cases where the user's historical profile can be used to personalise recommended places to see, visit, or attend.
3. **Routing and Transport:** Finally, a number of use cases have appeared in the literature that deal with recommending personalised *routes* to follow. While mainly focused on tourist routes, this use case responds to: how should *I* get from here to there? What route should I walk when I am visiting Barcelona, with my children? And so forth.

Beyond these, there are location-based social matching applications, tailored to find people of interest in particular locations, and behaviour-oriented applications, such as those related to sport and physical activity. While these are potentially amenable to personalisation and recommendation systems, this chapter focuses on those applications that are related to venues and places. The following published surveys review mobile recommender systems more broadly: [29, 42, 68].

14.2 Data for Mobile Recommender Systems

One of the key differences between mobile- and web-based recommender systems is that the former tend to have access to a broader set of data than the latter. Traditionally, web-based recommender systems' data is described as being either explicit (e.g., a rating or similar value derived from a user's evaluation of an item) or implicit (e.g., a purchase or click; a value derived from the user's behaviour). Mobile systems can also collect these, and more. While recent systems have particularly focused on location and mobility data, mobile systems can collect:

1. **Explicit Data:** Mobile users can, as they do on the web, rate, tag, share, 'like,' or otherwise score an item while on the go. Beyond this, the most prominent explicit action that has emerged across mobile services (e.g., Foursquare, Facebook Places, Google+, Yelp) is the *check-in*: users share their current location with their friends by finding and selecting the venue they are in. In the following, we describe how these relate to preference.
2. **Implicit Data:** As above, users may provide similar implicit data as they do on the web by clicking links, streaming videos, making purchases, or otherwise engaging in an action that is not limited to mobile only. However, the mobile device does provide some differences: there are behaviours (e.g., taking a photo, tracking physical exercise) that are exclusive to mobile devices.
3. **Sensor Data:** Modern smartphones are increasingly sensor-rich. These typically include sensors that can measure location and mobility, co-location, and other facets that describe users' context [47].

Moreover, many mobile systems inherently collect multiple kinds of data at once. Consider, for example a check-in on a location-based social network (e.g., Foursquare). When checking in, users' sensor data is used to identify nearby venues [74]: their check-in action is an explicit signal of presence at that venue;

multiple check-ins at the same venue may be considered as an implicit confidence metric of preference for that venue [36], and the timestamp of their check-in implicitly uncovers features of the place where they are [8].

One of the most notable differences between web- and mobile-based recommender system data is that the *item set* that the recommender uses is often dynamic; to follow from the example above, not all possible venues that a user may like to check-in to may be known to the system. A key facet of building a mobile recommender therefore is using the available data in order to learn about *both* items and users. In the following, we describe a number of examples from the literature where data derived from mobile devices is used to build databases that could suitably underpin a recommender system. In particular, we focus on finding and inferring points of interest, learning and modelling mobility data, analysing check-ins, and inferring context and activities from sensors.

14.2.1 Uncovering Points of Interest and Location Preferences

As mobile devices are used on the go, they become an ideal source of location data. In this section, we describe how this data can be used to learn about both *users* and *items* in a recommender system, and the relations between them.

Location-based recommender systems rely on having a database of Points-of-Interest (POIs) from which to source recommendations. The recent literature has described a number of means of finding and inferring POIs from users' data. A number of systems (e.g., Foursquare) maintain their POI database via crow sourcing; the explicit check-ins that users provide can then be used to uncover venues' spatio-temporal patterns [57]. Others, instead, infer them from implicit data. These include, for example, sourcing POIs by clustering geo-tagged photographs that users upload to services like Flickr [20, 51]. These datasets can be used to automatically extract features of places and events [66], and have also been applied to image search result diversification [40]. Further information about the inferred items can be gathered by intersecting the location data with any available content and tags [41].

While the methods above can be used to populate information about items, geo-tagged photos have also been used to make inferences about users' behaviours. These include identify trips [60], analysing how tourists navigate a city [31], and predicting how people travel [18]. In essence, the seemingly meaningless act of taking a photograph from a geo-aware device can be used to find that (a) the targets of photographs are items that are of interest to users and (b) the users who took those photos are interested in, and have travelled between, those targets that they have captured.

Mobility data has more traditionally been sourced from mobile phones. These include the phones' Global Position System (GPS) [88], sensors, GSM traces [76], as well as the Call Detail Records (CDRs) that are created when devices pair with cellular network communication towers [9]. A full review of the literature analysing these data sources is beyond the scope of this chapter [11, 33]. However, these sources of data uncover a vast range of features about users' behaviours, including how far they tend to travel, their likely mode of travel, and the urban areas they frequent [67]. Clearly, these sources of data encode users' daily routines: the open question, related to recommender systems, is the extent that these also signal users' tastes. Few historical studies shed some light on this issue. Froehlich et al. [25] found that mobility patterns correlate with users' preferences: people tend to frequent those places that they like; similarity between users can also be measured from location histories [48]. However, other studies uncover that between 50 and 70 % of users' mobility captures routine behaviours [14]. The fact that such a large proportion of the user data contains places that users will, by definition, be very familiar with challenges the perspective of building recommender systems to facilitate *discovery* of new places. Yet this kind of data has been used to design location-based social activity recommendations [62]. Moreover, GPS traces can be mined for 'interesting' locations [89] in order to recommend locations and activities [86]; further details of the algorithmic approaches appear in the following section.

All of the above data sources share the common trait of requiring processing prior to being used as signals of users' mobility and/or preference. They differ from one another, instead, in how easily and accurately they may be collected. Typically, sources such as GSM and CDRs are only available to mobile operators; GPS and similar on-board location services require a tailor made app-based data collector. While the former kind of data is typically coarse-grained, and GPS can provide much finer-grained samples (both spatially and temporally), fully efficient implementations are dependent on the needs on the underlying application. In particular, continuously querying a phone's GPS sensor will quickly degrade the device's battery: system designers need to trade-off between the sampling accuracy that they seek and the energy efficiency of their application [64]. On the other hand, many applications collect data explicitly from their users, such as via location check-ins. These sorts of systems surface a variety of issues that reflect on data quality, such as the incentives and reasons that users have for contributing at all. Lindqvist et. al [49] explored a host of reasons why people participate in these location-based services (often, at the expense of their own privacy). These include: personal tracking, gaming, and social signalling with friends; moreover, they also uncover that there are many places that people proactively chose to *do not* check-in to.

14.2.2 Behavioural Inferences from Smartphone Sensors

While the previous section mainly dealt with what systems can learn about users and items from mobility data (including smartphone sensors, like GPS), there is a growing field of research that focuses on further behavioural aspects that can be inferred from sensors [43]. To date, these have not been widely applied to recommender systems. We include this brief review here since (a) these inferences provide insights into users, and is thus relevant to user modelling using smartphones, and (b) to highlight future opportunities that may emerge from applying these inferences to personalised systems.

1. **Activity Recognition.** Data from smartphone sensors (e.g., the accelerometer) has been used to monitor and detect users' current activities. These include whether the user is walking, sitting, driving, or talking [16]. Moreover, smartphone sensors have been used to detect users' contexts, including whether they are in an environment where music is being played [50].
2. **Transportation Modes.** Combinations of accelerometer and GPS data have been used to infer how users are moving between places, detecting transportation modes such as bicycles, cars, buses, or subways [77]. These kinds of inferences have, more broadly, been used to monitor users' 'green' behaviours [26], indicating how inferences from sensor states can be used to profile users' behaviours.
3. **Sociability.** Smartphone sensors have also been used to detect users' social networks and interactions [24]. A mixture of Bluetooth, accelerometers, and microphone sensors has been applied to detect users' collocations and interactions [65], both to quantify those users who are more sociable and provide feedback to users. Other work takes similar data into the domain of recommendation, by recommending online contacts based on physically sensed collocations [61].

There are a number of challenges related to the above, which include collecting data *efficiently*, without overly draining devices' batteries, designing *accurate* inference algorithms in order to infer the higher-level behaviours that are relevant to the user-modelling task at hand. However, these methods promise to deliver highly granular data about users: where they go, whom they interact with, their activities and routines, and more: just as locations reflect preference, future mobile recommender systems may use sensor inferences to augment user profiles.

14.3 Computing Recommendations in Mobile Applications

In this section, we describe approaches that have been proposed in order to compute recommendations for mobile users. In particular, we focus on how the problem of generating recommendations related to venues (e.g., restaurants, shops) has been formulated into well-defined machine learning problems, that can then be tackled by learning from the kinds of data described in the previous section.

We begin by briefly reviewing the equivalent in traditional recommender systems. In general, a recommender system will have a set of *items* and *users*; any given user may have rated a fraction of the items (or performed equivalent actions, if the system deals with implicit data: we use the term 'rating' to generically mean a preference value). The task of the system is to recommend, to each user, those items that he/she will be interested in—perhaps with a number of constraints. To do so, the system computes personalised *predictions* for those items that a user has not rated. These predictions can then be used to *rank* items according to estimated preference; the user is presented with a list of items ordered according to how interested the system has forecasted that user will be in them. Broadly, therefore, the two main approaches to web recommendation focus on rating prediction and item ranking

[21] (see also Chap. 7). In mobile recommender systems, some of these principles continue to apply: in the following, we review variants of them that have been tailored to particular mobile recommendation scenarios.

These variants have emerged for two reasons: first, those tasks that users seek to accomplish in mobile settings often differ from what people do on the web, and it is questionable as to whether the problem of information overload is applicable at all. Further, there are a variety of challenges related to applying machine learning to tasks related to mobile scenarios. These include limitations that are a result of the data itself (e.g., inferring preference from mobility, differentiating between positive and negative experiences from implicit datasets), as well as our current understanding of the limits to the predictability of any data that can be collected [14, 33]. Finally, there are also differences in the users themselves, who may be locals or tourists and may be interested in geographical regions of varying size.

14.3.1 Overview of Recommendation Formulations

In this section, we examine how the problem of recommending places to mobile users has been defined as a formal prediction problem. In particular, we consider four variants of the broad problem: (1) recommending venues of particular categories, (2) recommending the *next* place that a user may like to visit, (3) recommending *new* places that users have yet to visit, and (4) recommending *routes* that users may like to take as they navigate a particular space. While each of these can generally be considered as place-focused recommendation problems, they each capture differences in users' needs from a mobile recommender.

1. **Categorical Recommendation.** The setting that is likely to mirror 'traditional' single-category online recommendation is that of recommending venues of a particular type (e.g., restaurants). Systems described in the literature focus on shops [78, 82] restaurants [69, 81], and cultural/tourist travel [5, 83]. Much like movie recommendation (see Chap. 7), the items in this setting tend to all be the same—the task is therefore to rank them appropriately, perhaps with the only added constraint of being within a particular radius of the user's current location. In [69], items are described with n-dimensional vectors that include further attributes of each venue (e.g., average cost); this way of representing the data allows for the system which takes a conversational approach to recommending the best restaurant.
2. **Predicting the Next Place.** Let us assume that a user having dinner at a restaurant; she now would like a recommendation for bars or clubs to go to once she has finished eating. This is an example of seeking a recommendation for the *next* place to visit: the relevant inputs to this query are (a) the user and her preferences/location history, (b) the current location of the user, and (c) the current time of day. Formally, let us represent a user's location history as a time series of venues that end at the current venue V_n at time t_n:

$$P_u = \big((V_0, t_0), (V_1, t_1), \ldots, (V_{n-1}, t_{n-1}), (V_n, t_n)\big) \tag{14.1}$$

Given a set of candidate venues L, the prediction task is thus to predict which venue V_{n+1} the user should visit. More broadly, the goal is to *rank* venues such that the venue V_{n+1} that the user would like to visit next is placed as highly as possible within the recommendation list [56]. To do so, a ranking score $\hat{r}_{u,v}$ is computed for every venue v in $(L \backslash \{V_n\})$ (i.e., all the venues except the one where the user currently is) using features from all users' location histories (as described below).

$$\hat{r}_{u,v} = P(v = V_{n+1} | u, V_n) \tag{14.2}$$

This problem has been tackled in the literature using both Foursquare check-in data [56] and GPS and WiFi log data (although not from the perspective of recommendation) [53, 71]. Successfully predicting next places with these datasets, however, highlights one of the open challenges of this method when applied to a recommendation scenario: part of the success may be attributed to the habitual or otherwise routine mobility that is captured in the data [33]; in essence, predicting that a user will go from home to work and back again seems to have little value from the perspective of a recommender system. To tackle this shortcoming, researchers have narrowed the scope of what venues in L are candidate for recommendation: the following section focuses on one subset of these.

3. **Predicting New Venues.** Since recommender systems are often described as tools to facilitate discovery, another problem that mobile systems may tackle is that of predicting the *previously unvisited* venues that a user may like to go to. This problem has been formally defined by Noulas et. al [55] as follows. Given the set of venues U that a user u has historically visited over a period of time $(t - \Delta, t)$, the aim is to predict those venues in $(L \setminus U)$ that the user may like to visit in time $(t, t + \Delta)$. The choice of time period Δ is a parameter that determines the extent that this approach may be amenable to venue *rediscovery*, e.g. predicting venues that the user has not been to yesterday, last week, last month, or ever at all.

   Like above, this approach has its own shortcomings. Most notably, this approach can only predict and recommend novel locations that the system already knows about (i.e., that are available in the training data set), which is a particular instance of the cold-start problem.

4. **Recommending Routes to Follow.** Research that has focused on recommending to tourists often deals with personalised routes that this kind of user may follow as they explore a new area [15]; tourists' digital footprints can be directly uncovered from the photographs they take while on tour [30, 32], which can then be used to construct personalised tours [1, 12]. The idea here is somewhat akin to recommending a playlist of tracks [6], albeit with added geographic constraints: the formal task is to compute a sorted list of places to visit that optimises against both the user's preference, the time to travel between stop points, and any other contextual factors.

In essence, this setting may be viewed as an instance of the 'next place' problem, where the task is to recommend the next N places based on a number of constraints. For example, the system in [73] considers the time since a user has visited a place of a particular category, in order to diversify results. Similarly, the system in [13] also considers venue opening/closing times, the routes between places, and the 'best' times to visit particular venues. Finally, the system in [4] also considers the kinds of tourists groups that are requesting recommendations—including, for example, whether the group includes children.

We note that a number of other variant prediction problems that are relevant to mobile recommendations exist; the above are a selection that have appeared in the recent literature. These include, for example, discovering new events [75].

14.3.2 Algorithmic Approaches to Venue Recommendation

In this section, we review some of the algorithmic approaches that have been adopted for mobile recommendation. Many of these leverage the principles underlying collaborative filtering [28, 87]: a full review of collaborative filtering is beyond the scope of this chapter (see Chap. 7). Broadly speaking, when users can be represented as vectors of the venues that they have a preference for, and venues ('items') can be represented as vectors of the users who have a preference for them, the entire family of collaborative filtering approaches can be applied.

A particular characteristic of location-based recommender systems is that recommendation results may need to be pre- and/or post-filtered in order to localise the results to a particular geographic area [2]. These approaches are, more generally, typically applied in *context-aware* recommender systems: in the location-based domain, this may, for example, entail pre-filtering by only training on those ratings that match the current target one and/or post-filtering by removing some of the ranked items (e.g., "only show me recommendations within a 5 kilometre radius").

We begin by describing baseline approaches that may be suitable to compare any recommendation algorithm against. The include:

- **Popularity.** Although non-personalised, popularity is a strong baseline to consider when recommending venues. Popularity may be defined in a number of ways: geographically, by absolute number of visitors, by visitors' frequency of visits, or by category. While this approach does not personalise results, it captures the fact that popular venues are—by definition—places that many people will like to go to. A personalised variant of popularity could, for example, rank places based on a user's historical patterns (e.g., ranking coffee shops highly if a user tends to visit this category often).
- **Proximity.** Since the 'items' in venue recommender systems have an inherent geographical layout, another baseline to compare against is that of simply recommending venues by geographical distance from the user's current position [62].

This baseline does not consider preference, historical mobility, or any other contextual factors—yet captures users' tendency to travel over short distances [54].

An approach that has emerged in the recent literature [55, 56] revolves around extracting features from the data, creating binary-labelled datasets, and applying supervised learning in order to learn the likelihood that a user visit a particular venue. There are three kinds of features that can be extracted from mobility preference data. These include:

- **Place Features.** Beyond any categorical/attribute data that is available for venues, mobility data can be used to infer aspects of places that are, more broadly, related to the behaviours of those people who attend them. These include (a) the overall popularity of the venue, (b) the popularity of that venue at a particular time of day, or day of week, (c) the popularity of the venue within its particular category or geographic space. Popularity can be defined both in terms of absolute visits or the unique number of users who have visited a place.
- **User Features.** As above, beyond any attribute data available for a user, the mobility data can expose a number of features about preference for venues. These include (a) the frequency or proportion of times that the user has historically visited a place, (b) the user's prior likelihood of visiting a place of a particular category, and (c) the distance of a venue from the geographic centroid of a users' historical mobility. If a social network is also available, similar features can be extracted for a user's friends for each venue—capturing the importance of friend's mobility in determining how users navigate places [23].
- **Structural Features.** Finally, mobile data about users and places also inherently encodes a number of structural properties that are a result of both places and users combined. These include geographic features: the distance between places, and the *rank* distance between neighbouring venues. A sizeable amount of data about users' mobility allows for features relating to transition probabilities: what is the likelihood that a person go from venue A to venue B, or from category A to category B? The benefit of these features is that they are not solely based on geography; they uncover features that relate places without needing to know about the spatial layout of the items.

Using any of the available features described above, each visit by a user to a venue can be turned into a positively labelled *instance* that can be used to train any supervised learning approach (e.g. linear regression and decision trees [56]). However, doing so using only positively labelled instances will lead to poor results, as the training data is highly skewed. To overcome this, researchers have augmented their training data by randomly selecting unvisited venues to construct negatively labelled instances. This approach effectively reduces the problem of ranking into one of training a regression model with binary data [19]; learning on extracted features seeks to determine what aspects of venues attract users to them—to then be able to compute ranking scores for other venues that can be provided as recommendations.

A second approach that has been recently applied to recommending venues is by using *random walks* (often, with restart [80]), which is well-known in the context of web search [58]. This approach is suitable for a dataset that can be represented as a graph; broadly, the algorithm begins at node i and moves across the graph's nodes with particular transition probabilities: eventually, the steady-state of this walk is reached, and defines the probability of being at any particular node j, or, put another way, the relevance of j with respect to i. In the case of venue recommendation, the graph we have at hand contains nodes of users and venues. Links between users and venues define the preference (e.g., historical visits) of a user to a venue, and weights on those links are the transition probabilities. If we have a social network, there are also links between users; this approach has been used both the recommend places [55] as well as recommend links to be added to the social network [7]. While powerful, this method suffers from the perspective of scalability: for example, in [55], a separate random walk was computed for each user.

14.4 Evaluating Mobile Recommendations

A critical step of all recommender system research is applying a methodology to evaluate the quality of the recommendations [35]. Mobile recommender systems are no exception; in fact, many of the techniques that have been applied to evaluate recommendation quality can be similarly applied to this domain. For a full review of recommender system evaluation, please refer to Chap. 8. Broadly speaking, just like in web settings, mobile recommendation evaluations can be conducted using *quantitative* and *qualitative* methods.

Quantitative methods mirror precisely what is traditionally done with web data: data sets are split into appropriate training and test sets, and the predictive power of learning algorithms is measured, after they have been given the training set, on the hidden test set. However, while many web experiments focus on prediction accuracy, since mobile data is often unary (i.e., a check-in) or implicit (e.g., from location traces), then *ranking* metrics are more often appropriate. For example, in [62] the percentile-ranking metric is used to evaluate the quality of recommended events, a metric that was previously used with implicit data [36]. In this case, a successful recommendation would highly rank those events that users subsequently attended. It therefore defines $gone_{u,j}$ as a binary flag that reflects whether user u attended event j, and $rank_{u,j}$ as the normalised rank of the event j in u's recommendations. The percentile-rank is defined as:

$$\overline{rank} = \frac{\sum_{u,j} gone_{u,j} \times rank_{u,j}}{\sum_{u,j} gone_{u,j}} \tag{14.3}$$

A number of recent studies have also provided *qualitative* evaluations of their systems [13]. Much like their web-based equivalents, these studies entail building a system, recruiting participants, and evaluating the recommendations using surveys, interviews, or similar methods. While offering similar benefits, such as a finer grained understanding of user experience, they do also tend to suffer from similar drawbacks; for example, they often face cold-start settings and are relatively small-scale. For example, Tintarev et al. [79] evaluated a mobile tourist recommender by having recruited participants complete a questionnaire. This questionnaire was used to generate personalised points of interest, and the system was then evaluated by examining the number of venues visited, as well as their popularity and novelty. Similarly, the Magitti system [10] was evaluated in the field, allowing the researchers to understand concepts such as omissions, distance to recommended places, and the transparency/explainability of the recommendations.

All of the studies above indicate that evaluating a mobile recommender system begins by evaluating the recommender system as it would be evaluated on the web. However, limiting studies to these evaluations alone will not expose the complex mesh of values that users seek in a successful recommendation, including aspects that are also applicable to the web (novelty, diversity, explainability) as well as aspects that are unique to mobile settings (distance, time of day, geographic representativity, venue opening hours, etc.).

14.5 Conclusions and Future Directions

In this chapter, we have reviewed the basic components of mobile location-based recommender systems: the tasks that these systems seek to support, the (explicit, implicit, or sensor) data that can be used to build them, how these kinds of recommendations are defined as formal prediction problems, the algorithms that have been applied to them in the recent literature, and how these systems are both quantitatively and qualitatively evaluated. In doing so, a number of themes have emerged; a number of open challenges remain as we look forward to the future research in this domain. We close this chapter by describing a number of these challenges:

1. **Context.** Mobile recommender systems are, arguably, even more tied to users' current context than their web-based equivalents: those venues that people seek to discover will be highly dependent on (beyond their preferences) where they are, the time of day, who they are with, and perhaps even how they feel. While the concept of context is emergent in the recommender system literature [2, 3], fitting it appropriately into mobile recommender systems requires revisiting how context can be defined, collected, and applied to this domain.
2. **Hierarchical Item Sets.** In traditional recommender systems, 'items' are well-defined entities (books, e-commerce items) that often do not overlap, and may be 'dynamic' in terms, for example, their stockroom availability [37]. In mobile recommender systems, 'items' are dynamic in that they may be venues that are open, closed, or permanently moved; they may be events that have varying temporal qualities (e.g., a theatre production that lasts for 1 month vs. a rock concert that only happens on one night); or indeed they may have varying

geographic spans (such as a venue vs. a neighbourhood [85]). In essence, the items in mobile recommenders are strongly structured and relate to one another both hierarchically and spatio-temporally. One problem that emerges here is that historical mobility-preference data detracts from these system's ability to recommend upcoming events of interest, that will have no associated data. Future work can explore how these dynamics may be learned or detected, and, perhaps more importantly, how to appropriately structure a recommender system that balances between distance and preference: should such a system recommend that the user travel to somewhere distant in exchange for a high preference match, or recommend somewhere nearby that does not fully fit their profile?

3. **Privacy.** All of the potential that mobile recommender systems uncover seems to conflict with users' privacy: the data that we have described above includes instances of both users' selective exposure of their location as well as passive location tracking. Future systems may consider including obfuscation mechanisms that re-introduce certain levels of privacy into the collected data [63]: more work is required to understand how this would impact users' recommendations, and how to overcome any shortcomings.
4. **Proactivity and Interruptions.** As smartphones accompany their owners throughout their daily life, and are often within arms reach of their owners [22], mobile location recommender systems can also proactively send notifications to their users about places of potential interest that are around them [27]. The challenge with this feature is understanding the balance between pushing relevant information to users and not overly burdening them with a constant stream of interruptions. Recent work [59] has analysed interruptions within the context of mobile experience-sampling: future work could focus on whether a system could similarly learn about how to appropriately interrupt users to deliver recommendations.
5. **Different Users and Items.** This chapter has focused on recommending places to people. Future mobile systems need not limit themselves to this paradigm. For example, recent work has used mobility patterns to recommend public transport fares [44] and personalise service status updates [45]. Similarly, recent work has recommended passenger pick-up locations to cab drivers (and vice versa) [84], recommended where to place new retail stores in a city [38], and recommended places to groups of people [70]; the definition of what constitutes a 'user' and an 'item' is open to many further interpretations.

The list above constitutes a brief set of ideas about future directions for mobile recommender systems. As smartphones' ability to collect valuable data increases, these devices are beginning to draw the interest of researchers beyond the computer sciences [46]; the future work in this domain has the potential of having far-reaching implications across both research and practical applications.

References

1. Abowd, G., Atkeson, C., Hong, J., Long, S., Kooper, R., Pinkerton, M.: Cyberguide: a Mobile Context-Aware Tour Guide. Wireless Network **3** (2007)
2. Adomavicius, G., Tuzhilin, A.: Context-Aware Recommender Systems. In: ACM Recommender Systems, pp. 335–336. Lausanne, Switzerland (2008)
3. Adomavicius, G., Tuzhilin, A.: Context-aware recommender systems. In: Recommender systems handbook, pp. 217–253. Springer (2011)
4. Ardissono, L., Goy, A., Petrone, G., Segnan, M., Torasso, P.: Intrigue: Personalized Recommendation of Tourist Attractions for Desktop and Handset Devices. Applied Artificial Intelligence **17** (2003)
5. Ardissono, L., Kuflik, T., Petrelli, D.: Personalization in Cultural Heritage: The Road Travelled and the One Ahead. User Modelling and User-Adapted Interaction **22**(1), 73–99 (2012)
6. Baccigalupo, C., Plaza, E.: Case-Based Sequential Ordering of Songs for Playlist Recommendation. Lecture Notes in Computer Science **4106**, 286 – 300 (2006)
7. Backstrom, L., Leskovec, J.: Supervised Random Walks: Predicting and Recommending Links in Social Networks. In: ACM WSDM. Hong Kong, China (2011)
8. Bawa-Cavia, A.: Sensing the Urban: Using Location-Based Social Network Data in Urban Analysis. In: Workshop on Pervasive Urban Applications. San Francisco, USA (2011)
9. Becker, R., Caceres, R., Hanson, K., Isaacman, S., Loh, J., Martonosi, M., Rowland, J., Urbanek, S., Varshavsky, A., Volisky, C.: Human Mobility Characterization from Cellular Network Data. Communications of the ACM **56**(1), 74–82 (2013)
10. Bellotti, V., Begole, B., Chi, E., et al.: Activity-Based Serendipitous Recommendations with the Magitti Mobile Leisure Guide. In: ACM CHI. Florence, Italy (2008)
11. Blondel, V. (ed.): 3rd Conference on the Analysis of Mobile Phone Datasets. Boston, USA (2013)
12. C.H. Tai D.N. Yang, L.L., Chen, M.S.: Recommending Personalized Scenic Itinerary with Geo-Tagged Photos. In: ICME. Hannover, Germany (2008)
13. Cheverst, K., Davies, N., Mitchell, K., Friday, A., Efstratiou, C.: Developing a Context-Aware Electronic Tourist Guide: Some Issues and Experiences. In: ACM CHI. The Hague, The Netherlands (2000)
14. Cho, E., Myers, S., Leskovec, J.: Friendship and Mobility: User Movement in Location-Based Social Networks. In: ACM KDD. San Diego, USA (2011)
15. Choudhury, M., Feldman, M., Amer-Yahia, S., Golbandi, N., Lempel, R., Yu, C.: Automatic Construction of Travel Itineraries using Social Breadcrumbs. In: ACM Hypertext. Ontario, Canada (2010)
16. Choudhury, T., Borriello, G., Consolvo, S., Haehnel, D., Harrison, B., Hemingway, B., Hightower, J., Klasnja, P., Koscher, K., LaMarca, A., LeGrand, L., Lester, J., Rahimi, A., Rea, A., Wyatt, D.: The Mobile Sensing Platform: An Embedded Activity Recognition System. IEEE Pervasive Computing **7**(2), 32–41 (2008)
17. Church, K., Smyth, B.: Understanding the Intent Behind Mobile Information Needs. In: International Conference on Intelligent User Interfaces, pp. 247–256. Sanibel Island, FL, USA (2009)
18. Clements, M., Serdyukov, P., deVries, A.P., M.J.T.Reinders: Using Flickr Geotags to Predict User Travel Behaviour. In: ACM SIGIR. Geneva, Switzerland (2010)
19. Cohen, W., Schapire, R., Singer, Y.: Learning to Order Things. Journal of Artificial Intelligence Research **10**(1), 243–270 (1999)
20. Crandall, D., Backstrom, L., Huttenlocher, D., Kleinberg, J.: Mapping the World's Photos. In: WWW. Madrid, Spain (2009)
21. Deshpande, M., Karypis, G.: Item-Based Top-N Recommendation Algorithms. ACM Transactions on Information Systems **22**(1), 143–177 (2004)
22. Dey, A., Wac, K., Ferreira, D., Tassini, K., Hong, J., Ramos, J.: Getting Closer: An Empirical Investigation of the Proximity of Users to their Smartphones. In: ACM Ubicomp. Beijing, China (2011)

23. Domenico, M.D., Lima, A., Musolesi, M.: Interdependence and Predictability of Human Mobility and Social Interactions. In: Nokia Mobile Data Challenge Workshop. Newcastle, United Kingdom (2012)
24. Eagle, N., Pentland, A.: Reality Mining: Sensing Complex Social Systems. Personal and Ubiquitous Computing **10**(4), 255–268 (2006)
25. Froehlich, J., Chen, M., Smith, I., Potter, F.: Voting With Your Feet: An Investigative Study of the Relationship Between Place Visit Behavior and Preference. In: ACM Ubicomp (2006)
26. Froehlich, J., Dillahunt, T., Klasnja, P., Mankoff, J., Consolvo, S., Harrison, B., Landay, J.: UbiGreen: Investigating a Mobile Tool for Tracking and Supporting Green Transportation Habits. In: ACM CHI. Boston, USA (2009)
27. Gallego-Vico, D., Woerndl, W., Bader, R.: A Study on Proactive Delivery of Restaurant Recommendations for Android Smartphones. In: ACM RecSys Workshop on Personalization in Mobile Applications. Chicago, USA (2011)
28. Gao, H., Tang, J., Hu, X., Liu, H.: Exploring Temporal Effects for Location Recommendation on Location-Based Social Networks. In: ACM Recommender Systems. Hong Kong, China (2013)
29. Gavalas, D., Bellavista, P., Cao, J., Issarny, V.: Mobile Applications: Status and Trends. Journal of Systems and Software **84**(11), 1823–1826 (2011)
30. Girardin, F., Blat, J., Calabrese, F., Fiore, F.D., Ratti, C.: Digital Footprinting: Uncovering Tourists with User-Generated Content. IEEE Pervasive Computing **7**(4), 36–43 (2008)
31. Girardin, F., Calabrese, F., Fiore, F.D., Ratti, C., Blat, J.: Digital Footprinting: Uncovering Tourists with User-Generated Content. IEEE Pervasive Computing **7**(4), 36–43 (2008)
32. Girardin, F., Fiore, F.D., Ratti, C., Blat, J.: Leveraging Explicitly Disclosed Location Information to Understand Tourist Dynamics: A Case Study. Journal of Location-Based Services **2**(1), 41–54 (2008)
33. Gonzalez, M., Hidalgo, C., Barabasi, A.L.: Understanding Individual Human Mobility Patterns. Nature **453**(5) (2008)
34. van der Heijden, H., Kotsis, G., Kronsteiner, R.: Mobile Recommendation Systems for Decision Making on the Go. In: IEEE ICMB (2005)
35. Herlocker, J., Konstan, J., Terveen, L., Riedl, J.: Evaluating Collaborative Filtering Recommender Systems. ACM Transactions on Information Systems **22**, 5–53 (2004)
36. Hu, Y., Koren, Y., Volinsky, C.: Collaborative Filtering for Implicit Feedback Datasets. In: IEEE ICDM, pp. 263–272. Pisa, Italy (2008)
37. Jambor, T., Wang, J.: Optimizing Multiple Objectives in Collaborative Filtering. In: ACM Recommender Systems, pp. 55–62. Barcelona, Spain (2010)
38. Karamshuk, D., Noulas, A., Scellato, S., Nicosia, V., Mascolo, C.: Geo-Spotting: Mining Online Location-Based Services for Optimal Retail Store Placement. In: ACM KDD. Chicago, USA (2013)
39. Karatzoglou, A., Baltrunas, L., Church, K., Bohmer, M.: Climbing the App Wall: Mobile App Discovery through Context-Aware Recommendations. In: ACM CIKM. Maui, Hawaii (2012)
40. Kennedy, L., Naaman, M.: Generating Diverse and Representative Image Search Results for Landmarks. In: WWW. Madrid, Spain (2008)
41. Kennedy, L., Naaman, M., Ahern, S., Nair, R., Rattenbury, T.: How Flickr Helps us Make Sense of the World: Context and Content in Community-Contributed Media Collections. In: ACM MM. Augsburg, Germany (2007)
42. Kenteris, M., Gavalas, D., Economou, D.: Electronic Mobile Guides: A Survey. Personal and Ubiquitous Computing **15**(1), 97–111 (2011)
43. Lane, N., Miluzzo, E., Lu, H., Peebles, D., Choudhury, T., Campbell, A.: A Survey of Mobile Phone Sensing. IEEE Communications Magazine (2010)
44. Lathia, N., Capra, L.: Mining Mobility Data to Minimise Travellers' Spending on Public Transport. In: ACM KDD. San Diego, California (2011)
45. Lathia, N., Froehlich, J., Capra, L.: Mining Public Transport Usage for Personalised Intelligent Transport Systems. In: IEEE ICDM. Sydney, Australia (2010)

46. Lathia, N., Pejovic, V., Rachuri, K., Musolesi, M., Rentfrow, P.: Smartphones for Large-Scale Behaviour Change Interventions. IEEE Pervasive Computing, Special Issue on Understanding and Changing Behaviour **12**(3) (2013)
47. Lathia, N., Rachuri, K., Mascolo, C., Rentfrow, P.: Contextual Dissonance: Design Bias in Sensor-Based Experience Sampling Methods. In: ACM Ubicomp. Zurich, Switzerland (2013)
48. Li, Q., Zheng, Y., Xie, X., Chen, Y., Liu, W., Ma, W.: Mining User Similarity Based on Location History. In: Intl. Conf. on Advances in Geographic Information Systems. Santa Ana, USA (2008)
49. Lindqvist, J., Cranshaw, J., Wiese, J., Hong, J., Zimmerman, J.: I'm the Mayor of My House: Examining Why People Use Foursquare - a Social-Driven Location Sharing Application. In: ACM CHI. Vancouver, Canada (2011)
50. Lu, H., Pan, W., Lane, N., Choudhury, T., Campbell, A.: SoundSense: Scalable Sound Sensing for People-Centric Applications on Mobile Phones. In: ACM MobiSys. Krakow, Poland (2009)
51. Marlow, C., Naaman, M., Boyd, D., Davis, M.: Position Paper, Tagging, Taxonomy, Flickr, Article, ToRead. In: Collaborative Web Tagging Workshop (WWW) (2006)
52. Miller, B., Konstan, J., Riedl, J.: PocketLens: Toward a Personal Recommender System. In: ACM TOIS (2005)
53. Monreale, A., Pinelli, F., Trasarti, R., Giannotti, F.: WhereNext: A Location Predictor on Trajectory Pattern Mining. In: ACM SIGKDD, pp. 637–646. Paris, France (2009)
54. Noulas, A., Scellato, S., Lambiotte, R., Pontil, M., Mascolo, C.: A Tale of Many Cities: Universal Patterns in Human Urban Mobility. PLoS ONE **7**(5) (2012)
55. Noulas, A., Scellato, S., Lathia, N., Mascolo, C.: A Random Walk Around the City: New Venue Recommendation in Location-Based Social Networks. In: IEEE International Conference on Social Computing. Amsterdam, The Netherlands (2012)
56. Noulas, A., Scellato, S., Lathia, N., Mascolo, C.: Mining User Mobility Features for Next Place Prediction in Location-based Services. In: IEEE Internationcal Conference on Data Mining. Brussels, Belgium (2012)
57. Noulas, A., Scellato, S., Mascolo, C., Pontil, M.: An Empirical Study of Geographic User Activity Patterns in Foursquare. In: AAAI ICWSM. Barcelona, Spain (2011)
58. Page, L., Brin, S., Motwani, R., Winograd, T.: The PageRank Citation Ranking: Bringin Order to the Web. In: Technical Report Stanford InfoLab. Stanford, USA (1999)
59. Pejovic, V., Musolesi, M.: InterruptMe: Designing Intelligent Prompting Mechanisms in Pervasive Applications. In: ACM Ubicomp. Seattle, USA (2014)
60. Popescu, A., Grefenstette, G.: Deducing Trip Related Information from Flickr. In: WWW. Madrid, Spain (2009)
61. Quercia, D., Capra, L.: FriendSensing: Recommending Friends Using Mobile Phones. In: ACM RecSys. New York, USA (2009)
62. Quercia, D., Lathia, N., Calabrese, F., Lorenzo, G.D., Crowcroft, J.: Recommending Social Events from Mobile Phone Location Data. In: IEEE ICDM. Sydney, Australia (2010)
63. Quercia, D., Leontiadis, I., McNamara, L., Mascolo, C., Crowcroft, J.: SpotME If You Can: Randomized Responses for Location Obfuscation on Mobile Phones. In: ICDCS. Minneapolis, USA (2011)
64. Rachuri, K., Mascolo, C., Musolesi, M.: Energy-Accuracy Trade-offs of Sensor Sampling in Smart Phone based Sensing Systems. In: Mobile Context Awareness: Capabilities, Challenges and Applications Workshop. Springer, Copenhagen, Denmark (2010)
65. Rachuri, K., Mascolo, C., Musolesi, M., Rentfrow, P.: SociableSense: Exploring the Trade-offs of Adaptive Sampling and Computation Offloading for Social Sensing. In: ACM MobiCom. Las Vegas, USA (2011)
66. Rattenbury, T., Good, N., Naaman, M.: Toward Automatic Extraction of Event and Place Semantics from Flickr Tags. In: ACM SIGIR, pp. 103–110 (2007)
67. Ratti, C., Pulselli, R., Williams, S., Frenchman, D.: Mobile Landscapes: Using Location Data from Cell Phones for Urban Analysis. Environment and Planning B **33**(5), 727–748 (2006)
68. Ricci, F.: Mobile Recommender Systems. Journal of IT & Tourism **12**(3), 205–231 (2011)
69. Ricci, F., Nguyen, Q.N.: Critique-Based Mobile Recommender Systems. OGAI Journal (2005)

70. Salamo, M., McCarthy, K., Smyth, B.: Generating Recommendations for Consensus Negotiation in Group Personalization Services. Personal and Ubiquitous Computing **16**(5), 597–610 (2012)
71. Scellato, S., Musolesi, M., Mascolo, C., Latora, V., Campbell, A.: NextPlace: A Spatio-Temporal Prediction Framework for Pervasive Systems. In: Ninth International Conference on Pervasive Computing. San Francisco, USA (2011)
72. Schiller, J., Voisard, A. (eds.): Location-Based Services. Morgan Kaufman Publishers (2004)
73. van Setten, M., Pokraev, S., Koolwaaij, J.: Context- Aware Recommendations in the Mobile Tourist Application COMPASS. In: Adaptive Hypermedia and Adaptive Web-Based Systems. Eindhoven, The Netherlands (2004)
74. Shaw, B., Shea, J., Sinha, S., Hogue, A.: Learning to Rank for Spatiotemporal Search. In: ACM WSDM. Rome, Italy (2013)
75. Sklar, M., Shaw, B., Hogue, A.: Recommending Interesting Events in Real Time with Foursquare Checkins. In: ACM Recommender Systems. Dublin, Ireland (2012)
76. Sohn, T., Varshavky, A., LaMarca, A., Chen, M., Choudhury, T., Smith, I., Consolvo, S., Hightower, J., Grisworld, W., de Lara, E.: Mobility Detection Using Everyday GSM Traces. In: ACM Ubicomp. Orange County, USA (2006)
77. Stenneth, L., Wolfson, O., Yu, P., Xu, B.: Transportation Mode Detection using Mobile Phones and GIS Information. In: ACM SIGSPATIAL. Chicago, USA (2011)
78. Takeuchi, Y., Sugimoto, M.: CityVoyager: an Outdoor Recommendation System Based on User Location History. Ubiquitous Intelligence and Computing (2006)
79. Tintarev, N., Amatriain, X., Flores, A.: Off the Beaten Track: A Mobile Field Study Exploring the Long Tail of Tourist Recommendations. In: MobileHCI. Lisbon, Portugal (2010)
80. Tong, H., Faloutsos, C., Pan, J.: Fast Random Walk with Restart and Its Applications. In: IEEE International Conference on Data Mining. Hong Kong, China (2006)
81. Tung, H., Soo, V.: A Personalized Restaurant Recommender Agent for Mobile E-Service. In: Proceedings of IEEE International Conference on e-Technology, e-Commerce, and e-Services, pp. 259–262. Washington DC, USA (2004)
82. Yang, W., Cheng, H., Dia, J.: A Location-Aware Recommender System for Mobile Shopping Environments. Expert Systems with Applications (2008)
83. Yoon, H., Zheng, Y., Xie, X., Woo, W.: Social Itinerary Recommendation from User-Generated Digital Trails. Personal and Ubiquitous Computing **16**(5), 469–484 (2012)
84. Yuan, N., Zheng, Y., Zhang, L., Xie, X.: T-Finder: A Recommender System for Fidning Passengers and Vacant Taxis. IEEE Transactions on Knowledge and Data Engineering **25**(10) (2013)
85. Zhang, A., Noulas, A., Scellato, S., Mascolo, C.: Hoodsquare: Modeling and Recommending Neighborhoods in Location-Based Social Networks. In: SocialCom. Washington DC, USA (2013)
86. Zheng, V., Zheng, Y., Xie, X., Yang, Q.: Collaborative Location and Activity Recommendations with GPS History Data. In: WWW. Raleigh, North Carolina (2010)
87. Zheng, V.W., Cao, B., Zheng, Y., Xie, X., Yang, Q.: Collaborative filtering meets mobile recommendation: A user-centered approach. In: AAAI (2010)
88. Zheng, Y., Li, Q., Chen, Y., Xie, X., Ma, W.: Understanding Mobility Based on GPS Data. In: ACM Ubicomp. Seoul, Korea (2008)
89. Zheng, Y., Zhang, L., Xie, X., Ma, W.: Mining Interesting Locations and Travel Sequences From GPS Trajectories. In: WWW. Madrid, Spain (2008)

Chapter 15
Social Recommender Systems

Ido Guy

15.1 Introduction

The recent decade introduced the "social web" social web or "Web 2.0" [54] , a web where people play a central role by creating content, annotating it with tags, votes (or 'likes'), or comments, joining communities, and connecting to friends. *Social media* websites are proliferating and attract millions of users who author content, post messages, share photos with their friends, and engage in many other types of activities. This rapid growth intensifies the phenomenon of *social overload*, where users of social media are exposed to a huge amount of information and participate in vast amounts of interactions. Social overload makes it harder on the one hand for social media users to choose which sites to engage in and for how long and on the other hand makes it more challenging for social media websites to attract users and retain them.

Social Recommender Systems (SRS) are recommender systems that target the social media domain. They aim at coping with the social overload challenge by presenting the most relevant and attractive data to the user, typically by applying personalization techniques. The "marriage" between recommender systems (RS) and social media has many potential benefits for both sides. On the one hand, social media introduces many new types of data and meta-data, such as tags and explicit online relationships, which can be used in a unique manner by RS to enhance their effectiveness. On the other hand, recommender systems are crucial for social media websites to enhance the adoption and engagement by their users and thus play an important role in the overall success of social media. It should be noted that traditional RS, such as user-based collaborative filtering, are social in their nature since they mimic the natural process where we seek advice or suggestions from

I. Guy (✉)
Yahoo Labs, Haifa, Israel
e-mail: idoguy@acm.org

F. Ricci et al. (eds.), *Recommender Systems Handbook*,
DOI 10.1007/978-1-4899-7637-6_15

other people [59]. Yet, in this chapter we focus on those recommender systems that are aimed for the social media domain, which we term *social recommender systems* [31].

This chapter focuses on two key areas of SRS, social media content recommendation and people recommendation. We dedicate a section to each of these areas, reviewing the different sub-domains, their unique characteristics, the applied methods, case studies in the enterprise, and open challenges. SRS consist of more areas, such as recommendation of tags and groups (communities), however, these are left beyond the scope of this chapter. The remainder of the chapter is organized as follows: the next two sections discuss in detail content and people recommendation. The following section discusses key aspects characterizing SRS as raised throughout its preceding two sections. The chapter concludes by reviewing emerging SRS domains and open challenges.

15.2 Content Recommendation

Social media introduced many new types of content that can be created and shared by any user in a way that has never been possible before. Users became the center of every social media website and in many cases were the ones creating the actual content of the site: textual content as in Wikipedia and WordPress; photos as in Flickr and Facebook; and video as in YouTube. Users also have a key role in providing feedback and annotating existing content on social media websites. Comments allow users to add their own opinion; votes and ratings allow them to 'like' (or dislike) favourite posts; and tags allow them to annotate the content with keywords that reflect their own viewpoint. These new types of feedback forms allow RS to implicitly infer user preferences and content popularity by analyzing the crowd's feedback.

In the social media era, articulated relationships have become available through social network sites (SNSs) [7] and changed the world of content recommendation. While in the past such relationships could only be partially extracted by surveys and interviews, and later by mining communication patterns from phone logs or email that are highly sensitive privacy-wise, the availability of relationships in social networks allows tapping into one's network of familiar people (Facebook, LinkedIn) or people of interest (Twitter) in a simpler way without infringing privacy. The use of the friend list instead of or alongside the list of similar people as in traditional CF has been broadly proven to be productive for enhancing content recommendations. Sinha and Swearingen [66] were among the first to compare friend-based recommendation with traditional methods and showed their effectiveness for movie and book recommendation. Golbeck [26] showed that friends can be a trusted source for movie recommendation. Groh and Ehmig [28] compared collaborative filtering with friend-based "social filtering" and showed the advantage of the latter for club recommendation within a German SNS. Overall, recommendation based on friends enhance recommendations' accuracy; allow the user to better judge the recommendations since s/he is familiar with the respective people; spare the need for explicit feedback from the user in order to calculate similarity; and help cope with the cold-start problem for new users.

The remainder of this section reviews key domains of social media content recommendation, such as blogs, microblogs, news, and multimedia. We then briefly discuss group recommendation, which is especially relevant for recommendation of social media content. Following, a case study of social media recommendation within the enterprise is presented in detail. The section concludes with a summary of key points.

15.2.1 Key Domains

Blogs Blogs are one of the classic social media applications and a natural ground for recommendation techniques. They typically consist of inherent hierarchy that SRS need to take into account. At the top of this hierarchy is the blog itself, which may be owned by an individual user or a community, and is often focused on a topic or domain. The blog includes different blog posts (or blog entries) that include one article by a single author. The author (and sometimes other users) can usually annotate the post with appropriate tags, which also serve for dissemination to relevant populations. The post's readers can add comments and can often also vote for (or 'like') the post; other authors can use a trackback to reference the post from their own post. In one of the early studies of blog recommendation, Arguello et al. [2] explored personalized recommendation of whole blogs (as opposed to blog posts) using the TrecBlog06 dataset [50]. Given a query that represented the user's topical interests, two document models were explored: the first included a single large document that was based on concatenation of all the blog's posts and the second was based on smaller documents, each representing a single post, while aggregation was made at ranking time. Evaluation indicated that both models performed equally well and that hybridization of both further improved the results.

Multimedia Multimedia recommendation is challenging due to the lower amounts of textual data and the extremely large size of the content. One of the most popular social media websites, YouTube, includes an advanced recommender system that drives a large portion of the user traffic and helps direct users to more relevant videos. Davidson et al. [16] stated that the goals of the YouTube recommendations are to be recent and fresh, diverse, and relevant to the user's recent actions. They also stated that users should understand why a video was recommended to them, thus incorporating explanations in the YouTube RS. As described in their paper, YouTube recommendations are based on the user's personal activity on the site and are expanded by a variant of collaborative filtering (CF) over the co-visitation graph. Ranking is done based on a variety of signals for relevance and diversity.

Community Question and Answering. Social or community question-and-answering (SQA or CQA) websites, such as StackOverflow, Quora, and Yahoo

Answers, allow users to ask various types of questions and receive (and vote for) answers from the crowd. As such, they also serve as a fertile ground for different types of recommender systems for both question askers and answerers. The challenge here is twofold: on the one hand, recommend to askers similar previously-asked questions to avoid redundant burden on answerers and spread of similar information in many question pages; on the other hand, recommend answerers with questions they may want to answer and increase overall answer engagement on the website. As one example, Szpektor et al. [67] experimented with recommendation of questions to potential answerers on the Yahoo Answers website. They discovered that topic relevance was not a good enough basis for recommendation. Diversity and freshness also played a key role: on the one hand, a novel and somewhat different question was more likely to arouse answerer's attention and on the other hand it was extremely important for answerers to receive questions that are very fresh, typically only a few minutes old.

Jobs LinkedIn is one of the most successful SNSs and as the world's largest professional network it has many unique recommendation challenges, such as of companies and of professional groups. Another specifically interesting example is the recommendation of job opportunities. Such recommendation can have a tremendous influence on people's lives as it can ultimately lead to a career change. Recommendation needs to take into account many aspects, such as location alternatives, candidate's experience, and timing. Wang et al. [70] shed some light on the job recommendation task at LinkedIn and particularly focus on the timing of recommendation. Their statistical model considered the tenure between two successive decisions to estimate the likelihood of a user's decision to make a job transition at a given point. Evaluation used the real-world job application data and demonstrated the effectiveness of their model and the importance of considering the time factor as part of the recommendation process.

News Social news aggregators such as Digg, Google Reader, Reddit, and Slashdot, allow users to post and rate news articles and surface the most interesting and trending stories. News recommendation is especially challenging due to the need for freshness. Old stories or stories to which the user has already been exposed will be considered bad recommendations, even when relevant to the user's tastes and preferences. The pace of news appearance is very high, while different users have different news consumption rates, which personalization techniques need to take into account. Digg used to be a popular social news aggregation service, allowing its users to submit links to news stories, vote, and discuss them. Aside from promoting the most popular stories to users (by votes), Lerman [46] described the personalized recommender system implemented for Digg that was based on friends and "diggers like me". Recommendations for another popular news website, Google Reader, were described by Liu et al. [49]. They combined CF techniques with "individual filtering" techniques. Evaluation, based on a live trial, indicated that the hybrid approach performed best and improved 38 % over a popularity-based baseline. Pure CF was only able to improve 31 % on top of the baseline. An increase in return rate was observed due to the hybrid recommendations, however, interestingly, there was no effect on the overall number of stories read on the homepage.

Microblogs Microblogging, most famously brought into attention by Twitter, allows user to broadcast short messages. Those messages are typically propagated across a network of followers and "followees", built by the user's ability to follow any another user. On twitter, each message is limited to 140 characters and is called a 'tweet'. The high pace of messages (over half a billion tweets per day), their real-time nature, their concise content, and the lack of metadata and structure, make the challenge of filtering and personalizing the Twitter firehose of unique nature. In one of the earlier studies, Chen et al. [12] explored content recommendation through URLs shared in tweets. They compared 12 algorithms that differed in the following aspects: (1) candidate selection was either based on popular tweets or on tweets from followees and followees-of-followees (FoF); (2) topic relevance was based on cosine similarity between the user and the URL. The user's representation was based on self-tweets or on followees' tweets; (3) social voting was based on the number of user's followees who also follow the author and on author's frequency of tweeting. Results, based on a field study with 44 subjects, indicated that social voting worked better than topic relevance; FoF candidate selection outperformed popularity; and using self tweets for user modeling performed better than using the followees' tweets. The introduction of the 'retweet' feature, which allows user to share another user's tweet with their own audience of followers, provided researchers with direct feedback about the level of interest in an individual tweet. Many studies followed that attempted to use this information to predict "good" tweets. As one example, Chen et al. [13] suggested a model for personalized tweet recommendation using "collaborative ranking". The model was based on both explicit and latent features and considered a wide variety of topic-level, social relations, and global factors. Evaluation was based on re-tweet prediction and showed the superiority of the collaborative ranking method over various baselines, such as Latent Dirichlet Allocation and Support Vector Machine. It also indicated that all the three factors are important to consider.

15.2.2 Group Recommendation

Groups and communities play a central role in social media and often times form the entry gate for participation [60]. This makes group recommendation techniques highly relevant for the SRS domain. Due to this relevance, we briefly review the broad area of group recommendation in this sub-section; in the following section, as part of the enterprise case study, we describe in more detail an example of SRS aimed for communities.

Group recommendation targets a group of individuals rather than a single one (Chap. 22). Example scenarios for group recommendation include friends planning together their "perfect" vacation; a family selecting a movie or a television show to watch together; a group of colleagues choosing a restaurant for an evening outside (or looking for a recipe for a joint meal); or the classic (and less relevant in the era of personal music players) gym problem [51]: selection of a playlist based on the current group of trainees in a fitness center.

Group recommendation poses new challenges compared to individual recommendations. Two of the prominent challenges are the specification of preferences by members and the recommendation generation. Jameson et al. [40] suggested a collaborative interface for members to specify their preferences in a group recommender system for travel, which allowed collaborative editing of the members' preferences. Such an interface holds various benefits: it allows members to persuade others to specify a similar preference to their own, perhaps by giving them information they had previously lacked; it enables to explain and justify a member's preference (e.g., "I can't go hiking due to an injury"); it allows taking into account attitudes and anticipated behavior of other members; and it encourages assimilation to facilitate the reaching of agreement.

The most studied challenge of group recommendation is the generation of recommendations themselves. The two main techniques are profile aggregation and recommendation aggregation. Profile aggregation produces a single profile representative of the group by aggregating the preferences of the different group members. Recommendation aggregation generates a recommendation list for each of the group members and aggregates the list into one single list for the group, typically by using rank aggregation techniques. Berkovsky et al. [6] experimented with these two approaches for recipe recommendation to groups and found that the profile aggregation method was superior over the recommendation aggregation method.

There are various approaches for aggregating member preferences into a single community profile, each with its own pros and cons. Among the prominent approaches are: (1) least misery, which seeks to maximize the minimum ranking of any group member. Obviously, this approach can lead to a recommendation that does not maximize the average rating or the maximum benefit; (2) fairness, which aims at the most equal rating balance across group members. This can lead to a recommendation that gets a low rating by all members of the group; (3) and fusion, which aggregates individual rankings (e.g., by Borda count). Baltrunas et al. [3] compared several techniques for group recommendation using the MovieLens dataset. They examined both profile aggregation and rank aggregation techniques and found the optimal one given a set of parameters, such as the group's size and the similarity among group members.

15.2.3 Case Study: Social Media Recommendation in the Enterprise

In this section, we review a body of research that explored recommendation of mixed social media items within the enterprise, and included three main studies. The first study [34] focused on recommendation based on social relationships. As previously mentioned, social media enables the exposure of different types of social relationships in a way that has never been possible before. The study explored a rich set of indicators for social relationships based on social media data and compared two types of networks as basis for recommendation: familiarity and similarity. The familiarity network was built based on explicit and implicit signals from enterprise social media, such as articulated connection within an enterprise SNS, tagging one another, or co-authorship of the same wiki page. The similarity network was based on common activity in enterprise social media, such as membership in the same communities, usage of the same tags, or commenting on the same blog posts. An "overall" network was also examined, combining the two types of relationships. The recommendation score of item i to user u was determined by the following formula:

$$RS(u,i) = e^{-\alpha t(i)} \sum_{v \in N^T(u)} S^T[u,v] \sum_{r \in R(v,i)} W(r[v,i]) \tag{15.1}$$

where $t(i)$ is the number of days passed since the creation date of i; α is a decay factor; $N^T(u)$ is the set of users within u's network of type T ($T \in \{\text{familiarity,similarity,overall}\}$); $S^T[u,v]$ is the relationship score between u and v based on the network of type T; $R(v,i)$ is the set of all relationship types between user v and item i (authorship, membership, etc.); and $W(r[v,i])$ is the corresponding weight for the user-item relationship type between user v and item i. Ultimately, the recommendation score of an item, reflecting its likelihood to be recommended to the user, may increase due to the following factors: more people within the user's network are related to the item, stronger relationships of these people to the user, stronger relationships of these people to the item, and freshness of the item.

The recommendation widget, depicted in Fig. 15.1, presents the recommendations with explanations, which displays the people who served as the "implicit recommenders" and how they were related to both the user and the recommended item. One of the key research questions of the study was whether explanations influence the instant interest in the recommended items. This was examined by comparing recommendations with and without explanations.

The evaluation was primarily based on a user survey with 290 participants. Figure 15.2 shows the portion of items rated "interesting" for each of the three network types: familiarity, similarity, and overall. Recommendations from familiar people were found significantly more accurate than recommendations from similar people. The overall network did not improve accuracy on top of the familiarity network. That said, recommendations from similar people were found more diverse and less expected, indicating that the similarity network contributes on other dimensions than accuracy to the recommendation quality [53].

Figure 15.3 displays the effect of explanations. While explanations have been previously shown to have positive effect on recommendation in the long term, by providing transparency and building trust with the user [37], it was found that recommendations with explanations in this case also increase their instant effectiveness: when the people who serve as implicit recommenders were shown, interest rate in the recommendations grew. This was particularly true for familiar people, following the intuition that seeing a familiar person who is related to a recommended item may increase the likelihood of the user's interest in that item (e.g., "if John has bookmarked the page, there must have been something interesting in it").

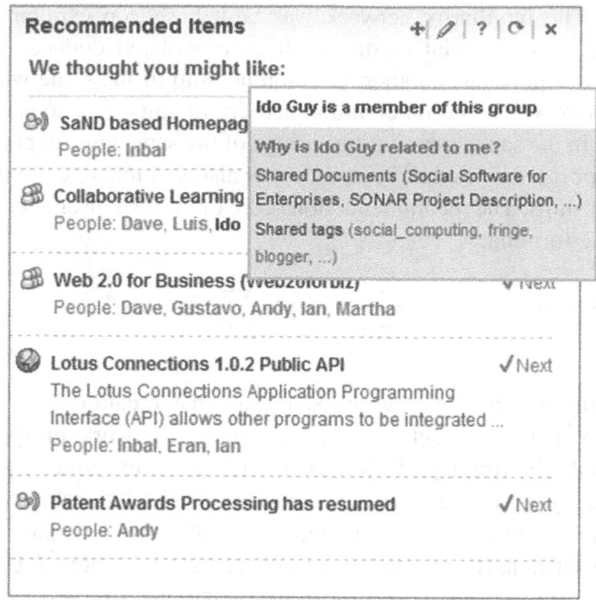

Fig. 15.1 Widget for social media item recommendation based on related people

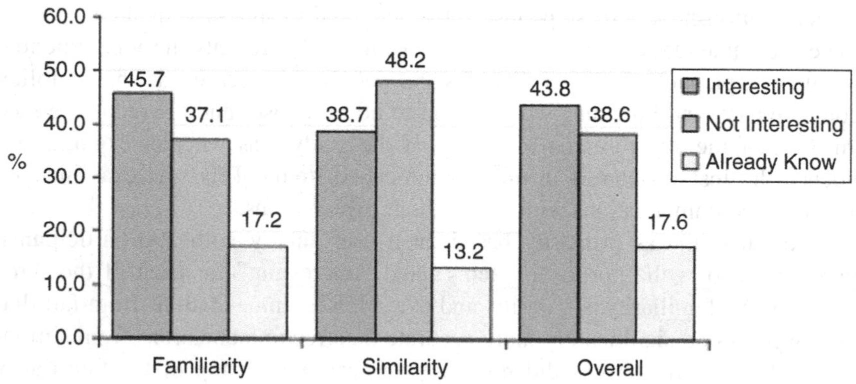

Fig. 15.2 Rating results across the three network types

After establishing understanding of people-based recommendation, a second study explored the use of tags for the recommendation task and compared tag-based with people-based recommendation [35]. The people-based recommendations were calculated based on a combined network of familiarity and similarity, with a triple-boost given to the familiarity network based on the results of the previous study.

A preliminary study was conducted to evaluate the use of four types of tags for recommendation: (1) used tags—tags that the user used to annotate artifacts with; (2) incoming tags—tags applied to the user by other individuals within a people tagging application; (3) direct tags—a combination of used and incoming

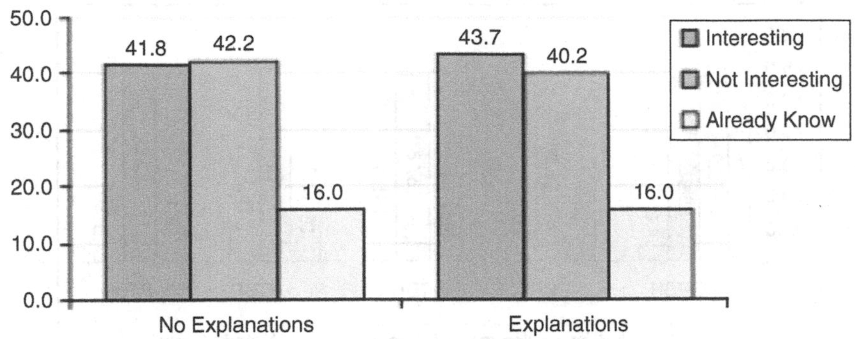

Fig. 15.3 Rating results with and without explanations

Table 15.1 Rating results of tags as topics of interest

%	Not interested (%)	Interested (%)	Highly interested (%)
Used	16.84	38.25	44.91
Incoming	15.48	31.75	52.78
Direct	7.46	22.81	69.74
Indirect	35.38	45.38	19.23

tags; and (4) indirect tags—tags applied on artifacts the user has tagged, but not necessarily those s/he used. Results, depicted in Table 15.1, indicated that direct tags, when available, achieve the most accurate results. Interestingly, incoming tags were slightly more accurate than used tags, indicating that the wisdom of the crowd reflected in tags applied by others may be more indicative of the user's interests than her own used tags. Indirect tags were found to be noisy and significantly less accurate.

Based on the results of the preliminary study, direct tags, combining used and incoming tags with equal weight, were chosen for the task of producing the tag-based recommendations. Experimentation was made with a pure people-based recommender (PBR), a pure tag-based recommender (TBR), two hybrid people-tag recommenders (or-PTBR and-PTBR), and a popularity baseline (POPBR). Given a user profile $P(u) = (N(u), T(u))$, where $N(u)$ is the set of u's related people and $T(u)$ is the set of u's related tags, the recommendation score of a social media item i for user u was calculated as follows:

$$RS(u,i) = e^{-\alpha t(i)} \left[\beta \sum_{v \in N(u)} w(u,v) \cdot w(v,i) + (1-\beta) \sum_{t \in T(u)} w(u,t) \cdot w(t,i) \right] \tag{15.2}$$

where $t(i)$ is the number of days passed since the creation date of i; α is a decay factor; β is a parameter that controls the relative weight between people and tags and was used to set the different types of personalized recommenders; $w(u, v)$ and

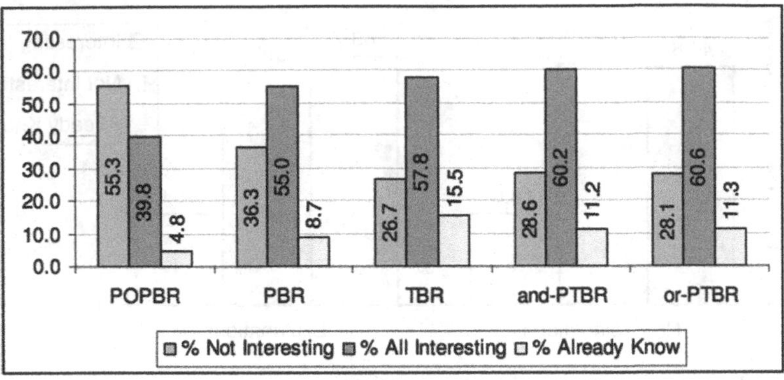

Fig. 15.4 Rating results for five different recommenders

$w(u, t)$ are the relationship strengths of u to user v and tag t, given as part of the user profile; and $w(v, i)$ and $w(t, i)$ are the relationship strengths between v and t, respectively, to item i. Ultimately, the recommendation score of an item, reflecting its likelihood to be recommended to the user, increased due to the following factors: more people and/or tags within the user's profile were related to the item; stronger relationships of these people and/or tags to the user; stronger relationships of these people and/or tags to the item; and freshness of the item.

Comparing people-based and tag-based recommendations produced the results shown in Fig. 15.4. In general, all personalization techniques outperformed the popularity-based recommender. In terms of accuracy (interest rate), tag-based recommenders significantly outperformed people-based recommenders. Yet, people-based recommenders showed other benefits, such as increased diversity across item types (tags substantially favored bookmarks), less expected results reflected in lower rates of already-known items, and more effective explanations. Specifically regarding explanations, the effect found for people-based explanations in increasing interest rates was not found for tag-based recommenders. Apparently, seeing the related tags to a recommended item does not have the effect (or extra value) that viewing the related people has. Hybrid recommendations, combining people-based and tag-based approaches, were shown to take the good of both worlds and also achieved the best accuracy with a ratio of around 70 % interesting items for the top 16 recommendations.

The third study in the series explored recommendation for online communities rather than for individuals [60]. As mentioned before, online communities have become central to social media experience and much of the social media content is created in the context of a community. In that work, recommendations were generated using group recommendation techniques, but were targeted to the community owners (moderators) only, so that they can share the content with the rest of the members as appropriate. Recommendations were generated using two main techniques. The first considered the members of the communities or a subset of them, and applied profile aggregation using the fusion approach (with advanced scoring) to generate a community profile that included both topics and people.

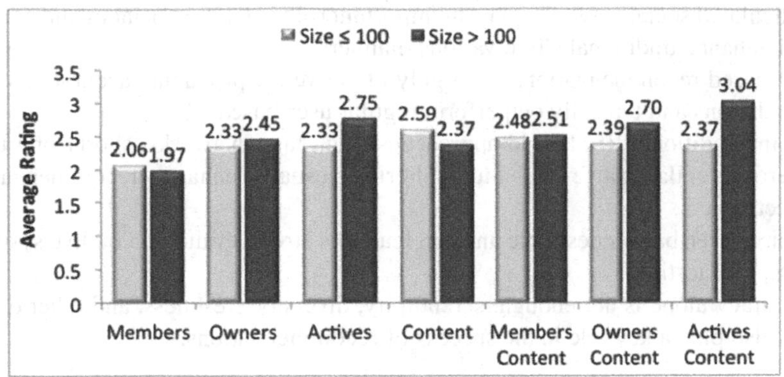

Fig. 15.5 Average rating for small vs. large communities across seven community profiles

These topics and people in turn served as the basis for recommendation: their most related content items were recommended. In particular, three subsets of the members were examined: all members, all owners, and active members. The second technique was content-based (CB): it considered the title, description, and tags of the community to generate recommendations. Hybrid approaches were also considered, by combining the topics and people from the member-based recommenders with the topics extracted by the content-based recommender into one community profile.

Evaluation was conducted using a large user survey of enterprise community owners and results are summarized in Fig. 15.5. Hybrid recommenders were generally found to perform better than the pure recommenders. For large communities (100 members or more), it was found that the hybrid profile that considered both active members and community's content performed significantly better than all other profiles. The pure active member-based profile was second best for large communities. For small communities (less than 100 members), the pure content profile was the best, followed by the hybrid profile considering all members and the content. These results indicate that for small communities, the content is a strong basis for recommendation and all members are a good representative group for profile aggregation. But for large communities, the content is less effective on its own and the group of all members becomes too disparate, while the group of only active members serves as the best basis for profile aggregation.

15.2.4 Summary

We reviewed different domains for recommendation of social media content and a case study for recommending mixed social media items in the enterprise. We also discussed the importance and relevance of group recommendation techniques when recommending social media content. Below are a few important points we wanted to re-iterate before moving to the next section:

- Articulated social networks play an important role in CF for social media content and enhance traditional CF in various manners.
- Tag-based recommendations are highly effective for producing accurate recommendations and typically outperform regular user-based CF.
- As in Traditional RS, hybrid approaches (e.g., tags+networks, short+long term interests, collaborative+individual filtering) usually enhance recommendation effectiveness.
- A large user-base is desirable and can lead to a strong evaluation on live systems (e.g., A/B testing).
- Accuracy alone is not enough: serendipity, diversity, freshness, and other qualities also play a key role in the success of recommendations.

15.3 People Recommendation

Social recommender systems span beyond content recommendation. As mentioned in the introduction, social overload originates from both information and interaction overload. Since people are the key element that makes the web "social", recommendation of people is a central pillar within the social recommender system domain. Terveen and McDonald [68] coined the term "social matching" for recommender systems that recommend people to people. In their work, they explained why a people recommender is a unique RS, which is different than recommendation of other artifacts, and thus deserves its own special attention. Among other aspects, trust, reputation, privacy, and personal attraction have greater importance when it comes to people recommendation. Please refer to Chap. 16 for further reading.

Social media sites and in particular SNSs define different types of explicit (or "articulated") relationships among their users. The main dimensions of the relationship types are:

- Symmetric vs. asymmetric. In some sites, such as Facebook and LinkedIn, a relationship between two users is reciprocated. In such a case, one user typically sends an invitation to connect to another user, who needs to accept the invitation. Once the other user accepts, the two are reciprocally connected on the site. On the other hand, asymmetric relationships, such as on Twitter or Pinterest, allow one user to "subscribe to" or "follow" another user. The other user does not necessarily need to follow the first user back and thus many asymmetric relationships are formed.
- Confirmed vs. non-confirmed. Some of the sites require the other side's agreement for connecting or following, while others do not. Typically, symmetric networks require such confirmation and as long as it has not been received, no connection exists. Asymmetric networks do not usually require a confirmation and any user can choose to follow any other user, however there are exceptions to these norms.

- Ad-hoc vs. permanent. Some of the sites encourage connection for an ad-hoc purpose, such as for people to meet at an event or partner for a joint task, while others encourage a long-term relationship that is meant to last over months and years.
- The site's domain. The domain of the SNS has an important influence on the formed network. For example, Facebook is typically used for maintaining social relationships with friends and acquaintances, while LinkedIn is a professional network meant for maintaining business relationships with colleagues and partners. The goals and characteristics of a connection in each of these sites are therefore different, as they would be in SNSs for other domains, such as travel, art, cooking, question and answering, etc.

The different characteristics of people relationships in the different sites require different recommendation techniques. For example, a recommender for people to connect with on Facebook may seek to recommend familiar people, while a recommender for people to follow on Twitter may recommend people the user is interested in, even if they are not familiar. Recommending "celebrities" or popular people is probably a better strategy for a follower-followee network than for a friendship network.

In the remainder of this section, we review three key types of people recommendation: recommending people to connect with, recommending people to follow, and recommending strangers to get to know. We describe the unique challenges and characteristics of each of these recommendation types and demonstrate how existing approaches handle them. Before summarizing the key aspects, we briefly discuss two closely related research areas to people recommendation: link prediction and expertise location.

15.3.1 Recommending People to Connect With

The first study that focused on people recommendation in an SNS introduced the "do you know?" (DYK) widget [33]. The widget recommended people to connect to within an enterprise SNS. The action the widget was targeting was clicking a 'connect' button that would trigger an invitation to connect within the SNS, which the other side would need to confirm for the connection to become public. Recommendations were made based on a variety of familiarity signals: org-chart relationships (peers, manager-employee, etc.), paper and patent co-authorship, project co-membership, blog commenting, person tagging, mutual connections, connection on another SNS, wiki co-editing, and file sharing. Figure 15.6 illustrates the widget, which included detailed explanations for each recommendation. The explanations indicated the counts per each of the signals mentioned above and further hovering over an evidence line allowed seeing the specific details (e.g., the wiki pages co-edited) and getting to the actual page of the evidence pieces.

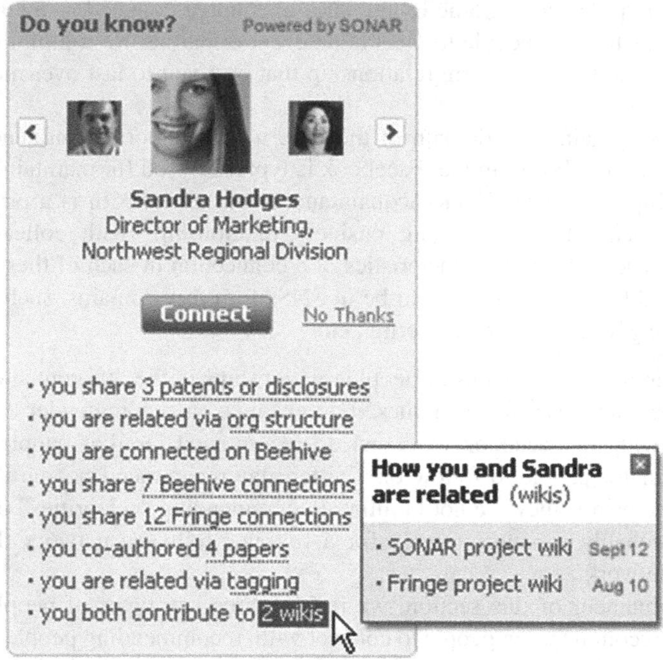

Fig. 15.6 The "Do You know?" (DYK) Widget

The evaluation of the widget was based on a field study of its use within the Fringe enterprise SNS. Fringe had the "friending" feature before, but did not have a people recommender. The inspected effect on the site was dramatic. Both the number of invitations sent and the number of users who send invitations significantly increased, as can be seen in Figs. 15.7 and 15.8. One of the users of the site explained: *"I must say I am a lazy social networker, but Fringe was the first application motivating me to go ahead and send out some invitations to others to connect."* Explanations increased user trust in the system and made them feel more comfortable sending invitations, as one user described: *"If I see more direct connections I'm more likely to add them [...] I know they are not recommended by accident."* Overall, there was a substantial increase in the number of connections per user on Fringe. However, a sharp decay of the widget usage was found over time, as excitement of the feature dropped and potential connections were exhausted.

In a follow-up study [11], conducted within a different enterprise SNS, nick-named Beehive, the aggregation algorithm used by the DYK widget (termed 'SONAR') was compared with three other algorithms for people recommendation: (1) Content Matching (CM)—based on cosine similarity of the content created by both users: profile entries, status messages, photos' text, shared lists, job title, location, description, and tags. Word vectors were created by a simple TF-IDF

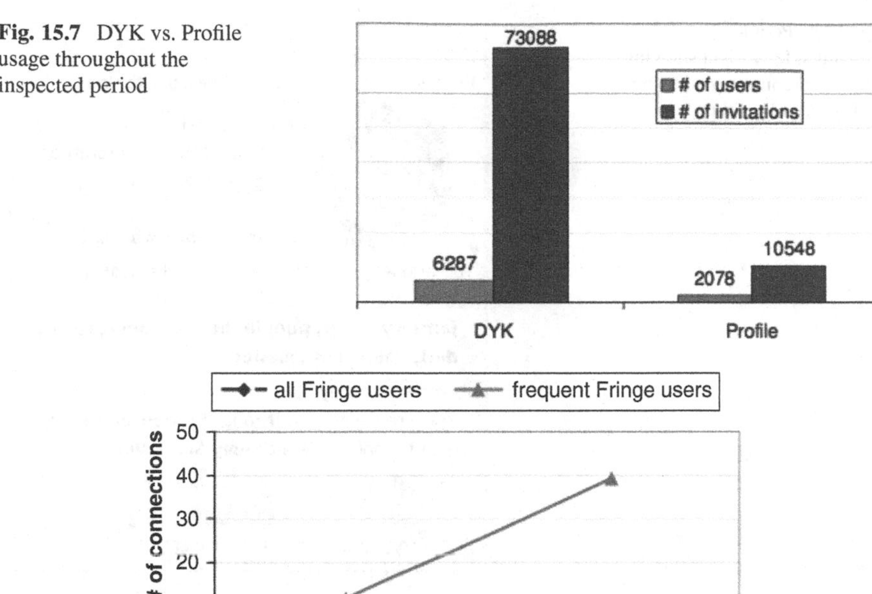

Fig. 15.7 DYK vs. Profile usage throughout the inspected period

Fig. 15.8 Average number of invitations per user before and after the inspected period

procedure. Latent semantic analysis (LSA) was not shown to produce better results and was not applied since it does not yield intuitive explanations; (2) Content plus Link (CplusL)—combined CM with social links. A social link was defined as a sequence of 3 or 4 users, where for each pair of users in the sequence u1 and u2, either u1 connects to u2, u2 connects to u1, or u1 commented on u2's content; (3) Friend of Friends (FoF)—based on the number of mutual friends, as done in many of the popular SNSs. The FoF algorithm was able to produce recommendations for only 57.2 % of the users (compared to 87.7 % for SONAR). Figure 15.9 shows the recommendation widget.

Evaluation was based on a user survey and a controlled field study. Figure 15.10 shows the main survey results. CM and CplusL produced mostly unknown people, while SONAR and FoF produced mostly known individuals. As could be expected, a higher portion of the recommended people who were familiar to the user were rated as good recommendations and resulted in a "connect" action. Yet, the unknown recommended individuals may help discover new potential friends. The overall superiority of algorithms that involve social links over content was clear: only 30.5 % of the CM recommendations resulted in a connect action, compared to 40 % for CplusL, 47.7 % for FoF, and 59.7 % for SONAR.

Fig. 15.9 People recommender widget showing a person recommended using the CplusL algorithm

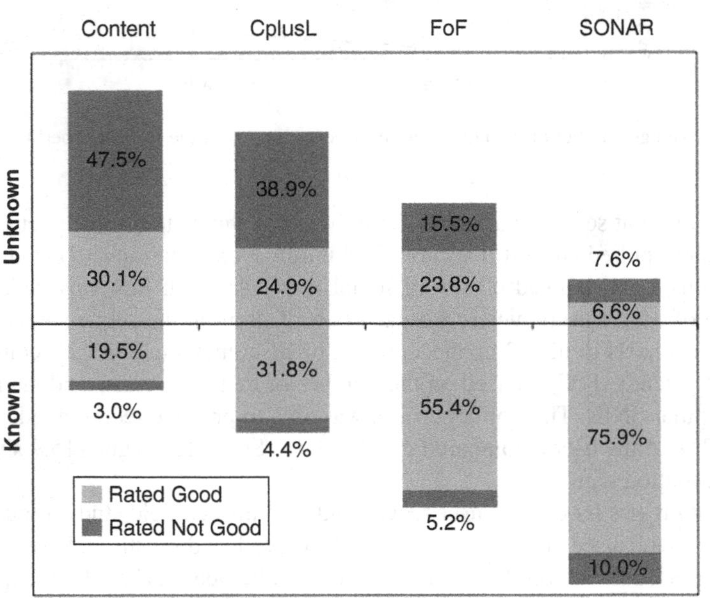

Fig. 15.10 Survey results for the four algorithms

A later study examined the recommendation impact on the network structure [15]. Since recommendations play such a key role in building the network during its early stages, they also substantially influence the structure of the generated network, its characteristics, and measurements. For example, Fig. 15.11 shows the average degree of recommended connections for each of the four algorithms. FoF is the

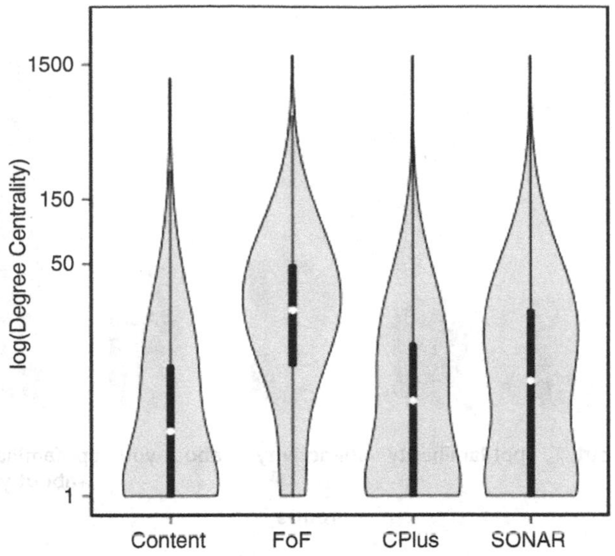

Fig. 15.11 Degree of recommended connections across the four algorithms

most biased towards high-degree connections, while CM does not have such bias: it often recommends users with few connections or even none at all. The high-degrees of FoF recommendations lead to a network with fewer nodes and higher average degree compared to the network created by CM recommendations. Another aspect of the effect of recommendations on the network is betweenness centrality, which measures the importance of nodes in the graph [8]: CM and SONAR generate the highest delta in betweenness compared to CplusL and FoF. Regarding demographic characteristics, CM is most biased towards the same country, but least biased towards the same organizational unit, while SONAR substantially increases cross-country and intra-unit connections. The network effects of people recommendations are an important global aspect of a people recommender and need to be considered when designing a new people recommender system.

Another related study by Freyne et al. focused on recommendation as a means to increase new users' engagement within an enterprise SNS [22]. That study used aggregated data external to the SNS in question to recommend both people and content to new users. Even brand new employees could still get recommendations based on their initial data, such as their org-chart information (indicating their peers), location, or organizational unit. The results indicated that combined recommendations have a significant effect in increasing users' visits to the site as well as their viewing activity and actual contributions to the site (the latter is depicted in Fig. 15.12). Interestingly, people recommendations were most effective when focusing on recommending the most active users, even if they had less familiarity signals with the user. Yet, as discussed, such recommendations can have a long-term effect on the network structure and lead to a less balanced degree distribution.

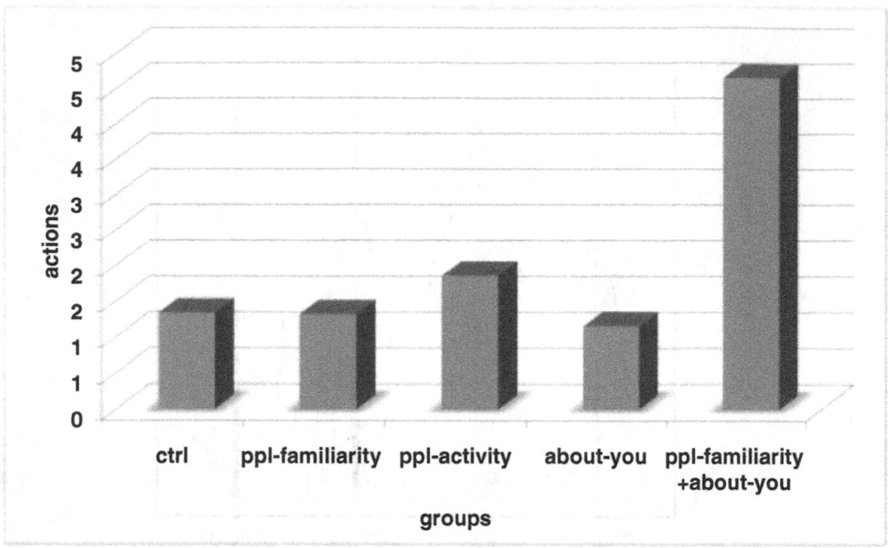

Fig. 15.12 Actions over 4 months

Friend recommendation has also become popular on mobile devices, where location often plays a role and makes the recommendations more transient or ad-hoc. Quercia et al. [58] discussed "friendsensing", sensing friends based on Bluetooth information on mobile devices. Friends were recommended based on co-location, while two basic approaches were attempted, taking into account the duration of co-location and its frequency, respectively. A weighted graph was built accordingly and recommendations were generated using that graph based on link analysis (shortest path, page rank, k-markov chain, and HITs). Simulation-based evaluation indicated both basic approaches perform similarly well and way beyond a random baseline.

15.3.2 Recommending Strangers

The focus of the work discussed thus far has been on recommending familiar people one can connect to. As already implied, there could also be value in recommending people the user does not know. StrangerRS [31] attempted to recommend people who are unknown yet interesting within the organization. Such recommendations can be useful in many potential manners, such as, for getting help or advice, reach new opportunities, discover new routes for career development, learn about new assets that can be leveraged, connect with subject-matter experts and influencers, cultivate one's organizational social capital, and grow own reputation and influence within the organization. As mentioned before, recommendation of people to connect to within an SNS is mostly effective for the network-building phase. Afterwards

Fig. 15.13 User Interface of the Stranger Recommender System

one's recommendations become staler, as the network becomes more stable and connection to others becomes less frequent. This is where stranger recommendation can become more relevant and complement the recommendation of familiar individuals, by suggesting interesting people the user does not know, but may want to start getting acquainted with.

Figure 15.13 shows the user interface of StrangerRS. Since it aimed at recommending strangers, more information about each person was presented, in the form of their full profile page (part A). Evidence for why this person may be interesting was also presented (part B). It included similarity points with that individual, such as common tags, common communities, common files, and others. The action suggested by the recommender was not a connection within the SNS, since it is likely to be too soon to connect to a stranger, but rather it was suggested to view the person's profile, read their blog, or follow them (part C).

A successful recommendation by StrangerRS was considered a recommendation of a stranger who might be interesting to the user. These two, almost contradicting, goals were not easy to satisfy and led to a much lower accuracy level than usual familiar people recommendation. Yet, supposedly, the value of a successful recommendation in this case is much higher, since this is no longer just about facilitating connection to a known person, but rather about exposing the user to a

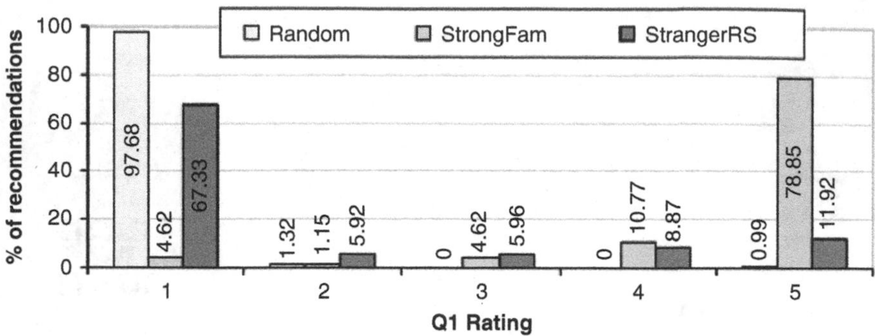

Fig. 15.14 Rating of "strangerness" for StrangerRS and two baselines: random and strong familiarity

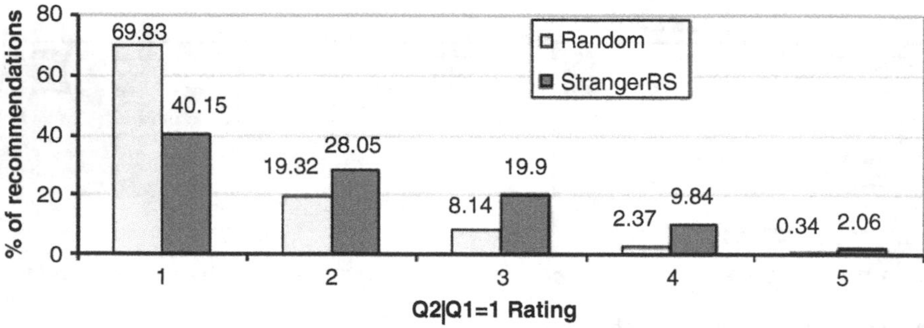

Fig. 15.15 Rating of interest in strangers for RandomRS vs. the random baseline

new interesting person s/he was not even aware of. The method used for producing the recommendations was based on network composition: the extracted familiarity network was subtracted from the extracted similarity network to produce the recommendations. Jaccard index was the main measure used for similarity between two individuals. Results, depicted in Figs. 15.14 and 15.15, indicated that two thirds of the recommended individuals were indeed strangers, yet strangers who were significantly more interesting than a random stranger. Out of 9 recommendations presented to each user, 67 % included at least one stranger rated 3 or above in terms of the user's interest, on a 5-point Likert scale.

Stranger recommendation is also a common feature of online dating websites. Pizzato et al. [57] introduced RECON, a reciprocal recommender for online dating. Similarly to the original social matching framework, they specified a few special characteristics of reciprocal recommendations, where people are both the subject and object of recommendations. These included the fact that success is dependent on both sides; the need for both sides to provide their profiles so that matching can occur; and the typical requirement that one individual will not be recommended to too many others. Their evaluation, conducted on a major Australian dating site, was based on 4 weeks of training and 2 weeks of testing, where success was determined based on previous user interaction. Generally they found that accounting for reciprocity features improves recommendation accuracy and helps address the cold-start problem.

15.3.3 Recommending People to Follow

Two studies were the earliest to explore recommendation of people to follow. Hannon et al. [36] used a CB-CF hybridization to recommend "followees" on Twitter. They examined several ways to generate user profiles, based on the user's own tweets, the user's followers, the user's followees, the user's followers' tweets, and the user's followees' tweets. The open source search engine Lucene was used to index users by their profile, after applying TF-IDF to boost distinctive terms or users within the profile. They applied an offline evaluation using a dataset with 20,000 Twitter users. 19,000 were used as a training set and the remaining 1000 were the test users. The different methods were compared based on their ability to predict the user's followees. A slight advantage was observed to profiles that were based on followers and followers' tweets. Hybrid profiles further improved the precision. A small-scale live trial was also conducted where users indicated whom they were likely to follow. On average, hybrid approached reached about 7 out of 30 accurate recommendations.

A second study was performed by Brzozowski and Romero [9], who experimented with the WaterCooler enterprise SNS. During a 24-day live trial period, they observed patterns of 110 users who followed 774 new individuals. The strongest pattern found was of the form $A \leftarrow X \rightarrow B$, meaning that sharing an audience (follower) with another person is a strong reason to follow that person. Most-replied was found as a strong global signal. Similarity and most-read were found as weaker signals for followee recommendation.

In a more recent study, Gupta et al. [29] revealed some details about the followee recommender systems in use by Twitter. From an architectural perspective, they noted the decision to process the entire Twitter follower-followee graph in memory using a single server, which contributed to the performance of the feature. They developed an open-source in-memory graph processing engine to traverse the Twitter graph and generate recommendations. The algorithm used was a combination of a random walk and SALSA [45], comparing two approaches: the first gives each user the same influence regardless of the number of users they follow or are followed by and the second gives equal influence to each follower-followee edge.

15.3.4 Related Research Areas

Link prediction in social networks is a fertile research area that is closely related to people recommendation and has often been offered to enhance it. The seminal work by Liben-Nowell and Kleinberg [48] formalized it as a task to predict new interactions within a social network based on the existing set of interactions. Experimentation with paper co-authorship networks showed, using an unsupervised learning approach, that the network topology can be effectively used to predict future collaboration. Moving to the social media domain, Leskovec et al. [47] developed models to determine the sign of links (positive or negative) in SNSs where interactions can be positive or negative (Epinions, Slashdot, Wikipedia). Fire et al. [19] experimented with five social media sites, including Facebook, YouTube, and Flickr, and proposed a set of graph-topology features for identifying missing links. This technique was shown to outperform common-friends and Jaccard's coefficient measures, implying it can be useful for recommending new connections. Scellato et al. [63] focused on location-based social networks and suggested a supervised learning framework to predict new links among users and places. In another study of mobile networks, Wang et al. [69] showed that combining network-based features with human mobility features (e.g., user movement across locations) can significantly improve link prediction performance using supervised learning.

It is also worth mentioning the research area of expertise location [43, 52] in the context of people recommendation. Expertise location deals with the problem of finding an expert in a given domain or technical area. It thus falls within the broad search domain, since it is triggered by a user query. Similarly to the difference between content and people recommendation, in expertise location the results are people rather than documents as in content search. For similar reasons to those already discussed in this section, the case of searching for people bears some unique characteristics compared to other content search scenarios and therefore forms its own area of research. A recent study has particularly focused on expertise location based on social media data, which serves as a good basis for expertise mining [30]. Despite its pertinence to the search field, expertise location is sometimes mixed with people recommendation and in many cases is termed "expert recommendation". It should be noted that a people recommender should be considered as such only when it does not involve a user query and is initiated by the system rather than by the user.

15.3.5 Summary

We have seen that people recommendation is a complex field of study. The fact that it deals with recommending people to themselves bring many interesting aspects to the table. For example, explanations may serve in this case to make users feel more comfortable accepting a recommendation and sending an invitation to connect or start following (in most cases, knowing that the user who has been followed will get a notification about it, even if their approval is not required). We reviewed three types of people recommendations: recommendation of familiar people, for example to connect with on an SNS; recommendation of interesting people, for example to follow in a social media site; and recommendation of strangers, for dating or for getting to know within a community or organization. A social website may transfer between these types of recommendations according to the user's phase within the site. For example, it may be desirable to recommend familiar and interesting people for users in their early stages, so they can build their network of friends or followees. In a later stage, when users start to exhaust their connections, stranger recommendations can help users get to know new individuals and increase their social capital.

15.4 Discussion

In this section, we summarize key SRS-related topics that were brought up throughout the previous two sections on people and content recommendation and suggest directions for future work.

Explanations The public nature of social media data enables to provide more transparency into recommendations by showing how they were formed. In some of the enterprise examples we reviewed for both content and people recommendations, explanations were found to have a key role in increasing the instant acceptance rate of recommendations [33, 34]. Beyond that, explanations in RS have been shown to have longer-term effects of building trust relationships with the user [37].

There are also a few challenges with regards to explanations. First, as we have seen, explanations do not always increase accuracy. For example, in our mixed content recommendation study, tag-based explanations did not increase recommendations' ratings. Second, not every recommendation method can provide intuitive explanations; there is usually a trade-off between the method's complexity and the clarity of explanations it can provide. For instance, recommendations that are based on clustering techniques are usually harder to explain. Third, explanations pose challenges in terms of privacy. For example, the YouTube explanations [16] explicitly show videos previously watched by the user, which directly expose information that might be sensitive if watched by another person. Fourth, explanations require extra real-estate on the user interface, which might be particularly challenging on mobile devices; therefore their cost-to-value ratio should be carefully considered when designing the recommender system.

Privacy As mentioned several times throughout this chapter, one of the key benefits of social media data is that large portions of it are public and thus can be used for analysis without infringing user privacy, as is the case, for example, with email or file system data (see Chap. 19). It should be noted, however, that in some countries, public social media information is still considered personal information (PI), when linked to an identity of a real person. This means that analysis and inference from such data may still require explicit user consent. Indeed, aggregation of public data, even if it was previously accessible, may reveal sensitive information the user did not intend to expose. In addition, as just mentioned, explanations aimed for a specific user might reveal very sensitive data, such as browsing or viewing history, when exposed to another person who may watch the screen alongside. Finally, there is much social media data that is still access-restricted. Recommender systems should pay special attention not to infringe the privacy model of the data, to avoid the exposure of sensitive information [18].

Tags The work we reviewed indicated that tags, a mechanism introduced by social media to annotate content, such as web pages, photos, or people, can be particularly effective as a basis for recommendation. Tags' ability to concisely summarize user perspective over large content pieces make them a highly valuable resource for producing recommendations [64]. Aside from recommendations, tags have been shown to be useful for other purposes, such as enhancing search or generating "tag clouds" that summarize the common topics of a group of items to the user [42]. Unfortunately, despite their value, tag usage is on the decrease in recent years, with sites such as Delicious becoming less popular and other sites giving less prominence to tags. Tag recommendation techniques [41, 65], which are another type of SRS not discussed in this chapter, should be used to promote tag usage and close the loop: tag recommendations help generate more tags, while these tags, in turn, used to produce other recommendations.

Social Relationships One of the most important contributions of social media to recommender systems is the introduction of the explicit (articulated) network. Social network sites, such as Facebook, LinkedIn, and Twitter, allow people to explicitly articulate their connections. As mentioned, there are two main types of connections, one expresses familiarity and the other expresses interest. Both of these articulated networks are very useful for content recommendation, and were shown to enhance traditional CF techniques. They also have other benefits: (1) sparing the need for explicit feedback in the form of ratings to determine the network of similarity, (2) help coping with the new-user cold start problem, in case the network can be used across social media websites, and (3) helping users judge the recommendations, since they originate from people they know or are interested in (also making explanations more effective). On the other hand, as we have seen, recommendations of people to connect with or to follow are essential for enhancing the formation of such explicit relationships. This is a classic demonstration of the mutual relationship between recommender systems and social media discussed in the introduction: on the one hand social media introduces a new type of data that enhances RS; on the other hand RS are essential for generating this type of data.

Trust and Reputation The topic of trust has a tremendous importance in the RS domain. Obviously, the best recommendations come from a trusted person. But on the other hand, trust is very challenging to compute as it represents a very abstract and subjective quality between two individuals. Reputation represents a more general concept about a person's perception by others [38]. One way to define it is the aggregation of trust in this person across the entire set of users. Social media and the "wisdom of the crowd" enable to estimate trust and reputation in ways that have not been possible before. Online social relationships and content feedback forms (comments, 'likes', etc.) introduce more signals that can be used to calculate trust and reputation. That said, many of the studies still use rough estimations that are based on controversial assumptions, for example, that a friend on an SNS is a trustworthy individual. Evaluation of trust and reputation is also particularly challenging, as even in the real world people have hard time figuring out who they trust or who has a good reputation. Assuming a network of trust is given, there are growing amounts of research that explore how to use it to enhance CF. The early work of Golbeck [27] suggested to adapt the CF formula in a way that would boost similar users whom the user trusts. More advanced approaches incorporate trust in matrix factorization techniques [39].

Evaluation As reviewed throughout this chapter, evaluation of SRS typically uses the common methods in the broader RS domain (see Chap. 8). These include offline evaluation, user studies (see Chap. 9) (especially common for SRS), and live field studies or A/B testing. Evaluation measures include RMSE, NDCG, precision, and other commonly used metrics from the RS domain. Looking forward, since social media is characterized by the "wisdom of the crowd", it will only be natural to see more crowdsourcing techniques used for evaluation of SRS. These have become common in many domains in the recent years, including information retrieval (e.g., [1, 10, 44]), however they are not as common yet in RS evaluation. Evaluation that goes beyond accuracy to include serendipity ("surprise"), diversity, novelty, coverage, and other factors is also due in the SRS area [24]. Finally, evaluation over time, which also examines the broader effect of the recommendation on the surrounding ecosystem of users, as demonstrated in [15], is a highly desirable direction. Rather than focusing mostly on recommendation effectiveness, their broader and longer-term influence on the environment should also be considered. As another example to such research, Said and Bellogin [62] started to explore the effect of recipe recommendation within the Allrecipes.com SNS on users' health. This kind of research requires new tools and creative thinking to be brought into the existing set of evaluation methods.

Recommending Content to Produce We extensively discussed content recommendation in Sect. 15.2. Our examples focused on content the user consumes: video, news, questions, social media items, etc. As explained in the introduction, one of the key characteristics of social media is that users are not just the consumers, but also the producers of content. There is a body of research that attempts to recommend users content they may want to produce. Question recommendation in CQA sites, which has already been mentioned in Sect. 15.2, has a role in encouraging users to produce content in the form of answers. Other works attempted to encourage users to create more profile entries [25], inspire users to write blogs [17], and prompt them to edit articles on Wikipedia [14]. Recommending content to generate is a particularly challenging task since the entry barrier is higher as many social media users are lurkers (only consume content). It is rooted in the area of persuasive technologies and theories such as self determination [61] and behavioral models [20]. Clearly, recommending content to produce has a central role in the symbiosis between recommender systems and social media.

15.5 Emerging Domains and Open Challenges

We conclude this chapter by pointing out potential emerging domains for SRS and a few open challenges on top of the topics discussed throughout this chapter and summarized in the previous section.

15.5.1 Emerging Domains

We enumerate four domains, which we think can serve as a fertile ground for SRS research in the years to come.

Mobile and Wearables Recommendations for mobile devices, such as PDAs, have been suggested since the beginning of the millennium. As smartphones and tablets with advanced technologies, such as high-resolution cameras, GPS, and touch screens started to prevail, recommendation technologies adapted themselves, for example, by taking into account the user's location (see Chap. 14). The combination of mobile and social (sometimes referred to as SoLoMo—social, mobile, and location) holds new opportunities for SRS, which will combine the advanced capabilities of mobile devices with social interaction across these devices. Looking further into the future, wearable devices, such as glasses and watches, are likely to have access to even more personal information that on the one hand will provide more data for SRS to work with, and on the other hand will require more advanced recommendation techniques, so these devices can work appropriately with minimum input from the user.

Smart TVs RS have been quite popular in the TV domain for many years. The Netflix prize advanced this domain even further [5]. However, as TVs continue to evolve into "smart TVs", they enable many more social elements, such as sharing and interaction between watchers, which make the new TVs a social medium on its own. This provides a highly interesting opportunity for SRS to make this new generation of televisions even smarter.

Automotive The automotive domain is also evolving in recent years. Self-driving cars is arguably the most exciting challenge on the table, but new car models allow more collaboration between cars and their drivers. Being such an advanced instrument, the car itself plays a special role and can sometimes be treated similarly to a person, given all the information gathered through its sensors. As more collaboration is expected to characterize the new generation of smart cars, SRS can play a key role in sparing extra work from drivers and providing cars with more necessary information. We start to see this in social navigation technologies, such as Waze, but this is likely only the beginning.

Healthcare The healthcare domain has always been slow to adopt "social", among other things due to the special privacy concerns it entails. On the other hand, it is not hard to imagine how much this domain can benefit from more sharing and collaboration, both among patients and among doctors. In recent years, we start to see a movement towards more openness to medical data sharing. As it seems that "social healthcare" starts to take off, the SRS community should consider how recommendations should be used in this domain, with all the complexities involved and the critical implications of a successful versus wrong recommendation.

15.5.2 Open Challenges

We finally highlight three more challenges for researchers in the SRS area to consider.

Social Streams Social streams, such as Twitter or the Facebook newsfeed, syndicate user activity within a social media site or a set of sites. Millions of users who share and interact in social media create a firehose of data in real-time that poses new types of challenges in terms of filtering and personalization. There are different types of streams in terms of the data they contain (homogenous as in Twitter or heterogeneous as in Facebook), the source of data (a single site or a group of sites), its access-control (public or friends-only), and subscription model (following or "friending"). As demonstrated in the Twitter-related work reviewed in this chapter, the stream's data is different than "traditional" social media content: it represents an activity rather than an artifact or an entity; it is more intensive as one entity (e.g., a wiki page) may have a large amount of activities (e.g., edits); it may be very noisy (e.g., multiple wiki edits might not be of interest); its freshness is key: items that are few days old might already be irrelevant; and it is sparse in content and metadata (e.g., Twitter messages are limited to 140 characters). Due to all these unique characteristics, recommending social stream items becomes a challenge on its own within the SRS domain, and as social information continues to grow, handling this task is becoming both more challenging and more important [21, 32, 55]. On the other hand, the stream data can also be used to model users' interests. Its fresh and concise nature can help build a user model that is up-to-date, identify changes in users' tastes and preferences in real-time, and detect global trends that may influence the recommendation strategy [23, 56].

Beyond Accuracy and Evaluation Over Time Many of the studies we reviewed focused on measuring the effectiveness of recommendation by their accuracy. As social recommendation proliferate, it is more important than ever to consider the bigger picture when evaluating the value of recommendation. Typical beyond-accuracy measures should be considered, including serendipity, diversity (see Chap. 26), novelty, and coverage [24, 53]. In addition, the effectiveness of recommendation should be compared against the case where no recommendation would have been provided [4]. Recommendations that can make the user discover and take action regarding an item s/he would not have noticed otherwise, are obviously more valuable. In many of the works we reviewed, evaluation was based on a one-time user survey. Longer term evaluation is required as the results may substantially change over time. Techniques that learn and adapt over time based on user behavior are going to be essential. Additionally, evaluation that examines the broader effect of the recommendation on the surrounding ecosystem of users, as demonstrated in [15, 62] is a highly desirable direction for SRS evaluation. This requires new tools and creative thinking to be brought into the existing evaluation methods.

Cross-Domain Analysis As we discussed, migrating data from one social media service to another may go a long way enhancing recommendations and help deal with the cold start problem for new users. Indeed, using another site's network, tags, and other types of information have been performed by various previous systems as mentioned in this chapter. Yet, social media sites differ in many aspects. It is not certain that one's travel network can serve as a reliable source of recommendation for recipes. Similarly, the tags used in a news site context are not necessarily valuable for video recommendation. More research is due to explore the common and different among social media systems and when information can effectively port from one application to another to be used for recommendation. Cross-domain recommendations in RS have always been harder to explore since they require richer datasets and involve more complex use cases and research questions (see Chap. 27). As social media continues to evolve, it will be more important to explore and better understand these complexities.

References

1. Alonso, O., Mizzaro, S.: Can we get rid of TREC assessors? Using Mechanical Turk for relevance assessment. In: Proceedings of the SIGIR 2009 Workshop on the Future of IR Evaluation, vol. 15, p. 16 (2009)
2. Arguello, J., Elsas, J.L., Callan, J., Carbonell, J.G.: Document Representation and Query Expansion Models for Blog Recommendation. Proceedings of the second AAAI conference on Weblogs and Social Media - ICWSM '08 (2008)
3. Baltrunas, L., Makcinskas, T., Ricci, F.: Group Recommendations with Rank Aggregation and Collaborative Filtering. In: Proceedings of the Fourth ACM Conference on Recommender Systems, RecSys '10, pp. 119–126. ACM, New York, NY, USA (2010). DOI 10.1145/1864708.1864733. URL http://doi.acm.org/10.1145/1864708.1864733
4. Belluf, T., Xavier, L., Giglio, R.: Case study on the business value impact of personalized recommendations on a large online retailer. In: Proceedings of the Sixth ACM Conference on Recommender Systems, RecSys '12, pp. 277–280. ACM, New York, NY, USA (2012). DOI 10.1145/2365952.2366014. URL http://doi.acm.org/10.1145/2365952.2366014
5. Bennett, J., Lanning, S.: The Netflix Prize. In: Proceedings of KDD cup and workshop, vol. 2007, p. 35 (2007)

6. Berkovsky, S., Freyne, J.: Group-based Recipe Recommendations: Analysis of Data Aggregation Strategies. In: Proceedings of the Fourth ACM Conference on Recommender Systems, RecSys '10, pp. 111–118. ACM, New York, NY, USA (2010). DOI 10.1145/1864708.1864732. URL http://doi.acm.org/10.1145/1864708.1864732
7. Boyd, D.M., Ellison, N.B.: Social Network Sites: Definition, History, and Scholarship. Journal of Computer-Mediated Communication (2007)
8. Brandes, U.: A faster algorithm for betweenness centrality. Journal of Mathematical Sociology **25**(2), 163–177 (2001)
9. Brzozowski, M.J., Romero, D.M.: Who Should I Follow? Recommending People in Directed Social Networks. In: ICWSM (2011)
10. Buhrmester, M., Kwang, T., Gosling, S.D.: Amazon's Mechanical Turk a New Source of Inexpensive, yet High-Quality, Data? Perspectives on Psychological Science **6**(1), 3–5 (2011)
11. Chen, J., Geyer, W., Dugan, C., Muller, M., Guy, I.: Make New Friends, but Keep the Old: Recommending People on Social Networking Sites. In: Proceedings of the SIGCHI Conference on Human Factors in Computing Systems, CHI '09, pp. 201–210. ACM, New York, NY, USA (2009). DOI 10.1145/1518701.1518735. URL http://doi.acm.org/10.1145/1518701.1518735
12. Chen, J., Nairn, R., Nelson, L., Bernstein, M., Chi, E.: Short and Tweet: Experiments on Recommending Content from Information Streams. In: Proceedings of the SIGCHI Conference on Human Factors in Computing Systems, CHI '10, pp. 1185–1194. ACM, New York, NY, USA (2010). DOI 10.1145/1753326.1753503. URL http://doi.acm.org/10.1145/1753326.1753503
13. Chen, K., Chen, T., Zheng, G., Jin, O., Yao, E., Yu, Y.: Collaborative Personalized Tweet Recommendation. In: Proceedings of the 35th International ACM SIGIR Conference on Research and Development in Information Retrieval, SIGIR '12, pp. 661–670. ACM, New York, NY, USA (2012). DOI 10.1145/2348283.2348372. URL http://doi.acm.org/10.1145/2348283.2348372
14. Cosley, D., Frankowski, D., Terveen, L., Riedl, J.: SuggestBot: Using Intelligent Task Routing to Help People Find Work in Wikipedia. In: Proceedings of the 12th International Conference on Intelligent User Interfaces, IUI '07, pp. 32–41. ACM, New York, NY, USA (2007). DOI 10.1145/1216295.1216309. URL http://doi.acm.org/10.1145/1216295.1216309
15. Daly, E.M., Geyer, W., Millen, D.R.: The Network Effects of Recommending Social Connections. In: Proceedings of the Fourth ACM Conference on Recommender Systems, RecSys '10, pp. 301–304. ACM, New York, NY, USA (2010). DOI 10.1145/1864708.1864772. URL http://doi.acm.org/10.1145/1864708.1864772
16. Davidson, J., Livingston, B., Sampath, D., Liebald, B., Liu, J., Nandy, P., Van Vleet, T., Gargi, U., Gupta, S., He, Y., et al.: The YouTube Video Recommendation System. Proceedings of the fourth ACM conference on Recommender systems - RecSys '10 pp. 293–296 (2010). DOI 10.1145/1864708.1864770. URL http://dx.doi.org/10.1145/1864708.1864770
17. Dugan, C., Geyer, W., Millen, D.R.: Lessons Learned from Blog Muse: Audience-based Inspiration for Bloggers. In: Proceedings of the SIGCHI Conference on Human Factors in Computing Systems, CHI '10, pp. 1965–1974. ACM, New York, NY, USA (2010). DOI 10.1145/1753326.1753623. URL http://doi.acm.org/10.1145/1753326.1753623
18. Dwyer, C.: Privacy in the age of Google and Facebook. Technology and Society Magazine, IEEE **30**(3), 58–63 (2011)
19. Fire, M., Tenenboim, L., Lesser, O., Puzis, R., Rokach, L., Elovici, Y.: Link Prediction in Social Networks using Computationally Efficient Topological Features. In: Privacy, security, risk and trust (passat), 2011 ieee third international conference on and 2011 ieee third international conference on social computing (socialcom), pp. 73–80. IEEE (2011)
20. Fogg, B.: A Behavior Model for Persuasive Design. In: Proceedings of the 4th International Conference on Persuasive Technology, Persuasive '09, pp. 40:1–40:7. ACM, New York, NY, USA (2009). DOI 10.1145/1541948.1541999. URL http://doi.acm.org/10.1145/1541948.1541999

21. Freyne, J., Berkovsky, S., Daly, E.M., Geyer, W.: Social Networking Feeds: Recommending Items of Interest. In: Proceedings of the Fourth ACM Conference on Recommender Systems, RecSys '10, pp. 277–280. ACM, New York, NY, USA (2010). DOI 10.1145/1864708.1864766. URL http://doi.acm.org/10.1145/1864708.1864766
22. Freyne, J., Jacovi, M., Guy, I., Geyer, W.: Increasing Engagement Through Early Recommender Intervention. In: Proceedings of the Third ACM Conference on Recommender Systems, RecSys '09, pp. 85–92. ACM, New York, NY, USA (2009). DOI 10.1145/1639714.1639730. URL http://doi.acm.org/10.1145/1639714.1639730
23. Garcia Esparza, S., O'Mahony, M.P., Smyth, B.: On the Real-time Web As a Source of Recommendation Knowledge. In: Proceedings of the Fourth ACM Conference on Recommender Systems, RecSys '10, pp. 305–308. ACM, New York, NY, USA (2010). DOI 10.1145/1864708.1864773. URL http://doi.acm.org/10.1145/1864708.1864773
24. Ge, M., Delgado-Battenfeld, C., Jannach, D.: Beyond accuracy: Evaluating recommender systems by coverage and serendipity. In: Proceedings of the Fourth ACM Conference on Recommender Systems, RecSys '10, pp. 257–260. ACM, New York, NY, USA (2010). DOI 10.1145/1864708.1864761. URL http://doi.acm.org/10.1145/1864708.1864761
25. Geyer, W., Dugan, C., Millen, D.R., Muller, M., Freyne, J.: Recommending Topics for Self-descriptions in Online User Profiles. In: Proceedings of the 2008 ACM Conference on Recommender Systems, RecSys '08, pp. 59–66. ACM, New York, NY, USA (2008). DOI 10.1145/1454008.1454019. URL http://doi.acm.org/10.1145/1454008.1454019
26. Golbeck, J.: Generating predictive movie recommendations from trust in social networks. In: Proceedings of the 4th International Conference on Trust Management, iTrust'06, pp. 93–104. Springer-Verlag, Berlin, Heidelberg (2006). DOI 10.1007/11755593_8. URL http://dx.doi.org/10.1007/11755593_8
27. Golbeck, J.A.: Computing and Applying Trust in Web-based Social Networks. Ph.D. thesis, College Park, MD, USA (2005). AAI3178583
28. Groh, G., Ehmig, C.: Recommendations in Taste Related Domains. Proceedings of the 2007 international ACM conference on Conference on supporting group work - GROUP '07 pp. 127–136 (2007). DOI 10.1145/1316624.1316643. URL http://dx.doi.org/10.1145/1316624.1316643
29. Gupta, P., Goel, A., Lin, J., Sharma, A., Wang, D., Zadeh, R.: WTF: The Who to Follow Service at Twitter. In: Proceedings of the 22Nd International Conference on World Wide Web, WWW '13, pp. 505–514. International World Wide Web Conferences Steering Committee, Republic and Canton of Geneva, Switzerland (2013). URL http://dl.acm.org/citation.cfm?id=2488388.2488433
30. Guy, I., Avraham, U., Carmel, D., Ur, S., Jacovi, M., Ronen, I.: Mining Expertise and Interests from Social Media. In: Proceedings of the 22Nd International Conference on World Wide Web, WWW '13, pp. 515–526. International World Wide Web Conferences Steering Committee, Republic and Canton of Geneva, Switzerland (2013). URL http://dl.acm.org/citation.cfm?id=2488388.2488434
31. Guy, I., Carmel, D.: Social Recommender Systems. Proceedings of the 20th international conference companion on World wide web - WWW '11 pp. 283—284 (2011). DOI 10.1145/1963192.1963312. URL http://dx.doi.org/10.1145/1963192.1963312
32. Guy, I., Ronen, I., Raviv, A.: Personalized Activity Streams: Sifting Through the River of News. In: Proceedings of the Fifth ACM Conference on Recommender Systems, RecSys '11, pp. 181–188. ACM, New York, NY, USA (2011). DOI 10.1145/2043932.2043966. URL http://doi.acm.org/10.1145/2043932.2043966
33. Guy, I., Ronen, I., Wilcox, E.: Do You Know?: Recommending People to Invite into Your Social Network. In: Proceedings of the 14th International Conference on Intelligent User Interfaces, IUI '09, pp. 77–86. ACM, New York, NY, USA (2009). DOI 10.1145/1502650.1502664. URL http://doi.acm.org/10.1145/1502650.1502664

34. Guy, I., Zwerdling, N., Carmel, D., Ronen, I., Uziel, E., Yogev, S., Ofek-Koifman, S.: Personalized Recommendation of Social Software Items Based on Social Relations. In: Proceedings of the Third ACM Conference on Recommender Systems, RecSys '09, pp. 53–60. ACM, New York, NY, USA (2009). DOI 10.1145/1639714.1639725. URL http://doi.acm.org/10.1145/1639714.1639725
35. Guy, I., Zwerdling, N., Ronen, I., Carmel, D., Uziel, E.: Social Media Recommendation Based on People and Tags. In: Proceedings of the 33rd International ACM SIGIR Conference on Research and Development in Information Retrieval, SIGIR '10, pp. 194–201. ACM, New York, NY, USA (2010). DOI 10.1145/1835449.1835484. URL http://doi.acm.org/10.1145/1835449.1835484
36. Hannon, J., Bennett, M., Smyth, B.: Recommending Twitter Users to Follow Using Content and Collaborative Filtering Approaches. In: Proceedings of the Fourth ACM Conference on Recommender Systems, RecSys '10, pp. 199–206. ACM, New York, NY, USA (2010). DOI 10.1145/1864708.1864746. URL http://doi.acm.org/10.1145/1864708.1864746
37. Herlocker, J.L., Konstan, J.A., Riedl, J.: Explaining Collaborative Filtering Recommendations. In: Proceedings of the 2000 ACM Conference on Computer Supported Cooperative Work, CSCW '00, pp. 241–250. ACM, New York, NY, USA (2000). DOI 10.1145/358916.358995. URL http://doi.acm.org/10.1145/358916.358995
38. Jacovi, M., Guy, I., Kremer-Davidson, S., Porat, S., Aizenbud-Reshef, N.: The perception of others: Inferring reputation from social media in the enterprise. In: Proceedings of the 17th ACM Conference on Computer Supported Cooperative Work & Social Computing, CSCW '14, pp. 756–766. ACM, New York, NY, USA (2014). DOI 10.1145/2531602.2531667. URL http://doi.acm.org/10.1145/2531602.2531667
39. Jamali, M., Ester, M.: A matrix factorization technique with trust propagation for recommendation in social networks. In: Proceedings of the Fourth ACM Conference on Recommender Systems, RecSys '10, pp. 135–142. ACM, New York, NY, USA (2010). DOI 10.1145/1864708.1864736. URL http://doi.acm.org/10.1145/1864708.1864736
40. Jameson, A., Baldes, S., Kleinbauer, T.: Two Methods for Enhancing Mutual Awareness in a Group Recommender System. In: Proceedings of the Working Conference on Advanced Visual Interfaces, AVI '04, pp. 447–449. ACM, New York, NY, USA (2004). DOI 10.1145/989863.989948. URL http://doi.acm.org/10.1145/989863.989948
41. Jäschke, R., Marinho, L., Hotho, A., Schmidt-Thieme, L., Stumme, G.: Tag Recommendations in Folksonomies. In: Knowledge Discovery in Databases: PKDD 2007, pp. 506–514. Springer (2007)
42. Kaser, O., Lemire, D.: Tag-cloud Drawing: Algorithms for Cloud Visualization. arXiv preprint cs/0703109 (2007)
43. Kautz, H., Selman, B., Shah, M.: Referral Web: Combining Social Networks and Collaborative Filtering. Commun. ACM **40**(3), 63–65 (1997). DOI 10.1145/245108.245123. URL http://doi.acm.org/10.1145/245108.245123
44. Kittur, A., Chi, E.H., Suh, B.: Crowdsourcing User Studies with Mechanical Turk. In: Proceedings of the SIGCHI Conference on Human Factors in Computing Systems, CHI '08, pp. 453–456. ACM, New York, NY, USA (2008). DOI 10.1145/1357054.1357127. URL http://doi.acm.org/10.1145/1357054.1357127
45. Lempel, R., Moran, S.: SALSA: The Stochastic Approach for Link-structure Analysis. ACM Trans. Inf. Syst. **19**(2), 131–160 (2001). DOI 10.1145/382979.383041. URL http://doi.acm.org/10.1145/382979.383041
46. Lerman, K.: Social Networks and Social Information Filtering on Digg. Proceedings of the first AAAI conference on Weblogs and Social Media - ICWSM '07 (2007)
47. Leskovec, J., Huttenlocher, D., Kleinberg, J.: Predicting Positive and Negative Links in Online Social Networks. In: Proceedings of the 19th International Conference on World Wide Web, WWW '10, pp. 641–650. ACM, New York, NY, USA (2010). DOI 10.1145/1772690.1772756. URL http://doi.acm.org/10.1145/1772690.1772756
48. Liben-Nowell, D., Kleinberg, J.: The Link-Prediction Problem for Social Networks. Journal of the American society for information science and technology **58**(7), 1019–1031 (2007)

49. Liu, J., Dolan, P., Pedersen, E.R.: Personalized News Recommendation based on Click Behavior. Proceedings of the 15th international conference on Intelligent user interfaces - IUI '10 pp. 31–40 (2010). DOI 10.1145/1719970.1719976. URL http://dx.doi.org/10.1145/1719970.1719976
50. Macdonald, C., Ounis, I.: The trec blogs06 collection: Creating and analysing a blog test collection. Department of Computer Science, University of Glasgow Tech Report TR-2006-224 **1**, 3–1 (2006)
51. McCarthy, J.F., Anagnost, T.D.: MusicFX: An Arbiter of Group Preferences for Computer Supported Collaborative Workouts. In: Proceedings of the 1998 ACM Conference on Computer Supported Cooperative Work, CSCW '98, pp. 363–372. ACM, New York, NY, USA (1998). DOI 10.1145/289444.289511. URL http://doi.acm.org/10.1145/289444.289511
52. McDonald, D.W., Ackerman, M.S.: Just Talk to Me: A Field Study of Expertise Location. In: Proceedings of the 1998 ACM Conference on Computer Supported Cooperative Work, CSCW '98, pp. 315–324. ACM, New York, NY, USA (1998). DOI 10.1145/289444.289506. URL http://doi.acm.org/10.1145/289444.289506
53. McNee, S.M., Riedl, J., Konstan, J.A.: Being Accurate is Not Enough: How Accuracy Metrics Have Hurt Recommender Systems. In: CHI '06 Extended Abstracts on Human Factors in Computing Systems, CHI EA '06, pp. 1097–1101. ACM, New York, NY, USA (2006). DOI 10.1145/1125451.1125659. URL http://doi.acm.org/10.1145/1125451.1125659
54. o'Reilly, T.: What is Web 2.0. O'Reilly Media, Inc. (2009)
55. Paek, T., Gamon, M., Counts, S., Chickering, D.M., Dhesi, A.: Predicting the Importance of Newsfeed Posts and Social Network Friends. In: AAAI, vol. 10, pp. 1419–1424 (2010)
56. Phelan, O., McCarthy, K., Smyth, B.: Using Twitter to Recommend Real-time Topical News. In: Proceedings of the Third ACM Conference on Recommender Systems, RecSys '09, pp. 385–388. ACM, New York, NY, USA (2009). DOI 10.1145/1639714.1639794. URL http://doi.acm.org/10.1145/1639714.1639794
57. Pizzato, L., Rej, T., Chung, T., Koprinska, I., Kay, J.: RECON: A Reciprocal Recommender for Online Dating. In: Proceedings of the Fourth ACM Conference on Recommender Systems, RecSys '10, pp. 207–214. ACM, New York, NY, USA (2010). DOI 10.1145/1864708.1864747. URL http://doi.acm.org/10.1145/1864708.1864747
58. Quercia, D., Capra, L.: FriendSensing: Recommending Friends using Mobile Phones. Proceedings of the third ACM conference on Recommender systems - RecSys '09 pp. 273–276 (2009). DOI 10.1145/1639714.1639766. URL http://dx.doi.org/10.1145/1639714.1639766
59. Resnick, P., Varian, H.R.: Recommender Systems. Communications of the ACM **40**(3), 56–58 (1997). DOI 10.1145/245108.245121. URL http://dx.doi.org/10.1145/245108.245121
60. Ronen, I., Guy, I., Kravi, E., Barnea, M.: Recommending Social Media Content to Community Owners. In: Proceedings of the 37th International ACM SIGIR Conference on Research and Development in Information Retrieval, SIGIR '14, pp. 243–252. ACM, New York, NY, USA (2014). DOI 10.1145/2600428.2609596. URL http://doi.acm.org/10.1145/2600428.2609596
61. Ryan, R.M., Deci, E.L.: Self-Determination Theory and the Facilitation of Intrinsic Motivation, Social Development, and Well-being. American psychologist **55**(1), 68 (2000)
62. Said, A., Bellogín, A.: You are What You Eat! Tracking Health Through Recipe Interactions. In: 6th RecSys Workshop on Recommender Systems and the Social Web, RSWeb '14, p. 4 (2014)
63. Scellato, S., Noulas, A., Mascolo, C.: Exploiting Place Features in Link Prediction on Location-based Social Networks. In: Proceedings of the 17th ACM SIGKDD International Conference on Knowledge Discovery and Data Mining, KDD '11, pp. 1046–1054. ACM, New York, NY, USA (2011). DOI 10.1145/2020408.2020575. URL http://doi.acm.org/10.1145/2020408.2020575
64. Sen, S., Vig, J., Riedl, J.: Tagommenders: Connecting users to items through tags. In: Proceedings of the 18th International Conference on World Wide Web, WWW '09, pp. 671–680. ACM, New York, NY, USA (2009). DOI 10.1145/1526709.1526800. URL http://doi.acm.org/10.1145/1526709.1526800

65. Sigurbjörnsson, B., van Zwol, R.: Flickr Tag Recommendation Based on Collective Knowledge. In: Proceedings of the 17th International Conference on World Wide Web, WWW '08, pp. 327–336. ACM, New York, NY, USA (2008). DOI 10.1145/1367497.1367542. URL http://doi.acm.org/10.1145/1367497.1367542
66. Sinha, R.R., Swearingen, K.: Comparing Recommendations Made by Online Systems and Friends. In: DELOS workshop: personalisation and recommender systems in digital libraries, vol. 106 (2001)
67. Szpektor, I., Maarek, Y., Pelleg, D.: When Relevance is Not Enough: Promoting Diversity and Freshness in Personalized Question Recommendation. In: Proceedings of the 22Nd International Conference on World Wide Web, WWW '13, pp. 1249–1260. International World Wide Web Conferences Steering Committee, Republic and Canton of Geneva, Switzerland (2013). URL http://dl.acm.org/citation.cfm?id=2488388.2488497
68. Terveen, L., McDonald, D.W.: Social Matching: A Framework and Research Agenda. ACM Trans. Comput.-Hum. Interact. **12**(3), 401–434 (2005). DOI 10.1145/1096737.1096740. URL http://doi.acm.org/10.1145/1096737.1096740
69. Wang, D., Pedreschi, D., Song, C., Giannotti, F., Barabasi, A.L.: Human Mobility, Social Ties, and Link Prediction. In: Proceedings of the 17th ACM SIGKDD International Conference on Knowledge Discovery and Data Mining, KDD '11, pp. 1100–1108. ACM, New York, NY, USA (2011). DOI 10.1145/2020408.2020581. URL http://doi.acm.org/10.1145/2020408.2020581
70. Wang, J., Zhang, Y., Posse, C., Bhasin, A.: Is It Time for a Career Switch? In: Proceedings of the 22Nd International Conference on World Wide Web, WWW '13, pp. 1377–1388. International World Wide Web Conferences Steering Committee, Republic and Canton of Geneva, Switzerland (2013). URL http://dl.acm.org/citation.cfm?id=2488388.2488509

Chapter 16
People-to-People Reciprocal Recommenders

Irena Koprinska and Kalina Yacef

16.1 Introduction

Recommending people to people is the core task of many social websites. Examples include finding friends, professional contacts and communities to follow on social networks; matching people in online dating websites, matching job applicants with employers and matching mentors with mentees. While social networks such as Facebook and LinkedIn aim at connecting people by creating *n*-to-*n* relationships, online dating websites aim at matching people to create 1-to-1 relationships.

Most people-to-people recommendations, and especially the 1-to-1 recommendations, involve creating relationships that are reciprocal, i.e. where both parties can express their likes and dislikes and a good match requires satisfying the preferences of both parties. For instance, in the process of hiring someone for a job, both the candidate and the company offering the job need to assess each other; deciding whether the candidate is fit for the position and vice-versa. In online dating, reciprocity is fundamental. Users will build a successful relationship only if both parties are interested in each other. Grouping students in education may require reciprocity in order to maximise learning benefits.

The key role of reciprocity for recommending people to people has only recently being recognised. In this paper we discuss the distinctive nature of reciprocal recommenders, review the previous work and present a case study in online dating.

I. Koprinska (✉) • K. Yacef
School of Information Technologies, University of Sydney, Sydney, NSW 2006, Australia
e-mail: irena.koprinska@sydney.edu.au; kalina.yacef@sydney.edu.au

F. Ricci et al. (eds.), *Recommender Systems Handbook*,
DOI 10.1007/978-1-4899-7637-6_16

16.2 Reciprocal vs Traditional Recommenders

Reciprocal recommenders must satisfy the preferences and needs of the two parties involved in the recommendation. In contrast, the traditional items-to-people recommenders are one-sided and must satisfy only the preference of the person for whom the recommendation is generated. Table 16.1 summarizes the differences between the two types of recommenders; a comprehensive comparison can be found in [1].

The user behaviour is highly dependent on whether the domain is reciprocal or not. The success of a traditional book recommender is dependent only on the person receiving the recommendation. On the other hand, in a reciprocal domain such as online dating, the user receiving the recommendation knows that the success depends on both parties and this influences his/her behaviour. In addition, users in reciprocal domains may choose to act proactively by taking the initiative to connect with other users or to remain reactive and wait for contact.

Another difference is that for traditional recommenders, users have no reason to provide detailed information about themselves (user profile). In contrast, for reciprocal recommenders, there is a clear need and benefit for providing rich user profiles. These profiles might be inaccurate (e.g. due to a lack of self-awareness or desire to have a more attractive profile) and reciprocal recommenders need to account for that.

In traditional recommenders, satisfied and loyal users are likely to repeatedly use the site, allowing it to build rich user model by exploiting the explicitly and implicitly stated user preferences. In contrast, in reciprocal domains people may leave the site permanently after a successful recommendation. For example, a person who successfully finds a lifelong spouse on a dating website or who finds a long term job on a job website may not need to use these sites after that. This creates a paradox for this service provides who want their service to be the best for their users and therefore achieve what they are set to do. But at the same time, if they do provide the best recommendations, users may not use their services for long, possibly affecting revenue. On the other hand, happy users will refer the services

Table 16.1 Main differences between reciprocal and traditional recommenders

Traditional recommenders	Reciprocal recommenders
Success is determined solely by the user seeking the recommendation.	Success is determined by both users—the subject and object of the recommendation.
Users have no reason to provide detailed explicit user profiles.	Users are expected to provide detailed self-profiles. Explicit profiles and preferences are often inaccurate.
Satisfied users are likely to return for more recommendations. Better recommendations mean more engagement.	Users may leave the system after a successful recommendation. Better recommendations might mean less engagement.
The same item can be recommended to all users.	Popular users should not be recommended to too many users.

to new users, and are likely to use the service again if there is a future need for it. This is a clear multi-objective optimization problem. However, it is important to highlight that both objectives, i.e. (1) good successful recommendations for users and (2) short term revenue goals, should not be optimized in equal weights, since an optimization for short-term revenue is likely to hurt the service in the long term, while optimizing for the goodness of users may actually benefit the whole service. The key to the multi objective optimization here is to keep short-term revenue high without decreasing user satisfaction.

Finally, in reciprocal domains it is important that users are not recommended to others in a way that may cause them to be over-loaded with recommendations. For instance, if a highly qualified person is recommended to every single job position that he/she fits, this person is likely to be burdened by the amount of contacts and leave the website. A similar situation can occur for popular users in a dating website. These users are important as they represent the best for each service, therefore they should only be recommended to other users when the recommender is absolutely sure that these users will reciprocate the contact. We note that the popularity bias may be an issue also for some traditional recommender systems but it is a bigger problem for reciprocal recommender systems.

16.3 Previous Work on People-to-People Recommenders

16.3.1 Social Networks

In the broad area of social matching, recommending people to other people [2] has a clear link with reciprocal recommenders because the quality of a match is determined by both parties involved in the match. However, some existing work on social matching tailors recommendations only to the needs of one party [3]. Just a few papers mention the need for reciprocity and even fewer attempt to act on it.

IBM's enterprise social networking service, Beehive [4], allows users to connect to friends and co-workers, post new information or comment on shared information. Two types of people recommender algorithms were compared: content-based and collaborative filtering. The content-based approach assumes that if two people post content on similar topics, they are likely to be pleased to get to know each other. It is based on similarity of textual content and uses content posted by the user on Beehive and additional information such as job description and location. The collaborative filtering is a typical friend-of-friend approach and uses only linking information from the social network. It is based on the intuition that if many of A's connections are connected to B, then A may like to connect to B too. The results show that all approaches increased the number of connections, compared to a control group that received no recommendations. The content-based approach was more successful in recommending contacts that were unknown to each other, while the collaborative filtering approach was more successful in finding known contacts. It is important to note that the befriending in Bee-hive is non-reciprocal, i.e. any user can connect with any other user without the consent of the other person. However, there are still important reciprocal social considerations as noted by the authors, e.g. before adding a contact, one has to consider how the other person would perceive this action and whether they will reciprocate the connection and also how the new contact will be perceived by the other people using the social network service.

Kim et al. [5] created a people recommender system for a social networking website where users can reply positively or negatively to messages from other users. The authors distinguish between recommender systems for one-way interaction and two-way interaction. They propose an approach for a two-way interaction that considers both the interest of the sender and the interest of the recipient of message, and makes recommendations by combining them with a weighted harmonic mean to preserve the importance of these ratios of interest. The method uses both user profiles and information about previous user interactions. For a given user, it finds the best matching values for every attribute and then combines them in a rule that can be used to generate recommendations. Their method yields a success rate of 21.5–22.6 %, improving slightly from the baseline success rate (where users were simply browsing the site to search for people to connect to).

The same research group also developed a collaborative filtering approach that was evaluated on same social networking website [6]. The algorithm is called SocialCollab and considers the preferences of both sides. It is based on similarity of users in terms of attractiveness and taste. Two users are similar in *attractiveness* if they are liked by a common group of users, and these two users are similar in *taste* if they like a common group of users. To generate a recommendation for a user A, the SocialCollab algorithm considers all potential candidates R. For each candidate in R it first finds two groups of similar users (in attractiveness and in taste); the candidate is added to the recommendation list for A if there is at least one similar user in both groups that reciprocally liked A. The recommendations are ranked according to the number of similar users. SocialCollab was shown to outperform standard collaborative filtering, confirming the importance of reciprocity in people-to-people recommenders. Cai et al. [7] improved on these results by using gradient descent to learn the relative contribution of similar users in the ranking of the recommendations given by SocialCollab. In the same domain, the work of Kutty et al. [8] have reported improvements over Cai et al. by using a model based on tensor decomposition to generate recommendations.

Fazel-Zarandi et al. [9] studied different social drivers to predict collaborators in scientific collaboration networks. These social drivers include level of expertise, friend-of-friends, homophily, social exchange, and contagion. Fazel-Zarandi et al. found that these models could be used in combination to better predict collaborations, and that aspects such as homophily, and expert qualifications have a stronger impact in predicting collaborators than the network structure (including reciprocity). However, many of the social drivers may be considered reciprocal as aspects such as homophily, friend-of-friend and even level of expertise can be reciprocal (e.g. the mutually beneficial relationship between students and mentors in scientific collaborations).

16.3.2 Mentor-Mentee Matching

The i-Help system [10] helped students find people who could assist them with university courses, e.g. first year computer science problems. A matchmaking system matched helpers with helpees by considering their attributes and preferences. For the helpers, it stored or inferred attributes such as knowledge of the topic, interests, cognitive style, eagerness to help, helpfulness, availability, and current load. The information was collected from several sources including self-evaluation and peer feedback in previous help sessions. An initial ranked list of potential helpers was produced. It was then refined by considering the preferences of the helpee, e.g. the importance of criteria such as helpfulness and urgency; the preferred and banned helpers. A final list of five potential helpers was compiled; the first of them to reply became the helper.

The PHelpS system [11] was an earlier prototype of i-Help. It was used in a workplace to train staff in how to use a new data management system. The candidate helpers were filtered based on their knowledge of the task, availability and load using a constraint solver. The list was presented to the helpee who chose the helper. Both i-Help and PHelpS relied on rich user models encoding the expertise and preferences of helpers and helpees.

16.3.3 Job Recommendation

Malinowski et al. [12] investigated the problem of matching people and jobs and argued that the matching should be reciprocal, considering the preferences of both the job seeker and the recruiter. They built two recommender systems. The first one recommended job seekers (i.e. their résumés/profiles) to job descriptions of a particular recruiter. To create training data, a recruiter manually labelled the resume of a set of people as either fit or not fit for a list of jobs. The attribute set included demographic, educational, job experience, language, technology skills and other attributes. The second system recommended jobs to job seekers. To create training data, the job candidates were asked to rank a set of job descriptions indicating how well the jobs fitted their preferences. In both cases the authors used the expectation maximisation algorithm to build the prediction model. The two recommender systems were evaluated separately and showed promising prediction accuracy results. Several methods for combining the two recommendations were proposed but were not implemented and evaluated. More broadly, methods for combining different recommenders have been summarised by Burke [13].

16.3.4 Online Dating

The reported research on building recommender systems for online dating is still limited, and most of the papers are published in the last few years.

One of the first studies of recommender systems for online dating [18] evaluated two collaborative filtering based approaches (item-to-item and user-to-user). A data sample from a commercial dating website was collected, where users rated the attractiveness of other users based on their photos. The predictive accuracy of the collaborative filtering algorithms was evaluated and the results showed that both algorithms outperformed the baselines based on random and mean predictions. The authors mentioned the need for reciprocity, but did not explore it.

In [15], we proposed a content-based system which used both user profiles and user interactions. To produce recommendations for a given user, it extracted his/her implicit preferences (i.e. the preferences that are inferred from the interactions with the other users) and then matched them with the profiles of the other users. We showed that reciprocity improved both the success rate and recall of the recommender (see further in the article how these are exactly computed). In [19], we proposed a recommender system for online dating that combined content-based and collaborative filtering approaches and utilised both user profiles and user interactions.

Alsaleh et al. [20] used clustering to group the male users based on their attributes and the female users based on their preferences. It then generated recommendations by matching the male clusters with the female clusters based on user interactions, and recommending cluster members based on compatibility scores. In their subsequent paper [21], the same research group proposed a tensor space model for finding latent relationships between users based on user attributes and interactions. The results showed that the proposed model was more accurate than SocialCollab [6, 7] and other recommendation methods and baselines.

Diaz et al. [16] formulated the matchmaking task as an information retrieval problem, where user profiles were ranked with respect to a given ideal partner profile (i.e. explicit user preferences). Using historical data, a training set of matches (pairs of users represented with their profile attributes) was created and labelled as relevant and non-relevant. A match was considered relevant if users exchanged contact information, and irrelevant if one of the users inspected the profile of the other user but did not send a message or if he/she sent a message but the other user did not reply. A machine learning classifier (ensemble of boosted regression trees) was built and used to predict the relevance of new matches; given a new user, the potential candidates were ranked based on their predicted score. The approach was evaluated using data from an online dating website. The authors described the reciprocal aspect of their work as two-sided relevance and stressed its usefulness for ranking candidates in matchmaking problems.

McFee and Lanckriet [17] proposed an approach for learning distance metrics that were optimised for different ranking evaluation measures, e.g. mean average precision and area under the curve. The metric learning task was cast as an information retrieval problem using a machine learning algorithm (structural support vector machine) to learn the metric, given a ranking. The method was evaluated using data from an online dating website, where the metric was used to calculate the distance between users. Similarly to [16], each training example was a pair of users represented with their profile features and labelled as a successful or unsuccessful match (the match was successful if the users had expressed mutual interest and unsuccessful otherwise). The results showed that the new method was slightly better than the baseline (Euclidean distance measure). Reciprocity was not discussed in the paper; its main focus was the new general algorithm for learning distance metrics rather than the online dating application.

16.4 A Case Study in Online Dating

Online dating websites, e.g. Match.com, eHarmony, RSVP, Zoosk, OkCupid and Meetic, are used by millions of people and their popularity is increasing. Their revenue is also steadily increasing; it is estimated that in 2014 the US and Australian online dating industries have reached $2 billion and $113 million dollars in revenue, respectively [14].

To find dating partners, users provide information about themselves (*user profile*) and their preferred partner (*user preferences*); an example using predefined attributes is shown in Table 16.2. The *explicit* user preferences are the preferences stated by the user as shown in Table 16.2. The *implicit* user preferences are inferred from the interactions of the user with other users and may be quite different to the explicit user preferences (e.g. when a user contacts exclusively short people who smoke in spite of stating in their preferences that they are looking for tall people who do not smoke).

We worked with a major Australian dating site where user interactions consist of four steps:

1. Creating a user profile and specifying the explicit user preferences—New user Bob creates an account on the website and provides information about himself (user profile) and his preferred dating partner (explicit user preferences) using a set of predefined attributes such as the ones shown in Table 16.2 and possibly adding some textual information to expand on their tastes and personality.
2. Browsing the user profiles of other users for interesting matches—Bob finds Alice and decides to contact her.
3. Mediated interaction—Bob chooses a message from a predefined list, e.g. *I'd like to get to know you, would you be interested?* We call these messages *Expressions of Interest (EOI)*. Alice can reply with a predefined message that is either positive

Table 16.2 User profile and explicit user preferences

Bob	My details (Who I am?)	My ideal partner details (Who I am looking for?)
Age	44 years old	35–46 years old
Location	Sydney	Within 20 km
Height	175 cm	At most 175 cm
Body type	Athletic	Slim, average, athletic
Smoking	Trying to quit	Trying to quit, don't smoke
Relationship status	Divorced	Single, divorced, widowed, separated
Have children	Have children who don't live at home How many: 2 Age range: 18–23 years old	Have children who don't live at home, have children living at home, have no children
Personality	Social	Social, average
Eye colour	Blue	–
Hair color	Brown	–
Nationality	Australian	–

(e.g. *I'd like to know more about you*) or negative (e.g. *I don't think we are a good match*) or may not reply at all. When an EOI receives a positive reply, we say that the interest is *reciprocated.*

We define an interaction between users *A* and *B* as *successful* if *A* has sent an EOI to *B* and *B* has responded positively to it. Similarly, we define an interaction between A and B as *unsuccessful* if *A* has sent an EOI to *B* and *B* has responded negatively to it.

4. Unmediated interaction—Typically after a successful interaction, Bob or Alice buys tokens from the website to send each other unmediated messages. This is the only way to exchange contact details and develop further their relationship.

Whilst the relationship, once taken offline, may or may not become a successful one for Bob and Alice, reaching the fourth stage is the crucial and necessary step that makes it possible for them to find out. It is also the extent to which the dating website can go.

A major hurdle for progressing through these steps is that users must find fairly quickly users that are relevant to them, among the hundreds of thousands available. Failure to do so can result in a loss of interest ("there is no-one that I like"), or a feeling of rejection when they contact people who don't reciprocate ("no one wants to talk to me"). Therefore, an efficient reciprocal recommender algorithm is essential for a good customer experience.

16.4.1 A Content-Collaborative Reciprocal Recommender for Online Dating

CCR is our Content-Collaborative Reciprocal recommender [19]. It uses information from the user profile and user interactions to recommend potential matches for a given user. The content-based part computes similarities between users based on their profiles. The collaborative filtering part uses the interactions of the set of similar users, i.e. who they like/dislike and are liked/disliked by, to produce the recommendation. The recommender is *reciprocal* as it considers the likes and dislikes of both sides of the recommendation and aims to match users so that the paring has a high chance of success.

16.4.1.1 Algorithm

The main assumption of CCR, reflected in steps 1 and 2 below, is that a pair of users who have similar profiles will reciprocally like the same type of people (in terms of user profiles), i.e. if U has a similar profile to K_1 and K_1 reciprocally likes A, B and C, then U will reciprocally like A, B and C. We tested this hypothesis in [19] using correlation analysis and a large dataset of more than 7000 users and 16,700 EOI, and found that indeed similar people are reciprocally liked by the same type of people.

Figure 16.1 shows the three main steps that CCR follows, in order to generate a recommendation list for a given user U.

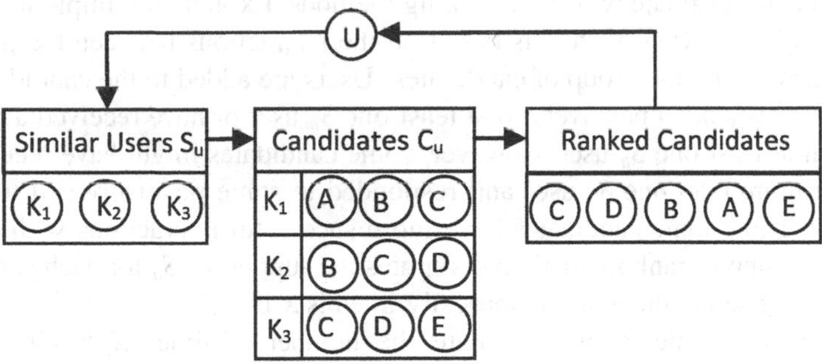

Fig. 16.1 The CCR recommender

1. **Generating similar users based on user profiles**
   This step produces a set of K users who have the most similar profile to U, i.e. that have the lowest possible distance to U. We use a modified version of the K-Nearest Neighbor algorithm, with seven attributes (*age, height, body type, education level, smoker, have children and marital status*) and a distance measure specifically developed for these attributes. For example, in Fig. 16.1 the set of similar users S_u for user U consists of K_1, K_2 and K_3.
2. **Generating recommendation candidates based on user interactions**
   This step produces a set C_u of candidate users for recommending to U. For every user K_i in S_u, we compute the list of all users with whom K_i had reciprocal interest with and add it to the set of candidates C_u. For example in Fig. 16.1, K_1 and A liked each other, so did K_1 and B, K_1 and C and so on, resulting in a recommendation candidate set for U of *{A, B, C, D, E}* with a frequency of 1, 2, 3, 2, 1 respectively.
3. **Ranking the candidates**
   This step uses a ranking method to order the candidates based on their desirability, and provide meaningful recommendations for U. Figure 16.1 shows a ranking method based on frequency—C is ranked the highest because it is the most frequent candidate in C_u.

16.4.1.2 Ranking Method Support

We have developed, implemented and compared a number of ranking methods [22]. Below we describe Support, which is CCR's core ranking method. We found Support to be the best method for our data in spite of its simplicity. In Sect. 16.4.2.5 we describe and evaluate two other ranking methods: Explicit and Implicit.

The Support ranking method is based on the interactions between the group of similar users S_u and the group of candidates. Users are added to the candidate pool if they have responded positively to at least one S_u user or have received a positive reply from at least one S_u user. However, some candidates might have received an EOI from more than one S_u user and responded to some positively and to others negatively. Thus, some candidates have more successful interactions with S_u than others. The Support ranking method computes the support of S_u for each candidate. The higher the score, the more reciprocally liked is X by S_u.

For each candidate X, we calculate the number of times X has responded positively or has received a positive response from S_u, see Table 16.3. We also calculate the number of times X has responded negatively or has received a negative response from S_u. The support score for X is the number of positive minus the number of negative interactions. The higher the score for X, the more reciprocally liked is X by S_u. The candidates are sorted in descending order based on their support score.

Table 16.3 Ranking method support

X	# Positive responses X →S_u	# Positive responses S_u →X	# Negative responses X →S_u	# Negative responses X →S_u	Score
A	10	1	4	2	5
B	4	2	4	1	1
C	5	1	1	1	4
D	2	0	6	1	−5

Table 16.4 Data characteristics

Total users	216,662
Male users	119,102 (54.97 %)
Female users	97,560 (45.03 %)
EOIs	167,810
Successful EOIs	24,079 (25.59 %)
Users sent/received at least 1 EOI	7322
Male users sent/received at least 1 EOI	3965
Female users sent/received at least 1 EOI	3357

16.4.1.3 Evaluation

Data

To evaluate the performance of CCR, we used real data from the Australian website we are working with. The data consists of user profiles and interactions for all active users in March 2010, i.e. all users who have sent or received at least 1 EOI in March 2010. Due to the size of the data we only considered users who reside in Sydney and interactions between people from different genders. The data characteristics are shown in Table 16.4. For each run of the experiment, the dataset is partitioned into two distinct sets, training and testing, containing approximately 2/3 and 1/3 of the users, respectively. Each training/testing partition contains an even distribution of males and females. Each set was also evenly assigned users who were more popular than their cohort in terms of EOI sent and/or received.

EOIs and their responses from users in the training set to users in the testing set and vice versa were removed to ensure fair evaluation. Users in either the testing or training set who no longer meet the minimum number of EOI required were removed. These processing resulted in the removal of less than 1 % of the users before the segmentation into training and test sets. Information about the interactions of the users from the testing set is never included when ranking the candidates for this user to ensure clear separation between the two sets.

Selected Attributes and Distance Measure

The original dataset consists of 39 user profile attributes. We conducted a preliminary data analysis of the distribution of these attributes to identify both the importance and suitability of each attribute. Using this analysis and after some trials of computing correlations, we manually selected the seven attributes: two numeric (*age and height*) and five nominal: *body type* (*values: slim, average, overweight*), *education level* (*secondary, technical, university*), *smoker* (*yes, no*), *have children* (*yes, no*) and *marital status* (*single, previously married*). Some attribute values were merged together during preprocessing, e.g. the values *overweight* and *largish* of *body type* were merged into *overweight*.

To measure the similarity between the user profiles of users *A* and *B*, we used a distance measure that considers the differences between all attributes, but weights higher the age difference. The distance between nominal attributes is calculated by using a reflected binary representation (Gray code) and the Hamming distance. The distance between the numeric attributes is calculated using a function of the absolute differences. For more details, see [19].

Performance Measure

For a user *U* we define the following sets:

- Successful EOI sent by *U*, *successful_sent*: The set of users who *U* has sent an EOI where the user has responded positively.
- Unsuccessful EOI sent by *U*, *unsuccessful_sent*: The set of users who *U* has sent an EOI where the user has responded negatively.
- Successful EOI received by *U*, *successful_recv*: The set of users who have sent an EOI to *U* where *U* has responded positively.
- Unsuccessful EOI received by *U*, *unsuccessful_recv*: The set of users who have sent an EOI to *U* where *U* has responded negatively.
- All successful EOI for *U*: *successful* = *successful_sent* + *successful_recv*.
- All unsuccessful EOI for *U*: *unsuccessful* = *unsuccessful_sent* + *unsuccessful_recv*.

For each user in the testing set, a list of *N* ordered recommendations *N_recommendations* is generated. We define the successful and unsuccessful EOI in the set of *N* recommendations as:

- Successful EOI for U that appear in the set of *N* recommendations: $successful@N = successful \cap N\_recommendations$.
- Unsuccessful EOI for *U* that appear in the set of *N* recommendations: $unsuccessful@N = unsuccessful \cap N\_recommendations$.
- Then, the *success rate* at *N* (i.e. given the *N* recommendations) is defined as:

$$successRate@N[\%] = \frac{\#successful@N}{\#successful@N + \#unsuccessful@N} \quad (16.1)$$

Hence, given a set of N ordered recommendations, the success rate at N is the number of correct recommendations over the number of interacted recommendations (correct or incorrect).

For comparison we use the following baseline: the success rate of the recommender using a random set of K users in S_u as opposed to K nearest neighbors in step 1 of the CCR algorithm (see Fig. 16.1). The random set of K users is used to generate candidates that are then ranked, i.e. there is no change in steps 2 and 3.

Each experiment has been run ten times; the reported success rate is the average over the ten runs.

Results

We evaluated the performance of CCR for different number of recommendations N (from 10 to 500) and different number of minimum number of EOI sent by a user *minEOI_sent* (from 1 to 20) and compared it to the baseline success rate of the recommender using a random set of K users in S_u as opposed to the K nearest neighbours. As an example, Fig. 16.2 shows the success rate result all N and *minEOI_sent* = 2. We found that CCR significantly outperforms the baseline for all cases. For example, for $N = 10$ and *minEOI_sent* = 2, the success rate of CCR is 69.26 % and the baseline success rate is 35.19 %.

As the number of recommendations N increases from 10 to 500, the success rate decreases by 10–20 %. This means that the best recommendations are at the top of the list and adding more recommendations only dilutes the success rate. Hence, our ranking criterion is useful and effective. In practice, the success rate for a smaller N, e.g. $N = 10 - -30$ is very important as this is the typical N presented to the user.

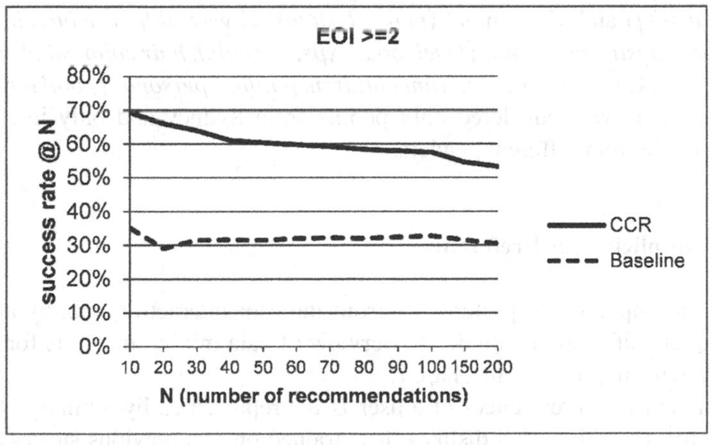

Fig. 16.2 CCR success rate results for *minEOI_sent* = 2

Unsuccessful recommendations, especially recommendations leading to rejection can be very discouraging.

Our results also show that as the number of *minEOI_sent* increases from 1 to 20, the success rate trends are very similar. However, for users who sent more EOIs, the success rate is slightly lower (e.g. 60.16 % for $minEOI\_sent = 10$ and 58.54 % $minEOI\_sent = 20$, for $N = 10$). This can be explained by the fact that the highly active users may be less selective.

In all experiments we used $K = 100$ and $C = 250$. With these parameters it took approximately 100 ms to generate the recommendation list for a user which confirms the efficiency of our algorithm for generation of similar users and candidate recommendations.

16.4.2 Explicit and Implicit User Preferences

In this section we firstly investigate the power of the explicit versus implicit user preferences in predicting the success of an interaction between two users. Then we use these preferences for ranking candidates in CCR. More details can be found in [22].

16.4.2.1 Explicit User Preferences

We define the explicit preferences of a user U as the vector of attribute values specified by U. The attributes and their possible values are predefined by the website.

In our study we used all attributes except *location*, i.e. 19 attributes—2 numeric (*age* and *height*) and 17 nominal (*marital status, have children, education level, occupation industry, occupation level, body type, eye color, hair color, smoker, drink, diet, ethnic background, religion, want children, politics, personality and have pets*).

For simplicity we considered only people from Sydney and only interactions between people from different genders.

16.4.2.2 Implicit User Preferences

We learn the implicit user preferences from the user interaction data by applying a Bayesian classification method; an overview of data mining methods for recommender systems in provided in Chap. 7.

The implicit user preferences of a user U are represented by a binary classifier which captures U's likes and dislikes. It is trained on U's previous successful and unsuccessful interactions. The training data consists of all users $U+$ with whom U had successful interactions and all users $U-$ with who U had unsuccessful interactions during a given time period. Each user from $U+$ and $U-$ is one training example; it is represented as a vector of user profile attribute values and labeled as either Success (successful interaction with U) or Failure (unsuccessful interaction with U). We used the same 19 user profile attributes as the explicit user preferences listed in the previous section. Given a new instance, user U_{new}, the classifier predicts how successful the interaction between U and U_{new} will be by outputting the probability for each class (*Success* or *Failure*) and assigning it to the class with higher probability.

As a classifier we employed NBTree [23] which is a hybrid classifier combining decision tree and Naïve Bayes classifiers. As in decision trees, each node of a NBTree corresponds to a test for the value of a single attribute. Unlike decision trees, the leaves of a NBTree are Naïve Bayes classifiers instead of class labels. We chose NBTree for two reasons. First, given a new instance, it outputs a probability for each class; we needed a probabilistic classifier as we use the probabilities for the ranking of the recommendation candidates. Second, NBTree was shown to be more accurate than both decision trees and Naïve Bayes, while preserving the interpretability of the two classifiers, i.e. providing an easy to understand output which can be presented to the user [23].

16.4.2.3 Are Explicit Preferences Good Predictors of User Interactions?

Data

To evaluate the predictive power of the explicit preferences we consider users who have sent or received at least 1 EOI during a 1-month period (March 2010). We further restrict this subset to users who reside in Sydney to simplify the dataset. These two requirements are satisfied by 8012 users (called *target users*) who had 115,868 interactions, of which 46,607 (40 %) were successful and 69,621 (60 %) were unsuccessful. Each target user U has a set of interacted users U_{int}, consisting of the users U had interacted with.

Method

We compare the explicit preferences of each target user U with the profile of the users in U_{int} by calculating the number of matching and non-matching attributes.

While the user can specify only a single value for a given attribute in his/her profile, e.g. *height* = *170* or *body* = *athletic*, he/she can specify more than one value in his/her preferences—a set of values for a nominal attribute, e.g. *body* = *slim* or *athletic*, and a range of values for a numeric attribute, e.g. height = 155–175. The matching between the preferences of U and the profile of U_{int} for a given attribute is done as follows.

For a numeric attribute, U_{int} matches U's preferences if U_{int}'s value falls within U's range or U_{int} has not specified a value (see the example in Table 16.5). For a

Table 16.5 Matching U's explicit preferences with U_{int}'s profile for numeric attributes

U's preference for *height*	155–175	155–175	155–175
U's value in profile for *height*	160	180	Unspecified
Matching outcome (U, U_{int})	Match	Non-match	Match

Table 16.6 Matching U's explicit preferences with U_{int}'s profile for nominal attributes

U's preference for *body type*	Slim, average	Slim, average	Slim, average	Slim, average
U_{int}'s value in profile for *body type*	Slim	Average	Overweight	Unspecified
Matching outcome (U, U_{int})	Match	Match	Non-match	Match

nominal attribute, U_{int} matches U's preferences if U_{int}'s value has been included in the set of values specified by U or U_{int} has not specified a value (see the example in Table 16.6). An attribute is not considered if U has not specified a value for it. The preferences of U_{int} match the profile of U if all attributes match; otherwise, they do not match.

Results

The results are shown in Table 16.7. They show that 59.40 % of all interactions occur between users with non-matching preferences and profiles. A further examination of the successful and unsuccessful interactions shows that:

- In 61.86 % of all successful interactions U's explicit preferences did not match U_{int}'s profile.
- In 42.25 % of all unsuccessful interactions U's explicit preferences matched the U_{int}'s profile.

Suppose that we use the matching of the user profiles and preferences to try to predict if an interaction between two users will be successful or not (if the profile and preferences match → successful interaction; if the profile and preferences do not match → unsuccessful interaction). The accuracy will be 49.43 % (17,775+39,998/115,868). This is lower than the baseline accuracy of always predicting the majority class (ZeroR baseline) which is 59.78 %. A closer examination of the misclassifications shows that the proportion of false positives is higher than the proportion of false negatives, although the absolute numbers are very similar.

In summary, the results show that the explicit preferences are not a good predictor of the success of interaction between users. This is consistent with [16].

Table 16.7 Explicit preferences—results

	U's preferences and U_{int}'s profile match	U's preferences and U_{int}'s profile do not match	Total
Successful interactions	17,775 (38.14 %)	28,832 (61.86 %) (false positives)	46,607 (all successful interactions)
Unsuccessful interactions	29,263 (42.25 %) (false negatives)	39,998 (57.75 %)	69,261 (all unsuccessful interactions)
Total	47,038 (40.60 %)	68,830 (59.40 %)	115,858 (all interactions)

16.4.2.4 Are Implicit Preferences Good Predictors of User Interactions?

Data

To evaluate the predictive power of the implicit preferences we consider users who have at least three successful and three unsuccessful interactions during a 1-month period (February 2010). This dataset was chosen so that we could test on the March dataset used in the study of the implicit preferences above. Here too, we restrict this subset to users who reside in Sydney. These two requirements are satisfied by 3881 users, called *target users*. The training data consists of the interactions of the target users during February; 113,170 interactions in total, 30,215 positive and 72,995 negative. The test data consists of the interactions of the target users during Match; 95,777 interactions in total, 34,958 positive (37 %, slightly less than the 40 % in the study above) and 60,819 negative (63 %, slightly more than the 60 % in the study above). Each target user U has a set of *interacted users* U_{int}, consisting of the users U had interacted with.

Method

For each target user U we create a classifier by training on U's successful and unsuccessful interactions from February as described in Sect. 16.3.2. We then test the classifier on U's March interactions. This separation ensures that we are not training and testing on the same interactions.

Results

Table 16.8 summarizes the classification performance of the NBTree classifier on the test data. It obtained an accuracy of 82.29 %, considerably higher than the ZeroR baseline of 63.50 % and the accuracy of the explicit preferences classifier. In comparison to the explicit preferences, the false positives drop from 61.86 to

Table 16.8 Classification performance of NBTree on test set

<– classified as	Successful interactions	Unsuccessful interactions	Total
Successful interactions	24,060 (68.83 %)	10,538 (30.14 %) (false positives)	34,958 (all successful interactions)
Unsuccessful interactions	6064 (9.97 %) (false negatives)	54,755 (90.03 %)	60,819 (all unsuccessful interactions)

Table 16.9 Ranking method Explicit

Candidate	# Matching attributes	# Non-matching attributes	Stage 1: non-match rank	Stage 2 (final ranking): match rank for ties
A	2	0	1	2
B	2	2	2	4
C	4	2	2	3
D	4	0	1	1

30.14 %, an important improvement in this domain since a recommendation that leads to rejection can be discouraging; the false negatives drop from 42.25 to 9.97 %.

In summary, the results show that the implicit preferences are a very good predictor of the success of user interactions, and considerably more accurate than the explicit preferences.

16.4.2.5 Using User Preferences for Ranking Candidates in CCR

Ranking Method Explicit

This is a content-based ranking method. It is based on minimising the number of non-matching attributes between the candidate profile and the explicit preferences of the target user; the lower the number of non-matches, the higher the candidate ranking. In addition to checking if the candidate satisfies the target user's explicit preferences it also checks the reverse: if the target user satisfies the candidate's explicit preferences. Thus, it minimises the number of reciprocal non-matches.

We compare each candidate (i.e. its profile) with the explicit preferences of the target user and each target user with the explicit preferences of the candidate. We tally the number of matches and non-matches from both comparisons. The candidates are first sorted in ascending order based on the non-match score (stage 1 ranking). After that candidates with the same non-match score are sorted in descending order based on their match score (stage 2 and final ranking). An example is shown in Table 16.9.

Ranking Method Implicit

This ranking method uses previous user interactions, and hence requires a history of previous usage of the recommender system.

It utilises the classifier generated for each target user U, based upon U's previous interactions. Given a candidate, the classifier gives a probability for the two classes *Success* and Failure (successful and unsuccessful interaction between the candidate and target user, respectively). Candidates are then ranked in descending order based on the probability of class *Success*.

Baseline

This ranking method assumes that all candidates have an equal chance of a successful pairing and that any one random selection will give the same chance of success as any other ranking approach. For each candidate pool the candidates are randomly shuffled before being presented to the target user.

Results

We used the same data as the data used to learn the implicit user preferences. As stated already, it consists of the profile attributes and user interactions of all users who had at least three successful and at least three unsuccessful interactions during February 2010 and reside in Sydney. We note that this dataset is a subset of the dataset from Table 16.4 which includes all users who have sent or received at least 1 EOI. A minimum number of positive and negative examples is required for the training of the NBTree classifier, hence the restriction for at least three successful and three unsuccessful interactions.

For each run of the experiment, the users who meet the two requirements listed above are considered as part of the test set. Information about a test user's interactions is never included when generating and ranking candidates for that user. This ensures a clean separation between testing and training data.

Figure 16.3 shows the success rate results for different number of recommendations N (from 10 to 200) and for *minEOI_sent* = 5. The main results are:

- The ranking methods Support (described in Sect. 16.4.1.2), Implicit and Explicit outperform the Random ranking method (baseline) for all N and all minimum number of EOI.
- The best ranking method is Support, followed by Implicit and Explicit. For a small number of recommendations ($N = 10 - -50$), Implicit performs similarly to Support. This is encouraging since the success rate for a small number of recommendations is very important in practical applications. As N increase the difference between Support and Implicit increases.

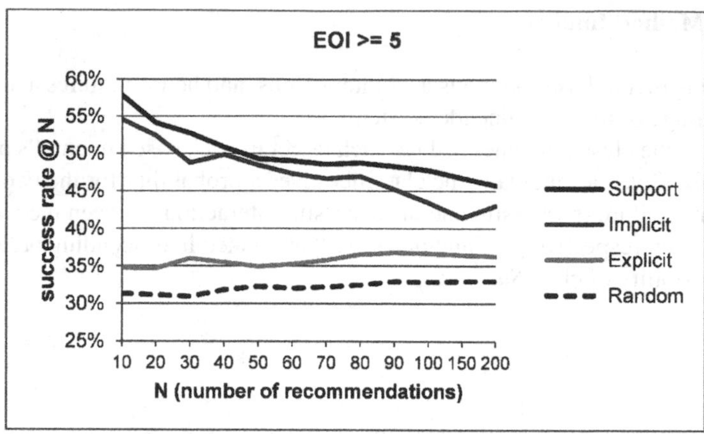

Fig. 16.3 Success rate of CCR using different ranking methods

- Implicit significantly outperforms Explicit for all N and minimum number of EOI. For instance, when the top ten recommendations are presented ($N = 10$), the success rates are: Implicit=54.59 %, Explicit=34.78 % for EOI=5; Implicit= 50.45 %, Explicit=36.05 % for EOI=10; Implicit=54.31 %, Explicit=32.95 % for EOI=20, i.e. the difference between the two methods is 14.4–21.4 %.
- As the number of recommendations N increases from 10 to 200, the success rate for Support and Implicit decreases with 8–12 %. This means that the best recommendations are already at the top. Hence, these ranking methods are useful and effective. For Explicit, as N increases the success rate does not change or even slightly increases in some cases. This confirms that the ranking function is less effective, although still better than the baseline.
- As the number of EOI_sent increases from 5 to 20, the success rate trends are very similar.

16.5 Conclusions and Future Work

People-to-people reciprocal recommenders are an important class of recommenders which have emerged fairly recently. In this paper we discussed their characteristics (a more comprehensive analysis is available in [1]) and the management of reciprocity.

To illustrate different aspects of this type of recommenders and how to take account of the reciprocity and build an effective reciprocal recommender, we presented a case study in online dating, using a large dataset from a major Australian online dating website.

We have developed CCR, a reciprocal recommender system for an online dating, that combines content-based and collaborative filtering, and utilises data from both user profiles and user interactions. It is based on our finding that people with similar profiles are reciprocally liked by people with similar profiles. CCR achieved success rate of 64.24–69.26 % for different number of EOI, significantly outperforming the baseline success rate of [23.44–35.19 %]. An important advantage of CCR is that it addresses the cold start problem of new users joining the website by being able to provide recommendations immediately, based on the profile of the new user, which is very important for engaging the new users.

We also studied the differences between the implicit and explicit user preferences. We found that the explicit user preferences, stated by the user, are not a good predictor of the success of user interactions, achieving an accuracy of 49.43 %. In contrast, the implicit user preferences, that are learned from successful and unsuccessful previous user interactions, using a probabilistic classifier, were a very good predictor of the success of user interactions, achieving an accuracy of 89.29 %. In addition we investigated the use of explicit and implicit user preferences for ranking of candidates in CCR and found that the ranking method using implicit preferences is more accurate than the one using explicit preferences.

There are many research questions that arise from designing reciprocal recommenders, some of which are the same as for standard recommenders, and others are inherent to the reciprocity aspect.

Some user profiles need to be handled with care in reciprocal recommender algorithms: for example, popular users should not be recommended too often, as they are likely to be overwhelmed and unresponsive. This problem does not normally occur in non-reciprocal domains or even people-to-people recommenders that are not reciprocal, e.g. Twitter.

Another issue is that popular users, in some cases, may even hide bait-profiles, created by criminals to lure people into trusting them in romance scams. The detection of scamming in the online dating industry is a high priority and requires the recommender systems to ensure they do not favour bait-profiles over authentic user profiles [21]. Although this issue is very important in online dating, where people are particularly vulnerable and seeking relationships, it can also be an issue in other people-to-people recommendations.

The predictive power of explicit and implicit user preferences needs further investigation. Not all explicit user preferences are equally important; if the user can specify the importance of the attributes in the explicit preferences, this information can be used to improve the prediction of successful and unsuccessful interactions. A comparison of the explicit and implicit user preferences would also be beneficial, e.g. (1) to find if there are some latent factors that are difficult to capture, and also (2) to make users aware when their stated explicit preferences are very different than their implicit preferences, and adjust the explicit preferences accordingly. It is also worth investigating if our findings about the explicit and implicit preferences carry over to other people-to-people reciprocal domains.

In order to increase the efficiency and relevance of reciprocal recommenders, a number of other data sources should also be explored: for instance the use of temporal information (e.g. how quickly users respond to EOIs), or the use of photos and free text to refine the quality of the implicit user profiles.

Although providing unexpected recommendations has been identified as a useful property of traditional recommender systems (Chap. 26), it is not clear how much novelty and serendipity is needed in reciprocal recommenders. In contrast with traditional domains, in reciprocal domains, users provide more information about themselves in their user profiles and explicit user preferences. Recommending surprising matches that do not satisfy these preferences may be seen as unacceptable by some users, and reduce their trust (Chap. 20) in the system. Some other users, however, may welcome suggestions of people different to the ones they think they like. One way to safely allow novelty and serendipity is to explicitly inform the users when the recommendations deviate from their explicit preferences.

Using user personality (Chap. 21) in reciprocal recommender systems is another interesting direction for future work. Some online dating website assess personality by asking users to complete long and intrusive questionnaires, and then match users based on personality type. It will be useful to acquire user personality implicitly in a non-obtrusive way, e.g. from free text comments in the user profile; book, movie and sport preferences; writing style, text sentiment, punctuation and grammar; user activity level and interactions.

Acknowledgements This work was supported by the Smart Services Cooperative Research Centre. We also thank Joshua Akehurst, Luiz Pizzato and Judy Kay for their contributions to this work.

References

1. L. Pizzato, T. Rej, J. Akehurst, I. Koprinska, K. Yacef, and J. Kay, "Recommending People to People: The Nature of Reciprocal Recommenders With a Case Study in Online Dating," *User Modeling and User-Adapted Interaction*, vol. 23, pp. 447–488, 2013.
2. L. Terveen and D. W. McDonald,"Social matching: A framework and research agenda," *ACM Transactions on Computer-Human Interaction*, vol. 12, pp. 401–434, 2005.
3. D. Richards, M. Taylor, and P. Busch, "Expertise recommendation: A two-way knowledge communication channel," presented at the International Conference on Autonomic and Autonomous Systems, 2008.
4. J. Chen, W. Geyer, C. Dugan, and M. G. I. Muller, "Make new friends, but keep the old: recommending people on social networking sites," presented at the International Conference on Computer-Human Interaction (CHI'2009), New York, 2009.
5. Y. S. Kim, A. Mahidadia, P. Compton, X. Cai, M. Bain, A. Krzywicki, and W. Wobcke, "People recommendation based on aggregated bidirectional intentions in social network site," presented at the Knowledge Management and Acquisition for Smart Systems and Services, 2010.
6. X. Cai, M. Bain, A. Krzywicki, W. Wobcke, Y. S. Kim, P. Compton, and A. Mahidadia, "Collaborative filtering for people to people recommendation in social networks," presented at the Advances in Artificial Intelligence, 2011.

7. X. Cai, M. Bain, A. Krzywicki, W. Wobcke, Y. S. Kim, P.Compton, and A. Mahidadia, "Collaborative filtering for people to people recommendation in social networks," presented at the Australian Joint Conference on Artificial Intelligence, 2010.
8. S. Kutty, L. Chen, and R. Nayak, "A people-to-people recommendation system using tensor space models," presented at the 27th Annual ACM Symposium on Applied Computing (SAC), 2012.
9. F.-Z. M., D. H.J., Y. Huang, and N. Contractor, "Expert recommendation based on social drivers, social network analysis, and semantic data representation," presented at the Second International Workshop on Information Heterogeneity and Fusion in Recommender Systems (HetRec).
10. S. Bull, J. E. Greer, G. I. McCalla, L. Kettel, and J. Bowes, "User Modelling in I-Help: What, Why, When and How," presented at the User Modeling, 2001.
11. J. Greer, G. McCalla, J. Collins, V. Kumar, P. Meagher, and J. Vassileva, "Supporting peer help and collaboration in distributed workplace environments," *International Journal on Artificial Intelligence in Education*, pp. 159–177, 1998.
12. J. Malinowski, T. Keim, O. Wendt, and T. Weitzel, "Matching People and Jobs: A Bilateral Recommendation Approach," presented at the 39th Annual Hawaii International Conference on System Sciences, 2006.
13. R. Burke, "Hybrid Recommender Systems: Survey and Experiments," *User Modeling and User-Adapted Interaction*, vol. 12, pp. 331–370, 2002.
14. IBISWorld. (2014, Dating Services in the US: Market Research Report, Apr 2014. Available: www.ibisworld.com.au/industry/dating-services.html
15. L. Pizzato, T. Rej, T. Chung, I. Koprinska, and J. Kay, "RECON: A Reciprocal Recommender for Online Dating," presented at the ACM Conference on Recommender Systems (RecSys'2010), Barcelona, Spain, 2010.
16. F. Diaz, D. Metzler, and S.Amer-Yahia., "Relevance and ranking in online dating systems," presented at SIGIR'2010, 2010.
17. B. McFee and G. R. G. Lanckriet, "Metric learning to rank," presented at the International Conference on Machine Learning (ICML), 2010.
18. L. Brozovsky and V. Petricek, "Recommender System for Online Dating Service," presented at the Procedings of Znalosti 2007 conference, Ostrava, 2007.
19. J. Akehurst, I. Koprinska, K. Yacef, L. Pizzato, J. Kay, and T. Rej, "CCR - a content-collaborative reciprocal recommender for online dating," in Peoc. 22nd *International Joint Conference on Artificial Intelligence (IJCAI)*, Barcelona, Spain, 2011.
20. S. Alsaleh, R. Nayak, Y. Xu, and L. Chen, "13th Asia-Pacific Conference on Web Technologies and Applications," 2011.
21. S. Kutty, L. Chen, and R. Nayak, "A people-to-people recommendation system using tensor space model," presented at the 27th Symposium on Applied Computing, 2012.
22. J. Akehurst, I. Koprinska, K. Yacef, L. Pizzato, J. Kay, and T. Rej, "Explicit and implicit user preferences in online dating," in *New Frontiers in Applied Data Mining*, L. Cao, J. Huang, J. Bailey, Y. Koh, and J. Luo, Eds., ed: Springer Lecture Notes in Computer Science, v. 7104, 2012, pp. 15–27.
23. R. Kohavi, "Scaling Up the Accuracy of Naive-Bayes Classifiers: a Decision-Tree Hybrid," presented at the Int. Conference on Knowledge Discovery in Databases (KDD), 1996.

Chapter 17
Collaboration, Reputation and Recommender Systems in Social Web Search

Barry Smyth, Maurice Coyle, Peter Briggs, Kevin McNally, and Michael P. O'Mahony

17.1 Introduction

The web is probably one of the most important and wide-spread information tools in use today. Many of us interact with general purpose search engines such as Goggle and Bing many times a day, while some of us use more specialized search services to cater for niche needs from time to time. Indeed mainstream search has become so much a part of everyday life that one would be forgiven for assuming that all of the major web search challenges have been overcome The reality is very different, however, and by some measures the pace of innovation in web search has never been greater as leading services continue to look for new ways to cope with the many challenges that remain in order to satisfy their users' changing needs and evolving expectations.

Recent research has highlighted how even the leading search engines suffer from low success rates when it comes to delivering relevant results to the average searcher. For example, in one study [24] of more than 20,000 search queries researchers found that, on average, Google delivered at least one result worth selecting only 48 % of the time. In other words, in 52 % of cases, searchers chose to select none of the results returned, a disappointing and somewhat surprising success rate by any standard. In large part this problem is as much due to the searcher as it is the search engine: our search queries tend to be vague and under-specified, and rarely provide a clear indication of our search needs [49, 113, 124–126]. Mostly we have adapted to these low success rates. We respond to poor result-lists with follow-up or alternative

B. Smyth (✉) • K. McNally • M.P. O'Mahony
Insight Centre for Data Analytics, University College Dublin, Dublin, Ireland
e-mail: barry.smyth@ucd.ie

M. Coyle • P. Briggs
HeyStaks Technologies Ltd, NovaUCD, University College Dublin, Dublin, Ireland
e-mail: Maurice.Coyle@heystaks.com

F. Ricci et al. (eds.), *Recommender Systems Handbook*,
DOI 10.1007/978-1-4899-7637-6_17

queries until we find what we are looking for. And while we usually do find what we are looking for it comes at a cost—wasted time and effort—and sometimes we may abandon our efforts altogether. At best this means that web search is far less efficient than it should be—indeed recent studies suggest that among information workers 10 % of salary costs are lost due to wasted search time [30]—and at worst a significant proportion of searchers may fail to find the information they need, even though it exists somewhere.

Thus, there remains plenty of scope for improvement in mainstream search. This is particularly true as the web evolves to become a more social and collaborative world, creating new opportunities to learn about and harness user preferences and relationships. In this chapter we will look into the future of web search by reviewing some of most promising research ideas that have the potential to bring game-changing innovation to this exciting technology sector. We will argue that the past is apt to repeat itself and just as Google's game-changing approach to web search led to its relentless rise over the past 15 years, so too will new search technologies emerge to have a similarly disruptive effect on the market over the next 15 years.

It can be useful to view modern search engines as a type of recommender system: they respond to user queries with a set of result-page recommendations. But unlike many conventional recommender systems, search engines have focused on text and link analysis rather than the user interactions and the similarity relationships that drive recommender systems. There is now an opportunity for recommendation technologies to play an increasingly important role in web search, by helping to address core web search challenges as well as contributing to the solution of a number of secondary search features.

For example, recently, modern search engines have added *query recommendation* services to supplement core search functionality. As the user enters their query, services like Google Suggest use recommendation techniques to identify, rank and recommend previously successful and relevant queries to the user; see [103]. In this chapter, we will focus on two promising and powerful new ideas in web search—personalization and collaboration—that can trace their origins to recent recommender systems research [5, 37, 59, 94, 105, 112]. They question the very core assumptions of mainstream web search engines and suggest important adaptations to conventional approaches to web search.

The first assumption concerns the *one-size-fits-all* nature of mainstream web search—two different users with the same query will, more or less, receive the very same result-list, regardless of their preferences—and argues that web search needs to become more *personalized* by considering the implicit needs and preferences of searchers. We will review a number of different approaches to personalizing web search which harness different types of user preference and context information to influence the search experience; see for example [2, 15, 20, 22, 23, 31, 33, 35, 53, 54, 85, 109, 123, 131]. That being said many mainstream search engines are beginning to adapt the results that they return to users, based on factors such as location, time of day etc. but less so based on an understanding of user preferences or needs. A valid concern when it comes to adapting or personalizing result-lists is the extent to which it may blinker the searcher and limit the possible views and opinions that the searcher is exposed to in the long-run; see [81]. However, personalization does not necessarily oblige a narrowing of results. And one of the most interesting dimensions to modern recommender systems is the extent to which they seek to explore issues such as diversity and novelty as well as relevance when it comes to evaluating the quality of result-lists; see for example, [7, 10, 36, 56, 60, 121]. In this sense the solution to Pariser's Filter Bubble is the recommendation of more diverse results and/or results that express novel and divergent viewpoints.

The second assumption to be questioned concerns the *solitary nature* of web search. By and large modern web search takes the form of an isolated interaction between a lone searcher and search engine. However, recent research suggests that there are many circumstances where the search for information can (and should) have a more collaborative flavour. Often it makes sense for groups of searchers (e.g., friends, colleagues, classmates) to cooperate in various ways as they search for and share results. We will describe recent work in the area of *collaborative information retrieval*, which attempts to capitalize on this potential for collaboration during a variety of information seeking tasks; see for example, [1, 69, 70, 87–90, 117].

In addition we will highlight a new breed of search service that combines elements of personalization and collaboration: so-called *social search* services take advantage of the recent evolution of the web as a social medium, one that promotes interaction and collaboration among individuals during search, so that searchers can benefit from the preferences and experiences of other like-minded individuals. This provides a new source of information for search engines to use during retrieval, specifically collaboration and reputation information. And this information can be used to drive recommendations at search time so that organic search results, based on term-overlap and link connectivity information, are complimented by additional result recommendations derived from the preferences and activities of searchers. In doing so we will bring together recommendation and search in a way that points to a new future for search engine development in the ongoing quest to deliver the right information to the right user at the right time.

17.2 A Brief History of Web Search

Before considering some of the emergent search technologies that have the potential to disrupt the search industry, it is first worth briefly reviewing the history of web search over the past 15 years, to better understand the evolution of modern web search. The early web was not a place of search. Instead if you wanted to get to a particular web page then you either typed the URL directly into your browser, or you used a portal like Yahoo as a starting point to navigate to this page. As the web grew (and grew, and grew) it became clear that portal browsing would not scale, and web search began to emerge in the guise of early search engines such as Lycos, Excite, and Altavista.

These search engines all relied on so-called information retrieval (IR) technologies that had been around since the 1970s [4, 96]. A simplified schematic of a

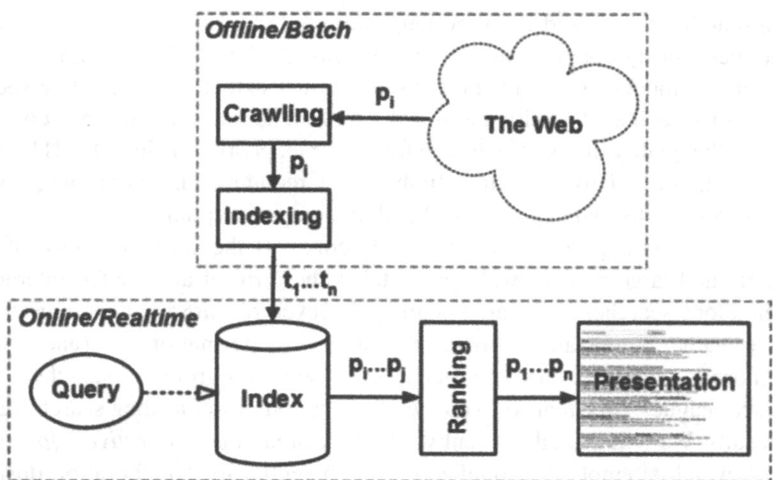

Fig. 17.1 Functional components of a typical web search engine. A page, p_i, is located on the web by the crawler and its content, the terms $t_1,\ldots,t_n$, are retrieved and indexed as part of an offline process. In response to a search query, the engine probes the index to retrieve results, $p_i,\ldots,p_j$, which match the query terms, which are then ranked by their relevance according to the search engine's particular ranking metrics, before being presented to the searcher as a result-list

typical search engine architecture is presented in Fig. 17.1. Briefly, early search engines constructed their own index of the web, by *crawling* the web's network of pages and analysing the content of each page in turn, recording the terms, and their frequencies, contained in each page. To respond to a search query, the search engine retrieves and ranks pages that contain query terms. During the early days of web search, the emphasis was very much on the size of the index, and search engines that had indexed more of the web had a clear coverage advantage over their rivals. Attention was also paid to the ranking of search results; for the most part, these search engines relied on the frequency of query terms in a web page (relative to the index as a whole) as the primary arbiter of relevance [122], preferring pages that contained frequent occurrences of distinctive query terms. While this approach worked reasonably well in the well-structured, closed-world of information retrieval systems, where information retrieval experts could be relied upon to submit detailed, well-formed queries, it did not translate well to the scale and heterogenous nature of web content or our vague search queries. The outcome was a poor search experience for most searchers, with relevant results hidden deep within result-lists dominated by results that were, at best, only superficially relevant to the query.

Improving the ranking of search results became the challenge for these early search engines and even the race for the largest search index took a back seat in the face of this more pressing need. It soon became clear, however, that relying solely on the terms in a page was not going to be sufficient, no matter how much time was invested in tweaking these early ranking algorithms. Simply put, there were lots of pages that scored equally well when it came to counting matching query and page terms, but few of these pages turned out to be truly relevant and authoritative. Although term matching information had a role to play in overall relevance, on its own it was insufficient, and it was clear that there was vital information missing from the ranking process.

The missing ingredient came about as a result of research undertaken by a number of groups during the mid 1990s. This included the work of Kleinberg [43] and, most famously, the work of Google founders Page and Brin [12]. These researchers were among the first to take advantage of the connectedness of web pages, and they used this information to evaluate the relative importance of individual pages. Kleinberg, Page, and Brin recognised the web as a type of *citation network* (for example, see [71]). Instead of one paper citing another through a bibliographic reference, on the web one page cited another page through a hyperlink connecting the two. Moreover, it seemed intuitive that the importance of a given page should be a function of the various pages that linked to it; the so-called *back-links* of the page. Thus a page could be considered important if lots of other important pages linked to it. This provided the starting point for a fundamentally new way to measure the importance of a page and, separately, the work of Kleinberg [43], Chakrabarti et al. [18] and Brin and Page [12] led to novel algorithms for identifying authoritative and relevant pages for even vague web search queries. By the late 1990s Page and Brin's so-called *PageRank* algorithm was implemented in the first version of Google, which combined traditional term-matching techniques with this new approach to link analysis, to provide search results that were objectively superior to the results of other search engines of the day. The rest, as they say, is history.

17.3 The Future of Web Search

There is no doubt that web search represents a very significant information discovery and recommendation challenge. The size and growth characteristics of the web, and the sheer diversity of content types on offer represent formidable information retrieval challenges in their own right. At the same time, as the demographics of the web's user-base continues to expand, search engines must be able to accommodate a diverse range of user types and search skill levels. In particular, most of us fail to live up to the expectations of the document-centric, term-based information retrieval engines that lie at the heart of modern search technology. These engines, and the techniques they rely upon, largely assume well-formed, detailed search queries, but such queries are far from common in web search today [38, 39, 49, 126]. Instead most web search queries are vague or ambiguous, with respect to the searcher's true information needs, and many queries can contain terms that are not even reflected in the target document(s).

Given that many queries fail to deliver the results that the searcher is looking for, there is considerable room for improvement in this most fundamental feature of the search experience. While the problem may reside, at least in part, with the nature of web search queries, as discussed above, it is unlikely that users will improve their query-skills any time soon. In response, researchers have begun to explore two complementary strands of research as a way to improve the overall searcher experience. One widely held view is that web search needs to become more personalized: additional information about users, their preferences and their current context, for example, should be used to deliver a more personalized form of web search by selecting and ranking search results that better match the preferences and context of the individual searcher (for example, see [2, 15, 22, 31, 53, 109]). Another view is that there is an opportunity for web search to become more collaborative, by allowing communities of users to co-operate (implicitly or overtly) as they search (for example, see [1, 69, 70, 87–90, 117]).

In the following sections we will review this research landscape, describing a number of initiatives that are attempting to transform static (non-personalized), solitary (non-collaborative), mainstream search engines into more personalized (see Sect. 17.3.1) or more collaborative (see Sect. 17.3.2) search services. These initiatives borrow ideas from recommender systems, user profiling, and computer-supported collaborative working research (for example, see [37, 44, 58, 107, 112]). We will also highlight recent research that seeks to bring both of these approaches together leading to a new generation of search services that are both collaborative and personalized. We will refer to these hybrid services as *social search* services and later in this chapter we will describe two detailed case-studies of two different approaches to social search.

17.3.1 Personalizing Web Search

Many recommender systems are designed to make suggestions to users that are relevant to their particular circumstances or their personal preferences; see Chaps. 13, 14, 22, and 27 in this volume. For example, recommender systems help users to identify personally relevant information such as news articles [8, 44, 82], books [51], movies [27, 45, 65], and even products to buy [21, 57, 91–93, 105]. The application of recommender technologies to web search allows for a departure from the conventional one-size-fits-all approach to mainstream web search. When it comes to delivering a more personalized search experience there are two key requirements: firstly, we must understand the needs of searchers (*profiling*); secondly, we must be able to use these profiles to influence the output of the search engine, for example by re-ranking results according to the profile, or, indeed, by influencing other components of the web search experience.

To put these research efforts into perspective it is useful to consider two important dimensions to personalizing web search. On the one hand we can consider the nature of the profiles that are learned: some approaches focus on *short-term* user profiles that capture features of the user's current search context [15, 31, 109], while others accommodate *long-term* profiles that capture the user's preferences over an extended period of time [2, 22, 53]. On the other hand, when it comes to harnessing these profiles during search, we can usefully distinguish between those approaches that are guided by an *individual* target user's profile (for example, see [16, 40, 46, 112]) versus those that are *collaborative*, in the sense that they are guided by the profiles of a group of users (for example, see [37, 44, 51, 108, 113]).

Generally speaking, user profiles can be constructed in two ways. *Explicit profiling* interrogates users directly by requesting different forms of preference information, from categorical preferences [22, 53] to simple result ratings [2]. In contrast, *implicit profiling* techniques attempt to infer preference information by monitoring user behaviour, and without interfering with users as they go about their searches [22, 52, 85].

With explicit profiling, the users themselves do the profiling work by either specifying search preferences up front, or by providing personal relevance feedback such as rating returned search results. Chirita et al. [22] use individual user profiles which are defined by the searcher through ODP[1] web directory categories to re-rank results according to the distance between the profile and ODP categories for each result. They investigate a number of different distance metrics, and report the findings of a live user evaluation that shows that their personalized approach is capable of more relevant result rankings than standard Google search. One of the drawbacks of relying on ODP categories in this way, however, is that only a small proportion of the web is categorised in the ODP and so many of the returned search results have no category information to base the re-ranking on. Ma et al. [53] propose a similar approach whereby user profiles are explicitly expressed through ODP categories, except they re-rank search results based on the cosine similarity between result-page content and the ODP directory category profiles. In this way the search results themselves are not required to be categorised in the ODP.

In contrast, *ifWeb* [2] builds user profiles using a less structured approach through keywords, free-text descriptions, and web page examples provided by the user to express their specific information needs, which are stored as a weighted semantic network of concepts. *ifWeb* also takes advantage of explicit relevance feedback where the searcher provides result ratings that are used to refine and update their profile. A similar approach is used by the *Wifs* system [66] in which profiles initially built using terms selected from a list can be subsequently improved with feedback on viewed documents provided by users. The major drawback with these types of explicit approaches to profiling is that the majority of users are reluctant to make the extra effort in providing feedback [17]. Furthermore, searchers may find it difficult to categorise their information needs and preferences accurately in the first place.

A potentially more successful approach to profiling is to infer user preferences implicitly (*implicit profiling*). As in the work of Chirita et al. [22], Liu et al. [52] also use hierarchical categories from the ODP to represent a searcher's profile, except in this work the categories are chosen automatically based on past search behaviour such as previously submitted queries and the content of selected result documents. A number of different learning algorithms are analysed for mapping this search

[1]The Open Directory Project, http://dmoz.org.

behaviour onto the ODP categories, including those based on Linear Least Squares Fit (LLSF) [130], the Rocchio relevance feedback algorithm [97], and k-Nearest Neighbor (kNN) [28]. In a related approach, statistical language methods are used [129] to mine contextual information from this type of long-term search history to build a language model based profile; similarly, user preferences are inferred [85] based on past behaviour, this time using the browser cache of visited pages to infer subject areas that the user is interested in. These subject areas, or categories, are combined into a hierarchical user profile where each category is also weighted according to the length of time the user spent viewing the pages corresponding to the category.

The above are all examples of long-term user profiles that seek to capture information about the user's preferences over an extended period of time, certainly beyond the bounds of a single search session. The alternative is to capture short-term profiling information, typically related to the particular context of the current information finding task. For example, the UCAIR system [109] concentrates on recently submitted queries and selected results to build a short-term profile that is used to personalize results for the current search task. When a new search session is initiated, a new profile for the user and their current information requirements is created. Similarly Watson [15] and IntelliZap [31] both generate short-term profiles from current context information. Watson identifies informative terms in local documents that the user is editing and web pages that are being browsed, and uses these to modify the user's search queries to personalize results. IntelliZap users initiate a search by selecting a textual query from within a document they are currently viewing, and the search is then guided by additional terms occurring in close proximity to the query terms in the document. In these examples, the profiles guiding the personalization of search results capture context which is pertinent to the users immediate, and possibly temporary, information needs.

The availability of profile and/or context information is the pre-requisite for personalization and there have been a wide range of techniques developed for utilizing profile information to influence different aspects of search experience. These techniques are not limited to influencing the retrieval and ranking of search results, for example, and in fact there has been research on how profiles can be used to influence many other stages in the web search pipeline including the spidering and indexing [29, 32, 34, 47] of raw page content and query generation [3, 6, 67]. For example, one common way to personalize search results based on a user profile involves using the profile to re-write, elaborate, or expand the original search query so that it returns more specific results that better reflect search interests or context. Koutrika and Ioannidis [46], for example, propose an algorithm they call *QDP* (Query Disambiguation and Personalization) to expand a query submitted by the user according to a user profile represented by weighted relationships between terms. These relationships take the form of logical operators (such as conjunction, disjunction, negation and substitution) between words and terms of interest to users. And so in effect the user's profile provides a set of personalized query rewriting rules, which can be applied to the submitted query before it is dispatched to the search engine, so that an initial query can be expanded or otherwise elaborated to capture the likely intent and interests of the searcher. Croft et al. [26] describe how individualized language models can be used as user profiles with a view to supporting query expansion and relevance feedback. There is also much research in the area of query expansion and disambiguation from the perspective of short term, session-based user profiles from a relevance feedback standpoint which is also highly relevant to work in personalized search [104]. This perspective is not so much targeted at personalizing search per se, but rather at improving search at the level of independent search sessions and many of these approaches can be expanded to encompass longer-term personalized search profiles.

However, perhaps the most popular way to personalize search through user profiles is to directly influence the *ranking* of search results. For example, Jeh and Widom [40] do this by introducing a personalized version of PageRank [13] for setting the query-independent priors on web pages based on user profiles. These profiles consist of a collection of *preferred* pages with high PageRank values which are explicitly chosen by the user, and are used to compute a personalized PageRank score for any arbitrary page based on how related it is to these highly scored preferred pages. Chirita et al. [23] build on this idea by automatically choosing these profile pages by analysing the searcher's bookmarked pages and past surfing behaviour, along with a *HubFinder* algorithm that finds related pages with high PageRank scores which are suitable for driving the personalized PageRank algorithm. Both of these approaches are based on long-term user profiles drawn from an extended period of the user's browsing history.

Chang et al. [20] propose a personalized version of Kleinberg's HITS [42] ranking algorithm. Their technique harnesses short-term feedback from the searcher, either explicitly or implicitly, to build a profile consisting of a personalized authority list which can then be used to influence the HITS algorithm to personalize the ranking of search results. Experimental results using a corpus of computer science research papers shows that personalized HITS is able to significantly improve result ranking in line with the searcher's preferences, even with only minimal searcher feedback.

Another popular ranking-based approach is the re-ranking of results returned from some underlying, generic web search engine according to searcher preferences without requiring access to the inner workings of the search engine. Speretta and Gauch [123] create individual user profiles by recording the queries and selected result snippets from results returned by Google which are classified into weighted concepts from a reference concept hierarchy. The results from future Google searches are then re-ranked according to the similarity between each result and the searcher's profile concept hierarchy. Rohini and Varma [98] also present a personalized search method where results from an underlying web search engine are re-ranked according to a collaborative filtering technique that harnesses implicitly generated user profiles.

All of the above techniques focus on harnessing single user profiles (the preferences of the target searcher) to personalize that user's search experience. In recommender systems research it is common to take advantage of groups of related profiles when it comes to generating recommendations for a target individual.

For instance, the well known *collaborative filtering* approach to recommendation explicitly uses the preferences of a group of users who are similar to the target user when it comes to generating recommendations [51, 94, 108]; see also [37, 37, 58]. Similar ideas are beginning to influence web search such as approaches that harness the preferences of communities of users; see [113, 114]. Sugiyama et al. [127] propose a method whereby long-term user profiles are constructed from similar searchers according to browsing history using a modified collaborative filtering algorithm. The idea is that searchers who issued similar queries and selected similar results in the past can benefit from sharing their search preferences. Sun et al. [128] propose a similar approach called CubeSVD which is also based on collaborative filtering to personalize web search results by analysing the correlation of users, queries and results in click-through data. Both these methods involve the identification of similar searchers to the current searcher in order to create a more comprehensive user profile for the individual. More recently, the work of Briggs and Smyth [11] describes a peer-to-peer approach to personalizing web search that also leverages the profiles of similar users during result recommendation. Each searcher is profiled in terms of their prior queries and result selections (once again these are long-term profiles). In response to a new target query, recommendations are derived from the user's own personal profile, but in addition, the query is propagated through the peer-to-peer search network so that connected users can also suggest relevant results based on their prior search behaviours. The resulting recommendations are aggregated and ranked according to their relevance to the target query and also in terms of the strength of the *trust* relationship between the target user and the relevant peer; see also recent trust-based recommendation techniques in [73–75, 78–80].

17.3.2 Collaborative Information Retrieval

Recent studies in specialised information seeking tasks, such as military command and control tasks or medical tasks, have found clear evidence that search-type tasks can be collaborative as information is shared between team members [87–90]. Moreover, recent work by Morris [68] highlights the inherently collaborative nature of more general purpose web search. For example, during a survey of just over 200 respondents, clear evidence for collaborative search behaviour emerged. More than 90 % of respondents indicated that they frequently engaged in collaboration at the level of the *search process*. For example, 87 % of respondents exhibited "backseat searching" behaviours, where they watched over the shoulder of the searcher to suggest alternative queries, while 30 % of respondents engaged in search coordination activities by using instant messaging to coordinate searches. Furthermore, 96 % of users exhibited collaboration at the level of *search products*, that is, the results of searches. For example, 86 % of respondents shared the results they had found during searches with others by email. Thus, despite the absence of explicit collaboration features from mainstream search engines there is clear evidence that users implicitly engage in many different forms of collaboration as they search, although, as reported by Morris [68], these collaboration "work-arounds" are often frustrating and inefficient. Naturally, this has motivated researchers to consider how different types of collaboration might be supported by future editions of search engines.

The resulting approaches to *collaborative information retrieval* can be usefully distinguished in terms of two important dimensions, *time*—that is, *synchronous* versus *asynchronous* search—and *place*—that is, *co-located* versus *remote* searchers. Co-located systems offer a collaborative search experience for multiple searchers at a single location, typically a single PC [1, 110], whereas remote approaches allow searchers to perform their searches at different locations across multiple devices [69, 70, 117]. The former enjoy the obvious benefit of an increased faculty for direct collaboration that is enabled by the face-to-face nature of co-located search, while the latter offer a greater opportunity for collaborative search. Alternatively, synchronous approaches are characterised by systems that broadcast a "call to search" in which specific participants are requested to engage in a well-defined search task for a well defined period of time [110]. In contrast, asynchronous approaches are characterised by less well-defined, ad-hoc search tasks and provide for a more open-ended approach to collaboration in which different searchers contribute to an evolving search session over an extended period of time [70, 114].

A good example of the co-located, synchronous approach to collaborative web search is given by the work in [1]. Their CoSearch system is designed to improve the search experience for co-located users where computing resources are limited; for example, a group of school children having access to a single PC. CoSearch is specifically designed to leverage peripheral devices that may be available (for example, mobile phones, extra mice etc.) to facilitate distributed control and division of effort, while maintaining group awareness and communication. For example, in the scenario of a group of users collaborating though a single PC, but with access to multiple mice, CoSearch supports a *lead searcher* or *driver* (who has access to the keyboard), with other users playing the role of search *observers*. The former performs the basic search task but all users can then begin to explore the results returned by independently selecting links so that pages of interest are added to a page queue for further review. The CoSearch interface also provides various opportunities for users to associate notes with pages. Interesting pages can be saved and as users collaborate a *search summary* can be created from the URLs and notes of saved pages. In the case where observers have access to mobile phones, CoSearch supports a range of extended interface functionality to provide observers with a richer set of independent functionality via a bluetooth connection. In this way observers can download search content to their mobile phone, access the page queue, add pages to the page queue and share new pages with the group.

The purpose of CoSearch is to demonstrate the potential for productive collaborative web search in resource-limited environments. The focus is very much on dividing the search labour while maintaining communication between searchers, and live user studies speak to the success of CoSearch in this regard [1]. The work in [111] is related in spirit to CoSearch but focuses on image search tasks using a table-top computing environment, which is well suited to supporting collaboration between co-located users who are searching together. Once again, preliminary studies speak to the potential for such an approach to improve overall search productivity and collaboration, at least in specific types of information access tasks, such as image search, for example. A variation on these forms of synchronous search activities is presented in [110], where the use of mobile devices as the primary search device allows for a remote form of synchronous collaborative search. The iBingo system allows a group of users to collaborate on an image search task with each user using an iPod touch device as their primary search/feedback device (although conventional PCs appear to be just as applicable). Interestingly, where the focus on CoSearch is largely on the division of search labour and communication support, iBingo offers the potential to use relevance feedback from any individual searcher to the benefit of others. Specifically, the iBingo collaboration engine uses information about the activities of each user in order to encourage other users to explore different information trails and different facets of the information space. In this way, the ongoing activities of users can have an impact on future searches by the group and, in a sense, the search process is being "personalized" according to the group's search behaviour.

Remote search collaboration (whether asynchronous or synchronous) is the aim of SearchTogether, which allows groups of searchers to participate in extended shared search sessions as they search to locate information on particular topics; see also [70]. In brief, the SearchTogether system allows users to create shared search sessions and invite other users to join in these sessions. Each searcher can independently search for information on a particular topic, but the system provides features to allow individual searchers to share what they find with other session members by recommending and commenting on specific results. In turn, SearchTogether supports synchronous collaborative search by allowing searchers to invite others to join in specific search tasks, allowing cooperating searchers to synchronously view the results of each others' searches via a split-screen style results interface. As with CoSearch above, one of the key design goals in SearchTogether is to support a division of labour in complex, open-ended search tasks. In addition, a key feature of the work is the ability to create a shared awareness among group members by reducing the overhead of search collaboration at the interface level. SearchTogether does this by including various features, from integrated messaging, query histories, and recommendations arising out of recent searches.

In the main, the collaborative information retrieval systems we have so far examined have been largely focused on supporting collaboration from a division of labour and shared awareness standpoint, separate from the underlying search process. In short, these systems have assumed the availability of an underlying search engine and provided a collaboration interface that effectively *imports* search results directly, allowing users to share these results. As noted in [83], one of the major limitations of these approaches is that collaboration is restricted to the interface in the sense that while individual searchers are notified about the activities of collaborators, they must individually examine and interpret these activities in order to reconcile their own activities with their co-searchers. Consequently, the work in [83] describes an approach to collaborative search that is more tightly integrated with the underlying search engine resource so that the operation of the search engine is itself influenced by the activities of collaborating searchers in a number of ways. For example, mediation techniques are used to prioritise, as yet, unseen documents, while query recommendation techniques are used to suggest alternative avenues for further search exploration.

17.3.3 On Reputation and Recommendation

Collaborative information retrieval has highlighted the importance of the searcher in web search tasks and the potential for groups of searchers to collaborate (implicitly or explicitly) during complex search tasks. This perspective suggests that the *reputation* of a user may have an important role to play in guiding collaboration; it seems natural to give greater emphasis to the opinions and/or suggestions of more reputable users.

Recently there has been considerable interest in *reputation systems* to evaluate user reputation and inter-user trust across social web and e-commerce applications. For example, the reputation system used by eBay has been examined by Jøsang et al. [41] and Resnick et al. [95]. Briefly, eBay elicits feedback from buyers and sellers regarding their interactions with each other, and that information is aggregated in order to calculate user reputation scores. The aim is to reward good behaviour on the site and to improve robustness by leveraging reputation to predict whether a vendor will honour future transactions.

The work of O'Donovan and Smyth [76] considers the role of reputation in recommender systems. In this case, a standard collaborative filtering algorithm is modified to add a trust score to complement the normal profile or item-based similarity score, so that recommendation partners are chosen from those users that are not only similar to the target user, but who have also had a successful recommendation history with that user. It is posited that this trust information can be estimated by measuring the accuracy of a profile at making predictions over time, and using this approach the average prediction error is improved significantly in comparison with conventional collaborative filtering approaches.

Other research has examined reputation systems employed in social networking platforms. Lazzari [50] performed a case study of the professional social networking site Naymz. He warns that calculating reputation on a global level allows users who have interacted with only a small number of others to accrue a high degree of reputation, making the system vulnerable to malicious use. Similar to Jøsang et al. [41], Lazzari [50] suggests that vulnerability lies in the site itself, allowing malicious users to game the reputation system for their own ends. However, applying reputation globally affords malicious users influence over the entire system, which adds to its vulnerability.

In this chapter we consider the role of reputation models in a social search service in order to capture the *quality* of search knowledge that is contributed by users and how this reputation data can be leveraged to improve overall recommendation quality.

17.3.4 Towards Social Search

So far we have touched on separate strands of complementary research in the field of web search, recommender systems and information finding, motivated by questions that cut to the very core of conventional web search. The one-size-fits-all nature of mainstream web search is questioned by researchers developing more personalized web search techniques, and the assumption that search is largely a solitary experience is undermined by recent studies that highlight the inherently collaborative nature of many search scenarios.

To date, these different strands of research have been separated by different motivations and objectives. The world of personalized search, for example, has been largely guided by the need to produce result-lists that are better targeted to the needs of the individual searcher, whereas collaborative information retrieval has focused on supporting groups of searchers by facilitating the division of search labour and by promoting shared awareness among cooperating searchers. However both of these research communities are linked by a common thread of research from the recommender systems field and this perspective has helped to identify opportunities to bring these two different strands of research together. In what follows we will describe two complementary case-studies that describe the evolution of one particular approach to making conventional web search more collaborative and personal.

To begin with we will describe the HeyStaks social search system [115, 120], which adds a layer of community-based collaboration atop conventional search services such as Google or Bing. HeyStaks is an example of a remote, asynchronous form of collaborative web search and we will summarize the results of recent live-user studies to highlight its potential end-user benefits. The second case-study will introduce the notion of *reputation* as a novel relevance signal that can further improve the quality of the HeyStaks suggestions, by weighting the influence of other searchers differently depending on their past search successes.

17.4 Case-Study 1: HeyStaks—A Social Search Utility

We describe a model of collaborative web search as implemented in a system called *HeyStaks*, which is novel in two important ways. First of all, HeyStaks adopts a more user-led approach to collaborative web search, one that is focused on helping users to better organise and share their search experiences. HeyStaks does this by allowing users to create, curate and share repositories of search experiences as opposed to coordinating the participation of search communities. Secondly, HeyStaks is tightly coupled to a mainstream search engine, such as Google, through a browser toolbar, which provides the collaborative search engine with the ability to capture and guide search activities. This means that users can enjoy the benefits of collaborative search while continuing to use their favourite search engine. Finally, we will also summarize the findings of a recent live-user study to investigate the nature of search collaboration that manifests within HeyStaks' user population.

17.4.1 The HeyStaks System

HeyStaks adds two basic features to a mainstream search engine. First, it allows users to create *search staks*, as a type of folder for their search experiences at search time. Staks can be shared with others so that their searches will also be added to the stak. Second, HeyStaks uses staks to generate recommendations that are added to the underlying search results that come from the mainstream search engine. These recommendations are results that stak members have previously found to be relevant for similar queries and help the searcher to discover results that friends or colleagues have found interesting, results that may otherwise be buried deep within Google's default result-list.

As shown in Fig. 17.2, HeyStaks takes the form of two basic components: a client-side *browser toolbar* and a back-end *server*. The toolbar allows users to create and share staks and provides a range of ancillary services, such as the ability to tag or vote for pages. The toolbar also captures search click-throughs and manages the integration of HeyStaks recommendations with the default result-list. The back-end server manages the individual stak indexes (indexing individual pages against query/tag terms and positive/negative votes), the stak database (stak titles, members, descriptions, status, etc.), the HeyStaks social networking service and, of course, the recommendation engine. In the following sections we will briefly outline the basic operation of HeyStaks and then focus on some of the detail behind the recommendation engine.

Consider, as a motivating example, the scenario of a group of friends planning a trip (to Canada, in this case). They know that during the course of their trip research they will use web search as their primary source of information about what to do and where to visit. So, one of the group creates a stak called "Canada Trip" and shares it with the other travellers, encouraging them to use this stak for all of their Canada-related searches regarding the trip.

Figure 17.3 shows one of the group searching for information related to "visa Canada"; the "Canada Trip" stak has been automatically suggested as their search context in the HeyStaks Toolbar based on their query. In addition to the expected Google search results, they also see a number of pages that have been recommended from this suggested stak. These are results that other travellers have found to be useful in their searches for related queries. These recommendations may have been

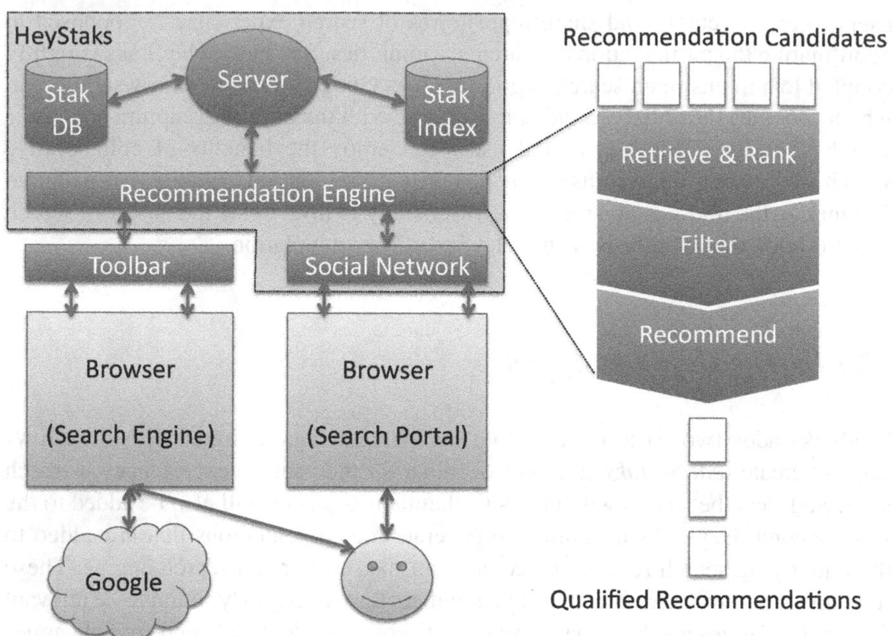

Fig. 17.2 The HeyStaks system architecture and outline recommendation model

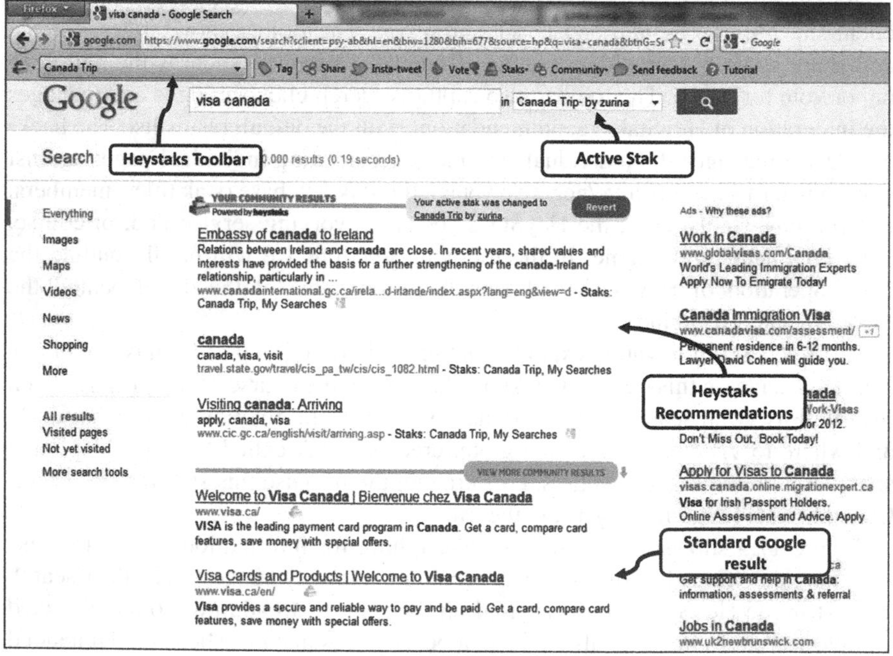

Fig. 17.3 Google search results with HeyStaks promotions

previously selected or tagged or otherwise shared during recent searches by group members. Moreover, these recommendations may have been promoted from much deeper within the Google result-list, or they may not even be present in Google's default results for the target query.

17.4.2 The HeyStaks Recommendation Engine

In HeyStaks each search stak (S) serves as a profile of the search activities of the stak members and HeyStaks combines a number of implicit and explicit profiling techniques to capture a rich history of search experiences. Each stak is made up of a set of result-pages ($S = \{p_1, \ldots, p_k\}$) and each page is anonymously associated with a number of implicit and explicit interest indicators, including the total number of times a result has been selected (*sel*), the query terms ($q_1, \ldots, q_n$) that led to its selection, the number of times a result has been tagged (*tag*), the terms used to tag it ($t_1, \ldots, t_m$), the votes it has received (v^+, v^-), and the number of people it has been shared with (*share*) as indicated by Eq. (17.1).

$$p_i^S = \{q_1, \ldots, q_n, t_1, \ldots, t_m, v^+, v^-, sel, tag, share\} \tag{17.1}$$

In this way, each page is associated with *term data* (query terms and/or tag terms) and *usage data* (the selection, tag, share, and voting count). The term data is represented as a Lucene[2] index table, with each page indexed under its associated query and tag terms, and provides the basis for retrieving and ranking *promotion candidates*. The usage data provides an additional source of evidence that can be used to filter results and to generate a final set of recommendations. At search time, a set of recommendations is produced in a number of stages: relevant results are retrieved and ranked from the Lucene stak index; these promotion candidates are filtered based on an *evidence model* to eliminate noisy recommendations; and the remaining results are added to the Google result-list according to a set of *recommendation rules*.

Briefly, there are two types of promotion candidates: *primary promotions* are results that come from the active stak S_t; whereas *secondary promotions* come from other staks in the searcher's stak-list. To generate these promotion candidates, the HeyStaks server uses the current query q_t as a probe into each stak index, S_i, to identify a set of relevant stak pages $P(S_i, q_t)$. Each candidate page, p, is scored using Lucene's *TF-IDF* retrieval function as per Eq. (17.2), which serves as the basis for an initial recommendation ranking.

$$rel(q_t, p) = \sum_{t \in q_t} tf(t \in p) \times idf(t)^2 \tag{17.2}$$

[2] http://lucene.apache.org.

Staks are inevitably noisy, in the sense that they will frequently contain pages that are not on topic. For example, searchers will often forget to set an appropriate stak at the start of a new search session and, although HeyStaks includes a number of automatic stak-selection techniques to ensure that the right stak is active for a given search, these techniques are not perfect, and misclassifications do inevitably occur; see also [19, 99–102, 119]. As a result, the retrieval and ranking stage may select pages that are not strictly relevant to the current query context. To avoid making spurious recommendations HeyStaks employs an *evidence filter*, which uses a variety of threshold models to evaluate the relevance of a particular result in terms of its usage evidence; tagging evidence is considered more important than voting, which in turn is more important than implicit selection evidence. For example, pages that have only been selected once, by a single stak member, are not automatically considered for recommendation and, all other things being equal, will be filtered out at this stage. In turn, pages that have received a high proportion of negative votes will also be eliminated. The precise details of this model are beyond the scope of this chapter but suffice it to say that any results which do not meet the necessary evidence thresholds are eliminated from further consideration.

After evidence pruning we are left with revised primary and secondary promotions and the final task is to add these *qualified recommendations* to the Google result-list. HeyStaks uses a number of different recommendation rules to determine how and where a promotion should be added. Once again, space restrictions prevent a detailed account of this component but, for example, the top three primary promotions are always added to the top of the Google result-list and labelled using the HeyStaks promotion icon. If a remaining primary promotion is also in the default Google result-list then this is labeled in place. If there are still remaining primary promotions then these are added to the secondary promotion list, which is sorted according to TF-IDF scores. These recommendations are then added to the Google result-list as an optional, expandable list of recommendations; for further details see [116, 118]

17.4.3 Evaluation

To gain an understanding of both how users are using HeyStaks, and whether they seem to be benefiting from its search promotions, we consider a subset of 95 HeyStaks users who remained active during the course of the early beta release of the toolbar and service. These users registered with HeyStaks during the period October to December 2008 and the results below represent a summary of their usage during the period October 2008 to January 2009. Because this is a study of live-users *in the wild* there are certain limitations about what we can measure. There is no control group, for example, and it has not been feasible, mainly for data privacy reasons, to analyse the relative click-through behaviour of users, by comparing their selections of default Google results to their selections of HeyStaks

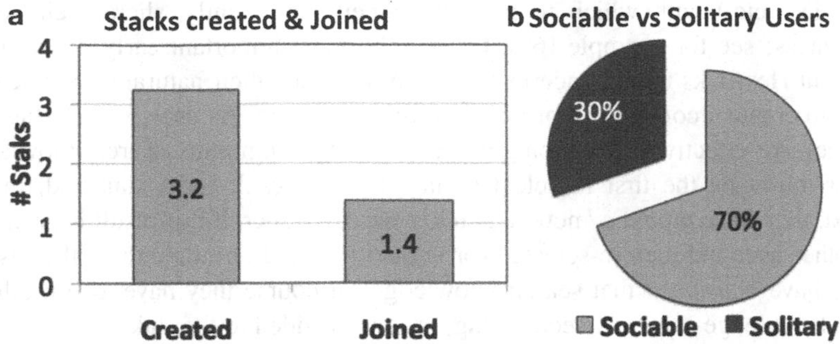

Fig. 17.4 (**a**) The average number of staks created and joined per user. (**b**) The percentage of *sociable* and *solitary* users

promotions. However, for the interested reader, other studies do report on this type of analysis in more conventional control-group laboratory studies [9, 25, 114, 120].

Key to the HeyStaks proposition is that searchers need a better way to organise and share their search experiences, as opposed to the largely ad-hoc and very manually mechanisms (email, word of mouth, face-to-face collaboration) that are currently the norm. HeyStaks provides these features but do users actually take the time to create staks as a gateway to better search collaboration? Do they share these staks or join those created by others?

During the course of the initial deployment of HeyStaks users did engage in a reasonable degree of stak creation and sharing activity. For example, as shown in Fig. 17.4, on average, beta users created just over 3.2 new staks and joined a further 1.4. Perhaps this is not surprising: most users create a few staks and share them with a small network of colleagues or friends, at least initially.

In total there were over 300 staks created on a wide range of topics, from broad topics such as travel, research, music and movies, to more niche interests including archaeology, black and white photography, and mountain biking. A few users were prolific stak creators and joiners: one user created 13 staks and joined another 11, to create a search network of 47 other searchers (users who co-shared the same staks). In fact, on average, each user was connected to a search network of just over five other searchers by the staks that they shared.

The vast majority of staks were created as public staks, although most (52 %) remained the domain of a single member, the stak creator. Thus 48 % of staks were shared with at least one other user and, on average, these staks attracted 3.6 members. Another way to look at this is as depicted in Fig. 17.4b: 70 % of users make the effort to share or join staks (*sociable* users); and only 30 % of users created staks just for their own personal use and declined to join staks created by others (*solitary* users).

At its core HeyStaks is motivated by the idea that web search is an inherently social or collaborative activity. And even though mainstream search engines do not support this, searchers do find alternative collaboration channels (for example, email, IM, etc.) with which to partially, albeit inefficiently, share their search experiences; see for example [68]. One of the most important early questions to ask about HeyStaks users concerns the extent to which their natural search activity serves to create a community of collaborating searchers. As users search, tag, and vote they are effectively producing and consuming community search knowledge. A user might be the first to select or tag a given result for a stak and, in this context, they have *produced* new search knowledge. Later, if this result is promoted to another user and then re-selected (or tagged or voted on), then this other user is said to have *consumed* that search knowledge; of course they have also produced search knowledge as their selection, tag, or vote is added to the stak.

We have found that 85 % of users have engaged in search collaborations. The majority have consumed results that were produced by at least one other user, and on average these users have consumed results from 7.5 other users. In contrast 50 % of users have produced knowledge that has been consumed by at least one other user, and in this case each of these producers has created search knowledge that is consumed by more than 12 other users on average.

Another matter we might consider is to what *degree* individual users tend to be producers or consumers of search knowledge. Are some searchers *net producers* of search knowledge, in the sense that they are more inclined to create search knowledge that is useful to others? Are other users *net consumers*, in the sense that they are more inclined to consume search knowledge that others have created? This data is presented in Fig. 17.5a. To be clear, a net producer is defined as a user who has helped more other users than they themselves have been helped by, whereas a net consumer is defined as a user who has been helped by more users than they themselves have helped. The chart shows that 47 % of users are net producers. Remember that, above, we noted how 50 % of users have produced at least *some* search knowledge that has been consumed by some other user. It seems that the vast majority of *these* users, 94 % of them in fact, are actually helping more people than they are helped by in return.

So, we have found that lots of users are helping other users, and lots of users are helped by other users. Perhaps this altruism is limited to a small number of

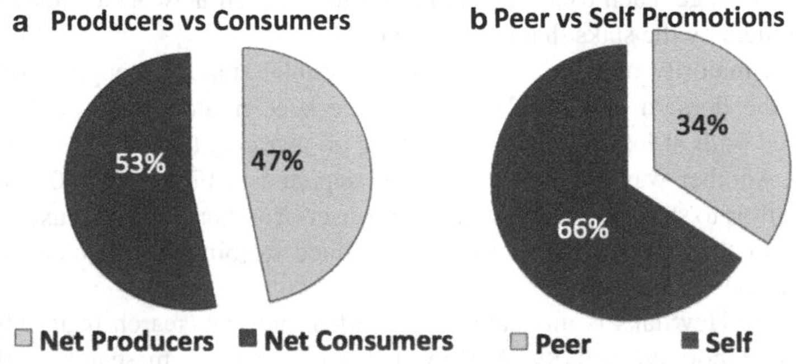

Fig. 17.5 (**a**) Net producers vs. consumers. (**b**) Promotion sources (self vs. peer)

searches? Perhaps, most of the time, at the level of individual searches, users are helping themselves? A variation on the above analysis can help shed light on this question by looking at the source of promotions that users judge to be relevant enough to select during their searches. Overall, the beta users selected more than 11,000 promotions during their searches. Some of these promotions will have been derived from the searcher's own past history; we call these *self* promotions. Others will have been derived from the search activities of other users who co-share staks with the searcher; we call these *peer* promotions. The intuition here is that the selection of self promotions corresponds to examples of HeyStaks helping users to *recover* results they have previously found, whereas the selection of promotions from peers corresponds to *discovery* tasks, where the user is benefiting from focused new content that might otherwise have been missed, or have been difficult to find; see [55, 72]. Thus Fig. 17.5b compares the percentage of peer and self promotions and shows that two-thirds of selected promotions are generated from the searcher's own past search activities; most of the time HeyStaks is helping searchers to recover previously found results. However, 33 % of the time peer promotions are selected (and we already know that these come from many different users), helping the searcher to discover new information that others have found.

The bias towards self promotions is perhaps not surprising, especially given the habits of searchers, and especially during the early stages of stak development. The growth of most staks is initially led by a single user, usually the creator, and so inevitably most of the promotions are generated in response to the creator's own search queries. And most of these promotions will be self promotions, derived from the leader's own search activities. Many staks are not shared and so are only capable of making self promotions. As staks are shared, however, and more users join, the pool of searchers becomes more diverse. More results are added by the actions of peers and more peer promotions are generated and selected. It is an interesting task for future work to explore the evolution of a search stak and to investigate how stak content and promotions are affected as more and more users participate. Are there well-defined stages in stak evolution, for example, as self promotions give way to peer promotions? For now it is satisfying to see that even in the early stages of stak evolution, where the average stak has between 3 and 4 members, that 34 % of the time members are benefiting from promotions that are derived from the activities of their peers.

17.5 Case-Study 2: A Reputation Model for Social Search

As described previously, the many and varied different types of activities that a HeyStaks user can perform (click-throughs, tagging, voting, sharing) on a web page are ultimately combined and leveraged by HeyStaks to make recommendations at search time. While the recommendation algorithm used differentially weights different activity types (so that tagging, for example, is considered a more reliable indicator of interest than a simple result click-through), the source of the activity (the user performing the activity) is not considered explicitly. Intuitively, we might expect that some users are more experienced searchers than others and, as such, perhaps their activities should be considered as more reliable at recommendation time. In other words promotion candidates that come from the activities of very experienced users might be considered ahead of candidates that come from the activity of less experienced users. This is particularly important given the potential for malicious users to disrupt stak quality by introducing dubious results to a stak; see also [78, 79] for related matters.

In this case-study we describe how user activities in HeyStaks can be harnessed to generate a computational model of searcher reputation, based on the collaboration events that naturally occur between HeyStaks users as they share their search experiences. We describe an algorithm for maintaining an up-to-date reputation model at search time and go on to propose a mechanism for incorporating reputation into the HeyStaks result recommendation subsystem.

17.5.1 From Activities to Reputation

It seems natural that the reputation of searchers should be linked to the search knowledge that they contribute. In simple terms this search knowledge is based on the creation and sharing of search staks and, ultimately, the web pages that are added to these staks according to a variety of different types of user activities (selections, voting, sharing, tagging). Each of these activities results in the creation of new search knowledge. If the target page is not present in a stak, then its selection, sharing, voting, or tagging will cause it to be added to the stak for the first time. If the page is already present, as a result of an earlier activity, then the page's stak record will be updated to reflect the additional activity.

What then is the relationship between search activity and searcher reputation? Under the heading of "more search knowledge is better than less search knowledge", it might make sense to model reputation as a direct function of the volume of activity that a given searcher has engaged in. This would be a mistake. For a start, just because a user is creating a lot of search knowledge, by adding many pages to many staks, it does not mean that this new knowledge is useful, especially to others. On the contrary, and as already mentioned, one of the major concerns in any social recommender is the potential for misuse through the actions of malicious users, a problem that would no doubt be exacerbated by valuing the contribution of very 'productive' malicious users.

Ultimately, in a social context, reputation is a form of *incentive*. It allows HeyStaks to capture and encode the value of user contributions [84, 86]. This is related to the concept of trust in recommender systems and social networks [48, 77] where, for example, the accumulation of trust scores can motivate users to enhance the quantity and quality of their contributions. But like any incentive, reputation can be *gamed* and so it is important that the incentive is correctly aligned with the sort of behaviour that benefits the system and its users as a whole. A reputation model that is the sum of all user activities does not meet this requirement since it is not necessarily to anyone's benefit to create a system that is measured simply by the volume of its search knowledge.

17.5.2 Reputation as Collaboration

Thus, our model of reputation must recognise the *quality* of *shared* search knowledge. To do this the key idea is that the quality of shared search knowledge can be estimated by looking at the frequency of *search collaborations* within HeyStaks. If HeyStaks recommends a result to a searcher, and the searcher chooses to act on (select, tag, vote on or share) this result, then we can view this as an instance of search collaboration (a *collaboration event*). The current searcher—the one who chooses to act on the recommendation—is known as the *consumer* and, in the simplest case, the original searcher—the one whose earlier activity caused this result to be added to the stak—is known as the *producer*. In other words, the producer creates search knowledge by adding the page to a stak, while the consumer consumes this knowledge by acting on the page when it is recommended.

The basic idea behind our reputation model is that this *implicit* collaboration between producer and consumer confers a *unit of reputation* on the producer (Fig. 17.6); incidentally, it is implicit because neither the producer nor the consumer are consciously or actively collaborating, rather the collaboration is a side-effect of recommendation, but a side-effect that creates a connection between the producer and consumer. If a given user is a regular producer of search knowledge (pages that are frequently recommended to, and acted on, by many other users) then this producer should enjoy a high reputation score. Moreover, if users create lots of staks and share these staks with many other users, or simply join staks that have been created by others, then they create an opportunity for more collaboration events to occur; and if users contribute good search knowledge to shared staks then their reputation score will benefit from the realisation of these frequent collaboration opportunities. In this way, this collaboration-based model of reputation is incentivizing users not just to create search knowledge but also to share it with others.

In reality the conferral of reputation by a consumer on a producer is more complicated than just described. In the general case, when a consumer acts on the promoted result, there may be many different relevant producers. One producer will have been the first to act on the result in question, causing it to be added to a stak,

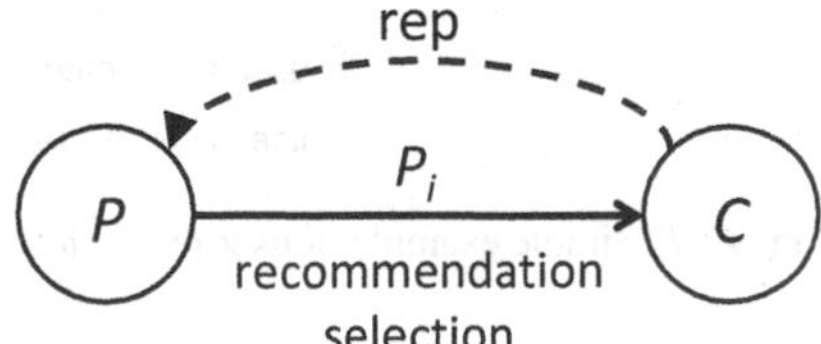

Fig. 17.6 Producer (P) and consumer (C) collaboration: C selects page p_i, which has been recommended to C based on P's previous activity. In turn, C confers reputation on P

but subsequent users may have (re)selected it for similar or different queries, or they may have voted on it or tagged it or shared it with others independently of its other producers. These other users are also producers in the sense that their actions will be considered at recommendation time. In this case we should share the unit of reputation between these multiple producers. We propose to do this using a simple model so that if, at time t, a consumer acts on a promoted result, then the reputation score of each of its k producers is incremented by $1/k$; that is, a single unit of reputation is shared equally among the producers. It is worth noting that although this approach shares out reputation equally at any given collaboration event, because producers accumulate over time, it will naturally be the case that early producers will tend to enjoy greater reputation if the result in question features in multiple collaboration events over an extended time period.

17.5.3 An Example

To illustrate our user reputation model, consider the simple scenario as depicted in Fig. 17.7. Here, the activity of four users, $\{u_1, \ldots, u_4\}$, with respect to a single search result-page r, is shown at four points in time t_i, where $t_4 > t_3 > t_2 > t_1$. Further, assume that all four users are members of a particular stak S, which is currently the active stak for each of these users. The sequence of events at each time step t_i is as follows:

$t1$: User u_1 organically selects result r for some search query q, causing result r to be added to stak S.

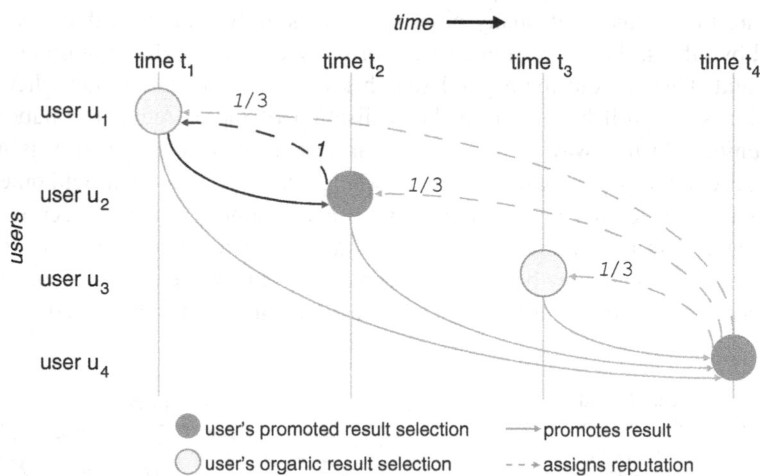

Fig. 17.7 Simple example of user reputation calculations in HeyStaks

*t*2: User u_2 selects result *r*, which has been promoted by HeyStaks, for a search query that is related to *q*. Since user u_1 is the only user to have previously selected result *r* in stak *S*, we say that user u_1 (the *producer*) has *promoted* result *r* to user u_2 (the *consumer*). Consequently, user u_2 assigns a *reputation* score of 1 to user u_1.

*t*3: User u_3 organically selects result *r* for an unrelated search query q'. This time, result *r* is not promoted by HeyStaks and hence no reputation is assigned by user u_3 to any of the other users.

*t*4: Finally, user u_4 selects result *r*, which has been promoted by HeyStaks, for a search query that is again related to *q*. Since users u_1, u_2 and u_3 have all previously selected (either organically or by promotion) result *r*, on this occasion reputation is assigned by user u_4 to each of these users. Thus, in Fig. 17.7, the reputation score is distributed equally among the three users, such that each user receives a score of $1/3$.

At the end of the time period, overall user reputation can be calculated, for example, by simply summing the individual reputation scores that each user has received. For example, in the above scenario, the overall reputation scores for users u_1, u_2, u_3 and u_4 are $4/3$, $1/3$, $1/3$ and 0, respectively.

17.5.4 Graph-Based Reputation Models

In fact we can treat the collaborations that occur among users as a type of graph, a *collaboration graph*. Each node represents a unique user and the edges represent collaboration events between pairs of users. These edges are directed to reflect the producer/consumer relationships and reputation flows along these edges, and is aggregated at the nodes. In the above example, user reputation was calculated as a simple weighted sum of collaboration events but we could so also consider other types of aggregation approaches. Below we formalise this model and also describe an alternative based on PageRank [14].

17.5.4.1 Reputation as a Weighted Sum of Collaboration Events

As previously described, according to this aggregation approach, producer reputation is calculated as a sum of the collaboration events in which they have participated. Consider the selection of result *r* by consumer *c* at time *t*. The producers responsible for this result recommendation are given by $producers(r,t)$ [Eq. (17.3)] such that each p_i denotes a specific user u_i in a specific stak S_j.

$$producers(r,t) = \{p_1, \ldots, p_k\} \,. \tag{17.3}$$

Then, for each producer of r, p_i, we update its reputation according to Eq. (17.4). In this way reputation is shared equally among its k contributing producers.

$$rep(p_i, t) = rep(p_i, t-1) + 1/k \;. \tag{17.4}$$

As users participate in more and more collaboration events, their reputation grows over time. See [61] for further details on this approach.

17.5.4.2 Reputation as PageRank

PageRank [14] can also be applied to compute the reputation of HeyStaks users, which take the place of web pages in the collaboration graph. When a collaboration event occurs, directed links are inserted from the consumer to each producer. Once all collaboration events up to some point in time, t, have been captured, the reputation of each user p_i at time t is given by:

$$PR(p_i) = \frac{1-d}{N} + d \sum_{p_j \in M(p_i)} \frac{PR(p_j)}{|L(p_j)|} \;, \tag{17.5}$$

where d is a damping factor, N is the number of users, $M(p_i)$ is the set of inlinks (from consumers) to (producer) p_i and $L(p_j)$ is the set of outlinks from p_j (i.e. the other users from whom p_j has consumed results).

17.5.5 From User Reputation to Result Promotion

In the previous case-study the standard HeyStaks recommendation engine scores each recommendation candidate based on how relevant it is to the target query ($rel(q_t, r)$ as per Eq. (17.2), but here with p replaced by r to avoid confusion between pages and producers). If reputation is to influence recommendation ranking, as well as relevance, then we need to transform the above user-based reputation measures into a page-based reputation measure, which can be incorporated into recommendation. Recommendation candidates can then be ranked according to a weighted score of *relevance* ($rel(q_t, r)$) and *reputation* ($rep(r, t)$) by Eq. (17.6), where w is used to adjust the relative influence of relevance and reputation.

$$score(r, q_t) = w \times rep(r, t) + (1-w) \times rel(q_t, r) \;. \tag{17.6}$$

Equation (17.6) describes one simple approach to combining result reputation and relevance at recommendation time and we now consider two ways to transform user reputation into a page reputation score; as mentioned above, here we use r to refer to a result-page instead of p since the latter is more conveniently associated with a producer. In what follows then we describe two alternative approaches to transferring reputation from producers to pages for the purpose of recommendation.

17.5.5.1 Max Reputation

The first page reputation score calculates the reputation of a result-page r (at time t) as the maximum reputation of its associated producers, $\{p_1, \ldots, p_k\}$; see Eq. (17.7). Scoring results in this way provides the advantage that the reputation of a page will not be prematurely decreased if, for example, many new, but not yet reputable, users have selected the page.

$$rep(r,t) = \max_{\forall p_i \in \{p_1,\ldots,p_k\}} \left(rep(p_i,t)\right) . \tag{17.7}$$

17.5.5.2 Hooper's Reputation

Hooper's *Rule for Concurrent Testimony* was proposed to calculate the credibility of human testimony [106]. Hooper gives to a report a credibility of $1 - (1 - c)^k$, assuming k reporters, each with a credibility of c ($0 \leq c \leq 1$). For HeyStaks, result reputation can be determined by performing a similar calculation across the reputation scores of its producers as in Eq. (17.8).

$$rep(r,t) = 1 - \prod_{i=1}^{k} (1 - rep(p_i,t)) . \tag{17.8}$$

17.5.6 Evaluation

The key hypothesis in this case-study has been that by allowing reputation, as well as relevance, to influence the ranking of result recommendations, we can improve the overall quality of search results. In this section we evaluate our reputation models using data generated during a closed, live-user trial of HeyStaks, designed to evaluate the utility of the HeyStaks approach to collaborative web search in fact-finding information discovery tasks.

17.5.6.1 Dataset and Methodology

Our live-user trial involved 64 first-year undergraduate university students with varying degrees of search expertise; see [63]. Users were asked to participate in a general knowledge quiz, during a supervised laboratory session, answering as many questions as they could from a set of 20 questions in the space of 1 h. Each student received the same set of questions which were randomly presented to avoid any ordering bias. See [63] for a list of questions used in the trial.

Each user was allocated a desktop computer with the Firefox web browser and the HeyStaks toolbar pre-installed; they were permitted to use Google, enhanced by HeyStaks functionality, as an aid in the quiz. The 64 students were randomly divided into search groups. Each group was associated with a newly created search stak, which would act as a repository for the group's search knowledge. We created 6 *solitary* staks, each containing just a single user, and four *shared* staks containing 5, 9, 19, and 25 users. The solitary staks served as a benchmark to evaluate the search effectiveness of individual users in a non-collaborative search setting, whereas the different sizes of shared staks provided an opportunity to examine the effectiveness of collaborative search across a range of different group sizes. All activity on both Google search results and HeyStaks recommendations was logged, as well as all queries submitted during the experiment. During the 1 h trial, some 3,124 queries and 1,998 result activities (selections, tagging, voting, popouts) were logged, and 724 unique results were selected.

While the reputation model was not used during this original live-user trial—recommendations were ranked based on relevance only—the data produced does make it possible for us to *replay* the trial to construct reputation models and use them to re-rank the recommendations made by HeyStaks. We can then retrospectively test the quality of re-ranked results versus the original ranking against a ground-truth relevance. As part of the post-trial analysis, each selected result was manually classified as *relevant* (the result contained the answer to a question), *partially relevant* (the result referred to an answer, but not explicitly), or *not-relevant* (the result did not contain an explicit or implicit reference to an answer) by experts.

17.5.6.2 User Reputation

To get a sense of how users were scored by the two reputation models described in Sect. 17.5.4, we now examine the type of user reputation values that are generated from the trial data. In Fig. 17.8, box-plots are shown for the reputation scores across the four shared staks and for each reputation model. Here we see that for the WeightedSum model there is a clear difference in the median reputation score for members of the five person stak when compared to members of the larger staks. This is not evident in results for the PageRank model, which shows very similar reputation scores, regardless of stak size.

Figure 17.9 shows the reputation scores (normalised by the maximum user reputation score for each model) that members of the 19-person stak had accumulated at the end of the trial. Users are ranked according to their WeightedSum score in descending order, and this ordering is maintained in both graphs. The long-tail distribution of reputation scores is representative of that found in the other staks, where a small number of users had accumulated high reputation scores and the remainder relatively low scores. Users with high reputation can be considered

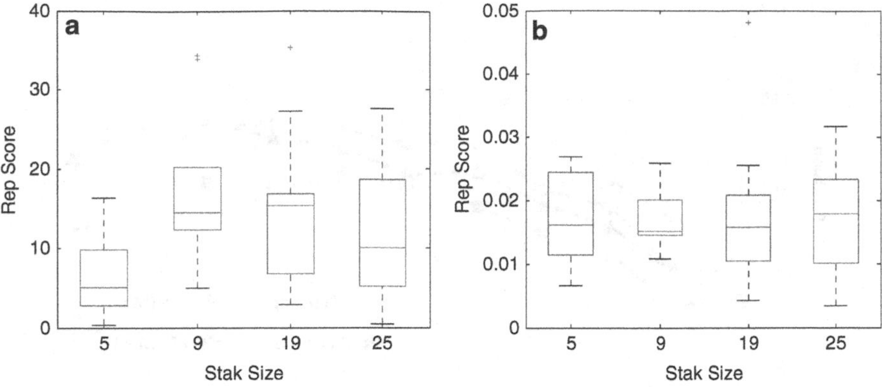

Fig. 17.8 User reputation scores: WeightedSum (**a**) and PageRank (**b**) reputation models

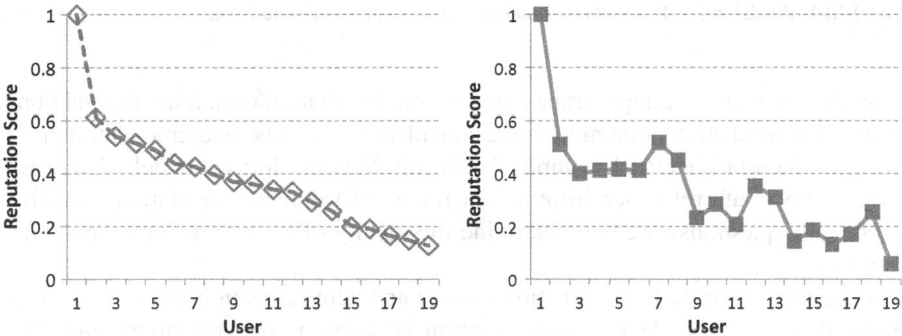

Fig. 17.9 User reputation scores for members of the 19-person stak: WeightedSum (**a**) and PageRank (**b**) reputation models

as *search leaders*, who are among the first to locate and add relevant results to staks, and whose search contributions are deemed to be particularly useful by other stak members. Further, the graphs indicate a strong correlation exists between reputation scores according to the WeightedSum and PageRank models (Spearman rank correlation of 0.91).

17.5.6.3 From Reputation to Quality

Of course the true test of the reputation models is the extent to which they improve the quality of results recommended by HeyStaks.

We have described how user reputation can be combined with term-based relevance to generate recommendations; see Eq. (17.6). Accordingly, as mentioned above, we re-rank each of the (relevance-based) recommendation lists produced during the trial using the result reputation models, based on the user reputation

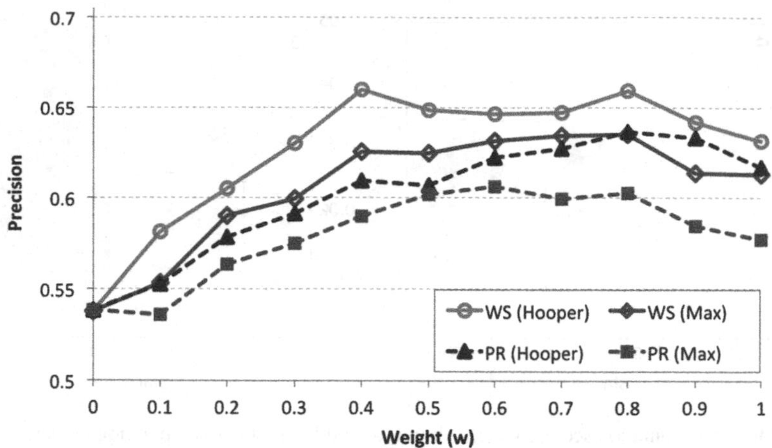

Fig. 17.10 Precision for different combinations of relevance and reputation

scores calculated at the appropriate point in time. In what follows, four combinations of user and result reputation models are considered to re-rank recommendation lists: WeightedSum or PageRank combined with the Max or Hooper models. Since we have ground-truth relevance information for all of the recommendations (relative to the quiz questions), we can determine the quality of the new recommendations rankings.

Specifically, for each combination of user and item reputation model, we count how often the top-ranked recommendation is relevant for each query and then compute a precision metric by dividing this count by the total number of queries considered. Thus, precision returns a value between 0 and 1 and a precision of 0.5, for example, means that 50 % of top-ranked results over all queries are relevant for a given condition.

Figure 17.10 shows precision versus the weighting (w) used in Eq. (17.6) to adjust the influence of term-based relevance versus reputation during recommendation. The results for each combination of user and result reputation model show an increase in precision when compared to recommendations based on relevance ranking only; at $w = 0$, reputation is not an influencing factor and in all cases the precision is 0.54. As the influence of reputation over relevance during recommendation is increased (by increasing w), an improvement in precision is seen up to values of w in the range 0.4–0.8. For example, at $w = 0.5$, the reputation models achieve a precision of 0.60–0.65 compared to 0.54 for the default HeyStaks relevance-only recommendations, a percentage improvement of 11–20 %. In all cases, precision decreases as w approaches 1, indicating that the relevance information HeyStaks uses to rank recommendations is needed in order to optimally rank recommendations; i.e. reputation alone does not provide best performance.

The WeightedSum user reputation model, when paired with the Hooper result reputation model, is the best performing technique, peaking at $w = 0.4$ and

$w = 0.8$, each time achieving a precision of approximately 0.66. Hooper's model also performed well when combined with PageRank, achieving a precision of 0.64 at $w = 0.8$. This leads us to believe that Hooper may be the most suitable option for result reputation. The score it produces for a result is a consensus based on the reputation of its producers. The model promotes the idea that a result will have a high score by way of reinforcement from its producers, assuming they are reputable; for further discussion and results see [61, 62, 64].

17.6 Search Futures

Mainstream search engines are evolving to offer users greater support when it comes to finding the right information at the right time, and recommendation technologies are set to play an important role in their evolution going forward. Researchers are continuing to explore how to make search engines more responsive to the particular needs and preferences of individuals, and how to introduce greater opportunity for collaboration into the standard search model. Where this might take us is a risky prediction to make other than to say that we can be certain that the way we search for information today is unlikely to be the way we will search for information in the near future. With this in mind, what follows is a consideration of two different pressures that will likely push search forward throughout the next decade.

17.6.1 From Search to Discovery

In the original version of this chapter, published as part of the first edition of this volume, we predicted that mainstream search engines would likely evolve to accommodate many elements of the personalization and collaboration ideas surveyed and presented. This prediction has come to pass, at least in part. Mainstream search engines such as Google and Bing are increasingly personalizing their results based on the searcher and her context. In some cases, mainstream search engines have also begun to incorporate social signals into their ranking engines. For example, Bing has partnered with social media services such as Twitter and Facebook to incorporate content and signals from these networks during result selection and ranking, while Google now emphasises content from its own social network (Google+) in similar ways. Indeed Google prioritises content from verified Google+ users, lending a form of reputation to its rankings.

Where today the burden of web search is still very much on the individual searcher, we believe that the introduction of recommendation technologies will provide search engines with the opportunity to function more proactively as they work to anticipate, rather than respond to, a user's information needs. For example, the Google Now service goes some way to realising this by making suggestions to users based on various signals that are relevant to their needs and context. But this is just the beginning, and as researchers address the challenges of profiling, privacy, and recommendation head-on (see also Chap. 19), search engines will provide a unique platform for the next generation of recommendation technologies. And just as e-commerce sites have served as an early platform for recommender systems, search engines will help to introduce a new era of recommendation technologies to a much wider audience.

For example, in the future we might reasonable expect that most of our information needs will be within the prediction capabilities of the "search services" of the day, as they analyse our online behaviours, capture our daily activities, and mine our social contexts to predict our need for information ahead of our desire to search, and so proactively recommend the right information when it is needed. This will fundamentally change the user-experience and invite new innovations when it comes not just to the presentation of information, but also how users are "interrupted" during their day by these proactive recommendations. In addition to predicting and fulfilling a user's information needs, search and discovery services of the future will need predict *when* to recommend, to carefully time their interventions. Our tolerance to these interruptions will change throughout the day depending on the context, activity, and even our emotional state. To deliver the right user experience it will not only be necessary to identify the right information but also to deliver it at the right time and in the right way.

17.6.2 Search in a Sensor-Rich, Mobile World

Perhaps the greatest opportunity for further innovation will occur as a direct response to what is surely an inexorable shift away from large-format computing devices (desktops and laptops) to mobile devices such as tablets, phones, a new generation of smart watches, and even smart spectacles such as Google Glass; see also Chap. 14. The shift from desktops and laptops to phones and tablets is now well documented and in the near future it is likely that the lion's share of information access will be conducted through such devices. These devices introduce an entirely new set of search and discovery constraints, such as restrictions on screen real-estate and text input capabilities. But far from being limitations these constraints serve only to create exciting new opportunities for innovation.

Already there is evidence that voice input is capable of taking over as a primary source of input for mobile devices. For example, at the time of writing Apple, Google, and Microsoft all offered mature speech recognition-based virtual assistants on their mobile platforms. Moreover, Apple have recently revealed some unique user-interface innovations, both display and input, for its new Apple Watch device. This includes a fluid, zoomable, scrollable UI combined with haptic feedback and a novel context-sensitive input device, called the *digital crown*, which echoes the click-wheel that distinguished the original iPod as a revolutionary music player more than a decade ago.

But mobile information and computing devices are just the tip-of the iceberg. We are living in a world that is increasingly instrumented with sensors that are capable of capturing events in the real-world. Indeed almost everything we do, whether buying groceries, exercising in the park, even taking a nap, can result in data being created and stored somewhere. Privacy and security issues aside, how will the availability of this data change the way we access information? At the very least it will provide a unique insight into our daily routines and the context (see also Chap. 6) of our lives and so provides a new set signals when it comes to anticipating our needs and the timing of recommendations.

In conclusion, it is probably fair to say that even though our need for information is unlikely to wane, our reliance on search probably will. It is more likely that search and recommendation capabilities will be part of the fabric of the web as it evolves. For certain the search engines of the future will understand us better than they do today and will serve us more accurately and more frequently. But we will probably not recognise many of these interactions as classical search sessions. The iconic query box and familiar "ten blue links" of search today will most likely fade away to reveal a more nuanced connection between users and information, where the right information is just there, when we need it, at a touch or at a glance.

Acknowledgements This work is supported by Science Foundation Ireland: through the CLARITY Centre for Sensor Web Technologies under grant number 07/CE/I1147; and through the Insight Centre for Data Analytics under grant number SFI/12/RC/2289.

References

1. Amershi, S., Morris, M.R.: CoSearch: A System for Co-Located Collaborative Web Search. In: Proceedings of the Annual SIGCHI Conference on Human Factors in Computing Systems (CHI), pp. 1647–1656 (2008). Florence, Italy
2. Asnicar, F.A., Tasso, C.: IfWeb: A Prototype of User Model-Based Intelligent Agent for Document Filtering and Navigation in the World Wide Web. In: Proceedings of the Workshop on Adaptive Systems and User Modeling on the World Wide Web at the Proceedings of the Annual SIGCHI Conference on Human Factors in Computing Systems (CHI), pp. 3–11 (1997). Chia Laguna, Sardinia
3. Baeza-Yates, R.A., Hurtado, C.A., Mendoza, M.: Query Recommendation Using Query Logs in Search Engines. In: Current Trends in Database Technology - EDBT 2004 Workshops, pp. 588–596 (2004). Heraklion, Greece
4. Baeza-Yates, R.A., Ribeiro-Neto, B.A.: Modern Information Retrieval. ACM Press / Addison-Wesley (1999)
5. Balabanovic, M., Shoham, Y.: FAB: Content-Based Collaborative Recommender. Communications of the ACM **40(3)**, 66–72 (1997)
6. Balfe, E., Smyth, B.: Improving Web Search through Collaborative Query Recommendation. In: Proceedings of the European Conference on Artificial Intelligence (ECAI), pp. 268–272 (2004)
7. Belém, F., Martins, E.F., Almeida, J.M., Gonçalves, M.A.: Exploiting novelty and diversity in tag recommendation. In: ECIR, pp. 380–391 (2013)
8. Billsus, D., Pazzani, M.J., Chen, J.: A learning agent for wireless news access. In: Proceedings of the 5th International Conference on Intelligent User Interfaces (IUI), pp. 33–36 (2000). DOI http://doi.acm.org/10.1145/325737.325768. New Orleans, Louisiana, United States
9. Boydell, O., Smyth, B.: Enhancing case-based, collaborative web search. In: Proceedings of International Conference on Case-Based Reasoning (ICCBR), pp. 329–343 (2007)

10. Bridge, D., Kelly, J.P.: Diversity-enhanced conversational collaborative recommendations. In: N. Creaney (ed.) Procs. of the Sixteenth Irish Conference on Artificial Intelligence and Cognitive Science, pp. 29–38 (2005)
11. Briggs, P., Smyth, B.: Provenance, Trust, and Sharing in Peer-to-Peer Case-Based Web Search. In: Proceedings of European Conference on Case-Based Reasoning (ECCBR), pp. 89–103 (2008)
12. Brin, S., Page, L.: The anatomy of a large-scale hypertextual web search engine. Computer Networks **30**(1–7), 107–117 (1998)
13. Brin, S., Page, L.: The anatomy of a large-scale hypertextual web search engine. Comput. Netw. ISDN Syst. **30**(1–7), 107–117 (1998). DOI http://dx.doi.org/10.1016/S0169-7552(98)00110-X
14. Brin, S., Page, L.: The anatomy of a large-scale hypertextual web search engine. In: Proceedings of the 7th International Conference on World Wide Web (WWW '98), pp. 107–117. ACM, Brisbane, Australia (1998)
15. Budzik, J., Hammond, K.J.: User interactions with everyday applications as context for just-in-time information access. In: Proceedings of the 5th International Conference on Intelligent User Interfaces (IUI), pp. 44–51 (2000). New Orleans, Louisiana, United States
16. Burke, R.: The Wasabi Personal Shopper: A Case-Based Recommender System. In: Proceedings of the 17th National Conference on Artificial Intelligence (AAAI) (1999). Orlando, Florida, USA
17. Carroll, J.M., Rosson, M.B.: Paradox of the active user. In: J.M. Carroll (ed.) Interfacing Thought: Cognitive Aspects of Human-Computer Interaction, chap. 5, pp. 80–111. Bradford Books/MIT Press (1987). URL citeseer.ist.psu.edu/carroll87paradox.html
18. Chakrabarti, S., Dom, B., Kumar, R., Raghavan, P., Rajagopalan, S., Tomkins, A., Gibson, D., Kleinberg, J.M.: Mining the Web's Link Structure. IEEE Computer **32**(8), 60–67 (1999)
19. Champin, P.A., Briggs, P., Coyle, M., Smyth, B.: Coping with Noisy Search Experiences. In: 29th SGAI International Conference on Artificial Intelligence (AI), pp. 5–18 (2009). Cambridge, UK
20. Chang, H., Cohn, D., McCallum, A.: Learning to Create Customized Authority Lists. In: ICML '00: Proceedings of the 17th International Conference on Machine Learning (ICML), pp. 127–134 (2000)
21. Chen, L., Pu, P.: Evaluating Critiquing-based Recommender Agents. In: Proceedings of the 21st National Conference on Artificial Intelligence (AAAI) (2006). Boston, Massachusetts
22. Chirita, P.A., Nejdl, W., Paiu, R., Kohlschütter, C.: Using ODP Metadata to Personalize Search. In: Proceedings of the 28th Annual International ACM Conference on Research and Development in Information Retrieval (SIGIR), pp. 178–185 (2005). Salvador, Brazil
23. Chirita, P.A., Olmedilla, D., Nejdl, W.: PROS: A Personalized Ranking Platform for Web Search. In: Proceedings of International Conference on Adaptive Hypermedia and Adaptive Web-Based Systems (AH), pp. 34–43 (2004). Eindhoven, The Netherlands
24. Coyle, M., Smyth, B.: Information Recovery and Discovery in Collaborative Web Search. In: Proceedings of the European Conference on Information Retrieval (ECIR), pp. 356–367. Rome, Italy
25. Coyle, M., Smyth, B.: Supporting Intelligent Web Search, volume = 7, year = 2007. ACM Trans. Internet Techn. (4)
26. Croft, W.B., Cronen-Townsend, S., Larvrenko, V.: Relevance Feedback and Personalization: A Language Modeling Perspective. In: DELOS Workshop: Personalisation and Recommender Systems in Digital Libraries (2001). URL citeseer.ist.psu.edu/article/croft01relevance.html
27. Dahlen, B., Konstan, J., Herlocker, J., Good, N., Borchers, A., Riedl, J.: Jump-Starting MovieLens: User Benefits of Starting a Collaborative Filtering System with "dead-data". In: University of Minnesota TR 98-017 (1998)
28. Dasarathy, B.V.: Nearest Neighbor (NN) Norms: NN Pattern Classification Techniques. IEEE Computer Society Press, Los Alamitos, CA (1991)

29. Dolin, R., Agrawal, D., Abbadi, A.E., Dillon, L.: Pharos: A Scalable Distributed Architecture for Locating Heterogeneous Information Sources. In: Proceedings of the International Conference on Information and Knowledge Management (CIKM), pp. 348–355 (1997). Las Vegas, Nevada, United States
30. Feldman, S., Sherman, C.: The High Cost of Not Finding Information. In: (IDC White Paper). IDC Group (2000)
31. Finkelstein, L., Gabrilovich, E., Matias, Y., Rivlin, E., Solan, Z., Wolfman, G., Ruppin, E.: Placing Search in Context: The Concept Revisited, url = citeseer.ist.psu.edu/finkelstein01placing.html, year = 2001, bdsk-url-1 = citeseer.ist.psu.edu/finkelstein01placing.html. In: Proceedings of the 10th International Conference on the World Wide Web (WWW), pp. 406–414. Hong Kong
32. Giles, C.L., Bollacker, K.D., Lawrence, S.: CiteSeer: An Automatic Citation Indexing System. In: Proceedings of the 3rd ACM Conference on Digital Libraries (DL), pp. 89–98 (1998). Pittsburgh, Pennsylvania, United States
33. Granka, L.A., Joachims, T., Gay, G.: Eye-Tracking Analysis of User Behavior in WWW Search. In: Proceedings of the 27th Annual International ACM Conference on Research and Development in Information Retrieval (SIGIR), pp. 478–479 (2004). Sheffield, United Kingdom
34. Gravano, L., García-Molina, H., Tomasic, A.: GlOSS: Text-Source Discovery Over the Internet. ACM Trans. Database Syst. **24**(2), 229–264 (1999). DOI http://doi.acm.org/10.1145/320248.320252
35. Hassan, A., White, R.W.: Personalized models of search satisfaction. In: CIKM, pp. 2009–2018 (2013)
36. Hurley, N., Zhang, M.: Novelty and diversity in top-n recommendation - analysis and evaluation. ACM Trans. Internet Techn. **10**(4), 14 (2011)
37. Jameson, A., Smyth, B.: Recommendation to Groups. In: P. Brusilovsky, A. Kobsa, W. Nejdl (eds.) The Adaptive Web, pp. 596–627. Springer-Verlag (2007)
38. Jansen, B.J., Spink, A.: An Analysis of Web Searching by European AlltheWeb.com Users. Inf. Process. Manage. **41**(2), 361–381 (2005). DOI http://dx.doi.org/10.1016/S0306-4573(03)00067-0
39. Jansen, B.J., Spink, A., Bateman, J., Saracevic, T.: Real life Information Retrieval: A Study of User Queries on the Web. SIGIR Forum **32**(1), 5–17 (1998)
40. Jeh, G., Widom, J.: Scaling Personalized Web Search. In: Proceedings of the 12th International conference on World Wide Web (WWW), pp. 271–279. ACM (2003). Budapest, Hungary
41. Jøsang, A., Ismail, R., Boyd, C.: A survey of trust and reputation systems for online service provision. Decision Support Systems **43**(2), 618–644 (2007)
42. Kleinberg, J.M.: Authoritative Sources in a Hyperlinked Environment. J. ACM **46**(5), 604–632 (1999). DOI http://doi.acm.org/10.1145/324133.324140
43. Kleinberg, J.M.: Hubs, Authorities, and Communities. ACM Comput. Surv. **31**(4), 5 (1999)
44. Konstan, J., Miller, B., Maltz, D., Herlocker, J., Gorgan, L., Riedl, J.: GroupLens: Applying Collaborative Filtering to Usenet News. Communications of the ACM **40(3)**, 77–87 (1997)
45. Koren, Y.: Tutorial on Recent Progress in Collaborative Filtering. In: Proceedings of the International Conference on Recommender Systems (RecSys), pp. 333–334 (2008)
46. Koutrika, G., Ioannidis, Y.: A Unified User-Profile Framework for Query Disambiguation and Personalization. In: Proc. of the Workshop on New Technologies for Personalized Information Access, pp. 44–53 (2005). Edinburgh, UK
47. Kruger, A., Giles, C.L., Coetzee, F.M., Glover, E., Flake, G.W., Lawrence, S., Omlin, C.: DEADLINER: Building a New Niche Search Engine. In: Proceedings of the 9th International Conference on Information and Knowledge Management (CIKM), pp. 272–281. New York, NY, USA (2000). McLean, Virginia, United States
48. Kuter, U., Golbeck, J.: SUNNY: A new algorithm for trust inference in social networks, using probabilistic confidence models. In: AAAI, pp. 1377–1382 (2007)

49. Lawrence, S., Giles, C.L.: Accessibility of Information on the Web. Nature **400(6740)**, 107–109 (1999)
50. Lazzari, M.: An experiment on the weakness of reputation algorithms used in professional social networks: The case of naymz. In: Proceedings of the IADIS International Conference e-Society 2010, pp. 519–522. IADIS, Freiburg, Germany (2010)
51. Linden, G., Smith, B., York, J.: Amazon.com Recommendations: Item-to-Item Collaborative Filtering. IEEE Distributed Systems Online **4**(1) (2003)
52. Liu, F., Yu, C., Meng, W.: Personalized Web Search by Mapping User Queries to Categories, year = 2002, bdsk-url-1 = http://doi.acm.org/10.1145/584792.584884. In: Proceedings of the 11th International Conference on Information and Knowledge Management (CIKM), pp. 558–565. ACM Press, New York, NY, USA. DOI http://doi.acm.org/10.1145/584792.584884. McLean, Virginia, USA
53. Ma, Z., Pant, G., Sheng, O.R.L.: Interest-Based Personalized Search. ACM Trans. Inf. Syst. **25**(1), 5 (2007). DOI http://doi.acm.org/10.1145/1198296.1198301
54. Makris, C., Panagis, Y., Sakkopoulos, E., Tsakalidis, A.: Category Ranking for Personalized Search. Data Knowl. Eng. **60**(1), 109–125 (2007). DOI http://dx.doi.org/10.1016/j.datak.2005.11.006
55. Marchionini, G.: Exploratory search: From Finding to Understanding. Communications of the ACM **49**(4), 41–46 (2006). DOI http://doi.acm.org/10.1145/1121949.1121979
56. McCarthy, K., Reilly, J., McGinty, L., Smyth, B.: An analysis of critique diversity in case-based recommendation. In: Proceedings of the International FLAIRS Conference, pp. 123–128 (2005)
57. McCarthy, K., Reilly, J., McGinty, L., Smyth, B.: Experiments in Dynamic Critiquing. In: Proceedings of the International Conference on Intelligent User Interfaces (IUI), pp. 175–182 (2005)
58. McCarthy, K., Salamó, M., Coyle, L., McGinty, L., Smyth, B., Nixon, P.: Cats: A synchronous approach to collaborative group recommendation. In: Proceedings of the International FLAIRS Conference, pp. 86–91 (2006)
59. McGinty, L., Smyth, B.: Comparison-Based Recommendation. In: S. Craw (ed.) Proceedings of the Sixth European Conference on Case-Based Reasoning (ECCBR 2002), pp. 575–589. Springer (2002). Aberdeen, Scotland.
60. McGinty, L., Smyth, B.: On The Role of Diversity in Conversational Recommender Systems. In: K.D. Ashley, D.G. Bridge (eds.) Proceedings of the 5th International Conference on Case-Based Reasoning, pp. 276–290. Springer-Verlag (2003)
61. McNally, K., O'Mahony, M.P., Coyle, M., Briggs, P., Smyth, B.: A case study of collaboration and reputation in social web search. ACM TIST **3**(1), 4 (2011)
62. McNally, K., O'Mahony, M.P., Smyth, B.: A model of collaboration-based reputation for the social web. In: ICWSM (2013)
63. McNally, K., O'Mahony, M.P., Smyth, B., Coyle, M., Briggs, P.: Social and collaborative web search: An evaluation study. In: Proceedings of the 15th International Conference on Intelligent User Interfaces (IUI '11), pp. 387–390. ACM, Palo Alto, California USA (2011)
64. McNally, K., O'Mahony, M.P., Smyth, B., Coyle, M., Briggs, P.: Social and collaborative web search: an evaluation study. In: IUI, pp. 387–390 (2011)
65. Meuth, R.J., Robinette, P., Wunsch, D.C.: Computational Intelligence Meets the NetFlix Prize. In: Proceedings of the International Joint Conference on Neural Networks (IJCNN), pp. 686–691 (2008)
66. Micarelli, A., Sciarrone, F.: Anatomy and Empirical Evaluation of an Adaptive Web-Based Information Filtering System. User Modeling and User-Adapted Interaction **14**(2–3), 159–200 (2004). DOI http://dx.doi.org/10.1023/B:USER.0000028981.43614.94
67. Mitra, M., Singhal, A., Buckley, C.: Improving Automatic Query Expansion. In: Proceedings of ACM SIGIR, pp. 206–214. ACM Press (1998)
68. Morris, M.R.: A Survey of Collaborative Web Search Practices. In: Proceedings of the Annual SIGCHI Conference on Human Factors in Computing Systems (CHI), pp. 1657–1660 (2008)

69. Morris, M.R., Horvitz, E.: SearchTogether: An Interface for Collaborative Web Search. In: UIST, pp. 3–12 (2007)
70. Morris, M.R., Horvitz, E.: S^3: Storable, Shareable Search. In: INTERACT (1), pp. 120–123 (2007)
71. Nerur, S.P., Sikora, R., Mangalaraj, G., Balijepally, V.: Assessing the Relative Influence of Journals in a Citation Network. Commun. ACM **48**(11), 71–74 (2005)
72. O'Day, V.L., Jeffries, R.: Orienteering in an Information Landscape: How Information Seekers Get from Here to There. In: Proceedings of the SIGCHI Conference on Human Factors in Computing Systems (CHI), pp. 438–445. ACM Press, New York, NY, USA (1993). DOI http://doi.acm.org/10.1145/169059.169365. Amsterdam, The Netherlands
73. O'Donovan, J., Evrim, V., Smyth, B.: Personalizing Trust in Online Auctions. In: Proceedings of the European Starting AI Researcher Symposium (STAIRS). Trento, Italy (2006)
74. O'Donovan, J., Smyth, B.: Eliciting Trust Values from Recommendation Errors. In: Proceedings of the International FLAIRS Conference, pp. 289–294 (2005)
75. O'Donovan, J., Smyth, B.: Trust in Recommender Systems. In: Proceedings of the International Conference on Intelligent User Interfaces (IUI), pp. 167–174 (2005)
76. O'Donovan, J., Smyth, B.: Trust in recommender systems. In: Proceedings of the 10th International Conference on Intelligent User Interfaces (IUI '05), pp. 167–174. ACM, San Diego, California, USA (2005)
77. O'Donovan, J., Smyth, B.: Trust in recommender systems. In: IUI, pp. 167–174 (2005)
78. O'Donovan, J., Smyth, B.: Trust No One: Evaluating Trust-based Filtering for Recommenders. In: Proceedings of the International Joint Conference on Artificial Intelligence (IJCAI), pp. 1663–1665 (2005)
79. O'Donovan, J., Smyth, B.: Is Trust Robust?: An Analysis of Trust-Based Recommendation. In: Proceedings of the International Conference on Intelligent User Interfaces, pp. 101–108 (2006)
80. O'Donovan, J., Smyth, B.: Mining trust values from recommendation errors. International Journal on Artificial Intelligence Tools **15**(6), 945–962 (2006)
81. Pariser, E.: The Filter Bubble : What the Internet is Hiding from You, year = 2011. Penguin Press
82. Pazzani, D.B.M.: A Hybrid User Model for News Story Classification. In: Proceedings of the 7th International Conference on User Modeling (UM) (1999). Banff, Canada
83. Pickens, J., Golovchinsky, G., Shah, C., Qvarfordt, P., Back, M.: Algorithmic Mediation for Collaborative Exploratory Search. In: Proceedings of the International Conference on Information retrieval Research and Development (SIGIR), pp. 315–322 (2008)
84. Preece, J., Shneiderman, B.: The reader to leader framework: Motivating technology-mediated social participation. AIS Trans. on Human-Computer Interaction **1**(1), 13–32 (2009)
85. Pretschner, A., Gauch, S.: Ontology Based Personalized Search. In: Proceedings of the 11th IEEE International Conference on Tools with Artificial Intelligence (ICTAI), p. 391. IEEE Computer Society, Washington, DC, USA (1999)
86. Rashid, A.M., Ling, K., Tassone, R.D., Resnick, P., Kraut, R., Riedl, J.: Motivating participation by displaying the value of contribution. In: CHI, pp. 955–958 (2006)
87. Reddy, M.C., Dourish, P.: A Finger on the Pulse: Temporal Rhythms and Information Seeking in Medical Work. In: CSCW, pp. 344–353 (2002)
88. Reddy, M.C., Dourish, P., Pratt, W.: Coordinating Heterogeneous Work: Information and Representation in Medical Care. In: CSCW, pp. 239–258 (2001)
89. Reddy, M.C., Jansen, B.J.: A model for understanding collaborative information behavior in context: A study of two healthcare teams. Inf. Process. Manage. **44**(1), 256–273 (2008)
90. Reddy, M.C., Spence, P.R.: Collaborative Information Seeking: A Field Study of a Multidisciplinary Patient Care Team. Inf. Process. Manage. **44**(1), 242–255 (2008)

91. Reilly, J., McCarthy, K., McGinty, L., Smyth, B.: Dynamic Critiquing. In: P. Funk, P.A.G. Calero (eds.) Proceedings of the 7th European Conference on Case-Based Reasoning, pp. 763–777. Springer-Verlag (2004)
92. Reilly, J., McCarthy, K., McGinty, L., Smyth, B.: Incremental critiquing. Knowl.-Based Syst. **18**(4–5), 143–151 (2005)
93. Reilly, J., Smyth, B., McGinty, L., McCarthy, K.: Critiquing with confidence. In: Proceedings of International Conference on Case-Based Reasoning (ICCBR), pp. 436–450 (2005)
94. Resnick, P., Varian, H.R.: Recommender systems. Commun. ACM **40**(3), 56–58 (1997). DOI http://doi.acm.org/10.1145/245108.245121
95. Resnick, P., Zeckhauser, R.: Trust among strangers in internet transactions: Empirical analysis of ebay's reputation system. Advances in Applied Microeconomics **11**, 127–157 (2002)
96. van Rijsbergen, C.J.: Information Retrieval. Butterworth (1979)
97. Rocchio, J.: Relevance Feedback in Information Retrieval. G. Salton (editor), The SMART Retrieval System: Experiments in Automatic Document Processing. Prentice–Hall, Inc., Englewood Cliffs, NJ (1971)
98. Rohini, U., Varma, V.: A novel approach for re-ranking of search results using collaborative filtering. In: Proceedings of the International Conference on Computing: Theory and Applications, vol. 00, pp. 491–496. IEEE Computer Society, Los Alamitos, CA, USA (2007). DOI http://doi.ieeecomputersociety.org/10.1109/ICCTA.2007.15
99. Saaya, Z., Rafter, R., Schaal, M., Smyth, B.: The curated web: a recommendation challenge. In: RecSys, pp. 101–104 (2013)
100. Saaya, Z., Schaal, M., Coyle, M., Briggs, P., Smyth, B.: A comparison of machine learning techniques for recommending search experiences in social search. In: SGAI Conf., pp. 195–200 (2012)
101. Saaya, Z., Schaal, M., Coyle, M., Briggs, P., Smyth, B.: Exploiting extended search sessions for recommending search experiences in the social web. In: ICCBR, pp. 369–383 (2012)
102. Saaya, Z., Schaal, M., Rafter, R., Smyth, B.: Recommending topics for web curation. In: UMAP, pp. 242–253 (2013)
103. Sahami, M., Heilman, T.D.: A web-based kernel function for measuring the similarity of short text snippets. In: Proceedings of the International World-Wide Web Conference, pp. 377–386 (2006)
104. Salton, G., Buckley, C.: Improving retrieval performance by relevance feedback. In: Readings in information retrieval, pp. 355–364. Morgan Kaufmann Publishers Inc., San Francisco, CA, USA (1997)
105. Schafer, J.B., Konstan, J., Riedi, J.: Recommender systems in e-commerce. In: EC '99: Proceedings of the 1st ACM conference on Electronic commerce, pp. 158–166. ACM Press, New York, NY, USA (1999). DOI http://doi.acm.org/10.1145/336992.337035. Denver, Colorado, United States
106. Shafer, G.: The combination of evidence. International Journal of Intelligent Systems **1**(3), 155–179 (1986)
107. Shardanand, U., Maes, P.: Social Information Filtering: Algorithms for Automating "Word of Mouth". In: Proceedings of the Conference on Human Factors in Computing Systems (CHI '95), pp. 210–217. ACM Press (1995). New York, USA
108. Shardanand, U., Maes, P.: Social Information Filtering: Algorithms for Automating "Word of Mouth". In: Proceedings of the SIGCHI Conference on Human Factors in Computing Systems (CHI), pp. 210–217 (1995)
109. Shen, X., Tan, B., Zhai, C.: Implicit User Modeling for Personalized Search. In: Proceedings of the Fourteenth ACM Conference on Information and Knowledge Management (CIKM 05) (2005). Bremen, Germany
110. Smeaton, A.F., Foley, C., Byrne, D., Jones, G.J.F.: ibingo mobile collaborative search. In: CIVR, pp. 547–548 (2008)
111. Smeaton, A.F., Lee, H., Foley, C., McGivney, S.: Collaborative video searching on a tabletop. Multimedia Syst. **12**(4–5), 375–391 (2007)

112. Smyth, B.: Case-Based Recommendation. In: P. Brusilovsky, A. Kobsa, W. Nejdl (eds.) The Adaptive Web, pp. 342–376. Springer-Verlag (2007)
113. Smyth, B.: A community-based approach to personalizing web search. IEEE Computer **40**(8), 42–50 (2007)
114. Smyth, B., Balfe, E., Freyne, J., Briggs, P., Coyle, M., Boydell, O.: Exploiting query repetition and regularity in an adaptive community-based web search engine. User Model. User-Adapt. Interact. **14**(5), 383–423 (2004)
115. Smyth, B., Briggs, P., Coyle, M., O'Mahony, M.P.: A case-based perspective on social web search. In: ICCBR '09: Proceedings of the 8th International Conference on Case-Based Reasoning: Case-Based Reasoning Research and Development, pp. 494–508. Springer-Verlag, Seattle, Washington, USA (2009)
116. Smyth, B., Briggs, P., Coyle, M., O'Mahony, M.P.: A case-based perspective on social web search. In: Proceedings of International Conference on Case-Based Reasoning (ICCBR) (2009)
117. Smyth, B., Briggs, P., Coyle, M., O'Mahony, M.P.: Google shared. A case study in social search. In: Proceedings of the 17th International Conference on User Modeling, Adaptation, and Personalization (UMAP '09), pp. 283–294. Springer-Verlag, Trento, Italy (2009)
118. Smyth, B., Briggs, P., Coyle, M., O'Mahony, M.P.: Google. Shared! A Case-Study in Social Search. In: Proceedings of the International Conference on User Modeling, Adaptation and Personalization (UMAP), pp. 494–508. Springer-Verlag (2009)
119. Smyth, B., Champin, P.A.: The Experience Web: A Case-Based Reasoning Perspective. In: Workshop on Grand Challenges for Reasoning from Experiences at the International Joint Conference on Artificial Intelligence (IJCAI) (2009)
120. Smyth, B., Coyle, M., Briggs, P.: Heystaks: a real-world deployment of social search. In: RecSys, pp. 289–292 (2012)
121. Smyth, B., McClave, P.: Similarity v's Diversity. In: D. Aha, I. Watson (eds.) Proceedings of the 3rd International Conference on Case-Based Reasoning, pp. 347–361. Springer (2001)
122. Sparck Jones, K.: A statistical interpretation of term specificity and its application in retrieval. In: Document retrieval systems, pp. 132–142. Taylor Graham Publishing, London, UK, UK (1988)
123. Speretta, M., Gauch, S.: Personalized search based on user search histories. In: WI '05: Proceedings of the 2005 IEEE/WIC/ACM International Conference on Web Intelligence, pp. 622–628. IEEE Computer Society, Washington, DC, USA (2005). DOI http://dx.doi.org/10.1109/WI.2005.114
124. Spink, A., Bateman, J., Jansen, M.B.: Searching Heterogeneous Collections on the Web: Behaviour of Excite Users. Information Research: An Electronic Journal **4**(2) (1998)
125. Spink, A., Jansen, B.J.: A Study of Web Search Trends. Webology **1**(2), 4 (2004). URL http://www.webology.ir/2004/v1n2/a4.html
126. Spink, A., Wolfram, D., Jansen, M.B.J., Saracevic, T.: Searching the Web: the Public and their Queries. Journal of the American Society for Information Science **52**(3), 226–234 (2001)
127. Sugiyama, K., Hatano, K., Yoshikawa, M.: Adaptive web search based on user profile constructed without any effort from users. In: WWW '04: Proceedings of the 13th international conference on World Wide Web, pp. 675–684. ACM Press, New York, NY, USA (2004). DOI http://doi.acm.org/10.1145/988672.988764. New York, NY, USA
128. Sun, J.T., Zeng, H.J., Liu, H., Lu, Y., Chen, Z.: Cubesvd: a novel approach to personalized web search. In: WWW '05: Proceedings of the 14th international conference on World Wide Web, pp. 382–390. ACM Press, New York, NY, USA (2005). DOI http://doi.acm.org/10.1145/1060745.1060803. Chiba, Japan
129. Tan, B., Shen, X., Zhai, C.: Mining long-term search history to improve search accuracy. In: KDD '06: Proceedings of the 12th ACM SIGKDD international conference on Knowledge discovery and data mining, pp. 718–723. ACM Press, New York, NY, USA (2006). DOI http://doi.acm.org/10.1145/1150402.1150493. Philadelphia, PA, USA

130. Yang, Y., Chute, C.G.: An example-based mapping method for text categorization and retrieval. ACM Trans. Inf. Syst. **12**(3), 252–277 (1994). DOI http://doi.acm.org/10.1145/183422.183424
131. Zhou, B., Hui, S.C., Fong, A.C.M.: An effective approach for periodic web personalization. In: WI '06: Proceedings of the 2006 IEEE/WIC/ACM International Conference on Web Intelligence, pp. 284–292. IEEE Computer Society, Washington, DC, USA (2006). DOI http://dx.doi.org/10.1109/WI.2006.36

Part IV
Human Computer Interaction

Chapter 18
Human Decision Making and Recommender Systems

Anthony Jameson, Martijn C. Willemsen, Alexander Felfernig, Marco de Gemmis, Pasquale Lops, Giovanni Semeraro, and Li Chen

18.1 Introduction and Preview

What is the function of recommender systems? There are various possible answers; but in this chapter, we view recommender systems as tools for helping people to make better choices—not large, complex choices, such as where to build a new airport, but the small- to medium-sized choices that people make every day: what products to buy, what documents to read, which people to contact.[1] From this perspective, recommender systems researchers and designers should have a

[1]There is no crisp distinction in English between "choosing" and "deciding". We will mostly use the former term, since "decision making" is often associated with complex problems requiring deep thought and analysis, whereas recommender systems are more commonly used in connection with smaller, less complex problems.

A. Jameson (✉)
DFKI, German Research Center for Artificial Intelligence, Saarbrücken, Germany
e-mail: jameson@dfki.de

M.C. Willemsen
Eindhoven University of Technology, Eindhoven, The Netherlands
e-mail: M.C.Willemsen@tue.nl

A. Felfernig
University of Graz, Graz, Austria
e-mail: afelfern@ist.tugraz.at

M. de Gemmis • P. Lops • G. Semeraro
Department of Computer Science, University of Bari "Aldo Moro", Bari, Italy
e-mail: marco.degemmis@uniba.it; pasquale.lops@uniba.it; giovanni.semeraro@uniba.it

L. Chen
Hong Kong Baptist University, Hong Kong, China
e-mail: lichen@comp.hkbu.edu.hk

F. Ricci et al. (eds.), *Recommender Systems Handbook*,
DOI 10.1007/978-1-4899-7637-6_18

solid broad understanding of how people make choices and how the process of making choices can be supported. The main reason is that it is often desirable or necessary to keep the chooser in the loop: Arriving at a choice is in general best seen as involving collaboration between the chooser and the recommender system. Leaving the chooser out of the loop makes sense in some extreme cases, as when a music recommender (see Chap. 13) chooses music and plays it without consulting the listener; or when an intelligent house automatically sets parameters such as temperature and air circulation. Note that in cases like these we would often speak not of a "recommender system" but of an agent that performs tasks on behalf of a person.

There are two basic ways in which a recommender system can keep the chooser in the loop:

1. Take over only a part of the processing that is required to make a choice, leaving the rest to the chooser.

   For example, many recommenders use their algorithms to reduce a very large number of options to a smaller subset but then leave it to the chooser to select an option from the subset (see Sect. 18.6).
2. Generate an overall recommendation and present it to the chooser; but also offer an *explanation* of how the recommendation was generated, so that the chooser can decide for himself whether he wants to (a) follow the recommendation[2]; (b) deviate from the system's line of reasoning while still using part of it; or (c) reject the system's recommendation entirely.

   A discussion of explanations from the point of view of choice support will be given in Sect. 18.4.2.

This chapter begins with a compact overview of the psychology of everyday choice and decision making—called the ASPECT model—that is based on a broad range of psychological research and formulated so as to be relevant and accessible to recommender systems people. We will see that considering these patterns one by one gives us new ideas about how recommender systems can support particular aspects of human choice. We then provide a high-level overview of strategies for helping people make better choices—the ARCADE model—discussing how recommender systems can make use of these various strategies.[3] The succeeding sections of the chapter consider in turn a number of general topics in recommender systems research and show how they can be better understood in terms of the models of choice and choice support.

As an idealization, we assume in this chapter that the main goal of a recommender system is to help people make choices that they themselves will ultimately be satisfied with. In particular, if a chooser decides to reject the system's

[2]To avoid clumsy formulations like "him- or herself" when using personal pronouns in a generic way, we will alternate between the masculine and feminine forms on an example-by-example basis.

[3]Much more detail on the ASPECT and ARCADE models will be found in the book-length monograph by Jameson et al. [39].

recommendations and choose differently, that's no problem as long as the chooser is ultimately satisfied with her choice. In practice, there can be reasons why a system designer does want the chooser to tend to accept the recommendations (e.g., if the recommender system is intended to persuade the chooser to eat healthier food or to buy a particular company's products). In these cases, designers are likely to want to introduce some forms of bias into the system (e.g., recommending a particular class of options especially often; or making the recommendations seem to be better founded than they really are). Since introducing bias is in general fairly easy to do, we will leave the determination of how to do so as an exercise for the interested reader, so as to be able to focus here on the core issues raised by the goal of choice support, which are quite complex enough in themselves.[4]

18.2 Choice Patterns and Recommendation

The question "How do people make choices?" is surprisingly hard to answer, even if you are familiar with the vast and impressive scientific literature on this topic in psychology, economics, and other fields. Recommender systems people are in a good position to understand why, since the same difficulty would arise with the question "How can a computer program make recommendations?" In both cases, the top-level answer is: "There are a number of different approaches, and they can be combined in various ways."

With regard to computational recommendation, the various different paradigms (content-based, knowledge-based, etc.) and the ways of combining them have been ably described in works like those of Burke [9, 10]. The ASPECT model [39, Sect. 3] aims to do something similar for human choice: It distinguishes six human *choice patterns*, which are summarized in Table 18.1.[5] Each of these patterns is sometimes found in its pure form, but they are often blended together in various ways (see Sect. 18.2.7).

An advantage of distilling out these six choice patterns is that it becomes possible to think in detail about how to support choice when it occurs according to each pattern. As can be seen in Table 18.1, each pattern comprises a set of typical processing steps that are mostly different from the steps found in the other patterns. With regard to each pattern, we can ask: What can a recommender system do to help people to execute these steps more successfully? In this way, we will be able to identify a number of possible applications of recommendation technology that would otherwise be more difficult to discern.

---

[4]More discussion of the distinction between the contrasting goals of *persuasion* and *choice support* is given in [39, Sect. 1.2].

[5]ASPECT is an acronym formed from the first letters of the six patterns.

Table 18.1 Overview of the six choice patterns that make up the ASPECT model (C = the chooser)

Attribute-based choice		**Consequence-based choice**	
Conditions of applicability	*Typical procedure*	*Conditions of applicability*	*Typical procedure*
– The options can be viewed meaningfully as items that can be described in terms of attributes and levels – The (relative) desirability of an item can be estimated in terms of evaluations of its levels of various attributes	– (Optional:) *C* reflects in advance about the situation-specific (relative) importance of attributes and/or values of attribute levels – *C* reduces the total set of options to a smaller *consideration set* on the basis of attribute information – *C* chooses from a manageable set of options	– The choices are among actions that will have consequences	– *C* recognizes that a choice about a possible action can (or must) be made – *C* assesses the situation – *C* decides when and where to make the choice – *C* identifies one or more possible actions (options) – *C* anticipates (some of) the consequences of executing the options – *C* evaluates (some of) the anticipated consequences – *C* chooses an option that rates (relatively) well in terms of its consequences
Experience-based choice		**Socially-based choice**	
Conditions of applicability	*Typical procedure*	*Conditions of applicability*	*Typical procedure*
– *C* has made similar choices in the past	– *C* applies recognition-primed decision making – or *C* acts on the basis of a habit – or *C* chooses a previously reinforced response – or *C* applies the affect heuristic	– There is some information available about what relevant other people do, expect, or recommend in this or similar situations	– *C* considers *examples* of the choices or evaluations of other persons – or *C* considers the *expectations* of relevant people – or *C* considers explicit advice concerning the options

(continued)

In this section, we will focus on the core functionality of recommender systems: their ability to suggest which of a set of options a person should choose or how a person should evaluate a particular option.[6]

[6]In the terminology of the ARCADE model (Sect. 18.3 below), this strategy is called *Evaluate on Behalf of the Chooser*. As we will see in that section, recommender systems typically also support choice with applications of other strategies that are not specifically associated with recommendation technology.

Table 18.1 (continued)

Policy-based choice	**Trial-and-error based choice**
Conditions of applicability	*Conditions of applicability*
– *C* encounters choices like this one on a regular basis	– The choice will be made repeatedly; or *C* will have a chance to switch from one option to another even after having started to execute the first option
Typical procedure	*Typical procedure*
– [Earlier:] *C* arrives at a policy for dealing with this type of choice – [Now:] *C* recognizes which policy is applicable to the current choice situation and applies it to identify the preferred option – *C* determines whether actually to execute the option implied by the policy	– *C* selects an option *O* to try out, either using one of the other choice patterns or (maybe implicitly) by applying an *exploration strategy* – *C* executes the selected option *O* – *C* notices some of the consequences of executing *O* – *C* learns something from these consequences – (If *C* is not yet satisfied:) *C* returns to the selection step, taking into account what has been learned

To give a more concrete idea of the choice patterns and the relationships among them, we will refer to the following situation: An English-speaking tourist who is about to visit France would like to buy a French-English dictionary for his or her smartphone from an app store that offers a number of relevant dictionaries.

18.2.1 Attribute-Based Choice

If a user applies the attribute-based pattern, he will view each dictionary as an object that can be described in terms of various evaluation-relevant attributes (e.g., number of entries, usability, and price), some of which are more important than others. Each object has a *level* with respect to each attribute, such as a particular number of entries, which the user may or not be aware of in advance. The chooser can assign a *value* to an object's level of an attribute. Roughly speaking, the chooser will tend to select a dictionary that seems attractive in terms of the values of the levels of (some of) its attributes, with the more important attributes influencing the choice relatively strongly. But there are many specific ways of applying the attribute-based pattern, ranging from thoroughly considering each object's levels on many of its attributes to considering only a small sample of the attribute information and selecting an object that looks (relatively) good in terms of the sample. Useful entry points to the literature on attribute-based choice include [36, 66], [67, Chap. 2], and [5].

In principle, it is possible for a recommender system to take over just about the entire process of attribute-based choice from the user if it can acquire some useful hypotheses about the chooser's evaluation criteria (i.e., the relative importances of attributes and the values of levels of attributes) But there are also ways in which a recommender can help even while keeping the chooser in the loop:

1. The first way concerns the first of the three main steps listed for this pattern in Table 18.1: People often do not bring stable and appropriate evaluation criteria to a choice problem but rather develop them while choosing (see Sect. 18.7.2). Hence it can be useful for a recommender system to tell the chooser something like "For a person in your situation, a French-English dictionary ought to have at least 30,000 entries". This strategy of recommending evaluation criteria is sometimes found in knowledge-based recommender systems (see Chap. 5). But on the whole, recommending evaluation criteria is much less common than recommending particular items.
2. An obvious and frequently applied way in which a recommender system can help with attribute-based choice is in the second main step: reducing a very large set of options to a smaller *consideration set*. The initial set of potentially choosable options (e.g., books sold via an e-commerce website) is often so large that a chooser could not possibly consider each item. When choosing without the help of a recommender system, people often apply very simple *winnowing strategies* (see, e.g., [20]) for this purpose, such as eliminating all options that fail to meet some threshold with regard to one important attribute. Even a highly imperfect recommendation algorithm can often do a better job of winnowing, while still leaving the final decision to the chooser (see Sect. 18.6 for further discussion).

18.2.2 Consequence-Based Choice

A different way of thinking about an option is to consider the concrete consequences of choosing it. So instead of contemplating the number of entries offered by a dictionary, our tourist might consider how successfully she is likely to be able to use the dictionary to order meals in restaurants during her vacation. Consequence-based choice involves a number of different issues than attribute-based choice: Among other things, the chooser needs to deal with uncertainty about what consequences will occur if she chooses a particular option and the fact that they may occur in the distant future. And there is often a considerable variety of possible consequences, ranging from objectively describable events to the chooser's affective responses, a fact that complicates the process of evaluating an option in terms of its anticipated consequences. Entry points to the literature on consequence-based choice include works on the most prominent descriptive model, *prospect theory* [44, 92] and works that focus on support for consequence-based choice (e.g., [28]).

Here again, looking at Table 18.1, we can see points at which a recommender system can support consequence-based choice:

1. The recommender system can help the chooser to recognize that a choice can be made and to decide when and where to make it. Consider, for example, a system like COMMUNITYCOMMANDS [49], which suggests commands that a user of a complex application could execute in the current situation. Regardless of the value of the specific recommendations, the system is in effect telling the user that there is more than one command that could be used in the current situation and that this is a good time to consider which one to use. A recommender could in principle focus entirely on this specific form of choice support, saying something like "I recommend thinking now about what command to use in this situation". This type of recommendation could be useful when (a) the recommender does not have good reasons for recommending any specific option; but (b) the recommender is able to determine in a personalized way when and where the user should think about a particular type of choice.
2. The recommender can help the user to identify one or more options he didn't know were available, such as obscure commands or configuration settings—a useful function even if the chooser ends up evaluating these options entirely on his own.
3. The recommender can help the chooser arrive at evaluations of particular consequences. Even if a chooser knows that a particular consequence will occur (e.g., having to download a high-quality French-speaking voice with a size of 100 MB), she may have a hard time anticipating accurately how good or bad this consequence will be for her. A recommender system could in effect "recommend"—or warn against—particular unfamiliar consequences instead of entire options (compare the approach mentioned in Sect. 18.2.1 of recommending particular evaluation criteria within the attribute-based pattern).

18.2.3 Experience-Based Choice

The two preceding patterns can involve some quite elaborate reasoning about the merits of the available options. The remaining four ASPECT patterns describe how people use quite different approaches to arrive at choices in ways that are typically quicker and less effortful.

Experience-based choice occurs when the chooser's past experience with the choice situation and/or with particular options directly suggests some particular option. For example, if the chooser has had positive experience with the dictionaries of a particular publisher, he is likely to have a good feeling when he thinks about purchasing another dictionary from the same publisher, even if he does not remember the previous experiences. Or he may have fallen into the habit of purchasing products from a particular publisher, even without any particularly rewarding experiences. In Table 18.1, four specific variants of this pattern are distinguished, which are discussed in [39, Sect. 7]. The principle that they have in common is that the chooser selects an option that has worked well (or adequately) in the past.

Entry points to the literature on experience-based choice include [3, 45, 70, 95] and [30].

On a high level, case-based [83] and content-based [53] recommender systems can be seen as taking over (part of) the process of experience-based choice by analyzing the chooser's relevant previous experiences to determine which of the currently available options they suggest. One way in which a recommender system can support experience-based choice while keeping the chooser more in the loop is by helping the chooser to remember and take into account relevant aspects of her previous experience, such as the specific actions that the chooser has performed in the past and the feelings that she had while performing them. The term *recomindation* [69] has been coined to refer to this approach.

18.2.4 Socially Based Choice

People often allow their choices to be influenced by the examples, expectations, or advice of others. If many other people have tried a given dictionary and rated it positively, their ratings can be seen as a summary of a great deal of relevant experience that it would be impractical for the current chooser to acquire himself. In addition to providing such *social examples*, other people can have *social expectations* (e.g., as to what is considered cool or politically incorrect) as well as explicit *advice*.

Entry points to the literature on socially based choice include [27], [16, Chaps. 4 and 6], and [87, Chap. 3].

Collaborative filtering can be seen as a way of automating the "follow social examples" subpattern of the socially based pattern; but a closer look at this pattern [39, Sect. 8] brings to light additional ways in which recommender systems can support it:

1. Whereas collaborative filtering normally (directly or indirectly) considers examples from people who are similar to the current chooser in some respects, the class of similar people is not always the most relevant class: Sometimes a chooser wants to make choices that are characteristic of a group of people to which she does not (yet) belong (for example, people who are more advanced in a particular domain or who enjoy higher prestige). Some trust-based recommender systems [91] take into account the social relationships between the chooser and the other persons whose opinions and choices are being considered.
2. What is interesting about other people is often not the examples that they provide but the *expectations* that they have. For example, for a user who wants to become a well-regarded member of an online community, recommendations about how to behave are often better based on the (explicit or implicit) expectations that

govern behavior in that community as opposed to the actual typical behavior of members, which may largely fail to conform to these expectations.

3. The third variant of the socially based pattern involves not following examples or expectations but rather taking explicit advice into account. One way in which a recommender system can support this pattern is by helping the chooser to find persons who can provide good advice, as is done in many expert finding systems (see, e.g., the summary in [40, p. 444]).
4. This *advice taking* subpattern of the socially based pattern is even more relevant to recommender systems on a different level: When the chooser is aware of the fact that he is being offered recommendations,[7] it is natural for him to consider (mostly quickly and intuitively) some of the same questions that he would consider when taking advice from a human advice giver (see, e.g., [8, 42]), some of which concern the advice giver's credibility (see Chap. 20). In fact, it is often appropriate to view the user of a recommender system as applying a *combination* of (a) the advice taking subpattern of the socially based pattern, with the difference that the advice giver is not a person but a recommender system; and (b) one or more other choice (sub)patterns (see Sect. 18.2.7 for a discussion of combinations of choice patterns). We will return to this point when discussing the topic of explanations (Sect. 18.4.2).

18.2.5 Policy-Based Choice

Sometimes, the choice process can be seen as comprising two phases, which may be separated considerably in time: In the first phase, the chooser arrives at a *policy* for making a particular type of choice (e.g., "When buying a dictionary for your smartphone, always choose the Oxford dictionary if one is available"). Later, when faced with a specific choice to make, the user applies the policy.

Policy-based choice has been discussed mainly in the literature on organizational decision making, where policies play a more obvious role than they do with individual choice (see, e.g., [59, Chap. 2]). Relevant research on individual choices has been conducted in connection with the concepts of *choice bracketing* [75] and *self-control* [73].

1. A relatively neglected way of supporting a policy-based choice is to recommend a policy to the chooser. An example would be a system that recommended a diet or an exercise regime for the user to follow. This type of recommendation can be especially valuable in that it is often difficult for a chooser to evaluate a possible policy, partly because of the difficulty of anticipating what consequences its application will have in the long run. To take a striking example: Camerer et al.

[7] This type of awareness is often absent, as when the recommender system adapts the order in which a list of options is presented to the user without announcing the fact that it is doing so.

[11] found that taxi drivers who can choose how many hours to drive each day often apply a simple policy ("Drive each day until you have earned a fixed target amount of money") that in practice tends to *minimize* rather than maximize their hourly earnings.

2. An easier and more frequently found type of support is for a system to help the user apply a particular policy (e.g., concerning what types of newspaper story to read each day) by (a) having the chooser formulate the policy somehow and (b) automatically executing the policy whenever a relevant case arises. An example is a system for personalized news reading that allows the user to assign priorities to particular types of news item so as to influence the news stories that are presented to her. Recommender systems that ask users to specify their general "preferences" explicitly and that then apply these evaluation criteria to subsequent choices can be seen as supporting policy-based choice; see Sect. 18.5.1 for more discussion of what "preferences" actually are.

18.2.6 Trial-and-Error-Based Choice

Especially if none of the other patterns leads readily to a choice, a chooser will sometimes simply (perhaps randomly) choose an option and see how well it works out. For example, our dictionary chooser might download the free dictionary and quickly look up a few words, judging whether it seems worthwhile to spend money on one of the other dictionaries.

It is useful to view the trial-and-error-based pattern as being applied even in some cases where the chooser does not go all the way in executing the chosen option. For example, our dictionary chooser might "try out" a dictionary in the weaker sense of closely examining its description in the app store and carefully reading the reviews. The choice process and the appropriate forms of support are in many ways similar to those that arise when more thorough trials are involved.

Trial-and-error-based choice has been studied from various perspectives in the psychological literature, mostly not associated with the term "trial and error" (see, e.g., [17, 51, 68, 74], and [97]).

1. One important way in which a recommender system can support trial-and-error-based choice is by helping the chooser to decide, at each point in the cycle, which option(s) to try out next—a type of decision which, upon close inspection, turns out to involve a surprising variety of considerations. A relatively novel approach would be for a recommender explicitly to recommend an *exploration strategy*: a strategy for choosing the next option to try out (e.g., "In this situation, it seems best to try out the highest-rated dictionaries first, even though they are the most expensive ones"). An approach more commonly taken by recommender systems is to support the *execution* of a particular exploration strategy; variants of this approach are discussed in Sect. 18.7.

2. Recommender systems can also support the second main part of the trial-and-error-based pattern: learning from the experience acquired in trying out an option. Among other things, a recommender system can suggest what aspects of the outcome of a trial to attend to—something that is often not at all obvious. For example, a dictionary user might be advised to pay attention to how long it takes him to look up a word, given that this factor will be more important in everyday use of the dictionary than it is while he is trying it out in an artificial situation.

18.2.7 Combinations of Choice Patterns

The six choice patterns are often used in combination, just as different recommendation techniques are often combined to create hybrid recommenders [9, 10]. Explicit discussions of forms of combination are rather rare [39, Sect. 3.3.7]. Many studies, however, indirectly yield ideas about forms of combination, as does everyday experience. Most people, for example, can remember choice situations in which our experience-based "gut feeling" conflicted with the result of a careful consequence-based analysis, indicating that the two patterns had been applied in parallel and perhaps largely independently of each other. Another common form of combination is a "cascade" in which one pattern (e.g., a simple attribute-based strategy) is used to generate a manageable number of options and then a different pattern is used to choose among these options.

Recommender systems can in principle recommend particular (combinations of) choice patterns as being suitable for a given choice situation; this idea is discussed in Sect. 18.3.2 below.

18.2.8 What Constitutes a Good Choice?

If our goal is to help people make better choices, we should have some idea of when people feel that they have chosen well. A number of researchers have investigated this question (see, e.g., [4, 32, 96]). Although specific answers vary, the following statements are widely accepted (for a more detailed discussion, see [39, Sect. 3.6]):

1. Choosers want their decisions to yield good outcomes.
   This point isn't as straightforward as it may seem, because what counts as a "good outcome" is in turn surprisingly complex. In this chapter, we will view a good outcome as one that the chooser is (or would be) satisfied with in retrospect, after having acquired the most relevant knowledge and experience. The emphasis in the recommender systems field on maximizing the accuracy of recommendations can be seen as an attempt to optimize the outcomes of choice processes.

2. Choosers don't want to invest time and effort in the choice process itself that is out of proportion to the resulting benefits.
   Note that a recommender system whose use yields only barely acceptable outcomes can still be considered worth using if it drastically reduces the time and effort required to find an acceptable outcome.
3. Choosers tend to prefer to avoid unpleasant thoughts.
   Some ways of thinking about a decision can involve distressing thoughts, as when a car buyer considers whether to save money by not purchasing an optional safety feature, noting that doing so will increase the likelihood that a member of her family will be injured. One benefit of outsourcing parts of the decision process to a recommender system (or to a human advisor) is that the chooser herself does not need to think about such matters.
4. Choosers often want to be able to justify the decision that they have made to other persons—or to themselves.
   An implication is that one way of supporting choice is to make it easy for the user to come up with a satisfying justification of whatever option is best for him, for example, by supplying a justification explicitly, as is done by many recommender systems that provide explanations for their recommendations (see Chap. 10 and Sect. 18.4.2.)

In sum, all of the four main quality criteria for choices are fairly straightforwardly served by recommender systems. This fact may help to explain their popularity relative to some other forms of choice support that fare poorly with respect to one or more of these criteria (e.g., decision support systems that call for effortful and often frustrating contemplation of trade-offs, which violates two of the four criteria; see [96]).

18.3 Choice Support Strategies and Recommendation

While discussing the six ASPECT choice patterns, we have focused on how their application can be supported by the technology that is most characteristic of recommender systems: technology for generating choices and evaluations on behalf of the chooser. But there are several other general approaches to supporting choice, all of which can sometimes be applied fruitfully within recommender systems. The ARCADE model (introduced in [39, Sect. 4]), is a high-level synthesis of approaches to choice support that have been discussed, studied, and applied both with and without support from computing technology. The bottom part of Fig. 18.1 gives a high-level overview of the six strategies.

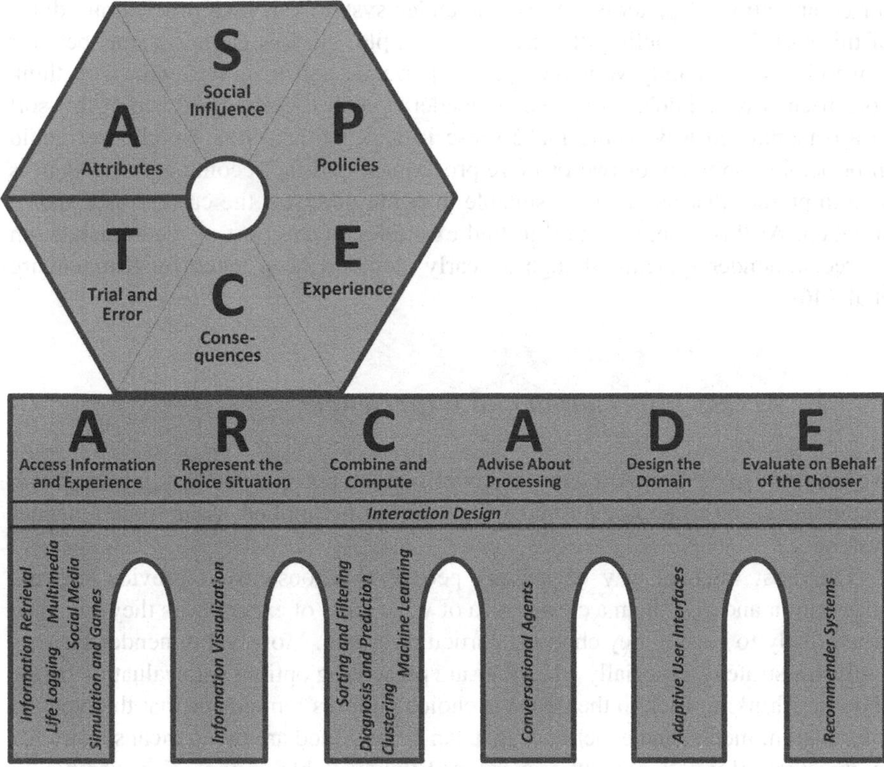

Fig. 18.1 High-level overview of the ARCADE model of choice support strategies, illustrating its relationship to the ASPECT model of choice patterns (The technologies shown in the pillars of the arcade are among those that can be deployed to realize the strategy in question.)

18.3.1 Evaluate on Behalf of the Chooser

The strategy that is typical of recommender systems is called within the ARCADE model *Evaluate on Behalf of the Chooser*. As is indicated in the bottom part of Fig. 18.1, the application of this strategy in interactive systems does not always require recommendation technology; straightforward interface design is often adequate, as when a generally relevant recommendation is offered to all choosers (e.g., "You are advised to close all open applications").

18.3.2 Advise About Processing

The second ARCADE strategy that involves a form of recommendation is the strategy *Advise About Processing*. The advice being given here concerns not particular options on the domain level but rather ways of applying a particular choice pattern (or combination of patterns). A recommender system can give procedural advice of this sort, in effect telling the user, for example, "In this case, it seems best for you to consider mainly your own past experience and to ignore what you think your friends would do".[8] For a recommender system to provide advice of this sort in a personalized way would make sense in a situation where the chooser could in principle apply any of two or more procedures and the recommender system is able to predict that one is more suitable than the other for the current user and/or situation. At this time, it is hard to find examples of this sort of recommendation by recommender systems, though an early step has been taken by Knijnenburg et al. [46].

18.3.3 Access Information and Experience

We now turn to the four ARCADE strategies that are not specifically connected with recommendation technology, though they can all be applied within recommender systems.

The most obvious way of helping people to choose is to provide relevant information and give them a clearer idea of what sorts of experiences they have had or are likely to have if they choose a particular option. Most recommender systems apply this strategy, especially when they are presenting options for evaluation by the chooser. Thinking back to the ASPECT choice patterns reminds us that the types of information, media, and experience that can be provided are by no means restricted to objective information about properties of the available options. For example, to support the consequence-based pattern, a system can give a preview of what it will feel like to watch a particular film; and to support the socially based pattern, it can inform the user about social examples and expectations.

18.3.4 Represent the Choice Situation

This high-level strategy takes into account the fact that the particular way in which information about a choice situation is organized (e.g., the way in which items are displayed on a computer screen) can make particular types of processing easier or more difficult. For example, it is easier to compare options with each other, as opposed to evaluating each option individually, if the options are displayed simultaneously and the information about them is organized so as to facilitate comparison. Shifting from *joint* to *separate evaluation* or vice-versa can have major consequences for processing (see, e.g., [36]).

[8]This type of advice is often given implicitly, in that the system provides support for one procedure but not for others (e.g., by reminding the chooser of her past experience but providing no information about what other people choose).

Since a recommender system almost inevitably contributes to the way in which the choice situation is represented to the chooser, recommender system designers should think about the consequences of particular forms of organization for the chooser's processing. Some issues of this sort are discussed in Sect. 18.8.

18.3.5 Combine and Compute

Even aside from the recommendation algorithms that it applies, a recommender system can make various types of computation on the basis of available information whose results can support the chooser's processing. Simple examples include functionality for allowing the user to sort or filter recommended items according to particular attributes. More sophisticated computation is involved, for example, when a set of items is automatically divided into clusters according to inter-item similarity so as to provide the user with a better overview of the set of options. As these examples show, this type of choice support can complement the core recommendation functionality of a recommender system.

18.3.6 Design the Domain

The basic idea with this strategy is to design the underlying reality that the chooser is making choices about in a way that makes it easier for the chooser to make the right choices—or for a recommender system to generate good recommendations. The difference from the strategy *Represent the Choice Situation* is that you are crafting the options and other aspects of the choice situation themselves, not just the way in which they are presented to the chooser.

Suppose, for example, that you are designing a recommender system that helps users to choose appropriate privacy settings within a particular social network site. Using the strategy *Represent the Choice Situation*, you would try to display the options to the user in a helpful way (e.g., grouping related options together). But if the privacy settings are inherently hard to deal with (for example, if there are a large number of settings that interact in complex ways), even the best representation may confront users with a challenging choice problem, and even the best recommendation algorithm can have a hard time determining which combinations of settings are likely to be best for the chooser. Applying the strategy *Design the Domain*, you would reconceptualize the set of privacy options themselves—and maybe also the underlying privacy management principles—so as to make the choice problem inherently easier for the chooser and/or for the recommender system. This idea of "designing for recommendability" is analogous to the idea of "designing for explanation", which was studied in connection with expert systems in the 1980s (see Chap. 10). We are aware of no explicit attempts to achieve this goal, but it appears to deserve some attention.

18.3.7 Concluding Remark on Support Strategies

This overview has shown that (a) recommendation technology makes it possible for recommender systems to support choice in ways that complement other technology-based forms of support but that (b) what a recommender system designer is designing is usually a hybrid system that incorporates other choice support strategies alongside the most relevant strategy *Evaluate on Behalf of the Chooser*.

18.4 Arguments and Explanations

So far, we have discussed individual applications of the ARCADE strategies. But a choice support agent will often present a coherent set of applications of such strategies, which may be called an *argument*. Arguments have a special role for recommender systems in that they often serve as part of an *explanation* of a recommendation (Sect. 18.4.2).

18.4.1 Arguments

A simple verbal argument within the attribute-based pattern would be "This product is the best one on the dimension which you consider most important [so it's worth considering seriously]". As this example shows, it is not always necessary or appropriate to formulate explicitly a conclusion that is implied by the argument. In discussions and models of argumentation (e.g., [89]), an argument is normally viewed as comprising purely verbal components; but with recommender systems, it can also include nonverbal elements such as tables and visualizations.

Almost all of the ARCADE strategies can be used (often in combination) to construct an argument for presentation to the chooser: *Access Information and Experience* and *Combine and Compute* determine what facts are presented. *Represent the Choice Situation* determines how they are presented. Arguments usually implicitly apply *Advise About Processing* in that they suggest that the particular type of processing embodied in the argument is appropriate for the current choice problem. *Evaluate on Behalf of the Chooser* is applied whenever an argument includes an evaluation made on behalf of the chooser (as happens twice in our example of "... the best product on the most important dimension ...").

Here are two points about arguments that are relevant to their use in a recommendation context:

1. Even a good argument does not *prove* that a particular option should be chosen but rather suggests reasons for choosing it, which may be overridden by other considerations (e.g., through the application of other choice patterns).

2. The chooser sometimes accepts some parts of an argument but not others. For example if he notices an incorrect statement being offered as one step in an argument, he can replace it with a correct statement and then try to work with the modified argument, seeing whether it leads to the same conclusion or to a different one.

18.4.2 *Explanations of Recommendations*

An argument can be presented as choice support independently of any recommendation technology, but it can also be provided as part of an explanation of a recommendation. The topic of explanations is treated thoroughly in Chap. 10, which covers their use for both choice support and persuasion; Table 10.2 of that chapter offers a convenient overview of examples of explanations, which the interested reader may want to consult at this point. As a supplement to that chapter, we provide, using concepts from the ASPECT and ARCADE models, a theoretical account of explanations seen as a form of choice support.

As can be seen from Chap. 10, the things that are called *explanations* come in a variety of forms, some of which do not involve actual explanations of how the recommender system arrived at its recommendation. We will consider three types that together represent most of the issues that arise:

18.4.2.1 Type 1: Direct Support for the Assessment of the Credibility of the Recommender System

For example, several of the "explanations" tested by Herlocker et al. [34] present only information that helps the chooser to assess the likelihood that the recommendation is accurate (e.g., "MOVIELENS has predicted correctly for you 80 % of the time in the past"). This type of information is comparable to information about the expertise of a human advice giver (e.g., references to academic degrees or job titles). So this type of explanation can be seen as support for the advice-taking subpattern of the socially based choice pattern (Sect. 18.2.4).[9]

Where the goal of the recommender system is choice support, the goal in providing this type of information should be to convey a *realistic* impression of the system's credibility (not to maximize apparent credibility).

[9] A thorough discussion of credibility in human and artificial advice giving can be found in Chap. 20.

18.4.2.2 Type 2: An Argument Coupled with a *Fidelity Claim*

Many explanations comprise two parts:

1. An argument (in the sense introduced above) that the chooser can consider when thinking about the choice problem.
   Example: "This movie stars your favorite actress, and it belongs to your favorite genre."
2. A *fidelity claim* to the effect that the argument reflects the system's reasoning in arriving at the recommendation.
   Example: "That's why this movie is being recommended."
   The fidelity claim is often implicit: The mere fact that the system accompanies a recommendation with an argument is likely to suggest the fidelity claim.

As was noted above, the argument can constitute useful choice support in its own right, regardless of whether it is offered as part of an explanation. But the fidelity claim adds an additional layer to the explanation in that it enables the chooser also to view the argument as (further) evidence concerning the recommender system's credibility (e.g., "If those are the only reasons why the system thinks I ought to like this movie, I can ignore this recommendation"). Hence this type of explanation supports the advice-taking subpattern of the socially based choice pattern as well as whatever choice patterns are represented in the argument itself (e.g., the attribute-based pattern in the example just given).

Accordingly, there are two different desiderata for this type of explanation: (a) that the argument should be useful for the chooser, whether she accepts it wholesale or makes selective, critical use of it; and (b) that the fidelity claim should be accurate and should help the chooser to make a realistic credibility assessment. In particular, if a fidelity claim is made even though the argument bears no relationship to the system's processing (a practice discussed in Sect. 10.3 of Chap. 10), any credibility assessment that the chooser makes will be based on a false premise. From the point of view of choice support, arguments that do not reflect the system's processing should be presented as arguments, not as explanations of the system's processing.

18.4.2.3 Type 3: An Explicit Description of the Recommender System's Processing

Often, an explanation consists of an explicit description of the system's processing, as with the "detailed process description" explanation of Herlocker et al. [34]: "To compute this prediction, MovieLens examined 1000 users and selected the 50 users whose ratings correlated closest to yours. Of these users, 33 had rated this movie. This prediction is based on those 33 ratings."

This type of explanation differs from the previous type in that it describes the system's processing rather than presenting an argument for consideration by the chooser; and indeed, the processing done by the recommender system will often be of a sort that could not be performed in the same way by a human chooser (e.g., because it requires data and computational capacity that are not available to the chooser). Still, it can suggest to the chooser a human-like argument (e.g., "people with tastes similar to mine apparently tend to like this movie") that he can make use of as part of his own thinking about the problem. And he can try to evaluate the credibility of the processing (e.g., "Is 1000 users a convincingly large number?"), subject to the limitations imposed by his lack of full understanding of how the processing works.

Hence this type of explanation has the same two-edged character as the previous type, and it should be designed with the same two basic desiderata in mind, even though they can be achieved only less directly: that a helpful argument should be suggested and that a realistic credibility assessment should be supported.

18.5 "Preferences" and Ratings

The picture of a chooser that has been presented in this chapter is that of a person who *makes choices* by applying one or more of the ASPECT choice patterns, a process that can be supported through application of one or more of the ARCADE choice support strategies, which can in turn involve the use of recommendation technology. A rather different conception, which is often expressed (mostly implicitly) in the recommender systems field and in economics and other areas (see, e.g., [33]), is that of a chooser who *has preferences* which determine what she chooses. According to this conception, the goal of a recommender system is to acquire information about the chooser's preferences so as to be able to create a *preference model* that can be used to predict what the chooser will like. To understand the relationship between these two conceptions, we need to understand what the term *preferences* refers to.

18.5.1 What Are "Preferences"?

The term *preferences* is used in a variety of senses in the recommender systems field to refer to something like the things in the chooser's head that determine how he will evaluate particular things and what choices he will make. As a way of teasing apart some of the senses that the term can have, consider a chooser who is answering the questions shown in Table 18.2.

Question 1, about a *specific, relative* preference, is fairly straightforward: The chooser is in effect being asked which of the two dictionaries she would choose in the current situation if there were no other dictionaries available. In economics, it is often assumed that exactly these "stated preferences" are what best expresses

Table 18.2 Illustration of four different senses of the term *preferences*

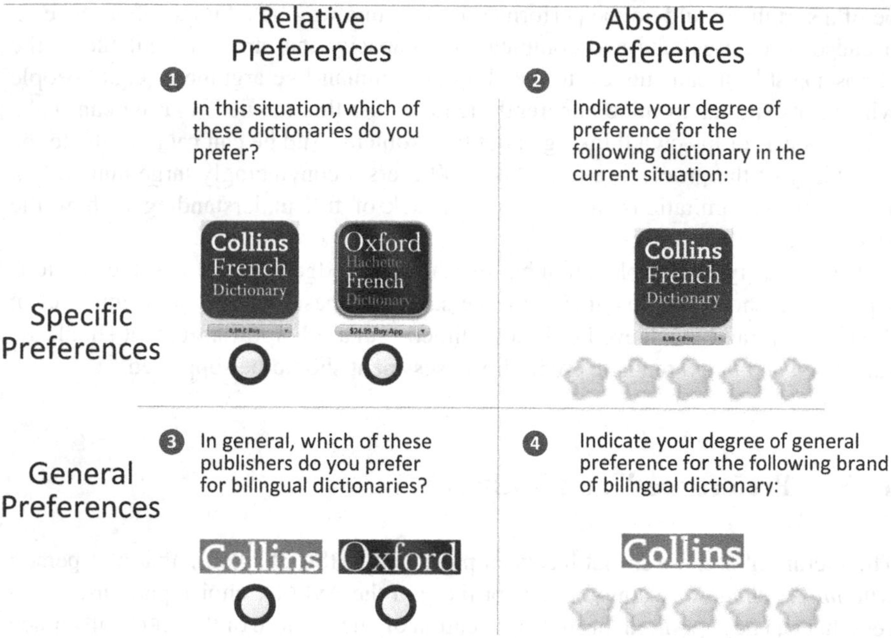

	Relative Preferences	Absolute Preferences
Specific Preferences	❶ In this situation, which of these dictionaries do you prefer? Collins French Dictionary / Oxford Hachette French Dictionary ($24.99 Buy App)	❷ Indicate your degree of preference for the following dictionary in the current situation: Collins French Dictionary
General Preferences	❸ In general, which of these publishers do you prefer for bilingual dictionaries? Collins / Oxford	❹ Indicate your degree of general preference for the following brand of bilingual dictionary: Collins

peoples likes and dislikes, and conjoint measurement methods [12] are used to build a general preference model from such specific choices.[10]

Question 2 differs from Question 1 in that it requires the chooser to express some sort of assessment of a dictionary independently of other dictionaries. Note that a chooser who answers Question 1 may or may not in any sense have made a separate evaluation of each of the dictionaries (See Sect. 18.3.3). For example, when applying the attribute-based pattern, the chooser may simply choose one dictionary because it seems better than the other one on the most important attribute. In this case, forcing the chooser to answer Question 2 would be to force him to produce assessments that he does not consider necessary for making his choice. Nevertheless, many recommender systems use such absolute specific preference statements, elicited as *ratings*, as input for creating a model to predict a chooser's choices and evaluations (see Sect. 18.5.2 below).

As is illustrated in the bottom row of Table 18.2, the term *preferences* is also often used to refer to (relative or absolute) evaluations that apply to categories or attributes of options, as opposed to specific options. Models in the recommender

[10] In the recommender systems field, relatively few attempts have been made to measure and model preferences in such a relative way, for example by using interfaces in which users rank a set of items; but see, for instance, the work of Boutilier and colleagues (e.g., [54]).

systems field, but also in fields such as economics and philosophy, often assume that people's specific preferences can be predicted and explained in terms of *general preferences*, though the latter can be conceptualized in many different ways. The relationship between general and specific preferences is complex, but the following points are relevant to our current discussion:

- The six ASPECT choice patterns cannot be reduced to straightforward processes of deriving specific preferences from general preferences (see Table 18.1 for a reminder of the typical steps of the patterns).
- Even when it is possible to induce a person to express a general preference by asking a question like those in the bottom row of Table 18.2, it cannot be assumed that the response corresponds to any previously existing predisposition that the person has (see, e.g., [26]).

Taken together, these points imply that we can avoid confusion by using the term *preferences*, if at all, only when referring to specific relative preferences. When we need a term to refer to the general predispositions that people have regarding a particular choice domain—for example, when we want to distinguish whether these predispositions change over time on the basis of experience (as in Sect. 18.7 below)—we can use the term *evaluation criteria*, which avoids most of the problems with the term *preferences*—as long as we remember that evaluation criteria can take very different forms depending on which choice pattern (or combination of choice patterns) is being applied.

Instead of saying that a recommender system models a chooser's preferences, we should say that it creates and uses a *preference model*, which we can define as a model that can be used to predict *specific preferences*. Preference models take different forms in different types of recommender system, and they do not necessarily describe anything like the "general preferences" illustrated in Table 18.2.

18.5.2 What Do Ratings Reflect?

Some widely adopted methods in recommender systems acquire input for their preference model by eliciting *ratings*, which are supposed to reflect people's absolute preferences for specific options (see the discussion of Table 18.2).

18.5.2.1 A Sketch of the Processing Underlying Ratings

Given the importance of ratings in the recommender systems field, it is important to have some idea of what goes on inside a person's head when she is asked to rate an item. There is no clear consensus on this question in relevant areas of psychology such as attitude research (see, e.g., [23, 29, 81]) and the measurement of "preferences" (see, e.g., [26, 43, 93]), but the following points would presumably be widely accepted:

Table 18.3 Types of association that can be evoked in a rater by an item *I* that is presented for rating, organized in terms of the corresponding ASPECT choice patterns

Choice pattern	Corresponding type(s) of association
Attribute-based	Levels of *I* on important attributes
Consequence-based	Consequences of dealing with *I*
Experience-based	Affective responses to, and stored evaluations of, *I* and/or similar options
Socially based	Social examples, advice, and perceived expectations relevant to *I*
Policy-based	Implications of policies relevant to *I*

An item *I* presented to a rater *R* will evoke various evaluation-relevant memories, beliefs, experiences, and affective responses (loosely called here *associations* for short), and the rating that *R* gives will be a summary of the overall positivity of these associations. As is shown in Table 18.3, these associations can be of different types, which can be organized according to the ASPECT choice patterns. As with the task of choosing, *R* will probably not be able to contemplate all possible relevant associations of these types; he may restrict himself to one or two of the ASPECT patterns and think selectively within each pattern (e.g., with a dictionary, thinking only of a relevant previous experience and a salient social example or two). Hence he can be seen as drawing a *sample* from the large set of possibly relevant associations. To express his rating on whatever scale is offered to him, he will choose the predefined scale value that seems best to summarize his sample; note that there is no obviously appropriate procedure for arriving at this summary, especially when different ASPECT patterns are being applied at the same time and the associations are diverse and maybe even contradictory (see, e.g., [18]).

A type of association that is of special importance is the *stored evaluation* that may be available if the rater has evaluated *I* in the past: Just as a person will often simply repeat previous choices, when rating an item *I* she will often just try to reproduce an evaluation of *I* that she has expressed in the past (see the entry for the experience-based pattern in Table 18.3). But even when *R* did evaluate *I* in the past, *R* may not actually retrieve a stored evaluation but rather infer (on the basis of associations that come to mind now) what her previous evaluation is likely to have been.

18.5.2.2 Implications for the Practice of Rating Elicitation

This picture of the activity of rating yields some implications concerning the ways in which it makes sense to elicit ratings:

1. It is not in general helpful to view a rating as reflecting a single, well-defined variable such as a degree of "liking" or "preference" that has a true value that is simply masked by "noise" that arises during the rating process

(e.g., because of the rater's inconsistent use of the rating scale).[11] Instead, the various samples of associations that a rater may summarize at different times can be viewed as the reflections of different *perspectives* on the item which arise under different conditions. As an analogy, note that a building (e.g., the White House) can look quite different when photographed from different angles; no single photograph, no matter how carefully taken, reflects or even approximates the "true appearance" of the building.

2. Which particular perspective the rater takes can depend on various factors, such as the following:

   - What specific question is asked (e.g., "How have you enjoyed your experience with the product so far?" vs. "How do you expect to enjoy the product from now on?") or how *R* interprets an unspecific question (e.g., "How do you rate the product?").
   - Other aspects of the way in which the rating is elicited, such as the rating questions that were asked previously [77] and reference points that are provided [1, 19, 65].
   - Other contextual factors that tend to increase attention to particular associations, such as the rater's current mood or recent experiences.
   - The temporal relationship between the rating event and the experience of the item. For example, Bollen et al. [6] showed that as the time between viewing a movie and rating it increases, movie ratings seem to regress toward the middle of the scale.

3. Although there is in general no single "true" perspective, some perspectives will in general be more *relevant* than others in view of the goal of the recommender system. For example, if the system's goal is to predict which meal a user is likely to be satisfied with immediately after eating it, then ratings of other meals that have been elicited immediately after consumption will be more relevant than ratings elicited the next day; and vice versa. Hence a way to go about structuring the rating situation is as follows:

   1. Imagine a user who has chosen and dealt with a recommended item *I*, and consider from what perspective you would like him to rate *I* in order to give you maximal information about whether the recommendation was successful.
   2. Try to create a rating situation now that is as similar as possible to that post hoc rating situation.

[11] See [2, 77] and [35] for discussions of rating noise.

18.6 Combating Choice Overload

As was noted in Sect. 18.2.1, one frequent function of recommender systems is to help the chooser to winnow a large option space down to a manageable consideration set. Recommender systems are especially well suited to this task, since they have more computational power than humans for dealing with very large item sets and can therefore mitigate the frequently discussed problem of *choice overload*. It is worthwhile to understand this problem so as to be able to think more precisely about how a recommender system can aim to mitigate it.

In the psychological literature, it is often argued that larger assortments offer important advantages for consumers (see, e.g., [15, 78]), as they make it more likely that the consumer will find a highly satisfactory option. Unfortunately, these benefits seem to occur mainly for choosers who have relatively stable and precise evaluation criteria [15] that enable them to identify especially suitable options quickly.

Choosers without such evaluation criteria—for example, consumers who are unfamiliar with the domain in question—can experience *choice overload* with a larger item set[12]: They may invest an inordinate amount of time in choosing, experience frustration, find it hard to justify any particular choice, and ultimately decide not to make a choice at all.

The most straightforward way for a recommender system to help is by applying the ARCADE strategy *Evaluate on Behalf of the Chooser* to take over from the chooser the subtask of winnowing a large set of options down to a consideration set which is so small that choice overload cannot arise. Even if this consideration set omits some of the options that the chooser would value highly, this drawback may be outweighed by the benefits of avoiding choice overload. For example, Bollen et al. [7] found that people were just as satisfied with choosing from a set of 5 recommendations as from a set of 20 recommendations, because the increased attractiveness and variety of the larger item set was counteracted by the increased choice difficulty.

If the recommender system designer for some reason does not want to have the system provide such a small consideration set, how can choice overload be combated? Possible remedies in this case are suggested by some of the specific factors that have been identified as contributing to choice overload (e.g., in the meta-analysis of 50 studies of Scheibehenne et al. [78]), which include the similarity and density of the items in the option set [22], the extent to which the option set is categorized [63], and individual characteristics such as a chooser's expertise and her tendency to *maximize* (i.e., look for the best possible option) or *satisfice* (i.e, be satisfied with an adequate option; see [80]). In contrast to the nonpersonalized option sets typically used in these studies, recommender systems can control many of these factors, applying one or more of the ARCADE strategies. For example,

[12]The most widely recounted—and most often overinterpreted—example of choice overload is the "jam study" of Iyengar and Lepper [38].

to combat the problem of high density, the recommender system can ensure a certain amount of diversity in the consideration set ([94] and Chap. 26). Or applying the strategy *Represent the Choice Situation*, the recommender system can arrange the consideration set in such a way that the options are clearly categorized and structured (e.g., divided into groups according to important attributes, possibly in a personalized way). Following the example of Schwartz [79, p. 231], the recommender system could apply the strategy *Advise About Processing*, recommending that choosers should adopt the standards of a satisficer rather than a maximizer.[13]

In sum, the problem of choice overload constitutes one of the justifications for the existence of recommender systems; but combating the problem effectively can require a variety of tactics based on a good understanding of the problem.

18.7 Supporting Trial and Error

It is sometimes useful to view a recommender system as supporting the trial-and-error-based choice pattern (Sect. 18.2.6). Examples of such situations are the following:

- In critique-based recommendation (see, e.g., the survey by McGinty and Reilly [62] and the further references below), the system presents one or more options, the chooser gives some sort of feedback on them, the system presents one or more further options, and so on until the chooser has found a satisfactory option.
- In systems that are explicitly designed to support exploration of unfamiliar options (e.g., some music recommender systems; see, e.g., [13]), the recommendations are most naturally seen as a way of encouraging the chooser to try out something new, even if the probability is not particularly high that the chooser will actually like it (see Chap. 26 for comments on the goal of helping users to discover new interests).

As was mentioned in Sect. 18.2.6, "trying out" an option may involve simply acquiring some more information about it than that chooser had initially (as is typical of critique-based recommender systems), but it can also involve fully experiencing the option (as is more typical of the second case).

The question of how a recommender system can support trial and error is conceptually tricky, because the relevant situations can differ along two dimensions:

1. Whether the chooser's evaluation criteria (in the sense defined in Sect. 18.5.1) are *stable* or *evolving*:
    - *Stable evaluation criteria:* The chooser's evaluation criteria cannot be expected to change significantly on the basis of the trials and their results.

[13]This sort of advice might be given selectively only to choosers who had been identified as likely maximizers with the help of one of the relevant testing scales [64, 80].

- *Evolving evaluation criteria:* The chooser's evaluations and choices can be expected to change systematically over time as the chooser gains more experience with the choice domain.
  For example, the chooser may become aware of important attributes and consequences that he was not previously aware of; he may acquire experience with particular options that influence his future experienced-based choices; or he may arrive at a new policy for making this type of choice. More fundamentally, his tastes and abilities may change.

2. Whether the recommender system attempts to improve its preference model (as defined in Sect. 18.5.1)
   - *No improvement of preference model:* The recommender system does *not* aim to improve its preference model by learning from the results of the chooser's observed responses to the results of her trials.
   - *Improvement of preference model:* The recommender system does aim to improve its preference model in this way.

18.7.1 Trial and Error with Stable Evaluation Criteria

When the chooser's evaluation criteria are *stable*, trial and error makes sense when the way in which the options are presented does not make it possible straightforwardly to identify a suitable option without acquiring further experience or information about one or more options. As was mentioned in Sect. 18.2.6, one main challenge facing the chooser concerns the choice of an (implicit or explicit) exploration strategy, which determines at each point which option(s) should be tried out next. Possible desiderata of an exploration strategy include (a) a tendency to lead the chooser to a satisfactory solution quickly and with little effort; (b) a tendency to yield a highly satisfactory outcome; and (c) a positive experience during the process of trial and error itself (see the discussion in Sect. 18.2.8 of the desiderata of choice processes in general). Since it is unlikely to be obvious which of these desiderata are most important to a given chooser, the question of how to recommend or support an exploration strategy is a challenging one for recommender system researchers.

In connection with systems that are not necessarily trying to improve their preference model, some research has looked at ways of helping choosers to arrive quickly at a satisfactory option. One general strategy applied by many critique-based systems (see, e.g., [21, 71]) is to provide a number of examples at once for the chooser to consider, so as to increase the likelihood that at least one of the presented options is found to represent a step in a good direction. A different approach that is completely infeasible for unaided choosers was introduced by McCarthy et al. [61] (and extended by Mandl and Felfernig [56]): Their critique-based recommender system compares the current chooser's critiquing history with the histories of previous choosers to identify previous choosers with similar histories; then it tries to recommend an item that has tended ultimately to be chosen by those previous choosers.

In the case where improvement of the preference model is desired, an additional goal is to have the chooser try out options that will yield informative feedback from the chooser, which is a form of *active learning* on the part of the recommender system (see Chap. 24). One of the earliest recommender systems that explicitly attempted to achieve this goal was the AUTOMATED TRAVEL ASSISTANT of Linden et al. [52], which sometimes proposed flights mainly because they seemed likely to elicit informative reactions from the chooser. An example of a more recent effort in the context of conversational recommender systems is the method presented by Viappiani and Boutilier [90], which tends to generate a diverse set of recommendations that is likely to contain suitable items for a wide range of evaluation criteria.

18.7.2 Trial and Error with Evolving Evaluation Criteria

When the chooser's evaluation criteria are *evolving*, there is an additional desideratum of an exploration strategy: that it should tend to yield information and experience that will cause the chooser's evaluation criteria to evolve in a desirable way. One complication is that there are various types of evolution of evaluation criteria that may be "desirable" from the chooser's point of view. For example, he may want to acquire new tastes, or he may aim to learn more reliable criteria for choosing options that he will find satisfactory according to his current tastes.

One general approach is to ensure that the chooser is repeatedly confronted with a broad variety of options, so that no a priori limits are placed on the evolution of her evaluation criteria. Hence this scenario provides yet another reason to consider diversity of recommendations as a desirable quality of recommendation lists (see Chap. 26).

A more specific strategy, introduced in the context of a critiquing system by McCarthy et al. [60] (see also Pu and Chen [72, pp. 96–98]), is to present pairs of recommendations each of which clearly illustrates a trade-off between two dimensions (e.g., the price and resolution of a digital camera); the chooser can then contemplate these examples to get a better idea of how he wants to handle such trade-offs.

18.8 Dealing with Potentially Distorting Influences on Choice Processes

Even when a recommender system reduces an initially large item set to a much more manageable consideration set, it usually does leave it to the chooser to make the final selection from this set (see Sect. 18.2.1). Research has shown repeatedly that the processing in this phase can depend on specific relationships among the options that are presented and on the exact way in which they are presented—often in ways that people are not aware of and would not acknowledge as being relevant.

For basic research on human choice, these effects are of interest in that they generate criteria for choosing among competing theories of unobservable choice processes (see, e.g., [76] and [5]). For those who work on recommender systems, these effects have practical significance in that they warn the system designer of unobvious drawbacks and benefits of particular ways of presenting options [57]. That is, a recommender system designer can apply the ARCADE strategy *Represent the Choice Situation* taking these effects into account when determining how options will be presented.

18.8.1 Context Effects

As an example of the class of *context effects*, we will first consider one that has especially clear practical implications for recommender systems: the *decoy effect* (or *asymmetric dominance* effect; see, e.g., [37]). Consider, for example, the choice alternatives shown in Table 18.4, which presents important attributes of monthly subscription plans to a mobile internet provider. If only the options A and B were available, some customers would choose A because of its higher download limit, while others would choose B because of its lower price. But suppose now that the third option D is introduced: This option is *dominated* by A: It is inferior with regard to both price and download limit. D is not, however, dominated by B. Hence the introduction of D introduces an asymmetry between A and B that is favorable to A: In essence, A looks good because it dominates something, whereas B doesn't dominate anything. In a situation where the chooser lacks predetermined, precise evaluation criteria and a predetermined choice strategy, this sort of consideration can be enough to influence the choice of some consumers. And indeed, empirical results (see, e.g., [37]) show that A will tend to be chosen more often once D has been introduced.

Marketers can and do introduce decoys in this way as a subtle way of promoting particular products. For the recommender system designer who is interested in supporting choice rather than influencing it in a particular direction, decoys are more naturally viewed as a sort of noise that ought to be avoided where it is feasible to do so. For example, a recommender system might, before presenting a set of options for

Table 18.4 Example illustrating the decoy effect (The options being compared are monthly subscriptions to a mobile internet provider.)

Item	A	B	D
Price per month	30 euros	20 euros	35 euros
Download limit	10 GB	6 GB	9 GB

consideration, check whether any option is dominated by any other option according to evaluation criteria of the sort that users are likely to have; and if so leave it out of the consideration set.

An analysis of decoy effects in financial service recommendation is presented by Teppan et al. [86], where decoy effects are documented in the context of real-world financial services. In a study of users' choice behavior when interacting with e-tourism recommenders, Teppan and Felfernig [84] showed that decoy effects are positively correlated with the chooser's decision confidence. Further potential impacts of decoy effects are the increased selection share of a target product and willingness to buy ([41, Sect. 10.2], [57]). An approach to minimizing decoy effects in attribute-based decision making is presented in [85]. Felfernig et al. [25] present a model that supports the identification of suitable decoy products by a recommender system that uses decoys for persuasive purposes.

Another type of context effect that has a similar sort of relevance to recommender systems design is the *compromise effect*: In situations such as the one considered in our examples so far, an option tends to be viewed relatively favorably if it can be seen as a compromise between two other options that are available at the same time. For example, in Table 18.5 the likelihood of choosing *A* over *B* is increased if *D* is added to the choice set. This effect tends to be stronger if the chooser expects to have to justify her decision to other persons [82], which is understandable in that the fact that a given option represents a compromise can be used as a justification (see Sect. 18.2.8).

Further discussion of context effects and their implications for recommender systems is provided in [41, Sect. 10.2].

18.8.2 Order Effects

Another relevant aspect of a representation of a choice situation is the order in which options—or types of information about options—are presented to the chooser. The order can have an effect for various different reasons:

1. There is often a general assumption on the part of the chooser that the most relevant and important information will be presented first: In particular, lists of recommendations and search results are typically ordered in this way.
2. Partly as a consequence of the first point, a chooser will often process options and other information in the order in which he encounters them. The order of processing might not be so important if the chooser exhaustively considered all available options and information. But in general a chooser will process

Table 18.5 Example illustrating the compromise effect

Item	*A*	*B*	*D*
Price per month	30 euros	20 euros	55 euros
Download limit	10 GB	6 GB	16 GB

information selectively, and it is easiest for him to do so in the order in which he encounters it. For example, a processing strategy that has been studied especially in connection with attribute-based and trial-and-error-based choice is *satisficing*: The chooser considers options one at a time until he has found one that seems satisfactory; at that point, he stops, even if he is aware that a better option might be found with additional effort (see, e.g., Payne et al. [66, Chap. 2]).

3. In cases where the chooser needs to store information in memory—for either a short time or a longer time—the *primacy* and *recency* effects that are found with both short- and long-term memory become relevant (see, e.g., [50, Chap. 8]). Hence presenting important information in the middle of a sequence makes it less likely to be remembered (see [24] for an examination of this phenomenon in a recommender system context).

18.8.3 Framing Effects

The importance of how a choice situation is represented has also been underscored by research on *framing effects*. Levin et al. [48] introduced an influential distinction between three categories of framing effect, which apply to different aspects of information presentation and which are associated with different explanations in terms of cognitive processes:

Attribute framing, which is most directly relevant to the attribute-based choice pattern, concerns the fact that an option's level of a particular attribute can often be described in either positive or negative terms; even if the information conveyed is exactly the same, the positive formulation tends to evoke a more positive evaluation of the option with respect to that attribute. To mention the best-known example: Beef described as being "75 % lean" was evaluated more positively than beef described as being "25 % fat" [47]. Analogous effects can be found within the consequence-based pattern. For example, a financial service with a 95 % probability of yielding a gain will typically be evaluated better than a service with a 5 % probability of yielding a loss.

Where the goal is to have a recommender system present options with minimal bias, one simple design strategy is to use the same type of framing (positive or negative) for all options that are being presented.

Analogous strategies can be applied to the other two types of framing distinguished by Levin et al. [48]: *risky choice framing* and *goal framing*. These types are relevant to the consequence-based pattern; they concern the effect of the way in which the anticipated consequences of performing particular actions are characterized in terms of gains or losses.

18.8.4 Priming Effects

A priming effect is found when exposure to some stimulus, called a *prime*, increases the accessibility of information already existing in memory [55]; this change in information accessibility in turn influences the way in which a person responds to a stimulus or task. Priming effects have been found in various areas of psychology; examples of practical relevance for recommender systems include the following:

1. In a widely cited study, Mandel and Johnson [55] showed that different web page backgrounds (e.g., clouds vs. coins) in an online store influenced the chooser's choices regarding the products offered for sale—even when the chooser had considerable experience in the product domain in question. Evidently, for example, the exposure to coins primed the choosers to attach more weight to the "price" attribute—though only about 14 % of participants acknowledged after the study that their choices might have been influenced by the web page background.
2. In a study by Haeubl and Murray [31], participants were first asked questions about different attributes of tents (e.g., durability, weight) and then asked to choose a tent from a given set. Participants tended (implicitly) to assign more weight to the attributes that they had been asked about.

The implications of results like these for recommender system designers who aim to support choice are less obvious than the implications for marketers. As with the other effects considered so far in this section, one strategy is to try to avoid the presentation of primes that introduce systematic distortion. A more active strategy is to deploy primes in a way that appears to be consistent with what the system knows about the chooser's evaluation criteria. For example, if the system has somehow determined that the chooser attaches high value to safety as an attribute of cars, the recommender can not only recommend safe cars and provide information about their safety but also adaptively use primes to increase the chooser's attention to safety. In fact, the system is likely to provide such primes even without any conscious effort by the designer to do so: The mere fact that information about safety is being presented can serve as a prime for the attribute of safety even if the chooser does not pay attention to the details of the information provided.

18.8.5 Defaults

Yet another surprisingly influential factor is whether a particular option constitutes the *default* option for the choice in question—that is, the option that will be executed if the chooser does nothing. There are various ways in which an option can constitute the default, and there are various reasons why choosers can be inclined to choose the default option:

1. Sometimes, the chooser is not even aware that there is a choice that she could make, as in the case of a configuration setting for a complex application that can

be changed only in a screen that the user is not aware of. In this case, the user does not choose the default option, but it in effect gets chosen anyway.

2. In other cases, the chooser sees that he has a choice and that one option is designated as the default. Here, there can be two possible reasons for being inclined to choose the default option:
   - The chooser may assume that this option is one that is in some sense recommended. This assumption is often—though not always—reasonable in view of efforts made by the system's designers to ensure that the default option is at least acceptable whenever it is chosen—efforts that these designers in turn often make because they know that the default is likely to be chosen.
   - It may simply be physically and/or mentally easier for the user to choose the default option (e.g., because no mouse clicks or text input are required; see, e.g., [58]).

The important role of the default option represents an opportunity for designers of recommender systems: One function of a recommender system can be to determine automatically which option ought to be the default for a given user in a given situation (see, e.g., [57, 88]); defaults determined in this way are sometimes called *dynamic defaults*.

Whether the default is determined dynamically or not, recommender systems designers should take into account, when designing for a particular choice situation, which option (if any) will serve as the default and which factors might cause users to be inclined to choose it. The designer can then determine whether these effects are consistent with the overall intent and strategy of the recommender system. In particular, if the overall intent is to keep the chooser tightly in the loop and have her explicitly approve the choice that is finally made, the designer may want to minimize the use of defaults; conversely, defaults can be a useful tool for reducing the need for the chooser to remain involved in the choice process.

18.9 Recapitulation and Concluding Remarks

The field of recommender systems has been exciting and successful. But what will recommender systems people be doing 20 years from now? The possibilities for improving algorithms technically may be unlimited; but if the algorithms continue to be applied to the same problems, there is a limit to what can be achieved. We therefore also need new ideas about how recommendation technology can be put to good use.

We hope to have shown in this chapter that such ideas can come from an unexpected source: the psychology of choice and choice support. By looking systematically at the diverse ways in which people make everyday choices, we identified a number of novel ways in which recommender systems can support these processes; and imaginative readers will be able to think of many more. While systematically viewing recommendation as essentially one of six high-level strategies for choice support, we saw new ways in which recommendation technology can be combined with applications of other choice support strategies. In the rest of the chapter, we showed that a number of familiar concepts and topics in the recommender systems field—explaining recommendations, eliciting "preferences", preventing information overload, supporting exploration, and appropriately presenting small numbers of recommended options—look quite different, and even more interesting, when viewed through the prism of an understanding of choice and choice support.

We therefore hope that this chapter will be found stimulating not only by readers interested in the psychology of choice but even more by those who are looking for new and powerful ways to apply recommendation technology.

Acknowledgements The preparation of this chapter benefited from a series of initiatives that have taken place since 2011 under titles similar to the title of this chapter: workshops at the conferences UMAP 2011[14] and ACM RecSys 2011,[15] 2012,[16] 2013,[17] and 2014[18]; a special issue of the ACM Transactions on Interactive Intelligent Systems [14]; and a workshop in September of 2014 at the University of Bolzano.[19]

References

1. Adomavicius, G., Bockstedt, J., Curley, S., Zhang, J.: Recommender systems, consumer preferences, and anchoring effects. In: Proceedings of the Workshop Decisions@RecSys, in Conjunction with the Fourth ACM Conference on Recommender Systems, pp. 35–42. Chicago (2011)
2. Amatriain, X., Pujol, J., Oliver, N.: I like it ... I like it not: Evaluating user ratings noise in recommender systems. In: G.J. Houben, G. McCalla, F. Pianesi, M. Zancanaro (eds.) Proceedings of the Seventeenth International Conference on User Modeling, Adaptation, and Personalization, pp. 247–258. Springer, Heidelberg (2009)
3. Betsch, T., Haberstroh, S. (eds.): The Routines of Decision Making. Erlbaum, Mahwah, NJ (2005)
4. Bettman, J., Luce, M.F., Payne, J.: Constructive consumer choice processes. Journal of Consumer Research **25**, 187–217 (1998)
5. Bhatia, S.: Associations and the accumulation of preference. Psychological Review **120**(3), 522–543 (2013)
6. Bollen, D., Graus, M., Willemsen, M.: Remembering the stars? Effect of time on preference retrieval from memory. In: P. Cunningham, N. Hurley, I. Guy, S.S. Anand (eds.) Proceedings of the Sixth ACM Conference on Recommender Systems, pp. 217–220. ACM, New York (2012)

[14] http://www.di.uniba.it/~swap/DM.

[15] http://recex.ist.tugraz.at:8080/RecSysWorkshop2011/.

[16] http://recex.ist.tugraz.at/RecSysWorkshop2012.

[17] http://recex.ist.tugraz.at/RecSysWorkshop/.

[18] http://recex.ist.tugraz.at/intrs2014/.

[19] http://dmrsworkshop.inf.unibz.it.

7. Bollen, D., Knijnenburg, B., Willemsen, M., Graus, M.: Understanding choice overload in recommender systems. In: X. Amatriain, M. Torrens, P. Resnick, M. Zanker (eds.) Proceedings of the Fourth ACM Conference on Recommender Systems, pp. 63–70. ACM, New York (2010)
8. Bonaccio, S., Dalal, R.: Advice taking and decision-making: An integrative literature review, and implications for the organizational sciences. Organizational Behavior and Human Decision Processes **101**, 127–151 (2006)
9. Burke, R.: Hybrid recommender systems: Survey and experiments. User Modeling and User-Adapted Interaction **12**(4), 331–370 (2002)
10. Burke, R.: Hybrid web recommender systems. In: P. Brusilovsky, A. Kobsa, W. Nejdl (eds.) The Adaptive Web: Methods and Strategies of Web Personalization, pp. 377–408. Springer, Berlin (2007)
11. Camerer, C., Babcock, L., Loewenstein, G., Thaler, R.: Labor supply of New York City cab drivers: One day at a time. In: D. Kahneman, A. Tversky (eds.) Choices, Values, and Frames. Cambridge University Press, Cambridge, UK (2000)
12. Carson, R., Louviere, J.: A common nomenclature for stated preference elicitation approaches. Environmental and Resource Economics **49**(4), 539–559 (2011)
13. Celma Herrada, O.: Music Recommendation and Discovery in the Long Tail (2008). PhD Thesis, University of Barcelona
14. Chen, L., de Gemmis, M., Felfernig, A., Lops, P., Ricci, F., Semeraro, G.: Human decision making and recommender systems. ACM Transactions on Interactive Intelligent Systems **3**(3) (2013)
15. Chernev, A.: When more is less and less is more: The role of ideal point availability and assortment in consumer choice. Journal of Consumer Research **30**(2), 170–183 (2003)
16. Cialdini, R.: Influence: The Psychology of Persuasion. HarperCollins, New York (2007)
17. Cohen, J., McClure, S., Yu, A.: Should I stay or should I go? How the human brain manages the trade-off between exploitation and exploration. Philosophical Transactions of the Royal Society **362**, 933–942 (2007)
18. Conner, M., Armitage, C.: Attitudinal ambivalence. In: W. Crano, R. Prislin (eds.) Attitudes and Attitude Change. Psychology Press, New York (2008)
19. Cosley, D., Lam, S., Albert, I., Konstan, J., Riedl, J.: Is seeing believing? How recommender systems influence users' opinions. In: L. Terveen, D. Wixon, E. Comstock, A. Sasse (eds.) Human Factors in Computing Systems: CHI 2003 Conference Proceedings, pp. 585–592. ACM, New York (2003)
20. Edwards, W., Fasolo, B.: Decision technology. Annual Review of Psychology **52**, 581–606 (2001)
21. Faltings, B., Torrens, M., Pu, P.: Solution generation with qualitative models of preferences. Computational Intelligence **20**(2), 246–263 (2004)
22. Fasolo, B., Hertwig, R., Huber, M., Ludwig, M.: Size, entropy, and density: What is the difference that makes the difference between small and large real-world assortments? Psychology and Marketing **26**(3), 254–279 (2009)
23. Fazio, R.: Attitudes as object-evaluation associations of varying strength. Social Cognition **25**(5), 603–637 (2007)
24. Felfernig, A., Friedrich, G., Gula, B., Hitz, M., Kruggel, T., Melcher, R., Riepan, D., Strauss, S., Teppan, E., Vitouch, O.: Persuasive recommendation: Exploring serial position effects in knowledge-based recommender systems. In: Y. de Kort, W. IJsselsteijn, C. Midden, B. Eggen, B. Fogg (eds.) Proceedings of the Second International Conference on Persuasive Technology, pp. 283–294. Springer, Heidelberg (2007)
25. Felfernig, A., Gula, B., Leitner, G., Maier, M., Melcher, R., Schippel, S., Teppan, E.: A dominance model for the calculation of decoy products in recommendation environments. In: AISB Symposium on Persuasive Technologies, pp. 43–50 (2008)
26. Fischhoff, B.: Value elicitation: Is there anything in there? American Psychologist **46**(8), 835–847 (1991)
27. Fishbein, M., Ajzen, I.: Predicting and Changing Behavior: The Reasoned Action Approach. Taylor & Francis, New York (2010)

28. French, S., Maule, J., Papamichail, N.: Decision Behaviour, Analysis, and Support. Cambridge University Press, Cambridge, UK (2009)
29. Gawronski, B., Bodenhausen, G.: Unraveling the processes underlying evaluation: Attitudes from the perspective of the APE model. Social Cognition **25**(5), 687–717 (2007)
30. Gigerenzer, G.: Gut Feelings: The Intelligence of the Unconscious. Penguin, London (2007)
31. Haeubl, G., Murray, K.: Preference construction and persistence in digital marketplace: The role of electronic recommendation agents. Journal of Consumer Psychology **13**, 75–91 (2003)
32. Hastie, R.: Problems for judgment and decision making. Annual Review of Psychology **52**, 653–683 (2001)
33. Hausman, D.: Preference, Value, Choice, and Welfare. Cambridge University Press, Cambridge, UK (2012)
34. Herlocker, J., Konstan, J., Riedl, J.: Explaining collaborative filtering recommendations. In: P. Dourish, S. Kiesler (eds.) Proceedings of the 2000 Conference on Computer-Supported Cooperative Work. ACM, New York (2000)
35. Herlocker, J., Konstan, J., Terveen, L., Riedl, J.: Evaluating collaborative filtering recommender systems. ACM Transactions on Information Systems **22**(1), 5–53 (2004)
36. Hsee, C.: Attribute evaluability: Its implications for joint-separate evaluation reversals and beyond. In: D. Kahneman, A. Tversky (eds.) Choices, Values, and Frames. Cambridge University Press, Cambridge, UK (2000)
37. Huber, J., Payne, W., Puto, C.: Adding asymmetrically dominated alternatives: Violations of regularity and the similarity hypothesis. Journal of Consumer Research **9**, 90–98 (1982)
38. Iyengar, S., Lepper, M.: When choice is demotivating: Can one desire too much of a good thing? Journal of Personality and Social Psychology **79**, 995–1006 (2000)
39. Jameson, A., Berendt, B., Gabrielli, S., Gena, C., Cena, F., Vernero, F., Reinecke, K.: Choice architecture for human-computer interaction. Foundations and Trends in Human-Computer Interaction **7**(1–2), 1–235 (2014)
40. Jameson, A., Gajos, K.: Systems that adapt to their users. In: J. Jacko (ed.) The Human-Computer Interaction Handbook: Fundamentals, Evolving Technologies and Emerging Applications, 3rd edn. CRC Press, Boca Raton, FL (2012)
41. Jannach, D., Zanker, M., Felfernig, A., Friedrich, G.: Recommender Systems: An Introduction. Cambridge, Cambridge, UK (2011)
42. Jungermann, H., Fischer, K.: Using expertise and experience for giving and taking advice. In: T. Betsch, S. Haberstroh (eds.) The Routines of Decision Making. Erlbaum, Mahwah, NJ (2005)
43. Kahneman, D., Ritov, I., Schkade, D.: Economic preferences or attitude expressions? an analysis of dollar responses to public issues. Journal of Risk and Uncertainty **19**, 203–235 (1999)
44. Kahneman, D., Tversky, A.: Prospect theory: An analysis of decision under risk. Econometrica **47**(2), 263–295 (1979)
45. Klein, G.: Sources of Power: How People Make Decisions. MIT Press, Cambridge, MA (1998)
46. Knijnenburg, B., Reijmer, N., Willemsen, M.: Each to his own: How different users call for different interaction methods in recommender systems. In: B. Mobasher, R. Burke, D. Jannach, G. Adomavicius (eds.) Proceedings of the Fifth ACM Conference on Recommender Systems. ACM, New York (2011)
47. Levin, I., Gaeth, G.: How consumers are affected by the framing of attribute information before and after consuming the product. Journal of Consumer Research **15**, 374–379 (1988)
48. Levin, I., Schneider, S., Gaeth, G.: All frames are not created equal: A typology and critical analysis of framing effects. Organizational Behavior and Human Decision Processes **76**, 90–98 (1998)
49. Li, W., Matejka, J., Grossman, T., Konstan, J., Fitzmaurice, G.: Design and evaluation of a command recommendation system for software applications. ACM Transactions on Computer-Human Interaction **18**(2) (2011)
50. Lieberman, D.: Human Learning and Memory. Cambridge University Press, Cambridge, UK (2012)

51. Lindblom, C.: Still muddling, not yet through. Public Administration Review **39**(6), 517–526 (1979)
52. Linden, G., Hanks, S., Lesh, N.: Interactive assessment of user preference models: The automated travel assistant. In: A. Jameson, C. Paris, C. Tasso (eds.) User Modeling: Proceedings of the Sixth International Conference, UM97, pp. 67–78. Springer Wien New York, Vienna (1997)
53. Lops, P., de Gemmis, M., Semeraro, G.: Content-based recommender systems: State of the art and trends. In: F. Ricci, L. Rokach, B. Shapira, P. Kantor (eds.) Recommender Systems Handbook, pp. 73–105. Springer, Berlin (2011)
54. Lu, T., Boutilier, C.: Learning Mallows models with pairwise preferences. In: L. Getoor, T. Scheffer (eds.) Proceedings of the 28th International Conference on Machine Learning, pp. 145–152. ACM, New York (2011)
55. Mandel, N., Johnson, E.: When web pages influence choice: Effects of visual primes on experts and novices. Journal of Consumer Research **29**, 235–245 (2002)
56. Mandl, M., Felfernig, A.: Improving the performance of unit critiquing. In: J. Masthoff, B. Mobasher, M. Desmarais, R. Nkambou (eds.) Proceedings of the Twentieth International Conference on User Modeling, Adaptation, and Personalization, pp. 176–187. Springer, Heidelberg (2012)
57. Mandl, M., Felfernig, A., Teppan, E., Schubert, M.: Consumer decision making in knowledge-based recommendation. Journal of Intelligent Information Systems **37**(1), 1–22 (2010)
58. Mandl, M., Felfernig, A., Tiihonen, J., Isak, K.: Status quo bias in configuration systems. In: Twenty-Fourth International Conference on Industrial, Engineering and Other Applications of Applied Intelligent Systems, pp. 105–114. Syracuse, New York (2011)
59. March, J.: A Primer on Decision Making: How Decisions Happen. The Free Press, New York (1994)
60. McCarthy, K., Reilly, J., McGinty, L., Smyth, B.: Experiments in dynamic critiquing. In: J. Riedl, A. Jameson, D. Billsus, T. Lau (eds.) IUI 2005: International Conference on Intelligent User Interfaces, pp. 175–182. ACM, New York (2005)
61. McCarthy, K., Salem, Y., Smyth, B.: Experience-based critiquing: Reusing critiquing experiences to improve conversational recommendation. In: I. Bichindaritz, S. Montani (eds.) Case-Based Reasoning Research and Development: Proceedings of ICCBR 2010, pp. 480–494. Springer, Berlin, Heidelberg (2010)
62. McGinty, L., Reilly, J.: On the evolution of critiquing recommenders. In: F. Ricci, L. Rokach, B. Shapira, P. Kantor (eds.) Recommender Systems Handbook, pp. 419–453. Springer, Berlin (2011)
63. Mogilner, C., Rudnick, T., Iyengar, S.: The mere categorization effect: How the presence of categories increases choosers' perceptions of assortment variety and outcome satisfaction. Journal of Consumer Research **35**(2), 202–215 (2008)
64. Nenkov, G., Morrin, M., Ward, A., Schwartz, B., Hulland, J.: A short form of the Maximization Scale: Factor structure, reliability and validity studies. Judgment and Decision Making **3**(5), 371–388 (2008)
65. Nguyen, T., Kluver, D., Wang, T.Y., Hui, P.M., Ekstrand, M., Willemsen, M., Riedl, J.: Rating support interfaces to improve user experience and recommender accuracy. In: Q. Yang, I. King, Q. Li, P. Pu, G. Karypis (eds.) Proceedings of the Seventh ACM Conference on Recommender Systems, pp. 149–156. ACM, New York (2013)
66. Payne, J., Bettman, J., Johnson, E.: The Adaptive Decision Maker. Cambridge University Press, Cambridge, UK (1993)
67. Pfeiffer, J.: Interactive Decision Aids in E-Commerce. Springer, Berlin (2012)
68. Pirolli, P.: Information Foraging Theory: Adaptive Interaction with Information. Oxford University Press, New York (2007)
69. Plate, C., Basselin, N., Kröner, A., Schneider, M., Baldes, S., Dimitrova, V., Jameson, A.: Recomindation: New functions for augmented memories. In: V. Wade, H. Ashman, B. Smyth (eds.) Adaptive Hypermedia and Adaptive Web-Based Systems: Proceedings of AH 2006, pp. 141–150. Springer, Berlin (2006)

70. Plessner, H., Betsch, C., Betsch, T. (eds.): Intuition in Judgement and Decision Making. Erlbaum, New York (2008)
71. Pu, P., Chen, L.: Integrating tradeoff support in product search tools for e-commerce sites. In: J. Riedl, M. Kearns, M. Reiter (eds.) Proceedings of the Sixth ACM Conference on Electronic Commerce, pp. 269–278. ACM, New York (2005)
72. Pu, P., Chen, L.: User-involved preference elicitation for product search and recommender systems. AI Magazine **29**(4), 93–103 (2008)
73. Rachlin, H.: The Science of Self-Control. Harvard, Cambridge, MA (2000)
74. Rakow, T., Newell, B.: Degrees of uncertainty: An overview and framework for future research on experience-based choice. Journal of Behavioral Decision Making **23**, 1–14 (2010)
75. Read, D., Loewenstein, G., Rabin, M.: Choice bracketing. Journal of Risk and Uncertainty **19**, 171–197 (1999)
76. Roe, R., Busemeyer, J., Townsend, J.: Multialternative decision field theory: A dynamic connectionist model of decision making. Psychological Review **108**(2), 370–392 (2001)
77. Said, A., Jain, B., Narr, S., Plumbaum, T.: Users and noise: The magic barrier of recommender systems. In: B. Masthoff Judith a., M.C. Desmarais, R. Nkambou (eds.) User Modeling, Adaptation, and Personalization, no. 7379 in Lecture Notes in Computer Science, pp. 237–248. Springer Berlin Heidelberg (2012)
78. Scheibehenne, B., Greifeneder, R., Todd, P.: Can there ever be too many options? A meta-analytic review of choice overload. Journal of Consumer Research **37**(3), 409–425 (2010)
79. Schwartz, B.: The Paradox of Choice: Why More Is Less. HarperCollins, New York (2004)
80. Schwartz, B., Ward, A., Monterosso, J., Lyubomirsky, S., White, K., Lehman, D.: Maximizing versus satisficing: Happiness is a matter of choice. Journal of Personality and Social Psychology **83**(5), 1178–1197 (2002)
81. Schwarz, N.: Attitude measurement. In: W. Crano, R. Prislin (eds.) Attitudes and Attitude Change, pp. 41–60. Psychology Press, New York (2008)
82. Simonson, I.: Choice based on reasons: The case of attraction and compromise effects. Journal of Consumer Research **16**(2), 158–174 (1989)
83. Smyth, B.: Case-based recommendation. In: P. Brusilovsky, A. Kobsa, W. Nejdl (eds.) The Adaptive Web: Methods and Strategies of Web Personalization, pp. 342–376. Springer, Berlin (2007)
84. Teppan, E., Felfernig, A.: The asymmetric dominance effect and its role in e-tourism recommender applications. In: Proceedings of the International Conference Wirtschaftsinformatik, pp. 791–800. Vienna (2009)
85. Teppan, E., Felfernig, A.: Minimization of product utility estimation errors in recommender result set evaluations. Web Intelligence and Agent Systems **10**(4), 385–395 (2012)
86. Teppan, E., Felfernig, A., Isak, K.: Decoy effects in financial service e-sales systems. In: Proceedings of the Workshop Decisions@RecSys, in Conjunction with the Fourth ACM Conference on Recommender Systems, pp. 1–8. Chicago (2011)
87. Thaler, R., Sunstein, C.: Nudge: Improving Decisions About Health, Wealth, and Happiness. Yale University Press, New Haven (2008)
88. Tiihonen, J., Felfernig, A.: Towards recommending configurable offerings. International Journal of Mass Customization **3**(4), 389–406 (2010)
89. Toulmin, S.: The Uses of Argument. Cambridge University Press, Cambridge, UK (1958)
90. Viappiani, P., Boutilier, C.: Regret-based optimal recommendation sets in conversational recommender systems. In: L. Bergman, A. Tuzhilin, R. Burke, A. Felfernig, L. Schmidt-Thieme (eds.) Proceedings of the Third ACM Conference on Recommender Systems, pp. 101–108. ACM, New York (2009)
91. Victor, P., Cock, M.D., Cornelis, C.: Trust and recommendations. In: F. Ricci, L. Rokach, B. Shapira, P. Kantor (eds.) Recommender Systems Handbook, pp. 645–675. Springer, Berlin (2011)
92. Wakker, P.: Prospect Theory for Risk and Ambiguity. Cambridge University Press, Cambridge, UK (2010)

93. Weber, E., Johnson, E.: Constructing preferences from memory. In: S. Lichtenstein, P. Slovic (eds.) The Construction of Preference. Cambridge University Press, Cambridge, UK (2006)
94. Willemsen, M., Knijnenburg, B., Graus, M., Velter-Bremmers, L., Fu, K.: Using latent features diversification to reduce choice difficulty in recommendation lists. In: Proceedings of the Second Workshop on User-Centric Evaluation of Recommender Systems and Their Interfaces, in Conjunction With the Fifth ACM Conference on Recommender Systems, *CEUR Workshop Proceedings*, vol. 811, pp. 14–20 (2011)
95. Wood, W., Neal, D.: A new look at habits and the habit-goal interface. Psychological Review **114**(4), 843–863 (2007)
96. Yates, J.F., Veinott, E., Patalano, A.: Hard decisions, bad decisions: On decision quality and decision aiding. In: S. Schneider, J. Shanteau (eds.) Emerging Perspectives on Judgment and Decision Research. Cambridge University Press, Cambridge, UK (2003)
97. Zwick, R., Rapoport, A., Lo, A.K., Muthukrishnan, A.: Consumer sequential search: Not enough or too much? Marketing Science **22**(4), 503–519 (2003)

Chapter 19
Privacy Aspects of Recommender Systems

Arik Friedman, Bart P. Knijnenburg, Kris Vanhecke, Luc Martens, and Shlomo Berkovsky

19.1 Introduction

The deluge of online products, services, and information has made recommender systems an inherent part of the Web realm. They are used in a variety of use cases and applications: from eCommerce sites, through the Social Web, to health mobile apps. The benefits of personalized recommendations, both for users and service providers, are numerous. However, they also bring to the fore some risks that may limit the uptake of recommenders, one of which is the risk of a privacy breach.

The privacy risk is mainly caused by the recommenders' need to collect and store personal information about their users. Indeed, in order to provide personalized recommendations, a recommender needs to possess some information about its users, encapsulated in user models. This information serves as the basis for generating the recommendations and, generally, the quality of the recommendations is correlated with the amount, richness, and freshness of the underlying user modeling data. On the other hand, the same factors drive the severity of the privacy risk and

The author contributed to this chapter while he was at the University of California, Irvine.

A. Friedman (✉)
NICTA, Sydney, NSW, Australia
e-mail: arik.friedman@nicta.com.au

B.P. Knijnenburg
Clemson University, Clemson, SC, USA
e-mail: bartk@clemson.edu

K. Vanhecke • L. Martens
iMinds - Ghent University, Ghent, Belgium
e-mail: kris.vanhecke@intec.ugent.be; luc.martens@intec.ugent.be

S. Berkovsky
CSIRO, Sydney, NSW, Australia
e-mail: shlomo.berkovsky@csiro.au

F. Ricci et al. (eds.), *Recommender Systems Handbook*,
DOI 10.1007/978-1-4899-7637-6_19

the damage that can be caused if the user modeling data is exposed to third parties. This is referred to as the *privacy-personalization trade-off* [10, 24, 37, 87, 98, 156], and it inevitably manifests once personalized recommendations are considered.

The privacy risks posed by personalization are aggravated when more sophisticated recommendation scenarios are deployed. For example, consider a recommender that, as part of the recommendation process, either augments its user models by extracting new features and populating their data, or cross-links multiple sources of user modeling data. In these scenarios, the recommender is likely to uncover additional information that was not readily accessible in the original user models, i.e., information that the users may not have consented to be released for the recommendation purposes. Having this information exposed and accessed by untrusted parties could lead to harmful consequences.

In this chapter we concentrate on the privacy challenge faced by recommender systems. We survey related work on privacy-enhanced recommenders and partition it into three broad categories. The first focuses on *architectures* that facilitate more private recommendations. These entail various decentralized solutions that eliminate a single repository of user modeling data, which would otherwise be the target for attacks on the recommender. The second category refers to *algorithmic* solutions, which either perturb the original user modeling data or apply formal encryption methods. These assure that, even if accessed by an untrusted party, only modified/encrypted user data would be exposed, rather than the original data. Lastly, the category of *policy* driven solutions addresses directives and legislation initiatives that limit the storage, transfer, and exploitation of personal user data. Clearly, these solutions are not mutually exclusive, and a recommender may—and often will—deploy solutions from multiple categories.

While these solutions may improve objective and measurable privacy aspects, an important question pertains to the users of the recommenders. They may have their own considerations regarding the sensitivity of their data, exposure/preservation of some information, and measures they are willing to take to protect their privacy [21]. Hence, users' perception of and reasoning about privacy deserves special attention. Therefore, we also discuss users' privacy attitudes and behaviors, as well as current practices and recent advances to support the users' privacy decision-making process.

This chapter is structured as follows. In Sect. 19.2 we give a broad definition of privacy and discuss the privacy risks faced by the users of recommender systems. In Sect. 19.3 we outline the three categories of solutions to these risks; namely, the architectural (Sect. 19.3.1), algorithmic (Sect. 19.3.2), and policy solutions (Sect. 19.3.3). We survey a number of papers implementing the solutions and summarize each category. In Sect. 19.4 we switch to the human aspects, and discuss users' perception of and attitude towards privacy, as well as privacy-related decision making. We conclude the chapter in Sect. 19.5, where we outline the achievements and shortcomings of privacy-enhanced recommender systems and discuss future research directions in light of emerging trends in recommendation technologies.

19.2 Privacy Risks in Recommender Systems

Most scholars argue that in the modern information age people regard their personal information as a *commodity*: they are willing to give up some personal information in return for personal gains. Recommender systems are a perfect example of this dynamic: They collect a wide variety of user data as input for their recommender systems, and in return provide their users with better services and products [10, 37, 44, 87, 139]. The information collected might include users' clicking or viewing behavior; contextual information like the location or mood; social information like user friends, family, or colleagues; as well as demographic parameters like age and occupation [72]. To make sure that data collectors treat the collected information responsibly, the OECD [114] has defined a set of Fair Information Practices (FIPS):

Collection Limitation Data should be collected within limits, by lawful and fair means and with consent (where appropriate).

Data Quality Data should be relevant, accurate, complete and kept up-to-date.

Purpose Specification The purposes of collection should be specified at the time of collection.

Use Limitation Data should not be used or disclosed for other purposes except with consent or by the authority of law.

Security Safeguards Personal data should be protected against unauthorized access, destruction, use, modification or disclosure.

Openness Users should be able to know what data is being collected, who controls the data, and for what purposes they are used.

Individual Participation An individual should be allowed to inspect the collected data about themselves, and have them erased, rectified, completed or amended.

Accountability The collector of the data should be accountable for complying with the above measures.

Generally speaking, privacy is breached when any of these principles are violated. Given their need to collect large amounts of information and innate capability to infer users' personal tastes from this data, recommender systems run a heightened risk to violate the Collection Limitation, Purpose Specification, Use Limitation, and Security Safeguards principles. In this light, we categorize privacy risks in Table 19.1 along two dimensions: whether the privacy breach is due to direct access to existing data (a violation of the Collection and Use Limitation principles) or due to inference of new data (a violation of the Purpose Specification principle), and who the adversary trying to uncover user information is. We consider three types of adversaries: (1) the *recommender system* interacts with the user, but it might operate in a way that is incompatible with the user's expectations of privacy (a violation of the Collection and Use Limitation principles); (2) *other users* of the system have no direct access to another user's private data, but they might exploit the outputs of the recommender to uncover the information of a target user (a violation of the Security Safeguards principle); and finally, (3) *external entities* are not users

Table 19.1 Privacy risks in recommender systems

Adversary	Direct access to existing data	Inference of new data
Recommender system	Unsolicited data collection	Exposure of sensitive information
	Sharing data with third parties	Targeted advertising
	Unsolicited access by employees	Discrimination
Other users	Leaks through shared device or service	Inference from the recommender output
External entities	Lawful data disclosure	Exposure of sensitive information
	Hacking	
	Re-identification of anonymized data	

of the recommender, but they may try to access the information retained by the system or intervene in the interaction between the system and its users to get access to such information (another violation of the Security Safeguards principle, but regarding a different type of security safeguard). We next look in detail at the risks imposed by each of these actors.

19.2.1 Risks Imposed by the Recommender System

19.2.1.1 Direct Access to Data

Recommender systems typically rely on a central entity, which accesses personal user data for the purpose of personalizing a service. However, the availability of this information, combined with commercial incentives, may result in this data being used in a way that violates the end-users' expectations of privacy, even when this use is consistent with the provider's privacy policy [46]. There are several ways in which direct access to data could expose users to privacy risks, including:

Unsolicited data collection As storage capabilities are cheap, online services are tempted to collect as much user data as possible, either because it might be useful at some point in the future (e.g., Chap. 6 discusses the value of rich contextual information), or because it can be monetized. However, collection of data that is not deemed necessary to provide a service may break user expectations of privacy. For example, in a survey that aimed to capture the expectations of what sensitive resources mobile apps use [99], Pandora Internet Radio was one of the apps singled out by the users for unexpected resource usage, since it accesses the contact list on the mobile device. In general, users seem particularly wary of "context tracking," arguably because unwanted or unexpected inferences can be made about such data [80].

Sharing data with third parties There are many scenarios in which recommender systems have incentives to share raw user data with third parties. For example:

- Companies that have access to such information may wish to share it to collaborate with the research community, as was the case when AOL released anonymized user search queries [12] and in the Netflix Prize competition [20].
- Companies may need to share data with third parties to outsource parts of their operation. Today, many companies offer so-called *recommendations as a service*. The third party receives user profiles and interaction logs from a website, processes them, generates recommendations, and sends them back to the website. While the user profiles may have been anonymized before transmission, a copy of the user profile now exists with the third party. Even if the user were to delete their account, they could not verify the deletion of their profile by the third party.
- Finally, service providers may be tempted to sell personal user data to data brokers, as this was shown to be a lucrative business [17]. Data may also change hands following acquisition of companies, or when liquidators sell off databases of bankrupt companies.

Ackerman et al. [1] and Krishnamurthy and Willis [92] highlighted that propagation to third parties and profile data that can be linked back to a user's identity are important concerns that users have when they consider releasing information online. Although the data custodian may take precautions and anonymize the data prior to release to safeguard user privacy, the released data may be subject to de-anonymization attacks, as will be discussed later.

Unsolicited access by employees While the recommender system may take precautions to ensure user data is maintained under its control, it is possible that employees, who need access to user data to fulfill their role, will abuse their privileges to snoop for data of people they know. Employees may also be tempted to steal the data of well-known people (celebrities) for curiosity or for money. This risk exists in any system that retains user information, and can be mitigated to some extent by ensuring appropriate access control and auditing mechanisms.

19.2.1.2 Inference from User Preference Data

Sophisticated manipulation of the data collected or processed by the recommender system (see Chap. 7 for an overview of data mining methods) could lead to additional privacy risks due to inference of new data, sometimes without the awareness or consent of the user:

Exposure of sensitive information Several recent works [36, 91, 147] have demonstrated the power of machine learning techniques in uncovering sensitive and private personal information, including personality traits (see Chap. 21). While such inferences are probabilistic in nature, they could be harmful even if wrong, particularly when judgments are based on risk (e.g., insurance decisions) or prejudice (e.g., workplace discrimination).

Targeted advertising In targeted advertising, the collected data is used to learn user interests and select advertisements that are most likely to result in conversion. The targeted ads may expose sensitive or embarrassing information—one prominent example is of a parent who learned that his teenager daughter was pregnant after Target started sending her coupons for baby clothes and cribs [47].

Discrimination Recent works [105, 106] have shown evidence of online price discrimination facilitated by personal information. Individuals may perceive this as a misuse of their information, and as overstepping the purposes specified for data collection.

Inference attacks exploit various aspects of user data to derive sensitive and private information. These attacks typically rely on correlations learned from other users' data, but can exploit them in various ways. For example, an adversary can rely solely on information contributed by the system users [147], leverage semantic relations between different attributes [36], cross-link the data with additional sources to extract more correlations [91], or exploit the structure of social links [157].

Weinsberg et al. [147] showed that demographic information such as age, gender, ethnicity, or political orientation can be inferred from information disclosed to recommender systems. Several classifiers were trained using the data contributed by the users, and inferred with high accuracy the demographic information of users who did not disclose similar data. Experiments conducted on the Flixster and Movielens datasets demonstrated the effectiveness of the approach. In fact, the mere act of watching a movie (regardless of the rating) conveys a lot of information, in the sense that classifiers trained over binary data (i.e., movie watched or not) performed only slightly worse than those trained on the complete rating data.

While Weinsberg et al. exploited structured data, Chaabane et al. [36] leveraged the ontologized version of Wikipedia to identify semantic relations between unstructured user interests, and showed how seemingly harmless interests, such as music interests, can leak sensitive information about users. They assigned the user interests into higher-level interest topics, and the interests of each user were mapped to these topics, allowing to identify users with similar tastes. Assuming that users with similar tastes are similar in multiple aspects, it was then possible to guess a user's private attribute based on the public attributes of similar users. The authors crawled public profiles from Facebook, and used the self-declared, publicly available music interests of users to infer their gender, relationship, age, and country attributes.

Kosinski et al. [91] conducted a large-scale study that correlated the Facebook 'likes' of users to a range of sensitive personal attributes, including sexual orientation, ethnicity, religious and political views, and personality traits using machine learning techniques. The authors generated predictors for these sensitive attributes and achieved remarkable results. For example, the model could distinguish between homosexual and heterosexual men in 88 % of cases, African Americans and Caucasian Americans in 95 % of cases, and between Democrats and Republicans in 85 % of cases. While some 'likes' were related to the attribute in question (e.g., liking pages related to homosexuality), some of the discovered correlations had no obvious connections.

The inference problem is exacerbated in online social networks, where friendship links and group membership can be leveraged to infer private information.

Zheleva and Getoor [157] considered the possibility that linked objects in a social network are correlated, i.e., that online friends share common characteristics. They proposed several inference attacks that exploit the structure of the network to predict private attributes. Based on evaluation of such inference using data from Flickr, Facebook, Dogster, and BibSonomy, the authors concluded that the performance of the predictors was dataset-dependent. For example, link-based methods did not perform well, since there was no strong correlation between the inferred attributes and the friends. On the other hand, group membership improved the inference, and some of the group memberships allowed to predict the user's attributes with high accuracy. Note that while users may have control over which attributes are made public, in some social networks (e.g., Facebook and Flickr) the user has limited control over the visibility of group membership information.

19.2.2 Risks Imposed by Other System Users

Since recommender systems leverage data collected from numerous users, they allow users to learn personal information about each other, even when such information is kept private. This problem is most evident when users share the same account on a device or a service: the recommendations for this account would be derived from the users' combined activities, and therefore the recommendations generated for one user provide insights on the activities of the other users. A similar problem can occur in group recommender systems (see Chap. 22).

A harder problem is imposed when the outputs of a recommender system leak private information of other unrelated users in the system. This problem is particular to collaborative filtering recommender systems (as opposed to content-based recommenders), since inherently these recommenders adapt the recommendations provided to each user based on data collected from other users. Ramakrishnan et al. [124] showed how the recommendations and their explanations can expose information of users who rate items across disparate domains. The recommendations allow an adversary to deduce connections between items. For example, given a certain item, an adversary can create a fake account and add item ratings to identify the smallest set of items that would result in a recommendation of the target item. This implies that there exists a set of users who rated both these items and the target item. This set of users is likely to be small when the items belong to different domains, making it easier to target these users in privacy attacks. For example, the revealed connections can be combined with additional data sources to compromise the identity of the users and uncover additional personal information.

A stronger attack that exploits the public outputs of item-to-item collaborative filtering systems was put forward by Calandrino et al. [31]. Public outputs of such recommenders typically contain item similarity lists or cross-item correlations. For example, Amazon provides the "customers who bought this item also bought…" lists, Hunch provides the entire item-to-item covariance matrix, and Last.fm provides an item similarity list. By passively observing the changes in these outputs over time, an attacker could infer private transactions of a target user, given background knowledge on some items previously rated by the user. In an item-to-item collaborative recommender, when a user makes a transaction involving an item, this results in an increase of the similarity of the item to other items in the user's transaction history. Therefore, the attacker can track the similarity lists of items known to be associated with the target user, and identify new items in the lists. When the same item appears in a number of tracked lists, the attacker can infer that the item was added to the target user's record. The authors successfully applied this approach to several real-world recommender systems, including Hunch, LibraryThing, Last.fm and Amazon. The attack exhibits a trade-off between the number of inferences and their accuracy (for example, inference results on LibraryThing ranged from 58 inferences per user with 50 % accuracy to six inferences per user with 90 % accuracy) and achieves the best results when applied to small or new sites.

In addition to the passive attack that Calandrino et al. presented in [31], they also described an active sybil attack that targets neighborhood-based collaborative filtering. Given background knowledge on some items previously rated by a user, the adversary creates fake users that are similar to the target user, and likely to be identified as neighbors of that user and of each other. A neighborhood-based recommender is therefore likely to provide to the fake users recommendations based on the other fake users and the target user. This allows to isolate the target user's data, as any recommended item that does not appear in the fake profiles is likely to originate from the target user.

19.2.3 Risks Imposed by External Entities

Data sharing and misuse are subject to the control of the recommender system, and may therefore be mitigated through regulation, or be disclosed to obtain the user's consent. In contrast, some scenarios may lead to unintended data disclosure. One risk is imposed by unlawful access to data by hackers (e.g., due to insufficient security safeguards), resulting in data theft. Another risk is due to court subpoenas and surveillance by law enforcement agencies. While such data access is lawful, it is often conducted without user awareness, and, in some cases, even without the service provider's awareness.

Third parties may also obtain personal information gathered by recommender systems after it was anonymized for privacy protection. However, even in the anonymized form, this data poses a serious privacy risk due to the possibility of de-anonymization. Narayanan and Shmatikov [108] demonstrated the difficulty of guaranteeing anonymity in transaction and preference records common in recommender systems. In general, the sparseness of large multi-dimensional data collections ensures that a record will not have many other "similar" records in the dataset, allowing to single it out and re-identify it with relatively little background information. The attack can be carried out by an adversary who knows a (possibly imprecise) subset of the target user's attributes, e.g., items that were rated by the user, ratings that were assigned, or the time of the ratings. The de-anonymization algorithms evaluate the similarity of each record in the anonymized dataset to the background information. Due to the sparseness of transaction and preference records, these algorithms are robust to imprecision and uncertainty in the background knowledge, as well as to a moderate level of perturbation in the published records. The authors conjectured that the amount of perturbation needed to defeat this de-anonymization approach would destroy the utility for collaborative filtering.

The effectiveness of this attack was demonstrated using the Netflix Prize dataset, containing anonymized ratings of 500K Netflix subscribers. The authors found that with background knowledge consisting of eight movie ratings (of which two may be wrong) and rating dates known within a 14-day error, 99 % of records can be uniquely re-identified in the dataset. Even without knowing the dates on which the items were rated, information about a few rated items may be sufficient. For example, 84 % of records can be uniquely re-identified if the adversary knows six out of eight movies rated outside the 500 most frequently rated movies. This background information may be relatively easy to obtain for most users, e.g., by observing their voluntary disclosure of information on social networks or on IMDB. It can be argued that the anonymized records may not contain sensitive data. However, even in these cases, re-identification carries a privacy risk: any information that can be traced back to a person can be leveraged in subsequent attacks, and provide additional hooks that the adversary could use to de-anonymize further data releases. An aggregate of such releases could lead to a "database of ruin" [115], which would tie together digital traces from different sources, exposing an elaborate picture on individuals' online and offline activities.

The possibility of re-identification of the Netflix dataset resulted in a lawsuit that was settled out of court, and subsequent cancelation of the second Netflix challenge [29]. To date, safe release of de-anonymized datasets for research purposes is still an open problem. As stated in [108], in such scenarios "*the purpose of the data release is to foster computations on the data that have not even been foreseen at the time of release, and are more sophisticated than the computations that we know how to perform in a privacy-preserving manner*." Inferences on this data, thus, pose privacy problems, because they almost definitely go beyond users' initial expectations of privacy.

19.2.4 Summary

Research conducted in recent years demonstrated the ability to infer highly sensitive information from user interest data, even when they express seemingly innocent information. Such information could be abused either by the systems that collect the data (e.g., inferring users' psychological traits and leveraging these for targeted advertising); by other users in the systems who may be exposed to the data (e.g., by default, public "likes" on Facebook) or may analyze the output of the recommender; or by external entities that access the user data.

These results stress that even privacy-conscious users who may withhold some of their information, cannot guarantee their privacy, since the withheld information could be inferred from other information disclosed to the recommender. Moreover, the privacy of a user does not solely depend on the user's personal choices and privacy preferences, but is also influenced by the data made available by other users, regardless of whether they are associated with the user. Therefore, the user may only have limited control over the privacy risks resulting from using the system. Instead, integrating privacy into the design of recommender systems may prove more effective in safeguarding users' privacy. In the next section we will discuss approaches that can be taken to mitigate the identified privacy risks.

19.3 Privacy Solutions

The discussion about the risks of personal data leakage through recommender systems naturally leads to the "defender" side, i.e., how can the recommender protect user privacy without compromising the quality of the recommendations. We consider three categories of approaches, which can address the privacy problem in recommender systems:

- The first category refers to *architectures*, *platforms*, and *standards* that minimize the data leakage threat. These include various protocols and certificates that guarantee to users that the recommendation provider adheres to privacy-preserving practices and protects the users' personal data with due diligence. This inherently limits the ability of external entities to access user data or to infer new data, other than the authorized and regulated data access methods. We classify into this category also the distributed architectures, which eliminate the single point of failure typical to centralized recommenders.
- The second deals with the *algorithmic techniques* for data protection. Here, we distinguish between several types of approaches. Some of them involve data modification approaches—either of user identities (identity anonymization or abstraction to stereotypes) or of the rating data (substituting or adding noise to true rating data). Others exploit provable privacy guarantees offered by the differential privacy framework or apply cryptographic tools to protect the data. The basic idea underpinning the algorithmic techniques is that even if the users' personal data leaked to an adversary or untrusted party, they would possess only modified or encrypted information, and would struggle to recover the original data.
- The third category refers to "top-down" *legislations*, *policies*, and *regulations*, which may be imposed on the recommendation services by their governments and legislative bodies, or adopted as self-regulatory industry practices. They may

preclude the services from manipulating, sharing, or trading the data. Although this category of approaches addresses outright many of the above privacy risks, the regulations vary significantly across countries and even states, and their enforcement is hard to validate in practice.

The main rationale for this categorization lies in the grouping of these three categories into technical and non-technical solutions. The former consist of the architectural and algorithmic solutions, whereas the latter includes only the policy solutions. The technical solutions either provide a general infrastructure that supports privacy, or offer specific algorithms for data protection. On the other hand, the non-technical solutions provide an umbrella that outlines the allowed and the prohibited activities with regards to personal user data. Another important observation stemming from this grouping is that although the three categories seem independent, many recommender systems may (and actually should) apply more than one approach to protect the privacy of their users. Hence, we propose recommender system designers to consider all three categories of solutions when devising their privacy-protection mechanisms.

For example, consider a use case of a large-scale eCommerce website providing personalized recommendations to users. The site may apply architectural solutions and distribute the data storage. At the same time, the site may exploit algorithmic techniques and allow only cryptography-protected data access. In addition, the site may want to increase user trust and declare that the collection and use of personal user data is done in compliance with privacy regulations. Many of these details, especially the architectural and the algorithmic solutions in place, are not disclosed by practical websites. Nevertheless, we refer the reader to several publicly accessible privacy policies (see those of eBay,[1] Amazon,[2] and Google.[3])

We would like to revisit the access and inference risks outlined in Table 19.1, and intersect these with the three categories of solutions. Clearly, the architectural and policy solutions better address the direct data access risk, as private protocols, distribution of the recommendation process, and data protecting regulations make unauthorized access to the data harder. The application of algorithmic approaches cannot eliminate this access, but reduces the value of the data if it gets accessed. However, the algorithmic approaches substantially minimize the risk of inferring new data, as the input to the inference attacks becomes unreliable. It should also be mentioned that the policy solutions are likely to address the data inference risk, as they often prohibit the use of the collected data for purposes that are beyond those declared by the data collector.

In the following sections we elaborate on each of the categories and on specific works that apply these approaches.

[1] http://pages.ebay.com/help/policies/privacy-policy.html.

[2] http://www.amazon.com/gp/help/customer/display.html?nodeId=468496.

[3] http://www.google.com/intl/en/policies/privacy/.

19.3.1 Architecture and System Design Solutions

In this section, we consider how the architecture underlying the recommender system can put hard limits on the disclosure, propagation and linkability [119] of profile data. In Sect. 19.3.1.1, we introduce a trusted component that is guaranteed to act in a certain way. Then, in Sect. 19.3.1.2, we look at an architecture for social networking websites that gives the user control over their profile data through standard technologies from the Semantic Web. Finally, in Sect. 19.3.1.3, we cover approaches that shift some of the workload of the recommender system to the client-side, thereby reducing the amount of user data that needs to be disclosed.

19.3.1.1 Trusted Software for Limiting Linkability and Propagation of User Data

As we saw in Sect. 19.2, a recommender system may cross-link data from multiple sources to create comprehensive user models. If the models are retained after the recommendation process terminates, or even disclosed to untrusted parties, this could pose a grave threat to the user's privacy. The recommender could therefore make certain claims regarding data storage, linkability, and disclosure, to put the user's mind at ease, e.g., "no disclosure of any profile data without explicit consent," "no linkability between individual user sessions," "no linkability between partial user profiles," or "temporal limits on the storage of user data."

But how can the user trust that the service actually complies with these principles? In researching privacy-preserving recommendation solutions, Cissée and Albayrak [39] identified three ways of establishing trust:

- Reputation [74]: Non-compliance would lead to negative user feedback and sentiment, which discourages other users from using the service.
- Certification [136]: A trusted third party performs a detailed technical audit, e.g., by analyzing the source code and performing tests, to verify that the software has all the qualities and properties that it claims to have.
- Trusted computing [56]: An application has the ability to verify that a system consists of specific hardware and software, e.g., the ability to encrypt data in a way that can only be decrypted in a particular configuration.

We will analyze two examples of trusted systems that restrict the linkability and propagation of profile data: a privacy-preserving event planner proposed in [39] and a privacy-friendly loyalty card and shopping assistant application for smartphones.

In [39], Cissée and Albayrak built a privacy-preserving event planner on top of a FIPA-compliant [137] multi-agent system (MAS). The authors list various properties of MAS entities that make them ideal for creating a privacy-preserving recommender system, in which only trusted parties can temporarily cross-link user profile data from multiple sources: entities are autonomous and can be deployed dynamically in the MAS environment; each entity can perform a well-defined task; entities can communicate with each other; and they can be tamper resistant.

With regard to user privacy, the purpose of the system is to ensure that disclosed user profile data is not stored permanently and cannot be linked to any particular user. A temporary filter agent (TFE), responsible for generating recommendations, is created, and a relay entity establishes control over the TFE's communication abilities on the user's behalf. This way, it can be ensured that only the recommendations will be propagated to other entities; user profile data will not be propagated because the relay does not provide the TFE with the means of communicating it to other parties. Controlling agents' communication abilities is not part of the standard MAS feature set, so the authors have implemented this aspect as trusted software. With control established, the user provides profile data (made up of behavior information, personal details and preferences) to the TFE and the service provider hands the TFE a set of items to recommend from. The TFE uses all data at its disposal to generate content-based recommendations for the user, which are then propagated to the service provider for visualization. Finally, the TFE is terminated by the relay entity, thereby destroying the linked dataset. The service provider can thus present the user with personalized recommendations without gaining permanent access to the profile data.

The MobCom project[4] explored the possibility of implementing various identity-based applications such as identity cards, membership cards, and customer loyalty cards on a smartphone, in a way that protects the privacy of the user. Put et al. [123] developed a shopping and loyalty card application that discloses only the minimal amount of information required, with user consent. The smartphone serves as a self-scanning device with secure local storage for the customer's personal information, shopping history, loyalty points and product vouchers. At the start of each shopping session, a temporary shopping basket is created under a new pseudonym, so that the store cannot track customer behavior across sessions. In exchange for disclosing profile data, e.g., product preferences, the retail store offers a more personalized service and additional loyalty points. This way, customers control their data and can weigh the benefits of releasing profile data against the loss of privacy. In this architecture, both the smartphone application and the in-store service are regarded as trusted software. At the start of the shopping session, the smartphone and the server can verify that each is running the trusted software and that it has not been tampered with. The smartphone does not release any profile data without the user's explicit consent. The shopping basket contents and any disclosed profile data are destroyed at the end of the session.

19.3.1.2 User-Managed Portable Profiles

Beyond the privacy risks originating from inference and profiling, which were discussed in Sect. 19.2, social networking websites (see also Chap. 15) tend to become data silos [27], with profile data either locked away or only partially

[4]http://www.mobcom.org.

accessible through proprietary APIs. If users were able to port profile data from one platform to another, they could receive better recommendations and more personalized service, alleviating the cold start issue when joining a new service. They could also allow access to specific profile information on a case by case basis. Currently, however, this scenario is not possible because users do not have such level of control over their data.

We focus here on an alternative architecture proposed by Heitmann et al. [64], which puts the user in charge of fully portable profile data through Semantic Web technologies and an access control system. Using this architecture, profile data can be shared between services and the users can decide what parts of their profiles are disclosed to each provider. Building on earlier work of Hollenbach et al. [66], Heitmann et al. base their architecture on three standards: (1) Friend-of-a-Friend [26]: a data format suitable for storing generalized user profile data, as well as social friendship relations; (2) WebID [32]: an SSL certificate that refers to the URI where the profile data can be found; and (3) a Web Access Control [66]: vocabulary for controlling access rights to resources. The authors also identify three distinct roles for entities that wish to participate in the architecture:

- *Profile stores* are tasked with storing the user profiles and providing access to data according to the access rules. They also allow users to manage these access rules. Notably, the user can perform this role by hosting his own profile.
- *Data consumers* are third-party services that wish to access the user profile data. Each time they request data from a profile store, data consumers authenticate themselves with their own unique WebID.
- *User agents* are responsible for authenticating the user with profile stores and data consumers through their WebIDs.

To summarize, users are able to port their profile data from one service to another. By using Semantic Web technologies, entities that wish to perform any of these roles, have an easy-to-use, stable, and non-proprietary interface to work with. Users can selectively disclose parts of their profiles to data consumers of their choice. Through the use of WebIDs, unlinkability of data is built-in: a user can have multiple identities, each with its own WebID. Data consumers are thus unable to link multiple WebIDs to a particular user and the framework assumes that the profile stores can be trusted to not maintain or disclose links between the users' multiple identities. We refer to Chap. 4 for more on Semantic Web technologies.

19.3.1.3 Generating Recommendations on the Client

Shifting some of the recommender's load to client devices allows to reduce the amount of information accessed and retained by a recommendation service, thereby mitigating any privacy risks that could result from the server's exposure to user data.

Several works proposed to implement the recommendation process as a pure peer-to-peer system, thereby eliminating the role of a centralized service [22, 94]. However, such systems could still expose user data to other users, who now interact directly with the user to generate the recommendations. Lathia et al. [94] addressed this risk by proposing a privacy-friendly measure of similarity that relies on the *concordance* between users, i.e., the proportion by which two user rating sets agree. This measure has the property that it can be evaluated by comparing the two sets of ratings to a third rating set, rather than directly to each other. Therefore, user similarity can be evaluated without exchanging user profiles. Berkovsky et al. [22] leveraged a hierarchical topology, in which peers are organized into peer-groups managed by super-peers. A user who seeks recommendations interacts with the super-peers. The super-peers select a random subset of the underlying peers, aggregate the results obtained from them, and return them to the querying user, who processes them to generate the recommendation.

In a hybrid approach proposed by Shokri et al. [131], each client interacts with a centralized server to obtain recommendations, but can also exchange information with other system users to enhance privacy. In this approach, each user maintains two profiles: an offline profile stored locally at the client, which is updated continuously, and an online profile at the server that is only synchronized occasionally. Users contact each other and exchange items, so that their offline and consequently the online profiles are a mix of each user's original ratings and ratings provided by other users. To maintain accurate recommendations, the exchange process favors ratings conducted by similar users.

One of the challenges in distributed architectures is that many recommendation algorithms are computationally intensive, and while mobile devices have recently become powerful, they are still ill-suited for heavy computations. This limitation gives rise to architectural approaches that divide work between a powerful back-end and a weaker end-user device. Such approaches allow for recommendations to be generated on the client, while disclosing less information to the centralized recommender back-end than in a centralized recommendation scenario. These approaches usually leverage the ability to break the recommendation generation into two stages: (1) modeling, for which the entire dataset is typically required, and (2) recommending, for which the models are used to compute the recommendations. Given an established model, recommending can be a relatively light-weight task.

For example, consider item-based collaborative filtering, where all the available user-item ratings are needed to construct the item-to-item similarity matrix. Recommendations are then generated by taking items that are similar to items that the user has previously consumed. In PocketLens [107], Miller et al. set out to build a portable collaborative filtering recommender system, where the similarity computation is separated from the recommendation stage. Through homomorphic encryption methods that are also applied in secure voting systems, the back-end constructs an item-to-item similarity matrix based on co-occurrence, without having to decrypt individual purchase records. A mobile client can retrieve this matrix and generate recommendations locally. After implementing and evaluating several architectures, the authors found that their best performing architecture could protect the user's privacy without compromising the recommendation accuracy.

The separation between the modeling and the recommendation stages is also evident in matrix factorization. The modeling stage that consists of the derivation of the latent factors, requires access to all the ratings and is computationally expensive. The recommendation generation then is realized as a product of two latent vectors and can be performed on the client. Moreover, since matrix factorization separates between the user and the item latent factors, the user data can be stored on the client side. Vallet et al. [141] explored this possibility in a semi-decentralized setting, in which the server maintains item factors, whereas user factors are stored and maintained on the client-side. The authors developed a streaming model, which performs incremental updates of the latent factors using only the data of the user interacting with the system, and without any server-side retention of user data. The predictive accuracy of this model was found comparable to that of a system that retains user data.

Isaacman et al. [70] leverage the same matrix factorization property in the context of a distributed system of content producers (e.g., bloggers) and consumers. To maintain privacy, information is exchanged only between the content producer and its subscribers, e.g., item ratings are shared only with the item's producer. The system computes the probability distribution of content ratings that is estimated with a low-rank latent model constructed by solving the factorization problem. Each producer maintains a factor vector that constitutes its "production profile." In addition, each consumer maintains for each possible rating value a factor vector, and these factor vectors constitute its "consumption profile." The client can compute the product of these vectors to estimate the probability that the consumer would provide a certain rating to any given producer's content, without disclosing all of the consumer's ratings to that producer.

To summarize, architectures that shift computation to the client side are particularly useful for mitigating privacy risks that follow from data retention on a centralized server. However, user data may still be exposed during the interaction with the server, or when interacting with other system users. Cryptographic protocols allow to address this deficiency, and are discussed in detail in Sect. 19.3.2.4.

19.3.2 Algorithmic Solutions

In this section, we discuss algorithmic solutions to recommender system privacy. We split them into four categories: algorithms based on pseudonyms or user anonymization, algorithms involving user data modification, differentially private algorithms, and cryptography-based algorithms. Similarly to what was discussed earlier, these categories are not mutually exclusive; a recommender may benefit from employing multiple solutions that belong to different categories.

19.3.2.1 Pseudonyms and Anonymization

Algorithmic approaches that mask the users of recommender systems through pseudonyms and anonymization were not received well initially. In particular, Schafer et al. [130] wrote in 2001 that "*anonymizing techniques are disasters for recommenders, because they make it impossible for the recommender to easily recognize the customer, limiting the ability even to collect data, much less to make accurate recommendations.*" More than a decade later, the topic still remains largely under-investigated and there are only several works in this direction.

An early proposal for a pseudonymity-based personalization framework was developed by Arlein et al. [9] and drew on the notion of 'personae.' The framework implied that users have in place a suite of abstractions of themselves, e.g., entertainment, medical, and shopping, and use these abstract entities when interacting with various websites and services. Each persona is linked across multiple services and exposes only the activities carried out by this persona. The services access only one user persona at a time and cannot link it to other personae, so they are unable to uncover additional information, while the users manage their own personae and set access rights for various services and abstractions.

Another pseudonimity framework for personalized systems was proposed by Kobsa and Schreck [89]. The framework includes a suite of privacy-preserving components: user anonymization, user data encryption, role-based access, and selective access permissions. Each component is managed by a dedicated server and the servers tune the overall level of user privacy to the user's privacy settings and the degree of cooperation between the services possessing the partial user models.

The approaches to user anonymization in recommender systems typically entail simple de-identification solutions. For example, in the Netflix Prize data, the identities of the users were replaced with random numbers. A major threat to this anonymization method lies in the high dimensionality and sparsity of the data [108], which is typical in recommender datasets. As discussed in Sect. 19.2.3, this sparsity can be exploited to thwart anonymization and re-identify the records.

19.3.2.2 Obfuscation

Application of data perturbation (or obfuscation) techniques to recommender systems was inspired by earlier works outside the field of recommender systems [7]. The basic idea underpinning this body of work is that modifying a certain number of data points in the user profiles, e.g., by adding noise to the real data, will have a limited effect on the recommendation accuracy. However, if adversaries or an untrusted party accessed the user profiles, they would only obtain the disguised profiles. This allows for "plausible deniability" [61, 142]: the adversary cannot prove whether a certain profile entry is accurate.

To the best of our knowledge, this idea was first proposed for recommender systems by Polat and Du [120]. They used a randomized data perturbation technique to mask ratings stored in the user profiles. The data is modified by adding random noise to the ratings, such that no certain information about the ratings can be derived. Since the recommendations are generated by aggregating user ratings, the overall impact of data perturbation on the recommendations is assumed to be minor. The authors compared the recommendations generated using the masked data with those using the original data, and showed that perturbed profiles could still generate reasonably accurate recommendations. The accuracy of the recommendations is inversely correlated with the magnitude of the noise, but the impact of noise decreases with the number of users and items accessible by the recommender.

Another variant of data perturbation was presented by Parameswaran and Bloug [118]. They proposed to mask auxiliary data pertaining either to users (e.g., demographic data) or to items (e.g., domain metadata), which are exploited by the similarity computation mechanism of collaborative filtering. The evaluation showed that the impact of masking auxiliary data on the accuracy of the recommendations is minor, although the direct contribution of this perturbation to user privacy was not explored.

Unfortunately, data perturbation through the addition of noise is inapplicable to binary data, which is prevalent in recommenders, as the systems increasingly rely on binary behavior logs (browsing logs, purchase data, listened songs, etc.). In this case, the addition of noise distorts the logs and can be easily identified. In [122], Polat and Du applied a different technique, called a randomized response, to the binary user profiles. This technique randomly chooses which bits of the binary profile are preserved and which are flipped. Two variants of randomized responses were evaluated and, as before, the accuracy was found to be correlated with the volume of training data.

The application of random perturbation has gone beyond the canonic collaborative filtering. Yakut and Polat [153] applied data perturbation also to the Eigenstate-based variant of CF that reduces the dimensionality of the rating matrix through Principal Component Analysis. Two distributions for generating the noise factors and several variants of privacy-enhanced Eigenstate CF were proposed and evaluated. Also, Kaleli and Polat [76] applied randomized response to a Naïve Bayes Classifier implementation of CF. That work primarily focused on tweaking the noise parameters for the purpose of maintaining reasonable levels of user privacy and recommendation accuracy at the same time.

Basu et al. [14] applied data perturbation to the Slope-One recommender [96], a highly scalable version of item-based collaborative filtering. It was found that Slope-One is robust to the noise and capable of delivering reasonable accurate recommendations despite the masking of user data. Polat and Du [121] applied data perturbation to an SVD-based CF recommender, which decomposes the masked ratings matrix into a product of three latent matrices. SVD recommendations were also found to be reasonably robust to random perturbation.

More recently, data perturbation was applied by Renckes et al. [126] to a hybrid graph-based recommender representing users as nodes and their similarity through the edges. The paper reaffirmed the findings of Polat and Du [120] relating to the impact of data availability on the accuracy of private recommendations, and practically demonstrated the privacy-accuracy trade-off. In a nutshell, privacy loss decreased with the level of perturbation, but the accuracy of the recommendations deteriorated too, such that privacy and accuracy conflicted with each other. To allow users more control over the privacy-accuracy trade-off, Kandappu et al. [77] have proposed an interactive obfuscation mechanism. The obfuscation is applied to ratings before they are shared with the system (input perturbation). Before sharing new ratings, the mechanism probes the recommender to obtain rating predictions over a hold-out set of items, which were rated by the user but were not disclosed to the recommender. The magnitude of obfuscation is then calibrated based on the accuracy of those predictions, such that privacy protection is maximized within the constraints of a target accuracy level.

Berkovsky et al. [23, 24] focused on the application of data perturbation to various ratings in collaborative profiles. They compared the impact of five data masking policies applied to both *moderate* (close to average) and *extreme* (positive or negative) ratings on the accuracy of the generated recommendations. Perturbation of the latter was found to have a higher impact on the accuracy of the recommendations than of the former. That is, extreme ratings bear more information than moderate ratings, and adding noise to these ratings deteriorates the accuracy of the recommendations. However, extreme ratings were perceived as more sensitive by the users. This gives a different perspective on the privacy-accuracy trade-off, as masking the sensitive ratings damages the recommendation accuracy.

Aside from a potential decrease in recommendation accuracy, data perturbation can also be problematic for legal and psychological reasons. A perturbed profile is essentially "incorrect data," which violates the Data Quality principle of the FIPS (see Sect. 19.2) as well as several European privacy laws that require data collectors to pursue the correctness of the collected data. Psychologically speaking, users may fear that this incorrect data may result in incorrect inferences (which is possible in specific instances even when the overall accuracy of the recommender does not decrease due to perturbation). Even worse, if users' data gets subpoenaed or stolen and published, they may have a hard time defending the claim that some of the data in their profile is incorrect. So while obfuscated data may afford users "plausible deniability," it does not offer them what we would like to call "deniable plausibility" (i.e., the ability to prove that certain items were in fact fabricated by the obfuscation mechanism). Indeed, a study by Chen et al. [38] on the application of obfuscation techniques in online social networks has indicated that users care about the impact of obfuscation on their visible profile, and suggested to incorporate such preferences into the obfuscation algorithms.

We summarize the surveyed works that apply data obfuscation techniques in Table 19.2. These are split into the basic Collaborative Filtering (based on either user-to-user or item-to-item similarity) and other CF algorithms.

19.3.2.3 Differential Privacy

Differential privacy [48] is a privacy model based on the principle that the output of a computation should not allow inference about any record in the input. This is achieved by requiring that the probability distribution over the possible

Table 19.2 Privacy-preserving recommendation algorithms with data obfuscation

Similarity-based collaborative filtering (CF)	User-to-user similarity [24, 120]
	Item-to-item similarity [118, 122]
Other CF algorithms	Eigenstate-based CF [153]
	Naïve Bayes CF [76]
	Slope-one [14]
	SVD-based CF [121]
	Graph-based recommender [126]

outcomes does not change significantly when any particular record is added to or removed from the input. Therefore, differential privacy provides the means to mitigate inference of private user data from the output of the recommender system. One of the commonly used approaches to obtain differential privacy is through the Laplace mechanism, in which carefully calibrated noise sampled from the Laplace distribution is added to a computation. The noise masks the influence that any difference in a particular record could have on the outcome of the computation.

McSherry and Mironov were the first to study the application of differential privacy to recommender systems, and in particular to collaborative filtering [103]. They used the Laplace mechanism to derive noisy counts and sums over the input ratings, and to compute a differentially-private variant of the item-to-item covariance matrix. The noisy covariance matrix could then be used to generate differentially-private k-Nearest Neighbors and SVD recommendations.

Zhu et al. [158] took a different approach to differentially private neighborhood-based collaborative recommendations, aiming specifically at the sybil attack presented by Calandrino et al. [31] (see Sect. 19.2.2). They considered a differentially-private k-nearest neighbors algorithm that operates in two steps: selection of the neighbors, and rating prediction based on the neighbors. They relied on the smooth sensitivity [112] of the similarity function, allowing to introduce lower levels of noise than those required by the Laplace mechanism. They also introduced randomness to the k nearest neighbors selection, while ensuring that, with high probability, the selected neighbors have high similarity scores.

Machanavajjhala et al. [101] studied privacy-preserving social recommendations on the basis of a graph linking users and items. Given the graph, they derived utility vectors that capture the utility of items for users, with the goal of inducing a probability distribution that maximizes the user's utility while keeping the utility vector private. The authors provided a theoretical analysis of the problem and concluded that good recommendations were achievable only under weak privacy parameters, or only for a small fraction of users, highlighting that the privacy-accuracy trade-off also exists in differential privacy based methods.

Riboni and Bettini [127] investigated the application of differential privacy to context-aware recommendations, and specifically to recommendations of Points of Interest (POI), where the spatial context is taken into account. The spatial domain of the service is partitioned into non-overlapping regions, and each POI belongs to a single region. In addition, each user belongs to a given stereotype, which represents semantic abstraction of profile data. The Laplace mechanism is used to capture the distribution of POI preferences for each stereotype. Consequently, when a user queries a region, the POIs best matching the user stereotype are recommended.

The research of differentially private recommender systems shows that while in some settings (e.g., social recommendations) it may be impossible to obtain privacy and accuracy guarantees simultaneously, in other cases privacy-preserving recommender systems can achieve reasonable accuracy. However, the works conducted so far assume a one-off computation, whereas re-calculation of recommendations when additional data becomes available may introduce additional privacy leaks. Therefore, maintaining privacy over multiple computations or data releases requires an increase in the amount of introduced noise, and leads to deterioration in accuracy. While there is a line of work studying efficient differential privacy in continual settings [49, 57], this has not been studied yet in recommender systems.

19.3.2.4 Cryptographic Solutions

Cryptographic solutions mitigate privacy risks triggered by the exposure of user data, like intentional misuse (e.g., sharing data with third parties or inferring sensitive information), as well as unintentional disclosure (e.g., data theft). Secure multi-party computation protocols allow to accurately compute recommendations, while keeping user input confidential. Unlike data obfuscation or differential privacy, secure computations produce the same recommendations as non-private protocols, but this comes at the cost of computational overhead, making these protocols suitable mainly for off-line recommendations.

The majority of the work in this area relies on additive homomorphic encryption schemes, such as the Paillier public-key cryptosystem [116]. Essentially, in such encryption schemes, any linear function of the inputs can be evaluated by manipulating their encryptions. This property has been leveraged in several recommendation algorithms and architectures, listed in Table 19.3. Below, we elaborate on the proposed architectures and provide examples of homomorphic encryption applications.

Distributed settings As detailed in Sect. 19.3.1.3, distributed architectures mitigate privacy risks by keeping the data on the client side. To the best of our knowledge, the protocol proposed by Canny [32] was the first application of secure multi-party computations to recommender systems. A partial singular value decomposition of the ratings data can be reduced to a series of additions of user inputs and carried out over encrypted inputs using an additive homomorphic encryption. Based on this, Canny proposed a peer-to-peer system, consisting of two types of nodes: "clients" who provide in each iteration their encrypted contribution to the gradient, and "talliers" who manipulate and aggregate these inputs to derive an encrypted total gradient. The encryption key is shared between the clients, and each client applies its share of the key to decrypt the total.

Table 19.3 Privacy-preserving recommendation algorithms with homomorphic encryption

Distributed	Weighted slope-one [13]
	Neighborhood-based [51]
	Trust networks [65]
	Partial SVD [32]
	Factor analysis model [33]
Cross-system collaboration	User-to-user similarity [71]
	Item-to-item similarity [154]
Client-server	Weighted slope-one in cloud setting [15]
Privacy service provider	General framework [8]
	Neighborhood-based [53]
	Trust networks [52]

If enough clients provide decryptions with their share of the key, then the talliers can reconstruct the new gradient. The result of the computation is guaranteed to be correct, even in the presence of malicious parties, as long as a sufficient portion of the nodes are trustworthy and follow the protocol.

Cross-system collaboration Distributed algorithms can also be carried out between service providers, allowing cross-system collaboration without disclosing clients' information to other systems, and thereby mitigating privacy risks due to sharing data with third parties. For example, Jeckmans et al. [71] studied how a company can generate recommendations based on its own customer data and data from other companies, while keeping customer data confidential. They relied on additive homomorphic encryption, as well as secure comparison, absolute value, and division protocols. The proposed two-party protocol, executed between a pair of servers, allows to generate predictions based on user-to-user similarity, which is evaluated using the ratings that the users have on both sites.

Client-server settings Encryption can keep user ratings confidential when the user interacts with the server in the prediction stage, as demonstrated in a Slope-One recommender that Basu et al. [15] studied. In a Slope-One predictor, predictions are based on the average deviations of item ratings, which are linear combinations of user ratings, making it suitable for secure evaluation with additive homomorphic encryption. In the learning phase, the users send their (obfuscated or anonymized) inputs to the cloud in the clear, and the cloud application produces the deviation matrix and the cardinality matrix for the Slope-One predictor. In the prediction stage, the target user sends a rating vector encrypted with a public key, which the cloud application manipulates with additive homomorphic encryption to produce an encrypted prediction vector. Finally, the user decrypts the vector to retrieve the prediction.

Privacy service provider Several works addressed the privacy risks in the client-server interaction by introducing a third party acting as a privacy service provider.

These solutions rely on the "division of trust" principle [8], i.e., no entity in the system holds the complete information. Aïmeur et al. [8] proposed a framework for privacy preserving recommenders based on this principle. Each merchant in the system is assigned to an agent that mediates the interaction with the clients. The client profiles are encrypted with the agent's public key, such that the agent can access them but the merchant cannot. On the other hand, the items are anonymized by a mapping known only to the merchant, so the agent cannot know the actual products purchased or rated by the customer. The agent maintains the list of products associated with a cluster of clients and a table of product similarities, uses these to generate recommendations, and can update them based on user inputs, but without knowing the actual products.

Homomorphic encryption is not the only approach to secure computation of recommendations. Nikolaenko et al. [109] proposed a privacy-preserving matrix factorization algorithm, in which the recommender profiles items without learning the users' ratings. In the proposed protocol, the recommender is assisted by a crypto-service provider, who prepares a Yao garbled circuit [155] that evaluates the item profiles given the encrypted rating inputs. The authors report a reasonably low running time and, since the described operations are parallelizable, they suggest that the algorithm may be suitable for batch processing of real large-scale datasets.

The extensive research on cryptographic solutions for privacy-preserving recommendations shows the feasibility of these solutions in diverse settings and with different recommendation algorithms. However, these solutions entail significant computational resources and time, as well as storage and communication overhead, which still impose a hurdle for their application in online recommender systems.

19.3.3 Policy Solutions

As Kobsa points out [87], many countries and states actively regulate consumers' privacy, and many industries adopt additional privacy guidelines. We refer to [144] for an overview of the impact of privacy laws and regulations on personalized systems up to 2006. Two important proposals since then are the U.S. Consumer Privacy Bill of Rights [67] and the 2012 revision of the European Privacy Directive [55].

Both of these proposals have a heavy emphasis on transparency and control. For example, the U.S. Consumer Privacy Bill of Rights suggests that "*companies should offer consumers clear and simple choices [...] about personal data collection, use, and disclosure*" and "*companies should provide clear descriptions of [...] why they need the data, how they will use it*" [67]. Under the European Privacy Directive, "personal data should be processed on the basis of the consent of the person concerned or some other legitimate basis" [55].

The U.S. privacy bill furthermore requires that consumers are able to access the personal data that companies collect about them, and correct it if necessary. It also requires that data collection is focused and limited to what is expected in the context in which the data was provided by the consumer. The European directive also requires that people are able to access their personal data. It additionally requires that they are allowed to transfer this data from one service to another, and that people are able to delete their data should they so desire.

The 2002 version of the European Union Privacy directive severely limited the use of non-essential cookies, often used for personalized advertising [54]. As a result, online advertising could not be targeted and became far less effective in the EU than in other countries [60]. The new directive requires websites to explicitly ask their users to accept its non-essential cookies. The Netherlands and the United Kingdom [69] have already implemented this directive as a national "cookie consent" law. However, to comply with the rules without losing advertising money, most sites give users only two options: leave the website or accept the cookies and continue. The resulting sprawl of consent-requesting pop-ups has caused much confusion among users, who typically accept the cookies without knowing what they really consent to, which arguably only increases their privacy concerns [140].

An alternative to privacy legislation is self-regulation via trust seals like the TRUSTe seal [19] or privacy standards like P3P [43]. Xu et al. [151] have shown that TRUSTe seals can be an effective substitute to legislation when it comes to reducing consumers' privacy concerns. TRUSTe seals have been shown to reduce perceived risk and increase trust, whereas P3P compliance increases trust but does not reduce perceived risk [150]. Self-regulation is not without problems, though. Research has shown that trust seals are only partially effective [50, 68, 128], and A/B tests on eCommerce websites have demonstrated that seals may lead to significantly lower conversion rates [30, 59]. This calls the benefits of "certification" (cf. [136]) into question. P3P, on the other hand, suffers from poor observability and complex user agents, which has led to a low level of adoption on the user-side [16].

In conclusion, privacy legislation and regulation has become more comprehensive over the last few decades. However, as Compañò and Lusoli point out, "*policy makers need to take into account that citizens do not always behave rationally*" [40], a topic we will cover in much more detail in the next section.

19.4 Human Aspects and Perception of Privacy

While we have mainly discussed the technical solutions to privacy risks in recommender systems, the concept of privacy is an inherently human attitude associated with the collection, distribution and use of disclosed data, and this disclosure is also a human behavior. Since recommenders critically rely on their users to disclose information about themselves, recommender system developers are advised to conduct user experiments to study users' information disclosure behavior and their privacy-related attitudes towards the recommender system (see Chap. 9).

This section discusses existing research concerning users' privacy attitudes and behaviors. The link between privacy attitudes and subsequent behaviors is not very clear: while several studies find this link to be significant [80, 88, 132] others find that it is not, or at least not very strong [2, 4, 58]. Due to this divergence, which Norberg et al. call the *privacy paradox* [113], developers of recommender systems are advised to study users' attitudes *and* behaviors regarding the privacy of their systems. The privacy paradox is a symptom of the fact that users' cognitive resources are in most cases insufficient to effectively take control over their privacy. The end of this section therefore discusses the importance of supporting users to make better privacy decisions, as well as an interesting new venue for recommender systems to provide such "privacy decision support."

Privacy Attitudes In studying privacy attitudes, one can make a distinction between privacy attitude as a personal trait or tendency, and as an attitude directed towards a specific system. General privacy concern was first measured by Westin and Harris and Associates, who classified people into three categories: privacy fundamentalists, pragmatists, and unconcerned [63, 148]. Researchers have since recognized that this personal trait consists of multiple dimensions. For example, the Concern For Information Privacy scale consists of four correlated factors: collection concerns, unauthorized access, fear of accidental errors, and secondary use [133]. Similarly, Malhotra et al. provide an Internet Users Information Privacy Concern scale measuring three factors: collection, control, and awareness [102].

Several works have highlighted the importance of measuring privacy concerns as a system/context-specific concept [6, 18, 132]. System-specific factors considered in previous work include "perceived privacy threats" [80, 88, 149], "perceived protection" [88], and "trust in the company" [80, 104]. These system-specific factors are usually better at predicting users' disclosure behavior than privacy concerns as a personal trait. Recommender system developers are thus advised to measure users' system-specific privacy attitudes. Moreover, they should not just focus on protecting users' privacy via the technical means described earlier in this chapter, but also to reduce the potential privacy threats to begin with (a philosophy called "privacy by design", cf. [34]) or to increase the reputation of their brand.

Privacy Behaviors Laufer and Wolfe were the first to argue that people trade off the risks and benefits of disclosure [95], a process that Culnan and Bies have called "privacy calculus" [45]. This term is commonly used to investigate information disclosure [62, 97, 149], and has become a well-established concept in privacy research [132]. In the field of recommender systems, several researchers have demonstrated that users indeed make this trade-off when deciding what information to disclose [10, 37, 58, 80, 85, 88, 90, 98]. The exact outcome of this trade-off depends on the context of the decision [81, 110]. Particularly, if users deem the requested information relevant to the purpose of the system, they will be more likely to disclose it. For example, it is reasonable to expect that a system for recommending nearby restaurants would collect street-level location information from the user device, but a user may be surprised to learn about such data being collected by a book recommender. This can be problematic for recommender systems, since they often use data from diverse application domains.

19.4.1 The Limits of Transparency and Control

Having a minimum level of control over one's disclosure is a necessary prerequisite for being able to engage in a privacy calculus. Moreover, people can only make an informed trade-off between benefits and risks if they are given adequate information. Based on this reasoning, advocates of transparency and control argue that they empower users to regulate their privacy at the desired level [35, 138, 152]. This advocacy for transparency and control has become a central part of the privacy directives proposed in the European Union and the United States [55, 67].

The call for control suggests that recommender systems should provide users advanced capabilities to manage their privacy. However, while users *claim* to want full control over their data, they typically eschew the hassle of actually exploiting this control [40]. While it is possible to overcome this control paradox [81], the privacy controls of systems like Facebook are so complex that they are overwhelming or confusing to most users [42]. As a result, Facebook users have severe misconceptions about the implications of their selected privacy settings [100].

Similarly, the call for transparency suggests that recommender systems should be forced to be open about their privacy practices, so that users can walk away if they do not like them (cf. "reputation" [74]). However, Bakos et al. demonstrate that only 0.2 % of all users read boilerplate documents such as End User License Agreements [11]. As noted earlier, "summarizing" this information with trust seals may actually impede rather than increase system usage [30, 59].

This ironic effect of trust seals on privacy concerns extends to other privacy-related situations as well. For example, John et al. demonstrate that even subtle privacy-minded designs and information may trigger users' privacy fears and reduce disclosure and participation [73]. They found that a professional looking site garners higher privacy concerns than an informal and unprofessional looking site, because the former design reminds users of privacy. While it is arguably more risky to entrust such an unprofessional-looking site with one's information, its appearance apparently downplays privacy concerns and increases disclosure.

Arguably, since even a professional looking site can instill privacy concerns, any reference to privacy will inadvertently prime users with privacy fears. This highlights a fundamental problem of any privacy-preserving architecture or algorithm: informing users about the superior privacy protection is likely to make them more concerned about their privacy [78, 80]. In some cases, this fear stems from concerns that the developers of these systems had not accounted for. For example, Kobsa et al. show that while client-side recommendation algorithms prevent the disclosure of personal information to third parties, users are concerned about their device getting lost or stolen [88]. Their user profile could then not only fall in the hands of a third party; they themselves would lose access to it. Users' lack of familiarity with a technology may exacerbate their privacy concerns. For example, Kobsa et al. show that users are rather skeptical about cloud-based recommendation services [88] like those proposed in [15].

The proponents of increasing transparency and control in information disclosure decisions assume that people are rational decision-makers who will use the provided information and controls to their best advantage. However, our decisions often do not follow rational economic principles [75] (see also Chap. 18), and this also holds true for information disclosure decisions [4, 5]. In fact, information disclosure decisions are among the hardest decisions to make, because they have delayed and uncertain repercussions that are difficult to trade-off with the possibly immediate gratification of disclosure [2, 5]. In this light, an abundance of information and control may only aggravate this problem, because it can lead to choice overload or information overload. Consequently, several researchers have recently questioned the effectiveness of the "transparency and control" paradigm [111, 135].

19.4.2 Privacy Nudges

The first step in supporting users' privacy decisions that does not require users to be rational decision-makers is to nudge these decisions into the "right direction" [3, 146] (see below for a discussion regarding what the "right direction" of privacy nudges could be). A nudge is a subtle yet persuasive cue that makes people more likely to decide in one direction or the other. Carefully designed nudges make it easier for people to make the right choice, without limiting their ability to choose freely. Broadly speaking, two types of nudges have been tried out in the field of privacy decision-making: justifications and defaults.

Justifications Justifications make it easier to rationalize decisions, and to minimize the regret associated with choosing the wrong option. Different types of justifications include providing a reason for requesting the information [41], highlighting the benefits of disclosure [90, 143], and appealing to the social norm [6, 25]. Justifications are especially useful in recommender systems, because recommenders are able to extract valuable taste information from seemingly irrelevant data. A good disclosure justification can nudge users to disclose these data, which helps to build their user model and improve the accuracy of the recommendations.

The effect of justifications seems to vary though. In a study by Kobsa and Teltzrow, users were 8.3 % more likely to disclose information when they knew the benefits of disclosure [90]. In a study by Acquisti et al. users were 27 % more likely to do this when they learned that many others decided to disclose the same information [6]. However, Besmer et al. found that social cues had barely any effect on users' Facebook privacy settings: only the small subset of users who take the time to customize their settings may be influenced by strong negative social cues [25]. Knijnenburg et al. tested a wide range of justifications in a demographics- and context-based mobile app recommender [80, 84]. They also found "fickleness" in the effects of justifications on users' disclosure to—and satisfaction with—the recommender. Users found these justifications helpful, but in contrast to some of the above findings, the justifications did not increase users' disclosure, trust, or satisfaction with the system, but rather decreased them. In line with Besmer et al. [25], Knijnenburg and Kobsa conclude in a follow-up analysis that only a subset of users is amenable to justifications [79].

Defaults The other approach to nudging users' privacy decisions is to ease their burden of making information disclosure decisions by providing sensible defaults (see Chap. 18). Providing a certain default option may nudge users in the direction of that default. For example, John et al. [73] show that people are more likely to admit to certain sensitive behaviors via an act of omission than via an act of commission. Similarly, Lai and Hui [93] show that defaults have a significant impact on user participation in an online newsletter. Recommender systems can manage privacy perceptions by carefully setting the defaults of optional features such as making one's taste profile public, or social network integration.

Another default that can be used to nudge privacy decisions is the order of the disclosure requests. Acquisti et al. demonstrated that people disclose less information when requests are made in increasing order of intrusiveness compared to a random order [6]. This effect is particularly pronounced for more intrusive questions: asking those questions upfront increases their likelihood of being answered. Arguably, people become more wary of disclosing very personal information as the disclosed information accumulates; the most relevant information should thus be requested upfront. Similarly, Knijnenburg and Kobsa manipulated the request order, and showed that any type of information enjoys higher disclosure when requested first rather than last [80, 84]. Note though, that although asking sensitive questions upfront increases disclosure in research settings, it may scare away new users when done in commercial applications. The order of disclosure requests arguably has a large impact in conversational recommender systems, where quick convergence on an accurate user model needs to be balanced with privacy concerns related to sensitive information requests. Disclosure request order strategies are thus an important topic for future research in recommender systems.

The problem with existing privacy nudging techniques is that they have to take an implicit stance on whether the purpose of the nudge should be to increase disclosure, or to decrease it. Recommender system developers may claim that it is in users' best interest to provide more data to the recommender, as it will improve their user model and, subsequently, the recommendations. They may thus argue to use nudges to increase disclosure, but these nudges may cause the more privacy-minded users to feel "tricked" into disclosing more information than they would like [28]. Others (e.g., privacy advocates, certain lawmakers) may instead believe that privacy is an absolute right that needs to be defended at all costs. But if the protective nudges they impose make it more difficult to disclose information, this would reduce the overall benefit of a recommender system, especially for less privacy-minded users.

19.4.3 Privacy Adaptation

Given these opposing forces, how can we nudge users in the "right direction?" This is a difficult question, because human decisions are highly dependent on the personal context in which they are made, and the same holds true for information disclosure decisions [5, 73, 97, 110]. For example, the fact that one person has no problems disclosing a certain item in a particular context does not mean that disclosure is equally likely for a different person, a different item, or in a different context [82, 97]. Likewise, a convincing justification to disclose a certain item in a particular context for a certain person, may be completely irrelevant for a different person, a different item, or a different context [25, 79]. The "right direction" of a privacy nudge thus depends on these contextual variables. This idea of context-dependent privacy nudges leads to a new application domain for recommender systems: *user-tailored privacy decision support* [86, 145]. Specifically, a recommender can be used to predict users' context-dependent privacy preferences based on their known characteristics and behaviors, and then provide automatic "smart default" settings [134] in line with their disclosure profiles. Below we outline the budding research in this new field of "privacy adaptation."

The first step towards privacy adaptation is to gain a deeper understanding of people's cognitive decision-making process: What kind of benefits and threats do users consider when making disclosure decisions? What is the relative weight of each of these aspects? Can the weights be influenced by a justification or a default, and if so, in what context(s)?

Some of the work by Knijnenburg et al. tries to measure these cognitive determinants and integrate them in behavioral models of information disclosure decisions. For example, they demonstrate that:

- the effect of justifications on information disclosure decisions is mediated by the user's perceptions of *help*, *trust* and *satisfaction* [80];
- the effect of decision context in a location-sharing service depends on users' perception of the *privacy* and *benefits* of the available options [83] (so-called "context effects;" cf. Chap. 18);
- perceived *risk* and *relevance* mediate user evaluation of the purpose-specificity of information disclosure requests [81].

The second step towards privacy adaptation is to determine how information disclosure depends on the recipient, item and type of user. This would allow to train a recommender that can tailor defaults and justifications to these contextual factors. Work in this direction shows that even though privacy preferences vary considerably across users, recommendation techniques can be used to predict these preferences quite accurately. For example, Knijnenburg et al. identify distinct subgroups of users with similar privacy preferences in many domains [82]. These subgroups can be mapped to demographics and other behaviors, allowing a recommender to classify users into a certain subgroup. Ravichandran et al. [125] apply k-means clustering to users' contextualized location sharing decisions to come up with a number of default policies. They show that a small number of default policies for the user to choose from could accurately capture a large part of their location sharing decisions. Sadeh et al. [129] apply a kNN algorithm and a random forest algorithm to learn users' privacy preferences in a location-sharing system. They show that the applied recommendation techniques can help users in specifying more accurate disclosure preferences. Pallapa et al. [117] propose context-aware approaches to privacy preservation in wireless and mobile pervasive environments. One of their solutions leverages the history of interaction between users to determine the level of privacy required in new situations. They demonstrate that this solution efficiently supports users in dealing with their privacy concerns. Finally, adaptive procedures also work for justifications: although justifications generally do not increase disclosure or satisfaction, Knijnenburg and Kobsa find that tailoring justifications to the user can reduce this negative effect [79].

In sum, privacy adaptation strikes a balance between giving users no control over, or information about, their privacy at all and giving them full control and information. It solves the problem of finding the "right direction" for nudges by using users' own preferences as a yardstick. At the same time, it gives users the right privacy-related information and the right amount of privacy control that is useful, but not overwhelming. It thereby enables users to make privacy-related decisions within the limits of their bounded rationality. In many systems, privacy concerns seem to rise in concert with the complexity of users' privacy decisions. "Privacy adaptation" may thus present a unique opportunity for recommender systems to help solving this problem.

19.5 Summary and Discussion

We conclude the chapter with a summary of the privacy-enhancing solutions that were outlined, along with their current shortcomings. Next, we discuss current and emerging trends in recommender systems and identify the key privacy issues associated with them. Lastly, we suggest research tracks to better address the privacy risks of today and those of the future.

In Sect. 19.2, we discussed various privacy risks originating from the recommender system itself, from other system users, or from third parties. The risks are highly diverse, but center around potential adversaries either directly accessing the existing user data or inferring new information through cross-linking multiple sources of user data. While they can be broadly categorized as either technical or non-technical, the solutions that were proposed in Sect. 19.3 are even more diverse than the challenges they seek to address.

The architectural solutions covered various protocols and certificates that guarantee that the recommender behaves in a way that preserves the users' privacy. Barriers are put up for untrusted parties that may want to access user profiles or infer non-disclosed sensitive data. Then, we proceeded to algorithmic solutions, which incorporate privacy into the recommendation generation process. Here, we partitioned prior works into four broad directions: to anonymize and/or abstract individual users; to introduce noise into the original user data, making it hard to uncover true user preferences; to use differential privacy, a widely-used model that offers provable privacy guarantees; and to exploit cryptography-based approaches to generate recommendations, while keeping user inputs confidential. Note that these directions are by no means mutually exclusive—a recommender may deploy algorithms from several groups to improve user privacy.

As discussed in Sect. 19.4, users have their own perceptions of privacy that do not necessarily align with the privacy assurances provided by the above solutions. Moreover, some of the proposed approaches may even have an opposite effect on users' behavior and their perception of privacy. We suggested that privacy solutions should be tailored to users' inherent privacy preferences. This results in a new opportunity for recommender systems: providing privacy decision support.

The field of recommender systems is still largely evolving, and is gaining emerging popularity in several relatively new use-cases and application domains. Some of these applications pose a significant risk to user privacy, and, therefore, the importance of privacy-preserving recommendations is paramount there. We will briefly discuss some of these cases and highlight their privacy implications.

Recommenders on the Social Web. Online social networks are tremendously popular these days. The social Web attracts billions of users, who not only expose unprecedented volumes of personal information, but also voluntarily cross-link data from a wide spectrum of sources. Various personalization and recommendation technologies have been developed for the social Web (Chap. 15), and these highlight the need for privacy-preserving solutions that will deliver user-tailored services without compromising user privacy.

Cross-Domain Recommender Systems. The challenge of generating recommendations by combining multiple sources of user modeling data, which potentially span several recommender systems and application domains, has recently attracted a lot of attention (Chap. 27). This poses a direct threat to privacy, as domain-specific user profiles are inherently linked, and cross-domain recommenders already apply the techniques mentioned in Sect. 19.2 for the inference of new undisclosed data. Hence, cross-domain recommenders call for a special focus on the preservation of user privacy.

Mobile and Context-Aware Recommendations. Users are increasingly surrounded by sensors and smart environments, which interact directly with the users' personal devices. This facilitates the collection of rich user profiles and opens the opportunity for the delivery of context-aware recommendations (Chaps. 6 and 14). Users have little control over these pervasive data collection procedures. Users may wish to control data access limitations and the invasiveness of the recommender, but since these recommenders typically operate in the background, the act of control itself may disrupt the users' primary workflow. Control mechanisms should thus be very lightweight, lest users simply ignore them.

Explanation of Recommendations. Recommendations are often accompanied by a textual description explaining why the items were recommended to the user (Chap. 10). Consider Amazon's "you were recommended X because you bought

Y" or the widely-used "people who examined X were also interested in Y." While this helps users to find related items and supports the vendors' cross-selling, these explanations can potentially compromise user privacy by leaking private information and revealing information to others watching over the user's shoulder.

Group Recommenders. Consumption of the recommended items is increasingly used in a group setting, where users' individual preferences are combined to provide recommendations that fit the entire group (Chap. 22). In these settings, users may infer the preferences of the members of their group from their combined recommendations. Group recommender systems may thus need to perturb recommendations in a way that allows users a certain level of "plausible deniability" regarding their specific tastes and preferences.

This chapter has presented a patchwork of technical and non-technical solutions that can each address *specific* privacy risks regarding current and future recommender system scenarios. However, it should be highlighted that most of the existing works in the recommender systems space are focused on a single solution and very little has been done on developing a *holistic* and encompassing solution. Hence, the challenge of integrating the diverse (and often conflicting) solutions from the architectural and algorithmic realms, and developing a recommender that is privacy-friendly at the core, user-friendly and maintainable from a development point of view, and, not the least, complies with existing privacy policies, is still open.

At the same time, recommender system developers should not forget that dealing with privacy extends beyond the technical aspects of their systems. The privacy attitudes among recommender system users—the yardstick against which privacy practices should be evaluated—vary considerably and evolve continuously. Therefore, industry players have to engage in an active conversation with their users about what are considered good privacy practices. As we ran a quick survey among industry contacts to get a basic understanding of prevalent industry privacy practices, it became painfully clear that companies do not feel comfortable to talk about even their basic approach to privacy. Moving forward, though, we predict that a more conscientious discussion about privacy in recommender systems will emerge, and we conjecture that the key challenges presented above will be addressed both by the research community and by industrial players concerned with improving the privacy of their customers.

References

1. Ackerman, M.S., Cranor, L.F., Reagle, J.: Privacy in e-commerce: Examining user scenarios and privacy preferences. In: Proceedings of the 1st ACM Conference on Electronic Commerce, EC '99, pp. 1–8. ACM, New York, NY, USA (1999). DOI 10.1145/336992.336995
2. Acquisti, A.: Privacy in electronic commerce and the economics of immediate gratification. In: Proceedings of the 5th ACM conference on Electronic commerce, EC '04, pp. 21–29. ACM, New York, NY (2004). DOI 10.1145/988772.988777
3. Acquisti, A.: Nudging privacy: The behavioral economics of personal information. IEEE Security and Privacy **7**, 82–85 (2009). DOI http://dx.doi.org/10.1109/MSP.2009.163

4. Acquisti, A., Grossklags, J.: Privacy and rationality in individual decision making. IEEE Security & Privacy **3**(1), 26–33 (2005). DOI 10.1109/MSP.2005.22
5. Acquisti, A., Grossklags, J.: What can behavioral economics teach us about privacy? In: A. Acquisti, S. De Capitani di Vimercati, S. Gritzalis, C. Lambrinoudakis (eds.) Digital Privacy: Theory, Technologies, and Practices, pp. 363–377. Auerbach Publications (2008)
6. Acquisti, A., John, L.K., Loewenstein, G.: The impact of relative standards on the propensity to disclose. Journal of Marketing Research **49**(2), 160–174 (2012). DOI 10.1509/jmr.09.0215
7. Agrawal, R., Srikant, R.: Privacy-preserving data mining. In: SIGMOD Conference, pp. 439–450 (2000)
8. Aïmeur, E., Brassard, G., Fernandez, J.M., Mani Onana, F.S.: Alambic: A privacy-preserving recommender system for electronic commerce. International Journal of Information Security **7**(5), 307–334 (2008). DOI 10.1007/s10207-007-0049-3
9. Arlein, R.M., Jai, B., Jakobsson, M., Monrose, F., Reiter, M.K.: Privacy-preserving global customization. In: Proceedings of the 2nd ACM Conference on Electronic Commerce, EC '00, pp. 176–184. ACM, New York, NY, USA (2000). DOI 10.1145/352871.352891
10. Awad, N.F., Krishnan, M.S.: The personalization privacy paradox: An empirical evaluation of information transparency and the willingness to be profiled online for personalization. MIS Quarterly **30**(1), 13–28 (2006)
11. Bakos, Y., Marotta-Wurgler, F., Trossen, D.R.: Does anyone read the fine print? testing a law and economics approach toStandard form contracts (2009). URL http://archive.nyu.edu/handle/2451/29503
12. Barbaro, M., Zeller Jr., T.: A face is exposed for AOL searcher no. 4417749. URL http://www.nytimes.com/2006/08/09/technology/09aol.html. [Online; accessed 22-January-2014]
13. Basu, A., Kikuchi, H., Vaidya, J.: Privacy-preserving weighted Slope One predictor for Item-based Collaborative Filtering. In: Proceedings of the international workshop on Trust and Privacy in Distributed Information Processing, Copenhagen, Denmark (2011)
14. Basu, A., Vaidya, J., Kikuchi, H.: Perturbation based privacy preserving slope one predictors for collaborative filtering. In: IFIPTM, pp. 17–35 (2012)
15. Basu, A., Vaidya, J., Kikuchi, H., Dimitrakos, T.: Privacy-preserving collaborative filtering on the cloud and practical implementation experiences. In: IEEE CLOUD, pp. 406–413 (2013)
16. Beatty, P., Reay, I., Dick, S., Miller, J.: P3P adoption on e-commerce web sites: A survey and analysis. IEEE Internet Computing **11**(2), 65–71 (2007). DOI 10.1109/MIC.2007.45
17. Beckett, L.: Big data brokers: They know everything about you and sell it to the highest bidder (18 March 2013).
18. Bélanger, F., Crossler, R.E.: Privacy in the digital age: A review of information privacy research in information systems. MIS Quarterly **35**(4), 1017–1042 (2011)
19. Benassi, P.: TRUSTe: an online privacy seal program. Commun. ACM **42**(2), 56–59 (1999)
20. Bennett, J., Lanning, S.: The netflix prize. In: KDD Cup (2007)
21. Berkovsky, S., Borisov, N., Eytani, Y., Kuflik, T., Ricci, F.: Examining users' attitude towards privacy preserving collaborative filtering. Proceedings of DM. UM **7** (2007)
22. Berkovsky, S., Eytani, Y., Kuflik, T., Ricci, F.: Hierarchical neighborhood topology for privacy enhanced collaborative filtering. Proceedings of PEP06, CHI 2006 Workshop on Privacy-Enhanced Personalization, Montreal, Canada pp. 6–13 (2006)
23. Berkovsky, S., Eytani, Y., Kuflik, T., Ricci, F.: Enhancing privacy and preserving accuracy of a distributed collaborative filtering. In: RecSys, pp. 9–16 (2007)
24. Berkovsky, S., Kuflik, T., Ricci, F.: The impact of data obfuscation on the accuracy of collaborative filtering. Expert Syst. Appl. **39**(5), 5033–5042 (2012)
25. Besmer, A., Watson, J., Lipford, H.R.: The impact of social navigation on privacy policy configuration. In: Proceedings of the Sixth Symposium on Usable Privacy and Security, p. Article 7. Redmond, Washington (2010). DOI 10.1145/1837110.1837120
26. Bojars, U., Passant, A., Breslin, J.G., Decker, S.: Social network and data portability using semantic web technologies. In: 2nd Workshop on Social Aspects of the Web (SAW 2008) at BIS2008, pp. 5–19 (2008)

27. Bonneau, J., Anderson, J., Danezis, G.: Prying data out of a social network. In: Social Network Analysis and Mining, 2009. ASONAM'09. International Conference on Advances in, pp. 249–254. IEEE (2009)
28. Brown, C.L., Krishna, A.: The skeptical shopper: A metacognitive account for the effects of default options on choice. Journal of Consumer Research **31**(3), 529–539 (2004). DOI 10.1086/425087
29. Buley, T.: Netflix settles privacy lawsuit, cancels prize sequel. Forbes (3 December 2010).
30. Bustos, L.: Best practice gone bad: 4 shocking A/B tests (2012). URL http://www.getelastic.com/best-practice-gone-bad-4-shocking-ab-tests/
31. Calandrino, J.A., Kilzer, A., Narayanan, A., Felten, E.W., Shmatikov, V.: "you might also like:" privacy risks of collaborative filtering. In: IEEE Symposium on Security and Privacy, pp. 231–246 (2011)
32. Canny, J.F.: Collaborative filtering with privacy. In: Proceedings of the IEEE Symposium on Security and Privacy, pp. 45–57. IEEE Computer Society, Washington, DC, USA (2002)
33. Canny, J.F.: Collaborative filtering with privacy via factor analysis. In: SIGIR, pp. 238–245 (2002)
34. Cavoukian, A.: Privacy by design: The 7 foundational principles. Tech. rep., Information and Privacy Commissioner of Ontario, Canada, Ontario, Canada (2009).
35. Cavusoglu, H., Phan, T., Cavusoglu, H.: Privacy controls and content sharing patterns of online social network users: A natural experiment. ICIS 2013 Proceedings (2013)
36. Chaabane, A., Acs, G., Kaafar, M.A.: You Are What You Like! Information Leakage Through Users' Interests. In: 19th Annual Network & Distributed System Security Symposium (2012)
37. Chellappa, R.K., Sin, R.G.: Personalization versus privacy: An empirical examination of the online consumer's dilemma. Information Technology and Management **6**(2), 181–202 (2005). DOI 10.1007/s10799-005-5879-y
38. Chen, T., Boreli, R., Kaafar, D., Friedman, A.: On the effectiveness of obfuscation techniques in online social networks. In: The 14th Privacy Enhancing Technologies Symposium, pp. 42–62 (2014)
39. Cissée, R., Albayrak, S.: An agent-based approach for privacy-preserving recommender systems. In: Proceedings of the 6th International Joint Conference on Autonomous Agents and Multiagent Systems, AAMAS '07, pp. 182:1–182:8. ACM, New York, NY, USA (2007)
40. Compañó, R., Lusoli, W.: The policy maker's anguish: Regulating personal data behavior between paradoxes and dilemmas. In: T. Moore, D. Pym, C. Ioannidis (eds.) Economics of Information Security and Privacy, pp. 169–185. Springer US, New York, NY (2010)
41. Consolvo, S., Smith, I., Matthews, T., LaMarca, A., Tabert, J., Powledge, P.: Location disclosure to social relations: why, when, & what people want to share. In: Proceedings of the SIGCHI Conference on Human Factors in Computing Systems, pp. 81–90. Portland, OR (2005). DOI 10.1145/1054972.1054985
42. Consumer Reports: Facebook & your privacy: Who sees the data you share on the biggest social network? (2012). URL http://www.consumerreports.org/cro/magazine/2012/06/facebook-your-privacy
43. Cranor, L.F.: Web Privacy with P3P. O'Reilly & Associates, Inc., Sebastopol, CA (2002)
44. Cranor, L.F.: 'I didn't buy it for myself': privacy and ecommerce personalization. In: WPES, pp. 111–117 (2003)
45. Culnan, M.J., Bies, R.J.: Consumer privacy: Balancing economic and justice considerations. Journal of Social Issues **59**(2), 323–342 (2003). DOI 10.1111/1540-4560.00067
46. Dhar, V., Hsieh, J., Sundararajan, A.: Comments on 'Protecting consumer privacy in an era of rapid change: Aproposed framework for businesses and policymakers'. NYU Working Paper CEDER-11-04, New York University, New York, NY (2011)
47. Duhigg, C.: How companies learn your secrets. New York Times Magazine (16 February 2012). URL http://www.nytimes.com/2012/02/19/magazine/shopping-habits.html. [Online; accessed 22-January-2014]
48. Dwork, C., McSherry, F., Nissim, K., Smith, A.: Calibrating noise to sensitivity in private data analysis. In: TCC, pp. 265–284 (2006)

49. Dwork, C., Pitassi, T., Naor, M., Rothblum, G.N.: Differential privacy under continual observation. In: STOC, pp. 715–724 (2010)
50. Egelman, S., Tsai, J., Cranor, L.F., Acquisti, A.: Timing is everything?: the effects of timing and placement of online privacy indicators. In: Proceedings of the 27th international conference on Human factors in computing systems, CHI '09, pp. 319–328. ACM (2009)
51. Erkin, Z., Beye, M., Veugen, T., Lagendijk, R.L.: Privacy enhanced recommender system. Thirty-first Symposium on Information Theory in the Benelux pp. 35–42 (2010)
52. Erkin, Z., Veugen, T., Lagendijk, R.L.: Generating private recommendations in a social trust network. In: CASoN, pp. 82–87 (2011)
53. Erkin, Z., Veugen, T., Toft, T., Lagendijk, R.L.: Generating private recommendations efficiently using homomorphic encryption and data packing. IEEE Transactions on Information Forensics and Security **7**(3), 1053–1066 (2012)
54. EU: Directive 2002/58/EC of the european parliament and of the council concerning the processing of personal data and the protection of privacy in the electronic communications sector. Tech. rep., European Commission (2002)
55. EU: Proposal for a directive of the european parliament and of the council on the protection of individuals with regard to the processing of personal data by competent authorities for the purposes of prevention, investigation, detection or prosecution of criminal offences or the execution of criminal penalties, and the free movement of such data. Tech. Rep. 2012/0010 (COD), European Commission (2012)
56. Felten, E.W.: Understanding trusted computing: Will its benefits outweigh its drawbacks? IEEE Security & Privacy **1**(3), 60–62 (2003)
57. Friedman, A., Sharfman, I., Keren, D., Schuster, A.: Privacy-preserving distributed stream monitoring. In: Proceedings of the 21st Annual Network & Distributed System Security Symposium, NDSS '14. Internet Society (2014)
58. van de Garde-Perik, E., Markopoulos, P., de Ruyter, B., Eggen, B., Ijsselsteijn, W.: Investigating privacy attitudes and behavior in relation to personalization. Social Science Computer Review **26**(1), 20–43 (2008). DOI 10.1177/0894439307307682
59. Gardner, J.: 12 surprising A/B test results to stop you making assumptions (2012). URL http://unbounce.com/a-b-testing/shocking-results/
60. Goldfarb, A., Tucker, C.E.: Privacy regulation and online advertising. Management Science **57**(1), 57–71 (2011). DOI 10.1287/mnsc.1100.1246
61. Hancock, J.T., Thom-Santelli, J., Ritchie, T.: Deception and design: the impact of communication technology on lying behavior. In: Proceedings of the SIGCHI conference on Human factors in computing systems, CHI '04, pp. 129–134. ACM, New York, NY, USA (2004)
62. Hann, I.H., Hui, K.L., Lee, S.Y., Png, I.: Overcoming online information privacy concerns: An information-processing theory approach. Journal of Management Information Systems **24**(2), 13–42 (2007). DOI 10.2753/MIS0742-1222240202
63. Harris, L., Westin, A.F., associates: Consumer privacy attitudes: A major shift since 2000 and why. Tech. Rep. 10, Harris Interactive, Inc. (2003)
64. Heitmann, B., Kim, J.G., Passant, A., Hayes, C., Kim, H.G.: An architecture for privacy-enabled user profile portability on the web of data. In: Proceedings of the 1st International Workshop on Information Heterogeneity and Fusion in Recommender Systems, HetRec '10, pp. 16–23. ACM, New York, NY, USA (2010). DOI 10.1145/1869446.1869449
65. Hoens, T.R., Blanton, M., Chawla, N.V.: A private and reliable recommendation system for social networks. In: Proceedings of the 2010 IEEE Second International Conference on Social Computing, SOCIALCOM '10, pp. 816–825. IEEE Computer Society, Washington, DC, USA (2010). DOI 10.1109/SocialCom.2010.124
66. Hollenbach, J., Presbrey, J., Berners-Lee, T.: Using rdf metadata to enable access control on the social semantic web. In: Proceedings of the Workshop on Collaborative Construction, Management and Linking of Structured Knowledge (CK2009), vol. 514 (2009)
67. House, W.: Consumer data privacy in a networked world: A framework for protecting privacy and promoting innovation in the global economy. Tech. rep., White House, Washington, D.C. (2012)

68. Hui, K.L., Teo, H.H., Lee, S.Y.T.: The value of privacy assurance: An exploratory field experiment. MIS Quarterly **31**(1), 19–33 (2007)
69. ICO: Guidance on the rules on use of cookies and similar technologies. Tech. rep., Information Commissioner's Office (2012)
70. Isaacman, S., Ioannidis, S., Chaintreau, A., Martonosi, M.: Distributed rating prediction in user generated content streams. In: RecSys, pp. 69–76 (2011)
71. Jeckmans, A., Tang, Q., Hartel, P.: Privacy-preserving collaborative filtering based on horizontally partitioned dataset. In: Collaboration Technologies and Systems (CTS), 2012 International Conference on, pp. 439–446 (2012). DOI 10.1109/CTS.2012.6261088
72. Jeckmans, A.J., Beye, M., Erkin, Z., Hartel, P., Lagendijk, R.L., Tang, Q.: Privacy in recommender systems. In: Social Media Retrieval, Computer Communications and Networks, pp. 263–281. Springer (2013)
73. John, L.K., Acquisti, A., Loewenstein, G.: Strangers on a plane: Context-dependent willingness to divulge sensitive information. Journal of consumer research **37**(5), 858–873 (2011)
74. Jøsang, A., Ismail, R., Boyd, C.: A survey of trust and reputation systems for online service provision. Decis. Support Syst. **43**(2), 618–644 (2007). DOI 10.1016/j.dss.2005.05.019
75. Kahneman, D., Tversky, A.: Prospect theory: An analysis of decision under risk. Econometrica **47**(2), 263–292 (1979). DOI 10.2307/1914185
76. Kaleli, C., Polat, H.: Providing private recommendations using naïve bayesian classifier. In: K.M. Wegrzyn-Wolska, P.S. Szczepaniak (eds.) Advances in Intelligent Web Mastering, *Advances in Soft Computing*, vol. 43, pp. 168–173. Springer Berlin Heidelberg (2007)
77. Kandappu, T., Friedman, A., Boreli, R., Sivaraman, V.: PrivacyCanary: Privacy-aware recommenders with adaptive input obfuscation. In: MASCOTS (2014)
78. Knijnenburg, B.P., Jin, H.: The persuasive effect of privacy recommendations. In: Twelfth Annual Workshop on HCI Research in MIS, p. Paper 16. Milan, Italy (2013)
79. Knijnenburg, B.P., Kobsa, A.: Helping users with information disclosure decisions: potential for adaptation. In: Proceedings of the 2013 ACM international conference on Intelligent User Interfaces, pp. 407–416. ACM Press, Santa Monica, CA (2013)
80. Knijnenburg, B.P., Kobsa, A.: Making decisions about privacy: Information disclosure in context-aware recommender systems. ACM Transactions on Interactive Intelligent Systems **3**(3), 20:1–20:23 (2013). DOI 10.1145/2499670
81. Knijnenburg, B.P., Kobsa, A., Jin, H.: Counteracting the negative effect of form autocompletion on the privacy calculus. In: ICIS 2013 Proceedings. Milan, Italy (2013)
82. Knijnenburg, B.P., Kobsa, A., Jin, H.: Dimensionality of information disclosure behavior. International Journal of Human-Computer Studies **71**(12), 1144–1162 (2013)
83. Knijnenburg, B.P., Kobsa, A., Jin, H.: Preference-based location sharing: are more privacy options really better? In: Proceedings of the SIGCHI Conference on Human Factors in Computing Systems, pp. 2667–2676. ACM, Paris, France (2013). DOI 10.1145/2470654.2481369
84. Knijnenburg, B.P., Kobsa, A., Saldamli, G.: Privacy in mobile personalized systems: The effect of disclosure justifications. In: Proceedings of the SOUPS 2012 Workshop on Usable Privacy & Security for Mobile Devices, pp. 11:1–11:5. Washington, DC (2012)
85. Knijnenburg, B.P., Willemsen, M.C., Hirtbach, S.: Receiving recommendations and providing feedback: The user-experience of a recommender system. In: EC-Web, pp. 207–216 (2010)
86. Kobsa, A.: Tailoring privacy to users' needs (invited keynote). In: M. Bauer, P.J. Gmytrasiewicz, J. Vassileva (eds.) User Modeling 2001, no. 2109 in Lecture Notes in Computer Science, pp. 303–313. Springer Verlag (2001).
87. Kobsa, A.: Privacy-enhanced web personalization. In: P. Brusilovsky, A. Kobsa, W. Nejdl (eds.) The Adaptive Web, pp. 628–670. Springer-Verlag, Berlin, Heidelberg (2007)
88. Kobsa, A., Knijnenburg, B.P., Livshits, B.: Let's do it at my place instead? attitudinal and behavioral study of privacy in client-side personalization. In: ACM CHI Conference on Human Factors in Computing Systems. Toronto, Canada (2014)
89. Kobsa, A., Schreck, J.: Privacy through pseudonymity in user-adaptive systems. ACM Trans. Internet Techn. **3**(2), 149–183 (2003)

90. Kobsa, A., Teltzrow, M.: Contextualized communication of privacy practices and personalization benefits: Impacts on users' data sharing and purchase behavior. In: D. Martin, A. Serjantov (eds.) Privacy Enhancing Technologies: Revised Selected Papers of the 4th International Workshop, PET 2004, Toronto, Canada, May 26–28, 2004, *LNCS*, vol. 3424, pp. 329–343. Springer Berlin Heidelberg (2005). DOI 10.1007/b136164
91. Kosinski, M., Stillwell, D., Graepel, T.: Private traits and attributes are predictable from digital records of human behavior. Proceedings of the National Academy of Sciences (2013)
92. Krishnamurthy, B., Wills, C.: Privacy diffusion on the web: A longitudinal perspective. In: Proceedings of the 18th International Conference on World Wide Web, WWW '09, pp. 541–550. ACM, New York, NY, USA (2009). DOI 10.1145/1526709.1526782
93. Lai, Y.L., Hui, K.L.: Internet opt-in and opt-out: Investigating the roles of frames, defaults and privacy concerns. In: Proceedings of the 2006 ACM SIGMIS CPR Conference on Computer Personnel Research, pp. 253–263. Claremont, CA (2006). DOI 10.1145/1125170.1125230
94. Lathia, N., Hailes, S., Capra, L.: Private distributed collaborative filtering using estimated concordance measures. In: Proceedings of the 2007 ACM Conference on Recommender Systems, RecSys '07, pp. 1–8. ACM, New York, NY, USA (2007)
95. Laufer, R.S., Proshansky, H.M., Wolfe, M.: Some analytic dimensions of privacy. In: R. Küller (ed.) Proceedings of the Lund Conference on Architectural Psychology. Dowden, Hutchinson & Ross, Lund, Sweden (1973)
96. Lemire, D., Maclachlan, A.: Slope one predictors for online rating-based collaborative filtering. In: SDM (2005)
97. Li, H., Sarathy, R., Xu, H.: Understanding situational online information disclosure as a privacy calculus. Journal of Computer Information Systems **51**(1), 62–71 (2010)
98. Li, T., Unger, T.: Willing to pay for quality personalization? trade-off between quality and privacy. European Journal of Information Systems **21**(6), 621–642 (2012)
99. Lin, J., Sadeh, N.M., Amini, S., Lindqvist, J., Hong, J.I., Zhang, J.: Expectation and purpose: understanding users' mental models of mobile app privacy through crowdsourcing. In: UbiComp, pp. 501–510 (2012)
100. Liu, Y., Gummadi, K.P., Krishnamurthy, B., Mislove, A.: Analyzing facebook privacy settings: user expectations vs. reality. In: Proceedings of the 2011 ACM SIGCOMM conference on Internet measurement conference, pp. 61–70. ACM, Berlin, Germany (2011)
101. Machanavajjhala, A., Korolova, A., Sarma, A.D.: Personalized social recommendations - accurate or private? PVLDB **4**(7), 440–450 (2011)
102. Malhotra, N.K., Kim, S.S., Agarwal, J.: Internet users' information privacy concerns (IUIPC): the construct, the scale, and a nomological framework. Information Systems Research **15**(4), 336–355 (2004). DOI 10.1287/isre.1040.0032
103. McSherry, F., Mironov, I.: Differentially private recommender systems: Building privacy into the netflix prize contenders. In: KDD, pp. 627–636 (2009)
104. Metzger, M.J.: Privacy, trust, and disclosure: Exploring barriers to electronic commerce. Journal of Computer-Mediated Communication **9**(4) (2004)
105. Mikians, J., Gyarmati, L., Erramilli, V., Laoutaris, N.: Detecting price and search discrimination on the internet. In: HotNets, pp. 79–84 (2012)
106. Mikians, J., Gyarmati, L., Erramilli, V., Laoutaris, N.: Crowd-assisted search for price discrimination in e-commerce: first results. In: CoNEXT, pp. 1–6 (2013)
107. Miller, B.N., Konstan, J.A., Riedl, J.: Pocketlens: Toward a personal recommender system. ACM Transactions on Information Systems **22**(3), 437–476 (2004)
108. Narayanan, A., Shmatikov, V.: Robust de-anonymization of large sparse datasets. In: IEEE Symposium on Security and Privacy, pp. 111–125 (2008)
109. Nikolaenko, V., Ioannidis, S., Weinsberg, U., Joye, M., Taft, N., Boneh, D.: Privacy-preserving matrix factorization. In: ACM Conference on Computer and Communications Security, pp. 801–812 (2013)
110. Nissenbaum, H.: Privacy as contextual integrity. Washington Law Review **79**(1), 101–139 (2004)
111. Nissenbaum, H.: A contextual approach to privacy online. Daedalus **140**(4), 32–48 (2011)

112. Nissim, K., Raskhodnikova, S., Smith, A.: Smooth sensitivity and sampling in private data analysis. In: Proceedings of the Thirty-ninth Annual ACM Symposium on Theory of Computing, STOC '07, pp. 75–84. ACM, New York, NY, USA (2007)
113. Norberg, P.A., Horne, D.R., Horne, D.A.: The privacy paradox: Personal information disclosure intentions versus behaviors. Journal of Consumer Affairs **41**(1), 100–126 (2007)
114. OECD: Recommendation of the council concerning guidelines governing the protection of privacy and transborder flows of personal data. Tech. rep., Organization for Economic Co-operation and Development (1980). Print file://Lit1/OECD-privacy-1980.htm
115. Ohm, P.: Broken promises of privacy: Responding to the surprising failure of anonymization. UCLA Law Review **57**, 1701 (2010)
116. Paillier, P.: Public-key cryptosystems based on composite degree residuosity classes. In: EUROCRYPT, pp. 223–238 (1999)
117. Pallapa, G., Das, S.K., Di Francesco, M., Aura, T.: Adaptive and context-aware privacy preservation exploiting user interactions in smart environments. Pervasive and Mobile Computing **12**, 232–243 (2014). DOI 10.1016/j.pmcj.2013.12.004. URL http://www.sciencedirect.com/science/article/pii/S1574119213001557
118. Parameswaran, R., Blough, D.M.: Privacy preserving collaborative filtering using data obfuscation. In: Proceedings of the IEEE Conference on Granular Computing, p. 380 (2007)
119. Pfitzmann, A., Hansen, M.: A terminology for talking about privacy by data minimization: Anonymity, unlinkability, undetectability, unobservability, pseudonymity, and identity management. http://dud.inf.tu-dresden.de/literatur/Anon_Terminology_v0.34.pdf (2010)
120. Polat, H., Du, W.: Privacy-preserving collaborative filtering using randomized perturbation techniques. In: ICDM, pp. 625–628 (2003)
121. Polat, H., Du, W.: Svd-based collaborative filtering with privacy. In: SAC, pp. 791–795 (2005)
122. Polat, H., Du, W.: Achieving private recommendations using randomized response techniques. In: PAKDD, pp. 637–646 (2006)
123. Put, A., Dacosta, I., Milutinovic, M., De Decker, B., Seys, S., Boukayoua, F., Naessens, V., Vanhecke, K., De Pessemier, T., Martens, L.: inshopnito: An advanced yet privacy-friendly mobile shopping application. In: Proceedings of 2014 IEEE World Congress on Services. IEEE Computer Society Press (2014). URL https://lirias.kuleuven.be/handle/123456789/454582
124. Ramakrishnan, N., Keller, B.J., Mirza, B.J., Grama, A., Karypis, G.: Privacy risks in recommender systems. IEEE Internet Computing **5**(6), 54–62 (2001)
125. Ravichandran, R., Benisch, M., Kelley, P., Sadeh, N.: Capturing social networking privacy preferences:. In: I. Goldberg, M. Atallah (eds.) Privacy Enhancing Technologies, *Lecture Notes in Computer Science*, vol. 5672, pp. 1–18. Springer Berlin / Heidelberg (2009).
126. Renckes, S., Polat, H., Oysal, Y.: A new hybrid recommendation algorithm with privacy. Expert Systems **29**(1), 39–55 (2012)
127. Riboni, D., Bettini, C.: Private context-aware recommendation of points of interest: An initial investigation. In: PerCom Workshops, pp. 584–589 (2012)
128. Rifon, N.J., LaRose, R., Choi, S.M.: Your privacy is sealed: Effects of web privacy seals on trust and personal disclosures. Journal of Consumer Affairs **39**(2), 339–360 (2005)
129. Sadeh, N., Hong, J., Cranor, L., Fette, I., Kelley, P., Prabaker, M., Rao, J.: Understanding and capturing people's privacy policies in a mobile social networking application. Personal and Ubiquitous Computing **13**(6), 401–412 (2009). DOI 10.1007/s00779-008-0214-3
130. Schafer, J.B., Konstan, J.A., Riedl, J.: E-commerce recommendation applications. Data Min. Knowl. Discov. **5**(1/2), 115–153 (2001)
131. Shokri, R., Pedarsani, P., Theodorakopoulos, G., Hubaux, J.P.: Preserving privacy in collaborative filtering through distributed aggregation of offline profiles. In: RecSys, pp. 157–164 (2009)
132. Smith, H.J., Dinev, T., Xu, H.: Information privacy research: An interdisciplinary review. MIS Quarterly **35**(4), 989–1016 (2011)
133. Smith, H.J., Milberg, S.J., Burke, S.J.: Information privacy: Measuring individuals' concerns about organizational practices. MIS Quarterly **20**(2), 167–196 (1996)

134. Smith, N.C., Goldstein, D.G., Johnson, E.J.: Choice without awareness: Ethical and policy implications of defaults. Journal of Public Policy & Marketing **32**(2), 159–172 (2013)
135. Solove, D.J.: Privacy self-management and the consent dilemma. Harvard Law Review **126**, 1880–1903 (2013)
136. Stafford, J., Wallnau, K.: Is third party certification necessary. In: Proceedings of the 4th ICSE Workshop on Component-based Software Engineering: Component Certification and System Prediction, pp. 13–17 (2001)
137. Suguri, H.: A standardization effort for agent technologies: The foundation for intelligent physical agents and its activities. In: HICSS (1999)
138. Taylor, D., Davis, D., Jillapalli, R.: Privacy concern and online personalization: The moderating effects of information control and compensation. Electronic Commerce Research **9**(3), 203–223 (2009). DOI 10.1007/s10660-009-9036-2
139. Toch, E., Wang, Y., Cranor, L.F.: Personalization and privacy: a survey of privacy risks and remedies in personalization-based systems. User Modeling and User-Adapted Interaction **22**(1–2), 203–220 (2012). DOI 10.1007/s11257-011-9110-z
140. TRUSTe: First in-depth analysis of the impact of EU cookie directive shows majority of users choosing to allow advertising cookies (2012).
141. Vallet, D., Friedman, A., Berkovsky, S.: Matrix factorization without user data retention. In: PAKDD (2014)
142. Walton, D.: Plausible deniability and evasion of burden of proof. Argumentation **10**(1), 47–58 (1996). DOI 10.1007/BF00126158
143. Wang, W., Benbasat, I.: Recommendation agents for electronic commerce: Effects of explanation facilities on trusting beliefs. Journal of Management Information Systems **23**(4), 217–246 (2007). DOI 10.2753/MIS0742-1222230410
144. Wang, Y., Kobsa, A.: Impacts of privacy laws and regulations on personalized systems. In: A. Kobsa, R. Chellappa, S. Spiekermann (eds.) Proceedings of PEP06, CHI 2006 Workshop on Privacy-Enhanced Personalization, pp. 44–46. Springer Verlag, Montréal, Canada (2006)
145. Wang, Y., Kobsa, A.: Respecting users' individual privacy constraints in web personalization. In: C. Conati, K. McCoy, G. Paliouras (eds.) User Modeling 2007, pp. 157–166. Springer Verlag (2007)
146. Wang, Y., Leon, P.G., Scott, K., Chen, X., Acquisti, A., Cranor, L.F.: Privacy nudges for social media: An exploratory facebook study. In: Second International Workshop on Privacy and Security in Online Social Media. Rio De Janeiro, Brazil (2013)
147. Weinsberg, U., Bhagat, S., Ioannidis, S., Taft, N.: Blurme: inferring and obfuscating user gender based on ratings. In: RecSys, pp. 195–202 (2012)
148. Westin, A.F., Harris, L., associates: The Dimensions of privacy : a national opinion research survey of attitudes toward privacy. Garland Publishing, New York (1981)
149. Xu, H., Luo, X.R., Carroll, J.M., Rosson, M.B.: The personalization privacy paradox: An exploratory study of decision making process for location-aware marketing. Decision Support Systems **51**(1), 42–52 (2011). DOI 10.1016/j.dss.2010.11.017
150. Xu, H., Teo, H.H., Tan, B.C.Y.: Predicting the adoption of location-based services: The role of trust and perceived privacy risk. In: Proceedings of the International Conference on Information Systems, pp. 861–874. Las Vegas, NV (2005)
151. Xu, H., Teo, H.H., Tan, B.C.Y., Agarwal, R.: Effects of individual self-protection, industry self-regulation, and government regulation on privacy concerns: A study of location-based services. Information Systems Research (2012). DOI 10.1287/isre.1120.0416
152. Xu, H., Wang, N., Grossklags, J.: Privacy-by-ReDesign: alleviating privacy concerns for third-party applications. In: ICIS 2012 Proceedings. Orlando, FL (2012)
153. Yakut, I., Polat, H.: Privacy-preserving eigentaste-based collaborative filtering. In: A. Miyaji, H. Kikuchi, K. Rannenberg (eds.) Advances in Information and Computer Security, *Lecture Notes in Computer Science*, vol. 4752, pp. 169–184. Springer Berlin Heidelberg (2007)
154. Yakut, I., Polat, H.: Arbitrarily distributed data-based recommendations with privacy. Data & Knowledge Engineering **72**(0), 239–256 (2012)

155. Yao, A.C.: Protocols for secure computations. In: Proceedings of the 23rd Annual Symposium on Foundations of Computer Science, SFCS '82, pp. 160–164. IEEE Computer Society, Washington, DC, USA (1982). DOI 10.1109/SFCS.1982.88
156. Zhang, A., Bhamidipati, S., Fawaz, N., Kveton, B.: Priview: Media consumption and recommendation meet privacy against inference attacks. In: W2SP (2014)
157. Zheleva, E., Getoor, L.: To join or not to join: the illusion of privacy in social networks with mixed public and private user profiles. In: WWW, pp. 531–540 (2009)
158. Zhu, T., Ren, Y., Zhou, W., Rong, J., Xiong, P.: An effective privacy preserving algorithm for neighborhood-based collaborative filtering. Future Generation Computer Systems (2013)

Chapter 20
Source Factors in Recommender System Credibility Evaluation

Kyung-Hyan Yoo, Ulrike Gretzel, and Markus Zanker

20.1 Introduction

Recommender systems are taking on an important role in supporting online users during complex decision-making processes by providing personalized advice [9, 73]. Yet, although recommender systems make recommendations based on often sophisticated data mining and analysis techniques, it cannot be automatically implied that the advice provided by a system will be accepted by its users. Whether a recommendation is seen as credible advice and actually taken into account not only depends on users' perceptions of the recommendation but also of the system as the advice-giver. The traditional persuasion literature suggests that people are more likely to accept recommendations from credible sources. It has recently been argued that creating a credible recommender system is important for increasing the likelihood of recommendation acceptance [32, 42, 69, 108, 162]. The question of how to actually translate credibility into system characteristics in the context of recommender systems remains, however, underexplored.

Recent research regarding the persuasiveness of technology suggests that technologies can be more credible and persuasive when leveraging social aspects that

K.-H. Yoo (✉)
William Paterson University, 300 Pompton Road, Wayne, NJ, USA
e-mail: yook2@wpunj.edu

U. Gretzel
University of Queensland, Sir Fred Schonell Drive,
St. Lucia, Brisbane, QLD 4072, Australia
e-mail: u.gretzel@business.uq.edu.au

M. Zanker
Alpen-Adria-Universitaet Klagenfurt, Universitaetsstrasse 65,
9020 Klagenfurt, Austria
e-mail: markus.zanker@aau.at

F. Ricci et al. (eds.), *Recommender Systems Handbook*,
DOI 10.1007/978-1-4899-7637-6_20

elicit social responses from their human users [42, 105]. This notion emphasizes the role of recommender systems as quasi-social actors, and thus, sources of advice whose characteristics influence the perceptions of their users. Various influential source factors have been investigated in the traditional persuasion literature based on human-human communication. Recent research in the context of human-computer interaction found that these factors are also important when humans interact with technologies [42, 43, 105, 124]. With regards to recommender systems, some studies exist that have investigated various influences of system characteristics when users evaluate systems as well as recommendations (e.g. [28, 91, 108, 121, 122]). While these findings provide good examples of source factors that help to develop more credible recommender systems, still many possibly influential source characteristics have not been examined. Consequently, this chapter seeks to provide a synopsis of credibility-related research to draw attention to source factors which likely play a role in recommender system credibility evaluations. For that purpose, this chapter will first give a brief overview of the source factors found influential in traditional interpersonal advice seeking relationships. Then, source characteristics which have been studied in the context of human and technology interaction and, in particular, in the recommender systems realm will be discussed. Finally, the chapter identifies research gaps in terms of source factors that have yet to be examined in the context of recommender systems. Overall, by exploring existing findings and identifying important knowledge gaps, this chapter seeks to provide insights for recommender system researchers as far as future research needs are concerned. It also aims at providing practical implications for recommender system designers who seek to enhance the credibility of the recommender systems they build. Note that this chapter focuses on the source characteristics of recommender systems that determine users' credibility perceptions. The issue of human users' decision-making and the role of recommender systems to support these processes is dealt with in Chap. 18. Furthermore, see Chap. 6 for discussions about contextual information in recommender systems.

20.2 Credibility Evaluation of Online Sources

With the plethora of information available online, a growing number of online users seeks an effective way to find information and evaluate its credibility. Past online credibility literature has identified a number of different ways that online information seekers use for their online credibility judgment. At the beginning of online credibility research, a number of research groups (e.g. [127, 142]) have identified five criteria that users should employ in their assessments of the credibility of online information: accuracy, authority, objectivity, currency, and coverage. Several subsequent empirical studies, however, have revealed that Internet users do not vigorously apply all five criteria in their judgment of online information credibility [39, 134]. Rather, recent studies found that most Internet users invoke cognitive heuristics and rely on others to evaluate the credibility of information and sources online [92]. This means that simple cues displayed by online sources (e.g. Website design/presentation, positive reviews from consumers, endorsements from a third party) can be the primary factor in users' online information credibility assessments. Indeed, a common finding in online credibility research is that online users often process the surface characteristics of Websites and sources when evaluating credibility [40, 42]. In the recommender system context, this suggests the need for research that examines the impacts of source characteristics on system credibility evaluation.

20.3 Recommender Systems as Social Actors

Most existing recommender system studies have viewed recommender systems as software tools and have largely neglected their social role in the interaction with users. A growing number of studies, however, argues that computer applications like recommender systems need to be understood as "social actors" [124]. Nass and Moon [105] urged that people construct social relationships with machines including computers, and apply social rules in their interactions with technology. Indeed, several past empirical studies have shown that individuals form social relationships with technology and that these social relationships form the basis for interactions with the technology [44, 96, 103, 106, 115, 123]. A good number of recommender system studies also support this "Computers as Social Actors" paradigm. Wang and Benbasat [154], for instance, found that users perceived human characteristics such as benevolence and integrity from recommender systems and treated systems as social actors. Zanker and his colleagues [165] argued that interactions with recommender systems should not only be seen from a technical perspective but should also be examined from social and emotional perspectives. The findings by Aksoy et al. [2] suggest that the similarity rule is also applied when humans interact with recommender systems. They found that a user is more likely to use a recommender agent when it generates recommendations in a way similar to the user's decision-making process. Morkes et al. [98] demonstrated that computer agents that use humor are rated as more likable, competent, and cooperative. More recently, Yoo [161] investigated how virtual agents embedded in system interfaces influence users when they evaluate systems. The study found that users socially interact with the systems and the social cues portrayed by the embedded virtual agents influence system users' evaluations of the agents as well as the overall system quality. These studies all support the notion of recommender systems as social actors and suggest a need for examining the social aspects of recommender systems. This implies that recommender systems can be understood as communication sources to which the communication theories developed for human-human communication apply. One set of such theories relates to the impact of source characteristics on persuasion likelihood and outcomes.

20.4 Source Factors in Human-Human Communication

There has been considerable research attention on investigating various communicator characteristics that influence the outcomes of the communicator's persuasive efforts in human-human interactions. This section provides a brief review of the most relevant source factors examined in the literature. Figure 20.1 provides an overview of influential source cues influencing credibility assessment in interpersonal communication.

20.4.1 Source Credibility

A good number of past studies have confirmed that a more credible source is preferred and also more persuasive [4, 49, 58, 78, 90, 136, 137]. Credibility is generally described as comprising multiple dimensions [16, 46, 119, 135] but most researchers agree that it consists of two key elements: expertise and trustworthiness [42, 43, 113, 126]. The dimension of expertise captures the perceived knowledge and skill of the source [85, 113] while trustworthiness of a source refers to aspects such as character or personal integrity [113]. Whether a source is perceived as having expertise and being trustworthy depends to a great extent on its characteristics.

20.4.2 Source Cues

20.4.2.1 Source Likeability

People mindlessly tend to agree with those who are seen as likable [18]. Research generally supports the assumption that liked communicators are more effective

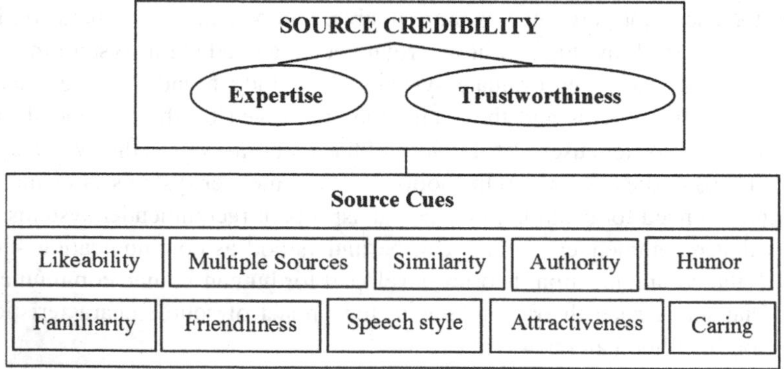

Fig. 20.1 Influential source cues in credibility evaluations

influence agents than disliked communicators [34, 47, 128]. O'Keefe [113] stressed enhanced liking for the source is commonly accompanied by enhanced judgments of the communicator's trustworthiness. Further, a number of studies found that similarity increases likeability [21, 23, 64].

20.4.2.2 Multiple Sources

Social impact theory [67, 79] explains that impact of a persuasive attempt depends on strength, immediacy and number of influencing sources. The theory predicts that the message will be more persuasive when it comes from multiple sources than from a single source. This prediction was supported by several studies that found that a message presented by several different sources was more persuasive than the same message presented by a single source [56, 57, 158]. Such social or group-based information evaluation and credibility assessment is increasingly critical within the context of recent sociotechnical developments. Online users today are naturally social and often access social collaborative efforts to evaluate online source and information credibility [92].

20.4.2.3 Similarity

In general, homophily theory [81] states that humans like similar others. However, the relation between similarity and the dimensions of credibility appears to be complex. Mills and Kimble [93] found that similar others are seen as having greater expertise than dissimilar others. However, Delia [31] observed that similarity between the source and the message receiver makes the receiver see the source less as an expert. In contrast, some studies found that similarity does not make any difference in source expertise judgments (e.g., [7, 147]). The perceived similarity of the message source also has varying effects on perceived trustworthiness of the communicator. O'Keefe [113] suggested that perceived attitudinal similarities can enhance liking for the source that is commonly accompanied by enhanced judgments of the communicator's trustworthiness. However, Atkinson et al. [7] found that ethnic similarity and dissimilarity did not influence the perceived trustworthiness of the source, while Delia [31] observed that similarity sometimes diminished trustworthiness perceptions. O'Keefe [113] noted that the effects of perceived similarities on judgments of communicator credibility depend on whether, and how, the receiver perceives these as relevant to the issue at hand. Thus, different types of similarity likely have different effects in different communication contexts.

20.4.2.4 Symbols of Authority

Evidence presented in the persuasion literature indicates that people often embrace the mental shortcut of assuming that sources who simply display symbols of authority such as titles, tailors and tone should be listened to [13, 48, 63, 120, 126].

A number of studies reported that cues like the communicator's education, occupation, training, amount of experience, and outfit influence a message receiver's perceptions of source credibility [62, 63].

20.4.2.5 Styles of Speech

Several studies suggest that the style of speech can influence speaker credibility judgments. Previous findings indicate that providing both sides of an argument can enhance the trustworthiness of communicators [35, 143] while using complex, difficult-to-understand terms can increase the perceived expertise of speakers [27]. In addition, the fluency of speech [17, 36, 88, 133], speaking rate [1, 53, 80, 83] and citing sources of evidence (e.g., [41, 87, 112]) appeared to influence source credibility evaluation.

20.4.2.6 Humor

Previous studies found effects of humor when message receivers evaluate a communicator's credibility. However, the specific effects varied across different studies. A number of studies found positive effects of humor on communicator trustworthiness judgments but rarely on judgments of expertise [24, 52, 149]. When positive effects of humor were found, the effects tended to enhance the audience's liking of the communicator and this liking helped increase perceptions of trustworthiness. In contrast, some researchers found that the use of humor can decrease the audience's liking for the communicator, the perceived trustworthiness, and even the perceived expertise of the source when the use of humor is perceived as excessive or inappropriate for the context [15, 100, 150].

20.4.2.7 Physical Attractiveness

A number of studies have found that physically attractive communicators are more persuasive [33, 66, 144]. Eagly et al. [33] explained that there appears to be a positive reaction to good physical appearance that generalizes to favorable trait perceptions such as a talent, kindness, honesty and intelligence. The effects of physical attractiveness are seen as influencing indirectly, especially by means of influence on the receiver's liking for the communicator [113].

20.4.2.8 Caring

Caring as a theoretical construct encompasses motives and intentions. Benevolence, which refers to concern about the message receiver's best interest, has been proposed as an underlying dimension of trust [8]. Delgado-Ballester [30] conceptualizes good intentions as an important factor that determines trustworthiness. Perloff [118] reports that communicators who have the recipient's interests at their heart and communicate goodwill are often evaluated as credible sources.

20.4.2.9 Familiarity and Friendliness

As a rule, individuals are more likely to comply with requests of someone they know in contrast to requests made by strangers [25]. Familiarity itself is very persuasive as people are more prone to like people they know personally [25, 82, 139]. However, also friendly strangers will get a head start. Praise and other forms of positive estimation stimulate liking [22]. Communicators who are nice and friendly can change attitudes because they make the recipient feel good, and the positive feeling becomes transferred to the message [126].

20.4.2.10 Discussion

While these source cues have been identified as influential factors for source credibility in interpersonal communication, the challenge is how these cues can be translated and implemented in the recommender systems context. This area remains underexplored but previous findings of recommender system studies indicate the relevance of interpersonal source cues to recommender systems. For example, a good deal of studies has found effectiveness of collaborative filtering (e.g. [116, 130]) in recommender systems. This implies that similarity and multiple source cues are influential factors in the recommender systems context but the cues are typically not well presented to users. Systems may enhance the impacts of these cues by explaining the similarity algorithm behind the recommendation (e.g. Amazon's explanation of "Customers who viewed this item also viewed"), integrating other users' ratings (e.g. MovieLens) or displaying the number of users who were satisfied with the recommended items. Similarly, symbols of authority could be implemented by displaying third party seals on the system interface or presenting the users' ratings of the system. Recent findings by Shani and his colleagues [138] indicate that users build trust when systems provide a display of confidence alongside a recommendation although the display does not help the users in identifying the recommendation quality and making decisions. Styles of speech cues could be translated into the system's recommendation generation process or presentation style. For instance, a good flow of process or informing users about the search progress could enhance users' overall satisfaction [94]. The format and layout of recommendation presentation also has been found to influence users' perception [141]. Further, styles of speech cues might be easily translated into real systems due to advances in voice technology.

The physical attractiveness of source cues can be related to overall system interface design and the perceived attractiveness of embodied agents. Implementing caring and friendliness cues into the systems is challenging but improved transparency and interactivity of recommender systems can express benevolence/caring towards users. Providing explanations of the reasoning mechanism that generates recommendations can help users to better understand the good intentions and efforts of the system, which helps to determine the trustworthiness of the source [154]. Likewise, systems can implement cues of caring or friendliness when interacting with users. For instance, Amazon's "Improve Your Recommendations" link allows users to be involved in the recommendation generation process and shows the system's concern about users' best interest. The conversation styles of systems or embodied agents can also convey caring and friendliness cues. In addition, familiarity cues could be translated into interface design (familiar interface vs. unfamiliar interface) or by integrating social technologies (recommend items that the users' social media friends have purchased or rated). When translating humor into systems one can benefit from the research on funology. Integrating humor or playfulness into the preference-measurement task might improve users' interaction experience with systems [14, 51]. Fun games can be designed to support the preference elicitation process or humorous virtual agents can be used. Khooshabeh and his colleagues [71] have found that individuals interacting with a humorous virtual agent were more likely persuaded by the agent's suggestions. As discussed above, there are potential approaches to implementing interpersonal source cues in recommender systems. However, many cues have not yet been implemented and empirically tested in the recommender system context. Findings from human-computer interaction studies can further inform such efforts. The following section discusses the source factors examined in human-technology interactions, followed by a systematic overview of source factor-related research in the recommender system realm.

20.5 Source Factors in Human-Technology Interactions

It seems obvious that a computer is a tool or medium and not an actor in social life. However, media equation theory suggests that individuals' interactions with computers, television sets, and new media are fundamentally social and natural, just like interactions in real life [124]. This theory thus argues that the technologies should be understood as social actors, not just tools or media. Based on this paradigm, a growing number of studies have investigated how certain social characteristics of the technologies influence their users' perceptions and behaviors. Similarity between a computer and its users was found to be important when computer users evaluated the computer and its contents [42, 105]. For example, Nass and Moon [105] report that computers conveying similar personality types are more persuasive. In their study, dominant participants were more attracted to, assigned greater intelligence to, and conformed more with a dominant computer compared to a submissive computer. Submissive participants reacted the same way to the submissive computer as opposed to the dominant computer, despite the essentially identical content. Nass et al. [104] also revealed the effects of demographic similarity. Their study found that computer users perceived computer agents as more attractive, trustworthy, persuasive and intelligent when same-ethnicity agents were presented.

Presenting authority symbols has also been identified as an influential factor when people interact with technology. Nass and Moon [105] found that a television set labeled as a specialist was perceived as providing better content than a television set labeled as a generalist. Fogg [42] also posited that computing technology that assumes roles of authority is more persuasive. He argued that websites displaying awards or third-party endorsements such as seals of approval will be perceived as more credible.

A number of studies [104, 107] argue that the demographic characteristics of computer agents influence users' perceptions. Nass et al. [107] illustrated that people apply gender and ethnicity stereotypes to computers. Specifically, their study found that people evaluated the tutor computer as significantly more competent and likeable when it was equipped with a male voice than a female voice. They also found that the female-voiced computer was perceived as a better teacher of love and relationships and a worse teacher of computing than a male-voiced computer, even though they performed identically. In addition, the use of language such as flattery [44], apology [152] and politeness [86] has been identified as factors which make a difference in computer users' perceptions and behaviors. Further, the physical attractiveness of computer agents was found to matter. The findings by Nass et al. [104] indicate that computer users prefer to look at and interact with computer agents that are more attractive. Finally, humor has also been tested in the human-computer interaction context. Morkes et al. [98] found that computers which display humor are rated as more likeable.

20.6 Source Factors in Human-Recommender System Interactions

A number of previous studies have investigated how specific characteristics of recommender systems influence users' evaluations of the system as well as its recommendations. Existing recommender system studies have examined some source factors identified as influential in traditional interpersonal relations and also identified important source factors that are prominent in recommender system contexts. Xiao and Benbasat [159, 160] classified the various source characteristics that have been studied as being associated with either recommender system type, input, process or output design. Also, with the increasing interest in and use of embodied agents in recommender systems, a considerable number of studies has investigated the effects of characteristics displayed by embodied virtual agents that often guide users through the various steps of the recommender process. More recently, there is growing research attention on factors that have emerged with the rise of social technology. Figure 20.2 provides an overview of source factors identified in contemporary recommender system research. See Chaps. 8–10 for

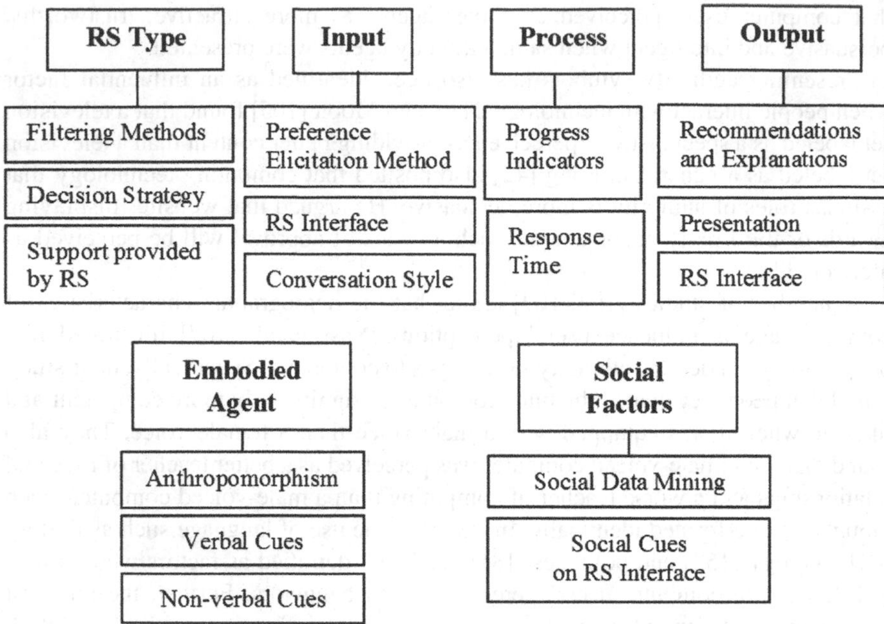

Fig. 20.2 Overview of source factors examined in recommender system research

additional discussions on how to assess the quality and value of recommender systems. For examples of recommender systems used in industrial settings, see Chap. 11.

20.6.1 Recommender System Type

Recommender systems come in different shapes and forms and can be classified based on filtering methods, decision strategies or amount of support provided [159]. A number of previous studies have discussed the advantages and disadvantages of these different types of recommender systems (e.g. [5, 19, 84]). Different filtering methods were compared and it was found that meta-recommender systems that combine collaborative filtering and content filtering are evaluated as more helpful than traditional systems that use a pure collaborative filtering technique [131, 132]. Burke [19] also confirmed that hybrid recommender systems provide more accurate predictions of users' preferences. Regarding the different decision strategies used in recommender systems, compensatory recommender systems have been suggested to lead to greater trust, perceived usefulness and satisfaction than non-compensatory recommender systems [159]. They have also been found to increase users' confidence in their product choices [37]. As far as the amount of support provided by the recommender system is concerned, Xiao and Benbasat

[159] argued that needs-based systems rather than feature-based systems help users to better recognize their needs and more accurately answer the preference-elicitation questions, thus resulting in better decision quality. Needs-based systems are therefore recommended for novice users [38].

20.6.2 Input Characteristics

Input characteristics of recommender systems include those cues that are related to the preference elicitation method, ease of generating new/additional recommendations and the amount of control users have when interacting with the recommender system's preference elicitation interface [159]. A number of previous findings suggest that characteristics associated with recommender system input design influence system users' evaluations. Xiao and Benbasat [159] specifically argued that the preference elicitation method (implicit vs. explicit) influences users' evaluation of the system. They proposed that an implicit preference elicitation method leads to greater perceived ease of use and satisfaction with the recommender system while explicit elicitation is considered to be more transparent by users and leads to better decision quality. Allowing users more control was also found to be an influential factor when evaluating systems. West et al. [157] posited that giving more control to system users will increase their trust and satisfaction with the system. Indeed, a study conducted by McNee et al. [91] found that users who used user-controlled interfaces reported higher user satisfaction than users who interacted with system-controlled and mixed-initiative recommender systems. In addition, users of user-controlled interfaces felt that recommender systems more accurately represented their tastes and showed the greatest loyalty to the systems. Similarly, Pereira [117] demonstrated that users showed more positive affective reactions to recommender systems when they had increased control over the interaction with the recommender system. Komiak et al. [76] also found that control over the process was one of the top contributors to users' trust in a virtual agent. Supporting the importance of user control, Wang [153] noted that more restrictive recommender systems were considered as less trustworthy and useful by their users.

In addition to control, the structural characteristics of the preference elicitation process (relevance, transparency and effort) have also been found to influence users' perceptions of the recommender system [51]. The specific study by Gretzel and Fesenmaier [51] found that topic relevance, transparency in the elicitation process and the effort required by users to provide inputs positively influence users' perceptions of the value of the elicitation process. The findings suggest that by asking questions, the system takes on a social role and communicates interest in the user's preferences, which is seen as valuable. The more questions it asks, the greater its potential to provide valuable feedback. Also, making intentions explicit in this interaction is important. Although trust was not specifically measured, benevolence and intentions are important drivers of trust and can be implied from the importance based on transparency. Further, McGinty and Smyth [89] suggested that the conversation style of recommender systems during the input process matters. In contrast to Gretzel and Fesenmaier [51], they argued that the comparison-based recommendation approach, which asks users to choose a preferred item from a list of recommended items instead of a deep dialogue approach that asks users a series of direct questions about the importance of product features, would minimize the cost to the user and maintain recommendation quality.

20.6.3 Process Characteristics

Characteristics of recommender systems displayed during the recommendation calculation process appear to influence users' perceptions of the systems [159]. Such process factors include information about the search process and about the system response time. Mohr and Bitner [94] noted that system users use various cues or indicators to assess the amount of effort saved by decision aids. Indicators that inform users about the search progress help them become aware of the efforts saved by the system. The higher users' perceptions of the effort saved by decision aids, the greater their satisfaction with the decision process [11]. Sutcliffe et al. [146] found that users reported usability/comprehension problems with information retrieval systems that did not provide a search progress indicator.

Influences of system response time, i.e. the time between the user's input and the system's response, have also been identified as important in a number of studies. Basartan [10] varied the response time from a simulated shopbot and found that users prefer those shopbots less that make them wait a long time before receiving recommendations. In contrast, Sinha and Swearingen [141, 148] found that the time taken by users to register and to receive recommendations from recommender systems did not have a significant effect on users' perceptions of the system. In the study by McNee et al. [91], the lengthier sign up process increased users' satisfaction with and loyalty toward the system. Xiao and Benbasat [159] explained that the contradicting findings of previous studies regarding response time may depend on users cost-benefit assessments. They suggest that users do not form negative evaluations of the recommender systems when they perceive the benefits of waiting as leading to high quality recommendations. The findings of Gretzel and Fesenmaier [51] regarding the relationship between elicitation effort and the perceived value of the elicitation process support this assumption.

20.6.4 Output Characteristics

Recommender system characteristics portrayed in the output stage of the recommendation process are related to the content and the format of the recommendations presented to users. Previous findings indicate that the content and the format of recommendations can have significant impact on users' evaluations of recommender systems (e.g. [28, 141, 155, 159]). Xiao and Benbasat [159] noted that three aspects of recommendation contents—the familiarity of the recommended option, the amount of information on recommended products, and the explanation on how the recommendation was generated—are especially relevant when users evaluate recommender systems. Some studies found that more familiar recommendations increase users' trust in the recommender system. Sinha and Swearingen [141] found that recommended products that were familiar to users were helpful in establishing users' trust in recommender systems. A study by Cooke et al. [26] also observed that unfamiliar recommendations lowered users' favorable evaluations of recommender systems. Further, the availability of product information appeared to positively influence users' perceptions of recommender systems. Sinha and Swearingen [141] suggest that detailed product information available on the recommendation page enhances users' trust in the recommender system. Cooke et al. [26] also explained that the attractiveness of unfamiliar recommendations can be increased if recommender systems provide detailed information about the new product.

The impacts of explanations on users' evaluations of recommender systems have been investigated in a considerable number of studies. Wang and Benbasat [154] found that explanations of the recommender system's reasoning logic strengthened users' beliefs in the recommender system's competence and benevolence. Herlocker et al. [60] also reported that explanations were important in establishing trust in systems since users were less likely to trust recommendations when they did not understand why certain items were recommended to them. Bonhared and Sasse [114] emphasized that recommender systems must establish a connection between the advice seeker and the system through explanation interfaces in order to enhance the user's level of trust in the system. Similarly, studies by Pu and Chen [121] and Tintarev and Masthoff [151] showed that system users exhibited more trust in the case of explanation interfaces.

The format in which recommendations are presented to the user also appears to influence users' evaluation of recommender systems. Sinha and Swearingen [141] found that navigation and layout of recommendation presentation interfaces significantly influence users' satisfaction with systems. Swearingen and Sinha [141] further found that interface navigation and layout influenced users' overall rating of systems. Consistent with these findings, Yoon and Lee [164] showed that interface design and display format influenced system users' behaviors. However, a study conducted by Bharti and Chaudhury [12] did not find any significant influence of navigational efficiency on users' satisfaction. In addition, Schafer [129] suggested that merging the preferences interface and the recommendation elicitation interface within a single interface can make the recommender system be seen as more helpful since this new "dynamic query" interface can provide immediate feedback regarding the effect caused by an individual's preference changes. Since this merges the input with the output interface, this suggestion touches upon cues such as transparency already discussed in the context of input characteristics.

20.6.5 Characteristics of Embodied Agents

Recommender systems often include virtual personas guiding the user through the process. It can be assumed that social responses are even more prevalent if the system is personified. Indeed, the important role and impacts of embodied interface agents in the context of recommender systems have recently been emphasized in a number of studies. For example, the presence of a humanoid virtual agent in the system interface was found to increase system credibility [99], to augment social interactions [122], to enhance the online shopping experience [65], as well as to induce trust [156]. With growing interests in such interface agents, a number of studies have started investigating if and how certain characteristics of the interface agent influence recommender system users' perceptions and evaluations.

One of the important identified characteristics of agents is anthropomorphism. Anthropomorphism is defined as the extent to which a character has either the appearance or behavioral attributes of a human being [74, 109–111]. Many researchers have found that anthropomorphism of embodied agents influences people's interactions with computers (e.g. [74, 109, 111]), and specifically with recommender systems [122]. Yet, the benefits and costs of anthropomorphic agents are debatable. For example, more anthropomorphic interface agents were rated as being more credible, engaging, attractive and likeable than less anthropomorphic agents in some studies [74, 110] while other studies found contrasting results [101, 109, 111]. The social cues communicated by the inclusion of such agents might create expectations in the users that cannot be met by the actual system functionalities.

Human voice is a very strong social cue that has been found to profoundly shape human-technology interactions [102]. However, findings in the context of embodied interface agents are not widely available and are currently inconclusive. The voice output of interface agents was found to be helpful in inducing social and affective responses from users in some studies [97, 122] but other studies found that sociability is higher when the system avatar only communicated with text [145].

The demographic characteristics of interface agents have also been found to influence system users' perceptions and behaviors. Qiu [122] reports that system users evaluated the system as more sociable, competent, and enjoyable when the agents were matched with them in terms of ethnicity and gender, thus supporting the homophily hypothesis. Cowell and Stanny [29] also observed that system users prefer to interact with interface characters that matched their ethnicity and were young looking. A study by Nowak and Rauh [110] indicated that people showed a clear preference for characters that matched their gender.

In addition to similarity cues, other source characteristics have also been investigated in the context of embodied interface agents. The effects of attractiveness and expertise of interface agents were tested by Holzwarth et al. [65]. They found that an attractive avatar is a more effective sales agent at moderate levels of product involvement while an expert agent is a more effective persuader at high levels of product involvement. Further, the potential impacts of nonverbal behavior cues including facial expression, eye contact, gestures, paralanguage and posture of interface agents were emphasized by Cowell and Stanney [29]. However, research in this area is still limited.

20.6.6 Impact of Emerging Social Technologies

Social technologies and recommender systems benefit mutually from each other [55]. On the one hand, recommender systems embedded in social technologies alleviate information overload for social technology users by presenting only relevant and personalized content [54, 55, 167]. On the other hand, recommender systems can integrate new social media-generated data such as tags, ratings and comments to enhance the quality of their recommendations. These social media-generated data can play an important role in recommender system credibility assessments.

Metzger and her colleagues [92] found that a growing number of online users make information evaluations and credibility assessments using cues provided by social technologies. They argued that, today, source credibility is no longer evaluated by just one person but rather collaboratively. Zhou and his team [167] specifically examined the benefits of exploiting social content/data in recommender systems. They explained that social technologies contain data that can be mined and analyzed to expand user profiles, and to build complex maps of user-to-user and user-to-interest relationships. Their argument is that recommender systems can generate high quality and reliable recommendations by incorporating social data more effectively via the use of the latest collaborative filtering approaches, data mining techniques, and trust/reputation management technology. Indeed, a study by Guy and his colleagues [55] found that recommender system users showed greater interest in items recommended by systems that combined related people and tags data in order to generate recommendations. In addition, Armentano et al. [6] found that system users often perceived recommendations as relevant when the system generated the recommendations using an algorithm based on the social network structure of users. Further, Guy and Carmel [54] noted that the system should provide explanations of how and why the specific recommendations were presented to users to increase the level of trust in the system. In summary, there is increasing evidence that social cues generated by social technology matter for credibility assessments. See Chap. 15 for additional discussions on social recommender systems.

20.7 Discussion

Swearingen and Sinha [141] noted that the ultimate effectiveness of a recommender system depends on factors that go beyond the quality of the algorithm. Nevertheless, recommender system features are oftentimes implemented because they can be implemented. They might be tested in the course of overall system evaluations or usability studies but are rarely assessed in terms of their persuasiveness. Häubl and Murray [59] demonstrated that recommender systems can indeed have profound impacts on consumer preferences and choice beyond the immediate recommendation. Thus, conceptualizing recommender systems not only as social but also as persuasive actors is crucial in understanding their potential impacts. The above review of the literature suggests a wide array of recommender system characteristics which could be influential.

Following the paradigm of "Computers as Social Actors" [42, 124], recent recommender system studies have started emphasizing the social aspects of recommender systems and stress the importance of integrating social cues to create more credible and persuasive systems [3, 122, 154]. This recognition of recommender systems as social actors has important implications for recommender systems research and design. Most importantly, conceptualizing human-recommender system interactions as social exchanges means that important source characteristics identified as influential in traditional advice seeking relationships can also be seen as potentially influential in human-recommender system interactions.

20.8 Implications

Understanding the influence of source characteristics when evaluating recommender systems has many implications of theoretical and practical importance. From a theoretical perspective, the classic interpersonal communication theories need to be expanded in scope and applied to understand human-recommender system relationships. By applying classic theories, researchers can test and examine various aspects of human-recommender system interactions. However, the unique qualities of human-recommender interactions should be considered when applying these theories and when developing methodologies to test them. Further, while some recommender system-related research exists with respect to source characteristics, the efforts are currently not very systematic and sometimes inconclusive. Clearly, more research is needed in this area so that a strong theoretical framework can be built.

From the practical perspective, understanding recommender systems as social actors whose characteristics influence user perceptions helps system developers and designers to better understand user interactions with systems. Social interactions thrive on trust and are also subject to persuasion. The way in which preferences are elicited, the way recommendations are derived, and the more insight users have in these processes, the greater perceptions of credibility and the greater the likelihood for a recommendation to be accepted [51]. Opposed to the common practice of one-shot interactions, recommender systems would be more probable to trigger a social frame in the minds of users if their conceptualization and design were more ambitious with respect to the consideration of the different source factors:

RS Type and Input Hybrid systems, explicit elicitation and generally giving users control over the process seem to be highly effective strategies [19, 77, 91, 117, 131, 132, 157, 159]. Seen from an abstract viewpoint two basic conversational strategies have been explored in recommender systems: asking and proposing. *Asking* denotes the explicit elicitation of user preferences in order to compute recommendations [166]. The *Proposing* conversation strategy is also known as critiquing, where one or more items are presented and the user can provide feedback why a specific item does not exactly match the user's preferences [20]. One of the earliest systems combining both strategies, i.e. first asking users about their preferences and then making several rounds of propositions which can be critiqued, is the ExpertClerk system [140]. Another system suggested by Schafer [129] has a dynamic query interface, that merges the preferences interface and the recommendation elicitation interface within a single user interface. This helps users feel that they have control over the system since the interface can provide immediate feedback regarding the effects caused by individuals' preference changes.

Process During interaction with recommender systems, response times needs to be kept short [10] and the specifics of the search process should be communicated to users [11, 94, 146] to demonstrate the system's efforts as this will influence credibility perceptions.

Output When generating recommendations, more familiar recommendations with detailed product descriptions [26, 141] and explanations regarding the underlying logic of how the recommendation was generated [45, 60, 154] would increase users' perceived credibility of the system. A good understanding of users' system use history and patterns using a sophisticated data mining technique would help the systems generate recommendations that are more familiar to users. Along with the text descriptions of recommended products, recommender system designers may consider providing virtual product experiences. Jiang and Benbasat [70] noted that a virtual product experience enhances consumers' product understanding, brand attitude, purchase intention as well as decreases the perceived risks. Adding virtual experiences of products enables the users not only to have a better understanding of the recommended products but also to inspire greater attention, interest and enjoyment.

Recommender system designers should also pay attention to the display format of the recommendations [141, 164]. Navigational efficacy, design familiarity and attractiveness need to be considered when the recommendations are presented to users. The challenge for design is to find ways in which source characteristics such as similarity, likeability and authority can be manipulated and translated into concrete design features that fit within the context of recommender systems. For instance, presenting third party seals signaling the authority of the system can increase the overall credibility of systems.

Embodied Agent One way in which some characteristics can be more easily implemented is by adding an embodied agent to the system interface. The embodied agent serves as the representative of the system and, thus, emphasizes the social role of the system as the advice giver [163]. Voice interfaces can be another way to translate source characteristics into credibility-evoking recommender system design, for instance one very recent work combines speech interaction with a conversational critiquing strategy [50]. Manipulating personalities (e.g. extraversion or introversion) of recommender systems to match with users' personalities by varying communication style and voice characteristics was also suggested by Hess et al. [61] and Moon [95].

Social Factors The first authors envisioning collaborative recommender systems [125] already had a clear social perspective of this technology in mind, which might influence the social structure among its users by fracturing the global village into smaller tribes. Since then the paradigm shift that came along with social web applications turns information seekers and consumers also into information contributors. The Social Web therefore not only became a rapidly growing application domain in order to support users in digging through the enormous information offerings, but also a precious source for making algorithms more accurate (see [68] for a quantitative survey on domains of interest to recommender systems research). However, purposefully exploiting social cues to develop more credible and persuasive recommender systems is still in its infancy. From the marketing point of view, creating recommender systems that play similar roles as human salespersons in physical stores who interact with consumers and advise consumers in terms of what to buy continues to be an important goal [75, 76].

20.9 Directions for Future Research

While existing studies have identified and tested a number of influential source characteristics in human-recommender system advice seeking relationships, many potential characteristics suggested by general communication theories such as authority, caring, non verbal behaviors like facial expression and gestures, and humor have not been examined. Those unexamined characteristics need to be successfully implemented and also empirically tested in future recommender system studies. The identified and tested source characteristics also need to be more precisely examined. The effects of source characteristics on judgments of source credibility are often found to be complex rather than linear in previous studies conducted in human-human advice seeking contexts [113]. Since situational factors, individual differences and product type can also play a significant role in determining the recommender system credibility, relationships will have to be specifically tested for specific recommender systems to provide accurate input for design considerations. The increasing use of recommender systems through mobile devices warrants particular attention in this context. In addition, there can be additional source characteristics that might not be prominent in influencing advice seeking relationships among human actors but are important aspects to be considered in the realm of recommender systems. For instance, anthropomorphism of the technology has been identified as an important characteristic that influences interactions with technologies [74, 111] while it is of course not a critical characteristic in interactions among human actors. The realness of interface agents can also be considered as a potentially influential source cue. There is some evidence that users are less likely to respond socially to a poor implementation of a human-like software character than to a good implementation of a dog-like character [72]. Cues generated by social technology also fall into this category. In future research, such additional source cues need to be identified and tested.

Some of the source characteristics have been tested in isolation from another. In order to investigate interaction effects, different source cues should be tested simultaneously if it is possible to implement them at the same time. This will help with understanding the relationships among various source factors.

Overall, the literature presented in this chapter suggests that there is a great need for research in this area. It also suggests that new methodologies might have to be developed to investigate influences that happen at a sub-conscious level. Especially a greater emphasis on behavioral measures of recommendation acceptance seems to be warranted if the persuasiveness of recommender systems is to be evaluated.

References

1. Addington, D.: The effect of vocal variations on ratings of source credibility. Speech Monographs **38**, 242–247 (1971)
2. Aksoy, L., Bloom, P.N., Lurie, N.H., Cooil, B.: Should recommendation agents think like people? Journal of Service Research **8**(4), 297–315 (2006)
3. Al-Natour, S., Benbasat, I., Cenfetelli, R.T.: The role of design characteristics in shaping perceptions of similarity: The case of online shopping assistants. Journal of Association for Information Systems **7**(12), 821–861 (2006)
4. Andersen, K.E., Clevenger T., J.: A summary of experimental research in ethos. Speech Monographs **30**, 59–78 (1963)
5. Ansari, A., Essegaier, S., Kohli, R.: Internet recommendation systems. Journal of Marketing Research **37**(3), 363–375 (2000)
6. Armentano, M.G., Godoy, D., Amandi, A.: Topology-based recommendation of users in micro-blogging communities. Journal of Computer Science and Technology **27**(3), 624–634 (2012)
7. Atkinson, D.R., Winzelberg, A., Holland, A.: Ethnicity, locus of control for family planning, and pregnancy counselor credibility. Journal of Counseling Psychology **32**, 417–421 (1985)
8. Bart, Y., Shankar, V., Sultan, F., Urban, G.L.: Are the drivers and role of online trust the same for all web sites and consumers?: A large scale exploratory and empirical study. Journal of Marketing **69**(4), 133–152 (2005)
9. Barwise, P., Elberse, A., Hammond, K.: Marketing and the internet: A research review. In: B. Weitz, R. Wensley (eds.) Handbook of Marketing, pp. 3–7. Russell Sage, New York, NY (2002)
10. Basartan, Y.: Amazon versus the shopbot: An experiment about how to improve the shopbots. Tech. rep., Carnegie Mellon University, Pittsburgh, PA (2001). Ph.D. Summer Paper

11. Bechwati, N.N., Xia, L.: Do computers sweat? the impact of perceived effort of online decision aids on consumers' satisfaction with the decision process. Journal of Consumer Psychology **13**(1–2), 139–148 (2003)
12. Bharti, P., Chaudhury, A.: An empirical investigation of decision-making satisfaction in web-based decision support systems. Decision Support Systems **37**(2), 187–197 (2004)
13. Bickman, L.: The social power of a uniform. Journal of Applied Social Psychology **4**, 47–61 (1974)
14. Blythe, M.A., Overbeeke, K., Monk, A., Wright, P. (eds.): Funology: From Usability to Enjoyment, *Human-Computer Interaction Series*, vol. 3. Kluwer (2003)
15. Bryant, J., Brown, D., Silberberg, A.R., Elliott, S.M.: Effects of humorous illustrations in college textbooks. Human Communication Research **8**, 43–57 (1981)
16. Buller, D.B., Burgoon, J.K.: Interpersonal deception theory. Communication Theory **6**, 203–242 (1996)
17. Burgoon, J.K., Birk, T., Pfau, M.: Nonverbal behaviors, persuasion, and credibility. Human Communication Research **17**, 140–169 (1990)
18. Burgoon, J.K., Dunbar, N.E., Segring, C.: Nonverbal influence. In: J.P. Dillard, M. Pfau (eds.) Persuasion Handbook: Developments in Theory and Practice, pp. 445–473. Sage Publications, Thousand Oaks, CA (2002)
19. Burke, R.: Hybrid recommender systems: Survey and experiments. User Modeling and User-Adapted Interaction **12**(4), 331–370 (2002)
20. Burke, R., Hammond, K., Young, B.: The findme approach to assisted browsing. IEEE Expert **4**(12), 32–40 (1997)
21. Byrne, D.: The attraction paradigm. Academic Press, New York (1971)
22. Byrne, D., Rhamey, R.: Magnitude of positive and negative reinforcements as a determinant of attraction. Journal of Personality and Social Psychology **2**, 884–889 (1965)
23. Carli, L.L., Ganley, R., Pierce-Otay, A.: Similarity and satisfaction in roommate relationships. Personality and Social Psychology Bulletin **17**(4), 419–426 (1991)
24. Chang, K.J., Gruner, C.R.: Audience reaction to self-disparaging humor. Southern Speech Communication Journal **46**, 419–426 (1981)
25. Cialdini, R.B.: Interpersonal influence. In: S. Shavitt, T.C. Brock (eds.) Persuasion: Psychological Insights and Perspective, pp. 195–217. Allyn and Bacon, Needhan Heights, Massachusetts (1994)
26. Cooke, A.D.J., Sujan, H., Sujan, M., Weitz, B.A.: Marketing the unfamiliar: The role of context and item-specific information in electronic agent recommendations. Journal of Marketing Research **39**(4), 488–497 (2002)
27. Cooper, J., Bennett, E.A., Sukel, H.L.: Complex scientific testimony: How do jurors make decisions? Law and Human Behavior **20** (1996)
28. Cosley, D., Lam, S.K., Albert, I., Konstan, J., Riedl, J.: Is seeing believing? how recommender systems influence users' opinions. In: Proceedings of ACM CHI: Human Factors in Computing Systems, pp. 585–592 (2003)
29. Cowell, A.J., Stanney, K.M.: Manipulation of non-verbal interaction style and demographic embodiment to increase anthropomorphic computer character credibility. International Journal of Human-Computer Studies **62**, 281–306 (2005)
30. Delgado-Ballester, E.: Applicability of a brand trust scale across product categories: A multi-group invariance analysis. European Journal of Marketing **38**(5–6), 573–592 (2004)
31. Delia, J.G.: Regional dialect, message acceptance, and perceptions of the speaker. Central States Speech Journal **26**, 188–194 (1975)
32. Dijkstra, J.J., Liebrand, W.B.G., Timminga, E.: Persuasiveness of expert systems. Behaviour & Information Technology **17**(3), 155–163 (1998)
33. Eagly, A.H., Ashmore, R.D., Makhijani, M.G., Longo, L.C.: What is beautiful is good, but . . . : A meta-analytic review of research on the physical attractiveness stereotype. Psychological Bulletin **110**, 109–128 (1991)
34. Eagly, A.H., Chaiken, S.: An attribution analysis of the effect of communicator characteristics on opinion change: The case of communicator attractiveness. Journal of Personality and Social Psychology **32**(1), 136–144 (1975)

35. Eagly, A.H., Wood, W., Chaiken, S.: Causal inferences about communicators and their effect on opinion change. Journal of Personality and Social Psychology **36**, 424–435 (1978)
36. Engstrom, E.: Effects of nonfluencies on speakers' credibility in newscast settings. Perceptual and Motor Skills **78**, 739–743 (1994)
37. Fasolo, B., McClelland, G.H., Lange, K.A.: The effect of site design and interattribute correlations on interactive web-based decisions. In: C.P. Haughvedt, K. Machleit, R. Yalch (eds.) Online Consumer Psychology: Understanding and Influencing Behavior in the Virtual World, pp. 325–344. Lawrence Erlbaum Associates, Mahwah, NJ (2005)
38. Felix, D., Niederberger, C., Steiger, P., Stolze, M.: Feature-oriented versus needs-oriented product access for non-expert online shoppers. In: B. Schmid, K. Stanoevska-Slabeva, V. Tschammer-Zurich (eds.) Towards the E-Society: E-Commerce, E-Business, and E-Government, pp. 399–406. Springer, New York (2001)
39. Flanagin, A. J., Metzger, M. J.:Perceptions of Internet Information credibility. Journalism & Mass Communication Quarterly, 77(3), 515–540 (2000)
40. Flanagin, A.J., Metzger, M.J.: The role of site features, user attributes, and information verification behaviors on the perceived credibility of web-based information. New Media & Society **9**, 319–342 (2007)
41. Fleshler, H., Ilardo, J., Demoretcky, J.: The influence of field dependence, speaker credibility set, and message documentation on evaluations of speaker and message credibility. Southern Speech Communication Journal **39**, 389–402 (1974)
42. Fogg, B.J.: Persuasive Technology: Using Computers to Change What We Think and Do. Morgan Kaufmann, San Francisco (2003)
43. Fogg, B.J., Lee, E., Marshall, J.: Interactive technology and persuasion: Developments in theory and practice. In: P. Dillard, M. Pfau (eds.) Persuasion handbook, pp. 765–797. Sage, London, United Kingdom (2002)
44. Fogg, B.J., Nass, C.: Silicon sycophants: Effects of computers that flatter. International Journal of Human-Computer Studies **46**(5), 551–561 (1997)
45. Friedrich, G., Zanker, M.: A taxonomy for generating explanations in recommender systems. AI Magazine **32**(3), 90–98 (2011)
46. Gatignon, H., Robertson, T.S.: Innovative Decision Processes. Prentice Hall, Englewood Cliffs, NJ (1991)
47. Giffen, K., Ehrlich, L.: Attitudinal effects of a group discussion on a proposed change in company policy. Speech Monographs **30**, 377–379 (1963)
48. Giles, H., Coupland, N.: Language: Contexts and Consequences. Brooks/Cole, Pacific Grove, CA (1991)
49. Gilly, M.C., Graham, J.L., Wolfinbarger, M.F., Yale, L.J.: A dyadic study of personal information search. Journal of the Academy of Marketing Science **26**(2), 83–100 (1998)
50. Grasch, P., Felfernig, A., Reinfrank, F.: Recomment: Towards critiquing-based recommendation with speech interaction. In: Proceedings of the 7th ACM Conference on Recommender Systems (RecSys), pp. 157–164 (2013)
51. Gretzel, U., Fesenmaier, D.R.: Persuasion in recommender systems. International Journal of Electronic Commerce **11**(2), 81–100 (2007)
52. Gruner, C.R., Lampton, W.E.: Effects of including humorous material in a persuasive sermon. Southern Speech Communication Journal **38**, 188–196 (1972)
53. Gundersen, D.F., Hopper, R.: Relationships between speech delivery and speech effectiveness. Communication Monographs **43**, 158–165 (1976)
54. Guy, I., Carmel, D.: Social recommender systems. In: Proceedings of the World-Wide-Web Conference (WWW), pp. 283–284 (2011)
55. Guy, I., Zwerdling, N., Ronen, I., Carmel, D., Uziel, E.: Social media recommendation based on people and tags. In: Proceedings of the ACM SIGIR Conference, pp. 194–201 (2010)
56. Harkins, S.G., Petty, R.E.: The multiple source effect in persuasion: The effects of distraction. Personality and Social Psychology Bulletin **4**, 627–635 (1981)
57. Harkins, S.G., Petty, R.E.: Information utility and the multiple source effect. Journal of Personality and Social Psychology **52**, 260–268 (1987)

58. Harmon, R.R., Coney, K.A.: The persuasive effects of source credibility in buy and lease situations. Journal of Marketing Research **19**(2), 255–260 (1982)
59. Häubl, G., Murray, K.: Preference construction and persistence in digital marketplaces: The role of electronic recommendation agents. Journal of Consumer Psychology **13**(1–2), 75–91 (2003)
60. Herlocker, J., Konstan, J.A., Riedl, J.: Explaining collaborative filtering recommendations. In: Proceedings of the ACM Conference on Computer Supported Cooperative Work, pp. 241–250. Philadelphia, PA (2000)
61. Hess, T., J. Fuller, M.A., Mathew, J.: Involvement and decision-making performance with a decision aid: The influence of social multimedia, gender, and playfulness. Journal of Management Information Systems **22**(3), 15–54 (2005)
62. Hewgill, M.A., Miller, G.R.: Source credibility and response to fear-arousing communications. Speech Monographs **32**, 95–101 (1965)
63. Hofling, C.K., Brotzman, E., Dalrymple, S., Graves, N., Pierce, C.M.: An experimental study of nurse-physician relationships. Journal of Nervous and Mental Disease **143**, 171–180 (1966)
64. Hogg, M.A., CooperShaw, L., Holzworth, D.W.: Group prototypically and depersonalized attraction in small interactive groups. Personality and Social Psychology Bulletin **19**(4), 452–465 (1993)
65. Holzwarth, M., Janiszewski, C., Neumann, M.M.: The influence of avatars on online cosumer shopping behavior. Journal of Marketing **70**, 19–36 (2006)
66. Horai, J., Naccari, N., Fatoullah, E.: The effects of expertise and physical attractiveness upon opinion agreement and liking. Sociometry **37**, 601–606 (1974)
67. Jackson, J.M.: Theories of group behavior, chap. Social impact theory: A social forces model of influence, pp. 111–124. Springer, New York (1987)
68. Jannach, D., Zanker, M., Ge, M., Groening, M.: Recommender systems in computer science and information systems - a landscape of research. In: Proceedings of the 13th International Conference on Electronic Commerce and Web Technologies (EC-Web), pp. 76–87 (2012)
69. Jiang, J.J., Klein, G., Vedder, R.G.: Persuasive expert systems: The influence of confidence and discrepancy. Computers in Human Behavior **16**, 99–109 (2000)
70. Jiang, Z., Benbasat, I.: Virtual product experience: Effects of visual and functional control of products on perceived diagnosticity and flow in electronic shopping. Journal of Management Information Systems **21**(3), 111–148 (2005)
71. Khooshabeh, J., McCall, P., Gratch, C., Blascovich, J., Gandhe, S.: Does it mater if a computer jokes? In: Proceedings of ACM CHI: Human Factors in Computing Systems, pp. 77–86. Vancouver, Canada (2011)
72. Kiesler, S., Sproull, L., Waters, K.: A prisoner's dilemma experiment on cooperation with people and human-like computers. Journal of Personality and Social Psychology **70**(1), 47–65 (1996)
73. Kim, B.D., Kim, S.O.: A new recommender system to combine content-based and collaborative filtering systems. Journal of Database Marketing **8**(3), 244–252 (2001)
74. Koda, T.: Agents with faces: A study on the effects of personification of software agents. Master's thesis, Massachusetts Institute of Technology, Boston, MA, USA (1996)
75. Komiak, S.X., Benbasat, I.: Understanding customer trust in agent-mediated electronic commerce, web-mediated electronic commerce and traditional commerce. Information Technology and Management **5**(1–2), 181–207 (2004)
76. Komiak, S.Y.X., Wang, W., Benbasat, I.: Trust building in virtual salespersons versus in human salespersons: Similarities and differences. e-Service Journal **3**(3), 49–63 (2005)
77. Konstan, J.A., Riedl, J.: Designing Information Spaces: The Social Navigation Approach, chap. Collaborative Filtering: Supporting Social Navigation in Large, Crowded Infospaces, pp. 43–82. Springer, London (2003)
78. Lascu, D.N., Bearden, W.O., Rose, R.L.: Norm extremity and personal influence on consumer conformity. Journal of Business Research **32**, 201–213 (1995)
79. Latané, B.: The psychology of social impact. American Psychologist **36**, 343–356 (1981)

80. Lautman, M.R., Dean, K.J.: Time compression of television advertising. In: L. Percy, A.G. Woodside (eds.) Advertising and consumer psychology, pp. 219–236. Lexington Books, Lexington, Ma (1983)
81. Lazarsfeld, P., Merton., R.K.: Friendship as a social process: A substantive and methodological analysis. In: M. Berger, T. Abel, C.H. Page (eds.) Freedom and Control in Modern Society, pp. 18–66. Van Nostrand, New York (1954)
82. Levine, R.V.: Whom do we trust? experts, honesty, and likability. In: R.V. Levine (ed.) The Power of Persuasion, pp. 29–63. John Wiley & Sons, Hoboken, NJ (2003)
83. MacLachlan, J.: Listener perception of time-compressed spokespersons. Journal of Advertising Research **22**(2), 47–51 (1982)
84. Maes, P., Guttman, R.H., Moukas, A.G.: Agents that buy and sell. Communications of the ACM **42**(3), 81–91 (1999)
85. Mayer, R.C., Davis, J.H., Schoorman, F.D.: An integrative model of organizational trust. Academy of Management Review **20**, 709–734 (1995)
86. Mayer, R.E., Johnson, W.L., Shaw, E., Sandhu, S.: Constructing computer-based tutors that are socially sensitive: Politeness in educational software. International Journal of Human-Computer Studies **64**(1), 36–42 (2006)
87. McCroskey, J.C.: The effects of evidence as an inhibitor of counter-persuasion. Speech Monographs **37**, 188–194 (1970)
88. McCroskey, J.C., Mehrley, R.S.: The effects of disorganization and nonfluency on attitude change and source credibility. Speech Monographs **36**, 13–21 (1969)
89. McGinty, L., B., S.: Deep dialogue vs casual conversation in recommender systems. In: F. Ricci, B. Smyth (eds.) Proceedings of the Workshop on Personalization in eCommerce at the Second International Conference on Adaptive Hypermedia and Web-Based Systems (AH), pp. 80–89. Springer, Universidad de Malaga, Malaga, Spain (2002)
90. McGuire, W.J.: The nature of attitudes and attitude change. In: G. Lindzey, E. Aronson (eds.) Handbook of Social Psychology. Addison-Wesley, Reading, MA (1968)
91. McNee, S.M., Lam, S.K., Konstan, J.A., Riedl, J.: Interfaces for eliciting new user preferences in recommender systems. In: User Modeling, LNCS 2702, pp. 178–187. Springer (2003)
92. Metzger, M.J., Flanagin, A.J., Medders, R.B.: Social and heuristic approaches to credibility evaluation online. Journal of Communication **60**, 413–439 (2010)
93. Mills, J., Kimble, C.E.: Opinion change as a function of perceived similarity of the communicator and subjectivity of the issue. Bulletin of the psychonomic society **2**, 35–36 (1973)
94. Mohr, L.A., Bitner, M.J.: The role of employee effort in satisfaction with service transactions. Journal of Business Research **32**(3), 239–252 (1995)
95. Moon, Y.: Personalization and personality: Some effects of customizing message style based on consumer personality. Journal of Consumer Psychology **12**(4), 313–326 (2002)
96. Moon, Y., Nass, C.: How "real" are computer personalities? psychological responses to personality types in human-computer interaction. Communication Research **23**(6), 651–674 (1996)
97. Moreno, R., Mayer, R.E., Spires, H.A., Lester, J.C.: The case for social agency in computer-based teaching: Do students learn more deeply when they interact with animated pedagogical agents? Cognition and Instruction **19**(2), 177–213 (2001)
98. Morkes, J., Kernal, H.K., Nass, C.: Effects of humor in task-oriented human-computer interaction and computer-mediated communication: A direct test of srct theory. Human-Computer Interaction **14**(4), 395–435 (1999)
99. Moundridou, M., Virvou, M.: Evaluation the persona effect of an interface agent in a tutoring system. Journal of Computer Assisted Learning **18**(3), 253–261 (2002)
100. Munn, W.C., Gruner, C.R.: "sick" jokes, speaker sex, and informative speech. Southern Speech Communication Journal **46**, 411–418 (1981)
101. Murano, P.: Anthropomorphic vs. non-anthropomorphic software interface feedback for online factual delivery. In: Proceedings of the Seventh International Conference on Information Visualization (2003)

102. Nass, C., Brave, S.: Wired for Speech: How Voice Activates and Advances the Human-Computer Relationship. MIT Press, Cambridge, MA (2005)
103. Nass, C., Fogg, B.J., Moon, Y.: Can computers be teammates? International Journal of Human-Computer Studies **45**(6), 669–678 (1996)
104. Nass, C., Isbister, K., Lee, E.J.: Truth is beauty: Researching embodied conversational agents. In: J. Cassell, J. Sullivan, S. Prevost, E. Churchill (eds.) Embodied conversational agents, pp. 374–402. MIT Pres, Cambridge, MA (2000)
105. Nass, C., Moon, Y.: Machines and mindlessness: Social responses to computers. Journal of Social Issues **56**(1), 81–103 (2000)
106. Nass, C., Moon, Y., Carney, P.: Are respondents polite to computers? social desirability and direct responses to computers. Journal of Applied Social Psychology **29**(5), 1093–1110 (1999)
107. Nass, C., Moon, Y., Green, N.: Are computers gender-neutral? gender stereotypic responses to computers. Journal of Applied Social Psychology **27**(10), 864–876 (1997)
108. Nguyen, H., Masthoff, J., P., E.: Persuasive effects of embodied conversational agent teams. In: Proceedings of 12th International Conference on Human-Computer Interaction, pp. 176–185. Springer-Verlag, Berlin, Beijing, China (2007)
109. Nowak, K.: The influence of anthropomorphism and agency on social judgment in virtual environments. Journal of Computer-Mediated Communication **9**(2) (2004)
110. Nowak, K., Rauh, C.: The influence of the avatar on online perceptions of anthropomorphism, androgyny, credibility, homophily, and attraction. Journal of Computer-Mediated Communication **11**(1) (2005)
111. Nowak, K.L., Biocca, F.: The effect of the agency and anthropomorphism on user's sense of telepresence, copresence, and social presence in virtual environments. Presence: Teleperators and Virtual Environments **12**(5), 481–494 (2003)
112. O'Keefe, D.J.: Justification explicitness and persuasive effect: A meta-analytic review of the effects of varying support articulation in persuasive messages. Argumentation and advocacy **35**, 61–75 (1998)
113. O'Keefe, D.J.: Persuasion: Theory & Research. Sage Publications, Thousand Oaks, CA (2002)
114. P., B., A., S.M.: I thought it was terrible and everyone else loved it - a new perspective for effective recommender system design. In: Proceedings of the 19th British HCI Group Annual Conference, pp. 251–261. Napier University, Edinburgh, UK (2005)
115. Parise, S., Kiesler, S., Sproull, L., Waters, K.: Cooperating with life-like interface agents. Computers in Human Behavior **15**, 123–142 (1999)
116. Pazzani, M.: A framework for collaborative, content-based and demographic filtering. Artificial Intelligence Review **13**, 393–408 (1999)
117. Pereira, R.E.: Optimizing human-computer interaction for the electronic commerce environment. Journal of Electronic Commerce Research **1**(1), 23–44 (2000)
118. Perloff, R.M.: The Dynamics of Persuasion, 2nd edition. Lawrence Erlbaum Associates, Mahwah, NJ (2003)
119. Petty, R.E., Cacioppo, J.T.: Attitudes and Persuasion: Classic And Contemporary Approaches. William C. Brown, Dubuque, IA (1981)
120. Pittam, J.: Voice in Social Interaction: An Interdisciplinary Approach. Sage, Thousand Oaks, CA (1994)
121. Pu, P., Chen, L.: Trust-inspiring explanation interfaces for recommender systems. Knowledge-Based Systems **20**, 542–556 (2007)
122. Qiu, L.: Designing social interaction with animated avatars and speech output for product recommendation agents in electronic commerce. Ph.D. thesis, University of British Columbia, Vancouver (2006)
123. Quintanar, L.R., Crowell, C.R., Pryor, J.B., Adamopoulos, J.: Human-computer interaction: A preliminary social psychological analysis. Behavior Research Methods & Instrumentation **14**(2), 210–220 (1982)

124. Reeves, B., Nass, C.: The Media Equation: How People Treat Computers, Television, and New Media Like Real People and Places. CSLI, New York, NY (1996)
125. Resnick, P., Iacovou, N., Suchak, M., Bergstrom, P., Riedl, J.: Grouplens: An open architecture for collaborative filtering of netnews. In: Proceedings of ACM Conference on Computer Supported Cooperative Work, pp. 175–186 (1994)
126. Rhoads, K.V., Cialdini, R.B.: The business of influence. In: J.P. Dillard, M. Pfau (eds.) Persuasion handbook: Developments in theory and practice, pp. 513–542. Sage, London, United Kingdom (2002)
127. Rosen, D.J.: Driver education for the information super-highway: How adult learners and practitioners use the internet. Literacy Leader Fellowship Program Reports **2**(2) (1998)
128. Sampson, E.E., Insko, C.A.: Cognitive consistency and performance in the autokinetic situation. Journal of Abnormal and Social Psychology **68**, 184–192 (1964)
129. Schafer, J.B.: Dynamiclens: A dynamic user-interface for a meta-recommendation system. In: Proceedings of the Workshop: Beyond Personalization at IUI'05. San Diego, CA (2005)
130. Schafer, J.B., Frankowski, D., Herlocker, J., Sen, S.: Collaborative filtering recommender systems. In: The Adaptive Web, LNCS 4321, pp. 291–324 (2007)
131. Schafer, J.B., Knostan, J.A., Riedl, J.: Meta-recommendation systems: User-controlled integration of diverse recommendations. In: Proceedings of the 11th international Conference on Information and Knowledge Management. McLean, VA (2002)
132. Schafer, J.B., Konstan, J.A., Riedl, J.: View through metalens: Usage patterns for a meta-recommendation system. IEE Proceedings-Software **151** (2004)
133. Schliesser, H.F.: Information transmission and ethos of a speaker using normal and defective speech. Central States Speech Journal **19**, 169–174 (1968)
134. Scholz-Crane, A.: Evaluating the future: A preliminary study of the process of how undergraduate students evaluate Web sources, Reference Services Review 26(3–4): 53–60, (1998)
135. Self, C.S.: Credibility. In: D.W. Stacks, M.B. Salwen (eds.) An integrated approach to communication theory and research, pp. 421–441. Lawrence Erlbaum, Mahwah, NJ (1996)
136. Sénécal, S., Nantel, J.: Online influence of relevant others: A framework. In: Proceedings of the Sixth International Conference on Electronic Commerce Research (ICECR-6). Dallas, Texas (2003)
137. Sénécal, S., Nantel, J.: The influence of online product recommendations on consumers' online choices. Journal of Retailing **80**(2), 159–169 (2004)
138. Shani, G., Rokach, L., Shapira, B., Hadash, S., Tangi, M.: Investigating confidence displays for top-n recommendations. Journal of the American Society for Information Science and Technology **64**(12), 2548–2563 (2013)
139. Shavitt, S., Brock, T.C.: Persuasion: Psychological Insights and Perspectives. Allyn and Bacon, Needham Heights, MA (1994)
140. Shimazu, H.: Expertclerk: A conversational case-based reasoning tool for salesclerk agents in e-commerce webshops. Artificial Intelligence Review **18**(3–4), 223–244 (2002)
141. Sinha, R., Swearingen, K.: Comparing recommendations made by online systems and friends. In: Proceedings of the 2nd DELOS Network of Excellence Workshop on Personalization and Recommender Systems in Digital Libraries, pp. 18–20. Dublin, Ireland (2001)
142. Smith, A.G.: Testing the surf: Criteria for evaluation internet information resources. Public-Access Computer System Review **8**(3), 5–23 (1997)
143. Smith, R.E., Hunt, S.D.: Attributional processers and effects in promotional situations. Journal of Consumer Research **5**, 149–158 (1978)
144. Snyder, M., Rothbart, M.: Communicator attractiveness and opinion change. Canadian Journal of Behavioural Science **3**, 377–387 (1971)
145. Sproull, L., Subramani, M., Kiesler, S., Walker, J.H., Waters, K.: When the interface is a face. Human-Computer Interaction **11**(1), 97–124 (1996)
146. Sutcliffe, A.G., Ennis, M., Hu, J.: Evaluating the effectiveness of visual user interfaces for information retrieval. International Journal of Human-Computer Studies **53**, 741–763 (2000)

147. Swartz, T.A.: Relationship between source expertise and source similarity in an advertising context. Journal of Advertising **13**(2), 49–55 (1984)
148. Swearingen, K., Sinha, R.: Beyond algorithms:an hci perspective on recommender systems. In: Proceedings of the ACM SIGIR Workshop on Recommender Systems. New Orleans, Louisiana (2001)
149. Tamborini, R., Zillmann, D.: College students' perceptions of lecturers using humor. Perceptual and Motor Skills **52**, 427–432 (1981)
150. Taylor, P.M.: An experimental study of humor and ethos. Southern Speech Communication Journal **39**, 359–366 (1974)
151. Tintarev, N., Masthoff, J.: Effective explanations of recommendations: User-centered design. In: Proceedings of the ACM Conference on Recommender Systems (RecSys), pp. 153–156. Minneapolis, USA (2007)
152. Tzeng, J.Y.: Toward a more civilized design: Studying the effects of computers that apologize. International Journal of Human-Computer Studies **61**(3), 319–345 (2004)
153. Wang, W.: Design of trustworthy online recommendation agents: Explanation facilities and decision strategy support. Ph.D. thesis, University of British Columbia, Vancouver (2005)
154. Wang, W., Benbasat, I.: Trust in and adoption of online recommendation agents. Journal of the Association for Information Systems **6**(3), 72–101 (2005)
155. Wang, W., Benbasat, I.: Recommendation agents for electronic commerce: Effects of explanation facilities on trusting beliefs. Journal of Management Information Systems **23**(4), 217–246 (2007)
156. Wang, Y.D., Emurian, H.H.: An overview of online trust: Concepts, elements and implications. Computers in Human Behavior **21**(1), 105–125 (2005)
157. West, P.M., Ariely, D., Bellman, S., Bradlow, E., Huber, J., Johnson, E., Kahn, B., Little, J., Schkade, D.: Agents to the rescue? Marketing Letters **10**(3), 285–300 (1999)
158. Wolf, S., Bugaj, A.M.: The social impact of courtroom witnesses. Social Behaviour **5**(1), 1–13 (1990)
159. Xiao, B., Benbasat, I.: E-commerce product recommendation agents: Use, characteristics, and impact. MIS Quarterly **31**(1), 137–209 (2007)
160. Xiao, B., Benbasat, I.: Handbook of Strategic e-Business Management, chap. Research on the Use, Characteristics, and Impact of e-Commerce Product Recommendation Agents: A Review and Update for 2007–2012, pp. 403–431. Springer, Berlin Heidelberg (2014)
161. Yoo, K.H.: Creating more credible and likable recommender systems. Ph.D. thesis, Texas A&M University, College Station, USA (2010)
162. Yoo, K.H., Gretzel, U.: The influence of perceived credibility on preferences for recommender systems as sources of advice. Information Technology & Tourism **10**(2), 133–146 (2008)
163. Yoo, K.H., Gretzel, U.: The influence of virtual representatives on recommender system evaluation. In: Proceedings of the 15th Americas Conference on Information Systems. San Francisco, California (2009)
164. Yoon, S.N., Lee, Z.: The impact of the web-based product recommendation systems from previous buyers on consumers' purchasing behavior. In: 10th Americas Conference on Information Systems. New York, New York (2004)
165. Zanker, M., Bricman, M., Gordea, S., Jannach, D., Jessenitschnig, M.: Persuasive online-selling in quality and taste domains. In: E-Commerce and Web Technologies, pp. 51–60. Springer (2006)
166. Zanker, M., Jessenitschnig, M.: Case-studies on exploiting explicit customer requirements in recommender systems. User Modeling and User-Adapted Interaction **19**(1–2), 133–166 (2009)
167. Zhou, X., Xu, Y., Li, Y., Josang, A., Cox, C.: The state-of-the-art in personalized recommender systems for social networking. Artificial Intelligence Review **37**, 119–132 (2012)

Chapter 21
Personality and Recommender Systems

Marko Tkalcic and Li Chen

21.1 Introduction

In recent years, there has been an increased research interest in more user-oriented approaches in recommender systems, where various psychological aspects have been investigated (e.g. personality [28] and emotions [70]) compared to the classical machine-learning approaches in recommender systems (i.e. classical ratings prediction from the user-item matrix, such as the Netflix-prize problem [36]). As argued in Chap. 18, an important function of recommender systems is to help people make better decisions. As personality plays an important role in decision-making [13] it should be taken into account. It has been also argued that an improvement in the rating prediction accuracy (usually measured with measures such as the Root Mean Square Error, see also Chap. 8) does not necessarily mean a better user experience [45]. As further discussed in Chap. 9, assessing the recommender systems from a user-centric perspective yields a better picture of the quality of the recommender system under study. Hence, when optimizing a recommender system for user-centric aspects one should take into consideration these aspects already in the design of the recommender systems. This is why personality, which by definition measures individual users' differences [33], should be taken into account in order for the recommender system to perform better in user-centric metrics.

The individual differences between users, as described by personality, are useful in a wide range of aspects of recommender systems. For example, music preferences

M. Tkalcic (✉)
Johannes Kepler University, Altenberger Strasse 69, Linz, Austria
e-mail: marko.tkalcic@jku.at

L. Chen
Hong Kong Baptist University, 224 Waterloo Road,
Kowloon Tong, Kowloon, Hong Kong, China
e-mail: lichen@comp.hkbu.edu.hk

F. Ricci et al. (eds.), *Recommender Systems Handbook*,
DOI 10.1007/978-1-4899-7637-6_21

have been shown to correlate with personality [55]. It has been shown that people with different personalities can be more or less inclined to consume novel items, so the degree of diversity in presenting recommended items can be personalized accordingly [74]. Personality has been used to improve user-similarity calculation in the new-user problem [29, 69]. Also, group modeling based on personality has improved the performance of group recommendations [35, 54, 56].

In this chapter we present personality-based recommender systems. We focus on the tools needed to design such systems, especially on (1) personality acquisition methods and (2) strategies for using personality in recommender systems.

From its definition in psychology, personality accounts for the individual differences in our enduring emotional, interpersonal, experiential, attitudinal and motivational styles [33]. Incorporating these differences in the recommender system appears to be a natural choice for delivering personalized recommendations. Furthermore, personality parameters can be quantified as feature vectors, which makes them suitable to use in computer algorithms. However, the acquisition of personality parameters for individual users could be, until recently, acquired only through extensive questionnaires, which was an obstacle in a day-to-day use of recommender systems. Examples of such questionnaires are the International Personality Item Pool (IPIP) [23] and the NEO Personality Inventory [43]. Recently, several investigations have been conducted to extract personality parameters in an implicit way from social media streams [22, 37, 53]. Valuable sources for assessing the personality of a user without bothering her/him with extensive questionnaires are social media streams (e.g. Facebook [37], blogs [32] or Twitter [53]) and other user-generated data streams (e.g. email [63]).

The chapter is organized as follows. In Sect. 21.2 we survey various models of personality that were developed and are suitable for recommender systems. In Sect. 21.3 we present various methods for acquiring personality, which fall in either of the two categories: implicit or explicit. In Sect. 21.4 we discuss various strategies that exploit personality and have been used so far in recommender systems. Further, in Sect. 21.5 we present the challenges that are still ahead in the domain of personality-based recommender systems. Finally we provide some conclusive thoughts in Sect. 21.6

21.2 What is Personality?

According to [44], personality accounts for the most important ways in which individuals differ in their enduring emotional, interpersonal, experiential, attitudinal and motivational styles. Translated into the recommender systems terminology, personality can be thought of as a user profile, which is context-independent (it does not change with time, location or some other context—see Chap. 6 for context in recommender systems) and domain-independent (it does not change through different domains, e.g. books, movies—see also Chap. 27 for personality in cross-domain recommender systems).

Historically, the first reports of studies of individual differences among humans go back to the ancient Greeks with the Hippocrates' Four Humours that eventually led to the personality theory known today as the four temperaments (Choleric, Sanguinic, Melancholic and Phlegmatic) [34].

Today, the Five Factor Model of personality (FFM) [44], is considered one of the most comprehensive and is the mostly used personality model in recommender systems [10, 18, 28–30, 48, 49, 67, 72, 74]. The FFM is sometimes referred to also as the Big-Five (Big5) model of personality.

21.2.1 The Five Factor Model of Personality

The roots of the FFM lie in the lexical hypothesis, which states that things that are most important in people's lives eventually become part of their language. Studying the usage of language, researchers extracted a set of adjectives that describe permanent traits (see Table 21.1). With further research, these adjectives were clustered into the five main dimensions: openness to experience, conscientiousness, extraversion, agreeableness, and neuroticism (the acronym OCEAN is often used) [44].

Openness to Experience (O), often referred to just as Openness, describes the distinction between imaginative, creative people and down-to-earth, conventional people. High O scorers are typically individualistic, non conforming and are very aware of their feelings. They can easily think in abstraction. People with low O values tend to have common interests. They prefer simple and straightforward thinking over complex, ambiguous and subtle. The sub-factors are imagination, artistic interest, emotionality, adventurousness, intellect and liberalism.

Conscientiousness (C) concerns the way in which we control, regulate and direct our impulses. People with high C values tend to be prudent while those with low values tend to be impulsive. The sub-factors are self-efficacy, orderliness, dutifulness, achievement-striving, self-discipline and cautiousness.

Extraversion (E) tells the degree of engagement with the external world (in case of high values) or the lack of it (low values). The sub-factors of E are friendliness, gregariousness, assertiveness, activity level, excitement-seeking and cheerfulness.

Table 21.1 Examples of adjectives related to the FFM [44]

Factor	Adjectives
Extraversion (E)	Active, assertive, energetic, enthusiastic, outgoing, talkative
Agreeableness (A)	Appreciative, forgiving, generous, kind, sympathetic, trusting
Conscientiousness (C)	Efficient, organized, planful, reliable, responsible, thorough
Neuroticism (N)	Anxious, self-pitying, tense, touchy, unstable, worrying
Openness (O)	Artistic, curious, imaginative, insightful, original, wide interest

Extrovert people (high score on the E factor) tend to react with enthusiasm and often have positive emotions while introverted people (low score on the E factor) tend to be quiet, low-key and disengaged in social interactions.

Agreeableness (A) reflects individual differences in concern with cooperation and social harmony. The sub-domains of the A factor are trust, morality, altruism, cooperation, modesty and sympathy.

Neuroticism (N) refers to the tendency of experiencing negative feelings. People with high N values are emotionally reactive. They tend to respond emotionally to relatively neutral stimuli. They are often in a bad mood, which strongly affects their thinking and decision making (see Chap. 18 for more on decision making). Low N scorers are calm, emotionally stable and free from persistent bad mood. The sub-factors are anxiety, anger, depression, self-consciousness, immoderation and vulnerability. The neuroticism factor is sometimes referred to as emotional stability [25].

The five factors and their respective adjectives are shown in Table 21.1.

21.2.2 Other Models of Personality

Other personality models that can be of interest to the recommender system community are the vocational RIASEC (with the main types *Realistic, Investigative, Artistic, Social, Enterprising* and *Conventional*) model [27], which was used in an e-commerce prototype [7] and the Bartle model (with the main types *Killers, Achievers, Explorers* and *Socializers*), which is suitable for the videogames domain [65].

The Thomas-Kilman conflict mode personality model has been developed to model group dynamics [66]. The model is composed of the following two dimensions that account for differences in individual behaviour in conflict situations[1]: *Assertiveness* and *Cooperativeness*. Within this two-dimensional space subjects are classified into any of these five categories: *Competing, Collaborating, Compromising, Avoiding* or *Accommodating*.

Although learning styles per se are not considered as a personality model they share with personality the quality of being time invariant. In the domain of e-learning (see also Chap. 12), models of learning styles have been used to recommend course material to students [17]. An example is the Felder and Silverman Learning Style Model [20] which measures four factors: *active/reflective, sensing/intuitive, visual/verbal* and *sequential/global*.

In addition, some ad-hoc personality models have been proposed in the recommender systems community. For a trendy pictures recommender system, a personality model with two types, the *trend-setters* and the *trend-spotters*, has been proposed, along with a methodology for predicting the personality types from

[1]The Thomas-Kilman conflict mode instrument is available at http://cmpresolutions.co.uk/wp-content/uploads/2011/04/Thomas-Kilman-conflict-instrument-questionaire.pdf.

Table 21.2 Main personality models

References	Model name	Primary domain	Domain types/traits
[44]	Five factor model	General	Openness, conscientiousness, extraversion, agreeableness, and neuroticism
[34]	Four temperaments	General	Choleric, sanguinic, melancholic and phlegmatic
[27]	RIASEC	Vocational	Realistic, investigative, artistic, social, enterprising and conventional
[65]	Bartle types	Video games	Killers, achievers, explorers and socializers
[20]	Felder and Silverman learning style model	Learning styles	Active/reflective, sensing/intuitive, visual/verbal, sequential/global
[66]	Thomas-Kilmann conflict model	Group/conflict modeling	Assertiveness, cooperativeness

social media networks [62]. Especially in the domain of social networks, there is a tendency to stress the *influence/susceptibility* aspects of users as the main personality traits (e.g. *leaders/followers*) [5] (Table 21.2).

21.2.3 How Does Personality Relate to User Preferences?

A number of studies showed that personality relates strongly with user preferences. Users with different personalities tend to prefer different kinds of content. These relations are domain dependant. Such an information is very valuable when designing a recommender system for a specific domain.

In their study, Rentfrow and Gosling [58] explored how music preferences are related to personality in terms of the FFM model. They categorized music pieces each into one of the four categories: reflective & complex, intense & rebellious, upbeat & conventional and energetic & rhythmic. The reflective & complex category was related to openness to new experience. Similarly, the intense & rebellious category was also positively related to openness to new experience. However, although this category contains music with negative emotions it was not related to neuroticism or agreeableness. The upbeat & conventional category was found to be positively related with extraversion, agreeableness, and Conscientiousness. Finally, they found that the energetic & rhythmic category is related to extraversion and agreeableness.

In a similar study, Rentfrow et al. [57], extended the domain to general entertainment, which included music, books, magazines, films and TV shows. They categorized the content into the following categories: aesthetic, cerebral, communal, dark and thrilling. The communal category was positively related to extraversion, agreeableness and conscientiousness while being negatively related to extraversion and neuroticism. The aesthetic category was positively related to agreeableness, extraversion and negatively to neuroticism. The dark category was positively related extraversion and negatively to conscientiousness and agreeableness. The cerebral category was related to extraversion while the thrilling category did not reveal any consistent correlation with personality factors.

The relation between music and personality was also explored by Rawlings et al. [55]. They observed that the Extraversion and Openness factors are the only ones that explain the variance in the music preferences. Subjects with high openness tend to prefer diverse music styles. Extraversion, on the other hand, was found to be strongly related to preferences to popular music.

Cantador et al. [9] presented the results of an experiment where they observed the relations between user preferences and personality in the domains of movies, TV shows, music and books. Their work is based on the myPersonality dataset [37]. They observe a large number of relations between personality traits and individual domains as well as in crossed domains.

In an experiment based on a contextual movie recommender system dataset (the CoMoDa dataset [50]), Odic et al. explored the relations between personality factors and the induced emotions in movies in different social context [51]. They observed different patterns in experienced emotions for users in different social contexts (i.e. alone vs. not alone) as functions of the extraversion, agreeableness and neuroticism factors. People with different values of the conscientiousness and openness factors did not exhibit different patterns in their induced emotions.

21.3 Personality Acquisition

The acquisition of personality parameters is the first major issue in the design of personality-based recommender systems. Generally, the acquisition techniques can be grouped into

- explicit techniques (questionnaires depending on the model)
- implicit techniques (regression/classification based on social media streams)

While explicit techniques provide accurate assessments of the users' personalities they are intrusive and time consuming. Hence, these techniques are useful only in laboratory studies and for the assessment of ground truth data for the later automatic extraction.

Implicit techniques, on the other hand, offer an unobtrusive way of acquiring personality parameters. However, the accuracy of these instruments is not high and depends heavily on the quality of the source information (e.g. how often does a user tweet).

In this section we survey existing techniques for the acquisition of personality in recommender system. Table 21.3 sums the methods described in this section.

Table 21.3 Personality acquisition methods

References	Method	Personality model	Source
[15, 23–26, 33]	Explicit	FFM	Questionnaires (from ten questions up)
[53]	Implicit	FFM	Micro-blogs (twitter)
[4, 37, 61]	Implicit	FFM	Social media (facebook)
[21]	Implicit	FFM	Social media (weibo)
[40]	Implicit	FFM	Role-playing game
[16]	Implicit	FFM	Game (Commons Fishing Game)
[11]	Implicit	FFM	Mobile phone logs
[63]	Implicit	FFM	Emails
[30]	Implicit	FFM	Ratings of products in a webstore
[14]	Implicit	FFM	Stories
[66]	Explicit	Thomas-Kilmann conflict model	Questionnaire
[64]	Explicit	Felder and Silverman learning style model	Questionnaire

21.3.1 Explicit Personality Acquisition

A widely used questionnaire for assessing the FFM factors is the International Personality Item Pool (IPIP) set of questionnaires [23]. The IPIP's web page[2] contains questionnaires with 50 and 100 items, depending on the number of questions per factor (10 or 20). The relatively high number of questions makes it an accurate instrument, although it's time consuming for end users. Furthermore, it has been translated in many languages and validated in terms of cross-cultural differences [42].

In the questionnaire defined by Hellriegel and Slocum [26], each factor is measured via five questions, so there are 25 questions in total regarding the five factors. Each factor's value is the average of user's scores on its related five questions. For example, the questions used to assess "Openness to Experience" include "imagination", "artistic interests", "liberalism", "adventurousness", and "intellect". Users are required to respond to every question on a 5-point Likert scale (for example, "imagination" is rated from 1 "no-nonsense" to 5 "a dreamer"). John and Srivastava [33] developed a more comprehensive list containing 44 items, called Big Five Inventory (BFI), by which each personality factor is measured by eight or nine questions. For example, the items related to "Openness to Experience" are "is original, comes up with new ideas", "is curious about many different things", "is ingenious, a deep thinker", "has an active imagination", etc. (each is rated on a 5-point Likert scale from "strongly disagree" to "strongly agree", under the

[2]http://ipip.ori.org/.

Table 21.4 The ten-items personality inventory questionnaire developed by Gosling et al. [25]

FFM factor	Statement: I see myself as
E	Extraverted, enthusiastic
A	Critical, quarrelsome
C	Dependable, self-disciplined
N	Anxious, easily upset
O	Open to new experiences, complex
E	Reserved, quiet
A	Sympathetic, warm
C	Disorganized, careless
N	Calm, emotionally stable
O	Conventional, uncreative

general question of "I see Myself as Someone Who ..."). This questionnaire has been recognized as a well-established measurement of personality traits. The other commonly used public-free instruments include the 100-item Big Five Aspect Scales (BFAS) [15] and the 100 trait-descriptive adjectives [24]). A super-short measure of the Big5 model is the Ten Item Personality Inventory (TIPI) in which each factor is only assessed by two questions (e.g., "Openness to Experiences" is assessed by "open to new experiences, complex" and "conventional, uncreative" on the same Likert scale used in BFI) [25]. This instrument can meet the need for a very short measure (e.g., when time is limited), although it may somewhat diminished psychometric properties. We provide the TIPI questionnaire in Table 21.4.

A typical example of a commercially controlled instrument is the NEO PI-R (with a 240-items inventory) [12], which can not only measure the five factors, but also the six facets (i.e. subfactors) of each factor. For example, "Extroversion" contains six facets: Gregariousness (sociable), Assertiveness (forceful), Activity (energetic), Excitement-seeking (adventurous), Positive emotions (enthusiastic), and Warmth (outgoing). The NEO-FFI instrument, which measures the five factors only (but not their related facets), is a 60-item truncated version of NEO PI-R [12].

A quasi-explicit instrument for measuring personality is the approach of using stories. In their work, Dennis et al. [14] developed a set of stereotypical stories where each one conveys a personality trait from the FFM. For each of the five FFM factors they devised a pair of stories, one for a high level of the observed factor and one for the low level of the observed factor. The subject then rates how well each story applies to her/him on a Likert scale from 1 (extremely inaccurate) to 9 (extremely accurate).

Though different instruments have been developed so far, the choice of instrument is highly application-dependent and there is no one-size-fits-all measure.

21.3.2 Implicit Personality Acquisition

In their work, Quercia et al. [53], present the outcomes of a study that shows strong correlations between features extracted from users' micro-blogs and their respective FFM factors. The authors used the myPersonality dataset of 335 users. The dataset contains the users' FFM personality factors and the respective micro-blogs. The authors extracted several features from the micro-blogs and categorized them into the following quantities: listeners, popular, highly-read and influential. Each of these quantities showed a strong correlation with at least one of the FFM factors. The authors went a step further into predicting the FFM factors. Using a machine learning approach (the M5 rules regression and the tenfold-cross validation scheme) they were able to achieve a predictability in RMSE ranging from 0.69 to 0.88 (on FFM factors ranging from 1 to 5).

Kosinski et al. [37] used the whole myPersonality dataset of over 58,000 subjects with their respective Facebook activity records to predict the FFM factors of the subjects. The source dataset was the user-like matrix of Facebook likes. The authors applied the Singular Value Decomposition method to reduce the number of features and used the logistic regression model to predict the FFM factors (along with other user parameters such as gender, age etc.). Their model was able to predict well the traits Openness and Extraversion while the other traits were predicted with lower accuracy.

An interesting approach was taken by van Lankveld et al. [40] who observed the correlation between FFM parameters and the users' behaviour in a videogame. They modified the Neverwinter Nights (a third-person role-playing video game) in order to store 275 game variables for 44 participants. They used variables that recorded conversation behavior, movement behavior and miscellaneous behaviors. They found significant correlations between all five personality traits and game variables in all groups.

Chittaranjan et al. [11] used mobile phone usage information for inferring FFM parameters. They used call logs (e.g. outgoing calls, incoming calls, average call duration etc.), SMS logs and application-usage logs as features for predicting the FFM factors. They observed that a number of these features have a significant correlations with the FFM factors. Using the Support Vector Machine classifier they achieved better results in the prediction of the traits than a random baseline although the difference was not always significant, which makes the task of inferring personality from call logs a hard one.

Shen et al. [63] attempted to infer the email writer's personality from her/his emails. To preserve privacy, they only extract high-level aggregated features from email contents, such as bag-of-word features (built from most commonly used words in daily life), meta features (such as TO/CC/BCC counts, importance of the email, count of different punctuation symbols, count of words, count of positive and negative numbers, count of attachments, month of the sent time, etc.), word statistics (through part-of speech tagging, sentiment analysis, and counting of pronouns and negations words), writing styles (in greeting patterns, closing patterns, wish patterns, and smiley words), and speech act scores (for detecting the purpose of work-related emails). These groups of features are then applied to train predictors of the writer's personality, through three different generative models: joint model, sequential model, and survival model. The function is formally represented as $f : X \rightarrow Y$, where X is the feature vector and $Y =< y_1, .., y_K >$ is the personality trait value vector (each element of Y corresponds to one personality trait, such as Extraversion, with either of three values "low", "medium" and "high"). The joint model takes all the personality traits as a single entity to jointly decide whether a feature is selected; sequential model first selects a personality trait, and then uses this trait to decide whether to select a feature; survival model allows all personality traits to decide whether to select a feature independently, then the feature selected by all traits will be get selected. The experiment done on over 100,000 emails showed that the survival model (with label-independence assumption) works best in terms of prediction accuracy and computation efficiency, while joint model performs worst in terms of inferring personality traits such as Agreeableness, Conscientiousness, and Extraversion. The results to some extend infer that the personality traits are relatively distinct and independent from each other. Furthermore, it was found that people with high Conscientiousness are inclined to write long emails and use more characters; people with high Agreeableness tend to use more "please" and good wishes in their emails; and people with high Neuroticism use more negations.

The set of studies by Oberlander et al. [32, 47] showed that personality can be inferred also from blog entries. In [32] they used features such as stemmed bigrams, no exclusion of stopwords (i.e. common words) or the boolean presence or absence of features noted (rather than their rate of use) in combination with the Support Vector Machines classifier. On a large corpus of blogs they managed to predict the FFM factors with an accuracy ranging from 70 % (for neuroticism) to 84 % (for openness).

With the development of social networking, some researchers have begun to study the correlation between users' personality and their social behavior on the web (e.g., Facebook, Twitter) [4, 59]. For example, [4] found strong connection between users' personality and their Facebook use through a user survey on 237 students. Participants' personality was self-reported through answering the NEO PI-R questionnaire. The collected personality data were then used to compute correlation with users' Facebook information (such as basic information, personal information, contact information and education, and work information). The results show that Extroversion has a positive effect on the number of friends. Moreover, individuals with high Neuroticism are more inclined to post their private information (such as photos). The factor Openness to Experience was found to have positive correlation with users' willingness to use Facebook as a communication tool, and the factor Conscientiousness is positively correlated with the number of friends. In [61], a similar experiment was performed. They verified again that Extroversion was significantly correlated with the size of a user's social network. Moreover, people tend to choose friends who are with higher Agreeableness but similar Extroversion and Openness.

In [22], the authors developed a method to predict users' personality from their Facebook profile. Among various features, they identified ones that have a significant correlation with one or more of the Big5 personality traits based on studying 167 subjects' public data on Facebook. These features include linguistic features (such as swear words, social processes, affective processes, perceptual processes, etc.), structural features (number of friends, egocentric network density), activities and preferences (e.g., favorite books), and personal information (relationship status, last name length in characters). Particularly, the linguistic analysis of profile text (which is the combination of status updates, About Me, and blurb text) was conducted through Linguistic Inquiry and Word Count (LIWC) program [52], which is a tool to produce statistics on 81 different text features in five psychological categories. They further proposed a regression analysis based approach to predict the personality, in two variations: M5'Rules, and Gaussian Processes. The testing shows that the prediction of each personality factor can be within 11 % of the actual values. Moreover, M5'Rules acts more effective than Gaussian Processes, with stronger connection to Openness, Conscientiousness, Extroversion, and Neuroticism.

Recently, Gao et al. [21] proposed a method for inferring the users' personality from their social media contents. To be specific, they obtained 1766 volunteers' personality values and Weibo behavior (which is a popular micro-blog site in China) to train the prediction model. Hundred and sixty eight features were extracted from these users' Weibo status, and then classified into categories including status statistics features (e.g., the total number of statuses), sentence-based features (the average number of Chinese characters per sentence), word-based features (the number of emotion words), character-based features (the number of commas, colons, etc.), and LIWC features. They then applied M5-Rules, Pace Regression and Gaussian process, to make prediction. The results show that the Pearson correlation between predicted personality and user self-reported personality can achieve 0.4 (i.e., fairly correlated), especially regarding the three traits Conscientiousness, Extroversion, and Openness to Experience.

Hu and Pu studied the effect of personality on users' rating behavior in recommender systems [30]. They obtained 86 participants' valid ratings on at least 30 items among a set of 871 products (from 44 primary categories). The rating behavior was analyzed from four aspects: number of rated items (NRI), percentage of positive ratings (PerPR), category coverage (CatCoverage), and interest diversity (IntDiversity). The CatCoverage is measured as the number of categories of rated items. The IntDiversity reveals the distribution of users' interests in each category, formally defined as the Shannon index according to information theory. They calculated the correlation between users' Big5 personality traits and the rating variables through Pearson product-moment. The results identify the significant impact of personality on the way users rate items. Particularly, Conscientiousness and gender were found negatively correlated with the number of ratings, category coverage and interest diversity, which indicates that conscientious and/or female users are more likely to prefer providing fewer ratings, lower level of category coverage, and lower interest diversity. In addition, Agreeableness is positively correlated with the percentage of positive ratings, implying that agreeable people tend to give more positive ratings. All these findings show correlations between personality and rating behaviour on the samples used. However, exploring whether it is possible to infer personality from rating behaviour is an open issue for future work.

Dunn et al. [16] proposed, beside an explicit questionnaire, a gamified user interface for the acquisition of personality for recommender systems. Through the Commons Fishing Game (CFG) interface the users were instructed to maximize the amount gathered from a common resource, which was shared amongst a group of players; collectively trying not to deplete this resource. The experiment showed that it is possible to predict Extraversion and Agreeableness with the described instrument.

21.3.3 Datasets for Offline Recommender Systems Experiments

Given that a number of research activities has already been published, there exist some datasets that can be used for personality-aware recommender systems experiments. The minimal requirements for such a dataset are (a) to include the user-item interaction data (e.g. ratings) and (b) to include the personality factors associated to the users. In this section we survey a number of such datasets, which are summarized in Table 21.5.

The first dataset containing personality parameters to be released was the LDOS-PerAff-1 [71]. Based on 52 subjects it contains ratings of images. The user-item matrix has all elements (i.e. sparsity is null). The dataset contains the corresponding FFM factors for each user. The FFM factors were acquired using the 50-items IPIP

Table 21.5 Overview of datasets

Name	References	Domain	Personality model	Number of subjects	Other metadata
LDOS-CoMoDa	[38]	Movies	FFM	95	Movie context metadata (location, weather, social state, emotions etc.)
LDOS-PerAff-1	[71]	Images	FFM	52	Item induced emotions in the VAD space
myPersonality	[37]	Social media (Facebook)	FFM	38,330	Twitter names
Chittaranjan	[11]	Mobile phone usage	FFM	117	Call logs, SMS logs, app logs

questionnaire [23]. Furthermore, all items were selected from the IAPS dataset of images [39] and are annotated with the values of the induced emotions in the valence-arousal-dominance (VAD) space.

The LDOS-CoMoDa (Context Movies Dataset) dataset [38] was developed for research on contextual recommender systems. A unique feature of the dataset is that it contains FFM parameters for each users. According to [38] it contains data for 95 users and 961 movies. The FFM factors were collected using the 50-items IPIP questionnaire [23]. The dataset is also rich in contextual parameters such as time, weather, location, emotions, social state etc.

A dataset that contains more users is the myPersonality dataset [37]. It contains FFM factors for 38,330 users. The dataset has been collected using a Facebook application. It contains the Facebook Likes for each of the users. Furthermore it also contains twitter names for more than 300 subjects which opens new possibilities for crawling these users' micro-blogs (as has been done in [53]).

Chittaranjan et al. [11] presented a dataset of mobile phone users logs along with the respective FFM values. The dataset contains information about 177 subjects and their daily phone usage activities (the CDR—call data record) over a period of 17 months on a Nokia N95 smartphone. The phone usage logs contain data related to calls, SMSs and application usage.

Furthermore, a number of datasets, not released as datasets per se, exist, as they have been used in the studies reported in this chapter.

21.4 How to Use Personality in Recommender Systems

In this section we provide an overview of how personality has been used in recommender systems. The most common issues addressed are the cold-start problem and the presentation of the recommended results in terms of diversity. Table 21.6 summarizes the various strategies described in this section.

21.4.1 Addressing the New User Problem

The new user problem occurs when the recommender system does not have enough ratings from a user that has just started to use the system [3]. The problem is present both in content-based recommender systems and in collaborative recommender systems although it is more difficult to solve within the latter. The system must first have some information about the user, which is usually in the form of ratings. In the case of content-based recommender systems, the lack of ratings implies that, for the observed user, the system does not know the preferences towards the item's features (e.g. the genre). In the case of collaborative filtering, especially in neighborhood methods, the lack of ratings for a new user implies that there are not enough overlapping ratings with other users, which makes it hard to calculate user

Table 21.6 Survey of recommender systems using personality

References	Recommender system's goal	Personality acquisition method	Approach
[72]	Cold-start problem	IPIP 50	User-user similarity measure based on personality
[29]	Cold-start problem	TIPI	User-user similarity measure based on personality
[8, 18]	Cold-start problem	TIPI	Active learning, matrix factorization
[74]	Diversity	TIPI	Personality-based diversity adjusting approach for movie recommendation
[67]	Diversity	NEO IPIP 20	Personality-based diversity adaptation
[9]	Cross-domain recommendations	NEO IPIP 20	Similarities between personality-based user stereotypes for genres in different domains
[54, 56]	Group recommendations	Thomas-Kilmann conflict model instrument	Combining assertiveness and cooperativeness into the aggregation function
[35]	Group recommendations	Thomas-Kilmann conflict model instrument and NEO IPIP 20	Group satisfaction modeling with a personality-based graph model

similarities. So far this problem has been tackled with various techniques such as hybrid methods [3], adaptive learning techniques [19] or simply by recommending popular items [3].

Personality is suitable to address the new-user problem. Given the assumption that the user's personality is available (e.g. from another domain) it can be used in collaborative filtering recommender systems.

Personality has been used in a memory-based collaborative filtering recommender system for images [69, 72]. In an offline experiment, the authors acquired explicit FFM parameters for each user and calculated the user distances (as opposed to similarities) using the weighted distance formula

$$d(b_i, b_j) = \sqrt{\sum_{l=1}^{5} w_l(b_{il} - b_{jl})^2} \quad (21.1)$$

where b_i and b_j are the FFM vectors for two arbitrary users (b_{il} and b_{jl} are the individual FFM factors) and w_l are the weights. The weights were computed as the eigenvalues from the principal component analysis on the FFM values of all users. On the given dataset, this approach was statistically equivalent to using standard rating-based user similarity measures.

A similar approach was taken by Hu and Pu [29] where they used a different formula to calculate the user similarities. They proposed to use the Pearson correlation coefficient to calculate the user similarities

$$sim(b_i, b_j) = \frac{\sum_l (b_{il} - \overline{b_i})(b_{jl} - \overline{b_j})}{\sqrt{\sum_l (b_{il} - \overline{b_i})^2}\sqrt{\sum_l (b_{jl} - \overline{b_j})^2}} \tag{21.2}$$

and they combined it with existing ratings by controlling the contribution of each similarity measure with the weight α. They compared the proposed approach to a rating-based user similarity metric collaborative filtering recommender system. On a dataset of 113 users and 646 songs the personality-based algorithm outperformed the rating-based in terms of mean absolute error, recall and specificity.

Their results showed that both personality-based similarity and the hybrid scheme lead CF recommender systems to generate more accurate recommendations than the traditional rating-based one in a sparse music dataset.

A standard approach to tackle the cold-start problem is to use the active learning approach (rating elicitation—see also Chap. 24) [19]. In their work, Elahi et al. [18], proposed an active learning strategy that incorporated user personality data. They acquired the personality information using the 10-items IPIP questionnaire through a mobile application. They formulated the rating prediction as a modified matrix factorization approach where the FFM factors are treated as additional users' latent factors:

$$\hat{r}_{ui} = b_i + b_u + q_i^T \cdot (p_u + \sum_l b_l) \tag{21.3}$$

where p_u is the latent factor of the user u, q_i is the latent factor o the item i, b_u and b_i are the user's and item's biases and b_l are the FFM factors. The proposed rating elicitation method outperformed (in terms of Mean Absolute Error) the baseline (the log(popularity)*entropy method) and the random method.

In these examples, personality has been acquired separately with questionnaires. With this approach the authors have just moved the burden of an initial questionnaire about user ratings to another initial questionnaire (for personality). However, the idea here is that personality is going to be available in advance, for example from other domains or acquired implicitly.

21.4.2 *Diversity/Serendipity*

Recently, the impact of personality on users' preferences on recommendation diversity has been investigated in [10, 67]. Diversity refers to recommending users a diverse set of items, so as to allow them to discover unexpected items more effectively [46] (see also Chap. 26). The existing approaches commonly adopt a fixed strategy to adjust the diversity degree within the set of recommendations [2, 31, 75], which however, does not consider that different users might possess different attitudes towards the diversity of items. The limitation motivates the authors of paper [10] to research whether and how personality might impact users' needs for diversity in recommender systems. They conducted a user survey (with 181 subjects) to know the causal relationship. For each user, they obtained her/his movie selections as well as personality values. Then, two levels of diversity were considered: the diversity in respect to individual attributes (such as the movie's genre, director, actor/actress, etc.); the overall diversity when all attributes are combined. The correlation analysis showed that some personality factors have a significant correlation with users' diversity preferences. For instance, it shows that more reactive, excited and nervous persons (high Neuroticism) are more inclined to choose diverse directors, and suspicious/antagonistic users (low Agreeableness) prefer diverse movie countries. As for the movie's release time, its diversity is preferred by efficient/organized users (high Conscientiousness), while for the movie's actor/actress, its diversity is preferred by imaginative/creative users (high Openness to experience). At the second level (i.e., overall diversity), no matter how the weights placed on attributes vary, Conscientiousness was shown significantly negatively correlated with it, which means that less conscientious people essentially prefer higher level of overall diversity.

Inspired by the user survey's findings, they developed a personality-based diversity adjusting approach for movie recommendation [74]. They have incorporated personality, as a moderating factor, into a content-based recommender system. Specifically, given the user's personality values in respect to the Big5 factors, they first identify her/his diversity needs. For example, since high Openness to Experience is linked to high need for diversity with regards to "actor/actress", in the case that the "actor/actress" is the current user's most important attribute and s/he possesses a high Openness to Experience value, the system will return movies with diverse actors/actresses to the user. In addition, if the user has a low Conscientiousness value, the system will further increase the recommendations' overall diversity degree, since low Conscientiousness is correlated with high need for the overall diversity. The number of diverse items within the whole recommendation set is accordingly adjusted to reflect the user's diversity needs. The proposed method was tested in a controlled user study (with 52 participants), by means of comparing it to a variant that incorporated personality in the contrary way (i.e., offering less diverse items to the user though s/he spontaneously requires a higher level of diversity given her/his personality values). The user evaluation demonstrated that their method can significantly increase users' perception of system competence and recommendation accuracy. Users were also more satisfied with the personality-based recommendation. The findings thus consolidate the previous survey's results. They also suggest an effective solution in terms of taking personality into account for generating personalized diversity in recommender systems.

Tintarev et al. applied a User-as-Wizard approach to study how people apply diversity to the set of recommendations [67]. Particularly, they emphasized the personality factor Openness to Experience as for its specific role in personalizing the recommendation diversity's level, because it describes users' imagination, aesthetic sensitivity, attentiveness to inner feelings, preference for variety, and intellectual curiosity (so they assumed that people with higher Openness to Experience would be more willing to receive novel items). Their experiment was in the form of an online questionnaire with the aid of Amazon's Mechanical Turk (MT) service. Hundred and Twenty users' responses were analyzed. Each of them was required to provide some recommendation to a fictitious friend who is in one of three conditions: high Openness to Experience, low Openness to Experience, no personality description (baseline). The results did not prove the effect of Openness to Experience on the overall diversity participants applied, but the authors observed that participants tend to recommend items with high categorical diversity (i.e., across genres) but low thematic diversity (inter-genre) to others who are more open to experience. In other words, users who are low on Openness to Experience might prefer thematic diversity to categorical variation. The observation is consistent with the finding from [1] that users generally prefer recommendations from diversified categories, but less diversity within one category.

21.4.3 Cross-Domain Recommendations

As we mentioned in the introduction, personality is domain-independent, i.e. when users are being recommended books or movies, we can use the same personality profile. This can be especially useful in cross-domain recommender systems (see also Chap. 27). In a study performed by Cantador et al. [9] personality factors are related to domain genres and similarities between personality-based user stereotypes for genres in different domains are computed. Among the many cross-domain-genres combinations we can find relations such as *salsa-music lovers are dissimilar to science-fiction-books lovers* or *news-tv-show lovers are similar to mystery-books lovers.*

21.4.4 Group Recommender Systems

Group recommendations are discussed in Chap. 22. Recommending items to groups of users is not the same as recommending items to individual users [41]. Beside having to choose among strategies that address users as individuals (e.g. least misery, most pleasure etc.—see Chap. 22 for an extensive overview), the relationships between group members play an important role. Personality is an important factor in group dynamics.

In their work, Recio-Garcia et al. [56] and Quijano-Sanchez et al. [54] propose to use the Thomas-Kilmann Conflict personality model [66] to model the relationships between group members in terms of *assertiveness* and *cooperativeness*. They applied the model to three group recommendation approaches (i.e. least misery, minimize penalization and average satisfaction). They collected ground truth data through a user study with 70 students who formed groups, discussed and decided which movies they would watch together in a cinema. The proposed approach showed an increase in prediction accuracy compared to the same techniques without taking into account the conflict personality model.

Similarly, Kompan et al. [35] used the Thomas-Kilmann model and the FFM to model individual users. They modeled the group satisfaction with a graph-based approach where vertices represent users and edges represent user influences based on relationship, personality and actual context. They performed a small-scale user study with users rating movies. The usage of the personality-based group satisfaction model in an average-aggregation strategy-based group recommender system outperformed the same algorithm without the proposed group satisfaction modeling.

21.5 Open Issues and Challenges

The usage of personality in recommender systems has just started, which makes it a very interesting research topic as there are quite some open issues and challenges that need to be addressed. In this section we survey these open issues.

21.5.1 Non-intrusive Acquisition of Personality Information

The limitation of traditional explicit acquisition approach is that the required user effort is usually high, especially if we want to obtain their accurate personality profile (e.g., through 100-item Big Five Aspect Scales (BFAS); see Sect. 21.3.1). Users might be reluctant to follow the time-consuming and tedious procedure to answer all questions, due to their cognitive or emotional reason. Thus, the implicit, unobtrusive approach might be more acceptable and effective to build their personality profile. The critical question is then how to accurately derive users' personality traits from the information they have provided. In Sect. 21.3.2, we discussed various methods, such as ones based on users' emails or their generated contents and behavior in social networking sites (e.g., Facebook, Twitter). However, the research is still at the beginning stage, and there is large room to improve the existing algorithms' accuracy. One possible solution is to explore other types of info as to their power of reflecting users' personality. For instance, since the significant correlation between users' personality and their rating behavior was proven in [30], the findings might be constructive for some researchers to develop the rating-based personality inference algorithm. The developed method might be further extended to consider the possible impacts of other actions, such as users' browsing, clicking, and selecting behavior in recommender systems. Indeed, it will be interesting to investigate the complementary roles of various resources to fulfill their combinative effect on deriving users' personality. To be specific, we may infer users' personality by integrating their history data left at different platforms (e.g., the integration of rating behavior, email, and social media content). The different types of info might be heterogenous in nature, so how to effectively fuse them together might be an open issue.

21.5.2 *Larger Datasets*

The recommender systems oriented datasets containing personality factors of users are very few (see Sect. 21.3.3). Furthermore the number of subjects in databases is very low, ranging from roughly 50 to a little more than 100, with the exception of the myPersonality dataset. Compared to the huge datasets that the recommender systems community is used to work with (e.g. the Netflix or the Yahoo! Music datasets) the lack of bigger datasets is an obvious issue that needs to be addressed.

21.5.3 *Cross-Domain Applications*

An unexplored area of recommender systems, where personality appears to be a natural fit, are cross-domain applications (see also Chap. 27). As personality is domain-independent it can be used as a generic user model. Cross-domain applications have been researched in the past and correlations of preferences among different domains have been identified. For example, Winoto et al. [73] observed the relations between the *games*, *TV series* and *movie* domains, while Tiroshi et al. [68] observed the relations between *music*, *movies*, *TV series* and *books*. The first to explore the potential role of personality in cross-domain applications were Cantador et al. [9] who observed the relations between the FFM factors and preferences in various domains (movies, TV shows, music, books). An intuitive continuation of this work is the application of the personalities learned in one domain to another domain to beat the cold-start problem.

Another aspect of cross-domain recommendations is cross-application recommendations. In order to be able to transfer the personality profiles between applications a standardized description of personality should be used. There has been an attempt, the *Personality Markup Language* (PersonalityML), to standardize the description of personality in user models across different domains [6].

21.5.4 *Diversity*

How to provide diverse and novel recommendations has increasingly become an important topic in the area of recommender systems. That is, we are no longer satisfied with providing items similar to what users preferred before, but showing ones that can be unexpected and surprising to users. The recent works [10, 67] have indicated the difference occurring among users in terms of their needs for recommendation diversity as influenced by their inherent personality. It hence comes to the question of how to enhance the existing diversity algorithm to make it more tailored to individual user's requirement. For example, in [74], the authors gave a preliminary attempt to solve this problem and obtain interesting results. The ideas might be further enhanced and consolidated from both aspects of algorithm development and user evaluation. Moreover, in addition to personality, it will be meaningful to study the potential influence of other personal factors such as demographic characteristics (e.g., age, gender, cultural background). According to [10], some demographical properties did show significant correlation with some diversity variables. For example, people who are younger and/or with lower education level are more likely to prefer diverse movies. It hence suggests that these factors could be considered together with personality for optimally adjusting the diversity degree within the list of recommendations.

21.5.5 Privacy Issues

Although all the research done so far on personality in recommender systems touched upon the sensitivity of the data, the issue of privacy has not been addressed properly yet. The fact that, in terms of personality, a user can be tagged as *neurotic* or otherwise with labels that suggest a negative trait makes these data very sensitive. Schrammel et al. [60] explored if there were any differences in the degree of disclosure acceptance among users with different personalities but found no significant differences. Some aspects are discussed in Chap. 19.

21.6 Conclusion

In this chapter we presented the usage of personality in recommender systems. Personality, as defined in psychology, accounts for the most important ways in which users differ in their preferences and behaviour. It can be acquired using either questionnaires or by inferring implicitly from other sources (e.g. social media streams). The most common model of personality is the Five Factor Model (FFM), which is composed of the factors openness, conscientiousness, extraversion, agreeableness and neuroticism. This model is suitable for recommender systems since it can be quantified with feature vectors that describe the degree each factor is expressed in a user. Furthermore, the FFM (and personality in general) is domain independent. We presented several methods for the acquisition of personality factors, with a special focus on implicit methods. We showcased a number of ways recommender systems have been shown to improve using personality models, especially in terms of the cold-start problem and diversity. Finally, we provided a list of open issues and challenges that need to be addressed in order to improve the adoption of personality in recommender systems.

Acknowledgements Part of the work presented in this chapter has received funding from the European Union FP7 programme through the PHENICX project (grant agreement no. 601166), China National Natural Science Foundation (no. 61272365), and Hong Kong Research Grants Council (no. ECS/HKBU211912).

References

1. Abbassi, Z., Mirrokni, V.S., Thakur, M.: Diversity maximization under matroid constraints. In: Proceedings of the 19th ACM SIGKDD International Conference on Knowledge Discovery and Data Mining, KDD '13, pp. 32–40. ACM, New York, NY, USA (2013). DOI 10.1145/2487575.2487636
2. Adomavicius, G., Kwon, Y.: Improving aggregate recommendation diversity using ranking-based techniques. Knowledge and Data Engineering, IEEE Transactions on **24**(5), 896–911 (2012). DOI 10.1109/TKDE.2011.15
3. Adomavicius, G., Tuzhilin, a.: Toward the next generation of recommender systems: a survey of the state-of-the-art and possible extensions. IEEE Transactions on Knowledge and Data Engineering **17**(6), 734–749 (2005). DOI 10.1109/TKDE.2005.99
4. Amichai-Hamburger, Y., Vinitzky, G.: Social network use and personality. Computers in Human Behavior **26**(6), 1289–1295 (2010)
5. Aral, S., Walker, D.: Identifying influential and susceptible members of social networks. Science (New York, N.Y.) **337**(6092), 337–41 (2012). DOI 10.1126/science.1215842
6. Augusta Silveira Netto Nunes, M., Santos Bezerra, J., Adicinéia, A.: PersonalityML: A Markup Language to Standardize the User Personality in Recommender Systems. Revista Gestão, Inovação e Tecnologia **2**(3), 255–273 (2012). DOI 10.7198/S2237-0722201200030006
7. Bologna, C., Rosa, A.C.D., Vivo, A.D., Gaeta, M., Sansonetti, G., Viserta, V., A, Q.G.S.: Personality-Based Recommendation in E-Commerce. EMPIRE 2013: Emotions and Personality in Personalized Services (2013)
8. Braunhofer, M., Elahi, M., Ge, M., Ricci, F.: Context Dependent Preference Acquisition with Personality-Based Active Learning in Mobile Recommender Systems. Learning and Collaboration Technologies. Technology-Rich Environments for Learning and Collaboration pp. 105–116 (2014). DOI 10.1007/978-3-319-07485-6_11
9. Cantador, I., Fernández-tobías, I., Bellogín, A.: Relating Personality Types with User Preferences in Multiple Entertainment Domains. EMPIRE 1st Workshop on "Emotions and Personality in Personalized Services", 10. June 2013, Rome (2013)
10. Chen, L., Wu, W., He, L.: How personality influences users' needs for recommendation diversity? CHI '13 Extended Abstracts on Human Factors in Computing Systems on - CHI EA '13 p. 829 (2013). DOI 10.1145/2468356.2468505
11. Chittaranjan, G., Blom, J., Gatica-Perez, D.: Mining large-scale smartphone data for personality studies. Personal and Ubiquitous Computing **17**(3), 433–450 (2011). DOI 10.1007/s00779-011-0490-1
12. Costa, P.T., Mccrae, R.R.: NEO PI-R professional manual. Odessa, FL (1992)
13. Deniz, M.: An Investigation of Decision Making Styles and the Five-Factor Personality Traits with Respect to Attachment Styles. Educational Sciences: Theory and Practice **11**(1), 105–114 (2011)
14. Dennis, M., Masthoff, J., Mellish, C.: The quest for validated personality trait stories. In: Proceedings of the 2012 ACM international conference on Intelligent User Interfaces - IUI '12, p. 273. ACM Press, New York, New York, USA (2012). DOI 10.1145/2166966.2167016
15. DeYoung, C.G., Quilty, L.C., Peterson, J.B.: Between facets and domains: 10 aspects of the Big Five. Journal of personality and social psychology **93**(5), 880–896 (2007). DOI 10.1037/0022-3514.93.5.880

16. Dunn, G., Wiersema, J., Ham, J., Aroyo, L.: Evaluating interface variants on personality acquisition for recommender systems. User Modeling, Adaptation, and Personalization pp. 259–270 (2009). DOI 10.1007/978-3-642-02247-0_25
17. El-Bishouty, M.M., Chang, T.W., Graf, S., Chen, N.S.: Smart e-course recommender based on learning styles. Journal of Computers in Education **1**(1), 99–111 (2014). DOI 10.1007/s40692-014-0003-0
18. Elahi, M., Braunhofer, M., Ricci, F., Tkalcic, M.: Personality-based active learning for collaborative filtering recommender systems. AI*IA 2013: Advances in Artificial Intelligence pp. 360–371 (2013). DOI 10.1007/978-3-319-03524-6_31
19. Elahi, M., Repsys, V., Ricci, F.: Rating elicitation strategies for collaborative filtering. E-Commerce and Web Technologies pp. 160–171 (2011)
20. Felder, R., Silverman, L.: Learning and teaching styles in engineering education. Engineering education **78**(June), 674–681 (1988)
21. Gao, R., Hao, B., Bai, S., Li, L., Li, A., Zhu, T.: Improving user profile with personality traits predicted from social media content. In: Proceedings of the 7th ACM Conference on Recommender Systems, RecSys '13, pp. 355–358. ACM, New York, NY, USA (2013). DOI 10.1145/2507157.2507219
22. Golbeck, J., Robles, C., Turner, K.: Predicting personality with social media. Proceedings of the 2011 annual conference extended abstracts on Human factors in computing systems - CHI EA '11 p. 253 (2011). DOI 10.1145/1979742.1979614
23. Goldberg, L., Johnson, J., Eber, H., Hogan, R., Ashton, M., Cloninger, C., Gough, H.: The international personality item pool and the future of public-domain personality measures. Journal of Research in Personality **40**(1), 84–96 (2006). DOI 10.1016/j.jrp.2005.08.007
24. Goldberg, L.R.: The Development of Markers for the Big-Five Factor Structure. Psychological assessment **4**(1), 26–42 (1992)
25. Gosling, S.D., Rentfrow, P.J., Swann, W.B.: A very brief measure of the Big-Five personality domains. Journal of Research in Personality **37**(6), 504–528 (2003). DOI 10.1016/S0092-6566(03)00046-1
26. Hellriegel Don, Slocum, J.: Organizational Behavior. Cengage Learning (2010)
27. Holland, J.L.: Making vocational choices: A theory of vocational personalities and work environments. Psychological Assessment Resources (1997)
28. Hu, R., Pu, P.: A Study on User Perception of Personality-Based Recommender Systems. User Modeling, Adaptation, and Personalization **6075**, 291–302 (2010). DOI 10.1007/978-3-642-13470-8_27
29. Hu, R., Pu, P.: Using Personality Information in Collaborative Filtering for New Users. Recommender Systems and the Social Web p. 17 (2010)
30. Hu, R., Pu, P.: Exploring Relations between Personality and User Rating Behaviors. EMPIRE 1st Workshop on "Emotions and Personality in Personalized Services", 10. June 2013, Rome (2013)
31. Hurley, N., Zhang, M.: Novelty and diversity in top-n recommendation – analysis and evaluation. ACM Trans. Internet Technol. **10**(4), 14:1–14:30 (2011). DOI 10.1145/1944339.1944341
32. Iacobelli, F., Gill, A.J., Nowson, S., Oberlander, J.: Large Scale Personality Classification of Bloggers. In: S. DMello, A. Graesser, B. Schuller, J.C. Martin (eds.) Affective Computing and Intelligent Interaction, *Lecture Notes in Computer Science*, vol. 6975, pp. 568–577. Springer Berlin Heidelberg, Berlin, Heidelberg (2011). DOI 10.1007/978-3-642-24571-8
33. John, O.P., Srivastava, S.: The Big Five trait taxonomy: History, measurement, and theoretical perspectives. In: L.A. Pervin, O.P. John (eds.) Handbook of personality: Theory and research, vol. 2, second edn., pp. 102–138. Guilford Press, New York (1999)
34. Keirsey, D.: Please Understand Me 2? Prometheus Nemesis pp. 1–350 (1998)
35. Kompan, M., Bieliková, M.: Social Structure and Personality Enhanced Group Recommendation. UMAP 2014 Extended Proceedings (2014)
36. Koren, Y., Bell, R., Volinsky, C.: Matrix Factorization Techniques for Recommender Systems. Computer **42**(8), 30–37 (2009). DOI 10.1109/MC.2009.263
37. Kosinski, M., Stillwell, D., Graepel, T.: Private traits and attributes are predictable from digital records of human behavior. Proceedings of the National Academy of Sciences pp. 2–5 (2013). DOI 10.1073/pnas.1218772110

38. Košir, A., Odić, A., Kunaver, M., Tkalčič, M., Tasič, J.F.: Database for contextual personalization. Elektrotehniški vestnik **78**(5), 270–274 (2011)
39. Lang, P.J., Bradley, M.M., Cuthbert, B.N.: International affective picture system (IAPS): Affective ratings of pictures and instruction manual. Technical Report A-8. Tech. rep., University of Florida (2005)
40. van Lankveld, G., Spronck, P., van den Herik, J., Arntz, A.: Games as personality profiling tools. 2011 IEEE Conference on Computational Intelligence and Games (CIG'11) pp. 197–202 (2011). DOI 10.1109/CIG.2011.6032007
41. Masthoff, J., Gatt, A.: In pursuit of satisfaction and the prevention of embarrassment: affective state in group recommender systems. User Modeling and User-Adapted Interaction: The Journal of Personalization Research **16**(3-4), 281–319 (2006). DOI 10.1007/s11257-006-9008-3
42. McCrae, R., Allik, I.: The five-factor model of personality across cultures. Springer (2002)
43. McCrae, R.R., Costa, P.T.: A contemplated revision of the NEO Five-Factor Inventory. Personality and Individual Differences **36**(3), 587–596 (2004). DOI 10.1016/S0191-8869(03)00118-1
44. McCrae, R.R., John, O.P.: An Introduction to the Five-Factor Model and its Applications. Journal of Personality **60**(2), p175–215 (1992)
45. McNee, S.M., Riedl, J., Konstan, J.A.: Being accurate is not enough. In: CHI '06 extended abstracts on Human factors in computing systems - CHI EA '06, p. 1097. ACM Press, New York, New York, USA (2006). DOI 10.1145/1125451.1125659
46. McNee, S.M., Riedl, J., Konstan, J.A.: Being accurate is not enough: How accuracy metrics have hurt recommender systems. In: CHI '06 Extended Abstracts on Human Factors in Computing Systems, CHI EA '06, pp. 1097–1101. ACM, New York, NY, USA (2006). DOI 10.1145/1125451.1125659
47. Nowson, S., Oberlander, J.: Identifying more bloggers: Towards large scale personality classification of personal weblogs. International Conference on Weblogs and Social Media. (2007)
48. Nunes, M.A.S., Hu, R.: Personality-based recommender systems. In: Proceedings of the sixth ACM conference on Recommender systems - RecSys '12, p. 5. ACM Press, New York, New York, USA (2012). DOI 10.1145/2365952.2365957
49. Nunes, M.A.S.N.: Recommender Systems based on Personality Traits: Could human psychological aspects influence the computer decision-making process? VDM Verlag (2009)
50. Odić, A., Tkalčič, M., Tasic, J.F., Košir, A.: Predicting and Detecting the Relevant Contextual Information in a Movie-Recommender System. Interacting with Computers **25**(1), 74–90 (2013). DOI 10.1093/iwc/iws003
51. Odić, A., Tkalčič, M., Tasič, J.F., Košir, A.: Personality and Social Context : Impact on Emotion Induction from Movies. UMAP 2013 Extended Proceedings (2013)
52. Pennebaker, J.W., Francis, M.E., Booth, R.J.: Linguistic inquiry and word count: Liwc 2001. Mahway: Lawrence Erlbaum Associates p. 71 (2001)
53. Quercia, D., Kosinski, M., Stillwell, D., Crowcroft, J.: Our Twitter Profiles, Our Selves: Predicting Personality with Twitter. In: 2011 IEEE Third Int'l Conference on Privacy, Security, Risk and Trust and 2011 IEEE Third Int'l Conference on Social Computing, pp. 180–185. IEEE (2011). DOI 10.1109/PASSAT/SocialCom.2011.26
54. Quijano-Sanchez, L., Recio-Garcia, J.a., Diaz-Agudo, B.: Personality and Social Trust in Group Recommendations. 2010 22nd IEEE International Conference on Tools with Artificial Intelligence (c), 121–126 (2010). DOI 10.1109/ICTAI.2010.92
55. Rawlings, D., Ciancarelli, V.: Music Preference and the Five-Factor Model of the NEO Personality Inventory. Psychology of Music **25**(2), 120–132 (1997). DOI 10.1177/0305735697252003
56. Recio-Garcia, J.A., Jimenez-Diaz, G., Sanchez-Ruiz, A.A., Diaz-Agudo, B.: Personality aware recommendations to groups. In: Proceedings of the third ACM conference on Recommender systems - RecSys '09, p. 325. ACM Press, New York, New York, USA (2009). DOI 10.1145/1639714.1639779

57. Rentfrow, P.J., Goldberg, L.R., Zilca, R.: Listening, watching, and reading: the structure and correlates of entertainment preferences. Journal of personality **79**(2), 223–58 (2011). DOI 10.1111/j.1467-6494.2010.00662.x
58. Rentfrow, P.J., Gosling, S.D.: The do re mi's of everyday life: The structure and personality correlates of music preferences. Journal of Personality and Social Psychology **84**(6), 1236–1256 (2003). DOI 10.1037/0022-3514.84.6.1236
59. Ross, C., Orr, E.S., Sisic, M., Arseneault, J.M., Simmering, M.G., Orr, R.R.: Personality and motivations associated with facebook use. Computers in Human Behavior **25**(2), 578–586 (2009)
60. Schrammel, J., Köffel, C., Tscheligi, M.: Personality traits, usage patterns and information disclosure in online communities. Proceedings of the 23rd British HCI ... pp. 169–174 (2009)
61. Selfhout, M., Burk, W., Branje, S., Denissen, J., van Aken, M., Meeus, W.: Emerging late adolescent friendship networks and Big Five personality traits: a social network approach. Journal of personality **78**(2), 509–38 (2010). DOI 10.1111/j.1467-6494.2010.00625.x
62. Sha, X., Quercia, D., Michiardi, P., Dell'Amico, M.: Spotting trends. In: Proceedings of the sixth ACM conference on Recommender systems - RecSys '12, p. 51. ACM Press, New York, New York, USA (2012). DOI 10.1145/2365952.2365967
63. Shen, J., Brdiczka, O., Liu, J.: Understanding Email Writers: Personality Prediction from Email Messages. User Modeling, Adaptation, and Personalization pp. 318–330 (2013). DOI 10.1007/978-3-642-38844-6_29
64. Soloman, B.A., Felder, R.M.: Index of Learning Styles Questionnaire (2014). URL http://www.engr.ncsu.edu/learningstyles/ilsweb.html
65. Stewart, B.: Personality And Play Styles: A Unified Model (2011)
66. Thomas, K.W.: Conflict and conflict management: Reflections and update. Journal of Organizational Behavior **13**(3), 265–274 (1992). DOI 10.1002/job.4030130307
67. Tintarev, N., Dennis, M., Masthoff, J.: Adapting Recommendation Diversity to Openness to Experience: A Study of Human Behaviour. User Modeling, Adaptation, and Personalization, Lecture Notes in Computer Science Volume 7899 (I), 190–202 (2013). DOI 10.1007/978-3-642-38844-6_16
68. Tiroshi, A., Kuflik, T.: Domain ranking for cross domain collaborative filtering. User Modeling, Adaptation, and Personalization pp. 328–333 (2012). DOI 10.1007/978-3-642-31454-4_30
69. Tkalcic, M., Kunaver, M., Košir, A., Tasic, J.: Addressing the new user problem with a personality based user similarity measure. Joint Proceedings of the Workshop on Decision Making and Recommendation Acceptance Issues in Recommender Systems (DEMRA 2011) and the 2nd Workshop on User Models for Motivational Systems: The affective and the rational routes to persuasion (UMMS 2011) (2011)
70. Tkalčič, M., Burnik, U., Košir, A.: Using affective parameters in a content-based recommender system for images. User Modeling and User-Adapted Interaction **20**(4), 279–311 (2010). DOI 10.1007/s11257-010-9079-z
71. Tkalčič, M., Košir, A., Tasič, J.: The LDOS-PerAff-1 corpus of facial-expression video clips with affective, personality and user-interaction metadata. Journal on Multimodal User Interfaces **7**(1-2), 143–155 (2013). DOI 10.1007/s12193-012-0107-7
72. Tkalčič, M., Kunaver, M., Tasič, J., Košir, A.: Personality Based User Similarity Measure for a Collaborative Recommender System. 5th Workshop on Emotion in Human-Computer Interaction-Real World Challenges p. 30 (2009)
73. Winoto, P., Tang, T.: If You Like the Devil Wears Prada the Book, Will You also Enjoy the Devil Wears Prada the Movie? A Study of Cross-Domain Recommendations. New Generation Computing **26**(3), 209–225 (2008). DOI 10.1007/s00354-008-0041-0

74. Wu, W., Chen, L., He, L.: Using personality to adjust diversity in recommender systems. Proceedings of the 24th ACM Conference on Hypertext and Social Media - HT '13 (May), 225–229 (2013). DOI 10.1145/2481492.2481521
75. Ziegler, C.N., McNee, S.M., Konstan, J.A., Lausen, G.: Improving recommendation lists through topic diversification. In: Proceedings of the 14th International Conference on World Wide Web, WWW '05, pp. 22–32. ACM, New York, NY, USA (2005). DOI 10.1145/1060745.1060754

Part V
Advanced Topics

Chapter 22
Group Recommender Systems: Aggregation, Satisfaction and Group Attributes

Judith Masthoff

22.1 Introduction

Most work on recommender systems to date focuses on recommending items to individual users. For instance, they may select a book for a particular user to read based on a model of that user's preferences in the past. The challenge recommender system designers traditionally faced is how to decide what would be optimal for an individual user. A lot of progress has been made on this, as evidenced by other chapters in this handbook (e.g. Chaps. 2, 4, 5, 7 and 27).

In this chapter, we go one-step further. There are many situations when it would be good if we could recommend to a group of users rather than to an individual. For instance, a recommender system may select television programmes for a group to view or a sequence of songs to listen to, based on models of all group members. Recommending to groups is even more complicated than recommending to individuals. Assuming that we know perfectly what is good for individual users, the issue arises how to combine individual user models. In this chapter, we will discuss how group recommendation works, what its problems are, and what advances have been made. Interestingly, we will show that group recommendation techniques have many uses as well when recommending to individuals. So, even if you are developing recommender systems aimed at individual users you may still want to read on (perhaps reading Sect. 22.8 first will convince you).

This chapter focuses on deciding what to recommend to a group, in particular how to aggregate individual user models or aggregate recommendations. There are

J. Masthoff (✉)
University of Aberdeen, AB24 3UE Aberdeen, UK
e-mail: j.masthoff@abdn.ac.uk

F. Ricci et al. (eds.), *Recommender Systems Handbook*,
DOI 10.1007/978-1-4899-7637-6_22

other issues to consider when building a group recommender system which are outside the scope of this chapter. In particular:

- *How to acquire information about individual users' preferences.* The usual recommender techniques can be used (such as explicit ratings and collaborative- and content-based filtering, see other handbook chapters). There is a complication in that it is difficult to infer an individual's preferences when a group uses the system, but inferences can be made during individual use combined with a probabilistic model when using it in company. An additional complication is that an individual's ratings may depend on the group they are in. For instance, a teenager may be very happy to watch a programme with his younger siblings, but may not want to see it when with his friends.
- *How will the system know who is present?* Different solutions exist, such as users explicitly logging in, probabilistic mechanisms using the time of day to predict who is present, the use of tokens and tags, etc. [28]. More sophisticated approaches have been used in recent years. For example, the GAIN system divides the group into a known subgroup (users which it knows are there) and an unknown subgroup (users that cannot be recognized but should be there statistically) [11]. A group recommender in a public display system recognizes the gender and emotions of people present and group structures (which people are alone and which with others) [25].
- *How to present and explain group recommendations?* As seen in this handbook's chapter on explanations, there are already many considerations when presenting and explaining *individual* recommendations. The case of group recommendations is even more difficult. More discussion on explaining group recommendations is provided in [23] and under Challenges in our final section.
- *How to help users to settle on a final decision?* In some group recommenders, users are given group recommendations, and based on these recommendations negotiate what to do. In other group recommenders this is not an issue (see Sect. 22.2.3 on the difference between passive and active groups). An overview of how users' decisions can be aided is provided in [23].

The next section highlights usage scenarios of group recommenders, and provides a classification of group recommenders inspired by differences between the scenarios. Section 22.3 discusses strategies for aggregating models of individual users to allow for group recommendation, what strategies have been used in existing systems, and what we and others have learned from experiments in this area. Section 22.4 deals with the issue of order when we want to recommend a sequence of items. Section 22.5 provides an introduction into the modeling of affective state, including how an individual's affective state can be influenced by the affective states of other group members. Section 22.6 explores how such a model of affective state can be used to build more sophisticated aggregation strategies. Section 22.7 discusses other group attributes (such as personality of users) that can be used in aggregation strategies. Section 22.8 shows how group modeling and group recommendation techniques can be used when recommending to an individual user. Section 22.9 concludes this chapter and discusses future challenges.

22.2 Usage Scenarios and Classification of Group Recommenders

There are many circumstances in which adaptation to a group is needed rather than to an individual. Below, we present two scenarios that inspired our own work in this area, discuss the scenarios underlying related work, and provide a classification of group recommenders inspired by differences between the scenarios.

22.2.1 Usage Scenario 1: Interactive Television

Interactive television offers the possibility of personalized viewing experiences. For instance, instead of everybody watching the same news program, it could be personalized to the viewer. For me, this could mean adding more stories about the Netherlands (where I come from), China (a country that fascinates me after having spent some holidays there) and football, but removing stories about cricket (a sport I hardly understand) and local crime. Similarly, music programs could be adapted to show music clips that I actually like.

There are two main differences between traditional recommendation as it applies to say PC-based software and the interactive TV scenarios sketched above. Firstly, in contrast to the use of PCs, television viewing is largely a family or social activity. So, instead of adapting the news to an individual viewer, the television would have to adapt it to the group of people sitting in front of it at that time. Secondly, traditional work on recommendation has often concerned recommending one particular thing to the user, so for instance, which movie the user should watch. In the scenarios sketched above, the television needs to adapt a sequence of items (news items, music clips) to the viewer. The combination of recommending to a group and recommending a sequence is very interesting, as it may allow you to keep all individuals in the group satisfied by compensating for items a particular user dislikes with other items in the sequence which they do like.

22.2.2 Usage Scenario 2: Ambient Intelligence

Ambient intelligence deals with designing physical environments that are sensitive and responsive to the presence of people. For instance, consider the case of a bookstore where sensors detect the presence of customers identified by some portable device (e.g. a Bluetooth-enabled mobile phone, or a fidelity card equipped with an active RFID tag). In this scenario, there are various sensors distributed among the shelves and sections of the bookstore which are able to detect the presence of individual customers. The bookstore can associate the identification of customers with their profiling information, such as preferences, buying patterns and so on.

With this infrastructure in place, the bookstore can provide customers with a responsive environment that would adapt to maximize their well-being with a view to increasing sales. For instance, the device playing the background music should take into account the preferences of the group of customers within hearing distance. Similarly, LCD displays scattered in the store show recommended books based on the customers nearby, the lights on the shop's display window (showing new titles) can be rearranged to reflect the preferences and interests of the group of customers watching it, and so on. Clearly, group adaptation is needed, as most physical environments will be used by multiple people at the same time.

22.2.3 Usage Scenarios Underlying Related Work

In this section we discuss the scenarios underlying some of the best known group recommender systems as well as some newer ones:

- MUSICFX [33] chooses a radio station for background music in a fitness center, to suit a group of people working out at a given time. This is similar to the Ambient Intelligence scenario discussed above.
- POLYLENS [36] is a group recommender extension of MOVIELENS. MOVIELENS recommends movies based on an individual's taste as inferred from ratings and social filtering. POLYLENS allows users to create groups and ask for group recommendations.
- INTRIGUE [2] recommends places to visit for tourist groups taking into account characteristics of subgroups within that group (such as children and the disabled).
- The TRAVEL DECISION FORUM [22] helps a group to agree on the desired attributes of a planned joint holiday. Users indicate their preferences on a set of features (like sport and room facilities). For each feature, the system aggregates the individual preferences, and users interact with embodied conversational agents representing other group members to reach an accepted group preference.
- The COLLABORATIVE ADVISORY TRAVEL SYSTEM (CATS) [34] also helps users to choose a joint holiday. Users consider holiday packages, and critique their features (e.g., 'like the one shown but with a swimming pool'). Based on these critiques, the system recommends other holidays to them. Users also select holidays they like for other group members to see, and these are annotated with how well they match the preferences of each group member (as induced from their critiques). The individual members' critiques results in a group preference model, and other holidays are recommended based on this model.
- YU'S TV RECOMMENDER [49] recommends a television program for a group to watch. It bases its recommendation on the individuals' preferences for program features (such as genre, actors, keywords).
- The GROUP ADAPTIVE INFORMATION AND NEWS system (GAIN) [11] adapts the display of news and advertisements to the group of people near it.

- The REMINISCENCE THERAPY ENHANCED MATERIAL PROFILING IN ALZHEIMERS AND OTHER DEMENTIAS system (REMPAD) [7] recommends multimedia material to be used by a facilitator in a group reminiscence therapy session, based on the suitability of material for individual participants as inferred from their date of birth, locations lived in, and interest vectors.
- HAPPYMOVIE [39] recommends movies to groups, using in the recommendation algorithm the individuals' personality (assertiveness and cooperativeness) and the relationship strengths (they call this social trust) between individuals.
- INTELLIREQ [14] supports groups in deciding which software requirements to implement. Users can view and discuss recommendations for group decisions based on already defined user preferences.

22.2.4 A Classification of Group Recommenders

The scenarios provided above differ on several dimensions, which provide a way to classify group recommender systems:

- *Individual preferences are known versus developed over time.* In most scenarios, the group recommender starts with individual preferences. In contrast, in CATS, individual preferences develop over time, using a critiquing style approach. Others have also adopted this critiquing approach (e.g., [17]). In [35] critiquing is discussed in detail including its role in group recommendation. In INTELLIREQ, preferences can be influenced by the group discussion and the group recommendation based on preferences defined so far.
- *Recommended items are experienced by the group versus presented as options.* In the Interactive TV scenario, the group experiences the news items. In the Ambient Intelligence, GAIN, and MUSICFX scenarios, they experience the music and advertisements. In contrast, in the other scenarios, they are presented with a list of recommendations. For example, POLYLENS presents a list of movies the group may want to watch.
- *The group is passive versus active.* In most scenarios, the group does not interact with the way individual preferences are aggregated. However, in the TRAVEL DECISION FORUM and CATS the group negotiates the group model. In INTELLIREQ, the group does not influence the aggregation, but may influence the ratings provided.
- *Recommending a single item versus a sequence.* In the scenarios of MUSICFX, POLYLENS, and YU'S TV RECOMMENDER it is sufficient to recommend individual items: people normally only see one movie per evening, radio stations can play forever, and YU'S TV RECOMMENDER chooses one TV program only. Similarly, in the TRAVEL DECISION FORUM and CATS users only go on one holiday. In contrast, in our Interactive TV scenario, a sequence of items is

recommended, for example making up a complete news broadcast. Similarly, in INTRIGUE, it is quite likely that a tourist group would visit multiple attractions during their trip, so would be interested in a sequence of attractions to visit. Also, in the Ambient Intelligence scenario it is likely that a user will hear multiple songs, or see multiple items on in-store displays. In GAIN, the display shows multiple items simultaneously; additionally, the display is updated every 7 min, so people are likely to see a sequence as well. In INTELLIREQ, the group needs to decide on which alternative to choose for multiple requirements.

In this chapter, we will focus on the case where individual preferences are known, the group directly experiences the items, the group is passive, and a sequence is recommended. Recommending a sequence raises interesting questions regarding sequence order (see Sect. 22.4) and considering the individuals' affective state (see Sects. 22.5 and 22.6). A passive group with direct experience of the items makes it even more important that the group recommendation is good.

de Campos et al.'s classification of group recommenders also distinguishes between passive and active groups [10]. In addition, it uses two other dimensions:

- *How individual preferences are obtained.* They distinguish between content-based and collaborative filtering. Of the systems mentioned above, POLYLENS and HAPPYMOVIE use collaborative filtering; the others tend to use content-based filtering (e.g. REMPAD or to let users state preferences explicitly (e.g. INTELLIREQ).
- *Whether recommendations or profiles are aggregated.* In the first case, recommendations are produced for individuals and then aggregated into a group recommendation. In the second case, individual preferences are aggregated into a group model, and this model is used to produce a group recommendation. They mention INTRIGUE and POLYLENS as aggregating recommendations, while the others tend to aggregate profiles. Aggregating profiles can happen in multiple ways. In this chapter, we will look at the aggregation of preference ratings. It is also possible to aggregate content: for example, GroupReM aggregates individuals' tag cloud profiles to produce a group tag cloud profile[37]. It is also possible to use a combination of aggregating profiles and aggregating recommendations: [6] proposes a hybrid switching approach that uses aggregated recommendations when user data is sparse and aggregated profiles otherwise. Following their example, [13] also uses a combination.

These two dimensions are related to how the group recommender is implemented rather than being inherent to the usage scenario. In this chapter, we focus on aggregating profiles, but the same aggregation strategies apply when aggregating recommendations. The material presented in this chapter is independent of how the individual preferences are obtained.

22.3 Aggregation Strategies

The main problem group recommendation needs to solve is how to adapt to the group as a whole based on information about individual users' likes and dislikes. For instance, suppose the group contains three people: Peter, Jane and Mary. Suppose a system is aware that these three individuals are present and knows their interest in each of a set of items (e.g. music clips or advertisements). Table 22.1 gives example ratings on a scale of 1 (really hate) to 10 (really like). Which items should the system recommend, given time for four items?

22.3.1 Overview of Aggregation Strategies

Many strategies exist for aggregating individual ratings into a group rating (e.g. used in elections and when selecting a party leader). For example, the Least Misery Strategy uses the minimum of ratings to avoid misery for group members (Table 22.2).

Eleven aggregation strategies inspired by Social Choice Theory are summarized in Table 22.3 (see [28] for more details).

In [42], aggregation strategies are classified into (1) *majority-based strategies* that use the most popular items (e.g., Plurality Voting), (2) *consensus-based strategies* that consider the preferences of all group members (e.g., Average, Average without Misery, Fairness), and (3) *borderline strategies* that only consider a subset (e.g., Dictatorship, Least Misery, Most Pleasure).

Table 22.1 Example of individual ratings for ten items (A–J)

	A	B	C	D	E	F	G	H	I	J
Peter	10	4	3	6	10	9	6	8	10	8
Jane	1	9	8	9	7	9	6	9	3	8
Mary	10	5	2	7	9	8	5	6	7	6

Table 22.2 Example of the Least Misery strategy

	A	B	C	D	E	F	G	H	I	J
Peter	10	4	3	6	10	9	6	8	10	8
Jane	1	9	8	9	7	9	6	9	3	8
Mary	10	5	2	7	9	8	5	6	7	6
Group rating	1	4	2	6	7	8	5	6	3	6

Table 22.3 Overview of aggregation strategies

Strategy	How it works	Example
Plurality voting	Uses 'first past the post': repetitively, the item with the most votes is chosen.	A is chosen first, as it has the highest rating for the majority of the group, followed by E (which has the highest rating for the majority when excluding A).
Average	Averages individual ratings	B's group rating is 6, namely (4 + 9 + 5)/3.
Multiplicative	Multiplies individual ratings	B's group rating is 180, namely 4*9*5.
Borda count	Counts points from items' rankings in the individuals' preference lists, with bottom item getting 0 points, next one up getting one point, etc.	A's group rating is 17, namely 0 (last for Jane) + 9 (first for Mary) + 8 (shared top 3 for Peter)
Copeland rule	Counts how often an item beats other items (using majority vote[a]) minus how often it looses	F's group rating is 5, as F beats 7 items (B,C,D,G,H,I,J) and looses from 2 (A,E).
Approval voting	Counts the individuals with ratings for the item above a approval threshold (e.g. 6)	B's group rating is 1 and F's is 3.
Least misery	Takes the minimum of individual ratings	B's group rating is 4, namely the smallest of 4,9,5.
Most pleasure	Takes the maximum of individual ratings	B's group rating is 9, namely the largest of 4,9,5.
Average without misery	Averages individual ratings, after excluding items with individual ratings below a certain threshold (say 4).	J's group rating is 7.3 (the average of 8,8,6), while A is excluded because Jane hates it.
Fairness	Items are ranked as if individuals are choosing them in turn.	Item E may be chosen first (highest for Peter), followed by F (highest for Jane) and A (highest for Mary).
Most respected person (or Dictatorship)	Uses the rating of the most respected individual.	If Jane is the most respected person, then A's group rating is 1. If Mary is most respected, then it is 10.

[a]If the majority of group members have a higher rating for an item X than for an item Y, then item X beats item Y

22.3.2 *Aggregation Strategies Used in Related Work*

Most of the related work uses one of the aggregation strategies in Table 22.3 (sometimes with a small variation), and they differ in the one used:

- INTRIGUE uses a weighted form of the Average strategy. It bases its group recommendations on the preferences of subgroups, such as children and the disabled. It takes the average, with weights depending on the number of people in the subgroup and the subgroup's relevance (children and disabled were given a higher relevance).

- POLYLENS uses the Least Misery Strategy, assuming groups of people going to watch a movie together tend to be small and that a small group tends to be as happy as its least happy member.
- MUSICFX uses a variant of the Average Without Misery Strategy. Users rate all radio stations, from +2 (really love this music) to −2 (really hate this music). These ratings are converted to positive numbers (by adding 2) and then squared to widen the gap between popular and less popular stations. An Average Without Misery strategy is used to generate a group list: the average of ratings is taken but only for those items with individual ratings all above a threshold. To avoid starvation and always picking the same station, a weighted random selection is made from the top stations of the list.
- YU'S TV RECOMMENDER uses a variant of the Average Strategy. It bases its group recommendation on individuals' ratings of program features: −1 (dislikes the feature), +1 (likes the feature) and 0 (neutral). The feature vector for the group minimizes its distance compared to individual members' feature vectors (see [49] for detail). This is similar to taking the average rating per feature.
- The TRAVEL DECISION FORUM has implemented multiple strategies, including the Average Strategy and the Median Strategy. The Median strategy (not in Table 22.1) uses the middle value of the ratings. So, in our example, this results in group ratings of 10 for A, and 9 for F. The Median Strategy was chosen because it is nonmanipulable: users cannot steer the outcome to their advantage by deliberately giving extreme ratings that do not truly reflect their opinions. In contrast, for example, with the Least Misery strategy devious users can avoid getting items they dislike slightly, by giving extremely negative ratings. The issue of manipulability is most relevant when users provide explicit ratings, used for group recommendation only, and are aware of others' ratings, all of which is the case in the TRAVEL DECISION FORUM. It is less relevant when ratings are inferred from user behavior, also used for individual recommendations, and users are unaware of the ratings of others (or even of the aggregation strategy used).
- In CATS, users indicate through critiquing which features a holiday needs to have. For certain features, users indicate whether they are required (e.g. ice skating required). For others, they indicate quantities (e.g. at least three ski lifts required). The group model contains the requirements of all users, and the item which fulfills most requirements is recommended. Users can also completely discard holidays, so, the strategy has a Without Misery aspect.
- GAIN uses a variant of the Average strategy, with different weights for users that the system knows are near the system and for unrecognized users who should be there statistically.
- REMPAD uses the Least Misery strategy.
- HAPPYMOVIE uses a variant of the Average strategy, with different weights for users based on their personality (assertiveness and cooperativeness) and users' ratings influenced by the ratings of others based on relationship strengths.
- INTELLIREQ uses Plurality Voting.

It should be noted that both YU'S TV RECOMMENDER and the TRAVEL DECISION FORUM aggregate preferences for each feature without using the idea of fairness: loosing out on one feature is not compensated by getting your way on another.

In addition to the strategies in Table 22.3, more complicated strategies have been used,[1] such as:

- the *graph-based ranking* algorithm in [24], which uses (1) a graph with users and items as nodes, with positive links between users and items rated above the user's average item rating, negative links for items rated below the user's average rating (with weights of how much above/below), (2) a user neighborhood graph linking users with similar rating patterns, and (3) an item neighborhood graph linking items that have been rated similarly. Recommendations for the group are based on two random walks over the graphs, with the idea that items that are highly visited by a random walk over positive links would tend to be liked by the group, and items highly visited by a random walk over negative links would tend to be disliked by the group.
- the *Spearman footrule rank* aggregation in [4], which uses as the aggregate list for the group a list with minimum distance to the individual lists. The Spearman footrule distance between two lists is the summation of absolute differences between the ranks of the items in the lists.
- the *Nash equilibrium* used by Carvalho and Macedo [9], who model group members as players in a non-cooperative game and players' actions as item recommendations (choosing from their top three items). Group satisfaction is achieved by finding the Nash equilibrium in the game.
- the *purity* and *completeness* strategies in [41]. The purity strategy is a statistical dispersion strategy just like the simpler average strategy. It tries to satisfy as many group members' preferences as possible (considering the deviation in preferences). The completeness strategy models group recommendation as a negotiation between group members, favoring high scores whilst penalizing large differences between members.

22.3.3 Which Strategy Performs The Best

Though some exploratory evaluation of MUSICFX, POLYLENS and CATS has taken place, for none of these systems it has been investigated how effective their strategy really is, and what the effect would be of using a different strategy. The experiments presented in this section shed some light on this question.

In contrast, some evaluation of YU'S TV RECOMMENDER has taken place [49]. They found that their aggregation worked well when the group was quite

[1] These strategies are too complicated to fully explain here, see the original papers for details.

Fig. 22.1 Experiment 1: which sequence of items do people select if given the system's task

homogenous, but that results were disliked when the group was quite heterogeneous. This is as we would expect, given the Average Strategy will make individuals quite happy if they are quite similar, but will cause misery when tastes differ widely.

We conducted a series of experiments to investigate which strategy from Table 22.3 is the best in terms of (perceived) group satisfaction (see [28] for details). In Experiment 1 (see Fig. 22.1), we investigated how people would solve the group recommendation problem, using the User as Wizard evaluation method [31]. Participants were given individual ratings identical to those in Table 22.1. These ratings were chosen to be able to distinguish between strategies. Participants were asked which items the group should watch, if there was time for one, two, .., seven items. We compared participants' decisions and rationale with those of the aggregation strategies. We found that participants cared about fairness, and about preventing misery and starvation ("this one is for Mary, as she has had nothing she liked so far"). Participants' behavior reflected that of several of the strategies (e.g. the Average, Least Misery, and Average Without Misery were used), while other strategies (e.g. Borda count, Copeland rule) were clearly not used.[2]

In Experiment 2 (see Fig. 22.2), participants were given item sequences chosen by the aggregation strategies as well as the individual ratings in Table 22.1. They rated how satisfied they thought the group members would be with those sequences, and explained their ratings. We found that the Multiplicative Strategy (which multiplies the individual ratings) performed the best, in the sense that it was the only strategy for which *all* participants thought its sequence would keep all members of the group satisfied. Borda count, Average, Average without Misery and Most Pleasure also performed quite well. Several strategies (such as Copeland rule, Plurality voting, Least misery) could be discarded as they clearly were judged to result in misery for group members.

[2]This does not necessarily mean that these strategies are bad, as complexity can also play a role. In fact, in Experiment 2 Borda count was amongst the best performing strategies.

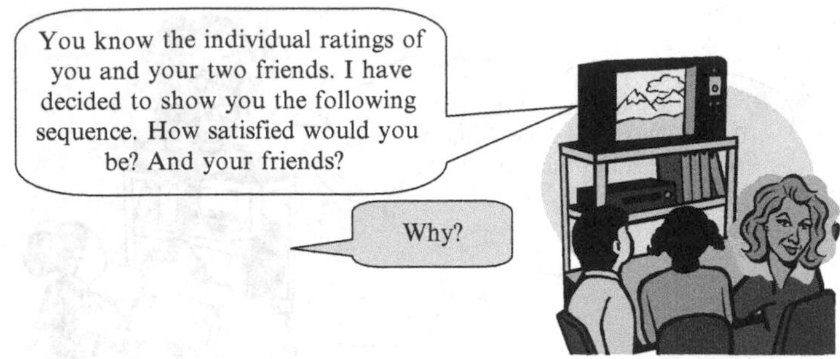

Fig. 22.2 Experiment 2: What do people like?

We also compared the participants' judgments with predictions by simple satisfaction modeling functions. Amongst other, we found that more accurate predictions[3] resulted from using:

- quadratic ratings,[4] which e.g. makes the difference between a rating of 9 and 10 bigger than that between a rating of 5 and 6
- normalization,[5] which takes into account that people rate in different ways, e.g., some always use the extremes of a scale, while others only use the middle of the scale.

In [30], we did a further study using simulated users based on models of affective state (see next Section). We found that the Multiplicative strategy performed the best.

There are also several studies by others investigating the effect of different aggregation strategies. Table 22.4 provides an overview of evaluations of aggregation strategies. Most studies compare group sizes and often also compare between homogeneous groups (where users' preferences are similar) and more heterogeneous groups. Studies typically find that aggregation strategies perform better for more homogeneous and smaller groups.

Unfortunately, most studies use synthetic groups: they have data about individual users' preferences (such as MovieLens data), produce synthetic groups of these individuals, use an aggregation strategy to recommend to the group, decide how satisfied each individual in the group would be with the recommendation (independent of the group), and then calculate the satisfaction of the group as a whole by averaging that

[3]In terms of satisfaction functions predicting the same relative satisfaction scores for group members as predicted by participants, see [28] for details.

[4]We transformed a rating r into (r-scale_midpoint)^2 if r$\geq$ scale_midpoint, and -(r-scale_midpoint)^2 if r<scale_midpoint.

[5]We transformed a rating r by a user u into r $\times$ (TotalRatingsAverage $\div$ TotalRatings(u)), where TotalRatingsAverage is the sum for all items of the average ratings by all users, and TotalRatings(u) is the sum for all items of u's rating.

Table 22.4 Evaluation of aggregation strategies

Who	Domain	Evaluation methodology	Groups	Strategies	Results
[28]	TV	Experiment 1 above User as Wizard	Size: 3 Friends Heterogeneous	All from Table 22.3	USED: Average, Average Without Misery, Least Misery. NOT USED: Borda, Approval, Plurality, Copeland.
[28]	TV	Experiment 2 above User as Wizard	Size: 3 Friends Heterogeneous	All from Table 22.3	BEST: Multiplicative. OK: Borda, Average, Average without Misery, Most Pleasure. WORST: Copeland, Plurality, Least misery.
[30]	TV	Simulated users Metric: Satisfaction functions.	Size: 3 Friends Heterogeneous	All from Table 22.3	BEST: Multiplicative. WORST: Borda, Plurality, Most Pleasure.
[42]	TV	Historic TV use, including individual and group data	Size: 2–5 Family groups	Plurality Voting, Least Misery, Most Pleasure, Dictatorship, Average	BEST: Average for most groups, Dictatorship in 20 % of groups. WORST: Most Pleasure, Least Misery.
[9]	Movies	MovieLens data. Metric: average	Size: 3,5,7 Types: homogeneous, heterogeneous	Least Misery, Average, Plurality Voting, Nash Equilibrium	BEST: Average. Equilibrium better than Least Misery and Plurality Voting in one scenario.

(continued)

Table 22.4 (continued)

[8]	TV movies	User study. Metric: average of individual satisfaction	Size: 3,5,10 Types: experts, high similarity, social relationships	Multiplicative, Borda, Approval Voting, Least Misery, Most Pleasure, Respect	BEST: Multiplicative and Respect. WORST: Most Pleasure. Least Misery better in larger groups than Most Pleasure.
[13]	Movies	Synthetic data Metric: average of individual satisfaction	Size: 2,5	Average, Average Without Misery, Dictatorship, Least Misery, Most Pleasure	BEST: Average and Average Without Misery. Dictatorship low accuracy when aggregating recommendations.
[4]	Movies	MovieLens data Metric: weighted average	Size: 2,3,4,8 Types: similarity high, random	Average, Borda, Least Misery, Random, Spearman footrule	WORST: Random. Others very similar.
[6]	Recipes	User study	Size: 2,3,4 Family Types: homogeneous, heterogeneous	Average, Weighted Average (based on activity, roles, etc)	BEST: Weighted average with weights based on activity.
[41]	Holidays	Synthetic groups and simulated critiquing Metric: average	Size: 3,4,6,8 Types: Similar, Mixed, Diverse	Average, Borda, Least Misery, Most Pleasure, Multiplicative, Random, Completeness, Purity	BEST: Multiplicative, Completeness, Borda.

of individuals. The problem with this approach is that it presumes that a group is as satisfied as the average person in the group, whilst the core reason for the existence of multiple aggregation strategies is that this may not be the case. Unsurprisingly, those studies tend to find that the Average strategy performs well (as do strategies that resemble it).

The notable exception to using synthetic groups is [42], which uses data both on what individuals watch and what those individuals watch in groups with others. This provides a more accurate view on what actually happens in groups. The only drawback of that approach is that what happens in real groups does not necessarily lead to optimal group satisfaction. For example, when a Dictatorship strategy is used (as seems to have happened in 20 % of their groups), this may have left others in the group unsatisfied, and it is possible that the group as a whole would have been more satisfied if a different approach had been used (though sometimes due to for example participant personality, individuals may well be satisfied when Dictatorship is used). This raises the question whether group recommenders should mimic what happens in real groups or should try to do better.

Sometimes these studies also investigated other aspects not reported here. For example, the study in [6] investigated the effect of aggregating ratings versus aggregating preferences.

22.4 Impact of Sequence Order

As mentioned in Sect. 22.2, we are particularly interested in recommending a *sequence* of items. The discussion in Sect. 22.3 has mainly focussed on what items to select if there is time for a certain number of items. For example, for a personalized news program on TV, a recommender may select seven news items to be shown to the group. To select the items, it can use an aggregation strategy (such as the Multiplicative Strategy) to combine individual preferences, and then select the seven items with the highest group ratings.

In this section, we are interested in the *order* of items in the sequence. For example, once seven news items have been selected, the question arises in what order to show them in the news program. Many options exist: for instance, the news program could show the items in descending order of group rating, starting with the highest rated item and ending with the lowest rated one. Or, it could mix up the items, showing them in a random order.

However, the problem is actually far more complicated than that. Firstly, in responsive environments, the group membership changes continuously, so deciding on the next seven items to show based on the current members seems not a sensible strategy, as in the worse case, none of these members may be present anymore when the seventh item is shown.

Secondly, overall satisfaction with a sequence may depend more on the order of the items than one would expect. For example, for optimal satisfaction, we may need to ensure that our news program has:

- *A good narrative flow.* It may be best to show topically related items together. For example, if we have two news items about Michael Jackson (say about his funeral and about a tribute tour) then it seems best if these items are presented together. Similarly, it would make sense to present all sports' items together.
- *Mood consistency.* It may be best to show items with similar moods together. For example, viewers may not like seeing a sad item (such as a soldier's death) in the middle of two happy items (such as a decrease in unemployment and a sporting victory).
- *A strong ending.* It may be best to end with a well-liked item, as viewers may remember the end of the sequence most.

Similar ordering issues arise in other recommendation domains. For example, a music programme may want to consider rhythm when sequencing items. The recommender may need additional information (such as items' mood, topics, rhythm) to optimize ordering. It is beyond the topic of this chapter to discuss how this can be done (and is very recommender domain specific). We just want to highlight that the items already shown may well influence what the best next item is. For example, suppose the top four songs in a music recommender were all Blues. It may well be that another Blues song ranked sixth may be a better next selection than a Classical Opera song ranked fifth. Similarly, the group may prefer something from a different music genre after a sequence of songs from one genre, even if the song ranked the best next is of the same genre.

In Experiment 3 (see Fig. 22.3 and more detail in [28]), we investigated, in the news domain, how a previous item may influence the impact of the next item. Participants rated a set of news items. They were then shown one news item[6] and

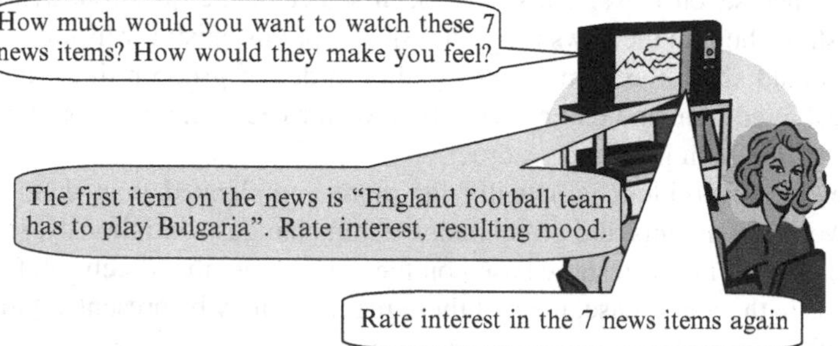

Fig. 22.3 Experiment 3: Investigating the effect of mood and topic

[6] In a between-subject design, two different topics were used evoking different moods.

rated how interested they were in it and how it made them feel, and re-rated the original items to see if their ratings would have changed. Amongst others, we found that mood (resulting from the previous item) and topical relatedness can influence ratings for subsequent news items.

This means that aggregating individual profiles into a group profile should be done repeatedly, every time a decision needs to be made about the next item to display. So, instead of first selecting say seven items to show and then deciding on the order, only one item is selected, and then it needs to be decided which item from *all*remaining ones is the best to show next, given that the first item may have an impact on the ratings of the remaining ones.

22.5 Modeling Affective State

When recommending to a group of people, you cannot give everybody what they like all of the time. However, you do not want anybody to get too dissatisfied. For instance, in a shop it would be bad if a customer were to leave and never come back, because they really cannot stand the background music. Many shops currently opt to play music that nobody really hates, but most people not love either. This may prevent loosing customers, but would not result in increasing sales. An ideal shop would adapt the music to the customers in hearing range in such a way that they get songs they really like most of the time (increasing the likelihood of sales and returns to the shop). To achieve this, it is unavoidable that customers will occasionally get songs they hate, but this should happen at a moment when they can cope with it (e.g. when being in a good mood because they loved the previous songs). Therefore, it is important to monitor continuously how satisfied each group member is. Of course, it would put an unacceptable burden on the customers if they had to rate their satisfaction (on music, advertisements etc.) all the time. Similarly, measuring this satisfaction via sensors (such as heart rate monitors or facial expression recognizers) is not yet an option, as they tend to be too intrusive, inaccurate or expensive. So, it was proposed to model group members' satisfaction; predicting it based on what we know about their likes and dislikes.

22.5.1 *Modeling an Individual's Satisfaction on Its Own*

In [30], we investigated four satisfaction functions to model an individual's satisfaction. We compared the predictions of these satisfaction functions with the predictions by the participants of Experiment 2 above. We also performed an

Fig. 22.4 Experiment 4: Measuring overall satisfaction during a series of tasks

experiment (see Fig. 22.4) to compare the predictions with the real feelings of users.[7]

The satisfaction function that performed the best defines the satisfaction of a user with a new item *i* after having seen a sequence *items* of items as:

$$Sat(items + < i >) = \frac{\delta \times Sat(items) + Impact(i, \delta \times Sat(items))}{1 + \delta}$$

with the impact on satisfaction of new item *i* given existing satisfaction *s* defined as

$$Impact(i, s) = Impact(i) + (s - Impact(i)) \times \varepsilon, \text{ for } 0 \leq \varepsilon \leq 1 \text{ and } 0 \leq \delta \leq 1$$

Parameter δ represents satisfaction decaying over time (with $\delta = 0$ past items have no influence, with $\delta = 1$ there is no decay).

Parameter ε represents the influence of the user's satisfaction after experiencing previous items on the impact of a new item. This parameter is inspired by the psychology and economics literature, which shows that mood impacts evaluative judgment [30]. For instance, half the participants answering a questionnaire about their TVs received a small present first to put them in a good mood. These participants were found to have televisions that performed better. So, if a user is in a good mood due to liking previous items, the impact of an item they normally dislike may be smaller (with how much smaller depending on ε).

Parameters δ and ε are user dependent (as confirmed in the experiment in [30]). We will not define *Impact*(*i*) in this chapter, see [30] for details, but it involves quadratic ratings and normalization as found in the experiment discussed above.

[7] For reasons explained in [30], a learning rather than recommender task was used, and satisfaction with performance measured. There was an easy (E), medium (M) and difficult (D) variant of the task, so we could predict accurately how satisfied participants would be with performance on an individual task, and could focus on modeling the effect of sequences on satisfaction. Half the participants did tasks in order E-D-M, the other half in order D-E-M.

Fig. 22.5 Types of relationship

22.5.2 Effects of the Group on an Individual's Satisfaction

The satisfaction function given does not take the satisfaction of other users in the group into account, which may well influence a user's satisfaction. As argued in [30] based on social psychology, two main processes can take place.

Emotional Contagion Firstly, the satisfaction of other users can lead to so-called emotional contagion: other users being satisfied may increase a user's satisfaction (e.g. if somebody smiles at you, you may automatically smile back and feel better as a result). The opposite may also happen: other users being dissatisfied may decrease a user's satisfaction. For instance, if you are watching a film with a group of friends then the fact that your friends are clearly not enjoying it may negatively impact your own satisfaction.

Emotional contagion may depend on your personality (some people are more easily contaged than others), and your relationship with the other person. Anthropologists and social psychologists have found substantial evidence for the existence of four basic types of relationships, see Fig. 22.5. In Experiment 5 (see Fig. 22.6), participants were given a description of a hypothetical person they were watching TV with (using the relationship types in Fig. 22.5) and asked how their own emotion would be impacted (on a scale from 'decrease a lot' to 'increase a lot') by that person's strong positive or negative emotions (see detail in [30]). Results confirmed that emotional contagion indeed depends on the relationship you have: you are more likely to be contaged by somebody you love (such as your best friend) or respect (such as your mother or boss) then by somebody you are on equal footing with or are in competition with.

Conformity Secondly, the opinion of other users may influence your own expressed opinion, based on the so-called process of conformity.

Think of somebody you share everything with (maybe your best friend). Assume you and this person are watching TV together. You are enjoying the program a little. How would it make you feel to know that the other person is enjoying it greatly / really hating it?

Fig. 22.6 Experiment 5: Impact of relationship type on emotional contagion

Fig. 22.7 Conformity experiment by Asch

Figure 22.7 shows the famous conformity experiment by Asch [3]. Participants were given a very easy task to do, such as decide which of the four lines has the same orientation as the line in Card A. They thought they were surrounded by other participants, but in fact the others where part of the experiment team. The others all answered the question before them, picking the same wrong answer. It was shown that most participants then pick that same wrong answer as well.

Two types of conformity exist: (1) normative influence, in which you want to be part of the group and express an opinion like the rest of the group even though inside you still belief differently, and (2) informational influence, in which your own opinion changes because you believe the group must be right. Informational influence would change your own satisfaction, while normative influence can change the satisfaction of others through emotional contagion because of the (insincere) emotions you are portraying.

More complicated satisfaction functions are presented in [30] to model emotional contagion and both types of conformity. These functions also serve as a basis for work in [47].

22.6 Using Satisfaction Inside Aggregation Strategies

Once you have an accurate model of the individual users' satisfaction, which predicts how satisfied each group member is after a sequence of items, it would be nice to use this model to improve on the group aggregation strategies. For instance, the aggregation strategy could set out to please the member of the group who is least satisfied with the sequence of items chosen so far. This can be done in many different ways, and we have only started to explore this issue. For example:

- *Strongly Support Grumpiest strategy.* This strategy picks the item which is *most liked* by the least satisfied member. If multiple of these items exist, it uses one of the standard aggregation strategies, for instance the Multiplicative Strategy, to distinguish between them.
- *Weakly Support Grumpiest strategy.* This strategy selects the items that are *quite liked* by the least satisfied member, for instance items with a rating of 8 or above. It uses one of the standard aggregation strategies, such as the Multiplicative Strategy, to choose between these items.
- *Weighted strategy.* This strategy assign weights to users depending on their satisfaction, and then use a weighted form of a standard aggregation strategy. For instance, Table 22.5 shows the effect of assigning double the weight to Jane when using the Average Strategy. Note that weights are impossible to apply to a strategy such as the Least Misery Strategy.

In [32], we discuss this in more detail, propose an agent-based architecture for applying these ideas to the Ambient Intelligence scenario, and describe an implemented prototype. Preliminary work in [38], also uses a strategy which

Table 22.5 Results of average strategy with equal weights and with twice the weight for Jane

	A	B	C	D	E	F	G	H	I	J
Peter	10	4	3	6	10	9	6	8	10	8
Jane	1	9	8	9	7	9	6	9	3	8
Mary	10	5	2	7	9	8	5	6	7	6
Average (equal weights)	7	6	4.3	7.3	8.7	8.7	5.7	7.7	6.7	7.3
Average (Jane twice)	5.5	6.8	5.3	8.3	8.3	8.8	5.8	8	5.8	7.5

balances user satisfaction. Clearly, empirical research is needed to investigate the best way of using affective state inside an aggregation strategy.

22.7 Incorporating Group Attributes: Roles, Personality, Expertise, Relationship Strength, Relationship Type and Personal Impact

Above, we discussed how an individual's satisfaction can be influenced by others in the group due to emotional contagion and normative behavior. Individuals' personality (e.g., propensity to emotional contagion) and social relationships between individuals played a role in this. These were incorporated into our models of satisfaction [30], which were then used in aggregation strategies [32]. Instead of using group attributes indirectly, via satisfaction models, it is also possible to incorporate them more directly into aggregation strategies.

Firstly, attributes can be used of individual group members, typically giving more weight to certain group members than others:

- *Demographics and Roles*. As mentioned above, INTRIGUE [2] distinguishes different user types (children, adults with and without disability), and uses higher weights for more vulnerable user types. The recipe group recommender in [6] distinguishes between user roles (applicant, partner, child) and varies the weights based on their presumed level of engagement with the system (lowest for child, highest for applicant). An analysis of groups whose behavior corresponded to a Dictatorship strategy in [42] showed many cases in which teenagers acted as dictator in the company of children and where adults acted as dictator in the company of teenagers or children. So, different roles may influence what happens in groups, though [42] does not present the group composition when Dictatorship is not used.
- *Personality: Assertiveness and Cooperativeness*. HAPPYMOVIE [39] uses how *assertive* (extent to which person attempts to satisfy own concerns) and how *cooperative* (extent to which person attempts to satisfy others concerns) group members are, and gives a higher weight to assertive members and a lower weight to cooperative members.
- *Expertise*. As reported in [19], according to Social Psychology expertise may provide influence, so in normal group processes experts may have more influence on the group's decision.[8] Gatrell et al. [15] apply higher weights to people with

[8] Additionally, it seems plausible (but requires investigation) that users would be more dissatisfied with disliked selected items when their expertise is higher than that of other group members.

more expertise.[9] They infer expertise from activity, namely the number of movies watched. The recipe group recommender in [6] also uses higher weights for family members who have engaged more.

- *Personal impact.*[10] Liu et al. [26] incorporate the concept of *personal impact* into their group recommender algorithm, to model that different members will have different impacts on group decisions. They consider decisions made in the past to decide on personal impact. Herr et al. [19] advocate using the social psychology concept of *cognitive centrality*: the degree to which a group member's cognitive information is shared within the group. They propose that the degree of centrality can be used to infer a person's importance and that more important members should be given higher weights.

Secondly, attributes can be used of the group as a whole, typically using a different aggregation strategy based on the type of group:

- *Relationship strength.* Gatrell et al. [15] advocate using different aggregation strategies depending on the group's relationship strength. They propose to use a Maximum Pleasure strategy for groups with a strong relationship (such as couples and close friends' groups), a Least Misery strategy for groups with a weak relationship (such as first-acquaintance groups), and an Average strategy for groups with an intermediate relationship (such as acquaintance groups).
- *Relationship type.* Wang et al. [47] distinguish between *positionally homogeneous*[11] and *positionally heterogeneous* groups. In positionally homogeneous groups, such as friend and tourist groups, the position of members is equal. In heterogeneous groups, such as family groups, the position of members is unequal. They also distinguish between *tightly-coupled* (strong relationship: members are close and intercommunication is important) and *loosely-coupled* (weak relationship: members are relatively estranged, and intercommunication is less frequent and less important) groups. Based on these two dimensions, Wang et al. define four different group types: tightly-coupled homogeneous (e.g. a friends' group), loosely coupled homogeneous (e.g. a tourist group), tightly-coupled heterogeneous (e.g. a family group), and loosely coupled heterogeneous (e.g. a staff group including managers).

Thirdly, attributes of people pairs in the group can be used, typically to adjust the ratings of an individual in light of the rating of the other person in the pair:

[9] This may work well when using an Additive or Multiplicative strategy, but does not really work for the Least Misery and Most Pleasure strategies used in [15], and hence unfortunately some of the formulas in [15] which incorporate expertise lack validity.

[10] Personal impact is not completely distinct from Role: somebody's role may influence their personal impact. However, it is still possible for people with the same official roles to have a different cognitive centrality.

[11] We have added the word positional to the terms homogeneous and heterogeneous used in [47] to avoid confusion with the earlier use of these words to indicate how diverse group preferences are.

- *Relationship strengths.* HAPPYMOVIE [39] uses relationship strengths (which they call *social trust*) into its aggregation strategy, adapting individuals' ratings based on the ratings of others depending on the relationship strength between individuals.
- *Personal impact.* The concept of personal impact from [26] mentioned above can also be used in this way. Ioannidis et al. [21] argue that people will be influenced by some people in their group more than others. Their group recommender uses a cascading process, where the group can see the votes that have already been cast and by whom, and can comment on alternatives. They and Ye et al. [48] learn social influence values for use in the group aggregation strategy.

22.8 Applying Group Recommendation to Individual Users

So, what if you are developing an application that recommends to a single user? Group recommendation techniques can be useful in three ways: (1) to aggregate multiple criteria, (2) to solve the so-called cold-start problem, (3) to take into account opinions of others. Chapter 23 also discusses how aggregation may be needed when recommending to individuals, and covers several specific aggregation functions [5].

22.8.1 Multiple Criteria

Sometimes it is difficult to give recommendations because the problem is multi-dimensional: multiple criteria play a role. For instance, in a news recommender system, a user may have a preference for location (being more interested in stories close to home, or related to their favorite holiday place). The user may also prefer more recent news, and have topical preferences (e.g. preferring news about politics to news about sport). The recommender system may end up with a situation such as in Table 22.6, where different news story rate differently on the criteria. Which news stories should it now recommend?

Table 22.6 resembles the one we had for group recommendation above (Table 22.1), except that now instead of multiple users we have multiple criteria to satisfy. It is possible to apply our group recommendation techniques to this problem. However, there is an important difference between adapting to a group

Table 22.6 Ratings on criteria for ten news items

	A	B	C	D	E	F	G	H	I	J
Topic	10	4	3	6	10	9	6	8	10	8
Location	1	9	8	9	7	9	6	9	3	8
Recency	10	5	2	7	9	8	5	6	7	6

Table 22.7 Average strategy ignoring unimportant criterion Location

	A	B	C	D	E	F	G	H	I	J
Topic	10	4	3	6	10	9	6	8	10	8
Recency	10	5	2	7	9	8	5	6	7	6
Group	20	9	5	13	19	17	11	14	17	14

Table 22.8 Average strategy with weights 3 for Topic and Recency and 1 for location

	A	B	C	D	E	F	G	H	I	J
Topic	30	12	9	18	30	27	18	24	30	24
Location	1	9	8	9	7	9	6	9	3	8
Recency	30	15	6	21	27	24	15	18	21	18
Group	61	36	23	48	64	60	39	51	54	50

of people and adapting to a group of criteria. When adapting to a group of people, it seems sensible and morally correct to treat everybody equally. Of course, there may be some exceptions, for instance when the group contains adults as well as children, or when it is somebody's birthday. But in general, equality seems a good choice, and this was used in the group adaptation strategies discussed above. In contrast, when adapting to a group of criteria, there is no particular reason for assuming all criteria are as important. It is even quite likely that not all criteria are equally important to a particular person. Indeed, in an experiment we found that users treat criteria in different ways, giving more importance to some criteria (e.g. recency is seen as more important than location) [29]. So, how can we adapt the group recommendation strategies to deal with this? There are several ways in which this can be done:

- Apply the strategy to the most respected criteria only. The ratings of unimportant criteria are ignored completely. For instance, assume criterion Location is regarded unimportant, then its ratings are ignored. Table 22.7 shows the result of the Average Strategy when ignoring Location.
- Apply the strategy to all criteria but use weights. The ratings of unimportant criteria are given less weight. For instance, in the Average Strategy, the weight of a criterion is multiplied with its ratings to produce new ratings. For instance, suppose criteria Topic and Recency were three times as important as criterion Location. Table 22.8 shows the result of the Average Strategy using these weights. In case of the Multiplicative Strategy, multiplying the ratings with weights does not have any effect. In that strategy, it is better to use the weights as exponents, so replace the ratings by the ratings to the power of the weight. Note that in both strategies, a weight of 0 results in ignoring the ratings completely, as above.
- Adapt a strategy to behave differently to important versus unimportant criteria: Unequal Average Without Misery. Misery is avoided for important criteria but not for unimportant ones. Assume criterion Location is again regarded as unimportant. Table 22.9 shows the results of the Unequal Average Without Misery strategy with threshold 6.

Table 22.9 Unequal Average Without Misery strategy with location unimportant and threshold 6

	A	B	C	D	E	F	G	H	I	J
Topic	10	4	3	6	10	9	6	8	10	8
Location	1	9	8	9	7	9	6	9	3	8
Recency	10	5	2	7	9	8	5	6	7	6
Group	21			22	26	26		23	20	22

Fig. 22.8 Cold-start problem in case of social-filtering

We have some evidence that people's behavior reflects the outcomes of these strategies [29], however, more research is clearly needed in this area to see which strategy is the best. Also, more research is needed to establish when to regard a criterion as "unimportant". The issue of multiple criteria is also the topic of Chap. 25 in this handbook.

22.8.2 Cold-Start Problem

A big problem for recommender systems is the so-called cold-start problem: to adapt to a user, the system needs to know what the user liked in the past. This is needed in content-based filtering to decide on items similar to the ones the user liked. It is needed in social filtering to decide on the users who resemble this user in the sense that they (dis)liked the same items in the past (see Fig. 22.8). So, what if you do not know anything about the user yet, because they only just started using the system? Recommender system designers tend to solve this problem by either getting users to rate items at the start, or by getting them to answer some demographic questions (and then using stereotypes as a starting point, e.g. elderly people like classical music).

Both methods require user effort. It is also not easy to decide which items to get a user to rate, and stereotypes can be quite wrong and offensive (some elderly people prefer pop music and people might not like being classified as elderly).

The group recommendation work presented in this chapter provides an alternative solution. When a user is new to the system, we simply provide recommendations to that new user that would keep the whole group of existing users happy. We assume

Fig. 22.9 Gradually learning about the user, and whom she resembles most

that our user will resemble one of our existing users, though we do not know which one, and that by recommending something that would keep all of them happy, the new user will be happy as well.[12]

Gradually, we will learn about the new user's tastes, for instance, by them rating our recommended items or, more implicitly, by them spending time on the items or not. We provide recommendations to the new user that would keep the group of existing users happy including the new user (or more precisely, the person we now assume the new user to be). The weight attached to the new user will be low initially, as we do not know much about them yet, and will gradually increase. We also start to attach less weight to existing users whose taste now evidently differs from our new user.

Figure 22.9 shows an example of the adaptation: the system is including the observed tastes of the new user to some extent, and has started to reduce the weights of some of the other users. After prolonged use of the system, the user's inferred wishes will completely dominate the selection.

We have done a small-scale study using the MovieLens dataset to explore the effectiveness of this approach. We randomly selected five movies, and twelve users who had rated them: ten users as already known to the recommender, and two as new users. Using the Multiplicative Strategy on the group of known users, movies were ranked for the new users. Results were encouraging: the movie ranked highest was in fact the most preferred movie for the new users, and also the rest of the ranking was fine given the new users' profiles. Applying weights led to a further improvement of the ranking, and weights started to reflect the similarity of the new users with known users. More detail on the study and on applying group adaptation to solve the cold-start problem is given in [27]. A follow on study in [12] confirmed

[12]This initially offers the user non-personalized recommendations, however not necessarily by purely using popularity (e.g. Average without Misery can be used and fairness principles can be applied towards the other group members when recommending a sequence).

the usefulness of this method. The use of aggregate ratings to solve the cold-start problem is also discussed in [46].

Another approach to solving the cold-start problem can be found in Chap. 24.

22.8.3 Virtual Group Members

Finally, group adaptation can also be used when adapting to an individual by adding virtual members to the group. For instance, parents may want to influence what television their children watch. They may not mind their children watching certain entertainment programmes, but may prefer them watching educational programmes. When the child is alone, a profile representing the parent's opinions (about how suitable items are for their child) can be added to the group as a virtual group member, and the TV could try to satisfy both, establishing a balance between the opinions of the parent and child. Similarly, a virtual group member with a profile produced by a teacher could be added to a group of learners.

22.9 Conclusions and Challenges

Group recommendation is a relatively new research area. This chapter is intended as an introduction in the area, in particular on aggregating individual user profiles. For more detail please see [22, 23, 27–30, 32].

22.9.1 Main Issues Raised

The main issues raised in this chapter are:

- Adapting to groups is needed in many scenarios such as interactive TV, ambient intelligence, recommending to tourist groups, etc. Inspired by the differences between scenarios, group recommenders can be classified using multiple dimensions.
- Many strategies exist for aggregating individual preferences (see Table 22.3), and some perform better than others. Users seem to care about avoiding misery and fairness.
- Existing group recommenders differ on the classification dimensions and in the aggregation strategies used. See Table 22.10 for an overview.
- When recommending a sequence of items, aggregation of individual profiles has to occur at each step in the sequence, as earlier items may impact the ratings of later items.

Table 22.10 Group recommender systems

System	Usage scenario	Classification				Strategy used
		Preferences known	Direct experience	Group active	Recommends sequence	
MUSICFX [33]	Chooses radio station in fitness center based on people working out	Yes	Yes	No	No	Average Without Misery
POLYLENS [36]	Proposes movies for a group to view	Yes	No	No	No	Least Misery
INTRIGUE [2]	Proposes tourist attractions to visit for a group based on characteristics of subgroups (such as children and the disabled)	Yes	No	No	Yes	Average
TRAVEL DECISION FORUM [22]	Proposes a group model of desired attributes of a planned joint vacation and helps a group of users to agree on these	Yes	No	Yes	No	Median
YU'S TV REC. [49]	Proposes a TV program for a group to watch based on individuals' ratings for multiple features	Yes	No	No	No	Average
CATS [34]	Helps users choose a joint holiday, based on individuals' critiques	No	No	Yes	No	Counts requirements met Uses Without Misery
MASTHOFF'S [28, 30]	Chooses a sequence of music video clips for a group to watch	Yes	Yes	No	Yes	Multiplicative etc
GAIN [11]	Displays information and advertisements adapted to the group present	Yes	Yes	No	Yes	Average
REMPAD [7]	Proposes multimedia material for a group reminiscence therapy session	Yes	No	No	No	Least Misery
HAPPYMOVIE [39]	Recommends movies to groups	Yes	No	No	No	Average
INTELLIREQ [14]	Supports groups in deciding which requirements to implement	No	No	Yes	Yes	Plurality Voting

- It is possible to construct satisfaction functions to predict how satisfied an individual will be at any time during a sequence. However, group interaction effects (such as emotional contagion and conformity) can make this complicated.
- It is possible to evaluate in experiments how good aggregation strategies and satisfaction functions are, though this is not an easy problem.
- Group aggregation strategies are not only important when recommending to groups of people, but can also be applied when recommending to individuals, e.g. to prevent the cold-start problem and deal with multiple criteria.

22.9.2 Caveat: Group Modeling

The term "group modeling" is also used for work that is quite different from that presented in this chapter. A lot of work has been on modeling common knowledge between group members (e.g. [20, 44], modeling how a group interacts (e.g. [18, 40]) and group formation based on individual models (e.g. [1, 40]).

22.9.3 Challenges

Compared to work on individual recommendations, group recommendation is still quite a novel area. The work presented in this chapter is only a starting point. There are many challenging directions for further research, including:

- *Recommending item sequences to a group.* Our own work and the preliminary work in [38] seem to be the only work to date on recommending balanced *sequences* that address the issue of fairness. Even though sequences are important for the usage scenario of INTRIGUE, their work has not investigated making sequences balanced nor has it looked at sequence order. Clearly, a lot more research is needed on recommending and ordering sequences, in particular on how already shown items should influence the ratings of other items. Some of this research will have to be recommender domain specific.
- *Modeling of affective state.* There is a lot more work needed to produce validated satisfaction functions. The work presented in this chapter and [30] is only the starting point. In particular, large scale evaluations are required, as are investigations on the affect of group size.
- *Incorporating satisfaction within an aggregation strategy.* As noted in Sect. 22.6, there are many ways in which satisfaction can be used inside an aggregation strategy. We presented some initial ideas in this area, but extensive empirical research is required to investigate this further.
- *Explaining group recommendations: Transparency and Privacy.* One might think that accurate predictions of individual satisfaction can also be used to improve the recommender's transparency: showing how satisfied other group members are

could improve users' understanding of the recommendation process and perhaps make it easier to accept items they do not like. However, users' need for privacy is likely to conflict with their need for transparency. An important task of a group recommender system is to avoid embarrassment. Users often like to conform to the group to avoid being disliked (we discussed normative conformity as part of Sect. 22.5.2 on how others in the group can influence an individual's affective state). In [30], we have investigated how different group aggregation strategies may affect privacy. More work is needed on explanations of group recommendations, in particular on how to balance privacy with transparency and scrutability. Chapter 10 provides more detail on the different roles of explanations in recommender systems [45].

- *User interface design.* An individual's satisfaction with a group recommendation may be increased by good user interface design. For example, when showing an item, users could be shown what the next item will be (e.g. in a TV programme through a subtitle). This may inform users who do not like the current item that they will like the next one better. There is also a need for additional research on good interfaces for supporting group decision making (for some initial research see [43]).
- *Group aggregation strategies for cold-start problems.* In Sect. 22.8.2, we have sketched how group aggregation can be used to help solve the cold-start problem. However, our study in this area was very small, and a lot more work is required to validate and optimize this approach.
- *Dealing with uncertainty.* In this chapter, we have assumed that we have accurate profiles of individuals' preferences. For example, in Table 22.1, the recommender knows that Peter's rating of item B is 4. However, in reality we will often have probabilistic data. For example, we may know with 80 % certainty that Peter's rating is 4. Adaptations of the aggregation strategies may be needed to deal with this. de Campos et al. try to deal with uncertainty by using Bayesian networks [10]. However, they have so far focused on the Average and Plurality Voting strategies, not yet tackling the avoidance of misery and fairness issues.
- *Dealing with group attributes.* In Sect. 22.7, we have discussed initial work on incorporating group attributes in group recommender systems. Additionally, as mentioned in [16], users may well have different preferences in the context of a particular group then when they are alone. Clearly more research is needed in this area.
- *Empirical studies.* More empirical evaluations are vital to bring this field forwards. It is a challenge to design well-controlled, large scale empirical studies in a real-world setting, particularly when dealing with group recommendations and affective state. It is likely that different aggregation strategies may be effective for different kinds of groups and for different application domains (see [43] for initial work on group recommender application domains). Almost all research so far (including my own) has either been on a small scale, in a contrived setting, using synthetic groups (with the problem of using an Average metric, see Sect. 22.3.3) or lacks control.

Acknowledgement Judith Masthoff's research has been partly supported by Nuffield Foundation Grant No. NAL/00258/G.

References

1. Alfonseca, E., Carro, R.M., Martín, E., Ortigosa, A., Paredes, P.: The Impact of Learning Styles on Student Grouping for Collaborative Learning: A Case Study. UMUAI 16 (2006) 377–401
2. Ardissono, L., Goy,A., Petrone, G., Segnan, M., Torasso, P.: Tailoring the Recommendation of Tourist Information to Heterogeneous User Groups. In S. Reich, M. Tzagarakis, P. De Bra (eds.), Hypermedia: Openness, Structural Awareness, and Adaptivity, International Workshops OHS-7, SC-3, and AH-3. Lecture Notes in Computer Science 2266, Springer Verlag, Berlin (2002) 280–295
3. Asch,S.E.:Studies of independence and conformity: a minority of one against a unanimous majority. Pschol. Monogr. 70 (1956) 1–70
4. Baltrunas, L., Makcinskas, T., Ricci, F.: Group recommendations with rank aggregation and collaborative filtering. In: Proceedings of the fourth ACM conference on Recommender systems (2010) 119–126. ACM.
5. Beliakov, G., Calvo, T., James, S.: Aggregation functions for recommender systems. In this handbook (2015).
6. Berkovsky, S., Freyne, J.: Group-based recipe recommendations: analysis of data aggregation strategies. In: Proceedings of the fourth ACM conference on Recommender systems 111–118. ACM.
7. Bermingham, A., O'Rourke, J., Gurrin, C., Collins, R., Irving, K., Smeaton, A. F.: Automatically recommending multimedia content for use in group reminiscence therapy. In: Proceedings of the 1st ACM international workshop on Multimedia indexing and information retrieval for healthcare (2013) 49–58. ACM.
8. Bourke, S., McCarthy, K., Smyth, B: Using social ties in group recommendation. In: Proceedings of the 22nd Irish Conference on Artificial Intelligence and Cognitive Science (2011) University of Ulster-Magee. Intelligent Systems Research Centre.
9. Carvalho, L. A., Macedo, H. T.: Users' satisfaction in recommendation systems for groups: an approach based on noncooperative games. In: Proceedings of the 22nd international conference on World Wide Web Companion (2013) 951–958.
10. de Campos, L.M., Fernandez-Luna, J.M., Huete, J.F., Rueda-Morales, M.A.: Managing uncertainty in group recommending processes. UMUAI 19 (2009) 207–242
11. De Carolis, B.: Adapting news and advertisements to groups. In: Pervasive Advertising (2011). 227–246. Springer. **CITED identification of people in group; GAIN system**
12. de Mello Neto, W. L., Nowé, A.: Insights on social recommender system. In: Proceedings of the Workshop on Recommendation Utility Evaluation: Beyond RMSE, at ACM RecSyS12 (2012) 33–38.
13. De Pessemier, T., Dooms, S., Martens, L.: Comparison of group recommendation algorithms. Multimedia Tools and Applications, (2013) 1–45.
14. Felfernig, A., Zehentner, C., Ninaus, G., Grabner, H., Maalej, W., Pagano, D., Reinfrank, F.: Group decision support for requirements negotiation. In: Advances in User Modeling (2012) 105–116. Springer.
15. Gatrell, M., Xing, X., Lv, Q., Beach, A., Han, R., Mishra, S., Seada, K.: Enhancing group recommendation by incorporating social relationship interactions. In: Proceedings of the 16th ACM international conference on Supporting group work (2010) 97–106. ACM.
16. Gorla, J., Lathia, N., Robertson, S., Wang, J.: Probabilistic group recommendation via information matching. In: Proceedings of the 22nd international conference on World Wide Web (2013) 495–504.

17. Guzzi, F., Ricci, F., Burke, R. Interactive multi-party critiquing for group recommendation. In: Proceedings of the fifth ACM conference on Recommender systems (2011) 265–268. ACM.
18. Harrer, A., McLaren, B.M., Walker, E., Bollen L., Sewall, J.: Creating Cognitive Tutors for Collaborative Learning: Steps Toward Realization. UMUAI 16 (2006) 175–209
19. Herr, S., Rösch, A., Beckmann, C., Gross, T.: Informing the design of group recommender systems. In: CHI12 Extended Abstracts on Human Factors in Computing Systems (2012) 2507–2512. ACM.
20. Introne, J., Alterman,R.: Using Shared Representations to Improve Coordination and Intent Inference. UMUAI 16 (2006) 249–280
21. Ioannidis, S., Muthukrishnan, S., Yan, J. (2013): A consensus-focused group recommender system. arXiv preprint arXiv:1312.7076.
22. Jameson, A.: More than the Sum of its Members: Challenges for Group Recommender Systems. International Working Conference on Advanced Visual Interfaces, Gallipoli, Italy (2004)
23. Jameson, A., Smyth, B.: Recommendation to groups. In: Brusilovsky, P., Kobsa, A., Njedl, W. (Eds). The Adaptive Web Methods and Strategies of Web Personalization. Springer (2007) 596–627
24. Kim, H. N., Bloess, M., El Saddik, A.: Folkommender: a group recommender system based on a graph-based ranking algorithm. Multimedia Systems (2013) 1–17
25. Kurdyukova, E., Hammer, S., André, E.: Personalization of content on public displays driven by the recognition of group context. In: Ambient Intelligence (2012) 272–287. Springer.
26. Liu, X., Tian, Y., Ye, M., Lee, W. C.: Exploring personal impact for group recommendation. In: Proceedings of the 21st ACM international conference on Information and knowledge management (2012) 674–683. ACM.
27. Masthoff, J.: Modeling the multiple people that are me. In: P. Brusilovsky, A.Corbett, and F. de Rosis (eds.) Proceedings of the 2003 User Modeling Conference, Johnstown, PA. Springer Verlag, Berlin (2003) 258–262
28. Masthoff, J.: Group Modeling: Selecting a Sequence of Television Items to Suit a Group of Viewers. UMUAI 14 (2004) 37–85
29. Masthoff, J.: Selecting News to Suit a Group of Criteria: An Exploration. 4th Workshop on Personalization in Future TV - Methods, Technologies, Applications for Personalized TV, Eindhoven, the Netherlands (2004)
30. Masthoff, J., Gatt, A.: In Pursuit of Satisfaction and the Prevention of Embarrassment: Affective state in Group Recommender Systems. UMUAI 16 (2006) 281–319
31. Masthoff, J.: The user as wizard: A method for early involvement in the design and evaluation of adaptive systems. Fifth Workshop on User-Centred Design and Evaluation of Adaptive Systems (2006)
32. Masthoff, J., Vasconcelos, W.W., Aitken, C., Correa da Silva, F.S.: Agent-Based Group Modelling for Ambient Intelligence. AISB symposium on Affective Smart Environments, Newcastle, UK (2007)
33. McCarthy, J., Anagnost, T.: MusicFX: An Arbiter of Group Preferences for Computer Supported Collaborative Workouts. CSCW, Seattle, WA. (1998) 363–372
34. McCarthy, K., McGinty, L., Smyth, B., Salamo, M.: The needs of the many: A case-based group recommender system. European Conference on Case-Based Reasoning, Springer (2006) 196–210
35. McGinty, L., Reilly, J. On the evolution of critiquing recommenders. In F. Ricci, L. Rokach, B. Shapira, and P.B. Kantor: Recommender Systems Handbook, First Edition, Springer (2011) 73–105
36. O' Conner, M., Cosley, D., Konstan, J.A., Riedl, J.: PolyLens: A Recommender System for Groups of Users. ECSCW, Bonn, Germany (2001) 199–218. As accessed on http://www.cs.umn.edu/Research/GroupLens/poly-camera-final.pdf
37. Pera, M. S., Ng, Y. K.: A group recommender for movies based on content similarity and popularity. Information Processing & Management. (2012)

38. Piliponyte, A., Ricci, F., Koschwitz, J. Sequential music recommendations for groups by balancing user satisfaction. In: Proceedings of the Workshop on Group Recommender Systems: Concepts, Technology, Evaluation at UMAP13.(2013) 6–11.
39. Quijano-Sanchez, L., Recio-Garcia, J. A., Diaz-Agudo, B., Jimenez-Diaz, G.: Social factors in group recommender systems. ACM Transactions on Intelligent Systems and Technology, 4(1) 8 (2013).
40. Read, T., Barros, B., Bárcena, E., Pancorbo, J.: Coalescing Individual and Collaborative Learning to Model User Linguistic Competences. UMUAI 16 (2006) 349–376
41. Salamó, M., McCarthy, K., Smyth, B.: Generating recommendations for consensus negotiation in group personalization services. Personal and Ubiquitous Computing, 16(5) (2012) 597–610.
42. Senot, C., Kostadinov, D., Bouzid, M., Picault, J., Aghasaryan, A., Bernier, C.: Analysis of strategies for building group profiles. In: Proceedings of User Modeling, Adaptation, and Personalization (2010) 40–51. Springer.
43. Stettinger, M., Ninaus, G., Jeran, M., Reinfrank, F., Reiterer, S.: WE-DECIDE: A decision support environment for groups of users. In: Recent Trends in Applied Artificial Intelligence (2013) 382–391. Springer.
44. Suebnukarn, S., Haddawy, P.: Modeling Individual and Collaborative Problem-Solving in Medical Problem-Based Learning. UMUAI 16 (2006) 211–248
45. Tintarev, N., Masthoff, J.: Explaining recommendations: Design and evaluation. In this handbook (2015).
46. Umyarov, A., Tuzhilin, A.: Using external aggregate ratings for improving individual recommendations. ACM Transactions on the Web 5 (2011) 1–45
47. Wang, Z., Zhou, X., Yu, Z., Wang, H., Ni, H.: Quantitative evaluation of group user experience in smart spaces. Cybernetics and Systems: An International Journal 41:2 (2010) 105–122
48. Ye, M., Liu, X., Lee, W. C.: Exploring social influence for recommendation: a generative model approach. In Proceedings of the 35th international ACM SIGIR conference on Research and development in information retrieval (2012) ACM: 671–680
49. Yu, Z., Zhou, X., Hao, Y. Gu, J.: TV Program Recommendation for Multiple Viewers Based on User Profile Merging. UMUAI 16 (2006) 63–82

Chapter 23
Aggregation Functions for Recommender Systems

Gleb Beliakov, Tomasa Calvo, and Simon James

23.1 Introduction

Aggregation functions are employed at various stages and for various purposes in recommender systems. From vast databases of electronic objects and information, recommender systems (RS) guide users to items that may be of interest which to date have included movies [39], web-pages [6], news articles [40], medical treatments [19, 36], tourist destinations [31], music and other products [37, 43]. Due to the sheer size of the data sets, aggregation becomes necessary to help summarize the extent to which an item satisfies a user's preferences, the similarity between users or items, or even the credibility of an online store.

The arithmetic mean or maximum/minimum functions are typically the default choice for such aggregation, however the user-specific and personalized aspects of RS suggests that the flexibility of some aggregation functions could lead to more relevant recommendations as opposed to a one-fits-all approach. In this chapter we will review the basics of aggregation functions and their properties, and present the most important families, including generalized means, Choquet and Sugeno integrals, ordered weighted averaging, triangular norms and conorms, as well as bipolar aggregation functions. Such functions can model various interactions between the inputs, conjunctive, disjunctive and mixed behavior. We will then present different methods of construction, based either on analytical formulas,

---

G. Beliakov • S. James (✉)
School of Information Technology, Deakin University,
221 Burwood Hwy, Burwood, VIC 3125, Australia
e-mail: gleb@deakin.edu.au; sjames@deakin.edu.au

T. Calvo
Departamento de Ciencias de la Computación, Universidad de Alcalá,
28871 Alcalá de Henares, Madrid, Spain
e-mail: tomasa.calvo@uah.es

F. Ricci et al. (eds.), *Recommender Systems Handbook*,
DOI 10.1007/978-1-4899-7637-6_23

algorithms, or empirical data. We discuss how parameters of aggregation functions can be fitted to observed data, while preserving the desirable properties that ensure consistency and robustness. By replacing the arithmetic mean with more sophisticated, adaptable functions, by canceling out redundancies in the inputs, one can improve the quality of automatic recommendations, and tailor recommender systems to specific domains.

23.2 Types of Aggregation in Recommender Systems

A key feature of recommender systems that traditionally distinguished them from other such as internet filtering is the targeted relationship between users and items. The sophistication of web applications today and the rise of Web 2.0 has resulted in this distinction becoming less pronounced, however we can still broadly categorize recommender systems based on how data is collected and used to form user-specific justifications to recommend items. Recommendations based on justifications concerning item features can be broadly classified as *content-based* (CB), whereas recommendations that utilize user similarity are referred to as *collaborative* (CF) [1, 2]. It is useful to further identify demographic (DF), utility-(UB) and knowledge-based (KB) methods [21] as distinct from the usual perception of CB recommendation as anything that uses item-item similarity. The more recent literature has been characterized by a focus on hybrid systems (HS), which combine two or more of these approaches. In particular, the phenomenon of social media has allowed RS to increasingly take advantage of such information to augment the accuracy and reliability of recommendations [17].

Collaborative methods use the item preferences or ratings of similar users as justification for recommendation. The recommendations built into *Amazon.com* [37] are an archetypical example of these methods. Aggregation functions (usually the simple or weighted average) are employed in CF to aggregate the ratings or preferences of similar users, however they can also be used to determine user similarity and help define *neighborhoods*.

Content-based filtering methods form justifications by matching item-features to user profiles. For instance, a news recommender may build a profile for each user that consists of *keywords* and the interest in an unseen news item can be predicted by the number of keywords in the story that correspond to those in the user's profile. The way aggregation functions are used (and whether they are used) for content-based methods depends on the nature of the profile that is given to each user and the description of items. We consider their use in item score computation, similarity computation and the construction of profiles.

Demographic filtering techniques assign each user to a demographic class based on their user profiles. Each demographic class has an associated user archetype or user stereotype that is then used to form justifications for recommendation. Rather than item history, user similarity here is more likely to be calculated from personal information and hence may be of lower dimension than most collaborative techniques. This makes nearest-neighbor or other classification and clustering tools particularly useful.

Rather than build long-term models, *utility-based* recommenders match items to the current needs of the users, taking into account their general tendencies and preferences. For instance, a user may be looking for a particular book, and it is known from past behavior that old hardback editions are preferred even if it takes longer to ship them. As is the case with content-based filtering, items can be described in the system by their features and, more specifically, the utility associated with each of those features. Aggregation can then be performed as it is with content-based filtering, although the user profiles and system information may differ.

Knowledge-based recommenders use background knowledge about associated and similar items to infer the needs of the user and how they can best be met. Knowledge-based methods will then draw not only on typical measures of similarity like correlation, but also on feature similarities that will interest the user. It is pointed out in [21] that KB recommenders often draw on case-based reasoning approaches.

Hybrid recommender systems are employed to overcome the inherent drawbacks of each recommendation method. Burke [21] distinguishes weighted, mixed, switching, feature combination, cascade, feature augmentation and meta-level HS. Aggregation functions may be involved in the hybridization process—e.g. to combine different recommender scores in weighted HS or the features in feature combination HS. On the other hand, some of these hybrid methods are particularly useful in improving the performance of aggregation functions used at different stages. For instance, cascade methods use one filtering technique to reduce the size of the dataset, while feature augmentation HS might use one method to reduce its dimension. Similarity measures used for CF could be based on the similarity between user-specific aggregation functions (e.g. the similarity between weights and parameters) constructed in UB and CB frameworks. Similar meta-level HS are described in [21]. The switching criteria in switching HS could be based to some degree on aggregation functions, however here, as with mixed HS, their use is less likely.

It is also worth making special mention of social media and trust, which play an increasingly important role in today's recommender systems. Systems of all types can now take advantage of the abundance of research concerning social networks and how users interact and influence one another, as well as the new platforms through which items can be shared and recommended. Aggregation functions can be used to indirectly establish trust patterns, preferences and relationships by summarizing network features and structures. They can also be used directly in the calculation of network or user similarities and trust/distrust measures [46].

Simple examples of aggregation functions include the arithmetic mean, median, maximum and minimum, each taking multiple inputs as arguments and combining them into a single representative output. The use of more complicated and expressive functions in RS would usually be motivated by the desire for more accurate recommendations, however in some circumstances aggregation functions might provide a practical alternative to other data processing methods. In the following subsections we will investigate the role of aggregation functions within different types of recommender system, indicating where they can be and have been applied.

23.2.1 Aggregation of Preferences in CF

Given a user u and a neighborhood of similar users $U_k = \{u_1, \ldots, u_k\}$, the preference of u for an unseen item d_i can be predicted by aggregating the scores given by U_k. We will denote the predicted degree of interest, rating or preference by $R(u, d_i)$.

$$R(u, d_i) = \sum_{j=1}^{k} sim(u, u_j) R(u_j, d_i) \tag{23.1}$$

The function can be interpreted as a weighted arithmetic mean (WAM) where similarities between the user and similar users $sim(u, u_j) = w_j$ are the weights and $R(u_j, d_i) = x_j$ are the inputs to be aggregated. Provided $w_j, x_j \geq 0$, the function $R(u, d_i)$ is an aggregation function. Whilst the WAM is simply interpreted, satisfies many useful properties and is computationally inexpensive, other aggregation functions including power means (which can be non-linear) or the Choquet integral (which accounts for correlated inputs) may give a more accurate prediction of the users' ratings.

23.2.2 Aggregation of Features in CB and UB Recommendation

Where the profile is representable as a vector of feature preferences, $P_u = (p_1, \ldots, p_n)$, items can then be described in terms of the degree to which they satisfy these features, i.e. $d_i = (x_1, \ldots, x_n)$. Here, a value of $x_j = 1$ indicates that the preference p_j is completely satisfied by the item. P_u could also be a vector of keywords, in which case $x_j = 1$ might simply mean that the keyword p_j is mentioned once. The overall rating $R(u, d_i)$ of an item is then determined by aggregating the x_j,

$$R(u, d_i) = f(x_1, \ldots, x_n) \tag{23.2}$$

Equation (23.2) is an aggregation function provided the function satisfies certain boundary conditions and is monotone with respect to increases in x_j. The $R(u, d_i)$ scores can be used to provide a ranking of unseen items, which can then be recommended. If the RS allows only one item to be shown, the how and why of this score evaluation becomes paramount. If the user is only likely to buy/view items when all of their preferences are satisfied, a *conjunctive* function like the *minimum* should be used. On the other hand, if some of the preferences are unlikely to be satisfied simultaneously, e.g. the user is interested in drama and horror films, an *averaging* or *disjunctive* function might be more reliable. We present many examples of these broad classes of aggregation functions in Sect. 23.3.

In situations where it is practical to calculate item-item similarity, content-based filtering could also be facilitated using methods that mirror those in collaborative filtering [2]. In this case, a user profile might consist of all or a subset of previously rated/purchased items, $D = \{d_1, \ldots, d_q\}$, and a measure of similarity is calculated between the unseen item d_i and those in D,

$$R(u, d_i) = \sum_{j=1,(j \neq i)}^{q} sim(d_i, d_j)R(u, d_j). \tag{23.3}$$

In this case, content-based methods can benefit from the use of aggregation functions in determining item similarity and item neighborhoods as in Sect. 23.2.3.

23.2.3 Item and User Similarity and Neighborhood Formation

The behavior and accuracy of recommendation when using Eq. (23.1) will be largely dependent on how similarity (the weighting vector) is determined. The similarity between one user and another can be measured in terms of items previously rated or bought, or may be calculated based on known features associated with each user—e.g. the age, location and interests of a user may be known. The most commonly used measures of similarity, i.e. the weights in Eq. (23.1), are based on the cosine calculation [42] and Pearson's correlation coefficient [40]. Recently, other similarity measures have emerged such as fuzzy distance [4] (or traditional distances such as the Euclidean or Manhattan distances) and other recommender-specific metrics, e.g. as in [3, 24], based on the distribution of user ratings or latent/implicit user and item feature spaces (see also Chap. 2 of this book).

Equation (23.1) can also be considered within the framework of a *k-nearest-neighbors* (kNN) approach. Aggregation functions have been used to enhance the accuracy and efficiency of nearest-neighbor rules, with the OWA and Choquet integral providing the framework to model decaying weights and neighbor interaction [14, 50]. In the nearest-neighbor setting, similarity is tantamount to multi-dimensional proximity or distance. Euclidean distance was considered for measuring similarity for recommenders that use both ratings and personal information as inputs in [45]. Euclidean distance is just one type of metric, and may not capture the concept of distance well—for instance, where the data dimensions are correlated to some degree or even incommensurable. Metrics defined with the help of certain aggregation functions, including the OWA operator and Choquet integral, have been investigated in [18, 44] and could potentially prove useful for measuring similarity in some RS.

If we regard each value $sim(u, u_j)$ in Eq. (23.1) as a weight rather than a similarity, we can keep in mind that the problem of weight identification for various aggregation functions has been studied extensively. One method is to learn the weights from a data subset by using least-squares fitting techniques. For instance, given a set of mutually rated items $D = \{d_1, \ldots, d_q\}$, the weights of a WAM can be fitted using the following program:

$$\text{minimize} \sum_{i=1}^{q} \left(R(u, d_i) - \sum_{j=1}^{k} w_j R(u_j, d_i) \right)^2$$

$$\text{s.t.} \qquad w_j \geq 0, \quad \forall j$$

$$\sum_{j=1}^{k} w_j = 1.$$

What is actually being determined is the vector of weights $\mathbf{w} = (w_1, \ldots, w_k)$ that minimizes the residual errors. Each weight is then the importance of a given user u_j in accurately predicting $R(u, d_i)$. Non-linear functions such as the weighted geometric mean can also be fitted in this way. Such algorithms are relatively efficient in terms of computation time, and could be calculated either offline or in real-time depending on the RS and size of the database.

Alternatively, aggregation functions can be used to combine differing measures of similarity. Given a number of similarity measures $sim_1(u, u_1)$, $sim_2(u, u_1)$ etc., an overall measure of similarity can be obtained. This type of aggregated similarity was used in [26] for the recommendation of movies. In this example, cosine and correlation scores were combined using the product, which is a non-linear and conjunctive aggregation function. In [2], the extension of recommendation techniques to multi-dimensional approaches was proposed, where a user might rate a movie in terms of its plot, visual effects and acting as well as providing an overall score. Two users may provide similar overall scores for a film, however may like the film for different reasons making this evaluation of similarity misleading. Aggregation functions can then be used to combine the measures of similarity in each dimension (also see Chap. 25 for more on recommendations based on multiple criteria).

23.2.4 Profile Construction for CB, UB

More sophisticated systems will assign a weight w_j to each of the preferences in P_u. To enhance the online-experience, many recommenders opt to learn the preferences (and weights) from online behavior, rather than ask the user to state them explicitly. The features of previously rated or purchased items can be aggregated to give an overall score for each preference. Given a preference p_j, let x_{ij} be the degree to which item d_i satisfies p_j, then the score $w(p_j)$ will be

$$w(p_j) = f(x_{1j}, \dots, x_{nj}). \tag{23.4}$$

Once all the preferences are determined, these $w(p_j)$ can be used to determine w_j for use in calculations such as Eq. (23.2).

Preferences can also be learned using programming methods of the form given above for similarity, e.g. in [47], the Choquet integral was used to detect customer preferences for tourism websites. This stands as an alternative approach to matrix reduction methods (e.g. principal component analysis, single value decomposition and use of latent factors) for handling implicit interactions between users' preferences and between item descriptors. The advantage with aggregation functions is that we still obtain data-based models with parameters that have direct interpretations, however it should be noted that they are less suited to dealing with sparse datasets.

23.2.5 Connectives in Case-Based Reasoning for RS

The approach of many researchers in the fuzzy sets community has been to frame the recommendation problem in terms of case-based reasoning [29] where aggregation functions can be used as connectives . This results in rules of the form,

$$\textbf{If } d_{i1} \textit{ is } A_1 \textbf{ AND } d_{i2} \textit{ is } A_2 \textbf{ OR } \dots\ d_{in} \textit{ is } A_n \textbf{ THEN} \dots \tag{23.5}$$

$x_1, x_2, \dots, x_n$ denote the degrees of satisfaction of the rule predicates d_{i1} is A_1, etc., and aggregation functions are used to replace the AND and OR operations. For instance, a user whose profile indicates a preference for comedies and action films might have a recommendation rule "IF the film is a comedy *OR* an action THEN recommend it."[1] Each genre can be represented as a fuzzy set with fuzzy connectives used to aggregate the degrees of satisfaction. The OR- and AND-type behavior are usually modeled by disjunctive and conjunctive aggregation functions respectively. In recommender systems, it has been shown that the property of noble reinforcement

[1] We note here also that such rules could be used in any RS to decide *when* to recommend items, e.g. "IF user is inactive THEN recommend *something*".

is desirable [11, 49]. This property allows many *strong* justifications to result in a *very strong* recommendation, or a number of *weak* justifications to reduce the recommendation if desired.

Functions that model Eq. (23.5) can be used to match items to profiles or queries in CB (content-based filtering), UB (utility-based recommendation) and KB (knowledge-based recommender system). In some demographic RS, items will be generically recommended to everyone in a given class, making the classification process the primary task of the RS. It may be desirable to classify users by the degree to which they satisfy a number of stereotypes, and in turn describe items in terms of their interest to each of these. For instance, a personal loan with an interest-free period could be very attractive to graduating students and somewhat attractive to new mothers, but of no interest to someone recently married. A user could partially satisfy each of these archetypes, requiring the system to aggregate the interest values in each demographic. This leads to rules similar to (23.5). "IF the item is interesting to students OR interesting to mothers THEN it will be interesting to user u" or "IF user u is unmarried AND either a student OR mother, THEN recommend the item".

23.2.6 Weighted Hybrid Systems

Given a number of recommendation scores obtained by using different methods, e.g. $R_{CF}(u,d_i)$, $R_{CB}(u,d_i)$, etc., an overall score can be obtained using

$$R(u,d_i) = f(R_{CF}(u,d_i), R_{CB}(u,d_i), \ldots) \tag{23.6}$$

with f an aggregation function. The P-Tango system [25] uses a linear combination of collaborative and content-based scores to make its recommendations, and adjusts the weight according to the inferred user preferences. Aggregation of two or more methods can be performed using a number of functions with different properties and behavior. Aggregation-based trust and distrust evaluations, degrees of affinity and social connectedness can also be incorporated at different levels of a hybrid RS in weight determination and to guide recommendation rules.

Although the standard operators can provide reasonable improvements to recommendation, the use of lesser known or sometimes more complicated functions could enable some recommenders to fine-tune the ranking process, creating less irrelevant and more accurate predictions.

23.3 Review of Aggregation Functions

The purpose of aggregation functions is to combine inputs that are typically interpreted as degrees of membership in fuzzy sets, degrees of preference, strength of evidence, or support of a hypothesis, and so on. In this section, we provide preliminary definitions and properties before giving an introduction to some well known families.

23.3.1 Definitions and Properties

We will consider aggregation functions defined on the unit interval $f : [0,1]^n \rightarrow [0,1]$, however other choices are possible. The input value 0 is interpreted as no membership, no preference, no evidence, no satisfaction, etc., and naturally, an aggregation of n 0s should yield 0. Similarly, the value 1 is interpreted as full membership or strongest preference, and an aggregation of 1s should naturally yield 1.

Aggregation functions also formally require monotonicity in each argument, where an increase to any input cannot result in a decrease in the overall score.

Definition 23.1 (Aggregation Function). An aggregation function is a function of $n > 1$ arguments that maps the (n-dimensional) unit cube onto the unit interval $f : [0,1]^n \rightarrow [0,1]$, with the properties

(i) $f(\underbrace{0,0,\ldots,0}_{n-times}) = 0$ and $f(\underbrace{1,1,\ldots,1}_{n-times}) = 1$.

(ii) $\mathbf{x} \leq \mathbf{y}$ implies $f(\mathbf{x}) \leq f(\mathbf{y})$ for all $\mathbf{x}, \mathbf{y} \in [0,1]^n$.

For some applications, the inputs may have a varying number of components (for instance, some values can be missing). Particularly in the case of automated systems, it may be desirable to utilize functions defined for $n = 2, 3, \ldots$ arguments with the same underlying property in order to give consistent aggregation results. One approach is to consider the class of *extended aggregation functions* [38], which can be expressed succinctly for all n, however more recently the notion of aggregation stability (see below) has received attention [16, 41].

Aggregation functions are classed depending on their overall behavior in relation to the inputs [23, 27, 28]. In some cases we require high inputs to compensate for low inputs, or that inputs may average each other. In other situations, it may make more sense that high scores reinforce each other and low inputs are essentially discarded.

Definition 23.2 (Classes). An aggregation function $f : [0,1]^n \rightarrow [0,1]$ is:

Averaging if it is bounded by $\min(\mathbf{x}) \leq f(\mathbf{x}) \leq \max(\mathbf{x})$;
Conjunctive if it is bounded by $f(\mathbf{x}) \leq \min(\mathbf{x})$;
Disjunctive if it is bounded by $f(\mathbf{x}) \geq \max(\mathbf{x})$;
Mixed otherwise.

The class of aggregation function to be used depends on how the inputs of the recommender system are interpreted and how sensitive or broad an output is desired. When aggregating recommendation scores in CF, the use of averaging functions ensures that the predicted interest in an item is representative of the central tendency of the scores. On the other hand, the semantics of some mixed aggregation functions makes their use appealing. For instance, MYCIN [19] is a classical expert system used to diagnose and treat rare blood diseases and utilizes a mixed aggregation function so that inputs of only high scores reinforce each other, while scores below a given threshold are penalized.

There are several studied properties that can be satisfied by aggregation functions, making them useful in certain situations. We provide descriptions for those that are frequently referred to in the literature.

Definition 23.3 (Properties). An aggregation function $f : [0, 1]^n \to [0, 1]$ is:

Idempotent if for every $t \in [0, 1]$ the output is $f(t, t \ldots, t) = t$;

Symmetric if its value does not depend on the permutation of the arguments, i.e.,$f(x_1, x_2, \ldots, x_n) = f(x_{P(1)}, x_{P(2)}, \ldots, x_{P(n)})$ for every $\mathbf{x}$ and every permutation $P = (P(1), P(2), \ldots, P(n))$ of $(1, 2 \ldots, n)$;

Associative if, for $f : [0, 1]^2 \to [0, 1], f(f(x_1, x_2), x_3) = f(x_1, f(x_2, x_3))$ holds for all x_1, x_2, x_3;

LR-stable if, for all $\mathbf{x} \in [0, 1]^{n-1}$ it holds that, $f(x_1, \ldots, x_{n-1}, f(x_1, \ldots, x_{n-1})) = f(f(x_1, \ldots, x_{n-1}), x_1, \ldots, x_{n-1}) = f(x_1, \ldots, x_{n-1})$;

Shift-invariant if for all $\lambda \in [-1, 1]$ and for all $\mathbf{x} = (x_1, \ldots, x_n), f(x_1+\lambda, \ldots, x_n+\lambda) = f(\mathbf{x}) + \lambda$ whenever $(x_1 + \lambda, \ldots, x_n + \lambda) \in [0, 1]^n$ and $f(\mathbf{x}) + \lambda \in [0, 1]$;

Homogeneous if for all $\lambda \in [0, 1]$ and for all $\mathbf{x} = (x_1, \ldots, x_n), f(\lambda x_1, \ldots, \lambda x_n) = \lambda f(\mathbf{x})$;

Strictly monotone if $\mathbf{x} \leq \mathbf{y}$ but $\mathbf{x} \neq \mathbf{y}$ implies $f(\mathbf{x}) < f(\mathbf{y})$;

Lipschitz continuous if there is a positive number M, such that for any two inputs $\mathbf{x}, \mathbf{y} \in [0, 1]^n$, $|f(\mathbf{x}) - f(\mathbf{y})| \leq Md(\mathbf{x}, \mathbf{y})$, where $d(\mathbf{x}, \mathbf{y})$ is a distance between $\mathbf{x}$ and $\mathbf{y}$. The smallest such number M is called the Lipschitz constant of f.

Has *neutral elements* if there is a value $e \in [0, 1]$ such that $f(e, \ldots, e, t, e, \ldots, e) = t$ for every $t \in [0, 1]$ in any position.

Has *absorbing elements* if there is a value $a \in [0, 1]$ such that for any $\mathbf{x}$ with an input $x_j = a$, it follows that $f(x_1, \ldots, x_{j-1}, a, x_{j+1}, \ldots, x_n) = a$.

23.3.1.1 Practical Considerations in RS

We will discuss some of the implications of each of these properties with some examples before providing the formal definitions of many important and extensively studied aggregation functions.

Idempotency All averaging aggregation functions, including the means, OWA and Choquet integral defined in Sect. 23.3.2, are idempotent.[2] The usual interpretation of this property is toward a representation of consensus amongst the inputs. However in some RS applications, e.g. when aggregating ratings in CF, the relative ranking of items is of more concern than the commensurability of input/output interpretations.

[2]Idempotency and averaging behavior are equivalent for aggregation functions due to the monotonicity requirement. This property is sometimes referred to as unanimity since the output agrees with each input when the inputs are unanimous.

Symmetry The use of symmetric aggregation functions implies equal importance or reliability with regard to the inputs. Non-symmetric weights can be used with quasi-arithmetic means if it is desired that particular inputs have more influence on the aggregated output. Although the ordered weighted averaging function (OWA) is defined with respect to a weighting vector, it is still considered a symmetric function since changing the order of the inputs will have no effect, i.e. they will be sorted into descending order regardless.

Example 23.1. A collaborative RS considers two items rated by three similar users $d_1 = (0.2, 0.7, 0.6), d_2 = (0.6, 0.2, 0.7)$. Aggregating these inputs using a WAM with symmetric weights would give the identical result $R(u, d_1) = R(u, d_2) = (0.2 + 0.7 + 0.6)/3 = 0.5$. Similarly, using an OWA with weights $\mathbf{w} = (0.5, 0.4, 0.1)$ will also give the same result for both items, with $R(u, d_1) = R(u, d_2) = 0.5(0.7) + 0.4(0.6) + 0.1(0.2) = 0.61$. However if it is known that u_1 is more similar to the user than u_2 or u_3, then we could use a weighted mean with $\mathbf{w} = (0.6, 0.2, 0.2)$ so that the rating of u_1 has more influence. This results in d_2 having a higher predicted suitability, with $R(u, d_1) = 0.6(0.2) + 0.2(0.7) + 0.2(0.6) = 0.38$ and $R(u, d_2) = 0.6(0.6) + 0.2(0.2) + 0.2(0.6) = 0.52$.

Associativity Associativity is a useful property for automatic computation as it allows functions to be defined recursively for any dimension. This is potentially useful for collaborative RS where data sparsity is a problem. The same function could be used to evaluate one item rated by 10 similar users, and another rated by 1000 similar users. T-norms and t-conorms, uninorms and nullnorms are associative, however the quasi-arithmetic means are not.

Example 23.2. A collaborative RS uses personal information to determine similarity between users (i.e. the values do not need to be reassessed every time a new item is rated). Rather than store an *items* × *users* matrix for each user, the system uses a uninorm $U(x, y)$ to aggregate the similar user ratings and stores a single vector of aggregated item scores $\mathbf{d} = (U(d_i), \ldots, U(d_n))$. When a new item score x_{ij} is added, the system aggregates $U(U(d_i), x_{ij})$ and stores this instead of $U(d_i)$. The advantage here is that neither the previous scores nor the number of times the item is rated is required in order to update the predicted rating.

LR-stability The concept of LR-stability [41] or stability with respect to any position [16] ensures that the function is consistently defined for any number of inputs. The idea is that if we append the output to the vector of inputs, the new output should not change. Functions which satisfy LR-stability are then useful for the sparse item×user matrices that recommender systems need to deal with.

Shift-invariance and homogeneity The main advantage of shift-invariant and homogeneous functions is that translating or dilating the domain of consideration will not affect relative orderings of aggregated inputs. The weighted arithmetic mean, OWA and Choquet integral are all shift invariant, so it makes no difference whether inputs are considered on [0,100] or [1,7], as long as the inputs are commensurable.

Strict monotonicity Strict monotonicity is desired in applications where the number of items to be shown to the user is limited. Weighted arithmetic means and OWA functions are strictly monotone when $w_j > 0, \forall j$, while geometric and harmonic means are strict for $\mathbf{x} \in]0,1]^n$. Aggregation functions which are not strict, the *maximum* function for instance, could not distinguish between an item $d_1 = (0.3, 0.8)$ and another $d_2 = (0.8, 0.8)$.

Example 23.3. A holiday recommendation site uses a utility-based RS where the Łukasiewicz t-conorm $S_L(x,y) = \min(x+y,1)$ is used to aggregate item features. It is able to show the user every item $S_L(d_i) = 1$ by notifications through e-mail. It doesn't matter that $d_1 = (0.3, 0.8)$ and $d_2 = (0.8, 0.8)$, since both of them are predicted to completely satisfy the user's needs.

Lipschitz continuity Continuity, in general, ensures that small input inaccuracies cannot result in drastic changes in output. Such a property is especially important in RS where the inputs, whether item descriptions or user ratings, are likely to be inexact. Some functions only violate this property on a small portion of the domain. As long as this is taken into account when the RS considers the recommendation scores, the function might still be suitable.

Neutral and absorbent elements Absorbent elements could be useful in RS to ensure that certain items always or never get recommended. For example, a UB recommender could remove every item from consideration which has any features that score zero, or definitely recommend items which completely satisfy one of the user preferences. T-norms and t-conorms each have absorbent elements. Incorporating functions with neutral elements into a recommender system that aggregates user ratings (in either a CF or CB framework) allows values to be specified which will not affect recommendation scores. A movie that is liked by many people, for instance, would usually have its overall approval rating reduced by someone who was indifferent toward it but still required to rate it. If a neutral value exists it will not influence the aggregated score.

23.3.2 Aggregation Families

23.3.2.1 Quasi-Arithmetic Means

The family of weighted quasi-arithmetic means generalizes the power mean, which in turn includes other classical means such as the arithmetic and geometric mean as special cases (see [20] for an overview of means).

Definition 23.4 (Weighted Quasi-Arithmetic Means). For a given strictly monotone and continuous function $g : [0, 1] \to [-\infty, +\infty]$, called a generating function or generator, and a weighting vector $\mathbf{w} = (w_1, \ldots, w_n)$, the weighted quasi-arithmetic mean is the function

$$M_{\mathbf{w},g}(\mathbf{x}) = g^{-1}\left(\sum_{i=1}^{n} w_j g(x_j)\right). \tag{23.7}$$

where $\sum w_j = 1$ and $w_j \geq 0 \; \forall \, j$.

Special cases include:

Arithmetic means	$WAM_{\mathbf{w}} = \sum_{j=1}^{n} w_j x_j,$	$g(t) = t;$
Geometric means	$G_{\mathbf{w}} = \prod_{j=1}^{n} x_j^{w_j},$	$g(t) = log(t);$
Harmonic means	$H_{\mathbf{w}} = \left(\sum_{j=1}^{n} \frac{w_j}{x_j}\right)^{-1},$	$g(t) = \frac{1}{t};$
Power means	$M_{\mathbf{w},[r]} = \left(\sum_{j=1}^{n} w_j x_j^r\right)^{\frac{1}{r}},$	$g(t) = t^r$

The term *mean* is usually used to imply averaging behavior. Quasi-arithmetic means defined with respect to a weighting vector with all $w_j = \frac{1}{n}$ are symmetric, and asymmetric otherwise. Usually the weight allocated to a particular input is indicative of the importance of that particular input. All power means (including $WAM_{\mathbf{w}}$, $G_{\mathbf{w}}$ and $H_{\mathbf{w}}$) are idempotent, homogeneous and strictly monotone on the open interval $]0, 1[^n$, however only the weighted arithmetic mean is shift-invariant. The geometric mean is not Lipschitz continuous.[3]

[3]The Lipschitz property for quasi-arithmetic means and other generated aggregation functions is explored in [13].

23.3.2.2 OWA Functions

Ordered weighted averaging functions (OWA) are also averaging aggregation functions, which associate a weight not with a particular input, but rather with its relative value or order compared to others. They have been introduced by Yager [48] and have become very popular in the fuzzy sets community.

Definition 23.5 (OWA). Given a weighting vector $\mathbf{w}$, the OWA function is

$$OWA_{\mathbf{w}}(\mathbf{x}) = \sum_{j=1}^{n} w_j x_{(j)},$$

where the (.) notation denotes the components of $\mathbf{x}$ being arranged in non-increasing order $x_{(1)} \geq x_{(2)} \geq \ldots \geq x_{(n)}$.

Special cases of the OWA operator, depending on the weighting vector $\mathbf{w}$ include:

Arithmetic mean where all the weights are equal, i.e. all $w_j = \frac{1}{n}$
Maximum function for $\mathbf{w} = (1, 0, \ldots, 0)$;
Minimum function for $\mathbf{w} = (0, \ldots, 0, 1)$;
Median function for $w_j = 0$ for all $j \neq m$, $w_m = 1$ if $n = 2m + 1$ is odd, and $w_j = 0$ for all $j \neq m, m+1$, $w_m = w_{m+1} = 0.5$ if $n = 2m$ is even.

The OWA function is a piecewise linear idempotent aggregation function. It is symmetric, homogeneous, shift-invariant, Lipschitz continuous and strictly monotone if $w_j > 0, \forall\, j$.

23.3.2.3 Choquet and Sugeno Integrals

Referred to as fuzzy integrals, the Choquet integral and the Sugeno integral are averaging aggregation functions defined with respect to a fuzzy measure. They are useful for modeling interactions between the input variables x_j.

Definition 23.6 (Fuzzy Measure). Let $\mathcal{N} = \{1, 2, \ldots, n\}$. A discrete fuzzy measure is a set function[4] $v : 2^{\mathcal{N}} \to [0, 1]$ which is monotonic (i.e. $v(A) \leq v(B)$ whenever $A \subseteq B$) and satisfies $v(\emptyset) = 0, v(\mathcal{N}) = 1$. Given any two sets $A, B \subseteq \mathcal{N}$, fuzzy measures are said to be:

Additive where $v(A \cup B) = v(A) + v(B)$, for $v(A \cap B) = \emptyset$;
Symmetric where $|A| = |B| \to v(A) = v(B)$;
Submodular if $v(A \cup B) - v(A \cap B) \leq v(A) + v(B)$;
Supermodular if $v(A \cup B) - v(A \cap B) \geq v(A) + v(B)$;

[4] A set function is a function whose domain consists of all possible subsets of $\mathcal{N}$. For example, for $n = 3$, a set function is specified by $2^3 = 8$ values at $v(\emptyset)$, $v(\{1\})$, $v(\{2\})$, $v(\{3\})$, $v(\{1, 2\})$, $v(\{1, 3\})$, $v(\{2, 3\})$, $v(\{1, 2, 3\})$.

Subadditive if $v(A \cup B) \leq v(A) + v(B)$ whenever $A \cap B = \emptyset$;
Superadditive if $v(A \cup B) \geq v(A) + v(B)$ whenever $A \cap B = \emptyset$;
Decomposable if $v(A \cup B) = f(v(A), v(B))$ whenever $A \cap B = \emptyset$, for a given function $f : [0,1]^2 \to [0,1]$;
Sugeno (λ-fuzzy measure) if v is *decomposable* with $f = v(A) + v(B) + \lambda v(A)v(B), \lambda \in]-1, \infty[$.

The behavior of the Sugeno and Choquet integral depends on the values and properties of the associated fuzzy measure. The fuzzy measure used to define the Choquet integral can be interpreted as a weight allocation, not merely to individual inputs but rather to each subset of inputs. It may be that there are redundancies among the inputs, or that certain inputs complement each other.

Definition 23.7 (Choquet Integral). The discrete Choquet integral with respect to a fuzzy measure v is given by

$$C_v(\mathbf{x}) = \sum_{j=1}^{n} x_{(j)}[v(\{k|x_k \geq x_{(j)}\}) - v(\{k|x_k \geq x_{(j+1)}\})], \tag{23.8}$$

where (.) in this case denotes the components of $\mathbf{x}$ being arranged in non-decreasing order such that $(x_{(1)} \leq x_{(2)} \leq \cdots \leq x_{(n)})$ (note that this is opposite to OWA).

Special cases of the Choquet integral include weighted arithmetic means and the OWA function where the fuzzy measure is additive or symmetric respectively. Submodular fuzzy measures result in Choquet integrals which are concave, the upshot of which is that increases to lower inputs affect the function more than increases to higher inputs. Conversely, supermodular fuzzy measures result in convex functions. Choquet integrals are idempotent, homogeneous, shift-invariant and strictly monotone where $A \subsetneq B \to v(A) < v(B)$. Where the fuzzy measure is symmetric, the function will obviously satisfy the symmetry property.

The Choquet integral has been predominantly used for numerical inputs, the Sugeno integral defined below is useful where the inputs are ordinal. It also uses fuzzy measures for its definition.

Definition 23.8 (Sugeno Integral). The Sugeno integral with respect to a fuzzy measure v is given by

$$S_v(\mathbf{x}) = \max_{j=1,\dots,n} \min\{x_{(j)}, v(H_j)\}, \tag{23.9}$$

where (.) denotes a non-decreasing permutation of the inputs such that $(x_{(1)} \leq x_{(2)} \leq \cdots \leq x_{(n)})$ (the same as with the Choquet integral), and $H_j = \{(j), \dots, (n)\}$.

Certain indices have been introduced in order to better understand the behavior of the Choquet and Sugeno integrals. In particular, the Shapley value gives an indication of the overall importance of a given input, while the interaction index between two inputs shows to what extent they are redundant or complimentary.

Definition 23.9 (Shapley Value). Let v be a fuzzy measure. The Shapley index for every $i \in \mathcal{N}$ is

$$\phi(i) = \sum_{A \subseteq \mathcal{N} \setminus \{i\}} \frac{(n - |A| - 1)!|A|!}{n!}[v(A \cup \{i\}) - v(A)].$$

The Shapley value is the vector $\phi(v) = (\phi(1), \ldots, \phi(n))$.

Definition 23.10 (Interaction Index). Let v be a fuzzy measure. The interaction index for every pair $i, j \in \mathcal{N}$ is

$$I_{ij} = \sum_{A \subseteq \mathcal{N} \setminus \{i,j\}} \frac{(n - |A| - 2)!|A|!}{(n-1)!}[v(A \cup \{i,j\}) - v(A \cup \{i\}) - v(A \cup \{j\}) + v(A)].$$

Where the interaction index is negative, there is some redundancy between the two inputs. Where it is positive, the inputs complement each other to some degree and their weight together is worth more than their combined individual weights.

23.3.2.4 T-Norms and T-Conorms

The prototypical examples of conjunctive and disjunctive aggregation functions are so-called triangular norms and conorms respectively (t-norms and t-conorms) [34]. Given any t-norm $T : [0, 1]^2 \to [0, 1]$, there is a dual function which is a t-conorm S, with

$$S(x, y) = 1 - T(1 - x, 1 - y)$$

and vice-versa. T-norms and t-conorms are hence often studied in parallel, as many properties concerning S can be determined from T. Triangular norms are associative, symmetric with the neutral element $e = 1$, whereas triangular conorms are associative, symmetric and have the neutral element $e = 0$. The definitions of the four basic t-norms and t-conorms are provided below.

Definition 23.11 (The Four Basic t-Norms). The two-variate cases for the four basic t-norms are given by

Minimum	$T_{min}(x, y)$	$= \min(x, y);$
Product	$T_P(x, y)$	$= xy;$
Łukasiewicz t-norm	$T_L(x, y)$	$= \max(x + y - 1, 0);$
Drastic Product	$T_D(x, y)$	$= \begin{cases} 0, & \text{if } (x, y) \in [0, 1[^2, \\ \min(x, y) & \text{otherwise.} \end{cases}$

Definition 23.12 (The Four Basic t-Conorms). The two-variate cases for the four basic t-conorms are given by

Maximum	$S_{max}(x,y)$	$= \max(x,y);$
Probabilistic Sum	$S_P(x,y)$	$= x+y-xy;$
Łukasiewicz t-conorm	$S_L(x,y)$	$= \min(x+y,1);$
Drastic Product	$S_D(x,y)$	$= \begin{cases} 1, & \text{if } (x,y) \in]0,1]^2, \\ \max(x,y) & \text{otherwise.} \end{cases}$

There are families of parameterized t-norms and t-conorms that include the above as special or limiting cases. These families are defined with respect to generating functions and are known as Archimedean t-norms.

Definition 23.13 (Archimedean t-Norm). A t-norm is called Archimedean if for each $(a,b) \in]0,1[^2$ there is an $n = \{1,2,\ldots\}$ with $T(\overbrace{a,\ldots,a}^{n-times}) < b$.

For t-conorms, the inequality is reversed, i.e. the t-conorm $S > b$. Continuous Archimedean t-norms can be expressed by use of their generators as

$$T(x_1,\ldots,x_n) = g^{(-1)}(g(x_1)+\ldots+g(x_n)),$$

where $g : [0,1] \to [0,\infty]$ with $g(1) = 0$ is a continuous, strictly decreasing function and $g^{(-1)}$ is the pseudo inverse of g, i.e.,

$$g^{(-1)}(x) = g^{-1}(\min(g(1), \max(g(0),x))).$$

Archimedean families include Schweizer-Sklar, Hamacher, Frank, Yager, Dombi, Aczel-Alsina, Mayor-Torrens and Weber-Sugeno t-norms and t-conorms.

23.3.2.5 Nullnorms and Uninorms

In some situations, it may be required that high input values reinforce each other whereas low values pull the overall output down. In other words, the aggregation function has to be disjunctive for high values, conjunctive for low values, and perhaps averaging if some values are high and some are low. This is typically the case when high values are interpreted as "positive" information, and low values as "negative" information.

In other situations, it may be that aggregation of both high and low values moves the output towards some intermediate value. Thus certain aggregation functions need to be conjunctive, disjunctive or averaging in different parts of their domain.

Uninorms and nullnorms are typical examples of such aggregation functions, but there are many others. We provide the following definitions.

Definition 23.14 (Nullnorm). A nullnorm is a bivariate aggregation function $V : [0,1]^2 \to [0,1]$ which is associative, symmetric, such that there exists an element a belonging to the open interval $]0,1[$ verifying

$$\forall t \in [0, a], \quad V(t, 0) = t,$$
$$\forall t \in [a, 1], \quad V(t, 1) = t.$$

Definition 23.15 (Uninorm). A uninorm is a bivariate aggregation function $U : [0, 1]^2 \rightarrow [0, 1]$ which is associative, symmetric and has a neutral element e belonging to the open interval $]0, 1[$.

Some uninorms can be built from generating functions in a similar way to quasi-arithmetic means and Archimedean t-norms. These are called representable uninorms.

Definition 23.16 (Representable Uninorm). Let $u : [0, 1] \rightarrow [-\infty, +\infty]$ be a strictly increasing bijection verifying $g(0) = -\infty, g(1) = +\infty$ such that $g(e) = 0$ for some $e \in]0, 1[$.

- The function given by

$$U(x, y) = \begin{cases} g^{-1}(g(x) + g(y)), & \text{if } (x, y) \in [0, 1]^2 \backslash \{(0, 1), (1, 0)\}, \\ 0, & \text{otherwise.} \end{cases}$$

  is a conjunctive uninorm with the neutral element e, known as a *conjunctive representable uninorm.*
- The function given by

$$U(x, y) = \begin{cases} g^{-1}(g(x) + g(y)), & \text{if } (x, y) \in [0, 1]^2 \backslash \{(0, 1), (1, 0)\}, \\ 1, & \text{otherwise.} \end{cases}$$

  is a disjunctive uninorm with the neutral element e, known as a *disjunctive representable uninorm.*

The $3 - \Pi$ function is an example of a representable uninorm [51]. It uses a generating function $g(x) = \ln(\frac{x}{1-x})$ and is used by the expert system PROSPECTOR [30] for combining uncertainty factors.

$$f(\mathbf{x}) = \frac{\prod_{i=1}^{n} x_i}{\prod_{i=1}^{n} x_i + \prod_{i=1}^{n} (1 - x_i)},$$

with the convention $\frac{0}{0} = 0$. It is conjunctive on $[0, \frac{1}{2}]^n$, disjunctive on $[\frac{1}{2}, 1]^n$ and averaging elsewhere. It is associative, with the neutral element $e = \frac{1}{2}$, and discontinuous on the boundaries of $[0, 1]^n$.

23.4 Construction of Aggregation Functions

There are infinitely many aggregation functions. The question is how to choose the most suitable aggregation function for a specific application. Sometimes one function may suffice for all components of the application, at other times a different type of aggregation may be employed at various stages. The following considerations should be helpful.

23.4.1 Data Collection and Preprocessing

The type of data, and how it is collected affects the way it can be aggregated to form justifications. If users could thoughtfully provide accurate scores on a consistent scale for each item, or numerical descriptions of themselves with their preferences expressed to a degree of certainty, an RS could quite comfortably make some relevant recommendations. Of course, the aesthetic preference is usually to limit the explicit information required from the user and hence enhance the interactive experience. We will briefly consider the different types of data that systems are able to obtain and how this might affect the suitability of certain aggregation functions.

Ordinal Data CF recommenders that ask for explicit ratings information will usually do so on a finite ordinal scale—e.g. {1 = *didn't like it!*,..., 5 = *loved it!*}. On the other hand, it may be possible to convert user actions into ordinal values as part of their profile—e.g. {*regularly views, sometimes views*, etc.}. Ordinal values can be approximated with values over a given numerical scale, however it can be problematic to determine whether, say, the step-size between *fair* and *good* should be the same as between *good* and *very good* or even *fair* and *poor*. The scale granularity may also make the difference between, say, the weighted arithmetic mean and the geometric mean negligible. The Sugeno integral is one such function that is particularly suited to handling ordinal information, since it is built from max and min operations, while the IOWA is able to deal with induced orderings according to an ordinal rather than numerically defined variable.

Numerical Data Where a system is capable of representing user inputs or actions as numerical data, it is useful to take into account whether these values are accurate, whether they are commensurate, and whether they are independent. Functions such as the geometric mean are more influenced by changes to low values than high values, while the arithmetic mean treats high and low inputs the same way. In CF, two users might have similar preferences however one may consistently overrate items. In these cases, it might make sense to standardize the ratings before aggregating so the values between users are comparable. The use of the WAM implies independence between inputs, however other averaging functions, especially the Choquet integral, can express interaction and correlation either among certain inputs or relative scores (see Sect. 23.4.3 below).

Interval or Multiset Data It may be more natural or convenient for information to be collected that incorporates some degree of uncertainty. For example, a user might provide the interval “6 to 8” as their rating for a film. In other circumstances, both positive and negative aspects may be considered as is the case with Atanassov’s extension of fuzzy sets [5]. Whereas a standard fuzzy set usually allocates the degree of membership to a given object, Atanassov’s so-called *intuitionistic* fuzzy sets (AIFS) allocate both a membership and non-membership degree. For example, both the suitable and unsuitable aspects of an item could be summarized with the pair $\langle 0.5, 0.2 \rangle$, where 0.5 is the extent to which it is known that it partially satisfies the buyer’s preferences, while the score of 0.2 is how much it is known that it does not. The gap of 0.3 can be interpreted as a degree of uncertainty. A number of aggregation functions have recently been extended to deal with interval and AIFS inputs (see [10, 15]). For intervals, the most common technique is to aggregate the endpoints of the intervals separately.

Categorical Data In some cases, the use of categorical data may make it impractical to use aggregation functions. If there is no order between categories, it is meaningless to take the *average* or *maximum*, and other techniques may be useful for establishing similarity between users etc. It may be possible to transform the categorical data, for example, by the degree to which it contributes towards a certain archetype in DF.

Data of Varying Dimension Some components of the vectors associated with d_i could be missing—e.g. ratings in CF, or the inputs $d_i = (x_1, \ldots, x_n)$ may have varying dimension by construction. Associativity, LR-Stability and the use of generating functions are all ways of dealing with the problem of varying dimension, whilst maintaining some level of consistency in the way inputs are treated.

23.4.2 Desired Properties, Semantics and Interpretation

The first step in choosing an aggregation function once the data structure is known is usually to decide which class of either averaging, conjunctive, disjunctive or mixed is desired. As discussed in Sect. 23.3.1.1, sometimes it will be more important to have a function which sorts items into order of preference than one which gives easily interpreted outputs. We consider four functions whose semantics can be used to decide which class of function is required:

Minimum (conjunctive) The minimum uses the minimum input as its output. This means the function can only return a high output if all the inputs are high. Such aggregation is useful for certain KB or UB systems using Eq. (23.5) or even CB where it is desired that all the inputs be satisfied. Functions such as the product (T_P) have an accumulative effect for any output which is not perfect, so might be less useful than the min when the dimension is high.

Maximum (disjunctive) Whereas the minimum models AND-like aggregation, disjunctive functions model OR. This type of aggregation results in outputs which are equal to or greater than the highest input. This is useful in KB, UB or CB as well if there are multiple preferences or criteria and one good score is enough justification for recommendation. Consider Example 23.4.

Example 23.4. A user of a CB news recommender has the keywords {*Haruki Murakami, X-Men, bushfires, mathematics, Jupiter orbit*} associated with her profile. It is unlikely that any one news story will be highly relevant to all or even any few of these keywords, so the RS uses disjunctive aggregation as a basis for recommendation.

Arithmetic Mean (averaging) When aggregating user ratings in CF or item features in CB it is reasonable to assume that although scores will vary, if enough inputs are used, the output will be reliable. We do not want the recommendations to be severely affected by an isolated user that is unsatisfied with every item he purchases, or a single feature among twenty or so that is completely satisfied.

Uninorm (mixed) In cases where different behavior is required on different parts of the domain, a mixed aggregation function may be required. This can be as straightforward as deciding that only values with *all* high inputs should be high, or it could be that the bounded behavior affects the accuracy of the function. The use of a uninorm, for instance, allows high values to push the score up and low values to push the score down. An item with consistently high scores would be preferred to one with mostly high scores but one or two low ones.

Certain properties of aggregation functions might also make them appealing. Table 23.1 lists the main aggregation functions we have presented and whether they always, or under certain circumstances, satisfy the properties in Definition 23.3.

23.4.3 Complexity and the Understanding of Function Behavior

In some cases, simple functions such as the WAM will be adequate to meet the goals of recommendation, with potential improvements to the RS lying in other directions. Due to its properties, the WAM is quite a robust and versatile function. It is not biased towards high or low scores, it does not accumulate the effects of errors, it is computationally inexpensive and its common use makes it well understood and easily interpreted. We present the power mean and Choquet integral as two example alternatives whose properties might make them more appropriate in certain situations.

Table 23.1 Aggregation functions and properties

Property	$WAM_\mathbf{w}$	$G_\mathbf{w}$	$H_\mathbf{w}$	$M_{\mathbf{w},[r]}$	C_v	S_v	$OWA_\mathbf{w}$	max	min	T_P	T_L	U	V
Idempotent	◆	◆	◆	◆	◆	◆	◆	◆	◆				
Symmetric	◇	◇	◇	◇	◇	◇	◆	◆	◆	◆	◆	◆	◆
Asymmetric	◇	◇	◇	◇	◇	◇							
Associative								◆	◆	◆	◆	◆	◆
LR-stable	◇	◇	◇	◇	◇	◇	◇	◆	◆				
Strictly monotone	◇			◇	◇	◇	◇						
Shift-invariance	◆			◇	◆	◆	◆	◆	◆				
Homogeneous	◆	◆	◆	◆	◆	◆	◆	◆	◆				
Lipschitz continuous	◆		◆	◇	◆	◆	◆	◆	◆	◆	◆		△
Neutral elements							◇	◆	◆	◆	◆	◆	
Absorbent elements		◆	◆				◇	◆	◆	◆	◆		◆

◆ = always; ◇ = depending on weights; △ = depends on T,S used

$WAM_\mathbf{w}$ weighted arithmetic mean, $G_\mathbf{w}$ weighted geometric mean, $H_\mathbf{w}$ weighted harmonic mean, $M_{\mathbf{w},[r]}$ weighted power mean, C_v Choquet integral, S_v Sugeno integral, $OWA_\mathbf{w}$ ordered weighted averaging operator, *max* maximum, *min* minimum, T_P product T-norm, T_L Łukasiewicz T-norm, U uninorm, V nullnorm

The power mean The power mean is a parameterized function, capable of expressing functions that graduate from the minimum to the maximum including the WAM. This makes it immediately useful when fitting techniques are at our disposal, since we can use the one process to identify any number of functions as the best candidate. Consider the harmonic mean $M_{\mathbf{w},[-1]}$ and the quadratic mean $M_{\mathbf{w},[2]}$. The harmonic mean cannot give an output greater than zero if even one of the inputs is zero. This has the nice interpretation of only allowing items to be considered that at least partially satisfy all criteria, however it is not conjunctive, so still gives a score somewhere between the highest and lowest inputs. The harmonic mean is also concave and its output is equal to or less than the WAM for any choice of d_i. This allows less compensation for low inputs, so items must satisfy more of the criteria overall to rate highly. On the other hand, the quadratic power mean tends more towards high scores, favoring items that have a few very high scores which compensate more for low-scoring features or ratings.

The Choquet integral As with the power mean, the Choquet integral is capable of expressing functions ranging between the minimum and maximum. The use of the Choquet integral is most interesting in asymmetric situations where there tends to be some correlation. For example, in a KB recommender, sometimes preferences will be contradictory while at other times one implies the other. In the case of Entree [21], it is noted that users might demonstrate a preference for *inexpensive* and *nice* restaurants. Since usually some trade-off is involved, a restaurant that does satisfy these criteria should be especially rewarded when it comes to recommendation. In the case of CB movie recommendation, it could be that a user likes *Johnny Depp* and *Tim Burton*. As there is a high frequency of films which are directed by Tim Burton that also star Johnny Depp, it might not make sense to *double-count* these features. The Choquet integral can account for a combination of these situations, since a weight is allocated to each subset of criteria. The subset of "stars Depp AND is directed by Burton" would be allocated less weight than the sum of its parts, while inexpensive and nice restaurants in the KB example would be allocated more.

Of course, sometimes the structure of the data might be difficult to understand and interpret towards the use of a particular function. In these cases, it might be worthwhile to check the accuracy of a number of functions on a subset of the data. A comparison of the minimum, maximum, arithmetic mean and harmonic mean could suggest much about which functions will be useful.

23.4.4 Penalty-Based Construction

The problem of choosing the most appropriate aggregation function can also be framed in terms of penalties [22]. For instance, the weighted arithmetic mean of an input set is the value y which minimizes,

$$P(\mathbf{x}, y) = \sum_{j=1}^{n} w_j (x_j - y)^2.$$

In this case, we use the squared distance for the partial penalty for each variable. If the squared distance is replaced with the absolute value $p(x_i, y) = |x_j - y|$ then we have a weighted median, and if we can use the generator transformations $p(x_i, y) = (g(x_j) - g(y))$, then we obtain the quasi-arithmetic means. In order for this minimization to result in aggregation functions, $P(\mathbf{x}, y)$ should satisfy the following definition.

Definition 23.17. A penalty function $P : [0, 1]^{n+1} \to [0, \infty)$ satisfies:

i) $P(\mathbf{x}, y) \geq 0$ for all $\mathbf{x}, y$;
ii) $P(\mathbf{x}, y) = 0$ if and only if $x_i = y \; \forall i$;
iii) For every fixed $\mathbf{x}$, the set of minimizers of $P(\mathbf{x}, y)$ is either a singleton or an interval.

The penalty based function is then given by

$$f(\mathbf{x}) = \arg\min_{y} P(\mathbf{x}, y),$$

if y is the unique minimizer, and $y = \frac{a+b}{2}$ if the set of minimizers is the interval (a, b) (open or closed).

The penalty-based framework also allows us to choose the output from a finite set of options. So in recommendation we can find the predicted rating $R(u, d_i)$ from a discrete rating scale, e.g. $\mathcal{R} = \{1, 2, \ldots, 7\}$ which minimizes our desired penalty. In collaborative filtering, this would be expressed,

$$\arg \min_{R(u,d_i) \in \mathcal{R}} \sum_{j=1}^{k} sim(u, u_j) p(R(u_j, d_i), R(u, d_i)).$$

The partial penalties p can also be chosen such that different penalties are used for different users or items depending on our knowledge about relationships in the rating patterns.

23.4.5 *Weight and Parameter Determination*

The determination of weights for use in ratings aggregation for CF is often understood in terms of the similarity between users and neighborhood formation. Weights in CB and UB are a measure of the importance of each feature to the user, while the weights in weighted HS are indicative of the reliability of each component in recommendation. Weights can be selected using predetermined measures like cosine, or might be decided in advance by the RS designers—e.g. we decide to weight the similar users with a decreasing weighting vector $\mathbf{w} = (0.4, 0.3, 0.2, 0.1)$. Some systems adjust weights incrementally according to implicit or explicit feedback concerning the quality of recommendation, for instance in the hybrid recommender system, P-Tango [25]. In Sect. 23.5, programming methods are discussed for determining weights from available data-sets.

23.5 Sophisticated Aggregation Procedures in Recommender Systems: Tailoring for Specific Applications

We consider the fitting problem in terms of a CF recommender, however it is also possible to fit weights in CB and UB recommender systems provided the system has access to input and output values so that the strength of fit can affirm the suitability of the weights or parameters. Fitting can be accomplished by means of interpolation or approximation. In the case of interpolation, the aim is to fit the specified output values exactly (in the case of aggregation functions, the pairs $((0, 0, \ldots, 0), 0)$ and $((1, 1, \ldots, 1), 1)$ should always be interpolated). In the case of RS, the data will normally contain some errors or degree of approximation, and therefore it may not be appropriate to interpolate the inaccurate values. In this case our aim is to stay close to the desired outputs without actually matching them. This is the approximation problem.

The selection of an aggregation function can be stated formally as follows:

Given a number of mathematical properties $P_1, P_2, \ldots$ and a dataset $D = \{(\mathbf{x}_k, y_k)\}_{k=1}^{K}$, choose an aggregation function f consistent with $P_1, P_2, \ldots$, and satisfying $f(\mathbf{x}_k) \approx y_k, k = 1, \ldots, K$.

We can also vary the problem to accommodate fitting to intervals, i.e. we require $f(\mathbf{x}_k) \in [\underline{y}_k, \overline{y}_k]$. How these values are specified will depend on the application. In some cases it may be possible to fit the function exactly without violating any of the desired properties, however most of the time we merely want to minimize the error of approximation. Mathematically, the satisfaction of approximate equalities $f(\mathbf{x}_k) \approx y_k$ can be translated into the following minimization problem.

$$\text{minimize } ||\mathbf{r}|| \tag{23.10}$$
$$\text{subject to } f \text{ satisfies } \mathcal{P}_1, \mathcal{P}_2, \ldots,$$

where $||\mathbf{r}||$ is the norm of the residuals, i.e., $\mathbf{r} \in R^K$ is the vector of the differences between the predicted and observed values $r_k = f(\mathbf{x}_k) - y_k$. There are many ways to choose the norm, and the most popular are the least squares norm and the least absolute deviation norm, respectively given by

Table 23.2 Example dataset for mutually rated items in CF

	Items $i = 1..10$ rated by user and neighbors										Unrated	
User ratings $R(u, d_i)$	6	4	6	8	10	5	7	7	5	5	?	?
Neighbor ratings												
$R(u_1, d_i)$	4	4	4	8	10	3	7	5	3	3	4	7
$R(u_2, d_i)$	6	0	6	4	6	1	3	3	1	5	8	7
$R(u_3, d_i)$	3	1	8	5	7	2	4	4	2	2	7	5
$R(u_4, d_i)$	6	5	6	8	8	6	5	5	3	5	3	8
$R(u_5, d_i)$	6	4	6	7	8	1	5	8	5	8	5	9

$$||\mathbf{r}||_2 = \left(\sum_{k=1}^{K} r_k^2\right)^{1/2}, \qquad ||\mathbf{r}||_1 = \sum_{k=1}^{K} |r_k|,$$

or their weighted analogues if some of the y_k are considered less reliable than others.

Consider Example 23.5.[5]

Example 23.5. In a CF recommending application we want to use five similar users to predict the ratings of new objects for a given user. At hand we have a data set of many items previously rated by the user and the five similar users or neighbors $\{(d_i, R(u, d_i))\}_{i=1}^{1}0$ where $d_i = (R(u_1, d_i), \ldots, R(u_5, d_i))$ denotes the ratings given by each of the neighbors $u_1, \ldots, u_5$ to a past item d_i, and the $R(u, d_i)$ are the user's actual ratings. I.e. $d_i = \mathbf{x}_k, R(u, d_i) = y_k$ from above. Table 23.2 shows an example data set with two items rated by the neighbors which the user is yet to rate and could be recommended. We want to define a weighted arithmetic mean using the least squares approach that assigns a weight w_i to each user. So we have

$$\text{minimize} \sum_{i=1}^{10} \left(\sum_{j=1}^{5} w_j R(u_j, d_i) - R(u, d_i) \right)^2$$

$$\text{subject to} \qquad \sum_{j=1}^{5} w_j = 1,$$

$$w_1, \ldots, w_5 \geq 0.$$

(continued)

[5]All examples in this section utilize the software packages *aotool* and *fmtools* [9]. Versions have also been created in the R programming language, available at *http://aggregationfunctions.wordpress.com/r-code* and *http://www.tulip.org.au/resources/rfmtool*.

Example 23.5 (continued)
This is a quadratic programming problem, which is solved by a number of standard methods. In the current example one resulting model allocates the weights $\mathbf{w} =< 0.27, 0.07, 0.06, 0.19, 0.41 >$ with recommendation scores of 4.7 and 7.9 for the unrated items. The maximum difference between observed and predicted ratings is 2.45 with an average of 0.98. If we had instead used the cosine calculation to define the weights, we would have $\mathbf{w} =< 0.19, 0.24, 0.23, 0.18, 0.17 >$ and recommendation scores of 5.6 and 7.1. The accuracy is similar for this method, with maximum error 2.48 and average error 1.6. Interestingly u_5 was least similar using this measure, but most important when accurately predicting the ratings for u.

As mentioned, if the number of items to be recommended is limited, the ranking, rather than the accuracy of prediction becomes crucial (see also [33]). In situations where it makes sense, the ranking of the outputs can be preserved with $f(R(u_1, d_k), \ldots, R(u_n, d_k)) \leq f(R(u_1, d_l), \ldots, R(u_n, d_l))$ if $R(u, d_k) \leq R(u, d_l)$ for all pairs k, l added as an extra constraint. In CF, imposing this condition weights the similar users higher who have rankings that better reflect the user's. This is useful when we know that some users might tend to overrate or underrate items, but will be consistent in terms of the items they prefer.

The approximation problem thus far described may turn out to be a general non-linear optimization problem, or a problem from a special class. Some optimization problems utilize a convex objective function, in which case the difficulty is not so much in finding a feasible solution, but rather in feasibly defining the constraints. Fitting the Choquet integral, for instance has an exponential number of constraints which need to be defined. Many problems, however can be specified as linear or quadratic programming problems, which have been extensively studied with many solution techniques available. Example 23.6 uses the same dataset (Table 23.2) with the Choquet integral as the desired function. In practice, it would be preferable to have a much larger data set for the Choquet integral (i.e. the number of instances should be well above the 2^n points required to define it to reduce the chance of overfitting).

Example 23.6. (Continued from Example 23.5)...The system designers decide that they would prefer to use a Choquet integral to predict the unknown ratings. To make the fitting process less susceptible to outliers, they decide to use the least absolute deviation norm and express the optimization process as the following.

(continued)

Example 23.6 (continued)

$$\text{minimize} \qquad \sum_{i=1}^{5} |C_v(d_i) - R(u, d_i)|$$

$$\text{subject to} \quad v(A) - v(B) \geq 0, \text{ for all } B \subseteq A,$$

$$v(A) \geq 0, \forall A \subset \mathcal{N}, v(\emptyset) = 0, v(\mathcal{N}) = 1$$

This results in a Choquet integral defined by a fuzzy measure with the following values

$$v(\{1\}) = 1, v(\{2\}) = 0.33, v(\{3\}) = 0, v(\{4\}) = v(\{5\}) = 0.67$$

$$v(\{2,3\}) = 0.33, v(\{2,4\}) = v(\{3,4\}) = v(\{3,5\}) = v(\{2,3,4\}) = 0.67$$

$$v(A) = 1 \text{ for all other subsets.}$$

The Shapley values provide a good indication of the influence of each of the neighbors, and are given as

$$\phi_1 = 0.39, \phi_2 = 0.11, \phi_3 = 0, \phi_4 = 0.22, \phi_5 = 0.28$$

As with the weighted arithmetic mean, the values suggest that neighbors 1, 4 and 5 are perhaps more similar to the given user. We also note the interaction indices for pairs, given as

$$I_{12} = I_{24} = I_{45} = -0.17, I_{14} = -0.33, I_{15} = -0.5$$

$$I_{ij} = 0 \text{ for all other pairs.}$$

This shows the redundancy between some of the neighbors. In particular, neighbors 1 and 5 are very similar. The maximum error in this case is 1.6 and the average error is 0.6, with resulting recommendations 6.0 and 8.7. Because of the substitutive variables, the function behaves similar to a maximum function. We see the high score given for the latter item, mainly due to the high ratings given by neighbors 4 and 5.

The families of aggregation functions defined in Sect. 23.3.2 are convenient to use when trying to understand and interpret the results. The weights and parameters have a tangible meaning and fitting these functions essentially involves finding the best values for each parameter to maximize the reliability of the RS.

In other situations however, the interpretation side of things may not be as important: we just want to predict the unknown ratings reliably and automatically. There are many non-parametric methods for building aggregation functions, which do not have the advantage of system interpretation, however can be constructed automatically and fit the data closely. One "black-box" type method is to build a general aggregation operator piecewise from the data. We can ensure that monotonicity and boundary conditions are specified by smoothing the data and ensuring these properties hold for each individual segment. We consider here, the construction of spline based aggregation functions [12].

Monotone tensor product splines are defined as

$$f_B(x_1,\dots,x_n) = \sum_{j_1=1}^{J_1}\sum_{j_2=1}^{J_2}\dots\sum_{j_n=1}^{J_n} c_{j_1 j_2 \dots j_n} B_{j_1}(x_1)B_{j_2}(x_2)\dots B_{j_n}(x_n).$$

If it is desired the built function belong to a particular class or hold certain properties, additional constraints can be added when fitting. In particular, we can ensure monotonicity holds by expressing linear conditions on the coefficients $c_{j_1 j_2 \dots j_n}$. The fitting of this function to data involves sparse matrices, their size increasing with the number of basis functions in respect to each variable and exponentially with n. We give an example of this fitting process in the Example 23.7.

Example 23.7. (Continued from Examples 23.5–23.6)... It is not necessary in our application that the weighting of similar users be known. We simply want automatically built functions that can predict the ratings of unseen items. We decide that we still desire the properties of monotonicity and idempotency to ensure reliable outputs, and build a general aggregation operator represented by tensor product splines. The following quadratic programming problem is used.

$$\text{minimize} \quad \sum_{i=1}^{5} (f_B(d_i) - R(u,d_i))^2$$

$$\text{subject to} \quad \sum_{j_1=1}^{J_1}\sum_{j_2=1}^{J_2}\dots\sum_{j_n=1}^{J_n} c_{j_1 j_2 \dots j_n} \geq 0,$$

$$f_B(0,\dots,0) = 0, f_B(1,\dots,1) = 0$$

Idempotency is also ensured by imposing a number of interpolation conditions such that $f_B(t_i,\dots,t_i) = t_i$. These conditions must be chosen in a certain way (see [7, 8]). The fitted non-parametric function gives resulting recommendation scores for the unrated items of 4.2 and 8.1 so it seems that the latter item should be suggested to the user.

Clearly it is the choice of system designers as to whether to use non-parametric or parametric methods, and how complex an aggregation function should be used. Recommender systems usually require timely decisions and deal with large data sets, so a compromise between expressibility and simplicity is usually sought.

23.6 Conclusions

The purpose of this chapter has been to present the state of the art in aggregation functions and introduce established families of these functions that have properties useful for the purposes of recommendation. This has included means defined with various weights, Choquet integrals defined with respect to fuzzy measures, t-norms/t-conorms which can be built from generators, and representable uninorms. Many of the current methods used in recommender systems involve constructing weighted arithmetic means where weights are determined by varying measures of similarity, however in many cases the accuracy and flexibility of functions could be improved with only slight increases to complexity. We have provided a number of illustrative examples of the different ways in which aggregation functions can be applied to recommendation processes including ratings aggregation, feature combination, similarity and neighborhood formation and component combination in weighted hybrid recommender system. We also referred to some current software tools which can be used to fit these functions to data (see also [32, 35]) when we are trying to find weights, similarity or the parameters used that best model the dataset.

References

1. Adomavicius, G., Sankaranarayanan, R., Sen, S., and Tuzhilin, A.: Incorporating contextual information in recommender systems using a multi-dimensional approach, ACM Transactions on information systems, **23**(1), 103–145 (2005)
2. Adomavicius, G. and Kwon, Y.: New Recommendation Techniques for Multicriteria Rating Systems. IEEE Intelligent Systems, **22**(3), 48–55 (2007)
3. Ahn, H.J.: A new similarity measure for collaborative filtering to alleviate the new user cold-starting problem. Information Sciences, **178**, 37–51 (2008)
4. Al-Shamri, M.Y.H. and Bharadwaj, K.K.: Fuzzy-genetic approach to recommender systems based on a novel hybrid user model. Expert Systems with Applications, **35**, 1386–1399 (2008)
5. Atanassov, K.: Intuitionistic fuzzy sets. Fuzzy Sets and Systems, **20**, 87–96 (1986)
6. Balabanovic, M. and Shoham, Y.: Fab: Content-Based, Collaborative Recommendation. Comm. ACM, **40**(3), 66–72 (1997)
7. Beliakov, G.: Monotone approximation of aggregation operators using least squares splines. Int. J. of Uncertainty, Fuzziness and Knowledge-Based Systems, **10**, 659–676 (2002)
8. Beliakov, G.: How to build aggregation operators from data? Int. J. Intelligent Systems, **18**, 903–923 (2003)
9. Beliakov, G.: FMTools package, version 1.0, http://www.deakin.edu.au/~gleb/aotool.html, (2007)
10. Beliakov, G., Bustince, H., Goswami, D.P., Mukherjee, U.K. and Pal, N.R.: On averaging operators for Atanassov's intuitionistic fuzzy sets. Information Sciences, **181**, 1116–1124 (2011)
11. Beliakov, G. and Calvo, T.: Construction of Aggregation Operators With Noble Reinforcement. IEEE Transactions on Fuzzy Systems, **15**(6), 1209–1218 (2007)
12. Beliakov, G., Pradera, A. and Calvo, T.: Aggregation Functions: A guide for practitioners. Springer, Heidelberg, Berlin, New York (2007)
13. Beliakov, G., Calvo, T. and James, S: On Lipschitz properties of generated aggregation functions. Fuzzy Sets and Systems, **161**, 1437–1447 (2009)

14. Beliakov, G. and James, S: Using Choquet Integrals for kNN Approximation and Classification. In Gary G. Feng (ed.), 2008 IEEE International Conference on Fuzzy Systems (FUZZ-IEEE 2008), 1311–1317 (2008)
15. Beliakov, G. and James, S: On extending generalized Bonferroni means to Atanassov orthopairs in decision making contexts, Fuzzy Sets and Systems, **211**, 84–98 (2013)
16. Beliakov, G. and James, S: Stability of weighted penalty-based aggregation functions, Fuzzy Sets and Systems, **226**, 1–18 (2013)
17. Bobadilla, J., Ortega, F., Hernando, A. and Gutiérrez, A.: Recommender systems survey, Knowledge-Based Systems, **46**, 109–132 (2013)
18. Bolton, J., Gader, P. and Wilson, J.N.: Discrete Choquet Integral as a Distance Metric. IEEE Trans. on Fuzzy Systems, **16**(4), 1107–1110 (2008)
19. Buchanan, B. and Shortliffe, E.: Rule-based Expert Systems: The MYCIN Experiments of the Stanford Heuristic Programming Project. Addison-Wesley, Reading, MA (1984)
20. Bullen, P.S.: Handbook of Means and Their Inequalities. Kluwer, Dordrecht (2003)
21. Burke, R.: Hybrid Recommender Systems: Survey and Experiments, User Modeling and User-adapted interaction, **12**(4), 331–370 (2002)
22. Calvo, T. and Beliakov, G.: Aggregation functions based on penalties, Fuzzy Sets and Systems, **161**, 1420–1436 (2010)
23. Calvo, T., Kolesárová, A., Komorníková, M. and Mesiar, R.: Aggregation operators: properties, classes and construction methods. In : Calvo, T., Mayor, G. and Mesiar, R. (eds.) Aggregation Operators. New Trends and Applications, pp. 3–104. Physica-Verlag, Heidelberg, New York (2002)
24. Chen, Y.-L. and Cheng, L.-C.: A novel collaborative filtering approach for recommending ranked items. Expert Systems with Applications, **34**, 2396–2405 (2008)
25. Claypool, M., Gokhale, A., Miranda, T., Murnikov, P., Netes, D. and Sartin, M.: Combining Content-Based and Collaborative Filters in an Online Newspaper. In Proceedings of SIGIR 99 Workshop on Recommender Systems: Algorithms and Evaluation, Berkeley, CA (1999)
26. Campos, L.M.d., Fernández-Luna, J.M. and Huete, J.F.: A collaborative recommender system based on probabilistic inference from fuzzy observations. Fuzzy Sets and Systems, **159**, 1554–1576 (2008)
27. Dubois, D. and Prade, H.: Fuzzy Sets and Systems: Theory and Applications. Academic Press, New York (1980)
28. Dubois, D. and Prade, H.: Fundamentals of Fuzzy Sets. Kluwer, Boston (2000)
29. Dubois, D., Hllermeier, E., and Prade, H.: Fuzzy methods for case-based recommendation and decision support. J. Intell. Inform. Systems, **27**(2), 95–115 (2006)
30. Duda, R. Hart, P. and Nilsson, N.: Subjective Bayesian methods for rule-based inference systems. In Proc. Nat. Comput. Conf. (AFIPS), volume 45, 1075–1082 (1976)
31. Garcia, I., Sebastia, L. and Onaindia, E.: On the design of individual and group recommender systems for tourism, Expert Systems with Applications, **38**, 7683–7692 (2011)
32. Grabisch, M., Kojadinovic, I., and Meyer, P.: A review of methods for capacity identification in Choquet integral based multi-attribute utility theory: Applications of the Kappalab R package. European Journal of Operational Research. **186**, 766–785 (2008)
33. Kaymak, U. and van Nauta Lemke, H.R.: Selecting an aggregation operator for fuzzy decision making. In 3rd IEEE Intl. Conf. on Fuzzy Systems, volume 2, 1418–1422 (1994)
34. Klement, E.P., Mesiar, R. and Pap, E.: Triangular Norms. Kluwer, Dordrecht, (2000)
35. Kojadinovic, I. and Grabisch, M.: Non additive measure and integral manipulation functions, *R* package version 0.2, http://www.polytech.univ-nantes.fr/kappalab, (2005)
36. Krawczyk, H., Knopa, R., Lipczynska, K., and Lipczynski, M.: Web-based Endoscopy Recommender System - ERS. In International Conference on Parallel Computing in Electrical Engineering (PARELEC'00), Quebec, Canada, 257–261 (2000)
37. Linden, G., Smith, B., and York, J.: Amazon.com recommendations: Item-to-item collaborative filtering. IEEE Internet Computing, **7**(1), 76–80 (2003)
38. Mayor, G., and Calvo, T.: Extended aggregation functions. In IFSA'97, volume 1, Prague, 281–285 (1997)

39. Miller, B.N., Albert, I., Lam, S.K., Konstan, J.A., and Riedl, J.: MovieLens unplugged: experiences with an occasionally connected recommender system. In Proceedings of the 8th international ACM conference on Intelligent user interfaces, Miami, USA, 263–266 (2003)
40. Resnick, P., Iakovou, N., Sushak, M., Bergstrom, P., and Riedl, J.: GroupLens: An open architecture for collaborative filtering of Netnews. In Proceedings of ACM conference on computer supported cooperative work, Chapel Hill, NC, 175–186 (1994)
41. Rojas, K., G6mez, D., Montero, J., and Rodríguez, J. T.: Strictly stable families of aggregation operators, Fuzzy Sets and Systems, **228**, 44–63 (2013)
42. Salton, G. and McGill, M.: Introduction to Modern Information retrieval. McGraw Hill, New York (1983)
43. Schafer, J.B., Konstan, J.A., and Riedl, J.: E-commerce recommendation applications, Data Mining and Knowledge Discover, **5**, 115–153 (2001)
44. Santini, S. and Jain, R.: Similarity Measures. IEEE Transactions on Pattern Analysis and Machine Intelligence, **21**(9), 871–883 (1999)
45. Ujjin, S., and Bentley, P.: Using evolutionary to learn user preferences. In: Tan, K., Lim, M., Yao, X. and Wang, L. (eds.). Recent advances in simulated evolution and learning, pp. 20–40. World Scientific Publishing (2004)
46. Victor, P., Cornelis, C., De Cock, M. and Herrera-Viedma, E.: Practical aggregation operators for gradual trust and distrust, Fuzzy Sets and Systems, **184**, 126–147 (2011)
47. Vu, H. Q., Beliakov, G., and Li, G.: A Choquet integral toolbox and its application in customers preference analysis, in Data Mining Applications with *R*, Elsevier (2013)
48. Yager, R.: On ordered weighted averaging aggregation operators in multicriteria decision making. IEEE Trans. on Systems, Man and Cybernetics, **18**, 183–190 (1988)
49. Yager, R.: Noble Reinforcement in Disjunctive Aggregation Operators. IEEE Transactions on Fuzzy Systems, **11(6)** 754–767 (2003)
50. Yager, R. R. and Filev, D. P.: Induced ordered weighted averaging operators. IEEE Transactions on Systems, Man, and Cybernetics – Part B: Cybernetics, **20**(2), 141–150 (1999)
51. Yager, R. and Rybalov. A.: Uninorm aggregation operators. Fuzzy Sets and Systems, **80**, 111–120 (1996)

Chapter 24
Active Learning in Recommender Systems

Neil Rubens, Mehdi Elahi, Masashi Sugiyama, and Dain Kaplan

24.1 Introduction

Recommender Systems (RSs) are often assumed to present items to users for one reason—to *recommend* items a user will likely be interested in. However, there is another reason for presenting items to users: to learn more about their preferences. This is where Active Learning (AL) comes in. Augmenting RSs with AL helps the user become more self-aware of their own likes/dislikes while at the same time providing new information to the system that it can analyze for subsequent recommendations. In essence, applying AL to RSs allows for personalization of the recommending process, a concept that makes sense as recommending is inherently geared towards personalization. This is accomplished by letting the system actively influence which items the user is exposed to (e.g. the items displayed to the user during sign-up or during regular use), and letting the user explore his/her interests freely.

Unfortunately, there are very few opportunities for the system to acquire information, such as when a user rates/reviews an item, or through a user's browsing history. Since these opportunities are few, we want to be as sure as possible that the data we acquire tells us something *important* about the user's preferences. After all, one of the most valuable assets of a company is user data.

N. Rubens (✉)
University of Electro-Communications, Tokyo, Japan
e-mail: rubens@hrstc.org

M. Elahi
Free University of Bozen-Bolzano, Bolzano, Italy
e-mail: mehdi.elahi@unibz.it

M. Sugiyama • D. Kaplan
Tokyo Institute of Technology, Tokyo, Japan
e-mail: sugi@cs.titech.ac.jp; dain@cl.cs.titech.ac.jp

F. Ricci et al. (eds.), *Recommender Systems Handbook*,
DOI 10.1007/978-1-4899-7637-6_24

For example, when a new user starts using a recommender system, very little is known about his/her preferences [2, 47, 55]. A common approach to learning the user's preferences is to ask him/her to rate a number of items (known as training points). A model that approximates their preferences is then constructed from this data. Since the number of items reviewed by the user cannot span the system's entire catalog (and indeed would make the task of AL as well as *recommending* moot points), the collection of items presented to the user for review must necessarily be very limited. The accuracy of the learned model thus greatly depends on the selection of good training points. A system might ask the user to rate *Star Wars I*, *II*, and *III*. By rating all three volumes of this trilogy, we will have a good idea of the user's preferences for *Star Wars*, and maybe by extension, an inclination for other movies within the Sci-Fi genre, but overall the collected knowledge will be limited. It is therefore unlikely that picking the three volumes of a trilogy will be informative.[1] Another issue with selecting a popular item such as *Star Wars* is that by definition the majority of people like them (or they would not be popular). It is not surprising then, that often little insight is gained by selecting popular items to learn about the user (unless the user's tastes are atypical).

There is a notion that AL is a bothersome, intrusive process, but it does not have to be this way [50, 66]. If the items presented to the user are interesting, it could be both a process of discovery and of exploration. Some Recommender Systems provide a "surprise me!" button to motivate the user into this explorative process, and indeed there are users who browse suggestions just to see what there is without any intention of buying. Exploration is crucial for users to become more self-aware of their own preferences (changing or not) and at the same time inform the system of what they are. Keep in mind that in a sense users can also be defined by the items they consume, *not* only by the ratings of their items, so by prompting users to rate different items it may be possible to further distinguish their preferences from one another and enable the system to provide better personalization and to better suit their needs.

This chapter is only a brief foray into Active Learning in Recommender Systems.[2] We hope that this chapter can, however, provide the necessary foundations.

For further reading, [57] gives a good, general overview of AL in the context of Machine Learning (with a focus on Natural Language Processing and Bioinformatics). For a theoretical perspective related to AL (a major focus in the field of Experimental Design), see [4, 7, 28]; there have also been recent works in Computer Science [5, 17, 62].

---

[1]Unless our goal is to learn a kind of micro-preference, which we can define as a person's tendency to be more "picky" concerning alternatives close to one another in an genre they like.

[2]Supplementary materials on Active Learning can be found at: http://ActiveIntelligence.org.

24.1.1 Objectives of Active Learning in Recommender Systems

Different RSs have different objectives (Chap. 8), which necessitate different objectives for their Active Learning components as well. As a result, one AL method may be better suited than another for satisfying a given task [46]. For example, what is important in the recommender system being built (Chap. 9)? The difficulty of signing-up (user effort)? If the user is happy with the service (user satisfaction)? How well the system can predict a user's preferences (accuracy)? How well the system can express a user's preferences (user utility)? How well the system can serve other users by what it learns from this one (system utility)? System functionality may also be important, such as when a user inquires about a rating for an item of interest the system has insufficient data to predict a rating for, what the system does in response. Does it in such a case give an ambiguous answer, allowing the user to train the system further if they have the interest and the time to do so? Or does it require them to rate several other items before providing a prediction? Perhaps the user has experienced the item (e.g. watched the movie or trailer) and thinks their rating differs substantially from the predicted one [11]. In all these cases how the system responds to the user is important for consideration.

Traditionally AL does not consider the trade-off of exploration (learning user's preferences) and exploitation (utilizing user's preferences), that is, it does not dynamically assign weights to exploitation/exploration depending on system objectives. This trade-off is important because for a new user about which nothing or little is known, it may be beneficial to validate the worth of the system by providing predictions the user is likely to be interested in (exploitation), while long-term users may wish to expand their interests through exploration [50, 52].

Though an objective of the RS will likely be to provide accurate predictions to the user, the system may also need to recommend items of high novelty/serendipity Chap. 26, improve coverage, maximize profitability, or determine if the user is even able to evaluate a given item, to name a few [27, 43, 55]. Multiple objectives may need to be considered simultaneously (Chap. 25), e.g. minimizing the net acquisition cost of training data *while* maximizing net profit, or finding the best match between the cost of offering an item to the user, the utility associated with expected output, and the alternative utility of inaction [50]. The utility of training may also be important, e.g. predicting ratings for exotic cars may not be so useful if the user is not capable of purchasing them and so should be avoided. It can be seen that the system objective is often much more complex than mere predictive accuracy, and may include the combination of several objectives.

While Recommender Systems often have an ill-defined or open-ended objective, namely to predict items a user would be "interested" in, Conversation-based AL [9, 42, 49], as the name suggests, engages in a conversation with the user as a goal oriented approach. It seeks to, through each iteration of questioning, elicit a response from the user to best reduce the search space for quickly finding what it is the user seeks (see Sect. 24.7).

The New User Problem When a user starts using a RS they expect to see interesting results after a minimal amount of training. Though the system knows little about their preferences, it is essential that training points are selected for rating by the user that will maximize understanding what the new user wants [46].

The New Product Problem As new products are introduced into the system, it is important to quickly improve prediction accuracy for these items by selecting users to rate them [30].

Cost of Obtaining an Output Value Different means of obtaining an output value come at different costs. Implicit strategies, such as treating a user click on a suggested item as positive output, or not clicking as negative, are inexpensive in relation to user effort. Conversely, asking the user to explicitly rate an item is more costly, though still dependent on the task. Watching a movie like Star Wars to rate may provide good results but requires substantial user effort [25]; rating a joke requires much less. This often dovetails the exploration/exploitation coupling and trade-offs between obtaining outputs from different inputs should also be considered (e.g. certainty/uncertainty, ease of evaluation, etc.)

Adaptation for Different AL Methods Though we focus on the traditional objective of reducing predictive error, it is equally plausible to construct a method for maximizing other goals, such as profitability. In this case a model would pick points that most likely increase profit rather than a rating's accuracy.

24.1.2 An Illustrative Example

Let's look at a concrete example of Active Learning in a Recommender System. This is only meant to demonstrate concepts, so it is oversimplified. Please note that the similarity metric may differ depending on the method used; here, movies are assumed to be close to one another if they belong to the same genre. Figure 24.1 on page 813 shows two charts, the leftmost is our starting state, in which we have already asked the user to rate a movie within the upper right group, which we will say is the Sci-Fi genre. The right chart shows us four possibilities for selecting our next training point: (a), (b), (c), or (d). If we select the training point (a) which is an obscure movie (like *The Goldfish Hunter*), it does not affect our predictions because no other movies (points) are nearby. If we select the training point (b), we can predict the values for the points in the same area, but these predictions are already possible from the training point in the same area (refer to the chart on the left). If training point (c) is selected, we are able to make new predictions, but only for the other

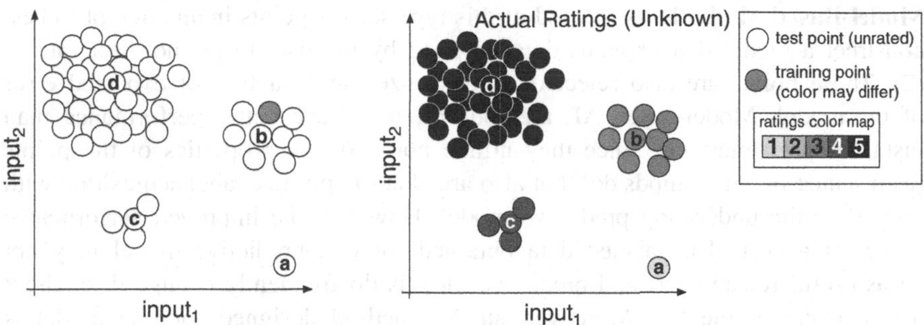

Fig. 24.1 Active Learning: illustrative example (See Sect. 24.1.2)

three points in this area, which happens to be Zombie movies. By selecting training point (d), we are able to make predictions for a large number of test points that are in the same area, which belong to Comedy movies. Thus selecting (d) is the ideal choice because it allows us to improve accuracy of predictions the most (for the highest number of training points).[3]

24.1.3 Types of Active Learning

AL methods presented in this chapter have been categorized based on our interpretation of their primary motivation/goal. It is important to note, however, that various ways of classification may exist for a given method, e.g. sampling close to a decision boundary may be considered as Output Uncertainty-based since the outputs are unknown, Parameter-based because the point will alter the model, or even Decision boundary-based because the boundary lines will shift as a result. However, since the sampling is performed with regard to decision boundaries, we would consider this the primary motivation of this method and classify it as such.

In addition to our categorization by primary motivation (Sect. 24.1), we further subclassify a method's algorithms into two commonly classified types for easier comprehension: instance-based and model-based.

Instance-Based Methods A method of this type selects points based on their properties in an attempt to predict the user's ratings by finding the closest match to other users in the system, without explicit knowledge of the underlying model. Other common names for this type include memory-based, lazy learning, case-based, and non-parametric [2].

[3]This may be dependent on the specific prediction method used in the RS.

Model-Based Methods A method of this type selects points in an attempt to best construct a model that explains data supplied by the user to predict user ratings [2]. These points are also selected to maximize the reduction of expected error of the model. Model-based AL methods often achieve better performance than instance-based methods, since they utilize not only the properties of the points (as instance-based methods do), but also are able to optimize label acquisition with regards to the underlying predictive model. However, the improved performance comes at a cost. The labeled data obtained for one predictive model may not be as useful for another; and predictive models do frequently change throughout the lifecycle of the RS. Moreover, an AL method designed for one model is often incompatible with a different model since model-based AL methods rely on access to specific parameters of a model and the model's estimates (e.g. not all of the models are able to provide a distribution of rating estimates, and models are parameterized differently); this might necessitate using a different AL method each time the predictive model changes.

Modes of Active Learning: Batch and Sequential Because users typically want to see the system output something interesting immediately, a common approach is to recompute a user's predicted ratings after they have rated a single item, in a sequential manner. It is also possible, however, to allow a user to rate several items, or several features of an item before readjusting the model. On the other hand, selecting training points sequentially has the advantage of allowing the system to react to the data provided by users and make necessary adjustments immediately. Though this comes at the cost of interaction with the user at each step. Thus a trade-off exists between Batch and Sequential AL: the usefulness of the data vs. the number of interactions with the user.

24.2 Properties of Data Points

When considering any Active Learning method, the following three factors should always be considered in order to maximize the effectiveness of a given point. Supplementary explanations are then given below for the first two. Examples refer to the Illustrative Example (Fig. 24.1 on page 813).

(R1) *Represented*: Is it already represented by the existing training set? E.g. point (b).

(R2) *Representative*: Is the point a good candidate for representing other data points? Or is it an outlier? E.g. point (a).

(R3) *Results*: Will selecting this point result in better prediction ratings or accomplish another objective? E.g. point (d), or even point (c).

(R1) Represented by the Training Data As explained in the introduction to this chapter, asking for ratings of multiple volumes from a trilogy, such as *Star Wars*, is likely not beneficial, as it may not substantially contribute to the acquisition of *new* information about the user's preferences. To avoid obtaining redundant information, therefore an active learning method should favor items that are not yet well represented by the training set [23].

(R2) Representative of the Test Data It is important that any item selected for being rated by an AL algorithm be as representative of the test items as possible (we consider all items as potentially belonging to the test set), since the accuracy of the algorithm will be evaluated based on these items. If a movie is selected from a small genre, like Zombie movies from the Illustrative Example (Fig. 24.1 on page 813), then obtaining a rating for this movie likely provides little insight into a user's preferences other, more prominent genres. In addition, users naturally tend to rate movies from genres they like, meaning that any genre that dominates the training set (which is likely composed of items the user likes) may be representative of only a small portion of all items [50]. In order to increase information obtained, it is important to select representative items which may provide information about the other yet unrated items [23, 58, 64].

(R3) Results Active learning methods are typically evaluated based on how well they assisted a recommender system in achieving its objectives (e.g. accuracy, coverage, precision, etc. (Chap. 8). A common objective of RSs is high predictive accuracy; hence active learning methods are primarily evaluated based on the same metric. There are also some AL-centric metrics. A common AL-centric metric reflects the number of acquired ratings. In addition to measuring the quantity of the elicited ratings, it is also important to measure the type of elicited ratings (e.g. ratings low/high, genre, etc.) [20]. Many of the objectives have also been adopted from other fields, in particular from the field of information retrieval: precision, cumulative gain[4] (a measure for ranking quality of an item based on its relevance and position in the list (i.e. high rated items should appear towards the top of the recommendation list)) (Chap. 8). Finally, it is important to closely emulate the actual settings in which results are obtained (Sect. 24.8).

24.2.1 Other Considerations

In addition to the three Rs listed in Sect. 24.2, it may also be desirable to consider other criteria for data points, such as the following.

[4]For comparing of recommendations with various lengths, normalized Discounted Cumulative Gain (NDCG) is frequently used.

Cost As touched upon in the introduction to this chapter, obtaining implicit feedback from user selections is cheaper than asking the user to explicitly rate an item [24]. This can be considered a variable cost problem. One approach for tackling this, is to take into account both the cost of labeling an item and the future cost of estimated misclassification were the item to be added to the training set [35]. Moreover, the cost may be unknown beforehand [59].

Ratability A user may not always be able to provide a rating for an item; you cannot properly rate a movie you have not seen! It is suggested therefore that the probability of a user being able to evaluate an item also be considered (Sect. 24.8.4).

Saliency Decision-centric AL places emphasis on items whose ratings are more likely to affect decision-making, and acquires instances that are related to decisions for which a relatively small change in their estimation can change the order of top rated predictions [54]. For example, unless labeling an item would result in displacing or rearranging a list of top 10 recommended movies on a user's home page (the salient items), it may be considered of little use. It is also possible to only consider the effect of obtaining an item's rating on items that are strongly recommended by the system [6].

Popularity It has also been suggested to take an item's popularity into account [46], i.e. how many people have rated an item. This operates on the principle that since a popular item is rated by many people, it may be rather informative. Conversely, an item's rating uncertainty should also be considered since popular items have a tendency to be rated highly by most users (the reason for it being popular), indicating that the item may not provide much discriminative power and thus not worth including in the training set. This limitation has been partially addressed in [36] by selecting popular items (in a personalized manner) among similar users.

Best/Worst The ratings with extreme values (best/worst) are often quite informative about both the user's and items' preferences [39]. One way to utilize this is to ask the user to rate items with the highest [20, 65] and lowest predicted ratings [18, 20]. Note that the highest-predicted is the default strategy used by RSs to acquire ratings. However, concentrating on obtaining only highly rated items could introduce a system-wide bias [21] and could result in degradation of predictive performance [20]. Highest-lowest strategy is more likely to present items that users are able to rate (likely to have experienced the highest-predicted items, and can probably easily express a negative opinion about the lowest-predicted items). A major drawback of this method is that the system tends to obtain new information when its predictions are wrong (which we would hope is not so frequent). We hypothesize that this problem could be alleviated by asking a user to provide his/her most liked/disliked items. However, this changes the type of the task from active learning (providing a label for an item), to *active class selection* [40] (providing an item with a certain label (liked/disliked)).

24.3 Active Learning in Recommender Systems

With traditional AL, users are asked to rate a set of preselected items. This is often at the time of enrollment, though a preselected list may be presented to existing users at a later date as well. It may be argued that since these items are selected by experts, they capture essential properties for determining a user's preferences. Conceptually this may sound promising, but in practice this often leads towards selecting items that best predict the preferences of only an *average* user. Since the idea of RS is to provide personalized recommendations, selecting items to rate in a personalized manner should readily make more sense. The following matrix (Table 24.1 on page 817) provides a summary of the methods overviewed in this chapter.

Table 24.1 Method summary matrix

Primary motivation of approach	Description/goal	Possible considerations
Uncertainty Reduction (Sect. 24.4)	Reducing uncertainty of: • rating estimates (Sect. 24.4.1), • decision boundaries (Sect. 24.4.2), • model parameters (Sect. 24.4.3).	Reducing uncertainty may not always improve accuracy; the model could simply be certain about the wrong thing (e.g. when the predictive method is wrong).
Error Reduction (Sect. 24.5)	Reducing the predictive error by utilizing the relation between the error and: • the changes in the output estimates (Sect. 24.5.1.1), • the test set error (Sect. 24.5.1.2), • changes in parameter estimates (Sect. 24.5.2.1), • the variance of the parameter estimates (Sect. 24.5.2.2).	Estimating reduction of error reliably could be difficult and computationally expensive.
Ensemble-based (Sect. 24.6)	Identifying useful training points based on consensus between: • models in the ensemble (Sect. 24.6.1), • multiple candidate models (Sect. 24.6.1).	The effectiveness depends on the quality of models/candidates, and could be computationally expensive since it is performed with regards to multiple models/candidates.

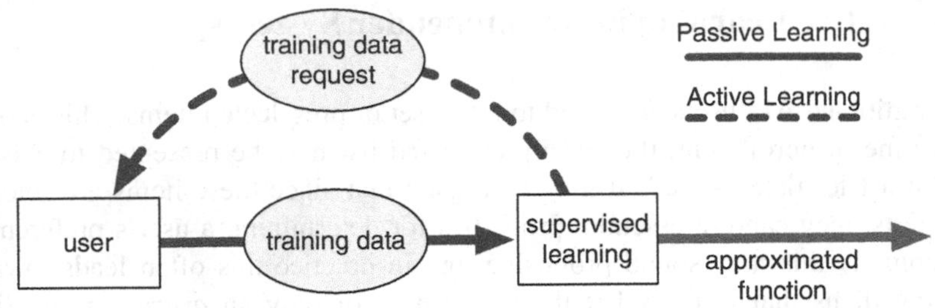

Fig. 24.2 Active learning employs an interactive/iterative process for obtaining training data, unlike passive learning, where the data is simply given

24.3.1 Active Learning Formulation

Passive Learning (see Fig. 24.2 on page 818) refers to when training data is provided beforehand, or when the system makes no effort to acquire new data (it simply accumulates through user activities over time). *Active Learning*, on the other hand, selects training points actively (the input) so as to observe the most informative output (user ratings, behavior, etc.).

Let us define the problem of active learning in a more formal manner (Table 24.2). An item is considered to be a multi-dimensional input variable and is denoted by a vector $\mathbf{x}$ (also referred to as a *data point*).[5] The set of all items is denoted by $\mathcal{X}$. The preferences of a user u are denoted by a function f_u (also referred to as a *target function*); for brevity, we use f when referring to a target user. A rating of an item $\mathbf{x}$ is considered to be an output value (or *label*) and is denoted as $y = f(\mathbf{x})$. Each item $\mathbf{x}$ could be rated on a finite scale $\mathcal{Y} = \{1, 2, \ldots, 5\}$.

In supervised learning, the items and corresponding user ratings are often partitioned into complementary subsets—a training set and a testing set (also called a validation set). The task of supervised learning is then too, given a training set (often supplemented by the ratings of all users), learn a function $\hat{f}$ that accurately approximates a user's preferences. Items that belong to the training set are denoted by $\mathcal{X}^{(Train)}$, and these items along with their corresponding ratings constitute a training set, i.e. $\mathcal{T} = \{(\mathbf{x}_i, y_i)\}_{\mathbf{x}_i \in \mathcal{X}^{(Train)}}$. We measure how accurately the learned function predicts the true preferences of a user by the generalization error:

$$G(\hat{f}) = \sum_{\mathbf{x} \in \mathcal{X}} \mathcal{L}\left(f(\mathbf{x}), \hat{f}(\mathbf{x})\right) P(\mathbf{x}). \qquad (24.1)$$

[5]The way in which an item is represented depends on the RS and the underlying predictive method. In Collaborative Filtering based approaches items could represented through the ratings of the users, or, in content based RSs, items could be represented through their descriptions.

Table 24.2 Summary of notation

$\mathbf{x}$	input (item)
$\mathcal{X}$	inputs (items)
y	output (item's rating)
$\mathcal{Y} = \{1, 2, \ldots, 5\}$	possible outputs (ratings), i.e. $y \in \mathcal{Y}$
f	user's preferences function (unknown to the system)
$\mathcal{X}^{(Train)}$	training inputs (rated items)
$\mathcal{T} = \{(\mathbf{x}_i, y_i\}_{\mathbf{x}_i \in \mathcal{X}^{(Train)}}$	training set (items and their ratings)
$\hat{f}$	approximated function of user's preferences (from training set)
G	generalization error (predictive accuracy) see (Eq. (24.1))
$\mathbf{x}_a$	item considered for rating
$\hat{G}(\mathbf{x}_a)$	active learning criterion (estimates the usefulness of an item $\mathbf{x}_a$)

In practice, however, $f(\mathbf{x})$ is not available for all $\mathbf{x} \in \mathcal{X}$; it is therefore common to approximate the generalization error by the test error:

$$\hat{G}(\hat{f}) = \sum_{\mathbf{x} \in \mathcal{X}^{(Test)}} \mathcal{L}\left(f(\mathbf{x}), \hat{f}(\mathbf{x})\right) P(\mathbf{x}), \tag{24.2}$$

where $\mathcal{X}^{(Test)}$ refers to the items in the *test set*, and prediction errors are measured by utilizing a loss function $\mathcal{L}$, e.g. mean absolute error (MAE):

$$\mathcal{L}_{MAE}\left(f(\mathbf{x}), \hat{f}(\mathbf{x})\right) = \left| f(\mathbf{x}) - \hat{f}(\mathbf{x}) \right|, \tag{24.3}$$

or mean squared error (MSE):

$$\mathcal{L}_{MSE}\left(f(\mathbf{x}), \hat{f}(\mathbf{x})\right) = \left(f(\mathbf{x}) - \hat{f}(\mathbf{x})\right)^2. \tag{24.4}$$

The active learning criterion is defined so as to estimate the usefulness of obtaining a rating of an item $\mathbf{x}$ and adding it to the training set $\mathcal{X}^{(Train)}$ for achieving a certain objective (Sect. 24.1.1). For simplicity, let us consider this objective to be the minimization of generalization error of a learned function with respect to the training set. We then denote the active learning criterion as:

$$\hat{G}(\mathcal{X}^{(Train)} \cup \{\mathbf{x}\}), \tag{24.5}$$

or for brevity, denote it as:

$$\hat{G}(\mathbf{x}). \tag{24.6}$$

The goal of active learning is to select an item $\mathbf{x}$ that would allow us to minimize the generalization error $\hat{G}(\mathbf{x})$:

$$\text{argmin}_{\mathbf{x}} \hat{G}(\mathbf{x}). \tag{24.7}$$

If we consider asking a user to rate an item $\mathbf{x}_j$ or an item $\mathbf{x}_k$, then we would estimate their usefulness by an active learning criterion, i.e. $\hat{G}(\mathbf{x}_j)$ and $\hat{G}(\mathbf{x}_k)$, and select the one that will result in a smaller generalization error. Note that we need to estimate the usefulness of rating an item without knowing its actual rating. To distinguish a candidate item to be rated from the other items we refer to it as $\mathbf{x}_a$. AL can be applied to any predictive method as long as it provides the required information, such as rating estimates [53] and their distribution [29, 31], closeness to the decision boundary [16, 67], method parameters [60], etc.

Regression and Classification The problem of predicting a user's ratings could be treated as both a regression and a classification problem. It is a regression problem since the ratings are discrete numerical values,such as if we consider their ordinal properties, meaning the ratings could be ordered (e.g. a rating of 4 is higher than a rating of 3). On the other hand, we can disregard the numerical properties of the ratings and treat the problem as a classification one by treating ratings as classes/labels.[6] For example, we can use a nearest-neighbor (NN) approach to do classification, e.g. pick the most frequent label of the neighbors; or we can use NN to do regression, e.g. calculate the mean of the ratings of the neighbors. Throughout the chapter we use both classification and regression in examples, selecting the one most appropriate for aiding the current explanation.

24.4 Uncertainty-Based Active Learning

Uncertainty-based AL tries to obtain training points so as to reduce uncertainty in some aspect, such as concerning output values [37], the model's parameters [29], a decision boundary [56], etc. A possible drawback to this approach is that reducing uncertainty may not always be effective. If a system becomes certain about user ratings, it does not necessarily mean that it will be accurate, since it could simply be certain about the wrong thing (i.e., if the algorithm is wrong, reducing uncertainty will not help). As an example, if the user has so far rated items positively, a system may mistakenly be certain that a user likes all of the items, which is likely incorrect.

[6]If the ordinal properties of the labels are considered, it is referred to as Ordinal Classification.

24.4.1 Output Uncertainty

In Output Uncertainty-based methods, an item to label (training point) is selected so as to reduce the uncertainty of rating predictions for test items. In Fig. 24.1 on page 813, with the assumption that the RS estimates the rating of an item based on the cluster to which it belongs (e.g. items in the same movie genre receive the same rating), if a user's rating for a movie from the Sci-Fi genre (upper-right) has already been obtained, then there is a higher likelihood that the RS may be more certain about the ratings of other movies in the Sci-Fi genre, likely making it more beneficial to obtain a user's preference for a movie from a genre (cluster) not yet sampled, i.e. a cluster that is still uncertain.

The difference between instance-based and model-based approaches for Output Uncertainty-based AL is primarily in how for an arbitrary item **x** the rating's distribution $P(Y_{\mathbf{x}})$ is obtained, where a rating's distribution is defined as the probability of an item being assigned a certain rating. For model-based methods it is possible to obtain the rating's distribution from the model itself. Probabilistic models are particularly well suited for this as they directly provide the rating's distribution [29, 31]. For instance-based methods, collected data is used to obtain the rating's distribution. As an example, methods utilizing nearest-neighbor techniques can obtain a rating's distribution based on the votes of its neighbors, where "neighbor" here means a user with similar preferences,[7] using a formula such as:

$$P(Y_{\mathbf{x}} = y) = \frac{\sum_{nn \in NN_{\mathbf{x},y}} w_{nn}}{\sum_{nn \in NN_{x}} w_{nn}}, \tag{24.8}$$

where NN_x are neighbors that have rated an item x, and $NN_{\mathbf{x},y}$ are neighbors that have given an item x a rating of y, and w_{nn} is the weight of the neighbor (such as similarity).

24.4.1.1 Active Learning Methods

Some AL methods [37] estimate the usefulness of a potential training point in a *local* (greedy) manner by measuring the uncertainty of its output value:

$$\hat{G}_{Uncertainty_{local}}(\mathbf{x}_a) = -Uncertainty(Y_a). \tag{24.9}$$

Since our goal is to minimize $\hat{G}$, rating an item with *high* uncertainty is useful; it will eliminate the uncertainty about the rating of the chosen item. However, labeling an item whose rating is uncertain does not necessarily accomplish the goal of reducing the uncertainty of ratings for other items (e.g. labeling an outlier may only reduce rating uncertainty for a few other similar items, such as when selecting item (c) in the Zombie genre, or even none as in (d), shown in Fig. 24.1 on page 813.

[7] Defining a neighbor as a similar item is also feasible depending on the method.

We may thus consider reducing uncertainty in a *global* manner by selecting an item which may reduce the uncertainty about *other* unrated items. One approach [51] for doing this is to define criteria by measuring the uncertainty of ratings over all of the test items $\mathcal{X}^{(Test)}$ with respect to a potential training input item $\mathbf{x}_a$:

$$\hat{G}_{Uncertainty}(\mathbf{x}_a) = \frac{1}{\left|\mathcal{X}^{(Test)}\right|} \sum_{\mathbf{x} \in \mathcal{X}^{(Test)}} \mathbb{E}_{\mathcal{T}^{(a)}} \left(Uncertainty(Y_{\mathbf{x}}) \right), \tag{24.10}$$

where $\frac{1}{\left|\mathcal{X}^{(Test)}\right|}$ is a normalizing factor, and $\mathbb{E}_{\mathcal{T}^{(a)}} \left(Uncertainty(Y_{\mathbf{x}}) \right)$ is the expected value of uncertainty with respect to adding an estimated rating y_a of a candidate item $\mathbf{x}_a$ to the training set $\mathcal{T}$; i.e. $\mathcal{T}^{(a)} = \mathcal{T} \cup (\mathbf{x}_a, y_a)$.

A possible drawback of this non-local approach is that while with the local approach it is only necessary to estimate the uncertainty of a single output value y_a, for the non-local approach uncertainty needs to be estimated for the output values of *all* the test points *with respect to* a potential training point $(\mathbf{x}_a, y_a)$; this may be difficult to estimate accurately and could be computationally expensive.

24.4.1.2 Uncertainty Measurement

Uncertainty of an item's rating (output value) is often measured by its variance, its entropy [37], or by its confidence interval [50]. Variance is maximized when ratings deviate the most from the mean rating, and entropy when all the ratings are equally likely.

Uncertainty of an output value could be calculated by using a definition of variance as follows:

$$Uncertainty(Y_a) = VAR(Y_a) = \sum_{y \in \mathcal{Y}} \left(y - \overline{Y_a} \right)^2 P(Y_a = y), \tag{24.11}$$

where $\overline{Y_a}$ is the mean rating of all users for an item $\mathbf{x}_a$ and $P(Y_a = y)$ is the probability of an items rating Y_a being equal to y, both being calculated based on either nearest-neighbors for instance-based, or obtained from the model for model-based approaches.

Uncertainty could also be measured by entropy as follows:

$$Uncertainty(Y_a) = ENT(Y_a) = -\sum_{y \in \mathcal{Y}} P(Y_a = y) \log P(Y_a = y). \tag{24.12}$$

In [58] a method is proposed for measuring the uncertainty of a rating based on the probability of the most likely rating:

$$Uncertainty(Y_a) = -P(Y_a = y^*), \tag{24.13}$$

where $y^* = \text{argmax}_y P(Y_a = y)$ is the most likely rating.

In [50] the confidence interval is used as a measure of uncertainty for selecting the training input point:

$$c = P(b_l(Y_a) < y_a < b_u(Y_a)), \tag{24.14}$$

where c is the confidence that the actual rating y_a will lie in the interval between the lower bound $b_l(Y_a)$ and the upper bound $b_u(Y_a)$. For example, it is possible for the system to be certain that an item will be assigned a rating between 3 and 5 with a probability $c = 90\%$. Many methods prefer items with a higher upper bound, indicating that an item may be rated highly (good for exploitation), and if the confidence interval is also wide then it may be good for exploration. In some cases where it is desirable to increase the number of items predicted to be more highly rated, it may be beneficial to use the expected change in the lower bound of the confidence interval for selecting an item [50], the higher the expected change the more desirable.

24.4.2 Decision Boundary Uncertainty

In Decision Boundary-based methods, training points are selected so as to improve decision boundaries. Often an existing decision boundary is assumed to be somewhat accurate, so points are sampled close to the decision boundary to further refine it (Fig. 24.3 on page 823). In a way this may also be considered Output Uncertainty-based, since the uncertainty of the points close to the decision boundary may be high. This method operates with the assumption that the decision boundary of the underlying learning method (e.g. Support Vector Machine) is easily accessible. A clear advantage of this method is that given a decision boundary, selecting training examples by their proximity to it is computationally inexpensive.

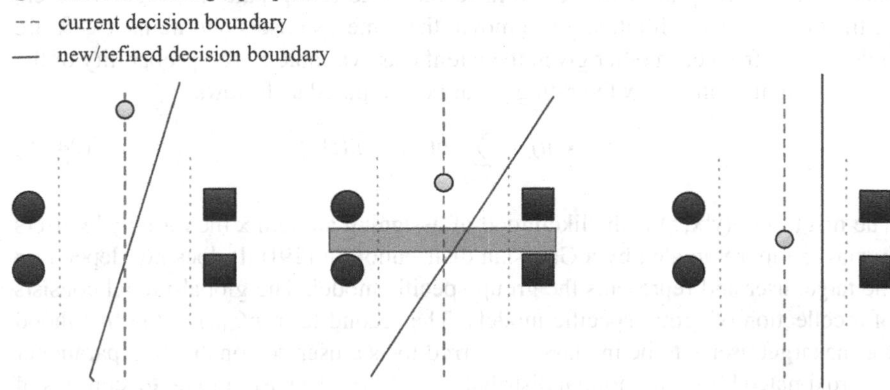

Fig. 24.3 Decision boundary uncertainty

As discussed in [56], training points may be selected for obtaining a more accurate dividing hyperplane (Fig. 24.3b on page 823), or if the direction of the hyperplane is already certain, input points may be selected for reducing the size of margin (Fig. 24.3c on page 823). While it may seem obvious to sample training points closest to the decision boundary [16, 67], there are also methods that select the items furthest away [16] that have potential advantages in scenarios involving several candidate classifiers, which are discussed in Sect. 24.6. This is because a classifier should be quite certain about any items far from a decision boundary, but if newly acquired training data reveals the classifier to be inaccurate, the classifier may not fit the user's preferences well, so it should be removed from the pool of candidate classifiers.

24.4.3 Model Uncertainty

Model Uncertainty-based methods select training points for the purpose of reducing uncertainty within the model, more specifically to reduce uncertainty about the model's parameters. The assumption is that if we improve the accuracy of the model's parameters the accuracy of output values will improve as well. If we were to predict a user's preferences based on membership in different interest groups [29], i.e. a group of people with a similar interest, then training points may be selected so as to determine to which groups the user belongs (Sect. 24.4.3.1).

24.4.3.1 Probabilistic Models

Probabilistic models are best explained with an example. The aspect model [29], a probabilistic latent semantic model in which users are considered to be a mixture of multiple interests (called aspects) is a good choice for this. Each user $u \in U$ has a probabilistic membership in different interest groups $z \in Z$. Users in the same interest group are assumed to have the same rating patterns (e.g. two users of the same aspect will rate a given movie the same), so users and items $\mathbf{x} \in \mathcal{X}$ are independent from each other given the latent class variable z. The probability of the user u assigning an item $\mathbf{x}$ the rating y can be computed as follows:

$$P(y|\mathbf{x}, u) = \sum_{z \in Z} p(y|\mathbf{x}, z) p(z|u). \tag{24.15}$$

The first term $p(y|\mathbf{x}, z)$ is the likelihood of assigning an item $\mathbf{x}$ the rating y by users in class z (approximated by a Gaussian distribution in [29]). It does not depend on the target user and represents the group-specific model. The global-model consists of a collection of group-specific models. The second term $p(z|u)$ is the likelihood for the target user u to be in class z, referred to as a user personalization parameter (approximated by a multinomial distribution in [29]). The user model $\boldsymbol{\theta_u}$ consists of one or more user personalization parameters, i.e. $\boldsymbol{\theta_u} = \{\theta_{u_z} = p(z|u)\}_{z \in Z}$.

A traditional AL approach would be to measure the usefulness of the candidate training input point $\mathbf{x}_a$ based on how much it would allow for reduction of the uncertainty about the user model's parameters $\boldsymbol{\theta}_u$ (i.e. the uncertainty about to which interest group z the user u belongs):

$$\hat{G}_{\theta Uncertainty}(\mathbf{x}_a) = Uncertainty(\boldsymbol{\theta}_u), \tag{24.16}$$

$$Uncertainty(\boldsymbol{\theta}_u) = -\left\langle \sum_{z \in Z} \theta_{u_z|\mathbf{x}_a,y} \log \theta_{u_z|\mathbf{x}_a,y} \right\rangle_{p(y|\mathbf{x}_a,\boldsymbol{\theta}_u)}, \tag{24.17}$$

where $\boldsymbol{\theta}_u$ denotes the currently estimated parameters of the user u and $\theta_{u_z|x,y}$ a parameter that is estimated using an additional training point $(\mathbf{x}_a, y)$. Since the goal of the above criterion is to reduce the uncertainty of which interest groups the target user belongs to, it favors training points that assign a user to a *single* interest group. This approach may not be effective for all models, such as with the aspect model, in which a user's preferences are better modeled by considering that a user belongs to *multiple* interest groups [29, 31].

Another potential drawback comes from the expected uncertainty being computed over the distribution $p(y|\mathbf{x}, \boldsymbol{\theta}_u)$ by utilizing the currently estimated model $\boldsymbol{\theta}_u$. The currently estimated model could be far from the true model, particularly when the number of training points is small, but the number of parameters to be estimated is large. Therefore, performing AL based only on a single estimated model can be misleading [31]. Let us illustrate this by the following example shown in Fig. 24.4 on page 825. The four existing training points are indicated by solid line contours, test points by dashed ones. Based on these four training examples, the most likely decision boundary is the horizontal line (dashed), even though the true decision boundary is a vertical line (solid). If we select training input points based only on the estimated model, subsequent training points would likely be obtained from areas along the estimated boundary, which are ineffective in adjusting the estimated

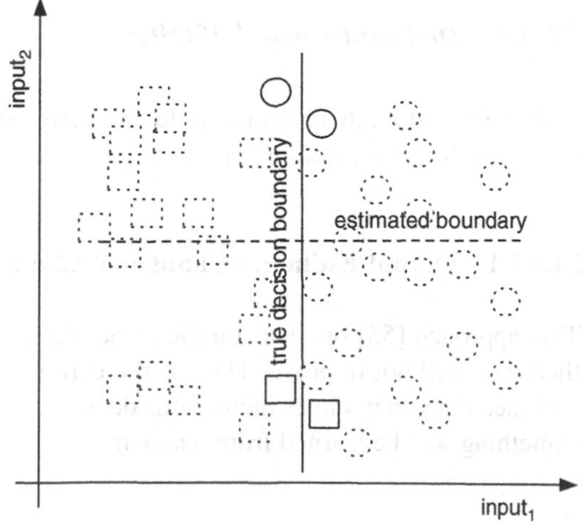

Fig. 24.4 A learning scenario when the estimated model is far from the true model. Training points are indicated by *solid contours*

decision boundary (horizontal line) towards the correct decision boundary (vertical line). This example illustrates that performing AL for the currently estimated model without taking into account the model's uncertainty can be very misleading, particularly when the estimated model is far from the true model. A better strategy could be to consider model uncertainty by utilizing the model distribution for selecting training input points [31]. This would allow for adjusting the decision boundary more effectively since decision boundaries other than the estimated one (i.e. horizontal line) would be considered for selecting the training input points. This idea is applied to probabilistic models in [31] as follows. The usefulness of the candidate training input point is measured based on how much it allows adjusting the model's parameters $\boldsymbol{\theta}_u$ towards the optimal model parameters $\boldsymbol{\theta}_u{}^*$:

$$\hat{G}_{\theta Uncertainty}(\mathbf{x}_a) = \left\langle \sum_{z \in Z} \theta_u{}^*_z \log \frac{\theta_{u_z|\mathbf{x}_a,y}}{\theta_u{}^*_z} \right\rangle_{p(y|\mathbf{x}_a,\boldsymbol{\theta}_u{}^*)} . \quad (24.18)$$

The above equation corresponds to Kullback–Leibler divergence which is minimized when the estimated parameters are equal to the optimal parameters. The true model $\boldsymbol{\theta}_u{}^*$ is not known but could be estimated as the expectation over the posterior distribution of the user's model i.e. $p(\boldsymbol{\theta}_u|u)$.

24.5 Error-Based Active Learning

Error-based Active Learning methods aim to reduce the predictive error, which is often the final goal. Instance-based approaches try to find and utilize the relation between the training input points and the predictive error. Model-based approaches tend to aim at reducing the model error (i.e. the error of model parameters), which is hoped would result in the improvement of predictive error.

24.5.1 Instance-Based Methods

Instance-based methods aim at reducing error based on the properties of the input points, such as are listed in Sect. 24.2.

24.5.1.1 Output Estimates Change (Y-Change)

This approach [53] operates on the principle that if rating estimates do not change then they will not improve. Thus, if the estimates of output values do change, then their accuracy may either increase or decrease. However, it is expected that at least something will be learned from a new training point, so it follows then that in many

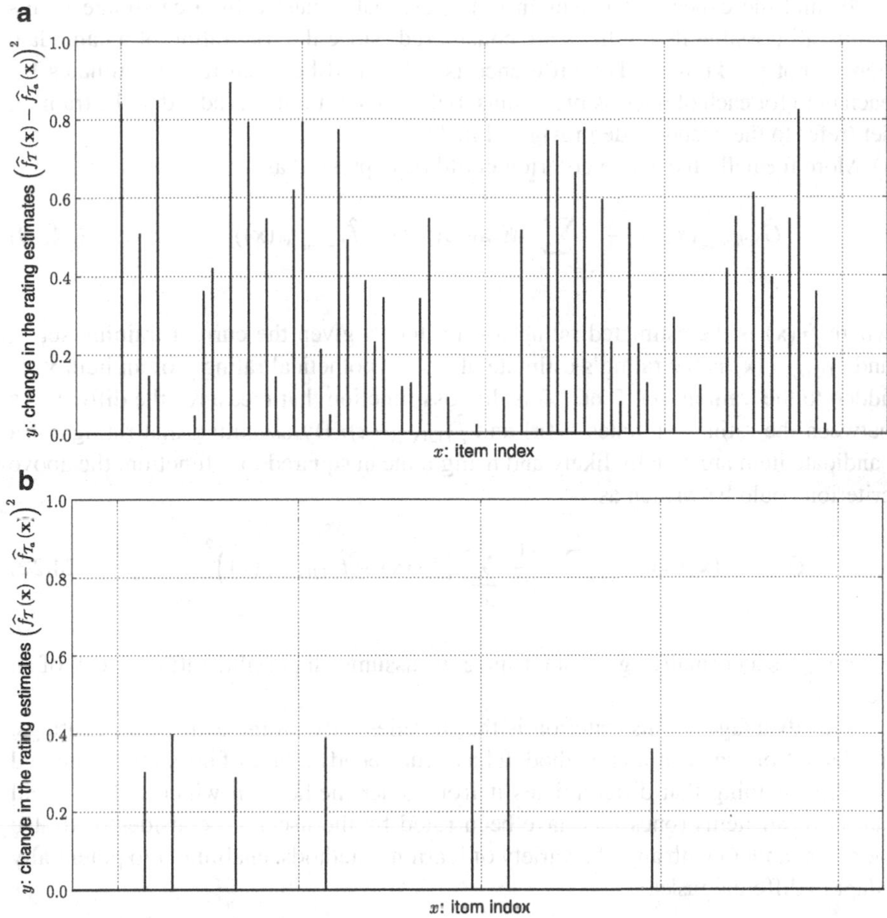

Fig. 24.5 Output estimate-based AL (Sect. 24.5.1.1). The x-axis corresponds to an item's index, and the y-axis to the changes in rating estimates with regard to a candidate training point. Training points that cause many changes in rating estimates are considered to be more informative (**a**) vs (**b**)

cases estimates do in fact become more accurate. Assuming that most changes in estimates are for the better, an item that causes many estimates to change will result in the *improvement* of many estimates, and is considered useful.

As an example (Fig. 24.5 on page 827), if a user rates an item that is representative of a large genre, such as the Sci-Fi movie *Star Wars*, then its rating (regardless of its value) will likely cause a change in rating estimates for many other related items (e.g. items within that genre), in other words, rating such a representative item is very informative about the user's preferences. On the other hand, the user rating an item without many other similar items, such as the movie *The Goldfish Hunter*, would change few rating estimates, and supply little information.

To find the expected changes in rating estimates caused by a candidate item's rating, all possible item ratings are considered (since the true rating of a candidate item is not yet known). The difference is calculated between rating estimates for each item for each of its possible ratings, before and after it was added to the training set (refer to the pseudocode in Algorithm 1).

More formally the above criterion could be expressed as:

$$\hat{G}_{Ychange}(\mathbf{x}_a) = -\sum_{\mathbf{x}\in\mathcal{X}^{(Test)}} \mathbb{E}_{y\in\mathcal{Y}} \mathcal{L}(\hat{f}_{\mathcal{T}}(\mathbf{x}), \hat{f}_{\mathcal{T}\cup(\mathbf{x}_a,y)}(\mathbf{x})), \tag{24.19}$$

where $\hat{f}_{\mathcal{T}}(\mathbf{x})$ is the estimated rating for an item $\mathbf{x}$ given the current training set $\mathcal{T}$, and $\hat{f}_{\mathcal{T}\cup(\mathbf{x}_a,y)}(\mathbf{x})$ is the rating's estimate after a hypothetical rating y of an item $\mathbf{x}_a$ is added to the training set $\mathcal{T}$, and $\mathcal{L}$ is the loss function that measures the differences between the rating estimates $\hat{f}_{\mathcal{T}}(\mathbf{x})$ and $\hat{f}_{\mathcal{T}\cup(\mathbf{x}_a,y)}(\mathbf{x})$. By assuming that ratings of a candidate item are equally likely and using a mean squared loss function, the above criterion could be written as:

$$\hat{G}_{Ychange}(\mathbf{x}_a) = -\sum_{\mathbf{x}\in\mathcal{X}^{(Test)}} \frac{1}{|\mathcal{Y}|} \sum_{y\in\mathcal{Y}} \left(\hat{f}_{\mathcal{T}}(\mathbf{x}) - \hat{f}_{\mathcal{T}\cup(\mathbf{x}_a,y)}(\mathbf{x})\right)^2 \tag{24.20}$$

where $\frac{1}{|\mathcal{Y}|}$ is a normalizing constant since we assume all possible ratings $y \in \mathcal{Y}$ of an item $\mathbf{x}_a$.

The advantage of this criterion is that it relies only on the *estimates* of ratings, available from any learning method. It has a further advantage of utilizing all unrated items, something that differentiates it from other methods in which only a small subset of all items (ones that have been rated by the user) are considered. It also works in tandem with any of a variety of learning methods, enabling it to potentially adapt to different tasks.

24.5.1.2 Cross Validation-Based

In this approach a training input point is selected based on how well it may allow for approximation of already known ratings, i.e. items in the training set [16]. That is, a candidate training point $\mathbf{x}_a$ with each possible rating $y \in \mathcal{Y}$ is added to the training set $\mathcal{T}$, then an approximation of the user's preferences $\hat{f}$ is obtained and its accuracy is evaluated (i.e. cross-validated) on the training items $\mathcal{X}^{(Train)}$. It is assumed that when the candidate training item is paired with its correct rating, the cross-validated accuracy will improve the most. The usefulness of the candidate training point is measured by the improvement in the cross-validated accuracy as following:

$$\hat{G}_{CV_{\mathcal{T}}}(\mathbf{x}_a) = -\max_{y\in\mathcal{Y}} \sum_{x\in\mathcal{X}^{(Train)}} \mathcal{L}(\hat{f}_{\mathcal{T}\cup(\mathbf{x}_a,y)}(x), f(x)), \tag{24.21}$$

Algorithm 1 Output estimates-based Active Learning (Sect. 24.5.1.1)

$\hat{G}$ estimates predictive error that rating an item $\mathbf{x}_a$ would allow to achieve
function $\hat{G}(\mathbf{x}_a)$
  # learn a preference approximation function $\hat{f}$ based on the current training set $\mathcal{T}$
  $\hat{f}_{\mathcal{T}}$ =learn($\mathcal{T}$)
    # for each possible rating of an item $\mathbf{x}_a$ e.g. $\{1, 2, \ldots, 5\}$
    for $y_a \in \mathcal{Y}$
      # add a hypothetical training point $(\mathbf{x}_a, y_a)$
      $\mathcal{T}^{(a)} = \mathcal{T} \cup (\mathbf{x}_a, y_a)$
      # learn a new preference approximation function $\hat{f}$ based on the new training set $\mathcal{T}^{(a)}$
      $\hat{f}_{\mathcal{T}^{(a)}}$ =learn($\mathcal{T}^{(a)}$)
      # for each unrated item
      for $\mathbf{x} \in \mathcal{X}^{(Test)}$
        # record the differences between ratings estimates
        # before and after a hypothetical training point $(\mathbf{x}_a, y_a)$ was added to the training set $\mathcal{T}$
        $\hat{G} = \hat{G} + \left(- \left(\hat{f}_{\mathcal{T}}(\mathbf{x}) - \hat{f}_{\mathcal{T}^{(a)}}(\mathbf{x}) \right)^2 \right)$
  return $\hat{G}$

where $\mathcal{L}$ is a loss function such as MAE or MSE (Sect. 24.3.1), and $f(x)$ is the actual rating of the item $\mathbf{x}$, and $\hat{f}_{\mathcal{T}\cup(\mathbf{x}_a,y)}(x)$ is the approximated rating (where a function $\hat{f}$ is learned from the training set $\mathcal{T} \cup (\mathbf{x}_a, y)$) .

A potential drawback is that training points selected by this AL method could be overfitted to the training set.

24.5.2 *Model-Based*

In model-based approaches training input points are obtained as to reduce the model's error, i.e. the error of the model's parameters. A potential drawback of this approach is that reducing the model's error may not necessarily reduce the prediction error which is the objective of AL.

24.5.2.1 Parameter Change-Based

Parameter Change-based AL [60] favors items that are likely to influence the model the most. Assuming that changes in the model's parameters are for the better, i.e. approach the optimal parameters, it is then beneficial to select an item that has the greatest impact on the model's parameters:

$$\hat{G}_{\theta change}(\mathbf{x}_a) = - \sum_{\theta} \mathbb{E}_{y \in \mathcal{Y}} \mathcal{L}(\theta_{\mathcal{T}}, \theta_{\mathcal{T}\cup(\mathbf{x}_a,y)}), \qquad (24.22)$$

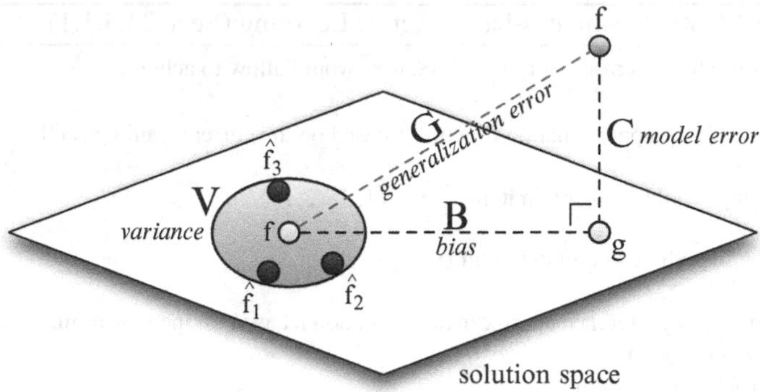

Fig. 24.6 Decomposition of generalization error G into model error C, bias B, and variance V, where g denotes optimal function, $\hat{f}$ is a learned function $\hat{f}_i$'s are the learned functions from a slightly different training set

where $\theta_{\mathcal{T}}$ are the model's parameters estimated from the current training set $\mathcal{T}$, and $\theta_{\mathcal{T}\cup(\mathbf{x}_a,y)}$ are the model's parameter estimates after a hypothetical rating y of an item $\mathbf{x}_a$ is added to the training set $\mathcal{T}$, and $\mathcal{L}$ is the loss function that measures the differences between the parameters.

24.5.2.2 Variance-Based

In this approach the error is decomposed into three components: model error C (the difference between the optimal function approximation g, given the current model, and the true function f), bias B (the difference between the current approximation $\hat{f}$ and an optimal one g), and variance V (how much the function approximation $\hat{f}$ varies). In other words, we have (Fig. 24.6):

$$G = C + B + V. \tag{24.23}$$

One solution [14] is to minimize the variance component V of the error by assuming that the bias component becomes negligible (if this assumption is not satisfied then this method may not be effective). There are a number of methods proposed that aim to select training inputs for reducing a certain measure of the variance of the model's parameters. The A-optimal design [12] seeks to select training input points so as to minimize the average variance of the parameter estimates, the D-optimal design [33] seeks to maximize the differential Shannon information content of the parameter estimates, and the Transductive Experimental design [68] seeks to find representative training points that may allow retaining most of the information of the test points. The AL method in [62], in addition to the variance component, also takes into account the existence of the model error component.

24.5.2.3 Image Restoration-Based

It is also possible to treat the problem of predicting the user's preferences as one of image restoration [44], that is, based on our limited knowledge of a user's preferences (a partial picture), we try to restore the complete picture of the user's likes and dislikes. The AL task is then to select the training points that would best allow us to restore the "image" of the user's preferences. It is interesting to note that this approach satisfies the desired properties of the AL methods outlined in Sect. 24.2. For example, if a point already exists in a region, then without sampling neighboring points the image in that region could likely be restored. This approach also may favor sampling close to the edges of image components (decision boundaries).

24.6 Ensemble-Based Active Learning

Sometimes instead of using a single model to predict a user's preferences, an ensemble of models may be beneficial (Chap. 22). In other cases only a single model is used, but it is selected from a number of candidate models. The main advantage of this is the premise that different models are better suited to different users or different problems. The preferences of one user, for example, could be better modeled by a stereotype model, while the preferences of another user may be better modeled by a nearest-neighbor model. The training input points for these AL methods must be selected with regards to multiple models (Sect. 24.6.1) or multiple model candidates (Sect. 24.6.2).

24.6.1 Models-Based

In Models-based approaches, the models form a "committee" of models that act, in a sense, cooperatively to select training input points [61]. Methods tend to differ with respect to: (1) how to construct a committee of models, and (2) how to select training points based on committee members [57]. As [57] explains thoroughly (please refer to it for more details), the Query by Committee approach (QBC) involves maintaining a committee of models which are all trained on the same training data. In essence, they represent competing hypotheses for what the data might look like (as represented by the model). The members of this committee then vote on how to label potential input points (the "query" in "QBC"). The input points for which they disagree the most are considered to be the most informative. The fundamental premise of QBC is minimizing the version space, or the subset of all hypotheses that are consistent with all the collected training data; we want to then constrain the size of this space as much as possible, while at the same time minimizing the number of training input points. Put a different way, QBC "queries" in controversial regions to refine the version space.

There are many ways to construct the committee of models; [57] provides numerous examples. It can, for example, be constructed through simple sampling [61]. With generative model classes, this can be achieved by randomly sampling an arbitrary number of models from some posterior distribution, e.g. using the Dirichlet distribution over model parameters for naive Bayes [41], or sampling Hidden Markov Models (HMMs) using the Normal distribution [15]. The ensemble can be constructed for other model classes (such as discriminative or non-probabilistic models) as well, e.g. query-by-boosting and query-by-bagging [1], which employ the boosting [22] and bagging [8] ensemble learning methods to construct the committees; there has also been research [13] on using a selective sampling algorithm for neural networks that utilizes the combination of the "most specific" and "most general" models (selecting the models that lie at two extremes of the current version space given the current training set).

The "committee is still out" on the appropriate number of models to use, but even small sizes have demonstrated good results [41, 58, 61].

Measuring the disagreement between models is fundamental to the committee approach; there are two main means for calculating disagreement: vote uncertainty [15] and average Kullback-Leibler (KL) divergence [41]. Vote uncertainty selects the point with the largest disagreement between models of the committee. KL divergence is an information-theoretic measure of the difference between two probability distributions. KL divergence selects the input point with the largest average difference between the distributions of the committee consensus and the most differing model.

24.6.2 Candidates-Based

Different models are better suited to different users or to different problems (Chap. 7). So both the choice of the training set (AL) and the choice of the model, called Model Selection (MS), affect the predictive accuracy of the learned function. There is in fact a strong dependency between AL and MS, meaning that useful points for one model may not be as useful for another (Fig. 24.9 on page 834). This section discusses how to perform AL with regards to multiple model candidates and the issues that may arise when doing so.

The concept of *model* has several different meanings. We may refer to a model as a set of functions with some common characteristic, such as a function's complexity, or the type of a function or learning method (e.g. SVM, Naive Bayes, nearest-neighbor, or linear regression). The characteristics of the functions that may differ are often referred to as parameters. Thus, given a model and training data, the task of MS is to find parameters that may allow for accurate approximation of the target function. All of the model's characteristics affect the predictive accuracy, but for simplicity we concentrate only on the complexity of the model.

As illustrated by Fig. 24.7 on page 833, if the model is too simple in comparison with the target function, then the learned function may not be capable of approximating the target function, making it under-fit (Fig. 24.7a on page 833). On the

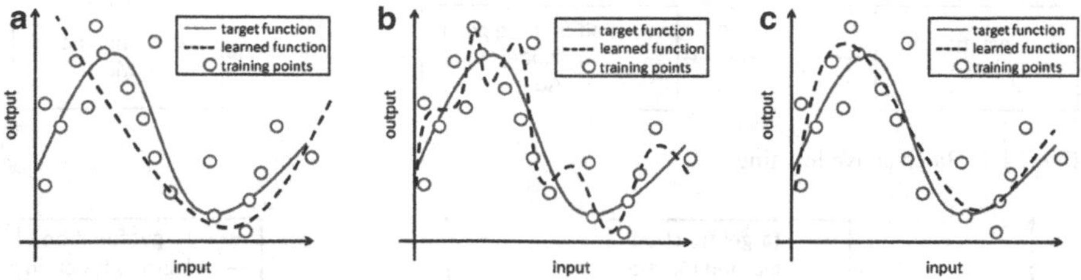

Fig. 24.7 Dependence between model complexity and accuracy. (**a**) Under-fit; (**b**) over-fit; (**c**) appropriate fit

other hand, if the model is too complex it may start trying to approximate irrelevant information (e.g. noise that may be contained in the output values) which will cause the learned function to over-fit the target function (Fig. 24.7b on page 833). A possible solution to this is to have a number of candidate models. The goal of model selection (MS) is thus to determine the weights of the models in the ensemble, or in the case of a single model being used, to select an appropriate one (Fig. 24.7c on page 833):

$$\min_{\mathcal{M}} G(\mathcal{M}). \tag{24.24}$$

The task of AL is likewise to minimize the predictive error, but with respect to the choice of the training input points:

$$\min_{\mathcal{X}^{(Train)}} G(\mathcal{X}^{(Train)}). \tag{24.25}$$

It would be beneficial to combine AL and MS since they share a common goal of minimizing the predictive error:

$$\min_{\mathcal{X}^{(Train)},\, \mathcal{M}} G(\mathcal{X}^{(Train)}, \mathcal{M}). \tag{24.26}$$

Ideally we would like to choose the model of appropriate complexity by a MS method and to choose the most useful training data by an AL method. However simply combining AL with MS in a batch manner, i.e. selecting all of the training points at once (Fig. 24.8), may not be possible due to the following paradox:

- To select training input points by a standard AL method, a model must be fixed. In other words, MS has already been performed (see Fig. 24.9 on page 834).
- To select the model by a standard MS method, the training input points must be fixed and corresponding training output values must be gathered. In other words, AL has already been performed (see Fig. 24.10 on page 834).

As a result Batch AL selects training points for a randomly chosen model, but after the training points are obtained the model is selected once again, giving rise to the possibility that the training points will not be as useful if the initial and final models differ. This means that the training points could be over-fitted to a possibly inferior model, or likewise under-fitted.

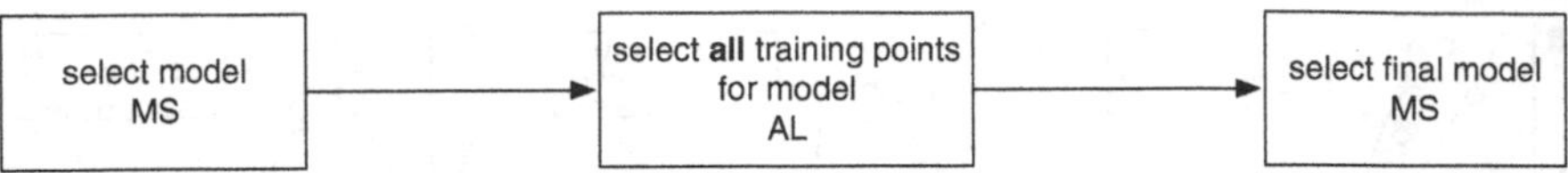

Fig. 24.8 Batch active learning

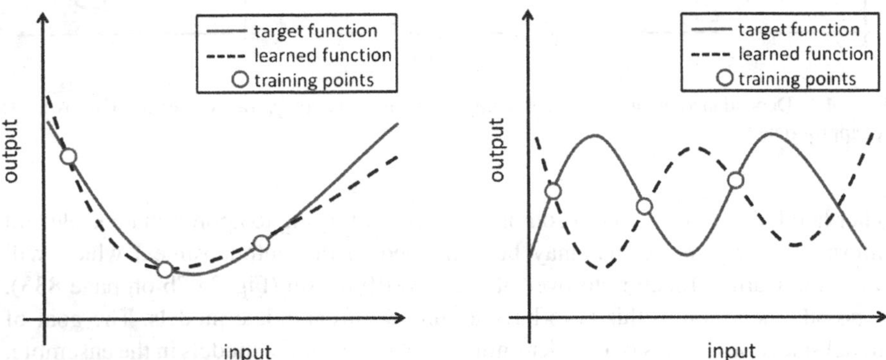

Fig. 24.9 Training input points that are good for learning one model, are not necessary good for the other

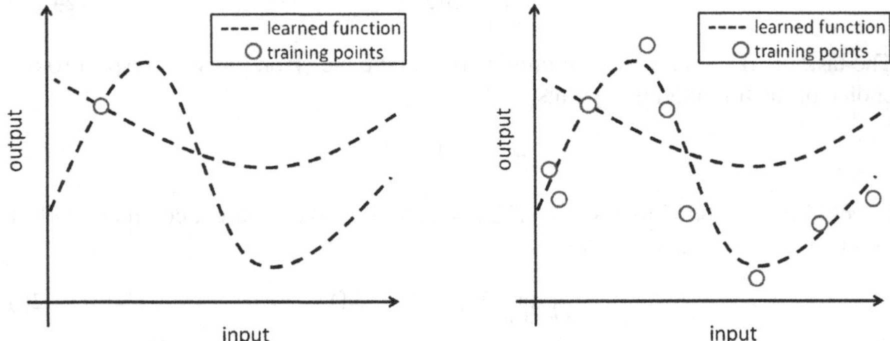

Fig. 24.10 Dependence of model selection on active learning. Unable to determine which model is more appropriate (Model Selection), until training points have been obtained (Active Learning)

With Sequential AL, the training points and models are selected incrementally in a process of selecting a model, then obtaining a training point for this model, and so on (Figs. 24.11). Although this approach is intuitive, it may perform poorly due to *model drift*, where a chosen model varies throughout the learning process. As the number of training points increases, more complex models tend to fit data better and are therefore selected over simpler models. Since the selection of training input points depends on the model, the training points chosen for a simpler model in the early stages could be less useful for the more complex model selected at the end of the learning process. Due to model drift portions of training points are gathered for different models, resulting in the training data being not well suited for any of the

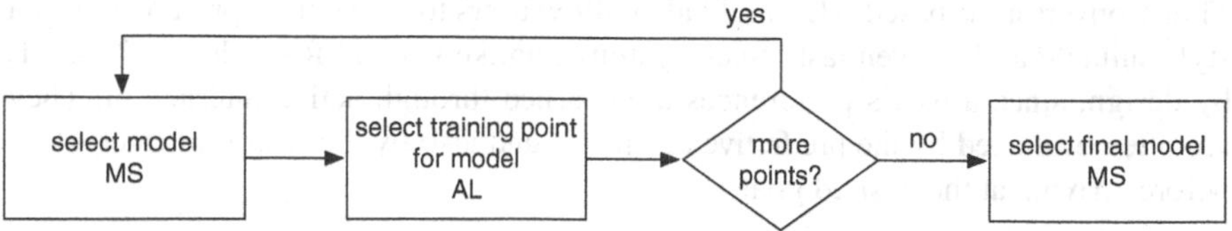

Fig. 24.11 Sequential active learning

models. However, because the selection of the final model is unclear at the onset, one possibility is to select training input points with respect to multiple models [63], by optimizing the training data for all the models:

$$\min_{\mathcal{X}^{(Train)}} \sum_{\mathcal{M}} \hat{G}(\mathcal{X}^{(Train)}, \mathcal{M}) w(\mathcal{M}), \tag{24.27}$$

where $w(\mathcal{M})$ refers to the weight of the model in the ensemble, or among the candidates. This allows each model to contribute to the optimization of the training data and thus the risk of overfitting the training set to possibly inferior models can be hedged.

24.7 Conversation-Based Active Learning

Preference elicitation [45], just as active learning, aims at constructing an accurate model of user preferences. However, unlike AL that elicits ratings to inductively model the user preferences, preference elicitation aims to lean about user preferences on a more abstract level e.g. by directly acquiring or deducting user's preferences (e.g. by asking users which genre of movies they like). Preference elicitation is often performed with the help of conversation-based AL that is goal oriented with the task of starting general and, through a series of interaction cycles, narrowing down the user's interests until the desired item is obtained [9, 42, 49], such as selecting a hotel to stay at during a trip. In essence, the goal is to supply the user with the information that best enables them to reduce the set of possible items, finding the item with the most utility. The system therefore aims at making accurate predictions about items with the highest utility for a potentially small group of items, such as searching for a restaurant within a restricted locale. A common approach is to iteratively present sets of alternative recommendations to the user, and by eliciting feedback, guide the user towards an end goal in which the scope of interest is reduced to a single item. This cycle-based approach can be beneficial since users rarely know all their preferences at the start (becoming self-aware), but tend to form and refine them during the decision making process (exploration).

Thus Conversation-based AL should also allow users to refine their preferences in a style suitable to the given task. Such systems, unlike general RSs, also include AL by design, since a user's preferences are learned through active interaction. They are often evaluated by the predictive accuracy, and also by the length of interaction before arriving at the desired goal.

24.7.1 Case-Based Critique

One means for performing a conversation with a user is the Case-based Critique approach, which finds cases similar to the user's query or profile and then elicits a critique for refining the user's interests [49]. As mentioned above (Sect. 24.7), the user is not required to clearly define their preferences when the conversation initiates; this may be particularly beneficial for mobile device-oriented systems. Each step of iteration displays the system's recommendations in a ranked list and allows for user critique, which will force the system to re-evaluate its recommendations and generate a new ranked list. Eliciting a user critique when a feature of a recommended item is unsatisfactory may be more effective in obtaining the end goal than mere similarity-based query revision combined with recommendation by proposing. As an example of a user critique, he/she may comment "I want a less expensive hotel room" or "I like restaurants serving wine."

24.7.2 Diversity-Based

While suggesting items to the user that are similar to the user query is important (Sect. 24.7.1), it may also be worthwhile to consider diversity among the set of proposed items [42]. This is because if the suggested items are too similar to each other, they may not be representative of the current search space. In essence, the recommended items should be as representative and diverse as possible, which should be possible without appreciably affecting their similarity to the user query. It is particularly important to provide diverse choices while the user's preferences are in their embryonic stages. Once the user knows what it is they want, providing items that match as closely as possible may be pertinent, and the AL technique used should attempt to make this distinction, i.e. if the recommendation space is properly focused, reduce diversity, and if incorrect, increase it.

24.7.3 Query Editing-Based

Another possibility is to allow a user to repeatedly edit and resubmit a search query until their desired item is found [9]. Since it is an iterative process, the objective is to minimize the number of queries needed before the user finds the item of highest utility. A query's usefulness is estimated based on the likelihood of the user submitting a particular query, along with its satisfiability, accomplished by observing user actions and inferring any constraints on user preferences related to item utility and updating the user's model. As an example, a user may query for hotels that have air-conditioning and a golf course. The RS can determine this to be satisfiable, and further infer that though the user is likely to add a restraint for the hotel being located in the city-center, no hotels match such criteria, so the system preemptively notifies the user that such a condition is unsatisfiable to prevent wasted user effort. The RS may also infer that for a small increase in price there are hotels with a pool and spa and a restaurant. Knowing the user's preferences for having a pool (and not for other options), the system would only offer adding the pool option, since it may increase the user's satisfaction, and not the others since they may overwhelm the user and decrease overall satisfaction.

24.8 Evaluation Settings

Proper evaluation of active learning is important for measuring how well the system meets given objectives, and investigating if there are any undesirable side effects. In experimental studies, evaluation setup should reflect as closely as possible the actual settings for which the system was designed. In Sect. 24.3.1 we briefly described machine learning-based settings under which active learning algorithms are typically evaluated. If one aims for a more realistic evaluation, other domain specific aspects must be considered (some of which are described below).

24.8.1 Scope

Traditionally, the evaluation of active learning strategies has been user-centered; that is, the usefulness of the elicited rating was judged based on the improvement in the user's prediction error. This is illustrated in Fig. 24.12a. In this scenario the system is supposed to have a large number of ratings from several users, and focusing on a new user (the first one in Fig. 24.12a) it first elicits ratings from this new user that are in X, and then system predictions for this user are evaluated on the test set T. Hence these traditional evaluations focussed on the new-user problem and measured how the ratings elicited from a new user may help the system to generate good recommendations for this particular user. Elahi et al. [20] noted that eliciting a rating from a user may improve not only the rating predictions for that user, but also the predictions for the other users, as is graphically illustrated in Fig. 24.12b. To illustrate this point, let us consider an extreme example in which a new item is added to the system. The traditional user-centered AL strategy, when trying to identify the items that a target user should rate, may ignore obtaining user's rating for that new item. In fact, this item has not been rated by any other user and

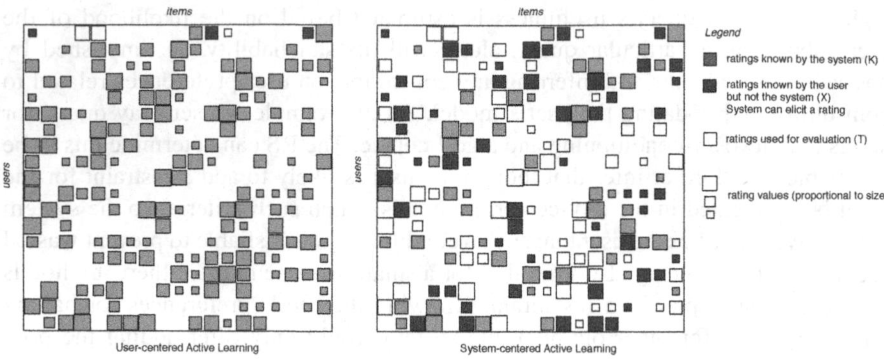

Fig. 24.12 Comparison of the scope of the ratings data configurations used for evaluating (**a**) user-centered and (**b**) system-centered active learning strategies (Sect. 24.8.1)

therefore its ratings cannot contribute to improving the rating predictions for the target user. However, the rating of the target user for the new item would allow to bootstrap the predictions[8] for the rest of the users in the system, and hence from the system's perspective the elicited rating is indeed very informative. Conversely, it was shown some user-centric strategies, while being beneficial for the target user, may increasing the system error. For instance, requesting to rate the items with the highest predicted ratings (an AL approach that is often adopted in real RSs), may generate a system-wide bias, and inadvertently increase the system error (especially at the early stages) by adding to the training set disproportionately more high ratings than low ones, and as a result biasing the rating prediction towards overestimating ratings. Elicited rating has effects across the system, so a typical user-centric evaluation which ignores any changes of rating prediction of other users also ignores these cumulative effects, which could be more influential on the performance of the system as a whole.

24.8.2 Natural Rating Acquisition

In RSs there are two primary ways in which ratings are acquired: (1) users are prompted to rate an item by an active learning method; (2) users provide ratings without being prompted (natural rating acquisition), e.g. while browsing items. Previous studies considered the situation where the active learning rating elicitation strategy was the only tool used to collect new ratings from the users. Recently, [20] has proposed a more realistic evaluation setting, where in addition to the ratings being acquired by the elicitation strategies, the ratings are also entered by the users

[8]Recently it has also been proposed to utilize transfer learning for leveraging pre-existing labeled data from related tasks to improve the performance of an active learning algorithm [34, 69].

(without being prompted), similarly to what happens in actual settings. Mixing in naturally acquired ratings significantly impacts the performance of some of the active learning methods (Sect. 24.8.5). For example, without mixing in naturally acquired ratings, highest-predicted AL is shown to acquire many new ratings. Yet, when the naturally acquired ratings are mixed in, highest-predicted AL acquires very few ratings since many of the ratings are already collected by the natural process (i.e. the user would rate these items on his own initiative).

24.8.3 Temporal Evolution

Ratings data changes with time: more ratings are added, new users and items appear, underlying recommendation and active learning algorithms change, as do user interfaces. While it is convenient to evaluate AL method on a snapshot of the database; it is also advisable to incorporate temporal aspects of RSs in order to obtain a more complete view of the algorithm's performance. proposed considering temporal aspects with a simulation loop that models the day-by-day process of rating elicitation and rating database growth (starting from an empty database); where users repeatedly come back to the system for receiving recommendations, while the system has possibly elicited ratings from other users. To achieve a realistic setting, only the items that users actually experienced during the following week (according to the timestamps) are added to the database for each time period. Elahi et al. [20] showed that different strategies improve different aspects of the recommendation quality at different stages of the rating database growth. Moreover, performance of AL varies significantly from week to week, caused by the fact that for every week system is trained on the data from previous weeks, and is evaluated on the next week's ratings. Hence, the quality of the training data and predictive difficulty of the test set can therefore change from week to week, and hence influence the performance of the AL strategies. Zhao et al. [70] proposed AL method that explicitly takes temporal changes into account, focusing on changes in users preferences over time.

Time-dependent evolution of predictive aspects of recommender systems has also received some attention. In [10] the author analyzes the temporal properties of a standard user-based collaborative filtering [26] and Influence Limiter [48], a collaborative filtering algorithm developed for counteracting profile injection attacks by considering the time at which a user has rated an item. These works evaluate the accuracy of prediction algorithms while the users are rating items and the database is growing. This is radically different from the typical evaluations that we mentioned earlier, where the rating dataset is decomposed into the training and testing sets without considering the timestamp of the ratings. In [10] it is argued that considering the time at which the ratings were added to the system gives a better picture of the real user experience during the interactions with the system in terms of recommendation accuracy. They discovered the presence of two time segments: the start-up period, until day 70 with MAE dropping gradually, and the remaining period, where MAE was dropping much slower.

24.8.4 Ratability

A user may not always be able to provide a rating for an item; e.g. you cannot rate a movie you have not seen [25, 38]. On the other hand, the system typically contains ratings for only a portion of items that users have experienced. This is a common problem of any offline evaluation of a recommender system, where the performance of the recommendation algorithm is estimated on a test set that is never coincident with the recommendations set. The recommendation set is composed of the items with the largest predicted ratings. But if such an item is not present in the test set, an offline evaluation will be never able to check if that prediction is correct [19]. Only a few evaluations simulated limited knowledge about the user's ratings [20, 25]; from the user and/or system perspective. The system is assumed to unaware about what items the simulated user has experienced, and may ask ratings for items that the user will not be able to provide. This better simulates a realistic scenario where not all rating requests can be satisfied by a user. It is important to note that the simulated application of an active learning strategy is able to add many fewer ratings than what could be elicited in a real setting. In fact, the number of ratings that are supposed to be known by the users in the simulated process is limited by the number of ratings that are present in the dataset. In [19] it has been estimated that the number of items that are really known by the user is more than 4 times larger than what is typically observed in the simulations. Hence, a lot of our elicitation request would be unfulfilled, even though the user in actuality would have been able to rate the item. To adjust for the discrepancy between the knowledge of the actual and simulated users, it is recommended to increase number of active learning requests by a factor of 4 [19].

24.8.5 Summary

In [20] performance of many of the common active learning methods has been evaluated considering many of the aspects mentioned above, as to more realistically simulate actual RS settings. The evaluation (summarized in Table 24.3 on page 841) has shown that the system-wide effectiveness of a rating elicitation strategy (Sect. 24.8.1) depends on the stage of the rating elicitation process (Sect. 24.8.3), and on the evaluation metrics (Sects. 24.2 and 24.1.1). Surprisingly, some common user-centric strategies (Sect. 24.8.1) may actually degrade the overall performance of a system. Finally, the performance of many common active learning strategies changes significantly when evaluated concurrently with e.g. the natural acquisition of ratings (Sect. 24.8.2).

Table 24.3 Summary of performance evaluation (performance: ✓—good, ×—bad)

	Metrics														
	MAE				NDCG			Elicited #			Inform.		Precision		
Strategies	Early stage	Late stage	Randomized	w/ natural	Early stage	Late stage	Randomized	Early stage	Late stage	w/ natural	Early stage	Late stage	Early Stage	Late stage	Randomized
variance	×	✓	✓	✓	×	×	✓	✓	✓	×	×	×	×	×	×
Popularity	×	✓	✓	✓	×	×	✓	✓	✓	×	×	×	×	×	✓
Lowest-pred	✓	✓	✓	×	×	×	×	×	×	×	✓	✓	×	✓	×
Lo-hi-pred	✓	✓	✓	×	×	×	✓	×	×	×	✓	✓	✓	✓	✓
Highest-pred	×	✓	✓	×	×	×	✓	×	×	×	×	×	✓	✓	✓
Binary-pred	×	✓	✓	×	×	×	✓	×	×	×	×	×	✓	✓	✓
Voting	✓	×	✓	✓	✓	✓	✓	×	×	×	✓	✓	×	×	✓
log(pop)*ent	×	✓	✓	✓	×	×	✓	✓	✓	✓	×	×	×	×	✓
Random	✓	×	NA	✓	✓	✓	NA	×	✓	×	✓	✓	×	×	NA
Natural	✓	✓	✓	NA	×	×	✓	✓	✓	NA	✓	✓	✓	✓	✓

24.9 Computational Considerations

It is also important to consider the computational costs of AL algorithms. Roy and Mccallum [51] have suggested a number of ways of reducing the computational requirements, summarized (with additions) below.

- Many AL select an item to be rated based on its expected effect on the learned function. This may require retraining with respect to each candidate training item, and so efficient incremental training is crucial. Typically this step-by-step manner has lower cost than starting over with a large set.
- New rating estimates may need to be obtained with respect to each candidate item. Likewise, this could be done in an incremental manner, since only the estimates that change would need to be obtained again.
- It is possible to incrementally update the estimated error only for items likely to be effected by the inclusion of a training point, which in practice is only nearby items or items without similar features. A common approach is to use inverted indices to group items with similar features for quick lookup.
- A candidate training item's expected usefulness can likely be estimated using a subset of all items.
- Poor candidates for training points can be partially pruned through a pre-filtering step that removes poor candidate items based on some criteria, such as filtering books written in a language the user cannot read. A suboptimal AL method may be a good choice for this task.

24.10 Discussion

Though very brief, hopefully the collection of Active Learning methods presented in this chapter has demonstrated that AL is indeed not only beneficial but also desirable for inclusion in many systems, namely Recommender Systems. It can be seen that due to individual characteristics, the AL method selected, in many cases, relies heavily on the specific objectives (Sect. 24.1.1) that must be satisfied, either due to business constraints, preferred system behavior, user experience, or a combination of these (and possibly others). In addition to AL objectives, it is also prudent to evaluate the computational costs (Sect. 24.9) of any methods under consideration for use, and their trade-offs. Despite the success that many of the methods discussed have received, there is also something to be said for abstracting the problem, or finding solutions to other problems that though seemingly unrelated, may have strikingly similar solutions (e.g. Image Restoration (Sect. 24.5.2.3)). We have also touched upon conversation-based systems (Sect. 24.7) which differ from traditional RSs, but include the notion of AL by design. Depending on the task at hand, such as specific goal oriented assistants, this may also be a nice fit for a Recommender System.

Some issues related to AL have already been well studied in Statistics; this is not the case in Computer Science, where research is still wanting. Recommender Systems are changing at a rapid pace and becoming more and more complex. An example of this is the system that won the NetFlix Recommendation Challenge, which combined multiple predictive methods in an ensemble manner (Chap. 3). Given the high rate of change in predictive methods of RSs, and their complex interaction with AL, there is an ever increasing need for new approaches.

Improving accuracy has traditionally been the main focus of research. Accuracy alone, however, may not be enough to entice the user with RSs (Chap. 8). This is because the system implementing AL may also need to recommend items of high novelty/serendipity, improve coverage, or maximize profitability, to name a few [27, 32, 43, 55]. Another aspect that is frequently overlooked by AL researchers is the manner in which a user can interact with AL to reap improvements in performance. Simply presenting items to the user for rating lacks ingenuity to say the least; surely there is a better way? One example of this is a work [3] which demonstrated that by using the right interface even such menial tasks as labeling images could be made fun and exciting. With the right interface alone the utility of an AL system may increase dramatically.

Many issues remain that must be tackled to ensure the longevity of AL in RSs; with a little innovation and elbow grease we hope to see it transform from a "bothersome process" to an enjoyable one of self-discovery and exploration, satisfying both the system objectives and the user at the same time.

References

1. Abe, N., Mamitsuka, H.: Query learning strategies using boosting and bagging. In: Proceedings of the Fifteenth International Conference on Machine Learning, vol. 388. Morgan Kaufmann Publishers Inc. (1998)
2. Adomavicius, G., Tuzhilin, A.: Toward the next generation of recommender systems: A survey of the state-of-the-art and possible extensions. IEEE Transactions on Knowledge and Data Engineering **17**(6), 734–749 (2005)
3. Ahn, L.V.: Games with a purpose. Computer **39**(6), 92–94 (2006). DOI 10.1109/MC.2006.196
4. Bailey, R.A.: Design of Comparative Experiments. Cambridge University Press (2008)
5. Balcan, M.F., Beygelzimer, A., Langford, J.: Agnostic active learning. In: ICML '06: Proceedings of the 23rd international conference on Machine learning, pp. 65–72. ACM, New York, NY, USA (2006). DOI http://doi.acm.org/10.1145/1143844.1143853
6. Boutilier, C., Zemel, R., Marlin, B.: Active collaborative filtering. In: Proceedings of the Nineteenth Annual Conference on Uncertainty in Artificial Intelligence, pp. 98–106 (2003). URL citeseer.ist.psu.edu/boutilier03active.html
7. Box, G., Hunter, S.J., Hunter, W.G.: Statistics for Experimenters: Design, Innovation, and Discovery. Wiley-Interscience (2005)
8. Breiman, L., Breiman, L.: Bagging predictors. In: Machine Learning, pp. 123–140 (1996)
9. Bridge, D., Ricci, F.: Supporting product selection with query editing recommendations. In: RecSys '07: Proceedings of the 2007 ACM conference on Recommender systems, pp. 65–72. ACM, New York, NY, USA (2007). DOI http://doi.acm.org/10.1145/1297231.1297243
10. Burke, R.: Evaluating the dynamic properties of recommendation algorithms. In: Proceedings of the fourth ACM conference on Recommender systems, RecSys '10, pp. 225–228. ACM, New York, NY, USA (2010). DOI http://doi.acm.org/10.1145/1864708.1864753. URL http://doi.acm.org/10.1145/1864708.1864753
11. Carenini, G., Smith, J., Poole, D.: Towards more conversational and collaborative recommender systems. In: IUI '03: Proceedings of the 8th international conference on Intelligent user interfaces, pp. 12–18. ACM, New York, NY, USA (2003). DOI http://doi.acm.org/10.1145/604045.604052
12. Chan, N.: A-optimality for regression designs. Tech. rep., Stanford University, Department of Statistics (1981)
13. Cohn, D.A.: Neural network exploration using optimal experiment design **6**, 679–686 (1994). URL citeseer.ist.psu.edu/article/cohn94neural.html
14. Cohn, D.A., Ghahramani, Z., Jordan, M.I.: Active learning with statistical models. Journal of Artificial Intelligence Research **4**, 129–145 (1996)
15. Dagan, I., Engelson, S.: Committee-based sampling for training probabilistic classifiers. In: Proceedings of the International Conference on Machine Learning (ICML), pp. 150–157. Citeseer (1995)
16. Danziger, S., Zeng, J., Wang, Y., Brachmann, R., Lathrop, R.: Choosing where to look next in a mutation sequence space: Active learning of informative p53 cancer rescue mutants. Bioinformatics **23(13)**, 104–114 (2007)
17. Dasgupta, S., Lee, W., Long, P.: A theoretical analysis of query selection for collaborative filtering. Machine Learning **51**, 283–298 (2003). URL citeseer.ist.psu.edu/dasgupta02theoretical.html
18. Diaz-Aviles, E., Drumond, L., Schmidt-Thieme, L., Nejdl, W.: Real-time top-n recommendation in social streams. In: Proceedings of the Sixth ACM Conference on Recommender Systems, RecSys '12, pp. 59–66. ACM, New York, NY, USA (2012). DOI 10.1145/2365952.2365968. URL http://doi.acm.org/10.1145/2365952.2365968
19. Elahi, M.: Adaptive active learning in recommender systems. In: User Modeling, Adaption and Personalization—19th International Conference, UMAP 2011, Girona, Spain, July 11–15, 2011. Proceedings, pp. 414–417 (2011)

20. Elahi, M., Ricci, F., Rubens, N.: Active learning strategies for rating elicitation in collaborative filtering: a system-wide perspective. ACM Transactions on Intelligent Systems and Technology **5**(11) (2013)
21. Ertekin, S., Huang, J., Bottou, L., Giles, L.: Learning on the border: active learning in imbalanced data classification. In: Proceedings of the sixteenth ACM conference on Conference on information and knowledge management, pp. 127–136. ACM (2007)
22. Freund, Y., Schapire, R.: A decision-theoretic generalization of on-line learning and an application to boosting. Journal of computer and system sciences **55**(1), 119–139 (1997)
23. Fujii, A., Tokunaga, T., Inui, K., Tanaka, H.: Selective sampling for example-based word sense disambiguation. Computational Linguistics **24**, 24–4 (1998)
24. Greiner, R., Grove, A., Roth, D.: Learning cost-sensitive active classifiers. Artificial Intelligence **139**, 137–174 (2002)
25. Harpale, A.S., Yang, Y.: Personalized active learning for collaborative filtering. In: SIGIR '08: Proceedings of the 31st annual international ACM SIGIR conference on Research and development in information retrieval, pp. 91–98. ACM, New York, NY, USA (2008). DOI http://doi.acm.org/10.1145/1390334.1390352
26. Herlocker, J.L., Konstan, J.A., Borchers, A., Riedl, J.: An algorithmic framework for performing collaborative filtering. In: Proceedings of the 22nd annual international ACM SIGIR conference on Research and development in information retrieval, SIGIR '99, pp. 230–237. ACM, New York, NY, USA (1999). DOI http://doi.acm.org/10.1145/312624.312682. URL http://doi.acm.org/10.1145/312624.312682
27. Herlocker, J.L., Konstan, J.A., Terveen, L.G., Riedl, J.T.: Evaluating collaborative filtering recommender systems. ACM Trans. Inf. Syst. **22**(1), 5–53 (2004). DOI http://doi.acm.org/10.1145/963770.963772
28. Hinkelmann, K., Kempthorne, O.: Design and Analysis of Experiments, Advanced Experimental Design. Wiley Series in Probability and Statistics (2005)
29. Hofmann, T.: Collaborative filtering via gaussian probabilistic latent semantic analysis. In: SIGIR '03: Proceedings of the 26th annual international ACM SIGIR conference on Research and development in informaion retrieval, pp. 259–266. ACM, New York, NY, USA (2003). DOI http://doi.acm.org/10.1145/860435.860483
30. Huang, Z.: Selectively acquiring ratings for product recommendation. In: ICEC '07: Proceedings of the ninth international conference on Electronic commerce, pp. 379–388. ACM, New York, NY, USA (2007). DOI http://doi.acm.org/10.1145/1282100.1282171
31. Jin, R., Si, L.: A bayesian approach toward active learning for collaborative filtering. In: AUAI '04: Proceedings of the 20th conference on Uncertainty in artificial intelligence, pp. 278–285. AUAI Press, Arlington, Virginia, United States (2004)
32. Johar, M., Mookerjee, V., Sarkar, S.: Selling vs. profiling: Optimizing the offer set in web-based personalization. Information Systems Research **25**(2), 285–306 (2014).
33. John, R.C.S., Draper, N.R.: D-optimality for regression designs: A review. Technometrics **17**(1), 15–23 (1975)
34. Kale, D., Liu, Y.: Accelerating active learning with transfer learning. In: Data Mining (ICDM), 2013 IEEE 13th International Conference on, pp. 1085–1090 (2013). DOI 10.1109/ICDM.2013.160
35. Kapoor, A., Horvitz, E., Basu, S.: Selective supervision: Guiding supervised learning with decision-theoretic active learning. In: Proceedings of International Joint Conference on Artificial Intelligence (IJCAI), pp. 877–882 (2007)
36. Karimi, R., Freudenthaler, C., Nanopoulos, A., Schmidt-Thieme, L.: Exploiting the characteristics of matrix factorization for active learning in recommender systems. In: Proceedings of the Sixth ACM Conference on Recommender Systems, RecSys '12, pp. 317–320. ACM, New York, NY, USA (2012). DOI 10.1145/2365952.2366031. URL http://doi.acm.org/10.1145/2365952.2366031
37. Kohrs, A., Merialdo, B.: Improving collaborative filtering for new users by smart object selection. In: Proceedings of International Conference on Media Features (ICMF) (2001)

38. Le, Q.T., Tu, M.P.: Active learning for co-clustering based collaborative filtering. In: Computing and Communication Technologies, Research, Innovation, and Vision for the Future (RIVF), 2010 IEEE RIVF International Conference on, pp. 1–4 (2010). DOI 10.1109/RIVF.2010.5633245
39. Leino, J., Räihä, K.J.: Case amazon: ratings and reviews as part of recommendations. In: RecSys '07: Proceedings of the 2007 ACM conference on Recommender systems, pp. 137–140. ACM, New York, NY, USA (2007). DOI http://doi.acm.org/10.1145/1297231.1297255
40. Lomasky, R., Brodley, C., Aernecke, M., Walt, D., Friedl, M.: Active class selection. In: In Proceedings of the European Conference on Machine Learning (ECML). Springer (2007)
41. McCallum, A., Nigam, K.: Employing em and pool-based active learning for text classification. In: ICML '98: Proceedings of the Fifteenth International Conference on Machine Learning, pp. 350–358. San Francisco, CA, USA (1998)
42. Mcginty, L., Smyth, B.: On the Role of Diversity in Conversational Recommender Systems. Case-Based Reasoning Research and Development pp. 276–290 (2003)
43. McNee, S.M., Riedl, J., Konstan, J.A.: Being accurate is not enough: how accuracy metrics have hurt recommender systems. In: CHI '06: CHI '06 extended abstracts on Human factors in computing systems, pp. 1097–1101. ACM Press, New York, NY, USA (2006). DOI http://doi.acm.org/10.1145/1125451.1125659
44. Nakamura, A., Abe, N.: Collaborative filtering using weighted majority prediction algorithms. In: ICML '98: Proceedings of the Fifteenth International Conference on Machine Learning, pp. 395–403. Morgan Kaufmann Publishers Inc., San Francisco, CA, USA (1998)
45. Pu, P., Chen, L.: User-Involved Preference Elicitation for Product Search and Recommender Systems. AI magazine pp. 93–103 (2009). URL http://www.aaai.org/ojs/index.php/aimagazine/article/viewArticle/2200
46. Rashid, A.M., Albert, I., Cosley, D., Lam, S.K., McNee, S.M., Konstan, J.A., Riedl, J.: Getting to know you: learning new user preferences in recommender systems. In: IUI '02: Proceedings of the 7th international conference on Intelligent user interfaces, pp. 127–134. ACM Press, New York, NY, USA (2002). DOI http://doi.acm.org/10.1145/502716.502737
47. Rashid, A.M., Karypis, G., Riedl, J.: Influence in ratings-based recommender systems: An algorithm-independent approach. In: SIAM International Conference on Data Mining, pp. 556–560 (2005)
48. Resnick, P., Sami, R.: The influence limiter: provably manipulation-resistant recommender systems. In: Proceedings of the 2007 ACM conference on Recommender systems, RecSys '07, pp. 25–32. ACM, New York, NY, USA (2007). DOI http://doi.acm.org/10.1145/1297231.1297236. URL http://doi.acm.org/10.1145/1297231.1297236
49. Ricci, F., Nguyen, Q.N.: Acquiring and revising preferences in a critique-based mobile recommender system. IEEE Intelligent Systems **22**(3), 22–29 (2007). DOI http://dx.doi.org/10.1109/MIS.2007.43
50. Rokach, L., Naamani, L., Shmilovici, A.: Pessimistic cost-sensitive active learning of decision trees for profit maximizing targeting campaigns. Data Mining and Knowledge Discovery **17**(2), 283–316 (2008). DOI http://dx.doi.org/10.1007/s10618-008-0105-2
51. Roy, N., Mccallum, A.: Toward optimal active learning through sampling estimation of error reduction. In: In Proc. 18th International Conf. on Machine Learning, pp. 441–448. Morgan Kaufmann (2001)
52. Rubens, N., Sugiyama, M.: Influence-based collaborative active learning. In: Proceedings of the 2007 ACM conference on Recommender systems (RecSys 2007). ACM (2007). DOI http://doi.acm.org/10.1145/1297231.1297257
53. Rubens, N., Tomioka, R., Sugiyama, M.: Output divergence criterion for active learning in collaborative settings. IPSJ Transactions on Mathematical Modeling and Its Applications **2**(3), 87–96 (2009)
54. Saar-Tsechansky, M., Provost, F.: Decision-centric active learning of binary-outcome models. Information Systems Research **18**(1), 4–22 (2007). DOI http://dx.doi.org/10.1287/isre.1070.0111

55. Schein, A.I., Popescul, A., Ungar, L.H., Pennock, D.M.: Methods and metrics for cold-start recommendations. In: SIGIR '02: Proceedings of the 25th annual international ACM SIGIR conference on Research and development in information retrieval, pp. 253–260. ACM, New York, NY, USA (2002). DOI http://doi.acm.org/10.1145/564376.564421
56. Schohn, G., Cohn, D.: Less is more: Active learning with support vector machines. In: Proc. 17th International Conf. on Machine Learning, pp. 839–846. Morgan Kaufmann, San Francisco, CA (2000). URL citeseer.ist.psu.edu/schohn00less.html
57. Settles, B.: Active learning literature survey. Computer Sciences Technical Report 1648, University of Wisconsin–Madison (2009)
58. Settles, B., Craven, M.: An analysis of active learning strategies for sequence labeling tasks. In: Proceedings of the Conference on Empirical Methods in Natural Language Processing (EMNLP), pp. 1069–1078. ACL Press (2008)
59. Settles, B., Craven, M., Friedland, L.: Active learning with real annotation costs. In: Proceedings of the NIPS Workshop on Cost-Sensitive Learning, pp. 1–10 (2008)
60. Settles, B., Craven, M., Ray, S.: Multiple-instance active learning. In: Advances in Neural Information Processing Systems (NIPS), vol. 20, pp. 1289–1296. MIT Press (2008)
61. Seung, H.S., Opper, M., Sompolinsky, H.: Query by committee. In: Computational Learning Theory, pp. 287–294 (1992). URL citeseer.ist.psu.edu/seung92query.html
62. Sugiyama, M.: Active learning in approximately linear regression based on conditional expectation of generalization error. Journal of Machine Learning Research **7**, 141–166 (2006)
63. Sugiyama, M., Rubens, N.: A batch ensemble approach to active learning with model selection. Neural Netw. **21**(9), 1278–1286 (2008). DOI http://dx.doi.org/10.1016/j.neunet.2008.06.004
64. Sugiyama, M., Rubens, N., Müller, K.R.: Dataset Shift in Machine Learning, chap. A conditional expectation approach to model selection and active learning under covariate shift. MIT Press, Cambridge (2008)
65. Sutherland, D.J., Póczos, B., Schneider, J.: Active learning and search on low-rank matrices. In: Proceedings of the 19th ACM SIGKDD International Conference on Knowledge Discovery and Data Mining, KDD '13, pp. 212–220. ACM, New York, NY, USA (2013). DOI 10.1145/2487575.2487627. URL http://doi.acm.org/10.1145/2487575.2487627
66. Swearingen, K., Sinha, R.: Beyond algorithms: An hci perspective on recommender systems. ACM SIGIR 2001 Workshop on Recommender Systems (2001). URL http://citeseer.ist.psu.edu/cache/papers/cs/31330/http:zSzzSzweb.engr.oregonstate.eduzSz~herlockzSzrsw2001zSzfinalzSzfull_length_paperszSz4_swearingenzPz.pdf/swearingen01beyond.pdf
67. Tong, S., Koller, D.: Support vector machine active learning with applications to text classification. In: P. Langley (ed.) Proceedings of ICML-00, 17th International Conference on Machine Learning, pp. 999–1006. Morgan Kaufmann Publishers, San Francisco, US, Stanford, US (2000). URL citeseer.ist.psu.edu/article/tong01support.html
68. Yu, K., Bi, J., Tresp, V.: Active learning via transductive experimental design. In: Proceedings of the 23rd Int. Conference on Machine Learning ICML '06, pp. 1081–1088. ACM, New York, NY, USA (2006). DOI http://doi.acm.org/10.1145/1143844.1143980
69. Zhao, L., Pan, S.J., Xiang, E.W., Zhong, E., Lu, Z., Yang, Q.: Active transfer learning for cross-system recommendation. In: AAAI (2013)
70. Zhao, X., Zhang, W., Wang, J.: Interactive collaborative filtering. In: Proceedings of the 22nd ACM international conference on Conference on information & knowledge management, CIKM '13, pp. 1411–1420. ACM, New York, NY, USA (2013). DOI 10.1145/2505515.2505690. URL http://doi.acm.org/10.1145/2505515.2505690

Chapter 25
Multi-Criteria Recommender Systems

Gediminas Adomavicius and YoungOk Kwon

25.1 Introduction

The research discipline of recommender systems arose to address the problem of information or choice over-abundance, i.e., to help users find information or items that are most likely to be interesting to them or to be relevant to their needs [4, 7, 12, 38, 39, 73, 74]. Typically, the recommendation problem assumes that there is set *Users* of all the users of a system and set *Items* of all possible items that can be recommended to them. Then, the utility function that measures the appropriateness of recommending item $i \in Items$ to user $u \in Users$ is often defined as $R : Users \times Items \rightarrow R_0$. R_0 typically represents users' possible *preference ratings* for items (e.g., non-negative integers or real numbers within a certain range). The goal of recommender systems is, for each user $u \in Users$, to be able to (a) accurately estimate (or approximate) utility function $R(u, i)$ for item $i \in Items$ for which $R(u, i)$ is not yet known, and then (b) select one or a set of items i for which the predicted value $R(u, i)$ is high (i.e., items that are predicted to be relevant for u) and also possibly satisfy some other desirable conditions (e.g., items with high novelty or diversity [31, 88]).

In most recommender systems, utility function $R(u, i)$ usually estimates a *single-criterion* value, e.g., an overall evaluation or rating of an item by a user. In some recent work, this assumption has been considered as limited [2, 4, 51], because the

G. Adomavicius (✉)
Department of Information and Decision Sciences, University of Minnesota,
321 19th Avenue South, Minneapolis, MN 55455, USA
e-mail: gedas@umn.edu

Y. Kwon
Sookmyung Women's University, Cheongpa-ro 47-gil 100,
Yongsan-gu, Seoul 140-742, Korea
e-mail: yokwon@sm.ac.kr

F. Ricci et al. (eds.), *Recommender Systems Handbook*,
DOI 10.1007/978-1-4899-7637-6_25

suitability of the recommended item for a particular user may depend on more than one utility-related aspect that the user takes into consideration when making the choice. Particularly in systems where recommendations are based on the opinion of others, the incorporation of multiple criteria that can affect the users' opinions may lead to more accurate recommendations.

Thus, the additional information provided by *multi-criteria ratings* could help to improve the quality of recommendations because it would be able to represent more complex preferences of each user. As an illustration, consider the following example. In a traditional single-rating movie recommender system, user u provides a single rating for movie i that the user has seen, denoted by $R(u, i)$. Specifically, suppose that the recommender system predicts the rating of the movie that the user has not seen based on the movie ratings of other users with similar preferences, who are commonly referred to as "neighbors" [12, 73, 74]. For example, if two users u and u' have seen three movies in common, and both of them rated their overall satisfaction from each of the three movies as 6 out of 10, the two users are considered as neighbors and the ratings of unseen movies for user u are predicted using the ratings of user u'. Therefore, the ability to correctly determine the users that are most similar to the target user is crucial in order to have accurate predictions or recommendations.

In contrast, in a multi-criteria rating setting, users can provide their subjective preference ratings on multiple attributes of an item. For example, a two-criterion movie recommender system allows users to specify their preferences on two attributes of a movie (e.g., story and visual effects). A user may like the story, but dislike the visual effects of a movie, e.g., $R(u, i) = (9, 3)$. If we simply aggregate the two individual criteria ratings by giving them the same weight in making recommendations, rating the user's overall satisfaction as 6 out of 10 in the single-rating application might correspond to a variety of situations in multi-rating application: (9, 3), (6, 6), (4, 8), etc. Therefore, although the ratings of the overall satisfaction are stated as 6, two users may show different rating patterns on each criterion of an item, e.g., user u gives ratings (9, 3), (9, 3), (9, 3), and user u' gives ratings (3, 9), (3, 9), (3, 9) to the same three movies. This additional information on each user's preferences would help to model users' preferences more accurately, and new recommendation techniques need to be developed to take advantage of this additional information. The importance of studying multi-criteria recommender systems has been highlighted as a separate strand in the recommender systems literature [2, 4, 51], and recently several recommender systems (as we present later in this chapter) have been adopting multiple criteria ratings, instead of traditional single-criterion ratings. Thus, the aim of this chapter is to provide an overview of *multi-criteria recommender systems*.

The use of multi-criteria recommender systems has been proposed for a wide range of applications. As mentioned above, for experiential products (such as movies, books, and music) users may have varying subjective tastes and preferences for multiple product dimensions, and richer information on user preferences helps to improve the quality of recommendations [2, 42, 43, 68]. Other popular domains where multi-criteria recommendation algorithms can be applied include travel and tourism domains. Customers can have different preferences on friendliness, room size, service quality, and tidiness about the hotel, in addition to an overall perspective [34]. Mobile banking business can also adopt the multi-criteria algorithms by tracking each user's behavior data on the mobile service, rather than obtaining explicit ratings [93]. Furthermore, restaurants [44, 83] can be considered with different aspects such as the quality of service, location, value for money, and an overall experience. Similarly, research papers [58, 99] can be recommended with the information on multiple dimensions such as title, keywords, authors, publication year, and the citation links (i.e., representing the papers that cite the target paper as well as the papers cited by the target paper). Multi-criteria recommendation algorithms have also been used to support clinical decision making by combining evidence-based (i.e., disease information) and patient-centric (i.e., patient preferences) information [22].

Generally, recommendation techniques are often classified based on the recommendation approach into several categories: content-based, collaborative filtering, knowledge-based, and hybrid approaches [4, 7]. Content-based recommendation techniques find the best recommendations for a user based on what the user liked in the past [48, 69], and collaborative filtering recommendation techniques make recommendations based on the information about other users with similar preferences [12, 41, 73, 74]. Knowledge-based approaches use knowledge about users and items to find the items that meet users' requirements [14, 17]. The bottleneck of this knowledge-based approach is that it needs to acquire a knowledge base beforehand, but the obtained knowledge base helps to avoid cold start or data sparsity problems that pure content-based or collaborative filtering systems encounter by relying on solely the ratings obtained by users. Hybrid approaches combine content-based, collaborative filtering, and knowledge-based techniques in many different ways [15, 16].

Multi-criteria recommender systems can employ any of these general approaches. However, it is important to note that "multi criteria" is a very generic term, and we observe that in research literature "multi-criteria recommender systems" may point to several substantially different ideas, including:

- Multi-attribute content search, filtering, and preference modeling;
- Multi-objective recommendation strategies;
- Multi-criteria rating-based preference elicitation.

Below we provide a brief overview of these three categories.

Multi-Attribute Content Search, Filtering, and Preference Modeling These approaches allow the user to specify her current preferences or needs based on various content-based attributes across all items, through searching or filtering processes (e.g., searching for only comedy movies) or by pre-specifying her "favorite" content attributes (e.g., indicating favorite actors or the fact that comedy movies are preferable to action movies), and recommend to the user the items that are the most similar to her preferences and satisfy specified search and/or filtering conditions. Therefore, even though there are some aspects of "multi-criteria" nature due to multiple content attributes, most of these approaches are well represented by the existing paradigms of content-based, hybrid, conversational, case-based reasoning, and some knowledge-based recommender systems as well as traditional information retrieval approaches. For example, several case-based travel recommender systems [76, 77] filter out unwanted items based on each user's preferences on multi-attribute content (e.g., locations, services, and activities), and find personalized travel plans for each user by ranking possible travel plans based on the user's preferences and past travel plans of this or similar users. In addition, some case-based recommender systems [14, 72] allow users to "critique" the recommendation results by refining their requirements as part of the interactive and iterative recommendation process, which uses various search and filtering techniques to continuously provide the user with the updated set of recommendations. For example, when searching for a desktop PC, users can critique the current set of provided recommendations by expressing their refined preferences on individual features (e.g., cheaper price) or multiple features together (e.g., higher processor speed, RAM, and hard-disk capacity). An entire research stream of *conversational recommender systems* is dedicated to these types of approaches [8, 9, 13, 37, 95–97]. Some additional examples of related approaches can be found in Chap. 5.

Multi-Objective Recommendation Strategies Traditionally, the main focus of recommender systems research has been on developing recommendation algorithms that provide *accurate* recommendations, where accuracy can be evaluated using a variety of different measures, such as MAE, RMSE, precision, recall, F-measure, normalized discounted cumulative gain (NDCG), and many others, depending on recommendation task. However, understanding that recommendation accuracy may not always completely align with recommendation usefulness, researchers have been proposing a number of alternative measures, including coverage, diversity, novelty, serendipity, and several others, to evaluate the performance of recommender systems. As a result, modern recommender systems implementations may use multiple *performance* criteria when deciding on the final set of recommendations to be shown to a given user, e.g., using accuracy, diversity, and freshness recommendation criteria in Netflix movie recommendations [6]. In summary, the "multi-criteria" nature in such approaches arises not from the attempts to represent more complex user preferences but rather from optimizing multiple different recommendation performance objectives. This type of work is well represented in recommender systems research stream on performance metrics and evaluation [31, 75, 88].

Multi-Criteria Rating-Based Preference Elicitation This category of recommender systems engage multi-criteria ratings, often by extending traditional collaborative filtering approaches, that represent users' *subjective* preferences for various *components* of individual items. For instance, such systems allow users to rate not only the overall satisfaction from a particular movie, but also the satisfaction from the various movie components (factors), such as the visual effects, the story, or the acting. In other words, these approaches allow a user to specify her individual preferences in a more precise and nuanced manner by rating each item on multiple criteria (e.g., rating the story of movie "Avatar" as 3, and the visual effects of the same movie as 5), and then are able to leverage this more sophisticated preference information in item recommendations. These approaches differ from the multi-attribute content approaches in that the users do not indicate their preference or importance weight on the visual effects component for movies in general or to be used in a particular user query, but rather *how much* they liked the visual effects of the *particular* movie. One example of early research in this area is the Intelligent Travel Recommender system [76], where users can rate multiple travel items within a "travel bag" (e.g., location, accommodation, etc.) as well as the entire travel bag. Then, candidate travel plans are ranked according to these user ratings, and the system finds the best match between recommended travel plans and the current needs of a user. These and similar types of multi-criteria rating-based systems are the focus of this chapter and more exemplar systems and techniques are provided in the later sections.

In summary, as seen above, a number of recommendation approaches that employ traditional content-based, knowledge-based, collaborative filtering, and hybrid techniques can be viewed as multi-criteria recommender systems in some way or another. Some of these approaches model user preferences based on multi-attribute content of items that users preferred in the past, others allow users to specify their current content-related preferences as search or filtering conditions, and yet others try to provide recommendations by balancing several performance metrics at once. However, as mentioned earlier, there is a recent trend in multi-criteria recommendation that studies innovative approaches in collaborative recommendation by attempting to capture and model user preferences in a more comprehensive, more nuanced manner by engaging multi-criteria ratings. We believe that this additional information on users' preferences offers many opportunities for providing novel recommendation support, creating a unique multi-criteria rating environment that has not been extensively researched. Therefore, in the following sections, we survey the state-of-the-art techniques on this particular type of systems that use individual ratings along multiple criteria, which we will refer to as *multi-criteria rating recommenders*.

The remainder of this chapter is organized as follows. In Sect. 25.2, we overview the particular type of multi-criteria recommender systems that use multi-criteria ratings, referred to as *multi-criteria rating recommenders*. In Sects. 25.3 and 25.4, we survey the state-of-the-art algorithms that are used in this type of recommenders for rating prediction and recommendation generation. Finally, Sect. 25.5 discusses research challenges and future research directions for multi-criteria recommender systems, followed by brief conclusions in Sect. 25.6.

25.2 Multi-Criteria Rating Recommendation

In this section, we define the multi-criteria rating recommendation problem by formally extending it from its single-rating counterpart (for more details on traditional single-rating recommender systems refer to Chaps. 2, 3 and 7), and provide some further discussion about the advantages that additional criteria may provide in recommender systems.

25.2.1 Traditional Single-Rating Recommendation Problem

Traditionally recommender systems operate in a two-dimensional space of *Users* and *Items*. The utility of items to users is generally represented by a totally ordered set of ratings R_0. The ratings can be unary (e.g., purchases), binary (e.g., like vs. dislike, high vs. low, good vs. bad), small set of ordered discrete values (e.g., 1-star, 2-stars, ..., 5-stars), or numbers within a certain range (e.g., $[-10, 10]$) [4]. In most recommendation applications, function R is explicitly known only for some subset of the $Users \times Items$ space, e.g., for the items that users have previously consumed and have provided their preference ratings for, and that the majority of the $Users \times Items$ space is unknown. Recommender systems aim to predict the utility of an item for a user. As mentioned earlier, a utility function R can be formally written as follows:

$$R : Users \times Items \rightarrow R_0 \tag{25.1}$$

The utility function is determined based on user inputs, such as numeric ratings that users explicitly give to items and/or transaction data that implicitly shows users' preferences (e.g., purchase history). The majority of traditional recommender systems use single-criterion ratings that indicate how much a given user liked a particular item in total (i.e., the overall utility of an item by a user). For example, in a movie recommender system, as shown in Fig. 25.1, user *Alice* may assign a single-criterion rating of 5 (out of 10) for movie *Wanted*, which can be denoted by $R(Alice, Wanted) = 5$. As an illustration, let us assume that the neighborhood-based collaborative filtering technique [73], i.e., one of the most popular heuristic-based recommendation techniques, is used for rating prediction. This technique predicts a user's rating for a given item based on the ratings of other users with similar preferences (i.e., neighbors). Particularly, in this example, the recommender system tries to predict the utility of movie *Fargo* for *Alice* based on the observed ratings. Since *Alice* and *John* show similar rating patterns on the four movies that both of them have previously seen and rated (see Fig. 25.1), for the purpose of this simple example the rating of movie *Fargo* for user *Alice* is predicted using *John*'s rating (i.e., 9), although we would like to note that it is more common to use the ratings of more than one neighbor in a real system.

	Wanted	WALL-E	Star Wars	Seven	Fargo	
Target user → Alice	5	7	5	7	?	← Ratings to be predicted
User most similar to the target user → John	5	7	5	7	9	← Ratings to be used in prediction
Mason	6	6	6	6	5	
:	:	:	:	:	:	

Fig. 25.1 Single-rating movie recommender system

25.2.2 Extending Traditional Recommender Systems to Include Multi-Criteria Ratings

With a growing number of real-world applications, extending recommendation techniques to incorporate multi-criteria ratings has been regarded as one of the important issues for the next generation of recommender systems [4]. Examples of multi-criteria rating systems include Zagat's Guide that provides three criteria for restaurant ratings (e.g., food, décor, and service), Buy.com that provides multi-criteria ratings for consumer electronics (e.g., display size, performance, battery life, and cost), and Yahoo! Movies that show each user's ratings for four criteria (e.g., story, action, direction, and visuals). This additional information about users' preferences provided by multi-criteria ratings (instead of a single overall rating) can potentially be helpful in improving the performance of recommender systems.

Some multi-criteria rating systems can choose to model a user's utility for a given item with an overall rating R_0 as well as the user's ratings $R_1, \ldots, R_k$ for each individual criterion c ($c = 1, \ldots, k$), whereas some systems can choose not to use the overall rating and focus solely on individual criteria ratings. Therefore, the utility-based formulation of the multi-criteria recommendation problem can be represented either with or without overall ratings as follows:

$$R : \mathit{Users} \times \mathit{Items} \rightarrow R_0 \times R_1 \times \cdots \times R_k \tag{25.2}$$

or

$$R : \mathit{Users} \times \mathit{Items} \rightarrow R_1 \times \cdots \times R_k \tag{25.3}$$

Given the availability of multi-criteria ratings (in addition to the traditional single overall rating) for each item, Figs. 25.1 and 25.2 illustrate the potential benefits of this information for recommender systems. While *Alice* and *John* have similar preferences on movies in a single-rating setting (Fig. 25.1), in a multi-criteria rating setting we could see that they show substantially different preferences on several movie aspects, even though they had the same overall ratings (Fig. 25.2). Upon further inspection of all the multi-criteria rating information, one can see that *Alice*

	Wanted	WALL-E	Star Wars	Seven	Fargo	
Alice (Target user)	5,2,2,8,8	7,5,5,9,9	5,2,2,8,8	7,5,5,9,9	?,?,?,?,?	← Ratings to be predicted
John	5,8,8,2,2	7,9,9,5,5	5,8,8,2,2	7,9,9,5,5	9,8,8,10,10	
Mason (User most similar to the target user)	6,3,3,9,9	6,4,4,8,8	6,3,3,9,9	6,4,4,8,8	5,2,2,8,8	← Ratings to be used in prediction
:	:	:	:	:	:	

Fig. 25.2 Multi-criteria movie recommender system (ratings for each item: overall, story, action, direction, and visual effects)

and *Mason* show very similar rating patterns (much more similar than *Alice* and *John*). Thus, using the same collaborative filtering approach as before, but taking into account multi-criteria ratings, *Alice*'s overall rating for movie *Fargo* would be predicted as 5, based on *Mason*'s overall rating for this movie.

This example implies that a single overall rating may hide the underlying heterogeneity of users' preferences for different aspects of a given item, and multi-criteria ratings may help to better understand each user's preferences, as a result enabling to provide users more accurate recommendations. It also illustrates how multi-criteria ratings can potentially produce more powerful and focused recommendations, e.g., by recommending movies that will score best on the story criterion, if this is the most important one for some user.

Therefore, new recommendation algorithms and techniques are needed that can utilize multi-criteria ratings in recommender systems. Since recommender systems typically calculate and provide recommendations using the following two-phase process, i.e., rating prediction phase and recommendation generation phase, multi-criteria rating information can be used in both of these phases in different ways. A number of approaches have been developed for the prediction or recommendation and there are already several systems implementing such algorithms, which we analyze in the next two sections.

- *Prediction*: the phase in which the prediction of a user's preference is calculated. Traditionally, it is the phase in which a recommender estimates the utility function R for the entire or some part of $Users \times Items$ space based on known ratings and possibly other information (such as user profiles and/or item content); in other words, it calculates the predictions of ratings for the unknown items.
- *Recommendation*: the phase in which the calculated prediction is used to support the user's decision by some recommendation process, e.g., the phase in which the user gets recommended a set of top-N items that maximize his/her utility (such as recommend N items with highly predicted ratings and that also satisfy some additional desirable requirements, e.g., related to item diversity or novelty).

We first classify the existing techniques for multi-criteria rating recommenders into two groups—techniques used during rating prediction and techniques used during recommendation generation—and describe these groups in more detail in the next two sections. The overview of these techniques is presented in Table 25.1.

Table 25.1 Techniques for multi-criteria rating recommenders

<table>
<tr><th>Phase of the recommendation process</th><th colspan="2">Recommendation techniques</th></tr>
<tr><td rowspan="2">Rating prediction</td><td>Heuristic-based approaches</td><td>Model-based approaches</td></tr>
<tr><td>Using multi-criteria ratings to improve user-user or item-item similarity calculation in neighborhood-based collaborative filtering:
• Calculate similarity values on each criterion, aggregate individual similarities into a single similarity (possibly using importance weights for each criterion)
• Calculate similarity values using multidimensional distance metrics directly on multi-criteria rating vectors
Heuristic rating prediction using fuzzy modeling:
• Fuzzy linguistic modeling
• Fuzzy multi-criteria preference aggregation</td><td>Building predictive models to estimate unknown ratings given multi-criteria rating data
• Typical approach: build models to aggregating individual criteria ratings into one overall rating
Representative model-based approaches:
• Simple aggregation functions: simple average, linear regression
• Probabilistic modeling: flexible mixture models, probabilistic latent semantic analysis
• Multi-linear singular value decomposition (MSVD)
• Complex aggregation functions: support vector regression (SVR)</td></tr>
<tr><td>Item recommendation (i.e., determining the best items)</td><td colspan="2">When the overall rating is available (among the multi-criteria ratings)
• Typical approach: rank items by their predicted overall rating
When the overall rating is not available:
• Design a total order for item recommendations, e.g., UTA approach
• Find Pareto optimal item recommendations, e.g., data envelopment analysis, skyline queries
• Use individual rating criteria as recommendation filters</td></tr>
</table>

25.3 Engaging Multi-Criteria Ratings During Prediction

This section provides an overview of the techniques that use multi-criteria ratings to predict an overall rating or individual criteria ratings (or both). In general, recommendation techniques can be classified by the formation of the utility function into two categories: heuristic-based (sometimes also referred to as memory-based) and model-based techniques [4, 12]. Heuristic-based techniques compute the utility of each item for a user on the fly based on the observed data of the user and are typically based on a certain heuristic assumption. For example, a neighborhood-based technique—one of the most popular heuristic-based collaborative filtering techniques—assumes that two users who show similar preferences on the observed items will have similar preferences for the unobserved items as well. In contrast, model-based techniques learn a predictive model, typically using statistical or machine-learning methods, that can best explain the observed data, and then use the learned model to estimate the utility of unknown items for recommendations. Following this classification, we also present the algorithms of multi-criteria rating recommenders by grouping them into heuristic and model-based approaches.

25.3.1 Heuristic Approaches

There has been some work done to extend the *similarity* computation of the traditional heuristic-based collaborative filtering technique to reflect multi-criteria rating information [2, 52, 92]. In this approach, the similarities between users are computed by aggregating traditional similarities from individual criteria or using multidimensional distance metrics. Note that this approach changes only the similarity calculation component of traditional recommendation algorithms; once the similarity is estimated, the overall rating calculation process remains the same.

In particular, the neighborhood-based collaborative filtering recommendation technique predicts unknown ratings for a given user, based on the known ratings of the other users with similar preferences or tastes (i.e., neighbors). Therefore, the first step of the prediction processes is to choose the similarity computation method to find a set of neighbors for each user. Various methods have been used for similarity computation in single-criterion rating recommender systems, and the most popular methods are correlation-based and cosine-based. $R(u, i)$ represents the rating that user u gives to item i, and $\overline{R(u)}$ represents the average rating of user u. Assuming that $I(u, u')$ represents the common items that two users u and u' rated, two popular similarity measures can be formally written as follows:

- *Pearson correlation-based*:

$$sim(u, u') = \frac{\sum_{i \in I(u,u')} (R(u, i) - \overline{R(u)})(R(u', i) - \overline{R(u')})}{\sqrt{\sum_{i \in I(u,u')} (R(u, i) - \overline{R(u)})^2} \sqrt{\sum_{i \in I(u,u')} (R(u', i) - \overline{R(u')})^2}} \tag{25.4}$$

- *Cosine-based*:

$$sim(u, u') = \frac{\sum_{i \in I(u,u')} R(u, i) R(u', i)}{\sqrt{\sum_{i \in I(u,u')} R(u, i)^2} \sqrt{\sum_{i \in I(u,u')} R(u', i)^2}} \tag{25.5}$$

Multi-criteria rating recommenders cannot directly employ the above formulas, because $R(u, i)$ contains an overall rating r_0, and k multi-criteria ratings $r_1, \ldots, r_k$, i.e., $R(u,i) = (r_0, r_1, \ldots, r_k)$.[1] Thus, there are k+1 rating values for each pair of (u, i), instead of a single rating. Two different similarity-based approaches that use $k+1$ rating values in computing similarities between users have been used. The first approach *aggregates traditional similarities that are based on each individual rating*. This approach first computes the similarity between two users separately on each individual criterion, using any traditional similarity computation, such as correlation-based and cosine-based similarity. Then, a final similarity between two users is obtained by aggregating $k+1$ individual similarity values. Adomavicius and Kwon [2] propose two aggregation approaches: an average and the worst-case (i.e., smallest) similarity, as specified in (25.6) and (25.7). As a general approach, Tang and McCalla [92], in their recommender system of research papers, compute an aggregate similarity as a weighted sum of individual similarities over several criteria of each paper (e.g., overall rating, value added, degree of being peer-recommended, and learners' pedagogical features such as interest and background knowledge) as specified in (25.8). In their approach, the weight of each criterion c, denoted by w_c, is chosen to reflect how important and useful the criterion is considered to be for the recommendation.

- *Average similarity*:

$$sim_{avg}(u,u') = \frac{1}{k+1}\sum\nolimits_{c=0}^{k} sim_c(u,u') \tag{25.6}$$

- *Worst-case(smallest) similarity*:

$$sim_{min}(u,u') = \min_{c=0,\ldots,k} sim_c(u,u') \tag{25.7}$$

- *Aggregate similarity*:

$$sim_{aggregate}(u,u') = \sum\nolimits_{c=0}^{k} w_c sim_c(u,u') \tag{25.8}$$

The second approach calculates similarity using *multidimensional distance metrics*, such as Manhattan, Euclidean, and Chebyshev distance metrics [2]. The distance between two users u and u' on item i, $d(R(u,i), R(u',i))$, can be calculated as:

- *Manhattan distance*:

$$\sum\nolimits_{c=0}^{k} |r_c(u,i) - r_c(u',i)| \tag{25.9}$$

---

[1] In some recommender systems, $R(u,i)$ might not contain the overall ratings r_0 in addition to k multi-criteria ratings, i.e., $R(u,i) = (r_1, \ldots, r_k)$. In this case, all the formulas in this subsection will still be applicable with index $c \in \{1, \ldots, k\}$, as opposed to $c \in \{0, 1, \ldots, k\}$.

- *Euclidean distance*:

$$\sqrt{\sum_{c=0}^{k} |r_c(u,i) - r_c(u',i)|^2} \tag{25.10}$$

- *Chebyshev (or maximal value) distance*:

$$\max_{c=0,\ldots,k} |r_c(u,i) - r_c(u',i)| \tag{25.11}$$

The overall distance between two users can be simply an average distance for all common items that both users rated, and it can be formally written as:

$$dist(u,u') = \frac{1}{|I(u,u')|} \sum_{i \in I(u,u')} d(R(u,i), R(u',i)) \tag{25.12}$$

The more similar two users are (i.e., the larger the similarity value between them is), the smaller is the distance between them. Therefore, the following simple transformation is needed because of the inverse relationship of the two metrics:

$$sim(u,u') = \frac{1}{1 + dist(u,u')} \tag{25.13}$$

Manouselis and Costopoulou [52] also propose three different algorithms to compute *similarities* between users in multi-criteria rating settings: similarity-per-priority, similarity-per-evaluation, and similarity-per-partial-utility. The similarity-per-priority algorithm computes the similarities between users based on importance weights $w_c(u)$ of user u for each criterion c (rather than ratings $R(u,i)$). In this way, it creates a neighborhood of users that have the same importance weights on multiple criteria with the target user. Then, it tries to predict the overall utility of an item for this user, based on the total utilities of the users in the neighborhood. In addition, the similarity-per-evaluation and similarity-per-partial-utility algorithms create separate neighborhoods for the target user for each criterion, i.e., they calculate the similarity with other users per individual criterion, and then predict the rating that the target user would provide upon each individual criterion. The similarity-per-evaluation algorithm calculates the similarity based on the non-weighted ratings that the users provide on each criterion. The similarity-per-partial-utility algorithm calculates the similarity based on the weighted (using $w_c(u)$ of each user u) ratings that the users provide on each criterion.

In such systems, the similarities between users are obtained using multi-criteria ratings, and the rest of the recommendation process can be the same as in single-criterion rating systems. The next step is, for a given user, to find a set of neighbors with the highest similarity values and predict unknown overall ratings of the user based on neighbors' ratings. Therefore, these similarity-based approaches are applicable only to neighborhood-based collaborative filtering recommendation techniques that need to compute the similarity between users (or items).

In summary, multi-criteria ratings can be used to compute the similarity between two users in the following two ways [2]: by (1) aggregating similarity values that are calculated separately on each criterion into a single similarity and (2) calculating the distance between multi-criteria ratings directly in the multi-dimensional space. Empirical results using a small-scale Yahoo! Movies dataset show that both heuristic approaches outperform the corresponding traditional single-rating collaborative filtering technique (i.e., that uses only single overall ratings) by up to 3.8 % in terms of precision-in-top-N metric, which represents the percentage of truly high overall ratings among those that the system predicted to be the N most relevant items for each user [2]. The improvements in precision depend on many parameters of collaborative filtering techniques, such as neighborhood sizes and the number of top-N recommendations. Furthermore, these approaches can be extended as suggested by Manouselis and Costopoulou [52] by computing similarities using not only known rating information, but also importance weights for each criterion. The latter approaches were evaluated in an online application that recommends e-markets to users, where multiple buyers and sellers can access and exchange information about prices and product offerings, based on users' multi-criteria evaluations on several e-markets. The similarity-per-priority algorithm using Euclidian distance performed the best among their proposed approaches in terms of the mean absolute error (MAE) (i.e., 0.235 on scale of 1–7) with a fairly high coverage (i.e., 93 % of items can be recommended to users) as compared to non-personalized algorithms, such as arithmetic mean and random, that produce higher MAE (0.718 and 2.063, respectively) with 100 % coverage [52].

Maneeroj et al. [50] further investigate the problem of finding the most appropriate neighbors in multi-criteria recommendation settings. In particular, based on the observation that different criteria may have varying importance for different users, they propose an approach that incorporates the individualized importance levels of each criteria into the user-user similarity calculation process. This approach may provide more appropriately chosen neighbors and, consequently, result in better recommendation results.

As mentioned earlier, once the similarity between users or items is computed, the standard neighborhood-based collaborative filtering recommendation technique generally estimates the rating that user u would give to item i by computing the weighted average of all known ratings $R(u', i)$, where user u' is "similar" to u. Two popular ways to compute this weighted average are as follows [12]:

- *Weighted sum approach*:

$$R(u,i) = \frac{\sum_{u' \in N(u,i)} sim(u,u')R(u',i)}{\sum_{u' \in N(u,i)} |sim(u,u')|} \tag{25.14}$$

- *Adjusted weighted sum approach*:

$$R(u,i) = \overline{R(u)} + \frac{\sum_{u' \in N(u,i)} sim(u,u')(R(u',i) - \overline{R(u')})}{\sum_{u' \in N(u,i)} |sim(u,u')|} \tag{25.15}$$

Here the value of rating $R(u', i)$ is weighted by the similarity of user u' to user u—the more similar the two users are, the more weight $R(u', i)$ will have in the computation of rating $R(u, i)$. $N(u, i)$ represents the set of users that are similar to user u among the ones who consumed item i, and the size of set $N(u, i)$ can range anywhere from 1 to all users in the dataset. Limiting the neighborhood size to some specific number (e.g., 3) will determine how many similar users will be used in the computation of rating $R(u, i)$.

In the similarity-based approach [2], the above two formulas are typically used to predict the *overall* ratings only, because the recommendations are usually based on the system's predictions of the overall user preferences for items. In other words, $R(u, i)$ here refers to r_0 and not to the entire multi-dimensional rating vector $R(u, i) = (r_0, r_1, \ldots, r_k)$. However, the same formulas can be used to predict each individual criteria rating r_i, if desired. Also, the heuristic similarity-based approach explained above represent the *user-based* approach that uses neighboring users to compute recommendations. As the user-based approach using single criterion ratings can be straightforwardly transformed to the item-based approach that uses neighboring items to compute recommendations [85], the formulas for the user-based approach in the multi-criteria rating settings can be straightforwardly rewritten for the item-based approach.

Furthermore, having to submit precise numeric ratings for multiple criteria of each individual item may represent an increased burden for users. Therefore, it may be advantageous to consider the subjective, imprecise, and vague nature of human ratings when collecting such information. Several studies propose to use fuzzy linguistic approaches for representing and collecting user ratings and to employ fuzzy multi-criteria decision making techniques to rank the relevant items for each user [10, 66]. More specifically, each user's relevance feedback can be collected in the qualitative form (in linguistic terms). For example, in the work of Boulkrinat et al. [10], each user evaluated six criteria of a hotel (i.e., Clean, Comfort, Location, Facilities, Staff, and Value-for-Money), and the user's preferences are expressed through linguistic terms on a scale of 7 levels (i.e., Very High, High, Medium High, Medium, Medium Low, Low and Very Low). The preference for each criterion is then modeled not by a single numeric value (i.e., single level) but rather by a "fuzzy number" (essentially, by a range of levels). The weight of each criterion can be provided by an individual user, representing his or her personal relative importance among the six criteria.

Other fuzzy-based algorithms for multi-criteria CF systems are introduced in the work of Nilashi et al. [61], including Weighted Fuzzy MC-CF and Fuzzy Euclidean MC-CF that use fuzzy-based average similarity and fuzzy-based Euclidean distance respectively, and Fuzzy Average MC-CF that uses a fuzzy-based user- and item-based predictions in a weighted approach. Palanivel and Sivakumar [68] also propose a fuzzy aggregation-based approach that finds preference criterion using a maximum operator, particularly from implicit interest indicators such as time spent on hearing a music item, number of accesses to a music item, and music download status. The use of such implicit interest indicators can further mitigate the burden for the users to keep providing multiple ratings for each consumed item.

25.3.2 Model-Based Approaches

Model-based approaches construct a predictive model to estimate unknown ratings by learning from the observed data. Several existing approaches for multi-criteria rating recommenders fall into this category, including simple aggregation functions, probabilistic modeling, multilinear singular value decomposition (MSVD), and support vector regression (SVR).

Aggregation Function Approach While overall rating r_0 is often considered simply as just another criterion rating in similarity-based heuristic approaches (as illustrated earlier), the aggregation function approach assumes that the overall rating serves as an aggregate of multi-criteria ratings [2]. Given this assumption, this approach finds aggregation function f that represents the relationship between overall and multi-criteria ratings, i.e.,

$$r_0 = f(r_1, \ldots, r_k) \tag{25.16}$$

For example, in a movie recommendation application, the story criteria rating may have a very high "priority," i.e., the movies with high story ratings are well liked overall by some users, regardless of other criteria ratings. Therefore, if the story rating of the movie is predicted high, the overall rating of the movie must also be predicted high in order to be accurate.

The aggregation function approach consists of three steps, as summarized in Fig. 25.3. First, this approach estimates k individual ratings using any recommendation technique. That is, the k-dimensional multi-criteria rating problem is decomposed into k single-rating recommendation problems. Second, aggregation function f is chosen using domain expertise, statistical techniques, or machine learning techniques. For example, the domain expert may suggest a simple average function of the underlying multi-criteria ratings for each item based on her prior experience and knowledge. An aggregation function also can be obtained by using statistical techniques, such as linear and non-linear regression analysis techniques, as well as various sophisticated machine learning techniques, such as artificial neural networks. Finally, the overall rating of each unrated item is computed based on the k predicted individual criteria ratings and the chosen aggregation function f.

While the similarity-based heuristic approaches described earlier apply to only neighborhood-based collaborative filtering recommendation techniques, the aggregation function approach can be used in combination with any traditional recommendation technique, because individual criteria ratings are used for the prediction in the first step. As one example of possible aggregation functions, Adomavicius and Kwon [2] use linear regression and estimate coefficients (i.e., importance weights of each individual criterion) based on the known ratings.

Adomavicius and Kwon [2] also note that the aggregation function can have different scopes: total (i.e., when a single aggregation function is learned based on the entire dataset), user-based or item-based (i.e., when a separate aggregation function is learned for each user or item).

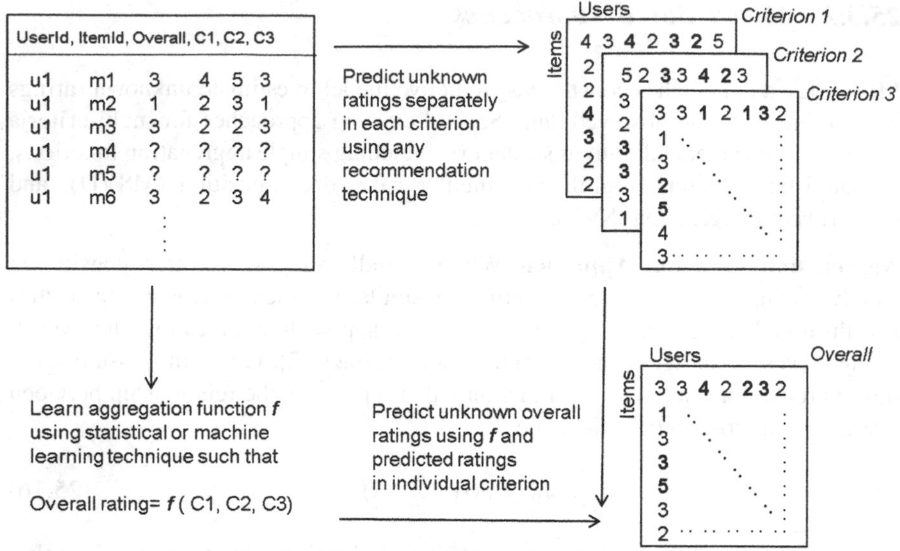

Fig. 25.3 Aggregation function approach (an example of a three-criteria rating system)

Empirical analysis using data from Yahoo! Movies shows that the aggregation function approach (using multi-criteria rating information) outperforms a traditional single-rating collaborative filtering technique (using only overall ratings) by 0.3–6.3 % in terms of precision-in-top-N ($N = 3, 5$, and 7) metric [2].

Probabilistic Modeling Approach Some multi-criteria recommendation approaches adopt probabilistic modeling algorithms that are becoming increasingly popular in data mining and machine learning. One example is the work of Sahoo et al. [80], which extends the flexible mixture model (FMM) developed by Si and Jin [89] to multi-criteria rating recommenders. The FMM assumes that there are two latent variables Z_u and Z_i (for users and items), and they are used to determine a single rating r of user u on item i, as shown in Fig. 25.4a. Sahoo et al. [80] also discover the dependency structure among the overall ratings (r_0) and multi-criteria ratings (r_1, r_2, r_3, and r_4), using Chow-Liu tree structure discovery [19], and incorporate the structure into the FMM, as shown in Fig. 25.4b.

The FMM approach is based on the assumption that the joint distribution of three variables (user u, rating r, and item i) can be expressed using the sum of probabilities over the all possible combinations of the two latent class variables Z_u and Z_i, as follows.

$$P(u, i, r) = \sum_{Z_u, Z_i} P(Z_u)P(Z_i)P(u|Z_u)P(i|Z_i)P(r|Z_u, Z_i) \qquad (25.17)$$

In summary, an overall rating of an unknown item for a target user is estimated with the following two steps: learning and prediction. In the first (learning) step, all

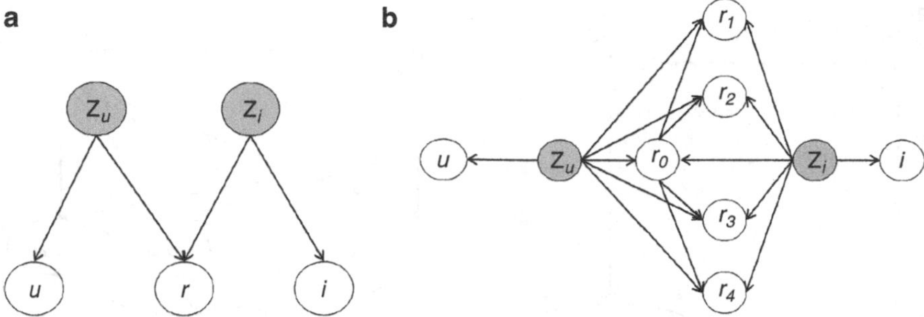

Fig. 25.4 Examples of probabilistic modeling approach in recommender systems. (**a**) Flexible Mixture Model for a single-rating recommender system [89]. (**b**) FMM with multi-criteria rating dependency structure [80]

the parameters of the FMM are estimated using the expectation maximization (EM) algorithm [21]. Using the obtained parameters, in the second (prediction) step, the overall rating of a given unknown item is predicted as the most likely value (i.e., the rating value with the highest probability). This approach has been extended to multi-criteria ratings, and the detailed algorithm can be found in [80].

Sahoo et al. [80] also compare their model in Fig. 25.4b with the model that assumes independence among multi-criteria ratings conditional on the latent variables, and found that the model with dependency structure performs better than the one with the independence assumption. This finding demonstrates the existence of the "halo effect" in multi-criteria rating systems. The "halo effect" is a phenomenon often studied in psychometric literature, which indicates a cognitive bias whereby the perception of a particular object in one category influences the perception in other categories [94]. In multi-criteria recommender systems, the individual criterion ratings provided by users are correlated due to the "halo effect", and particularly more correlated to an overall rating than to other individual ratings [80]. In other words, the overall rating given by the user to a specific item seems to affect how the user rates the other (individual) criteria of this item. Thus, controlling for an overall rating reduces this halo effect and helps to make individual ratings independent of each other, as represented in the Chow-Liu tree dependency structure (Fig. 25.4b).

Using data from Yahoo! Movies, Sahoo et al. [80] show that multi-criteria rating information is advantageous over a single rating when very little training data is available (i.e., less than 15 % of the whole data is used for training). On the other hand, when large training data is available, additional rating information does not seem to add much value. In this analysis, they measure the recommendation accuracy using the MAE metric. However, when they validate this probabilistic modeling approach using precision and recall metrics in retrieving top N items, their model performs better in all cases (i.e., both with small and large datasets) with a maximum of 10 % increase. With more training data, the difference between the model with multi-criteria ratings and the traditional single-rating model diminishes in terms of precision and recall metrics.

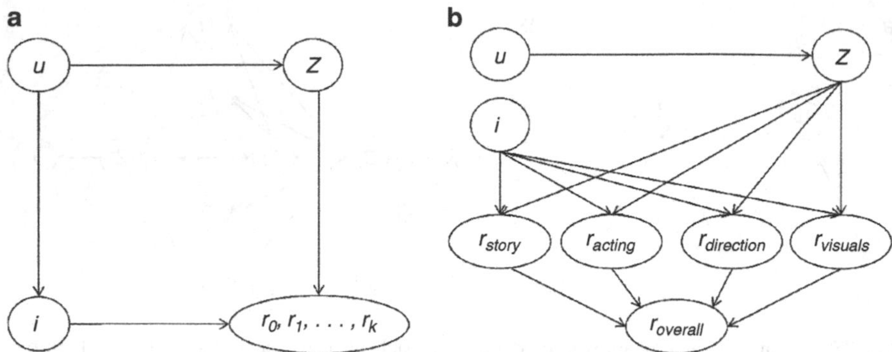

Fig. 25.5 Graphical model representation of multi-criteria PLSA algorithms. (**a**) Full Gaussian PLSA [100]. (**b**) Linear Gaussian Regression PLSA using Yahoo!Movies dataset [100]

Another probabilistic modeling approach was proposed by Zhang et al. [100], who extend the probabilistic latent semantic analysis (PLSA) approach used for single-criteria recommender systems [32] into multi-criteria rating settings. In particular, [100] investigate two multi-criteria PLSA algorithms, based on their modeling of the underlying multi-criteria rating distribution of each user: (1) using full multi-variate Gaussian distribution, and (2) using linear Gaussian regression model. Both proposed approaches provide accuracy improvements over several single-criteria and multi-criteria recommender systems baselines. Graphical model presentations of the two approaches are shown in Fig. 25.5a and b, where r represents a rating of item i by user u and Z is a latent variable. The full gaussian model uses multi-variable nodes $r_0, r_1, \ldots, r_k$ instead of uni-variate node r, and applies the same EM algorithm as used in the single-rating PLSA. Linear Gaussian regression model computes the overall preference (r_0) as the linear combination of preferences on individual criteria ($r_1, \ldots, r_k$). Furthermore, while the work of Sahoo et al. [80] does not employ any normalization scheme for ratings of each user (e.g., adjusting the neutral vote of the individuals to zero and standardizing the scale of all users to the same value), [100] shows that user normalization significantly affects the performance of the multi-criteria PLSA approaches.

Multilinear Singular Value Decomposition (MSVD) Approach Li et al. [46] propose an approach to improve a traditional collaborative filtering algorithm by utilizing the MSVD technique which is a particular realization of the Matrix Factorization approach in multi-criteria rating settings. Singular value decomposition (SVD) techniques have been extensively studied in numerical linear algebra and have also gained popularity in recommender systems applications because of their effectiveness in improving recommendation accuracy [28, 40, 84]. In single-rating recommender systems, these techniques are used to find a lower-dimensional feature space. For example, using K latent features (i.e., rank-K SVD), user u is associated with user-factor vector p_u (the user's preferences on K features), and item i is associated with item-factor vector q_i (the item's importance weights on K features).

After all the values in user- and item-factors vectors are estimated, the preference of how much user u likes item i, denoted by $R^*(u, i)$, is predicted by taking an inner product of the two vectors, i.e.,

$$R^*(u, i) = p_u^T q_i \tag{25.18}$$

More details on the basic SVD techniques can be found in Chap. 7. While the SVD techniques are commonly used as a decomposition method for two-dimensional data (i.e., single criterion ratings), they can be extended for multi-dimensional data (i.e., multi-criteria ratings), referred to as MSVD techniques [20]. For example, Li et al. [46] incorporate contextual information and multi-criteria ratings into recommendation processes. Based on the contextual information, the recommendation problem is defined as a 3-order tensor representing the rating of an item by a user on a criterion under a specific context, and the tensor approximation based on the truncated MSVD technique is then performed. The approximated tensor is finally used to improve neighborhood formation for later use in a neighborhood-based collaborative filtering approach, i.e., identifying the nearest neighbors of each user and computing top-N recommendations.

More specifically, Li et al. [46] use the MSVD to reduce the dimensionality of multi-criteria rating data and evaluate their approach in the context of a restaurant recommender system, where a user rates a restaurant on 10 criteria (i.e., cuisine, ambience, service, etc.). The results demonstrate that their approach improves the accuracy of recommendations (as measured by precision-in-top-N) by up to 5 %, as compared to the traditional single-rating model.

Support Vector Regression (SVR) Approach Several other studies also follow the general aggregation function approach; however, instead of using the traditional linear least squares regression method, they propose to use the Support Vector Regression (SVR) [23] to learn the regression-based rating aggregation functions [25, 34, 35, 81]. While all features can be considered in the regression, [34, 35] propose several ways to choose the most relevant features—by using the chi-squared statistics with respect to the overall ratings for each criterion, applying a genetic feature selection algorithm, or obtaining the advice from a domain expert—and highlight the importance of choosing an adequate subset of item dimensions since it affects the performance of recommendations.

In addition to the higher reported predictive accuracy, another advantage of the SVR technique is that it can be employed in settings with relatively few data points but many features (e.g., many rating dimensions). In particular, Jannach et al. [35] use both user- and item-based SVR approach, i.e., they estimate regression models R^*_{user} individually for each user and regression models R^*_{item} individually for each item. Then, the two predictions can be combined using item and user weights. As described in Fig. 25.6, user- and item-based SV-regression is learned from training data, and criteria ratings can be predicted using any CF technique. Then, overall ratings are estimated using the criteria predictions and SV-regression functions. The final prediction is computed as a weighted combination of the two

Step 1. For each user u and each item i, learn user and item SV-regression-based aggregation functions $R^*_{user}(u,i)$ and $R^*_{item}(u,i)$ from training data
Step 2. Predict individual ratings on multiple criteria for item i and user u (using some standard CF technique)
Step 3. Predict overall ratings using user and item SV-regression-based aggregation functions $R^*_{user}(u,i)$ and $R^*_{item}(u,i)$
Step 4. Use standard gradient descent to compute user and item weights (w_u, w_i)

```
require: #iterations, γ, λ
// Gradient descent iterations:
for 1 to #iterations do
  for each user u do
    for each rated item i of user u do
      // compute prediction with current weights
      R*(u,i) → w_u × R*_user(u,i) + w_i × R*_item(u,i)
      // compare with real rating R(u,i) and determine the error e(u,i)
      e(u,i) ← R(u,i) − R*(u,i)
      // Adjust w_u in gradient step
      w_u ← w_u + γ·(e(u,i) − λ·w_u)
      // Adjust w_i in gradient step
      w_i ← w_i + γ·(e(u,i) − λ·w_i)
return w_u for each user u, and w_i for each item i
```

Step 5. Combine the two predictions using user and item weights
$R^*(u,i) = w_u \times R^*_{user}(u,i) + w_i \times R^*_{item}(u,i)$

Fig. 25.6 Gradient descent algorithm for the weighted support vector regression (SVR) method [35]

overall predictions obtained from user and item-based SV-regression function. Step 4 of Fig. 25.6 describes how weights w_u and w_i are estimated (optimized) in a personalized manner for each user u and item i. A fast, heuristic gradient descent procedure is used to estimate parameters for each user and item by minimizing the prediction error calculated as the difference between the predicted and the actual rating. Here parameter γ determines the size of the correcting step, and λ is used as a regularization to avoid over-fitting.

The results show that the proposed approach using support vector regression with individual and optimized weights for each single user and item compares favorably against a number of existing approaches with respect to multiple evaluation metrics (RMSE, F-measure, precision-in-top-N) on hotel and movie rating datasets. In addition, [35] also evaluated several feature selection strategies that can be useful for multi-criteria recommendation settings with many rating dimensions and showed that using relative simple feature selection procedures (such as chi-square statistics) can lead to further improvements in recommendation accuracy.

In summary, the above approaches represent some of the initial attempts to apply sophisticated learning techniques to address multi-criteria recommendation problems, and we expect to see more such techniques in the future. In the next section, we discuss different approaches to recommending items to users, assuming that the unknown multi-criteria ratings have been estimated using any of the techniques discussed above.

25.4 Engaging Multi-Criteria Ratings During Recommendation

As mentioned above, multi-criteria recommender systems may choose to model a user's utility for a given item by including both the overall rating and ratings of individual item components/criteria or they may choose to include only ratings of individual criteria. If overall ratings are included as part of the model, the recommendation process in such cases is typically straightforward: after predicting all unknown ratings, the recommender system uses the overall rating of items to select the most highly predicted items (i.e., the most relevant items) for each user. In other words, the recommendation process is essentially the same as in traditional, single-criterion recommender systems.

However, without an overall rating the recommendation process becomes more complex, because it is less apparent how to establish the total order of the items. For example, suppose that we have a two-criterion movie recommender system, where users judge movies based on their story (i.e., plot) and visual effects. Further, suppose that one movie needs to be chosen for recommendation among the following two alternatives: (1) movie X, predicted as 8 in story and 2 in visuals, and (2) movie Y, predicted as 5 in story and 5 in visuals. Since there is no overall criterion to rank the movies, it is not easy to judge which movie is better, unless some other modeling approach is adopted, using some non-numerical (e.g., rule-based) way for expressing preferences. Several approaches have been proposed in the recommender systems literature to deal with this problem: some try to design a total order on items and obtain a single global optimal solution for each user, whereas others take one of the possible partial orders of the items and find multiple (Pareto optimal) solutions. Below we briefly mention related work on multi-criteria optimization, describe several approaches that have been used in the recommender systems literature, and discuss other potential uses of multi-criteria ratings in the recommendation process.

25.4.1 *Related Work: Multi-Criteria Optimization*

Multi-criteria optimization problems have been extensively studied in the operations research (OR) literature [24], although not in the context of recommender systems. This multi-criteria optimization approach assists a decision maker in choosing the best alternative when multiple criteria conflict and compete with each other. For example, various points of view, such as financial, human resources-related, and environmental aspects should be considered in organizational decision making. The following approaches are often used to address multi-criteria optimization problems, and can be applied to recommender systems, as discussed in [4]:

- Finding Pareto optimal solutions;
- Taking a linear combination of multiple criteria and reducing the problem to the single-criterion optimization problem;
- Optimizing only the most important criterion and converting other criteria to constraints;
- Consecutively optimizing one criterion at a time, converting an optimal solution to constraints and repeating the process for other criteria.

In multi-criteria rating recommenders, an item can be evaluated differently on a different criterion; thus, it is not an easy task to find the best item overall. Below we describe several recommendation approaches that have been used in the recommender systems literature, all of them having roots in multi-criteria optimization techniques, including: converting the multi-criteria optimization problem into single-criterion ranking problem (Sect. 25.4.2), finding Pareto optimal recommendations (Sect. 25.4.3), and using multiple criteria as constraints (Sect. 25.4.4).

25.4.2 Designing a Total Order for Item Recommendations

In the recommender systems literature there has been some work using multi-attribute utility theories from decision sciences, which can be described as one way to take a linear combination of multiple criteria and find an optimal solution [43], essentially reducing the multi-criteria optimization problem to a simple, single-criteria ranking problem. For example, the approach by Lakiotaki et al. [43] ranks the items by adopting the UTilités Additive (UTA) method proposed by Siskos et al. [90]. Their algorithm aims to estimate overall utility U of a specific item for each user by adding the marginal utilities of each criterion $c (c = 1, \ldots, k)$.

$$U = \sum\nolimits_{c=1}^{k} u_c(R_c) \tag{25.19}$$

which is subject to the following constraints: $u_c(R_c^{worst}) = 0, \forall c = 1, 2, \ldots, k$ and $\sum_{c=1}^{k} u_c(R_c^{best}) = u_1(R_1^{best}) + u_2(R_2^{best}) + \cdots + u_k(R_k^{best}) = 1$. Here R_c is the rating provided on criterion c, and $u_c(R_c)$ is a non-decreasing real-value function (marginal utility function) for a specific user. Assuming that $[R^{worst}, R^{best}]$ is the criterion evaluation scale, R_i^{worst} and R_i^{best} are the worst and the best level of the i-th criterion respectively. The decision maker is asked to provide her global evaluation so as to form a total pre-order of the alternatives (items): $i_1 \succ i_2 \succ \cdots \succ i_m$. The developed utility model is assumed to be consistent with the decision maker's judgment policy so that $U(i_1) > U(i_2) \cdots > U(i_m)$. In developing the global utility model to meet this requirement, there are two types of possible errors which may occur: (1) the under-estimation error when the developed model assigns an alternative to a lower (better) rank than the one specified in the given pre-order (the alternative is under-estimated by the decision maker), and (2) the over-estimation error when the developed model assigns an alternative to a higher (worse) rank than the one specified in the given pre-order (the alternative is over-estimated by the decision maker). The final model is chosen by minimizing the sum of these two errors. Given the estimated ratings on multiple criteria, this can be performed using linear programming techniques.

Since this approach uses the ranking information with ordinal regression techniques, Kendall's tau is used as a measure of correlation between two ordinal-level variables to compare an actual order and the predicted order. The empirical results obtained by using data from Yahoo! Movies show that 20.4 % of users obtain a Kendall's tau of 1 indicating a total agreement of the orders between the ones predicted by the recommender system and the ones stated by users, and the mean value of Kendall's tau across all users is 0.74. This approach is also evaluated using the Receiver Operating Curve (ROC), which depicts relative trade-offs between true positives and false positives. The obtained Area Under Curve (AUC) of 0.81, where 1 represents a perfect classifier and 0.5 represents the performance of a random classifier, demonstrates that multi-criteria ratings provide measurable improvements in modeling users' preferences.

Similarly, Manouselis and Costopoulou [52] propose a method that calculates total utility U either by summing the k predicted partial utilities u_c (in their similarity-per-partial-utility algorithm) or by weighting the predicted ratings that the user would give on each criterion c by the user's importance weights w_c (in their similarity-per-evaluation algorithm). In both cases, the total utility of a candidate item is calculated using an aggregate function of the following form:

$$U = \sum_{c=1}^{k} u_c = \sum_{c=1}^{k} w_c R_c \tag{25.20}$$

Here individual ratings on multiple criteria are used to rank the candidate items, rather than explicitly estimate overall ratings. Finally, once the total order on the candidate items is established using any of the above techniques, each user gets recommended the items that maximize this total utility.

Akhtarzada et al. [5] also use each user's ratings on items under multiple criteria to rank the items as a recommendation list. To do so, users are first assigned ideal values on each criterion as an average of their past ratings, and the rating on a new item for a specific user is predicted by calculating the distance between the ideal values for all users and the ideal values for the user. Then, when a user sees an item, the most similar item can be recommended based on the similarities between items for the user.

25.4.3 Finding Pareto Optimal Item Recommendations

This approach discovers several good items among large number of candidates (rather than arriving at a unique solution by solving a global optimization problem) when different items can be associated with multiple conflicting criteria and the total order on items is not directly available. *Data envelopment analysis* (DEA), often also called "frontier analysis", is commonly used to measure productive efficiency of decision making units (DMU) in operations research [18]. DEA computes the efficiency frontier, which identifies the items that are "best performers" overall, taking into account all criteria. DEA does not require *a priori* weights for each criterion, and uses linear programming to arrive more directly at the best set of weights for each DMU. Specifically, in the context of multi-criteria recommender systems, given all the candidate items that are available for recommendation to a given user (including the information about their predicted ratings across all criteria), DEA would be able to determine the reduced set of items (i.e., the frontier) that have best ratings across all criteria among the candidates. These items then can be recommended to the user.

While DEA has not been directly used in multi-criteria rating recommenders, the multi-criteria recommendation problem without overall ratings can also be formulated as a data query problem in the database field, using similar motivation [44]. Lee and Teng [44] utilize *skyline* queries to find the best restaurants across multiple criteria (i.e., food, décor, service, and cost). As Fig. 25.7 shows, skyline queries identify a few skyline points (i.e., Pareto optimal points) that are not dominated by any others from a large number of candidate restaurants in two-dimensional data space (food and décor). Here, for a given user, a candidate item is considered to be dominated, if there exists another candidate item that has better or equal ratings on all criteria.

Empirical results using multi-criteria ratings of Zagat Survey in [44] show that the recommender system using skyline queries helps to reduce the number

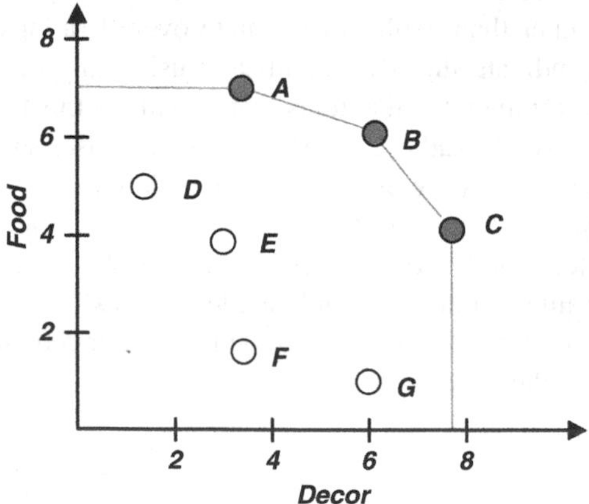

Fig. 25.7 An example of skyline points (the best candidate restaurants) in two-dimensional space

of choices that users should consider from their inquiries. For example, when a user searches for buffet restaurants which are located in New York City with a cost of no more than $30, the system recommends only two restaurants among twelve candidate restaurants, based on the ratings on four criteria. However, this preliminary work needs to be extended in several directions because the skyline queries may not scale well with the increasing number of criteria, resulting in a large number of skyline points with high computational cost.

25.4.4 Using Multi-Criteria Ratings as Recommendation Filters

Similar to how content attributes can be used as recommendation filters in recommender systems [45, 86], multi-criteria ratings can be used for similar purposes as well. For example, a user may want to specify that only the movies with an exceptionally good story should be recommended to her at a given time, regardless of other criteria, such as visual effects. Then, only the movies that are highly predicted in the story criterion (say, ≥ 9 out of 10) will be recommended to the user. In other words, the dimensionality of multi-criteria optimization problem can be reduced by converting some of the criteria to constraints (filters). This approach is also similar to how content-based [45, 86] or context-aware [3] recommendation approaches filter recommendations; however, it is also slightly different from them, because the filtering is done not based on objective content attributes (e.g., MovieLength < 120 min) or additional contextual dimensions (e.g., TimeOfWeek = weekend), but on the subjective rating criteria (e.g., Story $\geq$ 9), the predicted value of which is highly dependent on user's tastes and preferences.

25.5 Discussion and Future Work

Recommender systems represent a vibrant and constantly changing research area. Among the important recent developments, recommender systems have recently started adopting multi-criteria ratings provided by users, and in this chapter we explored algorithms and techniques for multi-criteria recommender systems. These relatively new systems have not yet been studied extensively, and in this section we present a number of challenges and future research directions for this category of recommender systems.

25.5.1 Developing New Approaches for Multi-Criteria Ratings

Modeling Multi-Criteria Ratings Traditionally, user preferences in recommender systems (including multi-criteria recommender systems) are expressed using simple numeric ratings. Recent work has started to explore alternative approaches for representing and collecting user ratings (e.g., using fuzzy techniques [10, 66]) as well as for modeling ratings in a more nuanced manner (e.g., taking into account semantic interval-scale characteristics of numeric ratings [57]). A comprehensive exploration of user preference modeling, especially in more complex multi-criteria settings, represents an interesting direction for future work.

Intelligent Data Pre-Processing and Segmentation It is well-known that many recommendation settings suffer from the data "sparsity" issue. One possible approach to alleviate this problem is to perform intelligent data segmentation or clustering, where the non-useful dimensions (criteria) are discarded or where data from similar users (or similar items) is merged and the resulting recommendations are calculated (and potentially improved) by taking this aggregation into account. In data mining literature, there has been some work on what the optimal customer segmentation should be [36]. Also, in multi-criteria recommender systems, several approaches have already used a wide variety of specialized user clustering procedures as part of the proposed recommendation algorithms (e.g., [42, 47, 49, 61, 62]). Some researchers have also explored different feature selection techniques for determining the best criteria to use in multi-criteria settings [35]. However, further studies are needed to examine various data pre-processing and segmentation approaches for multi-criteria recommender systems in a more systematic manner.

Predicting Relative Preferences An alternative way to define the multi-criteria recommendation problem could be formulated as predicting the *relative* preferences of users, as opposed to the *absolute* rating values. There has been some work on constructing the correct relative order of items using ordering-based techniques. For example, Freund et al. [26] developed the RankBoost algorithm based on the well-known AdaBoost method and, in multi-criteria settings, such algorithms could be adopted to aggregate different relative orders obtained from different rating criteria for a particular user. In particular, this is an approach taken by the DIVA system [59, 60].

Constructing the Item Evaluation Criteria More research needs to be done on choosing or constructing the best set of criteria for evaluating an item. For example, most of current multi-criteria rating recommenders require users to rate an item on multiple criteria at a single level (e.g., story and special effects of a movie). This single level of criteria could be further broken down into sub-criteria, and there could be multiple levels depending on the given problem. For example, in a movie recommender system, special effects could be again divided into sound and graphic effects. More information with multiple levels of criteria could potentially help to better understand user preferences, and various techniques, such as the analytic hierarchy process (AHP), can be used to consider the hierarchy of criteria [79], as Schmitt et al. [87] propose to do in their system. As we consider more criteria for each item, we may also need to carefully examine the correlation among criteria because the choice of criteria may significantly affect the recommendation quality. Furthermore, it is important to have a *consistent* family of criteria for a given recommender system application, which means that the criteria are monotonic, exhaustive, and non-redundant. In summary, constructing a set of criteria for a given recommendation problem is an interesting and important topic for future research.

Incorporating Domain-Specific Information Many multi-criteria recommender systems are designed without exploiting specific domain knowledge. For example, understanding not just the multiple hotel characteristics (such as cleanliness, location, service, etc.), but also the different segments of population that like to travel (e.g., business travellers, senior travellers, honeymoon/romantic travellers, spring-break travellers, etc.) can provide substantial advantages in designing better recommendation algorithms. Several studies have started exploring the models that can incorporate domain-specific information into multi-criteria recommender systems [11, 27], but there are a lot of further opportunities in this research direction. Similarly, many application domains have rich content information available, and taking advantage of this information (e.g., leveraging tag information for movie recommendation [29, 30] or leveraging job-seeking intent for talent recommendation [78]), can provide further improvements in multi-criteria recommender systems.

25.5.2 Extending Existing Techniques for Multi-Criteria Settings

Reusing Existing Single-Rating Recommendation Techniques A huge number of recommendation techniques have been developed for single-rating recommender systems over the last 15–20 years, and some of them have been extended to multi-criteria rating systems, as discussed in this chapter. For example, neighborhood-based collaborative filtering techniques can take into account multi-criteria ratings using the huge number of design options that Manouselis and Costopoulou [53] suggest (and as discussed in Sect. 25.3.1). There have also been multi-criteria SVD-based and PLSA-based recommendation approaches proposed (as discussed in Sect. 25.3.2), which stem from their single-criterion counterparts. However, among alternative approaches, there has been a number of sophisticated hybrid recommendation approaches developed in recent years [16], and some of them could potentially be adopted for multi-criteria rating recommenders. Finally, more sophisticated techniques, e.g., based on data envelopment analysis (DEA) or multi-criteria optimization, could be adopted and extended for choosing best items in the multi-criteria rating settings.

Investigating Group Recommendation Techniques for Multi-Criteria Settings Some techniques for generating recommendations to groups, as described in Chap. 22, can be adopted in multi-criteria rating settings. According to [33], a group preference model can be built by aggregating the diverse preferences of several users. Similarly, a user's preference for an item in multi-criteria rating settings can be predicted by aggregating the preferences based on different rating criteria. More specifically, there can be many different goals for aggregating individual preferences [55, 64], such as maximizing average user satisfaction, minimizing misery (i.e., high user dissatisfaction), and providing a certain level of fairness (e.g., low variance with the same average user satisfaction). Multi-criteria rating recommenders could investigate the adoption of some of these approaches for aggregating preferences from multiple criteria.

25.5.3 Managing Multi-Criteria Ratings

Managing Intrusiveness The extra information provided by multi-criteria ratings can give rise to an important issue of "intrusiveness", i.e., the requirement for the users to provide this extra information to the system. Specifically, for a recommender system to achieve good recommendation performance, users typically need to provide to the system a certain amount of feedback about their preferences (e.g., in the form of item ratings). This can be an issue even in single-rating recommender systems [39, 56, 63], and some less intrusive techniques to obtain user preferences in multi-criteria recommender systems have been explored [54, 65, 67, 71]. Multi-criteria rating systems are likely to require a more significant level of user involvement because each user would need to rate an item on multiple criteria. Therefore, it is important to measure the costs and benefits of adopting multi-criteria ratings and find an optimal solution to meet the needs of both users and system designers. Preference disaggregation methods could support the implicit formulation of a preference model based on a series of previous decisions. A characteristic example is the UTA (i.e., UTilités Additive) method, which can be used to extract the utility function from a user-provided ranking of known items [43]. Another example is the ability to obtain each user's preferences on several attributes of an item implicitly from the user's written comments, minimizing intrusiveness [1, 54, 70]. There are also some empirical approaches with less computational complexity [82]. Lastly, performing user studies on multi-criteria recommender systems would further examine the impact of having to submit more ratings on the overall user satisfaction.

Dealing with Missing Multi-Criteria Ratings Multi-criteria recommender systems typically would require the users to provide more data to such systems than their single-rating counterparts, thus increasing the likelihood of obtaining missing or incomplete data. One popular technique to deal with missing data is the expectation maximization (EM) algorithm [21] that finds maximum likelihood estimates for incomplete data. In particular, the probabilistic modeling approach for multi-criteria rating prediction proposed by Sahoo et al. [80] uses the EM algorithm to predict values of the missing ratings in multi-criteria rating settings. Similarly, Bayesian models are proposed to handle incomplete missing rating data, for example, missing ratings on one criterion with the ratings on other criteria [91]. The applicability of other existing techniques in this setting should be explored, and novel techniques could be developed by considering the specifics of multi-criteria information, such as the possible relationships between different criteria.

Collecting Large-Scale Multi-Criteria Rating Data Multi-criteria rating datasets that can be used for algorithm testing and parameterization are rare. For this new area of recommender systems to be successful, it is crucial to have a number of standardized real-world multi-criteria rating datasets available to the research community. Some initial steps towards a more standardized representation, reusability, and interoperability of multi-criteria rating datasets have been taken in other application domains, such as e-learning [98].

In this section we discussed several potential future research directions for multi-criteria recommenders that should be interesting to recommender systems community. This list is not meant to be exhaustive; we believe that research in this area is only in its preliminary stages, and there are a number of possible additional topics that could be explored to advance multi-criteria recommender systems.

25.6 Conclusions

In this chapter, we aimed to provide an overview of multi-criteria recommender systems. More specifically, we focused on the category of *multi-criteria rating recommenders*, i.e., techniques that provide recommendations by modelling a user's utility for an item as a vector of ratings along several criteria. We reviewed current techniques that use multi-criteria ratings for calculating the rating predictions and generating recommendations, and discussed open issues and future challenges for this class of recommender systems.

This survey provides a systematic view of multi-criteria recommender systems, a roadmap of relevant work, and a discussion of a number of promising future research directions. However, we believe that this sub-area of recommender systems is still in its early stages of development, and much more research is needed to unlock the full potential of multi-criteria recommenders.

References

1. Aciar, S., Zhang, D., Simoff, S., Debenham, J.: Informed recommender: Basing recommendations on consumer product reviews. IEEE Intelligent systems **22**(3), 39–47 (2007)
2. Adomavicius, G., Kwon, Y.: New recommendation techniques for multicriteria rating systems. IEEE Intelligent Systems **22**(3), 48–55 (2007)

3. Adomavicius, G., Sankaranarayanan, R., Sen, S., Tuzhilin, A.: Incorporating contextual information in recommender systems using a multidimensional approach. ACM Transactions on Information Systems (TOIS) **23**(1), 103–145 (2005)
4. Adomavicius, G., Tuzhilin, A.: Toward the next generation of recommender systems: A survey of the state-of-the-art and possible extensions. IEEE Transactions on Knowledge and Data Engineering **17**(6), 734–749 (2005)
5. Akhtarzada, A., Calude, C., Hosking, J.: A multi-criteria metric algorithm for recommender systems. Fundamenta Informaticae **110**(1), 1–11 (2011)
6. Amatriain, X., Basilico, J.: Netflix recommendations: Beyond the 5 stars. http://techblog.netflix.com/2012/04/netflix-recommendations-beyond-5-stars.html (2012). Accessed: 2014-06-28
7. Balabanovic, M., Shoham, Y.: Fab: content-based, collaborative recommendation. Communications of the ACM **40**(3), 66–72 (1997)
8. Blanco, H., Ricci, F.: Acquiring user profiles from implicit feedback in a conversational recommender system. In: Q. Yang, I. King, Q. Li, P. Pu, G. Karypis (eds.) RecSys, pp. 307–310. ACM (2013)
9. Blanco, H., Ricci, F., Bridge, D.: Conversational query revision with a finite user profiles model. In: G. Amati, C. Carpineto, G. Semeraro (eds.) IIR, *CEUR Workshop Proceedings*, vol. 835, pp. 77–88. CEUR-WS.org (2012)
10. Boulkrinat, S., Hadjali, A., Mokhtari, A.: Towards recommender systems based on a fuzzy preference aggregation. In: 8th conference of the European Society for Fuzzy Logic and Technology (EUSFLAT-13). Atlantis Press (2013)
11. Brandt, D.: How service marketers can identify value-enhancing service elements. Journal of Services Marketing **2**(3), 35–41 (1988)
12. Breese, J., Heckerman, D., Kadie, C.: Empirical analysis of predictive algorithms for collaborative filtering. In: Proc. of the 14th Conference on Uncertainty in Artificial Intelligence, vol. 461, pp. 43–52. San Francisco, CA (1998)
13. Bridge, D.: Towards conversational recommender systems: A dialogue grammar approach. In: ECCBR Workshops, pp. 9–22 (2002)
14. Burke, R.: Knowledge-based recommender systems. Encyclopedia of Library and Information Systems **69**(Supplement 32), 175–186 (2000)
15. Burke, R.: Hybrid recommender systems: Survey and experiments. User Modeling and User-Adapted Interaction **12**(4), 331–370 (2002)
16. Burke, R.: Hybrid web recommender systems. Lecture Notes in Computer Science **4321**, 377–408 (2007)
17. Burke, R., Ramezani, M.: Matching recommendation technologies and domains. In: Recommender Systems Handbook, pp. 367–386. Springer (2011)
18. Charnes, A., Cooper, W., Rhodes, E.: Measuring the efficiency of decision making units. European Journal of Operational Research **2**(6), 429–444 (1978)
19. Chow, C., Liu, C.: Approximating discrete probability distributions with dependence trees. IEEE Transactions on Information Theory **14**(3), 462–467 (1968)
20. De Lathauwer, L., De Moor, B., Vandewalle, J.: A multilinear singular value decomposition. SIAM Journal on Matrix Analysis and Applications **21**(4), 1253–1278 (2000)
21. Dempster, A., Laird, N., Rubin, D.: Maximum likelihood from incomplete data via the EM algorithm. Journal of the Royal Statistical Society.Series B (Methodological) **39**(1), 1–38 (1977)
22. Dolan, J.: Multi-criteria clinical decision support. The Patient: Patient-Centered Outcomes Research **3**(4), 229–248 (2010). DOI 10.2165/11539470-000000000-00000. URL http://dx.doi.org/10.2165/11539470-000000000-00000
23. Drucker, H., Burges, C., Kaufman, L., Smola, A., Vapnik, V.: Support vector regression machines. In: M. Mozer, M. Jordan, T. Petsche (eds.) NIPS, pp. 155–161. MIT Press (1996)
24. Ehrgott, M.: Multicriteria optimization. Springer Verlag (2005)
25. Fan, J., Xu, L.: A robust multi-criteria recommendation approach with preference-based similarity and support vector machine. In: Advances in Neural Networks–ISNN 2013, pp. 385–394. Springer (2013)

26. Freund, Y., Iyer, R., Schapire, R., Singer, Y.: An efficient boosting algorithm for combining preferences. The Journal of Machine Learning Research **4**, 933–969 (2003)
27. Fuchs, M., Zanker, M.: Multi-criteria ratings for recommender systems: An empirical analysis in the tourism domain. In: E-Commerce and Web Technologies, pp. 100–111. Springer (2012)
28. Funk, S.: Netflix update: Try this at home. http://sifter.org/ simon/journal/20061211.html (2006)
29. Gedikli, F., Jannach, D.: Rating items by rating tags. In: Proceedings of the 2010 Workshop on Recommender Systems and the Social Web at ACM RecSys, pp. 25–32 (2010)
30. Gedikli, F., Jannach, D.: Improving recommendation accuracy based on item-specific tag preferences. ACM Transactions on Intelligent Systems and Technology (TIST) **4**(1), 11 (2013)
31. Herlocker, J., Konstan, J., Terveen, L., Riedl, J.: Evaluating collaborative filtering recommender systems. ACM Transactions on Information Systems (TOIS) **22**(1), 5–53 (2004)
32. Hofmann, T.: Latent semantic models for collaborative filtering. ACM Trans. Inf. Syst. **22**(1), 89–115 (2004). DOI 10.1145/963770.963774. URL http://doi.acm.org/10.1145/963770.963774
33. Jameson, A., Smyth, B.: Recommendation to groups. Lecture Notes in Computer Science **4321**, 596–627 (2007)
34. Jannach, D., Gedikli, F., Karakaya, Z., Juwig, O.: Recommending hotels based on multidimensional customer ratings. In: Information and Communication Technologies in Tourism 2012, pp. 320–331. Springer (2012)
35. Jannach, D., Karakaya, Z., Gedikli, F.: Accuracy improvements for multi-criteria recommender systems. In: Proceedings of the 13th ACM Conference on Electronic Commerce, pp. 674–689. ACM (2012)
36. Jiang, T., Tuzhilin, A.: Segmenting customers from population to individuals: Does 1-to-1 keep your customers forever? IEEE Trans. on Knowl. and Data Eng. **18**(10), 1297–1311 (2006). DOI 10.1109/TKDE.2006.164. URL http://dx.doi.org/10.1109/TKDE.2006.164
37. Kelly, J., Bridge, D.: Enhancing the diversity of conversational collaborative recommendations: a comparison. Artif. Intell. Rev. **25**(1-2), 79–95 (2006)
38. Konstan, J.: Introduction to recommender systems: Algorithms and evaluation. ACM Transactions on Information Systems (TOIS) **22**(1), 1–4 (2004)
39. Konstan, J., Miller, B., Maltz, D., Herlocker, J., Gordon, L., Riedl, J.: Grouplens: applying collaborative filtering to usenet news. Communications of the ACM **40**(3), 77–87 (1997)
40. Koren, Y.: Collaborative filtering with temporal dynamics. In: Proc. of the 15th ACM SIGKDD international conference on Knowledge discovery and data mining, pp. 447–456. ACM New York, NY, USA (2009)
41. Koren, Y., Bell, R.: Advances in collaborative filtering. In: Recommender Systems Handbook, pp. 145–186. Springer (2011)
42. Lakiotaki, K., Matsatsinis, N., Tsoukias, A.: Multicriteria user modeling in recommender systems. IEEE Intelligent Systems **26**(2), 64–76 (2011). DOI http://doi.ieeecomputersociety.org/10.1109/MIS.2011.33
43. Lakiotaki, K., Tsafarakis, S., Matsatsinis, N.: UTA-Rec: a recommender system based on multiple criteria analysis. In: Proc. of the 2008 ACM conference on Recommender systems, pp. 219–226. ACM New York, NY, USA (2008)
44. Lee, H., Teng, W.: Incorporating multi-criteria ratings in recommendation systems. In: IEEE International Conference on Information Reuse and Integration, pp. 273–278 (2007)
45. Lee, W., Liu, C., Lu, C.: Intelligent agent-based systems for personalized recommendations in internet commerce. Expert Systems with Applications **22**(4), 275–284 (2002)
46. Li, Q., Wang, C., Geng, G.: Improving personalized services in mobile commerce by a novel multicriteria rating approach. In: Proc. of the 17th International World Wide Web Conference. Beijing, China (2008)
47. Liu, L., Mehandjiev, N., Xu, D.L.: Multi-criteria service recommendation based on user criteria preferences. In: Proceedings of the fifth ACM conference on Recommender systems, pp. 77–84. ACM (2011)

48. Lops, P., De Gemmis, M., Semeraro, G.: Content-based recommender systems: State of the art and trends. In: Recommender systems handbook, pp. 73–105. Springer (2011)
49. Lousame, F., Sánchez, E.: Multicriteria predictors using aggregation functions based on item views. In: Intelligent Systems Design and Applications (ISDA), 2010 10th International Conference on, pp. 947–952. IEEE (2010)
50. Maneeroj, S., Samatthiyadikun, P., Chalermpornpong, W., Panthuwadeethorn, S., Takasu, A.: Ranked criteria profile for multi-criteria rating recommender. In: Information Systems, Technology and Management, pp. 40–51. Springer (2012)
51. Manouselis, N., Costopoulou, C.: Analysis and classification of multi-criteria recommender systems. World Wide Web: Internet and Web Information Systems **10**(4), 415–441 (2007)
52. Manouselis, N., Costopoulou, C.: Experimental analysis of design choices in multiattribute utility collaborative filtering. International Journal of Pattern Recognition and Artificial Intelligence **21**(2), 311–332 (2007)
53. Manouselis, N., Costopoulou, C.: Overview of design options for neighborhood-based collaborative filtering systems. Personalized Information Retrieval and Access: Concepts, Methods and Practices pp. 30–54 (2008)
54. McAuley, J., Leskovec, J., Jurafsky, D.: Learning attitudes and attributes from multi-aspect reviews. In: Data Mining (ICDM), 2012 IEEE 12th International Conference on, pp. 1020–1025. IEEE (2012)
55. McCarthy, J.: Pocket restaurantfinder: A situated recommender system for groups. In: Proc. of the Workshop on Mobile Ad-Hoc Communication at the 2002 ACM Conference on Human Factors in Computer Systems. Minneapolis, MN (2002)
56. Middleton, S., Shadbolt, N., De Roure, D.: Ontological user profiling in recommender systems. ACM Transactions on Information Systems (TOIS) **22**(1), 54–88 (2004)
57. Mikeli, A., Apostolou, D., Despotis, D.: A multi-criteria recommendation method for interval scaled ratings. In: Web Intelligence (WI) and Intelligent Agent Technologies (IAT), 2013 IEEE/WIC/ACM International Joint Conferences on, vol. 3, pp. 9–12. IEEE (2013)
58. Naak, A., Hage, H., Aimeur, E.: A multi-criteria collaborative filtering approach for research paper recommendation in papyres. In: E-Technologies: Innovation in an Open World, pp. 25–39. Springer (2009)
59. Nguyen, H., Haddawy, P.: DIVA: applying decision theory to collaborative filtering. In: Proc. of the AAAI Workshop on Recommender Systems. Madison, WI (1998)
60. Nguyen, H., Haddawy, P.: The decision-theoretic video advisor. In: Proc. of the 15th Conference on Uncertainty in Artificial Intelligence (UAI'99), pp. 494–501. Stockholm, Sweden (1999)
61. Nilashi, M., Ibrahim, O., Ithnin, N.: Hybrid recommendation approaches for multi-criteria collaborative filtering. Expert Systems with Applications **41**(8), 3879–3900 (2014)
62. Nilashi, M., Ibrahim, O., Ithnin, N.: Multi-criteria collaborative filtering with high accuracy using higher order singular value decomposition and neuro-fuzzy system. Knowledge-Based Systems (2014)
63. Oard, D., Kim, J.: Modeling information content using observable behavior. In: Proc. of the Annual Meeting-American Society for Information Science, vol. 38, pp. 481–488. Washington DC. (2001)
64. O'Connor, M., Cosley, D., Konstan, J., Riedl, J.: PolyLens: A recommender system for groups of users. In: Proc. of the seventh conference on European Conference on Computer Supported Cooperative Work, pp. 199–218. Kluwer Academic Publishers (2001)
65. Oh, J., Jeong, O., Lee, E.: A personalized recommendation system based on product attribute-specific weights and improved user behavior analysis. In: Proceedings of the 4th International Conference on Ubiquitous Information Management and Communication, p. 57. ACM (2010)
66. Palanivel, K., Siavkumar, R.: Fuzzy multicriteria decision-making approach for collaborative recommender systems. International Journal of Computer Theory and Engineering **2**(1), 57–63 (2010)
67. Palanivel, K., Sivakumar, R.: A study on implicit feedback in multicriteria e-commerce recommender system. Journal of Electronic Commerce Research **11**(2) (2010)

68. Palanivel, K., Sivakumar, R.: A study on collaborative recommender system using fuzzy-multicriteria approaches. International Journal of Business Information Systems **7**(4), 419–439 (2011)
69. Pazzani, M., Billsus, D.: Learning and revising user profiles: The identification of interesting web sites. Machine Learning **27**(3), 313–331 (1997)
70. Plantie, M., Montmain, J., Dray, G.: Movies recommenders systems: automation of the information and evaluation phases in a multi-criteria decision-making process. Lecture Notes in Computer Science **3588**, 633–644 (2005)
71. Premchaiswadi, W., Poompuang, P.: Hybrid profiling for hybrid multicriteria recommendation based on implicit multicriteria information. Applied Artificial Intelligence **27**(3), 213–234 (2013)
72. Reilly, J., McCarthy, K., McGinty, L., Smyth, B.: Incremental critiquing. Knowledge-Based Systems **18**(4-5), 143–151 (2005)
73. Resnick, P., Iacovou, N., Suchak, M., Bergstrom, P., Riedl, J.: GroupLens: An open architecture for collaborative filtering of netnews. In: Proc. of the 1994 ACM conference on Computer supported cooperative work, pp. 175–186 (1994)
74. Resnick, P., Varian, H.: Recommender systems. Communications of the ACM **40**(3), 56–58 (1997)
75. Ribeiro, M., Lacerda, A., de Moura, E., Veloso, A., Ziviani, N.: Multi-objective pareto-efficient approaches for recommender systems. ACM Transactions on Intelligent Systems and Technology **9**(1), 1–20 (2013)
76. Ricci, F., Arslan, B., Mirzadeh, N., Venturini, A.: ITR: a case-based travel advisory system. Lecture Notes in Computer Science pp. 613–627 (2002)
77. Ricci, F., Venturini, A., Cavada, D., Mirzadeh, N., Blaas, D., Nones, M.: Product recommendation with interactive query management and twofold similarity. Lecture Notes in Computer Science pp. 479–493 (2003)
78. Rodriguez, M., Posse, C., Zhang, E.: Multiple objective optimization in recommender systems. In: Proceedings of the Sixth ACM Conference on Recommender Systems, RecSys '12, pp. 11–18. ACM, New York, NY, USA (2012). DOI 10.1145/2365952.2365961. URL http://doi.acm.org/10.1145/2365952.2365961
79. Saaty, T.: Optimization in integers and related extremal problems. McGraw-Hill (1970)
80. Sahoo, N., Krishnan, R., Duncan, G., Callan, J.: Research note-the halo effect in multicomponent ratings and its implications for recommender systems: The case of yahoo! movies. Information Systems Research **23**(1), 231–246 (2012)
81. Samatthiyadikun, P., Takasu, A., Maneeroj, S.: Bayesian model for a multicriteria recommender system with support vector regression. In: Information Reuse and Integration (IRI), 2013 IEEE 14th International Conference on, pp. 38–45. IEEE (2013)
82. Sampaio, I., Ramalho, G., Corruble, V., Prudencio, R.: Acquiring the preferences of new users in recommender systems: the role of item controversy. In: Proc. of the 17th European Conference on Artificial Intelligence (ECAI) Workshop on Recommender Systems, pp. 107–110. Riva del Garda, Italy (2006)
83. Sanchez-Vilas, F., Ismoilov, J., Lousame, F.P., Sanchez, E., Lama, M.: Applying multicriteria algorithms to restaurant recommendation. In: Proceedings of the 2011 IEEE/WIC/ACM International Conferences on Web Intelligence and Intelligent Agent Technology-Volume 01, pp. 87–91. IEEE Computer Society (2011)
84. Sarwar, B., Karypis, G., Konstan, J., Riedl, J.: Application of dimensionality reduction in recommender system - a case study. In: Proc. of the Workshop on Knowledge Discovery in the Web (WebKDD) (2000)
85. Sarwar, B., Karypis, G., Konstan, J., Riedl, J.: Item-based collaborative filtering recommendation algorithms. In: Proc. of the 10th International Conference on World Wide Web, pp. 285–295. ACM, New York, NY, USA (2001)
86. Schafer, J.: Dynamiclens: A dynamic user-interface for a meta-recommendation system. In: Proc. of the Workshop on the next stage of recommender systems research at the ACM Intelligent User Interfaces Conf. (2005)

87. Schmitt, C., Dengler, D., Bauer, M.: Multivariate preference models and decision making with the maut machine. In: Proc. of the 9th International Conference on User Modeling (UM 2003), pp. 297–302 (2003)
88. Shani, G., Gunawardana, A.: Evaluating recommendation systems. In: Recommender systems handbook, pp. 257–297. Springer (2011)
89. Si, L., Jin, R.: Flexible mixture model for collaborative filtering. In: Proc. of the 20th International Conference on Machine Learning, vol. 20, pp. 704–711. AAAI Press (2003)
90. Siskos, Y., Grigoroudis, E., Matsatsinis, N.: UTA methods. Springer (2005)
91. Takasu, A.: A multicriteria recommendation method for data with missing rating scores. In: Data and Knowledge Engineering (ICDKE), 2011 International Conference on, pp. 60–67. IEEE (2011)
92. Tang, T., McCalla, G.: The pedagogical value of papers: a collaborative-filtering based paper recommender. Journal of Digital Information **10**(2) (2009)
93. Tangphoklang, P., Tanchotsrinon, C., Maneeroj, S., Sophatsathit, P.: A design of multi-criteria recommender system architecture for mobile banking business in thailand. In: Proceedings of the Second International Conference on Knowledge and Smart Technologies, vol. 2010 (2010)
94. Thorndike, E.: A constant error in psychological ratings. Journal of applied psychology **4**(1), 25–9 (1920)
95. Trabelsi, W., Wilson, N., Bridge, D.: Comparative preferences induction methods for conversational recommenders. In: P. Perny, M. Pirlot, A. Tsoukiàs (eds.) ADT, *Lecture Notes in Computer Science*, vol. 8176, pp. 363–374. Springer (2013)
96. Viappiani, P., Craig, B.: Regret-based optimal recommendation sets in conversational recommender systems. In: D. Lawrence, A. Tuzhilin, R. Burke, A. Felfernig, L. Schmidt-Thieme (eds.) RecSys, pp. 101–108. ACM (2009)
97. Viappiani, P., Pu, P., Faltings, B.: Conversational recommenders with adaptive suggestions. In: J. Konstan, J. Riedl, B. Smyth (eds.) RecSys, pp. 89–96. ACM (2007)
98. Vuorikari, R., Manouselis, N., Duval, E.: Using metadata for storing, sharing, and reusing evaluations in social recommendation: the case of learning resources. Social Information Retrieval Systems: Emerging Technologies and Applications for Searching the Web Effectively pp. 87–107 (2008)
99. Zarrinkalam, F., Kahani, M.: A multi-criteria hybrid citation recommendation system based on linked data. In: Computer and Knowledge Engineering (ICCKE), 2012 2nd International eConference on, pp. 283–288. IEEE (2012)
100. Zhang, Y., Zhuang, Y., Wu, J., Zhang, L.: Applying probabilistic latent semantic analysis to multi-criteria recommender system. Ai Communications **22**(2), 97–107 (2009)

Chapter 26
Novelty and Diversity in Recommender Systems

Pablo Castells, Neil J. Hurley, and Saul Vargas

26.1 Introduction

Accurately predicting the users' interests was the main direct or implicit drive of the recommender systems field in roughly the first decade and a half of the field's development. A wider perspective towards recommendation utility, including but beyond prediction accuracy, started to appear in the literature by the beginning of the 2000s [36, 70], taking views that began to realize the importance of novelty and diversity, among other properties, in the added value of recommendation [53, 90]. This realization grew progressively, reaching an upswing of activity by the turn of the past decade [1, 3, 20, 39, 75]. Today we might say that novelty and diversity are becoming an increasingly frequent part of evaluation practice. They are being included increasingly often among the reported effectiveness metrics of new recommendation approaches, and are explicitly targeted by algorithmic innovations time and again. And it seems difficult to conceive progress in the recommender systems field without considering these dimensions and further developing our understanding thereof. Even though dealing with novelty and diversity remains an active area of research and development, considerable progress has been achieved in these years in terms of the development of enhancement techniques, evaluation metrics, methodologies, and theory, and we deem the area is therefore ripe for a broad overview as we undertake in this chapter.

In this chapter we analyze the different motivations, notions and perspectives under which novelty and diversity can be understood and defined (Sect. 26.2).

P. Castells (✉) • S. Vargas
Universidad Autonoma de Madrid, Madrid, Spain
e-mail: pablo.castells@uam.es; saul.vargas@uam.es

N.J. Hurley
University College Dublin, Dublin, Ireland
e-mail: neil.hurley@ucd.ie

F. Ricci et al. (eds.), *Recommender Systems Handbook*,
DOI 10.1007/978-1-4899-7637-6_26

We revise the evaluation procedures and metrics which have been developed in this area (Sect. 26.3), as well as the algorithms and solutions to enhance novelty and/or diversity (Sect. 26.4). We analyze the relationship with the recent and prolific stream of work on diversity in Information Retrieval, as a confluent area with recommender systems, and discuss a unifying framework that aims to provide a common basis as comprehensive as possible to explain and interrelate different novelty and diversity perspectives (Sect. 26.5). We show some empirical results that illustrate the behavior of metrics and algorithms (Sect. 26.6), and close the chapter with a summary and discussion of the progress and perspectives in this area, and directions for future research (Sect. 26.7).

26.2 Novelty and Diversity in Recommender Systems

Novelty can be generally understood as the difference between present and past experience, whereas diversity relates to the internal differences within parts of an experience. The difference between the two concepts is subtle and close connections can in fact be established, depending on the point of view one may take, as we shall discuss. The general notions of novelty and diversity can be particularized in different ways. For instance, if a music streaming service recommends us a song we have never heard before, we would say this recommendation brings some novelty. Yet if the song is, say, a very canonical music type by some very well known singer, the involved novelty is considerably less than we would get if the author and style of the music were also original for us. We might also consider that the song is even more novel if, for instance, few of our friends know about it. On the other hand, a music recommendation is diverse if it includes songs of different styles rather than different songs of very similar styles, regardless of whether the songs are original or not for us. Novelty and diversity are thus to some extent complementary dimensions, though we shall seek and discuss in this chapter the relationships between them.

The motivations for enhancing the novelty and diversity of recommendations are manifold, as are the different angles one may take when seeking these qualities. This is also the case in other fields outside information systems, where novelty and diversity are recurrent topics as well, and considerable efforts have been devoted to casting clear definitions, equivalences and distinctions. We therefore start this chapter by overviewing the reasons for and the possible meanings of novelty and diversity in recommender systems, with a brief glance at related perspectives in other disciplines.

26.2.1 Why Novelty and Diversity in Recommendation

Bringing novelty and diversity into play as target properties of the desired outcome means taking a wider perspective on the recommendation problem concerned with final actual recommendation utility, rather than a single quality side such as accuracy [53]. Novelty and diversity are not the only dimensions of recommendation utility one should consider aside from accuracy (see e.g. Chap. 8 for a comprehensive survey), but they are fundamental ones. The motivations for enhancing novelty and diversity in recommendations are themselves diverse, and can be founded in the system, user and business perspectives.

From the system point of view, user actions as implicit evidence of user needs involve a great extent of uncertainty as to what the actual user preferences really are. User clicks and purchases are certainly driven by user interests, but identifying what exactly in an item attracted the user, and generalizing to other items, involves considerable ambiguity. On top of that, system observations are a very limited sample of user activity, whereby recommendation algorithms operate on significantly incomplete knowledge. Furthermore, user interests are complex, highly dynamic, context-dependent, heterogeneous and even contradictory. Predicting the user needs is therefore an inherently difficult task, unavoidably subject to a non-negligible error rate. Diversity can be a good strategy to cope with this uncertainty and optimize the chances that at least some item pleases the user, by widening the range of possible item types and characteristics at which recommendations aim, rather than bet for a too narrow and risky interpretation of user actions. For instance, a user who has rated the movie "Rango" with the highest value may like it because—in addition to more specific virtues—it is a cartoon, a western, or because it is a comedy. Given the uncertainty about which of the three characteristics may account for the user preference, recommending a movie of each genre generally pays off more than recommending, say three cartoons, as far as three hits do not necessarily bring three times the gain of one hit—e.g. the user might rent just one recommended movie anyway—whereas the loss involved in zero hits is considerably worse than achieving a single hit. From this viewpoint we might say that diversity is not necessarily an opposing goal to accuracy, but in fact a strategy to optimize the gain drawn from accuracy in matching true user needs in an uncertain environment.

On the other hand, from the user perspective, novelty and diversity are generally desirable per se, as a direct source of user satisfaction. Consumer behaviorists have long studied the natural variety-seeking drive in human behavior [51]. The explanation of this drive is commonly divided into direct and derived motivations. The former refer to the inherent satisfaction obtained from "novelty, unexpectedness, change and complexity" [50], and a genuine "desire for the unfamiliar, for alternation among the familiar, and for information" [64], linking to the existence of an ideal level of stimulation, dependent on the individual. Satiation and decreased satisfaction results from the repeated consumption of a product or product characteristic in a decreasing marginal value pattern [25]. As preferences towards discovered products are developed, consumer behavior converges towards a balance between alternating choices and favoring preferred products [16]. Derived motivations include the existence of multiple needs in people, multiple situations, or changes in people's tastes [51]. Some authors also explain diversity-seeking as a strategy to cope with the uncertainty about one's own future preference when one will actually consume the choices [44], as e.g. when we choose books and music for a trip. Moreover, novel and diverse recommendations enrich the user experience over time, helping expand the user's horizon. It is in fact often the case that we approach a recommender system with the explicit intent of discovering something new, developing new interests, and learning. The potential problems of the lack of diversity which may result from too much personalization has recently come to the spotlight with the well-known debate on the so-called filter bubble [60]. This controversy adds to the motivation for reconciling personalization with a healthy degree of diversity.

Diversity and novelty also find motivation in the underlying businesses in which recommendation technologies are deployed. Customer satisfaction indirectly benefits the business in the form of increased activity, revenues, and customer loyalty. Beyond this, product diversification is a well-known strategy to mitigate risk and expand businesses [49]. Moreover, selling in the long tail is a strategy to draw profit from market niches by selling less of more and getting higher profit margins on cheaper products [9].

All the above general considerations can be of course superseded by particular characteristics of the specific domain, the situation, and the goal of the recommendations, for some of which novelty and diversity are indeed not always needed. For instance, getting a list of similar products (e.g. photo cameras) to one we are currently inspecting may help us refine our choice among a large set of very similar options. Recommendations can serve as a navigational aid in this type of situation. In other domains, it makes sense to consume the same or very similar items again and again, such as grocery shopping, clothes, etc. The added value of recommendation is probably more limited in such scenarios though, where other kinds of tools may solve our needs (catalog browsers, shopping list assistants, search engines, etc.), and even in these cases we may appreciate some degree of variation in the mix every now and then.

26.2.2 Defining Novelty and Diversity

Novelty and diversity are different though related notions, and one finds a rich variety of angles and perspectives on these concepts in the recommender system literature, as well as other fields such as sociology, economy, or ecology. As pointed out at the beginning of this section, novelty generally refers, broadly, to the difference between present and past experience, whereas diversity relates to the internal differences within parts of an experience. Diversity generally applies to a set of items or "pieces", and has to do with how different the items or pieces are with respect to each other. Variants have been defined by considering different pieces and sets of items. In the basic case, diversity is assessed in the set of items recommended to each user separately (and typically averaged over all users afterwards) [90]. But global diversity across sets of sets of items has also been considered, such as the recommendations delivered to all users [3, 4, 89], recommendations by different systems to the same user [11], or recommendations to a user by the same system over time [46].

The novelty of a set of items can be generally defined as a set function (average, minimum, maximum) on the novelty of the items it contains. We may therefore consider novelty as primarily a property of individual items. The novelty of a piece of information generally refers to how different it is with respect to "what has been previously seen" or experienced. This is related to novelty in that when a set is diverse, each item is "novel" with respect to the rest of the set. Moreover, a system that promotes novel results tends to generate global diversity over time in the user experience; and also enhances the global "diversity of sales" from the system perspective. Multiple variants of novelty arise by considering the fact that novelty is relative to a context of experience, as we shall discuss.

Different nuances have been considered in the concept of novelty. A simple definition of novelty can consist of the (binary) absence of an item in the context of reference (prior experience). We may use adjectives such as unknown or unseen for this notion of identity-based novelty [75]. Long tail notions of novelty are elaborations of this concept, as they are defined in terms of the number of users who would specifically know an item [20, 61, 89]. But we may also consider how different or similar an unseen item is with respect to known items, generally—but not necessarily—on a graded scale. Adjectives such as unexpected, surprising and unfamiliar have been used to refer to this variant of novelty. Unfamiliarity and identitary novelty can be related by trivially defining similarity as equality, i.e. two items are "similar" if and only if they are the same item. Finally, the notion of serendipity is used to mean novelty plus a positive emotional response—in other words, an item is serendipitous if it is novel—unknown or unfamiliar—and relevant [57, 88].

The present chapter is concerned with the diversity and novelty involved in recommendations, but one might also study the diversity (in tastes, behavior, demographics, etc.) of the end-user population, or the product stock, the sellers, or in general the environment in which recommenders operate. While some works in the field have addressed the diversity in user behavior [31, 72], we will mostly focus on those aspects a recommender system has a direct hold on, namely the properties of its own output.

26.2.3 Diversity in Other Fields

Diversity is a recurrent theme in several fields, such as sociology, psychology, economy, ecology, genetics or telecommunications. One can establish connections and analogies from some—though not all—of them to recommender systems, and some equivalences in certain metrics, as we will discuss.

Diversity is a common keyword in sociology referring to cultural, ethnic or demographic diversity [47]. Analogies to recommender system settings would apply to the user population, which is mainly a given to the system, and therefore not within our main focus here. In economy, diversity is extensively studied in relation to different issues such as the players in a market (diversity vs. oligopolies), the number of different industries in which a firm operates, the variety of products commercialized by a firm, or investment diversity as a means to mitigate the risk involved in the volatility of investment value [49]. Of all such concepts, product and portfolio diversity most closely relate to recommendation, as mentioned in Sect. 26.2.1, as a general risk-mitigating principle and/or business growth strategy.

Behaviorist psychology has also paid extensive attention to the human drive for novelty and diversity [51]. Such studies, especially the ones focusing on consumer behavior, provide formal support to the intuition that recommender system users may prefer to find some degree of variety and surprise in the recommendations they receive, as discussed in Sect. 26.2.1.

An extensive strand or literature is devoted to diversity in ecology as well, where researchers have worked to considerable depth on formalizing the problem, defining and comparing a wide array of diversity metrics, such as the number of species (richness), Gini-Simpson and related indices, or entropy [62]. Such developments connect to aggregate recommendation diversity perspectives that deal with sets of recommendations as a whole, as we shall discuss in Sects. 26.2.3 and 26.5.3.3.

Finally, the issue of diversity has also attracted a great deal of attention in the Information Retrieval (IR) field. A solid body of theory, metrics, evaluation methodologies and algorithms has been developed in this scope in the last decade [6, 17, 21, 22, 24, 67, 84], including a dedicated search diversity task in four consecutive TREC editions starting in 2009 [23]. Search and recommendation are different problems, but have much in common: both tasks are about ranking a set of items to maximize the satisfaction of a user need, which may or may not have been expressed explicitly. It has in fact been found that the diversity theories and techniques in IR and recommender systems can be connected [77, 78], as we will discuss in Sect. 26.5.4. Given these connections, and the significant developments on diversity in IR, we find it relevant to include an overview of this work here, as we will do in Sects. 26.3 (metrics) and 26.4 (algorithms).

26.3 Novelty and Diversity Evaluation

The definitions discussed in the previous sections can only get a full, precise and practical meaning when one has given a specific definition of the metrics and methodologies by which novelty and diversity are to be measured and evaluated. We review next the approaches and metrics that have been developed to assess novelty and diversity, after which we will turn to the methods and algorithms proposed in the field to enhance them.

26.3.1 Notation

As is common in the literature, we will use the symbols i and j to denote items, u and v for users, $\mathcal{I}$ and $\mathcal{U}$ for the set of all items and users respectively. By $\mathcal{I}_u$ and

$\mathcal{U}_i$ we shall denote, respectively, the set of all items u has interacted with, and the set of users who have interacted with i. In general we shall take the case where the interaction consists of rating assignment (i.e. at most one time per user-item pair), except where the distinction between single and multiple interaction makes a relevant difference (namely Sect. 26.5.2.1. We denote ratings assigned by users to items as $r(u,i)$, and use the notation $r(u,i) = \emptyset$ to indicate missing ratings, as in [5]. We shall use R to denote a recommendation to some user, and R_u whenever we wish or need to explicitly indicate the target user u to whom R is delivered—in other words, R will be a shorthand for R_u. By default, the definition of a metric will be given on a single recommendation for a specific target user. For notational simplicity, we omit as understood that the metric should be averaged over all users. Certain global metrics (such as aggregate diversity, defined in Sect. 26.3.5) are the exception to this rule: they directly take in the recommendations to all users in their definition, and they therefore do not require averaging. In some cases where a metric is the average of a certain named function (e.g. IUF for inverse user frequency, SI for self-information) on the items it contains, we will compose the name of the metric by prepending an "M" for "mean" (e.g. MIUF, MSI) in order to distinguish it from the item-level function.

26.3.2 Average Intra-List Distance

Perhaps the most frequently considered diversity metric and the first to be proposed in the area is the so-called average intra-list distance—or just intra-list diversity, ILD (e.g. [70, 85, 90]). The intra-list diversity of a set of recommended items is defined as the average pairwise distance of the items in the set:

$$\mathrm{ILD} = \frac{1}{|R|(|R|-1)} \sum_{i \in R} \sum_{j \in R} d(i,j) \tag{26.1}$$

The computation of ILD requires defining a distance measure $d(i,j)$, which is thus a configurable element of the metric. Given the profuse work on the development of similarity functions in the recommender systems field, it is common, handy and sensible to define the distance as the complement of well-understood similarity measures, but nothing prevents the consideration of other particular options. The distance between items is generally a function of item features [90], though the distance in terms of interaction patterns by users has also been considered sometimes [79].

The ILD scheme in the context of recommendation was first suggested, as far as we are aware of, by Smyth and McClave [70], and has been used in numerous subsequent works (e.g. [75, 79, 85, 90]). Some authors have defined this dimension by its equivalent complement intra-list similarity ILS [90], which has the same relation to ILD as the distance function has to similarity, e.g. ILD $= 1 -$ ILS if $d = 1 - sim$.

26.3.3 Global Long-Tail Novelty

The novelty of an item from a global perspective can be defined as the opposite of popularity: an item is novel if few people are aware it exists, i.e. the item is far in the long tail of the popularity distribution [20, 61]. Zhou et al. [89] modeled popularity as the probability that a random user would know the item. To get a decreasing function of popularity, the negative logarithm provides a nice analogy with the inverse document frequency (IDF) in the vector-space Information Retrieval model, with users in place of documents and items instead of words, which has been referred to as inverse user frequency (IUF) [15]. Based on the observed user-item interaction, this magnitude can be estimated as IUF $= -\log_2 |\mathcal{U}_i|/|\mathcal{U}|$, where by $\mathcal{U}_i \stackrel{\text{def}}{=} \{u \in \mathcal{U} | r(u,i) \neq \emptyset\}$ we denote the set of users who have interacted with item i. Thus the novelty of a recommendation can be assessed as the average IUF of the recommended items:

$$\text{MIUF} = -\frac{1}{|R|} \sum_{i \in R} \log_2 \frac{|\mathcal{U}_i|}{|\mathcal{U}|} \tag{26.2}$$

The IUF formula also has a reminiscence of the self-information measure of Information Theory, only for that to be properly the case, the probability should add to 1 over the set of items, which is not the case here. We discuss that possibility in Sect. 26.5.2.1.

26.3.4 User-Specific Unexpectedness

Long-tail novelty translates to non-personalized measures for which the novelty of an item is seen as independent of the target user. It makes sense however to consider the specific experience of a user when assessing the novelty carried by an item that is recommended to her, since the degree to which an item is more or less familiar can greatly vary from one user to the next.

Two perspectives can be considered when comparing an item to prior user experience: the item identity (was this particular item seen before?) or the item characteristics (were the attributes of the item experienced before?). In the former view, novelty is a Boolean property of an item which occurs or not in its totality, whereas the latter allows to appreciate different degrees of novelty in an item even if it was never, itself, seen before.

It is not straightforward to define identity-based novelty on an individual user basis. In usual scenarios, if the system observes the user interact with an item, it will avoid recommending her this item again.[1] This is a rather trivial feature and does not

[1]Of course, what “interaction” means and to what extent it will inhibit future recommendations is application-dependent, e.g. an online store may recommend an item the user has inspected but not bought.

need to be evaluated—if anything, just debugged (e.g. for near-duplicate detection). We may therefore take it for granted, except in particular scenarios where users recurrently consume items—where on the other hand a recommender system may have a more limited range for bringing added value. It would be meaningful though to assess the Boolean novelty of an item in probabilistic terms, considering the user activity outside the system, which in a detailed sense is of course impractical. Long tail novelty can be seen as a proxy for this notion: a user-independent estimate of the prior probability that the user—any user—has seen the item before. Finer, user-specific probability estimation approaches could be explored but have not, to the best of our knowledge, been developed in the literature so far.

An attribute-based perspective is an easier-to-compute alternative for a user-specific novelty definition. Taking the items the user has been observed to encounter, the novelty of an item can be defined in terms of how different it is to the previously encountered items, as assessed by some distance function on the item properties. This notion reflects how unfamiliar, unexpected and/or surprising an item may be based on the user's observed experience. The set-wise distance to the profile items can be defined by aggregation of the pairwise distances by an average, minimum, or other suitable function. For instance, as an average:

$$\text{Unexp} = \frac{1}{|R||\mathfrak{I}_u|} \sum_{i \in R} \sum_{j \in \mathfrak{I}_u} d(i,j)$$

where by $\mathfrak{I}_u \stackrel{\text{def}}{=} \{i \in \mathfrak{I} \mid r(u,i) \neq \emptyset\}$ we denote the set of items with which user u has interacted.

Some authors have generalized the notion of unexpectedness to the difference of a recommendation with respect to an expected set of items, not necessarily the ones in the target user profile, thus widening the perspective on what "expected" means [1, 32, 57]. For instance, Murakami et al. [57] define the expected set as the items recommended by a "primitive" system which is supposed to produce unsurprising recommendation. The difference to the expected set can be defined in several ways, such as the ratio of unexpected recommended items:

$$\text{Unexp} = |R - EX|/|R| \tag{26.3}$$

EX being the set of expected items. Other measures between the recommended and expected set include the Jaccard distance, the centroid distance, the difference to an ideal distance, etc. [1].

26.3.5 Inter-Recommendation Diversity Metrics

Adomavicius and Kwon [3, 4] recently proposed measuring the so-called aggregate diversity of a recommender system. This perspective is different from all the metrics described above in that it does not apply to a single set of recommended items, but to all the output a recommender system produces over a set of users. It is in fact a quite simple metric which counts the total number of items that the system recommends.

$$\text{Aggdiv} = \left| \bigcup_{u \in \mathcal{U}} R_u \right| \tag{26.4}$$

A version Aggdiv@k of the metric can be defined by taking R_u as the top k items recommended to u. Since it applies to the set of all recommendations, aggregate diversity does not need to be averaged over users, differently from most other metrics mentioned in these pages.

Aggregate diversity is a relevant measure to assess to what extent an item inventory is being exposed to users. The metric, or close variations thereof, have also been referred to as item coverage in other works [11, 32, 35, 36] (see also Chap. 8). This concept can be also related to traditional diversity measures such as the Gini coefficient, the Gini-Simpson's index, or entropy [62], which are commonly used to measure statistical dispersion in such fields as ecology (biodiversity in ecosystems), economics (wealth distribution inequality), or sociology (e.g. educational attainment across the population). Mapped to recommendation diversity, such measures take into account not just whether items are recommended to someone, but to how many people and how even or unevenly distributed. To this extent they serve a similar purpose as aggregate diversity as measures of the concentration of recommendations over a few vs. many items. For instance, Fleder and Hosanagar [31] measure sales concentration by the Gini index, which Shani and Gunawardana (See Chap. 8) formulate as:

$$\text{Gini} = \frac{1}{|\mathcal{I}| - 1} \sum_{k=1}^{|\mathcal{I}|} (2k - N - 1) p(i_k|s)$$

where $p(i_k|s)$ is the probability of the k-th least recommended item being drawn from the recommendation lists generated by a system s:

$$p(i|s) = \frac{|\{u \in \mathcal{U} \mid i \in R_u\}|}{\sum_{j \in \mathcal{I}} |\{u \in \mathcal{U} \mid j \in R_u\}|}$$

The Gini index and aggregate diversity have been used in subsequent work such as [42, 76]. Other authors (e.g. [72] or Chap. 8) suggest the Shannon entropy with similar purposes:

$$\text{H} = -\sum_{i \in \mathcal{I}} p(i|s) \log_2 p(i|s)$$

Related to this, Zhou et al. [89] observe the diversity of the recommendations across users. They define inter-user diversity (IUD) as the average pairwise Jaccard distance between recommendations to users. In a quite equivalent reformulation of this measure we may define the novelty of an item as the ratio of users to which it is not recommended[2]:

$$\text{IUD} = \frac{1}{|R|} \sum_{i \in R} \frac{|\{v \in \mathcal{U} \mid i \notin R_v\}|}{|\mathcal{U}| - 1} = \frac{1}{|\mathcal{U}| - 1} \sum_{v \in \mathcal{U}} |R - R_v| / |R| \tag{26.5}$$

Since $|R - R_v|/|R| = 1 - |R \cap R_v|/|R \cup R_v|$, it can be seen that the difference between this definition and the Jaccard-based formulation is basically that the latter has $|R|$ instead of $|R \cup R_v|$ in the denominator, but the above formulation is interesting because it connects to the Gini-Simpson index, as we will show in Sect. 26.5.3.3.

With a similar metric structure, Bellogin et al. [11] measure the inter-system diversity (ISD), i.e. how different the output of a system is with respect to other systems, in settings where several recommenders are operating. This can be defined as the ratio of systems that do not recommend each item:

$$\text{ISD} = \frac{1}{|R|} \sum_{i \in R} \frac{|\{s \in \mathcal{S} \mid i \notin R^s\}|}{|\mathcal{S}| - 1} = \frac{1}{|\mathcal{S}| - 1} \sum_{s \in \mathcal{S}} |R - R^s| / |R| \tag{26.6}$$

where $\mathcal{S}$ is the set of recommenders in consideration, and R^s denotes the recommendation to the target user by a system $s \in \mathcal{S}$. This metric thus assesses how different the output of a recommender system is with respect to alternative algorithms. This perspective can be useful, for instance, when an application seeks to distinguish itself from the competition, or when selecting an algorithm to add to an ensemble.

In a different angle, Lathia et al. [46] consider the time dimension in novelty and diversity. Specifically, they study the diversity between successive recommendations by a system to a user, as the ratio of items that were not recommended before:

$$\text{TD} = |R - R'| / |R| \tag{26.7}$$

The authors distinguish the difference between consecutive recommendations, and the difference between the last recommendation and all prior recommendations. In the former case (which they name "temporal diversity") R' is the recommendation immediately preceding R, and in the latter ("temporal novelty") R' is the union of all recommendations to the target user preceding R. In both cases, the metric gives a perspective of the ability of a recommender system to evolve with the changes in the environment in which it operates, rather than presenting users the same set of items over and over again.

[2]Note that we normalize IUD by $|\mathcal{U}| - 1$ because all items in R are recommended to at least one user (the target of R), therefore if we normalized by $|\mathcal{U}|$, the value of the metric for the optimal recommendation would be $(|\mathcal{U}| - 1)/|\mathcal{U}| < 1$. Put in another way, $v \in \mathcal{U}$ in the numerator could be as well written as $v \in \mathcal{U} - \{u\}$, which would call for normalizing by $|\mathcal{U} - \{u\}| = |\mathcal{U}| - 1$. The difference is negligible in practice though, and we believe both forms of normalization would be acceptable. The same rationale applies to Eq. (26.6) below.

Note that IUD, ISD and TD fit as particular cases under the generalized unexpectedness scheme [1] described in the previous section (Eq. (26.3)), where the set *EX* of expected items would be the items recommended to other users by the same system ($EX = R_v$), to the same user by other systems ($EX = R^s$), or to the same user by the same system in the past ($EX = R'$). One difference is that IUD and ISD take multiple sets *EX* for each target user (one per user v and one per system s respectively), whereby these metrics involve an additional average over such sets.

26.3.6 Specific Methodologies

As an alternative to the definition of special-purpose metrics, some authors have evaluated the novelty or diversity of recommendations by accuracy metrics on a diversity-oriented experimental design. For instance, Hurley and Zhang [39] evaluate the diversity of a system by its ability to produce accurate recommendations of difficult items, "difficult" meaning unusual or infrequent for a user's typical observed habits. Specifically, a data splitting procedure is set up by which the test ratings are selected among a ratio of the top most different items rated by each user, "different" being measured as the average distance of the item to all other items in the user profile. The precision of recommendations in such a setting thus reflects the ability of the system to produce good recommendations made up of novel items. A similar idea is to select the test ratings among cold, non-popular long tail items. For instance, Zhou et al. [89] evaluate accuracy on the set of items with less than a given number of ratings. Shani and Gunawardana also discuss this idea in Chap. 8.

26.3.7 Diversity vs. Novelty vs. Serendipity

Even though the distinction between novelty and diversity is not always a fully clean-cut line, We may propose a classification of the metrics described so far as either novelty or diversity measures. ILD can be considered the genuine metric for diversity, the definition of which it applies to the letter. We would also class inter-recommendation metrics (Sect. 26.3.5) in the diversity type, since they assess how different are recommendations to each other. They do so at a level above an individual recommendation, by (directly or indirectly) comparing sets of recommended items rather than item pairs.

On the other hand, we may consider that long tail and unexpectedness fit in the general definition of novelty: unexpectedness explicitly measures how different each recommended item is with respect to what is expected, where the latter can be related to previous experience. And long tail non-popularity defines the probability that an item is different (is absent) from what a random user may have seen before. The methodologies discussed in the previous section can also be placed in the novelty category, as they assess the ability to properly recommend novel items.

It should also be noted that several authors target the specific concept of serendipity as the conjunction of novelty and relevance [32, 39, 57, 87, 89]. In terms of evaluation metrics, this translates to adding the relevance condition in the computation of the metrics described in Sects. 26.3.3 and 26.3.4. In other words, taking the summations over $i \in R \wedge i$ relevant to u in place of just $i \in R$ turns a plain novelty metric (long tail or unexpectedness) into the corresponding serendipity metric.

26.3.8 Information Retrieval Diversity

Differently (at least apparently) from the recommender systems field, diversity in IR has been related to an issue of uncertainty in the user query. Considering that most queries contain some degree of ambiguity or incompleteness as an expression of user needs, diversity is posited as a strategy to cope with this uncertainty by answering as many interpretations of the query as early as possible in the search results ranking. The objective is thus redefined from returning as many relevant results as possible to maximizing the probability that all users (all query interpretations) will get at least some relevant result. This principle is derived from reconsidering the independence assumption on document relevance, whereby returning relevant documents for different query interpretations pays off more than the diminishing returns from additional relevant documents for the same interpretation. For instance a polysemic query such as "table" might be interpreted as furniture or a database concept. If a search engine returns results in only one of the senses, it will satisfy 100 % the users who were intending this meaning, and 0 % the rest of users. But combining instead a balanced mix of both intents, results will likely satisfy all users by far more than 50 %, in a typical search where a few relevant results are sufficient to satisfy the user need.

IR diversity metrics have been defined under the assumption that an explicit space of possible query intents (also referred to as query aspects or subtopics) can be represented. In general, the aspects for evaluation should be provided manually, as has been done in the TREC diversity task, where a set of subtopics is provided for each query, along with per-subtopic relevance judgments [23].

Probably the earliest proposed metric was subtopic recall [84], which simply consists in the ratio of query subtopics covered in the search results:

$$\text{S-recall} = \frac{|\{z \in \mathcal{Z} \mid d \in R \wedge d \text{ covers } z\}|}{|\{z \in \mathcal{Z} \mid z \text{ is a subtopic of } q\}|}$$

where $\mathcal{Z}$ is the set of all subtopics. Later on the TREC campaign popularized metrics such as ERR-IA [21] and α-nDCG [24], and a fair array of other metrics have been proposed as well. For instance, based on the original definition of ERR in [21], the intent-aware version ERR-IA is:

$$\text{ERR-IA} = \sum_z p(z|q) \sum_{d_k \in R} p(rel|d_k, z) \prod_{j=1}^{k-1} (1 - p(rel|d_j, z))$$

where $p(z|q)$ takes into account that not all aspects need to be equally probable for a query, weighting their contribution to the metric value accordingly. And $p(rel|d, z)$ is the probability that document d is relevant to the aspect z of the query, which can be estimated based on the relevance judgments. E.g. for graded relevance Chapelle [21] proposed $p(rel|d, z) = 2^{g(d,z)-1}/2^{g_{max}}$, where $g(d, z) \in [0, g_{max}]$ is the relevance grade of d for the aspect z of the query. It is also possible to consider simpler mappings, such as a linear map $g(d, z)/g_{max}$, depending on how the relevance grades are defined [75].

Novelty, as understood in recommender systems, has also been addressed in IR, though perhaps not to as much extent as diversity. It is mentioned, for instance, in [10] as the ratio of previously unseen documents in a search result. It is also studied at the level of document sentences, in terms of the non-redundant information that a sentence provides with respect to the rest of the document [7]. Even though the concept is essentially the same, to what extent one may establish connections between the sentence novelty techniques and methodologies, and item novelty in recommendation is not obvious, but might deserve future research.

26.4 Novelty and Diversity Enhancement Approaches

Methods to enhance the novelty and diversity of recommendations are reviewed in this section. It is noteworthy that research in this area has accelerated over the last number of years. The work can be categorized into methods that re-rank an initial list to enhance the diversity/novelty of the top items; methods based on clustering; hybrid or fusion methods; and methods that consider diversity in the context of optimization of learning to rank objectives.

26.4.1 Result Diversification/Re-ranking

One common approach to enhance the diversity of recommendation is the diversification or re-ranking of the results returned by an initial recommender system. In this approach, a set of candidate recommendations that have been selected on the basis of relevance, are re-ranked in order to improve the diversity or novelty of the recommendation, or the aggregate diversity of all recommendations offered by the system. Generally, work that has taken this approach[26, 28, 30, 85, 90] attempts to optimize the set diversity as expressed by the ILD measure defined in Sect. 26.3.2.

In the recommendation context, a personalized recommendation is formed for a given target user u, and the relevance of any particular item to the recommendation

Algorithm 2 Greedy selection to produce a re-ranked list R from an initial set C

$R \leftarrow \emptyset$
while $|R| < k$ **do**
  $i* \leftarrow \arg\max_{i \in C-R} g(R \cup \{i\}, \lambda)$
  $R \leftarrow R \cup \{i*\}$
end while
return R

depends on u. However, for notational simplicity, we will write $f_{rel}(i)$ for the relevance of item i, dropping the dependence on u. Given a candidate set C, the problem may be posed to find a set $R \subseteq C$ of some given size $k = |R|$, that maximizes $div(R)$ i.e.

$$R_{opt} = \arg\max_{R \subseteq C, |R|=k} div(R) \tag{26.8}$$

More generally, an objective to jointly optimize for relevance and diversity can be expressed as:

$$R_{opt}(\lambda) = \arg\max_{R \subseteq C, |R|=k} g(R, \lambda) \tag{26.9}$$

where

$$g(R, \lambda) = (1 - \lambda)\frac{1}{|R|}\sum_{i \in R} f_{rel}(i) + \lambda\, div(R)$$

and $\lambda \in [0, 1]$ expresses the trade-off between the average relevance of the items in the set and the diversity of the set. In information retrieval, a greedy construction approach to solving Eq. (26.9) is referred to as the maximum marginal relevance (MMR) approach in [17], where relevance is measured with respect to a given query. In the greedy approach, the recommended set R is built in an iterative fashion as follows. Let R^j be the set at iteration $j \in \{1, 2, \ldots, k\}$. The first item in the set is the one that maximizes $f_{rel}(i)$ and the j-th item is chosen to maximize $g(R^{j-1} \cup \{i\}, \lambda)$. Algorithm 2 summarizes this approach.

In the context of case-based reasoning, a greedy solution to Eq. (26.9) is proposed in [52, 70] as a means of selecting a set of cases to solve a given target problem. Using nearest-neighbor user- and item-based collaborative filtering methods to generate the initial candidate set, Ziegler et al. [90] also propose a greedy solution to Eq. (26.9), as a means of re-ranking the set, terming the method as topic diversification, as they employ a taxonomy-based distance metric. In the context of a publish-subscribe system, Drosou and Pitoura [28] use the formulation in Eq. (26.9) as a means of selecting a diverse set of relevant items to recommend to a user from a set of items gathered over a particular time window. The method is proposed in the context of image retrieval in [26] and an alternative method to optimize for Eq. (26.9) is studied in [85], again using an item-based kNN method to generate the candidate set. Also, in [27] a number of different heuristics for solving the maximum diversity problem (Eq. (26.8)) are evaluated and while none out-performs all others in all cases, several succeed in finding very good quality solutions in reasonable time. This work is followed up in [8], where a multiple-pass randomized greedy algorithm is shown to give better performance than the single-pass greedy algorithm.

Rather than maximize as a trade-off between relevance and diversity, [54] takes a more conservative approach of choosing the most diverse subset from a candidate set of items that have equal relevance, thereby maximizing diversity under a constraint of maintaining overall relevance. Similarly, [83] avoids using an explicit weighted trade-off between diversity and relevance and instead presents two algorithms that modify an initial relevance ranking of items to increase diversity.

Though it is difficult to compare directly across the different approaches, as the measures of relevance and pairwise distance differ, researchers have generally found the expected trade-off of increasing diversity and decreasing relevance of the retrieved set as λ is decreased towards 0. McGinty and Smyth [52, 70] evaluate the effect of diversifying the recommended set by counting the number of steps it takes a conversational recommender system to reach a given target item. Diversification always performs better than the algorithm that selects items using similarity only. An adaptive method that determines at each step whether or not to diversify gives even better performance. Evaluating on the Book-Crossing dataset, Ziegler et al. [90] found that the accuracy of their system, as measured by precision and recall, dropped with increasing diversification. Zhang and Hurley [85] evaluate on the Movielens dataset; they form test sets of increasing difficulty by splitting each user's profile into training a test sets of items and varying the average similarity of the items in the test set to the items in the training set, and find the diversified algorithm achieves better precision on the more difficult test sets.

Alternatives to MMR A number of alternative scoring functions for guiding re-ranking that capture the compromise between relevance and diversity or novelty have been proposed in the literature. For example, [82] computes a weighted sum of a global probability for including a candidate item in R and a local probability dependent on the set of items already in R. Definitions of novelty and diversity of news articles based on a distance between concepts in a taxonomy are given in [65] and a replacement heuristic is used to increase the novelty or diversity of the initial ranking by swapping in highly novel/diverse articles. To take account of mutual influence between items, [12] replace the pairwise diversity in the utility function by an estimate of the probability that the pair of items are both liked. Finally, an alternative formulation of the diversity problem, r-DisC diversity, is presented in [29] and solved using a greedy algorithm. In this formulation, the items in the set R are selected to cover the candidate, such that there is an item in R within a certain similarity threshold to each item in C, under a constraint that all items in R also have a certain minimum pairwise dissimilarity.

Aggregate Diversity Targeting aggregate diversity (Eq. (26.4) in Sect. 26.3.5), items are re-ranked in [2] using a weighted combination of their relevance and a score based on inverse popularity, or item likeability. Adomavicius and Kwon find that their re-ranking strategies succeed in increasing aggregate diversity at a small cost to accuracy as measured by the precision. A follow-up to this work is presented in [3], in which the aggregate diversity problem is shown to be equivalent to the maximum flow problem on a graph whose nodes are formed from the users and items of the recommendation problem. Other work [45] has investigated how neighborhood filtering strategies and multi-criteria ratings impact on aggregate diversity in nearest-neighbor collaborative filtering algorithms. In this line, Vargas and Castells [76] find out that aggregate diversity is considerably improved by transposing the kNN CF recommendation approach, swapping the role of users and items. The authors show the approach can be generalized to any recommendation algorithm based on a probabilistic reformulation of arbitrary user-item scoring functions which isolates a popularity component.

26.4.2 Using Clustering for Diversification

A method proposed in [86] clusters the items in an active user's profile, in order to group similar items together. Then, rather than recommend a set of items that are similar to the entire user profile, each cluster is treated separately and a set of items most similar to the items in each cluster is retrieved.

A different approach is presented in [14], where the candidate set is again clustered. The goal now is to identify and recommend a set of representative items, one for each cluster, so that the average distance of each item to its representative is minimized.

A nearest-neighbor algorithm is proposed in [48] that uses multi-dimensional clustering to cluster items in an attribute space and select clusters of items as candidates to recommend to the active user. This method is shown to improve aggregate diversity.

A graph-based recommendation approach is described in [69] where the recommendation problem is formulated as a cost flow problem over a graph whose nodes are the users and items of the recommendation. Weights in the graph are computed by a biclustering of the user-item matrix using non-negative matrix factorization. This method can be tuned to increase the diversity of the resulting set, or increase the probability of recommending long-tail items.

26.4.3 Fusion-Based Methods

Since the early days of recommender systems, researchers have been aware that no single recommendation algorithm will work best in all scenarios. Hybrid systems have been studied to offset the strengths of one algorithm against the weaknesses of another (see [68] for example). It may be expected that the combined outputs of multiple recommendation algorithms that have different selection mechanisms, may also exhibit greater diversity than a single algorithm. For example, in [66, 79], recommendation is treated as a multi-objective optimization problem. The outputs of multiple recommendation algorithms that differ in their levels of accuracy, diversity and novelty are ensemble using evolutionary algorithms. As another example, in a music recommendation system called Auralist [88], a basic item-based recommender system is combined with two additional algorithms, in order to promote serendipity (see section below).

26.4.4 Learning to Rank with Diversity

In the last few years, there is an increasing interest in learning to rank algorithms for recommender systems. These algorithms directly optimize an objective related to the ranking rather than forming the ranking in a post-processing step from a set of predicted ratings. To date, most such techniques do not take into account the dependencies between the items in the ranking. However, a small number of works have appeared in the literature that optimize a combined objective of ranking accuracy and set diversity. In [71], the concept of diversity is integrated into a matrix factorization model, in order to directly recommend item sets that are both relevant and diversified. A matrix factorization model is again used in [40] to optimize a ranking objective that is explicitly modified to account for the diversity of the ranking.

26.4.5 Serendipity: Enabling Surprising Recommendations

A number of algorithms have been proposed in the literature to recommend serendipitous items. For example, in a content-based recommender system, described in [41], a binary classifier is used to distinguish between relevant and irrelevant content. Those items for which the difference in the positive and negative class scores is smallest are determined to be the ones about which the user is most uncertain and therefore the ones that are likely to yield serendipitous recommendations.

Oku and Hattori [59] propose a method for generating serendipitous recommendations that, given a pair of items, uses the pair to generate a recommended set of serendipitous items. Several ways to generate the set are discussed and several ways to rank the items and hence select a top k are evaluated.

Utility theory is exploited in [1], where the utility of a recommendation is represented as a combination of its utility due to its quality and its utility due to its unexpectedness. A couple of different utility functions are proposed and ways to compute these functions on movie and book recommendation systems are discussed and evaluated.

Other recent work [13, 73] has investigated the use of graph-based techniques to make serendipitous recommendations in mobile app and music recommendation, respectively.

26.4.6 Other Approaches

A nearest neighbor algorithm called usage-context based collaborative filtering (UCBCF) is presented in [58], which differs from standard item-based CF in the calculation of item-item similarities. Rather than the standard item representation as a vector of user ratings, an item profile is represented as a vector of the k other items with which the item significantly co-occurs in user profiles. UCBCF is shown to obtain greater aggregate diversity than standard kNN and Matrix Factorization algorithms. A system described in [8] maps items into a utility space and maps a user's preferences to a preferred utility vector. In order to make a diverse recommendation, the utility space is split into m layers in increasing distance from the preferred utility and non-dominated items are chosen from each layer so as to maximize one dimension of the utility vector.

The works discussed so far have considered diversity in terms of the dissimilarity of items in a single recommendation set, or, in the case of aggregate diversity, the coverage of items in a batch of recommendations. Another approach is to consider diversity in the context of the behavior of the system over time. Temporal diversity (Eq. (26.7) in Sect. 26.3.4) is investigated by Lathia et al. [46] in a number of standard CF algorithms, and methods for increasing diversity through re-ranking or hybrid fusion are discussed. In a related vein, Mourao et al. [56] explore the "oblivion problem", that is, the possibility that in a dynamic system, items can be forgotten over time in such a way that they recover some degree of the original novelty value they had when they were discovered.

26.4.7 User Studies

It is one thing to develop algorithms to diversify top k lists, but what impact do these algorithms have on user satisfaction? A number of user studies have explored the impact of diversification on users. Topic diversification is evaluated in [90] by carrying out a user survey to assess user satisfaction with a diversified recommendation. In the case of their item-based algorithm, they find that satisfaction peaks around a relevance/diversity determined by $\lambda = 0.6$ in Eq. (26.9) suggesting that users like a certain degree of diversification in their lists.

While much of the work in diversifying top k lists does not consider the ordering of items in the recommended list, provided an overall relevance is attained, Ge et al. [32, 33] look at how this ordering affects the user's perception of diversity. In a user study, they experiment with placing diverse items—ones with low similarity to the other items in the list—either in a block or dispersed throughout the list and found that blocking the items in the middle of the list reduces perceived diversity.

The work of Hu and Pu [37] addresses user-interface issues related to augmenting users' perception of diversity. In a user study that tracks eye movements, they find that an organizational interface where items are grouped into categories is better than a list interface in supporting perception of diversity. In [19], 250 users are surveyed and presented with 5 recommendation approaches, with varying degrees of diversity. They find that users perceive diversity and that it improves their satisfaction but that diverse recommendations may require additional explanations to users who cannot link them back to their preferences.

26.4.8 Diversification Approaches in Information Retrieval

Most diversification algorithms proposed in IR follow the same greedy re-ranking scheme as described earlier for recommender systems in Sect. 26.4.1. The algorithms distinguish from each other in the greedy objective function and the theory behind it. They can be classed into two types based on whether or not the algorithms use an explicit representation of query aspects (as introduced earlier in Sect. 26.3.8). Explicit approaches draw an approximation of query aspects from different sources, such as query reformulations suggested by a search engine [67], Wikipedia disambiguation entries [81], document classifications [6], or result clustering [34]. Based on this, the objective function of the greedy re-ranking algorithms seeks to maximize the number of covered aspects and minimize the repetition of aspects already covered in previous ranking positions. For example xQuAD [67], the most effective algorithm in TREC campaigns, defines its objective function as:

$$f(d_k|S,q) = (1-\lambda)\, p(q|d_k) + \lambda \sum_{z} p(z|q)\, p(d_k|q,z) \prod_{j=1}^{k-1} (1 - p(d_j|q,z))$$

where $p(q|d_k)$ stands for the initial search system score, z represents query aspects, $p(z|q)$ weights the contribution on each aspect by its relation to the query, $p(d_k|q,z)$ measures how well document d_k covers aspect z, the product after that penalizes the redundancy with previous documents in the ranking covering the same aspect, and $\lambda \in [0,1]$ sets the balance in the intensity of diversification.

Diversification algorithms that do not explicitly deal with query aspects generally assess diversity in terms of the content of documents. For instance Goldstein and Carbonell [17] greedily maximize a linear combination of similarity to the query (the baseline search score) and dissimilarity (minimum or average distance) to the documents ranked above the next document. Other non-aspect approaches formulate a similar principle in more formal probabilistic terms [22], or in terms of the trade-off between risk and relevance, in analogy to Modern Portfolio Theory [80] on the optimization of the expected return for a given amount of risk in financial investment. Vargas et al. [77, 78] show that IR diversity principles and techniques make sense in recommender systems and can be adapted to them as well, as we discuss in Sect. 26.5.4.

26.5 Unified View

As the overview through this chapter shows, a wide variety of metrics and perspectives have been developed around the same concepts under different variants and angles. It is natural to wonder whether it is possible to relate them together under a common ground or theory, establishing equivalences, and identifying fundamental differences. We summarize next a formal foundation for defining, explaining, relating and generalizing many different state of the art metrics, and defining new ones. We also examine the connections between diversity as researched and developed in the Information Retrieval field, and the corresponding work in recommender systems.

26.5.1 General Novelty/Diversity Metric Scheme

As shown in [75] it is possible indeed to formulate a formal scheme that unifies and explains most of the metrics proposed in the literature. The scheme posits a generic recommendation metric m as the expected novelty of the items it contains:

$$m = \frac{1}{|R|} \sum_{i \in R} nov(i|\theta)$$

An item novelty model $nov(i|\theta)$ at the core of the scheme determines the nature of the metric that will result. The scheme further emphasizes the relative nature of novelty by explicitly introducing a context θ. Novelty is relative to a context of experience: (what we know about) what someone has experienced somewhere sometime, where "someone" can be the target user, a set of users, all users, etc.; "sometime" can refer to a specific past time period, an ongoing session, "ever", etc.; "somewhere" can be the interaction history of a user, the current recommendation being browsed, past recommendations, recommendations by other systems, "anywhere", etc.; and "what we know about that" refers to the context of observation, i.e. the available observations to the system. We elaborate next on how such models can be defined, computed, and packed into different metrics.

26.5.2 Item Novelty Models

As discussed in Sect. 26.3.4, the novelty of an item can be established in terms of whether the item itself or its attributes have been experienced before. The first case, which we may refer to as an issue of simple item discovery, calls for a probabilistic formulation, whereas feature-based novelty, which we shall refer to as an issue of item familiarity, can be more easily defined in terms of a distance model.

26.5.2.1 Item Discovery

In the simple discovery approach, $nov(i|\theta)$ can be expressed in terms of the probability that someone has interacted with the item [75]. This probability can be defined from two slightly different perspectives: the probability that a random user has interacted with the item (to which we shall refer as forced discovery) as in IUF (Eq. (26.2)), or the probability that the item is involved in a random interaction (free discovery). Both can be estimated based on the amount of interactions with the item observed in the system, as a sample of all the interaction the item may have received in the real world. We shall use the notation $p(known|i,\theta)$—the probability that "i is known" by any user given a context θ—for forced discovery, and $p(i|known,\theta)$ for free discovery. Note that these are different distributions, e.g. the latter sums to 1 over the set of all items, whereas the former sums to 1 with $p(\neg known|i,\theta)$. Forced discovery reflects the probability that a random user knows a specific item when asked about it, whereas free discovery is the probability that "the next item" someone discovers is precisely the given item. It is shown in [75] that the metrics induced by either model are quite equivalent in practice, as the two distributions are approximately proportional to each other (exactly proportional if the frequency of user-item pairs is uniform, as is the case e.g. with one-time ratings). In Sect. 26.7 we shall show some empirical results which confirm this near equivalence in practice.

Now depending on how we instantiate the context θ, we can model different novelty perspectives. For instance, if we take θ to be the set of available observations of user-item interaction (to be more rigorous, we take θ to be an unknown user-item interaction distribution of which the observed interactions are a sample), maximum-likelihood estimates of the above distributions yield:

$$\begin{aligned} p(known|i,\theta) &\sim |\{u \in \mathcal{U} \mid \exists t\ (u,i,t) \in \mathcal{O}\}| \ / \ |\mathcal{U}| = |\mathcal{U}_i|/|\mathcal{U}| \\ p(i|known,\theta) &\sim |\{(u,i,t) \in \mathcal{O}\}| \ / \ |\mathcal{O}| \end{aligned} \tag{26.10}$$

where $\mathcal{U}_i$ denotes the set of all users who have interacted with i, and $\mathcal{O} \subset \mathcal{U} \times \mathcal{I} \times \mathcal{T}$ is the set of observed item-user interactions with i (each labeled with a different timestamp $t \in \mathcal{T}$). If the observations consist of ratings, user-item pairs occur only once, and we have:

$$\begin{aligned} p(known|i,\theta) &\sim |\mathcal{U}_i|/|\mathcal{U}| = |\{u \in \mathcal{U} \mid r(u,i) \neq \emptyset\}| \ / \ |\mathcal{U}| \\ p(i|known,\theta) &\sim |\{u \in \mathcal{U} \mid r(u,i) \neq \emptyset\}| \ / \ |\mathcal{O}| = |\mathcal{U}_i|/|\mathcal{O}| \end{aligned} \tag{26.11}$$

Both $p(i|known, \theta)$ and $p(known|i, \theta)$ make sense as a measure of how popular an item is in the context at hand. In order to build a recommendation novelty metric based on this, we should take $nov(i|\theta)$ to be a monotonically decreasing function of these probabilities. The inverse probability, dampened by the logarithm function (i.e. $-\log_2 p$) is frequent in the literature [75, 89], but $1 - p$ is also reported as "popularity complement" [75, 79]. The latter has an intuitive interpretation when applied to forced discovery: it represents the probability that an item is not known to a random user. The former also has interesting connections: when applied to forced discovery, it gives the inverse user frequency IUF (see Sect. 26.3.3). When applied to free discovery, it becomes the self-information (also known as surprisal), an information theory measure that quantifies the amount of information conveyed by the observation of an event.

26.5.2.2 Item Familiarity

The novelty model scheme defined in the previous section considers how different an item is from past experience in terms of strict Boolean identity: an item is new if it is absent from past experience ($known = 0$) and not new otherwise ($known = 1$). There are reasons however to consider relaxed versions of the Boolean view: the knowledge available to the system about what users have seen is partial, and therefore an item might be familiar to a user even if no interaction between them has been observed in the system. Furthermore, even when a user sees an item for the first time, the resulting information gain—the effective novelty—ranges in practice over a gradual rather than binary scale (consider for instance the novelty involved in discovering the movie "Rocky V").

As an alternative to the popularity-based view, we consider a similarity-based model where item novelty is defined by a distance function between the item and a context of experience [75]. If the context can be represented as a set of items, for which we will intentionally reuse the symbol θ, we can formulate this as the distance between the item and the set, which can be defined as an aggregation of the distances to the items in the set, e.g. as the expected value:

$$nov(i|\theta) = \sum_{j \in \theta} p(j|\theta)\, d(i,j)$$

The $p(j|\theta)$ probability enables further model elaborations, or can be simply taken as uniform thus defining a plain distance average.

In the context of distance-based novelty, we find two useful instantiations of the θ reference set: (a) the set of items a user has interacted with—i.e. the items in his profile—and (b) the set R of recommended items itself. In the first case, we get a user-relative novelty model, and in the second case, we get the basis for a generalization of intra-list diversity. The notion of expected set in [1] plays a similar role to this idea of θ context. It is possible to explore other possibilities for θ, such as groups of user profiles, browsed items over an interactive session, items recommended in the past or by alternative systems, etc., which might motivate future work.

26.5.3 Resulting Metrics

As stated at the beginning of this section, having defined a model of the novelty of an item, the novelty or diversity of a recommendation can be defined as the average novelty of the items it contains [75]. Each novelty model, and each context instantiation produce a different metric. In the following we show some practical instantiations that give rise to (hence unify and generalize) metrics described in the literature and covered in Sect. 26.3.

26.5.3.1 Discovery-Based

A practical instantiation of the item discovery models described in Sect. 26.6 consists of taking the novelty context θ to be the set of user-item interactions observed by the system. The different discussed variants in the novelty model result in the following practical metric combinations (mean IUF, mean self-information, mean popularity complement):

$$\text{MIUF} = -\frac{1}{|R|}\sum_{i \in R} \log_2 p(known|i,\theta)$$

$$\text{MSI} = -\frac{1}{|R|}\sum_{i \in R} \log_2 p(i|known,\theta)$$

$$\text{MPC} = \frac{1}{|R|}\sum_{i \in R} (1 - p(known|i,\theta))$$

where the probabilities are estimated by Eq. (26.10) or (26.11) depending on the nature of the data. MPC has the advantage of simplicity, a clear interpretation (the ratio of unknown recommended items), and ranges in [0, 1]. MIUF generalizes the metric proposed by Zhou et al. [89] (Eq. (26.2) in Sect. 26.3.3), and MSI provides a nice connection to information theory concepts. MPC has the potential shortcoming of a tendency to concentrate its values in a small range near 1, whereas MIUF and MSI deliver less clumped values. We might as well consider the expected popularity complement of free discovery, but that does not have a particularly interesting interpretation or property with respect to the other metrics. In fact, given the discussed near equivalence of free and forced discovery, the three above metrics behave quite similarly to each other, as we will illustrate in Sect. 26.6 for MSI and MPC.

26.5.3.2 Familiarity-Based

Distance based item novelty models give rise to intra-list diversity and unexpectedness metrics. As mentioned in Sect. 26.5.2.2, these metrics simply result from taking, respectively, the recommended items or the target user's profile as the θ novelty context. The complement of any similarity function between items is potentially suitable to define the distance measure. For instance, with feature-based similarity we may define $d(i,j) = 1 - \cos(i,j)$ for numeric item features, $d(i,j) = 1 - \text{Jaccard}(i,j)$ for Boolean (or binarized) features, and so forth. The distinction between collaborative and content-based similarity deserves attention though, and care should be taken to make a meaningful choice between these two alternatives. Content-based similarity compares items by their intrinsic properties, as described by the available item features. Even though a collaborative similarity measure (which compares items by their common user interaction patterns) might make sense in some particular cases, we would contend that content-based similarity is generally more meaningful to assess the diversity in a way that users can perceive.

26.5.3.3 Further Unification

By explicitly modeling novelty as a relative notion, the proposed framework has a strong unifying potential of further novelty and diversity conceptions. Take for instance the notion of temporal diversity [46] discussed in Sect. 26.3.5. The metric can be described in the framework in terms of a discovery model where the source of discovery is the past recommendations of the system $\theta \equiv R'$, and novelty is defined as the complement of forced discovery given this context:

$$\frac{1}{|R|}\sum i \subset R(1 - p(known|i,R') = \frac{1}{|R|}\sum_{i\in R}(1 - [i \in R']) = \frac{1}{|R|}|R - R'| = \text{TD}$$

Similarly, for inter-user diversity (Eq. (26.5) in Sect. 26.3.5), we take as context the set of recommendations to all users in the system, $\theta \equiv \{R_v | v \in \mathcal{U}\}$. By marginalization over users, and assuming a uniform user prior $p(v) = 1/|\mathcal{U}|$ we have:

$$\frac{1}{|R|}\sum_{i\in R}(1 - p(known \mid i, \{R_v | v \in \mathcal{U}\}) = \frac{1}{|R|}\sum_{i\in R}\sum_{v\in\mathcal{U}}(1 - p(known|i,R_v))p(v)$$

$$= \frac{1}{|R||\mathcal{U}|}\sum_{v\in\mathcal{U}}\sum_{i\in R}(1 - p(known|i,R_v)) = \frac{1}{|R||\mathcal{U}|}\sum_{v\in\mathcal{U}}|R - R_v| = \text{IUD}$$

Inter-system novelty can be obtained in a similar way. So can generalized unexpectedness metrics, in their set difference form (Eq. (26.6) in Sect. 26.3.5), by using the expected set as context θ in place of R', R_v or R_s above.

Biodiversity measures from ecology can also be directly related to some of the recommendation metrics we have discussed. The equivalences hold by equating items to species, and the occurrence of an item in a recommendation as the existence of an individual of the species. In particular, stated in this way, aggregate diversity is the direct equivalent of so called richness, the number of different species that are present in an ecosystem [62]. On the other hand, it can be seen that the Gini-Simpson index (GSI) [62] is exactly equivalent to inter-user diversity. GSI is defined as the probability that two items (individuals) picked at random from the set of recommendations (ecosystem) are different items (species), which can be expressed as a sum over items, or as an average over pairs of recommendations:

$$\text{GSI} = 1 - \sum_{i \in \mathcal{I}} \frac{|\{u \in \mathcal{U} \mid i \in R_u\}|^2}{|\mathcal{U}|(|\mathcal{U}|-1)k^2} = 1 - \frac{1}{|\mathcal{U}|(|\mathcal{U}|-1)} \sum_{u \in \mathcal{U}} \sum_{v \in \mathcal{U}} \frac{|R_u \cap R_v|}{|R_u||R_v|}$$

where $k = |R_u|$ assuming they are the same size, or equivalently, considering we are computing GSI@k, and we assume item pairs are not sampled from the same recommendation. On the other hand, the average value of IUD over all users is:

$$\text{IUD} = \frac{1}{|\mathcal{U}|(|\mathcal{U}|-1)} \sum_{u \in \mathcal{U}} \sum_{v \in \mathcal{U}} \frac{|R_u - R_v|}{|R_u|} = 1 - \frac{1}{|\mathcal{U}|(|\mathcal{U}|-1)} \sum_{u \in \mathcal{U}} \sum_{v \in \mathcal{U}} \frac{|R_u \cap R_v|}{|R_u|}$$
$$= 1 - k(1 - \text{GSI}) \propto \text{GSI} \qquad \square$$

Table 26.1 summarizes some of the metrics that can be obtained in the unified framework by different instantiations of θ and item novelty models.

Table 26.1 Some item novelty and context model instantiations, and the metric they result into

Metric	Used in	Item novelty model	Context
ILD	[70, 75, 79, 85, 90]	$\sum_{j \in \theta} p(j \mid \theta)\, d(i,j)$	$\theta \equiv R$
Unexp	[1, 32, 57, 75]		$\theta \equiv$ items in user profile
MIUF	[89]	$-\log_2 p(known \mid i, \theta)$	$\theta \equiv$ all observed user-item interaction data
MSI	[75]	$-\log_2 p(i \mid known, \theta)$	
MPC	[66, 75, 79]	$1 - p(known \mid i, \theta)$	
TD	[46]		$\theta \equiv$ items recommended in the past
IUD/GSI	[89]		$\theta \equiv \{R_u \mid u \in \mathcal{U}\}$
ISD	[11]		$\theta \equiv \{R^s \mid s \in \mathcal{S}\}$

26.5.3.4 Direct Optimization of Novelty Models

The metric scheme described in the previous sections enables the definition of novelty or diversity enhancement re-ranking methods by the greedy optimization of an objective function combining the initial ranking score and the novelty model value:

$$g(i, \lambda) = (1 - \lambda) f_{rel}(i) + \lambda \, nov(i|\theta)$$

By taking a particular novelty model $nov(i|\theta)$, one optimizes for the corresponding metric that takes the model at its core. This is an approach to diversity enhancement which is by definition difficult to overcome—in terms of the target metrics—by other re-ranking means.

26.5.4 Connecting Recommendation Diversity and Search Diversity

Recommendation can be formulated as an information retrieval task, one where there is no explicit user query. To this extent, and in the aim to find a perspective as comprehensive as possible on the topic at hand in this chapter, it is natural to wonder whether it is possible to establish a connection between the work on diversity in both fields. This question finds affirmative answers in many senses [75, 77, 78]. We summarize here what we find to be the main considerations in this direction: (a) recommendation novelty and diversity can be extended to be sensitive to relevance and rank, (b) IR diversity principles, metrics and algorithms can be adapted to a recommendation setting, and (c) personalized search diversity can be formalized as a link between search and recommendation diversity.

26.5.4.1 Rank and Relevance

The novelty and diversity metrics described so far generally lack two aspects: they consider neither the relevance nor the rank position of the items when assessing their contribution to the novelty value of the recommendation. This is in contrast to IR metrics such as ERR-IA and α-nDCG which add up the novelty contribution of items only when they are relevant to the query, and apply a rank discount reflecting the assumption that lower ranking positions are less likely to be actually reached by users. Some authors in the recommender systems domain have also proposed to take relevance into account [32, 39, 57, 87, 89], though it is most often not the case, and rank position is generally not taken into account in the reported metrics.

Vargas and Castells [75] show that it is possible to deal with relevance and novelty or diversity together by introducing relevance as an intrinsic feature to the unified metric scheme described in the previous section. This can be done by just replacing "average" by "expected" item novelty at the top level of the scheme, where the novelty of a recommended item should only count when it is actually seen and consumed (chosen, accepted) by the user. The expected novelty is then computed in terms of the probability of choice. If we make the simplifying assumptions that (a) the user chooses an item if and only if she discovers it and likes it, and (b) discovery and relevance are independent, the resulting scheme is:

$$m = C \sum_{i \in R} p(seen \mid i, R)\, p(rel \mid i)\; nov(i \mid \theta)$$

where $p(rel|i)$ estimates the probability that i is relevant for the user, achieving the desired effect that only relevant novel items count, and $p(seen|i,R)$ estimates the probability that the user will get to see the item i while browsing R.

The probability of relevance can be defined based on relevance judgments (test ratings), for instance as $p(rel|i) \sim r(u,i)/(r_{max})$, where r_{max} is the maximum possible rating value. Assessing relevance and diversity together has several advantages. It allows for a unified criteria to compare two systems, where separate relevance and novelty metrics may disagree. Furthermore, assessing relevance and novelty together allows distinguishing, for example, between recommendations A and B in Table 26.2: B can be considered better (relevance-aware MPC = 0.5) since it

Table 26.2 Toy example recommendations of size two by three systems A, B, C

		Rank	A	B	1
		1	✓✗	✓✓	✗✗
		2	✗✓	✗✗	✓✓
Metric	$p(seen \mid i_k, R)$	$p(rel \mid i)$	A	B	C
Plain MPC	1	1	1	0.5	0.5
Relevance-aware MPC	1	$r(u,i)/r_{max}$	0	0.5	0.5
Zipfian MPC	$1/k$	1	0.25	0.5	0.25
Precision	1	$r(u,i)/r_{max}$	1	0.5	0.5
H(Plain MPC, Precision)	–	–	1	0.5	0.5

For each item, the pairs of check and cross marks indicate whether or not the item is relevant (left) and novel (right) to the user (e.g. item 1 of A is relevant and not novel). Below this, the values of MPC are shown with different combinations of rank discount and relevance awareness: plain MPC without relevance or rank discounts, relevance-weighted MPC (without rank discount), and MPC with a Zipfian rank discount (without relevance). The specific expression of the discount function $p(seen|i_k,R)$ and the relevance weight $p(rel|i)$ is shown for each metric variant. The last two rows show the precision of each recommendation, and the harmonic mean of precision and plain MPC recommends one useful item (relevant and novel), whereas the items recommended by A (relevance-aware MPC $=$ 0) lack either relevance or novelty. Note that an aggregation of separate novelty and relevance metrics would not catch this difference—e.g. the harmonic mean of MPC and precision is 0.5 for both A and B.

On the other hand, the $p(seen|i,R)$ distribution allows the introduction of a browsing model of a user interacting with the ranked recommendations, thus connecting to work on the formalization of utility metrics in IR [18, 21, 55]. The browsing model results in a rank discount which reflects the decreasing probability that the user sees an item as she goes down the ranking. Different models result in discount functions such as logarithmic $p(seen|i_k,R) = 1/\log_2 k$ as in nDCG, exponential p^{k-1} as in RBP [55], Zipfian $1/k$ as in ERR [21], and so forth (see [18] for a good compendium and formalization of alternatives). Rank discount allows distinguishing between recommendations B and C in Table 26.2: B is better (Zipfian MPC $=$ 0.5) since it ranks the relevant novel item higher than C (Zipfian MPC $=$ 0.25), with higher probability to be seen by the user.

26.5.4.2 IR Diversity in Recommendation

Vargas et al. [77, 78] have shown that the IR diversity principles, metrics and algorithms can be directly applied to recommendation. At a theoretical level, the evidence of user needs implicit in user actions is generally even more ambiguous and incomplete to a recommender system than an explicit query can be to a search system, whereby the rationale of diversifying retrieved results to increase the chances of some relevant result applies here as well. At a practical level, it makes as much sense to consider the different aspects of a user's preferences (there are different sides to a person's interests) as it can make for an expressed query. A user interest aspect representation can be drawn from item features in some suitable, meaningful space. This can be done in analogy to the document categories as handled in [6]. From this point on, IR diversity metrics such as ERR-IA [21] or subtopic recall [84] can be applied, and aspect-based algorithms such as xQuAD [67] or IA-Select [6] can be adapted, equating users to queries and items to documents.

Non-aspect based diversification methods are applied even more straightforwardly to recommendation, as proved by the equivalence between MMR [17] and methods in the recommender systems field [70, 90] (Sect. 26.4.1), or the adaptation of the Modern Portfolio Theory from IR [80] to recommendation [69].

26.5.4.3 Personalized Diversity

Recommender and search systems can be seen as extremes in the explicit vs. implicit spectrum of the available evidence of user needs: a recommender system takes no explicit query and relies on observed user choices—implicit evidence of user preferences—as input, whereas basic search systems use just an explicit query. Personalized search represents a middle ground in this spectrum, using both an explicit user query and implicit user feedback and observed actions.

The possibility to consider diversity in the presence of both a query and a user profile has been researched as well [63, 74]. This standpoint has interesting philosophical implications, since personalization can also be seen as a strategy to cope with the uncertainty in a user query. While in a diversification approach the system accepts a situation of uncertainty and adapts its behavior to it, personalization tries to reduce the uncertainty by enhancing the system knowledge about the user need.

Diversity and personalization do not necessarily exclude each other, and can in fact be combined into personalized diversification, as shown in [74]. Vallet and Castells developed and tested a full framework that generalizes IR diversification methods (including xQuAD [67] and IA-Select [6]) into a personalized diversification scheme, by introducing the user as a random variable in the probabilistic formalization of the diversity algorithm [74]. In addition to bridging two theories, the scheme compared favorably empirically to personalization and diversity alone.

26.6 Empirical Metric Comparison

We illustrate the metrics and some of the algorithms described along this chapter with some empirical measurements for a few recommendation algorithms on MovieLens 1M. In the tests we present, ERR-IA and subtopic recall are defined using movie genres as user aspects; ILD and unexpectedness take Jaccard on genres as the distance measure; and aggregate diversity is presented as a ratio over the total number of items, for a better appreciation of differences.

Table 26.3 shows the metric values for some representative recommendation algorithms: matrix factorization (MF) recommender, based on [38]; a user-based kNN algorithm using the Jaccard similarity, and omitting the normalization by the sum of similarities in the item prediction function; a content-based recommender using movie tags; a most-popular ranking; and random recommendation. We may mainly notice that matrix factorization stands out as the most effective in aggregate diversity and ERR-IA. The latter can be attributed to the fact that this metric takes relevance into account, a criteria on which MF achieves the best results of this set (as seen in nDCG).

Table 26.3 Novelty and diversity metrics (at cutoff 10) on a few representative recommendation algorithms in the MovieLens 1M dataset.

	nDCG	ILD	Unexp	MSI	MPC	Aggdiv	IUD	Entropy	ERR-IA	S-recall
MF	**0.3161**	0.6628	0.7521	9.5908	0.8038	**0.2817**	**0.9584**	**8.5906**	**0.2033**	0.5288
u-kNN	0.2856	0.6734	0.7785	9.0716	0.7361	0.1589	0.8803	7.1298	0.1800	**0.5422**
CB	0.1371	**0.6825**	0.7880	**9.7269**	**0.8101**	0.1650	0.7762	6.2941	0.1001	0.5378
PopRec	0.1415	0.6624	**0.8451**	8.5793	0.6514	0.0183	0.4943	4.5834	0.0773	0.5253
Random	0.0043	**0.7372**	0.8304	**13.1067**	**0.9648**	**0.9647**	**0.9971**	**11.7197**	0.0034	0.5055

The highest value of each metric is shown in boldface and table cells are colored in shades of green, darker representing higher values (the values of random recommendation are disregarded in the color and bold font of the rest of rows—though not vice versa—to allow the appreciation of differences excluding the random recommendation)

Content-based recommendation procures the best long tail novelty metrics, confirming a well-known fact [20]. It is not comparably as bad in unexpectedness as one might expect, and this can be attributed to the fact that movie genres (the basis for the unexpectedness distance) and movie tags (the basis for CB similarity) seem not to correlate that much. This, and the good results in terms of ILD can also be related to the suboptimal accuracy of this algorithm as a standalone recommender, which may lend it, albeit to a small degree, some of the flavor of random recommendations. We have checked (outside the reported results) that CB naturally gets the lowest ILD value of all recommenders if the metric uses the same features as the CB algorithm (i.e. movie tags).

Popularity has (almost by definition) the worst results in terms of most novelty and diversity metrics; except in terms of unexpectedness (distance to user profile), which makes sense since this algorithm ignores any data of target users and thus delivers items that are weakly related to the individual profiles. Random recommendation is naturally optimal at most diversity metrics except the one that takes relevance into account (it has low subtopic recall though, because of a bias in MovieLens whereby genre cardinality—therefore subtopic coverage—correlates negatively with popularity). And kNN seems to achieve a good balance of the different metrics. We may also notice that aggregate diversity, IUD and entropy go hand in hand, as one would expect.

In order to give an idea of how related or different the metrics are, Table 26.4 shows the pairwise Pearson correlation of the metrics on a user basis for the MF recommender. We see that ILD, unexpectedness and subtopic recall tend to go hand in hand, even though they capture different properties as seen previously in the comparison of recommenders in Table 26.3 (e.g. popularity has very good unexpectedness but very poor ILD). MSI and MPC confirm to be quite equivalent, and IUD (which is equivalent to Gini-Simpson) goes strongly along with these long tail metrics. Note that aggregate diversity and entropy do not have a definition for individual users, and therefore they cannot be included in this table. However, as mentioned before, these measures show strong system-wise correspondence with IUD in Table 26.3 and, by transitivity, can be expected to correlate with long-tail metrics as well. The correlation between ERR-IA and nDCG reflects the fact that in addition to aspect diversity ERR-IA takes much into account relevance, which is what nDCG measures.

Table 26.4 Pearson correlation between different metrics (on a user basis) applied to a matrix factorization algorithm on MovieLens 1M.

nDCG							
0.64	**ERR-IA**						
0.03	-0.02	**S-recall**					
0.03	-0.09	0.71	**ILD**				
0.07	-0.06	0.62	0.85	**Unexp**			
0.02	0.09	-0.21	-0.21	-0.20	**MSI**		
0.02	0.10	-0.19	-0.21	-0.19	0.97	**MPC**	
0.06	0.14	-0.20	-0.27	-0.23	0.87	0.93	**IUD**

The shades of color (red for negative, green for positive) highlight the magnitude of values

Table 26.5 Novelty and diversity metrics (at cutoff 10) on a few novelty and diversity enhancement algorithms applied to the matrix factorization algorithm on MovieLens 1M

	nDCG	ILD	Unexp	MSI	MPC	Aggdiv	ERR-IA	S-recall
MF	**0.3161**	0.6628	0.7521	9.5908	0.8038	0.2817	0.2033	0.5288
+MMR	0.2817	**0.7900**	0.8089	9.6138	0.8054	0.2744	0.1897	**0.6814**
+Unexp	0.2505	0.7588	**0.8467**	9.6011	0.8029	0.2483	0.1431	0.6439
+MSI	0.2309	0.6130	0.7384	**10.6995**	**0.8961**	**0.4700**	0.1583	0.4483
+MPC	0.2403	0.6233	0.7389	10.3406	0.8818	0.3683	0.1622	0.4696
+xQuAD	0.2726	0.6647	0.7596	9.5784	0.8034	0.2292	**0.2063**	0.6370
+Random	0.0870	0.6987	0.7698	10.2517	0.8670	**0.4836**	0.0623	0.5561

The diversifiers are denoted either by their common name, or by the name of the metric (the item novelty model) they target in their objective function

Finally, and just for the sake of illustration, we see in Table 26.5 the effect of different novelty/diversity enhancers, applied to the best performing baseline in nDCG, namely matrix factorization. The diversifiers labeled as MMR, Unexp, MSI and MPC are greedy optimizations of the corresponding item novelty model of each metric. xQuAD is an implementation of the algorithm described in [67] using movie genres as aspects, an algorithm which implicitly targets ERR-IA. We arbitrarily set $\lambda = 0.5$ for all algorithms, without a particular motive other than illustrative purposes. We can see that each algorithm maximizes the metric one would expect. The fact that MSI appears to optimize MPC better than MPC itself is because (a) both metrics are almost equivalent, and (b) $\lambda = 0.5$ is not the optimal value for optimization, whereby a small difference seems to tip the scale towards MSI by pure chance. Please note that these results are in no way aiming to approximate optimality or evaluate an approach over another, but rather to exemplify how the different models, metrics and algorithms may work and relate to each other in a simple experiment.

26.7 Conclusion

The consensus is clear in the community on the importance of novelty and diversity as fundamental qualities of recommendations, and it seems difficult to make progress in the field without considering these dimensions. Considerable progress has been achieved in the area in defining novelty and diversity from several points of view, devising methodologies and metrics to evaluate them, and developing different methods to enhance them. This chapter aims to provide a wide overview on the work so far, as well as a unifying perspective linking them together as developments from a few basic common root principles.

It is our perception that work in this area is far from being finished. There is still room for further understanding the role of novelty and diversity, as well as theoretical, methodological and algorithmic developments around them. For instance, modeling feature-based novelty in probabilistic terms in order to unify discovery and familiarity models would be an interesting line for future work.

Aspects such as the time dimension, along which items may recover part of their novelty value [43, 56], or the variability among users regarding their degree of novelty-seeking trend, are examples of issues that require further research. Last but not least, user studies would bring considerable light as to whether the described metrics match the actual user perception, as well as the precise extent and conditions in which users appreciate novelty and diversity versus accuracy and other potential dimensions of recommendation effectiveness.

References

1. Adamopoulos, P., Tuzhilin, A.: On unexpectedness in recommender systems: Or how to better expect the unexpected. ACM Transactions on Intelligent Systems and Technology 4(5), Special Section on Novelty and Diversity in Recommender Systems, **54**:1–54-32 (2015)
2. Adomavicius, G., Kwon, Y.: Maximizing aggregate recommendation diversity: A graph-theoretic approach. In: Proceedings of the 1st ACM RecSys Workshop on Novelty and Diversity in Recommender Systems, DiveRS 2011, pp. 3 10 (2011)
3. Adomavicius, G., Kwon, Y.: Improving aggregate recommendation diversity using ranking-based techniques. IEEE Transactions on Knowledge and Data Engineering **24**(5), 896–911 (2012)
4. Adomavicius, G., Kwon, Y.: Optimization-based approaches for maximizing aggregate recommendation diversity. INFORMS Journal on Computing **26**(2), 351–369 (2014)
5. Adomavicius, G., Tuzhilin, A.: Toward the next generation of recommender systems: A survey of the state-of-the-art and possible extensions. IEEE Transactions on Knowledge and Data Engineering **17**(6), 734–749 (2005)
6. Agrawal, R., Gollapudi, S., Halverson, A., Ieong, S.: Diversifying search results. In: Proceedings of the 2nd ACM Conference on Web Search and Data Mining, WSDM 2009, pp. 5–14. ACM, New York, NY, USA (2009)
7. Allan, J., Wade, C., Bolivar, A.: Retrieval and novelty detection at the sentence level. In: Proceedings of the 26th ACM SIGIR Conference on Research and Development in Information Retrieval, SIGIR 2003, pp. 314–321. ACM, New York, NY, USA (2003)
8. Alodhaibi, K., Brodsky, A., Mihaila, G.A.: COD: Iterative utility elicitation for diversified composite recommendations. In: Proceedings of the 43rd Hawaii International Conference on System Sciences, HICSS 2010, pp. 1–10. IEEE Computer Society, Washington, DC, USA (2010)
9. Anderson, C.: The Long Tail: Why the Future of Business Is Selling Less of More. Hyperion (2006)
10. Baeza-Yates, R., Ribeiro-Neto, B.: Modern Information Retrieval, 2nd edn. Addison-Wesley Publishing Company, USA (2008)
11. Bellogín, A., Cantador, I., Castells, P.: A comparative study of heterogeneous item recommendations in social systems. Information Sciences **221**, 142–169 (2013)
12. Bessa, A., Veloso, A., Ziviani, N.: Using mutual influence to improve recommendations. In: O. Kurland, M. Lewenstein, E. Porat (eds.) String Processing and Information Retrieval, *Lecture Notes in Computer Science*, vol. 8214, pp. 17–28. Springer International Publishing (2013)
13. Bhandari, U., Sugiyama, K., Datta, A., Jindal, R.: Serendipitous recommendation for mobile apps using item-item similarity graph. In: R.E. Banchs, F. Silvestri, T.Y. Liu, M. Zhang, S. Gao, J. Lang (eds.) Information Retrieval Technology, *Lecture Notes in Computer Science*, vol. 8281, pp. 440–451. Springer Berlin Heidelberg (2013)
14. Boim, R., Milo, T., Novgorodov, S.: Diversification and refinement in collaborative filtering recommender. In: Proceedings of the 20th ACM Conference on Information and Knowledge Management, CIKM 2011, pp. 739–744. ACM, New York, NY, USA (2011)

15. Breese, J.S., Heckerman, D., Kadie, C.: Empirical analysis of predictive algorithms for collaborative filtering. In: Proceedings of the 14th Conference on Uncertainty in Artificial Intelligence, UAI 1998, pp. 43–52. Morgan Kaufmann Publishers Inc., San Francisco, CA, USA (1998)
16. Brickman, P., D'Amato, B.: Exposure effects in a free-choice situation. Journal of Personality and Social Psychology **32**(3), 415–420 (1975)
17. Carbonell, J., Goldstein, J.: The use of MMR, diversity-based reranking for reordering documents and producing summaries. In: Proceedings of the 21st Annual International ACM SIGIR Conference on Research and Development in Information Retrieval, SIGIR 1998, pp. 335–336. ACM, New York, NY, USA (1998)
18. Carterette, B.: System effectiveness, user models, and user utility: A conceptual framework for investigation. In: Proceedings of the 34th Annual International ACM SIGIR Conference on Research and Development in Information Retrieval, SIGIR 2011, pp. 903–912. ACM, New York, NY, USA (2011)
19. Castagnos, S., Brun, A., Boyer, A.: When diversity is needed... but not expected! In: Proceedings of the 3rd International Conference on Advances in Information Mining and Management, IMMM 2013, pp. 44–50. IARIA, Lisbon, Portugal (2013)
20. Celma, O., Herrera, P.: A new approach to evaluating novel recommendations. In: Proceedings of the 2nd ACM Conference on Recommender Systems, RecSys 2008, pp. 179–186. ACM, New York, NY, USA (2008)
21. Chapelle, O., Ji, S., Liao, C., Velipasaoglu, E., Lai, L., Wu, S.L.: Intent-based diversification of web search results: Metrics and algorithms. Information Retrieval **14**(6), 572–592 (2011)
22. Chen, H., Karger, D.R.: Less is more: Probabilistic models for retrieving fewer relevant documents. In: Proceedings of the 2nd Annual International ACM SIGIR Conference on Research and Development in Information Retrieval, SIGIR 2006, pp. 429–436. ACM, New York, NY, USA (2006)
23. Clarke, C.L., Craswell, N., Soboroff, I., Cor: Overview of the TREC 2010 web track. In: Proceedings of the 19th Text REtrieval Conference, TREC 2010. National Institute of Standards and Technology (NIST) (2010)
24. Clarke, C.L., Kolla, M., Cormack, G.V., Vechtomova, O., Ashkan, A., Büttcher, S., MacKinnon, I.: Novelty and diversity in information retrieval evaluation. In: Proceedings of the 31st Annual International ACM SIGIR Conference on Research and Development in Information Retrieval, SIGIR 2008, pp. 659–666. ACM, New York, NY, USA (2008)
25. Coombs, C., Avrunin, G.S.: Single peaked preference functions and theory of preference. Psychological Review **84**(2), 216–230 (1977)
26. Deselaers, T., Gass, T., Dreuw, P., Ney, H.: Jointly optimising relevance and diversity in image retrieval. In: Proceedings of the ACM International Conference on Image and Video Retrieval, CIVR 2009, pp. 39:1–39:8. ACM, New York, NY, USA (2009)
27. Drosou, M., Pitoura, E.: Comparing diversity heuristics. Tech. rep., Technical Report 2009–05. Computer Science Department, University of Ioannina (2009)
28. Drosou, M., Pitoura, E.: Diversity over continuous data. IEEE Data Engineering Bulleting **32**(4), 49–56 (2009)
29. Drosou, M., Pitoura, E.: Disc diversity: Result diversification based on dissimilarity and coverage. Proceedings of the VLDB Endowment **6**(1), 13–24 (2012)
30. Drosou, M., Stefanidis, K., Pitoura, E.: Preference-aware publish/subscribe delivery with diversity. In: Proceedings of the 3rd ACM Conference on Distributed Event-Based Systems, DEBS 2009, pp. 6:1–6:12. ACM, New York, NY, USA (2009)
31. Fleder, D.M., Hosanagar, K.: Blockbuster culture's next rise or fall: The impact of recommender systems on sales diversity. Management Science **55**(5), 697–712 (2009)
32. Ge, M., Delgado-Battenfeld, C., Jannach, D.: Beyond accuracy: evaluating recommender systems by coverage and serendipity. In: Proceedings of the 4th ACM Conference on Recommender systems, RecSys 2010, pp. 257–260. ACM, New York, NY, USA (2010)

33. Ge, M., Jannach, D., Gedikli, F., Hepp, M.: Effects of the placement of diverse items in recommendation lists. In: Proceedings of the 14th International Conference on Enterprise Information Systems, ICEIS 2012, pp. 201–208. SciTePress (2012)
34. He, J., Meij, E., de Rijke, M.: Result diversification based on query-specific cluster ranking. Journal of the Association for Information Science and Technology **62**(3), 550–571 (2011)
35. Herlocker, J.L., Konstan, J.A., Borchers, A., Riedl, J.: An algorithmic framework for performing collaborative filtering. In: Proceedings of the 22nd Annual International ACM SIGIR Conference on Research and Development in Information Retrieval, SIGIR 1999, pp. 230–237. ACM, New York, NY, USA (1999)
36. Herlocker, J.L., Konstan, J.A., Terveen, L.G., Riedl, J.T.: Evaluating collaborative filtering recommender systems. ACM Transactions on Information Systems **22**(1), 5–53 (2004)
37. Hu, R., Pu, P.: Enhancing recommendation diversity with organization interfaces. In: Proceedings of the 16th International Conference on Intelligent User Interfaces, IUI 2011, pp. 347–350. ACM, New York, NY, USA (2011)
38. Hu, Y., Koren, Y., Volinsky, C.: Collaborative filtering for implicit feedback datasets. In: Proceedings of the 8th IEEE International Conference on Data Mining, ICDM 2008, pp. 263–272. IEEE Computer Society, Washington, DC, USA (2008)
39. Hurley, N., Zhang, M.: Novelty and diversity in top-N recommendation – analysis and evaluation. ACM Transactions on Internet Technology **10**(4), 14:1–14:30 (2011)
40. Hurley, N.J.: Personalised ranking with diversity. In: Proceedings of the 7th ACM Conference on Recommender Systems, RecSys 2013, pp. 379–382. ACM, New York, NY, USA (2013)
41. Iaquinta, L., de Gemmis, M., Lops, P., Semeraro, G., Filannino, M., Molino, P.: Introducing serendipity in a content-based recommender system. In: Proceedings of the 8th Conference on Hybrid Intelligent Systems, HIS 2008, pp. 168–173. IEEE (2008)
42. Jannach, D., Lerche, L., Gedikli, G., Bonnin, G.: What recommenders recommend - an analysis of accuracy, popularity, and sales diversity effects. In: Proceedings of the 21st International Conference on User Modeling, Adaptation and Personalization, pp. 25–37. Springer (2013)
43. Jeuland, A.P.: Brand preference over time: A partially deterministic operationalization of the notion of variety seeking. In: Proceedings of the Educators' Conference, 43, pp. 33–37. American Marketing Association (1978)
44. Kahn, B.E.: Consumer variety-seeking among goods and services: An integrative review. Journal of Intelligent Information Systems **2**(3), 139–148 (1995)
45. Kwon, Y.: Improving neighborhood-based CF systems: Towards more accurate and diverse recommendations. Journal of Intelligent Information Systems **18**(3), 119–135 (2012)
46. Lathia, N., Hailes, S., Capra, L., Amatriain, X.: Temporal diversity in recommender systems. In: Proceedings of the 33rd Annual International ACM SIGIR Conference on Research and Development in Information Retrieval, SIGIR 2010, pp. 210–217. ACM, New York, NY, USA (2010)
47. Levinson, D.: Ethnic Groups Worldwide: A ready Reference Handbook. Oryx Press (1998)
48. Li, X., Murata, T.: Multidimensional clustering based collaborative filtering approach for diversified recommendation. In: Proceedings of the 7th International Conference on Computer Science & Education, ICCSE 2012, pp. 905–910. IEEE (2012)
49. Lubatkin, M., Chatterjee, S.: Extending modern portfolio theory into the domain of corporate diversification: Does it apply? The Academy of Management Journal **37**(1), 109–136 (1994)
50. Maddi, S.R.: The pursuit of consistency and variety. In: R.P. Abelson, E. Aronson, W.J. McGuire, T.M. Newcomb, M.J. Rosenberg, P.H. Tannenbaum (eds.) Theories of Cognitive Consistency: A Sourcebook. Rand McNally (1968)
51. McAlister, L., Pessemier, E.A.: Variety seeking behaviour: and interdisciplinary review. Journal of Consumer Research **9**(3), 311–322 (1982)
52. McGinty, L., Smyth, B.: On the role of diversity in conversational recommender systems. In: Proceedings of the 5th International Conference on Case-based Reasoning, ICCBR 2003, pp. 276–290. Springer-Verlag, Berlin, Heidelberg (2003)

53. McNee, S.M., Riedl, J., Konstan, J.A.: Being accurate is not enough: How accuracy metrics have hurt recommender systems. In: CHI 2006 Extended Abstracts on Human Factors in Computing Systems, CHI EA 2006, pp. 1097–1101. ACM, New York, NY, USA (2006)
54. McSherry, D.: Diversity-conscious retrieval. In: S. Craw, A. Preece (eds.) Advances in Case-Based Reasoning, *Lecture Notes in Computer Science*, vol. 2416, pp. 219–233. Springer Berlin Heidelberg (2002)
55. Moffat, A., Zobel, J.: Rank-biased precision for measurement of retrieval effectiveness. ACM Transactions on Information Systems **27**(1), 2:1–2:27 (2008)
56. Mourão, F., Fonseca, C., Araújo, C., Meira, W.: The oblivion problem: Exploiting forgotten items to improve recommendation diversity. In: Proceedings of the 1st ACM RecSys Workshop on Novelty and Diversity in Recommender System, DiveRS 2011 (2011)
57. Murakami, T., Mori, K., Orihara, R.: Metrics for evaluating the serendipity of recommendation lists. In: K. Satoh, A. Inokuchi, K. Nagao, T. Kawamura (eds.) New Frontiers in Artificial Intelligence, *Lecture Notes in Computer Science*, vol. 4914, pp. 40–46. Springer Berlin Heidelberg (2008)
58. Niemann, K., Wolpers, M.: A new collaborative filtering approach for increasing the aggregate diversity of recommender systems. In: Proceedings of the 19th ACM SIGKDD Conference on Knowledge Discovery and Data Mining, KDD 2013, pp. 955–963. ACM, New York, NY, USA (2013)
59. Oku, K., Hattori, F.: Fusion-based recommender system for improving serendipity. In: Proceedings of the 1st ACM RecSys Workshop on Novelty and Diversity in Recommender Systems, DiveRS 2011 (2011)
60. Pariser, E.: The Filter Bubble: How the New Personalized Web Is Changing What We Read and How We Think. Penguin Books (2012)
61. Park, Y.J., Tuzhilin, A.: The long tail of recommender systems and how to leverage it. In: Proceedings of the 2th ACM Conference on Recommender Systems, RecSys 2008, pp. 11–18. ACM, New York, NY, USA (2008)
62. Patil, G.P., Taillie, C.: Diversity as a concept and its measurement. Journal of the American Statistical Association **77**(379), 548–561 (1982)
63. Radlinski, F., Dumais, S.: Improving personalized web search using result diversification. In: Proceedings of the 29th Annual International ACM SIGIR Conference on Research and Development in Information Retrieval, SIGIR 2006, pp. 691–692. ACM, New York, NY, USA (2006)
64. Raju, P.S.: Optimum stimulation level: Its relationship to personality, demographics and exploratory behavior. Journal of Consumer Research **7**(3), 272–282 (1980)
65. Rao, J., Jia, A., Feng, Y., Zhao, D.: Taxonomy based personalized news recommendation: Novelty and diversity. In: X. Lin, Y. Manolopoulos, D. Srivastava, G. Huang (eds.) Web Information Systems Engineering – WISE 2013, *Lecture Notes in Computer Science*, vol. 8180, pp. 209–218. Springer Berlin Heidelberg (2013)
66. Ribeiro, M.T., Lacerda, A., Veloso, A., Ziviani, N.: Pareto-efficient hybridization for multi-objective recommender systems. In: Proceedings of the 6th ACM Conference on Recommender Systems, RecSys 2012, pp. 19–26. ACM, New York, NY, USA (2012)
67. Santos, R.L., Macdonald, C., Ounis, I.: Exploiting query reformulations for web search result diversification. In: Proceedings of the 19th International Conference on World Wide Web, WWW 2010, pp. 881–890. ACM, New York, NY, USA (2010)
68. Schafer, J.B., Konstan, J.A., Riedl, J.: Meta-recommendation systems: User-controlled integration of diverse recommendations. In: Proceedings of the 11th ACM Conference on Information and Knowledge Management, CIKM 2002, pp. 43–51. ACM, New York, NY, USA (2002)
69. Shi, L.: Trading-off among accuracy, similarity, diversity, and long-tail: a graph-based recommendation approach. In: Proceedings of the 7th ACM Conference on Recommender Systems, RecSys 2013, pp. 57–64. ACM, New York, NY, USA (2013)
70. Smyth, B., McClave, P.: Similarity vs. diversity. In: Proceedings of the 4th International Conference on Case-Based Reasoning, ICCBR 2001, pp. 347–361. Springer-Verlag, London, UK, UK (2001)

71. Su, R., Yin, L., Chen, K., Yu, Y.: Set-oriented personalized ranking for diversified top-N recommendation. In: Proceedings of the 7th ACM Conference on Recommender Systems, RecSys 2013, pp. 415–418. ACM, New York, NY, USA (2013)
72. Szlávik, Z., Kowalczyk, W., Schut, M.: Diversity measurement of recommender systems under different user choice models. In: Proceedings of the 5th AAAI Conference on Weblogs and Social Media, ICWSM 2011. The AAAI Press (2011)
73. Taramigkou, M., Bothos, E., Christidis, K., Apostolou, D., Mentzas, G.: Escape the bubble: Guided exploration of music preferences for serendipity and novelty. In: Proceedings of the 7th ACM Conference on Recommender Systems, RecSys 2013, pp. 335–338. ACM, New York, NY, USA (2013)
74. Vallet, D., Castells, P.: Personalized diversification of search results. In: Proceedings of the 35th Annual International ACM SIGIR Conference on Research and Development in Information Retrieval, SIGIR 2012, pp. 841–850. ACM, New York, NY, USA (2012)
75. Vargas, S., Castells, P.: Rank and relevance in novelty and diversity metrics for recommender systems. In: Proceedings of the 5th ACM Conference on Recommender Systems, RecSys 2011, pp. 109–116. ACM, New York, NY, USA (2011)
76. Vargas, S., Castells, P.: Improving sales diversity by recommending users to items. In: Proceedings of the 8th ACM Conference on Recommender Systems, RecSys 2014, pp. 145–152. ACM, New York, NY, USA (2014)
77. Vargas, S., Castells, P., Vallet, D.: Intent-oriented diversity in recommender systems. In: Proceedings of the 34th Annual International ACM SIGIR Conference on Research and Development in Information Retrieval, SIGIR 2011, pp. 1211–1212. ACM, New York, NY, USA (2011)
78. Vargas, S., Castells, P., Vallet, D.: Explicit relevance models in intent-oriented information retrieval diversification. In: Proceedings of the 35th Annual International ACM SIGIR Conference on Research and Development in Information Retrieval, SIGIR 2012, pp. 75–84. ACM, New York, NY, USA (2012)
79. Ribeiro, M.T., Ziviani, N., Silva De Moura, E., Hata, I., Lacerda, A., Veloso, A.: Multiobjective pareto-efficient approaches for recommender systems. ACM Transactions on Intelligent Systems and Technology 4(5), Special Section on Novelty and Diversity in Recommender Systems, **53**:1–53-20 (2015)
80. Wang, J.: Mean-variance analysis: A new document ranking theory in information retrieval. In: Proceedings of the 31th European Conference on Information Retrieval, ECIR 2009, pp. 4–16. Springer-Verlag, Berlin, Heidelberg (2009)
81. Welch, M.J., Cho, J., Olston, C.: Search result diversity for informational queries. In: Proceedings of the 20th International Conference on World Wide Web, WWW 2011, pp. 237–246. ACM, New York, NY, USA (2011)
82. Wu, Q., Tang, F., Li, L., Barolli, L., You, I., Luo, Y., Li, H.: Recommendation of more interests based on collaborative filtering. In: Proceedings of the 26 IEEE Conference on Advanced Information Networking and Applications, AINA 2012, pp. 191–198. IEEE (2012)
83. Yu, C., Lakshmanan, L., Amer-Yahia, S.: It takes variety to make a world: Diversification in recommender systems. In: Proceedings of the 12th International Conference on Extending Database Technology, EDBT 2009, pp. 368–378. ACM, New York, NY, USA (2009)
84. Zhai, C.X., Cohen, W.W., Lafferty, J.: Beyond independent relevance: Methods and evaluation metrics for subtopic retrieval. In: Proceedings of the 26th Annual International ACM SIGIR Conference on Research and Development in Information Retrieval, SIGIR 2003, pp. 10–17. ACM, New York, NY, USA (2003)
85. Zhang, M., Hurley, N.: Avoiding monotony: Improving the diversity of recommendation lists. In: Proceedings of the 2nd ACM Conference on Recommender Systems, RecSys 2008, pp. 123–130. ACM, New York, NY, USA (2008)

86. Zhang, M., Hurley, N.: Novel item recommendation by user profile partitioning. In: Proceedings of the IEEE/WIC/ACM International Joint Conference on Web Intelligence and Intelligent Agent Technology, WI-IAT 2009, pp. 508–515. IEEE Computer Society, Washington, DC, USA (2009)
87. Zhang, Y., Callan, J., Minka, T.: Novelty and redundancy detection in adaptive filtering. In: Proceedings of the 25th Annual International ACM SIGIR Conference on Research and Development in Information Retrieval, SIGIR 2002, pp. 81–88. ACM, New York, NY, USA (2002)
88. Zhang, Y.C., Séaghdha, D.O., Quercia, D., Jambor, T.: Auralist: Introducing serendipity into music recommendation. In: Proceedings of the 5th ACM Conference on Web Search and Data Mining, WSDM 2012, pp. 13–22. ACM, New York, NY, USA (2012)
89. Zhou, T., Kuscsik, Z., Liu, J.G., Medo, M., Wakeling, J.R., Zhang, Y.C.: Solving the apparent diversity-accuracy dilemma of recommender systems. Proceedings of the National Academy of Sciences **107**(10), 4511–4515 (2010)
90. Ziegler, C.N., McNee, S.M., Konstan, J.A., Lausen, G.: Improving recommendation lists through topic diversification. In: Proceedings of the 14th International Conference on World Wide Web, WWW 2005, pp. 22–32. ACM, New York, NY, USA (2005)

Chapter 27
Cross-Domain Recommender Systems

Iván Cantador, Ignacio Fernández-Tobías, Shlomo Berkovsky, and Paolo Cremonesi

27.1 Introduction

Nowadays, the majority of recommender systems offer recommendations for items belonging to a single domain. For instance, Netflix recommends movies and TV programs, Barnes&Noble recommends books, and Last.fm recommends songs and music albums. These domain-specific systems have been successfully deployed by numerous websites, and the single-domain recommendation functionality is not perceived as a limitation, but rather pitched as a focus on a certain market.

Nonetheless, large e-commerce sites like Amazon and eBay often store user feedback for items from multiple domains, and in social media users often express their tastes and interests for a variety of topics. It may, therefore, be beneficial to leverage all the available user data provided in various systems and domains, in order to generate more encompassing user models and better recommendations. Instead of treating each domain (e.g., movies, books, and music) independently, knowledge acquired in a *source* domain could be transferred to and exploited in another *target* domain. The research challenge of transferring knowledge, and the business potential of delivering recommendations spanning across multiple domains, have triggered an increasing interest in *cross-domain recommendations.*

I. Cantador (✉) • I. Fernández-Tobías
Universidad Autónoma de Madrid, Madrid, Spain
e-mail: ivan.cantador@uam.es; ignacio.fernandezt@uam.es

S. Berkovsky
CSIRO, Sydney, NSW, Australia
e-mail: shlomo.berkovsky@csiro.au

P. Cremonesi
Politecnico di Milano, Milan, Italy
e-mail: paolo.cremonesi@polimi.it

F. Ricci et al. (eds.), *Recommender Systems Handbook*,
DOI 10.1007/978-1-4899-7637-6_27

Consider two motivating use cases for cross-domain recommendations. The first refers to the well known cold-start problem, which hinders the recommendation generation due to the lack of sufficient information about users or items. In a cross-domain setting, a recommender may draw on information acquired from other domains to alleviate such problem, e.g., a user's favorite movie genres may be derived from her favorite book genres. The second refers to the generation of personalized cross-selling or bundle recommendations for items from multiple domains, e.g., a movie accompanied by a music album similar to the soundtrack of the movie. This recommendation may be informed by the user's movie tastes, but may not be extracted from rating correlations within a joined movie-music rating matrix.

These use cases are underpinned by an intuitive assumption that there are correspondences between user and item profiles in the source and target domains. This assumption has been validated in several marketing, behavioral, and data mining studies, which uncover strong dependencies between different domains [58, 66]. Cross-domain recommender systems leverage these dependencies through considering, for example, overlaps between the user or item sets, correlations between user preferences, and similarities of item attributes. Then, they apply a variety of techniques for enriching the knowledge in the target domain, and improving the quality of recommendations generated therein.

Cross-domain recommendation is a challenging and still largely under-explored topic. Although it has been studied from several angles, an agreed upon definition of the cross-domain recommendation problem has not emerged yet, and no work has analyzed and classified the existing cross-domain recommendation techniques. In this chapter we survey the state of the art in cross-domain recommender systems, categorize the methods for establishing and exploiting links between diverse domains, compare the outcomes of prior work, and outline future research directions.

The chapter is structured as follows. In Sect. 27.2 we formulate the cross-domain recommendation problem, describing its main tasks and goals. In Sect. 27.3 we present a general categorization of cross-domain recommendation techniques. In Sects. 27.4 and 27.5 we review cross-domain recommendation approaches, distinguishing between knowledge aggregation and knowledge linkage/transfer approaches. In Sect. 27.6 we overview cross-domain recommendation evaluation. In Sect. 27.7 we discuss practical considerations about cross-domain recommender systems. Finally, in Sect. 27.8 we discuss open research issues in cross-domain recommendation.

27.2 Formulation of the Cross-Domain Recommendation Problem

The cross-domain recommendation problem has been addressed from various perspectives in different research areas. It has been handled by means of user preference aggregation and mediation strategies for the cross-system personalization problem in user modeling [2, 8, 58], as a potential solution to mitigate the cold-start and sparsity problems in recommender systems [16, 59, 64], and as a practical application of knowledge transfer in machine learning [26, 40, 51].

Aiming to unify perspectives, we provide a generic formulation of the cross-domain recommendation problem, focusing on existing domain notions (Sect. 27.2.1) and cross-domain recommendation tasks (Sect. 27.2.2) and goals (Sect. 27.2.3), and discuss the possible scenarios of data overlap between domains (Sect. 27.2.4).

27.2.1 Definition of Domain

In the literature researchers have considered distinct notions of domain. For instance, some have treated items like *movies* and *books* as belonging to different domains, while others have considered items such as *action movies* and *comedy movies* as different domains. To the best of our knowledge, in the context of recommender systems research, there have been no attempts to define the concept of *domain*. Here we distinguish between several domain notions according to the attributes and types of recommended items. Specifically, we consider that *domain* may be defined at four levels (see illustration in Fig. 27.1):

- *(Item) Attribute level.* Recommended items are of the same type, having the same attributes. Two items are considered as belonging to distinct domains if they differ in the value of certain attribute. For instance, two movies belong to distinct domains if they have different genres, like action and comedy movies. This definition of domain is rather borderline, and is mainly used as a way to increase the diversity of recommendations (e.g., we may wish to recommend some thriller movies even to users who only watch comedy movies).
- *(Item) Type level.* Recommended items are of similar types and share some attributes. Two items are considered as belonging to distinct domains if they have different attribute subsets. For instance, movies and TV shows belong to distinct domains, since although they have several attributes in common (title, genre), they still differ with respect to some others (e.g., the live attribute for TV shows).
- *Item level.* Recommended items are not of the same type, differing in most, if not all, of their attributes. For instance, movies and books belong to different domains, even though they have some attributes in common (title, release/publication year).

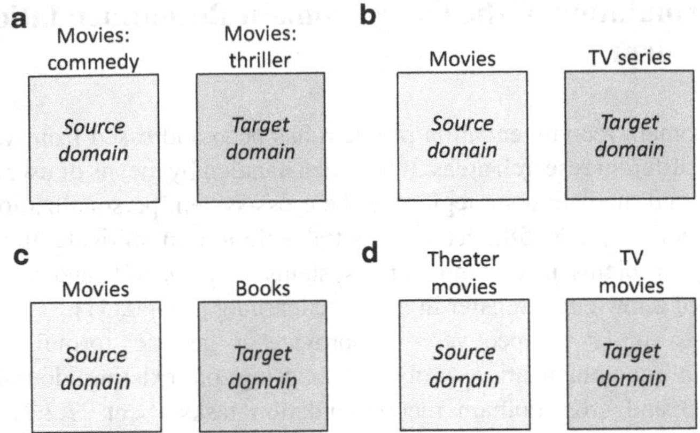

Fig. 27.1 Notions of domain according to attributes and types of recommended items. (**a**) *Attribute level*: same type of items (movies) with different values of certain attribute (genre). (**b**) *Type level*: similar types of items (movies and TV shows), sharing some of their attributes. (**c**) *Item level*: different types of items (books and movies). (**d**) *System level*: same type of items (movies) on different systems (theater and TV)

- *System level.* Recommended items belong to distinct systems, which are considered as different domains. For instance, movies rated in the MovieLens recommender, and movies watched in the Netflix video streaming service.

In Table 27.1 we summarize the considered notions of domains, addressed domains, and used datasets/systems in a significant number of prior works on cross-domain user modeling and recommendation. It can be seen that the majority of the papers considers domains at the item (about 55 %) and system (24 %) levels. The most frequently addressed domains are movies (75 %), books (57 %), music (39 %) and TV (18 %). In this context, we note that around 10 % of the papers addresses various domains, by exploiting user preference data from multi-domain systems like Amazon and Facebook. Analyzing the pairs of domains frequently addressed, we observe that movies are often crossed with books (33 %), music (19 %), and TV (7 %), whereas books are crossed with music (14 %) and TV (10 %).

The table also shows the utilized types of user preferences: ratings (61 %), tags (29 %), thumbs up (14 %), transaction history (7 %), and click-through data (4 %). Although only a few papers use semantic concepts as user preferences, in some papers, social tags are transformed into concepts from WordNet or Wikipedia. Overall, about 14 % of the papers use semantic-based user preferences.

27.2.2 Cross-Domain Recommendation Tasks

The research on cross-domain recommendation generally aims to exploit knowledge from a source domain $\mathcal{D}_S$ to perform or improve recommendations in a target

Table 27.1 Summary of domain notions, domains, and user preference datasets/systems used in the cross-domain user modeling and recommendation literature

Domain notion	Domains	User preferences—*datasets/systems*	References
Item attribute	Book categories	Ratings—*BookCrossing*	Cao et al. [13]
	Movie genres	Ratings—*EachMovie*	Berkovsky et al. [7]
		Ratings—*MovieLens*	Lee et al. [38] Cao et al. [13]
Item type	Books, movies, music	Ratings—*Amazon*	Hu et al. [31] Loni et al. [44]
	Books, games, music, movies and TV shows	Ratings	Winoto and Tang [66]
Item	Books, movies	Ratings—*BookCrossing, MovieLens/EachMovie*	Li et al. [40, 41] Gao et al. [26]
		Ratings, tags—*LibraryThing, MovieLens*	Zhang et al. [67] Shi et al. [59] Enrich et al. [20]
		Ratings, transactions	Azak [3]
		Ratings—*Imhonet*	Sahebi and Brusilovsky [55]
		Ratings—*Douban*	Zhao et al. [69]
	Movies, music	Thumbs up—*Facebook*	Shapira et al. [58]
	Books, movies, music	Tags—*MovieLens, Last.fm, LibraryThing*	Fernández-Tobías et al. [23]
	Books, movies, music, TV shows	Thumbs up—*Facebook*	Tiroshi and Kuflik [65] Cantador et al. [10] Tiroshi et al. [64]
	Music, tourism	Semantic concepts	Fernández-Tobías et al. [21] Kaminskas et al. [35]
	Restaurants, tourism	Ratings, transactions	Chung et al. [14]
	Various domains	Tags—*Delicious, Flickr*	Szomszor et al. [61, 62]
System	Movies	Ratings—*Netflix*	Cremonesi et al. [16] Zhao et al. [69]
		Ratings—*Douban, Netflix*	Zhao et al. [69]
		Ratings—*MovieLens, Moviepilot, Netflix*	Pan et al. [52] Pan et al. [53]
	Music	Tags—*Delicious, Last.fm*	Loizou [43]
		Tags—*Blogger, Last.fm*	Stewart et al. [60]
	Various domains	Tags—*Delicious, Flickr, StumbleUpon, Twitter*	Abel et al. [1] Abel et al. [2]
		Click-through data—*Yahoo! services*	Low et al. [45]

domain $\mathcal{D}_T$. Analyzing the literature, we observe that the addressed tasks are diverse, and a consensual definition of the cross-domain recommendation problem has not been formulated yet. Hence, some researchers have proposed models aimed to provide jointly diverse recommendations of items belonging to multiple domains, whereas others have developed methods to alleviate cold-start and sparsity situations in a target domain by using information from source domains.

Aiming to provide a unified formulation of the cross-domain recommendation problem, we define the tasks we identify as providing recommendations across domains. Without loss of generality, we consider two domains $\mathcal{D}_S$ and $\mathcal{D}_T$ (the definitions are extensible to more source domains). Let $\mathcal{U}_S$ and $\mathcal{U}_T$ be their sets of users, and let $\mathcal{I}_S$ and $\mathcal{I}_T$ be their sets of items. The users of a domain are those who expressed preferences (e.g., ratings, reviews, tags, and consumption logs) for the domain items. The items do not necessarily have preferences from users of the domain, but may have content-based attributes that establish their membership to the domain.

Sorted in increasing order of complexity, we distinguish between the following three recommendation tasks (see Fig. 27.2):

- *Multi-domain recommendation*: recommend items in both the source and target domains, i.e., recommend items in $\mathcal{I}_S \cup \mathcal{I}_T$ to users in $\mathcal{U}_S$ (or, equivalently, in $\mathcal{U}_T$ or $\mathcal{U}_S \cup \mathcal{U}_T$).
- *Linked-domain recommendation*: recommend items in the target domain by exploiting knowledge from the source and target domains, i.e., recommend items in $\mathcal{I}_T$ to users in $\mathcal{U}_S$ by exploiting knowledge about $\mathcal{U}_S \cup \mathcal{U}_T$ and/or $\mathcal{I}_S \cup \mathcal{I}_T$.
- *Cross-domain recommendation*: recommend items in the target domain by exploiting knowledge from the source domain, i.e., recommend items in $\mathcal{I}_T$ to users in $\mathcal{U}_S$ by exploiting knowledge about $\mathcal{U}_S$ and/or $\mathcal{I}_S$.

Multi-domain approaches have mainly focused on the provision of cross-system recommendations, by jointly considering user preferences for items in various systems. To perform this type of recommendations, a significant overlap between user preferences in distinct domains is needed. This is becoming more and more

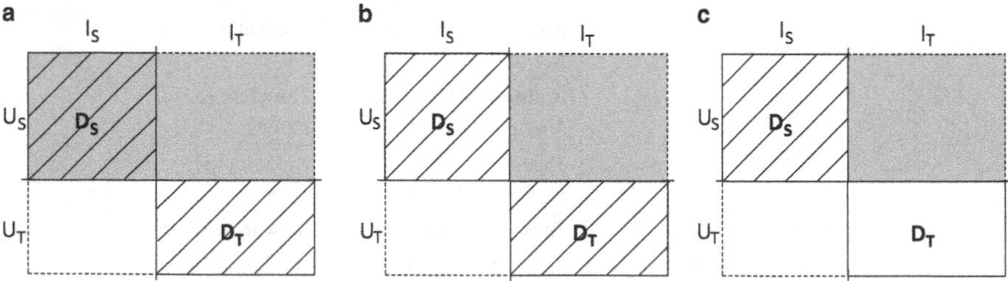

Fig. 27.2 Cross-domain recommendation tasks. *Grey* filled areas represent the target users and recommended items, and *hatched* areas represent the exploited data for generating recommendations (**a**) Multi-domain. (**b**) Linked-domain. (**c**) Cross-domain

feasible, since users maintain profiles in various social media, and there are interconnecting mechanisms for both cross-system interoperability [12] and cross-system user identification [11]. In addition to social media, the benefits of multi-domain recommendations also come through in e-commerce sites, where personalized cross-selling [19, 36] can increase customer satisfaction, and consequently, their loyalty and the businesses profitability. For such purposes, in general, approaches aim to aggregate knowledge from the source and target domains.

Linked-domain approaches have been mainly applied to improve the recommendations in a target domain where there is a scarcity of user preferences, either at the user level (the cold-start problem) or at the community level (the data sparsity problem). To deal with these situations, a common solution is to enrich or enhance the available knowledge in the target domain with knowledge from the source domain. Hence, to perform this type of recommendations, some data relations or overlaps between domains are needed, and approaches aim to establish explicit or implicit knowledge-based links between the domains.

Finally, cross-domain approaches have been proposed to provide recommendations in a target domain where there is no information about the users. In this case, there is no assumption of data relations and/or overlaps between domains, and approaches aim to establish knowledge-based links between domains or to transfer knowledge from the source domain to the target domain.

For the sake of simplicity, we consider the three recommendation tasks together, as a single formulation of the cross-domain recommendation problem, although in Sects. 27.4 and 27.5 we review specific approaches for each task.

27.2.3 Cross-Domain Recommendation Goals

From both the research and practical perspectives, it is important to match the recommendation algorithms to the task in hand. For this reason, we initially present a taxonomy of cross-domain recommendation goals. The taxonomy is described in a solution-agnostic way: each problem is defined based solely on its goals—without discussing how they are solved, which will be done in Sect. 27.3.

At the first level of the taxonomy, we consider the three recommendation tasks presented in Sect. 27.2.2, namely *multi-domain*, *linked-domain*, and *cross-domain* tasks, which are the columns of Table 27.2. At the second level, we distinguish between the specific goals addressed by cross-domain recommenders, which are the rows of Table 27.2. We identify the following goals:

- *Addressing the system cold-start problem* (*system bootstrapping*). This is related to situations in which a recommender is unable to generate recommendations due to an initial lack of user preferences. One possible solution is to bootstrap the system with preferences from another source outside the target domain.

Table 27.2 Summary of cross-domain recommendation approaches based on goals and tasks

Goal	Multi-domain task	Linked-domain task	Cross-domain task
Cold start			Shapira et al. [58]
New user		Winoto et al. [66] Cremonesi et al. [16] Low et al. [45] Hu et al. [31] Sahebi et al. [55]	Berkovsky et al. [6, 7] Berkovsky et al. [8] Nakatsuji et al. [47] Cremonesi et al. [16] Tiroshi et al. [65] Braunhofer et al. [9]
New item			Kaminskas et al. [35]
Accuracy	Cao et al. [13] Zhang et al. [67] Li et al. [42] Tang et al. [63] Zhang et al. [68]	Li et al. [40, 41] Moreno et al. [46] Shi et al. [59] Pan et al. [52] Gao et al. [26] Pan et al. [53] Zhao et al. [69]	Pan et al. [48] Stewart et al. [60] Pan et al. [51] Tiroshi et al. [64] Loni et al. [44]
Diversity		Winoto et al. [66]	
User model		Szomszor et al. [61] Abel et al. [1] Abel et al. [2] Fernández-Tobías [23] Goga et al. [28] Jain et al. [32]	

- *Addressing the new user problem.* When a user starts using a recommender, this has no knowledge of the user's tastes and interests, and cannot produce personalized recommendations. This may be solved by exploiting the user's preferences collected in a different source domain.
- *Addressing the new item problem (cross-selling of products).* When a new item is added to a catalog, it has no prior ratings, so it will not be recommended by a collaborative filtering system. This problem is particularly evident when cross-selling new products from different domains.
- *Improving accuracy (by reducing sparsity).* In many domains, the average number of ratings per user and item is low, which may negatively affect the quality of the recommendations. Data collected outside the target domain can increase the rating density, and thus may upgrade the recommendation quality.
- *Improving diversity.* Having similar, redundant items in a recommendation list may not contribute much to the user's satisfaction (Chap. 26). The diversity of recommendations can be improved by considering multiple domains, as this may provide a better coverage of the range of user preferences.

- *Enhancing user models*. The main goal of cross-domain user modeling applications is to enhance user models. Achieving this goal may have personalization-oriented benefits such as (1) discovering new user preferences for the target domain [60, 62], (2) enhancing similarities between users and items [1, 8], and (3) measuring vulnerability in social networks [28, 32].

Table 27.2 shows the mapping between the above recommendation tasks and goals. Cross-domain tasks are mainly used to address the cold start problem boosting data density, while linked-domain tasks are used to improve accuracy and diversity.

27.2.4 Cross-Domain Recommendation Scenarios

As discussed by Fernández-Tobías et al. [22], in the context of a cross-domain recommendation task, domains can be explicitly or implicitly linked by means of content-based (CB) or collaborative filtering (CF) characteristics associated with users and/or items, such as ratings, social tags, semantic relations, and latent factors.

Let $\mathcal{X}^{\mathcal{U}} = \{x_1^{\mathcal{U}}, \cdots, x_m^{\mathcal{U}}\}$ and $\mathcal{X}^{\mathcal{I}} = \{x_1^{\mathcal{I}}, \cdots, x_n^{\mathcal{I}}\}$ be the sets of characteristics utilized to represent the users and items, respectively. Two domains $\mathcal{D}_S$ and $\mathcal{D}_T$ are linked if $\mathcal{X}_S^{\mathcal{U}} \cap \mathcal{X}_T^{\mathcal{U}} \neq \varnothing$ or $\mathcal{X}_S^{\mathcal{I}} \cap \mathcal{X}_T^{\mathcal{I}} \neq \varnothing$, i.e., if they share user or item characteristics. In a realistic setting, due to the heterogeneity of domain representations, one may need to set functions that map characteristics between domains, i.e., $f : \mathcal{X}_S^{\mathcal{U}} \rightarrow \mathcal{X}_T^{\mathcal{U}}$ and $g : \mathcal{X}_S^{\mathcal{I}} \rightarrow \mathcal{X}_T^{\mathcal{I}}$. For instance, to link movies and books, a mapping function could identify users registered in two systems, $f(u_{l,movie\ system}) = u_{j,book\ system}$, or could link related genres, $g(comedy_{movie\ system}) = humor_{book\ system}$.

Next, we describe representative examples of user and item characteristics, as well as their inter-domain relations and data overlap scenarios.

- *Content-based relations between domains*. In CB systems, a set of content or metadata features $\mathcal{F} = \{F_1, \cdots, F_n\}$—e.g., keywords, properties, and categories—describes both user preferences and item attributes, i.e., $\mathcal{X}^{\mathcal{U}} \subseteq \mathcal{F}, \mathcal{X}^{\mathcal{I}} \subseteq \mathcal{F}$. In general, a user profile is composed of a vector, where each component reflects the degree to which the user likes or is interested in a specific feature, and similarly, an item profile is composed of a vector whose components reflect the relevance of the features to the item. An overlap between domains $\mathcal{D}_S$ and $\mathcal{D}_T$ occurs when $\mathcal{X}_S^{\mathcal{U}} \cap \mathcal{X}_T^{\mathcal{U}} \neq \varnothing$ and $\mathcal{F}_S \cap \mathcal{F}_T \neq \varnothing$.
- *Collaborative filtering-based relations between domains*. In CF systems, user preferences are modeled as a matrix $R \in \mathbb{R}^{|\mathcal{U}| \times |\mathcal{I}|}$, in which an element $r_{u,i}$ is the rating assigned by user u to item i. Thus, $\mathcal{X}^{\mathcal{U}} = \mathcal{I}$ ($\mathcal{I}$ being the rated items), and domains $\mathcal{D}_S$ and $\mathcal{D}_T$ overlap when $\mathcal{X}_S^{U} \cap \mathcal{X}_T^{U} \neq \varnothing$, i.e., $\mathcal{I}_S \cap \mathcal{I}_T \neq \varnothing$. An equivalent reasoning can be done for items, to derive that $\mathcal{X}^{\mathcal{I}} = \mathcal{U}$ ($\mathcal{U}$ being the users with ratings), and that $\mathcal{D}_S$ and $\mathcal{D}_T$ overlap when $\mathcal{X}_S^{\mathcal{I}} \cap \mathcal{X}_T^{\mathcal{I}} \neq \varnothing$, i.e., $\mathcal{U}_S \cap \mathcal{U}_T \neq \varnothing$.

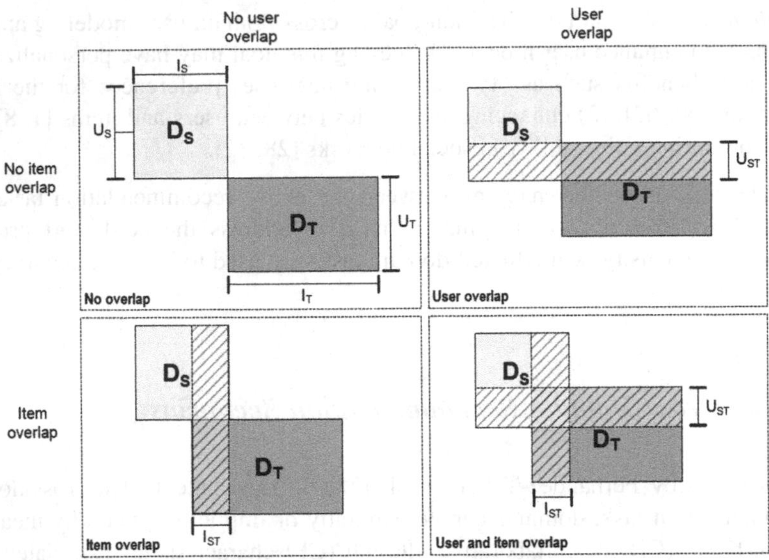

Fig. 27.3 Scenarios of data overlap between user and item sets in two domains $\mathcal{D}_S$ and $\mathcal{D}_T$: *no overlap*, *user overlap*, *item overlap*, and *user and item overlap*

Moreover, as explained in subsequent sections, approaches have been proposed to represent users and/or items in lower dimension spaces, called *latent factors*, in which the above vector representations are valid. In these cases, if $\mathbf{U}$ and $\mathbf{I}$ denote the sets of user and item latent factors, respectively, then $\mathcal{X}^{\mathcal{U}} = \mathbf{U}$ and $\mathcal{X}^{\mathcal{I}} = \mathbf{I}$.

As shown in Fig. 27.3, for the above types of relations, and generalizing the possible cross-domain CF cases identified by Cremonesi et al. [16], four scenarios of data overlap between two domains $\mathcal{D}_S$ and $\mathcal{D}_T$ can exist:

- *No overlap*. There is no overlap between users and items in the domains, i.e., $\mathcal{U}_{ST} = \mathcal{U}_S \cap \mathcal{U}_T = \varnothing$ and $\mathcal{I}_{ST} = \mathcal{I}_S \cap \mathcal{I}_T = \varnothing$.
- *User overlap*. There are some common users who have preferences for items in both domains, i.e., $\mathcal{U}_{ST} \neq \varnothing$, but every item belongs to a single domain. This is the case, for instance, where some users rated movies and books.
- *Item overlap*. There are some common items that have been rated by users from both domains, i.e., $\mathcal{I}_{ST} \neq \varnothing$. This is the case, for instance, where two IPTV providers share a catalog of TV programs, which may be rated in each system.
- *User and item overlap*. There is overlap between both the users and items, i.e., $\mathcal{U}_{ST} \neq \varnothing$ and $\mathcal{I}_{ST} \neq \varnothing$.

27.3 Categorization of Cross-Domain Recommendation Techniques

As discussed in Sect. 27.2, cross-domain recommendation has been addressed from various perspectives in distinct research areas. This has entailed the development of a wide array of recommendation approaches, which in many cases are difficult to compare due to the user preferences they use, the cross-domain scenario they deal with, and the algorithms and data on which they are based. Moreover, published reviews of the research literature and categorizations of existing approaches [16, 22, 33, 39] have not reflected the entire complexity of the space. In this section, we categorize and propose a unifying schema for the existing cross-domain recommendation techniques.

Chung et al. presented in their seminal research [14] a framework that provides integrated recommendations for items that may be of different types, and may belong to different domains. The framework accounts for three levels of recommendation integration: *single item type recommendations*, which consist of items of the same type, *cross item type recommendations*, which consist of items of different types that belong to the same domain, and *cross domain recommendations*, which consist of items whose types belong to different domains. The authors stated that integrated recommendations can be generated by following at least three approaches:

- General filtering: instantiating a recommendation model for multiple item types that may belong to different domains.
- Community filtering: utilizing ratings shared among several communities or systems that may deal with different item types and domains.
- Market basket analysis: applying data mining to extrapolate hidden relations between items of different types/domains and to build a model for item filtering.

In [43], Loizou identified three main trends in cross-domain recommendation research. The first focuses on compiling unified user profiles appropriate for cross-domain recommendations [29]. This is considered as an integration of domain-specific user models into a single, unified multiple-domain user model, which is subsequently used to generate recommendations. The second involves profiling user preferences through monitoring their interactions in individual domains [34], which can be materialized through agents that learn single-domain user preferences and gather them from multiple domains to generate recommendations. The third deals with combining (or mediating) information from several single-domain recommender systems [6]. A number of strategies for mediating single-domain CF systems were considered: exchange of ratings, exchange of user neighborhoods, exchange of user similarities, and exchange of recommendations.

Based on these trends, Cremonesi et al. surveyed and categorized cross-domain CF systems [16]. They enhanced Loizou's categorization by considering a more specific grouping of approaches:

- Extracting association rules from rating behavior in a source domain, and using extracted rules to suggest items in a target domain, as proposed by Lee et al. [38].
- Learning inter-domain rating-based similarity and correlation matrices, as proposed by Cao et al. [13] and Zhang et al. [67].
- Combining estimations of rating probability distributions in source domains to generate recommendations in a target domain, as proposed by Zhuang et al. [70].
- Transferring knowledge between domains to address the rating sparsity problem in a target domain, as proposed by Li et al. [40, 41] and Pan et al. [50, 51].

For the last group, Li presented a survey of transfer learning techniques in cross-domain CF [39]. There, Li proposed an alternative categorization based on types of domain. Specifically, the author distinguished between (1) *system domains* that are associated with different recommenders, and represent a scenario where the data in a target recommender are very sparse, while the data in related recommenders are abundant; (2) *data domains* that are associated with multiple sources of heterogeneous data, and represent a scenario where user data in source domains (e.g., binary ratings) can be obtained easier than in a target domain (e.g., five-star ratings); and (3) *temporal domains* that are associated with distinct data periods, and represent a scenario where temporal user preference dynamics can be captured. For these categories, Li considered three recommendation strategies differing in the knowledge transferred between domains:

- Rating pattern sharing, which aims to factorize single-domain rating matrices utilizing user/item groups, encode group-level rating patterns, and transfer knowledge between domains through the encoded patterns [40–42].
- Rating latent feature sharing, which aims to factorize single-domain rating matrices using latent features, share latent feature spaces across domains, and transfer knowledge between domains through the latent feature matrices [50–53].
- Domain correlating, which aims to factorize single-domain rating matrices using latent features, explore correlations between latent features in single domains, and transfer knowledge between domains through such correlations [13, 59, 67].

Pan and Yang identified in a survey of transfer learning for machine learning applications [49] three main questions to be faced: (1) *what* to transfer—which knowledge should be transferred between domains; (2) *how* to transfer—which learning algorithms should be exploited to transfer the discovered knowledge; and (3) *when* to transfer—in which situations the knowledge transfer knowledge is beneficial. Focusing on the what and how questions, Pan et al. proposed in [50, 51] a two-dimensional categorization of transfer learning-based approaches for cross-domain CF. The first dimension takes the type of transferred knowledge into account, e.g., latent rating features, encoded rating patterns, and rating-based correlations and covariances. The second dimension considers the algorithm, and distinguishes between adaptive and collective approaches, assuming, respectively, the existence of rating data only in the source domain, and in both the source and target domains.

In a more recent survey, Fernández-Tobías et al. went beyond CF recommendations, taking into account approaches that establish cross-domain relationships not necessarily based on ratings [22]. They identified three directions to address the cross-domain recommendation problem. The first is through the integration of single-domain user preferences into a unified cross-domain user model, which implies aggregating user profiles from multiple domains ("compile unified profiles" in [43]), and the mediation of user models across domains ("profile through monitoring" in [43]). The second direction aims to transfer knowledge from a source domain to a target domain, and includes approaches that exploit recommendations generated for a source domain in a target domain ("mediating information" in [43]), and approaches based on transfer learning, surveyed in [39]. The third direction is about establishing explicit relations between domains, which may be based either on content-based relations between items or on rating-based relations between users/items. The authors then proposed a two-dimensional categorization of cross-domain recommendation approaches: (1) according to the type of inter-domain relations: *content-based relations* (item attributes, tags, semantic properties, and feature correlations) vs. *rating-based relations* (rating patterns, rating latent factors, and rating correlations); and (2) according to the goal of the recommendation task: *adaptive models*, which exploit knowledge from a source domain to generate recommendations in a target domain, vs. *collective models*, which are built using data from several domains to improve recommendations in a target domain.

As can be seen from the previous discussion, the existing categorizations of cross-domain recommendation techniques are diverse. We aim to reconcile these categorizations in a way that captures and unifies their core ideas. For this, we focus on the exploitation of knowledge in cross-domain recommendation, which dictates the following two-level taxonomy:

- *Aggregating knowledge*. Knowledge from various source domains is aggregated to perform recommendations in a target domain (Fig. 27.4a). Three use cases are considered, which will be analyzed in Sect. 27.4:

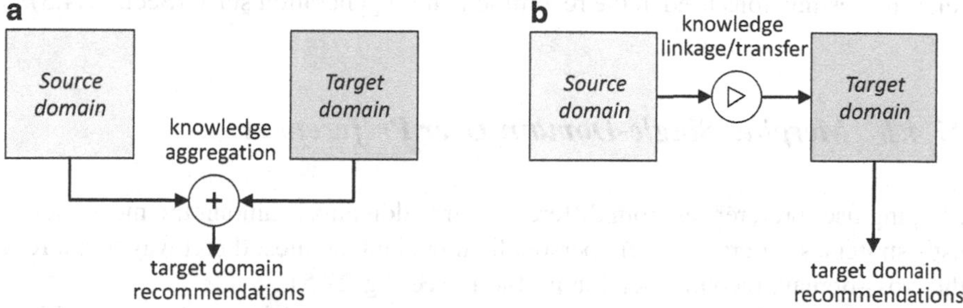

Fig. 27.4 Exploitation of knowledge in cross-domain recommendation. (**a**) Aggregating knowledge. (**b**) Linking/transferring knowledge

  - *Merging user preferences*—the aggregated knowledge consists of user preferences, e.g., ratings, tags, transaction logs, and click-through data.
  - *Mediating user modeling data*—the aggregated knowledge comes from user modeling data exploited by various recommender systems, e.g., user similarities and user neighborhoods.
  - *Combining recommendations*—the aggregated knowledge is composed of single-domain recommendations, e.g., rating estimations and rating probability distributions.

- *Linking and transferring knowledge*. Knowledge linkage or transfer between domains is established to support recommendations (Fig. 27.4b). Three variants are considered, which will be analyzed in Sect. 27.5:
  - *Linking domains*—linking domains by a common knowledge, e.g., item attributes, association rules, semantic networks, and inter-domain correlations.
  - *Sharing latent features*—the source and target domains are related by means of implicit latent features.
  - *Transferring rating patterns*—explicit or implicit rating patterns from source domains are exploited in the target domain.

27.4 Knowledge Aggregation for Cross-Domain Recommendations

In this section, we survey cross-domain recommendation approaches that aggregate knowledge from source domains to perform or improve recommendations in a target domain. The aggregated knowledge can be obtained at any stage of the recommendation process. In particular, it can be obtained from user preferences acquired at the user modeling stage (Sect. 27.4.1), from intermediate user modeling data utilized at the item relevance estimation stage (Sect. 27.4.2), or from item relevance estimations used at the recommendation generation stage (Sect. 27.4.3).

27.4.1 Merging Single-Domain User Preferences

Merging user preferences from different source domains is among the most widely used strategies for cross-system personalization, and the most direct way to address the cross-domain recommendation problem (see Fig. 27.5).

Research has shown that richer profiles can be generated for users when multiple sources of personal preferences are combined, revealing tastes and interests not captured in isolated domains [2, 61]. It has been also shown that enriching sparse user preference data in a certain domain by adding user preference data from other

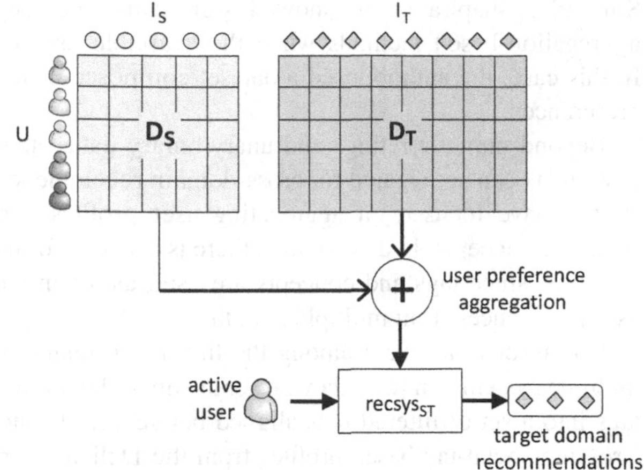

Fig. 27.5 *Merging user preferences.* Data sources from different domains are merged, and a traditional single-domain recommender system is used on the merged data

domains, can significantly improve the generated recommendations under cold-start and sparsity conditions [55, 58]. These benefits, however, are accompanied by the need for having a significant amount of user preferences in multiple domains, and methods for accessing and merging the user profiles from different systems, which may have distinct types and/or representations of user preferences.

The most favorable scenario for aggregation-based methods implies that different systems share user preferences of the same type and representation. This scenario was addressed by Berkovsky et al. with a mediation strategy for cross-domain CF [6, 7]. The authors considered a domain-distributed setting where a global rating matrix R is split, so that single-domain recommenders store local rating matrices R_d having the same structure. In this setting, a target domain recommender imports rating matrices R_d from the source domains, integrates the local and remote rating data into the unified rating matrix R, and applies CF to R. Note that this approach can be seen as a centralized CF with ratings split across multiple domains. Nonetheless, in this approach, smaller rating matrices are more efficiently maintained by local systems, and the data is shared with the target system only when needed.

Berkovsky et al. [6, 7] showed an improvement in the accuracy of target domain recommendations when aggregating ratings from several domains. This was also observed by Winoto and Tang [66]. The authors collected ratings for items in several domains and conducted a study that revealed that even when there exists significant overlap and correlation between domains, recommendation accuracy in the target domain is higher if only ratings in such domain are used. Despite these findings, Winoto and Tang stated that cross-domain recommendations may have alternative benefits, in particular, serendipity and diversity.

Apart from serendipity and diversity, other benefits of cross-domain recommendations have been identified. Sahebi and Brusilovsky [55] examined the impact of the size of user profiles in the source and target domains on the quality of CF, and showed that aggregating ratings from several domains allows increasing the accuracy of recommendations in the target domain under cold-start conditions.

Similarly, Shapira et al. showed significant accuracy improvements by using aggregation-based methods when the available user preferences are sparse [58]. In this case, the authors used a dataset composed of unary Facebook *likes* as user preferences.

Beyond numeric ratings and unary/binary data, other types of user preferences have also been aggregated for cross-domain recommendations. In particular, several studies have focused on aggregating user profiles composed of social tags and semantic concepts. In this context, there is no need for user or item overlap between domains, since tags and concepts are used as a common representation to merge user preferences from multiple domains.

Szomszor et al. were among the first to correlate tag-based user profiles from multiple systems. In [62], they presented an architecture that transforms a set of raw tags into a set of filtered tags aligned between folksonomies in different domains. Crossing social-tag based profiles from the Delicious and Flickr folksonomies, the authors showed that filtered tags increase the overlap between domains, and allows discovering prominent user interests, locations, and events. In a follow-up work [61], Szomszor et al. extended their framework to map social tags to Wikipedia concepts, and build cross-domain user profiles composed of Wikipedia categories. An evaluation showed that new concepts of interest were learnt when expanding a user tag cloud with an external repository. Related to these works, Abel et al. [1] investigated the aggregation of a user's tag clouds from multiple systems. They evaluated a number of methods for semantic enrichment of tag overlap between domains, via tag similarities and via association rules deduced from the tagging data across systems. Aiming to analyze commonalities and differences among tag-based profiles, in Abel et al. [2] mapped tags to WordNet categories and DBpedia concepts. They used the mapped tags to build category-based user profiles, which revealed significantly more information about the users than the profiles available in specific systems. Also in the context of tag-based user profile aggregation, Fernández-Tobías et al. [23] presented an approach that maps tags to emotional categories, under the assumption that emotions evoked by items in an entertainment domain can be represented through tags of folksonomies in which the items are annotated. Hence, emotions assigned to preferred items would be the bridge to merge user profiles across domains.

Regarding the use of semantic concepts as user preferences, Loizou [43] presented an approach that builds a graph where the nodes are associated with Wikipedia concepts describing items liked by the users, and the edges encode the semantic relationships between those concepts, obtained by integrating user ratings and Wikipedia hyperlinks. Using such a graph, a Markov chain model was used to produce recommendations by assessing the probability of traversing the graph towards a particular item, using the nodes in the user's profile as starting points. A related approach was studied by Fernández-Tobías et al. [21] and by Kaminskas et al. [35]. The authors presented a knowledge-based framework of semantic networks that link concepts from different domains. These networks are weighted graphs, in which nodes with no incoming edges represent concepts belonging to the source domain, and nodes with no outgoing nodes represent concepts belonging to the target domain. The framework provides an algorithm that propagates the node weights, in order to identify target concepts that are most related to the source concepts. Implemented on top of DBpedia, the framework was evaluated for recommending music suited to places of interest, which were related through concepts from several domains and contextual dimensions of location and time.

Instead of aggregating user preferences directly, several researches have focused on directed weighted graphs that link user preferences from multiple domains. In [47], Nakatsuji et al. presented an approach that builds domain-specific user graphs whose nodes are associated with users, and whose edges reflect rating-based user similarities. Domain graphs are connected via users who either rated items from several domains or shared social connections, to create a cross-domain user graph. Over this graph, a random walk algorithm retrieves items most liked by the users associated with the extracted nodes. Cremonesi et al. [16] built a graph whose nodes are associated with items and whose edges reflect rating-based item similarities. In this case, the inter-domain connections are the edges between pairs of items in different domains. The authors also proposed to enhance inter-domain edges by discovering new edges and strengthening existing ones, through strategies based on the transitive closure. Using the built multi-domain graph, several neighborhood- and latent factor-based CF techniques were evaluated. In [64], Tiroshi et al. collected a dataset containing user preferences in multiple domains extracted from social network profiles. The data was merged into a bipartite user-item graph, and various statistical and graph-based features of users and items were extracted from the graph. These features were exploited by a machine learning algorithm that addressed the recommendation problem as a binary classification problem.

The last type of cross-domain recommendation based on user preference aggregation is formed by the approaches that map user preferences from multiple domains to domain-independent features, and use the mapped feature-based profiles to build machine learning models that predict a user's preferences in the target domain. Although not conducting evaluations, González et al. [29] proposed an approach for unifying single domain user models by interoperability and coordination of several agents. In addition to user tastes and interests, the unified model is composed of the user's socio-demographic and emotional features. Focusing on user personality features, Cantador et al. [10] studied the relations that exist between personality types and user preferences in multiple entertainment domains, namely movies, TV, music, and books. They analyzed a large number of Facebook user profiles composed of both Big Five personality trait scores [15] and explicit preferences for 16 genres in each of the above domains. As a result, the authors inferred similarities between personality-based user stereotypes in different domains. Finally, Loni et al. [44] presented an approach that encodes rating matrices from multiple domains as real-valued feature vectors. With these vectors, an algorithm based on factorization machines [54] finds patterns between features from the source and target domains, and outputs preference estimations associated with the input vectors.

We summarize the discussed aggregation-based methods in Table 27.3. Aggregating ratings from several CF systems is the simplest method, but requires access to user profiles, and a significant rating overlap between domains, which

Table 27.3 Summary of cross-domain user modeling and recommendation approaches based on merging single-domain user preferences where (*N*) no overlap, (*U*) user overlap, (*I*) item overlap, (*UI*) user and item overlap

Cross-domain approach	Inter-domain relationships	References
Aggregating user ratings into a single multi-domain rating matrix	Rating correlations	Berkovsky et al. [7] ^{UI} Sahebi and Brusilovsky [55] ^{U} Shapira et al. [58] ^{U}
	Rating correlations and relations between domain categories	Winoto and Tang [66] ^{U}
Using a common representation for user preferences from multiple domains	Social tag overlap	Szomszor et al. [62] ^{N} Szomszor et al. [61] ^{N} Abel et al. [1] ^{N} Abel et al. [2] ^{N} Fernández-Tobías et al. [23] ^{N}
	Semantic relationships between domain concepts	Loizou [43] ^{N} Fernández-Tobías et al. [21] ^{N} Kaminskas et al. [35] ^{N}
Linking user preferences via a multi-domain graph	Rating-based user/item similarities	Nakatsuji et al. [47] ^{U} Cremonesi et al. [16] ^{U}
	Patterns of user-item graph-based features	Tiroshi et al. [64] ^{U}
Mapping user preferences to domain-independent features	Socio-demographic and emotional features	González et al. [29] ^{N}
	Personality features	Cantador et al. [10] ^{N}
	User-item interaction features	Loni et al. [44] ^{U}

may not be achievable in real situations. Thus, most aggregation-based methods transform user preferences from multiple domains into a common representation, independent of the domains of interest, and usable for establishing inter-domain data relations and overlaps. For this purpose, social tags and semantic concepts serve as the main types of user preferences. More recent methods focus on aggregating several sources of user preferences from multiple domains into a single graph. Due to the increasing use of social media, we envision that novel cross-domain recommendation approaches that both unify user preferences and aggregate them into multi-domain graphs will be developed.

27.4.2 Mediating Single-Domain User Modeling Data

Not only immediate user preferences, but also other recommendation-related information about users, items, and domains may be aggregated or mediated (see Fig. 27.6). An early approach for cross-domain recommendation through mediation was proposed by Berkovsky et al. [8]. The central idea behind user model mediation is that importing any user modeling data from source recommenders may benefit

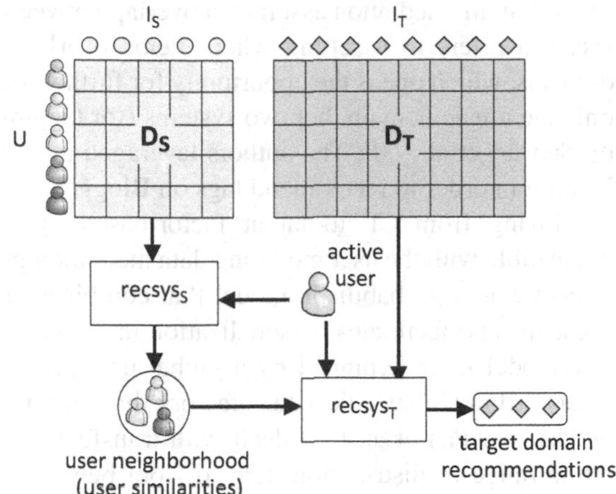

Fig. 27.6 *Mediating user modeling data.* A model is learnt in the source domain (e.g., the neighborhood of a user) and used in the target domain

a target recommender [4]—the mediation can enrich the user models of the target recommender, and yield more accurate recommendations. What data can be mediated between the source and the target recommenders? The most simple scenario covered in Sect. 27.4.1 includes importing the user models, whereas more complex scenarios include mediating specific recommendation data.

For example, in a CF system, cross-domain mediation may import the list of nearest neighbors. This is underpinned by two assumptions: (1) there is overlap of users between domains, and (2) user similarity spans across domains, i.e., if two users are similar in a source domain, they are similar also in the target domain. This idea was leveraged in the heuristic variant of cross-domain mediation developed by Berkovsky et al. [7]. There, it was shown that importing nearest neighbors, and computing their similarity with the target domain data only, can produce more accurate recommendations than single domain recommendations. A similar idea was formulated by Shapira et al. [58] as the *k* nearest neighbors (*k*-NN) source aggregation. They used multi-domain Facebook data to produce the set of candidate nearest neighbors, and compute their local similarity degree in the source domain. This allowed overcoming the new user problem and the lack of ratings in the target domain. Another attempt to use multi-domain Facebook data was done by Tiroshi and Kuflik [65]. They applied random walks to identify source domain-specific neighbor sets, which were used to generate recommendations in the target domain.

Aggregating the lists of nearest neighbors relies on their data in the target domain only, which may be too sparse and result in noisy recommendations. Thus, one could consider importing and aggregating also the degree of their similarity in the source domain. This approach was referred to in [7] as cross-domain mediation. A content-based and a statistical variant of domain distance metrics were evaluated in [5], producing comparable results and outperforming single-domain recommendations. The weighted k-NN aggregation was further enhanced by Shapira et al. [58]. The authors compared several weighting schemes, the performance of which was consistent across several metrics and recommendation tasks. The above scenarios of cross-domain mediation assume an overlap between the sets of users. An analogous scenario refers to a setting where items overlap between the source and target domains, which opens the opportunity for further mediation. One of them, involving only the music domain, but two systems (for tagging and for blogging) was studied by Stewart et al. [60]. The authors leveraged the tags assigned by similar users on Last.fm in order to recommend tags on Blogger.

Moving from CF to latent factor-based methods, we highlight two works compatible with the user modeling data mediation pattern. Low et al. [45] developed a hierarchical probabilistic model that combines user information across multiple domains, and facilitates personalization in domains with no prior user interactions. The model is underpinned by a global user profile based on a latent vector, and a set of domain-specific latent factors that eliminate the need for common items or features. Pan et al. [52] dealt with transferring uncertain ratings, i.e., expected rating range or distribution derived from behavioral logs, using latent features of both users and items. The uncertain ratings were transferred from the source to the target domain, and leveraged there as constraints for the matrix factorization model.

We summarize the mediation-based approaches in Table 27.4. As can be seen, they all imply either user- or item-overlap between the source and target domains. These are necessary for identifying high-level user preferences spanning across domains. This often requires sharing of user data between several systems, which is avoided due to commercial competition and conflicts with privacy regulations. However, it is usual for a user to utilize multiple systems (or, in a more common use-case, to have accounts on multiple social networks), and thus cross-domain recommendations through mediation is a feasible scenario. Most of the surveyed approaches apply simple mediation methods, whereas the last two are based on latent representations, and apply probabilistic or transfer learning models. None

Table 27.4 Summary of cross-domain recommendation approaches based on mediating single-domain user modeling data, where (*N*) no overlap, (*U*) user overlap, (*I*) item overlap, (*UI*) user and item overlap

Cross-domain approach	Inter-domain relationships	References
Aggregating neihgbourhoods to generate recommendations	Rating-based user similarities	Berkovsky et al. [7] ^{U} Tiroshi and Kuflik [65] ^{UI} Shapira et al. [58] ^{U}
Aggregating user-to-user similarities to generate recommendations	Content- and rating-based user similarities	Berkovsky et al. [7] ^{U} Shapira et al. [58] ^{U}
Exploiting user neighborhoods to enhance target user models	User overlap	Stewart et al. [60] ^{I}
Combining probabilistic user models	Latent features of domains and global user preferences	Low et al. [45] ^{U}
Combining heterogeneous user preferences	Domain-dependent constraints on matrix factorization	Pan et al. [52] ^{UI}

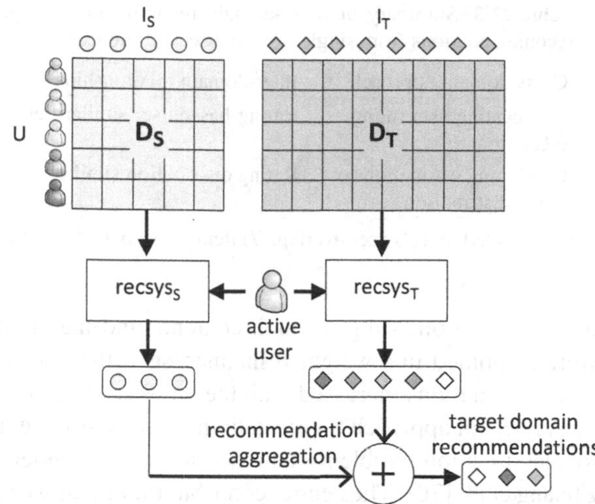

Fig. 27.7 *Combining single-domain recommendations.* Recommendations are generated independently for each domain and later merged for the final recommendation

of these works counts on explicit domain distance or similarity, which will be elaborated in Sect. 27.5.1). Hence, we conjecture that more future work will address cross-domain recommendation by mediating richer user modeling data.

27.4.3 Combining Single-Domain Recommendations

Overlap of both user and item sets allows aggregating ready-made single-domain recommendations (see Fig. 27.7). Contrarily to the mediation-based cross-domain recommendation scenarios, the predicted recommendations from the source domain may inform on their own to the target domain recommender. Hence, the central question in combining single-domain recommendation refers to the weights assigned to recommendations coming from the source domains, which reflect their importance for the target domain. These weights may be computed through various factors, such as the reliability of each recommender, distance between the domains, and so forth.

The idea of combining single-domain recommendations was referred to in [6, 7] as remote-average mediation. There, movie ratings were partitioned into domains according to the genres of the movies. Since movies combine elements from multiple genres, and users watch movies from various genres, the user- and item-overlap are both present. This allows computing stand-alone recommendations in the source domains, and aggregating them for the target domain. Weighted aggregation of single-domain recommendations also was studied by Givon and Lavrenko [27]. The authors focused on the book recommendation task, accomplished using two different methods. Standard CF recommendations were complemented by relevance model-based recommendations, relying on the similarity of a book and the user's

Table 27.5 Summary of cross-domain recommendation approaches based on combining recommendations from single-domain user preferences

Cross-domain approach	Inter-domain relationships	References
Aggregating user rating predictions	Rating-based user similarities	Berkovsky et al. [7] *UI* Givon and Lavrenko [27] *UI*
Combining estimations of rating distribution	Rating distribution similarities	Zhuang et al. [70] *N*

(*N*) no overlap, (*U*) user overlap, (*I*) item overlap, (*UI*) user and item overlap

model, both consisting of book contents and tags assigned to the book. The two were combined in a weighted manner, such that the relative importance of the CF recommendations increased with the number of ratings available.

A relevant approach for cross-domain consensus regularization, although applied to classification problems and not to recommender systems, was proposed by Zhuang et al. [70]. The central contribution of that work is a framework for learning from multiple source domains, and reconciling discrepancies between the classifiers using the local data of the target domain. One of the advantages of the framework is that it does not require overlaps in either the user or item sets.

The overviewed approaches that combine single-domain recommendations are summarized in Table 27.5. Clearly, the key point for this group of cross-domain recommenders refers to the way the stand-alone source domain recommendations are combined. This is touched upon in [70], but also addressed in numerous researches outside the recommender systems space. It should be highlighted that the single-domain recommenders can use various techniques, and the combination of their outputs is independent of other components, e.g., user modeling, contextualization, and presentation, which makes this cross-domain aggregation variant attractive for practical recommenders.

27.5 Knowledge Linkage and Transfer for Cross-Domain Recommendation

In this section, we survey cross-domain recommendation approaches that link or transfer knowledge between domains, enhancing the information available in the target domain for the generation of recommendations. The knowledge linkage and transfer can be done explicitly—e.g., via common item attributes, semantic networks, association rules, and inter-domain user preference similarities (Sect. 27.5.1)—implicitly by means of latent features shared by domains (Sect. 27.5.2), or by means of rating patterns transferred between domains (Sect. 27.5.3).

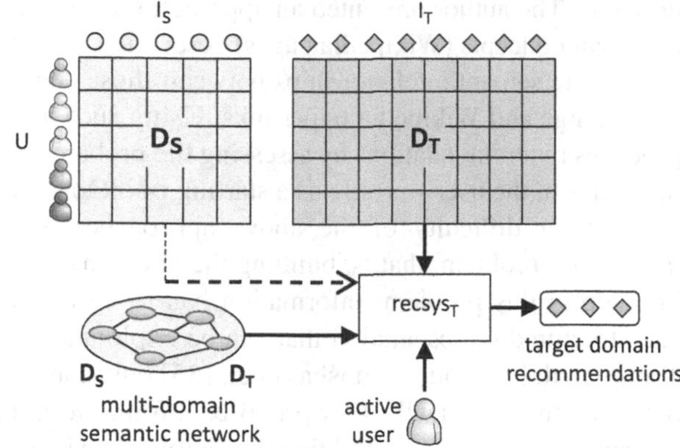

Fig. 27.8 *Linking domains.* An external knowledge source is used to link items from different domains. User preferences in the source domain may be used to adapt the item linkage

27.5.1 Linking Domains

A natural approach to address the heterogeneity of several domains is to identify correspondences between their characteristics. For instance, we may link a particular movie and a book because both belong to genres that can be semantically mapped, e.g., comedy movies and humorous books. In general, such inter-domain correspondences may be established directly using some kind of common knowledge between domains, e.g., item attributes, semantic networks, association rules, and inter-domain preference-based similarities or correlations (see Fig. 27.8).

These links are valuable sources of information for reasoning across domains. A recommender system could identify potentially relevant items in the target domain by selecting those that are related to others in the source domains, and for which the user has expressed a preference in the past. Besides, inter-domain similarities and correlations can be exploited to adapt or combine knowledge transferred from different domains. One of the earliest approaches for linking domains was explored by Chung et al. [14]. Aiming to support the decision making process in recommendation, they proposed a framework for designing personalized filtering strategies. In the framework, relevant items in the target domain are selected according to the attributes they have in common with items in the source domain the user is interested in. That is, the inter-domain links are established through the overlap of item attributes, and no user or item overlap between the domains is required.

Conversely to the use case of Chung et al. [14], in a realistic setting, items are highly heterogeneous, and often no common attributes between domains can be found. To address this situation, we may establish more complex, likely indirect relations between items in different domains. Hence, when suitable knowledge repositories are available, concepts from several domains can be connected by the means of semantic properties, forming semantic networks that explicitly link the domains of interest. Along these lines, Loizou [43] proposed to use Wikipedia as a universal vocabulary to express and relate user preferences across multiple domains. The author presented an approach that builds a graph, the nodes of which represent concepts (Wikipedia pages) describing items liked by the users, and edges encode the semantic relationships between those concepts, obtained by integrating user ratings and Wikipedia hyperlinks. Using such a graph, a Markov chain model produces recommendations by assessing the probability of traversing the graph from the nodes in the user's profile as a starting point toward the recommendable items.

A major difficulty of the above approaches is the well known *knowledge acquisition* problem, that is, building the above mentioned knowledge repositories. To address this problem, information has to be extracted and stored in a formal and structured representation that can be exploited by a recommender. Fernández-Tobías et al. [21] and Kaminskas et al. [35] envisioned Linked Data as a solution to the problem. Specifically, they proposed a framework for extracting a multi-domain semantic network from the DBpedia ontology, which links items and concepts in the source and target domains. Over the extracted network, a constrained spreading algorithm computes semantic similarities to rank and filter items in the target domain.

Inter-domain association rules have also been explored as an alternative to relate various types of items. In this direction, Azak [3] presented a framework for cross-domain recommendation in which knowledge-based rules defined by domain experts facilitate mapping between attributes in distinct domains, e.g., "people who like romance drama movies also like dramatic poetry books." These rules are then used to enhance CB and CF recommendations, adjusting the predicted ratings whenever rule conditions hold. In [10], Cantador et al. related user personality types with domain-dependent preferences by means of automatically generated association rules. The authors also extracted personality stereotypes for sets of domain genres. Based on these stereotypes, inter-domain similarities were computed between genres, which may be used to support knowledge transfer between domains.

Instead of linking domains by mapping attributes, an alternative way to transfer knowledge is to compute similarities or correlations between domains based on user preference or item content analysis. In an early work, Berkovsky et al. [5] explored this idea aiming to identify related domains, from which user data would be imported and utilized to enrich the user model in the target domain. The proposed approach makes use of web directories to identify websites that characterize the domains of interest. Then, the approach establishes domain similarities by computing the cosine similarity between the TF-IDF term vectors of the domains' websites. We note that this method requires no overlap of users or items, but rather an external source of representative documents classified to several domains.

Another way of exploiting inter-domain similarities for cross-domain recommendation consists of integrating them into the matrix factorization method [56]. Specifically, such similarities are imposed as constraints over user or item latent factors when jointly factorizing rating matrices. For instance, Cao et al. [13] proposed an approach in which inter-domain similarities are implicitly learnt from data, as model parameters in a non-parametric Bayesian framework. Since user feedback is used to estimate the similarities, user overlap between the domains is required.

Addressing the sparsity problem, Zhang et al. [67] adapted the probabilistic matrix factorization method to include a probability distribution of user latent factors that encodes inter-domain correlations. One strength of this approach is that user latent factors shared across domains are not needed, allowing more flexibility in capturing the heterogeneity of domains. Instead of automatically learning implicit correlations in the data, Shi et al. [59] argued that explicit common information is more effective, and relied on shared social tags to compute cross-domain user-to-user and item-to-item similarities. Similarly to previous approaches, rating matrices from the source and target domains are jointly factorized; but in this case user and item latent factors from each domain are restricted, so that their product is consistent with the tag-based similarities.

We have reviewed approaches that establish links and compute similarities between domains, which are summarized in Table 27.6. We observe that the majority of the proposed methods do not require inter-domain user or item overlap. Instead, linking approaches exploit content information to establish the inter-domain relationships. Likewise, in [5, 59], similarities are computed based on common text and social tags. For these approaches, it is also worth noticing that no one clearly outperforms the others, since most of them are designed for particular cross-domain scenarios and, to the best of our knowledge, have not been compared empirically.

27.5.2 Sharing Latent Features by Domains

Latent factor models are among the most popular CF techniques [37]. In these models, user preferences and item attributes, which are typically very sparse, are characterized through a reduced set of latent factors discovered from data, to obtain

Table 27.6 Summary of cross-domain user modeling and recommendation approaches based on linking domains, where (*N*) no overlap, (*U*) user overlap, (*I*) item overlap, (*UI*) user and item overlap

Cross-domain approach	Inter-domain relationships	References
Relating and filtering items via common attributes	Item attribute overlap	Chung et al. [14] ^{N}
Building semantic network linking domain concepts	Semantic relationships between domain concepts	Loizou [43] ^{N} Fernández-Tobías et al. [21] ^{N} Kaminskas et al. [35] ^{N}
Relating item types via knowledge-based rules	Inter-domain knowledge-based rules	Azak et al. [3] ^{N} Cantador et al. [10] ^{N}
Computing inter-domain similarities	Text overlap	Berkovsky et al. [5] ^{N}
Constraining matrix factorization with inter-domain similarities	Rating overlap	Cao et al. [13] ^{U} Zhang et al. [67] ^{N}
	Social tag overlap	Shi et al. [59] ^{N}

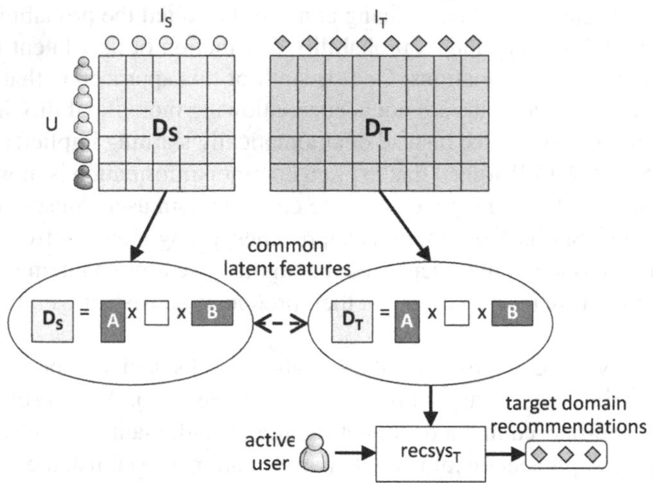

Fig. 27.9 *Sharing latent features.* Latent features models are learnt simultaneously on both the source and target domains, constraining user and/or item features to be the same across the domains

a denser representation. The assumption is that using the new representation, latent user preferences and item attributes are better captured and matched.

Related to the *what to transfer* aspect of transfer learning [49], latent factors shared between domains can be exploited to support cross-domain recommendations (see Fig. 27.9). Also, as pointed in Sect. 27.3, two types of approaches have been studied to address the *how to transfer* aspect; namely, *adaptive* and *collective* models. In the former, latent factors are learnt in the source domain, and are integrated into a recommendation model in the target domain, while in the latter, latent factors are learnt simultaneously optimizing an objective function that involves both domains.

In [51], Pan et al. addressed the sparsity problem in the target domain following the adaptive approach, proposing to exploit user and item information from auxiliary domains where user feedback may be represented differently. In particular, they studied the case in which users express binary like/dislike preferences in the source domain, and utilize 1–5 ratings in the target domain. Their approach performs singular value decomposition (SVD) in each auxiliary domain, in order to separately compute user and item latent factors, which are then shared with the target domain. Specifically, transferred factors are integrated into the factorization of the rating matrix in the target domain and added as regularization terms so that specific characteristics of the target domain can be captured.

Latent factors can also be shared in a collective way, as studied by Pan et al. [50]. In this case, instead of learning latent features from the source domains and transferring them to the target domain, the authors proposed to learn the latent features simultaneously in all the domains. Both user and item factors are assumed to generate the observed ratings in every domain, and, thus, their corresponding random variables are shared between the probabilistic factorization models of each rating matrix. Moreover, the factorization method is further extended by incorporating another set of factors that capture domain-dependent information, resulting in a tri-factorization scheme. A limitation of the proposed approach is that the users and items from the source and target domains have to be identical.

Instead of focusing on sharing latent factors, Enrich et al. [20] and Fernández-Tobías and Cantador [24] studied the influence of social tags on rating prediction, as a knowledge transfer approach for cross-domain recommendations. The authors presented a number of models based on the SVD++ algorithm [37] to incorporate the effect of tag assignments into rating estimation. The underlying hypothesis is that information about item annotation in a source domain can be exploited to improve rating prediction in a target domain, as long as a set of common tags between the domains exists. In the proposed models, tag factors are added to the latent item vectors, and are combined with user latent features to compute rating estimations. The difference between these models is in the set of tags considered for rating prediction. In all the models knowledge transfer is performed through the shared tag factors in a collective way, since these are computed jointly for the source and the target domains.

In [31], Hu et al. presented a more complex approach that takes domain factors into account. There, the authors argue that user-item dyadic data cannot fully capture the heterogeneity of items, and that modeling domain-specific information is essential to make accurate predictions in a setting, where users typically express their preferences in a single domain. They referred to this problem as the *unacquainted world*, and proposed a tensor factorization algorithm to exploit the triadic user-item-domain data. In that method, rating matrices from several domains are simultaneously decomposed into shared user, item, and domain latent factors, and genetic algorithm automatically estimates optimal weights of the domains.

Table 27.7 summarizes the described approaches sharing latent factors across domains. In contrast to the methods presented in Sect. 27.5.1, these approaches require inter-domain user or item overlap to extract shared latent factors, unless shared content information is available [20, 24]. As in the previous section, it is worth noticing the lack of a comparative study of the approaches. Again, the reason for this may be that the considered cross-domain task and data overlap scenarios vary among works.

27.5.3 Transferring Rating Patterns Between Domains

Rather than sharing user or item latent factors for knowledge transfer, a different set of approaches analyzes the structure of rating data at the community level. These methods are based on the hypothesis that even when their users and items are different, close domains are likely to have user preferences sampled with the same population. Therefore, latent correlations may exist between preferences of groups of users for groups of items, which are referred to as *rating patterns*. In this context,

Table 27.7 Summary of cross-domain recommendation approaches based on latent features shared by domains, where (*N*) no overlap, (*U*) user overlap, (*I*) item overlap, (*UI*) user and item overlap

Cross-domain approach	Inter-domain relationships	References
Using user and item latent features of source domains to regularize latent features in a target domain	Shared latent user preferences and latent item attributes	Pan et al. [51] *UI*
Using the same latent factors to jointly factorize the rating matrices in the source and target domains	User and item overlap	Pan et al. [50] *UI*
Extending matrix factorization with a vector of latent factors associated to social tags	Social tag overlap	Enrich et al. [20] *N* Fernández-Tobías and Cantador [24] *N*
Sharing latent features via a user-item-domain tensor factorization	Rating overlap	Hu et al. [31] *U*

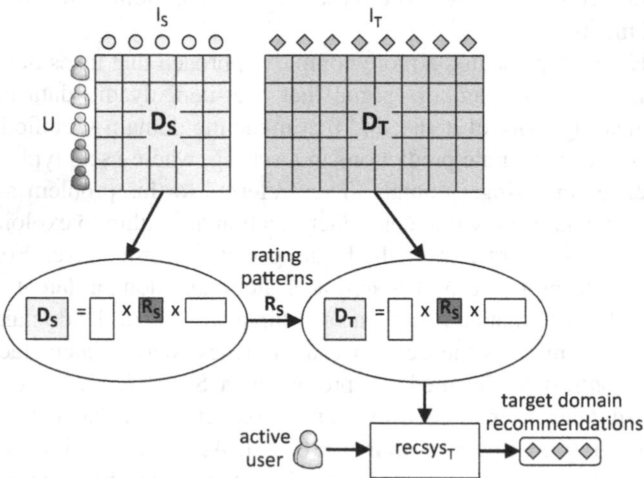

Fig. 27.10 *Transferring rating patterns.* A co-clustering model is learnt on the source domain to obtain rating patterns, which are used to cluster users and items in the target domain

rating patterns can act as a bridge that relates the domains (see Fig. 27.10), such that knowledge transfer can be performed in either adaptive or collective manners. In the adaptive setting, rating patterns are extracted from a dense source domain. In the collective setting, data from all the domains are pulled together and jointly exploited, even though users and items do not overlap across domains.

Lee et al. [38] proposed one of the first approaches to exploit rating patterns for cross-domain recommendation. Similarly to the cross-domain mediation proposed by Berkovsky et al. [6], global nearest neighbors are identified by adding the similarity scores from each domain. Then, patterns of items commonly rated together by a set of neighbors are discovered using association rules. Finally, in the recommendation stage, rating predictions are computed with the standard user-based CF algorithm, but enhanced with the user's rules that contain the target items.

Li et al. [40] proposed an adaptive method based on simultaneously co-clustering users and items in the source domain, to extract rating patterns. Clustering is performed using a tri-factorization of the source rating matrix [18]. Then, knowledge is transferred through a *codebook*, a compact cluster-level matrix computed in the source domain taking the average rating of each user-item cluster. In the target domain, missing ratings are predicted using the codebook. Moreno et al. [46] extended the codebook idea to a scenario in which various source domains contribute to the target domain. The approach is based on a linear combination of codebooks, where the weights are learnt by minimizing the prediction error in the target domain.

In a related work [41], Li et al. extended the same idea to a collective approach using a probabilistic framework. Instead of relying on an dense source domain data to build the codebook, all rating matrices are pulled together to extract the shared patterns. Furthermore, rather than having each user/item belonging to a single cluster, a probability distribution is introduced to allow users and items belong to multiple clusters, with distinct membership degrees. In the same fashion, the ratings associated with each user-item cluster are also given by a conditional probability distribution. In this way, a generative rating model is obtained, since the ratings of each domain can be recovered by drawing users and items from the shared cluster-level model, and then drawing the expected rating conditioned to the user-item cluster.

A strength of both approaches is that neither overlap of users nor of items is required. However, Cremonesi and Quadrana [17] partially disproved it, showing that the *codebook* does not transfer knowledge when source and target domains do not overlap. They provided an alternative explanation to the accuracy increase using a codebook that does not involve knowledge transfer between domains.

Finally, Gao et al. [26] followed the idea of extracting rating patterns by co-clustering rating matrices, and addressed two limitations of previous methods. First, they argued that some domains are more related to the target domain than others, and this cannot be captured using identical rating patterns. Second, they hypothesized that performance may suffer when the domains are diverse, and do not share common rating patterns. To overcome these limitations, the authors proposed a model capable of controlling the amount of knowledge transferred from each domain. Specifically, they used a co-clustering algorithm of Li et al. [40], but split the extracted rating patterns into a shared part and a domain-specific part. In contrast to [40], optimization is performed in a collective way, since the shared part of the rating patterns is learnt simultaneously from all the domains.

Table 27.8 summarizes the described cross-domain approaches based on transferring rating patterns between domains. We observe that more recent methods based on clustering do not rely on any overlap between domains. However, as discussed in [26], care must be taken in order not to degrade performance by transferring noisy

Table 27.8 Summary of cross-domain recommendation approaches based on transferring rating patterns between domains, where (*N*) no overlap, (*U*) user overlap, (*I*) item overlap, (*UI*) user and item overlap

Cross-domain approach	Inter-domain relationships	References
Extracting association rules from user rating behavior	Rating overlap	Lee et al. [38] ^{U}
Transferring implicit cluster-level rating patterns between domains	Rating patterns	Li et al. [40] ^{N} Li et al. [41] ^{N} Moreno et al. [46] ^{N} Cremonesi and Quadrana [17] ^{N}
	Domain-independent parts of rating patterns	Gao et al. [26] ^{N}

patterns from unrelated domains. We therefore conjecture that further research on the *when to transfer* aspect [49] will be conducted, to identify valuable information from source domains.

27.6 Evaluation of Cross-Domain Recommender Systems

In this section, we discuss the methods used to evaluate cross-domain recommender systems. The focal point is that such systems cannot be evaluated in a problem-independent way; whether a cross-domain recommender system is an appropriate solution cannot be evaluated without taking into account for what it is intended. The nature of the evaluation must be connected to the purpose for which the recommendations are required. Thus, we compare the corresponding evaluation methods based on the cross-domain recommendation goals addressed in the literature (see Sect. 27.2.3).

Three types of evaluations can be used to compare cross-domain recommender systems [25, 57]. *Offline experiments* evaluate a system by analyzing past user preferences. They are typically the easiest to conduct, as they require no interaction with real users. With *online studies*, a small group of subjects is asked to use the system in a controlled environment, and to report on the experience. Finally, *live trials* evaluates the system based on feedback from real users. As most cross-domain recommendation works use offline experiments (with a few performing online studies, and no live trials, see Table 27.9), we focus on offline experiments. The reader is referred to Chap. 8 for an extensive discussion on methodologies and metrics used to evaluate recommender systems.

The decision regarding the evaluation method is often critical, as each one reflects a specific task or goal. Many offline evaluation schemes exist, which differ in a number of aspects: *data partitioning*, *metrics*, and *sensitivity analysis* (e.g., relative density of domain datasets, and degree of overlap between domains), as discussed respectively in the next sections.

Table 27.9 Summary of cross-domain recommendation approaches based on the technique used to partition the data into training and test sets

Data partitioning	References	
Online studies	Braunhofer et al. [9] Fernandez-Tobias et al. [23] Shapira et al. [58]	Szomszor et al. [61] Winoto et al. [66]
Leave-all-users-out	Cremonesi et al. [16] Goga et al. [28] Hu et al. [31] Jain et al. [32]	Kaminskas et al. [35] Loni et al. [44] Shapira et al. [58] Tiroshi et al. [65]
Leave-some-users-out	Abel et al. [1] Abel et al. [2]	Li et al. [40, 41] Stewart et al. [60]
Hold-out	Li et al. [42] Nakatsuji et al. [47] Pan et al. [48] Pan et al. [51] Pan et al. [52] Pan et al. [53]	Sahebi et al. [55] Shi et al. [59] Tang et al. [63] Zhang et al. [67] Zhang et al. [68] Zhao et al. [69]

27.6.1 Data Partitioning

In order to evaluate algorithms offline, it is necessary to simulate the process where the system makes recommendations, and users evaluate them. This requires pre-recorded datasets of interactions between users and items. In cross-domain applications, there are (at least) two potentially overlapping datasets: the source dataset $\mathcal{D}_S$ and the target dataset $\mathcal{D}_T$.

We assume $\mathcal{D}_S$ and $\mathcal{D}_T$ are chosen according to the recommendation task and goal in hand. For instance, if we are evaluating a cross-selling recommender, $\mathcal{D}_S$ and $\mathcal{D}_T$ are set at the *item level* as described in Sect. 27.2.1, contain items of different nature, like movies and books, and have overlapping users. On the contrary, if we are evaluating a cross-domain recommender as a tool to increase recommendation diversity, $\mathcal{D}_S$ and $\mathcal{D}_T$ are set at the *item attribute level*, with items of the same type, but differ in the value of certain attribute, as comedy and drama movies.

In offline evaluations, a portion of $\mathcal{D}_T$ is hidden to facilitate prediction of the available knowledge, and gauge the quality of the recommendations. There is a number of ways to choose the ratings to be hidden. The most general approach creates three subsets of ratings from the original datasets: (1) $\mathcal{D}_{\text{training\_profiles}}$, which contains the set of ratings from users $\mathcal{U}_{\text{training\_profiles}}$ for items $\mathcal{I}_{\text{training\_profiles}}$ that are used to train the algorithms under evaluation; (2) $\mathcal{D}_{\text{test\_profiles}}$, which contains the set of users $\mathcal{U}_{\text{test\_profiles}}$ and their known ratings for items $\mathcal{I}_{\text{test\_profiles}}$ that are used as input profiles for the trained recommender; and (3) $\mathcal{D}_{\text{test\_ratings}}$, which contains the set of users $\mathcal{U}_{\text{test\_profiles}}$ and their hidden ratings for items $\mathcal{I}_{\text{test\_ratings}}$ that are used as the ground truth to evaluate the recommendations.

Depending on the choice of the $\mathcal{D}_{\text{training\_profiles}}$, $\mathcal{D}_{\text{test\_profiles}}$, and $\mathcal{D}_{\text{test\_ratings}}$ subsets, different evaluation data partitions can be designed.

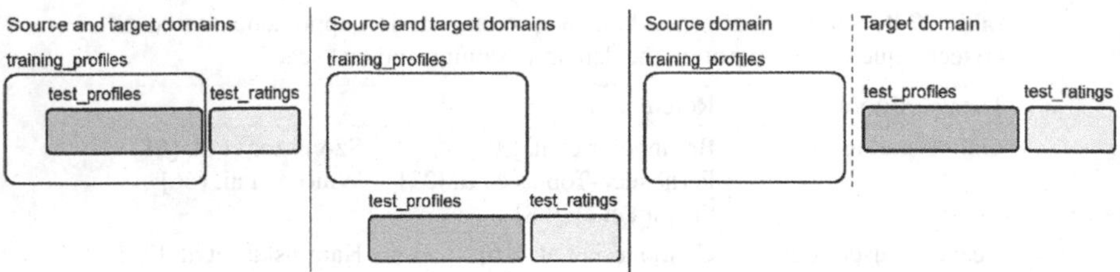

Fig. 27.11 Partitioning of $\mathcal{D}$: *(left) hold-out*—test ratings sampled and hidden without partitioning the users; *(middle) leave-some-users-out*—users split into disjoint training/test sets; *(right) leave-all-users-out*—ratings in the target dataset used as test profiles and ratings

- *Hold-out* (Fig. 27.11-left) is implemented when $\mathcal{D}_{\text{test\_profiles}} \subseteq \mathcal{D}_{\text{training\_profiles}}$, i.e., test ratings are sampled and hidden from the original dataset without partitioning the users. This partition is suitable to evaluate linked- and multi-domain recommenders with the accuracy goal, and is applicable to memory-based recommenders, which are unable to provide recommendations to new users.
- *Leave-some-users-out* (Fig. 27.11-middle) is implemented when $\mathcal{U}_{\text{training\_profiles}} \cap \mathcal{U}_{\text{test\_profiles}} = \emptyset$, i.e., the users are split into two disjoint subsets: one for training and one for testing. This partition is suitable to evaluate a cross-domain recommender with the new user goal.
- *Leave-all-users-out* (Fig. 27.11-right) is implemented when $\mathcal{D}_{\text{training\_profiles}} \cap \mathcal{D}_T = \emptyset$, i.e., the ratings in the target dataset are used only as profile and test ratings. This partition is suitable to evaluate a cross-domain recommender with the cold-start and new item goals.

27.6.2 Metrics

The notion of relevance of recommendations and the ways to measure it have been debated in numerous works on recommender systems. Generally speaking, there are three categories of evaluation metrics: *predictive metrics*, *ranking metrics*, and *classification metrics* [30].

Theoretical debates surround the distribution of the missing ratings. Because of the data sparsity, offline evaluations are performed on a small fraction of the available items. Each metric makes implicit assumptions regarding the value and the distribution of the missing ratings, which impact the interpretation of obtained results. For instance, predictive metrics like *MAE* and *RMSE* assume that the unknown ratings are missing at random, the classification metric of *precision* assumes that all missing ratings are irrelevant for the user, whereas *recall*, *fallout*, and *ROC* assume that non-relevant ratings are missing with a higher probability than relevant ratings. Practical debates also consider the recommendation goal. Prediction metrics are to be preferred when the goal is to reduce the sparsity of the

Table 27.10 Summary of metrics used for the evaluation of cross-domain recommender system

Category	Metric	References	
Predictionmetrics	*MAE*	Berkovsky et al. [6, 7] Berkovsky et al. [8] Cao et al. [13] Hu et al. [31] Li et al. [40, 41] Moreno et al. [46] Loni et al. [44] Nakatsuji et al. [47]	Pan et al. [48] Pan et al. [51] Pan et al. [52] Pan et al. [53] Shapira et al. [58] Shi et al. [59] Winoto et al. [66]
	RMSE	Li et al. [42] Loni et al. [44] Pan et al. [51] Pan et al. [52]	Pan et al. [53] Sahebi et al. [55] Zhang et al. [67] Zhao et al. [69]
Ranking metrics	*ROC*	Goga et al. [28]	
	MRR	Abel et al. [1]	Abel et al. [2]
	nDCG	Zhang et al. [68]	
	AUC	Fernandez-Tobias et al. [23] Hu et al. [31]	Tiroshi et al. [65]
	MAP	Fernández-Tobías et al. [23] Shapira et al. [58] Jain et al. [32]	Shapira et al. [58] Zhang et al. [68]
Classificationmetrics	*Precision*	Kaminskas et al. [35] Tiroshi et al. [64]	Stewart et al. [60]
	Recall	Stewart et al. [60]	Nakatsuji et al. [47]
	F-measure	Cremonesi et al. [16]	Gao et al. [26]

target domain; ranking metrics are adopted when testing user models, especially in cold-start situations; and classification metrics are best-suited for the top-N recommendation task.

Table 27.10 summarizes the offline evaluation metrics exploited in cross-domain recommenders. The majority of works adopts prediction metrics. This is motivated by the fact that the addressed goal is to reduce sparsity and increase accuracy, and the algorithms designed for this are often based on error-metric optimization techniques, which are naturally evaluated using the category of predictive metrics.

27.6.3 Sensitivity Analysis

The performance of a cross-domain recommender system is mainly affected by three parameters: the overlap between the source and target domains, the density of the target domain data, and the size of the target user's profile. Thus, the evaluation of a cross-domain recommendations mostly considered the sensitivity of the corresponding algorithms with respect to these three parameters.

Most works have assumed an overlap of users between the source and target domains. They all conducted evaluations with 100 % of overlap, except for two works. Cremonesi et al. [16] analyzed the behavior of various cross-domain recommenders by varying the percentage of user-overlap in the range 0–50 %, and Zhao et al. [69] adopted a similar evaluation by varying the percentage of user overlap in the range 0–100 %. Fewer works [8, 16, 53, 69] studied the case of item overlap, and they all assume to have the same catalog of items across domains. Some works [2, 9, 23, 35, 60, 61] studied the case of overlapping features, especially social tags. Shi et al. [59] studied the sensitivity of the cross-domain recommender by varying the number of overlapping tags between 5 and 50.

Some works [8, 40, 41, 55, 59] have studied the sensitivity of recommendations as a function of the user profile size, i.e., the number of ratings provided by the user receiving the recommendations. This is particularly important for the cold-start and new user goals. Both Pan et al. [51] and Abel et al. [2] developed tag-based recommenders, and performed their analysis by varying the number of tags in the user profile in the 10–40 and 0–150 ranges, respectively. Others conducted a similar analysis on rating-based recommenders: Shi et al. [59] varied the profile size from 20 to 100 ratings, Berkovsky et al. [8] varied the profile size from 3 to 33 % of ratings, and Li et al. [40, 41] and Sahebi et al. [55] varied the profile size in the range of 5–15 and 1–20 ratings, respectively.

Finally, some works [13, 16, 51, 58] have studied the quality of recommendations as a function of the dataset density. This is important for the cold-start and accuracy goals. Cao et al. [13] varied the density of the multi-domain dataset, i.e., the union of source and target datasets, between 0.2 and 1 %. Shapira et al. [58] varied the density of the dataset between 1 and 40 %, but only for the baseline single-domain algorithms, while evaluating cross-domain algorithms at the 1 % density. Cremonesi et al. [16] varied the density of the target domain between 0.1 and 0.9 %. The sensitivity analyses performed in the above works are summarized in Table 27.11.

Table 27.11 Summary of variables for sensitivity analysis of cross-domain recommender systems

Parameter	References	
Overlap between domains	Abel et al. [2] Cremonesi et al. [16]	Shi et al. [59] Zhao et al. [69]
Target domain density	Cao et al. [13] Cremonesi et al. [16] Pan et al. [48]	Pan et al. [51] Shapira et al. [58]
User profile size	Berkovsky et al. [6, 7] Berkovsky et al. [8] Li et al. [40, 41]	Sahebi et al. [55] Shi et al. [59]

27.7 Practical Considerations in Cross-Domain Recommendation

We have covered so far a wide spectrum of models and techniques applicable to cross-domain recommendation. Recommender system practitioners may find this variety of options overwhelming, when materializing a cross-domain recommender. Therefore, we list several practical considerations that drive the choice of the appropriate recommendation solution.

The first set of considerations deals with the pivotal questions of "*what, when,* and *how to transfer?*" that have already been raised in Sect. 27.3. The term 'transfer' refers in the following discussion to both the knowledge aggregation (Sect. 27.4) and the knowledge transfer (Sect. 27.5) approaches.

- *What to transfer?* Single-domain recommenders may gather different types of user data: explicit ratings, unary purchase lists, browsing logs, and many others. They are also likely to store domain metadata and recommendation method-specific data, e.g., collaborative neighborhoods of similar users and matrix factorization latent vectors. It cannot be determined in advance what knowledge from the source domain recommenders can benefit the target domain recommender, and some form of information gain analysis needs to be done. This may be a complex process, in which the target recommendation method and the recommendation task in hand should be taken into consideration .
- *When to transfer?* Deciding what information should be transferred is tightly bound to the consideration of conditions under which the transfer is beneficial. It is clear that at the initial deployment period of the target domain recommender, the transfer will enrich the recommender. On the contrary, no transfer is needed when the target domain recommender possesses complete and up-to-date information. But what happens in-between? This depends not only on the sparsity of the target domain data, but also on factors like the overlap of ratings between the domains, and freshness of data in the source domains.
- *How to transfer?* The answer to the 'how' question deals with the implementation of the knowledge transfer. Two high-level options are possible: either to implement direct one-to-one mappings between the source and the target recommenders, or to leverage a common representation that will facilitate the transfer. The downside of the former is that the number of possible combinations is quadratic and will grow if new recommenders are being introduced. The latter requires only a single transfer mechanism from/to the common representation, but an agreed upon representation is hard to achieve in practice. Some rules for reconciling conflicts in the transferred data should also be put in place.

Additional question that needs to be dealt with is "*where from to transfer?*" This question is peripheral in transfer learning since any available information is considered relevant, but this is not the case in cross-domain recommenders. The main indicator here is the distance between domains. Some pairs of domains, e.g., movies and TV, are inherently closer than others, e.g., games and tourism.

The close domains have a greater potential to benefit the target recommender, and are naturally the preferred sources. Contextual factors (location, temporal closeness) and the overlaps of user and item sets are also important in answering this question. We believe that practical cross-domain recommenders need to thoroughly examine the sources of the transferred knowledge.

Knowledge transfer between domains typically requires some *auxiliary information*. We highlight here two types of such information, which actually underpin the transfer. These are semantic networks like WordNet and DBpedia, and open or crowdsourced knowledge references like Wikipedia and Open Directory. The auxiliary information is critical for the knowledge transfer, since it links the domains and informs the answer to the 'how' question. Hence, important considerations faced by a practical cross-domain recommender deal with the availability and reliability of the auxiliary information. Chapters 4 and 15 address such issues in semantic-aware and social recommender systems.

The next set of considerations deals with the target *recommendation task*. Many options exist here: best item vs. top-K, one-off vs. sequential interaction, single product vs. bundle of products, recommendation to individual users vs. to a group of a users. Every recommendation scenario implies a different algorithm in place, and also distinct types of knowledge that can be transferred from the source domains. Related to this, the *metric* of recommendation success should be considered. Do the recommendations need to discover all the relevant items, match as many aspects of user interests as possible, or provide a surprising recommendation? Likewise, *technical constraints* may be an important factor. For instance, are the recommendations computed offline or delivered live to users? Is it a server-side recommendation which can be resource intense, or a lightweight client-side recommendation? These considerations cannot be discarded, as answers to the above questions may affect the choice of the knowledge transfer and of the cross-domain recommendation approach.

Last but not the least, special attention should be paid to *ethical* and *privacy aspects* (Chap. 19) in cross-domain recommenders. Transferring data and knowledge between single-domain recommenders may contradict privacy policies of the recommenders and existing privacy regulations. Moreover, it may allow malicious attackers not only to get access to a larger volume of user data, but also to apply data mining to the combined knowledge, uncovering (potentially sensitive) information. With respect to this, knowledge transfer methods are generally more robust than the aggregation methods, although they still cannot completely eliminate the data mining risk. Developers of a cross-domain recommender should keep the privacy consideration in mind, when selecting their knowledge transfer method.

27.8 Open Research Issues

This section provides an overview of new requirements and applications emerging from the landscape of cross-domain recommender systems. One interesting issue that deserves more attention in the future is the synergy between contextual and cross-domain recommendations: different contexts (e.g., location, time, and mood) can be treated as different domains (see Chap. 6 for details on context-aware recommendation). This opens interesting scenarios in which context-aware techniques can be applied to cross-domain recommendations, and vice versa. Moreover, context can be treated as a bridge between different domains, and seminal work has already been carried out in this direction [9, 23].

Another important issue concerns the metrics adopted for the evaluation of the recommendations. A common practice with cross-domain recommender systems is to evaluate their relevance through predictive accuracy metrics, such as MAE and RMSE, which capture the error between the actual and predicted ratings. However, in many commercial systems only a small number of best recommendations is shown, while the predicted ratings are not. That is, the system suggests a few items that are likely to be very appealing for users. Direct evaluation of top-N recommendation performance must be accomplished by means of alternative methodologies based either on classification metrics (e.g., recall and fallout) or ranking metrics (e.g., average reciprocal hit-rank and average relative position), as explained in Chap. 8.

We can push this idea further, by considering that accuracy is not sufficient to provide useful recommendations. Other criteria have been proposed to augment the evaluation dimensions, such as diversity, novelty, and serendipity (see Chap. 26). As one can expect, cross-domain recommendations would be less accurate than those based on the same amount of user data pertaining to the target domain. However, the true advantage of cross-domain recommendations is not necessarily in their accuracy, but rather in their novelty and diversity, which may lead to a higher satisfaction and utility for the user. In this context, the recently proposed novelty and diversity metrics could be taken into consideration [57].

The next open research issue deals with the use of cross-domain recommender systems as a means to reduce the user model elicitation effort. The preference elicitation process is important for the recommenders (Chap. 24), but it may pose two conflicting requirements. On the one hand, the system must collect "enough" ratings in order to learn the users' preferences and improve the accuracy of recommendations. On the other hand, gathering ratings imposes a burden on the users, which may negatively affect their experience. Cross-domain recommender systems could be used as alternative elicitation tools able to build detailed user profiles without the need to collect explicit user preferences.

Finally, the importance of real life datasets needs to be stressed (Chap. 11). These are necessary for evaluations of new cross-domain approaches, but are quite scarce and hard to reach in practice. Large-scale cross-domain datasets are gathered by big industry players, like Amazon, eBay, and Yelp, but these datasets rarely become available to the broader research community. We would like to encourage industry researchers to cooperate with the academic researchers and share their data. This could boost both the research in cross-domain recommendation and the deployment of practical cross-domain recommenders.

References

1. Abel, F., Araújo, S., Gao, Q., Houben, G.-J.: Analyzing Cross-system User Modeling on the Social Web. *11th International Conference on Web Engineering*, pp. 28–43 (2011)
2. Abel, F., Helder, E., Houben, G.-J., Henze, N., Krause, D.: Cross-system User Modeling and Personalization on the Social Web. *User Modeling and User-Adapted Interaction* 23(2-3), pp. 169–209 (2013)
3. Azak, M.: Crossing: A Framework to Develop Knowledge-based Recommenders in Cross Domains. *MSc thesis, Middle East Technical University* (2010)
4. Berkovsky, S., Kuflik, T., Ricci, F.: Entertainment Personalization Mechanism through Cross-domain User Modeling. *1st International Conference on Intelligent Technologies for Interactive Entertainment*, pp. 215–219 (2005)
5. Berkovsky, S., Goldwasser, D., Kuflik, T., Ricci, F.: Identifying Inter-domain Similarities through Content-based Analysis of Hierarchical Web-Directories. *17th European Conference on Artificial Intelligence*, pp. 789–790 (2006)
6. Berkovsky, S., Kuflik, T., Ricci, F.: Cross-Domain Mediation in Collaborative Filtering. *11th International Conference on User Modeling*, pp. 355–359 (2007)
7. Berkovsky, S., Kuflik, T., Ricci, F.: Distributed Collaborative Filtering with Domain Specialization. *1st ACM Conference on Recommender Systems*, pp. 33–40 (2007)
8. Berkovsky, S., Kuflik, T., Ricci, F.: Mediation of User Models for Enhanced Personalization in Recommender Systems. *User Modeling and User-Adapted Interaction* 18(3), pp. 245–286 (2008)
9. Braunhofer, M., Kaminskas, M., Ricci, F.: Location-aware Music Recommendation. *International Journal of Multimedia Information Retrieval* 2(1), pp. 31–44 (2013)
10. Cantador, I., Fernández-Tobías, I., Bellogín, A., Kosinski, M., Stillwell, D.: Relating Personality Types with User Preferences in Multiple Entertainment Domains. *1st Workshop on Emotions and Personality in Personalized Services*, CEUR workshop Proceedings, vol. 997 (2013)
11. Carmagnola, F., Cena, F.: User Identification for Cross-system Personalisation. *Information Sciences* 179(1–2), pp. 16–32 (2009)
12. Carmagnola, F., Cena, F., Gena, C.: User Model Interoperability: A Survey. *User Modeling and User-Adapted Interaction* 21(3), pp. 285–331(2011)
13. Cao, B., Liu, N. N., Yang, Q.: Transfer Learning for Collective Link Prediction in Multiple Heterogeneous Domains. *27th International Conference on Machine Learning*, pp. 159–166 (2010)
14. Chung, R., Sundaram, D., Srinivasan, A.: 2007. Integrated Personal Recommender Systems. *9th International Conference on Electronic Commerce*, pp. 65–74 (2007)
15. Costa, P. T., McCrae, R. R.: Revised NEO Personality Inventory (NEO-PI-R) and NEO Five-Factor Inventory (NEO-FFI) Manual. *Psychological Assessment Resources* (1992)
16. Cremonesi, P., Tripodi, A., Turrin, R.: Cross-domain Recommender Systems. *11th IEEE International Conference on Data Mining Workshops*, pp. 496–503 (2011)
17. Cremonesi, P., Quadrana, M.: Cross-domain recommendations without overlapping data: myth or reality? *8th ACM Conference on Recommender Systems* (2014)
18. Ding, C., Li, T., Peng, W., Park, H.: Orthogonal Nonnegative Matrix Tri-factorizations for Clustering. *12th ACM SIGKDD Conference on Knowledge Discovery and Data Mining)*, pp. 126–135 (2006)
19. Driskill, R., Riedl, J.: Recommender Systems for E-Commerce: Challenges and Opportunities. *AAAI'99 Workshop on Artificial Intelligence for Electronic Commerce*, pp. 73–76 (1999)
20. Enrich, M., Braunhofer, M., Ricci, F.: Cold-Start Management with Cross-Domain Collaborative Filtering and Tags. *14th International Conference on E-Commerce and Web Technologies*, pp. 101–112 (2013)
21. Fernández-Tobías, I., Cantador, I., Kaminskas, M., Ricci, F.: 2011. A Generic Semantic-based Framework for Cross-domain Recommendation. *2nd International Workshop on Information Heterogeneity and Fusion in Recommender Systems*, pp. 25–32 (2011)

22. Fernández-Tobías, I., Cantador, I., Kaminskas, M., Ricci, F.: Cross-domain Recommender Systems: A Survey of the State of the Art. *2nd Spanish Conference on Information Retrieval*, pp. 187–198 (2012)
23. Fernández-Tobías, I., Cantador, I., Plaza, L.: An Emotion Dimensional Model Based on Social Tags: Crossing Folksonomies and Enhancing Recommendations. *14th International Conference on E-Commerce and Web Technologies*, pp. 88–100 (2013)
24. Fernández-Tobías, I., Cantador, I.: Exploiting Social Tags in Matrix Factorization Models for Cross-domain Collaborative Filtering. *1st International Workshop on New Trends in Content-based Recommender Systems* (2013)
25. Freyne, J., Berkovsky, S., Smith, G.: Evaluating Recommender Systems for Supportive Technologies. *User Modeling and Adaptation for Daily Routines*, pp. 195–217 (2013)
26. Gao, S., Luo, H., Chen, D., Li, S., Gallinari, P., Guo, J.: Cross-Domain Recommendation via Cluster-Level Latent Factor Model. *17th and 24th European Conference on Machine Learning and Knowledge Discovery in Databases*, pp. 161–176 (2013)
27. Givon, S., Lavrenko, V.: Predicting Social-tags for Cold Start Book Recommendations. *3rd ACM Conference on Recommender Systems*, pp. 333–336 (2009)
28. Goga, O., Lei, H., Parthasarathi, S. H. K., Friedland, G., Sommer, R., Teixeira, R.: Exploiting Innocuous Activity for Correlating Users across Sites. *22nd International Conference on World Wide Web*, pp. 447–458 (2013)
29. González, G., López, B., de la Rosa, J. LL.: A Multi-agent Smart User Model for Cross-domain Recommender Systems. In: *Beyond Personalization 2005 - The Next Stage of Recommender Systems Research*, pp. 93–94 (2005)
30. Helocker, J.L., Konstan, J.A., Terveen, L.G., Riedl, J.: Evaluating Collaborative Filtering Recommender Systems. *ACM Transations on Information Systems* 22(1), pp. 5–53 (2004)
31. Hu, L., Cao, J., Xu, G., Cao, L., Gu, Z., Zhu, C.: Personalized Recommendation via Cross-domain Triadic Factorization. *22nd International Conference on World Wide Web*, pp. 595–606 (2013)
32. Jain, P., Kumaraguru, P., Joshi, A.: @i seek 'fb.me': Identifying Users across Multiple Online Social Networks.*22nd International Conference on WWW Companion*, pp. 1259–1268 (2013)
33. Jialin Pan, S., Yang, Q.: A Survey on Transfer Learning. *IEEE Transactions on Knowledge and Data Engineering* 22(10), pp. 1345–1359 (2010)
34. Joon Kook, H.: Profiling Multiple Domains of User Interests and Using them for Personalized Web Support. *1st International Conference on Intelligent Computing)*, pp. 512–520 (2005)
35. Kaminskas, M., Fernández-Tobías, I., Ricci, F., Cantador, I.: Ontology-based Identification of Music for Places. *13th International Conference on Information and Communication Technologies in Tourism*, pp. 436–447 (2013)
36. Kitts, B., Freed, D., Vrieze, M.: Cross-sell: A Fast Promotion-tunable Customer-item Recommendation Method based on Conditionally Independent Probabilities. *6th ACM SIGKDD Conference on Knowledge Discovery and Data Mining*, pp. 437–446 (2000)
37. Koren, Y.: Factorization Meets the Neighborhood: A Multifaceted Collaborative Filtering Model. *14th ACM SIGKDD Conference on Knowledge Discovery and Data Mining*, pp. 426–434 (2008) Ë
38. Lee, C. H., Kim, Y. H., Rhee, P. K.: Web Personalization Expert with Combining Collaborative Filtering and Association Rule Mining Technique. *Expert Systems with Applications* 21(3), pp. 131–137 (2001)
39. Li, B.: Cross-Domain Collaborative Filtering: A Brief Survey. *23rd IEEE International Conference on Tools with Artificial Intelligence*, pp. 1085–1086 (2011)
40. Li, B., Yang, Q., Xue, X.: Can Movies and Books Collaborate? Cross-domain Collaborative Filtering for Sparsity Reduction. *21st International Joint Conference on Artificial Intelligence*, pp. 2052–2057 (2009)
41. Li, B., Yang, Q., Xue, X.: Transfer Learning for Collaborative Filtering via a Rating-matrix Generative Model. *26th International Conference on Machine Learning*, pp. 617–624 (2009)
42. Li, B., Zhu, X., Li, R., Zhang, C., Xue, X., Wu, X.: Cross-domain Collaborative Filtering over Time. *22nd International Joint Conference on Artificial Intelligence*, pp. 2293–2298 (2011)

43. Loizou, A.: How to Recommend Music to Film Buffs: Enabling the Provision of Recommendations from Multiple Domains. *PhD thesis, University of Southampton* (2009)
44. Loni, B, Shi, Y, Larson, M. A., Hanjalic, A.: Cross-Domain Collaborative Filtering with Factorization Machines. *36th European Conference on Information Retrieval* (2014)
45. Low, Y., Agarwal, D., Smola, A. J.: Multiple Domain User Personalization.*17th ACM SIGKDD Conference on Knowledge Discovery and Data Mining*, pp. 123–131 (2011)
46. Moreno, O. Shapira, B. Rokach, L. Shani, G.: TALMUD: transfer learning for multiple domains. *21st ACM Conference on Information and Knowledge Management*, pp. 425–434 (2012)
47. Nakatsuji, M., Fujiwara, Y., Tanaka, A., Uchiyama, T., Ishida, T.: Recommendations Over Domain Specific User Graphs. *19th European Conference on Artificial Intelligence*, pp. 607–612 (2010)
48. Pan, S. J., Kwok, J. T., Yang, Q.: Transfer Learning via Dimensionality Reduction. *23rd AAAI Conference on Artificial Intelligence*, pp. 677–682 (2008)
49. Pan, S. J., Yang, Q.: A Survey on Transfer Learning. *IEEE Transactions on Knowledge and Data Engineering* 22(10), pp. 1345–1359 (2010)
50. Pan, W., Liu, N. N., Xiang, E. W., Yang, Q.: Transfer Learning to Predict Missing Ratings via Heterogeneous User Feedbacks. *22nd International Joint Conference on Artificial Intelligence*, pp. 2318–2323 (2011)
51. Pan, W., Xiang, E. W., Liu, N. N., Yang, Q.: Transfer Learning in Collaborative Filtering for Sparsity Reduction. *24th AAAI Conference on Artificial Intelligence*, pp. 210–235 (2010)
52. Pan, W., Xiang, E. W., Yang, Q.: Transfer Learning in Collaborative Filtering with Uncertain Ratings. *26th AAAI Conference on Artificial Intelligence*, pp. 662–668 (2012)
53. Pan, W., Yang, Q.: Transfer Learning in Heterogeneous Collaborative Filtering Domains. *Artificial Intelligence* 197, pp. 39–55 (2013)
54. Rendle, S.: Factorization Machines with libFM. *ACM Transactions on Intelligent Systems and Technology* 3(3), pp. 1–22 (2012)
55. Sahebi, S., Brusilovsky, P.: Cross-Domain Collaborative Recommendation in a Cold-Start Context: The Impact of User Profile Size on the Quality of Recommendation. *21st International Conference on User Modeling, Adaptation, and Personalization*, pp. 289–295 (2013)
56. Salakhutdinov, R., Mnih, A.: Probabilistic Matrix Factorization. *Advances in Neural Information Processing Systems* 20, pp. 1257–1264 (2008)
57. Shani, G., Gunawardana, A.: Evaluating Recommendation Systems. *Recommender Systems Handbook*, pp. 257–297 (2011)
58. Shapira, B., Rokach, L., Freilikhman, S.: Facebook Single and Cross Domain Data for Recommendation Systems. *User Modeling and User-Adapted Interaction* 23(2–3), pp. 211–247 (2013)
59. Shi, Y., Larson, M., Hanjalic, A.: Tags as Bridges between Domains: Improving Recommendation with Tag-induced Cross-domain Collaborative Filtering. *19th International Conference on User Modeling, Adaption, and Personalization*, pp. 305–316 (2011)
60. Stewart, A., Diaz-Aviles, E., Nejdl, W., Marinho, L. B., Nanopoulos, A., Schmidt-Thieme, L.: Cross-tagging for Personalized Open Social Networking. *20th ACM Conference on Hypertext and Hypermedia*, pp. 271–278 (2009)
61. Szomszor, M. N., Alani, H., Cantador, I., O'Hara, K., Shadbolt, N.: Semantic Modelling of User Interests Based on Cross-Folksonomy Analysis. *7th International Semantic Web Conference*, pp. 632–648 (2008)
62. Szomszor, M. N., Cantador, I., Alani, H.: Correlating User Profiles from Multiple Folksonomies. *19th ACM Conference on Hypertext and Hypermedia*, pp. 33–42 (2008)
63. Tang, J., Yan, J., Ji, L., Zhang, M., Guo, S., Liu, N., Wang, X., Chen, Z.: Collaborative Users' Brand Preference Mining across Multiple Domains from Implicit Feedbacks. *25th AAAI Conference on Artificial Intelligence*, pp. 477–482 (2011)
64. Tiroshi, A., Berkovsky, S., Kaafar, M. A., Chen, T., Kuflik, T.: Cross Social Networks Interests Predictions Based on Graph Features. *7th ACM Conference on Recommender Systems*, pp. 319–322 (2013)

65. Tiroshi, A., Kuflik, T.: Domain Ranking for Cross Domain Collaborative Filtering. *20th International Conference on User Modeling, Adaptation, and Personalization*, pp. 328–333 (2012)
66. Winoto, P., Tang, T.: If You Like the Devil Wears Prada the Book, Will You also Enjoy the Devil Wears Prada the Movie? A Study of Cross-Domain Recommendations. *New Generation Computing* 26, pp. 209–225 (2008)
67. Zhang, Y., Cao, B., Yeung, D.-Y.: Multi-Domain Collaborative Filtering. *26th Conference on Uncertainty in Artificial Intelligence*, pp. 725–732 (2010)
68. Zhang, X., Cheng, J., Yuan, T., Niu, B., Lu, H.: TopRec: Domain-specific Recommendation through Community Topic Mining in Social Network. *22nd International Conference on World Wide Web*, pp. 1501–1510 (2013)
69. Zhao, L., Pan, S. J., Xiang, E. W., Zhong, E., Lu, X., Yang, Q.: Active Transfer Learning for Cross-System Recommendation. *27th AAAI Conference on Artificial Intelligence*, pp. 1205–1211 (2013)
70. Zhuang, F., Luo, P., Xiong, H., Xiong, Y., He, Q., Shi, Z.: Cross-domain Learning from Multiple Sources: A Consensus Regularization Perspective. *IEEE Transactions on Knowledge and Data Engineering* 22(12), pp. 1664–1678 (2010)

[illegible]

Chapter 28
Robust Collaborative Recommendation

Robin Burke, Michael P. O'Mahony, and Neil J. Hurley

28.1 Introduction

Collaborative recommender systems are dependent on the goodwill of their users. There is an implicit assumption—note the word "collaborative"—that users are in some sense "on the same side", and at the very least, that they will interact with the system with the aim of getting good recommendations for themselves while providing useful data for their neighbors. Herlocker et al. [14] use the analogy of the "water-cooler chat", whereby co-workers exchange tips and opinions.

However, as contemporary experience has shown, the Internet is not solely inhabited by good-natured collaborative types. Users will have a range of purposes in interacting with recommender systems, and in some cases, those purposes may be counter to those of the system owner or those of the majority of its user population. To cite a well-known example, the Google search engine finds itself engaging in more-or-less continual combat against those who seek to promote their sites by "gaming" its retrieval algorithm.

In search engine spam, the goal for an attacker is to make the promoted page "look like" a good answer to a query in all respects that Google cares about. In the case of collaborative recommendation, the goal for an adversary is to make a particular product or item look like a good recommendation for a particular user (or maybe all users) when really it is not. Alternatively, the attacker might seek to prevent a particular product from being recommended when really it is a good

---

R. Burke (✉)
Center for Web Intelligence, School of Computer Science, Telecommunication and Information Systems, DePaul University, Chicago, IL, USA
e-mail: rburke@cs.depaul.edu

M.P. O'Mahony • N.J. Hurley
Insight Centre for Data Analytics, University College Dublin, Dublin, Ireland
e-mail: michael.omahony@ucd.ie; neil.hurley@ucd.ie

F. Ricci et al. (eds.), *Recommender Systems Handbook*,
DOI 10.1007/978-1-4899-7637-6_28

choice. If we assume that a collaborative system makes its recommendations purely on the basis of user profiles, then it is clear what an attacker must do—add user profiles that push the recommendation algorithm to produce the desired effect. A single profile would rarely have this effect, and in any case, fielded systems tend to avoid making predictions based on only a single neighbor. What an attacker really needs to do is to create a large number of psuedonomous profiles designed to bias the system's predictions. Site owners try to make this relatively costly, but there is an inherent tension between policing the input of a collaborative system and making sure that users are not discouraged from entering the data that the algorithm needs to do its work. The possibility of designing user rating profiles to deliberately manipulate the recommendation output of a collaborative filtering system was first raised in [31]. Since then, research has focused on attack strategies, detection strategies to combat attacks and recommendation algorithms that have inherent robustness against attack.

A framework for understanding this research is sketched in Fig. 28.1. First, we demonstrate the extent of the problem by modeling *efficient* attacks, attacks that can with relatively low cost produce a large impact on system output. This enables us to understand the shape of the impact curve for efficient attacks. Research on detection attempts to identify groups of profiles that make up an attack and to eliminate them from the database. Attacks that are not efficient are more difficult to detect, but because they are inefficient, must be very large to have an impact. A large influx of ratings for a particular item is easy to detect with standard system monitoring procedures. Research on detection therefore focuses on how to detect efficient attacks and variants of them, seeking to increase the size of the "detectable"

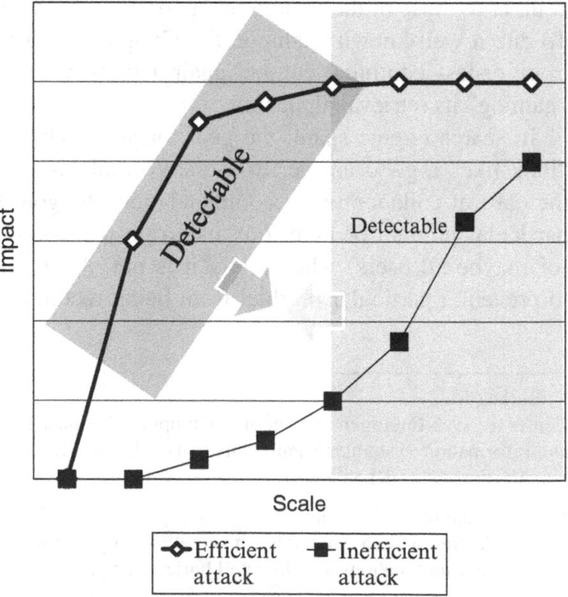

Fig. 28.1 *Curves* show the theoretical impact of attacks of different degrees of efficiency. The *shaded areas* shows attacks that can be detected

boxes in the diagram, and thereby limiting the impact that an attacker can have. At the same time, researchers have studied a number of algorithms that are intended to be robust against attack, having lower impact curves relative to efficient attacks. With the combination of these techniques, researchers have sought, not to eliminate attacks, but to control their impact to the point where they are no longer cost-effective.

This chapter looks at each of these points in turn. In Sect. 28.3, we look at research that aims to identify the most efficient and practical attacks against collaborative recommender systems, establishing the shape of the impact curve suggested above. Section 28.5 looks at the problem of detection: in particular, the left-most shaded area for detecting efficient attacks. Lastly, in Sect. 28.7, we examine attempts to reduce the impact of attacks through robust algorithms.

28.2 Defining the Problem

A collaborative recommender is supposed to change its recommendations in response to the profiles that users add. It is somewhat counter-intuitive to suppose that "robustness" or "stability" is a desirable property in a system that is supposed to be adaptive. The goal of robust recommendation is to prevent attackers from manipulating the system through large-scale insertion of user profiles, a *profile injection* attack.

We assume that any user profile is feasible. That is, we do not want to demand that users' ratings fit with those that have been entered previously or that they make any kind of objective sense. Users are entitled to their idiosyncratic opinions and there is always the possibility that what is an unusual user today may be more typical tomorrow as new users sign up. So, a profile, taken by itself, cannot constitute an attack. Also, it is important to note that some web phenomena that look like attacks are not considered such within this definition. For example, in the Fall of 2008, numerous videogame fans converged on the page for the game *Spore* on Amazon.com, using it as a vehicle for airing their complaints about the digital rights management software included with the game. Presumably these were a large number of authentic individuals, and while their ratings no doubt skewed the recommendations for *Spore* for some time, their actions would not be considered an attack as we define it here. It is not clear that any automated technique can identify when a real user posts a rating to make a political statement or as a prank, rather than to reflect an honest preference.[1]

For the purposes of this research, an attack is a concerted effort to bias the results of a recommender system by the insertion of a large number of profiles using false identities. Each of the separate identities assumed by the attacker are referred to as

---

[1]It could be argued that even such a technique did exist, it would not be in the interest of a collaborative system to deploy it.

an *attack profile*. Once created, these profiles are used to insert preference data into the system. The most dangerous attacks are those that are crafted for maximum impact on the system, so much research has been devoted to finding the most effective and practical attacks against different algorithms.

While random vandalism surely does occur, research in this area has concentrated on attacks designed to achieve a particular recommendation outcome. The objectives of *product push* and *product nuke* attacks are to promote or demote the recommendations made for items, respectively. For example, the goal of an attacker might be to force a system to output poor recommendations for his competitors' products (nuke) while attempting to secure positive recommendations for his own (push).

From the perspective of the attacker, the best attack against a system is one that yields the biggest impact for the least amount of effort, under the constraint of remaining undetectable. There are two types of effort involved in mounting an attack. The first is the effort involved in crafting profiles. On of the crucial variables here is the amount of knowledge that is required to put together an attack. A *high-knowledge attack* is one that requires the attacker to have detailed knowledge of the ratings distribution in a recommender system's database. Some attacks, for example, require that the attacker know the mean rating and standard deviation for every item. A *low-knowledge attack* is one that requires system-independent knowledge such as might be obtained by consulting public information sources.

We assume that the attacker will have a general knowledge of the type of algorithm being employed to produce recommendations. An attacker that has more detailed knowledge of the precise algorithm in use would be able to produce an *informed attack* that makes use of the mathematical properties of the algorithm itself to produce the greatest impact.

The second aspect of effort is the number of profiles that must be added to the system in order for it to be effective. The ratings are less important since the insertion of ratings can be easily automated. Most sites employ online registration schemes requiring human intervention, and by this means, the site owner can impose a cost on the creation of new profiles. This is precisely why, from an attacker's perspective, attacks requiring a smaller number of profiles are particularly attractive.

28.2.1 An Example Attack

To illustrate the basic idea of a profile injection attack, consider the simplified recommender system database that is presented in Fig. 28.2. In this example, the objective is to demote the recommendations that are made for item 7 (i.e. a product nuke attack), and a number of attack profiles (users i through m) have been inserted into the system to target this item.

In particular, consider the binary recommendation problem in which the task is to predict whether or not user h likes item 7. In the first instance, let the attack profiles be ignored and consider only the authentic profiles (users a through g) as

Items

Users	1	2	3	4	5	6	7	
a	+	−		+	+		+	Authentic profiles
b	−	+	+	−	−		−	
c	+	−	+		−	−	−	
d	−	+	+	−				
e	−		−	−	−		−	
f	+	−	+	+	+		+	
g		−	+	+	−	−	+	
h	+	−	+	+	+		?	Target profile
i	+	−	+		−	−	−	Attack profiles
j	−	+	+	−			−	
k	−		−	−	−		−	
l	+	−	+	+	+		−	
m		−	+	+	−	−	−	

Fig. 28.2 Simplified system database showing authentic user profiles and a number of attack profiles inserted. In this example, user h is seeking a prediction for item 7, which is the subject of a product nuke attack

possible neighbours for the target user, h. Regardless of the specific recommendation algorithm used, presumably the algorithm would determine that users a and f have similar tastes to the active user, and since both of these users like item 7, a positive recommendation for the item follows.

When the attack profiles are also considered as possible neighbours, the situation is significantly altered. Several of these attack profiles are also similar to user h, and, since all of these profiles rate item 7 poorly, the system is now likely to recommend a negative rating for the item. Thus, the objective of the attack is realised. The next section discusses how these attack profiles must be crafted to work well in a realistic setting.

28.3 Characterising Attacks

A profile-injection attack against a recommender system consists of a set of profiles added to the system by the attacker. A profile consists of a set of rating/item pairs, or alternately, we can think of the profile being a vector of all items, with a rating value for each item, but allowing the *null* value for unrated items. For the attacks that we are discussing, there will always be a target item i_t that the attacker is interested in promoting or demoting. There will generally also be a set of *filler items*, that are chosen randomly from those available. We will denote this set I_F. Some attack models also make use of a set of items that are selected out of the database. The small set usually has some association with the target item (or a targeted segment of users). For some attacks, this set is empty. This will be the set I_S. Finally, for completeness, the set $I_\emptyset$ contains those items not rated in the profile. Since the selected item set is usually small, the size of each profile (total number of ratings) is determined mostly by the size of the filler item set. Some of the experimental results report filler size as a proportion of the size of I (i.e., the set of all items).

28.3.1 Basic Attacks

Two basic attack models, introduced originally in [18], are the random and average attack models. Both of these attacks involve the generation of profiles using randomly assigned ratings to the filler items in the profile.

28.3.1.1 Random Attack

Random attack profiles consist of random ratings distributed around the overall mean assigned to the filler items and a prespecified rating assigned to the target item. In this attack model, the set of selected items is empty. The target item i_t is assigned the maximum rating (r_{max}) or the minimum rating (r_{min}) in the case of push or nuke attacks, respectively.

The knowledge required to mount such an attack is quite minimal, especially since the overall rating mean in many systems can be determined by an outsider empirically (or, indeed, may be available directly from the system). However, this attack is not particularly effective [7, 18].

28.3.1.2 Average Attack

A more powerful attack described in [18] uses the individual mean for each item rather than the global mean (except for the pushed item). In the average attack, each assigned rating for a filler item corresponds (either exactly or approximately) to the mean rating for that item, across the users in the database who have rated it.

As in the random attack, this attack can also be used as a nuke attack by using r_{min} instead of r_{max}. It should also be noted that the only difference between the average attack and the random attack is in the manner in which ratings are computed for the filler items in the profile.

The average attack might be considered to have considerable knowledge cost of order $|I_F|$ (the number of filler items in the attack profile) because the mean and standard deviation of these items must be known. Experiments, however, have shown that the average attack can be just as successful even when using a small filler item set. Thus the knowledge requirements for this attack can be substantially reduced, but at the cost of making all profiles contain the same items, possibly rendering them conspicuous [5].

28.3.2 *Low-Knowledge Attacks*

The average attack requires a relatively high degree of system-specific knowledge on the part of attackers. A reasonable defense against such attacks would be to make it very difficult for an attacker to accumulate the required distribution data. The next set of attack types are those for which the knowledge requirements are much lower.

28.3.2.1 Bandwagon Attack

The goal of the bandwagon attack is to associate the attacked item with a small number of frequently rated items. This attack takes advantage of the Zipf's distribution of popularity in consumer markets: a small number of items, bestseller books for example, will receive the lion's share of attention and also ratings. The attacker using this model will build attack profiles containing those items that have high visibility. Such profiles will have a good probability of being similar to a large number of users, since the high visibility items are those that many users have rated. It does not require any system-specific data, because it is usually not difficult to independently determine what the "blockbuster" items are in any product space.

The bandwagon attack uses selected items which are likely to have been rated by a large number of users in the database. These items are assigned the maximum rating value together with the target item i_t. The ratings for the filler items are determined randomly in a similar manner as in the random attack. The bandwagon attack therefore can be viewed as an extension of the random attack.

As we show in Sect. 28.4, the bandwagon attack is nearly as effective as the average attack against user-based algorithms, but without the knowledge requirements of that attack. Thus it is more practical to mount. However, as in the case of the average attack, it falls short when used against an item-based algorithm [18].

28.3.2.2 Segment Attack

Mobasher et al. [26] introduced the segment attack and demonstrated its effectiveness against the item-based algorithm. The basic idea behind the segment attack is to push an item to a targeted group of users with known or easily predicted preferences. For example, the producer of a horror movie might want to get the movie recommended to viewers who have liked other horror movies. In fact, the producer might prefer not to have his movie recommender to viewer who do not enjoy the horror genre, since these users might complain and thereby reveal his attack.

To mount this attack, the attacker determines a set of segment items that are likely to be preferred by his intended target audience. Like the bandwagon attack, it is usually fairly easy to predict what the most popular items in a user segment would be. These items are assigned the maximum rating value together with the target item. To provide the maximum impact on the item-based CF algorithm, the minimum rating is given to the filler items, thus maximising the variations of item similarities.

28.3.3 Nuke Attack Models

All of the attack models described above can also be used for nuking a target item. For example, as noted earlier, in the case of the random and average attack models, this can be accomplished by associating rating r_{min} with the target item instead of r_{max} . However, the results presented in Sect. 28.4 suggest that attack models that are effective for pushing items are not necessarily as effective for nuke attacks. Thus, researchers have designed additional attack models designed particularly for nuking items.

28.3.3.1 Love/Hate Attack

The love/hate attack is a very simple attack, with no knowledge requirements. The attack consists of attack profiles in which the target item it is given the minimum rating value, r_{min}, while other ratings in the filler item set are the maximum rating value, r_{max}. This can be seen as a very low-knowledge version of the Popular Attack below. Surprisingly, this is one of the most effective nuke attacks against the user-based algorithm.

28.3.3.2 Reverse Bandwagon Attack

The reverse bandwagon attack is a variation of the bandwagon attack, discussed above, in which the selected items are those that tend to be rated poorly by many users. These items are assigned low ratings together with the target item. Thus the target item is associated with widely disliked items, increasing the probability that the system will generate low predicted ratings for that item. This attack was designed to reduce the knowledge required by selecting only a handful of known disliked items. For example, in the movie domain, these may be box office flops that had been highly promoted prior to their openings.

In Sect. 28.4, we show that although this attack is not as effective as the more knowledge-intensive average attack for nuking items in the user-based system, it is a very effective nuke attack against item-based recommender systems.

28.3.4 *Informed Attack Models*

The low-knowledge attacks above work by approximating the average attack, concentrating on items that are expected to be rated because of their popularity. The average attack in turn is a natural choice for an attacker with a basic intuition about collaborative recommendation, namely that users will be compared on the basis of similarity, so the incentive is to make the profiles similar to the average user. Of course, should detailed knowledge be available concerning the rating distributions of particularly influential users in the system, the potential exists for more sophisticated attacks. In addition, knowledge of the precise algorithm, if available, can likewise be applied to mount more powerful attacks. In the following sections, informed attacks in the context of knowledge about the recommendation algorithm are discussed.

28.3.4.1 Popular Attack

Let us assume that the recommender system uses the widely studied user-based algorithm proposed in [35], where similarities between users are calculated using Pearson correlation.[2] In a similar manner to the bandwagon attack, attack profiles are constructed using popular (i.e. frequently rated) items from the domain under attack.

A high degree of overlap does not, however, guarantee high similarities between attack and authentic profiles. The bandwagon attack used random filler items to generate variation among ratings with the aim of producing at least some profiles that correlate correctly with any given user. The Popular Attack makes use of average rating data and rates the filler items either $r_{min} + 1$ and r_{min}, according to whether the average rating for the item is higher or lower. Linking the rating value to the average rating is likely to result in positive correlations between attack and authentic profiles and furthermore also maximises the prediction shift (see Sect. 28.4) of attack profiles as computed by the algorithm under consideration (see [32] for details).[3]

The ratings strategy described above applies to push attacks; this strategy can easily be adjusted for nuke attacks. For example, positive correlations but negative prediction shifts can be achieved by assigning the target item a rating of r_{min}, and ratings of r_{max} and $r_{max} - 1$ to the more- and less-liked selected items.

The knowledge requirement here is intermediate between the bandwagon attack and the average attack. Like the bandwagon attack, the popular items can usually

---

[2]See [32] for a discussion on informed attacks in cases where alternative similarity metrics are employed. Note that none of the metrics considered provided robustness against attack.

[3]Note that an optimal push attack strategy is also presented in [25]. In this case, it is concluded that maximising the correlation between authentic and attack profiles is the primary objective. While this conclusion makes sense, it is important to select attack profile ratings that also maximise prediction shift, as is the case with the popular attack described here.

be easily estimated from outside the system because there are no filler items, the Popular Attack will need more such items. The attacker then needs to guess at the relative average preferences between these items in order to provide the correct rating. It might be possible to extract such distinctions from the system itself, or if not, to mine them from external sources; for example, counting the number of positive and negative reviews for particular items to find general trends.

28.3.4.2 Probe Attack Strategy

A strategy that is less conspicuous to the popular attack is to obtain items and their ratings from the system itself via the probe attack. To perform this strategy, the attacker creates a seed profile and then uses it to generate recommendations from the system. These recommendations are generated by the neighboring users and so they are guaranteed to be rated by at least some of these users and the predicted ratings will be well-correlated with these users' opinions. One could imagine probing narrowly in order to influence a small group as in the segment attack, or probing more broadly to construct an average attack. In a sense, the probe attack provides a way for the attacker to incrementally learn about the system's rating distribution.

This strategy also has another advantage over the popular attack, since less domain knowledge is required by an attacker. Only a small number of seed items need to be selected by the attacker, thereafter the recommender system is used to identify additional items and ratings. In the experiments conducted in Sect. 28.4, seed items are selected and assigned ratings in a similar manner as in the popular attack.

28.3.4.3 Power User Attack

It is well known that certain users in the system have considerable influence on the recommendations made for others [13, 34]. Accordingly, the power user attack has been proposed [43]. Power users are identified as those (genuine) users in the dataset which, for example, appear in the highest number of neighbourhoods or have the largest number of ratings. The effectiveness of such users as attackers is demonstrated by selecting a group of genuine power users to act as attackers. Their ratings for the attacked item is set to the maximum or minimum depending on whether a push or nuke attack is intended, but otherwise their profile is left unchanged. The challenge remains as to how power user attack profiles could be synthesised by an actual attacker and the degree of knowledge required to so do, which is left to future work.

28.3.5 Obfuscated Attacks

The above attacks were proposed from the point-of-view of finding effective strategies to manipulate a CF system under certain constraints of knowledge available to the attacker. They give little attention to the issue of how conspicuous an attack is. However, if a CF system takes counter-measures to filter out attacks, then the attacker must in turn put effort into hiding the attack. Obfuscated attacks attempt to manipulate ratings using profiles that are difficult to distinguish from genuine profiles. In [17], an Average over Popular (AoP) attack is proposed that modifies the Average attack, so that filler items are chosen from a set of the most popular items. This circumvents detection strategies that depend on the difference between the way that filter items are chosen in the Average attack and the way that genuine users choose items to rate. Another obfuscation method is proposed in [8], where attack profiles are constructed to be highly diverse and so circumvent detection strategies that use clustering (see Sect. 28.5.3). Furthermore, attackers can exploit knowledge of the detection strategy. For example, [30] shows that if the attacker is aware of the criteria used to decide if an attack profile exists in the user's neighbourhood, then the attacker can construct profiles which, although somewhat less effective than the standard attacks, can circumvent detection. An evaluation of the effectiveness of various types of attack profile obfuscation is carried out in [42].

28.4 Measuring Robustness

Collaborative recommendation algorithms can be categorised into two general classes, which are commonly referred to as memory-based and model-based algorithms [3]. Memory-based algorithms utilise all available data from a system database to compute predictions and recommendations. In contrast, model-based algorithms operate by first deriving a model from the system data, and this model is subsequently used in the recommendation process.

A wide range of collaborative recommendation algorithms have been proposed in the literature, and a comprehensive analysis of the robustness of all of these algorithms is beyond the scope of this chapter. Here, we focus on two widely implemented and studied algorithms, the *user-based* and *item-based* algorithms [35, 39]. The reader is referred to [27, 28, 38] for a robustness analysis of some other collaborative recommendation algorithms.

28.4.1 Evaluation Metrics

Since the objective of push and nuke attacks is to promote and demote target items, we need to evaluate how successfully they do so. Evaluation metrics for robustness need to capture the differences in the predicted ratings and recommended status (i.e. whether or not the target item in included in a top N recommended list) of target items pre- and post-attack.

Many researchers have used average prediction shift to evaluate the changes in predicted ratings. Let U_T and I_T be the sets of users and items, respectively, in the test data. For each user-item pair (u, i), the prediction shift denoted by $\Delta_{u,i}$ can be measured as $\Delta_{u,i} = p'_{u,i} - p_{u,i}$, where p' is the post-attack prediction and p before. A positive value means that the attack has succeeded in making the pushed item more positively rated. The average prediction shift for an item i over all users can be computed as $\Delta_i = \sum_{u \in U_T} \Delta_{u,i}/|U_T|$. Similarly the average prediction shift for all items tested can be computed as $\bar{\Delta} = \sum_{i \in I_T} \Delta_i/|I_T|$.

Prediction shift is a good indicator that an attack is having the desired effect of making a pushed item appear more desirable. However, it is possible that an item could be strongly shifted on average, but still not make it onto a recommendation list. For example, the item's initial average prediction could be so low that even a strong boost is insufficient. To capture the impact of an attack on prediction lists, another metric has been proposed: hit ratio. Let R_u be the set of top N recommendations for user u. If the target item appears in R_u, for user u, the scoring function H_{ui} has value 1; otherwise it is zero. Hit ratio for an item i is given by $HitRatio_i = \sum_{u \in U_T} H_{ui}/|U_T|$. Average hit ratio can then calculated as the sum of the hit ratio for each item i following an attack on i across all items divided by the number of items: $\overline{HitRatio} = \sum_{i \in I_T} HitRatio_i/|I_T|$.

Many experimenters make use of the publicly available MovieLens 100K dataset.[4] This dataset consists of 100,000 ratings made by 943 users on 1682 movies. Ratings are expressed on an integer rating scale of 1–5 (the higher the score, the more liked an item is). Results below should be assumed to be relative to this dataset unless otherwise stated.

28.4.2 Push Attacks

To get a sense for the impact that a push attack can have, we will look at results originally reported in [27]. In these figures, the user-based algorithm is subjected to various attacks of different sizes (attack size is measured as a percentage of the total number of authentic profiles in the system; thus an attack of 1 % equates to the insertion of ten attack profiles into the MovieLens dataset). Figure 28.3 (left) shows the average attack (3 % filler size), the bandwagon attack (using one frequently rated item and 3 % filler size), and the random attack (6 % filler size). These parameters were selected as they are the versions of each attack that were found to be most effective. Not surprisingly, the most knowledge-intensive average attack achieved the best performance in terms of prediction shift. This attack works very well.

[4] http://www.cs.umn.edu/research/GroupLens/data/.

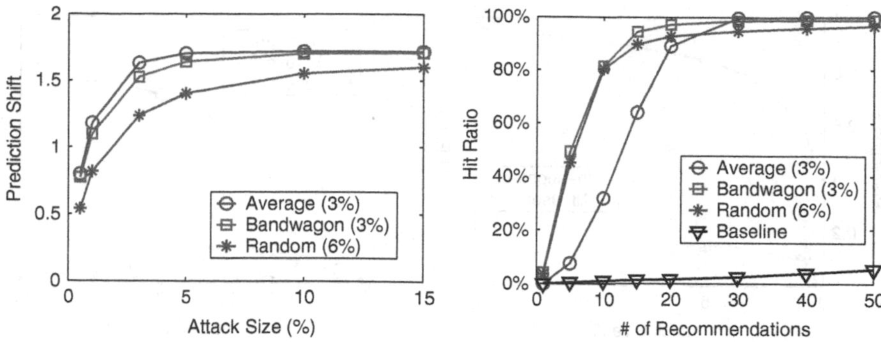

Fig. 28.3 Prediction shift (*left*) and hit ratio (*right*) for product push attacks mounted against the user-based collaborative recommendation algorithm. Hit ratio results relate to a 10 % attack size

It is capable of moving an average-rated movie (3.6 is the mean) to the top of the five point scale. The performance of the bandwagon attack was quite comparable, despite having a minimal knowledge requirement. In addition, the bandwagon attack was clearly superior to the random attack, which highlights the significance of including the selected items that are likely to be rated by many users.

Interestingly, Fig. 28.3 (right) shows that the largest hit ratios were achieved by the bandwagon attack, indicating that prediction shift does not necessarily translate directly into top N recommendation performance. This result is particularly encouraging from the attacker's perspective, given that the required knowledge to implement such attacks is low. Note that all attacks significantly outperform the pre-attack hit ratio results (indicated by "base line" in the figure).

The item-based algorithm was shown in [18] to be relatively robust against the average attack. The segment attack was introduced in [26] specifically crafted as a limited-knowledge attack for the item-based algorithm. It aims to increase the column-by-column similarity of the target item with the users preferred items. If the target item is considered similar to something that the user likes, then its predicted rating will be high—the goal of the push attack. The task therefore for the attacker is to associate her product with popular items considered similar. The users who have a preference for these similar items are considered the target segment. The task for the attacker in crafting a segment attack is therefore to select items similar to the target item for use as the segment portion of the attack profile I_S. In the realm of movies, we might imagine selecting films of a similar genre or those containing the same actors.

In [26], user segments are constructed by looking at popular actors and genres. For the results shown in Fig. 28.4, the segment is all users who gave above average ratings (4 or 5) to any three of the five selected horror movies, namely, Alien, Psycho, The Shining, Jaws, and The Birds. For this set of five movies, the researchers selected all combinations of three movies that had at least 50 users support, and chose 50 of those users randomly and averaged the results.

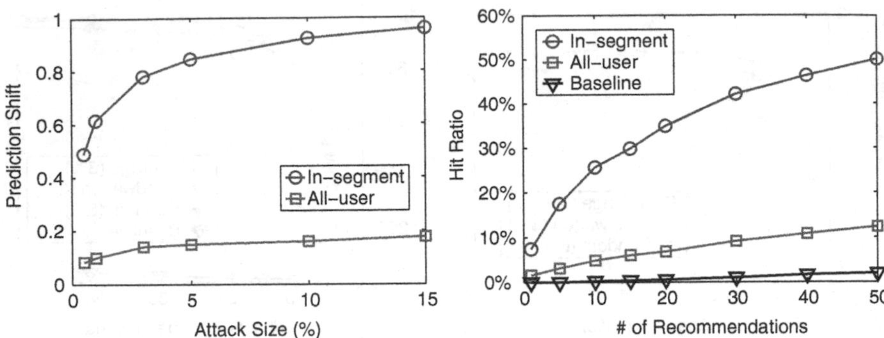

Fig. 28.4 Prediction shift (*left*) and hit ratio (*right*) for product push attacks mounted against the item-based collaborative recommendation algorithm. Hit ratio results relate to a 10 % attack size

The power of the segmented attack is demonstrated in the figure, which contrasts the horror movie fans against the set of all users. While the segmented attack shows some impact against all users, it is clearly very successful in pushing the attacked movie precisely to those users defined by the segment. Further, in the context of the item-based algorithm, the performance of this attack compares very favourably to that of the high-knowledge average attack. For example, the average attack achieved a hit ratio of 30 % against all users for top *N* lists of size 10 and an attack size of 10 %. In contrast, the segmented attack achieved approximately the same hit ratio for the same size top *N* list, but using an attack size of only 1 %.

It should also be noted that, although designed specifically as an attack against the item-based algorithm, the segment attack is also effective against the user-based algorithm. Due to limitations of space, we do not show these results here—refer to [27] for details.

28.4.3 Nuke Attacks

It might be assumed that nuke attacks would be symmetric to push attacks, with the only difference being the rating given to the target item and hence the direction of the impact on predicted ratings. However, our results show that there are some interesting differences in the effectiveness of models depending on whether they are being used to push or nuke an item. In particular, the rating distribution should be taken into account: there are in general relatively few low ratings in the MovieLens database, so low ratings can have a big impact on predictions. Furthermore, if we look at the top *N* recommendations, the baseline (the rate at which an average movie makes it into a recommendation list) is quite low, less than 0.1 even at a list size of 50. It does not take much to make an item unlikely to be recommended.

In the love/hate attack, the randomly selected 3 % of filler items were assigned the maximum rating while the target item was given the minimum rating. For the

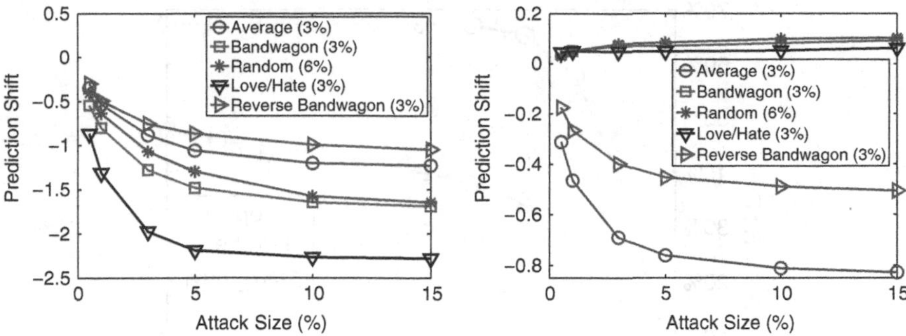

Fig. 28.5 Prediction shifts achieved by nuke attacks against the user-based (*left*) and item-based (*right*) algorithms

reverse bandwagon attack (designed to attack the item-based algorithm), items with the lowest average ratings that meet a minimum threshold in terms of the number of user ratings in the system are selected as the selected item set, as described in detail in Sect. 28.3. The experiments were conducted using $|I_S| = 25$ with a minimum of ten users rating each movie.

Results are shown in Fig. 28.5 for all attack models. Despite the minimal knowledge required for the love/hate attack, this attack proved to be the most effective against the user-based algorithm. Among the other nuke attacks, the bandwagon attack actually surpassed the average attack, which was not the case with the push results discussed above.

The asymmetry between these results and the push attack data is somewhat surprising. For example, the love/hate attack produced a positive prediction shift slightly over 1.0 for a push attack of 10 % against the user-based algorithm, which is much less effective than even the random attack. However, when used to nuke an item against the user-based algorithm, this model was by far the most effective model we tried, with a prediction shift of almost twice that of the average attack. For pushing items, the average attack was the most successful, while it proved to be one of the least successful attacks for nuking items. The bandwagon attack, on the other hand, performed nearly as well as the average attack in pushing items, and had superior overall performance for nuking, despite its lower knowledge requirement.

Overall, the item-based algorithm proved to be far more robust. The average attack was the most successful nuke attack here, with reverse bandwagon close behind. The asymmetries between push and nuke continue as we examine the item-based results. The random and love/hate attacks were poor performers for push attacks, but as nuke attacks, they actually failed completely to produce the desired effect. Reverse bandwagon (but not bandwagon) proved to be a reasonable low-knowledge attack model for a nuke attack against the item-based algorithm.

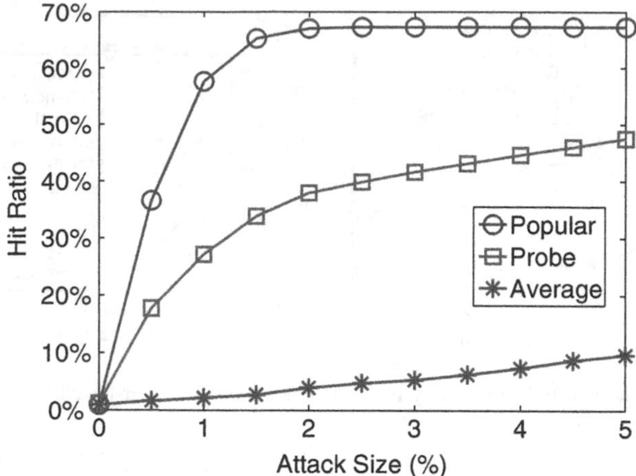

Fig. 28.6 Hit ratios achieved by the popular, probe and average push attacks against the user-based algorithm

28.4.4 Informed Attacks

Finally, we turn to the evaluation of the informed attack strategies against the user-based algorithm. In particular, we compare the performance of the informed popular and probe push attacks to the average attack as seen above.

The attacks were implemented as follows. Popular attack profiles consisting of a total of 100 items (including the target item) were selected and assigned ratings as described in Sect. 28.3. For the probe attack, 10 seed items were selected at random from the 100 most frequently rated items from the system. Thereafter the system was interrogated to discover additional profile items and ratings. In total, probe attack profiles consisted of 100 items. Likewise, the benchmark average attack profiles consisted of 100 items, which corresponds to a filler size of approximately 1.7 %. For the purposes of comparison, the 100 most frequently-rated items were chosen for average attack profiles (and not selected randomly, as before).

Figure 28.6 shows the hit ratios achieved by the three attacks. It is clear from the figure that the impact of the informed attacks was significantly greater than that of the average attack. For example, for an attack size of only 2 %, the hit ratios achieved by the popular, probe and average attacks were 65 %, 34 % and 3 %, respectively, for top N lists of size 10. Thus the advantage of creating attacks that consider particular features of the algorithm under attack is clearly demonstrated.

The main drawback associated with the informed attacks lies in the high degree of domain knowledge that is required in order to select the appropriate items and ratings with which to create the attack profiles. As discussed in Sect. 28.3, however, such knowledge is often made directly available to attackers by recommender system applications. Further, the knowledge required can often be obtained from other sources, e.g. by examining best seller lists and the number of positive and negative reviews received by items, etc. Even in situations where such data is only partially available, previous work demonstrates that these informed attacks retain their strong performance [33].

28.4.5 Attack Impact

It is clear from the research summarized above that the memory-based algorithms that form the core of collaborative recommendation research and practice are highly vulnerable to manipulation. An attacker with fairly limited knowledge can craft attacks that will make any item appear well liked and promote it into many users' recommendation lists. The "efficient" attacks that have been developed clearly are a threat to the stability and usability of collaborative systems and thus we see the justification for the low-scale/high-impact portion of the theoretical curve shown in Fig. 28.1.

To respond to this threat, researchers have examined two complementary responses. The shaded "detection" areas in Fig. 28.1 point towards the first response, which is to detect the profiles that make up an attack and eliminate them. The second approach is to design algorithms that are less susceptible to the types of attacks that work well against the classic algorithms.

28.5 Attack Detection

Figure 28.7 summarises the steps involved in attack detection. This is a binary classification problem, with two possible outcomes for each profile, namely, *Authentic*, meaning that the classifier has determined that the profile is that of a genuine system user or *Attack*, meaning that the classifier has determined that this is an instance of an attack profile. One approach to the detection problem, followed by work such as [1, 11], has been to view it as a problem of determining independently for each profile in the dataset, whether or not it is an attack profile. This is the 'single profile' input shown in Fig. 28.7. The input is a single rating vector $\mathbf{r}_u$, for some user u from the dataset. Before processing by the classifier, a *feature extraction* step may extract a set of features, $\mathbf{f}_u = (f_1, \ldots, f_k)$ from the raw rating vector $\mathbf{r}_u$. The classifier takes $\mathbf{f}_u$ as input and outputs, "*Attack*" or "*Authentic*". If the classifier is a *supervised* classifier, then a training phase makes use of annotated dataset of profiles, i.e. a set of profiles labelled as Authentic or Attack, in order to learn the classifier parameters.

Because most attack scenarios consist of groups of profiles working *in concert* to push or nuke a particular item, work such as [23, 30] has suggested that there is benefit to considering groups of profiles *together* when making the classification. This is represented by the 'Group of Profiles' input, in which the classifier considers an entire group of profiles, possibly after some feature extraction, and outputs a label for each profile in the group. Note that not all steps may take place in any particular

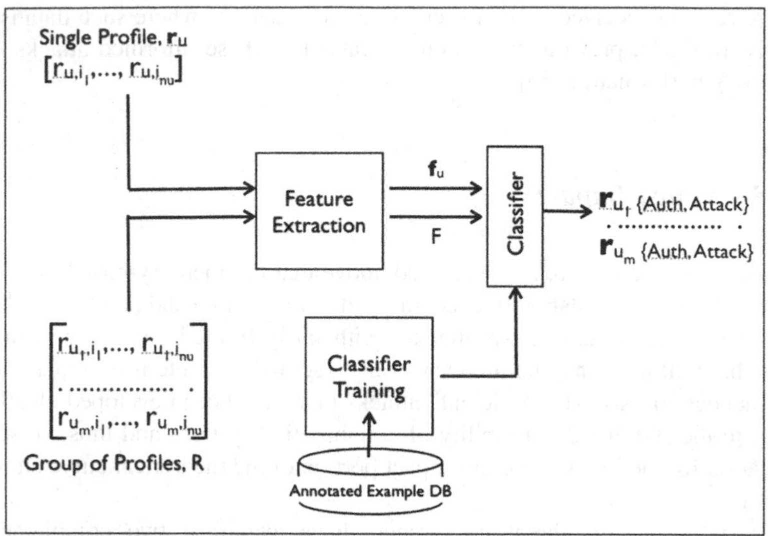

Fig. 28.7 The detection process

scenario. For instance, there may be no feature extraction, in which case, $\mathbf{f} = \mathbf{r}$ and if *unsupervised* classifiers are used, then there is no need for a training phase.

28.5.1 Evaluation Metrics

To compare different detection algorithms, we are interested primarily in measures of classification performance. Taking a 'positive' classification to mean the labeling of a profile as Attack, a confusion matrix of the classified data contains four sets, two of which—the true positives and true negatives—consist of profiles that were correctly classified as Attack or Authentic, respectively; and two of which—the false positives and false negatives—consist of profiles that were incorrectly classified as Attack or Authentic, respectively. Various measures are used in the literature to compute performance based on the relative sizes of these sets. Unfortunately, different researchers have used different measures, making direct comparison of results sometimes difficult.

Precision and *recall* are commonly used performance measures in information retrieval. In this context, they measure the classifier's performance in identifying attacks. Each measure counts the number of attack profiles correctly classified. Recall which is also called *sensitivity* presents this count as a fraction of the total number of actual attacks in the system. Precision, which is also called the *positive predictive value* (PPV), presents this count as a fraction of the total number of profiles labelled as Attack:

$$recall \equiv sensitivity = \frac{\#\text{ true positives}}{\#\text{ true positives} + \#\text{ false negatives}}, \tag{28.1}$$

$$precision \equiv PPV = \frac{\#\text{ true positives}}{\#\text{ true positives} + \#\text{ false positives}}.$$

Analogous measures can be given for performance in identifying authentic profiles. *Specificity* presents the count of authentic profiles correctly classified as a fraction of the total number of authentic profiles in the system. *Negative predictive value* (NPV), presents the count as a fraction of the total number of profiles labelled Authentic:

$$specificity = \frac{\#\text{ true negatives}}{\#\text{ true negatives} + \#\text{ false positives}}, \tag{28.2}$$

$$NPV = \frac{\#\text{ true negatives}}{\#\text{ true negatives} + \#\text{ false negatives}}.$$

In detection results below, we use the terms *precision*, *recall*, *specificity* and *NPV*.

28.5.1.1 Impact on Recommender and Attack Performance

The misclassification of authentic profiles results in the removal of good data from the ratings database, which has the potential to impact negatively on the overall performance of the recommender system. One way to assess this impact is to compute the MAE of the system before and after detection and filtering. On the positive side, the removal of attack profiles reduces attack performance. Assuming the attack is a push or nuke attack, the degree to which attack performance is affected can be assessed by computing the prediction shift on the targeted item before and after detection and filtering.

28.5.2 Single Profile Detection

The basis of individual profile detection is that the distribution of ratings in an attack profile is likely to be different to that of authentic users and therefore each attack profile can be distinguished by identification of these differences. As such, individual profile detection is an instance of a *statistical detection* problem. It should be noted that it is in the interest of the attacker to minimise the statistical differences between attack and authentic profiles, in order to minimise the probability of detection. On the other hand, a cost-effective attack is likely to consist of unusually influential profiles—e.g., a targeted pushed item will have unusually high ratings and filler items may have been chosen to support the influence of the profile towards high ratings for the target. As a result, distinctive characteristics are likely to exist and may be manifested in many ways, including an abnormal deviation from the system average rating, or an unusual number of ratings in a profile [1].

28.5.2.1 Unsupervised Detection

An unsupervised individual profile detection algorithm is described in [11]. Detection is based on certain common generic attributes of attack profiles, for example that there is a higher than usual rating deviation from mean in such profiles and that such profiles are likely to have a higher than usual similarity to their closest neighbours. Measures of these attributes are proposed and these are applied to compute a probability that a profile is an attack profile. This method is adapted to take into account the timestamps of when ratings are made in [41].

28.5.2.2 Supervised Detection

Supervised detection algorithms have focussed on the selection of attributes of attack profiles from which to build a feature vector for input to a classifier. Generally, such features have been selected by observation of *generic* attributes that are common across attack profiles of a number of different attack strategies and also *model specific* attributes that are common across profiles that have been generated for a specific type of attack.

In [6] profile attributes based to those proposed in [11] and others along similar lines were developed into features for inclusion in a feature vector input to a supervised classifier. Moreover, other features based on the statistics of the filler and target items in the user profile, rather than the entire profile, were proposed. For example, the *filler mean variance* feature is defined as the variance of the ratings in the filler partition of the profile and is used to detect average attacks; the *filler mean target difference* feature, defined as the difference between the means of the target items and the means of the filler items, is used to detect bandwagon attacks.

The authors looked at three supervised classifiers: kNN, C4.5, and SVM. The kNN classifier uses detection attributes of the profiles to find the $k = 9$ nearest neighbors in the training set using Pearson correlation for similarity to determine the class. The C4.5 and SVM classifiers are built in a similar manner such that they classify profiles based on the detection attributes only. The results for the detection of a 1 % average attack over various filler sizes are reproduced in Fig. 28.8. SVM and C4.5 have near perfect performance on identifying attack profiles correctly, but on the other hand, they also misclassify more authentic profiles than kNN. SVM has the best combination of recall and specificity across the entire range of filler sizes for a 1 % attack.

The effect of misclassification of authentic profiles is assessed by examining the MAE of the system before and after detection and filtering. The increase in MAE is observed to be less than 0.05 on a rating scale of 1–5. Finally the effectiveness of

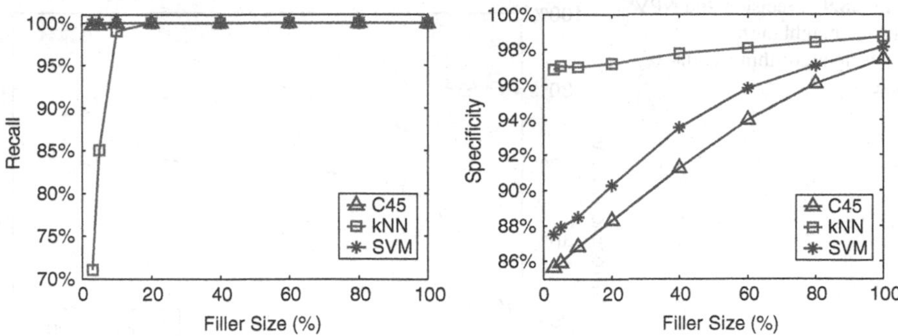

Fig. 28.8 Recall (*left*) and specificity (*right*) vs filler size for three classifiers trained on a 1 % average attack

the attack as measured by the prediction shift on the targeted item is shown to be significantly reduced when detection is used. All three classifiers reduce the range of attacks that are successful, particularly at low attack sizes. The SVM algorithm, in particular, dominates for attack sizes less than 10 %, allowing no resulting prediction shift over that entire range.

Hurley et al. [17] took a statistical approach to attack detection, by building statistical models of attack and genuine profiles, whose parameters are learned from a training set. This strategy proved highly successful in identifying the average, random and bandwagon attacks.

28.5.3 Group Profile Detection

A number of unsupervised algorithms that try to identify groups of attack profiles have been proposed [25, 30, 40]. Generally, these algorithms rely on clustering strategies that attempt to distinguish clusters of attack profiles from clusters of authentic profiles.

28.5.3.1 Neighbourhood Filtering

In [30] an unsupervised detection and filtering scheme is presented. Rather than filtering profiles from the dataset in a preprocessing step, in this method, filtering is applied *to the profiles in the active user's neighbourhood* during prediction for a particular item. This approach has the advantage of identifying just those attack profiles that are targeting the active item. The strategy is based on an algorithm proposed in [12] in the context of reputation reporting systems that aims to provide a reputation estimate for buyers and sellers engaged in on-line marketplaces that is robust to malicious agents who attempt to fraudulently enhance

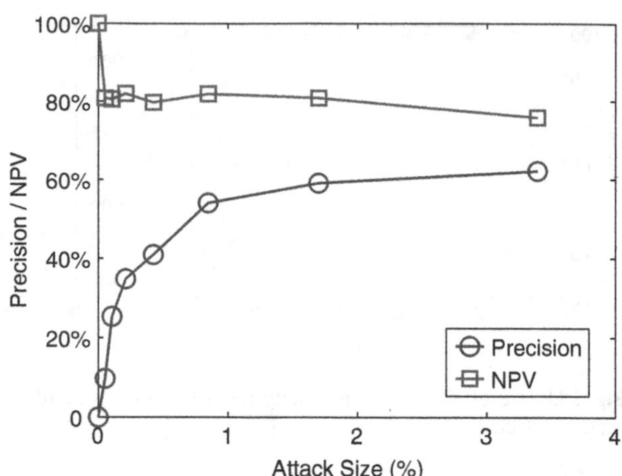

Fig. 28.9 Precision and NPV for the neighbourhood filtering algorithm vs attack size

their own reputations. The approach involves the clustering of neighbourhoods into two clusters. Analysing the statistics of the clusters, a decision is made as to whether an attack is present and, if so, which cluster contains the attack profiles. *All* profiles in the cluster are removed.

Clustering is performed using the Macnaughton-Smith et al. [20] divisive clustering algorithm. The rating distributions for the active item over each of the clusters are then compared. Since the goal of an attacker is to force the predicted ratings of targeted items to a particular value, it is reasonable to expect that the ratings for targeted items that are contained in any attack profiles are centered on the attack value, which is likely to deviate significantly from the mean of the authentic neighbours' ratings. Thus an attack is deemed to have taken place if the difference in the means for the two clusters is sufficiently large. The cluster with the smaller standard deviation is determined to be the attack cluster.

Results for this algorithm (using *precision* and *NPV*) applied to an informed nuke attack on the Movielens dataset are reproduced in Fig. 28.9. The fraction of authentic users contained in the cluster identified as the cluster of authentic users is at least 75 % for all attack sizes tested, so attack profiles are being effectively filtered from the system. However, particularly for small attack sizes, a significant proportion of the attack cluster is made up of authentic users. The cost of removing malicious profiles is to also lose authentic profiles that may have contributed to the accuracy of the prediction. Results show that filtering a system that has not been attacked leads to an increase of around 10 % in the MAE.

28.5.3.2 Detecting Attacks Using Profile Clustering

In [25] the observation is made that attacks consist of multiple profiles which are highly correlated with each other, as well as having high similarity with a large number of authentic profiles. This insight motivates the development of a clustering approach to attack detection, using Probabilistic Latent Semantic Analysis (PLSA) and Principal Component Analysis (PCA).

In the PLSA model [15], an unobserved factor variable $Z = \{z_1, \ldots z_k\}$ is associated with each observation. In the context of collaborative recommendation, an observation corresponds to a rating for some user-item pair and ratings are predicted using

$$\Pr(u,i) = \sum_{i=1}^{k} \Pr(z_i)\Pr(u|z_i)\Pr(i|z_i)\,.$$

The parameters of this expression are chosen to maximise the likelihood of the observed data, using the Expectation Maximisation algorithm. As discussed in [28], the parameters $\Pr(u|z_i)$ can also be used to produce a clustering of the users by assigning each user u to each cluster C_i such that $\Pr(u|z_i)$ exceeds a certain threshold μ or to the cluster that maximises $\Pr(u|z_i)$ if μ is never exceeded.

It is noted in [25] that all or most attack profiles tend to be assigned to a single cluster. Identifying the cluster containing the attack profiles provides an effective strategy for filtering them from the system. Using the intuition that clusters containing attack profiles will be 'tighter' in the sense that the profiles are very similar to each other, the average Mahalanobis distance over the profiles of each cluster is calculated and that with the minimum distance is selected for filtering. Experiments show that PLSA based attack detection works well against strong attacks. However, for weaker attacks the attack profiles tend to be distributed across different clusters.

A second strategy to exploit the high similarity between attack profiles proposed in [25] is to base a clustering on a PCA of the covariance matrix of the user profiles. Essentially this strategy attempts to identify a cluster where the sum of the pair-wise covariances between profiles in the cluster is maximised. PCA has been widely used as a dimension reduction strategy for high-dimensional data. Identifying profiles with dimensions, the method is explained intuitively in [25] as a method of identifying those highly-correlated dimensions (i.e. profiles) that would safely be removed by PCA. Alternatively, a cluster C can be defined by an indicator vector $\mathbf{y}$ such that $y(i) = 1$ if user $u_i \in C$ and $y(i) = 0$ otherwise. With S defined as the covariance matrix, the sum of the pair-wise covariances of all profiles in C, may be written as the quadratic form

$$\mathbf{y}^T \mathrm{S}\mathbf{y} = \sum_{i \in C, j \in C} S(i,j)\,.$$

Moreover, for the normalised eigenvectors $\mathbf{x}_i$ of S, associated with eigenvector λ_i such that $\lambda_1 \le \cdots \le \lambda_m$, the quadratic form evaluates as

$$\mathbf{y}^T \mathrm{S}\mathbf{y} = \sum_{i=1}^{m} (\mathbf{y}.\mathbf{x_i})^2 (\mathbf{x}_i^T \mathrm{S}\mathbf{x}_i) = \sum_{i=1}^{m} (\mathbf{y}.\mathbf{x_i})^2 \lambda_i\,.$$

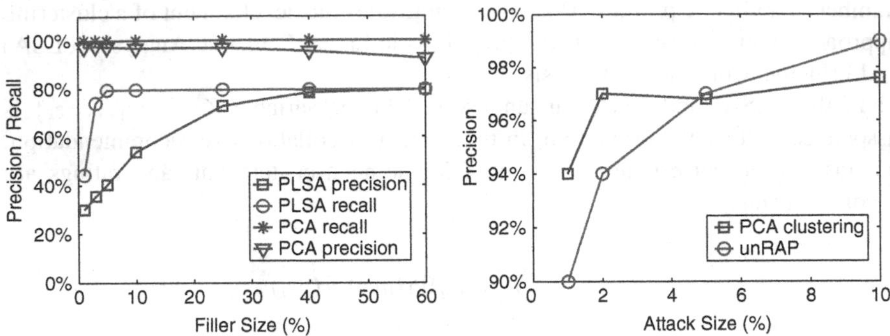

Fig. 28.10 Precision and recall for the PLSA and PCA clustering strategies vs filer size for a 10 % average attack (*left*). Precision vs attack size for PCA clustering and UnRAP on an average attack, with filler size=10 % (*right*)

With this observation, the method described in [25] may be understood as a method that seeks the binary vector **y** that maximises the quadratic form by choosing **y** so that it has small correlation with those 3–5 eigenvectors corresponding to the smallest eigenvalues and hence correlates strongly with the eigenvectors corresponding to large eigenvalues.

Precision and recall results for the PLSA and PCA clustering strategies are reproduced in Fig. 28.10 for an average attack of size 10 %. Similar results have been obtained for random and bandwagon attacks. The PLSA and PCA clustering strategies require that the size of the filtered cluster be specified and, in these results, the cluster size is taken to be the actual number of inserted attack profiles. This point should be taken into account in comparing the results with those obtained with the neighbourhood filtering strategy (Fig. 28.9), in which no such control on the cluster size was applied. The 80 % maximum recall obtained for the PLSA strategy is due to the fact that the wrong cluster is selected approximately 20 % of the time. The PCA clustering strategy shows very good performance, even in the case of attacks consisting of a mixture of random, average and bandwagon profiles.

In [17], this unsupervised clustering strategy is compared with detection that exploits statistical models of the attack. It is pointed out that the clustering succeeds by exploiting the difference in genuine rating behaviour, in terms of the selection of which items to rate, and the choice of ratings in the random and average attacks. This motivates the AoP attack, which in turn is detected, through both an unsupervised and supervised mixture of Gaussian model of rating behaviour. This is a good illustration of the attack/detection game in which attacks motivate detection strategies, which again motivate more sophisticated attacks and in turn detection strategies to combat these attacks. Work in a similar spirit is reported in [19], in which a latent statistical model is proposed for rating behaviour, where the latent variables encode different rating types. One of the learned rating types—the one that maximises the entropy of the distribution of item selection—is selected as an attack type. Again, this is exploiting the difference between the item selection strategies of the attack and genuine profiles.

The UnRAP algorithm [4] also uses clustering to distinguish attack profiles. This algorithm uses a measure called the H_v score which has proved successful in identifying highly correlated biclusters in gene expression data. In the context of attack detection, the H_v score measures for each user, a sum of the squared deviations of its ratings from the user mean, item mean and overall mean ratings:

$$H_v(u) = \frac{\sum_{i \in I}(r_{u,i} - \bar{r}_i - \bar{r}_u + \bar{r})^2}{\sum_{i \in I}(r_{u,i} - \bar{r}_u)^2},$$

where $\bar{r}_i$ is the mean over all users of the ratings for item i, $\bar{r}_u$ is the mean over all items of the ratings for user u and $\bar{r}$ is the mean over users and items.

A H_v score is assigned to all users in the database and users are sorted according to this score. The top $r = 10$ users with highest score are identified as potential attackers and are examined to identify a target item. The target is identified as that which deviates most from the mean user rating. Next, a sliding window of r users is passed along the sorted user list, shifting the window by one user each iteration. The sum of the rating deviation for the target item is calculated over the window and a stopping point is reached when this sum reaches zero. The users traversed during this process become candidate attack profiles, which are then further filtered by removing any that have not rated the item or whose rating deviation is in the opposite direction to the attack. Precision results for this method on an average attack are reproduced in Fig. 28.10, compared with the PCA clustering strategy. In general, the authors report that this method performs well particularly for mid-size attacks, in which other methods show a dip in performance.

A graph-based detection strategy is proposed in [48] where the problem is posed as finding a maximum submatrix in the profile similarity matrix. The problem is transformed into a graph and node-merging heuristics are applied. Evaluation on the Movielens 100k dataset, shows better performance than UnRAP, including good performance on the obfuscated AoP attack.

28.5.3.3 Hybrid Attack Detection

Hybrid has been used in the literature to refer to detection methods that combine two or more base detection methods. In this sense, a hybrid method combining both the PCA and UnRAP measures has been proposed in [50]. Another method that combines the UnRAP score with two scores proposed in [11] is described in [16]. Alternatively, hybrid attack detection has been used to refer to methods that detect a number of different attack types simultaneously. In particular, in [44], a semi-supervised method is presented to detect a mixture of average and random attacks. A key feature of this system is its ability to work with a small seed set of labelled data, using a classification method that extends Naive-Bayes to situation where both labelled and unlabelled data are present.

28.5.4 Detection Findings

For both supervised and unsupervised detection, it has proved possible to achieve reasonably good performance against the attack types discussed in Sect. 28.3. Perhaps this is not so surprising, since the assumption is that these attacks are crafted according to a fairly regular pattern and thereby vary substantially from the real users of the system. The extent to which real-life attacks against recommender systems correspond to these idealized models is not known, since e-commerce companies have been reluctant to reveal vulnerabilities that they have identified in their own systems.

Going back to the framework in Fig. 28.1, these findings give us some optimism that the shaded area at the upper left exists. That is, it is possible to detect attacks that are crafted to be optimal against the well-known memory-based algorithms. It remains an open question to what extent these detection measures extend downward and to the right, into regions where attacks differ from the optimal and have correspondingly less impact, but still remain a source of profit for the attacker.

28.6 Beyond Memory-Based Algorithms

Much of the early research on robustness focussed on attacks tailored to memory-based algorithms. Looking beyond such algorithms, we can ask whether model-based algorithms are inherently more robust to attack and whether it is possible to develop attacks that are effective on these algorithms.

28.6.1 Model-Based Recommendation

It was shown in [28] that model-based recommendation algorithms provide a greater degree of robustness to attack strategies that have proven highly effective on memory-based algorithms. Moreover, this robustness does not come at a significant cost in terms of recommendation accuracy. This work has been followed up in [22, 24], which surveys model-based attack resistant algorithms and proposes a robust matrix factorisation strategy.

A model-based recommendation strategy based on clustering user profiles is analysed in [28]. In this strategy, similar users are clustered into segments and the similarity between the target user and a user segment is calculated. For each segment, an aggregate profile, consisting of the average rating for each item in the segment is computed and predictions are made using the aggregate profile rather than individual profiles. To make a recommendation for a target user u and target item i, a neighbourhood of user segments that have a rating for i and whose

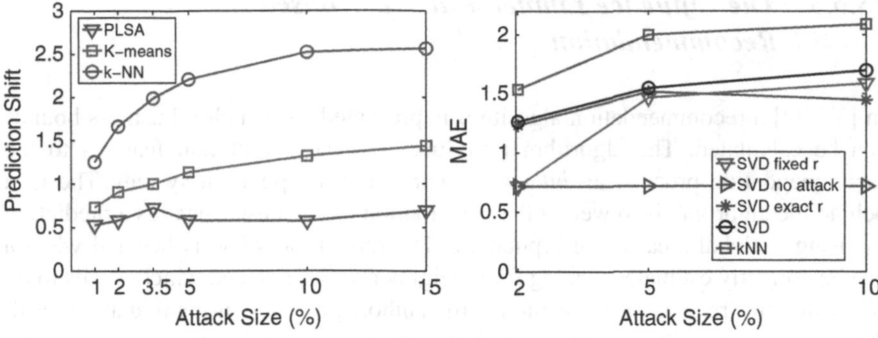

Fig. 28.11 Prediction shift vs attack size for an average attack at 5 % filler for segment recommendation (*left*). MAE on the attacked item vs attack size for filler size of 10 % using RMF (*right*)

aggregate profile is most similar to u is chosen. A prediction for item i is made using the k nearest segments and associated aggregate profiles, rather than the k nearest neighbours. Both k-means clustering and PLSA-based clustering, as described in Sect. 28.5.3.2, are evaluated. The prediction shift achieved by an average attack on these algorithms, compared with the standard kNN algorithm, is shown in Fig. 28.11 (left). The model-based algorithms are considerably more robust and not significantly less accurate, since, according to [28], PLSA and k-means clustering achieve an MAE of 0.75 and 0.76 using 30 segments, in comparison to a value of 0.74 for kNN. On the other hand, the high diversity attack proposed in [8] directly tailors the construction of the attack set to make clustering less-effective. Evaluated on the Movielens dataset, using an attack of size 5 % of the user base size, the high diversity average attack achieves a 40 % increase in the number of rating predictions of at least four compared to the non-attacked system, in comparison to about a 10 % increase when a simple average attack is used.

28.6.2 Privacy-Preserving Algorithms

An evaluation of the robustness of four different privacy-preserving recommendation algorithms using six standard attack models is carried out in [2]. In general, it is found that model-based privacy-preserving algorithms are very robust to these attacks. On the other hand, a robustness study of a specific privacy-preserving recommender algorithm is carried out in [9], in which it is shown that the public information made available by the distributed recommender system can be exploited in the development of an attack that is specifically focussed towards this algorithm.

28.6.3 The Influence Limiter and Trust-Based Recommendation

In [36, 37] a recommendation algorithm is presented for which robustness bounds can be calculated. The algorithm introduces two key additional features to the recommendation process, an *influence limiter* and a reputation system. The idea behind the algorithm is to weight the contribution of each user towards a prediction by using a global measure of reputation. The reputation value is boosted when a profile correctly estimates a rating for a neighbor and is reduced which it fails to do so. Within this recommendation model, the authors prove a non-manipulation result that shows that any attack strategy involving up to n attack users, the negative impact due to the attacker is bounded by a small amount. They also show that a user seeking to maximize influence has a strict incentive to rate honestly. Other properties of this algorithm, such as its accuracy, are still under study.

The influence limiter is just one algorithm that takes into account *trust* and *reputation* in order to build recommendations. In recent years, there has been increasing focus on incorporating trust models into recommender systems [21, 29, 47, 49]. In [21], trust propagation is used to increase the coverage of recommender systems while preserving accuracy. In [29] it is argued that the reliability of a profile to deliver accurate recommendations in the past should be taken into account by recommendation algorithms. An algorithm that uses trust as a means of filtering profiles prior to recommendation so that only the top k most trustworthy profiles participate in the prediction process is presented in [47]. The trust associated with a user for making predictions for an item is computed based on the users' accuracy on predicting their own ratings for that item. The robustness achieved by such algorithms is a function of how difficult it would be for an attacker to become trusted. Finally, [49] show that average attack profiles receive low trust values in their model, compared to genuine profiles. But, again, there is some research [8, 46], that exploits the vulnerabilities of trust-based systems, to develop attacks specifically for these systems.

28.7 Robust Algorithms

An alternative (or perhaps a complement) to filtering and detection is to develop recommendation algorithms that are intrinsically robust to attack.

28.7.1 Robust Matrix Factorisation (RMF)

One model-based approach to collaborative recommendation which has proven very successful recently, is the application of matrix factorisation approaches based on singular value decomposition (SVD) and its variants. Cheng and Hurley [10] showed that standard matrix factorisation algorithms can be made more robust through the use of trimmed least squares, that removes outliers during the fitting of the model. In [22] a robust factorisation strategy is proposed in which the clustering strategy of Sect. 28.5.3.2 is used in conjunction with the training phase of the factorisation procedure. For example, the PLSA clustering strategy can be applied in conjunction with the PLSA recommendation algorithm. After elimination of attack clusters, the $\Pr(z_i|u)$ distribution of the remaining clusters should be renormalised and the last few steps of training should be re-run, to maintain the predictive accuracy of the standard PLSA algorithm and significantly reduce prediction shift.

Another strategy proposed in [25] is in the context of the application of *Generalized Hebbian Learning* algorithm to compute a rank-1 SVD factorisation:

$$\mathrm{R} \approx \mathrm{GH},$$

where R is the rating matrix and G and H are matrices of rank 1. Again, the algorithm is modified so that the contribution of the suspicious users towards the prediction model is zero, once suspicious users have been identified. Results from this strategy are reproduced in Fig. 28.11 (right). The MAE for the attacked algorithm is shown when the number of suspicious users r is set to the exact number of attack profiles inserted, and when it is given a fixed value of 7 % of the user base. Also shown for reference is the MAE on the kNN algorithm and standard SVD, with and without attack.

Theoretical results have also been derived to support the robustness of particular classes of model-based algorithm. In [45], a manipulation-resistant class of collaborative filtering algorithm is proposed for which robustness is proved, in the sense that the effect of any attack on the ratings provided to an end-user diminishes with increasing number of products rated by the end-user. Here, effectiveness is measured in terms of a measure of the average distortion introduced by the attack to the ratings provided to the user. The class of algorithms for which the proof holds is referred to as a *linear* probabilistic collaborative filtering. In essence, the system is modelled as outputting a probability mass function (PMF) over the possible ratings and in linear algorithms, the PMF of the attacked system can be written as a weighted sum of the PMF obtained considering only genuine profiles and that obtained considering only attack profiles. Robustness is obtained, because, as the user supplies more ratings, the contribution of the genuine PMF to the overall PMF begins to dominate. The authors show that, while nearest neighbour algorithms are not linear in this sense, some well-known model-based algorithms such as the Naive-Bayes algorithm are asymptotically linear.

28.7.2 Other Robust Recommendation Algorithms

Attack profiles are ineffective if they do not appear in the neighborhoods of authentic users. By avoiding similarity as a criterion for neighbour selection, the recommendation algorithm can be made robust to attacks where the attack profiles are designed to have high similarity with authentic users. In [30] it is argued that the goal of neighbour selection is to select the most *useful* neighbours on which to base the prediction. While similarity is one measure of usefulness, the notion of neighbour utility can be extended to include other performance measures. A selection criterion is proposed based on a notion of *inverse popularity*. It is shown that, with this selection strategy, the same overall system performance in terms of MAE is maintained. Moreover, cost-effective attacks that depend on popular items to build highly influential profiles are rendered much less effective.

In [38], a robust algorithm is presented based on association rule mining. Considering each user profile as a transaction, it is possible to use the *A priori* algorithm to generate association rules for groups of commonly liked items. The support of an item set $X \subset I$ is the fraction of user profiles that contain this item set. An association rule is an expression of the form $X \Rightarrow Y(\sigma_r, \alpha_r)$, where σ_r is the support of $X \cup Y$ and α_r is the *confidence* for the rule, defined as $\sigma(X \cup Y)/\sigma(X)$. The algorithm finds a recommendation for a user u by searching for the highest confidence association rules, such that $X \subseteq P_u$ is a subset of the user profile and Y contains some item i that is unrated by u. If there is not enough support for a particular item, that item will never appear in any frequent item set and will never be recommended. This algorithm proves robust to the average attack. For attack sizes below 15 %, only 0.1 % of users are recommended an attacked item by the association rule algorithm, compared to 80–100 % of users for the *kNN* algorithm. The trade-off is that coverage of the association rule algorithm is reduced in comparison to kNN. However, the algorithm is not robust against the segment attack.

28.8 Practical Countermeasures to Recommender System Attack

The above discussion has assumed that malicious parties can access a recommender system, create multiple profiles and tailor them through the careful selection of item ratings. While this may represent a worst-case scenario against which algorithm designers can measure the robustness of their systems, it offers many practical challenges to a would-be attacker. These challenges can be made more difficult through system design choices that more carefully control the interactions with the user and make it harder for users to remain fully anonymous. For example, mobile based authentication or credit-card authentication can allow all profiles to be associated with a physical entity, increasing the risk of being exposed. The addition of new users and rating entry could be controlled, for example using Captchas, to make automatic user generation and rating submission difficult. Indeed, a cost is associated with rating entry, for example, if feedback can only be given upon purchase, this can act as an effective deterrent. Finally, systems can be made more open, by allowing ratings of users to be viewed by all others. In this way, malicious behaviour could be detected by the users themselves, although such exposure also introduces a risk of attacks that exploit open information.

28.9 Conclusion

Collaborative recommender systems are meant to be adaptive—users add their preferences to these system and their output changes accordingly. Robustness in this context must mean something different than the classical computer science sense of being able to continue functioning in the face of abnormalities or errors. Our goal is to have systems that adapt, but that do not present an attractive target to the attacker. An attacker wishing to bias the output of a robust recommender system would have to make his attack sufficiently subtle that it does not trigger the suspicion of an attack detector, sufficiently small that it does not stand out from the normal pattern of new user enrollment, and sufficiently close to real user distribution patterns that it is not susceptible to being separated out by dimensionality reduction. If this proves a difficult target to hit and if the payoff for attacks can be sufficiently limited, the attacker may not find the impact of his attack sufficiently large relative to the effort required to produce it. This is the best one can hope for in an adversarial arena.

It is difficult to say how close we have come to this ideal. If an attacker is aware that such detection strategies are being applied, then the attack can be modified to avoid detection. The general finding is that obfuscated attacks are not much less effective than optimal ones and much harder to detect. More research is needed in this area.

Similar issues apply in the context of attack resistant recommendation algorithms. While model-based algorithms show robustness to attacks that are effective on memory-based algorithms, it is possible to conceive of new attacks that target model-based algorithms. Sandvig et al. [38], for example, shows that association rule based recommendation is vulnerable to segment attacks.

Another way to view the problem is as a game between system designer and attacker. For each system that the designer creates, an optimal attack against it can be formulated by the attacker, which then requires another response from the designer, etc. What we would like to see is that there are diminishing returns for the attacker, so that each iteration of defense makes attacking more expensive and less effective. One benefit of a detection strategy is that a system with detection cannot be more vulnerable to attack than the original system, since in the worst case, the attacks are not detected. We do not yet know if the robust algorithms that have been proposed such as RMF have some as-yet-undiscovered flaw that could make them vulnerable to a sophisticated attack, perhaps even more vulnerable than the algorithms that they replace.

Acknowledgements The authors would like to thank the anonymous reviewer for some helpful suggestions. O'Mahony and Hurley are supported by Science Foundation Ireland under Grant Number SFI/12/RC/2289.

References

1. A.Williams, C., Mobasher, B., Burke, R.: Defending recommender systems: detection of profile injection attacks. Service Oriented Computing and Applications pp. 157–170 (2007)
2. Bilge, A., Gunes, I., Polat, H.: Robustness analysis of privacy-preserving model-based recommendation schemes. Expert Systems with Applications **41**(8), 3671–3681 (2014). DOI http://dx.doi.org/10.1016/j.eswa.2013.11.039. URL http://www.sciencedirect.com/science/article/pii/S0957417413009597
3. Breese, J.S., Heckerman, D., Kadie, C.: Empirical analysis of predictive algorithms for collaborative filtering. In Proceedings of the Fourteenth Annual Conference on Uncertainty in Artificial Intelligence pp. 43–52 (1998)
4. Bryan, K., O'Mahony, M., Cunningham, P.: Unsupervised retrieval of attack profiles in collaborative recommender systems. In: RecSys '08: Proceedings of the 2008 ACM conference on Recommender systems, pp. 155–162. ACM, New York, NY, USA (2008). DOI http://doi.acm.org/10.1145/1454008.1454034
5. Burke, R., Mobasher, B., Bhaumik, R.: Limited knowledge shilling attacks in collaborative filtering systems. In Proceedings of Workshop on Intelligent Techniques for Web Personalization (ITWP'05) (2005)
6. Burke, R., Mobasher, B., Williams, C.: Classification features for attack detection in collaborative recommender systems. In: Proceedings of the 12th International Conference on Knowledge Discovery and Data Mining, pp. 17–20 (2006)
7. Burke, R., Mobasher, B., Zabicki, R., Bhaumik, R.: Identifying attack models for secure recommendation. In: Beyond Personalization: A Workshop on the Next Generation of Recommender Systems (2005)
8. Cheng, Z., Hurley, N.: Effective diverse and obfuscated attacks on model-based recommender systems. In: Proceedings of the Third ACM Conference on Recommender Systems, RecSys '09, pp. 141–148. ACM, New York, NY, USA (2009). DOI 10.1145/1639714.1639739. URL http://doi.acm.org/10.1145/1639714.1639739
9. Cheng, Z., Hurley, N.: Trading robustness for privacy in decentralized recommender systems. In: IAAI, Proceedings of the Twenty-First Conference on Innovative Applications of Artificial Intelligence. AAAI (2009)
10. Cheng, Z., Hurley, N.: Robust collaborative recommendation by least trimmed squares matrix factorization. In: Proceedings of the 2010 22Nd IEEE International Conference on Tools with Artificial Intelligence - Volume 02, ICTAI '10, pp. 105–112. IEEE Computer Society, Washington, DC, USA (2010). DOI 10.1109/ICTAI.2010.90. URL http://dx.doi.org/10.1109/ICTAI.2010.90
11. Chirita, P.A., Nejdl, W., Zamfir, C.: Preventing shilling attacks in online recommender systems. In Proceedings of the ACM Workshop on Web Information and Data Management (WIDM'2005) pp. 67–74 (2005)
12. Dellarocas, C.: Immunizing on–line reputation reporting systems against unfair ratings and discriminatory behavior. In Proceedings of the 2nd ACM Conference on Electronic Commerce (EC'00) pp. 150–157 (2000)
13. Domingos, P., Richardson, M.: Mining the network value of customers. In: Proceedings of the Seventh ACM SIGKDD International Conference on Knowledge Discovery and Data Mining, KDD '01, pp. 57–66. ACM, New York, NY, USA (2001). DOI 10.1145/502512.502525. URL http://doi.acm.org/10.1145/502512.502525

14. Herlocker, J., Konstan, J., Borchers, A., Riedl, J.: An algorithmic framework for performing collaborative filtering. In Proceedings of the 22nd International ACM SIGIR Conference on Research and Development in Information Retrieval pp. 230–237 (1999)
15. Hofmann, T.: Collaborative filtering via gaussian probabilistic latent semantic analysis. In: SIGIR '03: Proceedings of the 26th annual international ACM SIGIR conference on Research and development in informaion retrieval, pp. 259–266. ACM, New York, NY, USA (2003). DOI http://doi.acm.org/10.1145/860435.860483
16. Huang, S., Shang, M., Cai, S.: A hybrid decision approach to detect profile injection attacks in collaborative recommender systems. In: L. Chen, A. Felfernig, J. Liu, Z. Raś (eds.) Foundations of Intelligent Systems, *Lecture Notes in Computer Science*, vol. 7661, pp. 377–386. Springer Berlin Heidelberg (2012). DOI 10.1007/978-3-642-34624-8_43. URL http://dx.doi.org/10.1007/978-3-642-34624-8_43
17. Hurley, N., Cheng, Z., Zhang, M.: Statistical attack detection. In: Proceedings of the Third ACM Conference on Recommender Systems, RecSys '09, pp. 149–156. ACM, New York, NY, USA (2009). DOI 10.1145/1639714.1639740. URL http://doi.acm.org/10.1145/1639714.1639740
18. Lam, S.K., Riedl, J.: Shilling recommender systems for fun and profit. In Proceedings of the 13th International World Wide Web Conference pp. 393–402 (2004)
19. Li, C., Luo, Z.: Detection of shilling attacks in collaborative filtering recommender systems. In: A. Abraham, H. Liu, F. Sun, C. Guo, S.F. McLoone, E. Corchado (eds.) SoCPaR, pp. 190–193. IEEE (2011). URL http://dblp.uni-trier.de/db/conf/socpar/socpar2011.html#LiL11
20. Macnaughton-Smith, P., Williams, W.T., Dale, M., Mockett, L.: Dissimilarity analysis – a new technique of hierarchical sub–division. Nature **202**, 1034–1035 (1964)
21. Massa, P., Avesani, P.: Trust-aware recommender systems. In: RecSys '07: Proceedings of the 2007 ACM conference on Recommender systems, pp. 17–24. ACM, New York, NY, USA (2007). DOI http://doi.acm.org/10.1145/1297231.1297235
22. Mehta, B., Hofmann, T.: A survey of attack-resistant collaborative filtering algorithms. Bulletin of the Technical Committee on Data Engineering **31**(2), 14–22 (2008). URL http://sites.computer.org/debull/A08June/mehta.pdf
23. Mehta, B., Hofmann, T., Fankhauser, P.: Lies and propaganda: Detecting spam users in collaborative filtering. In: Proceedings of the 12th international conference on Intelligent user interfaces, pp. 14–21 (2007)
24. Mehta, B., Hofmann, T., Nejdl, W.: Robust collaborative filtering. In: RecSys '07: Proceedings of the 2007 ACM conference on Recommender systems, pp. 49–56. ACM, New York, NY, USA (2007). DOI http://doi.acm.org/10.1145/1297231.1297240
25. Mehta, B., Nejdl, W.: Unsupervised strategies for shilling detection and robust collaborative filtering. User Modeling and User-Adapted Interaction **19**(1–2), 65–97 (2009). DOI http://dx.doi.org/10.1007/s11257-008-9050-4
26. Mobasher, B., Burke, R., Bhaumik, R., Williams, C.: Effective attack models for shilling item-based collaborative filtering system. In Proceedings of the 2005 WebKDD Workshop (KDD'2005) (2005)
27. Mobasher, B., Burke, R., Bhaumik, R., Williams, C.: Toward trustworthy recommender systems: An analysis of attack models and algorithm robustness. ACM Transactions on Internet Technology **7**(4) (2007)
28. Mobasher, B., Burke, R.D., Sandvig, J.J.: Model-based collaborative filtering as a defense against profile injection attacks. In: AAAI. AAAI Press (2006)
29. O'Donovan, J., Smyth, B.: Is trust robust?: an analysis of trust-based recommendation. In: IUI '06: Proceedings of the 11th international conference on Intelligent user interfaces, pp. 101–108. ACM, New York, NY, USA (2006). DOI http://doi.acm.org/10.1145/1111449.1111476
30. O'Mahony, M.P., Hurley, N.J., Silvestre, C.C.M.: An evaluation of neighbourhood formation on the performance of collaborative filtering. Artificial Intelligence Review **21**(1), 215–228 (2004)

31. O'Mahony, M.P., Hurley, N.J., Silvestre, G.C.M.: Promoting recommendations: An attack on collaborative filtering. In: A. Hameurlain, R. Cicchetti, R. Traunmüller (eds.) DEXA, *Lecture Notes in Computer Science*, vol. 2453, pp. 494–503. Springer (2002)
32. O'Mahony, M.P., Hurley, N.J., Silvestre, G.C.M.: An evaluation of the performance of collaborative filtering. In Proceedings of the 14th Irish International Conference on Artificial Intelligence and Cognitive Science (AICS'03) pp. 164–168 (2003)
33. O'Mahony, M.P., Hurley, N.J., Silvestre, G.C.M.: Recommender systems: Attack types and strategies. In Proceedings of the 20th National Conference on Artificial Intelligence (AAAI-05) pp. 334–339 (2005)
34. Rashid, A.M., Karypis, G., Riedl, J.: Influence in ratings-based recommender systems: An algorithm-independent approach. In: Proceedings of the 2005 SIAM International Conference on Data Mining, SDM 2005, pp. 556–560. SIAM (2005)
35. Resnick, P., Iacovou, N., Suchak, M., Bergstrom, P., J.Riedl: Grouplens: An open architecture for collaborative filtering of netnews. In Proceedings of the ACM Conference on Computer Supported Cooperative Work (CSCW'94) pp. 175–186 (1994)
36. Resnick, P., Sami, R.: The influence limiter: provably manipulation-resistant recommender systems. In: RecSys '07: Proceedings of the 2007 ACM conference on Recommender systems, pp. 25–32. ACM, New York, NY, USA (2007). DOI http://doi.acm.org/10.1145/1297231.1297236
37. Resnick, P., Sami, R.: The information cost of manipulation-resistance in recommender systems. In: RecSys '08: Proceedings of the 2008 ACM conference on Recommender systems, pp. 147–154. ACM, New York, NY, USA (2008). DOI http://doi.acm.org/10.1145/1454008.1454033
38. Sandvig, J.J., Mobasher, B., Burke, R.: Robustness of collaborative recommendation based on association rule mining. In: RecSys '07: Proceedings of the 2007 ACM conference on Recommender systems, pp. 105–112. ACM, New York, NY, USA (2007). DOI http://doi.acm.org/10.1145/1297231.1297249
39. Sarwar, B., Karypis, G., Konstan, J., Riedl, J.: Item–based collaborative filtering recommendation algorithms. In Proceedings of the Tenth International World Wide Web Conference pp. 285–295 (2001)
40. Su, X.F., Zeng, H.J., Chen, Z.: Finding group shilling in recommendation system. In: WWW '05: Special interest tracks and posters of the 14th international conference on World Wide Web, pp. 960–961. ACM, New York, NY, USA (2005). DOI http://doi.acm.org/10.1145/1062745.1062818
41. Tang, T., Tang, Y.: An effective recommender attack detection method based on time sfm factors. In: Communication Software and Networks (ICCSN), 2011 IEEE 3rd International Conference on, pp. 78–81 (2011). DOI 10.1109/ICCSN.2011.6013780
42. Williams, C., Mobasher, B., Burke, R., Bhaumik, R., Sandvig, J.: Detection of obfuscated attacks in collaborative recommender systems. In Proceedings of the 17th European Conference on Artificial Intelligence (ECAI'06) (2006)
43. Wilson, D.C., Seminario, C.E.: When power users attack: Assessing impacts in collaborative recommender systems. In: Proceedings of the 7th ACM Conference on Recommender Systems, RecSys '13, pp. 427–430. ACM, New York, NY, USA (2013). DOI 10.1145/2507157.2507220. URL http://doi.acm.org/10.1145/2507157.2507220
44. Wu, Z., Wu, J., Cao, J., Tao, D.: Hysad: a semi-supervised hybrid shilling attack detector for trustworthy product recommendation. In: Proceedings of the 18th ACM SIGKDD international conference on Knowledge discovery and data mining, pp. 985–993. ACM (2012)
45. Yan, X., Roy, B.V.: Manipulation-resistnat collaborative filtering systems. In: RecSys '09: Proceedings of the 2009 ACM conference on Recommender systems. ACM, New York, NY, USA (2009)
46. Zhang, F.G.: Preventing recommendation attack in trust-based recommender systems. J. Comput. Sci. Technol. **26**(5), 823–828 (2011). DOI 10.1007/s11390-011-0181-4. URL http://dx.doi.org/10.1007/s11390-011-0181-4

47. Zhang, F.G., Sheng-hua, X.: Analysis of trust-based e-commerce recommender systems under recommendation attacks. In: ISDPE '07: Proceedings of the The First International Symposium on Data, Privacy, and E-Commerce, pp. 385–390. IEEE Computer Society, Washington, DC, USA (2007). DOI http://dx.doi.org/10.1109/ISDPE.2007.55
48. Zhang, Z., Kulkarni, S.R.: Graph-based detection of shilling attacks in recommender systems. In: Machine Learning for Signal Processing (MLSP), 2013 IEEE International Workshop on, pp. 1–6. IEEE (2013)
49. Zheng, S., Jiang, T., Baras, J.S.: A robust collaborative filtering algorithm using ordered logistic regression. In: Proceedings of IEEE International Conference on Communications, ICC 2011, Kyoto, Japan, 5–9 June, 2011, pp. 1–6. IEEE (2011)
50. Zhou, Q., Zhang, F.: A hybrid unsupervised approach for detecting profile injection attacks in collaborative recommender systems. Journal of Information & Computational Science **9**(3), 687–694 (2012)

Index

F. Ricci et al. (eds.), *Recommender Systems Handbook*,
DOI 10.1007/978-1-4899-7637-6

Printed in the United States
By Bookmasters